THE COMPLETE GUIDE TO
THE NATIONAL PARKS
OF THE WEST

WELCOME TO THE NATIONAL PARKS OF THE WEST

Awe-inspiring, often remote landscapes and unlimited recreational opportunities make a trip to any western national park a grand adventure. You can raft the raging Colorado River as it pushes through the Grand Canyon, view wildlife in Yosemite while you hike, or watch Yellowstone's Old Faithful geyser in action. Places such as Mesa Verde also preserve the long history of life in the West. Wherever you explore in the parks, these sprawling treasures invite you to discover nature's stunning variety and reconnect with the great outdoors.

TOP REASONS TO GO

★ **Wildlife:** From bison to bald eagles to bears, the parks shelter amazing species.

★ **Hiking:** Countless scenic trails for all levels inspire and challenge walkers.

★ **Geology:** Unique formations like Oregon's Crater Lake and Utah's Arches astound.

★ **Great Views:** Mountain peaks and scenic overlooks reward climbers and drivers alike.

★ **History:** Monuments and outposts trace the settling of the former Wild West.

★ **Luxury Lodges:** Famous hotels pair old-school grandeur with splendid surroundings.

Fodor's THE COMPLETE GUIDE TO THE NATIONAL PARKS OF THE WEST

Publisher: Amanda D'Acierno, *Senior Vice President*

Editorial: Arabella Bowen, *Editor in Chief*; Linda Cabasin, *Editorial Director*

Design: Fabrizio La Rocca, *Vice President, Creative Director*; Tina Malaney, *Associate Art Director*; Chie Ushio, *Senior Designer*; Ann McBride, *Production Designer*

Photography: Melanie Marin, *Associate Director of Photography*; Jessica Parkhill and Jennifer Romains, *Researchers*

Maps: Rebecca Baer, *Senior Map Editor*; Mark Stroud, Moon Street Cartography *Cartographers*

Production: Linda Schmidt, *Managing Editor*; Evangelos Vasilakis, *Associate Managing Editor*; Angela L. McLean, *Senior Production Manager*

Sales: Jacqueline Lebow, *Sales Director*

Marketing & Publicity: Heather Dalton, *Marketing Director*; Katherine Fleming, *Senior Publicist*

Business & Operations: Susan Livingston, *Vice President, Strategic Business Planning*; Sue Daulton, *Vice President, Operations*

Fodors.com: Megan Bell, *Executive Director, Revenue & Business Development*; Yasmin Marinaro, *Senior Director, Marketing & Partnerships*

Copyright © 2014 by Fodor's Travel, a division of Random House LLC.

Writers: Shelley Arenas, Ricardo Baca, John Blodgett, Martha Schindler Connors, Cheryl Crabtree, Lindsay Galloway, Thomas D. Griffith, Aimee Heckel, Deb Hopewell, Kellee Katagi, Mara Levin, Johanna Love, Daniel Mangin, Debbie Olsen, Steve Pastorino, Marty Racine, Elise Riley, Christine Vovakes, Mike Weatherford, Sharron Wood.

Lead Editors: Salwa Jabado, Amanda Sadlowski

Editors: Bethany Beckerlegge, Denise Leto

Production Editor: Carrie Parker

4th Edition

ISBN 978-0-8041-4202-1

All details in this book are based on information supplied to us at press time. Always confirm information when it matters, especially if you're making a detour to visit a specific place. Fodor's expressly disclaims any liability, loss, or risk, personal or otherwise, that is incurred as a consequence of the use of any of the contents of this book.

SPECIAL SALES

This book is available at special discounts for bulk purchases for sales promotions or premiums. For more information, e-mail specialmarkets@randomhouse.com

PRINTED IN THE UNITED STATES OF AMERICA

10 9 8 7 6 5 4 3 2 1

CONTENTS

Fodor's Features

CONTENTS

CONTENTS

CONTENTS

MAPS

ABOUT THIS GUIDE

What's Inside

For each of the 38 national parks of the West, our writers have gathered comprehensive information on everything within the park and on the towns and attractions nearby. We have included as many sights, activities, lodging and dining options, and practical details as space allows, focusing on delivering the kind of in-depth, first-hand knowledge that you won't get elsewhere. Our first three chapters introduce you to the national parks of the West and provide tips on how to make the most of your visits to these national treasures. Following these insightful chapters is our suggested Great Itineraries that help you match parks together for regional road-trips. The bulk of the book are the chapters for each national park, listed alphabetically.

Fodor's Recommendations

Everything in this guide is worth doing— we don't cover what isn't—but exceptional sights, hotels, and restaurants are recognized with additional accolades. Fodor's Choice★ indicates our top recommendations. Care to nominate a new place? Visit Fodors.com/contact-us.

Trip Costs

Hotel and restaurant price categories from $ to $$$$ are noted alongside each recommendation. For hotels, we include the lowest cost of a standard double room in high season. For restaurants, we cite the average price of a main course at dinner, of if dinner isn't served, at lunch. For attractions, we always give standard adult admission fees; reductions are usually available for children, students, and senior citizens.

Top Picks		Hotels &
★ Fodor's Choice		Restaurants
	⌂	Hotel
Listings	⌷	Number of
✉ Address		rooms
✉ Branch address	⍾⍥	Meal plans
☎ Telephone	✗	Restaurant
🖷 Fax	⌕	Reservations
⊕ Website	🏛	Dress code
✍ E-mail	▭	No credit cards
🎟 Admission fee	$	Price
⊙ Open/closed		
times	**Other**	
Ⓜ Subway	⇨	See also
⊹ Directions or	☞	Take note
Map coordinates	⛳	Golf facilities

Restaurants

Unless we state otherwise, restaurants are open for lunch and dinner daily. We mention dress code only when there's a specific requirement and reservations only when they're essential or not accepted. **To make restaurant reservations, visit Fodors.com.**

Hotels

Our local writers vet every hotel to recommend the best overnights in each price category, from budget to expensive. Unless otherwise specified, you can expect private bath, phone, and TV in your room. **For expanded hotel reviews, facilities, and deals visit Fodors.com.**

Credit Cards

The hotels and restaurants in this guide typically accept credit cards. If not, we'll say so.

EXPERIENCE THE NATIONAL PARKS OF THE WEST

NATIONAL PARK SERVICE THEN AND NOW

Go West, Young Man

A romantic image of the West has gripped the American psyche since the nation's birth. As the frontier shifted from the Ohio River Valley to the Great Plains to the Rocky Mountains and finally to the Pacific coast, the land just over the horizon promised freedom, open space, self-sufficiency, and adventure. Manifest Destiny, gold rushes, and the Homestead Act of 1862—which offered 160-acre parcels of land to anyone 21 years or older with $18—spurred settlers, prospectors, soldiers, and laborers to tame the American West.

Vocal Pioneers

During this unprecedented land grab, interest in preserving scenic Western lands and archaeological sites emerged, along with a national sense of responsibility for the wilderness. While exploring the Dakotas in 1832, painter George Catlin noted the potential for loss of wildlife and wilderness. He wrote that they could be preserved "by some great protecting policy of government . . . in a magnificent park."

The tipping point came three decades later. In 1864, in the midst of the Civil War, President Lincoln set aside Yosemite Valley and the Mariposa Grove of giant sequoias as a public trust to preserve the land for future generations. This revolutionary federal preservation concept was just the beginning. When a handful of would-be entrepreneurs explored Yellowstone in 1870, dreaming up the possibilities for development of this fantastic land they'd found, a lawyer, Cornelius Hedges, made the bold suggestion that they preserve this geologically astounding land rather than capitalize on it.

Whatever persuasive prose Hedges used is not certain, but persuade them he did. A year later, one of these explorers was in the House of Representatives promoting the idea of preserving Yellowstone as a natural place. Also lobbying for the plan were artist Thomas Moran, photographer William Henry Jackson, and U.S. Geological Survey Director Ferdinand Hayden, who'd been appointed by Congress to lead an expedition to Yellowstone to validate the rumors of its otherworldly features. Congress was more than convinced of its merits (and the need to preserve them), and in early 1872, President Ulysses S. Grant signed into law the bill creating Yellowstone National Park.

The 1890s saw the creation of several more national parks, as well as the Forest Reserve Act of 1891, which led to the establishment of our first national forests. In 1906, the Antiquities Act passed, which allowed presidents to name national monuments. That same year, President Theodore Roosevelt established Devils Tower as the first such site, making Wyoming the home of both the first national park and first national monument.

Pioneering conservationists like Robert Underwood Johnson and John Muir advocated for further preservation of Western treasures. Muir, who founded the Sierra Club in 1892 and is often called the father of the National Park System, greatly influenced Theodore Roosevelt, who went on to establish five national parks.

The Birth of the National Park System

By 1916, the Interior Department was handling 14 national parks. In order to streamline the management of the national parks and monuments, President Woodrow Wilson approved legislation creating the National Park Service, or NPS, within the Department of the Interior. The mission of the new agency was "to conserve the scenery and the natural and historic objects and the wildlife therein and to provide for the enjoyment of the same in such manner and by such means as will leave them unimpaired for the enjoyment of future generations."

While Washington made these lands protected, railroads made them accessible. Thousands traveled west to such national parks as Grand Canyon, Glacier, Yosemite Valley, and Crater Lake, and stayed in the extravagant lodges constructed there by the railroad companies.

Growing Pains

The parks were initially established to ensure land preservation and visitor enjoyment, but by 1932, the park concept had expanded to include educational components with the formation of the NPS's Naturalist Division. The naturalists were assigned to interpret park features to the public through educational outreaches. The park system had also begun to rethink its wildlife management practices.

Between 1933 and 1942, thousands of hardy workers came to the nation's parks and forests through the Civilian Conservation Corps (CCC), part of President Franklin Delano Roosevelt's Works Progress Administration, established during the Great Depression. A total of 70 work camps were set up within the national parks.

WHAT'S NEW AT THE PARKS

A Call to Action. In anticipation of its 100-year anniversary in 2016, the National Park Service is implementing the Call to Action, a multipart initiative launched in 2011 and designed to help the service begin its second century in an even stronger position than at its founding. Specifically, the plan aims to boost public participation in the parks, advance the NPS's educational mission, and preserve the service's more than 400 sites through exemplary environmental protection, conservation, and resource management.

To achieve these ends, the Call to Action includes a variety of initiatives, such as providing transportation for 100,000 students to visit the parks each year and a pledge to reduce the parks' collective greenhouse gas emissions by 20%. In the West, plans are in place to restore wild bison populations and sponsor the country's first Dark Sky Cooperative on the Colorado Plateau.

New National Monuments. President Barack Obama designated three new national monuments in 2013—Charles Young Buffalo Soldiers NM in Wilberforce, Ohio; First State NM in Kent and New Castle Counties, Delaware; and the Harriet Tubman Underground Railroad NM in Dorchester County, Maryland—and a fourth, Cesar E. Chavez NM in Keene, California in 2012.

As the country's population continued to grow, and society learned more about the environment and the effects of pollution and increasing demands on natural resources, there was a need to take additional steps to maintain pristine wilderness and historic areas. Congress addressed this in the 1960s and early '70s with a host of legislative measures: the Clean Air Act (1963), Wilderness Act (1964), National Historic Preservation Act (1966), Wild and Scenic Rivers Act (1968), National Environmental Policy Act (1969), and the Endangered Species Act (1973).

The NPS Today

The National Park Service now manages more than 400 natural, cultural, and recreational sites on some 84 million acres. These sites include national parks as well as monuments, memorials, historic parks, and national preserves. The NPS defines these lands as follows:

National Park: A natural place, generally large in size, that possesses an array of attributes, such as providing an outstanding example of a particular type of resource and great opportunities for public use and enjoyment (or for scientific study). It may also be historically significant. National parks are protected from hunting, mining, logging, and other consumptive activities.

National Historic Park: A historic site that extends beyond single properties.

National Historic Site: Usually containing a single historic feature directly associated with its subject. Derived from the Historic Sites Act of 1935, a number of historic sites were established by secretaries of the Interior, but most have been authorized by acts of Congress. They appear on the National Register of Historic Places.

National Memorial: A site that is commemorative of a historic person or episode.

National Monument: A landmark, structure, or other object of historic or scientific interest situated on lands owned or controlled by the government.

National Preserve: An area having characteristics associated with national parks, but in which oil and gas exploration and extraction, hunting, and trapping are allowed. Many existing national preserves, without sport hunting, would qualify for national park designation.

NATIONAL PARKS TIMELINE

1872	Yellowstone National Park becomes the world's first national park.
1890	Sequoia, Yosemite, and General Grant (later part of Sequoia and Kings Canyon) become national parks.
1902	President Theodore Roosevelt establishes the first of his five parks, Crater Lake.

National Recreation Area: Places with this designation include reservoirs used for water-based activities and urban parks that combine outdoor recreation with the preservation of significant historic resources and important natural areas.

Hot Issues

More than a century ago, conservationists were instrumental in establishing the national parks as preserved areas; their efforts continue today, as these set-aside areas face a host of challenges, including overcrowding, noise and light pollution, and wildlife management. And, of course, funding is always a concern.

Here are a few of the issues facing the National Park Service today:

Attendance. Although the parks must compete for our attention with an ever-expanding range of entertainment options, attendance has been holding steady for the past several years, with close to 282 million recreational visits last year. A major challenge for the coming century is convincing an increasingly busy, plugged-in population to visit the wilderness. Paradoxically, the most popular parks are facing the opposite prob-lem: making sure huge seasonal crowds don't negatively impact the parks.

Funding. Tight budgets force the parks to consider alternative revenue sources, including corporate sponsorships. But you won't be seeing "McDonald's Grand Canyon" or "Half Dome, brought to you by Coca-Cola" anytime soon. In recent years, the NPS was able to more than double the federal dollars it received through matching donations made by private companies and individuals.

Migration Patterns. Managing wildlife is an increasingly complex responsibility. The parks' animal inhabitants don't recognize political boundaries: for example, elk stray into unprotected areas around Rocky Mountain National Park, where they wreak havoc on the native vegetation, and wolves hunt beyond the confines of Yellowstone, sometimes killing livestock on nearby ranches.

Pollution. Standing in a pristine natural paradise like Yellowstone or the Grand Canyon, you're not likely to think about pollution—but the problem encompasses more than just visible smog. As development encroaches on the parks, it brings the bright lights of the city one step

1903	Theodore Roosevelt makes Wind Cave the country's seventh national park, and the first dedicated to preserving a cave.
1906	Congress designates Mesa Verde as a national park. It is the first cultural park in the system.
1916	President Woodrow Wilson signs the Organic Act, creating the National Park Service.
1919	The Grand Canyon goes from a national monument to a national park.

1933	Franklin Delano Roosevelt develops the Civilian Conservation Corps, which works in national parks and forests, planting close to three billion trees in nine years.
1951	After much debate, the National Park Service adopts its official emblem: the outline of an arrowhead surrounding a mountain, a sequoia tree, a river, and a bison. The arrowhead represents historical and archaeological values, the tree and bison represent vegetation and wildlife, and the mountains and water represent scenic and recreational values.

closer to the wilderness. The resulting light pollution causes overly illuminated skies with fewer visible stars, which can be disappointing for visitors and deadly for disoriented birds and other animals.

Meanwhile, noise pollution, much of it from aircraft, threatens to break the silence that many visitors seek in the parks. This is especially troublesome at the Grand Canyon. There are also other factors putting the parks' air, water, and land at risk. High ozone levels in Sequoia and Kings Canyon National Park, for example, can cause respiratory irritation and are damaging the native Jeffrey pines.

Conservation Efforts

The NPS is continuing its efforts to sustain and recover in-park populations of threatened and endangered plant and animal species. More than 200 of the 401 NPS units (including national parks, national monuments, and other designated areas) are home to at least one endangered species (the system as a whole contains 421 threatened species that used to live in park areas but have been lost due to human activities.

The NPS has had several successes in recent years, including the dramatic recovery of endangered island foxes within the Channel Islands National Park. There are now more than 1,800 foxes on the islands, up from fewer than 500 animals in 1999, and the population is on the road to recovery. Meanwhile, a project in Olympic National Park has reintroduced endangered fishers—rare, reclusive mammals related to minks and otters—which were once plentiful in the area but had disappeared due to habitat loss and over-trapping.

Acknowledgments: We thank the Department of the Interior for their helpful resources, including *A Brief History of the National Park Service.*

1967	Congress establishes the National Park Foundation as a separate, fund-raising arm for the parks.
1984	The fossils of one of the oldest dinosaurs ever unearthed, *Chindesaurus bryansmalli* (nicknamed "Gertie"), are found in Petrified Forest National Park.
1987	Annual recreational visitors to the parks hits an all-time high: 287,244,998.
1988	Devastating fires rage through Yellowstone National Park, spreading to 793,000 of the park's 2.2 million acres.

1994	Death Valley and Joshua Tree National Monuments become national parks.
2001	The National Parks Legacy Project is established to provide funds to restore and improve park facilities and landscapes, increase park trails, and uphold existing initiatives to protect parkland from fires as well as mining and drilling operatives.

Resources

National Park Foundation. This is the nonprofit, fundraising arm of the National Park Service, administering grants and programs designed to support the parks. ☎ *202/354–6460* ⊕ *www.nationalparks.org.*

National Park Service. A bureau within the Department of the Interior, the NPS manages 401 sites, including the national parks, as well as battlefields, monuments, seashores, and other important areas. ☎ *202/208–3818* ⊕ *www.nps.gov.*

National Park System: Map and Guide. This two-part map and guide, published by the NPS, includes a full-color map and listing of activities at more than 300 parks and other federal lands. You can get it free online (PDF) from the Federal Citizen Information Center (FCIC) website. ☎ *719/295–2675* ⊕ *www.publications.usa.gov* ✉ *Free.*

National Parks Conservation Association. The NPCA is a nonpartisan advocacy group that raises awareness of the parks and the issues that face them through public, media, and government education. ☎ *800/628–7275* ⊕ *www.npca.org.*

Parks Canada. The Canadian equivalent of the U.S. National Park Service, this agency runs Canada's 215 national parks, historic sites, and marine conservation areas. ☎ *888/773–8888, 613/860–1251* ⊕ *www.pc.gc.ca.*

2007	Congress is presented with a record $2.4-billion budget for the parks, plus a $100-million donation match program as part of the Centennial Initiative.
2009	President Barack Obama signs the American Recovery and Reinvestment Act (ARRA), which allocates $3 billion to the Interior Department, including $750 million to restore and protect America's national parks.
2010	The Department of the Interior spends almost $270 million to enhance the infrastructure, facilities, and overall user experience within the National Parks and Wildlife Refuges under the AARA. At the one-year mark, the DOI had completed more than 80 projects within the NPS and was continuing work on another 243.
2011	The NPS announces its new Call to Action program, aimed at improving the parks without requiring additional federal funding.
2013	Pinnacles National Monument in California gains national park designation, becoming the newest national park.

FOUNDING FATHERS OF THE PARKS

Without Theodore Roosevelt and Franklin Delano Roosevelt, many of America's natural treasures would have ceased to exist. A generation apart, the two men were moved by the dire state of their nation's wilderness areas to make monumental changes in how the country preserved its outdoor wonders.

For Theodore, the impetus was the disappearance of the bison and rampant misuse of the land in the western United States. For Franklin, it was the needs of an unemployed population—and the need to save the country's ravaged forestland. Both men, through sheer force of will, drove their ideals into law.

Theodore, who believed America had an almost divine responsibility for proper stewardship of its ample resources, brought his conservationist leanings to the presidency in 1901. As part of his revolutionary administration, he established the U.S. Forest Service, along with 150 national forests, the first national wildlife refuge, 51 bird preserves, four game preserves, five national parks, and 18 national monuments, including four that became national parks—Grand Canyon, Petrified Forest, Lassen Peak, and Mount Olympus (now Olympic). His efforts accounted for more than half the lands that would be managed by the National Park Service when it was created in 1916—seven years after his presidency ended.

Franklin, who believed the president was called to lead with character and morality (and to rescue the country from the throes of the Great Depression), created millions of jobs on public works projects—including many in the national parks. Almost immediately after his inauguration in 1933, he developed the Civilian Conservation Corps. Over nine years,

DYNAMIC DUO

THEODORE ROOSEVELT
Lifespan: 1858–1919
Saying: "Speak softly and carry a big stick."
Regulated: Railroads
Unique qualities: Youngest president (age 42); won Nobel Peace Prize (for mediating the Russo-Japanese War)

FRANKLIN DELANO ROOSEVELT
Lifespan: 1882–1945
Saying: "The only thing we have to fear is fear itself."
Regulated: Wall Street
Unique qualities: Only president with polio; only four-term president; established the WPA (Works Progress Administration)

it employed 5% of American males and planted about 3 billion trees. The corps was instrumental in suppressing forest fires, clearing campgrounds, constructing roads and trails, controlling floods and soil erosion, and eradicating undesirable plants. The CCC also enabled the NPS to improve existing public lands, establish new national parks, and guide the development of a system of state parks. Seven states gained their first state parks through the CCC's efforts, and at the project's end in 1942, a total of 711 state parks had been established. Additionally, Franklin's Hyde Park, New York, home was added to the NPS holdings as a National Historic Site in 1946.

Though the inspiration for each differed, their contributions were similar, as are their legacies. They stand as giants among American presidents and as standard-bearers for government-aided conservation.

WILDLIFE IN THE PARKS

(A) Bats: Caves within the national parks teem with bats, the only mammals that can fly. Enormous bat colonies can be observed whirling and flying out of caves en masse at dusk for feeding time, returning around sunrise. You also can observe bats when they roost in snags—dead, hollowed-out trees left standing in the forest after lightning strikes and wildfires.

(B) Bighorn Sheep: Clambering along rocky ledges, muscular bighorn sheep fascinate with their ability to travel so easily where the rest of us can't. In winter the docile herd animals descend to lower elevations. Like their fellow park residents, the mule deer and elk, bighorns rut in autumn, when antlered males fight each other dramatically over mates. Rams have heavy, curled horns, while ewes' horns are short and slightly bent. From afar it's easy to spot both sexes' white rumps, which stand out brightly against their furry brown coats.

(C) Bison: The nappy, grouchy bison, also known as the American buffalo, may not be the Western frontier's most charismatic ungulate, but it's certainly the most iconic. Yellowstone is the only place in the country where bison have lived continuously since prehistoric times (between 2,300 and 4,500 animals make up the park's two herds), though you also can see the large creatures in other national parks. A bison can reach six feet at the shoulder, and males can weigh a ton (females typically weigh about 1,000 pounds). Bulls and cows alike sport short, curved horns, which they'll use to gore predators (or tourists who invade their space).

(D) Black Bear: Don't kid yourself: these excellent sniffers can smell your freeze-dried dinner from a mile away. Though they naturally forage for acorns and berries, black bears are omnivores and can be aggressive, especially if they're protecting their cubs. The animals measure about 3

feet at the shoulder and weigh up to 300 pounds, depending on their age and sex. They hibernate for about five months in the winter, and at lower elevations that see more moderate winters they may not sleep much at all. Most have inky black fur, but a brown or cinnamon color is not uncommon, especially in the western United States.

(E) Bobcat: Bobcats are solitary, elusive cats with reddish-brown coats, streaked with black or dark brown. They have prominent, pointed ears with a tuft of black hair at the tip and typically weigh between 16 and 30 pounds.

(F) Coyote: Coyotes are highly adaptable, intelligent animals (their name is derived from the Aztec word meaning "trickster") whose indiscriminate diets include carrion, small mammals, insects, and grasses. About the size of a mid-size dog, weighing between 25 and 35 pounds (much less than a wolf), the gray-tan canines thrive throughout the western United States.

They travel most often alone or in pairs, but occasionally form small packs for hunting. Although coyotes generally pose little threat to humans, you should never feed or approach one.

(G) Eagles: With a wingspan of 6 to 8 feet, bald eagles are primarily fish eaters, but they will also take birds or small mammals when the opportunity presents itself. Bald eagles' unmistakable white heads distinguish them from golden eagles, which nest on cliffs and prey on small mammals and birds. With a wingspan of up to 7½ feet, the adult golden eagle has plumage that is entirely dark, except for a golden head.

(H) Elk: A bull's antlers can weigh 40 pounds and, in summer, shed a soft fur known as antler velvet. Elk congregate where forest meets meadows, summering at high elevations before migrating lower in winter. In September and October, bulls attract a "harem" of mating partners by bugling, a loud and surreal whistling.

(I) Gray Wolf: These impressive canines, listed as threatened or endangered in parts of the United States, form close-knit family packs, which may range from a few animals to more than 30. They communicate with each other through body language, barks, and howls. Gray wolves tend to be 70 to 120 pounds, much larger than coyotes.

(J) Grizzly Bear: These furry bogeymen alternately fascinate and frighten. A mature male grizzly can weigh 700 pounds and stand about 3½ feet at the shoulder (or reach a height of 8 feet when standing up on its hind legs). Whitish shoulder hairs give grizzlies their name and help distinguish them from black bears, as do a distinctive muscle mass on their back and the convex curve of their snout. Grizzlies are also much larger and less common than black bears.

(K) Jackrabbit: Unmistakable for its mule-like ears and swift, bounding gait, the jackrabbit can induce a brief case of heart failure if you happen upon one and startle it into an explosive escape.

(L) Marmot: A few species of marmot like to live high up among granite rock piles of talus slopes and along riverbanks, so if you see them, it's likely to be along high-country trails. The rocky strongholds help protect these furry ground squirrels—one of the largest rodents in North America—from such natural predators as eagles and hawks.

(M) Moose: Feeding on fir, willows, and aspens, the moose is the largest member of the deer family: the largest bulls stand 7 feet tall at the shoulders and weigh up to 1,600 pounds. The moose's distinctive characteristics include its antlers, which lay flat like palmate satellite dishes, and its pendulous (and prehensile) upper lip. The peak of breeding occurs in late September. Females give birth to calves in late May and early June; twins are the norm.

(N) Mountain Goat: Not really goats at all (they're actually related to antelope), these woolly mountaineers live in high elevations throughout the northwestern United States.

(O) Mountain Lion: Although mountain lions live throughout the American west (their range runs from northern Canada through the South American Andes), chances are you won't see them at most of the parks due to their elusive nature. Also called cougars, these enormous carnivores can be 8 feet long and weigh up to 200 pounds. They're capable of taking down a mule deer or elk.

(P) Mule Deer: Often seen grazing in meadows and forests are mule deer, with their black-tipped tails and distinctive mulelike ears. Mule deer can run like other deer or do what's known as stotting—springing gazelle-like with all four feet leaving the ground at once—which allows them to move change directions instantly and gives them an advantage over predators.

(Q) Prairie Dog: Called "petit chien" (little dog) by French explorers, the prairie dog is a prolific member of the squirrel family. They get their name from the way they communicate: It sounds like a bark.

Pronghorn: Pronghorns are North America's only native hooved mammals and are one of the fastest land animals in the world, capable of speeds of up to 70 mph. Often called "antelopes," even though they're technically a different species, pronghorns can be spotted in open grassland areas.

Rattlesnake: About a dozen species of rattlesnake live in the American West, where in cooler weather they enjoy sunning on rocks or coiling in other open spaces. A snake will typically strike only when it senses a threat, but when it does bite, it can deliver a lethal dose of venom.

FIELD GUIDE: GEOLOGY AND TERRAIN

Arches and Bridges

(A) An arch is a window in a rock wall that typically forms through erosion, when wind and/or water wear away the rock face to create a hole that extends all the way through the rock. A natural bridge is a type of arch that was created by rushing water. Together, the two types of forms are called windows.

Buttes and Spires

(B) A butte is an isolated hill with very steep sides and a flat top (it's defined as a hill that's higher than it is wide). Buttes are formed in sedimentary (layered) rock by erosion, when wind or water wear away softer layers to leave a section of harder rock behind. As a butte erodes, it may become one or more spires, which look like giant stone columns (with a uniform thickness and smooth profile that tapers slightly at the top).

Canyons

(C) A canyon, also known as a gorge, forms when water (usually a river or glacier) erodes soft layers of Earth's crust. The hardness of the rock determines the shape of the canyon: a narrow, or slot, canyon generally results when the rock is the same composition all the way down and water runs through the crack. A stepped canyon, such as the Grand Canyon, forms when alternating soft and hard layers are eroded by wind and water, with a river cutting a groove at the bottom.

Caves

Caves—or caverns—are natural underground chambers that give you an opportunity to descend below Earth's surface and learn about the forces of heat and water upon rocks and minerals.

Craters and Calderas

(D) A crater is a bowl-shape depression that's left behind when a volcano erupts. A caldera (Spanish for "cooking pot" or "cauldron") is essentially a big, sunken crater in which the volcano's inner magma chamber has also collapsed.

Desert Pavement

(E) High winds can scour away sand, silt, and other small particles of soil, leaving behind a densely packed layer of coarse pebbles and gravel known as desert pavement. This surface acts as a protective crust and is fragile, so you shouldn't walk on it.

Desert Varnish

(F) This reddish-brown or black coating, sometimes called rock varnish, seems to drip down arid canyon walls as if from a spilled can of paint. Windblown dust or rain containing iron and manganese, along with microorganisms living on the rock's surface, create the color. Ancestral Puebloans and other ancient American Indians scratched drawings, called petroglyphs, into it.

Erosion and Weathering

(G) The mechanical wearing away of Earth's surface by water, ice, or wind, which use abrasive elements like sand or small rocks to remove the material. Weathering often accompanies and assists erosion by using chemical action (from things like water, air, plants, and bacteria) and temperature changes (freeze/thaw cycles).

Fault Zones

(H) Shifting underground land masses such as those of California's famous San Andreas Fault have helped create many of the dramatic elevations in the parks, and this same geologic upheaval has shifted and cracked underground rocks, damming up the flow of groundwater and forcing it to the surface, making precious moisture available to wildlife and plants.

Geothermal Features

(I) Hissing geysers, burbling mudpots, and steaming hot springs have fascinated travelers ever since mountain man John Coulter described them to an unbelieving public in 1810. Today, these "freaks of a fiery nature," as Rudyard Kipling described them, are created when superheated water rises to Earth's surface from a magma chamber below. In the case of geysers, the water is trapped under the surface until the pressure is so great that it bursts through. Mudpots, also known as paint pots, are a combination of hot water, hydrogen sulfide gas, and dissolved volcanic rock. The mixture looks like a hot, smelly, burping pudding.

Glaciers and Glacial Features

(J) Heavy snow compacted by centuries of pressure forms the slow-moving river of ice known as a glacier. Although most of the glaciers of North America have retreated, you can still see them in some of the Western parks.

Mesas and Cuestas

(K) A mesa ("table" in Spanish) is an isolated hill with a smooth, flat top and steeply sloping sides. Its topmost layer is comprised of rock that is much harder than the rocks below, which protects the lower layers from erosion. A cuesta is essentially a mesa that dips slightly to one side. A single mesa or cuesta may cover hundreds of square miles.

Monument

(L) This general term applies to two distinct geologic formations: those that are much taller than they are wide, and those that resemble man-made structures.

Peaks

A peak is what most people picture when they think "mountain"—a horn-shape formation created by ancient ice that juts up into the sky, generally surrounded by smaller peaks and gentler foothills.

Playas

(M) Shallow lake beds known as playas ("beaches" in Spanish) commonly lie in the low points of arid Southwestern valleys. These sedimentary basins often fill with rainwater, then dry again as the water evaporates.

Spheroidal Weathering

This unique type of chemical weathering is similar to exfoliation. It typically affects sandstone and intrusive igneous rock (the kind that's created when superheated molten rock seeps up from beneath Earth's crust to reach the surface).

Volcanoes and Volcanism

(N) Volcanoes are openings in Earth's crust where magma reaches the surface. Volcanic activity, or volcanism, can create many geologic formations beyond the lava-spewing, cone-shape mountains most of us think of as volcanoes. For example, volcanic intrusions, which are formed where magma pushes up between sections of existing rock, can create formations such as batholiths (large rounded domes), dikes and sills (banded, sheetlike formations), and laccoliths (domes created when magma pushes up on existing rock layers instead of erupting out). Geothermal features occur when water enters the picture.

GREAT LODGES
OF THE NATIONAL PARKS

by Marge Peterson

"IF YOU BUILD IT, THEY WILL COME" could apply to the railroad barons who laid track in the early 1900s to lure wealthy Easterners westward. But these scrappy companies took the declaration an inspired step further by building luxury hotels at the end of the line.

In 1901 the Atchison, Topeka, and Santa Fe Railway finished a 65-mi railroad spur from Williams, Arizona, to the South Rim of the Grand Canyon, and soon after built the spectacular Arizona lodge El Tovar. Union Pacific helped finance lodges at Bryce and Zion, Northern Pacific was behind the hotels in Yellowstone, and the Great Northern Railway built Glacier Park Lodge, and many other Glacier hotels. Today, the rails don't drive

tourism to the parks all that much. But the lodges still do. And you don't have to be wealthy to stay in one.

What makes them great? Unlike previous wilderness accommodations, which were built like city hotels so guests would feel safe, these new lodges incorporated materials from the environment like the lodgepole pines and Rhyolite stone used in building Old Faithful Inn. As long as these nature-inspired structures had creature comforts—which then, and in some cases now, doesn't include in-room televisions—architects felt guests would be happy.

> Architects felt guests would be happy as long as the lodges had creature comforts.

Opposite: Balconies claw skyward in the Old Faithful Inn's 76-foot-high lobby. *Above:* The historic El Tovar Hotel sits at the edge of the Grand Canyon's South Rim.

TOP LODGES

EL TOVAR, GRAND CANYON

"In the Grand Canyon, Arizona has a natural wonder, which, so far as I know, is in kind unparalleled throughout the rest of the world," said Teddy Roosevelt in 1903, speaking from the area where the El Tovar would open two years later. "What you can do is to keep it for your children, your children's children, and for all who come after you, as one of the great sights which every American if he can travel at all should see."

Set atop the South Rim of the Grand Canyon, El Tovar so blends into the landscape, with its stone foundation and rugged beams, that it looks almost like another tier of the multilayered, multihued canyon. With the elegance of a European villa and warm atmosphere of a rustic log cabin, it is arguably the most luxurious of the lodges.

Opened in 1905, El Tovar was named for Spanish explorer Don Pedro de Tobar (the "b" was changed to "v" to avoid people saying "to the bar") and was designed by architect Charles Whittlesey. Built for $250,000, it had 95 rooms, electricity, indoor plumbing, steam heat, solariums, and lounges. Originally, Jersey cows and poultry grazed on site, and greenhouses provided fresh herbs and flowers for guests feasting in the dining room. One of its most famous diners and overnight guests was **Teddy Roosevelt**, who came to dinner in muddy boots and dusty riding gear—or so says local lore. In addition to Roosevelt, seven other presidents have stayed here. For its 100th birthday, the hotel received a $4.6 million restoration.

Ahwahnee Hotel

AHWAHNEE HOTEL, YOSEMITE

Blending into a backdrop of granite cliffs, the elegant Ahwahnee Hotel, which opened in 1927, is six stories tall with three wings in a "Y" layout. Then-NPS Director Stephen Mather believed that attracting wealthy, influential folks into Yosemite would lend support and congressional funding to the national parks system.

Architect Gilbert Stanley Underwood was commissioned to build a first-class fireproof hotel that blended in with the landscape. In order to resist fire, concrete was formed within timbers and then dyed to resemble redwood. The motifs and patterns found in the basketry of the local Indian tribes were used on the ceiling beams, stained-glass windows, and concrete floors. Luminaries who have signed the lodge guest book include Franklin and Eleanor Roosevelt, John F. Kennedy, Queen Elizabeth, and Clark Gable.

Right, president Teddy Roosevelt.

OLD FAITHFUL INN, YELLOWSTONE

Amazement and awe may best describe the reaction of people entering the lobby of Old Faithful Inn for the first time. Its 76-foot high lobby has four levels of balconies with supports created from a tangle of gnarled branches reaching the ceiling. It was built in 1903–1904 at a cost of $140,000. Wings were added to the hotel in 1915 and 1927—it would be difficult to duplicate the inn's construction today, as cutting down trees, gathering wood, and quarrying rock inside the park are now illegal.

The park's most famous geyser, Old Faithful, is less than 100 yards from the inn. Approximate times for its eruptions are posted in the lobby.

WHAT TO EXPECT

Some lodges were built more than 100 years ago, when rooms and beds were smaller. However, the difference in room size is more than offset by the huge amount of public space offered on the properties. The availability of television and Internet access varies from lodge to lodge.

BRYCE CANYON LODGE

Bryce Canyon Lodge was the second structure built in the Union Pacific's Loop Tours building program, which included lodges in Zion and the Grand Canyon National Parks. In a grove of ponderosa pines within walking distance of the rim, the lodge opened in 1925 and expanded throughout the late 1920s. It now has 70 guest rooms, three deluxe suites, one studio room, and 40 log cabins. The property was known for its sing-aways, where employees lined up in front of the lodge and sang a farewell to departing guests. When plans to build a second lodge on the rim didn't materialize, a gift shop, soda fountain, barbershop, and auditorium were added.

Above, Old Faithful Inn. Top, Bryce Canyon Lodge.

Crater Lake Lodge

CRATER LAKE LODGE

When Crater Lake Lodge opened in 1915, it was anything but grand: the exterior was covered in tarpaper, fiberboard separated the guest rooms, bathrooms were shared, and the electricity seldom worked. But visitors loved it anyway because of the lake view. Due to its structural defects and lack of funding, the building was closed to the public in 1989. Public pressure convinced the National Park Service to spend $15 million for renovations, and the lodge was completely rebuilt and reopened in May 1995. Perched on the rim of a defunct caldera filled with cobalt blue water, the lodge has a fantastic deck, as well as an architectural trademark, a massive stone fireplace.

GLACIER PARK LODGE

An eclectic interior design with towering tree trunks highlights Glacier Park Lodge. Samuel L. Bartlett was the architect of record, but Louis Hill, president of the Great Northern Railway, controlled every aspect of the design. Hill based the lodge, which opened in 1913, on a Christian basilica, creating a rustic, cathedral-like building. He had 60 Douglas firs (averaging 40 feet high and 40 inches in diameter) shipped in from the Pacific Northwest for the construction.

When rail passengers arrived at Glacier Park Station, they saw Indian teepees scattered across the lawn as part of a show presented to visitors, along with colorful banks of flowers surrounding the majestic lodge.

The park and lodge were heavily promoted. On top of the half a million dollars it took to build and furnish Glacier Park Lodge, Hill spent $300,000 on artists, filmmakers, calendars, playing cards, and a special train car with a public exhibit. *The New York Times* said, "Next to Col. Roosevelt, L.W. Hill is about the best advertising man in the United States."

Glacier Park Lodge

LAKE LOUISE & BANFF SPRINGS LODGES

In the late 1800s, William Cornelius Van Horne, general manager of the Canadian Pacific Railway, said, "Since we can't export the scenery, we will have to import the tourists." And so they did. The railroad developed Fairmont Banff Springs Hotel and the Fairmont Chateau Lake Louise, both of which opened their doors in 1890.

While the great lodges of America's national parks have a comfortable hunting-lodge aura, Canada's Banff and Lake Louise accommodations have a stately, opulent ambience.

Banff Springs Hotel

Fairmont Banff Springs, a mile walk from downtown Banff, is styled after a Scottish baronial castle. Combining the best of the past with the amenities sought by modern-day travelers, the hotel offers tennis, golf, bowling, horseback rides, indoor and outdoor swimming, and one of the largest spas in Canada.

Surrounded by snow-tipped mountain peaks and the majestic Victorian Glacier, Chateau Lake Louise is on the shore of pristine Lake Louise, where you can hike, downhill or cross-country ski, cycle, and canoe.

TO RESERVE A ROOM

Reservations at historic lodges should be made six months to a year in advance (for Yellowstone, definitely 12 months in advance) directly with the lodge's websites; however, you can always check for last-minute cancellations. Be wary of other Internet reservation services that charge a non-refundable fee of up to 12 percent to book the lodging. ■ TIP➔ Dining reservations at lodge restaurants often can be made when you book your room.

OTHER GREAT LODGES

Zion Park Lodge.

GLACIER NATIONAL PARK
Belton Chalet, Lake McDonald Lodge, Many Glacier Hotel, Sperry & Granite Park Chalets

GRAND CANYON NATIONAL PARK
Grand Canyon Lodge—North Rim

MOUNT RAINIER NATIONAL PARK
Paradise Inn

WATERTON LAKES NATIONAL PARK
Prince of Wales Hotel

ZION NATIONAL PARK
Zion Park Lodge

CHOOSING
A PARK

WHAT'S WHERE

Parks in this section are organized by state; numbers refer to chapters in the book.

Canada

7 Banff. The Canadian Rockies are one of the most beautiful ranges on Earth, and Canada's first national park is nestled among these mountains, glaciers, and forests. It also has some of the world's best skiing. **Best Paired With:** Jasper

23 Jasper. One of the largest protected mountain ecosystems in the world and the largest of the Canadian Rocky Mountain parks, Jasper woos visitors with its lakes, glaciers, waterfalls, and mountains. **Best Paired With:** Banff

Washington

27 Mount Rainier. The fifth-highest mountain in the Lower 48, Mt. Rainier is so massive that the summit is rarely visible—but when conditions are right, the image of the entire mountain is unforgettable. Hikes cover temperate rainforest, old-growth forests of hemlock and fir, high meadows, and tundra—not to mention hot springs, glaciers, lakes, and waterfalls. **Best Paired With:** North Cascades and Olympic

28 North Cascades. Hiking on a real glacier is a memorable experience—especially if you add in marmots, golden eagles, and coyotes—and North Cascades is home to several hundred of them. **Best Paired With:** Mt. Rainier and Olympic

29 Olympic. Centered on Mt. Olympus and framed on three sides by water, this park is known for its temperate rain forests, rugged coastal expanses, Sol Duc hot springs, and hiking (or skiing) at Hurricane Ridge. **Best Paired With:** North Cascades and Mt. Rainier

Oregon

15 Crater Lake. Crater Lake is a geological marvel—the 21-square-mile sapphire-blue lake inside a caldera is the nation's deepest. The park itself includes about 90 miles of trails. **Best Paired With:** Mt. Rainier and Olympic or Redwood and Lassen Volcanic

Montana

17 Glacier–Waterton Lakes. The rugged mountains that weave their way through the Continental Divide in northwest Montana are the backbone of Glacier and its sister park in Canada, Waterton Lakes. The park's Going-to-the-Sun Road is a spectacular drive that crosses the crest of the Continental Divide. **Best Paired With:** Glacier and Waterton Lakes are best visited together.

North Dakota

36 Theodore Roosevelt. Theodore Roosevelt is known for chunks of badlands on the Little Missouri River and the 26th president's beloved Elkhorn Ranch. This is one of the most isolated parks in the country.

Wyoming

19 Grand Teton. With no foothills, the unimpeded view of the Teton Range rising out of Jackson Hole is stunning. Wildlife from short-tailed weasels to grizzly bears abound. **Best Paired With:** Yellowstone

38 Yellowstone. Best known for Old Faithful, the world's most famous geyser, flowing hot springs, and mudpots, Yellowstone is the oldest national park in the world. Spotting the abundant wildlife, like bison, elk, moose, and bears is the other main draw. **Best Paired With:** Grand Teton

South Dakota

6 Badlands. The park's eroded buttes and spires cast amazing shades of red and yellow across the South Dakota prairie. In addition to scenery, it has some of the world's richest mammal fossil beds. **Best Paired With:** Wind Cave

37 Wind Cave. One of the largest caves in the world, with beautiful cave formations including boxwork (3-D calcite honeycomb patterns on cave walls and ceilings), Wind Cave is the place to go spelunking. **Best Paired With:** Badlands

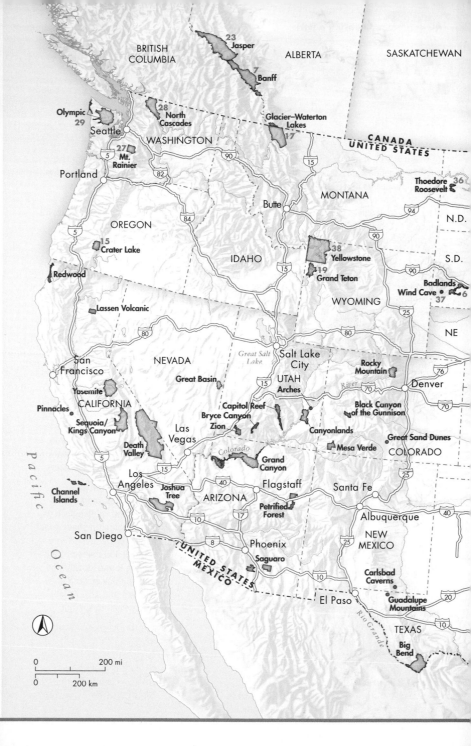

WHAT'S WHERE

Nevada

20 Great Basin. It may be one of the nation's least visited national parks (there isn't even an entrance fee), but the stalactites, stalagmites, and popcorn in Lehman Caves and the solitude of backcountry treks are big draws.

Utah

5 Arches. Four hours (235 miles) from Salt Lake City, this park has the world's largest concentration of natural sandstone arches, including that most-famous symbol of Utah, Delicate Arch. Nearby is Moab, an adventure hotspot, with world-class white-water rafting on the Colorado River, rock climbing, four-wheeling, and mountain biking. **Best Paired With:** Canyonlands

10 Bryce Canyon. Exploring the hoodoos (spectacular columns of rock) at this park is like wandering through a giant maze. Bryce is within a few hours of Utah's other national parks and near Kodachrome Basin State Park and Grand Staircase–Escalante National Monument. **Best Paired With:** Capitol Reef and Zion

11 Canyonlands. Biking on White Rim Road, whitewater rafting in Cataract Canyon—plus spires, pinnacles, cliffs, and mesas as far as the eye can see are the top reasons to go. **Best Paired With:** Arches

12 Capitol Reef. Seven times larger than nearby Bryce Canyon and much less crowded, Capitol Reef is known for its 100-mile-long Waterpocket Fold, a monocline (or "wrinkle" in the Earth's crust). It has many options for day hikes as well as backcountry trips into slot canyons, arches, cliffs, domes, and slickrock. **Best Paired With:** Bryce Canyon and Zion

40 Zion. Sheer 2,000-foot cliffs and river-carved canyons are what Zion is all about, and hiking the Narrows and the Subway are on many an adventurer's bucket-list. Zion is right next to hospitable Springdale, which is full of amenities and charm. **Best Paired With:** Bryce Canyon and Grand Canyon

Colorado

9 Black Canyon of the Gunnison. This steep and narrow river gorge has sheer cliffs and a drop twice as high as the Empire State Building.

21 Great Sand Dunes. The 30 square miles of landlocked dune fields are an impressive sight. Aside from the dunes there are eight different life zones to explore, ranging from salty wetlands to alpine peaks.

26 Mesa Verde. Located in the Four Corners region—the junction of Utah, Colorado, New Mexico, and Arizona—this park houses an amazing collection of Ancestral Puebloan dwellings, some carved directly into cliff faces, and ancient artifacts.

33 Rocky Mountain. Alpine lakes, mountain peaks, and wildlife such as elk and bighorn sheep draw visitors to the park. There are also 355 miles of trails leading to meadows filled with wildflowers and crystal lakes and 14,259-foot Long's Peak to summit.

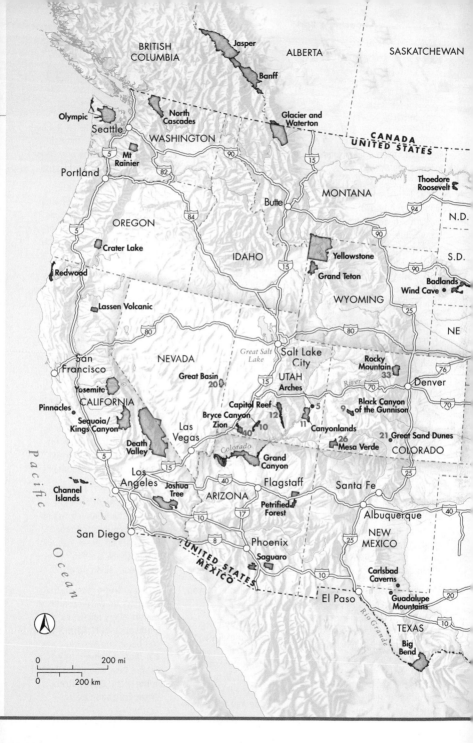

WHAT'S WHERE

California
14 Channel Islands.
You must take a boat or plane to reach the five islands, which are home to 145 species of terrestrial plants and animals found nowhere else on Earth. You're bound to see wildlife such as dolphins, sea lions, island foxes, and pelicans and can kayak, dive, and go whale-watching. **Best Paired With:** Yosemite and Sequoia and Kings Canyon

16 Death Valley. This is a vast, lonely, beautiful place with breathtaking vistas, blasting 120-degree heat, and mysterious moving rocks. The desert landscape is surrounded by majestic mountains, dry lakebeds, spring wildflowers, and Wild West ghost towns. **Best Paired With:** Joshua Tree and Zion

24 Joshua Tree. Large stands of Joshua trees gave the park its name, but it's also a great spot for bouldering and rock climbing. Brilliant wildflower displays and starry nights add to the draw. **Best Paired With:** Death Valley

25 Lassen Volcanic. Lassen Peak, a dormant plug dome volcano that last erupted in 1915, and every other type of known volcano (shield, cinder cone, and composite) are here, as well as roiling mud pots and hissing steam vents. **Best Paired With:** Redwood and Crater Lake or Yosemite

31 Pinnacles. Hiking among volcanic spires is a popular activity at Pinnacles, and the best chance you'll have at encountering one of the rare California condors that make their home here. **Best Paired With:** Yosemite

32 Redwood. Home to the world's tallest trees: giant coast redwoods, which grow to more than 300 feet tall. **Best Paired With:** Lassen Volcanic and Crater Lake

35 Sequoia and Kings Canyon. Sequoias are the big trees here, which have huge trunks and branches. The Generals Highway features these natural marvels. The Kings Canyon Scenic Byway offers views into a canyon deeper than the Grand Canyon. **Best Paired With:** Yosemite National Park

39 Yosemite. Dozens of famed features, from the soaring granite monoliths of Half Dome and El Capitan, to shimmering waterfalls like Yosemite Falls and Bridalveil Fall, lie within reach in the Yosemite Valley. **Paired With:** Sequoia and Kings Canyon

Arizona
18 Grand Canyon. The Grand Canyon exalts and humbles the human spirit. You can view the spectacle from the South Rim, the North Rim, or hike or take a mule ride into the canyon for a richer experience. Rafting the Colorado River through the canyon can't be beat. **Best Paired With:** Petrified Forest

30 Petrified Forest. This park is known for fallen and fossilized trees, which look like they are made of colorful stone. **Best Paired With:** Grand Canyon

34 Saguaro. The park takes its name from the saguaro cactus, found here. The park is split into two districts bookending Tucson (about 30 miles apart); the better collection of cacti is found in the west district.

New Mexico
13 Carlsbad Caverns.
The park's 113 caves, bizarre underground rock formations, and 400,000 diving, dipping, sonar-blipping bats are the main draws. **Best Paired With:** Guadalupe Mountains

Texas
8 Big Bend. In a remote location, with the Rio Grande River along its southern border, its limitless skies and ample space are two of its strongest selling points.

22 Guadalupe Mountains. This park draws thousands of visitors every fall, when the hardwoods of McKittrick Canyon burst into flaming color. The park is home to the Guadalupe Peak, the highest point in the state. **Best Paired With:** Carlsbad Caverns

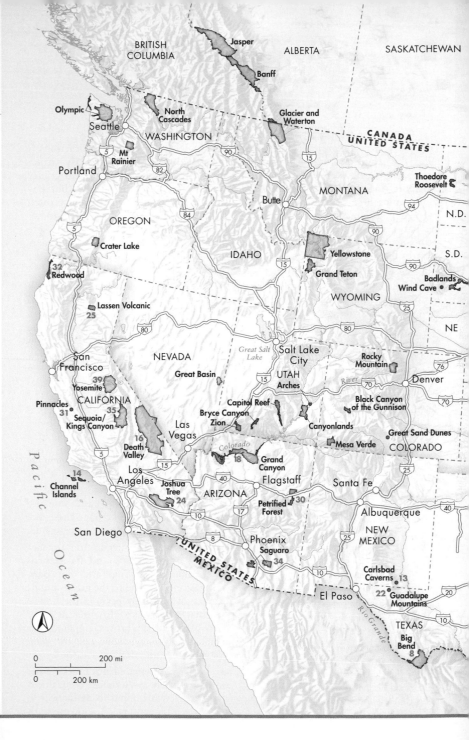

THE BEST OF THE NATIONAL PARKS

Best Parks for Accessibility

The best way to get an in-depth look at the parks is by exploring them on foot, horseback, or via some other mode of transportation, but sometimes physical conditioning or time prevents this from happening. The main sites at the following parks aren't too far off the beaten path—many are even visible from the comfort of your car.

■ **Badlands.** Drive slowly on the two-lane loop through the park, setting aside plenty of time for stopping at the overlooks. The view changes as you drive, moving from rocky formations to prairie.

■ **Bryce.** The 18-mile road along Plateau Rim has numerous overlooks and a handful of spurs, and provides fabulous views of this park's famous red-orange hoodoos and points beyond. If you want to journey beyond the overlooks, several nearby trailheads offer quick escapes into the park's interior.

■ **Crater Lake.** View the lake from various perspectives along the 33-mile loop Rim Drive. Though you can see much without pulling over, take the time to stop at a few overlooks off the road. The drive will take two or more hours.

■ **Mesa Verde.** Once the main park road passes the Morefield Campground, it forks, and the two branches lead to the archaeological treasures of the Wetherill and Chapin Mesas, respectively. Most sites are close enough to be viewed from the road, but short trails lead in for a closer look (and a few sites are wheelchair accessible).

■ **Petrified Forest.** Whether you enter from the north or the south entrance, the 28-mile park road leads to both visitor centers and a handful of quick and easy trails that meander among petrified trees.

Best Parks for Bear Spotting

One of the parks' greatest attractions is their wildlife, and few animals attract as much attention as black and grizzly bears. Cubs are cute and playful, but they shouldn't be approached—Mama is often close and will view you as a threat to her little ones. Still, when seen from a safe distance, bears serve as great reminders of the wildness that the national parks are meant to preserve and protect.

■ **Glacier.** There are so many black and grizzly bears in this part of Montana that they often come onto people's property, getting inside homes and causing general mayhem—though attacks on humans are rare. When hiking, make noise, especially when about to turn a corner or bend in the road. Say "Hey, bear!" and clap your hands.

■ **Waterton.** In this Canadian national park, grasslands sweep up the lower slopes of the mountains providing a unique topography that lends itself well to wonderful wildlife viewing. Grizzlies and black bears can be seen from park roads and watched safely from the inside of a vehicle. Bears are plentiful in the park, so make sure you always hike in groups and make enough noise that you won't surprise one.

■ **Yellowstone.** The inspiration for fictional Jellystone Park and its anthropomorphic bears Yogi and Boo-Boo, Yellowstone is home to the greatest concentration of grizzly bears in the Lower 48. Black bears are also present here. They can be blond, brown, cinnamon, or black. If you see a bear in the park, keep your distance and don't give it food.

■ **Yosemite.** American black bears are the only bruins left in Yosemite (the California grizzly was hunted to extinction in the early 20th century). Today, the park

is home to between 300 and 500 black bears; most are brown. If a bear threatens you, make noise and look big.

Best Parks for Burning Calories

The national parks are great places for a workout. Whether you walk, run, ski, paddle, or bike, you'll rarely have an excuse not to keep up with your exercise regimen while you're on vacation here. Hard-core fitness junkies should check out the following parks, which are particularly well suited for extreme exertion.

■ **Canyonlands.** Three distinct areas, or districts—Island in the Sky, the Maze, and the Needles—comprise this popular but spacious national park; each one offers plenty of opportunities to put boot (or mountain bike) to sandstone and become totally immersed in sun and solitude. The Maze is your best bet for getting away from it all—you can reach it only by driving at least 20 miles on lonely dirt roads.

■ **Channel Islands.** Kayakers can explore 175 miles of picturesque coastline around this island park, including one of the world's largest sea caves. Marine mammal sightings are common, and below the waves a kelp forest makes for some of the best scuba diving in the world. On land, take a hike to discover nearly 150 species of plants and animals that exist nowhere else on earth.

■ **Mount Rainier.** This Washington park is encircled by the aptly named Wonderland Trail—a whopping 93-mile trek that takes 10–14 days to complete. It's as rugged as it is long; elevation gains and losses of 3,500 feet in a day are not uncommon. Snow hangs around higher elevations into June and even July, and rain can appear at almost any time. The faint of heart and tender of sole should tramp elsewhere.

Best Parks for Cultural History

When you're surrounded by such overwhelming natural beauty, and so many opportunities to take part in outdoor activities, it's easy to overlook the parks' cultural attractions. But it would be a shame to miss out on a history lesson during your visit, whether it's touring an ancient dwelling, witnessing a historical reenactment, or visiting a great American icon.

■ **Mesa Verde.** Established in 1906, Mesa Verde was the first national park to "preserve the works of man," according to President Theodore Roosevelt. The ancestral Pueblo people lived here from AD 550 to AD 1300, and to date more than 4,000 archaeological sites— including 600 cliff dwellings—have been unearthed. Today, researchers continue to discover and catalog artifacts at Mesa Verde on a regular basis.

■ **Petrified Forest.** The roots at this park aren't just from its ancient trees: the area's human history and culture extend back more than 13,000 years, from prehistoric people to the more modern travelers of Route 66. You can still see petroglyphs scratched and carved into stone, as well as many other artifacts, from the ancestors of the Hopi, Zuni, and Navajo.

■ **Theodore Roosevelt.** It's fitting that Theodore Roosevelt—a major proponent of preservation who signed into law five national parks—should have a national park named in his honor. This North Dakota gem contains land that was once part of Roosevelt's Dakota Territory ranch. Visitors can step inside the former president's log cabin or peruse the visitor center's wide selection of books, posters, audio recordings, and videos dedicated to telling his many stories.

Best Parks for Day-Trippers

Some urbanites are fortunate to live just a short drive away from a national park. For those who live elsewhere, these parks have large gateway cities nearby that are served by major airports with plenty of car rental agencies, making a trip to a park a surprisingly quick getaway.

■ **Joshua Tree.** A quick two- or three-hour drive east from the urban sprawl of Los Angeles brings you to the junction of the Mojave and Colorado deserts. Joshua Tree National Park, named for extensive stands of the gnarled tree, is home to one of the finest wildflower displays in Southern California each spring.

■ **Mount Rainier.** Why just stare at the elusive, majestic mountain from afar? Seattle residents and visitors can easily make their way to Mt. Rainier National Park, just 60 miles away. You can pack a lot in a day: gawk at glaciers, hike one of the trails (the park has more than 240 miles of maintained trails), and poke around the Longmire historic district.

■ **Rocky Mountain.** It's about a 1½-hour drive from Denver up to one of the most visited national parks in the country, where you can view elk, enjoy alpine scenery, and myriad flora and fauna. Hiking and picnicking along its lakes make perfect activities for a day retreat.

■ **Saguaro.** You'll find the largest concentration of the towering saguaro cactus, famed emblem of the desert southwest, just minutes outside Tucson. The park is divided into two sections: the Rincon Mountain District to the east and the Tucson Mountain District to the west.

Best Parks for Desert Solitude

America's national parks run the gamut in terms of cultural, geographic, and geological attractions, but the desolate, arid environs offer a unique experience often colored by our nation's romantic notion of the desert. If you're seeking peace and quiet, you'll likely find it here.

■ **Arches.** Edward Abbey wrote his seminal *Desert Solitaire,* the book that defined the term, while stationed here as a park ranger in the 1960s. Though most often seen by car these days, Arches has an uncrowded backcountry that Abbey—were he alive—would argue is the best way to experience the place anyhow.

■ **Big Bend.** Even in West Texas—a region known for wide-open and silent spaces—Big Bend is quite remote. Among the least visited of the nation's national parks, it was dubbed El Despoblado (The Unpopulated Place), by early Spanish explorers, and has changed little since then. This is a great place to lose yourself among cacti and sprawling mountains.

■ **Death Valley.** With its inhospitable environment and forbidding name, Death Valley has come to epitomize the desert of the American Southwest. It attracts only one million visitors a year, mainly outside the scorching summer months—but even in the high season, the park's vast 3.4 million acres of space guarantee peace and solitude.

■ **Joshua Tree.** This south-central California park is prime hiking, rock-climbing, and exploring country, where you can have a close-up encounter with coyotes, desert pack rats, golden eagles, rattlers, and exotic plants like the creamy white yucca, crimson-tipped ocotillo, and spiny cholla cactus.

Best Parks for Fun and Funky Activities

All the national parks exist for a reason: to protect something that was deemed worthy of recognition and preservation. Still, a few have such unusual and unique features, or unusual surroundings, that they stand out from the rest.

■ **Badlands.** The park and surrounding Black Hills are perfect for family getaways, and you can't get much funkier than Wall Drug on Main Street in nearby Wall, South Dakota. It even has an animated T. rex in the yard. In the park itself, visiting the prairie-dog towns and seeing these creatures' antics can bring laughter to your carload of people.

■ **Carlsbad Caverns.** From mid-May to mid-October, watch thousands of bats spiral up into the evening sky from deep within the earth as they set out on their nightly hunt. If possible, get in on the ranger-led discussion beforehand in the nearby amphitheater.

■ **Crater Lake.** Take a boat tour on the clearest, deepest lake in the United States (and the seventh deepest in the world). Formed by volcanic activity, Crater Lake's deepest point is 1,943 feet down, and the sapphire-blue water is so clear that sunlight can penetrate to a depth of 400 feet.

■ **Lassen Volcanic.** Though dormant since 1921, activity around volcanic Lassen Peak makes it clear that there's still a lot going on beneath the ground. Fumaroles, mudpots, and bubbling hot springs dot the landscape. It's a fun and sometimes-smelly place to explore, but beware of the scalding water.

Best Parks for Getting a Taste of the Wild West

The American West isn't as wild as it once was, but you can find traces of its storied past. From small preserved towns to vast desert spaces, it's still possible to feel like you've stepped into a Western movie.

■ **Badlands.** Few words conjure up images of the old Wild West better than the word "Badlands"—except maybe "Deadwood," a town 100 miles northwest of the park. Once an infamous gold camp, the entire town of Deadwood has been named a National Historic Landmark. A nearby cemetery is the final resting place of Wild Bill Hickok and Calamity Jane.

■ **Big Bend.** Far from civilization, this West Texas park can easily bring out the John Wayne or Clint Eastwood in you. The desert environs are exactly where a Hollywood cowboy would feel at home. Try a tour by horseback to complete the experience.

■ **Death Valley.** Death Valley is not the most hospitable place—at least during certain times of the year—but the climate isn't as horrible as the park's reputation would suggest. Still, the name and the location have long epitomized the very idea of the desert in American literature, film, and television.

■ **Zion.** Thirty miles southeast of Zion's east entrance is the small city of Kanab, Utah, famously known as Little Hollywood for all the old Westerns shot in its environs. Downtown hotels still highlight the rooms where John Wayne and other film stars slept. This area of southern Utah has also served as the backdrop for TV shows (including *Gunsmoke*) and many Jeep commercials.

Best Parks for Inspiration

It's hard to not be inspired when you're at a national park. Natural wonders, peace and quiet, and ancient sites will likely leave you awestruck, no matter where you visit. These five parks, however, have left their mark on some famous visitors and influenced their subsequent work.

■ **Glacier.** It took a lot to impress pioneering naturalist John Muir, who once called Glacier a "precious reserve" and "the best care-killing scenery on the continent." Take a boat ride on one of the lakes for particularly inspiring views.

■ **Great Basin.** Among America's least visited national parks, Great Basin is also one of the most beautiful. Tucked away on Nevada's eastern border, far from major population centers, the park is a great place to hide from life and work back home.

■ **North Cascades.** Jack Kerouac, Gary Snyder, and Philip Whalen, fixtures of the Beat scene, all worked as National Park Service fire lookouts in the 1950s at Desolation Peak in North Cascades. Portions of Kerouac's *Desolation Angels* and *The Dharma Bums* chronicle his experiences on the mountain.

■ **Rocky Mountain.** With more than 60 mountains 12,000 feet or higher, 355 miles of hiking trails, 150 lakes, 450 miles of streams, and countless far-reaching vistas, Rocky Mountain has plenty to keep you inspired (and off the phone).

■ **Yosemite.** Ansel Adams's repeated visits to Yosemite provided him with the intimate understanding necessary to pre-visualize many of the famous images he captured here. His exposures of Half Dome are particularly noteworthy and are among his best-known works.

Best Parks to Pitch a Tent in

The national parks offer myriad options for sleeping close to nature, whether you rest your head on the plush bunks of an RV or beneath a tree separated from the stars by just a thin sheet of nylon. The facilities may vary, but many campers agree that the best way to see the parks is to get out into the undeveloped wilderness.

■ **Banff.** You'll be camping in bear country, but Parks Canada takes precautions to separate the humans and the animals—a protective electrical fence with a Texas gate (cattle guard) surrounds the wooded Lake Louise campground, which is open year-round (with restrictions in spring and fall). Many sites are great for families.

■ **Capitol Reef.** Remote and wide-open Cathedral Valley, accessible by crossing the Fremont River in a high-clearance vehicle, is filled with stunning monoliths and silence. First-come, first-served primitive backcountry campsites provide a base for exploration.

■ **Olympic.** Don't be deterred by the very real threat of rain at this mossy, misty, and wonderfully undeveloped national park. With the Pacific Ocean and temperate rain forests to the west and craggy peaks scattered throughout its interior, Olympic is a backpacker's delight. Its designated campgrounds are popular, too. Several have water views and kid's activities.

■ **Yosemite.** Beyond the Yosemite Valley and iconic sites like Half Dome, this park has a huge, almost secret backcountry perfect for backpackers and horseback riders wishing to embark on extended trips. In fact, 94.5% of the park is undeveloped wilderness. If you choose instead one of the developed campgrounds, book early—at least three months in advance.

Best Parks for Romantics

One of the marks of a great relationship is the ability to travel together. And while getting there may induce some stress, once you're at a national park, your spirits should lighten. The beauty and serenity of the parks can help you focus on each other, not your Day-Timer. Each of these national parks is a destination well suited for celebrating your bond with that special someone.

■ **Banff.** There is no shortage of escapist lodging at Banff, regardless of your budget or interests. There are more than 100 accommodation options around Lake Louise alone, from cozy little cottages to large historic lodges. And when you're not gazing into each other's eyes, you can stare at the breathtaking mountain scenery. Any one of the scenic drives can also help you relax and unwind.

■ **Channel Islands.** The mountains that dot this park off the coast of California are often obscured by mists, and animals found nowhere else on earth add to the park's otherworldly feel. The Pacific Ocean is the main attraction here: play on its beaches, ply its waters on a kayak, or tour it by boat as you enjoy an island escape for two—albeit one totally different from a typical Caribbean trip.

■ **Grand Canyon.** For couples who don't mind sweating a little to get to a romantic destination, the depths of the Grand Canyon offer the quintessential Western camping experience. Sleeping at the base of this massive canyon under a clear black sky blazing with bright stars is something to add to your life's to-do list. (After a long hike—or mule ride—it is also the perfect occasion for a massage!)

Best Parks for Scenic Drives

Sometimes the road to the trailhead is as, or even more, amazing than the trail itself. For those who want to experience the parks from behind the wheel, these drives are top-notch.

■ **Glacier.** Even the hardiest hiker will admit that there's something special about speeding along a road named Going-to-the-Sun. Every year the local newspapers chronicle the road's opening for the season, when big snowplows finally clear its high passes. The 50-mile stretch of road crosses the Continental Divide at Logan Pass, and is one of America's most beautiful drives. There's even a tour you can sign up for, so everyone in your group can ooh and aah without one of you having to focus on the driving.

■ **Jasper.** The Icefields Parkway is one of the world's most spectacular drives, winding its way for 230 km (143 miles) between Banff and Jasper past powerful rugged mountain scenery, massive glaciers, rushing waterfalls, icefalls and wildlife.

■ **Redwood.** Keeping your eyes on the road can be a challenge when you're passing 300-foot-tall trees. The 8-mile Coastal Drive is especially wonderful, offering views of the Pacific Ocean, with glimpses of sea lions and pelicans likely, and access to a section of the Coastal Trail, with turnouts for picnicking and gawking in wonder at majestic redwoods.

■ **Rocky Mountain.** The 48-mile Trail Ridge Road is the world's highest continuously paved road, with a maximum elevation of 12,183 feet. Connecting the park's east and west entrances, the road crosses the Continental Divide at Milner Pass, and it can take up to two months to clear off snow for its Memorial Day opening. The entire drive can be done in a couple of hours, but allow more time to stop and gaze out from the many turnouts.

Best Parks for Spotting Bald Eagles

It may sound clichéd, but you'll never forget the first time you see a bald eagle in person, soaring on the wing or diving into an icy stream to snatch up a fish with its talons. The national icon's white head and tail, set against a dark body, are not its only points of distinction—eagles are huge, far larger than even the biggest hawk. You can view these amazing birds at many of the national parks, but visit one of the following for your best chance at a sighting.

■ **North Cascades.** Bald eagles are so much a part of this region that an annual festival is held in their honor along the Upper Skagit River, where hundreds of the regal birds gather each winter. Highlights include American Indian music and dancing and bluegrass workshops. In the park itself, look for them along the Skagit River and various lakes.

■ **Olympic.** A coastal section of this park protects a stunning 65-mile stretch of Pacific Ocean coastline, providing an ideal environment for the fish-loving bald eagle. Another fish lover, the osprey, is also commonly found here—and from a distance, these birds look a lot like bald eagles. Up close, there's is no resemblance whatsoever, so use your binoculars to be sure. You're most likely to spot an eagle on the Shi Shi or Rialto beaches or the Ozette Loop hiking trail.

■ **Yellowstone.** As much a part of Yellowstone as the grizzly bear and bison, bald eagles can usually be seen in the vicinity of Yellowstone Lake—though you may see them in the park's interior as well, especially around the Madison River or the Hayden Valley. Greater Yellowstone provides habitat for more than 100 breeding pairs of bald eagles.

Best Parks for Train Travel

Traveling by train to and from a national park is a rare treat, harking back to the days when most visitors arrived by rail. Fortunately, two of the nation's grandest and most historic national parks are still fully accessible via trains coming from a handful of major metropolitan areas.

■ **Glacier.** Amtrak's Empire Builder stops at the east and west sides of Glacier on its way from Chicago to either Seattle or Portland. Shuttle service is available from either station to lodging in the park (with a prior reservation). The train also stops to the west in Whitefish, Montana, where there are additional lodging options.

■ **Grand Canyon.** Grand Canyon Railway offers a variety of daily train services from Williams, Arizona, to the park's South Rim. The adults-only Sunset Limited runs during weekends in the fall, allowing passengers to witness one of Grand Canyon's unmatched sunsets while enjoying appetizers and full bar service. From November through January, the Polar Express train reenacts the classic children's book (make sure to reserve far in advance). Amtrak's Southwest Chief stops in Williams on its Chicago-to-Los Angeles run, making Grand Canyon one of the few national parks fully accessible by rail transportation.

■ **Rocky Mountain.** Amtrak's California Zephyr line, running from San Francisco to Chicago, covers some of the West's most beautiful terrain, including the Rockies and Sierra Nevada. It stops at Granby, Colorado, the western gateway to Rocky Mountain National Park. The local Avalanche Car Rentals (☎ 970/887–3908 ⊕ *www.avscars.com*) can meet you at the station.

NATIONAL PARKS OF THE WEST BEST BETS

BEACHES
Channel Islands
Olympic
Redwood

BIRDS
Big Bend
Carlsbad Caverns
Great Sand Dunes
Guadalupe Mountains
Joshua Tree
Mount Rainier
Pinnacles
Rocky Mountain
Theodore Roosevelt

BISON
Grand Teton
Great Sand Dunes
Theodore Roosevelt
Yellowstone

BOATING
Big Bend
Channel Islands
Glacier-Waterton
Grand Canyon
Grand Teton
Lassen Volcanic
North Cascades
Olympic
Redwood
Theodore Roosevelt
Yellowstone
Yosemite

CAVES AND CAVERNS
Carlsbad Caverns
Channel Islands
Great Basin
Sequoia and Kings Canyon
Wind Cave

FISHING
Big Bend
Black Canyon of the Gunnison
Capitol Reef
Channel Islands
Glacier-Waterton
Grand Canyon
Grand Teton
Great Basin
Mount Rainier
North Cascades
Olympic
Redwood
Rocky Mountain
Sequoia and Kings Canyon
Theodore Roosevelt
Yellowstone
Yosemite

GEOLOGICAL GREATS
Arches
Bryce Canyon
Canyonlands
Carlsbad Caverns
Crater Lake
Grand Canyon
Lassen Volcanic
Petrified Forest
Yellowstone

GEYSERS
Death Valley
Lassen Volcanic
Mount Rainier
Olympic
Yellowstone

GLACIERS AND ICE FIELDS
Banff
Glacier-Waterton
Grand Teton
Jasper
Mount Rainier
North Cascades
Olympic

HORSEBACK RIDING
Banff
Glacier
Jasper
Lassen Volcanic
Mount Rainier
Olympic
Rocky Mountain
Theodore Roosevelt
Yosemite

MOUNTAINS
Big Bend
Capitol Reef
Glacier
Grand Teton
Guadalupe Mountains
Jasper
Lassen Volcanic
North Cascades
Olympic
Rocky Mountain
Sequoia and Kings Canyon
Yosemite

TREES AND FORESTS
Joshua Tree
North Cascades
Olympic
Petrified Forest
Redwood

Sequoia and Kings Canyon
Yosemite

VOLCANOES
Crater Lake
Death Valley
Lassen Volcanic
Mount Rainier
Yellowstone

WATERFALLS
Banff
Crater Lake
Jasper
Great Sand Dunes
Lassen Volcanic
Mount Rainier
Olympic
Rocky Mountain
Yellowstone
Yosemite

WINTER SPORTS
Bryce Canyon
Jasper
Joshua Tree
Mount Rainier
Olympic
Rocky Mountain
Yellowstone
Yosemite
Zion

PLANNING
YOUR VISIT

3

PARK PASSES

Nationwide Passes

If you're going to visit several American national parks in one vacation or over the course of a year, you can save money by investing in an annual pass. Each of these passes admits the cardholder and others in the vehicle (or up to three others at places that charge per person) to more than 2,000 sites managed by the NPS and four other federal agencies including national parks as well as national wildlife refuges, forests, and grasslands (find participating areas at ⊕ *www.store.usgs.gov/pass*).

You must have photo identification with you when presenting your pass at any park entrance. All passes are nontransferable and nonrefundable. If they are lost or stolen, they will need to be repurchased.

See ⊕ *www.nps.gov/findapark/passes.htm* for additional information.

America the Beautiful Annual Pass. Also known as the Interagency Annual Pass, this pass costs $80 and is valid for a year from the date of purchase. Buy online (⊕ *www.store.usgs.gov/pass*), by phone (✆ *888/275–8747 Ext. 1*), or in person.

America the Beautiful Senior Pass. If you're 62 or older, you can purchase this pass for $10, and it is valid for a lifetime. You may purchase it in person or by mail (download the application at ⊕ *www.nps.gov/findapark/passes*). Passes purchased through the mail cost an extra $10 in processing fees.

America the Beautiful Access Pass. Those with permanent disabilities may acquire a parks pass that is free and valid for a lifetime. The pass can be obtained in person or by mail (there's a $10 fee for passes issued by mail).

America the Beautiful Volunteer Pass. Volunteer 500 or more service hours in national parks or other participating federal agencies and you'll be eligible for this free pass, which is valid for one year from the date of acquisition. Go to ⊕ *www.store.usgs.gov/pass/volunteer* for more information.

Canadian Park Passes

Canada also offers annual passes to its parks. In Canada, an individual pass is good only for the pass holder, not for everyone in the vehicle. For a carload of people, you need the family/group pass (covers up to seven people in one vehicle). Passes may be purchased online at ⊕ *www.pc.gc.ca* or in person at one of the participating parks, conservation areas, or historic sites.

The pass must be signed by the cardholder and is nontransferable. Retain your receipt/proof of purchase in case you lose your pass and need to have it replaced.

Parks Canada Discovery Pass. Good for entrance to Canada's national parks and national historic sites (more than 100 in all) for a year, this pass costs $66 for individuals, $56 for those 65 and older, and $32 for youths up to age 16. A family/group package pass is $132.

Other Annual Passes

Most individual national parks also offer an annual pass for unlimited access to that particular park. Prices vary, but hover around $30 to $50. In a few cases these passes include admission to two parks that are near each other, such as Grand Teton and Yellowstone. If you think you might be back to a park within a year, ask the gate attendant how much the annual pass is. In some parks, there's only a small difference between a single day's admission and the cost of a year's worth of visits.

WHAT TO PACK

Top 10 Essentials

Packing lists for any trip vary according to the individual and his or her needs, of course, but here are 10 essential things to include in your luggage for a national parks vacation.

1. Binoculars. Many of the parks are a bird- (and animal-) watcher's dream. A pair of binos will help you spot feathered friends as well as larger creatures. Binoculars are sold according to power, or how much the objects you're viewing are magnified (i.e., 7x, 10x, 12x), and the diameter of objective lens, which is the one on the fat end of the binoculars; 10x is a good choice for magnification, field of view, and steadiness.

2. Clothes that layer. In much of the West (especially at higher elevations), days are often warm while nights turn chilly. The weather also can change quickly, with things going from dry and sunny to windy and wet in a matter of minutes. This means you need to pack with both warm and cold (as well as wet and dry) weather in mind. The easiest solution is to dress in layers. Experts suggest synthetics such as polyester (used in Coolmax and other "wicking" fabrics that draw moisture away from your skin, and fleece, which is an insulator) and lightweight merino wool. Look for socks in wicking wool or polyester. Don't forget a waterproof poncho or jacket.

3. Long pants and long-sleeve shirts. It's wise to minimize exposed skin when hiking, especially in areas with poison ivy and/ or ticks and at higher elevations, where the sun's radiation is much stronger. Convertible pants (the bottom portion zips off, leaving you in a pair of shorts) are another good option—they're often made of quick drying and rugged material and allow you the flexibility of pants or shorts at a moment's notice.

4. Sturdy shoes or sandals. If you plan to do any hiking, be sure your footwear has rugged soles, a necessity on unpaved trails. Be sure to break in your shoes before the trip.

5. Insect repellent. If you're hiking or camping in an area with lots of mosquitoes, a good bug spray can help keep your trip from being a swatting marathon. A repellent also helps deter ticks. Most experts recommend repellents with DEET (N,N-diethyl-m-toluamide); the higher the level of DEET, the longer the product will be effective. Just be sure to use a separate sunscreen, not a single product with both ingredients (this is because you're supposed to reapply sunscreen every few hours, but doing so with DEET could deliver a dangerous dose of the chemical).

6. Skin moisturizer, sunscreen, and lip balm. In the parks, you're likely to be outside for longer—and in higher altitudes and drier climates—than you're used to. All of this can leave your skin and lips parched and burned. Sunscreen should provide both UVA and UVB protection, with an SPF of at least 15; look for a lotion marked "sweatproof" or "sport" and be sure to reapply throughout the day.

7. Sunglasses and hat. Higher elevation means more ultraviolet radiation; research shows there's an 8% to 10% increase in UV intensity for every 1,000 feet in elevation gain. Look for sunglasses that provide 100% UV protection.

8. Journal and camera. When your jaw drops at the glorious vistas and your head clears from all the fresh air, you may want to try your hand at sketching what you see or jotting down your thoughts. And of course, you'll want to get photographs.

9. Snacks and water. National parks by their nature are remote, and some are lacking in services. Bring plenty of water, along with healthy snacks (or meals, depending on how long you plan to be out and what you're likely to find in the park). When hiking in hot weather, experts recommend ½ to 1 quart of water (or another fluid) per person, per hour, to prevent potentially dangerous dehydration. The risk of dehydration is greater at elevations above 8,000 feet. Even if you're not hiking, have some water and food in the car for long drives through the park, where facilities might be scarce.

10. First-aid kit. A solid kit should contain a first-aid manual, aspirin (or ibuprofen), razor blades, tweezers, a needle, scissors, adhesive bandages, butterfly bandages, sterile gauze pads, 1-inch-wide adhesive tape, an elastic bandage, antibacterial ointment, antiseptic cream or spray, antihistamines, calamine lotion, and moleskin (for blisters).

Hiking Items

For vacations where you'll be going on hiking trips longer than an hour or two, consider investing in the following:

- a **compass and map**
- a **daypack** with enough room for everybody's essentials
- **energy bars** (they may not be five-star dining, but they do give you energy and keep your kids—and you—from getting cranky)
- a **hiking stick or poles,** especially if you've got bad knees
- a **water filter** to treat water in the backcountry
- **bear bells** if you're in bear country
- **reusable water bottles**

MAPS

If you plan to do a lot of hiking or mountaineering, especially in the backcountry, invest in detailed maps and a compass. Topographical maps are sold in well-equipped outdoor stores (REI and Cabela's, for example). Maps in different scales are available from the U.S. Geological Survey. To order, go to ⊕ *www.usgs.gov/pubprod/maps.html* or call ☎ *888/275-8747.*

Camping Gear

Planning on roughing it on your national parks vacation? In addition to a working tent (check the zipper before you go!), sleeping bags and pillows, and, of course, the ingredients for s'mores (graham crackers, chocolate bars, and marshmallows), here are some things veteran campers recommend be among your gear:

- **camping chairs** (folding or collapsible)
- **camp stove and fuel**
- **cooking and eating utensils, plates, and cups**
- **duct tape** (great for covering tears)
- **flashlight, headlamp,** and **lantern**
- **matches**
- **paper towels, napkins, wet wipes**
- a **multipurpose knife** and **cutting board**
- a **rope** (for laundry or to help tie things down; pack clothespins, too)
- a **sleeping pad** or **air mattress**
- a **tarp** (will help keep the bottom of your tent—and you—dry)
- a **cooler**
- **toilet paper**
- a **shovel** (to bury waste) or **plastic bags** (to haul it out)

FAMILY FUN

Top 5 Tips

1. Plan ahead. At many parks, rooms and campsites fill up fast, so make your reservations as early as you can. Many parks will have every room and campsite booked several months in advance (weekends are especially popular). We recommend booking at least six months ahead, and more if you plan to visit one of the more popular parks, such as Grand Canyon, Grand Teton, Rocky Mountain, Yellowstone, or Yosemite. If you plan on staying outside the park, check with the hotels you're considering as far ahead as you can, as these places can fill up fast as well. You also can go online. All the national parks have websites—links to all of them are at the National Park Service page, ⊕ *www.nps.gov.*

2. Get the kids involved. It might seem easier to do the planning yourself, but you'll probably have a better time—and your kids definitely will—if you involve them. No matter how old they are, children ought to have a good idea of where you're going and what you're about to experience. It will help get them excited beforehand and will likely make them feel like they have a say and a stake in the trip. Discuss the park's attractions and give your kids a choice of two or three options (that are all amenable to you, of course). Many of the parks' web pages have a "For Kids" link, with helpful advice and suggestions.

3. Know your children. Consider your child's interests. This will help you plan a vacation that's both safe and memorable (for all the right reasons). For starters, if you have kids under 4, be honest with yourself about whether the national park itself is an appropriate destination. Parents are notorious for projecting their awe for majestic scenery and overall enthusiasm for sightseeing on their younger kids, who might be more interested in cataloging the snacks in the hotel room's minibar. Likewise, be realistic about your child's stamina and ability. If your children have never been hiking, don't expect them to be able to do a long hike at a higher altitude than they are used to. Remember: A child's first experience hiking can make them a lover or a hater of the activity, so start off slow and try some practice hikes near home.

4. Pack wisely. Be sure you're bringing kid-size versions of the necessities you'll pack for yourself. Depending on the park you're visiting (and the activities you're planning), that will probably include sturdy sandals or hiking shoes, sunglasses, sunscreen, and insect repellent. You'll almost certainly need a few layers of clothing and plenty of water and snacks. Kids can be more susceptible to heat stress and dehydration than adults, meaning they need plenty of water when exercising. The American Academy of Pediatrics recommends giving your child about five ounces of water or another beverage every 20 minutes during strenuous exercise.

5. Develop a Plan B. National parks are natural places, meaning they change dramatically with the seasons and the weather, so you should plan on alternate activities if Mother Nature isn't cooperative. And if you've already talked with your kids about your options, you can pick a new plan that appeals to everyone.

SAMPLE BUDGET FOR FAMILY OF FOUR

Here is an idea of what a family of four might spend on a three-day trip to Grand Canyon National Park, during which they stay and eat all their meals within the park. Depending on your accommodations and dining-out options, the total you spend can vary dramatically.

Admission: $25 per car; admission covers seven days in the park.

Lodging: A standard double room in one of the in-park lodges on the popular South Rim ranges from approximately $70 to $190 a night. Total for three nights: $210 to $570; double that ($420 to $1,140) if you have older children in a separate room. Tent camping in one of the park's campgrounds averages $15 per night. Total: $45. Backpackers must pay $10 for a backcountry permit and $5 per person, per night to camp below the rim (or $5 per group, per night above the rim). Total: $45 to $90.

Meals: Dining options in the park range from no-frills snack bars to upscale restaurants. Per-meal costs run from $10 to $40 or more, per person (you might be able to spend less if you're cooking meals over your campfire or packing bag lunches). Total (three meals per person, per day for three days): $360 to $1,440.

Souvenirs: budget $5 to $10 per person per day for souvenirs so each person can get something small each day, or one or two larger items per trip. Total: $60 to $120.

TOTAL COST: $490 to $2,725

Budgeting Your Trip

Like most vacations, a trip to a national park can be as frugal, or as fancy, as you like. Here are a few things to consider:

Getting in. Individual admission to the national parks ranges from free to $25, depending on the park (⇨ *see our Essentials section at the beginning of each park chapter to learn individual rates*). You also can buy an America the Beautiful Pass for $80, which will get you and three other adults (kids 15 and under are free) into any national park (as well as other designated federal lands) for one year.

Sleeping. Fewer than half of the parks charge for camping; the cost is typically under $20 per night. In many parks, you also can stay at a lodge, where prices run from $100 to $500 a night. Most parks have several accommodation options outside the park, as well.

Eating. In each of the parks, all the in-park concessions are run by companies under contract with the National Park Service, meaning their prices are set by the government. Generally speaking, prices are a bit higher than what you'd pay outside the park, but not significantly so. You also can bring in your own food and eat at one of the park's picnic areas.

Entertainment. Just looking at the wonders of the park is entertainment enough for many youngsters, but the many sports and outdoor activities—from hiking and bicycling to horseback riding and cave touring, depending on the park—help children stay active while exploring. Many park visitor centers also have films; some parks, such as Grand Canyon and Zion, even have IMAX movies. Cost for these offerings varies, ranging from free to a couple hundred dollars for more involved programs, such as a white-water rafting trip.

Souvenirs. All the parks have gift shops, and many stock items that are actually useful. For example, you'll find things like kid-size binoculars, fanny packs, and magnifying glasses, all of which can make your child's visit even more enjoyable. Budget $5 or $10 to cover one item (maybe something you might have bought for your child anyway, like a new sun hat).

Kids Programs

More than half of the 401 U.S. National Park Service units (national parks as well as historic sites, national monuments, preserves, and other significant places) are part of the Junior Ranger Program, which offers school-age kids the opportunity to learn about individual parks by filling out a short workbook or participating in an activity such as taking a hike with a park ranger. After completing the program, kids get a badge (or a pin or patch, depending on the park). For availability, check with the ranger station or visitor center when you arrive. Kids can also complete Junior Ranger activities online (⊕ *www.nps.gov/webrangers*).

In addition to the Junior Ranger Program, kids can find a variety of activities in the parks designed just for them. Some parks, such as Canyonlands, Grand Canyon, and Saguaro, loan "Discovery Packs," backpacks filled with kid-friendly tools like magnifying glasses. Call ahead for availability.

Many parks also have general-interest programs for kids. For example, Rocky Mountain National Park offers "Skins and Skulls," where visitors can touch a bear's fur and a marmot's skull, among other things. It's a safe way to get hands-on with wildlife.

When you're through with the organized activities and are ready to head off on your own, remember that kids often take a shorter view of things than adults do, meaning they may need to be reminded once in a while of why you're there and what lies ahead (especially if it's a cool waterfall or swimming hole). Singing camp songs, playing games like I Spy, or staging scavenger hunts will help kids refocus if they get bored or whiny.

Pets in the Parks

Generally, pets are allowed only in developed areas of the national parks, including drive-in campgrounds and picnic areas. They must be kept on a leash at all times. With the exception of guide dogs, pets are not allowed inside buildings, on most trails, on beaches, or in the backcountry. They also may be prohibited in areas controlled by concessionaires, such as restaurants. Some national parks have kennels; call ahead to learn the details and to see if there's availability. Some of the national forests (⊕ *www.fs.fed.us*) surrounding the parks have camping and are more lenient with pets, although you should not plan to leave your pet unattended at the campsite.

OH STARRY NIGHT

TIPS FOR STARGAZING IN THE PARKS

If your typical view of the night sky consists of a handful of stars dimly twinkling through a hazy, light-polluted sky, get ready for a treat. In the parks, the night sky blazes with starlight—and with a little practice, you can give your family a memorable astronomical tour.

Constellations

Constellations are stories in the sky—many depict animals or figures from Greek mythology. Brush up on a few of these tales before your trip, and you'll be an instant source of nighttime entertainment.

The stars in the Northern Hemisphere appear to rotate around Polaris, the North Star, in fixed positions relative to one another. To get your celestial bearings, first find the bright stars of the Big Dipper. An imaginary line drawn through the two stars that form the outside edge of the cup (away from the handle) will point straight to Polaris (Polaris also serves as the last star in the handle of the Little Dipper). Once you've identified Polaris, you should be able to find the other stars on our chart. Myriad astronomy books and Web sites have additional star charts; *National Geographic* has a cool interactive version with images from the Hubble Space Telescope (⊕ *www.nationalgeographic.com/stars*).

Planets

Stars twinkle, planets don't (because they're so much closer to Earth, the atmosphere doesn't distort their light as much). Planets are also bright, which makes them fairly easy to spot. Unfortunately, we can't show their positions on this star chart, because planets orbit the sun and move in relation to the stars.

The easiest planet to spot is Venus, the brightest object in the night sky besides the moon and the Earth's closest planetary neighbor. Look for it just before sunrise or just after sunset; it'll be near the point where the sun is rising or setting. (Venus and Earth orbit the sun at different speeds; when Venus is moving away from Earth, we see it in the morning, and when it's moving toward us, we see it in the evening.) Like the moon, Venus goes through phases—check it out through a pair of binoculars. You can also spot Mars, Jupiter, Saturn, and Mercury—with or without the aid of binoculars.

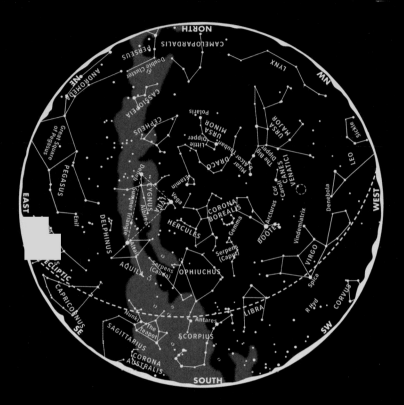

Meteors

It's hard to match the magic of a meteor shower, the natural fireworks display that occurs as Earth passes through a cloud of debris called meteoroids. These pieces of space junk—most the size of a pebble—hit our atmosphere at high speeds, and the intense friction produces brief but brilliant streaks of light. Single meteors are often called "shooting stars" or "falling stars."

Since our planet passes through the same patch of interstellar refuse each year, it's easy to roughly predict when the major meteor showers will occur. Notable ones include the Perseids (mid-August), the Orionids (late October), the Leonids (mid-November), and the Geminids (mid-December). Each shower is named after the point in the sky where meteors appear to originate. If you're not visiting during a shower, don't worry—you can spot individual meteors any time of the year.

Satellites

Right now, according to NASA, there are about 3,000 operative man-made satellites (along with 6,000 pieces of space junk) orbiting the Earth—and you can catch a glimpse of one with a little practice. Satellites look like fast-moving, non-blinking points of light; the best way to spot one is to lie on your back and scan the sky for movement. Be on the lookout for satellites an hour or two before or after sunset (though you may see them at other times as well).

You can take the guesswork out of the search with a few cool online tools (⊕ *www.nasa. gov* or *www.heavens-above.com*). Select your location, and these Web sites will help you predict—down to the minute—when certain objects will be streaking overhead. It's especially worthwhile to use these sites to look for the two brightest satellites: the International Space Station and the space shuttle.

OUTDOOR ADVENTURES

HIKING

Hiking in the national parks can mean many things, from a leisurely hour-long stroll along the rim of the Black Canyon of the Gunnison to a half-day scramble over ancient ruins at Mesa Verde to a multiday trek across Yellowstone. No matter what your fitness level, you'll find at least one hike that meets your needs.

Safety

Staying safe while hiking should be your number-one concern. While the vast majority of park visitors head off on hikes and return again unscathed, there is a handful each year that get hurt, some seriously. If your hike involves anything more strenuous than a short walk from the car to an observation area, check with a ranger to learn the special concerns for your planned adventure. Trails might be closed or rerouted, bad weather may be expected, or park wildlife may be causing problems on your route. Check the trail map carefully and pay attention to elevation changes, which make a huge difference in the difficulty of a hike (a steep 1-mile-long trail is much tougher to negotiate than a flat 2- or even 3-mile trail). And before you go, be sure to tell someone where you're going and how long you expect to be gone (if everyone in your group will be taking the hike, that someone should be a park ranger).

Best Hikes

Delicate Arch Trail, Arches National Park. This 3-mile round-trip hike takes you to the park's most famous sight and an iconic image of the American West, Delicate Arch. Hike over open, sun-baked slick-rock marked with cairns, then along a 200-yard stretch of rock ledge just before you reach the arch.

Highline Trail, Glacier National Park. The Garden Wall section of this popular trail takes you from Logan Pass to Granite Park Chalet. On the way, it passes over mostly open terrain, much of it just above the tree line, where you're likely to see lots of wildlife—bighorn sheep, mountain goats, ptarmigan, and even grizzly bears—along with mountain vistas. It's a challenging hike, with a few narrow sections only 3 to 5 feet wide.

The Narrows Trail, Zion National Park. Experience the thrill of walking in the Virgin River, peering up at millennia-old rock canyons, hanging gardens, and sandstone grottoes. To see the Narrows you must wade—and occasionally swim—upstream through chilly water and over uneven, slippery rocks, but the views are breathtaking. Unless you've got a wetsuit, plan to hike in the summer months, and even if you're hiking on a hot day, the water is likely to be very cold.

Panorama Trail, Yosemite National Park. If you're looking for eye-popping scenery and a heart-pounding hike, it doesn't get better than this. This 8-mile (one-way) trek is a doable, if strenuous, day trip, and delivers views of Yosemite Valley, several waterfalls, and the incomparable Half Dome. Take the hiker's bus ($25 one-way for adults) from Yosemite Lodge to the trailhead at Glacier Point and hike back down.

Widforss Trail, Grand Canyon National Park. Head to the less-crowded North Rim for this 10-mile round-trip hike that takes you along the canyon rim, through forests of aspen and Ponderosa pine, then out to Widforss Point, with incredible views of Haunted Canyon and its distinctive peaks, as well as a 10-mile stretch of the South Rim.

ROCK CLIMBING AND MOUNTAINEERING

Mountaineering can involve heavy traveling in the mountains, usually with the aim of reaching a summit. Mountaineers often employ rock climbing to reach their objectives, and the national parks are prime venues for both sports.

Getting Started

To get started in rock climbing, experts suggest taking an introductory course at an indoor climbing wall, which will give you a basic understanding of the techniques and equipment in a safe and controlled environment. After that, you can head out with a guide to try your skills on the real thing. A good guide will choose climbs that don't have a lot of exposure, so that you'll have time to get used to the sensation of climbing and being off the ground.

If you work with an instructor or go out with experienced friends, you'll only need a few items. Once you learn the basics and are ready to climb on your own, you'll need to invest in a lot more equipment. But getting started is easy and not terribly expensive. You'll need a harness, a helmet, rock shoes (special sticky, tight-fitting shoes), a locking carabiner, and a belay device.

American Alpine Institute (AAI). One of the premier rock-climbing and mountaineering schools in the United States, AAI offers courses all over the world in all types of climbing, from trekking and backpacking to high-altitude ascents. ☎ *360/671–1505, 800/424–4229* ⊕ *www. alpineinstitute.com.*

Best Climbs

Angel Wings, Sequoia and Kings Canyon National Park. Climbers flock to the sheer south face of this 1,800-foot granite wall, which offers several stellar climbs. Across the park, the west face of Moro Rock, a 6,725-foot granite monolith, provides another 1,000 vertical feet of cracks and knobs.

Longs Peak, Rocky Mountain National Park. At 14,255 feet, this is the tallest of Colorado's fourteeners. Take the Keyhole Route to the top for classic mountaineering challenges (steep cliffs, narrow ledges, and loose rocks) as well as spectacular views. The round-trip 7.5-mile trek takes between 10 to 15 hours, and late-afternoon thunderstorms are fairly common, so you should head out early (rangers recommend a presunrise start).

Mount Olympus, Olympic National Park. This 7,980-foot peak offers all the good parts of mountaineering (crossing snowfields and crevasses, ridges and moraine fields) without the expense of leaving the continental U.S. (or subalpine elevation).

Painted Wall, Black Canyon of the Gunnison National Park. A mecca for serious climbers, Painted Wall, on the north side of the canyon, is a jaw-dropping, 2,250-foot-high sheer cliff that's strictly for experts only.

Toulumne Meadows, Yosemite National Park. Yosemite Valley has El Capitan and Half Dome, but it's hot (and crowded) enough in the summer to send savvy climbers up to Toulumne Meadows, a spectacular subalpine playground studded with granite domes and cliffs, with multipitch face, knob, crack, and slab climbing routes for all levels.

RAFTING, KAYAKING, AND CANOEING

The national parks offer plenty of opportunity for aquatic adventures, from high-adrenaline trips through rapids (via raft or kayak) to more relaxing outings over gentler waters.

Getting Your Feet Wet

Unless you're a real pro at rafting or kayaking, with your own equipment and loads of experience under your belt, you're most likely going to hit the river with a guide, who will teach you the basics. Navigable rapids are typically classified from I to V, with V being the roughest. If you're interested in white water, and this is your first time, pick a trip on gentler waters (Class II or III). This will give you the chance to see some whitecaps without overwhelming you. This is also a good strategy if you're traveling with kids who may be frightened on more intense rapids.

Experts advise dressing for the temperature of the water, not the air (meaning you'll be bringing clothes that you wouldn't need if you were staying on dry land). Depending on where you are, you might want a few layers, with a sweatshirt or light jacket on top (fleece or another synthetic). Don't wear cotton or jeans: once they get wet, they stay wet (and will leave you chilled). Wear old tennis shoes, water shoes, or sandals that strap securely to your feet (not flip-flops). If you're wearing glasses or sunglasses, be sure you've got a "Croakie" or leash to keep them attached to you. The same goes for your hat (if yours doesn't have a chin strap, you can use a cord to tie it to your life jacket).

Be sure to apply plenty of water-resistant sunscreen. If yours is not the kind that dries completely, skip the backs of your legs: If your skin is slippery, you'll be sliding all over the place and have more trouble staying in the raft.

Best Places for Paddling

Colorado and Green Rivers, Canyonlands National Park. The Colorado and Green Rivers thread through the park, meeting at a confluence before spilling down Cataract Canyon and creating a 14-mile stretch of world-class white water. Upstream, you can hit the flat waters of either river (most launch locations are north of the park boundaries) in a kayak or canoe.

Colorado River, Grand Canyon National Park. You can tackle the rapids and smoother waters of the Colorado on both professionally guided and self-guided river trips.

East Santa Cruz Island, Channel Islands National Park. You'll find your sea kayaking nirvana here, with clear ocean waters and a spectacular shoreline with beautiful sea caves and cliffs to explore.

Kaweah River, Sequoia and Kings Canyon National Park. The middle fork of this river offers challenging Class IV rapids for expert kayakers.

Merced River, Yosemite National Park. A popular summer destination (and a designated Wild and Scenic River), the Merced offers white-water adventures for rafts and kayaks.

Snake River, Grand Teton National Park. The well-named Snake River winds its way through the southeast corner of Yellowstone before spilling into Jackson Lake in Grand Teton National Park, offering opportunities for both shooting some mild rapids and floating (or paddling) over more tranquil waters.

CAMPING

A night in a tent under the stars is the highlight of many trips to a national park.

Camping Tips

Ensuring a pleasant camping experience takes some preparation. Check the weather forecast—and your equipment—before you go. Test out a new tent to find out if there are any problems to contend with, like a faulty zipper, and be sure you know how to set it up.

If you can reserve your tent site ahead of time, take a look at the campground map and try to choose a site that meets your needs—nearer to a bathroom if you have small children, farther away if you want more privacy. The best sites, like ones with lake views, are often snapped up early, so try to reserve in advance.

Best Campgrounds

Fruita, Capitol Reef National Park. Here, there are cool, shady campsites near the orchards and the Freemont River.

Gold Bluffs Beach, Redwood National Park. Situated in nearby Prairie Creek Redwoods State Park on a stretch of rugged Pacific coastline, this campground has easy access to a beach and 70 miles of hiking and biking trails.

Manzanita Lake, Lassen Volcanic National Park. At Manzanita Lake, there are lots of ranger programs, plus fishing, swimming, and a boat launch. The camp store has food, hot showers, and a laundromat.

Mather, Grand Canyon National Park. These comfortable sites on the South Rim have all the comforts of home, including bathrooms, laundry, a cafeteria, and hot showers in nearby Grand Canyon Village.

Morefield, Mesa Verde National Park. Shady, pleasant campsites are adjacent to Morefield Village, a minicity with a café offering a daily all-you-can-eat pancake breakfast and free Wi-Fi, general store, and coin-operated laundry. They'll even rent you a tent, complete with cots and lanterns.

Sheep Creek, Sequoia and Kings Canyon National Park. This campground is nestled in the canyon near the middle fork of the Kings River, with groceries, showers, and other amenities about ¼ mile away, at Cedar Grove Village.

South Rim, Black Canyon of the Gunnison National Park. This conveniently located, fully loaded campground is open year-round.

Toulomne Meadows, Yosemite National Park. Large, private sites in a spectacular subalpine campground just south of the Toulomne Meadows and River have easy access to hiking and climbing and lots of ranger programs around the campfire.

Wheeler Peak, Great Basin National Park. Perched at 10,000 feet on Wheeler Peak Scenic Drive, the campground has spectacular views and a short commute to popular trailheads.

NATIONAL PARK TOURS

Whether you want an experienced guide for an active-sport trip or an educational but leisurely program that takes the planning out of your hands, tours can be ideal for all ages and life situations—families, outdoor enthusiasts, and retirees.

Adventure Trips

Many trip organizers specialize in only one type of activity, while a few companies guide several kinds of active trips. (In some cases, these larger companies also act essentially as a clearinghouse or agent for smaller trip outfitters.) Be sure to sign on with a reliable outfitter; getting stuck with a shoddy operator can be disappointing, uncomfortable, and even dangerous. Some sports—white-water rafting and mountaineering, for example—have organizations that license or certify guides, and you should be sure that the guide you're with is properly accredited.

Backroads. Arguably the best-known adventure travel company in the country, Backroads organizes trips to destinations all around the world—including the national parks of the West, Southwest, and Rocky Mountains. ☎ *510/527–1555, 800/462–2848* ⊕ *www.backroads.com.*

Off the Beaten Path. This company organizes trips throughout the U.S. and the world—including the national parks in the Rockies, desert Southwest, and Pacific coast—that combine outdoor activities with learning experiences. Their various National Parks Guided Group Journeys hit Arches, Canyonlands, Big Bend, Yellowstone, Glacier, Grand Canyon, Mount Rainier, and Zion national parks, among others. ☎ *800/445–2995* ⊕ *www. offthebeatenpath.com.*

REI Adventures. The outdoor outfitter also conducts trips to the national parks, among other destinations. Examples include hiking in Arches or Capitol Reef; cycling in Death Valley or Zion and Bryce Canyon; kayaking in Yellowstone or Channel Islands; rock climbing in Joshua Tree; and backpacking in the Grand Canyon, Rocky Mountain, or Yosemite National Park. ☎ *253/437– 1100, 800/622–2236* ⊕ *www.rei.com/ adventures.*

Sierra Club Outings. The travel arm of the iconic environmental organization, which was founded in 1892 by John Muir, organizes a variety of active trips (some of them service-oriented "volunteer vacations") to the national parks, including Grand Canyon, Guadalupe Mountains, Mesa Verde, North Cascades, Olympia, Rocky Mountain, Sequoia and Kings Canyon, and Yellowstone. ☎ *415/977– 5522* ⊕ *www.sierraclub.org/outings.*

The World Outdoors. This guide company offers hiking and multisport trips in Arches, Banff, Big Bend, Bryce Canyon, Canyonlands, Glacier, Grand Canyon, Grand Teton, Rocky Mountain, Sequoia and Kings Canyon, Yellowstone, Yosemite, and Zion national parks (and other places around the world). ☎ *303/413–0946, 800/488–8483* ⊕ *www.theworldoutdoors.com.*

Senior Tours

Those in their golden years can join special tours, some of which are quite adventurous, such as Road Scholar's intergenerational rafting trip on the Grand Canyon's Colorado River.

Road Scholar. This branch of the not-for-profit group Elderhostel, Inc., sends adult travelers on educational and adventurous trips all around the world. They've got offerings in many national parks, including less-visited parks like Big Bend, Channel Islands, and Lassen Volcanic. ☎ *800/454–5768* ⊕ *www.roadscholar.org.*

Walking the World. This tour company offers adventure travel for the 50+ crowd to U.S. and international destinations—including Arches, Capitol Reef, and Rocky Mountain national parks. ☎ *970/498–0500* ⊕ *www.walkingtheworld.com.*

Single-Park Tours

If you want to concentrate solely on one park, contact the park directly to learn about organized tours they may have. Or look into one of these organizations:

Glacier Park, Inc. This company offers a six-day Great Glacier Adventure tour that includes meals, accommodations in park lodges, guided hikes, fly-fishing lessons, white-water rafting—and time for play away from the group. They also offer a six-day tour of the park's great lodges, and half-day and full-day Red Bus tours of the park. ☎ *406/892–2525* ⊕ *www. glacierparkinc.com.*

Grand Canyon Tour Company. This operator provides tours of the park—by bus, helicopter, or plane—from nearby Las Vegas. They also offer guided rafting, hiking, and overnight camping trips in the park. ☎ *702/655–6060, 800/222–6966* ⊕ *www. grandcanyontourcompany.com.*

The Yellowstone Association Institute. The field institute of this nonprofit offers educational seminars and guided one-day and multiday tours and trips for adults and families in Yellowstone, ranging from backcountry expeditions to "Lodging and Learning" experiences. ☎ *406/848–2400* ⊕ *www.yellowstoneassociation.org.*

Tours with Accessibility

Access Tours. This group leads 8-to-12-day trips into U.S. and Canadian national parks (and other Western destinations) for people who use wheelchairs or have other mobility impairments; trips can be customized for small groups. ☎ *800/929–4811, 208/787–2338* ⊕ *www.accesstours.org.*

PHOTOGRAPHY TIPS

Today's digital cameras make it difficult to take a truly lousy picture, but there are still some things even the best models can't do on their own. The tips here (some of them classic photography techniques) won't turn you into the next Ansel Adams, but they might prevent you from being upstaged by your eight-year-old with her smart phone.

The Golden Hours. The best photos are taken when most of us are either snoozing or eating dinner: about an hour before and after sunrise and sunset. When the light is gentle and golden, your photos are less likely to be overexposed or filled with harsh shadows and squinting people.

Divide to Conquer. You can't go wrong with the Rule of Thirds: When you're setting up a shot, mentally divide your picture area into thirds, horizontally and vertically, which will give you nine squares. Any one of the four places where the lines intersect (the four corners of the center square) represents a good spot to place your primary subject. (If all this talk of imaginary lines makes your head spin, just remember not to automatically plop your primary focal point in the center of your photos).

Lock Your Focus. To get a properly focused photo using a camera with auto-focus, press the shutter button down halfway and wait a few seconds before pressing down completely. (On most cameras, a light or a beep will indicate that you're good to go).

Circumvent Auto-Focus. If your camera isn't homing in on your desired focal point, center the primary subject smack in the middle of the frame and depress the shutter button halfway, allowing the camera to focus. Then, without lifting your finger, compose your photo properly (moving your camera so the focal point isn't in the center of the shot), and press the shutter all the way down.

Jettison the Jitters. Shaky hands are among the most common causes of out-of-focus photos. If you're not good at immobility, invest in a tripod or rest the camera on something steady—such as a wall, a bench, or a rock—when you shoot. If all else fails, lean against something sturdy to brace yourself.

Consider the Imagery. Before you press that shutter button, take a moment or two to consider *why* you're shooting what you're shooting. Once you've determined this, start setting up your photo. Look for interesting lines that curve into your image—such as a path, the shoreline, or a fence—and use them to create the impression of depth. You can do the same thing by photographing people with their bodies or faces positioned at an angle to the camera.

Ignore All the Rules. Sure, thoughtful contemplation and careful execution are likely to produce brilliant images, but there are times when you just need to capture the moment. If you see something wonderful, grab your camera and just get the picture. If the photo turns out to be blurry, off-center, or over- or underexposed, you can always Photoshop it later.

Special Considerations. If you're going to any Indian reservations (many are near national parks), check the rules before you take photographs. In many cases you must purchase a permit.

STAYING HEALTHY, PLAYING IT SAFE

Altitude Sickness

Altitude sickness can result when you've moved to high elevations without having time to adjust. When you're at a mile (5,280 feet) or more above sea level, and especially when you're higher than 8,500 feet, you may feel symptoms of altitude sickness: shortness of breath, light-headedness, nausea, fatigue, headache, and insomnia. To help your body adjust, drink lots of water, avoid alcohol, and wait a day or two before attempting vigorous activity. If your symptoms are severe, last several days, or worsen, seek medical attention.

Animal Bites

Although animals abound in the national parks, the odds of your meeting one face to face, let alone sustaining a bite, are slim (especially if you follow the rules about not feeding them). But if you are bitten or scratched by any wild animal—even a small one—seek medical attention. You may need stitches and antibiotics, or a rabies or tetanus shot. If that animal is a snake, stay calm (if the snake is venomous, a lot of movement can spread the poison). Have someone else get medical help for you right away.

Dehydration

If your body doesn't have the fluids it needs, you're dehydrated. Symptoms can range from minor (a dull headache) to life threatening (seizures, coma). Dehydration is often caused by excessive sweating coupled with inadequate fluid intake, and is a real concern in the national parks, where visitors are generally active (hiking, climbing) but not good at carrying and drinking water. Dehydration is a particular problem for children and seniors and for anyone exercising in dry climates; it's also more likely at high altitudes. To counter a mild case, drink water or another beverage. Take small sips over a period of time instead of trying to force down a large amount. A serious case requires immediate medical attention. To prevent dehydration, be sure to bring and consume enough water: ½ to 1 quart per person for each hour of exercise.

Don't Feed the Animals

It's dangerous—and illegal (you'll be fined). Animals in many national parks are used to humans being around and may not flee at your presence. But feeding wild animals habituates them to humans and teaches them to look to us for food. When that happens, they lose the ability to hurt or forage on their own, meaning they might starve to death or be hit by cars when looking for handouts. Feeding animals also causes them to be more aggressive, and thus more dangerous, to future visitors. Aggressive animals are removed from areas where they'll have contact with people; in some cases, they're relocated, but in others, they're put down.

Heat-Related Illness

Typically caused by excessive exertion in high temperatures such as a strenuous hike in the desert, heat exhaustion or more serious heat stroke can cause nausea, headaches, and dizziness—and even seizures, unconsciousness, and death. If you suspect heat-related illness, rest in a cool, shady place and drink water. Dehydration is often a factor in heat exhaustion and heat stroke. Apply cool compresses to the head, forehead, and trunk. If the victim is unconscious or confused, seek medical help immediately.

GREAT
ITINERARIES

Updated
by Martha
Connors

Due to their grand size and endless recreation opportunities, visitors can easily spend an entire trip exploring just one national park. But adventurous travelers looking to discover more of the West can take on a bigger itinerary involving several parks, plus a couple of other destinations (national monuments, state parks, scenic byways, and the like) that show off some of the most impressive scenery America has to offer. We've put together a collection of these itineraries, aimed at the most popular (and feasible) routes taken by curious explorers.

Most of the national parks are so large you need a vehicle to properly explore, so planning a driving trip to visit them is a no-brainer. Whether you fly into the nearest airport and rent a car or drive all the way in your own vehicle, these itineraries can help you plan your route—and your time in the parks—to give you the best experience possible. Each itinerary is meant to be used for inspiration in planning your own trip, tailored to your interests and your travel style. We suggest you pick the parks that most appeal to you and linger a little longer there. That being said, those who want to see more in less time will prefer the tours just as they are.

We've developed these itineraries based on the idea that you'll be traveling during the summer, when you'll find most roads and facilities open in the parks. If you'll be traveling at another time of year, be sure to check with the park(s) you'll be visiting about road conditions and closures. Many of the parks included in this guide are in remote and/or mountainous areas, accessible by roads that are subject to seasonal closures.

You should also note that "summer" can mean something different in different parts of the West; warm weather typically arrives much later in the year in Canada and the northern United States than it

does in Arizona and New Mexico. Additionally, we're assuming you'll be traveling in a passenger car. If you're driving an RV (or pulling a trailer), check with the park(s) ahead of time to see if they have any restrictions on these vehicles.

WASHINGTON STATE: NORTH CASCADES, MOUNT RAINIER, AND OLYMPIC NATIONAL PARKS, 8 DAYS

A trip to Washington's three national parks—plus a visit to Mount St. Helen's National Volcanic Monument—takes you through rugged Pacific coastline and high alpine terrain as well as lush temperate rainforest, glaciers, waterfalls, and some of the largest remnants of ancient forests in the U.S.

DAY 1: WELCOME TO WASHINGTON STATE

For those coming from out of state, the nearest airport is ❶ **Seattle-Tacoma International,** where you can start your journey by picking up a rental car. Depending on when your flight gets in, you can rest up at a nearby hotel for the night or make the 85-mile, 1½-hour drive to ❷ **Sedro-Woolley,** Washington, where you can gather information at the park headquarters and spend the night.

DAY 2: NORTH CASCADES NATIONAL PARK
46 miles or about an hour drive from Sedro-Woolley.

From Sedro-Woolley, drive along Route 20 to the entrance of ❸ **North Cascades National Park.** Take your first stroll through an old-growth forest on the Skagit River Loop (1.8 miles), which starts at the visitor center near the town of Newhalem, about 9 miles from the entrance, then devote the rest of the day to driving through the park on Route 20, stopping at various overlooks. Exit the park and continue through the scenic Methow Valley and on to ❹ **Chelan** (about 72 miles from the park's western boundary) to stay the night. Another option would be to exit the park the way you came in, at the western entrance near Newhalem, then head west toward Arlington (about 60 miles away).

DAYS 3 AND 4: MT. RAINIER NATIONAL PARK
205 miles or a 3-hour, 45-minute drive from Chelan; 136 miles or a 2-hour, 45-minute drive from Arlington.

From Chelan, get an early start to drive to Ohanapecosh, the southeastern entrance to ❺ **Mt. Rainier National Park.** When you arrive, take a drive on the spectacular Sunrise Road (about 30 miles round-trip), which reveals the "back" (northeast) side of Rainier. A room at the Paradise Inn in nearby ❻ **Ashford** (about 19 miles east of the park's Nisqually entrance) is your base for the next two nights.

The next day, energetic hikers will want to tackle one of the four- to six-hour trails that scale the park's many peaks. Less ambitious visitors can take one of the shorter hikes in the Paradise Inn area or join a ranger-led walk through wildflower meadows. Another option is to hike to Panorama Point (a strenuous 4-mile round trip), near the foot of the Muir Snowfield, for breathtaking views of the glaciers and high ridges of Rainier. After dinner at the inn, watch the sunset's alpenglow on the peak from the back porch.

DAY 5: MOUNT ST. HELENS AND
THE OLYMPIC FOOTHILLS
120 miles or a 2½-hour drive from Mt. Rainer.

Today, drive south to spend the day visiting the ❼ **Mount St. Helens National Volcanic Monument,** where you can enter from the west side via Route 504 and see the destruction caused by the 1980 eruption. After leaving the monument, follow Route 504 back to I–5 and head north to Olympia, winding through scenic Puget Sound countryside, skirting the Olympic foothills, and periodically dipping down to the waterfront en route to ❽ **Port Angeles,** where you'll spend the night.

DAYS 6 AND 7: OLYMPIC NATIONAL PARK
212 miles or a 4-hour drive from Mount St. Helens to Port Angeles.

The next morning, launch into a full day at ❾ **Olympic National Park.** From the Port Angeles entrance, drive 17 miles south to Hurricane Ridge, where you'll find several trails taking you through meadows and subalpine forest. The Hurricane Hill Trail (3.2 miles round-trip) delivers panoramic views of the mountains and ocean. Afterward, head back to Port Angeles for the night.

On Day 7, follow U.S. 101 west to ⑩ **La Push,** a skinny satellite of coastal land that's part of the national park (69 miles from Port Angeles). From La Push, hike 1.4 miles to Third Beach for a taste of the wild Pacific coastline. Back on U.S. 101, head south to the town of Forks and then east to the ⑪ **Hoh Rain Forest,** also part of Olympic National Park. Explore the moss-covered alders and big-leaf maples, then follow a circular route on U.S. 101 to ⑫ **Lake Quinault,** winding west toward the coast, then back to the lake and the national park. Check into the Lake Quinault Lodge, then drive up the river to access one of several trails—the Graves Creek Trail is a popular choice—through the lush Quinault Valley.

DAY 8: HEADING HOME
Catch your flight back home from Seattle-Tacoma International, about 130 miles (a 2½-hour drive) from Olympic.

THE CANADIAN ROCKIES: JASPER AND BANFF NATIONAL PARKS, 8 DAYS

A few hundred miles from the U.S. border, the national parks of Jasper and Banff offer spectacular scenery like glaciers, hot springs, and snow-capped peaks, along with the incomparable blue waters of Lake Louise.

DAY 1: WELCOME TO THE CANADIAN ROCKIES
Most visitors will arrive at ❶ **Edmonton International Airport.** You can spend your first night in a hotel close to the airport or make the drive to Jasper right away.

DAYS 2 AND 3: JASPER NATIONAL PARK
396 km (246 miles) or a 4-hour drive from Edmonton International.

Begin your trip to ❷ **Jasper National Park** with a tour of the historic Jasper Townsite; be sure to stop at the Jasper Information Centre to get trail maps and information about free park interpretive programs. Then take a drive to ❸ **Disaster Point,** about 40 km (24 miles) east of Jasper on Highway 16 (Yellowhead Highway) while keeping an eye out for bighorn sheep and other wildlife. Stop at nearby ❹ **Miette Hot Springs,** 61 km (37 miles) east of Jasper, to enjoy a swim in the hot mineral pools. Book a room in Jasper (Alpine Village is a cozy favorite) for the next two nights.

Spend the next morning exploring ❺ **Mt. Edith Cavell** located off Highway 93 (the Icefields Parkway) and Cavell Road about 28 km (17 miles) south of Jasper. The 1-km (0.5-mile) trail from the parking lot leads to the base of an imposing cliff, where you can see the stunning Angel Glacier. A steep 3-km (2-mile) trail climbs up the valley to Cavell Meadows, which are carpeted with wildflowers from mid-July to mid-August. There are many options for the afternoon: hiking in nearby ❻ **Maligne Canyon,** kayaking in Maligne Lake, horseback riding, or mountain biking (the park has 300 km [186 miles] of trails with options for riders of all levels).

4

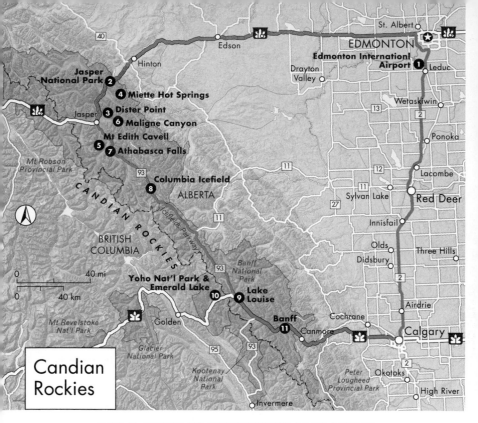

DAY 4: ICEFIELDS PARKWAY TO LAKE LOUISE
230 km (140 miles) or a 3-hour drive to Lake Louise.

From Jasper, head south 31 km (19 miles) on Highway 93, otherwise known as the Icefields Parkway, to ❼ **Athabasca Falls.** The 75-foot falls are some of the most powerful in the Canadian national parks. Continue along the Parkway until you reach the Athabasca Glacier, one of the eight major glaciers making up the ❽ **Columbia Icefield.** This incredible icefield covers an area of approximately 325 square km (125 square miles) and is one of the largest accumulations of ice and snow south of the Arctic Circle. Enjoy lunch at the Icefield Centre, and then experience an ice explorer bus tour or a guided hike of the Athabasca Glacier. ⚠ **For safety reasons, do not venture onto the glacier without a guide.** Continue driving along the Icefields Parkway and into Banff National Park, passing the Weeping Wall and stopping to stretch your legs at the Saskatchewan River Crossing and scenic Bow Lake, before stopping for the night at ❾ **Lake Louise.**

DAY 5: LAKE LOUISE
Spend the morning enjoying the scenery at beautiful Lake Louise, snapping a few pictures of the impressive Victoria Glacier flowing off the mountain at the lake's end. You can enjoy afternoon tea at the classy Fairmont Chateau Lake Louise Hotel adjacent to the lake,

then ride the Lake Louise Sightseeing Gondola to the Interpretive Centre at the top, where you can participate in a guided hike or presentation (or just have lunch) on an alpine plateau with a view of a dozen-plus glaciers. If time permits, take a drive 40 km (24 miles) west to **❿ Yoho National Park** and **Emerald Lake,** where you can rent a canoe, have dinner, or just take a stroll. Afterward, head back to Lake Louise for the night.

DAYS 6 AND 7: BANFF NATIONAL PARK
57 km (36 miles) or an hour drive from Lake Louise.

Spend the morning of Day 6 exploring the quaint shops and restaurants crammed together on Banff Avenue in the town of **⓫ Banff.** Stop at the Fairmont Banff Springs Hotel, a National Historic Site, and stroll the grounds or take a guided horseback ride from the on-site stables. Finish your day with a late-night dip in the Banff Upper Hot Springs. Spend the next two nights at the gorgeous Fairmont Banff Springs; there are plenty more affordable lodging options in the park as well.

On your second day in Banff, hike around Vermillion Lakes, off Highway 1. Common wildlife sightings in this wetlands setting include elk, bighorn sheep, muskrats, and the occasional moose. Then hop on the Banff Gondola to enjoy the view from the 7,500-foot summit of Sulfur Mountain. Later on, you can hike the 3-km (1-mile) trail around Johnson Lake or hit the water in a canoe or kayak.

DAY 8: HEADING HOME
It's 355 km (221 miles), about 3½ hours of driving, from Banff back to Edmonton International Airport.

YELLOWSTONE AND GRAND TETON, 7 DAYS

A visit to these two parks takes you through one of the last remaining natural ecosystems in this region of the world. Here, you'll see wildlife ranging from beavers, bison and bears to weasels and wolves, plus pristine mountain lakes, bubbling mud pots, and the world's biggest collection of geysers.

DAY 1: WELCOME TO YELLOWSTONE
If you'll be flying, the **❶ Jackson Hole Airport** in Jackson, Wyoming, is probably the best place to start, as it's only an hour from the southern entrance of Yellowstone. You'll find plenty of lodging options in Jackson for your first night, or you can book a room at one of the park's nine lodges—the centrally located Lake Hotel or the iconic Old Faithful Inn. Depending on your arrival time, you can spend the rest of your first day exploring the town of Jackson or, if you're staying in the park, taking a short driving tour around the lodge area.

DAYS 2–4: YELLOWSTONE NATIONAL PARK
Dedicate the next three days to **❷ Yellowstone National Park,** which because of its sheer size and incredible diversity of wildlife and scenery, could take a lifetime to fully explore its 2.2 million acres. Spend your first day on the park's 140-mile Grand Loop Road. This road forms a big figure-eight as it passes nearly every major Yellowstone attraction, and offers interpretive displays, overlooks, and short trails along the way.

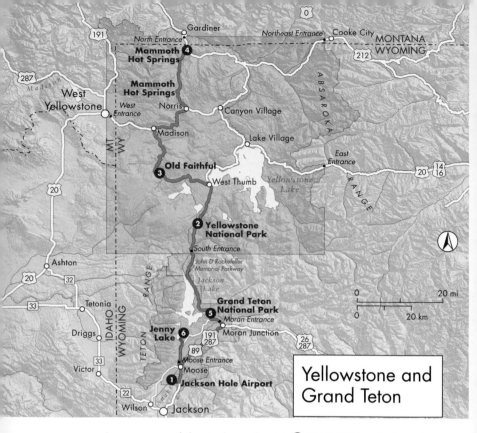

Yellowstone and Grand Teton

On your second day in the park, visit ❸ **Old Faithful** and take a short hike (about 2.5 miles round-trip) around Mystic Falls, then up head to the Canyon Village section of the park for a look at the Grand Canyon of Yellowstone, with its two separate waterfalls. For a more strenuous option, hike from Dunraven Pass to the summit of Mt. Washburn for wildflowers, wildlife, and panoramic views (6.2 miles round-trip).

For your third day, explore the northern part of the park, starting with the ❹ **Mammoth Hot Springs** area, with its terraced limestone formations. From there, head past Tower-Roosevelt to the Lamar Valley in the far northeast corner of the park for gorgeous mountain views, enormous herds of bison, and your best chance to spot wolves. Then check out the Mud Volcano and Sulphur Caldron in the Hayden Valley area, just south of Canyon Village.

DAYS 5 AND 6: GRAND TETON NATIONAL PARK
8 miles from Yellowstone's southern entrance to the northern boundary of Grand Teton.

Leaving Yellowstone, drive south into ❺ **Grand Teton National Park.** Stop in at the Flagg Ranch Information Station, about 2 miles from Yellowstone's southern boundary, to pick up a map and other information.

The largest hot spring in the country, the striking Grand Prismatic Spring, is located in Yellowstone, just north of Old Faithful.

The sheer ruggedness of the Tetons makes them seem imposing and unapproachable, but a drive on Teton Park Road, with frequent stops at scenic turnouts, will get you up close and personal with the peaks. The Jenny Lake Scenic Drive delivers fantastic views as well; just north of ❻ **Jenny Lake,** pull over to the Leigh Lake Trailhead for a hike. You can take the 3.7-mile loop around String Lake, or head north, then take the right-hand branch of the trail and follow the eastern shore of the lake (turn around at the campground on Trapper Lake) for a 9-mile hike. Spend your two nights at any of the excellent lodges or cabins in the park.

Your second day in the park, head back to Jenny Lake and catch a ferry across to the western side, where you can take either a short hike along the Cascade Canyon Trail (2 miles round-trip) or hike the Forks of Cascade Canyon, a 9.6-mile trip that's well worth the effort. If you'd rather explore Jenny Lake from the water, rent a canoe or kayak or take a guided tour.

DAY 7: HEAD HOME
When your visit to Grand Teton is complete, getting back to the Jackson Hole airport couldn't be simpler: it's actually inside the park boundary, about 4 miles from the southern entrance.

THE BLACK HILLS OF SOUTH DAKOTA: WIND CAVE AND BADLANDS NATIONAL PARKS, 6 DAYS

The national parks of southwestern South Dakota—along with the state park and two national memorials nearby—deliver a surprising variety of sights: the swaying grasses and abundant wildlife of one of the country's few remaining intact prairies, the complex labyrinth of passages and unique geologic formations in one of the world's longest caves, and some of the richest fossil beds on earth.

DAY 1: WIND CAVE NATIONAL PARK

The closest commercial airport is ❶ **Rapid City Regional Airport,** about 70 miles from Wind Cave. Arrive in the morning to pick up your rental car and make the 1½-hour drive to ❷ **Wind Cave National Park,** with more than 33,000 acres of wildlife habitat above ground (home to bison, elk, pronghorn, and coyotes) and one of the world's longest caves (featuring several types of rare rock formations) below. Take an afternoon cave tour and a short drive through the park. Spend the night in one of the B&Bs around ❸ **Hot Springs,** 11 miles away.

DAY 2: CUSTER STATE PARK

20 miles or a 50-minute drive from Wind Cave.

Spend today at ❹ **Custer State Park,** 31 miles north of Hot Springs. The 71,000-acre park has exceptional drives, lots of wildlife (including a herd of 1,300 bison), and fingerlike granite spires rising from the forest floor (they're the reason this is called the Needles region of South Dakota). While you're in the park, be sure to visit Limber Pine Natural Area, a National Natural Landmark containing spectacular ridges of granite. If you have time, check out the Cathedral Spires trail, 2.5 miles round trip. Overnight in one of four mountain lodges at the Custer State Park Resort.

DAY 3: JEWEL CAVE NATIONAL MONUMENT AND CRAZY HORSE MEMORIAL

30 miles or about an hour drive from Custer State Park.

Today, venture down U.S. 16 to ❺ **Jewel Cave National Monument,** 13 miles west of Custer, an underground wilderness where you can see beautiful nailhead and dogtooth spar crystals lining its more than 168 miles of passageways.

After visiting Jewel Cave, head back to Custer and take U.S. 16/385 to ❻ **Crazy Horse Memorial** (19 miles north of Jewel Cave), home to a colossal mountain carving of the legendary Lakota leader and the Indian Museum of North America. Afterward, head 10 miles north to the former gold and tin mining town of ❼ **Hill City,** where you'll spend the night.

DAY 4: MT. RUSHMORE NATIONAL MEMORIAL

23 miles or about a half an hour drive from the Crazy Horse Memorial.

This morning, travel 12 miles to ❽ **Mt. Rushmore National Memorial,** where you can view the huge carved renderings of presidents Washington, Jefferson, Theodore Roosevelt, and Lincoln. Afterward, head northwest for 23 miles back to Rapid City, the eastern gateway to the Black Hills. Spend the night here.

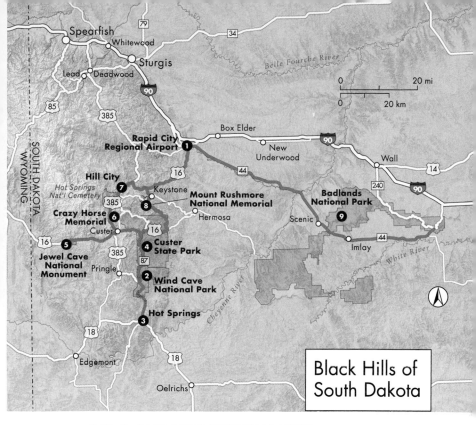

Black Hills of
South Dakota

DAY 5: BADLANDS NATIONAL PARK
79 miles or a 1-hour, 15-minute drive from Rapid City to the northeast entrance of Badlands.

Begin your day early and drive west (75 miles via I–90) to **⑨ Badlands National Park,** a 244,000-acre geologic wonderland. The Badlands Highway Loop Road (Highway 240) wiggles through the moonlike landscape of the park's north unit for 32 miles. Stop in at the Ben Riefel Visitor Center, at the far northeastern edge of the park, to pick up a trail map and head out on a hike. The Notch Trail, 1.5 miles round-trip, offers spectacular views of the White River Valley, but is definitely not for anyone with a fear of heights. The Cliff Shelf trail, 0.5 mile round-trip, is a more mellow option that showcases rock formations and juniper forest as well as occasional wildlife sightings (bighorn sheep is a frequent favorite).

After you leave the park, head back to Rapid City to spend the night.

DAY 6: HEADING HOME
The airport in Rapid City is 20 minutes east of town.

BEST OF CALIFORNIA: YOSEMITE, SEQUOIA AND KINGS CANYON, AND DEATH VALLEY, 9 DAYS

This trip takes you to California's most popular national parks. Yosemite is a nearly 1,200-square-mile expanse in the western Sierras filled with meadows, waterfalls, and spectacular granite domes and canyons. Nearby Sequoia and Kings Canyon parks deliver spectacular alpine scenery along with the world's largest trees. And Death Valley is a land of extremes, with its impossibly dry (and hot) below-sea-level basin alongside high mountain peaks and diverse wildlife.

DAY 1: WELCOME TO CALIFORNIA

If you're planning to start this trip with a flight, your best bet would be to arrive at ❶ **Fresno Yosemite International Airport,** which is reasonably close to Yosemite (your first stop) and Sequoia and Kings Canyon (your last), 70 miles (1½ hours) from Sequoia and Kings Canyon.

From the airport, head east toward ❷ **Yosemite National Park** and its ❸ **Arch Rock Entrance,** on the eastern side on El Portal Road. Depending on how much time you've got, either do some exploring (head for the Yosemite Valley Visitor Center, 16 miles from the entrance) or look for lodging. You can stay in the park (there are several options, from primitive camping to luxury rooms at the Ahwahnee Hotel) or in ❹ **Mariposa,** about 32 miles (45 minutes) southwest of the Arch Rock Entrance on Route 140.

DAYS 2–4: YOSEMITE NATIONAL PARK

64 miles or about a 1-hour, 15-minute drive from the airport.

Early in the morning of Day 2, head into Yosemite Valley, near the center of the park, and take a hike on Lower Yosemite Fall Trail, an easy 1.1-mile loop. If you've got more time and ambition, continue on for the first mile of the Upper Fall Trail to Columbia Rock, where you'll be rewarded with spectacular views of both the upper and lower sections of the highest waterfall in North America. Afterward, stop in at the historic Ahwahnee Hotel, then attend one of the ranger programs or a presentation at Yosemite Theater.

On your second day in the park, head back to the Yosemite Valley area and take an easy hike around Mirror Lake (5 miles round-trip) or a more strenuous trek to Vernal Fall (2.4 miles round-trip), then drop in at the Yosemite Museum (next to the visitor center) and the nearby reconstructed Indian Village. Drive up to Glacier Point for a valley-wide view, timing your arrival for sunset.

On your last day in the park, head east to Tuolumne Meadows, where you can stretch your legs with a hike (an easy option is the 1.5-mile round-trip trail to Soda Springs and historic Parsons Lodge). Then take a drive on Tioga Road, a 59-mile stretch through the high country that takes you over Tioga Pass (9,941 feet) and along the highest stretch of road in California. Leave the park through the ❺ **Tioga Pass Entrance,** then drive south 134 miles (about 2 hours, 15 minutes) to the town of ❻ **Lone Pine,** where you'll spend the night.

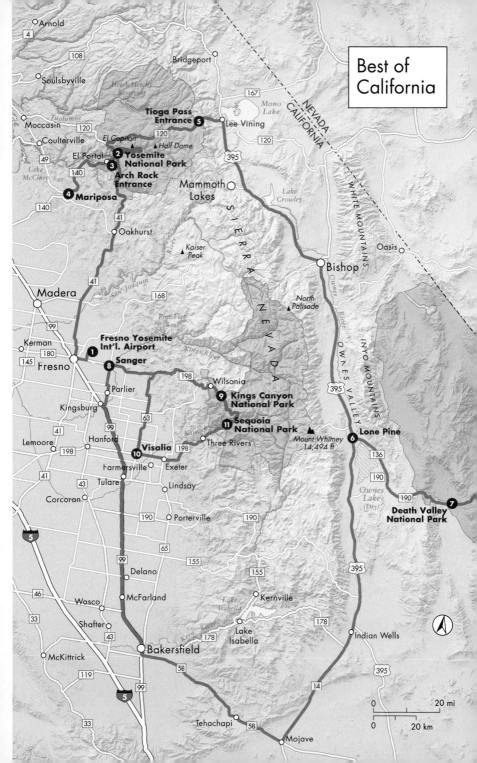

DAYS 5 AND 6: DEATH VALLEY NATIONAL PARK
37 miles or a 40-minute drive from Lone Pine.

On Day 5, drive to ❼ **Death Valley National Park,** known as the lowest, driest, and hottest place in North America. Covering more than 5,300 square miles, it's also the biggest national park in the lower 48, with vast expanses of desert and mountain ranges extending as far as the eye can see. But heat here is brutal (summer temperatures often exceed 120 degrees), so you should follow the park's guidelines carefully: do not hike when temperatures are high (especially in the lower parts of the park), always carry water (even when you're in a car), and keep your speed down when driving (and be sure to stay on paved roads).

Begin in the Furnace Creek area, roughly in the middle of the park. If you're getting an early start, hike into Golden Canyon by taking the 1-mile-long interpretive trail, which starts 2 miles south of Highway 190 on Badwater Road. From there, head to Devil's Golf Course (11 miles south of Furnace Creek) to see millions of tiny salt pinnacles and, if you get up close, a mass of perfectly round holes. Badwater Basin, 8 miles farther south, has expansive saltwater flats and the lowest point in the park, which is 282 feet below sea level. Then go to the highest spot—Dante's View, 5,000 feet above the valley floor—for the best views and blessedly cooler temperatures (the lookout is about 20 miles southeast of Furnace Creek). If you want to hike, there's a trail leading from the parking area onto Dante's Ridge that offers even more spectacular vistas (it's ½ mile to the first summit, then another 4 miles to Mt. Perry).

On your second day in Death Valley, explore the northern section of the park, near Grapevine Canyon (about 52 miles north of Furnace Creek). Uhebe Crater is visible from a turnout on the road. From there, if your car has high clearance and good tires, you can drive 27 miles southwest on a rough dirt road to the Racetrack, a phenomenal dry lakebed famous for its mysterious moving rocks (to see the rocks, drive 2 miles past the Grandstand parking area). From there, double back and drive another 3 miles east to Scotty's Castle, a quirky historic mansion.

Leave the park and head toward Sequoia and Kings Canyon. Stop in ❽ **Sanger,** 280 miles (about 4½ hours) from Death Valley, to spend the night.

DAYS 7 AND 8: SEQUOIA AND KINGS CANYON NATIONAL PARKS
41 miles or a 45-minute drive from Sanger.

From Sanger, drive east to the Big Stump Entrance of ❾ **Kings Canyon National Park.** Inside the park, head to Grant Grove Village and stop at the visitor center there, then take the Kings Canyon Scenic Byway (Route 180) along the Kings River and its giant granite canyon that is well over a mile deep at some points. Stop along the way at pullouts for long vistas of some of the highest mountains in the United States. Hike the Zumwalt Meadow Trail (1.5 miles), which starts just before the end of the road, 4.5 miles from Cedar Grove Village, for gorgeous views of the park's largest meadow, plus high granite walls, talus, and the river below. At the end of the day, follow Route 180 back to Grant Grove Village and take Generals Highway south into Sequoia National Park. Leave through the Ash Mountain Entrance and head to the nearby town of ❿ **Visalia** (35 miles, about 46 minutes away) for the night.

Spend the next day exploring ⓫ **Sequoia National Park**, where some of the world's oldest and largest trees stand. Driving the winding, 40-mile-long Generals Highway takes about two hours. Be sure to stop at the Redwood Mountain Overlook, just outside Cedar Grove Village, for terrific views of the world's largest sequoia grove. Take a hike on the Congress Trail (2 miles), which starts at the General Sherman Tree, the world's largest tree, just off the Generals Highway near Wolverton Road. At the end of the day, head back to Sanger for the night.

DAY 9: HEADING HOME

From Sanger, it's a short 13-mile drive (about 16 minutes) to the Fresno airport.

CANYON COUNTRY: ZION, BRYCE CANYON, AND GRAND CANYON, 9 DAYS

This itinerary takes you through Zion's massive sandstone cliffs and narrow slot canyons, the hoodoos (odd-shape pillars of rock left by erosion) of Bryce Canyon, and the overwhelming majesty of the Grand Canyon, close to 300 river miles long, 18 miles wide, and a mile deep.

DAYS 1: WELCOME TO CANYON COUNTRY

Plan to fly into and out of ❶ **St. George Municipal Airport** in St. George, Utah. It's close to all three parks, with Zion a little more than an hour away.

From the airport, head east toward ❷ **Zion National Park**. Depending on how much daylight you've got, you can start exploring the park—enter at the South Entrance and head to the Zion Canyon Visitor Center—or find a room for the next three nights in ❸ **Springdale**, the bustling town just outside the park (1.1 miles from the East Entrance).

DAYS 2 AND 3: ZION NATIONAL PARK

Start Day 1 at the Visitor Center, just south of the junction of the Zion–Mount Carmel Highway and the Zion Canyon Scenic Drive. Then explore the Drive, either in your own vehicle or via the park's free shuttle, which runs during the summer months (a round-trip ride takes about 80 minutes). Intrepid hikers will want to tackle the Narrows, Zion's infamous 16-mile-long gorge cut by the Virgin River, which requires hikers to spend more than half of their time walking, wading, or swimming in the fast-flowing river. For everyone else, Zion offers plenty of other hiking options. The Emerald Pool Trails (about 1 mile each) take you on a fairly easy hike from Zion Lodge, about 3 miles from Canyon Junction, to Lower and Upper Emerald Pool and waterfalls.

Spend the next day exploring the Kolob Canyons, in the northwestern corner of the park about 40 miles from Canyon Junction. Take the Kolob Canyons Road 5 miles to its end at the Kolob Canyons Viewpoint, where you'll get fabulous views of the surrounding red rock canyons. For a spectacular 5-mile hike, drive about 2 miles back on the Kolob Canyons Road to the Taylor Creek Trail, which takes you past historic homesteaders' cabins and through a narrow box canyon to the Double Arch Alcove, a large arched grotto.

At the end of the day, leave the park via the beautiful Zion–Mount Carmel Highway and its historic mile-long tunnel. You'll pass through slickrock country, with huge, petrified sandstone dunes etched by ancient waters, and head to Bryce Canyon, where you'll spend the night (you've got a few lodging options, both inside and just outside the park).

DAY 4: BRYCE CANYON NATIONAL PARK
74 miles or about a 1-hour, 25-minute drive from the East Entrance of Zion.

Start your tour of ❹ **Bryce Canyon National Park** at the visitor center, about 1 mile past the park entrance. Central to your tour of Bryce Canyon is the 18-mile-long main park road, where numerous scenic turnouts reveal vistas of bright red-orange rock. ■TIP→ If you're visiting in the summer, the free Bryce Canyon Shuttle will take you to many of the park's most popular attractions. Trails worth exploring include the 1-mile Bristlecone Loop Trail and the 1.3 mile Navajo Loop Trail, both of which will get you into the heart of the park.

At the end of the day, leave the park and head toward ❺ **Kanab,** 78 miles (about 1 hour, 25 minutes) away, to spend the night en route to the Grand Canyon.

DAY 5: EN ROUTE TO THE GRAND CANYON
284 miles or a 5-hour, 25-minute drive from Bryce Canyon to the South Rim of the Grand Canyon.

Today, you'll drive from Kanab to ❻ **Grand Canyon National Park.** Check into a hotel in Grand Canyon Village on the ❼ **South Rim** or in ❽ **Tusayan,** a few miles to the south, for the next two nights. If you've got time, hike (or take the shuttle) to Yavapai Point, just west of the visitor center in the South Rim Village, to catch the sunset.

DAYS 6–8: GRAND CANYON NATIONAL PARK
If you didn't make it yesterday, begin today's tour with a stop at the Grand Canyon Visitor Center, near Mather Point in the South Rim Village, for the latest maps and information. While you're there, check out the Historic District, with its early-19th-century train depot and other buildings, many built by the Santa Fe Railroad. Get your bearings with a drive (or, if you're visiting early spring–late fall, a free shuttle ride) on the 7-mile-long Hermit Road. Take a hike on the Rim Trail, a nearly flat path (much of which is paved) that hugs the edge of the canyon from the Village to Hermit's Rest, 2.8 miles to the west.

On your second day in the park, tackle the upper section of one of the "Corridor Trails"—South Kaibab or Bright Angel—which start at the South Rim and meet in the Bright Angel Campground at the bottom

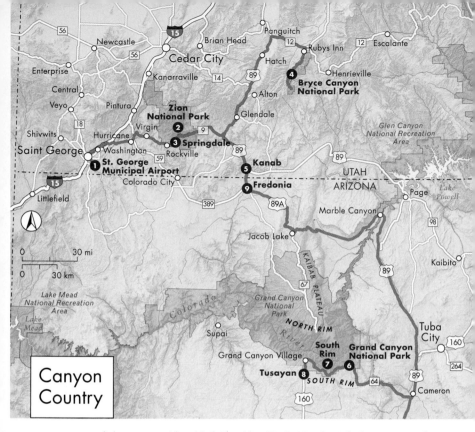

Canyon
Country

of the canyon (the third Corridor Trail, North Kaibab, connects the bottom of the canyon to the North Rim). Bright Angel, the easier of the two, is one of the most scenic paths into the canyon; the trailhead is near Kolb Studio, at the western end of the Village.

Note that visitors are strongly advised against attempting to hike to the bottom of the canyon and back in one day, which means you'll have to pick a place to turn around before you reach the end of the trail. On Bright Angel, that spot would be Indian Garden Campground, about 4.8 miles from the trailhead, or Plateau Point, which is another 1.5 miles past Indian Garden.

For your last day in the park, take an interpretive ranger-led program; they cover a wide variety of subjects, including geology, history, and wildlife so pick up a list at the Grand Canyon Visitor Center. Afterward, you can spend the night in (or near) the park again, or start your drive back toward the airport in St. George. The town of **❾ Fredonia, Arizona** (200 miles; 3 hours, 40 minutes from the South Rim), would be a good stopping point for the night.

DAY 9: HEADING HOME
The St. George Municipal Airport is 74 miles (1 hour, 22 minutes) from Fredonia.

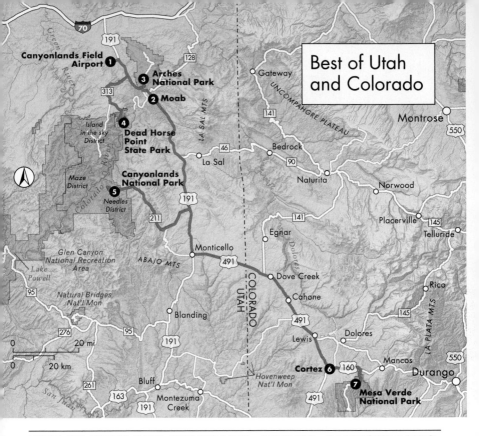

BEST OF UTAH AND COLORADO: ARCHES, CANYONLANDS, AND MESA VERDE NATIONAL PARKS, 6 DAYS

With this itinerary, you'll get to experience two of Utah's best parks. There's Arches, famous for its spectacular colors and unique landforms—natural stone arches, soaring pinnacles, plus giant fins and balanced rocks—and Canyonlands, with a wilderness of canyons and buttes carved by the Colorado River and its tributaries. A few hours away, Colorado's Mesa Verde offers a peek into the lives of the Ancestral Puebloan people, who made it their home from AD 600 to 1300.

DAY 1: WELCOME TO UTAH

The closest airport to your first two destinations is **❶ Canyonlands Field,** also known as Moab Airport, where you can get flights to and from Denver. After you land and get your rental car, head into **❷ Moab** (18 miles; 25 minutes away), where you'll find plenty of options for food and lodging. Book yourself a room for the next two nights.

"Every turn on the Fiery Furnace Trail in Arches brought views of unbelievable natural sculptures, including this double arch." –photo by CarlB9090, Fodors.com member

DAYS 2 AND 3: ARCHES NATIONAL PARK
5 miles from Moab.

Your trip begins at ❸ **Arches National Park,** which holds the world's largest concentration of natural rock windows or "arches." Start with a guided hike in the Fiery Furnace, a maze of sandstone canyons and fins that is considered one of the most spectacular hikes in the park. On your second day, take a detour to the mesa top at ❹ **Dead Horse Point State Park,** about 30 miles west of Moab, for magnificent views of the Colorado River as it goosenecks through the canyons below.

DAYS 4 AND 5: CANYONLANDS
29 miles or about a 48-minute drive from Arches.

From Moab, head to ❺ **Canyonlands National Park.** Start at the park's Island in the Sky District, 11 miles from the state park entrance. Explore the area from the road, which has many overlooks, or hike the first section of the Upheaval Dome Trail, an 8.3-mile loop that starts at Whale Rock, about 11 miles from the visitor center and spotlights an enormous syncline, or downward fold in the Earth's crust (there are overlooks ½ mile and 1 mile from the trailhead).

On Day 5, head to the Needles District, at the southwest corner of the park, and hike the Slickrock Trail (2.4 miles round-trip), keeping an eye out for bighorn sheep. At the end of the day, drive east about 110 miles (2 hours) to ❻ **Cortez,** where you can find a hotel for the night.

DAY 6: MESA VERDE NATIONAL PARK
120 miles or a 2-hour, 12-minute drive from Canyonlands.

From Coretz, drive about 11 miles east to ❼ **Mesa Verde National Park,** with 5,000 archaeological sites (including 600 cliff dwellings) left behind by the Ancestral Puebloan people, who lived here more than 1,000 years ago. Begin your visit at the visitor center, just before the entrance station, to get the latest park information and purchase tour tickets for some of the more popular tours (to get the most out of your visit, plan to take at least one ranger-led tour). Inside the park, stop at the Chapin Mesa Museum, then hike the 0.5-mile Spruce Tree House Trail for a glimpse of the best-preserved cliff dwelling in the park.

After exploring Mesa Verde, you can spend the night at the Far View Lodge inside the park or spend the night in Cortez again. If you've got an early flight in the morning, you'll probably want to head back to Moab.

DAY 6: HEADING HOME
From Mesa Verde, it's a 143-mile (2½-hour) drive back to Canyonlands Field airport.

ARCHES
NATIONAL PARK

Visit Fodors.com for advice, updates, and bookings

WELCOME TO ARCHES

TOP REASONS TO GO

★ **Arch appeal:** Nowhere in the world has such a large array and quantity of natural arches.

★ **Legendary landscape:** This section of Utah is every photographer's dream. No wonder it's been the backdrop for Hollywood legends from John Wayne to Indiana Jones and *Thelma & Louise.*

★ **Treasures hanging in the balance:** Landscape Arch and Balanced Rock look like they might topple tomorrow and they could! Come quick as the features in this park erode and evolve constantly.

★ **Fins and needles:** Fins are parallel vertical shafts of eroding rock that slowly disintegrate into towerlike "needles." The spaces around and between them will carve their way into your memories like the wind and water that formed them.

★ **Moab:** Utah's alternative town is a great base from which to explore by foot, bicycle, balloon, watercraft, and four-wheeler.

1 Devils Garden. About 18 miles from the visitor center, this is the end of the paved road in Arches. The park's only campground, a picnic area, and access to drinking water give way to several trails, including the incomparable Landscape Arch.

2 Fiery Furnace. This forbiddingly named area about 14 miles from the visitor center is so labeled because its orange spires of rock look much like tongues of flame, especially in the late-afternoon sun. Reservations are required weeks in advance to join the twice-daily ranger-guided treks here from March to October. Otherwise you need a permit and canyoneering savvy.

3 The Windows. Reached on a spur 9.2 miles from the visitor center, this area of the park is where visitors with little time stop. Here you can see many of the park's natural arches from your car or on an easy rolling trail.

4 Balanced Rock. This is the kind of landmark only nature can conjure up—a giant rock teetering atop a pedestal, creating a 128-foot formation of red rock grandeur right along the roadside, 9.2 miles from the visitor center.

5 Petrified Dunes. Just a tiny pull-out about 5 miles from the visitor center, this scenic stop is where you can take pictures of acres and acres of petrified sand dunes.

6 Courthouse Towers. The Three Gossips, Sheep Rock, and Tower of Babel are the rock formations to see here. Enter this section of the park 3 miles past the visitor center. The Park Avenue Trail winds through the area, which was named for its steep walls and towers that look like buildings.

7 Moab. A river-running, mountain-biking, canyoneering hub, unconventional Moab is the can't-miss base for all your adventures—and comforts—about 5 miles south of the park.

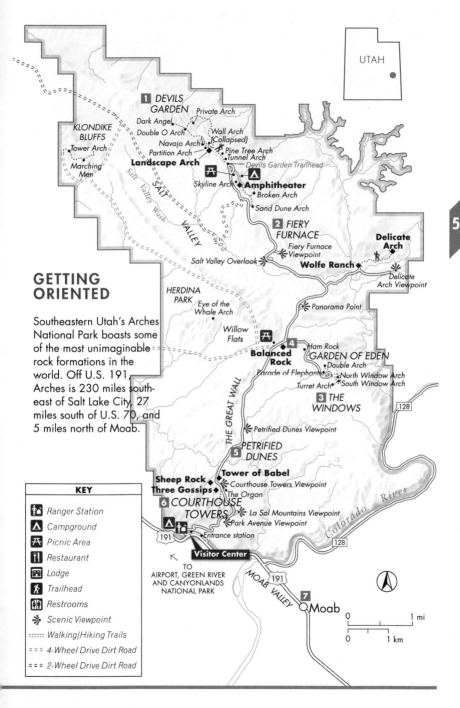

UTAH

1 DEVILS GARDEN

Private Arch

Dark Angel

KLONDIKE BLUFFS

Double O Arch

Navajo Arch

Tower Arch

Partition Arch

Wall Arch (Collapsed)

Pine Tree Arch

Tunnel Arch

Landscape Arch

Marching Men

Devils Garden Trailhead

Skyline Arch

Amphitheater

Broken Arch

Sand Dune Arch

SALT VALLEY

Salt Valley Wash

2 FIERY FURNACE

Fiery Furnace Viewpoint

Delicate Arch

Salt Valley Overlook

Wolfe Ranch

Delicate Arch Viewpoint

GETTING ORIENTED

HERDINA PARK

Eye of the Whale Arch

Panorama Point

Southeastern Utah's Arches National Park boasts some of the most unimaginable rock formations in the world. Off U.S. 191, Arches is 230 miles southeast of Salt Lake City, 27 miles south of U.S. 70, and 5 miles north of Moab.

Willow Flats

Balanced Rock

Ham Rock

GARDEN OF EDEN

Double Arch

North Window Arch

Parade of Elephants

South Window Arch

Turret Arch

3 THE WINDOWS

128

THE GREAT WALL

Petrified Dunes Viewpoint

5 PETRIFIED DUNES

Tower of Babel

Sheep Rock

Three Gossips

Courthouse Towers Viewpoint

The Organ

6 COURTHOUSE TOWERS

La Sal Mountains Viewpoint

Park Avenue Viewpoint

191

Entrance station

128

Colorado River

KEY	
🏕	*Ranger Station*
⛺	*Campground*
🎋	*Picnic Area*
🍴	*Restaurant*
🏠	*Lodge*
🥾	*Trailhead*
🚻	*Restrooms*
⇌	*Scenic Viewpoint*
⋯⋯	*Walking/Hiking Trails*
= = =	*4-Wheel Drive Dirt Road*
= = =	*2-Wheel Drive Dirt Road*

Visitor Center

TO AIRPORT, GREEN RIVER AND CANYONLANDS NATIONAL PARK

MOAB VALLEY

191

7 Moab

0   1 mi

0   1 km

5

Updated by
Steve Pastorino

More than 1 million visitors come to Arches annually, drawn by the red rock landscape and its teasing wind- and water-carved rock formations. The park is named for the 2,500-plus sandstone arches that frame horizons, cast precious shade, and nobly withstand the withering forces of nature and time. Fancifully named attractions like Three Penguins, Queen Nefertiti, and Tower of Babel stir the curiosity, beckoning even the most delicate of travelers from roadside locales. Immerse yourself in this 73,379-acre park, but don't lose yourself entirely—summer temperatures frequently crack 100°F, and water is hard to come by inside the park boundaries.

ARCHES PLANNER

WHEN TO GO

The busiest times of year are spring and fall. In the spring blooming wildflowers herald the end of winter, and temperatures in the 70s bring the year's largest crowds. The crowds remain steady in summer as the thermostat approaches 100°F and above in July and August. Sudden dramatic cloudbursts create rainfalls over red rock walls in late-summer "monsoon" season.

Fall weather is perfect—clear, warm days and crisp, cool nights. The park is much quieter in winter, and from December through February you can hike any of the trails in relative solitude. Snow seldom falls in the valley beneath La Sal Mountains, and when it does, Arches is a photographer's paradise, as snow drapes slickrock mounds and natural rock windows.

AVG. HIGH/LOW TEMPS.

JAN.	FEB.	MAR.	APR.	MAY	JUNE
44/19	53/25	64/33	76/39	84/49	98/58

JULY	AUG.	SEPT.	OCT.	NOV.	DEC.
100/62	99/61	86/50	77/40	58/32	48/21

Note: Extreme highs often exceed 100°F in July and August.

FESTIVALS AND EVENTS

SPRING **Moab Art Walk.** Moab galleries, shops, and cafés celebrate the perfect weather of spring and fall with a series of exhibits. Art Walks are held the second Saturday of the month from March through June and September through November. Stroll the streets to see and purchase original works by Moab artists. ☎ *435/259–4446* ⊕ *www.moabartwalk.com.*

Moab Arts Festival. Every Memorial Day weekend, artists from across the West gather at Moab's Swanny City Park to show their wares, including pottery, photography, and paintings. This fun festival is small enough to be manageable, charges no admission, and offers an array of affordable artwork. There's live music, cultural entertainment, a kids' tent, and lots of food. ☎ *435/259–2742 for Moab Arts Council* ⊕ *www. moabartsfestival.org.*

SUMMER **Canyonlands PRCA Rodeo.** Cowboys come to the Old Spanish Trail Arena (just south of Moab) for three days in late May or early June to try their luck on thrashing bulls and broncs at this annual Western tradition. Tickets start at $10 for adults. ⊠ *3641 S. U.S. 191* ☎ *435/259–6226* ⊕ *www.moabcanyonlandsrodeo.com.*

4th of July Celebration. Moab community residents and organizations unite for some old-fashioned Fourth fun with baking contests, fireworks, a parade, a kiddie carnival, watermelon-eating contests, the mayor's address, and local bands and dance groups. The free community festivities fill Swanny City Park and end with a traditional bang: fireworks. ☎ *435/259–7814.*

FALL **Green River Melon Days.** The town claims its melon festival, dating to 1906, is the world's oldest. All the watermelon you can eat, an old-fashioned parade, 5k run, and other small-town-America activities await you on the third Saturday of September. ☎ *435/564–3448* ⊕ *melon-days.com.*

Moab Music Festival. Moab's red rocks resonate with world-class music—classical, jazz, and traditional—during this annual festival that takes place in the city park, in private homes, or floating along the Colorado River. Musicians from all over the globe perform, and it's one of the West's top music showcases. The festival starts the Thursday before Labor Day and runs about two weeks. ☎ *435/259–7003* ⊕ *www. moabmusicfest.org.*

PLANNING YOUR TIME

There's no food service within the park, so you'll need to pack snacks, lunch, and plenty of water each day before you head into the park. You'll also need to plan ahead to get tickets to the daily Fiery Furnace walk with a ranger. It's a highlight for those who are adventurous and in good shape, but during most of the year, you must reserve your spot in advance at ⊕ *www.recreation.gov.* If you don't have a reservation, you can check for spots at the visitor center (make that your very first stop). The one-day itinerary *(⇨ below)* is based on what to do if you can't take the walk or what to do on a different day. On the day of your Fiery Furnace walk, you can fill in your spare time with a walk on the Park Avenue trail. And if you have a third day, take a rafting trip on the Colorado River, which runs along the park's boundary.

ARCHES IN ONE DAY

Start as early as sunrise for cool temperatures and some of the best natural light, and head out on the 3-mile round-trip hike on the **Delicate Arch Trail.** The route is strenuous but quite rewarding. Pause for a healthy snack before heading to **Devils Garden,** another great spot for morning photography, where you'll also find the easy, primarily flat trail to **Landscape Arch,** the second of the park's two must-see arches. If you're accustomed to hiking, continue on to **Double O,** but be aware that this portion of the trail is strenuous. Along the way, picnic in the shade of a juniper or in a rock alcove. By the time you return you'll be ready to see the rest of the park by car, with some short strolls on easy paths.

In the mid- to late afternoon, drive to **Balanced Rock** for photos, then on to the **Windows.** Wander around on the easy gravel paths for more great photo ops. Depending on what time the sun is due to set, go into town for dinner before or after you drive out to Delicate Arch or the Fiery Furnace and watch the sun set the rocks on fire.

GETTING HERE AND AROUND

AIR TRAVEL

The nearest airport is Canyonlands Field (aka Grand County Airport ☎ *435/259–4849*), 18 miles north of Moab. Great Lakes Airlines flies daily to and from Denver and Las Vegas. Grand Junction Airport (GJT) is 110 miles away in Colorado.

CAR TRAVEL

Interstate 70 is the highway that gets you across Utah from Denver. To dip southeast toward Moab, exit the interstate onto U.S. 191, a main artery running all the way south to the Arizona border, skirting Arches' western border, Moab, and the Manti–La Sal National Forest along the way. Alternatively, you can take Route 128, Colorado River Scenic Byway, traveling just east of Arches. On either road, services can be far apart.

Branching off the main, 18-mile park road are two spurs, one 2½ miles to the Windows section and one 1.6 miles to the Delicate Arch trailhead and viewpoint. There are several four-wheel-drive roads in the park; always check at the visitor center for conditions before attempting to drive them. U.S. 191 tends to back up midmorning to early afternoon. There's likely to be less traffic at 8 am or sunset.

TRAIN TRAVEL

The "California Zephyr," operated by Amtrak (☎ *800/872–7245*), stops daily in Green River, about 50 miles northwest of Moab.

PARK ESSENTIALS
PARK FEES AND PERMITS

Admission to the park is $10 per vehicle and $5 per person on foot, motorcycle, or bicycle, good for seven days. You must pay admission to Canyonlands separately. A $25 local park pass grants you admission to both Arches and Canyonlands parks as well as Natural Bridges and Hovenweep national monuments for one year.

Fees are required for the Fiery Furnace ranger-led hike ($10 per adult, $5 per child ages 7–12) and for a permit to hike without a park ranger in the Fiery Furnace ($4 per adult, $2.50 per child).

PARK HOURS

Arches National Park is open year-round, seven days a week, around the clock. It's in the Mountain time zone.

CELL-PHONE RECEPTION

Cell-phone reception is available intermittently in the park. You can find a public telephone at the park's visitor center.

RESTAURANTS

Because most people come to Arches to play outside, casual trekking-wear rules—sandals, shorts, and T-shirts in the very hot summers. Whether you select an award-winning Continental restaurant in Moab, a nearby resort, or the tavern in Green River, you can dress comfortably in shorts or jeans. But don't let the relaxed attire fool you. There are some wonderful culinary surprises waiting for you, a few with spectacular views as a bonus.

In the park itself, there are no dining facilities and no snack bars. Supermarkets, bakeries, and delis in downtown Moab will be happy to make you food to go. If you bring a packed lunch, there are several picnic areas from which to choose.

Prices in the reviews are the average cost of a main course at dinner, or if dinner is not served, at lunch.

HOTELS

Though there are no hotels or cabins in the park itself, in the surrounding area every type of lodging is available, from economy chain motels to B&Bs and high-end, high-adventure resorts. It's important to know when popular events are held, however, as accommodations can, and do, fill up weeks ahead of time.

Prices in the reviews are the lowest cost of a standard double room in high season. For expanded reviews, facilities, and current deals, visit Fodors.com.

VISITOR INFORMATION
PARK CONTACT INFORMATION

Arches National Park ⊠ *N. U.S. 191, Moab* ☎ *435/719–2299* ⊕ *www. nps.gov/arch.*

VISITOR CENTER

Arches Visitor Center. It's definitely worth stopping to see the interactive displays both inside and outside the building. Take time to view the 15-minute park film "Secrets of Red Rock"; inquire about camping, hiking, and ranger-led programs; fill up water bottles; and shop the bookstore for trail guides, books, and maps to enhance your visit. Exhibits inform you about geology, natural history, and human presence (from Anglo ranchers to Ancestral Puebloan and Fremont) in the Arches area. ⊠ *At park entrance* ☎ *435/719–2299* ⊕ *www.nps. gov/arch* ⊗ *Hrs vary but generally Nov.–Mar., daily 9–5; Apr.–Oct., daily 8–7.*

EXPLORING

SCENIC DRIVES

Arches Main Park Road. Although they are not formally designated as such, the main park road and its two short spurs are scenic and allow you to enjoy many park sights from your car. The main road leads through Courthouse Towers, where you can see Sheep Rock and the Three Gossips, then alongside the Great Wall, the Petrified Dunes, and Balanced Rock. A drive to the Windows section takes you to attractions like Double Arch, and you can see Skyline Arch along the roadside as you approach the campground. The road to Delicate Arch is not particularly scenic, but it allows hiking access to one of the park's main features. Allow about two hours to drive the 36-mile round-trip, more if you explore the spurs and their features and stop at viewpoints along the way.

HISTORIC SITES

Wolfe Ranch. Built in 1906 out of Fremont cottonwoods, this rustic one-room cabin housed Civil War veteran John Wesley Wolfe and his family after their first cabin was lost to a flash flood. Look for remains of a root cellar and a corral as well. Even older than these structures is the nearby Ute rock-art panel by the Delicate Arch trailhead. About 150 feet past the footbridge and before the trail starts to climb, you can see images of bighorn sheep and figures on horseback, as well as some smaller images believed to be dogs. To reach the panel, follow the narrow dirt trail along the rock escarpment until you see the interpretive sign. ⊠ *12.9 miles from park entrance, 1.2 miles off main road.*

SCENIC STOPS

It's easy to spot some of the arches from your car, but you should really take the time to step outside and walk beneath the spans and giant walls of orange rock. This gives you a much better idea of their proportion. No doubt you will feel as writer Edward Abbey did when he awoke on his first day as a park ranger in Arches: that you're walking in the most beautiful place on Earth.

■ TIP➜ **Visit as the sun goes down.** At sunset, the rock formations in Arches glow like fire, and you'll often find photographers behind their tripods waiting for magnificent rays to descend on Delicate Arch or other popular park sites. The Fiery Furnace earns its name as its narrow

CLOSE UP

Plants and Wildlife in Arches

As in any desert environment, the best time to see wildlife in Arches is early morning or evening. Summer temperatures keep most animals tucked away in cool places, though ravens and lizards are exceptions. If you happen to be in the right place at the right time, you may spot one of the beautiful turquoise-necklace-collared lizards. It's more likely you'll see the western whiptail. Mule deer, jackrabbits, and small rodents are usually active in cool morning hours or near dusk. You may spot a lone coyote foraging day or night. The park protects a small herd of desert bighorns, and some of their tribe are seen early in the morning grazing beside U.S. 191 south of the Arches entrance. If you encounter bighorn sheep, do not approach them. They have been known to charge people who attempt to get too close. The park's mule deer and small mammals such as chipmunks are very used to seeing people and may allow you to get close—but don't feed them.

5

fins glow red just before the sun dips below the horizon. Full-moon nights are particularly dramatic in Arches as the creamy white Navajo sandstone reflects light, and eerie silhouettes are created by towering fins and formations.

Balanced Rock. One of the park's favorite sights, this rock is visible for several minutes as you approach—and just gets more impressive and mysterious as you get closer. The formation's total height is 128 feet, with the huge balanced rock rising 55 feet above the pedestal. Be sure to hop out of the car and walk the short loop (0.3 miles) around the base. ⊠ *9.2 miles from park entrance, off main road.*

Fodor's Choice
★
Delicate Arch. The iconic symbol of the park and the state (it appears on many of Utah's license plates), the Delicate Arch is frankly tall and muscular compared to many of the spans in the park—and it's big enough to shelter a four-story building. The arch is a remnant of an Entrada Sandstone fin; the rest of the rock has eroded and now frames the La Sal Mountains in the background. Drive 2.2 miles off the main road to view the arch from a distance, or hike right up to it. The trail is a moderately strenuous 3-mile round-trip hike. ⊠ *13 miles from park entrance, 2.2 miles off main road.*

Double Arch. In the Windows section of the park, Double Arch has appeared in several Hollywood movies, including *Indiana Jones and the Last Crusade.* The northern arch is visible from the parking lot, but walk the short trail to see the southern one, as well as Turret Arch. ⊠ *11.7 miles from park entrance, off main road.*

Fiery Furnace. Fewer than 10% of the park's visitors ever descend into the chasms and washes of Fiery Furnace (a permit or a ranger-led hike is the only way to go), but you can gain an appreciation for this twisted, unyielding landscape from the Overlook. At sunset, the rocks glow a vibrant flame-like red, which gives the formation its daunting moniker. ⊠ *miles from park entrance, off main road.*

Skyline Arch. A quick walk from the parking lot at Skyline Arch gives you closer views and better photos. The short trail is 0.4 miles round-trip and only takes a few minutes to travel. ⊠ *16½ miles from park entrance, off main road.*

FAMILY **The Windows.** As you head north from the park entrance, turn right at Balanced Rock to find this concentration of natural windows, caves, and needles. Stretch your legs on the easy paths that wind between the arches and soak in a variety of geological formations. ⊠ *11.7 miles from park entrance, 2½ miles off main road.*

EDUCATIONAL OFFERINGS

RANGER PROGRAMS

As you explore Arches, look for sandwich boards announcing "Ranger Sightings" and stop for a 3- to 10-minute program led by park staff. Topics range from geology and desert plants to mountain lions and the Colorado River. Most nights, spring through fall, more in-depth campfire programs are available at Devils Garden Campground amphitheater. You may also find guided walks (in addition to the beloved Fiery Furnace walk) during your visit. For information on current schedules and locations of park programs, contact the visitor center (☎ *435/719-2299*) or check the bulletin boards throughout the park.

FAMILY **Fiery Furnace Walk.** Join a park ranger on a two- or three-hour walk
Fodor'sChoice through a labyrinth of rock fins and narrow sandstone canyons. You'll
★ see arches that can't be viewed from the park road and spend time listening to the desert. You should be relatively fit and not afraid of heights if you plan to take this moderately strenuous walk. Wear sturdy hiking shoes, sunscreen, and a hat, and bring at least a liter of water. Walks into the Fiery Furnace are usually offered twice a day (hours vary) and leave from Fiery Furnace Viewpoint. Tickets may be reserved up to six months in advance at ⊕ *www.recreation.gov*, or purchased at the visitor center. Children ages 7–12 pay half price; children under 5 are not recommended. ■ TIP➜ **Book early as the program usually fills several days (or sometimes weeks) prior to each walk.** ⊠ *Fiery Furnace trailhead, off the main road, about 15 miles from park visitor center* 🎟 *$10* ⊙ *Mid-Mar.–Oct., daily (hrs vary).*

FAMILY **Junior Ranger Program.** Kids 2 through 12 can pick up a Junior Ranger booklet at the visitor center. It's full of activities, word games, drawings, and thought-provoking material about the park and the wildlife. To earn your Junior Ranger badge, you must complete several activities in the booklet, attend a ranger program, or watch the park film and pick up some trash in the park. ■ TIP➜ **For ranger program veterans ages 8 and up, ask about the "extra credit" Red Rock Ranger Program.** ⊠ *Visitor center* ☎ *435/719-2299* 🎟 *Free.*

GOOD READS

Arches Visitor Center Bookstore.
Operated by Canyonlands Natural
History Association, Arches Visitor
Center Bookstore is the place in the
park to buy maps, guidebooks, driving tours on CD, and material about
the natural and cultural history of
Arches National Park. ⊠ *At the park
entrance* ☎ *435/259–6003.*

■ *127 Hours: Between a Rock and
a Hard Place* by Aron Ralston. This
true story—made into a movie of
the same name starring James
Franco—took place southeast of
Arches and is a modern-day survivor story of solitary man in nature.

■ *A Naturalist's Guide to Canyon
Country,* by David Williams and Gloria Brown, is an excellent, compact
field guide for both Arches and
Canyonlands national parks.

■ *Best Easy Day Hikes: Arches and
Canyonlands,* by Bill Schneider, is a
pocket-size trail guide that should
boost your confidence as you hit
the trails.

■ *Canyon Country Wildflowers,* by
Damian Fagan, can help you name
the colorful blossoms you see

during wildflower season (spring
and early summer).

■ *Desert Solitaire.* Eminent naturalist Edward Abbey's first ranger
assignment was Arches; this classic
is a must-read.

■ *Exploring Canyonlands and
Arches National Parks,* by Bill
Schneider, provides comprehensive
advice on hiking trails, backcountry
roads, and trip planning.

■ *Hiking Guide to Arches National
Park,* by Damian Fagan, details all of
the park's hiking trails.

■ *Road Guide to Arches National
Park,* by Peter Anderson, has basic
information about the geology and
natural history in the park.

■ *Moab Classic Hikes,* by Damian
Fagan, succinctly gives the skinny
on 40 area hikes and includes maps
and photos.

■ *Self-Guided Driving Tour CD,* produced by the Canyonlands History
Association, is like having a ranger
in your car; CDs can be rented or
purchased.

LEARNING RESOURCES

FAMILY **Red Rock Explorer Pack.** Better than borrowing from a library, families
can check out a youth backpack filled with tools for learning about
both Arches and Canyonlands national parks. Four books, a 3-ring
binder of activities, hand lens magnifier and binoculars are just some
of the loaner items. Backpacks can be returned to either Arches or
Island in the Sky visitor center. Use of the backpack is free with a
credit-card imprint in case of loss or damage to the pack or enclosed
items. ☎ *435/719–2299* ⊠ *Free.*

SPORTS AND THE OUTDOORS

Arches National Park lies in the middle of one of the adventure capitals of the United States. Deep canyons and towering walls are everywhere you look. Slick sandstone surfaces, known as slickrock, make for some of the world's best mountain biking. Thousand-foot sandstone walls draw rock climbers from across the globe. Hikers can choose from shady canyons or red rock ridges that put you in the company of the West's big sky. The Colorado River forms the southeast boundary of the park and can give you every grade of white-water adventure.

> **NOTABLE QUOTE**
>
> "You can't see *anything* from a car; you've got to get out and walk, better yet crawl, on hands and knees, over the sandstone and through the thornbush and cactus. When traces of blood begin to mark your trail you'll see something, maybe."
>
> —Edward Abbey, *Desert Solitaire*

Moab-based outfitters can set you up for any sport you may have a desire to try: mountain biking, ATVs, dirt bikes, four-wheel-drive vehicles, kayaking, climbing, stand-up paddleboarding, and even skydiving. Within the park, it's best to stick with basics such as hiking, sightseeing, and photography. Climbers and other adventure seekers should always inquire at the visitor center about restrictions.

MULTISPORT OUTFITTERS

Adrift Adventures. This outfitter takes pride in well-trained guides who can take you via foot, raft, kayak, 4X4, horse, and more, all over the Moab area, including the Colorado and Green rivers. They also offer history, movie, and rock-art tours. They've been in business since 1978 and have a great reputation around town. ⊠ *378 N. Main St., Moab* ☏ *435/259–8594, 800/874–4483* ⊕ *www.adrift.net.*

Dual Sport Utah. If you're into dirt biking, Dual Sport Utah is the only outfitter in Moab specializing in street-legal, off-road dirt-bike tours and rentals. Follow the Klondike Bluffs trail to Arches, or negotiate the White Rim Trail in Canyonlands in a fraction of the time you would spend on a mountain bike. ⊠ *197 W. Center St., Moab* ☏ *435/260–2724* ⊕ *www.dualsportutah.com.*

Moab Adventure Center. This reputable company has been offering river rides since 1961. Their prominent storefront on Main Street has tons of info about rafting, 4x4 tours, scenic flights, hikes, balloon rides, and much, much more. ⊠ *225 S. Main St., Moab* ☏ *435/259–7019, 866/904–1163* ⊕ *www.moabadventurecenter.com.*

NAVTEC. Doc Williams was the first doctor in Moab in 1896, and some of his descendants have never left, sharing his love for the area through this rafting, canyoneering, and 4x4 company. Whether you want to explore by boat, boots, or wheels, Navtec gives you a multitude of one-day and multiday options. ⊠ *321 N. Main St., Moab* ☏ *435/259–7983, 800/833–1278* ⊕ *www.navtec.com.*

SHUTTLES

Coyote Shuttle. If you need a ride to or from your hike or bike trailhead or river trip, call the Coyote. ■TIP→ Their website is a wealth of knowledge on trail and river conditions, and you can connect with others to carpool and save money. ✉ 55 W. 300 S, Moab ☎ 435/260–2097, 435/259–8656 ⊕ www.coyoteshuttle.com.

Roadrunner Shuttle. With vehicles that seat up to 24 people, Roadrunner is a great resource for groups large and small to get to trailheads or put-in spots. ✉ 197 W. Center St., Moab ☎ 435/259–9402 ⊕ www. roadrunnershuttle.com.

BICYCLING

There's world-class biking all around Arches National Park, but the park proper is not the best place to explore on two wheels. Bicycles are allowed only on established roads, and because there are no shoulders cyclists share the roadway with drivers and pedestrians gawking at the scenery. If you do want to take a spin in the park, try the dirt-and-gravel Willow Flats Road, the old entrance to the park. The road is about 6½ miles long one-way and starts directly across from the Balanced Rock parking lot. It's a pretty mountain-bike ride on dirt and sand through slickrock, pinyon, and juniper country. You must stay on the road with your bicycle or you chance steep fines.

TOURS AND OUTFITTERS

Chile Pepper Bikes. For mountain bike rentals, sales, service, and gear, plus espresso, stop at Chile Pepper Bikes before you hit the trails. ✉ 702 S. Main St., Moab ☎ 435/259–4688, 888/677–4688 ⊕ www. chilebikes.com.

Poison Spider Bicycles. This fully loaded shop serves the thriving road-cycling community as well as mountain bikers. Rent, buy (including Trek, Kona, Yeti, and Cervelo), or service your bike here. You can also arrange for shuttle service and purchase merchandise. ✉ 497 N. Main St., Moab ☎ 435/259–7882, 800/635–1792 ⊕ www. poisonspiderbicycles.com.

Rim Cyclery. The oldest bike shop in town, Rim Cyclery has offered mountain bike rentals and sales, trail advice, equipment, and gear since 1983. They have expertise in Specialized bikes. ✉ 94 W. 100 N, Moab ☎ 435/259–5333, 888/304–8219 ⊕ www.rimcyclery.com.

Rim Tours. Reliable, friendly, and professional, Rim Tours has been taking guests on guided one-day or multiday mountain-bike tours, including Klondike Bluffs (which enters Arches) and the White Rim Trail (inside Canyonlands) since 1985. Road-bike tours as well as bike rentals (and some sales) are also available. ✉ 1233 S. U.S. 191, Moab ☎ 435/259–5223, 800/626–7335 ⊕ www.rimtours.com.

Western Spirit Cycling. Head here for fully supported, go-at-your-own-pace, multiday bike tours throughout the western states, including trips to Canyonlands and the 140-mile Kokopelli Trail, which runs from Grand Junction, Colorado, to Moab. Guides versed in the geologic wonders of the area cook up meals worthy of the scenery each night.

5

Ask about family rides, too. There's also the option to combine a Green River kayak trip with the three-night bike route. ✉ *478 Mill Creek Dr., Moab* ☎ *435/259–8732, 800/845–2453* ⊕ *www.westernspirit.com.*

BIRD-WATCHING

Within the park you'll definitely see plenty of the big, black, beautiful raven. Look for them perched on top of a picturesque juniper branch or balancing on the bald knob of a rock. The noisy black-billed magpie populates the park, as do the more melodic canyon and rock wrens. Lucky visitors will spot a red-tailed hawk and hear its distinctive call.

Serious birders will have more fun visiting the **Scott M. Matheson Wetlands Preserve** *(⇨ Bird-watching, under Area Activities in the What's Nearby section)* 5 miles south of the park. The wetlands is home to more than 225 species of birds including the wood duck, western screech owl, indigo bunting, and plumbeous vireo.

BOATING AND RIVER EXPEDITIONS

Although the Colorado River runs along the border of the park, there is no boating within the park proper. You can, however, enjoy a splashy ride nearby on the Fisher Towers stretch of the river north of Moab, and there are plenty of fine outfitters in Moab that can set you up for expeditions. *⇨ For rafting outside the park, see Rafting, under Area Activities in the What's Nearby section.*

TOURS AND OUTFITTERS

Canyon Voyages Adventure Co. Since 1991, Canyon Voyages has been an excellent choice for rafting or kayaking adventures on the Colorado or Green rivers. Don and Denise Oblak run a friendly, professional company that's open year-round. While the majority of their customers take one-day trips, they also offer multiday itineraries, guided tours, and rentals. It's also the only company that operates a kayak school for those who want to learn how to run the rapids on their own. Ask about stand-up paddleboarding, biking, and horseback riding, too. Inside the booking office is a great shop that sells outdoor essentials, including clothing, hats, footwear, and backpacks. ✉ *211 N. Main St., Moab* ☎ *435/259–6007, 800/733–6007* ⊕ *www.canyonvoyages.com.*

Holiday River Expeditions. Since 1966, Holiday River Expeditions has offered one- to eight-day adventures on the Green and Colorado rivers, including inside Canyonlands National Park. Located behind the Comfort Inn in Green River, they also offer multisport trips, women's retreats, and bike adventures including the White Rim Trail. ✉ *2075 E. Main St., Green River* ☎ *435/564–3273, 800/624–6323* ⊕ *www.bikeraft.com.*

Tex's Riverways. The knowledgeable folks at Tex's Riverways shuttle hikers and boaters up, down, to, and from the Green and Colorado rivers. You can also rent canoes, kayaks, and gear from coolers to portable toilets (which are required on Utah rivers) for your backpacking or river adventure. Friendly expert advice based on more than 50 years of experience is included, but Tex's doesn't do guided tours. ✉ *691 N. 500 W, Moab* ☎ *435/259–5101, 877/662–2839* ⊕ *www.texsriverways.com.*

FISHING

There is no fishing in Arches National Park, and the Colorado River is too silty to offer good fishing. The nearby La Sal Mountains are dotted with small lakes that are stocked with small trout, but finding good native trout fishing in the area will take some effort.

FOUR-WHEELING

With thousands of acres of nearby Bureau of Land Management lands to enjoy, it's hardly necessary to use the park's limited trails for four-wheel adventures. You can, however, go backcountry in Arches on the Willow Flats Road and the Salt Valley Road—just don't set out for this expedition without first stopping at the visitor center to learn of current conditions. Salt Valley Road is very sandy and requires special driving skills.

TOURS AND OUTFITTERS

Coyote Land Tours. The imposing Mercedes Benz Unimog trucks (which dwarf Hummers) of this tour company take you to parts of the backcountry where you could never wander on your own. They offer technical tours (challenging drives over and through imposing rock formations, washes, and assorted obstacles), plus tamer sunset excursions, and camp-style ride-and-dine trips. They stand by their money-back "great time" guarantee. ☎ *435/259–6649 ⊕ www.coyotelandtours.com.*

High Point Hummer & ATV. "Moab's backcountry is our church," says enthusiastic, wilderness-loving owner Lori McFarland. Along with husband Scott, the family has operated High Point Hummer & ATV since 1996. Tour the backcountry in open-air Hummer vehicles, ATVs, dirt bikes, or dune buggy–like "side-by-sides" that seat up to six people. They love families and small, intimate groups, and they offer hiking and canyoneering as well. ⊠ *281 N. Main St., Moab* ☎ *435/259–2972, 877/486–6833 ⊕ www.highpointhummer.com.*

HIKING

Getting out on any one of the park trails will surely cause you to fall in love with this Mars-like landscape. But remember, you are hiking in a desert environment and approximately 1 mile above sea level. Many people succumb to heat and dehydration because they do not drink enough water. Park rangers recommend a gallon of water per day per person.

EASY

FAMILY **Balanced Rock Trail.** You'll want to stop at Balanced Rock for photo opportunities, so you may as well walk the easy, partially paved trail around the famous landmark. This is one of the most accessible trails in the park and is suitable for small children and folks who may have difficulty walking. The trail is only 0.3 mile round-trip; you should allow 15 minutes for the walk. *Easy.* ⊠ *Trailhead approximately 9 miles from park entrance.*

Broken Arch Trail. An easy walk across open grassland, this loop trail passes Broken Arch, which is also visible from the road. The arch gets its name because it appears to be cracked in the middle, but it's not really broken. The trail is 1.3 miles round-trip, and you should allow about an hour for the walk. *Easy.* ✉ *Trailhead at end of Sand Dune Arch trail, 0.3 mile off main road, 11 miles from park entrance.*

Double Arch Trail. If it's not too hot, anyone can walk here from Windows Trail. This relatively flat trail leads you to two massive arches that make for great photo opportunities. The 0.8-mile round trip gives you a good taste of desert flora and fauna. *Easy.* ✉ *Trailhead 2½ miles from main road, on the Windows Section spur road.*

PAW PRINTS

If Fido is along for the Arches adventure, keep in mind that pooches aren't allowed onnational park trails and must be on leash in the Devils Garden Campground. However, canines can join you on Bureau of Land Management trails, such as Negro Bill Canyon (named for one of the town's first nonnative settlers, William Granstaff), which match the beauty of in-park hikes. The heat can be stifling, so remember to bring enough water for you and your four-legged friend, hit the trails in the early morning hours, and avoid midsummer scorchers.

Landscape Arch. This natural rock opening competes with Kolob Arch at Zion for the title of largest geologic span in the world. Measuring 306 feet from base to base, it appears as a delicate ribbon of rock bending over the horizon. In 1991, a slab of rock about 60 feet long, 11 feet wide, and 4 feet thick fell from the underside, leaving it even thinner. You can reach it by walking a rolling, gravel 1.4-mile-long trail. *Easy.* ✉ *Trailhead at Devils Garden, off main road, 18 miles north of park entrance.*

Park Avenue Trail. The first named trail that park visitors encounter, Park Avenue Trail is an easy, 2-mile round-trip walk (with only one small hill) amidst walls and towers that resemble a New York City skyline. You'll walk under the gaze of Queen Nefertiti, a giant rock formation that some observers think has Egyptian-looking features. If you are traveling with companions, make it a one-way, 1-mile downhill trek by having them pick you up at the Courthouse Towers Viewpoint. Allow about 45 minutes for the one-way journey. *Easy.* ✉ *Trailhead off main road, 2 miles from park entrance.*

FAMILY **Sand Dune Arch Trail.** Your kids will return to the car with shoes full of bright red sand from this giant sandbox in the desert and will love exploring in and around the rock. ⚠ **Do not climb or jump off the arch, as doing so has frequently resulted in injuries.** Set aside five minutes for this shady, 0.3-mile walk and as much time as your children's imaginations allow for play. The trail intersects with the Broken Arch Trail, so if you visit both arches it's a 1½-mile round trip. *Easy.* ✉ *Trailhead off main road, about 15½ miles from park entrance.*

FAMILY **Windows Trail.** The first stop for many visitors to the park, Windows Trail gives you an opportunity to get out and enjoy the desert air. Here you'll see three giant openings in rock and walk on a trail that leads you

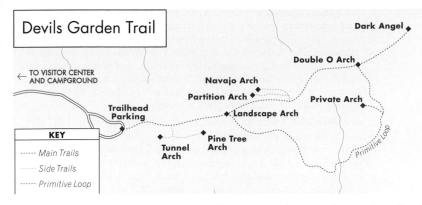

right through the holes. Allow about an hour on this gently inclined, 1-mile round-trip hike. As 90% of visitors won't follow the "primitive" trail around the backside of the two windows, take advantage if you want some desert solitude. The primitive trail adds an extra half hour to the trip. *Easy.* ⊠ *Trailhead off main road, 9½ miles from park entrance.*

MODERATE

Fodor's Choice
★ **Delicate Arch Trail.** To see the park's most famous freestanding arch up close takes effort and won't offer you much solitude—but it's worth every step. The 3-mile round-trip trail ascends via steep slickrock, sandy paths, and along one narrow ledge (at the very end) that might give pause to anyone afraid of heights. Plus, there's almost no shade. First-timers should start early to avoid the mid-day heat in summer. Still, at sunrise, sunset, and every hour in between, it's the park's most popular and busiest trail. ■TIP➜ The reward is not just the view, but the opportunity for photo ops directly under the span, so be sure to bring your camera. Allow two to three hours for this hike, depending on your fitness level and how long you plan to linger at the arch. If you go at sunset or sunrise, bring a headlamp or flashlight. Don't miss Wolfe Ranch and some ancient rock art near the trailhead. *Moderate.* ⊠ *Trailhead 2.2 miles off main road, 13 miles from park entrance.*

Fodor's Choice
★ **Devils Garden Trail.** Landscape Arch is the highlight of this trail but is just one of several arches within reach depending on your ambitions and the heat. It's an easy 0.8-mile one-way trip (mostly gravel, relatively flat) to Landscape Arch, one of the longest stone spans in the world at 306 feet and one of the most fragile-looking. In fact, you can see where a 60-foot-long piece fell off the underside in 1991, leading to the closure of the trail that used to go under the span. This serves as a reminder of the impermanence of the features in the park. Beyond Landscape Arch the scenery changes dramatically, and you must climb and straddle slickrock fins and negotiate some short, steep inclines. Finally, the stacked spans that compose Double O Arch come into view around a sharp bend. Allow up to three hours for this round-trip hike of just over 4 miles. For a still longer hike, venture on to see a formation called Dark Angel and then return to the trailhead on the primitive loop. The hike to Dark Angel is a difficult route through fins

with a short side trip to Private Arch. If you hike all the way to Dark Angel and return on the primitive loop, the trail is 5.9 miles round-trip, not including possible (and worthwhile) detours to Navajo Arch, Partition Arch, Tunnel Arch, and Pine Tree Arch. Allow about five hours for this adventure, take plenty of water, and watch your route carefully. ■TIP→ **Pick up the park's useful guide to Devils Garden, or download it from the website before you go.** *Moderate.* ⊠ *Trailhead off main road, 18 miles from park entrance.*

Tower Arch Trail. Check with park rangers before attempting the dirt road to Klondike Bluffs parking area. If rains haven't washed out the road, a trip to this seldom-visited area provides a solitude-filled hike climaxed with a giant rock opening. Allow from two to three hours for this 3.4-mile round-trip hike, not including the drive. *Moderate.* ⊠ *Trailhead 24½ miles from park entrance, 7.7 miles off main road, Klondike Bluffs parking area.*

DIFFICULT

Fiery Furnace. This area of the park has taken on a near-mythical lure for park visitors, who are drawn to the forbidden nature of Fiery Furnace. Rangers strongly discourage inexperienced hikers from entering here—in fact, you can't enter without watching a safety video and getting a permit ($4). As a result, up to one month's advance reservations are now required to get a spot on the 2-mile round-trip ranger-led hikes ($10) through this unique formation. *(⇨ Ranger Programs)* A hike here is a challenging but fascinating trip amidst rugged rocks and sandy washes into the heart of Arches. The trek may require the use of hands and feet to scramble up and through narrow cracks and along vertigo-inducing ledges above drop-offs and there are no trail markings. If you're not familiar with the Furnace you can easily get lost and cause resource damage, so watch your step and use great caution. ■TIP→ **Call or visit the park website for reservations, which are a must.** The less intrepid should look into Fiery Furnace from the Overlook off the main road. *Difficult.* ⊠ *Trailhead off main road, about 15 miles from visitor center.*

ROCK CLIMBING AND CANYONEERING

Rock climbers travel from across the country to scale the sheer red rock walls of Arches National Park and surrounding areas. Most climbing routes in the park require advanced techniques. Permits are not required, but you are responsible for knowing park regulations and restricted routes. Two popular routes ascend Owl Rock in the Garden of Eden (about 10 miles from the visitor center); the well-worn route has a difficulty of 5.8, while a more challenging option is 5.11 on a scale that goes up to 5.13 plus. Many climbing routes are available in the Park Avenue area, about 2.2 miles from the visitor center. These routes are also extremely difficult climbs. No commercial outfitters are allowed to lead rock-climbing excursions in the park, but guided canyoneering (which involves ropes, rappelling, and some basic climbing) is permitted. Before climbing, it's imperative that you stop at the visitor center and check with a ranger about climbing regulations.

DID YOU KNOW?

"I happened to catch this beautiful light on the back side of Pine Tree Arch on the Devils Garden Trail."
—photo by Merryl Edelstein, Fodors.com member

TOURS AND OUTFITTERS

Desert Highlights. This guide company takes adventurous types on descents and ascents through canyons (with the help of ropes), including those found in the Fiery Furnace. Full-day and multiday canyoneering treks are available to destinations both inside and outside the national parks. Desert Highlights does not offer guided rock climbing. ⊠ *50 E. Center St., Moab* ☎ *435/259–4433, 800/747–1342* ⊕ *www. deserthighlights.com.*

Moab Cliffs & Canyons. In a town where everyone seems to offer rafting and 4X4 expeditions, Moab Cliffs & Canyons focuses exclusively on canyoneering, climbing, and rappelling—for novice and veteran adventurers. This is the outfitter that provided technical assistance to the crew on the movie *127 Hours.* ⊠ *253 N. Main St., Moab* ☎ *435/259–3317, 877/641–5271* ⊕ *www.cliffsandcanyons.com.*

WHAT'S NEARBY

NEARBY TOWNS

Moab is the primary gateway to both Arches and Canyonlands national parks. Don't let its outsize image and status as Grand County seat fool you: only about 5,000 people live here year-round—compared with the 1 million who visit annually. Near the Colorado River in a beautiful valley between red rock cliffs, Moab is an interesting, eclectic place to visit, especially if you're looking for a variety of restaurants, shopping for Southwestern-inspired souvenirs, art galleries, and a plethora of lodging options. Also, here you'll find an array of sports outfitters to help you enjoy the parks. For those who want civilization and a sprinkling of culture with their outdoor itineraries, Moab is the place to be.

The next-closest town to Arches, about 47 miles to the northwest, is **Green River.** Unlike hip Moab, this dusty highway outpost is off the tourists' radar screen, except for boaters headed Moab's way on the Green. It's worth a visit for Ray's Tavern. Also, each September the fragrance of fresh cantaloupe, watermelon, and honeydew fills the air, especially during Melon Days, a family-fun event celebrating the harvest on the third weekend of September.

VISITOR INFORMATION

Green River Information Center ⊠ *John Wesley Powell River History Museum, 1765 E. Main St., Green River* ☎ *435/564–3427.*

Moab Information Center. A veritable gold mine, the Moab Information Center is located on the southeast corner of Main and Center streets. Stop here for brochures, books, and knowledgeable locals representing the travel industry, the nationals parks, and the Bureau of Land Management, which oversees non–national park land such as the Slickrock Trail and Colorado River campgrounds. ⊠ *25 E. Center St., Moab* ☎ *435/259–8825, 800/635–6622* ⊕ *www.discovermoab.com.*

NEARBY ATTRACTIONS

Courthouse Wash. Although this rock-art panel fell victim to an unusual case of vandalism in 1980, when someone scoured the petroglyphs and pictographs that had been left by four cultures, you can still see ancient images if you take a short walk from the parking area on the left-hand side of the road, heading south. ⊠ *U.S. 191, about 2 miles south of park entrance.*

John Wesley Powell River History Museum. At this riverfront museum you can see what it was like to travel down the Green and Colorado rivers in the 1800s. A series of displays tracks the Powell Party's arduous, dangerous 1869 journey, and visitors can watch the award-winning film *Journey Into the Unknown* for a cinematic taste of the white-water adventure. The center also houses the River Runner's Hall of Fame, a tribute to those who have followed in Powell's wake. An art gallery reserved for works thematically linked to river exploration is also on site. ⊠ *1765 E. Main St., Green River* ☎ *435/564-3427* ⊕ *www.jwprhm.com* ⊠ *$4* ☉ *Apr.–Oct., daily 8–7; Nov.–Mar., Tues.–Sat. 9–5.*

Museum of Moab. For a small taste of history in the Moab area and a chance to test out an old player piano, stop by this museum. In addition to settler-era antiques, ancient and historic American Indians are remembered in exhibits of baskets, pottery, sandals, and other artifacts. Displays also chronicle early Spanish expeditions into the area, regional dinosaur finds, and the history of uranium discovery and exploration. ⊠ *118 E. Center St., Moab* ☎ *435/259-7985* ⊕ *www.moabmuseum.org* ⊠ *$5 suggested donation, free Mon.* ☉ *Apr.–Oct., weekdays 10–5, Sat. noon–5; Nov.–Mar., Mon.–Sat. noon–5.*

Sego Canyon. About 39 miles from Moab, this is one of the most dramatic and mystifying rock-art sights in the area. On the canyon walls you can see large, ghostlike rock-art figures etched by American Indians approximately 4,000 years ago. There's also art left by the Ute Indians 400–700 years ago. This canyon is a little out of the way, but well worth the drive. ⊠ *About 4 miles off I-70, exit 187, Moab* ⊕ *www. blm.gov/utah/moab.*

⇨ *See Canyonlands National Park (Chapter 11) for additional area listings.*

AREA ACTIVITIES

SPORTS AND THE OUTDOORS
BIRD-WATCHING

Scott M. Matheson Wetlands Preserve. Three fires since 2009 have tested the fortitude of this special landscape and its management, but despite temporary closures it remains one of Moab's treasures. The best place around for bird-watching, this 894-acre desert oasis is home to hundreds of species of birds, including such treasures as the pied-billed grebe, the cinnamon teal, and the northern flicker. It's possible that you might even spot beaver and muskrat playing in the water. The preserve is home to several bat species such as the western pipistrelle, the pallid bat, and the hoary bat. A boardwalk winds through the preserve to a viewing shelter. ✉ *Near the intersection of 500 W and Kane Creek Blvd., Moab* ☎ *435/259–4629* ⊕ *nature.org.*

GOLF

Moab Golf Club. A favorite public golf course in Utah, this 18-hole, par-72 municipal course has lush greens set against a red rock sandstone backdrop, a breathtaking combination. It is open year-round and a relative bargain at $46 per round. ✉ *2705 S. East Bench Rd., Moab* ☎ *435/259–6488* ⊕ *www.moabcountryclub.com* ⅄ *18 holes. 6819 yards. Par 72. Slope 130. Green fee: $46* ⌂ *Facilities: driving range, golf carts, pro-shop, lessons, restaurant, bar.*

RAFTING

Fisher Towers. On the Colorado River northeast of Arches and very near Moab, you can take one of America's most scenic—yet unintimidating—river-raft rides. ■ TIP→ This is the perfect place to take the family or to learn to kayak with the help of an outfitter. The river rolls by the red Fisher Towers as they rise into the sky in front of the La Sal Mountains. A day trip on this stretch of the river will take you about 14 miles. Outfitters offer full- or half-day adventures here. Those who don't like water can enjoy some nice hikes in this area as well. ✉ *17 miles upriver from Rte. 128 near Moab.*

Gray–Desolation Canyon. Desolation is not really a fair name for this beautiful, lush canyon along the Green River. It's a favorite destination of canoe paddlers, kayakers, and beginning rafters. There are lots of rapids on this stretch of the Green; they are on the small side but deliver lots of laughs. Families with children of almost any age can share this adventure and even paddle on their own under the watchful eyes of a guide. This trip requires four or five days to complete. This is one of the favorite destinations for all of the outfitters in the region, but it's possible to do it on your own with a permit from Bureau of Land Management, available up to five months in advance. ✉ *On the Green River.*

Westwater Canyon. In this narrow, winding canyon near the Utah–Colorado border, the Colorado River cuts through the oldest exposed geologic layer on earth. The result is craggy black granite jutting out of the water with red sandstone walls towering above. This section of the river is rocky and considered highly technical for rafters and kayakers, but it dishes out a great white-water experience in a short period of time. Just 18 outfitters have permits to offer this trip; private permits are also available but recommended only for experienced boaters. ■ TIP→ Reserve well in advance as this is one of the most popular river routes in Utah. ✉ *About 51 miles northeast of Moab on the Colorado River* ⊕ *www.blm.gov/utah/moab.*

Sheri Griffith Expeditions. Moab outfitter Sheri Griffith Expeditions has offered trips through the white water of Cataract, Westwater, and Desolation canyons, on the Colorado and Green rivers since 1971. Specialty expeditions include river trips for women, writers, and families. You might also enjoy one of their more luxurious expeditions, which make roughing it a little more comfortable. ✉ *2231 S. U.S. 191, Moab* ☎ *435/259–8229, 800/332–2439* ⊕ *www.griffithexp.com.*

Tag-A-Long Expeditions. Celebrating 50 years in 2014, this outfitter has been taking people into the white water of Cataract Canyon and Canyonlands longer than any other outfitter in Moab. It also runs four-wheel-drive expeditions into the backcountry of the park plus calm-water excursions on the Colorado and Green rivers. Trips run from a half day to six days, and groups are kept small, from 3 to 11 passengers. ⊠ *452 N. Main St., Moab* ☎ *435/259–8946, 800/453–3292* ⊕ *www.tagalong.com.*

ARTS AND ENTERTAINMENT

Canyonlands by Night. From April to October, take a two-hour boat ride on the Colorado River after dark. While illuminating the canyon walls with 40,000 watts, the trip includes music and narration highlighting Moab's history, American Indian legends, and geologic formations along the river. You can combine the boat trip with a Dutch-oven dinner, too. Family pricing is available. ⊠ *1861 U.S. 191., Moab* ☎ *435/259–5261* ⊕ *www.canyonlandsbynight.com*

Moab Arts and Recreation Center. For a slice of Moab's arts scene, from "Quick Draw Sales" where artists have three hours to create pieces, to dance and fitness classes, this has been the spirited hub of arts activities in Moab since 1997. ⊠ *111 E. 100 N, Moab* ☎ *435/259–6272* ⊕ *www. moabcity.org/marc.*

SHOPPING

ART GALLERIES

Lema's Kokopelli Gallery. The folks at Lema's Kokopelli Gallery have built a reputation for fair prices on a giant selection of American Indian and Southwest-themed jewelry, art, pottery, rugs, and more. Everything for sale here is authentic. ⊠ *70 N. Main St., Moab* ☎ *435/259–5055* ⊕ *www.kokopellioutlet.com.*

Overlook Gallery. Fine art oil paintings of canyon country comprise the core and spirit of Overlook Gallery, an elegant little gallery just a short walk from Main Street. ⊠ *83 E. Center St., Moab* ☎ *435/259–3861* ⊕ *theoverlookgallery.com.*

Tom Till Gallery. After you visit Arches and Canyonlands, stop at Tom Till Gallery to buy stunning original photographs of the parks by one of the nation's best-loved landscape photographers. ⊠ *61 N. Main St., Moab* ☎ *435/259–9808* ⊕ *www.tomtillphotography.com.*

BOOKS

FAMILY **Back of Beyond Books.** A Main Street treasure, this comprehensive bookstore features an excellent selection of books on the American West, environmental studies, American Indian cultures, water issues, and Western history, as well as a collection of rare antiquarian books on the Southwest. There's also a nice nook for kids lit by a skylight. ⊠ *83 N. Main St., Moab* ☎ *435/259–5154, 800/700–2859* ⊕ *www. backofbeyondbooks.com.*

WESTERN GOODS

Western Image. A fun place to browse for a flavor of the Old West, Western Image has antiques, Western art, cowboy hats, boots, belts, coins, badges, and other favorite but classy souvenirs. ⊠ *39 N. Main St., Moab* ☎ *435/259–3006.*

SCENIC DRIVES

Colorado River Scenic Byway—Route 128. One of the most scenic drives in the country, Route 128 intersects U.S. 191 3 miles south of Arches. The 44-mile highway runs along the Colorado River with 2,000-foot cliffs rising on both sides. The gorgeous Castle Valley is home to a winery, orchards, and a couple of luxury lodging options. It also passes through world-class climbing destination Fisher Towers before winding north to Interstate 70. The drive from Moab to I–70 takes at least an hour.

WHERE TO EAT

IN THE PARK

PICNIC AREAS

Balanced Rock. The view is the best part of this picnic spot. There are no cooking facilities or water, but there are tables. If you sit just right you might find some shade under a small juniper; otherwise, this is an exposed site. Pit toilets are nearby. ⊠ *Opposite the Balanced Rock parking area, entrance on the main road, 9.2 miles from the park.*

Devils Garden. There are grills, water, picnic tables and restrooms here, and depending on the time of day, some shade from junipers and rock walls. It's a good place for lunch before or after a hike. ⊠ *On the main road, 18 miles from the park entrance.*

OUTSIDE THE PARK

GREEN RIVER

$$
MEXICAN

✕ **La Veracruzana.** The Polito family continues the long tradition of good food in this older, unassuming building on Green River's main drag. Couples and families should try the *molcajete,* a two-person entrée with meat, chicken, shrimp, and *nopal* (cactus) served on a volcanic-rock stone mortar. Savory pork and chile verde combinations also impress on a menu that offers enchiladas, tacos, and other standard Mexican fare. $ *Average main: $15* ⊠ *125 Main St., Green River* ☎ *435/564–3257.*

$
AMERICAN

✕ **Ray's Tavern.** Ray's is something of a Western legend and a favorite hangout for river runners. The bar that runs the length of the restaurant reminds you this is still a tavern and a serious watering hole—but all the photos and rafting memorabilia make it comfortable for families as well. It's worth stopping in for the great tales about working on the river and the coldest beer and the best hamburger in two counties. ■ **TIP➜ For dessert, owner Cathy Gardner makes homemade apple pie daily.** $ *Average main: $10* ⊠ *25 S. Broadway, Green River* ☎ *435/564–3511.*

MOAB

$$ SOUTHWESTERN Fodor's Choice ★ 🍴 **Buck's Grill House.** The raves continue for a spot that inspires near-unanimous acclaim from Moab locals as the town's best restaurant. Chef and owner Tim Buckingham pushes the envelope on Southwestern food with standards like buffalo meat loaf and elk stew, and new favorites like Utah trout (with chimichurri, rice verde, and grilled vegetables). Steaks are thick and tender, gravies will have you licking your fingers, and delicious burgers are made from ground chuck, buffalo, or vegetables. Vegetarian diners shouldn't despair with tasty choices like polenta lasagne. A good wine list complements the meal. The 21-plus crowd can hang out in the contemporary Vista Lounge. For a Zen-like end to your day, dine on the shady patio to the sound of water trickling down the outdoor sculptures. To take some of the Southwest with you, buy a bottle of Buck's Grillin Sauce on your way out. [$] *Average main: $19* ✉ *1393 N. U.S. 191, Moab* ☎ *435/259–5201* 🌐 *www.bucksgrillhouse.com* 🕑 *Limited menu late Nov.–mid-Feb.*

$$$$ AMERICAN Fodor's Choice ★ 🍴 **Desert Bistro.** The runaway choice for "Moab's finest restaurant" for a decade, Desert Bistro has settled into a 19th-century dance hall off Main Street where the ambience matches the cuisine. Chef/owner Karl Kelley innovates seasonally with cosmopolitan pairings like *gyozas* (Japanese dumplings) stuffed with tofu, tahini, and Anasazi bean hummus. Carnivores and vegans alike will find something memorable on this menu, and the presentation is exemplary. Whether you're in the warm adobe dining room or on one of the quiet cozy patios, you'll find the staff attentive and unpretentious. [$] *Average main: $32* ✉ *36 S. 100 W, Moab* ☎ *435/259–0756* 🌐 *www.desertbistro.com* 🕑 *No lunch. Closed Nov.–Mar.*

$$ AMERICAN 🍴 **Eddie McStiff's.** This sprawling restaurant and microbrewery tries (mostly successfully) to have something for everyone. Options include a full page of burger combinations, organic-flour brick-oven pizza, and pricier options like orange roughy. Start with a drink from an ambitious full bar or proprietary microbrewed beer, and cap your meal off with a decadent dessert. Set back off Main Street behind a busy parking lot, Eddie McStiff's seems to attract more tourists than locals. [$] *Average main: $14* ✉ *57 S. Main St., Moab* ☎ *435/259–2337* 🌐 *www.eddiemcstiffs.com.*

$ ECLECTIC 🍴 **Eklecticafe.** The eclectic font on the sign makes this place easy to miss but worth finding for one of the more creative, healthy menus in Moab. Breakfast and lunch items include a variety of burritos and wraps, scrambled tofu, salmon cakes, Indonesian satay kebabs, and many fresh, organic salads. On nice days you can take your meal outside to the large covered patio. In winter you'll want to stay inside by the wood-burning stove. [$] *Average main: $9* ✉ *352 N. Main St., Moab* ☎ *435/259–6896* 🕑 *No dinner.*

$ AMERICAN FAMILY 🍴 **Jail House Café.** Locals love the eggs Benedict, pancakes, and waffles galore in this 100-year-old cozy corner building that used to be the county courthouse. Dine outside if it's a typically crisp and cool Moab morning, but peek inside for historic photos and to imagine the prisoners that the jail once housed. [$] *Average main: $10* ✉ *101 N. Main St., Moab* ☎ *435/259–3900* 🕑 *Closed Tues. and Nov.–Feb. No lunch or dinner.*

5

$ ✕ **La Hacienda.** This family-run local favorite serves good south-of-the-
MEXICAN border meals at an equally good price. Enjoy flavorful seasoned pork carnitas with peppers, onions, and tomatoes with warm tortillas. The helpings are generous and the service is friendly. And yes, you can order a margarita. $ *Average main: $12* ✉ *574 N. Main St., Moab* ☎ *435/259–6319.*

$$ ✕ **Miguel's Baja Grill.** Great northern Mexican food, including fresh
MODERN Pacific seafood and massive flour tortillas, is served in this colorful
MEXICAN alleyway and restaurant on the heart of Moab's Main Street. Try the Mariscos La Paz, featuring shrimp, scallops, fish, and clams in a spicy tomato sauce bursting with arbol chilis. Don't be deterred by the closed wrought-iron doors during the day—the margaritas, chips, and salsa start flowing daily at 5. $ *Average main: $18* ✉ *51 N. Main St., Moab* ☎ *435/259–6546* ⊕ *www.miguelsbajagrill.com.*

$ ✕ **Milt's Stop and Eat.** Since 1954, Milt's has offered delicious burgers and
FAST FOOD shakes from an unassuming drive-up stand off Main Street. About all
FAMILY that's changed is that the buffalo burger is now nearly as popular as the beef version. Hand-cut fries, tater tots, and onion rings are among the sides. If you love milk shakes, these are the best in town— especially peach and raspberry in season. Grilled sandwiches and salads are also available. $ *Average main: $6* ✉ *356 Millcreek Dr., Moab* ☎ *435/259–7424* ⊕ *www.miltsstopandeat.com* ⊘ *Closed Mon.*

$ ✕ **Moab Brewery.** Southern Utah's award-winning brewery is known
AMERICAN for its Scorpion Pale Ale, Dead Horse Amber Ale, and an assortment
FAMILY of other brews from light to dark. Their on-site restaurant is spacious and comfortable and decorated with kayaks, bikes, and other adventure paraphernalia. You can always find someone to talk to about canyon-country adventure, since river runners, rock climbers, and locals all hang out here. There's a wide selection of menu choices, including fresh salads (try the gazpacho spinach salad), poultry (honey almond), vegetarian pasta, and fish (including fish tacos). The house-made gelato is rich but not as good as their beer. $ *Average main: $12* ✉ *686 S. Main St., Moab* ☎ *435/259–6333* ⊕ *www. themoabbrewery.com.*

$ ✕ **Moab Diner.** For breakfast, lunch, and dinner, this is the place where
AMERICAN old-time Moabites go. Go for the dishes smothered in green chile (bur-
FAMILY ritos, burgers, omelets, and more), which they claim is Utah's best. Breakfast is served all day and the ice-cream counter is as popular as ever—the diner did start out as an ice-cream parlor after all. $ *Average main: $10* ✉ *189 S. Main St., Moab* ☎ *435/259–4006* ⊕ *www. moabdiner.com.*

$$ ✕ **Pasta Jay's.** Mountain bikers, families, and couples pack this down-
ITALIAN town restaurant's patio from noon until well into the evening. This
FAMILY bustling spot's friendly servers rapidly dish up a dozen kinds of pasta in an equal number of preparations, perfect for hungry adventurers. If ravioli and manicotti aren't your thing, there's pizza, sandwiches, and salads, too. Linger over your meal and enjoy the people-watching on Moab's main drag. $ *Average main: $15* ✉ *4 S. Main St., Moab* ☎ *435/259–2900* ⊕ *www.pastajays.com.*

$$ ✕**Peace Tree Juice Cafe.** Start with your choice of a dozen smoothies,
CAFÉ then select from a menu that ranges from wraps to sandwiches to full
entrées prepared primarily from local, natural, and organic ingre-
dients for a healthy, filling meal. Try the quinoa-stuffed red pepper,
Mediterranean penne, or sweet-and-salty beet salad for interesting
new flavor combinations. Peace Tree's downtown location is as clean
and contemporary as its food. For dinner, you may have to wait for a
table on the patio. There's another location in Monticello, Utah. $ *Av-
erage main: $15* ⊠ *20 S. Main St., Moab* ☎ *435/259–8101* ⊕ *www.
peacetreecafe.com.*

$$$ ✕**Sorrel River Grill.** The most scenic dining experience in the area is 17
AMERICAN miles upstream from Moab at the Sorrel River Ranch. Both the casual
dining room and the swankier upstairs have outdoor seating, which
makes the most of views of the Colorado River, the La Sal Mountains,
and the red rock spires and towers surrounding the ranch. The seasonal
menu changes regularly but look for local options like buffalo, pheasant, lamb, and trout as well as vegetarian entrées. Even if you don't
splurge on a fall wine dinner, know that the wine list is high-quality
and fairly priced. $ *Average main: $28* ⊠ *Mile marker 17.5, Rte. 128,
Moab* ☎ *435/259–4642* ⊕ *www.sorrelriver.com* ✍ *Reservations essential* ☉ *Lunch for take-out only, Nov.–Mar.*

$$ ✕**Sunset Grill.** Once upon a time, this cliffside home of former uranium
AMERICAN kingpin Charlie Steen housed Moab's finest view, dining experience, and
prime rib; today, the exterior and interior need a face-lift. Unquestion-
ably, the magnificent aspect of this restaurant is the view of the Colo-
rado River, especially at sunset. Filet mignon, roasted duck, and prime
rib are some of the old standbys on the menu. $ *Average main: $20*
⊠ *900 N. Main St., Moab* ☎ *435/259–7146* ⊕ *www.sunsetgrillmoab.
com* ☉ *Closed Sun. No lunch.*

$ ✕**Sweet Cravings Bakery + Bistro.** Cinda Culton has created a sensation
BAKERY in Moab with some of the largest and most delicious cookies and cin-
FAMILY namon rolls you've ever seen, but the secret here is an amazing roster of
breakfast and lunch panini, wraps, and sandwiches, and daily comfort
foods like pot pies and soups. Everything is available to go, but the Can-
yon Ham with spinach and tarragon aioli on marbled rye is so good it
might not make it to the trail. Gluten-free options abound. $ *Average
main: $10* ⊠ *550 N. Main St., #C, Moab* ☎ *435/259–8983* ⊕ *www.
cravemoab.com* ☉ *Closed Mon. and Tues. No dinner. Nov.–Mar.*

$$ ✕**Zax.** Wood-fired pizza ovens are the focal point of this downtown eat-
AMERICAN ery and sports bar, where baseball bats double as door handles. For $14
FAMILY you can try the pizza-salad-soup buffet (a popular choice, so the pies
are constantly coming out of the oven), but while the pizza is a grand
slam, the salad bar is dull as a 1–0 game. The best seats in the house are
out on the patio for people-watching. Burgers, sandwiches, and salads
make up most of the rest of the menu, but there are pasta and steaks,
too. $ *Average main: $15* ⊠ *96 S. Main St., Moab* ☎ *435/259–6555*
⊕ *www.zaxmoab.com.*

5

WHERE TO STAY

For expanded hotel reviews, visit Fodors.com.

OUTSIDE THE PARK

Some of the best nightly lodging values in the area are rental condominiums and homes. Accommodations Unlimited is a great place to start, with units ranging from in-town studios to private homes. ☎ 435/259–6575 ⊕ *www.moabcondorentals.com.*

GREEN RIVER

$$
HOTEL

☷ **Green River Comfort Inn.** Right off Interstate 70, this clean, updated motel is convenient if you're staying for only one night, as many do on family rafting outings. **Pros:** convenient, clean, and comfortable; close to town's premier rafting outfitter, Holiday River Expeditions; kids under 18 stay for free. **Cons:** remote, barren town; no elevator to second-floor rooms; Green River's two best restaurants are not in walking distance. ⑤ *Rooms from: $109* ✉ *1975 E. Main St., Green River* ☎ *435/564–3300* ⊕ *www.comfortinn.com* ↝ *54 rooms, 3 suites* ⑩ *Breakfast.*

MOAB

$$$
HOTEL

☷ **Aarchway Inn.** You'll see the adobe-painted walls and red-tiled roof of the big, family-oriented Aarchway Inn—complete with playground, barbeque pavilion, and one of Moab's largest hotel swimming pools—soon after crossing the Colorado River and entering town. **Pros:** one of the closest properties to the parks; lots of room to spread out in suites, rooms, and on the property; family-friendly; big pool. **Cons:** one of the closest properties to the river, so it can be buggy; front-desk service is inconsistent; no elevator. ⑤ *Rooms from: $169* ✉ *1151 U.S. 191, Moab* ☎ *435/259–2599, 800/341–9359* ⊕ *www.aarchwayinn.com* ↝ *91 rooms, 6 suites* ⑩ *Breakfast.*

$$
B&B/INN

☷ **Adobe Abode.** A lovely B&B near the nature preserve, this one-story inn surrounds you with solitude. **Pros:** relaxing in the beautifully decorated common area; the entrée-of-the-day (sometimes ham and eggs or waffles) accompanying the Continental breakfast; peace and quiet. **Cons:** you can bicycle to town, but it's too far to walk; no children under 16. ⑤ *Rooms from: $139* ✉ *778 W. Kane Creek Blvd., Moab* ☎ *435/260–2932 innkeeper's cell, 435/259–7716* ⊕ *www.adobeabodemoab.com* ↝ *4 rooms, 2 suites* ⑩ *Breakfast.*

$$$$
HOTEL
FAMILY

☷ **Best Western Canyonlands Inn.** The intersection of Main and Center streets is the epicenter of Moab, and this comfortable, contemporary, impeccably clean hotel anchors the intersection, providing a perfect base camp for families just a few feet from the Moab Information Center, the Mill Creek Parkway Trail, and all downtown shops, outfitters, and restaurants (plus two restaurants are on the property). **Pros:** downtown location; smiling and helpful staff; updated, sparkling rooms; breakfast alfresco on new outdoor patio. **Cons:** pricier than comparable properties due to its location; for those seeking solitude, family-friendliness means the property bustles with happy children. ⑤ *Rooms from: $229* ✉ *16 S. Main St., Moab* ☎ *435/259–2300, 800/649–5191* ⊕ *www.canyonlandsinn.com* ↝ *34 rooms, 46 suites* ⑩ *Breakfast.*

CLOSE UP

Best Campgrounds In and Around Arches

Campgrounds in and around Moab range from sprawling RV parks with myriad amenities to quaint, shady retreats near a babbling brook. The Devils Garden Campground in the park is a wonderful spot to call home for a few days, though it is often full and does not provide an RV dump station. More than 350 campsites are operated in the vicinity by the Bureau of Land Management—their sites on the Colorado River and near the Slickrock Trail are some of the nicest (and most affordable) in the area. The most centrally located campgrounds in Moab will generally provide services needed by RV travelers.

IN THE PARK

Devils Garden Campground. This campground is one of the most unusual—and gorgeous— in the West, and in the national park system, for that matter. ✉ *Off main road, 18 miles from park entrance* ☎ *435/719–2299, 435/259–4351 for group reservations, 877/444–6777 for NRRS reservations* 🌐 *www.recreation.gov.*

OUTSIDE THE PARK

Bureau of Land Management Campgrounds. Most of the 350 sites at 25 different BLM campgrounds are in the Moab area, including some stunning sites along the Colorado River (Route 128 and Route 279), Sand Flats Recreation Area (near the Slickrock Trail), and Canyon Flats Recreation Area (outside Needles District of Canyonlands). ☎ *435/259–2100* 🌐 *www.blm.gov/utah/moab.*

Canyonlands Campground. Although this camping park is in downtown Moab, the campground is astride Mill Creek and has many shade trees. ✉ *555 S. Main St., Moab* ☎ *435/259–6848 or 888/522–6848* 🌐 *www.canyonlandsrv.com.*

Moab Valley RV Resort. Near the Colorado River, this campground with an expansive view feels more like a mall than a campground with its abundant space, activities, and services. ✉ *1773 N. U.S. 191, Moab* ☎ *435/259–4469* 🌐 *www.moabvalleyrv.com.*

Slickrock Campground. At one of Moab's older campgrounds you find lots of mature shade trees and all the basic amenities—plus three hot tubs where adults have priority. ✉ *1301½ N. U.S. 191, Moab* ☎ *435/259–7660 or 800/448–8873* 🌐 *www.slickrockcampground.com.*

Up the Creek Campground. Perhaps the quietest of the in-town campgrounds, Up the Creek lies under big cottonwoods on the banks of Mill Creek. ✉ *210 E. 300 S, Moab* ☎ *435/260–1888* 🌐 *www.moabupthecreek.com.*

5

$$ B&B/INN

Cali Cochitta Bed & Breakfast. One of the first homes built in Moab, this 19th-century Victorian in the heart of town, two blocks from Main Street shops and restaurants, has been restored to its classic style by owners David and Kim Boger. **Pros:** gracious owners pay attention to the details; easy walk to the hub of town; accomplished chef means scrumptious breakfast in the garden. **Cons:** given its historic construction, some quarters may feel a little tight. $ *Rooms from: $140* ✉ *110 S. 200 E, Moab* ☎ *435/259–4961, 888/429–8112* 🌐 *www.moabdreaminn.com* 🛏 *3 rooms, 1 suite, 2 cottages* 🍴 *Breakfast.*

$$$ HOTEL

[hotel icon] **Gonzo Inn.** Unconventional Moab's most original hotel property, this eclectic inn stands out for its design, color, art, and varnished adobe construction. **Pros:** unique, spotless, and hip; steps to Main Street but still one of downtown's quietest properties; friendly staff. **Cons:** interior hallways can be dark; no elevator. [$] *Rooms from: $169* ✉ *100 W. 200 S, Moab* ☎ *435/259–2515, 800/791–4044* 🌐 *www.gonzoinn.com* 🛏 *21 rooms, 22 suites* 🍴 *Breakfast.*

$$$ HOTEL

[hotel icon] **Hampton Inn.** Moab's newest property is sparkling clean and features a huge lobby with plenty of room to spread out. **Pros:** reliably clean; walking distance from downtown. **Cons:** the complimentary breakfast pales compared with others in town. [$] *Rooms from: $189* ✉ *488 N. Main St., Moab* ☎ *435/259–3030* 🌐 *hamptoninn.hilton.com* 🛏 *73 rooms, 6 suites* 🍴 *Breakfast.*

$$$$ RENTAL

[hotel icon] **Moab Springs Ranch.** First developed by William Granstaff in the late 19th century, this 18-acre property about 3 miles from Arches and 2 miles from downtown Moab features comfortable and spotless hotel rooms and one-, two-, and three-bedroom condos set by a meandering spring and decades-old sycamores, mulberries, and cottonwoods. **Pros:** large, green, shaded space filled with a natural spring and ponds; new, comfortable condos. **Cons:** more expensive than your average Moab accommodation; some U.S. 191 traffic noise; little within walking distance. [$] *Rooms from: $224* ✉ *1266 N. Main St., Moab* ☎ *435/259–7891, 888/259–5759* 🌐 *www.moabspringsranch.com* 🛏 *3 rooms, 14 condos* 🍴 *No meals.*

$$$$ RESORT

[hotel icon] **Red Cliffs Lodge.** There are few settings in the world that match this gorgeous, classically Western lodge where the Colorado River rolls by right outside your door and canyon walls reach for the sky in all their red glory. **Pros:** ranch setting on the river; a smorgasbord of adventures; afternoon wine tasting. **Cons:** the setting is stunning, but 14 miles from town. [$] *Rooms from: $239* ✉ *Rte. 128, mile marker 14, Moab* ☎ *435/259–2002, 866/812–2002* 🌐 *www.redcliffslodge.com* 🛏 *80 suites, 30 cabins* 🍴 *Breakfast.*

$$ HOTEL

[hotel icon] **Red Stone Inn.** One of the best bargains in town, this timber-framed motel offers small, clean rooms on the Moab strip near restaurants and shops. **Pros:** walking distance to Moab restaurants and shops; the price is right. **Cons:** pool is at sister property across busy Main Street; no frills. [$] *Rooms from: $105* ✉ *535 S. Main St., Moab* ☎ *435/259–3500, 800/722–1972* 🌐 *www.moabredstone.com* 🛏 *52 rooms* 🍴 *No meals.*

$$$$ RESORT

Fodor's Choice ★

[hotel icon] **Sorrel River Ranch Resort & Spa.** One of the premier, full-service luxury resorts in the Southwest, this lodge on the banks of the Colorado River, 17 miles north of Moab, is the ultimate getaway. **Pros:** swanky grounds and dining; comfortable, luxurious rooms; red rock setting away from town on the Colorado River. **Cons:** more than 17 miles from Moab; prices befitt the luxury (i.e., steep). [$] *Rooms from: $429* ✉ *Rte. 128, mile marker 17.5, Moab* ☎ *435/259–4642, 877/359–2715* 🌐 *www.sorrelriver.com* 🛏 *26 rooms, 32 suites, 1 3-bedroom house* 🍴 *No meals.*

Salinas Public Library
salinaspubliclibrary.org

Cesar Chavez Library
615 Williams Road
Salinas, CA 93905
831-758-7345

Fodor's the complete guide to the national parks of the
33550030860709
Due: 09/05/2015

Renew online:
salinas.kohalibrary.com

Snappy is coming to town for a visit!
See him Saturday, Aug. 29, at 11am
at the Steinbeck branch

BADLANDS NATIONAL PARK

WELCOME TO BADLANDS

TOP REASONS TO GO

★ **Fossils:** From the mid-1800s, the fossil-rich Badlands area has welcomed paleontologists, research institutions, and fossil hunters who have discovered the fossil remnants of numerous species from ancient days.

★ **A world of wildlife:** Badlands National Park is home to a wide array of wildlife: bison, pronghorn, deer, black-footed ferrets, prairie dogs, rabbits, coyotes, foxes, badgers.

★ **Missiles:** The Minuteman Missile National Historic Site, north of the entrance to the park, represents the only remaining intact components of a nuclear-missile field that consisted of 150 Minuteman II missiles and 15 launch control centers, and covered more than 13,500 square miles of southwestern South Dakota.

★ **Stars aplenty:** Due to its remote location and vastly open country, Badlands National Park contains some of the clearest and cleanest air in the country, which makes it perfect for viewing the night sky.

1 North Unit. This is the most easily accessible of the three units and attracts the most visitors. It includes the Badlands Wilderness Area.

2 Palmer Creek Unit. This is the most isolated section of the park—no recognized roads pass through its borders. You must obtain permission from private landowners to pass through their property (contact the White River Visitor Center on how to do so). If you plan on exploring here, count on spending two days—one day to hike in and one day out.

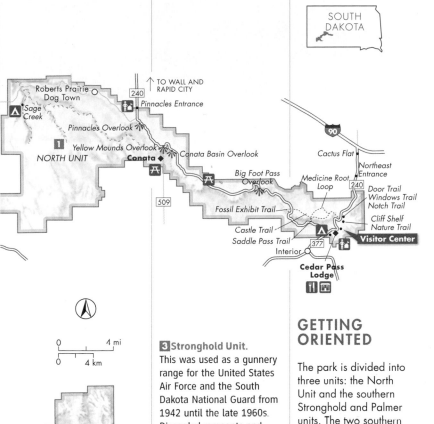

SOUTH
DAKOTA

0 4 mi
0 4 km

2
PALMER CREEK UNIT

↘ TO WOUNDED KNEE

KEY

- 👫 *Ranger Station*
- 🔺 *Campground*
- 🎪 *Picnic Area*
- 🍴 *Restaurant*
- 🖼 *Lodge*
- 🚶 *Trailhead*
- 🚻 *Restrooms*
- ⇗ *Scenic Viewpoint*
- ⋯ *Walking/Hiking Trails*

3 **Stronghold Unit.**
This was used as a gunnery range for the United States Air Force and the South Dakota National Guard from 1942 until the late 1960s. Discarded remnants and unexploded ordnance make this area potentially dangerous, so mind your step here. If you do find fragments of this era, do not handle them. Report the location to a ranger.

GETTING ORIENTED

The park is divided into three units: the North Unit and the southern Stronghold and Palmer units. The two southern units are within Pine Ridge Indian Reservation and are jointly managed by the National Park Service and the Oglala Sioux Tribe. Much of the southern park is accessible only on foot or horseback, or by a high-clearance four-wheel-vehicle drive.

6

Updated by
T.D. Griffith

So stark and forbidding are the chiseled spires, ragged ridgelines, and deep ravines of South Dakota's badlands that Lieutenant Colonel George Custer once described them as "hell with the fires burned out." Although a bit more accessible than the depths of the underworld, the landscape is easily the strangest in the Great Plains. Ruthlessly ravaged over the ages by wind and rain, the 380 square miles of wild terrain continue to erode and evolve, sometimes visibly changing shape in a few days. Prairie creatures thrive on the untamed territory, and animal fossils are in abundance.

BADLANDS PLANNER

WHEN TO GO

Most visitors see the park between Memorial Day and Labor Day. The park's vast size and isolation prevent it from ever being too packed—though it is usually crowded the first week of August, when hundreds of thousands of motorcycle enthusiasts flock to the Black Hills for the annual Sturgis Motorcycle Rally. In summer, temperatures typically hover around 90°F—though it can get as hot as 116°F—and sudden midafternoon thunderstorms are not unusual. Storms put on a spectacular show of thunder and lightning, but it rarely rains for more than 10 or 15 minutes (the average annual rainfall is 16 inches). Autumn weather is generally sunny and warm. Snow usually appears by late October. Winter temperature can be as low as –40°F. Early spring is often wet, cold, and unpredictable. By May the weather usually stabilizes, bringing pleasant 70°F days.

AVG. HIGH/LOW TEMPS.

JAN.	FEB.	MAR.	APR.	MAY	JUNE
34/11	40/16	48/24	62/33	72/44	82/56
JULY	AUG.	SEPT.	OCT.	NOV.	DEC.
91/60	92/55	81/46	65/34	48/21	39/17

FESTIVALS AND EVENTS

JANUARY–
FEBRUARY
Black Hills Stock Show and Rodeo. Watch world-champion wild-horse races, bucking horses, timed sheepdog trials, draft-horse contests, and steer wrestling during this two-week-long professional rodeo at the Rushmore Plaza Civic Center in Rapid City. Don't miss the stockman's banquet and ball. ☎ *605/258–2863* ⊕ *www.blackhillsstockshow.com.*

MARCH
Badlands Quilters Weekend Getaway. A display of the region's finest hand-and machine-made quilts, plus quilting classes by expert quilters, demonstrations, and sales are held in Wall's community center. A local church hosts the Saturday night banquet. ☎ *605/279–2889.*

JUNE–AUGUST
Red Cloud Indian Art Show. American Indian paintings and sculptures are the focus of this 11-week-long exhibition, beginning on the second Sunday in June, at the Red Cloud Indian School in Pine Ridge. ☎ *605/867–5491* ⊕ *www.redcloudschool.org.*

PLANNING YOUR TIME
BADLANDS IN ONE DAY

With a packed lunch and plenty of water, arrive at the park via the northeast entrance (off I–90 at exit 131) and follow Route 240 (Badlands Loop Road) southwest toward the **Ben Reifel Visitor Center.** You can pick up park maps and information here, and also pay the park entrance fee (if the booth at the entrance was closed).

Next, stop at the **Big Badlands Overlook,** just south of the northeast entrance, to get a good feel for the landscape. As you head toward the visitor center, hike any one of several trails you'll pass, or if you prefer guided walks, arrive at the visitor center in time to look at the exhibits and talk with rangers before heading down to the Fossil Exhibit Trail. The badlands are one of the richest fossil fields in the world, and along the trail are examples of six extinct creatures, now protected under clear plastic domes. After your walk, drive a couple of miles to the **Big Foot Pass Overlook,** up on the right. Here you can enjoy a packed lunch amid grassy prairies, with the rocky badland formations all around you.

After lunch, continue driving along Badlands Loop Road, stopping at the various overlooks for views and a hike or two. Near the Conata Picnic Area, you'll find the **Big Pig Dig,** a fossil site that was excavated by paleontologists through the summer of 2008. When you reach the junction with **Sage Creek Rim Road,** turn left and follow it along the northern border of the 100-square-mile **Badlands Wilderness Area,** which is home to hundreds of bison. Provided the road is dry, take a side trip 5 miles down Sage Creek Rim Road to **Roberts Prairie Dog Town,** inhabited by a huge colony of the chattering critters. Children will love to watch these small rodents, which bark warning calls and dive underground if you get too close to their colony. The animals built burrow networks that once covered the Great Plains, but since European settlers established ranches in the region during the late 19th century, prairie dogs have become a far rarer sight. The park is less developed the farther you travel on Sage Creek Rim Road, allowing you to admire the sheer isolation and untouched beauty of badlands country. Hold out for a glorious sunset over the shadows of the nearby Black Hills, and keep your eyes open for animals stirring about.

GETTING HERE AND AROUND
CAR TRAVEL

The North Unit of Badlands National Park is 75 miles east of Rapid City and about 140 miles northeast of Wind Cave National Park in western South Dakota. It's accessed via exit 110 or 131 off Interstate 90, or Route 44 east to Route 377. Few roads, paved or otherwise, pass within the park. Badlands Loop Road (Route 240) is the most traveled and the only one that intersects I–90. It's well maintained and rarely crowded. Parts of Route 44 and Route 27 run at the fringes of the badlands, connecting the visitor centers and Rapid City. Unpaved roads should be traveled with care when wet. Sheep Mountain Table Road, the only public road into the Stronghold Unit, is impassable when wet, with deep ruts—sometimes only high-clearance vehicles can get through. Off-road driving is prohibited. There's free parking at visitor centers, overlooks, and trailheads.

PARK ESSENTIALS
PARK FEES AND PERMITS

The entrance fee is $7 per person or $15 per vehicle, and is good for seven days. An annual park pass is $30. A backcountry permit isn't required for hiking or camping in Badlands National Park, but it's a good idea to check in at park headquarters before setting out on a backcountry journey. Backpackers may set up camps anywhere except within a half mile of roads or trails. Open fires are prohibited.

PARK HOURS

The park is open 24/7 year-round and is in the Mountain time zone.

CELL-PHONE RECEPTION

Cell-phone service has improved measurably over the last decade in western South Dakota, but you may not get a signal in much of the park. The closest pay phone you'll find will likely be in Wall.

RESTAURANTS

Dining on the prairies of South Dakota has always been a casual and family-oriented experience, and in that sense little has changed in the past century. Even the fare, which consists largely of steak and potatoes, has stayed consistent (in fact, in some towns, "vegetarian" can be a dirty word). But for its lack of comparative sophistication, the grub in the restaurants surrounding Badlands National Park is typically very good. You'll probably never have a better steak—beef or buffalo—outside this area. You should also try cuisine influenced by American Indian cooking. The most popular (and well-known) is the Indian taco, made from spiced meat and flat bread. In the park itself there's only one restaurant. The food is quite good, but don't hesitate to explore other options farther afield. You'll find the most choices in Wall.

Prices in the reviews are the average cost of a main course at dinner, of if dinner is not served, at lunch.

HOTELS

Badlands National Park is often visited by families on a vacation to see the American West, but few opt to stay overnight here, especially when there's a profusion of accommodations in the Black Hills, situated a mere 50 miles east. As a result, there are few lodging options in and around the park, and if you're determined to bed down within park boundaries, you have only one choice: Cedar Pass Lodge. Though rustic, it's comfortable, inexpensive, and has new cabins.

The rustic-but-comfy formula is repeated by the area's few motels, hotels, and inns. Most are chain hotels in Wall, grouped around the interstate. Whether you stay inside or outside the park, you shouldn't have to worry about making reservations very far in advance, except during the first full week of August, when the entire region is inundated with more than half a million motorcyclists for the annual Sturgis Motorcycle Rally. Rooms for miles around book up more than a year in advance.

Prices in the reviews are the lowest cost of a standard double room in high season. For expanded reviews, facilities, and current deals, visit Fodors.com.

TOURS

Affordable Adventures Badlands Tour. Take a seven-hour narrated tour through the park and surrounding badlands for $115 per person. Tours can easily be customized and are available year-round. ⊠ *5542 Meteor St.* ☎ *605/342–7691, 888/888–8249* ⊕ *www.affordableadventuresbh.com* 🖾 *$115.*

Golden Circle Tours. This company gives a seven- to nine-hour narrated van tour out of Custer to several venues, including Mount Rushmore, Crazy Horse Memorial, and Custer State Park. Other Black Hills tours are available. ⊠ *Box 4033, 12198 Hwy. 16, Custer* ☎ *605/673–4349* ⊕ *www.goldencircletours.com* 🖾 *$99–$125* ☉ *Mid-Apr.–Oct.*

Gray Line of the Black Hills. This outfit offers bus tours from Rapid City to Mt. Rushmore, Black Hills National Forest, Custer State Park, and the Crazy Horse Memorial, as well as other tours tied to special events such as the Mt. Rushmore Independence Day festivities and the Custer State Park Buffalo Roundup. ⊠ *1600 E. St. Patrick St., Rapid City* ☎ *800/456–4461* ⊕ *www.blackhillsgrayline.com* 🖾 *$68–$88* ☉ *May–Oct.*

FAMILY **Mount Rushmore Tours.** Beginning at Fort Hayes on the *Dances with Wolves* film set and then moving to Mt. Rushmore, Custer State Park, and Crazy Horse Memorial, this nine-hour trip around the Black Hills includes a cowboy show plus breakfast and dinner as options. Guests are responsible for their own lunch at the State Game Lodge. ⊠ *2255 Fort Hayes Dr., Rapid City* ☎ *888/343–3113* ⊕ *www.mountrushmoretours.com* 🖾 *$60–$80* ☉ *Mid-May–mid-Oct.*

VISITOR INFORMATION

PARK CONTACT INFORMATION

Badlands National Park. ☎ *605/433–5361* ⊕ *www.nps.gov/badl.*

VISITOR CENTERS

Ben Reifel Visitor Center. Open year-round, this is the park's main information hub. Stop here to pick up brochures and maps. A 22-minute video about geology and wildlife runs continually. The facility is named for a Sioux activist and the first Lakota to serve in Congress. Born on the nearby Rosebud Indian Reservation, Ben Reifel also served in the army during World War II. ✉ *Badlands Loop Rd., near Rte. 377 junction, 8 miles from northeast entrance* ☎ *605/433–5361* ⊙ *June–mid-Aug., daily 7 am–8 pm; mid-Aug.–mid-Sept., daily 8–6; mid-Sept.–May, daily 9–4.*

White River Visitor Center. Open in summer, this small center almost exclusively serves serious hikers and campers venturing into the Stronghold or Palmer units. If that's you, stop here for maps and details about road and trail conditions. The center is located on the Pine Ridge Indian Reservation. While you're here you can see fossils and Lakota artifacts, and learn about Sioux culture. ✉ *25 miles south of Rte. 44 via Rte. 27* ☎ *605/455–2878* ⊙ *June–Aug., daily 10–4.*

EXPLORING

SCENIC DRIVES

For the average visitor, a casual drive is the essential means by which to see Badlands National Park. To do the scenery justice, drive slowly, and don't hesitate to get out and explore on foot when the occasion calls for it.

Badlands Loop Road. The simplest drive is on two-lane Badlands Loop Road. The drive circles from exit 110 off Interstate 90 through the park and back to the interstate at exit 131. Start from either end and make your way around to the various overlooks along the way. Pinnacles and Yellow Mounds overlooks are outstanding places to examine the sandy pink-and-brown-toned ridges and spires distinctive to the badlands. At a certain point the landscape flattens out slightly to the north, revealing spectacular views of mixed-grass prairies. The Cedar Pass area of the drive has some of the park's best trails. ✉ *Badlands National Park, I–90, exit 110.*

HISTORIC SITES

Big Pig Dig. Until August 2008, paleontologists dug for fossils at this site named for a large fossil originally thought to be of a prehistoric pig (it actually turned out to be a small, hornless rhinoceros). Visitors will find interpretive signage detailing fossils discovered at the site. ✉ *Conata Picnic Area, 17 miles northwest of the Ben Reifel Visitor Center.*

Stronghold Unit. With few paved roads and no campgrounds, the park's southwest section is difficult to access without a four-wheel-drive

Peter Norbeck's Park

Much of the credit for setting aside South Dakota's badlands as public lands is owed to Peter Norbeck, a powerful politician who was also largely responsible for establishing nearby Custer State Park and obtaining federal funding for Mount Rushmore National Memorial. Convinced that the state's badlands formations were more distinctive than those in other parts of the American West, Norbeck began lobbying for a new national park almost immediately after he was elected a U.S. senator in 1920. Political maneuvering tied up the proposal in Congress for nearly 10 years, and land issues delayed the measure for another decade. Finally, on March 4, 1939, the region was declared Badlands National Monument by President Calvin Coolidge. It was re-designated as a national park in 1978.

vehicle. If you're willing to trek, its isolation provides a rare opportunity to explore badlands rock formations and prairies completely undisturbed. From 1942 to 1968, the U.S. Air Force and South Dakota National Guard used much of the area as a gunnery range. Hundreds of fossils were destroyed by bomber pilots, who frequently targeted the large fossil remains of an elephant-size titanothere (an extinct relative of the rhinoceros). Beware of unexploded bombs, shells, rockets, and other hazardous materials. Steer clear of it and find another route.

Within the Stronghold Unit, the **Stronghold Table**, a 3-mile-long plateau, can be reached only by crossing a narrow land bridge just wide enough to let a wagon pass. It was here, just before the Massacre at Wounded Knee in 1890, that some 600 Sioux gathered to perform one of the last known Ghost Dances, a ritual in which the Sioux wore white shirts that they believed would protect them from bullets. ⊠ *North and west of White River Visitor Center; entrance off Rte. 27.*

SCENIC STOPS

Badlands Wilderness Area. Covering about a quarter of the park, this 100-square-mile area is part of the country's largest prairie wilderness. About two-thirds of the Sage Creek region is mixed-grass prairie, making it the ideal grazing grounds for bison, pronghorn, and many of the park's other native animals. The Hay Butte Overlook (2 miles northwest on Sage Creek Rim Road) and the Pinnacles Overlook (1 mile south of the Pinnacles entrance) are the best places to get an overview of the wilderness area. Feel free to park at an overlook and hike your own route into the untamed, unmarked prairie. ⊠ *25 miles northwest of Ben Reifel Visitor Center.*

Big Badlands Overlook. From this spot just south of the park's northeast entrance, the vast majority of the park's 1 million annual visitors get their first views of the White River Badlands. ⊠ *5 miles northeast of the Ben Reifel Visitor Center.*

FAMILY **Roberts Prairie Dog Town.** Once a homestead, the site today contains one of the country's largest (if not the largest) colonies of black-tailed prairie dogs. ⊠ *Sage Creek Rim Rd., 5 miles west of Badlands Loop Rd.*

Yellow Mounds Overlook. Contrasting sharply with the whites, grays, and browns of the badlands pinnacles, the mounds viewed from here greet you with soft yet vivid yellows, reds, and purples. ⊠ *16 miles northwest of the Ben Reifel Visitor Center.*

> **TIPS FOR MULTIDAY TRIPS**
>
> Before you begin a multiday visit to the badlands, stock up on enough drinking water and food; both resources are hard to come by in the park. This is especially true in the backcountry, where water is so laden with silt and minerals that it's impossible to purify. Also bring a compass, topographical map, and rain gear.

EDUCATIONAL OFFERINGS

RANGER PROGRAMS

Evening Program. Watch a 40-minute outdoor audiovisual presentation on the wildlife, natural history, paleontology, or another aspect of the badlands. The shows typically begin around 9 pm. Check with a ranger for exact times and topics. ⊠ *Cedar Pass Campground amphitheater, 20681 Rte. 240* ⊗ *Mid-June–mid-Aug., daily around 9.*

Fossil Talk. What were the badlands like many years ago? This talk about protected fossil exhibits will inspire and answer all your questions. ⊠ *Fossil Exhibit Trail, 5 miles west of the Ben Reifel Visitor Center* ⊗ *Mid-June–mid-Aug., daily at 10:30, 1:30, and 3:30.*

Geology Walk. Learn the geologic story of the White River badlands in a 45-minute walk. The terrain can be rough in places, so be sure to wear hiking boots or sneakers. A hat is a good idea, too. ⊠ *Door and Window trails parking area, 2 miles east of the Ben Reifel Visitor Center* ⊗ *Mid-June–mid-Aug., daily at 8:30 am.*

FAMILY **Junior Ranger Program.** Children ages 5–12 can join in this 45-minute adventure, typically a short hike, game, or other hands-on activity focused on badlands wildlife, geology, or fossils. Parents are welcome. ⊠ *Cedar Pass Campground amphitheater, 20681 Rte. 240* ☎ *605/433-5361* ⊗ *June–Aug., daily at 10:30.*

SPORTS AND THE OUTDOORS

Pure, unspoiled, empty space is the greatest asset of Badlands National Park, and it can only be experienced to its highest degree if you're on foot. Spring and autumn are the best times of the year to do wilderness exploring, because the brutal extremes of summer and winter can—and do—kill. In fact, the two biggest enemies to hikers and bicyclists in the badlands are heat and lightning. Before you venture out, make sure you have at least one gallon of water per person per day, and be prepared to take shelter from freak thunderstorms, which often strike in the late afternoon with little warning.

Plants and Wildlife in Badlands

The park's sharply defined cliffs, canyons, and mesas are near-deserts with little plant growth. Most of the park, however, is made up of mixed-grass prairies, where more than 460 species of hardy grasses and wildflowers flourish in the warmer months. Prairie coneflower, yellow plains prickly pear, pale-green yucca, buffalo grass, and sideoats grama are just a few of the plants on the badlands plateau. Trees and shrubs are rare and usually confined to dry creek beds. The most common trees are Rocky Mountain junipers and plains cottonwoods.

It's common to see pronghorn antelope and mule deer dart across the flat plateaus, bison grazing on the buttes, prairie dogs and sharp-tailed grouse, and, soaring above, golden eagles, turkey vultures, and hawks. Also present are coyotes, swift foxes, jackrabbits, bats, gophers, porcupines, skunks, bobcats, horned lizards, bighorn sheep, and prairie rattlers. The latter are the only venomous reptiles in the park—watch for them near rocky outcroppings and in prairie-dog towns. Backcountry hikers might consider heavy boots and long pants reinforced with leather or canvas. Although rarely seen, weasels, mountain lions, and the endangered black-footed ferret roam the park.

AIR TOURS

Black Hills Balloons. Based in Custer, Black Hills Balloons provides amazing bird's-eye views of some of the Black Hills' most picturesque locations. Reservations are essential. ✉ *25158 Little Teton Rd.* ☎ *605/673–2520* ⊕ *www.blackhillsballoons.com* 💲 *$245–$500.*

BICYCLING

Bicycles are permitted only on designated roads, which may be paved or unpaved. They are prohibited from closed roads, trails, and the backcountry. Flat-resistant tires are recommended.

Sheep Mountain Table Road. This 7-mile dirt road in the Stronghold Unit is ideal for mountain biking, but should be attempted only when dry. The terrain is level for the first 3 miles, then it climbs and levels out again. At the top you can take in great views of the area. ✉ *About 14 miles north of the White River Visitor Center.*

OUTFITTERS

Two Wheeler Dealer Cycle and Fitness. Family-owned and -operated Two Wheeler Dealer Cycle and Fitness, based in Rapid City, with a second store on Colorado Boulevard in Spearfish, stocks more than 1,000 new bikes for sale or rent. The service is exceptional. Get trail and route information for Badlands National Park and the Black Hills at the counter. ✉ *1800 Haines Ave.* ☎ *605/343–0524* ⊕ *www. twowheelerdealer.com.*

BIRD-WATCHING

Especially around sunset, get set to watch the badlands come to life. More than 215 bird species have been recorded in the area, including herons, pelicans, cormorants, egrets, swans, geese, hawks, golden and bald eagles, falcons, vultures, cranes, doves, and cuckoos. Established roads and trails are the best places from which to watch for nesting species. The Cliff Shelf Nature Trail and the Castle Trail, which both traverse areas with surprisingly thick vegetation, are especially good locations. You may even catch sight of a rare burrowing owl at the Roberts Prairie Dog Town. Be sure to bring along a pair of binoculars.

HIKING

The isolation and otherworldliness of the badlands are best appreciated with a walk through them. Take time to examine the dusty rock beneath your feet, and be on the lookout for fossils and animals. Fossil Exhibit Trail and Cliff Shelf Nature Trail are must-dos, but even these popular trails tend to be primitive. You'll find bathrooms at Fossil Exhibit Trail. Both trails feature boardwalks, so you won't be shuffling through dirt and gravel. Because the weather here can be so variable, rangers suggest that you be prepared for anything. Wear sunglasses, a hat, and long pants, and have rain gear available. It's illegal to interfere with park resources, which includes everything from rocks and fossils to plants and artifacts. Stay at least 100 yards away from wildlife. Due to the dry climate, open fires are never allowed. Tell friends, relatives, and the park rangers if you're going to embark on a multiday expedition. Assume that your cell phone, if you've brought one, won't get a signal in the park. But most important of all, be sure to bring your own water. Sources of water in the park are few and far between, and none of them are drinkable. All water in the park is contaminated by minerals and sediment, and park authorities warn that it's untreatable. If you're backpacking into the wilderness, bring at least a gallon of water per person per day. For day hikes, rangers suggest you drink at least a quart per person per hour.

EASY

FAMILY **Fossil Exhibit Trail.** The trail, in place since 1964, has fossils of early
Fodor's Choice mammals displayed under glass along its ¼-mile length, which is now
★ completely wheelchair accessible. Give yourself at least an hour to fully enjoy this popular hike. *Easy.* ⊠ *Trail begins 5 miles northwest of the Ben Reifel Visitor Center, off Rte. 240.*

Window Trail. This 200-yard round-trip trail ends at a natural hole, or window, in a rock wall. Looking though, you'll see more of the distinctive badlands pinnacles and spires. *Easy.* ⊠ *Trail begins 2 miles north of the Ben Reifel Visitor Center, off Rte. 240.*

MODERATE

Cliff Shelf Nature Trail. This 0.5-mile loop winds through a wooded prairie oasis in the middle of dry, rocky ridges and climbs 200 feet to a peak above White River Valley for an incomparable view. Look for chipmunks, squirrels, and red-winged blackbirds in the wet wood, and eagles, hawks, and vultures at hilltop. Even casual hikers can complete this trail in far less than an hour, but if you want to observe the true diversity of wildlife present here, stay longer. *Moderate.* ⊠ *Trail begins 1 mile east of the Ben Reifel Visitor Center, off Rte. 240.*

BEST BETS FOR FAMILIES

- Badlands Loop Tour
- Fossil Exhibit Trail
- Mount Rushmore
- Robert's Prairie Dog Town
- Wall Drug

Notch Trail. One of the park's more interesting hikes, this 1.5-mile round-trip trail takes you over moderately difficult terrain and up a ladder. Winds at the notch can be fierce, but it's worth lingering for the view of the White River Valley and the Pine Ridge Indian Reservation. If you take a couple of breaks and enjoy the views, you'll probably want to plan on spending a little more than an hour on this hike. *Moderate.* ⊠ *Trail begins 2 miles north of the Ben Reifel Visitor Center, off Rte. 240.*

DIFFICULT

Saddle Pass Trail. This route, which connects with Castle Trail and Medicine Root Loop, is a steep, 0.25-mile climb up and down the side of "The Wall," an impressive rock formation. Plan on spending about an hour on this climb. *Difficult.* ⊠ *Trail begins 2 miles west of the Ben Reifel Visitor Center, off Rte. 240.*

HORSEBACK RIDING

The park has one of the largest and most beautiful territories in the state in which to ride a horse. Riding is allowed in most of the park except for some marked trails, roads, and developed areas. The mixed-grass prairie of the Badlands Wilderness Area is especially popular with riders. However, note that the weather in the Badlands Wilderness Area can be very unpredictable. Only experienced riders or people accompanied by experienced riders should venture far from more developed areas.

There are several restrictions and regulations that you must be aware of if you plan to ride your own horse. Potable water for visitors and animals is a rarity. Riders must bring enough water for themselves and their stock. Only certified weed-free hay is approved in the park. Horses are not allowed to run free within the borders of the park.

WHAT'S NEARBY

Badlands National Park is off Interstate 90 with two separate entrances. Badlands can be a one- or two-day stop for visitors who are traveling through the area or a place of frequent visits to locals. Located 50 miles east of the edge of the Black Hills (and Rapid City, the largest community on this side of the state), Badlands allows travelers a unique stop in a highly dense area of national parks, monuments, and memorials. Its close proximity to national treasures such as Mount Rushmore National Memorial, Wind Cave National Park, Jewel Cave National Monument, Devils Tower National Monument, and Custer State Park allow visitors to take in a wealth of sightseeing excursions in a relatively small area. The Black Hills provide a wonderful backdrop for the dry canyon and dusty buttes of the badlands.

NEARBY TOWNS

Built against a steep ridge of badland rock, **Wall** was founded in 1907 as a railroad station, and is among the closest towns to Badlands National Park, 8 miles from the Pinnacles entrance to the North Unit. Wall is home to about 850 residents and the world-famous Wall Drug Store, best known for its fabled jackalopes and free ice water. **Pine Ridge,** about 35 miles south of the Stronghold Unit, is on the cusp of Pine Ridge Indian Reservation. The town was established in 1877 as an Indian agency for Chief Red Cloud and his band of followers. With 2,800 square miles, the reservation, home, and headquarters of the Oglala Sioux, is second in size only to Arizona's Navajo Reservation. **Rapid City,** in the eastern buttes of the Black Hills, is South Dakota's second-largest city and a good base from which to explore the treasures of the state's southwestern corner, including the neighboring Black Hills National Forest, the badlands 75 miles to the east, and Mount Rushmore and Wind Cave National Park, 25 miles and 140 miles to the southwest respectively.

VISITOR INFORMATION

Oglala Sioux Tribe (Pine Ridge). The Pine Ridge Reservation is home to more than 35,000 Oglala Lakota, members of a major Sioux division known as the Western or Teton Sioux, who live in nine tribal districts on nearly 2 million acres of land. They are led by a Tribal Council President who is advised by an executive committee and a tribal council. ☎ *605/867–5821* ⊕ *www.oglalalakotanation.org.*

Rapid City Chamber of Commerce, and Convention and Visitors Bureau. ⊠ *444 Mt. Rushmore Rd. N, Rapid City* ☎ *605/343–1744, 800/487–3223* ⊕ *www.visitrapidcity.com.*

Wall–Badlands Area Chamber of Commerce. ⊠ *501 Main St., Wall* ☎ *605/279–2665, 888/852–9255* ⊕ *www.wall-badlands.com.*

NEARBY ATTRACTIONS

Main Street Square. Since opening in 2011, this attractive plaza in downtown Rapid City has become a focal point for a wide array of special events throughout the year, including movies under the stars, food festivals, a farmers' market, musical performances, and ice skating. At various times of the year, the square features interactive fountains, gardens, a fire pit, and a large oval lawn. ⊠ *Destination Rapid City, 512 Main St., Rapid City* ☎ *605/716–7979* ⊕ *www.mainstreetsquarerc.com.*

CLOSE UP

Wounded Knee Massacre

In late December 1890 the men of the Seventh Cavalry, armed with a federal mandate (and some light artillery), intercepted a group of 350 Lakota in southwest South Dakota with the intention of disarming them and marching them to Nebraska, where they would be forced onto scattered reservations. The disarming process was remarkably peaceful—that is, until soldiers approached a warrior named Black Coyote. According to several accounts, Black Coyote wouldn't relinquish his weapon without compensation, since he had bought the firearm himself. Somehow, a weapon was discharged, and at least one soldier ordered the troops to open fire. Fearful of an impending attack, the cavalry did so, even bringing their artillery to bear on the Lakota camp. Warriors scrambled to retrieve their seized rifles to re-arm themselves. By the time the smoke had cleared, about 150 Lakota and 25 U.S. soldiers lay dead. Although most of the remaining Lakota managed to escape, the majority perished in the elements, the victims of a sudden blizzard. When a burial party returned to the site after the storm, they found the frozen and contorted bodies of nearly 300 Lakota, mostly women and children, which they placed in a common grave.

In the following days, newspapers and government officials referred to the confrontation as a "battle," but it was none other than wholesale slaughter. Within a year, the army had awarded 23 Medals of Honor to members of the Seventh Cavalry for "valor" shown in the carnage (modern-day activists are seeking to have them rescinded). Even so, there was no cover-up of this affair. The American people were incensed, and from this point on, any government-led extermination of the Indian people ended. The blood in the snow at Wounded Knee melted in the spring of 1891, and as it thawed and ran across the prairie in a thousand rivulets, it carried with it a way of life for the American Indian.

Fodor's Choice ★ **Mount Rushmore National Memorial.** One of the nation's most iconic attractions, the giant likenesses of Washington, Jefferson, Lincoln, and Theodore Roosevelt, lie just 65 miles west of Badlands. An excellent interpretive center, trail network, and patriotic night lighting ceremony make the trip even more memorable. ⊠ *Rte. 244, Keystone* ☎ *605/574–2523* ⊕ *www.nps.gov/moru* 🅿 *Parking $11* ☉ *Monument daily 24 hrs; visitor facility and museum hrs vary.*

Outdoor Campus West. A project of South Dakota Game, Fish, and Parks, this attractive education center opened in 2011. It couples a hands-on museum featuring native habitats and wildlife with a 32-acre outdoor campus offering classes in hunting, fishing, camping, and snowshoeing. Nearby are several miles of hiking trails. ⌧ *4130 Adventure Trail, Rapid City* ☎ *605/394–2310* ⊕ *www.outdoorcampus.org* ☉ *Weekdays 8–5, Sat. 10–4, Sun. 1–4.*

FAMILY

Fodor's Choice

★

Wall Drug Store. This South Dakota original got its start in 1931 by offering free ice water to road-weary travelers. Today its four dining rooms seat 520 visitors at a time. A life-size mechanical Cowboy Orchestra and Chuckwagon Quartet greet you inside, and in the back you'll see an animated T. rex and replicas of Mt. Rushmore and a native village. The attached Western Mall has 14 shops selling all kinds of keepsakes from cowboy hats, boots and Black Hills gold jewelry to T-shirts and fudge. But don't skip the doughnuts. ⌧ *510 Main St., Wall* ☎ *605/279–2175* ⊕ *www.walldrug.com* 🍽 *Free* ☉ *Late May–early Sept., daily 6 am–10 pm; early Sept.–late May, daily 7–6.*

Wounded Knee Historical Site. A solitary stone obelisk commemorates the site of the 1890 massacre at Wounded Knee, the last major conflict between the U.S. military and American Indians. Only a handful of visitors make pilgrimages to the remote site today, which is simple and largely unchanged from its 1890 appearance. ⌧ *U.S. 18, 12 miles northwest of Pine Ridge* 🍽 *Free* ☉ *Daily 24 hrs.*

Wounded Knee: The Museum. This modern facility interprets the history of the December 29, 1890, Wounded Knee Massacre through interactive exhibits with historical photos and documents. Although a tour of the museum is an excellent companion to a visit to the actual site of the massacre, many visitors choose to stop at this convenient location off Interstate 90 in lieu of a stop at the isolated battleground 80 miles to the south. ⌧ *600 Main St., Wall* ☎ *605/279–2573* ⊕ *www.woundedkneemuseum.org* 🍽 *$6* ☉ *Apr.–mid-Oct., daily 9–5:30.*

WHERE TO EAT

IN THE PARK

$

AMERICAN

FAMILY

✕ **Cedar Pass Lodge Restaurant.** Cool off within dark, knotty-pine walls under an exposed-beam ceiling, and enjoy a hearty meal of steak, trout, or Indian tacos and fry bread. 💲 *Average main: $9* ⌧ *1 Cedar St., Interior* ☎ *605/433–5460* ⊕ *www.cedarpasslodge.com* ☉ *Closed Nov.–Mar.*

PICNIC AREAS

Bigfoot Pass Overlook. There is only a handful of tables here and no water, but the incredible view makes it a lovely spot to have lunch. Restrooms are available. ⌧ *Badlands Loop Rd., 7 miles northwest of the Ben Reifel Visitor Center.*

Conata Picnic Area. A half-dozen or so covered picnic tables are scattered over this area, which rests against a badlands wall ½ mile south of Badlands Loop Road. There's no potable water, but there are bathroom

Best Campgrounds in Badlands

Pitching a tent and sleeping under the stars is one of the greatest ways to fully experience the sheer isolation and unadulterated empty spaces of Badlands National Park. You'll find two relatively easy-access campgrounds within park boundaries, but only one has any sort of amenities. The second is little more than a flat patch of ground with some signs. Unless you desperately need a flush toilet to have an enjoyable camping experience, you're just as well off hiking into the wilderness and choosing your own campsite. The additional isolation will be well worth the extra effort. You can set up camp anywhere that's at least a half mile from a road or trail and is not visible from any road or trail.

Cedar Pass Campground. With tent sites and 20 new RV sites as well as coin-operated showers, this is the most developed campground in the park, and it's near the Ben Reifel Visitor Center, Cedar Pass Lodge, and a half-dozen hiking trails. ⊠ *Rte. 377, ¼ mile south of Badlands Loop Rd.* ☎ *605/433–5361* ⊕ *www.cedarpass-lodge.com.*

Sage Creek Primitive Campground. The word to remember here is primitive. If you want to get away from it all, this lovely, isolated spot surrounded by nothing but fields and crickets is the right camp for you. ⊠ *Sage Creek Rim Rd., 25 miles west of Badlands Loop Rd.* ☎ *No phone.*

facilities and you can enjoy your lunch in peaceful isolation at the threshold of the Badlands Wilderness Area. The Conata Basin area is to the east, and Sage Creek area is to the west. ⊠ *Conata Rd., 15 miles northwest of the Ben Reifel Visitor Center.*

OUTSIDE THE PARK

WALL

$
AMERICAN
✕ **Cactus Family Restaurant and Lounge.** Delicious hotcakes and pies await you at this restaurant in downtown Wall. In summer you'll find a buffet large enough to satisfy any appetite. $ *Average main: $10* ⊠ *519 Main St., Wall* ☎ *605/279–2561* ⊕ *www.cactuscafeandlounge.com.*

$
AMERICAN
✕ **Western Art Gallery Restaurant.** More than 200 original oil paintings, all with a Western theme, line the dining room of this eatery in the Wall Drug building. For a tasty meal, try a hot beef sandwich or a buffalo burger. The old-fashioned soda fountain has milk shakes and homemade ice cream. The place serves the area's best donuts. $ *Average main: $10* ⊠ *510 Main St., Wall* ☎ *605/279–2175* ⊕ *www.walldrug.com.*

WHERE TO STAY

IN THE PARK

$ HOTEL **Cedar Pass Lodge.** Besides impressive views of the badlands, these all-new in 2013 cabins include modern touches like flat-screen TVs and Wi-Fi connections. **Pros:** new cabins; the best stargazing in South Dakota. **Cons:** remote location; long drive to other restaurants. [$] *Rooms from: $85* ✉ *20681 Rte. 240, Interior* ☎ *605/433–5460, 877/386–4383* 🌐 *www.cedarpasslodge.com* 🛏 *24 cabins* 🕒 *Closed Oct.–Apr.*

OUTSIDE THE PARK

INTERIOR

$ HOTEL **Badlands Budget Host Motel.** Every room in this motel has views of the nearby Buffalo Gap National Grasslands. **Pros:** clean and comfortable; close to the national park. **Cons:** standard rooms with no frills. [$] *Rooms from: $65* ✉ *900 Rte. 377, Interior* ☎ *605/433–5335, 800/388–4643* 🌐 *www.budgethost.com* 🛏 *21 rooms, 70 campsites* 🕒 *Closed Oct.–Apr.* 🍴 *No meals.*

$ B&B/INN FAMILY **Circle View Guest Ranch.** Located in the heart of the badlands, this B&B has spectacular views. **Pros:** friendly people; beautiful views; great for groups. **Cons:** small and isolated. [$] *Rooms from: $95* ✉ *20055 Rte. 44 E, Interior* ☎ *605/433–5582* 🌐 *www.circleviewranch.com* 🛏 *8 rooms, 3 cabins.*

RAPID CITY

$ B&B/INN **Coyote Blues Village B&B.** This European-style lodge on 30 acres displays an unusual mix of antique furnishings and contemporary art. **Pros:** tucked away from the highway; exceptional food. **Cons:** not within walking distance of other restaurants. [$] *Rooms from: $65* ✉ *23165 Horseman's Ranch Rd., Rapid City* ☎ *605/574–4477, 888/253–4477* 🌐 *www.coyotebluesvillage.com* 🛏 *10 rooms.*

BANFF NATIONAL PARK

WELCOME TO BANFF

TOP REASONS TO GO

★ **Scenery:** Visitors are often unprepared for the sheer scale of the Canadian Rockies. Scattered between the peaks are glaciers, forests, valleys, meadows, rivers, and the bluest lakes of the planet.

★ **Spectacular ski slopes:** Lake Louise Mountain Resort is Canada's largest single ski area, with skiing on four mountain faces, 4,200 skiable acres, and 113 named trails—and that's only one of the three ski resorts in Banff.

★ **Trails galore:** More than 1,600 km (1,000 miles) of defined hiking trails in the park lead to scenic lakes, alpine meadows, glaciers, forests, and deep canyons.

★ **Banff Upper Hot Springs:** Relax in naturally hot mineral springs as you watch snowflakes swirl around you, gaze at the stars as you "take the waters" on a cool summer's evening.

★ **Icefields Parkway:** One of the most scenic drives on the continent, this 230-km (143-mile) roadway links Banff and Jasper.

1 Icefields Parkway. There are many sites to be seen along this spectacular 230-km (143-mile) stretch of road. The Crowfoot Glacier, Bow Pass, Mistaya Canyon, Saskatchewan Crossing, and the Columbia Icefield are the primary highlights in the Banff section.

2 Lake Louise, Moraine Lake, and the Bow Valley Parkway. Backed by snowcapped mountains, fantastically ice-blue, Lake Louise is one of the most photographed lakes in the world. Lake Louise, Moraine Lake and the Valley of the Ten Peaks, and stunning Johnston Canyon are highlights of this region.

3 Banff Townsite. The hub of the park, Banff Townsite is the place to go to find shops, restaurants, hotels, and other facilities. Highlights of the townsite: Banff Information Centre, Whyte Museum, Banff Centre, Upper Hot Springs Pool, Sulphur Mountain Gondola, and the Hoodoos.

↑ TO JASPER AND JASPER NATIONAL PARK

Sunwapta Pass

◆ **Columbia Icefield/ Athabasca Glacier**

93

BRITISH COLUMBIA

ALBERTA

Saskatchewan Crossing

◆ **Mistaya Canyon**

Stephen Lake

11

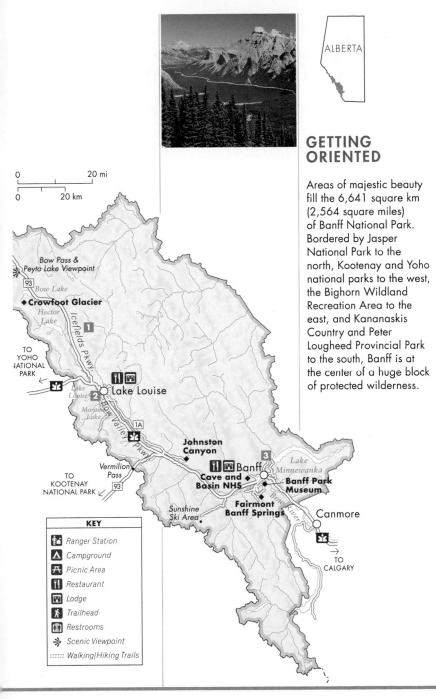

ALBERTA

GETTING ORIENTED

Areas of majestic beauty fill the 6,641 square km (2,564 square miles) of Banff National Park. Bordered by Jasper National Park to the north, Kootenay and Yoho national parks to the west, the Bighorn Wildland Recreation Area to the east, and Kananaskis Country and Peter Lougheed Provincial Park to the south, Banff is at the center of a huge block of protected wilderness.

7

0   20 mi

0   20 km

Bow Pass & Peyto Lake Viewpoint

93   Bow Lake

◆ **Crowfoot Glacier**

Hector Lake

Icefields Pkwy

1

TO YOHO NATIONAL PARK

Lake Louise

2   Lake Louise

Moraine Lake

Bow Valley Pkwy

1A

Johnston Canyon

Vermilion Pass

TO KOOTENAY NATIONAL PARK

93

Sunshine Ski Area

Cave and Basin NHS

Banff

3

Lake Minnewanka

Banff Park Museum

Bow River

Fairmont Banff Springs

Canmore

TO CALGARY

KEY

👫	Ranger Station
⛰	Campground
⛱	Picnic Area
🍴	Restaurant
🏠	Lodge
🥾	Trailhead
🚻	Restrooms
⇘	Scenic Viewpoint
⋯⋯	Walking/Hiking Trails

Updated by
Debbie Olsen

Comparing mountains is a subjective and imprecise business. Yet few would deny that the Canadian Rockies are one of the most extravagantly beautiful ranges on Earth. The mountains and vast stretches of wilderness that make up the birthplace of Canada's first national park offer stunning scenery of glaciers, lakes, valleys, and snowcapped mountain peaks. Large mammals such as deer and elk can be observed in all seasons from the roadside.

BANFF PLANNER

WHEN TO GO

Banff National Park is an all-season destination. Visit in summer to hike the mountain trails or go in winter to enjoy some of the world's best skiing. Millions of people visit the park every year with the vast majority traveling during July and August, the warmest and driest months in the park. ■TIP➔ **If you can visit in late spring (May to June) or early fall (September), you will be in shoulder season when prices are lower, crowds are fewer, and the temperatures are usually still comfortable.** The downside to an off-season visit is the fact that you miss the summer interpretive programs and the wildflowers that reach their peak from early July to mid-August.

Both of the park's information centers are open all year, with extended hours during the summer months.

AVG. HIGH/LOW TEMPS.

JAN.	FEB.	MAR.	APR.	MAY	JUNE
22/5	32/12	39/18	48/30	58/35	66/42
JULY	AUG.	SEPT.	OCT.	NOV.	DEC.
71/45	71/44	61/37	50/30	33/17	22/7

FESTIVALS AND EVENTS

WINTER **Snow Days.** A highlight of this monthlong winter celebration is the Ice Magic winter festival, which features world-class ice carving and outdoor events. There's also a 3-on-3 ball hockey tournament and a Mountain Adventure Weekend, where you can try ice climbing and other exhilarating outdoor activities and watch mountain films. The festival begins in early January each year. ☎ *403/762–8421* ⊕ *www.banfflakelouise.com.*

Christmas in the Rockies and Santa Claus Parade. Banff welcomes the holiday season with a one-day event featuring photos with that jolly old elf in Central Park, craft shows, children's ice-carving stations, and an evening parade of lights. On Christmas Day, Santa shows off his downhill skills at the three area ski resorts. ☎ *403/762–8421* ⊕ *www. banfflakelouise.com.*

SUMMER **Banff Summer Arts Festival.** The longest running arts festival in Canada takes place every summer at the Banff Centre and features film screenings, visual-art displays, theater, opera, dance, literary readings, speakers, and musical productions. ☎ *403/762–6300* ⊕ *www.banffcentre.ca/bsaf.*

Canada Day. This holiday on July 1 means free admission to the national park, as well as big celebrations in Canmore and Banff that include parades, fireworks, and live music. ☎ *403/762–0285* ⊕ *www.banff.com.*

PLANNING YOUR TIME

BANFF NATIONAL PARK IN ONE DAY

Start with a visit to the **Banff Information Centre** to pick up maps and information on the major sites. Buy lunch provisions and drive to beautiful **Lake Louise.** Walk the flat shoreline trail and venture upward along the **Lake Agnes Trail** to the teahouse (or turn back once you get a lofty view of Lake Louise). On the drive back to Banff Townsite, stop at Johnston Canyon and allow an hour for the easy round-trip hike to the dramatic waterfall. Have dinner at **Fairmont Banff Springs Hotel.** Afterward, explore the hotel's interior, then end the day with an evening dip in the **Banff Upper Hot Springs.**

GETTING HERE AND AROUND

Banff National Park, in west-central Alberta, is 128 km (80 miles) west of Calgary, 401 km (249 miles) southwest of Edmonton, and 850 km (528 miles) east of Vancouver.

AIR TRAVEL

The closest international airports are in Calgary and Edmonton. Major airlines serve both airports.

BUS TRAVEL

For travel within the towns of Banff and Lake Louise, there is a public transit system, as well as several local taxi companies to choose from. Public buses also run between Banff and Lake Louise, and in winter there is a ski shuttle service that picks up at most area hotels and transports guests to the park's three ski resorts.

Bus Contact Information Canadian Rockies Brewster Shuttle. Deluxe motorcoach bus transportation connects Calgary International Airport with Kananaskis, Banff, Lake Louise, and Jasper. ✉ *100 Gopher St., Banff* ☎ *403/762–6700* ⊕ *www.explorerockies.com* 🎫 *C$54–C$124* 🕐 *Nov.–Apr.*

7

CAR TRAVEL

A car allows the most flexible travel in the Canadian Rockies, and the easiest way to get from Calgary to Banff is by car on Trans-Canada Highway 1. Use Icefields Parkway (Highway 93) to get from Jasper to Banff. International car rental agencies are available at Edmonton and Calgary airports and in Canmore, Banff, Lake Louise, and Jasper.

PARK ESSENTIALS

PARK FEES AND PERMITS

Note that all prices in this chapter are in Canadian dollars, unless stated otherwise. A park entrance pass is C$9.80 per person or C$19.60 maximum per vehicle per day. An annual pass will cost C$67.70 per adult or C$136.40 per family or group. Larger buses and vans pay a group commercial rate. If you're planning to stay a week or more, your best bet is an annual pass.

Permits are required for backcountry camping and some other activities in the park. Backcountry camping permits (C$9.80 per day), fire permits (C$8.80 per day), dumping station permits (C$8.80 per day), and fishing permits (C$9.80 per day) are available at the park visitor information center or at some campgrounds. In some cases a fire permit is included in your camping fees. Be sure to check with campground staff.

PARK HOURS

The park is open 24/7 year-round. It's in the Mountain time zone.

CELL-PHONE RECEPTION

Cell-phone service in the park is sometimes unpredictable, but is fairly good near the Banff Townsite. Public telephones can be found at the information centers, at most hotels and bars, and at several key spots around the townsite of Banff and the village of Lake Louise.

RESTAURANTS

There are more than 100 eateries in Banff National Park, and visitors have a wide range of dining options—from fast-food outlets to chain restaurants to award-winning fine-dining experiences. Eating out is, for the most part, a casual affair with an emphasis on local foods served in large quantities. Trout, venison, elk, moose, and bison appear on the menus of even the most modest establishments. It's a good idea to make reservations at popular restaurants in advance, especially during the peak summer and ski seasons. Like most national parks, prices are slightly inflated.

Prices in the reviews are the average cost of a main course at dinner, or if dinner is not served, at lunch. Prices are in Canadian dollars unless otherwise stated.

HOTELS

The lodgings in Banff comprise an eclectic list that includes backcountry lodges without electricity or running water, campgrounds, hostels with shared bathroom facilities, standard roadside motels, quaint B&Bs, supremely luxurious hotels, and historic mountain resorts. Most accommodations do not provide meal plans, but some include breakfast.

With just a few exceptions, room rates are often highest from mid-June to late September and between Christmas and New Year's. In many cases, the best accommodation rates can be found during the months of October to mid-November and May to mid-June when rates can drop by half.

More accommodations and restaurants can be found just outside the national park in Canmore and in Kananaskis Country, a large multiuse provincial recreation area.

Prices in the reviews are the lowest cost of a standard double room in high season. Prices are in Canadian dollars unless otherwise stated. For expanded reviews, facilities, and current deals, visit Fodors.com.

PARK PUBLICATIONS

The Mountain Guide is distributed by parks staff upon entry to Banff National Park. It contains maps and good general park information such as points of interest, safety messages, programs and events, camping information, and fees. If you want to use it for advance planning, it is also available on the Parks Canada website (⊕ *www.pc.gc.ca/banff*) under "Visitor Information."

VISITOR INFORMATION

PARK CONTACT INFORMATION
Banff National Park ☎ *403/762–1550* ⊕ *www.explorerockies.com.*

VISITOR CENTERS
Banff Information Centre. This information center is jointly run by Parks Canada and Banff Lake Louise Tourism (BLLT). Parks Canada is on one side of the building and BLLT is on the other. Parks Canada staff can provide excellent information on camping, hiking, interpretive programs, and sightseeing. BLLT counselors can provide information on restaurants, tour operators, and accommodations. Be sure to check here in spring for information on which hiking trails are open—many remain closed into May due to avalanche risk. ⊠ *224 Banff Ave., Banff* ☎ *403/762–8421* ⊕ *www.explorerockies.com; www.banfflakelouise. com* ☉ *Jan.–mid-May, daily 9–5; mid-May–mid-June and Sept., daily 8–6; mid-June–Aug., daily 8–8.*

Lake Louise Visitor Centre. Stop here to get maps and information about area attractions and trails. The Banff Lake Louise Tourism desk can provide information on area accommodations and amenities, and you can purchase educational books and other materials from the Friends of Banff National Park. ⊠ *Village of Lake Louise, next to Samson Mall* ☎ *403/522–3833* ⊕ *www.banfflakelouise.com* ☉ *Mid-Sept.–Apr., daily 9–4; May–mid-June, daily 9–5; mid-June–mid-Sept., daily 9–8.*

7

EXPLORING

SCENIC DRIVES

Fodor's Choice ★ **Icefields Parkway.** Powerfully rugged mountain scenery, glaciers, waterfalls and icefalls, and wildlife: the Icefields Parkway reveals all of these and more as it snakes its way along 230 km (143 miles) connecting Banff National Park with Jasper National Park. It is an absolute highlight of the Canadian Rockies.

There aren't any gas stations along the route, so be sure to check the gas gauge before setting out. Although you could drive this winding road in three to four hours, it's more likely to be a full-day trip when you add in stops (⇨ *Scenic Stops Along Icefields Parkway*). The road rises to near the tree line at several points, and the weather can be chilly and unsettled at these high elevations, even in midsummer, so it's a good idea to bring warm clothing along.

Elk, moose, deer, and bighorn sheep are fairly common along this route, and occasionally you can see bears and mountain goats. In summer, alpine wildflowers carpet Bow Pass and Sunwapta Pass.

The most dramatic scenery is in the north end of Banff National Park and the south end of Jasper National Park, where ice fields and glaciers become common on the high mountains flanking the route (icefields are massive reservoirs of ice; glaciers are the slow-moving rivers of ice that flow from the icefields). Scenic overlooks and signposted hiking trails abound along the route.

Lake Minnewanka Loop. It's easy to spend the day along this 25-km (15-mile) loop. Traveling clockwise, you can explore Lower Bankhead and Upper Bankhead, an abandoned coal mine and mining community. Just 3 km (2 miles) farther you come to Lake Minnewanka, the largest lake in the park. Boat and fishing rentals are available. Farther along are more lakes and picnic areas.

Mount Noquay Drive. The highlight of this 6½-km (4-mile) route is the viewpoint near the top over Banff. Bighorn sheep and mule deer are often sighted along the twisting road. Trailheads at the top lead to Stoney Squaw Summit and Cascade Amphitheatre.

Tunnel Mountain Drive. On the east side of Banff, Tunnel Mountain Drive makes a scenic 5-km (3-mile) loop. It's closed in winter, but just off the drive, the hoodoos—fingerlike, eroded rock formations—are accessible year-round (signs on Banff's main street direct you there).

HISTORIC SITES

Banff Park Museum National Historic Site of Canada. This National Historic Site, made for the 1893 World Exhibition in Chicago, is western Canada's oldest natural-history museum. Most of the animals at the museum, fondly referred to as the "stuffed animal museum," were collected between 1890 and 1930, when the park was still open to hunting. You can get up close and personal with some of Banff's largest mammals, including a grizzly bear, bison, mountain goats, and bighorn sheep.

CLOSE UP

Plants and Wildlife in Banff

Awesome forces of nature combined to thrust wildly folded sedimentary and metamorphic rock up into ragged peaks and high cliffs. Add glaciers and snowfields to the lofty peaks, carpet the valleys with forests, mix in a generous helping of small and large mammals, wildflowers, rivers, and crystal-clear lakes, and you've got the recipe for Banff National Park.

This diverse topography has resulted in three complex life zones in Banff: montane, subalpine, and alpine. Each zone has characteristic physical environments along with its own species of plants and animals. The montane zone features valleys and grasslands as well as alders, willows, birches, and cottonwoods. The Douglas firs and lodgepole pines that cover the lower slopes of the mountains are also in the montane

zone. Subalpine forest extends from the montane to about 6,500 feet and is made up of mostly spruce and pine trees. The fragile alpine zone is found at the highest elevations in the park. The rocky terrain and cold, howling winds mean far fewer plants and animals can survive there.

Most of the wildlife is found in the montane zone, where bighorn sheep, deer, elk, and caribou abound. Moose and mountain goats can also be seen, as well as the occasional black bear. Other animals in the park include grizzly bears, wolves, coyotes, and cougars, as well as smaller mammals such as squirrels, marmots, muskrats, porcupines, and beavers. Birds commonly spotted are grouse, larks, finches, ptarmigans, bald eagles, golden eagles, loons, and Canada geese.

7

⌧ *91 Banff Ave.* ☎ *403/762–1558* ⊕ *www.pc.gc.ca/banff* ✉ *C\$3.90* ⊙ *Mid-May–Sept., daily 10–6; Oct.–mid-May, daily 1–5.*

FAMILY **Banff Upper Hot Springs.** Discovered in 1884, Banff's natural hot mineral springs were the impetus for the development of Canada's first national park. Early travelers to Banff came primarily to experience the "healing waters," and today they can still be experienced at the Banff Upper Hot Springs pools. The hot springs are a popular activity and are child-friendly during the day—think family swimming pool rather than couples' hot tub vibe. The water is especially inviting on a dull, cold day or when it's snowing, and views of the mountains are spectacular. Lockers, bathing suits (circa 1920s or modern), and towels can be rented, and spa services are available. Even though the recommended limit is 20 minutes in the water, you'll likely want to stay an hour or two. The springs can be reached via a short uphill walk from the parking lot. ⌧ *3 km (2 miles) south of downtown, 1 Mountain Ave.* ☎ *403/762–1515, 800/767–1611* ⊕ *www.hotspring.ca* ✉ *C\$7.30* ⊙ *Mid-May–mid-Oct., daily 9 am–11 pm; mid-Oct.–mid-May, Sun.–Thurs. 10–10, Fri. and Sat. 10 am–11 pm.*

FAMILY
Fodor's Choice
★

Cave and Basin National Historic Site. This site commemorates the birthplace of Canada's national parks system, which began with the protection of the Banff hot springs in 1885. The site underwent a three-year, C\$13.8-million renovation and reopened in May 2013. You'll find restored historic buildings, a new plaza, and great interpretive displays about Banff and the other national parks in Canada. An interpretive trail explains the area's geology and plant life and offers information on the wildlife and history of Banff national park. While visiting the cave and walking past the warm mineral pools, keep an eye out for the most endangered species in the park, the Banff snail, which makes its home in the warm mineral waters and cannot be found anywhere else in the world. ⊠ *2 km (1 mile) west of downtown, 311 Cave Ave.* ☎ *403/762–1566* ⊕ *www.pc.gc.ca/banff* ☎ *C\$3.90* ⊙ *Mid-May–Sept., daily 9–6; Oct.–mid-May, weekdays 11–4, weekends 9:30–5.*

Fairmont Banff Springs. This hotel, 2 km (1 mile) south of downtown Banff, is the town's architectural showpiece and a National Historic Site. Built in 1888, the hotel is easily recognized by its castle-like exterior. Heritage Hall, a small, free museum above the Grand Lobby, has rotating exhibits on the area's history and is open daily from 9 to 9. Historical tours are offered Tuesday through Saturday at 3 pm and are free for hotel guests or C\$15 for nonguests. ⊠ *405 Spray Ave.* ☎ *403/762–2211, 800/441–1414* ⊕ *www.fairmont.com.*

Lake Louise. This is one of the most photographed spots in the park. In summer, you can walk around the lake and enjoy the nearby hiking trails. Winter offers skating on the ice and sleigh rides. The Fairmont Château Lake Louise hotel sits on the edge of the lake and has several on-site restaurants. The lake is also a departure point for several short, moderately strenuous, well-traveled hiking routes, including the popular 3-km (2-mile) trail to Lake Agnes. The tiny lake hangs on a mountain-surrounded shelf that opens to the east with a bird's-eye view of the Beehives and Mount Whitehorn. At the teahouse (cash only) by Lake Agnes you can enjoy a variety of soups, sandwiches, and snacks. ⊠ *Fairmont Château Lake Louise, 111 Lake Louise Dr., Lake Louise* ☎ *403/522–3511.*

SCENIC STOPS

ALONG ICEFIELDS PARKWAY
The sights are organized from south to north.

Bow Summit. At 6,787 feet, Bow Summit is the highest drivable pass in the national parks of the Canadian Rockies. It is famous for its postcard viewpoint of Peyto Lake. To reach the summit viewpoint, park in the lot on the west side of the Icefields Parkway and take the trail from there that leads 1½ km (1 mile) through alpine forest to a scenic point above the timberline. On the south side of the pass is Bow Lake, source of the Bow River, which flows through Banff. ⊠ *Icefields Parkway (Hwy. 93), 40 km (25 miles) north of Lake Louise, 190 km [118 miles) south of Jasper.*

Simpson's Num-Ti-Jah Lodge. You may wish to stop for lunch or supper at Simpson's Num-Ti-Jah Lodge at Bow Lake. This rustic lodge with simple guest rooms specializes in excellent regional Canadian cuisine. Outside, walking paths circle the lake. ⊠ *Icefields Parkway (Hwy. 93), 40 km (25 miles) north of Lake Louise* ☎ *403/522–2167* ⊕ *www.sntj.ca.*

Above Bow Lake hangs the Crowfoot Glacier, so named because of its resemblance to a three-toed crow's foot. At least that's how it looked when it was named at the beginning of the 20th century. In the

Canadian Rockies, glaciers, including Crowfoot, have been receding. The lowest toe completely melted away 50 years ago, and now only the upper two toes remain. On the north side of Bow Pass is **Peyto Lake**; its startlingly intense aqua-blue color comes from the minerals in glacial runoff. Wildflowers blossom along the pass in summer, but note that it can be covered with snow as late as May and as early as September.

Parker Ridge Trail. The short (2½ km [1½ miles]), steep Parker Ridge Trail is one of the easiest hikes in the national parks to bring you above the tree line. There's an excellent view of the Saskatchewan Glacier, where the river of the same name begins, though you've got to make it to the top of the ridge to get the view. Snowbanks can persist into early summer, but carpets of wildflowers cross the trail in late July and August. Stay on the path to keep erosion to a minimum. The trailhead is about 4 km (2½ miles) south of the boundary between Banff and Jasper parks on the Icefields Parkway.

Sunwapta Pass. Marking the border between Banff and Jasper national parks, Sunwapta is the second-highest drivable pass—6,675 feet—in the national parks. Wildlife is most visible in spring and autumn after a snowfall, when herds of bighorn sheep come to the road to lick up the salt used to melt snow and ice. Be prepared for a series of hairpin turns as you switchback up to the pass summit. ⊠ *Icefields Parkway (Hwy. 93), 122 km (76 miles) north of Lake Louise, 108 km (67 miles) south of Jasper.*

Fodor's Choice   **Athabasca Glacier.** This is a 7-km (4½-mile) tongue of ice flowing from the
★   immense Columbia Icefield almost to the Icefields Parkway. A century ago the ice flowed over the current location of the highway; signposts depict the gradual retreat of the ice since that time. Several other glaciers are visible from here; they all originate from the Columbia Icefield, a giant alpine lake of ice covering 325 square km (125 square miles) whose edge is visible from the highway. You can hike up to the toe of the glacier, but venturing farther without a trained guide is extremely dangerous because of hidden crevasses. **Athabasca Glacier Ice Walks** (☎ 800/565–7547 ⊕ *www.icewalks.com*) offers three-, five-, and six-hour guided walks (C$36–C$45), which can be reserved at the Icefield Centre or through **Jasper Adventure Centre** (☎ 780/852–5595 or 800/565–7547 ⊕ *www. jasperadventurecentre.com*), in Jasper (⇨ *Chapter 23*). You can also take a trip onto the Athabasca Glacier in **Brewster Tours' Ice Explorers,** which have been modified to drive on ice (tickets are available at the Icefield Centre for C$29.86). ⊠ *Icefields Parkway (Hwy. 93), 127 km (79 miles) north of Lake Louise, 103 km (64 miles) south of Jasper.*

Columbia Icefield Discovery Centre. Opposite the Athabasca Glacier, this facility houses interpretive exhibits, a gift shop, and two dining facilities (one cafeteria-style, one buffet-style). The summer midday rush between 11 and 3 can be intense. The Glacier View Inn is opposite the icefield and has 32 hotel rooms, available from early May to mid-October. ⊠ *Icefields Pkwy., 127 km (79 miles) north of Lake Louise, 103 km (64 miles) south of Jasper* ☎ 877/423–7433 ⊕ *www.explorerockies. com* ⌨ *Free* ☉ *Late May–mid-June and Sept.–early Oct., daily 10–5; mid-June–Aug., daily 10–7.*

7

Catching a view from Moraine Lake as the sunlight plays on the snow-drizzled mountains around it.

Brewster Sightseeing Excursions. Book sightseeing excursions in Banff, Lake Louise, and Jasper and admission tickets and value passes, which include admission to multiple attractions, at a savings here. ☎ 800/760–6934 ⊕ *www.explorerockies.com*

Glacier Skywalk. Opening in May 2014, this fully accessible cliff-edge walkway will lead to a glass-floored observation platform 280 metres (918 feet) above the Sunwapta Valley. From this unique vantage point, visitors can get a bird's-eye view of the surrounding ice-capped mountain peaks and deep glacier carved valleys of the Canadian Rockies. ☎ 866/606–6700, 403/762–6700 ⊕ *www.glacierskywalk.ca*.

As you continue north from the Icefield Centre through Jasper National Park toward Jasper Townsite, you'll see some of the most spectacular scenery in the Canadian Rockies. One of the most stunning sites is the **Stutfield Glacier,** 95 km (57 miles) south of Jasper Townsite. The glacier stretches down 3,000 feet of cliff face, forming a set of double icefalls visible from a roadside viewpoint. Continuing along the parkway, you'll pass the access to spectacular **Sunwapta Falls,** 57 km (33 miles) south of the town of Jasper. You'll also want to stop at **Athabasca Falls,** 31 km (19 miles) south of Jasper Townsite. These powerful falls are created as the Athabasca River is compressed through a narrow gorge, producing a violent torrent of water. The falls are especially dramatic in early summer. Trails and overlooks provide good viewpoints.

OTHER SCENIC STOPS

FAMILY **Banff Gondola.** Views during the steep eight-minute ride to and from the 7,500-foot summit of Sulphur Mountain are spectacular in the enclosed four-person gondolas. From the upper gondola terminal you can hike the short distance to the true summit of Sulphur Mountain on the South East Ridge Trail and perhaps catch sight of grazing bighorn sheep, or visit the gift shop or the reasonably priced restaurant. Be sure to walk the easy 1-km (0.6-mile) skywalk to the Sanson's Peak Meteorological Station for excellent views and to break away from the crowds. Norman Bethune Sanson hiked up to this station more than 1,000 times during his life to record the weather. The gondola is south from the center of Banff; you can catch a Roam public transit bus. ■TIP→ This is a very popular activity—go early or late to avoid crowds. ✉ *Mountain Ave., 3 km (2 miles) south of downtown Banff* ☎ *403/762–5438, 403/762–2523* ⊕ *www. banffgondola.com* ✉ *C$34.95 round-trip* ☉ *Late May–late Aug., daily 8 am–9 pm; late Aug.–mid-Oct., daily 8–8; mid-Oct.–early Nov., daily 8:30–4:30; early Nov.–early Dec., daily 10–6.*

FAMILY **Lake Louise Sightseeing Gondola.** Ride this to an alpine plateau for a stunning view that includes more than a dozen glaciers. The deck of the Wildlife Interpretive Centre is a good place to enjoy an ice-cream cone, a cold drink, or a picnic lunch, or you can buy a ticket that includes buffet breakfast or buffet lunch that is enjoyed at the lodge near the base of the gondola. Guided interpretive walks take place at 10:30, 12:30, and 2:30 daily and last about 45 minutes. ✉ *Whitehorn Rd., off Hwy. 1 (Lake Louise exit)* ☎ *403/522–3555* ⊕ *www.lakelouisegondola.com* ✉ *C$28.75 ride only, C$30.95 with breakfast, $35.25 with lunch* ☉ *May 15–June 12, daily 9–4:30; June 13–Sept. 7, daily 9–5; Sept. 8–30, daily 9–4:30.*

Moraine Lake. This beauty, 11 km (7 miles) south of Lake Louise, is a photographic highlight of Banff National Park. Set in the Valley of the Ten Peaks, the lake reflects the snow-clad mountaintops that rise abruptly around it. The lake is a major stop for tour buses as well as a popular departure point for hikers and a place to canoe. Visit early or late in the day to avoid crowds. Moderate hiking trails lead from the lodge at Moraine Lake into some spectacular alpine country. Call ahead for special trail restrictions.

EDUCATIONAL OFFERINGS

There is a wide range of park interpretive programs in Banff. At the Banff Information Centre and at Cave and Basin, there are slide shows and presentations throughout the year. In the summer months you can enjoy campground interpretive programs, guided hikes, bicycle tours, film showings, and adventure games at Banff Avenue Square.

FAMILY

Fodor'sChoice

★

Friends of Banff National Park. This nonprofit group provides roving nature walks, guided hikes, and junior naturalist programs designed especially for children. The junior naturalist programs take place at Tunnel Mountain Campground, Johnston Canyon Campground, Two Jack Lakeside Campground, and Lake Louise Campground Theatre. ✉ *224 Banff Ave., Banff* ☎ *403/760–5331* ⊕ *www.friendsofbanff.com* ✉ *Free or nominal fee.*

SPORTS AND THE OUTDOORS

MULTISPORT OUTFITTERS

Abominable Ski & Sportswear. Rent or buy ski and snowboarding equipment in winter and bikes and accessories in summer. ⊠ *229 Banff Ave., Banff* ☎ *403/762–2905* ⊕ *www.abominablesports.com.*

Bactrax Bike Rentals. This supplier has Banff's largest selection of rental skis and snowboards. It also rents bikes in the summer and arranges one- to four-hour guided interpretive bike tours on local Banff trails, which are suitable for any age or physical ability. ⊠ *225 Bear St., Banff* ☎ *403/762–8177* ⊕ *www.snowtips-bactrax.com.*

Banff Adventures Unlimited. Rent bikes here, or come by to sign up for almost any area activity. ⊠ *211 Bear St., Banff* ☎ *403/762–4554, 800/644–8888* ⊕ *www.banffadventures.com.*

Discover Banff Tours. Sign up here for guided sightseeing, wildlife safaris, nature walks, ice walks, and snowshoeing adventures. ⊠ *Sundance Mall, 215 Banff Ave., Banff* ☎ *403/760–5007, 877/565–9372* ⊕ *www. banfftours.com.*

Great Divide Nature Interpretation. Guided interpretive hikes and snowshoeing trips are the specialty here. ⊠ *Lake Louise, Banff* ☎ *403/522–2735, 866/522–2735* ⊕ *www.greatdivide.ca.*

Mountain Magic Equipment. Canada's largest independent climbing outfitter has three floors of hiking, climbing, skiing, running, and biking gear and a 30-foot indoor climbing wall for testing equipment. ⊠ *216 Banff Ave., Banff* ☎ *403/762–2591, 877/665–9921* ⊕ *www.mountainmagic.com.*

Soul Ski & Bike. This great spot sells, rents, and services bicycles, skis, and snow boards. They are well known for their custom ski boot–fitting service, and they rent and retail standard, deluxe, and premium equipment. ⊠ *203A Bear St., Banff* ☎ *403/760–1650* ⊕ *www.soulskiandbike.com.*

White Mountain Adventures. Daily guided hikes, backpacking, and heli-hiking can be arranged through this outfitter. In winter, you can try snowshoeing, cross-country skiing, or a guided ice walk. ⊠ *120A Eagle Cresent, Banff* ☎ *403/760–4403, 800/408–0005* ⊕ *www.whitemountainadventures.com.*

Yamnuska. Canada's largest mountain-guide company has programs for groups and individuals. ⊠ *50 Lincoln Park, Canmore* ☎ *403/678–4164, 866/678–4164* ⊕ *www.yamnuska.com.*

AIR TOURS

TOURS AND OUTFITTERS

Alpine Helicopters. Helicopter sightseeing and heli-hiking in the Canadian Rockies are the specialty at Alpine Helicopters. ⊠ *91 Bow Valley Tr., Canmore* ☎ *403/678–4802* ⊕ *www.alpinehelicopter.com.*

CMH. This company can arrange multiday heli-hiking, heli-mountaineering, and heli-skiing with accommodation in remote mountain lodges. ⊠ *217 Bear St., Banff* ☎ *403/762–7100, 800/661–0252* ⊕ *www. canadianmountainholidays.com.*

BEST BETS FOR FAMILIES

■ **Athabasca Glacier.** This glacier is the most accessible one in the park, and a short walk leads you right to its toe. You can explore the free displays at the Icefield Centre and even take an Ice Explorer vehicle onto the ice.

■ **Canoe adventure.** Rent a canoe at Lake Minnewanka, Moraine Lake, or Lake Louise and learn to paddle like early explorers once did.

■ **Enjoy the view.** You can't beat the views from the Banff Gondola

during the steep eight-minute ride to the 7,500-foot summit of Sulphur Mountain. From the main deck you can hike the short distance to the summit of Samson Peak and perhaps catch sight of grazing bighorn sheep.

■ **Take a Hike.** The park's extensive network of trails is appropriate for hikers of all ages. There are even stroller-friendly hikes. Some favorites with families include Johnston Canyon Lower Falls, Moraine Lake Lakeshore Trail, and Bow Summit Lookout.

Icefield Helicopter Tours. Soar above the Columbia Icefields with Icefield Helicopter Tours, an outfitter that not only offers helicopter tours but has heli-yoga, heli-horseback riding, heli-hiking, and heli-fishing. Flights take off from the company's base in the Kootenay Plains area of Alberta, just north of Lake Louise. ☎ *403/721–2100* ⊕ *www.icefieldheli.com* 🖎 *Tours $59–$589 per person.*

BICYCLING

Some of the most spectacular road and mountain biking in the world can be found in Banff, and several world-class cycling events take place here. The biking season typically runs from May through October, and there are mountain-bike trails and paved multiuse trails as well as a wide variety of excellent routes for road biking. The newest trail development is the Legacy Trail, which was completed in 2010 to commemorate the 125th anniversary of the establishment of Banff National Park. This 17-km (11-mile), paved trail is part of the Trans Canada Trail and allows users to travel safely between Banff and Canmore without having to use the Trans-Canada Highway. You can ride the trail in either direction, but the route going from Banff to Canmore is slightly more downhill. There are more than 189 km (118 miles) of mountain-bike trails including those suitable for beginners and advanced bikers. Bikers and hikers often share the trails in the park, with hikers having the right of way. Those who wish to enjoy free riding or downhilling should go to nearby areas like Calgary's Canada Olympic Park, Fernie, or Golden. Those riders who like road biking can choose from a wide variety of scenic rides that run from a few hours to several days in length. Shorter rides include the Bow Lake Trail, Vermillion Lakes Drive, and the loop around Tunnel Mountain.

7

BIRD-WATCHING

Birdlife is abundant in the montane and wetland habitats of the lower Bow Valley, and more than 260 species of birds have been recorded in the park. Come in the spring to observe the annual migration of waterfowl, including common species of ducks and Canada geese as well as occasional tundra swans, cinnamon teal, Northern shovelers, white-winged and surf scoters, and hooded and common mergansers. Bald eagles are also seen regularly. Come in mid-October if you want to observe the annual migration of golden eagles along the "super flyway" of the Canadian Rockies. Interpreters and guides are on hand to explain the phenomenon.

BOATING

Lake Minnewanka, near town, is the only place in Banff National Park that allows private motorboats. Aluminum fishing boats with 8-horse-power motors can be rented at the dock (call Lake Minnewanka Boat Tours ☏ 403/762–3473).

Canoe rentals are available at Lake Louise, Moraine Lake, and in Banff, where you launch along the Bow River and explore the waterways of the Bow Valley.

Rafting options range from scenic float trips to family-friendly white-water excursions on the Kananaskis River to the intense white water of the Kicking Horse River, with its Class IV rapids.

TOURS

Banff Rafting Centre. Here you can book half-day or full-day rafting adventures suitable for families, as well as some for truly adventurous adults. ☏ 403/760–2007, 866/330–7238 ⊕ www.chinookrafting.com.

Blue Canoe Rentals. Explore the waterways of Bow Valley with Blue Canoe Rentals, paddling 40 Mile Creek, Vermillion Lakes, or the Bow River. ☏ 403/760–5007, 877/565–9372 ⊕ www.banfftours.com.

Canadian Rockies Rafting. Scenic floats and thrilling white-water rafting tours on the Bow and Kananaskis rivers are available with the local experts at Canadian Rockies Rafting. Pickups in Banff and Canmore are included. ✉ 701 Bow Valley Trail, Canmore ☏ 403/678–6535, 877/226–7625 ⊕ www.rafting.ca.

Fairmont Château Lake Louise Voyageur Canoe Experience. Paddle the tranquil waters of Lake Louise in a 26-foot cedar strip and canvas canoe with the Fairmont Château Lake Louise Voyageur Canoe Experience. The experience includes the services of a guide who shares stories of the history of canoes in Canada from the perspectve of First Nations people, voyagers, explorers, and fur traders. The boathouse also has regular canoes that rent for C$45 per hour. ☏ 403/522–3511, 800/441–1414 ⊕ www.fairmont.com/lake-louise/promotions/canoeing ⊟ C$39.

Hydra River Guides. This is the place to go for thrills. The guides here take you through the Class IV rapids on the Kicking Horse River. ☏ 403/762–4554, 800/644–8888 ⊕ www.raftbanff.com.

Kootenay River Runners. A variety of boating trips, ranging from scenic raft floats on the Toby or Kootenay to Class IV white-water rafting on the Kicking Horse, are available through Kootenay River Runners. A unique Voyageur Canoe Experience is also an option. For white-water rafting on the Kicking Horse, guests meet at the boat launch about 90 minutes from Banff Townsite. ☎ *250/347–9210, 800/599–4399* ⊕ *www.raftingtherockies.com.*

FAMILY **Minnewanka Lake Cruise.** From mid-May to mid-October, Minnewanka Lake Cruise offers 1½-hour, C$44.95 tours on the lake. ☎ *403/762–3473, 800/760–6934* ⊕ *www.explorerockies.com/minnewanka.*

Moraine Lake Lodge. Moraine Lake is one of the most photographed spots in the Canadian Rockies. From June through September, you can paddle on beautiful Moraine Lake with a canoe rental from the Moraine Lake Lodge, at the end of Moraine Lake Road in Lake Louise. Canoes can be rented right from the dock area. If you don't plan to canoe, there are several great hikes around this scenic lake. ☎ *403/522–3733, 877/522–2777* ⊕ *www.morainelake.com.*

FAMILY **Rocky Mountain Raft Tours.** Banff-based Rocky Mountain Raft Tours specializes in one- and two-hour float trips on the Bow River, starting at C$45. ☎ *403/762–3632* ⊕ *www.banffrafttours.com.*

Wild Water Adventures. Based 40 km (25 miles) north of Lake Louise, this outfitter has trips ranging from gentle floats to intense white-water experiences. Single-day and multiday trips are available. ☎ *403/522–2212, 888/647–6444* ⊕ *www.wildwater.com.*

FISHING

You can experience world-class trout fishing on the Bow River in Banff and enjoy fishing for trophy lake trout on Lake Minnewanka and several other mountain lakes. You will need a national park fishing permit to fish within the park and must follow strict fishing regulations, including no use of live bait. Some waterways are permanently closed to anglers, while others are open only at certain times of the year. Before heading out on your own, read the regulations or speak to the park staff.

TOURS AND OUTFITTERS

Alpine Anglers. This full-service fly shop has spin- and fly-rod rentals, float trips, and a fly-fishing guide service. Choose from full-day or multiday guided trout-fishing trips. ✉ *225 Bear St., Banff* ☎ *403/762–8223, 877/740–8222* ⊕ *www.alpineanglers.com.*

Banff Fishing Unlimited. A wide variety of fishing experiences from trolling for trophy lake trout to fly-fishing on the Bow River are available from the experienced guides at Banff Fishing Unlimited. In the winter, the outfitter also offers ice-fishing excursions. ☎ *403/762–4936, 866/678–2486* ⊕ *www.banff-fishing.com.*

Hawgwild Fly Fishing Guides. Learn how to fly-fish with a local guide by signing up with Hawgwild Fly Fishing Guides. ☎ *403/760–2446* ⊕ *www.flyfishingbanff.com.*

7

Tightline Adventures. Daylong and multiday fly-fishing trips can be arranged through Tightline Adventures. ✉ *129 Banff Ave., Banff* ☎ *403/762–4548, 800/644–8888* ⊕ *www.tightlineadventures.com.*

GOLF

Banff Springs Golf Course. The Stanley Thompson–designed championship course has breathtaking views in every direction. Its challenging 27 holes wind along the Bow River beneath snowcapped mountain peaks. ✉ *405 Spray Ave.* ☎ *403/762–6801, 877/591–2525* ⊕ *www. fairmontgolf.com* ⚑ *Original course: 18 holes. 6938 yards. Par 71. Slope 135. Green fee: $235. Tunnel course: 9 holes. 3287 yards. Par 36. Slope 129. Green fee: $80* ⚲ *Facilities: Driving range, putting green, golf carts, rental clubs, lessons, pro-shop, restaurant, bar.*

HIKING

The trail system in Banff National Park allows you to access the heart of the Canadian Rockies. The scenery is spectacular and you can see wildlife such as birds, squirrels, deer, and sheep along many of the trails. Make noise as you travel the trails, so you don't surprise a bear or other large animal. Also, prepare for any and all weather conditions by dressing in layers and bringing at least a half-gallon of drinking water along per person on all full-day hikes. Get a trail map at the information center. Some of the more popular trails have bathrooms or outhouses at the trailhead. Dogs should be leashed at all times, and hikers should carry bear spray.

EASY

FAMILY **Discovery Trail and Marsh Trail.** On a hillside above the Cave and Basin Centennial Centre, this 0.8-km (0.5-mile) boardwalk takes you past the vent of the cave to a spring flowing out of the hillside. Interpretive signage explains the geology and history of the Cave and Basin. Follow the Marsh Trail to get a good view of the lush vegetation that is fed by the mineral water and to see the birdlife. Along the boardwalk are telescopes, benches, and interpretive signage as well as a bird blind on the marsh itself. Wheelchairs have limited access to the boardwalk. *Easy.* ✉ *Trailhead at the parking lot of Cave and Basin National Historic Site.*

FAMILY **Fenland Trail.** It will take about an hour round-trip to walk the 2-km (1-mile) trail that slowly changes from marsh to dense forest. Watch for beavers, muskrat, and waterfowl. The trail is popular with joggers and cyclists. *Easy.* ✉ *Trailhead at 40 Mile Picnic Area.*

Surprise Corner to Hoodoos. This 4.8-km (3-mile) trail feels as if it is a world away from the busy townsite. It begins with a view of a waterfall on Bow River and then leads through meadows and forests and past sheer cliffs, ending at the hoodoos in the east part of Banff Townsite. *Easy.* ✉ *Trailhead at the Bow Falls Overlook on Tunnel Mountain Dr.*

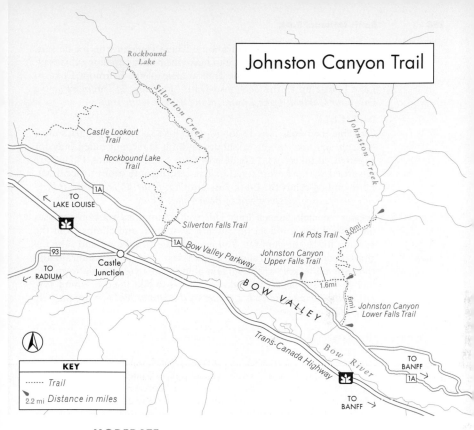

Johnston Canyon Trail

Rockbound Lake

Silverton Creek

Castle Lookout Trail

Rockbound Lake Trail

Johnston Creek

TO LAKE LOUISE

1A

Silverton Falls Trail

1A

Ink Pots Trail

3.0 mi

Bow Valley Parkway

Johnston Canyon Upper Falls Trail

93

Castle Junction

1.6 mi

TO RADIUM

BOW VALLEY

.6 mi

Johnston Canyon Lower Falls Trail

Trans-Canada Highway

Bow River

TO BANFF

1A

TO BANFF

KEY

······· *Trail*

2.2 mi *Distance in miles*

MODERATE

Boom Lake Trail. This 5-km (3.2-mile) hike climbs through a forest of pine, fir, and spruce. Surrounded by mountains and glaciers, the waters of the lake are crystal clear. The trail will take a half day round-trip. *Moderate.* ⊠ *Trailhead off Hwy. 93 S, 7 km (4½ miles) west of Castle Junction.*

Castle Lookout Trail. Outstanding views of Castle Mountain and the mountains above the Bow River Valley are the highlight of this 3.7-km (2.3-mile) one-way trail that is somewhat steep. *Moderate.* ⊠ *Trailhead off Hwy. 1A at the parking lot on the north side of Bow Valley Pkwy., 5 km (3.1 miles) west of Castle Junction.*

Fodor'sChoice **Johnston Canyon Trail.** Rushing water has carved a path through this
★ limestone canyon that is a must-see stop. The first 1.1 km (0.7 miles) is a paved walkway that leads to the 33-foot Lower Falls. From here a slightly more rugged 2.7-km (1.75-mile) trail leads to the almost 100-foot Upper Falls and a 5-km (3-mile) trail to the Ink Pots. The Ink Pots are six green pools filled with springwater. It will take four to five hours to complete the return trip. Trails begin off Highway 1A. *Moderate.* ⊠ *Trailhead at the Johnston Canyon parking lot.*

Lake Agnes Teahouse Trail. Winding north of Lake Louise, this 7-km (4.5-mile) trail has stunning views of Lake Agnes and Mirror Lake. The trail passes through an old-growth forest and comes up the right side of a waterfall before ending at a teahouse where you can stop for dessert. It will take four hours or more to make the return trip along this trail. Follow Lake Louise Shoreline Trail in front of the Fairmont Château Lake Louise up to the Teahouse Trail. *Moderate.* ⊠ *Trailhead at the Fairmont Château Lake Louise, along the shoreline trail.*

DIFFICULT

Cory Pass Loop Trail. This 13-km (8-mile) hike is one of the park's most difficult and takes about six hours to do; it is recommended only for experienced hikers who are able to trace a difficult route. Hikers are rewarded with awesome views. The return route loops around Mt. Edith and descends the Edith Pass Trail. *Difficult.* ⊠ *Trailhead at Fireside picnic area, eastern end of Bow Valley Pkwy.*

Sulphur Mountain Summit Trail. This well-maintained trail crisscrosses underneath the gondola on Sulphur Mountain and climbs from the parking lot to the summit. You may choose to hike up and take the gondola down, but you should check schedules first. A restaurant and cafeteria are located at the summit along with a viewing platform and interpretive signage. It will take four hours to hike the trail round-trip. *Difficult.* ⊠ *Trailhead at the corner of the Upper Hot Springs parking lot closest to the pool.*

HORSEBACK RIDING

Experiencing the Canadian Rockies on horseback takes you back to the era of Banff's early explorers. One-hour, half-day, full-day, and multiday guided trips within the park are offered by several outfitters. Make your reservations well in advance, especially during the peak summer months and for multiday journeys. Hourly rides start at $45 per person. Short-term boarding is available in Canmore and a few other communities outside Banff.

TOURS AND OUTFITTERS

Brewster Adventures. Experience the "cowboy way of life" by moving cattle and doing chores on overnight mountain pack tours with Brewster Adventures, a Banff company that also has daily summer trail rides to the Plain of Six Glaciers, Lake Agnes Tea House, Paradise Valley, and the Giant Steps. In the winter, sleigh rides are available at Brewster's Lake Louise Stable, which is near the Fairmont Château Lake Louise. ☎ *403/762–5454, 800/691–5085* ⊕ *www.brewsteradventures.com.*

FAMILY **Holiday on Horseback.** Banff-based Holiday on Horseback arranges hourly or daily rides, as well as lessons and multiday backcountry trips. The company operates out of three different locations in Banff (the main stable is located at the Fairmont Banff Springs). It also offers carriage rides in summer and sleigh rides in winter. ⊠ *132 Banff Ave., Banff* ☎ *403/762–4551, 800/661–8352* ⊕ *www.horseback.com.*

Outpost at Warden Rock. Multiday all-inclusive horseback, stagecoach, and bring-your-own horse holidays can be had at the Outpost at Warden Rock. The outpost is open mid-May to mid-October and is located 50 miles north of Banff. ⊠ *On the Red Deer River, bordering Banff* ☎ *403/762–2767, 877/762–2767* ⊕ *www.outpostatwardenrock.com.*

Timberline Tours. Trail rides ranging from 10 minutes to 10 days can be arranged with Timberline Tours. ⊠ *Lake Louise Dr., Lake Louise* ☎ *403/522–3743, 888/858–3388* ⊕ *www.timberlinetours.ca.*

SWIMMING

FAMILY **Banff Centre.** Amenities here include a 25-meter swimming pool, a wading pool, an outdoor sundeck, a climbing wall, fitness center, gymnasium, and squash center, as well as fitness classes. ⊠ *107 Tunnel Mountain Rd., Banff* ☎ *403/762–6100* ⊕ *www.banffcentre.ca* ⬚ *C$5.00 public swim* ◔ *Weekdays 6 am–10 pm, weekends 7 am–10 pm.*

WINTER SPORTS

Whether you're driving a dogsled across a frozen lake, ice climbing, snowshoeing, skiing at one of the world's top mountain ski resorts— or simply taking in the northern lights—there's no shortage of winter activities to choose from in Banff.

Skis and snowboards can be rented on the slopes or at many shops in town, concentrated along Bear Street and Banff Avenue.

For ski or boarding instruction, consider booking the program called Club Ski (⊕ *www.skibig3.com*). Participants get one day of instruction at each of the three resorts with the same instructor, guided tours of each resort, lift-line priority, and a souvenir photo for C$299. Lift tickets are not included.

■ TIP→ A good bargain is a C$265.80, three-day pass that allows you to ski at Sunshine Village, Mount Norquay, and Lake Louise ski area. It includes free shuttle service to the slopes. You can purchase the pass at the ski areas or at Banff Ski Hub store.

CROSS-COUNTRY SKIING

Canmore Nordic Centre. The best way to learn how to cross-country ski is with a lesson at this center, built for the 1988 Winter Olympic Games. It has rental equipment, a day lodge, and miles of trails to enjoy. ⊠ *1988 Olympic Way, Canmore* ☎ *403/678–2400.*

DOWNHILL SKIING

FAMILY **Lake Louise Ski Area.** The downhill terrain is expansive and varied, with a fairly even spread of novice, intermediate runs, 139 in all, on four mountain faces and north-facing back bowls. The vertical drop is 3,257 feet, and there are 11 lifts and a terrain park. ⊠ *1 Whitehorn Rd., off Lake Louise Dr., Lake Louise* ☎ *403/522–3555, 877/956–8473* ⊕ *www.skilouise.com.*

Ski Banff at Norquay. Locals like this five-lift, 28-run mountain, and so do Olympic and World Cup trainees. It has night skiing and tubing, too. The vertical drop is 1,650 feet. ☎ *403/762–4421* ⊕ *www. banffnorquay.com.*

Sunshine Village. About 8 km (5 miles) west of Banff, the terrain here offers options for all levels of skiers. The vertical drop is 3,514 feet, and there are 107 trails and 12 lifts. ⊠ *1 Sunshine access rd. (off Hwy. 1), Banff* ☎ *403/762–6500, 877/542–2633* ⊕ *www.skibanff.com.*

ARTS AND ENTERTAINMENT

ARTS VENUES

Banff Centre. Most of the cultural activities in the Canadian Rockies take place in and around Banff, and the hub of that activity is at these 16 buildings spread across 43 acres. The center presents a performing-arts grab bag of pop and classical music, theater, and dance throughout the year. The season peaks in summer with the monthlong Banff Arts Festival, with concerts, performances, films, and discussions. The free Walter Phillips Gallery, part of the Banff Centre, showcases contemporary artworks by Canadian and international artists. ☒ *107 Tunnel Mountain Dr.* ☎ *403/762–6100, 800/413–8368 in Alberta and British Columbia, 403/762–6301 Banff Arts Festival, 403/762–6281 Walter Phillips Gallery* ⊕ *www.banffcentre.ca* ☉ *Gallery Tues., Wed., and Fri.–Sun. noon–5, Thurs. noon–9.*

WHAT'S NEARBY

NEARBY TOWNS

About 25 km (15 miles) southeast of Banff, **Canmore** became a modest boomtown with the 1988 Olympic Games. It attracts a mix of tourists and locals who feel that the commuting from Calgary is a fair trade-off for living in the mountains. Canmore makes a good base for exploring both Kananaskis Country and Banff National Park, without the crowds or cost of Banff.

Three provincial parks make up the 4,200-square-km (1,600-square-mile) recreational region known as **Kananaskis Country,** whose northern entrance is 26 km (16 miles) southeast of Canmore. The area includes grand mountain scenery, though it's not quite a match for that in the adjacent national parks. Kananaskis allows some activities that are prohibited within the national-park system, such as snowmobiling, motorized boating, and off-road driving. It is also home to some spectacular cross-country and mountain biking trails. The main route through Kananaskis Country is Highway 40, also known as the Kananaskis Trail. It runs north–south through the front ranges of the Rockies. Only the northern 40 km (25 miles) of the road remain open from December 1 to June 15, in part because of the extreme conditions of Highwood Pass (at 7,280 feet, the highest drivable pass in Canada), and in part to protect winter wildlife habitats in Peter Lougheed Provincial Park. Highway 40 continues south to join Highway 541 west of Longview. Access to East Kananaskis Country, a popular area for horseback trips, is on Highway 66, which heads west from the town of Priddis.

VISITOR INFORMATION

Banff Lake Louise Tourism ☒ *224 Banff Ave., Banff* ☎ *403/762–8421* ⊕ *www.banfflakelouise.com.* **Tourism Canmore** ☒ *907 7th Ave., Canmore* ☎ *403/678–1295, 866/226–6673* ⊕ *www.tourismcanmore.com.*

AREA ACTIVITIES

SPORTS AND THE OUTDOORS

Many of the outfitters and operators who run tours in Banff National Park are based in Canmore, so if you're staying here, you can often join the tour from Canmore rather than having to drive to the park. Equipment for activities can be rented at most sports shops in Canmore.

GOLF

Silvertip Golf Course. Eighteen-hole, par-72 Silvertip Golf Course offers spectacular elevation changes and views of the valley and mountains from most holes. ⊠ *2000 Silvertip Tr.* ☎ *403/678–1600, 877/877–5444* ⊕ *www.silvertipresort.com* ⅄. *18 holes. 6646 yds. Par 72. Slope 139. Green Fee: $165* ☞ *Facilities: Driving range, putting green, golf carts, rental clubs, pro-shop, lessons, restaurant, bar.*

HIKING

There are many spectacular hikes inside Banff National Park, but there are also wonderful excursions just outside the borders that are often overlooked by visitors. Near Canmore, the two-hour hike to Grassi Lakes is one of the better ones. This scenic hike climbs through the forest to two beautiful spring-fed lakes and gives you the choice between an easy route and a more scenic moderate one. The trail passes by a waterfall, and at the far end of the second lake you'll find ancient pictographs.

SPELUNKING

FAMILY **Canmore Caverns.** If you have ever wanted to don a headlamp and explore an undeveloped cave, you can have Canmore Caverns arrange a suitable caving experience. The outfitter supplies the equipment and you bring the enthusiasm. Children should be at least 9 years of age to participate. ⊠ *112 Kananaskis Way, #107* ☎ *403/678–8819, 877/317–1178* ⊕ *www.canadianrockies.net/wildcavetours.*

WATER SPORTS

FAMILY **Blast Adventures.** Unique guided kayak adventures using inflatable vessels on white water are available through Blast Adventures. Transportation from Banff or Canmore is included. ⊠ *120 B Rundle Dr.* ☎ *403/609–2009, 888/802–5278* ⊕ *www.blastadventures.com.*

WINTER SPORTS

FAMILY **Canmore Nordic Centre.** Built for the 1988 Olympic Nordic skiing events, Canmore Nordic Centre has 70 km (43 miles) of groomed cross-country trails in winter that become mountain-biking trails in summer. Some trails are lighted for night skiing, and a 1.5-km (1-mile) paved trail is open in summer for roller skiing and rollerblading. This state-of-the-art facility is in the northwest corner of Kananaskis Country, south of Canmore. In late January, an international biathalon and dogsled races take place here as part of the annual **Canmore Winter Carnival.** ⊠ *1988 Olympic Way* ☎ *403/678–2400* ▨ *Trails free Apr.–Oct., C$7.50 per day Nov.–Mar.* ☉ *Lodge daily 9–5:30; trails open 7 am–11 pm, some trails illuminated until 9 pm.*

Nakiska. The site of the 1988 Olympic alpine events, Nakiska is 45 minutes southeast of Banff and has wide-trail intermediate skiing and a sophisticated snowmaking system. The vertical drop is 2,412 feet, and there are four lifts and a new tube park. ⊠ *3 Mount Allen Dr. (off Hwy. 40), Kananaskis Village* ☎ *403/591–7777* ⊕ *www. skinakiska.com.*

WHERE TO EAT

IN THE PARK

$$ ╳ **Banff Ave. Brewing Co.** Creating the highest-quality beer and serving it with classic Canadian pub food designed to complement it is the guiding philosophy of this family-friendly brewpub on Banff's busiest street. Impromtu free tours of the on-site brewery are commonplace. The flagship beer is a heavily hopped pale ale made with water from the Canadian Rockies. The restaurant is large and open, with plenty of windows and a patio overlooking Banff Avenue—ideal for people-watching. On the menu is classic pub fare, including burgers, steaks, and grilled fish served with fries in paper cones. The pulled pork poutine goes well with any drink. $ *Average main: C$18* ⊠ *Clock-tower Village Mall, 110 Banff Ave., Banff* ☎ *403/762–1003* ⊕ *www. banffavebrewingco.ca.*
CANADIAN

$$$$ ╳ **Banffshire Club.** The intimate signature restaurant of the "Castle in the Rockies" has a Scottish influence with vaulted ceilings, oak panel-ing, tartan drapes, and reproduction Stuart-era furniture, but the menu is filled with creative gourmet Canadian cuisine made from the finest seasonal ingredients. Entrées include line-caught Vancouver albacore tuna seared rare and served with baby artichokes and lavender essence, Alberta bison tenderloin with smoked corn and buffalo jerky popcorn, or the ever classic dry-aged Alberta strip steak with smoked scallions and king oyster mushrooms. Staff members are all sommelier-trained to help you choose from the extensive wine cellar, or you may choose to go with the chef's tasting menu with wine pairings. While some people may choose to dress for dinner, the dress code is resort casual. $ *Average main: C$45* ⊠ *Fairmont Banff Springs, 405 Spray Ave., Banff* ☎ *403/762–6860* ⊕ *www.fairmont.com/banffsprings* ⚠ *Reservations essential* ⊘ *Closed Sun. and Mon. No lunch.*
MODERN CANADIAN

$$$$ ╳ **The Bison.** "Rocky Mountain comfort food" made with organically grown local ingredients is on the menu, and as the name implies, bison is a specialty here. There is an emphasis on slow cooking and making everything from scratch—even the ketchup and mustard for the bison burgers are made in house. The decor is modern and contemporary, with hardwood floors, vaulted ceilings, and an open kitchen. The bison onion soup and bison short ribs with roasted potatoes are specialties, but you'll also find wild BC steelhead trout, poached halibut, and Alberta lamb on the menu. This is a popular spot for Sunday brunch. $ *Average main: C$36* ⊠ *211 Bear St., Banff* ☎ *403/762–5550* ⊕ *www.thebison.ca* ⚠ *Reservations essential* ⊘ *No lunch weekdays.*
CANADIAN

7

$$$$ CANADIAN

🍴 **Bow Valley Grill.** Serving breakfast, lunch, and dinner in a relaxed dining room with magnificent views of the Fairholme Mountain Range and the Bow Valley, this is one of the most popular restaurants in the Fairmont Banff Springs. You can choose between à la carte or buffet dining. There's a tantalizing selection of rotisserie-grilled meats, salads, and seafood, plus bread from an on-site bakery. The weekend brunches are legendary, with a wonderful selection of breakfast and dinner favorites including made-to-order omelets, prime rib, smoked salmon, and a wide selection of tantalizing desserts. [$] *Average main: C$38* ✉ *Fairmont Banff Springs, 405 Spray Ave., Banff* ☎ *403/762–6860* 🌐 *www.fairmont.com* ✍ *Reservations essential.*

$$$ SOUTHWESTERN

🍴 **Coyotes Southwestern Grill.** Fresh, healthy ingredients are used to create a wide array of Southwestern-style dishes for breakfast, lunch, and dinner. Breakfast favorites include scrambled eggs and salmon, stuffed French toast, and warm seven-grain cereal topped with fresh berries, pecans, and yogurt. For lunch or dinner you can't go wrong with the spicy black-bean burrito, the Southwestern polenta with ratatouille, or the pan-roasted honey-glazed salmon. There are a good number of vegetarian selections, and the in-house deli can prepare picnic lunches to go. The small restaurant is decorated with log beams and warm Santa Fe colors. [$] *Average main: C$25* ✉ *206 Caribou St., Banff* ☎ *403/762–3963* 🌐 *coyotesbanff.com.*

$$$$ FRENCH
Fodor's Choice ★

🍴 **Eden.** Luxurious decor and magnificent mountain views form the backdrop for a dinner of fine, regionally influenced French cuisine. Dining here is an experience that should be savored—plan to spend at least three hours. Food is prepared à-la-minute from fresh ingredients, and the menu is constantly changing. There are four fixed dining options, but the main courses constantly change; previous entrées have included BC sablefish with tomato, watermelon, and onion; rabbit with nuts, wild berries, and foraged mushrooms; and cinnamon-smoked short ribs. The prix-fixe menu is C$76 for two courses, C$84 for three courses, or C$99 for four courses. The eight-course grand degustation costs C$197. The wine cellar is spectacular, and customized wine pairings from an extensive wine collection can be added. [$] *Average main: C$76* ✉ *Rimrock Resort Hotel, 100 Mountain Ave., Banff* ☎ *403/762–1865* 🌐 *www.rimrockresort.com* ✍ *Reservations essential* 🕒 *Closed Mon. and Tues. No lunch.*

$$ CANADIAN

🍴 **Elk & Oarsman.** This second-floor, family-friendly casual pub is popular with locals and serves quality pub fare such as elk burgers, Tuscan-sausage pizzas, fish-and-chips, and steaks. All pizzas are C$10 on Monday, and you can get a steak sandwich on Tuesday for only C$8. There's a gluten-free menu, a vegeterian menu, and a wide selection of beverages. Ask for a table by the window so you can watch the action along Banff Avenue, or snag a seat near one of the flat-screen TVs and cheer for your favorite sports team. [$] *Average main: C$18* ✉ *119 Banff Ave., Banff* ☎ *403/762–4616* 🌐 *www.elkandoarsman.com.*

$$$$ FRENCH

🍴 **Le Beaujolais.** This French restaurant is a classic where you can expect to find wonderful wines, great service, and fine French cuisine served in a quiet upper-floor dining room. The relaxed atmosphere created by soft music, white tablecloths, and fresh flowers is a sharp contrast

Often found nibbling, elk like to eat such plants as beargrass, aspen leaves, sagebrush, and chokecherries.

to the busy main street of Banff. This is the place to sample French classics such as whole Dover sole meunière served tableside, steak au poivre, or roasted duck breast with seared foie gras. Three-course set dinner menus start at C$50 per person. The wine list is the size of a phone book, but the attentive servers are adept at recommending wine pairings. For a less costly and slightly more casual dining experience, try dining in the on-site bistro Café de Paris. $ *Average main: C$32 ⊠ Banff Ave. and Buffalo St., Banff ☎ 403/762–2712 ⊕ www. lebeaujolaisbanff.com.*

$$$$
EUROPEAN
Fodor's Choice
★
✕ **Post Hotel.** One of the true epicurean experiences in the Canadian Rockies, the Post delivers daring, regionally inspired, fresh-market cuisine accompanied by an excellent selection of wines. A low, exposed-beam ceiling and a stone, wood-burning hearth in the corner lend an in-from-the-cold atmosphere; white tablecloths and fanned napkins provide an elegant touch. Look for innovative dishes prepared with fresh fish, game, or Alberta beef. The menu changes regularly, but past menus included such items as warm Alaskan king crab drizzled with lemongrass-ginger butter served with gold beets, and Alberta beef tenderloin with Bordelaise sauce and buttermilk red-skin potatoes. There's a 2,200-label wine list and an incredible cellar that boasts more than 24,000 bottles. For a unique dining experience with a group of six or more, inquire about the private cellar dining room. $ *Average main: C$39 ⊠ 200 Pipestone Rd., Lake Louise ☎ 403/522–3989, 800/661–1586 ⊕ www.posthotel.com ⟁ Reservations essential.*

$$$
CANADIAN
✕ **The Sleeping Buffalo.** Located in the main building of the Buffalo Mountain Lodge, this rustic dining room serves Rocky Mountain cuisine for breakfast, lunch, and dinner made from fresh berries, regional

vegetables, fresh herbs, wild game, and locally produced meats. Historic photos and native artifacts adorn the pale-green walls, and there are plenty of windows to let in natural light. The lodge maintains an on-site garden and a game farm just outside Calgary, and smoked, cured, or roasted wild game is a specialty. Try the Reuben made with grilled elk ham, Appenzeller cheese, and house-made sauerkraut for lunch or the elk striploin with root vegetable fricassee for dinner. The wine list is extensive. $ *Average main: C$30* ⊠ *Buffalo Mountain Lodge, 700 Tunnel Mountain Rd., Banff* ☎ *403/762–2400* ⊕ *www.crmr.com.*

$$$$ ✕ **Three Ravens.** In the corner of the Sally Borden Building at the Banff
ECLECTIC Centre with floor-to-ceiling windows and spectacular mountain views on all sides, this restaurant is a great spot to watch the sun setting behind the mountains while enjoying fresh, seasonal, creatively prepared cuisine. There are several on-site eateries in this arts complex, but Three Ravens is the place to go for fine dining. Everything is prepared in-house from the breads and spiced butters to the fruit sorbets. Menus change twice per year, but past menus have included items like herb-crusted Alberta lamb rack, honey-and-ginger-glazed duck breast, and seared steelhead trout with cinnamon-infused black Thai rice. The wine list is easy to navigate with some nice selections at reasonable prices. $ *Average main: C$33* ⊠ *Sally Borden Bldg., 107 Tunnel Mountain Dr., Banff* ☎ *403/762–6300* ⊕ *www.banffcentre. ca/dining.*

$$$$ ✕ **Walliser Stube.** For something that's fun and a little different, try this
SWISS Swiss eatery's large selection of fondues and raclettes—they claim to serve the best cheese and chocolate fondues outside of Switzerland. Choose from bison, beef, tuna, or seafood in broth, or classic cheese fondues. Meat and seafood fondues are served with young vegetables, steamed potatoes, mushrooms, and a selection of sauces. Be sure to save room for dessert: a Swiss chocolate dessert fondue served with banana bread, fresh fruit, marshmallows, and whipped cream. There is also an excellent selection of fine wines kept in the back room, which is affectionately known as the wine library because the floor-to-ceiling shelves are lined with wine, not books. $ *Average main: C$43* ⊠ *Fairmont Château Lake Louise, Lake Louise Dr., Lake Louise* ☎ *403/522–1818* ⊕ *www.fairmont.com/lakelouise* ⌦ *Reservations essential* ⊗ *Closed Sun.*

$ ✕ **Wild Flour Bakery.** Banff's artisan bakery is also a great spot to enjoy
BAKERY breakfast or lunch without breaking the bank. Breakfast choices include items like waffles, toast, and house-made granola served with espresso, hot chocolate, and a wide variety of teas from the local Banff Tea Company. The lunch menu includes a great selection of salads, soups, wraps, and sandwiches. The menu is wholesome and innovative with items like quinoa salad made with fresh mint, blueberries, almonds, and raspberry vinaigrette or chicken wraps with spinach, tomatoes, cucumbers, peach salsa, and honey-soy dressing. This place is a favorite with locals, so it's often busy, but the lines move quickly. $ *Average main: C$10* ⊠ *101, 211 Bear St., Banff* ☎ *403/760–5074* ⊕ *www. wildflourbakery.ca* ⊗ *No dinner.*

PICNIC AREAS

🍴 **Bow Lake.** Situated on the shores of stunning Bow Lake, on the Icefields Parkway, this picnic area has a kitchen shelter, five tables, toilets, and fireboxes. ✉ *Icefields Pkwy., at edge of Bow Lake.*

🍴 **Cascade.** This spot has 60 tables, a kitchen shelter, fireplaces, and flush toilets. ✉ *Off Lake Minnewanka Rd.*

🍴 **Fireside.** Located on the Bow Valley Parkway, this picnic area has picnic tables and toilets nearby. ✉ *Off Bow Valley Pkwy.*

FAMILY 🍴 **Lake Minnewanka.** This popular picnic area has three picnic shelters, 35 tables, flush toilets, two fire rings, and six fireplaces. Hike, rent a boat, or try your luck at fishing. ✉ *10 km (6 miles) from Banff on Minnewanka Loop.*

🍴 **Moraine Lake.** One of the most beautiful lakes in the Canadian Rockies is the setting for this picnic area near Lake Louise. There are two kitchen shelters, eight tables, and toilets at this site. ✉ *Off Moraine Lake Rd., 5 km (3 miles) from village of Lake Louise.*

OUTSIDE THE PARK

$$$$ ECLECTIC 🍴 **The Trough Dining Co.** Fine dining without the attitude is the theme for this intimate Canmore restaurant with hardwood floors, a glass waterfall, and orange terra-cotta walls. The Trough has an ever-changing menu that features fresh, locally grown ingredients that are carefully prepared and creatively displayed. Signature items that appear often on Trough menus include the bruschetta appetizer and the jerk spiced Alberta baby back ribs. Slow cooking is the norm—the ribs are marinated for four days. There's a good selection of wines, and a palate-cleansing sorbet is served between the appetizer and the main course. If you choose to dine on the outdoor patio and get a touch chilly, your server can provide a fleece blanket. [$] *Average main: C$37* ✉ *725 B 9 St., Canmore* ☎ *403/678–2820* 🌐 *www.thetrough.ca.*

7

WHERE TO STAY

For expanded hotel reviews, visit Fodors.com.

IN THE PARK

$$$$ HOTEL 🏨 **Banff Caribou Lodge & Spa.** A great location close enough to the hustle and bustle of downtown but just far enough away makes this hotel with one of the largest spas in town a top pick. **Pros:** close to downtown; large lobby; excellent spa. **Cons:** average rooms; no a/c. [$] *Rooms from: C$229* ✉ *521 Banff Ave., Banff* ☎ *403/762–5887, 800/563–8764* 🌐 *www.bestofbanff.com/banff-caribou-lodge* 🛏 *190 rooms, 6 suites.*

$$$$ HOTEL 🏨 **Delta Banff Royal Canadian Lodge.** A grotto-style indoor mineral pool intended to mimic natural hot springs is a highlight of this stone-and-wood lodge set among the evergreens. **Pros:** intimate property; 10-minute walk to downtown; mineral pool and steam room. **Cons:** fee for parking; gym is very small. [$] *Rooms from: C$359* ✉ *459 Banff Ave., Banff* ☎ *403/762–3307, 800/661–1379* 🌐 *www.deltahotels.com* 🛏 *99 rooms.*

Best Campgrounds in Banff

Parks Canada operates 13 campgrounds in Banff National Park (not including backcountry sites for backpackers and climbers). The camping season generally runs from mid-May through October, although the Tunnel Mountain and Lake Louise campgrounds remain open year-round. Hookups are available at most of the campgrounds and at four of the 31 Kananaskis Country campgrounds. In 2013, Parks Canada built a new type of camping facility known as an oTENTik. A cross between a cabin and a tent, each oTENTik can sleep up to six people on foam mattresses. Each unit has a heater inside, a fire pit, a bear locker, a picnic table, and a barbecue. Prices for a one-night stay range from C$16 to C$28 for a tent site or C$120 for an oTENTik.

If you want to experience camping without the hassle of bringing sleeping bags and other supplies, try the BacTrax rental service (⊕ *www.campingbanff.com*). For $50 per day, you can rent camping equipment for up to six people. They also offer a setup and pack down service, so you can arrive at your campsite to find everything already set up.

Castle Mountain Campground.
This campground is in a beautiful wooded area close to a small store, a gas bar, and a restaurant. ⊠ *34 km (21 miles) from Banff on Bow Valley Pkwy.* ☎ *403/762–1550 or 877/737–3783* ⊕ *www.pccamping.ca.*

Johnston Canyon Campground.
The scenery is spectacular and the wildlife abundant in and around this campground, which is across from Johnston Canyon. A small creek flows right by the camping area. ⊠ *25 km (15½ miles) from Banff on Bow Valley Pkwy.* ☎ *403/762–1550 or 877/737–3783* ⊕ *www.pccamping.ca.*

Lake Louise Campground.
This forested area next to the Bow River is open year-round, but in early spring and late fall tents and soft-sided trailers are not permitted in order to protect both people and bears. ⊠ *1 km (½ mile) from Lake Louise Village and 4 km (2½ miles) from the lake* ☎ *905/566–4321 or 877/737–3783* ⊕ *www.pccamping.ca.*

Tunnel Mountain Campground.
Situated close to the townsite, this campground has a great view of the valley, hoodoos, and the Banff Springs golf course. ⊠ *2½ km (1½ miles) from Banff Townsite on Tunnel Mountain* ☎ *905/566–4321 or 877/737–3783* ⊕ *www.pccamping.ca.*

Two Jack Lakeside Campground.
This secluded campground is on the shores of beautiful Two Jack Lake—one of the most scenic areas in the park. There are on-site interpretive programs, and Parks Canada recently built 10 new lakefront oTENTiks that visitors can also rent. ⊠ *12 km (7½ miles) from Banff on the Minnewanka Loop* ☎ *403/762–1550 or 877/737–3783* ⊕ *www.pccamping.ca.*

$$$$
RESORT
FAMILY
🏨 **Douglas Fir Resort & Chalets.** A top pick with families, this resort has condo-style and chalet-style accommodations with fully equipped kitchens, a huge indoor water park, and an indoor playground. **Pros:** large indoor playground and water park; kitchen facilities. **Cons:** you need to drive to town; rustic older accommodation, abundance of children. $ *Rooms from: C$239* ⊠ *Tunnel Mountain Rd., Banff National*

Park ☎ *403/762–5591, 800/661–9267* ⊕ *www.douglasfir.com* ↪ *119 condo rooms, 11 chalets.*

$$$$ 🖵 **Fairmont Banff Springs.** Affectionately known as "The Castle in the
RESORT Rockies," this massive hotel built by the Canadian Pacific Railway in
Fodor's Choice 1888 marked the beginning of Banff's tourism boom and remains an
★ oasis of historic elegance. **Pros:** ultraluxurious; many amenities; historical property. **Cons:** costly rooms and dining. 💲 *Rooms from: C$459*
✉ *405 Spray Ave., Banff National Park* ☎ *403/762–2211, 800/441–
1414* ⊕ *www.fairmont.com/banffsprings* ↪ *770 rooms, 70 suites.*

$$$$ 🖵 **Fairmont Château Lake Louise.** There's a good chance that no hotel any-
RESORT where has a more dramatic view out its back door than this one, with
terraces and lawns that reach to the famous aquamarine lake, backed by
the Victoria Glacier. **Pros:** stunning setting; abundant amenities; luxurious accommodations. **Cons:** costly rooms and dining; farther away from
the townsite than some of the other lodging options. 💲 *Rooms from:
C$399* ✉ *Lake Louise Dr., Lake Louise* ☎ *403/522–3511, 800/441–
1414* ⊕ *www.fairmont.com/lakelouise* ↪ *433 rooms, 54 suites.*

$$$$ 🖵 **Fox Hotel & Suites.** The Fox is close enough to downtown that you
HOTEL can walk to most of the shopping and nightlife, but far enough away
that you won't be bothered by the noise while staying in its comfortable hotel or suite-style rooms with kitchenettes and separate living
areas. **Pros:** kitchen facilities; free Internet; artifical hot springs pool.
Cons: small fitness facility; parking is tight. 💲 *Rooms from: C$299*
✉ *461 Banff Ave., Banff* ☎ *403/760–8500, 800/563–8764* ⊕ *www.
bestofbanff.com/fox-hotel-suites* ↪ *116 rooms, 66 suites.*

$$$$ 🖵 **Hidden Ridge Resort.** Located on a secluded road on Tunnel Moun-
HOTEL tain, this resort has incredible views of the surrounding landscape as
FAMILY well as large, well-appointed accommodations with wood-burning
fireplaces, full kitchens with granite countertops, and flatscreen TVs
with DVD players. **Pros:** large units; great views; nice extras. **Cons:**
on a secluded road; long walk to town; parking can be tight during
peak times. 💲 *Rooms from: C$249* ✉ *901 Hidden Ridge Way, Banff*
☎ *403/762–3544, 800/563–8764* ⊕ *www.bestofbanff.com/hidden-
ridge-resort* ↪ *104 rooms.*

$$$ 🖵 **Paradise Lodge & Bungalows.** In a secluded forest setting near beauti-
HOTEL ful Lake Louise, this property offers comfortable suites and cute cabins
that were originally built in the 1930s and have been in the same family
for more than 50 years. **Pros:** comfortable, well-appointed cabins; good
value; picturesque setting. **Cons:** frontage road busy during daytime;
need to drive to get to lake or townsite. 💲 *Rooms from: C$189* ✉ *105
Lake Lousie Dr., Lake Louise* ☎ *403/522–3595* ⊕ *www.paradiselodge.
com* ↪ *21 cabins, 24 suites* ⊘ *Closed Oct.–Apr.*

$$$$ 🖵 **Post Hotel.** One of the finest retreats in the Rocky Mountains, this
HOTEL Swiss chalet–style lodging has an understated elegance, outstanding
dining, and many wonderful amenities that have garnered awards and
international attention. **Pros:** gourmet dining on-site with famous wine
menu; on-site spa; understated elegance. **Cons:** train nearby; costly
rooms and dining. 💲 *Rooms from: C$345* ✉ *200 Pipestone Rd., Lake
Louise* ☎ *403/522–3989, 800/661–1586* ⊕ *www.posthotel.com* ↪ *69
rooms, 26 suites, 3 cabins.*

7

$$$$ ⛄ **Rimrock Resort Hotel.** This luxurious nine-story hotel is perched on the
RESORT steep slope of Sulphur Mountain and has some of the best views of any
hotel in Banff along with one of the finest restaurants in all of Canada.
Pros: spectacular views; close to hot springs and gondola; world-class
gourmet dining. **Cons:** farther from townsite than some other options;
parking costs C$16 per day. $ *Rooms from: C$228 ✉ 300 Mountain
Ave., Banff National Park* ☎ *403/762–3356, 888/746–7625* ⊕ *www.
rimrockresort.com* ⌁ *346 rooms, 6 suites.*

OUTSIDE THE PARK

$$$$ ⛄ **Delta Lodge at Kananaskis.** The location of this lodge in Kananaskis
RESORT Country is second to none and the numerous on-site amenities such
as the large indoor pool, the indoor/outdoor hot tub, tennis courts,
eucalyptus-infused steam room, large fitness area, and spa make it a
destination in itself. **Pros:** beautiful mountain setting; family-friendly
resort; hiking, biking, golf, and skiing nearby. **Cons:** isolated: 30-min-
ute drive to Canmore; rooms could use an update; no a/c. $ *Rooms
from: C$249 ✉ Hwy. 40, 28 km (17 miles) south of Hwy. 1, Kanan-
askis Village* ☎ *403/591–7711, 888/244–8666* ⊕ *www.deltahotels.
com* ⌁ *412 rooms.*

$$$ ⛄ **Falcon Crest Lodge.** Just outside the national park in nearby Canmore,
HOTEL these modern condos are ideal if you enjoy cooking some of your own
meals, as the rooms have fully equipped kitchens with granite counter-
tops. **Pros:** feels like a home away from home; great views; free Wi-Fi.
Cons: 20-minute drive to Banff; no pool; small gym. $ *Rooms from:
C$155 ✉ 190 Kananaskis Way, Canmore* ☎ *403/678–6150, 866/609–
3222* ⊕ *www.falconcrestlodge.ca* ⌁ *46 1-bedroom condos, 8 2-bed-
room condos, 6 studio suites, 12 deluxe suites.*

BIG BEND
NATIONAL PARK

WELCOME TO BIG BEND

TOP REASONS TO GO

★ **Varied terrain:**
Visit thorny desert, a fabled river, bird-filled woods, and mountain spirals all in the same day.

★ **Wonderful wildlife:**
Catch sight of the park's extremely diverse animals, including bands of swarthy javelinas, reclusive mountain lions, and lumbering black bears.

★ **Bird-watching:**
Spy a pied-billed grebe or another member of the park's more than 400 bird species, including the Lucifer hummingbird and the unique-to-this-area *pato mexicano* (Mexican duck).

★ **Hot spots:** Dip into the natural hot springs (105°F) near Rio Grande Village.

★ **Mile-high mountains:**
Lace up those hiking boots and climb the Chisos Mountains, reaching almost 8,000 feet skyward in some places and remaining cool even during the most scorching Southwest summer.

1 North Rosillos. Dinosaur fossils have been found in this remote, northern portion of the park. Comprising primarily back roads, this is where nomadic warriors traveled into Mexico via the Comanche Trail.

2 Chisos Basin.
This bowl-shape canyon amid the Chisos Mountains is at the heart of Big Bend. It's a trailhead for numerous hikes and a prime place to watch a sunset through a "fracture" in the bowl known as the Window.

3 Castolon. Just east of Santa Elena Canyon, this cluster of adobe dwellings was once used by ranchers and the U.S. military, earning it a spot on the National Register of Historic Places.

4 Rio Grande Village.
Tall, shady cottonwoods highlight the park's eastern fringe along the Mexican border and Rio Grande. It's popular with RVers and bird-watchers.

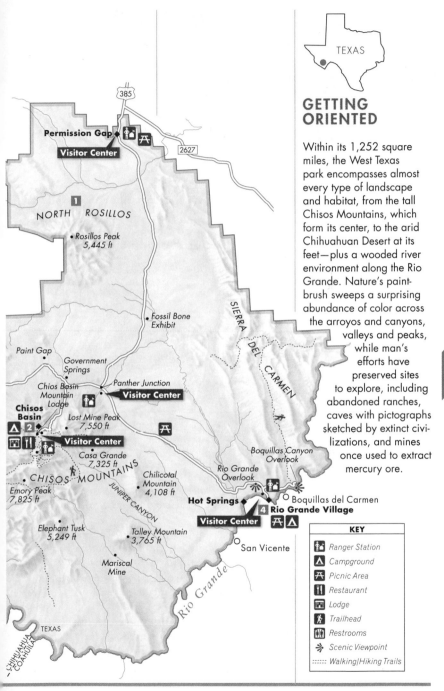

TEXAS

GETTING ORIENTED

Within its 1,252 square miles, the West Texas park encompasses almost every type of landscape and habitat, from the tall Chisos Mountains, which form its center, to the arid Chihuahuan Desert at its feet—plus a wooded river environment along the Rio Grande. Nature's paint-brush sweeps a surprising abundance of color across the arroyos and canyons, valleys and peaks, while man's efforts have preserved sites to explore, including abandoned ranches, caves with pictographs sketched by extinct civilizations, and mines once used to extract mercury ore.

8

Map labels

385

Permission Gap

Visitor Center

2627

1 NORTH ROSILLOS

• Rosillos Peak
5,445 ft

• Fossil Bone Exhibit

SIERRA DEL CARMEN

Paint Gap

Government Springs

Chios Basin Mountain Lodge

Panther Junction
Visitor Center

Chisos Basin

2

Visitor Center

Lost Mine Peak
7,550 ft

Casa Grande
7,325 ft

CHISOS MOUNTAINS

Chilicotal Mountain
4,108 ft

Boquillas Canyon Overlook

Rio Grande Overlook

Emory Peak
7,825 ft

JUNIPER CANYON

Hot Springs ◆ **4** Rio Grande Village

Visitor Center

Elephant Tusk
5,249 ft

Talley Mountain
3,765 ft

○ Boquillas del Carmen

Mariscal Mine

○ San Vicente

Rio Grande

TEXAS

CHIHUAHUA
COAHUILA

KEY

👫	Ranger Station
⛺	Campground
⛱	Picnic Area
🍴	Restaurant
🏨	Lodge
🚶	Trailhead
🚻	Restrooms
☀	Scenic Viewpoint
⋯⋯⋯	Walking/Hiking Trails

Updated by
Marty Racine

Cradled in the warm, southwestern elbow of Texas, the 801,163 acres of Big Bend National Park hang suspended above the deserts of northern Mexico. From the craggy, forested Chisos Mountains rising up to almost 8,000 feet to the flat, stark plains of the Chihuahuan Desert, Big Bend is one of the nation's most geographically diverse parks, with the kind of dramatic backdrop that inspired Hollywood's first Western sets. Visitors can ride the rapids of the Rio Grande, trek through the classic, Old West landscape, and marvel at the moonscape that skirts Boquillas, Mexico.

BIG BEND PLANNER

WHEN TO GO

There is never a bad time to make a Big Bend foray—except during Thanksgiving, Christmas, and spring break. During these holidays, competition for rooms at the Chisos Mountains Lodge and campsites is fierce—with reservations for campsites and rooms needed up to a year in advance.

Depending on the season, Big Bend sizzles or drizzles, steams up collars or chills fingertips. Many shun the park in the summer, because temperatures skyrocket (up to 120°F), and the Rio Grande lowers.

In winter, temperatures rarely dip below 30°F. During those few times the mercury takes a dive, visitors might be rewarded with a rare snowfall.

The mountains routinely are 5 to 20 degrees cooler than the rest of the park, while the sweltering stretches of Rio Grande are 5 to 10 degrees warmer.

AVG. HIGH/LOW TEMPS.

JAN.	FEB.	MAR.	APR.	MAY	JUNE
61/35	66/38	77/45	81/52	88/59	94/65

JULY	AUG.	SEPT.	OCT.	NOV.	DEC.
93/68	91/66	86/62	79/53	69/42	62/36

FESTIVALS AND EVENTS

FEBRUARY **Texas Cowboy Poetry Gathering.** Every February, generally toward the end of the month, ranchers and cowboys congregate for three days at Sul Ross State University to regale audiences with original poetry and washtub-bass tributes to singers like Bob Wills. The idea is to preserve the traditions of the West in words and song. ■TIP➔ **More on-site information is available on the second floor of the University Center.** ⊠ *Hwy. 90, Alpine* ☎ *432/837–2326, 800/561–3712* ⊕ *www. cowboy-poetry.org.*

JULY **Viva Big Bend.** After only two years, the annual Viva Big Bend music festival in July has established a West Texas showcase for Lone Star music. The action—rock, blues, country, Latin, and beyond—takes stage in Alpine, Fort Davis, Marathon, and Marfa, both in large paid-admission venues and free concerts in hotel patios. A shuttle service connecting the four cities is available for those consuming alcohol. The 2013 festival spanned four days. With all the talent within striking range, look for this event to become a regional fixture for live-music fans. ⊠ *Alpine* ⊕ *www.vivabigbend.com.*

SEPTEMBER **Big Bend Balloon Bash.** Brightly colored hot-air balloons dot the Alpine skies each Labor Day weekend. When the sun goes down, the balloons light up, and the flames are choreographed to music. ⊠ *Alpine-Casparis Municipal Airport, N. Rte. 118, Alpine* ☎ *432/837–7486* ⊕ *www. bigbendballoonbash.com.*

Marfa Lights Festival. This Labor Day weekend event celebrates the nighttime, multicolor mystery lights that appear in the Chinati Mountains east of U.S. 67 and south of U.S. 90 from 10 to 20 times a year. Do they result from pockets of atmospheric gas? The spirits of dead Apaches? Overdriven imaginations? Whatever they are, they draw curious visitors to the center of Marfa for a parade, live music, and food. ⊠ *Presidio County Courthouse lawn, Marfa* ☎ *800/650–9696, 432/729–4942 Marfa Chamber of Commerce* ⊕ *www.marfacc.com/ todo/marfalights.php.*

NOVEMBER **Alpine Gallery Night Artwalk.** For two days each November, the peculiar mix of ranching and artist culture that inhabits Alpine overflows the galleries and seeps into the town's main drag, Holland Avenue. Musicians play at the train depot, barbecue vendors crowd the streets, and local artists display their works in many downtown businesses. ⊠ *Holland Ave., Alpine* ☎ *432/837–2326 or 800/561–3712 for Alpine Chamber of Commerce* ⊕ *www.artwalkalpine.com.*

Terlingua International Chili Championship. On the first Saturday of November, top chefs spice up cooling weather with four days of chili cooking, bragging, and partying at Rancho CASI, on the north side of Route

8

170, 11 miles west of Study Butte. Some of the prize-winning cooks dole out samples. And this is Texas, pardner: no beans allowed. ⌧ *Rte.170, Terlingua* ☎ *210/887–8827* ⊕ *www.chili.org/terlingua.html.*

PLANNING YOUR TIME
BIG BEND IN ONE DAY

You can drive the paved roads of the park in a day, but you miss the striking details if you don't get out and hike. Two trails that are feasible on a one-day drive—if you start out early—are those through the rifts and boulders of **Santa Elena Canyon**, carved by the Rio Grande, and the rocky pinnacles of **Chisos Basin.** From Chisos Mountains Lodge, drive 7 miles north on **Chisos Basin Road**, turn west on Route 118 and connect with **Ross Maxwell Scenic Drive** at Santa Elena Junction. Explore as many overlooks and historical sites as time allows on this 30-mile stretch until you reach Santa Elena Canyon at the southwestern rim of the park. From there, take the **Santa Elena Canyon Trail** (1.7 miles round-trip). You might need to wade Terlingua Creek, and then ascend a steep trail cut into the canyon wall, which eventually steps down to a sandy clearing by the river. The majestic canyon is framed by gargantuan rock formations, with the Rio Grande sandwiched between sheer cliffs. Back at the trailhead, return to Route 118 via Ross Maxwell Scenic Drive or unpaved Old Maverick Road (12.8 miles) and turn east toward **Rio Grande Village.** Stroll through the tall, shady cottonwoods in the picnic area, home to many birds, including roadrunners. A convenience store is available for a midday snack. If you have the time, follow the signs to the natural hot spring and take a dip. Before calling it a day, drive east to the **Boquillas Canyon** overlook and view the Mexican village of Boquillas on the south side of the Rio Grande.

Return 25 miles on Route 118 to **Chisos Basin Junction** and head back to the lodge for a leisurely hike on the paved, quarter-mile **Window View Trail,** where prime-time views are captured at sunset.

A second one-day option is to explore the east side of the park from Chisos Mountains Lodge: Head east on Route 118 toward Rio Grande Village and explore Dugout Wells, Mariscal Mine, Hot Springs, Rio Grande Village, Glenn Spring, Daniels Ranch, and Boquillas Canyon. Return by the same route.

GETTING HERE AND AROUND
AIR TRAVEL

The nearest major airport is in Midland, 3½ hours north of the park.

BUS TRAVEL

The bus takes you only as far as Marathon.

CAR TRAVEL

Big Bend is 39 miles south of Marathon, off U.S. 385; 81 miles south of Alpine, off Route 118; and 69 miles east of Presidio, off Route 170. Paved park roads have twists and turns, some very extreme in higher elevations; if you have an RV longer than 24 feet or a trailer longer than 20 feet, you should avoid the Chisos Basin Road into higher terrain in Big Bend's central portion. Four-wheel-drive vehicles are needed for many of the backcountry roads. At parking areas take valuables with you.

PARK ESSENTIALS
PARK FEES AND PERMITS
It costs $20 to enter at the gate by car, and your pass is good for seven days. Entry on foot, bicycle, motorcycle, or commercial vehicle is $10. A Big Bend Annual Pass is $40. Camping fees in developed campgrounds are $14 per night, while backcountry camping is $10 for up to 14 days. Mandatory backcountry camping, boating, and fishing permits are available at visitor centers.

PARK HOURS
Big Bend National Park never closes. Visitor centers may be closed Christmas Day. Visitor centers at Rio Grande Village and the Castolon Historic District close in summer. The park is in the central time zone.

CELL-PHONE RECEPTION
Cell phones do not often work in the park, though service is generally more reliable in flat, open country. Public telephones can be found at the visitor centers.

RESTAURANTS
One word sums up the fare available in the park: casual. You can wear shorts and sneakers to the one park restaurant, which has American-style fare. North of the park, Alpine and Marfa have the biggest selection, while Terlingua, just outside the west park entrance, has a few eateries.

Prices in the reviews are the average cost of a main course at dinner, or if dinner is not served, at lunch.

HOTELS
At the Chisos Mountains Lodge, the only hotel in the park, you can select from a freestanding stone cottage or a motel-style room, both within a pace or two of spectacular views—Chisos sunsets are not to be missed. It's convenient to stay here because it's close to trails, and there is a gift shop, general store, visitor center, and the park's only restaurant. Even if you don't stay here, go just to see the stunning view through the wall-sized dining room windows. The Big Bend area retains its grand historic hotels, like the glamorous Hotel Paisano in Marfa, the Gage Hotel in Marathon, the Limpia in Fort Davis, and the Holland Hotel in Alpine, but it also boasts the Lajitas Resort and some more moderately priced hotels.

Prices in the reviews are the lowest cost of a standard double room in high season. For expanded reviews, facilities, and current deals, visit Fodors.com.

VISITOR INFORMATION
PARK CONTACT INFORMATION
Big Bend National Park ✉ *Headquarters 70 miles south of Marathon* ☎ *432/477–2251* ⊕ *www.nps.gov/bibe.*

VISITOR CENTERS
Castolon Visitor Center. Here you'll find some of the most hands-on exhibits the park has to offer, with touchable fossils, plants, and implements used by the farmers and miners who settled here in the 1800s and early 1900s. The center closes in summer. ✉ *In Castolon Historic District, southwest side of park, on Ross Maxwell Scenic Dr.* ☎ *432/477–2666* 🖷 *432/477–2666* ⊕ *www.nps.gov/bibe* ⊗ *Nov.–Apr., daily 10–5 (closed for lunch).*

Fodor's Choice
★
Chisos Basin Visitor Center. The center, located at the park's only lodge, is one of the better equipped, as it offers an interactive computer exhibit and a bookstore. An adjacent general store has camping supplies, picnic fare, and some produce. There are plenty of nods to the wild, with natural resource and geology exhibits and a larger-than-life representation of a mountain lion. The center sponsors educational activities here and at the nearby Chisos Basin Amphitheater. ■TIP➔ If you are traveling just to see the visitor center, call ahead; opening and closing times are subject to change due to staffing and seasonal transitions. ⊠ *Off Chisos Basin Rd., 7 miles southwest of Chisos Basin Junction and 9 miles southwest of Panther Junction* 🕾 *432/477–2264* ⊕ *www.nps. gov/bibe* ⊗ *Nov.–Mar., daily 8:30–5; Apr.–Oct., daily 8:30–4; closed for lunch.*

FAMILY
Fodor's Choice
★
Panther Junction Visitor Center. The park's main visitor center, near the base of the Chisos Mountains, includes a bookstore and exhibits on the park's mountain, river, and desert environments. One exhibit poses this question: What is the most dangerous animal in the park? When you open the panel, you're staring into a mirror. A new, elegantly produced 22-minute film detailing the wonders of the park shows on request in the theater, and there's a sprawling board replica of the park's topographical folds. Nearby, a gas station offers limited groceries such as chips, sandwiches, and other picnic items. ⊠ *Rte. 118 near the junction of U.S. 385, 30 miles south of park's northern entrance* 🕾 *432/477– 1158* ⊕ *www.nps.gov/bibe* ⊗ *Daily 9–5.*

Persimmon Gap Visitor Center. Complete with exhibits and a bookstore, this visitor center is the northern gateway into miles of flatlands that surround the more scenic heart of Big Bend. Dinosaur fossils have been found here; the **Fossil Bone Exhibit** is on the road between Persimmon Gap and Panther Junction. Depending on volunteer help, the center might stay open past posted hours during the busy winter season. ⊠ *U.S. 385, 2 miles south of the park's northern entrance* 🕾 *432/477– 2393* ⊕ *www.nps.gov/bibe* ⊗ *Daily 9–4.*

Rio Grande Village Visitor Center. Opening days and hours are sporadic and it's closed in summer, but if it's open you can take in the videos of Big Bend's geological and natural features at the minitheater. There are also exhibits dealing with the Rio Grande. ⊠ *22 miles southeast of Panther Junction* 🕾 *432/477–2271* ⊗ *Nov.–Apr., daily 8:30–4; closed for lunch.*

EXPLORING

SCENIC DRIVES

Chisos Basin Road. Ever changing, this 7-mile road climbs south from Chisos Basin Junction, ending at Chisos Mountains Lodge, with a spur leading to a campground. By driving into higher elevations (the heart of Big Bend), you're more likely to spot lions and bears as well as white-tailed deer amid juniper trees and pinyon pines. You'll also see lovely, red-barked Texas madrone along with some Chisos oaks and Douglas fir trees. Several roadside exhibits along the way explain the various ecosystems. Avoid this drive if you are in an RV longer than 24 feet, because of sharp curves. ⊕ *www.nps.gov/bibe.*

Fodor's Choice ★ **Ross Maxwell Scenic Drive.** Although it extends only 30 miles, you can easily spend a full day on this aptly named route admiring the views, visiting historic sites, taking short hikes, and getting a Big Bend education. There are scenic overlooks, a backside perspective of the Chisos Mountains, plenty of exhibits, and the ruins of old homesteads. If you don't mind a little grit in your gait from the gravel that blankets the road, you can make this drive a loop by reconnecting with Route 118 from Santa Elena Canyon via unpaved Old Maverick Road for 12.8 miles. ■ **TIP→ If you're in an RV, don't even attempt Old Maverick Road. The road isn't paved and is rough going in some spots.** ⊕ *www.nps.gov/bibe.*

HISTORIC SITES

Castolon Historic District. Adobe buildings and wooden shacks serve as reminders of the farming and military community of Castolon, near the banks of the Rio Grande. The Magdalena House has historical exhibits. A general store, housed in an old adobe and fronted by shaded picnic tables, is good for drinks, snacks, and a friendly face. The nearby Castolon Visitor Center closes in summer. ⊠ *On Ross Maxwell Scenic Dr., southwest portion of the park* ☎ *432/477–2225 ranger station* ⊕ *www.nps.gov/bibe.*

Hot Springs. Hikers soak themselves in the 105°F waters alongside the Rio Grande, where petroglyphs (rock art) coat the canyon walls nearby. The remains of a post office, motel, and bathhouse point to the old commercial establishment operating here in the early 1900s. The 1.6-mile dirt road leading to the Hot Springs trailhead from Route 118 is not suggested for RVs or trailers. Nor would it be wise to negotiate it in a rainstorm. Don't leave valuables in your car, as thefts sometimes occur, especially during the slow season. ⊠ *15 miles southeast of Panther Junction, near Rio Grande Village* ⊕ *www.nps.gov/bibe.*

Mariscal Mine. Hardy, hard-working men and women once coaxed cinnabar, or mercury ore, from the Mariscal Mine, located at the north end of Mariscal Mountain. They left the mines and surrounding stone buildings behind for visitors to explore. If you stop here, take care not to touch the timeworn stones, as they may contain poisonous mercury residue. ⊠ *5 miles west of Rio Grande Village, on River Rd. E* ⊕ *www. nps.gov/bibe/historyculture/mariscalmine.htm.*

8

West Texas fauna include prairie dogs, jackrabbits, and roadrunners, while its flora include yuccas.

SCENIC STOPS

Chisos Basin. Panoramic vistas, a restaurant with an up-close view of jagged mountains, and glimpses of the Colima warbler (which summers in Big Bend) await in the forested Chisos Basin. This central site, considered the spiritual heart of Big Bend at an elevation of 5,400 feet, is ringed by taller peaks and also has hiking trails, a lodge, a campground, a grocery store, a gift shop, the famous Window rock formation, and one of five park visitor centers. ⊠ *Off Chisos Basin Rd., 7 miles southwest of Chisos Basin Junction and 9 miles southwest of Panther Junction* ⊕ *www.nps.gov/bibe.*

Fodor's Choice
★ **Santa Elena Canyon.** The finale of a short but vigorous hike (1.7 miles round-trip) over a steep slope is a spectacular view of the Rio Grande and sheer cliffs that rise 1,500 feet to create a natural box. ■ **TIP**➜ **Summer can feel like a sauna, but you might have the place to yourself.** ⊠ *30 miles southwest of Santa Elena Junction via Ross Maxwell Scenic Dr.; 14 miles southwest of Rte. 118 via Old Maverick Rd.* ⊕ *www.nps.gov/bibe.*

EDUCATIONAL OFFERINGS

CLASSES AND SEMINARS

Big Bend Seminars. The Big Bend National History Association offers one- and two-day seminars covering subjects such as wildflowers, geology, and desert survival. Classes are generally limited to 15 people and are operated by Far Flung Outdoor Center outside Terlingua. ☎ *877/839–5337 or 800/839–7238 for Far Flung Outdoor Center* ⊕ *www.ffoc.net* ⊠ *Fees vary.*

RANGER PROGRAMS

Birding Talks. Rangers lead two-hour birding tours; binoculars are needed. ⊠ *Chisos Basin Visitor Center* ☎ *432/477–2264* ⊕ *www.nps.gov/bibe* ☉ *Nov.–Mar., daily 8–3:30; Apr.–Oct., daily 9–4; closed for lunch.*

Interpretive Activities. Ranger-guided activities are held throughout the park, indoors and outdoors, and include slide shows, talks, and walks on natural and cultural history. Check visitor centers and campground bulletin boards for event postings, which are usually updated on a two-week rotation. ☎ *432/477–2251* ⊕ *www.nps.gov/bibe.*

FAMILY **Junior Ranger Program.** This self-guided program for kids of all ages is taught via a $2 booklet of nature-based activities (available at visitor centers). Upon completion of the course, kids are given a Junior Ranger badge or patch, a certificate, and a bookmark. ☎ *432/477–2251* ⊕ *www.nps.gov/bibe.*

SPORTS AND THE OUTDOORS

Spectacular and varied scenery plus more than 300 miles of road spell adventure for hikers, bikers, horseback riders, or those simply in need of a ramble on foot or by Jeep. A web of dusty, unpaved roads lures adventuresome drivers and experienced hikers deep into the backcountry, while paved roads make shorter trails and scenic overlooks more accessible. Because the park has nearly half of the bird species in North America, birding ranks high. Boating is also popular, because some of the park's most striking features are accessible only via the Rio Grande.

MULTISPORT OUTFITTERS

Big Bend River Tours. Exploring the Rio Grande is this outfitter's specialty. Custom tours can be half a day up to three weeks and include rafting, canoeing, and hiking and horseback trips combined with a river float. Rafting tours include gourmet or music themes. ⊠ *FM 170, Terlingua* ☎ *800/545–4240, 432/371–3033* ⊕ *www.bigbendrivertours.com.*

Desert Sports. From rentals—mountain bikes, boats, rafts, and inflatable kayaks—to experienced guides for mountain-bike touring, boating, and hiking, this outfitter has it covered. The company prides itself on its small size and personal touch. ☎ *432/371–2727, 888/989–6900* ⊕ *www.desertsportstx.com.*

Far Flung Outdoor Center. Call these pros for personalized nature, historical, and geological trips via rafts, ATVs, and 4X4s. Trips include gourmet rafting tours with cheese and wine served on checkered tablecloths alongside the river, and sometimes spectacular star viewing at night. The property offers overnight "casitas" with kitchenettes and a full range of amenities. ⊠ *FM 170, Terlingua* ☎ *800/839–7238* ⊕ *www.ffoc.net.*

Red Rock Outfitters. This outfitter sells clothing and gear and arranges river-rafting, canoeing, horseback-riding, and mountain-biking excursions, as well as Jeep and ATV tours. ⊠ *Lobby of Badlands Hotel, 100 Main St./FM 170, Lajitas* ☎ *432/424–5170, 432/424–5000* ⊕ *www. lajitasgolfresort.com/default.aspx?pg=activity_center.*

8

Plants and Wildlife in Big Bend

Because Big Bend contains habitats as diverse as spent volcanoes, slick-sided canyons, and the Rio Grande, it follows that species here are extremely diverse, too. Among the park's most notable residents are endangered species like the agave- and cactus-eating Mexican long-nosed bat, shadow-dappled peregrine falcon, and fat-bellied horned lizard (Texans call them "horny toads"). More than 450 species of birds wing throughout the park, including the black-capped vireo and the turkey vulture, which boasts a 6-foot wingspan.

In the highlands mountain lions lurk, while black bears loll in the crags and valleys. Your chances of spotting the reclusive creatures are slim, though greater at dusk and dawn. If you do encounter either, don't run away. Instead, stand tall, shout, throw rocks if necessary, and look as scary as possible.

If the winged, furred, and legged denizens of Big Bend are watch-worthy, so, too, are the plants populating the region. Supremely adapted to the arroyos, valleys, and slopes, the plants range from the endangered Chisos Mountains hedgehog cactus (found only in the park) to the towering rasp of the giant dagger yucca. Also here are 60 types of cacti—so be careful where you tread.

BICYCLING

Mountain biking the backcountry roads can be so solitary that you're unlikely to encounter another human being. However, the solitude also means you should be extraordinarily prepared for the unexpected with ample supplies, especially water and sun protection (summer heat is brutal, and you're unlikely to find shade except in forested areas of Chisos Basin). Biking is recommended only during the cooler months (October–April).

On paved roads, a regular road bike should suffice, but you'll have to bring your own—outfitters tend to stock only mountain bikes. Off-road cycling is not allowed in the park. For an easy ride on mostly level ground, try the 13-mile (one-way) unpaved **Old Maverick Road** on the west side of the park off Route 118. For a challenge, take the unpaved **Old Ore Road** for 27 miles from the park's north area to near Rio Grande Village on the east side.

BIRD-WATCHING

Situated on north–south migratory pathways, Big Bend is home to approximately 450 species of birds—more than any other national park. In fact, the birds that flit, waddle, soar, and swim in the park represent more than half the bird species found in North America, including the Colima warbler, found nowhere else in the United States. To glimpse darting hummingbirds, turkey vultures, golden eagles, and the famous Colima, look to the Chisos Mountains. To spy woodpeckers and scaled quail (distinctive for dangling crests), look to the desert scrub. And for cuckoos, cardinals, and screech owls, you must prowl along the river. Rangers lead birding talks.

FAMILY

Fodor's Choice

★

Chisos Basin. Known as a "sky island" towering over the surrounding desert, Chisos Basin shelters the only lodge in the park and is etched by numerous hiking trails of varying difficulty. One takes you to the top of Emory Peak, the highest point in Big Bend. You'll have to hike the high country (above 5,400 feet elevation) to spy the Colima warbler and Lucifer hummingbird, but bear, deer, javelina, and even mountain lions have been known to range closer to the lodge grounds. Your chances of encountering them are rather small, especially during the day. If you do, the animals will likely shy away. ■TIP→ At more than a mile high, the basin floor is an especially inviting destination during summer. ⊠ *Chisos Basin Rd., 9 miles southwest of Panther Junction* ☎ *432/477–2291* ⊕ *www.nps.gov/bibe.*

FAMILY

Fodor's Choice

★

Rio Grande Village. Considered the best birding habitat in Big Bend, this river wetland has summer tanagers and vermilion flycatchers among many other species. The trail's a good one for kids, and a portion is wheelchair accessible. ⊠ *22 miles southeast of Panther Junction* ⊕ *www.nps.gov/bibe.*

BOATING AND RAFTING

Much is made of the park's hiking trails and the exquisite views they offer. Likewise, the watery pathway that is the Rio Grande should be mentioned for the spectacular views it affords. The 118 miles of the Rio Grande that border the park form its backbone, defining the vegetation, landforms, and animals found at the park's southern rim. By turns shallow and deep, the river flows through stunning canyons and picks up speed over small and large rapids.

Alternately soothing and exciting (Class II and III rapids develop here, particularly after the summer rains), the river can be traversed in several ways, from guided rafting tours to more strenuous kayak and canoe expeditions. In general, rafting trips spell smoother sailing for families, though thrills are inherent when soaring over the river's meringuelike tips and troughs. Always respect this river, however, for fatalities have occurred. ■TIP→ Be sure to check the river levels before planning an outing—many times during the year the river's too low to get a decent rafting experience. Conversely, during an especially wet monsoon season (as in 2013), the river rises to levels that even guides won't challenge.

You can bring your own raft to the boat launch at the Rio Grande, but you must obtain a $10 river-use permit (which allows you to camp along the river) from a visitor center. Leave the Jet Skis at home; no motorized vehicles are allowed on the Rio Grande. For less fuss, go with a tour guide or outfitter on trips that range from a few hours to several days. Most outfitters are in the communities of Study Butte, Terlingua, and Lajitas, just west of the park boundary off Route 170. They rent rafts, canoes, kayaks, and inflatable kayaks (nicknamed "duckies") for when the river is low. Their guided trips cost in the tens of dollars to thousands of dollars. Personalized river tours are available all year, and because this is the Lone Star State, they might include gourmet rafting tours that end with beef Wellington and live country music. Though many of the rafting trips are relatively smooth, thus safe for younger boaters, be sure to tell the equipment-rental agent or guide if a party member weighs less than 100 pounds or more than 200, because special life jackets may be necessary.

> **NOTABLE QUOTE**
>
> "I'd rather be broke down and lost in the wilds of Big Bend, any day, than wake up some morning in a penthouse suite high above the megalomania of Dallas or Houston."
> —Environmental writer Edward Abbey

FISHING

You can cast a line into the Rio Grande all year for free, as long as you obtain a permit from one of the park's visitor centers. You cannot use jug lines, traps, or other nontraditional fishing methods.

HIKING

Each of the park's zones has its own appeal. The east side offers demanding mountain hikes, border canyons, limestone aplenty, and sandy washes with geographic spectacles. Westside trails go down into striking scenery in the Santa Elena Canyon and up into towering volcanic landforms. Descend into gorges, arroyos, and springs or ascend into the must-see scenic windows of Grapevine Hills. The heart of the park has abandoned mines, pine-topped vistas, scrub vegetation around the Chisos, and deserts lying just below soaring Chisos Mountain aeries. ■TIP➔ **Carry enough drinking water—a gallon per person daily (more when extremely hot).**

While Big Bend certainly has "expedition level" trails to test the most veteran backpacker, many are very demanding and potentially dangerous (sometimes resulting in fatalities). So no "difficult" trails are noted here. Instead, the ones included here are representative of trails at Big Bend that most physically fit people can accomplish.

EASY

FAMILY **Chihuahuan Desert Nature Trail.** A windmill and spring form a desert oasis, a refreshing backdrop to a 0.5-mile, hot and flat nature trail; wild doves are abundant, the hike is pleasant, and kids will do just fine. While you're there, keep an eye out for the elf owl, one of the sought-after birds on the Big Bend's "Top 10" list. *Easy.* ✉ *Trailhead at Dugout Wells, 5 miles southeast of Panther Junction.*

FAMILY **Rio Grande Village Nature Trail.** Down by the Rio Grande, this short, 0.75-mile trail packs a powerful wildlife punch. The village is considered one of the best spots in the park to see rare birds, and other wildlife isn't in short supply either. Keep a lookout for coyotes, javelinas (they look like wild pigs), and other mammals. This is a good trail for kids, so expect higher traffic. Restrooms are nearby, and the

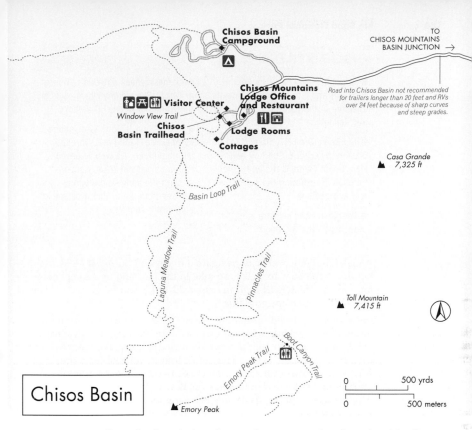

Chisos Basin

trail can be done in less than an hour, even when lingering. The first 0.25 mile is wheelchair accessible. *Easy.* ✉ *Trailhead 22 miles southeast of Panther Junction.*

FAMILY **Window View Nature Trail.** This 0.3-mile paved nature trail is wheelchair accessible and great for little ones. Take in the beautiful, craggy-sided Chisos and look through the V-shape rock-sided "Window" framing the desert below. This self-guided trail, which is especially captivating at sunset, is easily accomplished in half an hour. ■TIP→ Be on the lookout for wild javelina, which occasionally root through here. They're not normally aggressive, but give them a respectful distance. *Easy.* ✉ *Trail begins in Chisos Basin, west of lodge parking lot.*

MODERATE

Chisos Basin Loop Trail. A forested area and higher elevations give you some sweeping views of the lower desert and distant volcanic mountains on this 1.6-mile round trip. The elevation at the trailhead is 5,400 feet. Set aside about an hour. *Moderate.* ✉ *Trailhead 7 miles southwest of Chisos Basin Junction.*

Hot Springs Trail. An abandoned motel and a bathhouse foundation are among the sights along this 2-mile loop hike. The Rio Grande is heard at every turn, and trees occasionally shelter the walkway. The trailhead is accessed via a 1.6-mile dirt road. It's not passable for large

GOOD READS

■ *Naturalist's Big Bend*, by Roland H. Wauer and Carl M. Fleming, paints a picture of the park's diverse plants and animals.

■ *Big Bend, The Story Behind the Scenery*, by Carol E. Sperling and Mary L. Van Camp, is rife with colorful photos illustrating the park's history and geology.

■ For gleeful and awestruck thoughts on the Big Bend

wilderness, check out *God's Country or Devil's Playground*, which collects the writing of nearly 60 authors.

■ The Natural History Association's *Road Guide* ($1.95) gives in-depth information on the web of paved and improved dirt roads running through the park—and the views you can see from them. Find it on sale at park visitor centers.

vehicles, but most cars can navigate it in dry conditions. ■ TIP→ **Temperatures can soar to 120°F, so hike in the morning or during cooler months.** *Moderate.* ⊠ *Trail accessed 22 miles southeast of Panther Junction* ⊕ *www.nps.gov/bibe.*

Lost Mine Trail. Set aside about three hours to leisurely explore the nature of the Chisos Mountains along this elevation-climbing trail. It starts at 5,700 feet, one of the highest elevations in the park, and climbs to an even loftier vantage point. The entire length is 4.8 miles round-trip. ■ TIP→ **If fatigue or time constraints become a factor, the breathtaking view at marker 10, about halfway up, is a worthy destination in itself.** *Moderate.* ⊠ *Trail begins at mile marker 5 on the Chisos Basin Rd., 2 miles from lodge.*

Fodor's Choice   **Santa Elena Canyon Trail.** A 1.7-mile round trip crosses marshy Terlingua
★   Creek, scales a rocky staircase, and deposits you on the banks of the Rio Grande for a cathedral-like view of cliff walls boxing in the river. Try to end up here near sunset, when the sun stains the cliffs a rich red-brown chestnut. ■ TIP→ **An overlook on the Ross Maxwell Scenic Drive affords a panoramic view of Santa Elena Canyon from miles away.** *Moderate.* ⊠ *Trail accessed 8 miles west of Castolon via Ross Maxwell Scenic Dr. or Old Maverick Rd.*

JEEP TOURS

Wheeled traffic is welcome in the park, up to a point. RVs, trucks, cars, and Jeeps are allowed in designated areas, though personal ATV use is prohibited. Jeep rental isn't available inside the park, but Jeep, SUV, and ATV tours just outside the park are possible through outfitters. Jeep tours can cost as little as $49 for a two-hour tour, while ATV tours ring up at about $135 for the first person, with reduced rates for a second rider.

SWIMMING

Though it might be tempting to doff sweat-drenched T-shirts in favor of bathing suits, be careful where you take your dips. The Rio Grande has ample waters, but swimming isn't recommended due to dangerous currents and high pollution levels.

WHAT'S NEARBY

Just as many of Big Bend's zones are geographically remote, the park itself is isolated among hundreds upon hundreds of miles of West Texas desert and scrub. The nearest metropolis is El Paso, 329 miles away, while the nearest sizable cities are Odessa and Midland, 222 and 242 miles, respectively, to the northeast.

NEARBY TOWNS

Marathon, just 39 miles to the north, is one of the closest towns to Big Bend. Once a shipping hub, the population-500 town still contains reminders of its Old West railroad days. **Alpine,** a town of about 6,000, hunkers down among the Davis Mountains 81 miles north of the park. The town is known for its extensive college agriculture program at Sul Ross State University. It also attracts celebrities like Will Smith and Jada Pinkett-Smith, who have been spotted at its historic Holland Hotel. About 26 miles west of Alpine is **Marfa,** a population-2,000, middle-of-nowhere West Texas city known for its art scene and spooky, unexplained "Marfa lights," attributed to everything from atmospheric disturbances to imagination.

Once the headquarters of quicksilver mining (now defunct), **Terlingua** is 7 miles from the park's west entrance on Route 118. Four miles east of Terlingua is **Study Butte,** which also has its roots in the old quicksilver-mining industry. The combined Terlingua–Study Butte population is about 300, many of them iconoclasts and big-city refugees. Follow Route 170 west from Terlingua for 13 miles and you come upon the flat-rock formations of tiny **Lajitas** (pop. 75). Once a U.S. Cavalry outpost, Lajitas, which means "little flat stones," has been converted into a resort area offering plenty of golf and equestrian activities. The border town of **Presidio,** 69 miles from the park's west exit, is regarded as the gateway to northern Mexico. Across the border from Presidio is a spring-break favorite, **Ojinaga, Mexico,** famous for its partylike atmosphere. It's also a springboard to Copper Canyon, a striking series of canyons that run down the west side of the Sierra Tarahumara.

Big Bend residents are thrilled that the border crossing of **Boquillas, Mexico** (closed since 9/11) has finally reopened to U.S. citizens. Residents of both countries can now use the crossing, about 2 miles north of Rio Grande Village, from 9 to 6, Wednesday through Sunday. A passport or birth certificate is required. Once a mining boomtown that fed off rich minerals and silver, Boquillas has shrunk to a small pool of families due in part to the closed border crossing, but there is a restaurant and bar on the other side, plus some shopping. U.S. citizens are allowed to

8

bring back up to $200 in merchandise duty-free. Drive to the crossing from Rio Grande Village, which sells a $5 round-trip boat-ride ticket. The remaining ¾ mile to the village can be made on donkey or horseback. ⚠ **If you do not return to the border by 6 pm, Sunday, you'll have an "extended stay" in Mexico until Wednesday.**

VISITOR INFORMATION

Alpine Chamber of Commerce ⊠ *106 N. 3rd St., Alpine* ☎ *432/837–2326, 800/561–3712* ⊕ *www.alpinetexas.com.* **Big Bend Chamber of Commerce** ⊠ *P.O. Box 607, Terlingua* ☎ *432/371–2320* ⊕ *bigbendchamber.homestead.com.* **Del Rio Chamber of Commerce** ⊠ *1915 Veterans Blvd., Del Rio* ☎ *800/889– 8149* ⊕ *www.drchamber.com.* **Fort Davis Chamber of Commerce** ⊠ *No. 4 Memorial Sq., Fort Davis* ☎ *432/426–3015, 800/524–3015* ⊕ *www.fortdavis.com.* **Marathon Chamber of Commerce** ⊠ *105 Hwy. 90 W, Marathon* ☎ *432/386– 4516* ⊕ *www.marathontexas.com.* **Marfa Chamber of Commerce** ⊠ *207 N. Highland St., Marfa* ☎ *800/650–9696* ⊕ *www.marfacc.com.* **Presidio Tourism Department** ⊠ *507 O'Reilly St., Presidio* ☎ *432/229–3199* ⊕ *www.presidiotx.us.*

NEARBY ATTRACTIONS

Barton Warnock Environmental Education Center. Afflilated with Big Bend Ranch State Park of Texas, this visitor center offers a self-guided walking tour through a 2.5-acre landscaped desert garden. It's a good way to get acquainted with the Trans-Pecos region before adventuring to either the national or state park. Also on the grounds are an interpretive center, a covered picnic area, a bookstore and a gift shop. ⊠ *Rte. 170, 1 mile east of Lajitas* ☎ *432/424–3327* ⊕ *www.tpwd.state.tx.us/ state-parks* 🖾 *$5 Nov.–Apr.; $3 May–Oct.* ◷ *Daily 8–4:30.*

Big Bend Ranch State Park. As a western buffer to Big Bend National Park, this rugged desert wilderness extends along the Rio Grande across more than 300,000 acres from east of Lajitas to Presidio. It's less developed than the national park (if that seems possible), but you can hike, mountain bike, backpack, raft, and even round up longhorn steers on the biannual cattle drive in April and October of each year. A collection of hiking trailheads spoke off from FM 170 across from the Barton Warnock Environmental Education Center at Lajitas, which serves as the park's eastern visitor center. The western visitor center is at Fort Leaton State Historical Site near Presidio. ⊠ *Rte. 170, 4 miles southeast ofPresidio* ☎ *432/229–3613* ⊕ *www. tpwd.state.tx.us/state-parks* 🖾 *Nov.–Apr. $5; May–Oct. $3* ◷ *Park 24 hrs; visitor centers daily 8–4:30.*

Fort Leaton State Historic Site. The 23-acre site in Presidio County contains a thick-walled adobe trading post that dates back to pioneer days. There are exhibits, a 0.5-mile nature trail, picnic sites, guided tours and a store. The park is day-use only—no camping is available. The fort also doubles as a visitor center for Big Bend Ranch State Park. ⊠ *Rte. 170, 4 miles south of Presidio* ☎ *432/229–3613* ⊕ *www.tpwd. state.tx.us/state-parks* 🖾 *Nov.–Apr. $5; May–Oct. $3* ◷ *Daily 8–4:30.*

FAMILY **McDonald Observatory Visitors Center.** Check out exhibits, examine sunspots and flares safely via film, or peer into the workings of giant research telescopes. Guided bus tours of the domed observatories depart daily following programs at 11 and 2. After nightfall, the observatory offers public observing activities at star parties. The drive from Fort Davis to the visitor center at 6,235 feet is worth the trip. ■TIP➔ The observatory encourages online reservations due to limited tour-group size. Therefore, tickets for all events are slightly cheaper online. ✉ *3640 Dark Sky Dr., off Rte. 118, Fort Davis* ☎ *432/426–3640, 877/984– 7827* ⊕ *www.mcdonaldobservatory.org* ✉ *Programs $9, star parties $14* ☼ *Observatory programs, 11 am and 2 pm daily; star parties, after nightfall Tues., Fri., and Sat.*

FAMILY **Museum of the Big Bend.** With 5,000 square feet of space, this history-lover's haven has exhibits representing the life and cultures of the region and sponsors an annual show on ranching handiwork (such as saddles, reins, and spurs) held in conjunction with the Cowboy Poetry Gathering each February. The map collection is renowned. ✉ *Sul Ross State University, Hwy. 90, Alpine* ☎ *432/837–8730, 432/837–8143* ⊕ *ww2.sulross.edu/museum* ✉ *Free, donations accepted* ☼ *Tues.–Sat. 9–5, Sun. 1–5.*

> **BEST BETS FOR FAMILIES**
>
> ■ **Cowboy Poetry.** Cowboys and cowgirls regale with tales at Sul Ross State University's annual event.
>
> ■ **McDonald Observatory's Star Parties.** Guides lead observers on a tour of the celestial bodies.
>
> ■ **Overnight Rafting Trips.** Far Flung Outdoor Center sometimes offers spring-break trips for families with kids under 12. Trips include short hikes, goggles for stargazing, and canoeing.

ARTS AND ENTERTAINMENT

While recreation and the outdoor adventures are alive inside the park, the arts are vibrant outside it. Activities include live poetry readings, an annual four-day music festival, and Cinco de Mayo celebrations that fill up streets and shut down towns.

Ballroom Marfa. Ballroom Marfa is part gallery, part live-music venue. Young, hip, modern, and undeniably cool, the Ballroom welcomes visitors Wednesday through Saturday from 10 to 6 and Sunday 10 to 3. Performers take the stage on many Friday and Saturday evenings. Ballroom Marfa closes periodically for new installations; see the website for closures and the latest concert information. ✉ *108 E. San Antonio St., Marfa* ☎ *432/729–3600* ⊕ *www.ballroommarfa.org.*

8

BORDER CROSSING AT BIG BEND

Once upon a time, Big Bend visitors could splash across the Rio Grande and into the confines of Boquillas and Santa Elena, small Mexican towns that buttered their bread by selling Americans handicrafts. Now, if you want to visit one of the border towns, you must do so by entering official checkpoints in Texas; closed since 9/11, the Boquillas Crossing, at the park's southeastern edge, was reopened in 2013.

Once you're ready to cross, you'll be faced with a few options: hail a cab, park and walk, or drive your vehicle across. Many people choose to go by public transportation or by foot, because in order to drive your car into Mexico you may need a permit, Mexican auto insurance, and a tourist card. To reenter the United States, you'll need a passport, while children 16 and under will also need birth certificates. ⚠ **Most U.S. car rentals are not covered in Mexico, and you may be liable if anything happens to the car on the other side of the border.**

Once you get to Mexico, don't fret about language difficulties or money incompatibility. Border towns are very tourist-friendly, and most there speak English. American money is accepted, so it probably won't be necessary to get your greenbacks exchanged. Most Mexican border towns are easy to get to and can be explored in as little as one or two days.

Chinati Foundation. The Chinati Foundation, occupying 15 buildings on a 340-acre campus, changes its exhibits regularly and has a well-attended annual open house. People fly from all over the country to view the collection, and the foundation conducts guided tours Wednesday through Sunday of its huge contemporary-art holdings. **■ TIP→ Guided tour times are subject to change based on availability. Advance reservations are encouraged via website, email, or phone.** ✉ *1 Cavalry Row, Marfa* ☎ *432/729–4362* 🌐 *www.chinati.org* 🎟 *Up to $10 for self-guided tours; up to $25 for guided tours* 🕓 *Wed.–Sun. 9–5.*

WHERE TO EAT

IN THE PARK

$$$ SOUTHWESTERN Fodor's Choice ★ 🍴 **12 Gage Restaurant.** When the sun sets, this intimate indoor–outdoor restaurant, aka Cafe Cenizo, is the best place to eat and socialize in Marathon. The innovative menu, featuring fresh produce from the Gage Hotel Garden across the railroad tracks, changes with the season but always has a Southwestern flair. Entrées sizzle with prime steaks, smoked cabrito tacos, and roasted game. The chicken-fried steak, a Lone Star staple, is a cut above. Choose from the extensive wine cellar. After dinner you can belly up to the bar at the White Buffalo, where people-watching is always a kick. [$] *Average main: $26* ✉ *101 N.W. 1st St. (U.S. 90), Marathon* ☎ *432/386–4205* 🌐 *www.gagehotel.com.*

Bluebonnets: the Pride of Texas

Ever since men first explored the prairies of Texas, the bluebonnet has been revered. American Indians wove folktales around this bright bluish-violet flower; early-day Spanish priests planted it thickly around their newly established missions; and the cotton boll and cactus competed fiercely with it for the state flower—the bluebonnet won the title in 1901.

Nearly half a dozen varieties of the bluebonnet, distinctive for flowers resembling pioneers' sunbonnets, exist throughout the state. From mid-January until late March, at least one of the famous flowers carpets the park: the Big Bend (also called Chisos) bluebonnet has been described as the most majestic species, as its deep-blue flower spikes can shoot up to three feet in height. The Big Bend bluebonnets can be found beginning in late winter on the flats of the park as well as along the El Camino del Rio (Route 170), which follows the legendary Rio Grande between Lajitas and Presidio, Texas.

—Marge Peterson

$$

AMERICAN

✗ **Chisos Mountains Lodge Restaurant.** The decor of this comfy and casual eatery is unassuming, maybe because the star attraction is the signature view through a wall of windows that brings the craggy Chisos Mountains to your table. Breakfast offers the locally inspired Santa Elena Huevos Rancheros and Emory Peak Omelet. Later, choose from dishes like the Poco Caliente Burger, Rio Grande Chicken-Fried Steak, or Pine Canyon Mango Spinach Salad. There's a soup of the day, and if you're lucky, it'll be the thick and silky Cream of Potato. Each table has an informational booklet about the Big Bend region. ■ **TIP→** Arrive around sunset to catch the fading rust-color rays through the Window rock formation at the opposite end of the basin. $ *Average main:* $15 ⌧ *7 miles southwest of Chisos Basin Junction and 9 miles southwest of Panther Junction* ☎ *432/477–2292, 855/584–5295* ⊕ *www. chisosmountainslodge.com.*

PICNIC AREAS

Chisos Basin Area. There are several tables scattered off the parking lot near the visitor center and convenience store. If you want to put something to flame, though, you'll have to bring your own grill. For dessert, you get dramatic views of the Chisos Mountains. ⌧ *Off Chisos Basin Rd., 7 miles southwest of Chisos Basin Junction and 9 miles southwest of Panther Junction.*

Dugout Wells Area. There is a picnic table under the shady cottonwoods off the Dugout Wells Trail loop. There is also a vault toilet here (this type of facility is more pleasant than pit toilets). However, as with all vault toilets in the park, there is no running water to wash your hands. ⌧ *6 miles southeast of Panther Junction.*

Persimmon Gap Area. Quiet and remote, this relatively new picnic area has tables shaded by metal roofs called ramadas. There are no grills, but there is a pit toilet. ⌧ *North entrance to Big Bend, on U.S. 385.*

8

Rio Grande Village Area. Half a dozen picnic tables are scattered under cottonwoods south of the convenience store. Half a mile away at Daniels Ranch there are two tables and a grill. Wood fires aren't allowed (charcoal and propane are). ✉ *Rte. 118., 22 miles southeast of Panther Junction.*

Santa Elena Canyon Area. Two tables sit in the shade next to the parking lot at the trailhead. There is a vault toilet. ✉ *8 miles west of Castolon, accessible via Ross Maxwell Scenic Dr. or Old Maverick Rd.*

OUTSIDE THE PARK

$$ SOUTHWESTERN

🍴 **Candelilla Cafe and Thirsty Goat Saloon.** Southwestern dishes, Mexican-inspired fare, and sizzling steaks are the specialties at Candelilla, within walking distance if you're parked at the Lajitas Resort. Order the cream of avocado if it happens to be the soup of the day. The complimentary chips are freshly made, accompanied by a rich, garlicky salsa that's not too hot. Glass walls in this understated yet elegant room give you unobstructed views of sunsets, and a quick stroll next door finds you a nightcap at the Thirsty Goat Saloon, named for a legendary goat who liked Lone Star beer and was even elected "mayor" of Lajitas. [$] *Average main: $20* ✉ *Lajitas Resort, FM 170, 17 miles west of Rte. 118, Lajitas* ☎ *432/424–5000, 877/525–4827* 🌐 *www.lajitasgolfresort.com.*

$$ MODERN ITALIAN Fodor's Choice ★

🍴 **La Trattoria.** A classy if unpretentious bistro and espresso bar, La Trattoria opens at 11 for lunch specials ranging from panini sandwiches to freshly made soups and salads. Candlelight dinners offer antipasti and pasta dishes with an authentic tomato-basil sauce that lend a taste of Italy to the Chihuahuan Desert. If you prefer more traditional West Texas fare, there's Black Angus ribeye. There's a full wine and beer selection, and the restaurant is also vegetarian- and vegan-friendly. ■ **TIP→ It's a good idea to reserve a table on Friday and Saturday and during special events.** [$] *Average main: $18* ✉ *901 E. Holland Ave., Alpine* ☎ *432/837–2200* 🌐 *www.latrattoriacafe.com* 🕒 *Closed Sun. and Mon.*

$$ PIZZA FAMILY

🍴 **Pizza Foundation.** A funky gas-station-turned-pizza-joint that has been recently remodeled, the Pizza Foundation appeals to families because of its casual atmosphere, aromatic interior, and, most of all, the quality thin-crust pizza the native Rhode Island owners turn out. Kids will dig the fun pizza names such as the Faux Caesar, as well as several varieties of fruit punch, including blueberry and melon. They close for the evening when they run out of pizza, so you might call ahead to see if they're still making pies. [$] *Average main: $15* ✉ *100 E. San Antonio St., Marfa* ☎ *432/729–3377* 🌐 *www.pizzafoundation.com* 🕒 *Closed Mon.–Thurs.*

$$$ SOUTHWESTERN Fodor's Choice ★

🍴 **Reata.** A favorite of many West Texans spending the day in Alpine, the Reata ("rope" in Spanish) feels both welcoming and upscale, with lots of big, wooden tables and a pleasant rancher/cowboy vibe. It's a "howdy"-type place with a touch of discretion. Service is prompt but down-home. The menu features Tex-Mex accents such as tortilla soup and carne asada, while reflecting its Texas roots with dishes like calf fries and gravy. Of course, here's the beef—from a legendary ranch in the nearby Davis Mountains. The dessert tray is simply a work of art. [$] *Average main: $22* ✉ *203 N. 5th St., Alpine* ☎ *432/837–9232* 🌐 *www.reata.net* 🕒 *No dinner Sun.*

CLOSE UP

Best Campgrounds in Big Bend

The park's copious campsites are separated, roughly, into two categories—frontcountry and backcountry. Each of its four frontcountry sites, except Rio Grande Village RV Campground, has toilet facilities at a minimum. Far more numerous are the primitive backcountry sites, which require $10 permits from the visitor center. Primitive campsites with spectacular views are accessed via River Road, Glenn Springs, Old Ore Road, Paint Gap, Old Maverick Road, Grapevine Hills, Pine Canyon, and Croton Springs.

Chisos Basin Campground. Scenic views and cool shade are the highlights here. ✉ *7 miles southwest of Chisos Basin Junction* ☎ *432/477–2251* 🌐 *www.reserveusa.com.*

Cottonwood Campground. This Castolon-area campground is a popular bird-watching spot near the Rio Grande. ✉ *Off Ross Maxwell Scenic Dr., 22 miles southwest of Santa Elena Junction* ☎ *432/477–2251* 🌐 *www.reserveusa.com.*

Maverick Ranch RV Park. Owned by Lajitas Golf Resort, this layout has 101 RV sites and 18 primitive camping sites. RV connections are 30/50 amps, and there is a clubhouse, deli, hot showers, laundry facilities, picnic area, and hiking trails. It's also pet-friendly. ✉ *FM 170* ☎ *432/424-5180* 🌐 *www.lajitasgolfresort.com*

Rio Grande Village Campground. A shady oasis, this campground is a birding hot spot. It's also a great site for kids and seniors, due to the ease of accessing facilities. ✉ *22 miles southeast of Panther Junction* ☎ *432/477–2293* 🌐 *www.reserveusa.com.*

Rio Grande Village RV Park. Often full during holidays, this is one of the best sites for families because of the minitheater and proximity to the hot spring, which is fun to soak in at night. ✉ *22 miles southeast of Panther Junction* ☎ *432/477–2293* 🌐 *www.reserveusa.com.*

8

WHERE TO STAY

For expanded hotel reviews, visit Fodors.com.

IN THE PARK

$$ RESORT FAMILY Fodor's Choice ★ **Chisos Mountains Lodge.** With ranger talks just next door at the visitor center, miles of hiking trails to suit all levels of fitness, and plenty of wildlife nearby, these comfortable rooms—some of which have been nicely remodeled—are a great place for families with kids. **Pros:** refrigerators; central location for numerous hiking trails and scenic drives; free Wi-Fi in most rooms. **Cons:** no phones or TVs. [$] *Rooms from: $138* ✉ *7 miles southwest of Chisos Basin Junction and 9 miles southwest of Panther Junction* ☎ *432/477–2291 for desk, 877/386–4383 for reservations* 🌐 *www.chisosmountainslodge.com* 🛏 *72 rooms* 🍴 *No meals.*

$$ HOTEL **Hotel El Capitan.** Famed architect Henry Trost designed this Spanish Revival hotel, which takes its place among such other glamorous Trost landmarks as the Hotel Paisano (Marfa), the Holland Hotel (Alpine) and the Gage Hotel (Marathon). **Pros:** lovely architecture;

freeway accessible; pet-friendly. **Cons:** a little farther from the park than some other towns. $\boxed{\$}$ *Rooms from: $119* ✉ *100 E. Broadway, Van Horn* ☎ *432/283–1220* ⊕ *www.hotelelcapitan.net* ⤳ *30 rooms, 6 suites* ⫬❂⫭ *Breakfast.*

OUTSIDE THE PARK

$$$ ⫸ **Gage Hotel.** Cowboy, Indian, and Hispanic cultures are reflected in
HOTEL the furnishings of this picturesque, historic hotel, built in the 1920s facing the life-sustaining railroad tracks. **Pros:** amazing architecture; swimming pool; health center and spa; an intimate bar and restaurant. **Cons:** very popular in spring and fall, so it's often booked in advance. $\boxed{\$}$ *Rooms from: $156* ✉ *102 N.W. 1st St., Marathon* ☎ *432/386–4205, 800/884–4243* ⊕ *www.gagehotel.com* ⤳ *36 rooms, 9 with shared bath; 3 houses* ⫬❂⫭ *Breakfast.*

$$ ⫸ **Holland Hotel.** Once just a stop on the transcontinental railroad, the
HOTEL rancher-theme Holland Hotel is now a historic landmark still hung with its original sign on the main, bustling drag in downtown Alpine— just doors down from shops, cafés, and galleries. **Pros:** complimentary breakfast; elevator (not common to historic properties); pet-friendly; swimming pool available at the co-owned Maverick Inn. **Cons:** noise from nearby trains (earplugs provided in rooms). $\boxed{\$}$ *Rooms from: $115* ✉ *209 W. Holland Ave., Alpine* ☎ *432/837–2800, 800/535–8040* ⊕ *www.hollandhotel.net* ⤳ *14 rooms, 11 suites* ⫬❂⫭ *Breakfast.*

$$$ ⫸ **Hotel Paisano.** Once the playground of Liz Taylor, Rock Hudson,
HOTEL and James Dean, who stayed here while filming *Giant,* the Paisano
Fodor's Choice has maintained its glamour with beautiful Mediterranean architecture,
★ a fountain in the courtyard dining area, and dress and jewelry shops in downstairs hallways. **Pros:** Hollywood nostalgia; in the center of town. **Cons:** no elevator. $\boxed{\$}$ *Rooms from: $159* ✉ *207 N. Highland St., Marfa* ☎ *432/729–3669* ⊕ *www.hotelpaisano.com* ⤳ *33 rooms, 10 suites* ⫬❂⫭ *Breakfast.*

$$$ ⫸ **Lajitas Golf Resort & Spa.** The former-cavalry-post-turned-ghost-town
RESORT is now a privately owned collection of Western-theme tourist attractions
Fodor's Choice with a golf resort, spa, riding stables, convenience store, RV park, and
★ hiking trails, adding up to make this the nicest place to eat, shop, and overnight within 25 miles of the park. **Pros:** resort is a town unto itself, with many luxury activities. **Cons:** quite expensive. $\boxed{\$}$ *Rooms from: $199* ✉ *FM 170, 18 miles west of Rte. 118, Lajitas* ☎ *432/424–5000, 877/525–4827* ⊕ *www.lajitasgolfresort.com* ⤳ *101 rooms on 5 properties* ⫬❂⫭ *No meals.*

BLACK CANYON
OF THE GUNNISON
NATIONAL PARK

WELCOME TO BLACK CANYON OF THE GUNNISON

TOP REASONS TO GO

★ **Sheer of heights:**
Play it safe, but edge as close to the canyon rim as you dare and peer over into an abyss that's more than 2,700 feet deep in some places.

★ **Rapids transit:**
Experienced paddlers can tackle Class V rapids and 50°F water with the occasional portage past untamable sections of the Gunnison River.

★ **Fine fishing:** Fish the rare Gold Medal Waters of the Gunnison. Of the 9,000 miles of trout streams in Colorado, only 168 miles have this "gold medal" distinction.

★ **Triple-park action:**
Check out Curecanti National Recreation Area and Gunnison Gorge National Conservation Area, which bookend Black Canyon.

★ **Cliff-hangers:**
Watch experts climb the Painted Wall—Colorado's tallest vertical wall at 2,250 feet—and other challenging rock faces.

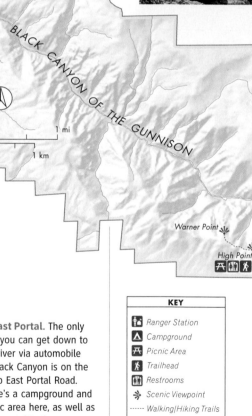

BLACK CANYON OF THE GUNNISON

0 — 1 mi
0 — 1 km

Warner Point ⚜

High Point
🏕 👪 🧍

1 East Portal. The only way you can get down to the river via automobile in Black Canyon is on the steep East Portal Road. There's a campground and picnic area here, as well as fishing and trail access.

KEY	
🛈	Ranger Station
⛺	Campground
🌲	Picnic Area
🧍	Trailhead
🚻	Restrooms
⚜	Scenic Viewpoint
......	Walking/Hiking Trails

2 **North Rim.** If you want to access this side of the canyon from the south, expect a drive of up to three hours as you wind around the canyon. The area's remoteness and difficult location mean the North Rim is never crowded; the road is partially unpaved and closes in the winter. There's also a small ranger station here.

3 **South Rim.** This is the main area of the park. The park's only visitor center is here, along with a camp-ground and a few picnic areas. The South Rim Road closes at Gunnison Point in the winter, when skiers and snowshoers take over.

COLORADO

GETTING ORIENTED

Black Canyon of the Gunnison is a park of extremes—great depths, narrow widths, tall cliffs, and steep descents. It is not a large park, but it offers incredible scenery and unforgettable experiences, whether you're hiking, fishing, or just taking it all in from the car. The adjacent parks and other open spaces offer even more opportunity for adventure.

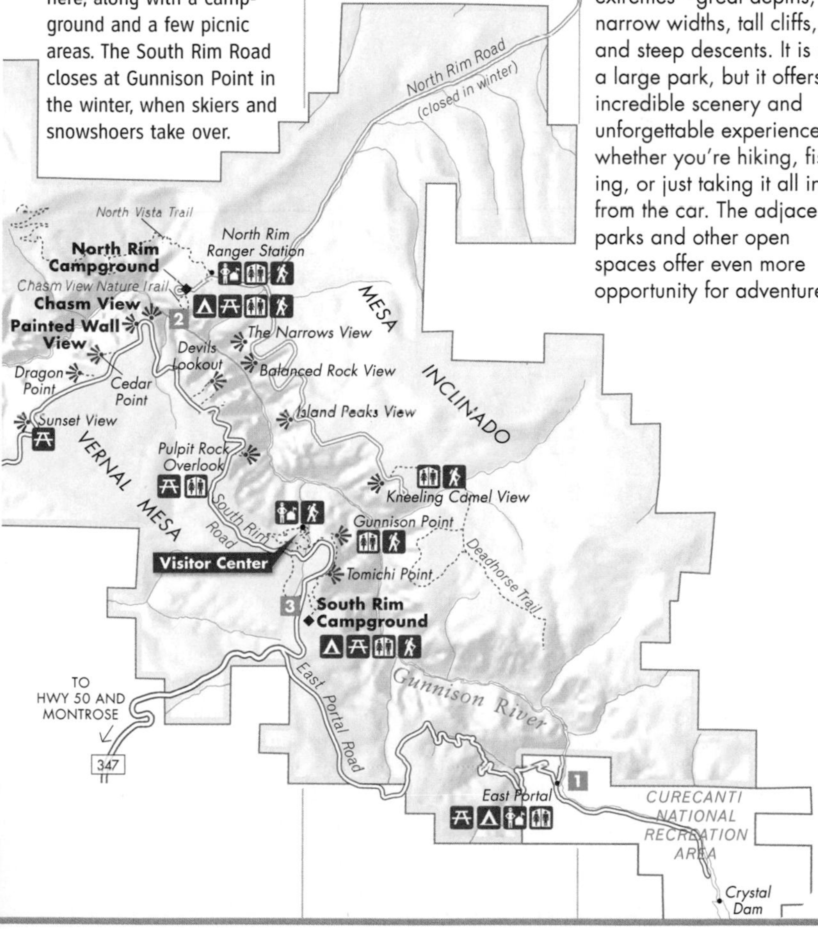

9

North Vista Trail

North Rim Campground
North Rim Ranger Station

Chasm View Nature Trail

Chasm View
Painted Wall View

Dragon Point

Cedar Point

Sunset View

MESA

INCLINADO

Devils Lookout

The Narrows View

Balanced Rock View

Island Peaks View

VERNAL MESA

Pulpit Rock Overlook

South Rim Road

Kneeling Camel View

Gunnison Point

Visitor Center

Tomichi Point

Deadhorse Trail

3 **South Rim Campground**

TO
HWY 50 AND
MONTROSE

347

East Portal Road

Gunnison River

East Portal

1

CURECANTI
NATIONAL
RECREATION
AREA

Crystal
Dam

Updated by
Kellee Katagi

The Black Canyon of the Gunnison River is one of Colorado's—and indeed the West's—most awe-inspiring places. A vivid testament to the powers of erosion, the canyon is roughly 2,000 feet deep. At its narrowest point, it spans 1,000 feet at the rim and only 40 feet at the bottom. The steep angles of the cliffs make it difficult for sunlight to fully break through during much of the day, and ever-present shadows blanket the canyon walls, leaving some places in almost perpetual darkness. No wonder it's called the "Black Canyon."

BLACK CANYON OF THE GUNNISON PLANNER

WHEN TO GO

Summer is the busiest season, with July experiencing the greatest crowds. However, a spring or fall visit gives you two advantages: fewer people and cooler temperatures. In summer, especially in years with little rainfall, daytime temperatures can reach into the 90s. A winter visit to the park brings even more solitude, as all but one section of campsites are shut down and only about 2 miles of South Rim Road, the park main road, are plowed.

November through March is when the snow hits, with an average of about 3 to 8 inches of it monthly. April through May and September and October are the rainiest, with about an inch of precipitation each month. June is generally the driest month. Temperatures at the bottom of the canyon are about 8 degrees warmer than at the rim.

AVG. HIGH/LOW TEMPS.

JAN.	FEB.	MARCH	APRIL	MAY	JUNE
37/14	42/16	50/18	47/23	67/37	75/44

JULY	AUG.	SEPT.	OCT.	NOV.	DEC.
84/51	81/50	72/42	62/31	48/23	37/12

FESTIVALS AND EVENTS

JULY–AUGUST **Main in Motion.** From 6–8:30 every Thursday in the summer, Main Street in Montrose is the place to be. Street performers and other artisans join Historic Downtown Montrose restaurants and shops to make for a pleasant evening stroll. ☎ 970/964–9304 ⊕ *www.maininmotion.com.*

JULY **Paonia Cherry Days.** One of Colorado's longest-running annual events, this small-town festival on the 4th of July includes a parade, food, crafts, sidewalk sales, and a variety of entertainment celebrating local cherry crops (and the other fruits that have made Paonia famous). ☎ 970/527–3886 ⊕ *www.paoniacherrydays.com.*

PLANNING YOUR TIME

BLACK CANYON OF THE GUNNISON IN ONE DAY

Pack a lunch and head to the canyon's South Rim, beginning with a stop at the **South Rim Visitor Center.** Before getting back into the car, take in your first view of Black Canyon from **Gunnison Point,** adjacent to the visitor center. Then set out on a driving tour of the 7-mile **South Rim Road,** allowing the rest of the morning to stop at the various viewpoints that overlook the canyon. Don't miss **Chasm View** and **Painted Wall View,** and be sure to stretch your legs along the short (0.4 miles round-trip) **Cedar Point Nature Trail.** If your timing is good, you'll reach **High Point,** the end of the road, around lunchtime.

After lunch, head out on **Warner Point Nature Trail** for an hour-long hike (1.5 miles round-trip). Then retrace your drive along South Rim Road back to the visitor center.

GETTING HERE AND AROUND

AIR TRAVEL

The Black Canyon of the Gunnison lies between the cities of Gunnison and Montrose, both of which have small regional airports.

CAR TRAVEL

The park has three roads. South Rim Road, reached by Route 347, is the primary thoroughfare and winds along the canyon's South Rim. From about late November to early April, the road is not plowed past the visitor center at Gunnison Point. North Rim Road, reached by Route 92, is usually open from May through Thanksgiving; in winter, the road is unplowed. On the park's south side, the serpentine East Portal Road descends abruptly to the Gunnison River below. The road is usually open from the beginning of May through the end of November. Because of the grade, vehicles or vehicle-trailer combinations longer than 22 feet are not permitted. The park has no public transportation.

9

PARK ESSENTIALS

PARK FEES AND PERMITS

Entrance fees are $15 per week per vehicle. Visitors entering on bicycle, motorcycle, or on foot pay $7 for a weekly pass. To access the inner canyon, you must pick up a wilderness permit (no fee).

PARK HOURS

The park is open 24/7 year-round. It's in the mountain time zone.

CELL-PHONE RECEPTION

Cell-phone reception in the park is unreliable and sporadic. There are public telephones at South Rim Visitor Center and South Rim Campground.

RESTAURANTS

The park itself has no eateries, but nearby towns have choices ranging from traditional American to an eclectic café and bakery.

> WILDLIFE IN
> BLACK CANYON
>
> You may spot peregrine falcons nesting in May and June, or other birds of prey such as red-tailed hawks, Cooper's hawks, and golden eagles circling overhead at any time of year. In summer, turkey vultures join the flying corps, and in winter, bald eagles. Mule deer, elk, and the very shy bobcat also call the park home. In spring and fall, you may see a porcupine among pinyon pines on the rims. Listen for the high-pitched chirp of the yellow-bellied marmot, which hangs out on sunny, rocky outcrops. Though rarely seen, mountain lions and black bears also live in the park.

Prices in the reviews are the average cost of a main course at dinner or, if dinner is not served, at lunch.

HOTELS

Black Canyon is devoid of hotels. Smaller hotels, some excellent B&Bs, and rustic lodges are nearby, as are a few of the larger chains.

Prices in the reviews are the lowest cost of a standard double room in high season. For expanded reviews, facilities, and current deals, visit Fodors.com.

VISITOR INFORMATION

PARK CONTACT INFORMATION

Black Canyon of the Gunnison National Park ⊠ *102 Elk Creek, Gunnison* ☏ *970/641–2337* ⊕ *www.nps.gov/blca.*

VISITOR CENTERS

North Rim Ranger Station. This small facility on the park's North Rim is open only in summer. Rangers can provide information and assistance and can issue permits for wilderness use and rock climbing. ⊠ *North Rim Rd., 11 miles from Rte. 92 turnoff* ☏ *970/641–2337* ☉ *Late May–Labor Day, daily 8–6.*

South Rim Visitor Center. The park's only visitor center offers interactive exhibits and introductory films detailing the park's geology and wildlife. Inquire at the center about free guided tours and informational ranger programs. ⊠ *1½ miles from the entrance station on South Rim Rd.* ☏ *970/249–1914* ☉ *Late May–early Sept., daily 8–6; early Sept.–late May, daily 8:30–4.*

EXPLORING

SCENIC DRIVES

The scenic South and North Rim roads offer deep and distant views into the canyon. Both also offer several lookout points and short hiking trails along the rim. The trails that go down into the canyon are steep and strenuous, and essentially unmarked, and so are reserved for experienced (and very fit) hikers.

East Portal Road. The only way to access the Gunnison River from the park by car is via this paved route, which drops approximately 2,000 feet down to the water in only 5 miles, giving it an extremely steep grade. Vehicles longer than 22 feet are not allowed on the road. If you're towing a trailer, you can unhitch it near the entrance to South Rim campground. The bottom of the road is actually in the adjacent Curecanti National Recreation Area. A tour of East Portal Road, with a brief stop at the bottom, takes about 45 minutes.

North Rim Road. Black Canyon's North Rim is much less frequented, but no less spectacular—the walls here are near vertical—than the South Rim. To reach the 15½-mile-long North Rim Road, take the signed turnoff from Route 92 about 3 miles south of Crawford. The road is paved for about the first 4 miles; the rest is gravel. After 11 miles, turn left at the intersection (the North Rim Campground is to the right). There are six overlooks along the road as it snakes along the rim's edge. Kneeling Camel, at the road's east end, provides the broadest view of the canyon. Set aside about two hours for a tour of the North Rim.

South Rim Road. This paved 7-mile stretch from Tomichi Point to High Point is the park's main road. The drive follows the canyon's level South Rim; 12 overlooks are accessible from the road, most via short gravel trails. Several short hikes along the rim also begin roadside. Allow between two and three hours round-trip.

9

SCENIC STOPS

The vast depths that draw thousands of visitors each year to Black Canyon have also historically prevented any extensive human habitation from taking root, so cultural attractions are largely absent here. But what the park lacks in historic sites it more than makes up for in scenery.

Chasm and Painted Wall Views. At the heart-in-your-throat Chasm viewpoint, the canyon walls plummet 1,820 feet to the river, but are only 1,100 feet apart at the top. As you peer down into the depths, keep in mind that this section is where the Gunnison River descends at its steepest rate, dropping 240 feet within the span of a mile. A few hundred yards farther is the best place from which to see Painted Wall, Colorado's tallest cliff. Pinkish swaths of pegmatite (a crystalline, granitelike rock) give the wall its colorful, marbled appearance. ⊠ *Approximately 3½ miles from the visitor center on South Rim Rd.*

Narrows View. Look upriver from this North Rim viewing spot and you'll be able to see into the canyon's narrowest section, just a slot really, with only 40 feet between the walls at the bottom. The canyon is also taller (1,725 feet) here than it is wide at the rim (1,150 feet). ⊠ *North Rim Rd., first overlook past the ranger station.*

Warner Point. This viewpoint, at the end of the Warner Point Nature Trail, delivers awesome views of the canyon's deepest point (2,722 feet), plus the nearby San Juan and West Elk mountain ranges. ⊠ *End of Warner Point Nature Trail, westernmost end of South Rim Rd.*

GOOD READS

■ *The Gunnison Country,* by Duane Vandenbusche, contains nearly 500 pages of historical photographs and essays on the park.

■ *The Essential Guide to Black Canyon of the Gunnison National Park,* by John Jenkins, is one of the definitive guides to the park.

■ The *South Rim Driving Tour Guide* is enlivened by David Halpern's evocative black-and-white images.

■ *A Kid's Guide to Exploring Black Canyon of the Gunnison National Park,* by Renee Skelton, is perfect for the 6–12 set.

EDUCATIONAL OFFERINGS

RANGER PROGRAMS

FAMILY **Junior Ranger Program.** Kids of all ages can participate in this program with an activities booklet to fill in while exploring the park. Inquire at the South Rim Visitors Center.

SPORTS AND THE OUTDOORS

Recreational activities in Black Canyon run the gamut from short and easy nature trails to world-class (and experts-only) rock climbing and kayaking. The cold waters of the Gunnison River are well known to trout anglers.

BIRD-WATCHING

The sheer cliffs of Black Canyon, though not suited for human habitation, provide a great habitat for birds. Peregrine falcons, white-throated swifts, and other cliff-dwelling birds revel in the dizzying heights, while at river level you'll find American dippers foraging for food in the rushing waters. Canyon wrens, which nest in the cliffs, are more often heard than seen, but their hauntingly beautiful songs are unforgettable. Dusky grouse are common in the sagebrush areas above the canyon, and red-tailed and Cooper's hawks and turkey vultures frequent the canyon rims. The best times for birding are spring and early summer.

BOATING AND KAYAKING

Fodor'sChoice
★

With Class V rapids, the Gunnison River is one of the premier kayak challenges in North America. The spectacular 14-mile stretch of the river that passes through the park is so narrow in some sections that the rim seems to be closing up above your head. Once you're downstream from the rapids (and out of the park), the canyon opens up into what is called the Gunnison Gorge. The rapids ease considerably, and the trip becomes more of a quiet float on Class I to Class IV water.

Kayaking the river through the park requires a wilderness use permit (and lots of expertise), and rafting is not allowed. Access to the Gunnison Gorge is only by foot or horseback. However, several outfitters offer guided raft and kayak trips in the Gunnison Gorge and other sections of the Gunnison River.

⇨ *For kayaking and rafting outfitters, see Area Activities in the What's Nearby section.*

FISHING

The three dams built upriver from the park in Curecanti National Recreation Area have created prime trout fishing in the waters below. Certain restrictions apply: Only artificial flies and lures are permitted, and a Colorado fishing license is required for people aged 16 and older. Rainbow trout are catch-and-release only, and there are size and possession limits on brown trout (check at the visitor center). Most anglers access the river from the bottom of East Portal Road; an undeveloped trail goes along the riverbank for about three-quarters of a mile.

HIKING

All trails can be hot in summer and most don't receive much shade, so bring water, a hat, and plenty of sunscreen. Dogs are permitted, on leash, on Rim Rock, Cedar Point Nature, and Chasm View Nature trails, and at any overlook. Hiking into the inner canyon, while doable, is not for the faint of heart—or slight of step. Six named routes lead down to the river, but they are not maintained or marked. In fact, the park staff won't even call them trails; they refer to them as "controlled slides." These supersteep, rocky routes vary in one-way distance from 1 to 2.75 miles, and the descent can be anywhere from 1,800 to 2,722 feet. Your reward, of course, is a rare look at the bottom of the inner-canyon and the fast-flowing Gunnison. ■TIP→ **Don't attempt an inner-canyon hike without plenty of water (the park's recommendation is one gallon per person, per day).** For descriptions of the routes and the necessary permit to hike them, stop at the visitor center at the South Rim or North Rim ranger station. Dogs are not permitted in the inner canyon.

EASY

FAMILY **Cedar Point Nature Trail.** This 0.4-mile round-trip interpretive trail leads out from South Rim Road to two overlooks. It's an easy stroll, and signs along the way detail the surrounding plants. *Easy.* ⊠ *Trailhead off South Rim Rd., 4.2 miles from South Rim Visitor Center.*

Deadhorse Trail. Despite its name, the 5-mile Deadhorse Trail is actually a pleasant hike, starting on an old service road from the Kneeling Camel View on the North Rim Road. The trail's farthest point provides the park's easternmost viewpoint. From this overlook, the canyon is much more open, with pinnacles and spires rising along its sides. *Easy.* ⊠ *Trailhead at the southernmost end of North Rim Rd.*

MODERATE

Chasm View Nature Trail. The park's shortest trail (0.3 mile round-trip) starts at North Rim Campground and offers an impressive 50-yard walk right along the canyon rim as well as an eye-popping view of Painted Wall and Serpent Point. This also an excellent place to spot raptors, swifts, and other birds. *Moderate.* ⊠ *Trailhead at North Rim Campground, 11¼ miles from Rte. 92.*

North Vista Trail. The round-trip hike to Exclamation Point is 3 miles; a more difficult foray to the top of 8,563-foot Green Mountain (a mesa, really) is 7 miles. The trail leads you along the North Rim; keep an eye out for especially gnarled pinyon pines—the North Rim is the site of some of the oldest groves of pinyons in North America, between 400 and 700 years old. *Moderate.* ⊠ *Trailhead at North Rim ranger station, off North Rim Rd., 11 miles from Rte. 92 turnoff.*

Fodor'sChoice ★ **Warner Point Nature Trail.** The 1.5-mile round-trip hike starts from High Point. It provides fabulous vistas of the San Juan and West Elk Mountains and Uncompahgre Valley. Warner Point, at trail's end, has the steepest drop-off from rim to river: a dizzying 2,722 feet. *Moderate.* ⊠ *Trailhead at the end of South Rim Rd.*

DIFFICULT

Oak Flat Loop Trail. This 2-mile loop is the most demanding of the South Rim hikes, as it brings you about 400 feet below the canyon rim. In places, the trail is narrow and crosses some steep slopes, but you won't have to navigate any steep drop-offs. Oak Flat is the shadiest of all the South Rim trails; small groves of aspen and thick stands of Douglas fir along the loop offer some respite from the sun. *Difficult.* ⊠ *Trailhead just west of the South Rim Visitor Center.*

HORSEBACK RIDING

Although its name might indicate otherwise, Deadhorse Trail is actually the only trail in the park where horses are allowed. The trail is an easy-to-moderate 5-mile loop that begins east of North Rim Road. Horses are not allowed on the South Rim, and can be on the North Rim only on the Deadhorse Trail, in the North Rim Campground, or on the North Rim Road during transport in a trailer.

Black Canyon of the Gunnison has no facilities geared toward horses. If you bring your own horse, go to the end of North Rim Road and park your trailer at Kneeling Camel Overlook to access Deadhorse Trail. No permit is required.

TOURS

Elk Ridge Ranch and Trail Rides. You can take 90-minute and two-hour rides at this ranch. Elk Ridge also offers a half-day ride to the rim of the Black Canyon. ✉ *10203 Bostwick Park Rd., Montrose* ☎ *970/240–6007* ⊕ *www.elkridgeranchinc.com* ⊗ *May–Sept., daily.*

ROCK CLIMBING

Fodor's Choice
★

For expert rock climbers, the sheer cliffs of the Black Canyon represent one of Colorado's premier big-wall challenges. Some routes can take several days to complete, with climbers sleeping on narrow ledges, or "portaledges." Though there's no official guide to climbing in the park, reports from individual climbers are kept on file at the South Rim Visitor Center. Nesting birds of prey may lead to wall closure at certain times of year.

Rock climbing in the park is for experts only, but you can do some bouldering at the Marmot Rocks area, about 100 feet south of South Rim Road between Painted Wall and Cedar Point overlooks (park at Painted Wall). Four boulder groupings offer a variety of routes rated from easy to very difficult; a pamphlet with a diagrammed map of the area is available at the South Rim Visitor Center.

TOURS AND OUTFITTERS

Crested Butte Mountain Guides. Intermediate and expert climbers can take a full-day rock- or ice-climbing guided tour for $395. ✉ *218 Maroon Ave., Crested Butte* ☎ *970/349–5430* ⊕ *www.crestedbutteguides.com.*

Skyward Mountaineering. Intermediate and advanced climbers can take lessons and guided tours on the Black Canyon's fabled climbs with this internationally certified guide and outfitter. ✉ *2392 Ridgeway Ct., Grand Junction* ☎ *970/209–2985* ⊕ *www.skywardmountaineering.com* ⊗ *Mar.–Nov.*

WINTER SPORTS

From late November to early April, South Rim Road is not plowed past the visitor center, offering park guests a unique opportunity to cross-country ski or snowshoe on the road. The Park Service also grooms a cross-country ski trail and marks a snowshoe trail through the woods, both starting at the visitor center. It's possible to ski or snowshoe on the unplowed North Rim Road, too, but it's about 4 miles from where the road closes, through sagebrush flats, to the canyon rim.

WHAT'S NEARBY

While not totally out of the way, Black Canyon of the Gunnison and its two neighboring recreation playgrounds—the Curecanti National Recreation Area and the Gunnison Gorge National Conservation Area—are far enough removed from civilization (i.e., big cities) to maintain a sense of getting-away-from-it-all isolation. They're a good 250 miles from Denver, and 240 miles from Colorado Springs, and touristy towns such as Durango and Telluride are 120 miles and 80 miles away, respectively. Colorado National Monument is about 85 miles distant.

NEARBY TOWNS

The primary gateway to Black Canyon is **Montrose,** 15 miles west of the park. The legendary Ute chief, Ouray, and his wife, Chipeta, lived near here in the late 1800s. Today, Montrose straddles the important agricultural and mining regions along the Uncompahgre River, and is the area's main shopping hub. The closest town to Black Canyon's North Rim is **Crawford,** about 3 miles from the entrance to the North Rim Road, a small hillside enclave amid the sheep and cattle ranches of the North Fork Valley with a small downtown area. Northeast on Route 92 (20 miles) is **Paonia,** a unique and charming blend of the old and new West. Here, career environmentalists and hippie types who have escaped the mainstream mingle with longtime ranchers, miners, and fruit growers. Eleven miles northwest of Crawford on Route 92 is the small ranching and mining community of **Hotchkiss.** The trappings and sensibilities of the Old West are here, from cowboy bars and fields of livestock to the annual summertime rodeo.

VISITOR INFORMATION
Crawford Area Chamber of Commerce ☎ 970/921–4000 ⊕ *www.crawfordcountry.org.* **Hotchkiss Community Chamber of Commerce** ☎ 970/872–3226 ⊕ *www.hotchkisschamber.com.* **Paonia Chamber of Commerce** ✉ *130 Grand Ave., Paonia* ☎ 970/527–3886 ⊕ *www.paoniachamber.com.*

NEARBY ATTRACTIONS

Colorado National Monument. Sheer red-rock cliffs open to 23 miles of steep canyons and thin monoliths that sprout as high as 450 feet from the floor of Colorado National Monument. This vast tract of rugged, ragged terrain was declared a national monument in 1911 at the urging of an eccentric visionary named John Otto. Now it's popular for rock climbing, horseback riding, cross-country skiing, biking, and camping. Cold Shivers Point is just one of the many dramatic overlooks along **Rim Rock Drive,** a 23-mile scenic route with breathtaking views. The town of Fruita, at the base of Colorado National Monument, is a haven for mountain bikers and hikers. It makes a great center for exploring the area's canyons—whether from the seat of a bike or the middle of a raft, heading for a leisurely float trip. ✉ *Fruita* ☎ *970/858–3617* ⊕ *www. nps.gov/colm* 🖫 *$10 per wk per vehicle. Visitors entering on bicycle, motorcycle, or foot pay $5 per wk* ☉ *Daily.*

Crawford State Park. The focus of this 337-acre park is Crawford Reservoir, created in 1963 when a dam was built to increase the supply of irrigated water to the surrounding ranches and farms. Boating and waterskiing are permitted on the reservoir, as are swimming and fishing (the lake is stocked with rainbow trout). The park has a 1-mile wheelchair-accessible hiking trail along with the primitive 0.5-mile Indian Fire Nature Trail, which runs along the reservoir on the park's west side. ✉ *40468 Rte. 92, 1 mile south of Crawford* ☎ *970/921–5721* ⊕ *parks. state.co.us/Parks/crawford* 🖫 *$7.*

Curecanti National Recreation Area. This nature preserve, named in honor of a Ute Indian chief, encompasses 40 miles of striking eroded volcanic landscape along U.S. 50, between Gunnison and Montrose. Three reservoirs were created by dams built on the Gunnison River in the 1960s: Morrow Point, Crystal Dam, and Blue Mesa, Colorado's largest lake at almost 20 miles long. You can windsurf, swim, fish, and boat in all three, although only Blue Mesa offers boat ramps. You'll find excellent fly-fishing at the east end of the recreation area, near Gunnison. Camping and hiking are also available. The Elk Creek Visitor Center on U.S. 50 provides more information. The Cimarron Visitor Center—at the western entrance to the recreation area, near the Morrow Point Dam—is more sporadically open, but if you catch it at the right time, you can view relics from the narrow-gauge Cimarron Canyon Railroad, including cars and livestock chutes. Call the Elk Creek Visitor Center for hours. Entrance to the recreation area is free, unless you use the east entrance, which is inside Black Canyon of the Gunnison National Park ($15 entrance fee). ⊠ *102 Elk Creek, Gunnison* ☎ *970/641–2337* ⊕ *www.nps.gov/cure* ⌑ *Free.*

AREA ACTIVITIES

SPORTS AND THE OUTDOORS
BOATING

TOURS AND
OUTFITTERS
Lake Fork Marina. Located on the western end of Blue Mesa Reservior off U.S. 92, the Lake Fork Marina rents all types of boats. If you have your own, there's a ramp at the marina and slips for rent. ⊠ *Off U.S. 92, near Lake Fork Campground, Gunnison* ☎ *970/641–3048* ⊕ *www. bluemesares.com.*

Morrow Point Boat Tours. Starting in neighboring Curecanti National Recreation Area, these guided tours run twice daily (except Tuesdays) in the summer, at 10 and 12:30. Morrow Point Boat Tours take passengers on a 90-minute tour via pontoon boat, and require a 1-mile walk to the boat dock. The cost is $16, and reservations are required. ⊠ *Pine Creek Trail and Boat Dock, U.S. 50, milepost 130, 25 miles west of Gunnison* ☎ *970/641–2337.*

KAYAKING AND RAFTING

TOURS AND
OUTFITTERS
Dvorak Expeditions. This outfitter offers rafting trips on the Dolores River that cover Class II to Class IV rapids and last up to 10 days. Or you can book a "Build-Your-Own-Adventure" trip that pairs rafting with other adventurous options, including ziplining, mountain biking, horseback riding, and rock climbing. ⊠ *17921 U.S. 285, Nathrop* ☎ *719/539–6851, 800/824–3795* ⊕ *www.dvorakexpeditions.com.*

SHOPPING

FOOD
Montrose Farmer's Market. Pack a picnic lunch for the Black Canyon from the Montrose Farmer's Market. ⊠ *S. 1st St. and S. Uncompahgre Ave., Montrose* ☎ *970/209–8463* ⊕ *www.montrosefarmersmarket.com* ⊗ *May–Oct., Sat. 8:30–1; Nov.–Apr., Sat. 8:30–1.*

CLOSE UP

Best Campgrounds in Black Canyon of the Gunnison

There are three campgrounds in Black Canyon National Park. The small North Rim Campground is first-come, first served, and is closed in the winter. Vehicles longer than 35 feet are discouraged from this campground. South Rim Campground is considerably larger, and has a loop that's open year-round. Reservations are accepted in South Rim Loops A and B. Power hookups only exist in Loop B. The East Portal campground is at the bottom of the steep East Portal Road and is open whenever the road is open. It offers 15 first-come, first-serve tent sites in a pretty setting. Water has to be trucked up to the campgrounds, so use it in moderation; it's shut off in mid-to-late September. Generators are not allowed at South Rim and are highly discouraged on the North Rim.

East Portal Campground. Its location next to the Gunnison River makes it perfect for fishing. ✉ *East Portal Rd., 5 miles from the main entrance.*

North Rim Campground. This small campground, nestled amid pine trees, offers the basics along the quiet North Rim. ✉ *North Rim Rd., 11¼ miles from Rte. 92.*

South Rim Campground. Stay on the canyon rim at this main campground right inside the park entrance. Loops A and C have tent sites only. The RV hookups are in Loop B, and those sites are priced higher than those in other parts of the campground. It's possible to camp here year-round (Loop A stays open all winter), but the loops are not plowed, so you'll have to hike in with your tent. ✉ *South Rim Rd., 1 mile from the visitor center.*

Russell Stover Factory Outlet. South of downtown Montrose, this outlet sells ice cream and fresh chocolates made right across the street. ✉ *2146 S. Townsend Ave., Montrose* ☎ *970/249–5372* ⊕ *www.russellstover.com.*

9

WHERE TO EAT

IN THE PARK

PICNIC AREAS

There are a variety of picnic areas at Black Canyon of the Gunnison, all with pit toilets; all are closed when it snows.

East Portal. This picnic area, located at the bottom of the canyon, accommodates large groups. There are tables, fire grates, bathrooms, and a large shaded shelter. ✉ *East Portal Rd. at the Gunnison River.*

High Point. When the sun is unforgiving, this overlook offers more shade than most of the other picnic areas. There are tables and bathrooms but no fire grates. ✉ *West end of South Rim Rd.*

North and South Rim campgrounds. Feel free to use unoccupied camping sites for picnicking. There are tables, fire grates, and bathrooms. ✉ *North Rim: west end of North Rim Rd.; South Rim: about 1 mile east of South Rim Visitor Center on South Rim Rd.*

OUTSIDE THE PARK

MONTROSE

$$ ✕ **Camp Robber.** This chic restaurant serves Montrose's most creative
SOUTHWESTERN   cuisine. Start with the famous green chili chicken and potato soup,
and follow with entrées such as Southwest chicken linguine or the
house specialty: pork medallions covered with pistachios. At lunch,
salads, hearty sandwiches, and blue-corn enchiladas fuel hungry hik-
ers. The Sunday brunch will leave you happily stuffed. When the
weather permits, you can sit on the shaded patio. $ *Average main: $15*
✉ *1515 Ogden Rd., Montrose* ☎ *970/240–1590* ⊕ *www.camprobber.
com* ⊙ *No dinner Sun.*

PAONIA

$$ ✕ **Flying Fork Café & Bakery.** This charming café serves tasty Italian fare in
ECLECTIC   a comfortable dining room and, in the summer, a shady outdoor garden.
An assortment of artisan breads and pastries is sold in the small bakery at the front of the building, with a growing selection of gluten-free
items. Local ingredients are used whenever possible to create dishes like
braised Colorado lamb shank or farfalle in a sauce of smoked chicken,
pear, and Gorgonzola. The individual pizzas, made with whole-wheat
flour and fresh basil and mozzarella, are good for smaller appetites.
$ *Average main: $18* ✉ *101 3rd St., Paonia* ☎ *970/527–3203* ⊕ *www.
flyingforkcafe.com* ⊙ *Closed Mon.*

WHERE TO STAY

OUTSIDE THE PARK

MONTROSE

$ ▦ **Best Western Red Arrow Motor Inn.** This low-key establishment is one
HOTEL   of the nicest lodgings in the area, mainly because of the large, pretty
rooms filled with handsome wood furnishings. **Pros:** spacious and
comfortable rooms; good breakfast, pleasant pool. **Cons:** pets add an
extra $10 per day; next to busy street. $ *Rooms from: $110* ✉ *1702
E. Main St., Montrose* ☎ *970/249–9641, 800/780–7234* ⊕ *www.
bestwesterncolorado.com* ⤢ *57 rooms, 2 suites.*

BRYCE CANYON
NATIONAL PARK

WELCOME TO BRYCE CANYON

TOP REASONS TO GO

★ **Hoodoo heaven:**
The brashly colored, gravity-defying limestone tentacles reaching skyward—known locally as "hoodoos"—are the main attraction of Bryce Canyon.

★ **Famous fresh air:**
With some of the clearest skies anywhere, the park offers views that, on a clear day, extend 200 miles and into three states.

★ **Spectacular sunrises and sunsets:** The deep orange and crimson hues of the park's hoodoos are intensified by the light of the sun at either end of the day.

★ **Dramatically different zones:** From the highest point of the rim to the canyon base, the park spans 2,000 feet, so you can explore three unique climatic zones: spruce-fir forest, ponderosa-pine forest, and pinyon pine–juniper forest.

★ **Snowy fun:** Bryce gets 200 inches of snowfall a year, and is a popular destination for skiers and snowshoe enthusiasts.

1 Bryce Amphitheater.
It's the heart of the park. From here you can access the historic Bryce Canyon Lodge as well as Sunrise, Sunset, and Inspiration points. Walk to Bryce Point at sunrise to view the mesmerizing collection of massive hoodoos known as Silent City.

2 Under-the-Rim Trail.
This 23-mile trail is the best way to reach Bryce Canyon backcountry. It can be a challenging three-day adventure or a half day of fun via one of the four access points from the main road. A handful of primitive campgrounds lines the route.

3 Rainbow and Yovimpa Points. The end of the scenic road, but not of the scenery, here you can hike a trail to see some ancient bristlecone pines and look south into Grand Staircase–Escalante National Monument.

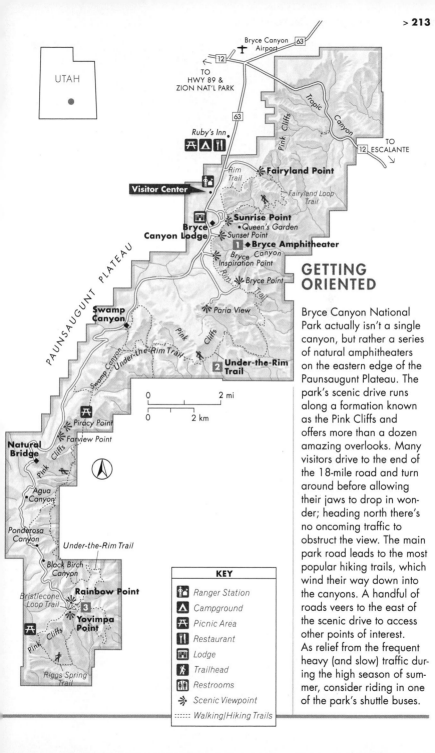

UTAH

Bryce Canyon Airport 63

TO
HWY 89 &
ZION NAT'L PARK

12

63

TO
12 ESCALANTE

Ruby's Inn

Fairyland Point

Rim Trail

Visitor Center

Fairyland Loop Trail

Bryce Canyon Lodge

Sunrise Point
Queen's Garden
Sunset Point
Bryce Amphitheater

PAUNSAUGUNT PLATEAU

Bryce Canyon Inspiration Point

Bryce Point

Rim Trail

Paria View

Swamp Canyon

Pink Cliffs

Under-the-Rim Trail

Swamp Canyon

Under-the-Rim Trail

0   2 mi
0   2 km

Piracy Point
Fairview Point

Natural Bridge

Pink Cliffs

Agua Canyon

Ponderosa Canyon

Under-the-Rim Trail

Black Birch Canyon

Bristlecone Loop Trail

Rainbow Point

Yovimpa Point

Pink Cliffs

Riggs Spring Trail

KEY

🏚	Ranger Station
🛆	Campground
🌲	Picnic Area
🍴	Restaurant
🏠	Lodge
🥾	Trailhead
🚻	Restrooms
⚓	Scenic Viewpoint
⋯⋯	Walking/Hiking Trails

GETTING ORIENTED

Bryce Canyon National Park actually isn't a single canyon, but rather a series of natural amphitheaters on the eastern edge of the Paunsaugunt Plateau. The park's scenic drive runs along a formation known as the Pink Cliffs and offers more than a dozen amazing overlooks. Many visitors drive to the end of the 18-mile road and turn around before allowing their jaws to drop in wonder; heading north there's no oncoming traffic to obstruct the view. The main park road leads to the most popular hiking trails, which wind their way down into the canyons. A handful of roads veers to the east of the scenic drive to access other points of interest. As relief from the frequent heavy (and slow) traffic during the high season of summer, consider riding in one of the park's shuttle buses.

10

Updated by Mike Weatherford

A land that captures the imagination and the heart, Bryce is a favorite among Utah's national parks. Although its splendor had been well known for decades, Bryce Canyon wasn't designated a national park until 1928. The park is named for Ebenezer Bryce, a pioneer cattleman and the first permanent settler in the area. His description of the landscape not being hospitable to cows has oft been repeated. Even more than his famous quote, however, Bryce Canyon is known for its fanciful "hoodoos," best viewed at sunrise or sunset, when the light plays off the red rock.

In geological terms, Bryce is actually an amphitheater, not a canyon. The hoodoos in the amphitheater took on their unusual shapes because the top layer of rock—"cap rock"—is harder than the layers below it. If erosion undercuts the soft rock beneath the cap too much, the hoodoo will tumble. Bryce continues to evolve today, but the hoodoos are a permanent feature; old ones may die, but new ones are constantly forming as the amphitheater rim recedes.

BRYCE CANYON PLANNER

WHEN TO GO
Around Bryce Canyon National Park and the nearby Cedar Breaks National Monument area, elevations approach and surpass 9,000 feet, making for temperamental weather, intermittent and seasonal road closures due to snow, and downright cold nights well into June. The air is cooler on the rim of the canyon than it is at lower altitudes. ■TIP→ **If you choose to see Bryce Canyon in summer, you'll be visiting with the rest of the world. During these months, traffic on the main road can be crowded with cars following slow-moving RVs, so consider taking one of the park shuttle buses.**

If it's solitude you're looking for, come to Bryce any time between October and March. The park is open all year long, so if you come during the cooler months you might just have a trail all to yourself.

AVG. HIGH/LOW TEMPS.

JAN.	FEB.	MAR.	APR.	MAY	JUNE
39/8	41/13	48/17	56/25	68/31	75/38

JULY	AUG.	SEPT.	OCT.	NOV.	DEC.
83/47	80/45	74/37	63/29	51/19	42/11

FESTIVALS AND EVENTS

FEBRUARY **Bryce Canyon Winter Festival.** This event at the Best Western Ruby's Inn features cross-country ski races, snow-sculpting contests, ski archery, and ice skating. Clinics to hone skills such as snowshoeing and photography also take place. ☎ *435/834–5341* ⊕ *www.rubysinn.com.*

JUNE **Panguitch Valley Balloon Rally.** The population of tiny Panguitch triples
FAMILY every year with this annual festival, which includes a morning launch of about 35 hot-air balloons, an evening balloon-glow, bands, food vendors, and a Harley-Davidson parade. ☎ *866/590–4134* ⊕ *www. panguitch.org.*

Quilt Walk Festival. During the bitter winter of 1864, Panguitch residents set out over the mountains to fetch provisions from the town of Parowan, 40 miles away. Legend says the men, frustrated and ready to turn back, laid a quilt on the snow and knelt to pray. Soon they realized the quilt had kept them from sinking into the snow. Spreading quilts before them as they walked, leapfrog style, the men traveled to Parowan and back. This three-day event in June commemorates the event with quilting classes, a tour of pioneer homes, and a dinner-theater production. ☎ *435/676–2651* ⊕ *www.quiltwalk.org.*

Utah Shakespearean Festival. For more than 50 years Cedar City has gone Bard-crazy, staging summer productions of Shakespeare's plays in theaters both indoors and outdoors at Southern Utah University. The Tony award–winning regional theater offers literary seminars, backstage tours, cabarets featuring festival actors, and an outdoor preshow with Elizabethan performers. Modern plays and musicals are also staged, and upcoming construction of a new open-air theater and a season now extending into fall are signs that all the world truly is a stage in little Cedar City. ☎ *435/586–7878* ⊕ *www.bard.org.*

PLANNING YOUR TIME

BRYCE CANYON IN ONE DAY

Begin your day at the **visitor center** to get an overview of the park and to purchase books and maps. Watch the video and peruse exhibits about the natural and cultural history of Bryce Canyon. Then, drive to the historic **Bryce Canyon Lodge.** From here, stroll along the relaxing **Rim Trail.** If you have the time and stamina to walk into the amphitheater, the portion of the Rim Trail near the lodge gets you to the starting point for either of the park's two essential hikes, the **Navajo Loop Trail** from **Sunset Point** or the **Queen's Garden Trail** that connects Sunset to **Sunrise Point.**

10

Afterward (or if you skip the hike), drive the 18-mile **main park road,** stopping at the overlooks along the way. Allowing for traffic, and if you stop at all 13 overlooks, this drive will take you between two and three hours.

If you have the time for more walking, a short, rolling hike along the **Bristlecone Loop Trail** at Rainbow Point rewards you with spectacular views and a cool walk through a forest of bristlecone pines. If you don't have time to drive the 18 miles to the end of the park, skip Bryce Canyon Lodge and drive 2 miles from the visitor center **to Inspiration Point** and then to the next overlook, **Bryce Point.**

End your day with sunset at Inspiration Point ordinner at Bryce Canyon Lodge. As you leave the park, stop at **Ruby's Inn** for American Indian jewelry, souvenirs for the kids, and groceries or snacks for the road.

GETTING HERE AND AROUND
AIR TRAVEL
The nearest commercial airport to Bryce Canyon is 80 miles west in Cedar City, Utah.

BUS TRAVEL
A shuttle bus system operates in Bryce Canyon from mid-May through September. Buses run every 12 to 15 minutes, and are free with your admission fee. The route stops at all the major hotels and campgrounds, as well as the visitor center and the main trailheads.

CAR TRAVEL
The closest major cities to Bryce Canyon are Salt Lake City and Las Vegas, each about 270 miles away. The park is reached via Route 63, just 3 miles south of the junction with Highway 12. You can see the park's highlights by driving along the well-maintained road running the length of the main scenic area. Bryce has no restrictions on automobiles on the main road, but in the summer you may encounter heavy traffic and full parking lots.

PARK ESSENTIALS
PARK FEES
The entrance fee is $25 per vehicle for a seven-day pass and $12 for pedestrians or bicyclists. The entrance fee includes unlimited use of the park shuttle. An annual Bryce Canyon park pass, good for one year from the date of purchase, costs $30. If you leave your private vehicle outside the park—at the shuttle staging area or Ruby's Inn— the one-time entrance fee, including transportation on the shuttle, is $25 per party.

A $5 backcountry permit, available from the visitor center, is required for camping in the park's interior, allowed only on Under-the-Rim Trail and Rigg's Spring Loop, both south of Bryce Point. Campfires are not permitted.

PARK HOURS
The park is open 24/7, year-round. It's in the Mountain time zone.

CLOSE UP

Plants and Wildlife in Bryce Canyon

Due to elevations approaching 9,000 feet, many of Bryce Canyon's 400 plant species are unlike those you'll see at less lofty places. Look at exposed slopes and you might catch a glimpse of the pygmy pinyon, or the gnarled, 1,000-year-old bristlecone pine. At lower altitudes are the Douglas fir, ponderosa pine, and the quaking aspen, sitting in groves of twinkling leaves. No fewer than three kinds of sagebrush—big, black, and fringed—grow here, as well as the blue columbine.

Mule deer and chipmunks are common companions on the trails and are used to human presence. You might also catch a glimpse of the endangered Utah prairie dog. Give them a wide berth; they may be cute, but they bite. Other animals include elk, black-tailed jackrabbits, and the desert cottontail. More than 170 species of bird live in the park or pass through as a migratory stop. Bird-watchers are often rewarded handsomely for their vigilance: eagles, peregrine falcons, and even the rare California condor have all been spotted in the park.

CELL-PHONE RECEPTION
Cell-phone reception is hit-and-miss in the park, with the visitor center and lodge your best bet. If you're getting reception, take advantage of it and make your calls; you may not have another chance. Bryce Canyon Lodge, Bryce Canyon Pines General Store, Ruby's Inn, Sunset Campground, and the visitor center all have public telephones.

RESTAURANTS
Dining options in the park proper are limited to Bryce Canyon Lodge; the nearby Ruby's Inn complex is your best eating bet before you pay to enter the park. The restaurants in nearby locales tend to be of the meat-and-potatoes variety. Utah's drinking laws can be confusing, so ask your server what is available: beer is more common than wine and spirits.

Prices in the reviews are the average cost of a main course at dinner, or if dinner is not served, at lunch.

10

HOTELS
Lodging options in and around Bryce Canyon include both rustic and modern amenities, but all fill up fast in summer. Bryce Canyon Lodge is the only hotel inside the park, but there are a number of options in Bryce Canyon City, just north of the park's entrance. Panguitch and Tropic are small towns nearby with good options for budget and last-minute travelers.

Prices in the reviews are the lowest cost of a standard double room in high season. For expanded reviews, facilities, and current deals, visit Fodors.com.

VISITOR INFORMATION
PARK CONTACT INFORMATION
Bryce Canyon National Park ☎ *435/834–5322* ⊕ *www.nps.gov/brca.*

VISITOR CENTER

Bryce Canyon Visitor Center. Even if you're anxious to hit the hoodoos, the visitor center is the best place to start if you want to know what you're looking at and how it got there. You can't miss the visitor center—the spacious building looks like a cross between a barn and a fire station. There are also multimedia exhibits, books, maps, and backcountry camping permits for sale. First aid, emergency, and lost-and-found services are offered here, along with free Wi-Fi. If you want coffee, head to nearby Ruby's Inn. ✉ *1 mile south of park entrance* ☎ *435/834–5322* ⊕ *www.nps.gov/brca* ☉ *Oct.–June, daily 8–4:30; July–Sept., daily 8–8.*

EXPLORING

SCENIC DRIVES

Fodor's Choice **Main Park Road.** Following miles of canyon rim, this thoroughfare gives
★ access to more than a dozen scenic overlooks between the park entrance and Rainbow Point. Major overlooks are rarely more than a few minutes' walk from the parking areas, and many let you see more than 100 miles on clear days. ■TIP→ Remember that all overlooks lie east of the road—to keep things simple, proceed to the southern end of the park and stop at the overlooks on your northbound return. Allow two to three hours to travel the entire 36 miles round-trip. The road is open year-round, but may close temporarily after heavy snowfalls. Keep your eyes open for wildlife as you drive. Trailers are not allowed beyond Sunset Campground, but you can park them at the visitor center. RVs can drive throughout the park, but vehicles longer than 25 feet are not allowed at Paria View.

HISTORIC SITES

Bryce Canyon Lodge. The lodge's architect, Gilbert Stanley Underwood, was a national park specialist, having designed lodges at Zion and Grand Canyon before turning his T-square to Bryce in 1923. The results are worth a visit, even if you plan to sleep elsewhere, as this National Historic Landmark has been faithfully restored, right down to the lobby's huge limestone fireplace and log and wrought-iron chandelier. The bark-covered hickory furniture isn't original, but renovators ordered it from the same company that created the originals. Inside the historic building are a restaurant and a gift shop, as well as plenty of information on park activities. Guests of the lodge can stay in the numerous log cabins on the wooded grounds. ✉ *Rte. 63, 2 miles south of park entrance* ☎ *435/834–8700.*

SCENIC STOPS

Agua Canyon. This overlook in the southern section of the park has a nice view of several standout hoodoos. Look for the top-heavy formation called The Hunter, which actually has a few small hardy trees

growing on its cap. As the rock erodes, the park evolves; snap a picture because The Hunter may look different the next time you visit. ⊠ *12 miles south of park entrance.*

Bryce Point. After absorbing views of the Black Mountains and Navajo Mountain, you can follow the Under-the-Rim-Trail and go exploring down in the amphitheater to the cluster of top-heavy hoodoos known collectively as the Hat Shop. Take a left and hike the challenging Peekaboo Loop Trail with its geological highlight, the **Wall of Windows.** Openings carved into a wall of rock illustrate the drama of erosion that formed Bryce Canyon. ⊠ *5½ miles south of park entrance on Inspiration Point Rd.*

GOOD READS

Bryce Canyon Auto and Hiking Guide, by Tully Stroud, includes information on the geology and history of the area.

Supplement the free park map with *Bryce Canyon Hiking Guide,* which includes an amphitheater hiking map and aerial photo.

To prepare kids ages 5–10 for a trip to the park, consider ordering the 32-page *Kid's Guide to Bryce Canyon.*

Fairyland Point. Just north of the visitor center, this scenic overlook atop Boat Mesa is a great first stop after you enter the park. There are splendid views of Fairyland Amphitheater and its delicate, fanciful forms. The Sinking Ship and other formations stand before the grand backdrop of the Aquarius Plateau and distant Navajo Mountain. Nearby is the Fairyland Loop trailhead; it's a stunning five-hour hike in summer and a favorite of cross-country skiers in winter. ⊠ *1 mile off main park road, 1 mile north of visitor center.*

Inspiration Point. Not far at all (0.3 miles) east along the Rim Trail from Bryce Point is Inspiration Point, site of a wonderful vista on the main amphitheater and one of the best places in the park to see the sunset. ⊠ *5 miles south of park entrance on Inspiration Point Rd.*

Natural Bridge. The Natural Bridge is an 85-foot arch formation—one of several rock arches in the park—and an essential photo op. The rusty-orange flying buttress formed over millions of years by wind, water, and chemical erosion. Beyond the parking lot lies a rare stand of aspen trees, whose leaves twinkle in the wind. ⚠ **Watch out for distracted drivers at this stunning viewpoint.** ⊠ *11 miles south of park entrance.*

Rainbow and Yovimpa Points. Separated by less than a mile, Rainbow and Yovimpa points offer two fine panoramas facing opposite directions. Rainbow Point's best view is to the north overlooking the southern rim of the amphitheater and giving a glimpse of Grand Staircase–Escalante National Monument. Yovimpa Point's vista spreads out to the south. On a clear day you can see all the way to Arizona, 100 miles away. Yovimpa Point also has a shady and quiet picnic area with tables and restrooms. Hike between them on the Bristlecone Loop Trail or take the more strenuous 8.5-mile Riggs Spring Loop Trail past the tallest point in the park. ⊠ *18 miles south of park entrance.*

Fodor's Choice
★
Sunrise Point. Named for its stunning views at dawn, this overlook is a short walk from the lodge and so one of the park's most popular stops. It's also the trailhead for the Queen's Garden Trail and the Fairyland Loop Trail. You have to descend the Queen's Garden Trail to get a regal glimpse of **Queen Victoria,** a hoodoo that appears to sport a crown and glorious full skirt. The trail is popular and marked clearly, but moderately strenuous with 300 feet of elevation change. ✉ *2 miles south of park entrance near Bryce Canyon Lodge.*

Sunset Point. Watch the late-day sun paint the hoodoos here. You can only see **Thor's Hammer,** a delicate formation similar to a balanced rock, when you hike 521 feet down into the amphitheater on the Navajo Loop Trail. ✉ *2 miles south of park entrance near Bryce Canyon Lodge.*

EDUCATIONAL OFFERINGS

RANGER PROGRAMS

Campfire and Auditorium Programs. Bryce Canyon's natural diversity comes alive in the park's North Campground, the adjacent amphitheaters, or at Bryce Canyon Lodge. Lectures, slide programs, and ranger walks introduce you to geology, astronomy, wildlife, history, and many other topics related to Bryce Canyon and the West. (In the winter, the programs move to the visitor center.) ☎ *435/834–5322.*

Canyon Hike. June to August, a ranger-led tour of the Queen's Garden or Navajo Loop Trail, stopping at multiple points along the way, explains the amphitheater's features and formations. The hike is 2–3 miles long and takes two to three hours to complete.

Full Moon Hike. Rangers lead guided hikes on the nights around each full moon (two in the summer, one in the winter). You must wear heavy-traction shoes, and you must reserve a spot at the visitor center on the day of the hike. ■ TIP→ **These free tours are a popular activity, so sign up early.**

Geology Talk. Rangers regularly host discussions about the long geologic history of Bryce Canyon; they are nearly always held at Sunset Point. Talks are free and last 30 minutes.

FAMILY **Junior Ranger Program.** Between Memorial Day and Labor Day, children ages 6 to 12 can sign up to be Junior Rangers at the Bryce Canyon Visitor Center. The park takes that title seriously, so kids have to complete several activities such as taking a hike or attending a lecture on fire safety, water conservation, or wildlife identification. Allow three to six hours for children to work their way through the requirements. Schedules of events and topics are posted at the visitor center, Bryce Canyon Lodge, and on North and Sunset campgrounds bulletin boards.

Fodor's Choice
★
Night Sky Program. Cityfolk are lucky to see 2,500 stars in their artificially illuminated skies. Among the hoodoos you see three times as many. The Night Sky Program includes low-key astronomy lectures and multimedia presentations, followed by telescope viewing. ☎ *435/834–4747.*

Rim Walk. Join a park ranger for a 1-mile stroll along the gorgeous rim of Bryce Canyon. The walk lasts about 90 minutes.

10

SPORTS AND THE OUTDOORS

Most visitors explore Bryce Canyon by car, but the hiking trails are far more rewarding. At these elevations, you'll have to stop to catch your breath more often than you're used to. It gets warm in summer but rarely uncomfortably hot, so hiking farther into the depths of the park is not difficult so long as you don't pick a hike that is beyond your abilities.

AIR TOURS

OUTFITTERS

Bryce Canyon Airlines & Helicopters. For a bird's-eye view of Bryce Canyon National Park, take a dramatic helicopter ride or airplane tour over the fantastic sandstone formations. Longer full-canyon tours and added excursions to sites such as the Grand Canyon, Monument Valley, or Zion are also offered. Flight time can last anywhere from 35 minutes to 4 hours; family and group rates are available. Tours start at $110. ☎ *435/834–8060* ⊕ *rubysinn.com/bryce-canyon-airlines.html.*

BIRD-WATCHING

More than 170 bird species have been identified in Bryce. Violet green swallows and white-throated swifts are common, as are Steller's jays, American coots, rufous hummingbirds, and mountain bluebirds. Lucky bird-watchers will see golden eagles floating across the skies above the pink rocks of the amphitheater, and experienced birders might spot an osprey nest high in the canyon wall. The best time in the park for avian variety is from May through July.

HIKING

To get up close and personal with the park's hoodoos, set aside a half day to hike into the amphitheater. There are no elevators, so remember that after you descend below the rim you'll have to get back up. The air gets warmer the lower you go, and the altitude will have you huffing and puffing unless you're a mountain native. The uneven terrain calls for lace-up shoes on even the well-trodden, high-traffic trails and sturdy hiking boots for the more challenging ones. No below-rim trails are paved. For trail maps, information, and ranger recommendations, stop at the visitor center. Bathrooms are at most trailheads but not down in the amphitheater.

EASY

Bristlecone Loop Trail. This 1-mile trail with a modest 100 feet of elevation gain alternates between spruce and fir forest and wide-open vistas of the Paunsaugunt Plateau and beyond. You might see yellow-bellied marmots and blue grouse, critters not found at lower elevations in the park. The most challenging part of the hike is ungluing your eyes from the scenery long enough to read the signage at the many trail forks. Plan on 45 minutes to an hour. *Easy.* ⊠ *Trailhead at Rainbow Point parking area, 18 miles south of park entrance.*

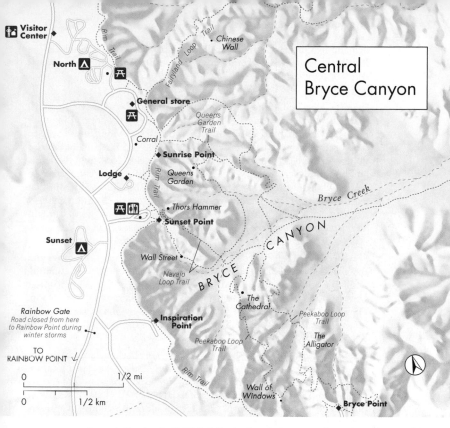

Central
Bryce Canyon

Visitor Center
North △
General store
Corral
Sunrise Point
Lodge ◆
Queens Garden
Thors Hammer
Sunset Point
Sunset △
Wall Street
Navajo Loop Trail
Rainbow Gate
Road closed from here to Rainbow Point during winter storms
TO RAINBOW POINT
Inspiration Point
Peekaboo Loop Trail
Rim Trail
Fairyland Loop Trail
Chinese Wall
Queens Garden Trail
Bryce Creek
BRYCE CANYON
The Cathedral
Peekaboo Loop Trail
The Alligator
Wall of Windows
Bryce Point

0   1/2 mi
0   1/2 km

FAMILY **Queen's Garden Trail.** This hike is the easiest way down into the amphitheater. Three hundred feet of elevation change will lead you to a short tunnel, quirky hoodoos, and lots of like minded hikers. Allow two hours total to hike the 1.5-mile trail plus the 0.5-mile rimside path back to the parking area. *Easy.* ⊠ *Trailhead at Sunrise Point, 2 miles south of park entrance.*

MODERATE

Navajo Loop Trail. One of Bryce's most popular and dramatic attractions is this steep descent via a series of switchbacks leading to Wall Street, a claustrophobic hallway of rock only 20-feet wide in places with walls 100-feet high. After a walk through the Silent City, the northern end of the trail brings Thor's Hammer into view. The trail leads to a well-marked intersection offering a shorter way back or continuing on the longer Queens Garden Trail to Sunset Point. For the short version allow at least an hour on this 1.5-mile trail with 500 feet of elevation change. *Moderate.* ⊠ *Trailhead at Sunset Point, 2 miles south of park entrance.*

Fodor's Choice **Navajo/Queen's Garden Combination Loop.** By walking this extended
★ 3-mile loop, you can see some of the best of Bryce; it takes more than two hours. The route passes fantastic formations and an open forest of pine and juniper on the amphitheater floor. Descend into the amphitheater from Sunset Point on the Navajo Trail and ascend via the less

10

demanding Queen's Garden Trail; return to your starting point via the Rim Trail. *Moderate.* ⊠ *Trailheads at Sunset and Sunrise points, 2 miles south of park entrance.*

DIFFICULT

Fairyland Loop Trail. Hike into whimsical Fairyland Canyon on this trail that gets more strenuous and less crowded as you progress along its 8 miles. It winds around hoodoos, across trickles of water, and finally to a natural window in the rock at Tower Bridge, 1.5 miles from Sunrise Point and 4 miles from Fairyland Point. The pink-and-white badlands and hoodoos surround you the whole way. Don't feel like you have to go the whole distance to make it worthwhile. But if you do, allow at least five hours for the round trip with 1,000 feet of elevation change. You can pick up the loop at Fairyland Point or Sunrise Point. *Difficult.* ⊠ *Trailhead at Fairyland Point, 1 mile off main park road, 1 mile south of park entrance; Sunrise Point, 2 miles south of park entrance.*

Peekaboo Loop. The reward of this steep trail is the Wall of Windows and the Three Wise Men. ■ TIP➔ Horses use this trail in spring, summer, and fall—and have the right-of-way. Start at Bryce, Sunrise, or Sunset Point and allow four to five hours to hike the 5-mile trail or 7-mile loop. *Difficult.* ⊠ *Trailheads at Bryce Point, 2 miles off main park road, 5 miles south of park entrance; Sunrise and Sunset points, 2 miles south of park entrance.*

Riggs Spring Loop Trail. One of the park's two true backpacker's trails, this rigorous 9-mile path has an overnight option at the Riggs Spring campsite. You'll journey past groves of twinkling aspen trees and the eponymous spring close to the campsite. Start at either Yovimpa or Rainbow points and be prepared for 1,500 feet of elevation change. Campers need to check in at the visitor center ahead of time for backcountry permits. *Difficult.* ⊠ *Trailheads at Yovimpa and Rainbow points, 18 miles south of park entrance.*

Tower Bridge. This short, uncrowded hike on the Fairyland Loop Trail takes you to a natural bridge deep in the amphitheater. Walk through pink and white badlands with hoodoos all around on this 3-mile trip that takes two to three hours. Some navigation required; it's not quite a loop. *Difficult.* ⊠ *Trailhead at Sunrise Point, 1 mile off the main park road, south of the park entrance.*

Trail to the Hat Shop. The sedimentary haberdashery sits 2 miles from the trailhead. Hard gray caps balance precariously atop narrow pedestals of softer, rust-colored rock. Allow three to four hours to travel this strenuous but rewarding 4-mile round-trip trail, the first part of the longer Under-the-Rim Trail. *Difficult.* ⊠ *Trailhead at Bryce Point, 2 miles off main park road, 5 miles south of park entrance.*

Under-the-Rim Trail. Starting at Bryce Point, the trail travels 22.5 miles to Rainbow Point, passing through the Pink Cliffs, traversing Agua Canyon and Ponderosa Canyon, and taking you by several springs. Most of the hike is on the amphitheater floor, characterized by up-and-down terrain among stands of ponderosa pine; the elevation change totals about 1,500 feet. Four trailheads along the main park road allow you to connect to the Under-the-Rim Trail and cover its length as a series of

Hikers in Bryce are rewarded with vistas highlighting the park's colorful landscape.

day hikes. Allow at least two days to hike the route in its entirety, and although it's not a hoodoo-heavy hike there's plenty to see to make it a more leisurely three-day affair. *Difficult.* ⊠ *Trailheads at Bryce Point, Swamp Canyon, Ponderosa Canyon, and Rainbow Point.*

HORSEBACK RIDING

Many of the park's hiking trails were first formed beneath the hooves of cattle wranglers. Today, hikers and riders share the trails. A number of outfitters can set you up with a gentle mount and lead you to the park's best sights. Not only can you cover more ground than you would walking, but equine traffic has the right-of-way at all times. Call ahead to the stables for reservations to find a trip that's right for you, from half an hour to overnight. The biggest outfitters have more than 100 horses and mules to choose from. People under the age of 7 or who weigh more than 220 pounds are prohibited from riding.

TOURS AND OUTFITTERS

Canyon Trail Rides. These rides descend to the floor of the Bryce Canyon amphitheater via horse or mule. Most visitors have no riding experience, so don't hesitate to join in. A $60 two-hour ride ambles along the amphitheater floor to the Fairy Castle before returning to Sunrise Point. The $80 half-day expedition follows Peekaboo Loop Trail, winds past the Fairy Castle and the Alligator, and passes the Wall of Windows before returning to Sunrise Point. Two rides a day of each type leave in the morning and early afternoon. Trips can now be booked online; there are no rides in winter. ⊠ *Bryce Canyon Lodge* ☎ *435/679–8665* ⊕ *www.canyonrides.com.*

FAMILY **Ruby's Horseback Adventures.** Mount up and retrace trails taken by out-law Butch Cassidy in Red Canyon National Forest, Bryce Canyon, or Grand Staircase–Escalante National Monument on Ruby's Horseback Adventures rides, which last from one hour to all day. Riders must be 7 or older. ☎ 866/782–0002 ⊕ *www.horserides.net.*

WINTER SPORTS

Unlike Utah's other national parks, Bryce Canyon receives plenty of snow, making it a popular cross-country ski area. Rim Trail, Paria Loop, and other paths above the canyon are popular destinations. The visitor center sells shoe-traction devices, and some of the ranger-guided snowshoe activities include snowshoes and poles.

OUTFITTERS

Ruby's Winter Activities Center. This facility grooms miles of private trails that connect to the ungroomed trails inside the park. Rental snowshoes, ice skates, and cross-country ski equipment are available. ⊠ *Rte. 63, 1 mile north of park entrance, Bryce* ☎ *435/834–5341* ⊕ *www.rubysinn. com/winter.html.*

WHAT'S NEARBY

Bryce Canyon is a bit off the beaten path, often a side trip for those who visit Zion National Park to the southwest, and far from major roads or large cities (both Las Vegas and Salt Lake City are approximately 270 miles away). The park is just one of a number of beautiful or unique natural areas in southern Utah worth exploring. Towns close to the park pulse with Western personality and are excellent bases for exploring the entire area. To the west, Red Canyon offers an array of activities not available inside the park, such as mountain biking. The expansive and remote Grand Staircase–Escalante National Monument is about an hour to the northeast. Nearby state parks are great side trips: Escalante Petrified Forest and Kodachrome Basin.

NEARBY TOWNS

Panguitch calls itself the "Center of Scenic Utah," and it's an accurate moniker. The small town, 25 miles from Bryce Canyon, boasts restaurants, motels, gas stations, and trinket shops. About 47 miles northeast of Bryce, **Escalante** has modern amenities and is a western gateway to the Grand Staircase–Escalante National Monument. If you're traveling through southwestern Utah on Interstate 15, **Cedar City** will be your exit to Bryce. The largest city you'll encounter in this part of Utah, it's 78 miles from Bryce Canyon. Southern Utah University is here, and the Utah Shakespeare Festival on its campus draws theater buffs from all over the country.

VISITOR INFORMATION

Garfield County Travel Council (Escalante, Panguitch) ⊠ *55 S. Main St., Panguitch* ☎ *435/676–1102, 800/444–6689* ⊕ *www.brycecanyoncountry.com.* **Cedar City/Brian Head Tourism Bureau** ⊠ *581 N. Main St., Cedar City* ☎ *800/354–4849, 435/586–5124* ⊕ *www.scenicsouthernutah.com.*

NEARBY ATTRACTIONS

Cedar Breaks National Monument. From the rim of Cedar Breaks, a natural amphitheater similar to Bryce Canyon plunges 2,000 feet into the Markagunt Plateau. Short alpine hiking trails along the rim make this a wonderful summer stop. ⊠ *Rte. 14, 23 miles east of Cedar City, Brian Head* ☎ *435/586–0787* ⊕ *www.nps.gov/cebr* ✉ *$4* ⊙ *Visitor center: late May–mid-Oct., daily 9–6; closed mid-Oct.–Apr.*

Dixie National Forest. This expansive natural area divided into four noncontiguous swaths covers a total of two million acres. Adjacent to three national parks, two national monuments, and several state parks, this area has 26 campgrounds in a variety of backdrops: lakeside, mountainside, in the depths of pine and spruce forests. Recreational opportunities abound, including hiking, camping, picnicking, horseback riding, and fishing. ⊠ *Dixie National Forest Headquarters, 1789 N. Wedgewood La., Cedar City* ☎ *435/865–3700, 800/280–2267 for campground information* ⊕ *www.fs.usda. gov/dixie* ✉ *Free.*

FAMILY **Escalante Petrified Forest State Park.** About 48 miles east of Bryce Canyon, this state park was created to protect a huge repository of petrified wood, which is easily spotted along two moderate-to-strenuous interpretive hiking trails. There's an attractive swimming beach at the park's Wide Hollow Reservoir, which is also good for boating, fishing, and birding, and a campground with hookup sites. ⊠ *710 N. Reservoir Rd., Escalante* ☎ *435/826–4466, 800/322-3770 for camping reservations* ⊕ *www.stateparks.utah.gov* ✉ *$7* ⊙ *Daily 6 am–10 pm.*

Grand Staircase–Escalante National Monument. In September 1996, President Bill Clinton designated 1.7 million acres in south-central Utah as Grand Staircase–Escalante National Monument. Its three distinct sections—the Grand Staircase, the Kaiparowits Plateau, and the Canyons of the Escalante—offer remote backcountry experiences hard to find elsewhere in the Lower 48. Waterfalls, shoulder-width slot canyons, and improbable colors all characterize this wilderness. Highway 12, which straddles the northern border of the monument, is one of the most scenic stretches in the Southwest. The small towns of Escalante and Boulder offer outfitters, lodging, and dining.

Larger than most national parks, this formidable monument is popular with backpackers, hikers, canyoneers, and hard-core mountain-bike enthusiasts. Views into the monument are most impressive from Highway 12 between Escalante and Boulder. Calf Creek Falls is an easy 6-mile round-trip hike from the trailhead at Calf Creek Recreation Area. At the end of your walk, a large waterfall explodes over a cliff hundreds of feet above. ⊠ *Kanab* ☎ *435/644–6400* ⊕ *www.blm. gov/ut/st/en/fo/grand_staircase-escalante.html* ✉ *Free.*

Kodachrome Basin State Park. As soon as you see it, you'll understand why the park earned this colorful photographic name from the National Geographic Society. The sand pipes here cannot be found anywhere else in the world. Hike any of the trails to spot some of the 67 pipes in and around the park. The short Angels Palace Trail takes you quickly

10

into the park's interior, up, over, and around some of the badlands. ✉ *Cottonwood Canyon Rd., Cannonville* ☎ *435/679–8562* ⊕ *www. stateparks.utah.gov* 🖅 *$6* ⊙ *Daily 6 am–10 pm.*

AREA ACTIVITIES

SPORTS AND THE OUTDOORS

BICYCLING

Hell's Backbone Road. This mountain-bike ride follows the 44-mile Hell's Backbone Road from Panguitch to the Escalante region and beyond. The route, also known as Highway 12, gives riders stunning views and a half dozen kitschy townships as a reward for the steep grades. The road begins 7 miles south of Panguitch.

TOURS AND OUTFITTERS

Excursions of Escalante. Hiking and canyoneering tours are custom-fit to your needs by Excursions of Escalante, whose specialty is taking canyoneers into the slot canyons to move through slot chutes or rappel down walls and other obstacles. All gear is provided, and trips last from one day to a week. Tours explore areas in and around Grand Staircase– Escalante, Glen Canyon, and the Death Hollow Wilderness area. ✉ *125 E. Main St., Escalante* ☎ *800/839–7567* ⊕ *www.excursionsofescalante. com* ⊙ *Mid-Apr.–mid-Nov.*

SCENIC DRIVES

Fodor'sChoice ★

Highway 12 Scenic Byway. Keep your camera handy and steering wheel steady along this route between Escalante and Loa, near Capitol Reef National Park. Though the highway starts at the intersection of U.S. 89, west of Bryce Canyon National Park, the stretch that begins in Escalante is one of the most spectacular. The road passes through Grand Staircase–Escalante National Monument and on to Capitol Reef along one of the most scenic stretches of highway in the United States. Be sure to stop at the scenic overlooks; almost every one will give you an eye-popping view. ⚠ Don't get distracted, though; the paved road is twisting and steep, and at times climbs over a hogback with sheer drop-offs on both sides.

U.S. 89/Utah's Heritage Highway. Winding north from the Arizona border all the way to Spanish Fork Canyon an hour south of Salt Lake City, U.S. 89 is known as the Heritage Highway for its role in shaping Utah history. At its southern end, Kanab is known as "Little Hollywood," having provided the backdrop for many famous Western movies and TV commercials. The town has since grown considerably to accommodate tourists who flock here to see where Ronald Reagan once slept and Clint Eastwood drew his guns. Other towns north along this famous road may not have the same notoriety in these parts, but they do provide a quiet, uncrowded, and inexpensive place to stay near Zion and Bryce Canyon National Parks. East of Kanab, U.S. 89 runs along the southern edge of the Grand Staircase–Escalante National Monument.

WHERE TO EAT

IN THE PARK

$$$ AMERICAN

🍴 **Bryce Canyon Lodge.** Set among towering pines, this rustic old lodge is the featured place to dine within the park. The menu changes each year, but always uses organic foods, emphasizing local choices such as Utah trout and ranging from prime rib to vegetarian-friendly quinoa primavera. A beer and wine selection includes Utah microbrews. No reservations are accepted, so you may encounter a wait. [$] *Average main: $24* ✉ *Rte. 63, 2 miles south of park entrance* ☎ *435/834–8700* 🌐 *www.brycecanyonforever.com* ✍ *Reservations not accepted* ⏲ *Closed Nov.–Mar.*

$ ITALIAN FAMILY

🍴 **Valhalla Pizzeria & Coffee Shop.** Addressing the need for a family-friendly, fast-casual alternative to Bryce Canyon Lodge's formal dining, a former recreation room across the parking lot from the lodge was converted into this 40-seat pizzeria and coffee shop. The patio is a nice place to have a beer or glass of wine in balmy weather (as long as you buy at least a banana to go with it, thanks to Utah liquor laws). In addition to pizza, the menu includes calzones, lasagna, salads, appetizers, and desserts. Valhalla lies on the edge of a parking lot south of the lodge. Hours are odd: daily 6–11:30 and 3–10. [$] *Average main: $10* ✉ *2 miles south of park entrance (shares parking with lodge)* ☎ *435/834–8709* 🌐 *www.brycecanyonforever.com/lodge-pizza* ✍ *Reservations not accepted.*

PICNIC AREAS

North Campground. On the south side of the campground, this picnic area in the shade of the ponderosa pines has tables and grills along with fresh-water taps. ✉ *About ¼ mile south of the visitor center.*

Yovimpa Point. At the southern end of the park, this shady, quiet spot looks out onto the 100-mile vistas from the rim. There are tables and restrooms. ✉ *18 miles south of the park entrance.*

10

OUTSIDE THE PARK

$ AMERICAN

🍴 **Bryce Canyon Restaurant.** Part of the Bryce Canyon Pines motel, this cozy eatery offers homemade soups like cream of broccoli and corn chowder, or settle down for a steak and mashed potatoes. They are known for their delicious homemade pies. [$] *Average main: $12* ✉ *Hwy. 12, about 15 miles west from Tropic* ☎ *800/892–7923* 🌐 *www.brycecanyonmotel.com.*

$ ITALIAN Fodor's Choice ★

🍴 **Centro Woodfired Pizzeria.** You can watch your handmade thin-crust pizza being pulled from the fires of the brick oven, then sit back and enjoy a seasonal pie layered with locally grown figs, prosciutto, and asiago cheese, or try year-round selections featuring roasted crimini mushrooms or Italian sopressata salami. The creamy vanilla gelato layered with a balsamic reduction and sea salt can actually be addictive. Wine and beer selections are offered as well. [$] *Average main: $12* ✉ *50 W. University Blvd., Cedar City* ☎ *435/867–8123* ✍ *Reservations not accepted* ⏲ *Closed Sun.*

$$ AMERICAN 🍴 **Cowboy Blues.** Step back into the Old West for basic but bountiful American food in this rustic restaurant adorned with ranching memorabilia. Steaks, ribs, and Utah trout dominate the dinner menu. The only full liquor license in Escalante allows beer, wine, and cocktails to be served. [$] *Average main: $13* ✉ *530 W. Main St., Escalante* ☎ *435/826–4577* 🌐 *www.cowboyblues.net* ✍ *Reservations not accepted.*

$$ AMERICAN 🍴 **Cowboy's Smokehouse Café.** This barbeque joint includes mesquite-smoked beef, pork, turkey, and chicken, and a secret sauce with no fewer than 15 ingredients. The menu is rounded out by burgers, salads, and homemade peach or blackberry cobbler—that is, if you have room for dessert. [$] *Average main: $20* ✉ *95 N. Main St., Panguitch* ☎ *435/676–8030* 🌐 *www.cowboyssmokehousecafe.com* 🕒 *Closed Sun.*

$$ CAFÉ 🍴 **Esca-Latte Internet Cafe & Pizza Parlor.** When you're spent after a day of exploration, there's no better place to sit back and relax with friends than this eatery at Escalante Outfitters. Try one of the pizzas, which are known for fresh, local ingredients such as applewood bacon and slow-roasted tomatoes, and pair it with an icy Utah microbrew. There are also sandwiches, salads, baked goods, and perhaps the best cup of coffee in town. [$] *Average main: $17* ✉ *310 W. Main St., Escalante* ☎ *435/826–4266* 🌐 *www.escalanteoutfitters.com/restaurant.*

$$ STEAKHOUSE 🍴 **Foster's Family Steakhouse.** This steak house is known for its prime rib and sautéed mushrooms, and a namesake mixed-berry pie that includes raspberries, rhubarb, and strawberries. Seafood dishes are also on the menu, as are beer and wine, and you can take home homemade breads and pastries. [$] *Average main: $15* ✉ *1150 Hwy. 12, 2 miles west of junction with Rte. 63, Panguitch* ☎ *435/834–5227* 🌐 *www.fostersmotel.com* 🕒 *Closed Mon.–Thurs. in Jan.*

$$ AMERICAN 🍴 **Harold's Place.** About 15 miles west of Bryce Canyon, this log cabin stands at the entrance to Red Canyon. It's the perfect pit stop, with a full-service restaurant, and no-frills rooms and cabins. The expansive dinner menu includes a variety of steaks, pork chops, and seafood, as well as tasty salads. Try Harold's Favorite for breakfast: eggs any way you like, potatoes, your choice of meat. [$] *Average main: $15* ✉ *3066 Hwy. 12, 7 miles south of Panguitch* ☎ *435/676–2350* 🌐 *www.haroldsplace.net* 🕒 *Closed mid-Oct.–mid-Mar. No lunch.*

$$$ AMERICAN Fodor's Choice ★ 🍴 **Milt's Stage Stop.** Locals and an increasing number of tourists have discovered the terrific food at this dinner spot in beautiful Cedar Canyon, about 78 miles from Bryce Canyon. It's known for ribeye steaks, prime rib, fajita platters, and seafood dishes. In winter, deer feed in front of the restaurant as a fireplace blazes away inside. A number of hunting trophies decorate the rustic building's interior, and splendid views of the surrounding mountains delight patrons year-round. The dining room serves beer, wine, and liquor. [$] *Average main: $25* ✉ *3560 E. Hwy. 14, Cedar City* ☎ *435/586–9344* 🌐 *www.miltsstagestop.com* ✍ *Reservations essential* 🕒 *No lunch.*

CLOSE UP

Best Campgrounds in Bryce Canyon

The two campgrounds in Bryce Canyon National Park fill up fast, especially in summer, and are family-friendly. All are drive-in, except for the handful of backcountry sites that only backpackers and gung-ho day hikers ever see. Both campgrounds completed a welcome renovation of their restrooms and shared facilities in 2012.

North Campground. A cool, shady retreat in a forest of ponderosa pines, this is a great home base for your exploration of Bryce Canyon. You're near the general store, trailheads, and the visitor center. ✉ *Main park rd. ½ mile south of visitor center* ☎ *435/834–5322.*

Sunset Campground. This serene alpine campground is within walking distance of Bryce Canyon Lodge and many trailheads. All sites are filled on a first-come, first-served basis. ✉ *Main park rd., 2 miles south of visitor center* ☎ *435/834–5322.*

WHERE TO STAY

IN THE PARK

$$$ HOTEL Fodor's Choice ★ 🏨 **Bryce Canyon Lodge.** A few feet from the amphitheater's rim and trailheads is this rugged stone-and-wood lodge with suites on the lodge's second level, motel-style rooms with balconies or porches in separate buildings, and cozy lodgepole-pine cabins, some with cathedral ceilings and gas fireplaces. **Pros:** only lodging inside the park; friendly and attentive staff; cabins have fireplaces. **Cons:** closed in the winter; books up fast; grounds can be dark at night, so bring a flashlight to dinner. [$] *Rooms from: $175* ✉ *2 miles south of park entrance* ☎ *435/834–8700, 877/386–4383* 🌐 *www.brycecanyonforever.com/lodging* 🛏 *70 rooms, 3 suites, 40 cabins* 🕓 *Closed Nov.–Mar.*

OUTSIDE THE PARK

$$ B&B/INN 🏨 **Bard's Inn Bed and Breakfast.** Rooms in this restored turn-of-the-20th-century house are named after famous females from Shakespeare's plays. **Pros:** immaculate rooms; good restaurant next door; enforced quiet at night. **Cons:** thin walls and creaky floors; Shakespeare is everywhere you look; books up fast for festival season. [$] *Rooms from: $119* ✉ *150 S. 100 West St., Cedar City* ☎ *435/586–6612* 🌐 *www.thebardsinn.com* 🛏 *12 rooms* 🍴 *Breakfast.*

$$$ HOTEL 🏨 **Best Western Bryce Canyon Grand Hotel.** If you're into creature comforts but can do without charm, this four-story hotel is the place: rooms are relatively posh, with comfortable mattresses, pillows, and bedding, spacious bathrooms, and modern appliances. **Pros:** clean and squared away; lots of indoor amenities. **Cons:** little personality; no pets allowed. [$] *Rooms from: $169* ✉ *30 N. 100 East, Bryce* ☎ *866/866–6636, 435/834–5700* 🌐 *www.brycecanyongrand.com* 🛏 *164 rooms* 🍴 *Breakfast.*

$$ ⛺ **Best Western Ruby's Inn.** As the park has grown more popular, so has
HOTEL   Ruby's Inn, expanding over the years to include various wings with
rooms that vary widely in terms of size and appeal but are consistently
comfortable. **Pros:** a good place to mingle with other park visitors and
swap canyon adventure stories. **Cons:** the lobby can get very busy,
especially when the big tour buses roll in. ⓢ *Rooms from: $110* ✉ *26
S. Main St., Bryce* ☎ *435/834–5341, 866/866–6616* ⊕ *www.rubysinn.
com* ⇆ *383 rooms, 2 suites.*

$$ ⛺ **Escalante's Grand Staircase Bed & Breakfast Inn.** Rooms are set apart
B&B/INN   from the main house, giving this property some motel privacy along
with B&B amenities. **Pros:** spacious rooms; wireless Internet; cute
back porch for horizon gazing. **Cons:** the rooms are packed in tight.
ⓢ *Rooms from: $142* ✉ *280 W. Main St., Escalante* ☎ *435/826–4890*
⊕ *www.escalantebnb.com* ⇆ *8 rooms* ⦿| *Breakfast.*

$ ⛺ **Escalante Outfitters.** This is a good option if you want a one-stop shop
HOTEL   to plan and gear up for your outdoor adventure or if you're on a budget
and don't care about amenities: the seven log bunkhouse cabins share
a single bathhouse. **Pros:** the food is a pleasant surprise; store and bike
rentals on site; pet friendly. **Cons:** right on the highway; communal
showers mean you may have to wait in line. ⓢ *Rooms from: $45* ✉ *310
W. Main St., Escalante* ☎ *435/826–4266* ⊕ *www.escalanteoutfitters.
com* ⇆ *7 cabins.*

$ ⛺ **Marianna Inn.** You can relax on the large covered patio at this motel,
HOTEL   which offers cabin-style lodging with rooms of one to four beds. **Pros:**
FAMILY   lovely cedar patio; cooling ceiling fans. **Cons:** tiny rooms. ⓢ *Rooms
from: $60* ✉ *699 N. Main St., Panguitch* ☎ *435/676–8844* ⊕ *www.
mariannainn.com* ⇆ *31 rooms.*

CANYONLANDS
NATIONAL PARK

WELCOME TO CANYONLANDS

TOP REASONS TO GO

★ **Endless vistas:** The view from the Island in the Sky stretches for miles as you look out over millennia of sculpting by wind and rain.

★ **Seeking solitude:** Needles, the most interesting part of the park to explore on foot, sees very few visitors, so you'll have it all to yourself.

★ **Radical rides:** The Cataract Canyon rapids and the White Rim Trail are world-class adventures by boat or bike.

★ **American Indian artifacts:** View rock art and Ancestral Puebloan dwellings in the park.

★ **Wonderful wilderness:** Some of the country's most untouched landscapes are within the park's boundaries, and they're worth the extra effort needed to get there.

★ **The night skies:** Far away from city lights, Canyonlands is ideal for stargazing.

1 Island in the Sky. From any of the overlooks here you can see for miles and look down thousands of feet to canyon floors. Chocolate-brown canyons are capped by white rock, and deep-red monuments rise nearby.

2 Needles. Pink, orange, and red rock is layered with white rock and stands in spires and pinnacles around grassy meadows. Extravagantly red mesas and buttes interrupt the horizon, as in a picture postcard of the Old West.

3 The Maze. Only the most intrepid adventurers explore this incredibly remote mosaic of rock formations. There's a reason Butch Cassidy hid out here.

4 Rivers. For many, rafting through the waterways is the best way to see the park. The Green and Colorado are as wild as when John Wesley Powell explored them in the mid-1800s.

5 Horseshoe Canyon. Plan on several hours of dirt-road driving to get here, but the famous rock art panel "Great Gallery" is a grand reward at the end of a long hike.

GETTING ORIENTED

Canyonlands National Park, in southeastern Utah, is divided into three distinct land districts and the river district, so it can be a little daunting to visit. It's exhausting, but not impossible, to explore the Island in the Sky and Needles in the same day.

KEY	
🏠	*Ranger Station*
⚠	*Campground*
🌲	*Picnic Area*
🍴	*Restaurant*
🏨	*Lodge*
🚶	*Trailhead*
🚻	*Restrooms*
⤳	*Scenic Viewpoint*
⋯	*Walking/Hiking Trails*

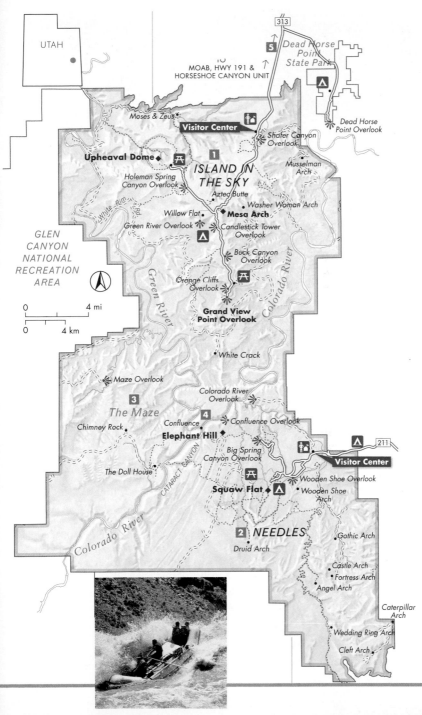

UTAH

313

5 Dead Horse Point State Park

TO
MOAB, HWY 191 &
HORSESHOE CANYON UNIT

Dead Horse Point Overlook

Moses & Zeus

Visitor Center

Shafer Canyon Overlook

Musselman Arch

Upheaval Dome

1 **ISLAND IN THE SKY**

Holeman Spring Canyon Overlook

Aztec Butte

Washer Woman Arch

GLEN CANYON NATIONAL RECREATION AREA

Willow Flat

Mesa Arch

Green River Overlook

Candlestick Tower Overlook

White Rim Rd.

Green River

Buck Canyon Overlook

Orange Cliffs Overlook

Colorado River

Grand View Point Overlook

0   4 mi
0   4 km

White Crack

Maze Overlook

Colorado River Overlook

3 **The Maze**

4 Confluence Overlook

Chimney Rock

Confluence

Elephant Hill

Big Spring Canyon Overlook

211

Visitor Center

The Doll House

CATARACT CANYON

Wooden Shoe Overlook

Squaw Flat

Wooden Shoe Arch

Colorado River

2 **NEEDLES**

Gothic Arch

Druid Arch

Castle Arch

Fortress Arch

Angel Arch

Caterpillar Arch

Wedding Ring Arch

Cleft Arch

Updated by
Steve Pastorino

Canyonlands is truly four parks in one, but the majority of visitors drive through the panoramic vistas of Island in the Sky and barely venture anywhere else. If you've come this far, plan a half-day to hike around the Needles district and see the park from the bottom up. To truly experience Canyonlands you should also float down the Green and Colorado rivers on a family-friendly rafting trip. (Rapids-lovers can take on the white water in the legendary Cataract Canyon.) The Maze is so remote that its river beds, slot canyons, and stark rock formations are only for the truly hardy.

CANYONLANDS PLANNER

WHEN TO GO

Gorgeous weather means that spring and fall are most popular for visitors. Canyonlands is seldom crowded, but in the spring backpackers and four-wheelers populate the trails and roads. During Easter week, some of the four-wheel-drive trails in the park are used for Jeep Safari, an annual event drawing thousands of visitors to town.

The crowds thin out by July as the thermostat approaches 100°F and beyond for about four weeks. It's a great time to get out on the Colorado or Green River winding through the park. October can be rainy, but the region receives only 8 inches of rain annually.

The well-kept secret is that winter is the best time in the park. Crowds are gone, roads are good, and snowcapped mountains stand in the background. Winter here is one of nature's most memorable shows, with red rock dusted white and low-floating clouds partially obscuring canyons and towers.

AVG. HIGH/LOW TEMPS.

JAN.	FEB.	MAR.	APR.	MAY	JUNE
44/22	52/28	64/35	71/42	82/51	93/60

JULY	AUG.	SEPT.	OCT.	NOV.	DEC.
100/67	97/66	88/55	74/42	56/30	45/23

PLANNING YOUR TIME

CANYONLANDS IN ONE DAY

Your day begins with a choice: Island in the Sky or Needles. If you want expansive vistas looking across southeast Utah's canyons, head for the island, where you stand atop a giant mesa. If you want to walk among Canyonlands' needles and buttes, Needles is your destination. If you have a second or third day in the area, consider contacting an outfitter to take you on a rafting or 4X4 trip. ■TIP➜ **Before venturing into the park, top off your gas tank, pack a picnic lunch, and stock up on plenty of water.**

ISLAND IN THE SKY Make your first stop along the main park road at **Shafer Canyon Overlook.** A short walk takes you out on a finger of land with views of the canyon over both sides. From here you can see Shafer Trail's treacherous descent as it hugs the canyon walls below.

Stop at the visitor center to learn about ranger talks or special programs, then drive to **Mesa Arch.** Grab your camera and water bottle for the short hike out to the arch perched on the cliff's edge. After your excursion, take the spur road to Upheaval Dome, with its picnic spot in the parking lot. A short walk takes you to the first viewpoint of this crater. If you still have energy, 30 more minutes and a little sense of adventure, continue to the second overlook.

Retrace your drive to the main park road and continue to **Grand View Point.** Stroll along the edge of the rim, and see how many landmarks you can spot in the distance. White Rim Overlook is the best of the scenic spots, particularly if you're not afraid of heights and venture all the way out to the end of the rocky cliffs (no guardrail here). On the way back to dinner in Moab, spend an hour in Dead Horse Point State Park.

NEEDLES If you can stay overnight as well, then begin today by setting up camp at Squaw Flat or one of the other wonderful campgrounds in Needles. Then hit the **Joint Trail,** or any of the trails that begin from Squaw Flat, and spend the day hiking in the backcountry of the park. Save an hour for the brief but terrific little hike to **Cave Springs.** Sleep under more stars than you've seen in a long time.

GETTING HERE AND AROUND

AIR TRAVEL

The nearest airport is Grand County Airport, 18 miles north of Moab. Great Lakes Airlines serves the area daily with flights from Denver. Colorado's Grand Junction Airport is 120 miles east of the park. Flights are limited.

CAR TRAVEL

Off U.S. 191, Canyonlands' Island in the Sky visitor center is 21 miles from Arches National Park and 32 miles from Moab on Route 313 west of U.S. 191; the Needles District is reached via Route 211, west of U.S. 191.

Before starting a journey to any of Canyonlands' three districts, make sure your gas tank is topped off, as there are no services inside the large park. Island in the Sky is 32 miles from Moab, Needles District is 80 miles from Moab, and the Maze is more than 100 miles from Moab. The Island in the Sky road from the district entrance to Grand View Point is 12 miles, with one 5-mile spur to Upheaval Dome. The Needles scenic drive is 10 miles with two spurs about 3 miles each. Roads in the Maze, suitable only for rugged, high-clearance, four-wheel-drive vehicles, wind for hundreds of miles through the canyons. Within the parks, safety and courtesy mandate that you always park only in designated pullouts or parking areas.

TRAIN TRAVEL

The nearest train "station" is a solitary Amtrak stop in Green River, about 50 miles northwest of Moab.

PARK ESSENTIALS

PARK FEES AND PERMITS

Admission is $10 per vehicle and $5 per person on foot, motorcycle, or bicycle, good for seven days. Your Canyonlands pass is good for all the park's districts. There's no entrance fee to the Maze District of Canyonlands. A $25 local park pass grants you admission to both Arches and Canyonlands as well as Natural Bridges and Hovenweep national monuments for one year.

You need a permit for overnight backpacking, four-wheel-drive camping, mountain-bike camping, four-wheel-drive day use in Horse and Lavender canyons, and river trips. Reservations need to be made at least two weeks (or more) in advance.

PARK HOURS

Canyonlands National Park is open 24 hours a day, seven days a week, year-round. It is in the Mountain time zone.

CELL-PHONE RECEPTION

Cell-phone reception may be available in some parts of the park, but not reliably so. Public telephones are at the park's visitor centers.

RESTAURANTS

There are no dining facilities in the park itself. Needles Outpost, just outside the entrance to the Needles District, has a small general store for picnicking necessities. Restaurants in Monticello and Blanding offer simple meals, and most do not serve alcohol. Moab has a multitude of options.

Prices in the reviews are the average cost of a main course at dinner, or if dinner is not served, at lunch.

Plants and Wildlife in Canyonlands

CLOSE UP

Wildlife is not the attraction in Canyonlands, as many of the creatures sleep during the heat of the day. On the bright side, there are fewer people and less traffic to scare the animals away. Cool mornings and evenings are the best time to spot them, especially in summer when the heat keeps them in cool, shady areas. Mule deer are nearly always seen along the roadway as you enter the Needles District, and you'll no doubt see jackrabbits and small rodents darting across the roadway. Approximately 250 bighorns populate the park in the Island in the Sky District, and the Maze shelters about 100 more. If you happen upon one of these regal animals, do not approach it even if it is alone, as bighorn sheep are skittish by nature and easily stressed. Also, report your sighting to a ranger.

HOTELS

There is no lodging inside Canyonlands. Most visitors use Moab as a base to explore the park. The towns of Monticello and Blanding offer basic motels, both family-owned and national chains. Bluff also has motels and B&Bs and offers a quiet place to stay.

Prices in the reviews are the lowest cost of a standard double room in high season. For expanded reviews, facilities, and current deals, visit Fodors.com.

VISITOR INFORMATION

PARK CONTACT INFORMATION

Canyonlands National Park ☎ *435/719–2313* ⊕ *www.nps.gov/cany.*

VISITOR CENTERS

Hans Flat Ranger Station. This remote outpost is a treasure trove of books, maps, and other documents about the unforgiving Maze District of Canyonlands. The slot canyons, pictographs, and myriad rock formations are tempting, but you need to know what you're doing. The rangers will be direct with you—inexperienced off-road drivers and backpackers can get themselves into serious trouble in the Maze. Just to get here you must drive 46 miles on a dirt road that is sometimes impassable even to 4X4 vehicles. There's a pit toilet, but no water, food, or services of any kind. If you're headed for the backcountry, inquire about new reservation policies effective beginning in 2013. ⊠ *46 miles east of Rte. 24; 21 miles south and east of the Y junction and Horseshoe Canyon kiosk on dirt road, Maze* ☎ *435/259–2652* ⊗ *Daily 8–4:30.*

Island in the Sky Visitor Center. The gateway to world-famous White Rim Road, this visitor center is often filled with a mix of mountain bikers, hikers, and tourists. Enjoy the orientation film, then browse the bookstore for information about the Canyonlands region. Exhibits help explain animal adaptations as well as some of the history of the park. Rangers give short talks twice a day. ⊠ *21 miles from U.S. 191, past park entrance off the main park road, Island in the Sky* ☎ *435/259–4712* ⊗ *Mar.–Oct., daily 8-6; Nov.–Feb., daily 9–4.*

Needles District Visitor Center. This gorgeous building is 34 miles from Highway 191. Needles is remote, so it's worth stopping to inquire about road, weather, and park conditions. You can also watch the interesting orientation film and get books, trail maps, and other information. ✉ *Less than 1 mile from park entrance off main park road, Needles* ☎ *435/259–4711* ⊙ *Mar.–May, Sept. and Oct., daily 8–5:30; June–Aug., daily 8–5; Nov.–Feb., daily 9–4:30.*

EXPLORING

SCENIC DRIVES

Island in the Sky Park Road. This 12-mile-long main road is bisected by a 5-mile side road to the Upheaval Dome area. To enjoy dramatic views, including the Green and Colorado rivers, stop at the overlooks and take the short walks. Once you get to the park, allow at least two hours to explore. ✉ *Island in the Sky.*

Needles District Park Road. You'll feel like you've driven into a Hollywood Western as you roll along the park road in the Needles District. Red mesas and buttes rise against the horizon, blue mountain ranges interrupt the rangelands, and the colorful red and white needles stand like soldiers on the far side of grassy meadows. You should get out of the car at a few of the marked roadside stops, including both overlooks at Pothole Point. Allow at least an hour in this less-traveled section of the park. ✉ *Needles.*

HISTORIC SITES

ISLAND IN THE SKY

Shafer Trail. This road was probably first established by ancient Native Americans, but in the early 1900s ranchers used it to drive cattle into the canyon. Originally narrow and rugged, it was upgraded during the uranium boom, when miners hauled ore by truck from the canyon floor. Check out the road's winding route down canyon walls from Shafer Canyon Overlook before you drive it to see why it's mostly used by daring four-wheelers and energetic mountain bikers. It descends 1,400 feet to the White Rim. ✉ *Off main road, less than 1 mile from park entrance, Island in the Sky.*

NEEDLES

FAMILY **Cowboy Line Camp.** This fascinating stop on the **Cave Springs Trail** is an authentic example of cowboy life more than a century ago. You do not need to complete the entire trail (which includes two short ladders and some rocky hiking) to see the 19th-century artifacts at the Cowboy Camp. ✉ *Off Cave Springs Rd., 2.3 miles from park entrance, Needles.*

SCENIC STOPS

ISLAND IN THE SKY

Grand View Point. This 360-degree view is the main event for many visitors to Island in the Sky. Look down on the Colorado and Green rivers and contemplate the power and persistence of water and the vast canyons carved over the millennia. Stretch your legs on the trails along the canyon edge. ⊠ *Off main road, 12 miles from park entrance, Island in the Sky.*

Mesa Arch. If you don't have time for the 2,000 arches in nearby Arches National Park, you should take the 0.5-mile walk to Mesa Arch. The arch is above a cliff that drops 800 feet to the canyon bottom. Views through Washerwoman Arch and surrounding buttes, spires, and canyons make this a favorite photo opportunity. ⊠ *Off main road, 6 miles from park entrance, Island in the Sky.*

Upheaval Dome. This mysterious crater is one of the wonders of Island in the Sky. Some geologists believe it's an eroded salt dome, but others have theorized that it was made by a meteorite. To see it, you'll have to walk about a mile, round-trip, to the first overlook. Energetic visitors should continue to the second overlook as well for a better perspective. ⊠ *Off Upheaval Dome Rd., 11 miles from park entrance, Island in the Sky.*

NEEDLES

Pothole Point Trail. Microscopic creatures lie dormant in pools that fill only after rare rainstorms. When the rains do come, some eggs hatch within hours and life becomes visible. If you're lucky, you'll hit Pothole Point after a storm. Otherwise, you'll have to use your imagination. The dramatic views of the Needles and Six Shooter Peak make this easy, 0.6-mile round-trip walk worthwhile in their own right. Plan for about 45 minutes. There's no shade, so wear a hat. ⊠ *Off main road, about 9 miles from Needles district park entrance, Needles.*

Wooden Shoe Arch. Kids will enjoy looking for the tiny window in the rock that looks like a wooden shoe with a turned-up toe. If you can't find it on your own; there's a marker to help you. ⊠ *Off main road, about 5 miles from Needles park entrance.*

EDUCATIONAL OFFERINGS

For more information on current schedules and locations of park programs, contact the visitor centers or check the bulletin boards throughout the park. Note that programs change periodically and may sometimes be canceled because of limited staffing.

FAMILY **Red Rock Explorer Pack.** Just like borrowing a book from a library, kids can check out a backpack filled with tools for learning about both Canyonlands and Arches national parks. The sturdy backpack includes binoculars, a magnifying glass, and a three-ring binder full of activities. It can be cumbersome to carry everything on a hike, but the backpack is great for around the campfire or back in your hotel room. ☏ *435/719–4712* ☎ *Free.*

RANGER PROGRAMS
Grand View Point Overlook Talk. Between April and October, rangers lead short geology presentations at Grand View Point. You'll learn something about the geology that created Utah's Canyonlands. ⊠ *Grand View Point, 12 miles from park entrance off the main park road, Island in the Sky* 🎫 *$10 per vehicle* ⊙ *Apr.–Oct., daily; check at park visitor centers for times and locations.*

FAMILY **Junior Ranger Program.** Kids ages 5 to 12 can pick up a Junior Ranger booklet at the visitor centers. It's full of puzzles, word games, and fun facts about the park and its wildlife. To earn the Junior Ranger badge, they must complete several activities in the booklet, attend a ranger program, watch the park film, and/or gather a bag of litter. ☎ *435/259–4712 for Island in the Sky, 435/259–4711 for Needles* 🎫 *Free.*

> ## MEET ME AT SUNSET
>
> Sunset is one of the picture-perfect times in Canyonlands, as the slanting sun shines over the vast network of canyons that stretch out below Island in the Sky. A moonlight drive to Grand View Point can also give you lasting memories as the moon drenches the white sandstone in the light. Likewise, late-afternoon color in the spires and towers at the Needles District is a humbling, awe-inspiring scene.

SPORTS AND THE OUTDOORS

Canyonlands is one of the world's best destinations for adrenaline junkies. You can rock climb, mountain bike treacherous terrain, tackle world-class white-water rapids, and make your 4X4 crawl over steep cliffs along precipitous drops. Compared with other national parks, Canyonlands allows you to enjoy an amazing amount of solitude while having the adventure of a lifetime.

BICYCLING

TOURS AND OUTFITTERS
Magpie Cycling Adventures. Seasoned bikers Mike Holme and Maggie Wilson lead groups (or lone riders) on daylong and multiday bike trips exploring the Moab region's most memorable terrain including the White Rim, Needles, and the Maze. If you need to rent a bike, Magpie will meet you at its preferred shop, Poison Spider Bicycles. ☎ *435/259–4464, 800/546–4245* ⊕ *www.magpieadventures.com.*

TRAILS
White Rim Road. Mountain bikers from all over the world like to brag that they've conquered this 100-mile ride. The trail's fame is well deserved: it traverses steep roads, broken rock, and dramatic ledges, as well as long stretches that wind through the canyons and look down onto others. If you're biking White Rim without an outfitter, you'll need careful planning, vehicle support, and much-sought-after backcountry reservations. ■TIP→ New in 2014, permits are available no more than four months, and no less than two days, prior to permit

start date. There is a 15-person, 3-vehicle limit for groups. You'll need a free day-use permit even if you don't stay overnight. Most White Rim Road journeys begin at the end of Shafer Trail. ⊠ *Off main park road about 1 mile from entrance, then about 11 miles on Shafer Trail, Island in the Sky* ☎ *435/259–4351* ⊕ *www.nps.gov/cany.*

BIRD-WATCHING

Without getting on the Colorado River, you can see a variety of wrens, including the rock wren, canyon wren, and Bewick's wren. Blue-gray gnatcatchers are fairly common in the summer, along with the solitary vireo and black-throated gray warbler and Virginia's warbler. You'll have the most fun spotting the American kestrel, peregrine falcon, or prairie falcon and watching golden and bald eagles soar overhead. The common raven is everywhere you look, as are the juniper titmouse, mountain chickadee, and a variety of jays. Once on the Colorado River, you'll stand a chance of glimpsing the elusive white-faced ibis, and you'll almost certainly see a great blue heron swooping along the water or standing regally on a sandbar.

BOATING AND RAFTING

Seeing Canyonlands National Park from the river is a great and rare pleasure. Long stretches of calm water on both the Green and Colorado rivers are perfect for lazy canoe or raft trips. Still, be sure to wear life preservers as drownings happen nearly every summer in the area. In Labyrinth Canyon, north of the park boundary, and in Stillwater Canyon, in the Island in the Sky District, the river is quiet and calm and there's plenty of shoreside camping. The Island in the Sky leg of the Colorado River, from Moab to its confluence with the Green River and downstream a few more miles to Spanish Bottom, is ideal for both canoeing and for rides with an outfitter in a large, stable jet boat. If you want to take a self-guided flat-water float trip in the park you must obtain a $30 permit, which you have to request by mail or fax. Make your upstream travel arrangements with a shuttle company before you request a permit. For permits, contact the reservation office at park headquarters (☎ *435/259–4351*).

Below Spanish Bottom, about 64 miles downstream from Moab, 49 miles from the Potash Road ramp and 4 miles south of the confluence, the Colorado churns into the first rapids of legendary Cataract Canyon. Home of some of the best white water in the United States, this piece of river between the Maze and the Needles districts rivals the Grand Canyon stretch of the Colorado River for adventure. During spring melt-off these rapids can rise to staggering heights and deliver heart-stopping excitement. The canyon cuts through the very heart of Canyonlands, where you can see this amazing wilderness area in its most pristine form. The water calms down a bit in summer but still offers enough thrills for most people. Outfitters will take you for the ride of your life in this wild canyon, where the river drops more steeply than anywhere else on the Colorado River (in ¾ mile, the river drops 39 feet). You can join an expedition lasting anywhere from one to six days, or you can purchase a $30 permit for a self-guided trip from park headquarters.

TOURS

Oars. This well-regarded outfitter can take you for several days of rafting and/or hiking through the Colorado and Green rivers. For those not into white water, it also offers calm-water rides. ✉ *Moab* ☎ *435/259–5865, 800/346–6277* ⊕ *www.oarsutah.com.*

FOUR-WHEELING

Nearly 200 miles of challenging backcountry roads lead to campsites, trailheads, and natural and cultural features in Canyonlands. All of the roads require high-clearance, four-wheel-drive vehicles, and many are inappropriate for inexperienced drivers. The 100-mile White Rim Trail, for example, can be extremely challenging, so make sure that your four-wheel-drive skills are well honed and that you are capable of making basic road and vehicle repairs. Carry at least one full-size spare tire, extra gas, extra water, a shovel, a high-lift jack, and—October through April—chains for all four tires. Double-check to see that your vehicle is in top-notch condition, for you definitely don't want to break down in the interior of the park: towing expenses can exceed $1,000.

For overnight four-wheeling trips you must purchase a $30 permit, which you can reserve no more than four months, and no fewer than two days in advance by contacting the Backcountry Reservations Office (☎ *435/259–4351*). Cyclists share all roads, so be aware and cautious of their presence. Vehicular traffic traveling uphill has the right-of-way. It's best to check at the visitor center for current road conditions before taking off into the backcountry. You must carry a washable, reusable toilet with you in the Maze District and carry out all waste.

ISLAND IN THE SKY

White Rim Road. Winding around and below the Island in the Sky mesa top, the dramatic, 100-mile White Rim Road offers a once-in-a-lifetime driving experience. As you tackle Murphy's Hogback, Hardscrabble Hill, and more formidable obstacles, you will get some fantastic views of the park. A trip around the loop can be done in one long day, or you can camp overnight with advance reservations. Campsite reservations open in July for the subsequent year, and popular spring and fall weekends fill up immediately. Bring plenty of water, a spare tire, and a jack, as no services are available on the road. White Rim Road starts at the end of Shafer Trail. ✉ *Off the main park road about 1 mile from the entrance, then about 11 miles on Shafer Trail, Island in the Sky* ☎ *435/259–4351* ⊕ *www.nps.gov/cany.*

THE MAZE

Flint Trail. This remote, rugged road is the most popular in the Maze District, but it's not an easy ride. It has 2 miles of switchbacks that drop down the side of a cliff face. You reach Flint Trail from the Hans Flat Ranger Station, 46 miles from the closest paved road. From Hans Flat to the end of the road at the Doll House it's 41 miles, a drive that takes at least six hours one way. The Maze is generally not a destination for a day trip, so you'll have to purchase an overnight backcountry permit for $30. ■ TIP→ **Despite its remoteness, the Maze District can fill to capacity during spring and fall, so plan ahead.** ✉ *Hans Flat Ranger Station, 46 miles east of Rte. 24, Maze.*

NEEDLES

Elephant Hill. The first 3 miles of this route are designated as passable by all vehicles, but don't venture out without asking about road conditions. For the rest of the trail, only 4WD vehicles are allowed. The route is so difficult that many people get out and walk—it's faster than you can drive it in some cases. From Elephant Hill Trailhead to Devil's Kitchen it's 3½ miles; from the trailhead to the Confluence Overlook, it's a 14½-mile round trip and requires at least eight hours. ⚠ **Don't attempt this without a well-maintained 4WD vehicle and spare gas, tires, and off-road knowledge.** ✉ *Off the main park road, 7 miles from park entrance, Needles.*

HIKING

Canyonlands National Park is a good place to saturate yourself in the intoxicating colors, smells, and textures of the desert. Many of the trails are long, rolling routes over slickrock and sand in landscapes dotted with juniper, pinyon, and sagebrush. Interconnecting trails in the Needles District provide excellent opportunities for weeklong backpacking excursions. The Maze trails are primarily accessed via four-wheel-drive vehicle. In the separate Horseshoe Canyon area, Horseshoe Canyon Trail takes a considerable amount of effort to reach, as it is more than 100 miles from Moab, 32 miles of which are a bumpy, and often sandy, dirt road.

ISLAND IN THE SKY

EASY

Aztec Butte Trail. The highlight of the 2-mile round-trip hike is the chance to see ancestral Puebloan granaries. *Easy.* ✉ *Trailhead on Upheaval Dome Rd., about 6 miles from park entrance, Island in the Sky.*

Grand View Point Trail. If you're looking for a level walk with some of the best scenery in the West, stop at Grand View Point and wander this 2-mile round-trip trail along the cliff edge. Many people just stop at the paved overlook and drive on, but you'll gain breathtaking perspective by strolling along this flat cliffside trail. On a clear day you can see up to 100 miles to the Maze and Needles districts of the park, the confluence of the Green and Colorado rivers, and each of Utah's major laccolithic mountain ranges: the Henrys, Abajos, and La Sals. *Easy.* ✉ *Trailhead on the main park road, 12 miles from park entrance, Island in the Sky.*

FAMILY **Mesa Arch Trail.** After the overlooks, this is most popular trail in the park.
Fodor's Choice A 0.5-mile loop acquaints you with desert plants and terrain and offers
★ vistas of the La Sal Mountains. The highlight of this hike is a natural arch window perched over an 800-foot drop, giving a rare downward glimpse through the arch rather than the usual upward view of the sky. Park rangers say this is one of the best spots to enjoy the sunrise. *Easy.* ✉ *Trailhead 6 miles from visitor center, Island in the Sky.*

11

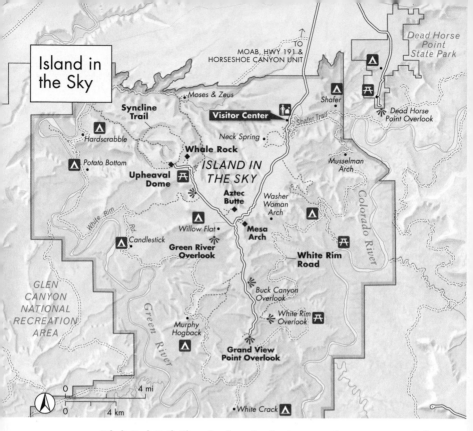

FAMILY **Whale Rock Trail.** If you've been hankering to walk across some of that pavement-smooth stuff they call slickrock, the hike to Whale Rock will make your feet happy. This 1-mile round-trip adventure, complete with handrails to help you make the tough final 100-foot climb, takes you to the very top of the whale's back. Once you get there, you are rewarded with great views of Upheaval Dome and Trail Canyon. *Easy.* ✉ *Trailhead on Upheaval Dome Rd., 11 miles from park entrance, Island in the Sky.*

MODERATE

Upheaval Dome Trail. It's fun to imagine that a giant meteorite crashed to earth here, sending shockwaves around the planet. But some people believe that salt, collecting and expanding upward, formed a dome and then exploded, causing the crater. Either way, it's worth the steep hike to see it and decide for yourself. You reach the main overlook after just 0.8 mile, but you can double your pleasure by going on to a second overlook for a better view. The trail is steeper and rougher after the first overlook. Round trip to the second overlook is 2 miles. *Moderate.* ✉ *Trailhead on Upheaval Dome Rd., 11 miles from park entrance, Island in the Sky.*

11

DIFFICULT

Syncline Loop Trail. If you're up for a strenuous day of hiking, try this 8-mile trail that circles Upheaval Dome. You get limited views of the dome itself as you actually make a complete loop around the outside of the crater. Stretches of the trail are rocky, rugged, and steep. *Difficult.* ⊠ *Trailhead on Upheaval Dome Rd., 11 miles from park entrance, Island in the Sky.*

THE MAZE

DIFFICULT

Horseshoe Canyon Trail. This remote region of Canyonlands National Park is accessible by dirt road, and then only in good weather. Park at the lip of the canyon and hike 6.5 miles round-trip to the Great Gallery, considered by some to be the most significant rock-art panel in North America. Ghostly life-size figures in the Barrier Canyon style populate the amazing panel. The hike is moderately strenuous, with a 750-foot descent. Allow at least six hours for the trip and take a gallon of water per person. There's no camping allowed in the canyon, although you can camp on top near the parking lot. *Difficult.* ⊠ *Trailhead 32 miles east of Rte. 24, Maze.*

NEEDLES

EASY

Slickrock Trail. Wear a hat if you're on this trail in summer, because you won't find any shade along the 2.4-mile round-trip trek. This is the rare frontcountry site where you might spot one of the few remaining native herds of bighorn sheep in the national park system. *Easy.* ⊠ *Trailhead on main park road, about 10 miles from park entrance, Needles.*

MODERATE

FAMILY **Cave Spring Trail.** One of the best, most interesting trails in the park takes you past a historic cowboy camp, prehistoric pictographs, and great views. Two wooden ladders and one short, steep stretch may make this a little daunting for the extremely young or old, but it's also a short hike, features some shade, and has many features packed into half a mile. Allow about 45 minutes. *Moderate.* ⊠ *Trailhead off the main park road on Cave Springs Rd., 2.3 miles from park entrance, Needles.*

DIFFICULT

Chesler Park Loop. Chesler Park is a grassy meadow dotted with spires and enclosed by a circular wall of colorful "needles." One of Canyonlands' more popular trails leads through the area to the famous Joint Trail. The trail is 6 miles round-trip to the viewpoint. The entire loop is 11 miles. *Difficult.* ⊠ *Accessed via the Elephant Hill Trailhead, off the main park road, about 7 miles from park entrance, Needles.*

Joint Trail. Part of the Chesler Park Loop, this well-loved trail follows a series of deep, narrow fractures in the rock. A shady spot in summer, it will give you good views of the Needles formations for which the district is named. The loop travels briefly along a four-wheel-drive road and is 11 miles round-trip; allow at least five hours to complete the hike. *Difficult.* ⊠ *Accessed via the Elephant Hill Trailhead, off the main park road, 7 miles from park entrance, Needles.*

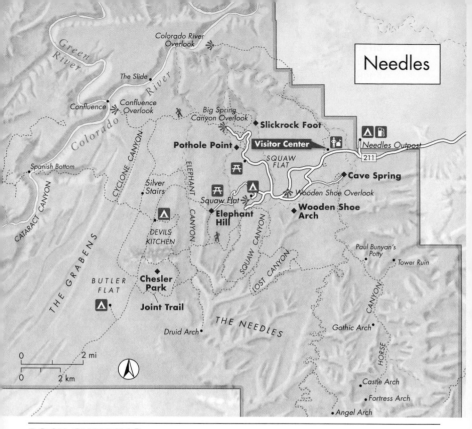

ROCK CLIMBING

Fodor's Choice ★ Canyonlands and many of the surrounding areas draw climbers from all over the world. Permits are not required, but because of the sensitive archaeological nature of the park, it's imperative that you stop at the visitor center to pick up regulations pertaining to the park's cultural resources. Popular climbing routes include Moses and Zeus towers in Taylor Canyon, and Monster Tower and Washerwoman Tower on the White Rim Road. Like most routes in Canyonlands, these climbs are for experienced climbers only. Just outside the Needles District, in Indian Creek, is one of the country's best traditional climbing areas.

WHAT'S NEARBY

NEARBY TOWNS

Moab is the major gateway to both Arches and Canyonlands national parks, with the most outfitters, shops, and lodging options of the area. A handful of communities that are much smaller and have fewer amenities is scattered around the Needles and Island in the Sky districts along U.S. 191.

Roughly 55 miles south of Moab is **Monticello.** Convenient to the Needles District, it lies at an elevation of 7,000 feet, making it a cool summer refuge from the desert heat. In winter, it gets downright cold and sees deep snow; the Abajo Mountains, whose highest point is 11,360 feet, rise to the west of town. Monticello motels serve the steady stream of tourists who venture south of Moab, but the town offers few dining or shopping opportunities. **Blanding,** 21 miles south of Monticello, prides itself on old-fashioned conservative values. By popular vote there's a ban on the sale of liquor, beer, and wine, so the town has no state liquor store and its restaurants do not serve alcoholic beverages. Blanding is a good resting point if you're traveling south from Canyonlands to Natural Bridges Natural Monument, Grand Gulch, Lake Powell, or the Navajo Nation. About 25 miles south of Blanding, tiny **Bluff** is doing its best to stay that way. It's a great place to stop if you aren't looking for many amenities but value beautiful scenery, silence, and starry nights. Bluff is the most common starting point for trips on the San Juan River, which serves as the northern boundary for the Navajo Reservation; it's also a wonderful place to overnight if you're planning a visit to Hovenweep National Monument, about 30 miles away.

VISITOR INFORMATION

Blanding Visitor Center ⊠ *12 N. Grayson Pkwy., Blanding* ☎ *435/678–3662* ⊕ *www.blanding-ut.gov.* **Monticello Welcome Center** ⊠ *216 S. Main St., Monticello* ☎ *435/587–3401* ⊕ *www.monticelloutah.org.* **San Juan County Community Development and Visitor Services** ⊠ *117 S. Main St., Monticello* ☎ *435/587–3235, 800/574–4386* ⊕ *www.utahscanyoncountry.com.*

NEARBY ATTRACTIONS

Colorado Riverway Scenic Byway. Spend a few hours along Route 279 if you're interested in Native American rock art. Look for signs for "Indian Writings," then park in designated areas to view the petroglyphs on the cliffs. At the 18-mile marker you'll reach Jug Handle Arch. A few miles later the road turns to four-wheel drive as it passes into the Island in the Sky District. If you start late in the afternoon, the cliffs will be glowing orange as the sun sets. Allow about two hours round-trip for the drive. ⊠ *Begins just north of Moab where U.S. 191 crosses the Colorado River, Moab.*

Dead Horse Point State Park. One of the gems of Utah's state park system, this nature preserve overlooks a sweeping oxbow of the Colorado River, some 2,000 feet below. Dead Horse Point itself is a small peninsula connected to the main mesa by a narrow neck of land. As the story goes, cowboys used to drive wild mustangs onto the point and pen them there with a brush fence. Some were forgotten and left to perish. There's a modern visitor center and museum as well as a 21-site campground with drinking water. Be sure to walk the 4-mile rim trail loop and drive to the park's eponymous point. ⊠ *34 miles west from Moab at end of Rte. 313* ☎ *435/259–2614, 800/322–3770* ⊕ *www.stateparks.utah.gov* 💲 *$10 per vehicle* ☉ *Park daily 6 am–10 pm. Visitor center Mar.–Oct., daily 8–6; Nov.–Feb., daily 9–5.*

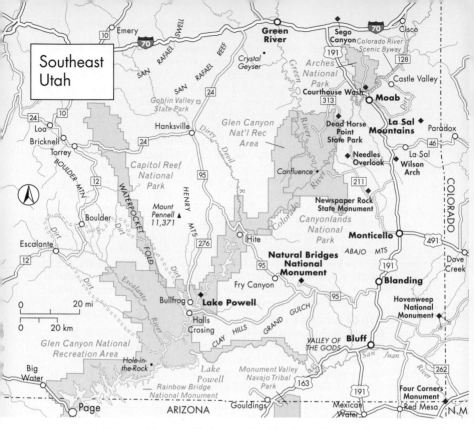

FAMILY **Dinosaur Museum.** Skeletons, fossils, footprints, and reconstructed dinosaur skins are all on display at this small museum. Hallways hold a collection of movie posters featuring Godzilla and other monsters dating back to the 1930s. ⊠ *754 S. 200 West St., Blanding* ☎ *435/678–3454* ⊕ *www.dinosaur-museum.org* ⊠ *$3.50* ⊙ *Apr.– Oct., Mon.–Sat. 9–5.*

Edge of the Cedars State Park Museum. Tucked away in Blanding is one of the nation's foremost museums dedicated to the Ancestral Puebloans. The museum displays a variety of pots, baskets, spear points, and rare artifacts, even a pair of sandals said to date back 1,500 years. Behind the museum, an interpretive trail leads to an Anasazi ruin. ⊠ *660 W. 400 North St., Blanding* ☎ *435/678–2238* ⊕ *stateparks.utah.gov/park/ edge-of-the-cedars-state-park-museum* ⊠ *$20 per vehicle or $5 per person* ⊙ *Mon.–Sat. 9–5.*

Natural Bridges National Monument. Sipapu is one of the largest natural bridges in the world, spanning 225 feet and standing more than 140 feet tall. You can take in the Sipapu, Owachomo, and Kachina bridges via an 8.6-mile round-trip hike that meanders around and under them. A 13-site primitive campground is an optimal spot for stargazing. The national monument is about 120 miles southwest of the Needles District visitor center at Canyonlands National Park. ⊠ *Rte. 275 off Rte.*

95, 35 miles west of Blanding, Lake Powell ☎ *435/692–1234* ⊕ *www. nps.gov/nabr* 🚗 *$6 per vehicle* ⊗ *May–Sept., daily 8–6; Oct. and Apr., daily 8–5; Nov.–Mar., daily 9–5.*

Newspaper Rock Recreation Site. On your drive into the Needles District, stop to admire one of the West's most famous rock-art sites. The Native American etchings span a period of about 2,000 years. Early explorers called the site Newspaper Rock because they believed that the rock, crowded with drawings, constituted a written language with which early people communicated. Archaeologists now agree the petroglyphs do not represent language. This is one of many "newspaper rocks" throughout the Southwest. ⊠ *Rte. 211, about 15 miles west of U.S. 191.*

Wilson Arch. Between Arches and the Needles District of Canyonlands, this roadside arch is popular with shutterbugs. In Moab, you can still find historical photos of an airplane flying through this arch. No one has tried the stunt lately, because it's now illegal. ⊠ *26 miles south of Moab on U.S. 191, Moab.*

SHOPPING

Thin Bear Indian Arts. The Hosler family has operated this tiny little trading post in the same location since 1973. Authentic jewelry, rugs, baskets, and pottery are for sale at this friendly spot. ⊠ *1944 S. Main St., Blanding* ☎ *435/678–2940.*

WHERE TO EAT

IN THE PARK

PICNIC AREAS

Grand View Point. It's hard to get a better view than from this point. It's a pleasant spot in which to recharge your energy and stretch your legs. There are picnic tables, grills, restrooms, and shade. ⊠ *12 miles from park entrance on the main road, Island in the Sky.*

Needles District. The most convenient picnic spot in the Needles District is a sunny location on the way to Big Spring Canyon Overlook. There are picnic tables, but no grills, restrooms, water, or other amenities. ⊠ *About 5 miles from the visitor center, Needles.*

OUTSIDE THE PARK

$$ ✕ **Homestead Steak House.** The folks here specialize in authentic Navajo
DINER fry bread and Navajo tacos. A variety of steaks, sandwiches, and pizza are also available, as is a salad bar. No alcohol is served. $ *Average main: $14* ⊠ *121 E. Center St., Blanding* ☎ *435/678–3456.*

Best Campgrounds in Canyonlands

Canyonlands campgrounds are some of the most beautiful in the National Park system. At the Needles District, campers will enjoy fairly private campsites tucked against red rock walls and dotted with pinyon and juniper trees. At Island in the Sky, starry nights and spectacular vistas make the small campground an intimate treasure. Hookups are not available in either of the park's campgrounds; however, the sites are long enough to accommodate units up to 28 feet long.

Squaw Flat Campground. The defining features of the camp sites at Squaw Flat are house-size red rock formations, which provide some shade, offer privacy from adjacent campers, and make this one of the more unique campgrounds in the National Park system. ⊠ *Off main road, about 5 miles from park entrance, Needles* ☎ *435/259–7164.*

Willow Flat Campground. From this little campground on a mesa top, you can walk to spectacular views of the Green River. Most sites have a bit of shade from juniper trees. ⊠ *Off main park road, about 9 miles from park entrance, Island in the Sky* ☎ *435/259–4712.*

WHERE TO STAY

OUTSIDE THE PARK

$$
HOTEL
 **Desert Rose Inn and Cabins.** Bluff's largest hotel is an attractive, wood-sided lodge with a huge two-story front porch. **Pros:** comfortable rooms; friendly staff. **Cons:** town has no historic charm; town not a culinary hub. $ *Rooms from: $135* ⊠ *701 W. Main St., Bluff* ☎ *435/672–2303, 888/475–7673* ⊕ *www.desertroseinn.com* ⌑ *30 rooms, 7 cabins* ⦿ *No meals.*

$
HOTEL
Inn at the Canyons. One of the largest properties in Monticello, this is also one of the nicest, with a heated indoor pool and a hot tub that's just what the doctor ordered for soaking adventure-weary bodies. **Pros:** management takes good care of the rooms; splashing about in the pool; close to Needles District of Canyonlands. **Cons:** sits near the highway, so might be noisy; in a sleepy town. $ *Rooms from: $94* ⊠ *533 N. Main St., Monticello* ☎ *435/587–2458* ⊕ *www.monticellocanyonlandsinn. com* ⌑ *43 rooms* ⦿ *Breakfast.*

$
HOTEL
Recapture Lodge. The knowledgeable owners of this family-owned and -operated inn known for its friendliness have detailed tips for exploring the surrounding canyon country and occasionally present slide shows about local geology, art, and history. **Pros:** set on shady grounds; owner is a wildlife biologist happy to share his knowledge; horses welcome. **Cons:** older property; small rooms and basic amenities; Bluff is about as small as it gets (which could be a pro). $ *Rooms from: $85* ⊠ *220 E. Main St. (U.S. 191), Bluff* ☎ *435/672–2281* ⊕ *www.recapturelodge. com* ⌑ *26 rooms, 2 houses* ⦿ *Breakfast.*

CAPITOL REEF
NATIONAL PARK

WELCOME TO CAPITOL REEF

TOP REASONS TO GO

★ **The Waterpocket Fold:** See an excellent example of a monocline—a fold in the earth's crust with one very steep side in an area that is otherwise horizontal. This one's almost 100 miles long.

★ **No crowds:** Experience the best of southern Utah weather, rock formations, and wide-open spaces without the crowds of nearby parks such as Zion and Bryce Canyon.

★ **Fresh fruit:** Pick apples, pears, apricots, and peaches in season at the pioneer-planted orchards at historic Fruita. These trees still produce plenty of fruit.

★ **Rock art:** View ancient pictographs and petroglyphs left by the Fremont people, who lived in this area from AD 700 to 1300.

★ **Pioneer artifacts:** Buy faithfully reproduced tools and utensils like those used by Mormon pioneers, at the Gifford Farmhouse.

1 Fruita. This historic pioneer village is at the heart of what most people see of Capitol Reef. The one and only park visitor center nearby is the place to get travel and weather information and maps. The scenic drive through Capitol Gorge provides a view of the Golden Throne.

2 Cathedral Valley. The views are stunning and the silence deafening in the park's remote northern section. High-clearance vehicles are required, as is a crossing of the Fremont River. Driving in this valley is next to impossible when the Cathedral Valley Road is wet, so ask at the visitor center about current weather and road conditions.

3 Muley Twist Canyon. At the southern reaches of the park, this canyon is accessed via Notom-Bullfrog Road from the north, and Burr Trail Road from the west and southeast. High-clearance vehicles are required for much of it.

GETTING ORIENTED

At the heart of this 378-square-mile park is the massive natural feature known as the Waterpocket Fold, which runs roughly northwest to southeast along the park's spine. Capitol Reef itself is named for a formation along the fold near the Fremont River. A historic pioneer settlement, the green oasis of Fruita is easily accessed by car, and a 9-mile scenic drive provides a good overview of the canyons and rock formations that populate the park. Colors here range from deep, rich reds to sage greens to crumbling gray sediments. The absence of large towns nearby ensures that night skies are brilliant starscapes.

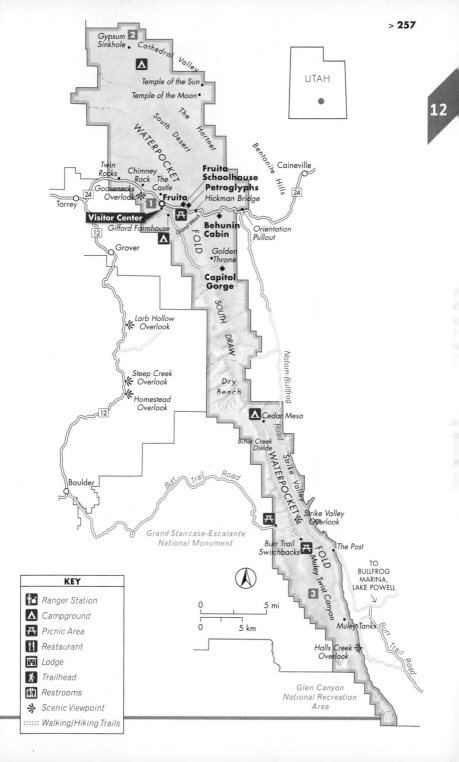

UTAH

12

Gypsum
Sinkhole 2
Cathedral Valley

WATERPOCKET

Temple of the Sun
Temple of the Moon

South Desert

The Hartnet

Bentonite Hills

Caineville

24

Twin
Rocks
Chimney
Rock
The
Castle

**Fruita
Schoolhouse
Petroglyphs**

Goosenecks
Overlook

24

Torrey

Visitor Center

Fruita

Hickman Bridge

Gifford Farmhouse

Grand Wash

FOLD

**Behunin
Cabin**

*Orientation
Pullout*

12

Grover

*Golden
Throne*

**Capitol
Gorge**

SOUTH

*Larb Hollow
Overlook*

DRAW

*Dry
Bench*

*Steep Creek
Overlook*

*Homestead
Overlook*

12

Cedar Mesa

Natom-Bullfrog

*Bitter Creek
Divide*

WATERPOCKET

Boulder

Burr Trail Road

Strike Valley

*Strike Valley
Overlook*

*Grand Staircase-Escalante
National Monument*

*Burr Trail
Switchbacks*

The Post

FOLD

Muley Twist Canyon

3

TO
BULLFROG
MARINA,
LAKE POWELL
↓

Muley Tanks

Burr Trail Road

*Halls Creek
Overlook*

*Glen Canyon
National Recreation
Area*

KEY	
🏠	*Ranger Station*
⛺	*Campground*
🧺	*Picnic Area*
🍴	*Restaurant*
🏨	*Lodge*
🚶	*Trailhead*
🚻	*Restrooms*
🌟	*Scenic Viewpoint*
┈┈	*Walking/Hiking Trails*

0   5 mi

0   5 km

Updated
by Mike
Weatherford

Your senses will be delighted by a visit to Capitol Reef National Park. Here, you are saturated in colors that are more dramatic than anywhere else in the West. The dominant Moenkopi rock formation is a rich, red-chocolate hue. Deep blue-green juniper and pinyon stand out against it. Other sandstone layers are gold, ivory, and lavender. Sunset brings out the colors in an explosion of copper, platinum, and orange, then dusk turns the cliffs purple and blue. The texture of rock deposited in ancient inland seas and worn by subsequent erosion is pure art.

The park preserves the Waterpocket Fold, a giant wrinkle in the earth that extends a hundred miles between Thousand Lake Mountain and Lake Powell. When you climb high onto the rocks or into the mountains, you can see this remarkable geologic wonder and the jumble of colorful cliffs, massive domes, soaring spires, and twisting canyons that surround it. It's no wonder American Indians called this part of the country the "land of sleeping rainbow."

But your eyes will not be alone in their joy. The fragrance of pine and sage rises from the earth, and canyon wrens sing to you as you sit by the water. Flowing across the heart of Capitol Reef is the Fremont River, a narrow little creek that can turn into a swollen, raging torrent during desert flash floods. The river sustains cottonwoods, wildlife, and verdant valleys rich with fruit. During the harvest, your sensory experience is complete when you bite into a perfect ripe peach or apple from the park's orchards. Your soul, too, will be gratified here. You can walk the trails in relative solitude and enjoy the beauty without confronting crowds on the roads or paths. All around you are signs of those who came before: ancient American Indians of the Fremont culture, Mormon pioneers who settled the land, and other courageous explorers who traveled the canyons. It is a rare thrill to feel the past overtake the present.

CAPITOL REEF PLANNER

12

WHEN TO GO

Spring and early summer are most bustling. Folks clear out in the midsummer heat, and then return for the apple harvest and crisp temperatures of autumn. Still, the park is seldom crowded—though the campground can fill quickly. Annual rainfall is scant, but when it does rain, flash floods can wipe out park roads. Snowfall is usually light. Sudden, short-lived snowstorms—and thunderstorms—are not uncommon in the spring.

AVG. HIGH/LOW TEMPS.

JAN.	FEB.	MAR.	APR.	MAY	JUNE
43/22	46/28	57/34	62/38	74/48	85/57

JULY	AUG.	SEPT.	OCT.	NOV.	DEC.
92/64	89/64	78/55	64/42	50/28	41/22

FESTIVALS AND EVENTS

JULY **Bicknell International Film Festival.** *Don't* get out your best black beret to attend this event—it's a spoof on serious film festivals. It begins with the world's fastest parade, a "55-mph" procession from Torrey to Bicknell. Past themes have included "UFO Flicks," "Japanese Monster Movies," and "Viva! Elvis." ⊕ *www.thebiff.org.*

AUGUST **Wayne County Fair.** The great American county-fair tradition is at its finest in Loa. Horse shows, demolition derby, rodeo, and a parade are part of the fun. There are also crafts such as handmade quilts, agricultural exhibits, children's games, and plenty of good food. ☏ 435/836–2765 ⊕ *www.waynecountyutah.org.*

PLANNING YOUR TIME

CAPITOL REEF IN ONE DAY

Pack a picnic lunch, snacks, and cold drinks to take with you, because there are no restaurants in the park. As you enter the park, look to your left for Chimney Rock; in a landscape of spires, cliffs, and knobs, this deep-red landmark is unmistakable. Start your journey at the **visitor center,** where you can study a three-dimensional map of the area, watch the short slide show, and browse the many books and maps related to the park. Then head for the park's scenic drive, stopping at the **Fruita Historic District** to see some of the sites associated with the park's Mormon history. Stop at the **Gifford Farmhouse** for a tour and a visit to the gift shop. That lunch you packed can be enjoyed at picnic tables on rolling green lawns lining both sides of the road between the orchard and Gifford Farmhouse.

As you continue on with your tour, check out the **Fremont Indian Petroglyphs,** and if you feel like some exertion, take a hike on the Hickman Bridge Trail. From the trail (or if you skip the hike, from Highway 24 about 2 miles east of the visitor center), you'll see **Capitol Dome.** Along this stretch of Highway 24 stop to see the old one-room **Fruita Schoolhouse,** the **petroglyphs,** and the **Behunin Cabin.** Next you'll have to backtrack a few miles on Highway 24 to find the **Goosenecks Trail.** At the same parking lot you'll find the trailhead for **Sunset Point Trail;** take this short hike in time to watch the setting sun hit the colorful cliffs.

Plants and Wildlife in Capitol Reef

The golden rock and rainbow cliffs are at their finest at sunset, when it seems as if they are lighted from within. That's also when mule deer wander through the orchards near the campground. The deer are quite tame, but do not feed them; their digestive systems are harmed by people food. Many of the park's animals move about only at night to escape the heat of the day, but pinyon jays and black-billed magpies flit around the park all day. The best place to see wildlife is near the Fremont River, where animals are drawn to drink. Ducks and small mammals such as the yellow-bellied marmot live nearby. Desert bighorn sheep also live in Capitol Reef, but they are elusive. Your best chance for spotting the sheep is during a long hike deep within the park. If you should encounter a sheep, do not approach it, as they've been known to charge human beings.

GETTING HERE AND AROUND

BUS TRAVEL

Once inside the park, there is no shuttle service as at nearby Zion and Bryce Canyon national parks.

CAR TRAVEL

Though far from big cities, Capitol Reef country can be reached by a variety of approaches. The main high-speed arteries through the region are Interstates 70 and 15, but any route will require travel of some secondary roads such as U.S. 50, U.S. 89, Highway 24, or Route 72. All are well-maintained, safe roads that bisect rich agricultural communities steeped in Mormon history (such as the nearby towns of Bicknell and Loa). Interstate 15 is the fastest way through central Utah, but U.S. 89 and the local roads that feed onto it will give you a more direct path into Utah's past and present-day character. Highway 24 runs across the middle of Capitol Reef National Park, so even those traveling between points west and east of the park with no intention of touring it get a scenic treat on their way.

PARK ESSENTIALS

PARK FEES AND PERMITS

There is no fee to enter the park, but it's $5 per vehicle (or $3 per bicycle) to travel on Scenic Drive beyond Fruita Campground; this fee is good for one week, paid via the "honor system" at a drop box versus a staffed entry gate. Backcountry camping permits are free; pick them up at the visitor center.

PARK HOURS

The park is open 24/7 year-round. It is in the Mountain time zone.

CELL-PHONE RECEPTION

Cell-phone reception is best near the visitor center and campground areas. Pay phones are at the visitor center and at Fruita Campground.

RESTAURANTS

There is no restaurant, just a small snack bar selling chips and ice cream inside Capitol Reef. But dining options exist close by in Torrey, where you can find everything from one of Utah's best restaurants serving high-end Southwestern cuisine to basic hamburger joints offering up consistently good food.

Prices in the reviews are the average cost of a main course at dinner, or if dinner is not served, at lunch.

HOTELS

There are no lodging options within Capitol Reef, but you'll have no problem finding clean and comfortable accommodations no matter what your budget in nearby Torrey and not far beyond in Bicknell and Loa. Drive farther into the region's towns, and you are more likely to find locally owned low- to moderate-priced motels and a few nice bed-and-breakfasts. Reservations are recommended in summer.

Prices in the reviews are the lowest cost of a standard double room in high season. For expanded reviews, facilities, and current deals, visit Fodors.com.

VISITOR INFORMATION

PARK CONTACT INFORMATION

Capitol Reef National Park ✉ *16 Scenic Dr., Torrey* ☎ *435/425–3791* ⊕ *www.nps.gov/care.*

VISITOR CENTERS

Capitol Reef Visitor Center. Watch a film, talk with rangers, or peruse the many books, maps, and materials offered for sale in the bookstore. Towering over the center is the Castle, one of the park's most prominent rock formations. ✉ *Hwy. 24, 11 miles east of Torrey* ☎ *435/425–3791* ☉ *Late May–Sept., daily 8–6; Oct. and mid-Apr.–late May, daily 8–5; Nov.–mid-Apr., daily 8–4:30.*

EXPLORING

SCENIC DRIVES

Capitol Reef Scenic Drive. This paved road starts at the visitor center and winds its way through the Fruita Historic District and colorful sandstone cliffs into Capitol Gorge; a side road, Grand Wash Road, provides access into the canyon. At Capitol Gorge, the canyon walls become steep and impressive but the route becomes unpaved, and road conditions may vary because of weather and amount of use. Check with the visitor center before entering Capitol Gorge. Capitol Reef Scenic Drive, called simply Scenic Drive by locals, is 9 miles long, with about the last quarter of it unpaved.

SCENIC STOPS

Behunin Cabin. Elijah Cutlar Behunin used blocks of sandstone to build this cabin in 1882. Floods in the lowlands made life too difficult, and he moved before the turn of that century. The house is empty, but you can peep through a window. ⊠ *Hwy. 24, 6.2 miles east of visitor center.*

Capitol Dome. One of the rock formations that gave the park its name, this giant, golden dome is visible in the vicinity of the Hickman Bridge trailhead. ⊠ *Hwy. 24, about 2 miles east of visitor center.*

Fodor's Choice **Capitol Gorge.** At the entrance to
★ this gorge Scenic Drive becomes unpaved. The narrow, twisting road on the floor of the gorge was a route for pioneer wagons traversing this part of Utah starting in the 1860s. After every flash flood, pioneers would laboriously clear the route so wagons could continue to go through. The gorge became the main automobile route in the area until 1962, when Highway 24 was built. The short drive to the end of the road has striking views of the surrounding cliffs and leads to one of the park's most popular walks, the hiking trail to the water-holding "tanks" eroded into the sandstone. ⊠ *Scenic Dr., 9 miles south of visitor center.*

> ### GEOLOGY BEHIND THE PARK'S NAME
>
> When water wears away layers of sandstone, basins can appear in the rock. These are called waterpockets. The 100-mile-long Waterpocket Fold—a massive rift in the Earth's crust, where geothermal pressure pushed one side 7,000 feet higher than the other (today it's settled to 2,600 feet)—is full of these waterpockets. Early explorers with seafaring backgrounds called the fold a reef, because it was a barrier to travel. Some of the rocks, due to erosion, also have domelike formations resembling capitol rotundas.

The Castle. This prominent geological landmark—sandstone that has taken the shape of a castle's spires—towers over the visitor center. ⊠ *Hwy. 24 at the visitor center.*

Chimney Rock. Even in a landscape of spires, cliffs, and knobs, this deepred landform is unmistakable. ⊠ *Hwy. 24, about 3 miles west of the visitor center.*

FAMILY **Fremont Indian Petroglyphs.** Nearly 1,000 years ago the Capitol Reef area was occupied by the Fremont Indians, whose culture was tied closely to the Ancestral Puebloan culture. A nice stroll along a boardwalk bridge allows close-up views of the Fremont rock art, which can be identified by the large trapezoidal figures often depicted wearing headdresses and ear baubles. ⊠ *Hwy. 24, 1.2 miles east of visitor center.*

FAMILY **Fruita Historic District.** In 1880 Nels Johnson became the first homesteader in the Fremont River Valley, building his home near the confluence of Sulphur Creek and the Fremont River. Other Mormon settlers followed and established small farms and orchards near the confluence, creating the village of Junction. The orchards thrived, and in 1902 the settlement's name was changed to Fruita. The orchards are preserved and protected as a Rural Historic Landscape. ⊠ *Scenic Dr., less than 1 mile from visitor center.*

Pioneer Register. Travelers passing through Capitol Gorge in the 19th and early 20th centuries etched the canyon wall with their names and the date they passed. Directly across the canyon from the Pioneer Register and about 50 feet up are signatures etched into the canyon wall by an early United States Geologic Survey crew. Though it's illegal to write or scratch on the canyon walls today, plenty of damage has been done by vandals over the years. You can reach the register via an easy hike from the sheltered trailhead at the end of Capitol Gorge Road; the register is about 10 minutes along the hike to the sandstone "tanks." ⊠ *Off Scenic Dr., 9 miles south of visitor center.*

The Waterpocket Fold. A giant wrinkle in the earth that extends almost 100 miles between Thousand Lake Mountain and Lake Powell, the Waterpocket Fold is not to be missed. You can glimpse the fold by driving south on Scenic Drive—after it branches off Highway 24—past the Fruita Historic District, but for complete immersion enter the park via the 66-mile Burr Trail from the town of Boulder. Travel through the southernmost reaches of the park requires a substantial amount of driving on unpaved roads. It's accessible to most vehicles during dry weather; check at the visitor center for road conditions.

EDUCATIONAL OFFERINGS

RANGER PROGRAMS

From late May to early September, ranger programs are offered at no charge. You can obtain current information about ranger talks and other park events at the visitor center or campground bulletin boards.

Evening Program. Learn about Capitol Reef's geology, American Indian cultures, wildlife, and more at a free lecture, slide show, or other ranger-led activities. A schedule of programs is offered from May to September on weekends, with the start times depending on the sunset. A schedule of topics and times is posted at the visitor center. ⊠ *Amphitheater, Loop C, Fruita Campground on Scenic Dr., about 1 mile from visitor center* ☎ *435/425–3791.*

Junior Ranger Program. Each child who participates in this self-guided, year-round program completes a combination of activities in the Junior Ranger booklet, attends a ranger program, interviews a park ranger, and/or picks up litter. ⊠ *Visitor center* ☎ *435/425–3791* 🖃 *Free.*

Ranger Talks. Each day at the visitor center—usually at 10—rangers give brief talks on park geology. Times can vary, so check for a current schedule. ⊠ *Visitor center* ☎ *435/425–3791* 🖃 *Free* ☉ *May–Sept., daily at 10.*

SPORTS AND THE OUTDOORS

The main outdoor activity at Capitol Reef is hiking. There are trails for all levels. Remember: Whenever you venture into the desert—that is, wherever you go in Capitol Reef—take, and drink, plenty of water.

MULTISPORT OUTFITTER

Hondoo Rivers & Trails. With a reputation for high-quality, educational trips into the backcountry of Capitol Reef National Park, these folks pride themselves on delivering a unique, private experience. From April to October, the company offers adventures on horseback, on foot, or via four-wheel-drive vehicle in Capitol Reef and the mountains and deserts surrounding it. Trips are designed to explore the geologic landforms in the area, seek out wildflowers in season, and to encounter free-roaming mustangs, bison, and bighorn sheep when possible. Single or multi-day trips can be arranged. ⊠ *90 E. Main St., Torrey* ☎ *435/425–3519, 800/332–2696* ⊕ *www.hondoo.com.*

BICYCLING

Bicycles are allowed only on established roads in the park. Highway 24 is a state highway and receives a substantial amount of through traffic, so it's not the best place to pedal. Scenic Drive is better, but the road is narrow, and you have to contend with drivers dazed by the beautiful surroundings. Four-wheel-drive roads are certainly less traveled, but they are often sandy, rocky, and steep. You cannot ride your bicycle in washes or on hiking trails.

Cathedral Valley Scenic Backway. In the remote northern end of the park you can enjoy solitude and a true backcountry ride on this trail. You'll be riding on surfaces that include dirt, sand, bentonite clay, and rock, and you will also ford the Fremont River; you should be prepared to encounter steep hills and switchbacks, wash crossings, and stretches of deep sand. Summer is not a good time to try this ride, as water is very difficult to find and temperatures may exceed 100°F. The entire route is about 58 miles long; during a multiday trip you can camp at the primitive campground with five sites, about midway through the loop. ⊠ *Off Hwy. 24 at Caineville, or at River Ford Rd., 5 miles west of Caineville on Hwy. 24.*

South Draw Road. This is a very strenuous ride that traverses dirt, sand, and rocky surfaces, and crosses several creeks that may be muddy. It's not recommended in winter or spring because of deep snow at higher elevations. If you like fast downhill rides, though, this trip is for you—it will make you feel like you have wings. The route starts at an elevation of 8,500 feet on Boulder Mountain and ends 15 miles later at 5,500 feet in the Pleasant Creek parking area at the end of Scenic Drive. ⊠ *At the junction of Bowns Reservoir Rd. and Hwy. 12, 13 miles south of Torrey.*

FOUR-WHEELING

You can explore Capitol Reef in a 4X4 on a number of exciting backcountry routes. Road conditions can vary greatly depending on recent weather patterns. Spring and summer rains can leave the roads muddy, washed out, and impassable even to four-wheel-drive vehicles. Always check at the park visitor center for current conditions before you set out, and take water, supplies, and a cell phone with you.

Cathedral Valley Scenic Backway. The north end of Capitol Reef, along this backcountry road, is filled with towering monoliths, panoramic vistas, and a stark desert landscape. The area is remote and the road through it unpaved, so do not enter without a high-clearance vehicle, some planning, and a cell phone (although reception is spotty). The drive through the valley is a 58-mile loop that you can begin at River Ford Road off Highway 24. From there, the loop travels northwest, giving you access to Glass Mountain, South Desert, and Gypsum Sinkhole. Turning southeast at the sinkhole, the loop takes you past the side road that accesses the Temples of the Moon and Sun, then becomes Caineville Wash Road before ending at Highway 24, 7 miles east of your starting point. Caineville Wash Road has two water crossings. Including stops, allow a half day for this drive. ■ TIP➔ **If your time is limited, you may want to tour only the Caineville Wash Road, which takes about two hours.** At the visitor center you can pick up a self-guided auto tour brochure for $2. ⊠ *River Ford Rd., 11.7 miles east of visitor center on Hwy. 24.*

HIKING

Many park trails in Capitol Reef include steep climbs, but there are a few easy-to-moderate hikes. A short drive from the visitor center takes you to a dozen trails, and a park ranger can advise you on combining trails or locating additional routes.

EASY

Goosenecks Trail. This nice little walk gives you a good introduction to the land surrounding Capitol Reef. Enjoy the dizzying views from the overlook. It's only 0.3 mile round-trip. *Easy.* ⊠ *Trailhead at Hwy. 24, about 3 miles west of the visitor center.*

Grand Wash Trail. At the end of unpaved Grand Wash Road you can continue on foot through the canyon to its end at the Fremont River. You're bound to love the trip. This flat hike takes you through a wide wash between canyon walls. It's an excellent place to study the geology up close. The round-trip hike is 4.5 miles; allow two to three hours for your walk. Check at the ranger station for flash-flood warnings before entering the wash. *Easy.* ⊠ *Trailhead at Hwy. 24, east of Hickman Bridge parking lot, or at end of Grand Wash Rd., off Scenic Dr. about 5 miles from visitor center.*

Sunset Point Trail. The trail starts from the same parking lot as the Goosenecks Trail. Benches along this easy, 0.7 mile round-trip invite you to sit and meditate surrounded by the colorful desert. At the trail's end, you will be rewarded with broad vistas into the park; it's even better at sunset. *Easy.* ⊠ *Trailhead at Hwy. 24, about 3 miles west of visitor center.*

GOOD READS

■ *Capitol Reef: Canyon Country Eden,* by Rose Houk, is an award-winning collection of photographs and lyrical essays on the park.

■ *Dwellers of the Rainbow, Fremont Culture in Capitol Reef National Park,* by Rose Houk, offers a brief background of the Fremont culture in Capitol Reef.

■ *Explore Capitol Reef Trails,* by Marjorie Miller and John Foster, is a comprehensive hiking guide.

■ *Geology of Capitol Reef National Park,* by Michael Collier, teaches the basic geology of the park.

■ *Red Rock Eden,* by George Davidson, tells the story of historic Fruita, its settlements, and orchards.

MODERATE

Capitol Gorge Trail and the Tanks. Starting at the Pioneer Register, about a mile from the Capitol Gorge parking lot, is a trail that climbs to the Tanks, two holes in the sandstone, formed by erosion, that hold water after it rains. After a scramble up about 0.2 mile of steep trail with cliff drop-offs, you can look down into the Tanks and can also see a natural bridge below the lower tank. Including the walk to the Pioneer Register, allow an hour or two for this interesting hike, one of the park's most popular. *Moderate.* ⊠ *Trailhead at end of Scenic Dr., 9 miles south of visitor center.*

FAMILY **Cohab Canyon Trail.** Children particularly love this trail for the geological features and native creatures, such as rock wrens and Western pipistrelles (canyon bats), that you see along the way. One end of the trail is directly across from the Fruita Campground on Scenic Drive, and the other is across from the Hickman Bridge parking lot. The first ¼ mile from Fruita is pretty strenuous, but then the walk becomes easy except for turnoffs to the overlooks, which are strenuous but short. Along the way you'll find miniature arches, skinny side canyons, and honeycombed patterns on canyon walls where the wrens make nests. The trail is 3.2 miles round-trip to the Hickman Bridge parking lot. The Overlook Trail adds 2 miles to the journey. Allow one to two hours to overlooks and back; allow two to three hours to Hickman Bridge parking lot and back. *Moderate.* ⊠ *About 1 mile south of visitor center on Scenic Dr., or about 2 miles east of visitor center on Hwy. 24.*

Fremont River Trail. What starts as a quiet little stroll beside the river turns into an adventure. The first 0.5 mile of the trail is wheelchair accessible as you wander past the orchards next to the Fremont River. After you pass through a narrow gate, the trail changes personality and you're in for a steep climb on an exposed ledge with drop-offs. The views at the top of the 770-foot ascent are worth it as you look down into the Fruita Historic District. The trail is 2.5 miles round-trip; allow two hours. *Moderate.* ⊠ *Trailhead near amphitheater off Loop C of Fruita Campground, about 1 mile from visitor center.*

Temple of the Sun, a monolith in Capitol Reef's Cathedral Valley, is a favorite with photographers.

Golden Throne Trail. As you hike to the base of the Golden Throne, you may be fortunate enough to see one of the park's elusive desert bighorn sheep. You're more likely, however, to spot their small, split-hoof tracks in the sand. The trail itself is 2 miles of gradual elevation gain with some steps and drop-offs. The Golden Throne is hidden until you near the end of the trail, then suddenly you find yourself looking at a huge sandstone monolith. If you hike near sundown the throne burns gold, salmon, and platinum. The round-trip hike is 4 miles and you should allow two to three hours. *Moderate.* ✉ *Trailhead at end of Capitol Gorge Rd., at Capitol Gorge trailhead, 9 miles south of visitor center.*

Hickman Bridge Trail. This trail is a perfect introduction to the park. It leads to a natural bridge of Kayenta sandstone, which has a 135-foot opening carved by intermittent flash floods. Early on, the route climbs a set of steps along the Fremont River, and as the trail tops out onto a bench, you'll find a slight depression in the earth. This is what remains of an ancient Fremont pit house, a kind of home that was dug into the ground and covered with brush. The trail splits, leading along the right-hand branch to a strenuous uphill climb to the Rim Overlook and Navajo Knobs. Stay to your left to see the bridge, and you'll encounter a moderate up-and-down trail. As you continue up the wash on your way to the bridge, you'll notice a Fremont granary on the right side of the small canyon. Allow about 1½ hours to walk the 2-mile round trip. The walk to the bridge is one of the most popular trails in the park, so expect lots of company along the way. *Moderate.* ✉ *Hwy. 24, 2 miles east of visitor center.*

DIFFICULT

Chimney Rock Trail. You're almost sure to see ravens drifting on thermal winds around the deep red Mummy Cliff that rings the base of this trail. This loop trail begins with a steep climb to a rim above Chimney Rock. The trail is 3.5 miles round-trip, with a 600-foot elevation change. Allow three to four hours. *Difficult.* ✉ *Hwy. 24, about 3 miles west of visitor center.*

WHAT'S NEARBY

NEARBY TOWNS

Probably the best home base for exploring the park, the pretty town of **Torrey,** just outside the park, has lots of personality. Giant old cottonwood trees make it a shady, cool place to stay, and the townspeople are friendly and accommodating. A little farther west on Highway 24, tiny **Teasdale** is a charming settlement cradled in a cove of the Aquarius Plateau. The homes, many of which are well-preserved older structures, look out onto brilliantly colored cliffs and green fields. **Bicknell** lies another few miles west of Capitol Reef. Not much happens here, making it a wonderfully quiet place to rest your head. The Wayne County seat of **Loa,** 10 miles west of Torrey, was settled by pioneers in the 1870s. If you head south from Torrey instead of west, you can take a spectacular 32-mile drive along Highway 12 to **Boulder,** a town so remote that its mail was carried on horseback until 1940. Nearby is Anasazi State Park. In the opposite direction, 51 miles east, **Hanksville** is more a crossroads than anything else.

VISITOR INFORMATION
Wayne County Office of Tourism (Bicknell, Hanksville, Loa, Teasdale, Torrey) ☎ *800/858–7951* ⊕ *www.capitolreef.org.* **Garfield County Office of Tourism (Boulder)** ✉ *55 S. Main St., Panguitch* ☎ *800/444–6689* ⊕ *www.brycecanyoncountry.com.*

NEARBY ATTRACTIONS

Anasazi State Park. *Anasazi* is a Navajo word interpreted to mean "ancient enemies." What the Anasazi called themselves we will never know, but their descendants, the Hopi people, prefer the term "Ancestral Puebloan." This state park is dedicated to the study of that mysterious culture, with a largely unexcavated dwelling site, an interactive museum, and a reproduction of a pueblo. ✉ *460 N. Hwy. 12, Boulder* ☎ *435/335–7308* ⊕ *www.stateparks.utah.gov* 💲 *$5* 🕙 *Mar.–Oct., daily 8–6; Nov.–Feb., daily 9–5.*

FAMILY **Goblin Valley State Park.** All of the landscape in this part of the country is surreal, but Goblin Valley takes the cake as the weirdest of all. It's full of hundreds of gnomelike rock formations colored in a dramatic orange hue. Short, easy trails wind through the goblins, which delight children. ✉ *Hwy. 24, 12 miles north of Hanksville* ☎ *435/564–3633* ⊕ *www.stateparks.utah.gov* 💲 *$8 per vehicle* 🕙 *Mar.–Nov., daily 8 am–10 pm; Dec.–Feb., daily 8–5.*

San Rafael Swell. About 80 miles long and 30 miles wide, this massive fold and uplift in the Earth's crust rises 2,100 feet above the desert. The Swell, as it is known locally, is northeast of Capitol Reef, between Interstate 70 and Highway 24. You can take photos from several viewpoints. ✉ *125 S. 600 West, Price* ☎ *435/636–3600* ⊕ *www.blm.gov/ut/st/en/fo/price/more/san_rafael_swell.html.*

12

AREA ACTIVITIES

SPORTS AND THE OUTDOORS
FISHING
Fishlake National Forest. Sitting at an elevation of 8,800 feet is Fish Lake, which lies in the heart of its namesake, 1.4-million-acre forest. The area has several campgrounds and wonderful lodges. The lake is stocked annually with lake and rainbow trout, mackinaw, and splake. A large population of brown trout is native to the lake. The Fremont River Ranger District office can provide all the information you need on camping, fishing, and hiking in the forest. ✉ *138 S. Main St., Loa* ☎ *435/836–2811* ⊕ *www.fs.usda.gov/fishlake.*

TOURS **Alpine Adventures.** With a stellar reputation for personalized attention during fly-fishing trips into the high backcountry around Capitol Reef and the Fremont River, Alpine Adventures also leads trophy hunting and horseback tours. ✉ *Torrey* ☎ *435/425–3660* ⊕ *www.alpineadventuresutah.com.*

SCENIC DRIVES

Burr Trail Scenic Backway. Branching east off Highway 12 in Boulder, Burr Trail travels through the Circle Cliffs area of Grand Staircase–Escalante National Monument into Capitol Reef. The views are of backcountry canyons and gulches. The road is paved between Boulder and the eastern boundary of Capitol Reef. It leads into a hair-raising set of switchbacks—not suitable for RVs or trailers—that ascends 800 feet in ½ mile. Before attempting to drive this route, check with the Capitol Reef Visitor Center for road conditions. From Boulder to its intersection with Notom-Bullfrog Road the route is 36 miles long.

Fodor's Choice **Utah Scenic Byway 12.** Named as one of only 20 All-American Roads in
★ the United States by the National Scenic Byways Program, Highway 12 is not to be missed. The 32-mile stretch between Torrey and Boulder winds through alpine forests and passes vistas of some of America's most remote and wild landscape. It is not for the faint of heart or those afraid of narrow, winding mountain roads.

Utah Scenic Byway 24. For 62 miles between Loa and Hanksville, you'll cut right through Capitol Reef National Park. Colorful rock formations in all their hues of red, cream, pink, gold, and deep purple extend from one end of the route to the other. The closer you get to the park the more colorful the landscape becomes. The vibrant rock finally gives way to lush green hills and the mountains west of Loa.

ARTS AND ENTERTAINMENT

ART GALLERIES

Gallery 24. This pleasing space sells contemporary fine art from Southern Utah–based artists that includes paintings, photography, and ceramics. ✉ *135 E. Main St., Torrey* ☎ *435/425–2124* ⊕ *www.gallery24.biz* ⊙ *Easter–mid-Oct., Mon.–Sat. 11–5:30.*

Torrey Gallery. At this lovely gallery, the art on display from regional artists includes oil paintings, photographs, Navajo rugs, and sculptures. ✉ *80 E. Main St. (Hwy. 24), Torrey* ☎ *435/425–3909* ⊕ *www.torreygallery.com* ⊙ *Mid-Mar.–late Nov., Mon.–Sat. 10–6.*

PERFORMING ARTS

Robber's Roost Bookstore. Open April to October, this shop named after Butch Cassidy's hideout is an excellent place to stop to browse, talk about trails, or find out what's going on around town. It's part coffee bar, part bookstore, and part performance space, all contained in the late Utah writer Ward Roylance's practically teepee-shape house. Robber's Roost is home base for the Entrada Institute, an alliance of arts and outdoor lovers that holds musical events and talks, usually on Saturday nights, from May through October. ✉ *185 W. Main St. (Hwy. 24), Torrey* ☎ *435/425–3265* ⊕ *www.robbersroostbooks.com.*

SHOPPING

Flute Shop Trading Post. Unique and unexpected, the nifty Flute Shop is open year-round and sells Native American–style flutes, rocks, and fossils. ✉ *1705 Scenic Rte. 12, 4 miles south of junction of hwys. 12 and 24, Torrey* ☎ *435/425–3144* ⊕ *www.vancesflutes.blogspot.com* ⊙ *Closed Sun.*

Robber's Roost Books and Beverages. The quiet little Robber's Roost Books and Beverages has books by regional authors, guidebooks, maps, T-shirts, and unique art items. The shop is only open from April to October. ✉ *185 W. Main St., Torrey* ☎ *435/425–3265* ⊕ *www.robbersroostbooks.com.*

WHERE TO EAT

IN THE PARK

PICNIC AREA

✗ **Gifford Farmhouse.** In a grassy meadow with the Fremont River flowing by, this is an idyllic shady spot in the Fruita Historic District for a sack lunch. Picnic tables, drinking water, grills, and a convenient restroom make it perfect. ✉ *On Scenic Dr., 1 mile south of visitor center*

OUTSIDE THE PARK

$$$ ✗ **Cafe Diablo.** This restaurant is one of the state's best. White plaster
AMERICAN walls are a perfect setting for the local art on display in the intimate
Fodor'sChoice dining room. Innovative Southwestern entrées include marinated Utah
★ lamb, and beef tenderloin medallions topped with roasted-shallot

CLOSE UP

Best Campgrounds in Capitol Reef

Campgrounds in Capitol Reef fill up fast between Memorial Day and Labor Day, though that goes mainly for the superconvenient Fruita Campground and not the more remote backcountry sites. Most of the area's state parks have camping facilities, and the region's two national forests offer many wonderful sites.

Cathedral Valley Campground. You'll find this primitive (no water, pit toilet) campground, about 30 miles from Highway 24, in the park's remote northern district. ✉ *Hartnet Junction, on Caineville Wash Rd.* ☎ *435/425–3791.*

Cedar Mesa Campground. Wonderful views of the Waterpocket Fold and Henry Mountains surround this primitive campground in the park's southern district. ✉ *Notom-Bullfrog Rd., 22 miles south of Hwy. 24* ☎ *435/425–3791.*

Fruita Campground. Near the orchards and the Fremont River, the park's developed (flush toilets, running water), shady campground is a great place to call home for a few days. The sites nearest the river or the orchards are the very best. ✉ *Scenic Dr., about 1 mile south of visitor center* ☎ *435/425–3791.*

butter. The rattlesnake cakes, made with free-range desert rattler and served with ancho-rosemary aioli, are delicious and a steadfast menu item. Try the pastries and ice cream made with fruits picked at nearby Fruita. [$] *Average main: $26* ✉ *599 W. Main St. (Hwy. 24), Torrey* ☎ *435/425–3070* 🌐 *www.cafediablo.net* 🕓 *Closed late Oct.–early Apr.*

$$ AMERICAN 🍴 **Capitol Reef Café.** For a varied selection of solid fare, visit this unpretentious eatery. Favorites include the vegetable salad and the flaky smoked or grilled fillet of rainbow trout, and the breakfasts are both delicious and hearty. There are a handful of vegetarian offerings—including mushroom lasagna—and a surprisingly expansive beer and wine list. Earth tones and Native American flute music make for a truly laid-back vibe, and the attached gift shop has an eclectic selection of books about the Southwest. [$] *Average main: $13* ✉ *360 W. Main St. (Hwy. 24), Torrey* ☎ *435/425–3271* 🌐 *www.capitolreefinn.com* 🕓 *Closed Nov.–Mar.*

$$$ ECLECTIC 🍴 **Hell's Backbone Grill.** One of the best restaurants in southern Utah, this remote spot is well worth the drive. The menu is inspired by American Indian, Western range, Southwestern, and Mormon pioneer recipes. The owners, who are also the chefs, have a historical connection to the area, and many of the ingredients they use come directly from their own organic farm. Because they insist on fresh ingredients, the menu changes weekly. The restaurant closes between lunch and dinner, 2:30 to 5. [$] *Average main: $25* ✉ *20 N. Hwy. 12, Boulder* ☎ *435/335–7464* 🌐 *www.hellsbackbonegrill.com* 🕓 *Closed Dec.–mid-Mar.*

$ AMERICAN 🍴 **Little L's Bakery.** If you are traveling by way of Panguitch, stop by this charming bakery for the homemade cheddar-and-bacon muffins, pot pies, or a raspberry donut and your favorite coffee drink priced at half the big-city version. The surroundings alone are worth a peek at this roomy bakery-coffeehouse, with tabletops made from antique doors and a counter area reminiscent of an old-time grocery. [$] *Average main: $5* ✉ *32 N. Main St., Panguitch* ☎ *435/676–8750.*

$ FAST FOOD 🍴 **Stan's Burger Shak.** This is the traditional pit stop between Lake Powell and Capitol Reef, featuring great burgers, fries, and shakes—and the only homemade onion rings you'll find for miles and miles. Keep in mind it generally closes for the winter in early December and reopens in February. [$] *Average main: $8* ✉ *140 S. Hwy. 95, Hanksville* ☎ *435/542–3330.*

NOTABLE QUOTE

"The colors (at Capitol Reef) are such as no pigments can portray. So luminous are they that the light seems to flow or shine out of the rock rather than to be reflected from it."

—Clarence Dutton

WHERE TO STAY

OUTSIDE THE PARK

$ HOTEL 🏨 **Aquarius Inn.** Large, comfortable rooms and recreational facilities such as an indoor pool and basketball and volleyball courts make this an attractive place for families. **Pros:** not too far from Torrey and Capitol Reef. **Cons:** Bicknell might be too tiny and quiet for some; can fill quickly on summer weekends. [$] *Rooms from: $57* ✉ *240 W. Main St., Bicknell* ☎ *435/425–3835, 800/833–5379* 🌐 *www.aquariusinn.com* 🛏 *28 rooms, 1 suite* 🍽 *No meals.*

$$$ HOTEL 🏨 **Boulder Mountain Lodge.** If you're traveling between Capitol Reef and Bryce Canyon national parks, don't miss this wonderful lodge with a fireplace in the great room and a remarkably good restaurant on the premises, right on scenic Highway 12. **Pros:** a perfect spot for peace and solitude; the service and care given to guests is impeccable. **Cons:** some might find the middle-of-nowhere location too remote. [$] *Rooms from: $160* ✉ *Hwy. 12 at Burr Trail, Boulder* ☎ *435/335–7460, 800/556–3446* 🌐 *www.boulder-utah.com* 🛏 *20 rooms, 2 suites* 🍽 *No meals.*

$ RESORT 🏨 **Fish Lake Resorts.** Here you can find everything from rustic cabins that sleep two to deluxe rental cabins with six bedrooms, all of which focus on function rather than cute amenities. **Pros:** great place for families and groups to congregate. **Cons:** some cabins are a little close together—so not the best for solitude. [$] *Rooms from: $65* ✉ *HC80, Rte. 25, Loa* ☎ *435/638–1000* 🌐 *www.fishlake.com* 🛏 *41 cabins* 🍽 *No meals.*

$$$ HOTEL Fodor's Choice ★ 🏨 **Lodge at Red River Ranch.** You'll swear you've walked into one of the great lodges of Western legend when you walk through the doors at Red River Ranch. **Pros:** furnishings and artifacts so distinctive they could grace the pages of a design magazine. **Cons:** rooms are on the small side. [$] *Rooms from: $160* ✉ *2900 W. Hwy. 24, Teasdale* ☎ *435/425–3322, 800/205–6343* 🌐 *www.redriverranch.com* 🛏 *15 rooms* 🍽 *No meals.*

$$ B&B/INN **Muley Twist Inn.** This gorgeous inn sits on 15 acres of land, with expansive views of the colorful landscape in just about every direction. **Pros:** dramatic setting against a beautiful rock cliff; a place you can slow down and unwind; all rooms have private baths. **Cons:** might be too far away from it all for some. [$] *Rooms from: $135* ✉ *249 W. 125 S., Teasdale* ☎ *435/425–3640, 800/530–1038* 🌐 *www.muleytwistinn.com* 🛏 *5 rooms* 🕒 *Closed Nov.–Mar.* 🍴 *Breakfast.*

$ HOTEL **Rim Rock Inn.** On a bluff with outstanding views into the desert, this motel was the first one to accommodate visitors to Capitol Reef. **Pros:** stunning views in every direction; reasonably priced. **Cons:** predictable motel-style rooms; no shade on property. [$] *Rooms from: $64* ✉ *2523 E. Hwy. 24, Torrey* ☎ *435/425–3398* 🌐 *www.therimrock.net* 🛏 *19 rooms* 🕒 *Closed Nov.–Mar.* 🍴 *Breakfast.*

$ B&B/INN **Snuggle Inn.** Individually decorated rooms, with features such as four-poster beds and pieces of Western artwork culled from the proprietor's personal collection, give this family-owned inn a homey feel. **Pros:** lots of character; modern amenities. **Cons:** few off-site restaurants nearby. [$] *Rooms from: $65* ✉ *55 S. Main St., Loa* ☎ *435/836–2898, 877/505–1936* 🌐 *www.thesnuggleinn.com* 🛏 *11 rooms, 4 suites* 🍴 *No meals.*

$ HOTEL **Sunglow.** This well-maintained and inexpensive motel in the heart of Bicknell has rooms that are clean, nicely furnished, and inexpensive. **Pros:** amazing pies in restaurant; new owners are giving rooms a face-lift. **Cons:** few amenities, either at this motel or in this small town. [$] *Rooms from: $58* ✉ *91 E. Main St., Bicknell* ☎ *435/425–3821* 🌐 *www.sunglowmotel.com* 🛏 *15 rooms* 🍴 *No meals.*

CARLSBAD CAVERNS NATIONAL PARK

WELCOME TO CARLSBAD CAVERNS

TOP REASONS TO GO

★ **400,000 hungry bats:** From mid-May to late October, bats wing to and from the caverns in a swirling, visible tornado.

★ **Take a guided tour through the underworld:** Plummet 75 stories underground and step into enormous caves hung with stalactites and bristling with stalagmites.

★ **Living Desert Zoo and Gardens:** More preserve than zoo, this 1,500-acre park houses scores of rare species, including endangered Mexican wolves, Bolson tortoises, and black bears.

★ **Birding at Rattlesnake Springs:** Nine-tenths of the park's 330 bird species, including roadrunners, golden eagles, and acrobatic cave swallows, visit this green desert oasis.

★ **Pecos River:** A Southwest landmark and recreational oasis, the Pecos River flows through the heart of nearby Carlsbad.

1 Bat Flight. Cowboy Jim White discovered the caverns after noticing that a swirling smokestack of bats appeared there each morning and evening. White is long gone, but the 400,000-member bat colony is still here, snatching up 3 tons of bugs a night. Watch them leave at dusk from the amphitheater near the park visitor center.

2 Carlsbad Caverns Big Room Tour. Travel 75 stories below the surface to visit the Big Room, where you can traipse beneath a 255-foot-tall ceiling and take in immense and eerie cave formations. Situated directly beneath the park visitor center, the room can be accessed via quick-moving elevator or the natural cave entrance.

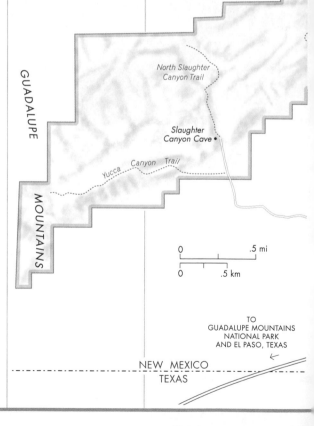

GUADALUPE

MOUNTAINS

North Slaughter
Canyon Trail

Slaughter
Canyon Cave

Yucca Canyon Trail

0   .5 mi

0   .5 km

TO
GUADALUPE MOUNTAINS
NATIONAL PARK
AND EL PASO, TEXAS

NEW MEXICO

TEXAS

**3 Living Desert Zoo
& Gardens State Park.**
Endangered river cooters,
Bolson tortoises, and Mexican wolves all roam in this
sprawling hilltop preserve.
You can skip alongside
roadrunners and slim wild
turkeys in the park's aviary,
visit a small group of cougars, and view exhibits of
the area's smaller creatures.
The Living Desert is on the
west side of Carlsbad, New
Mexico, 27 miles north of
the park.

4 The Pecos River.
Running through the town of
Carlsbad, the Pecos River is
a landmark of the Southwest
that gives life to boating,
water-skiing, and fishing. In
winter, residents gussy up
dozens of riverside homes
for the holiday season.

NEW
MEXICO

13

GETTING
ORIENTED

To reach the essence of
Carlsbad Caverns National
Park, you have to delve
below the surface—literally. Most of the park's key
sights are underground
in a massive latticework
of caves (there are 117
known caves in all,
although not all are open
to visitors; a variety of
tours leave from the visitor center). The park also
has a handful of trails and
scenic drives aboveground,
where you can experience
the Chihuahuan Desert
and some magnificent
geological formations.

TO
CARLSBAD,
LIVING DESERT
ZOO AND GARDENS,
AND PECOS RIVER

3 4

Walnut Canyon Desert Dr.

7

2 1
• Cavern Entrance
Visitor Center

Whites
City

Rattlesnake
Canyon Trail

62
180

**Rattlesnake
5 Springs**

418

62
180

5 Rattlesnake Springs.
Despite 30,000-plus acres in
which to roam, nine-tenths
of the park's 330-plus species of birds show up at
Rattlesnake Springs at one
time or another—probably
because it's one of the few
water sources in this area.

Updated by
Marty Racine

On the surface, Carlsbad Caverns National Park is deceptively normal—but all bets are off once visitors set foot in the elevator, which plunges 75 stories underground. The country beneath the surface is part silky darkness, part subterranean hallucination. The snaky, illuminated walkway seems less like a trail and more like a foray across the River Styx and into the underworld. Within more than 14 football fields of this netherworld are hundreds of formations that alternately resemble cakes, soda straws, ocean waves, and the large, leering face of a mountain troll.

CARLSBAD CAVERNS PLANNER

WHEN TO GO

While the desert above may alternately bake or freeze, the caverns remain in the mid-50s. If you're coming to see the Brazilian free-tailed bat, come between spring and mid-fall.

AVG. HIGH/LOW TEMPS.

JAN.	FEB.	MAR.	APR.	MAY	JUNE
57/27	63/32	70/38	79/47	87/56	95/64

JULY	AUG.	SEPT.	OCT.	NOV.	DEC.
95/67	93/66	87/59	79/47	67/35	59/29

FESTIVAL AND EVENTS

Star Parties. Coinciding with the new or first-quarter moon of every other month, star parties are held outside Living Desert Zoo & Gardens State Park about six times a year. A laser tour and powerful telescope bring the heavens closer. Call for exact scheduling. ⊠ *1504 Miehls Dr., Carlsbad* ☎ *575/887–5516* ⊕ *www.emnrd.state.nm.us.*

MAY **Mescal Roast and Mountain Spirit Dances.** This May celebration at Living Desert Zoo & Gardens State Park commemorates the connection that indigenous Mescalero Apaches have long had with the Guadalupe Mountains, where mescal plants were gathered for food. Descendants of the original Mescaleros perform a blessing in their native language, and everyone gets to taste the fruit from the mescal-baking pits. Fruit and candy is available as well. ⊠ *1504 Miehls Dr., Carlsbad* ☎ *575/887–5516* ⊕ *www.emnrd.state.nm.us.*

JULY/AUGUST **Bat Flight Breakfast.** In mid-summer once each year, early risers gather at the cave's entrance to eat breakfast and watch tens of thousands of bats return home from their nocturnal search for food. The breakfast is held either in July or August; check with the park for the 2014 date. ⊠ *727 Carlsbad Caverns Hwy., Carlsbad* ☎ *575/785–2232* ⊕ *www.nps.gov/cave.*

DECEMBER **Christmas on the Pecos.** Magical Christmas displays decorate Carlsbad mansions along a 3-mile-plus stretch of the Pecos River in a fairyland of seasonal delight. Boat tours ($17.50 Friday and Saturday, $12.50 Sunday to Thursday) run from Thanksgiving night through New Year's Eve except Christmas Eve, beginning at 5:30. Vessels depart from the Pecos River Village Conference Center. Purchase tickets there or at the Carlsbad Chamber of Commerce (⊠ *302 S. Canal Street*). ⊠ *Pecos River Village Conference Center, 711 Muscatel Dr., Carlsbad* ☎ *575/887–6516, 575/628–0952 after Oct. 1* ⊕ *www.christmasonthepecos.com.*

PLANNING YOUR TIME

CARLSBAD CAVERNS IN ONE DAY

In a single day, visitors can easily view both the eerie, exotic caverns and the volcano of bats that erupts from the caverns each evening. Unless you're attending the annual Bat Flight Breakfast, when visitors have the morning meal with rangers and then view the early-morning bat return, go ahead and sleep past sunrise and then stroll into the caves.

For the full experience, begin by taking the **Natural Entrance Route Tour,** which allows visitors to trek into the cave from surface level. This tour winds past the Boneyard, with its intricate ossifications and a massive boulder called the Iceberg. After 1¼ miles, or about an hour, the route links up with the **Big Room Route.** If you're not in good health or are traveling with young children, you might want to skip the Natural Entrance and start with the Big Room Route, which begins at the foot of the elevator. This underground walk extends 1¼ miles on level, paved ground, and takes about 1½ hours to complete. There is a shortcut option that's about two-thirds as long. If you have made reservations in advance or happen on some openings, you also can take the **King's Palace** guided tour for 1 mile and an additional 1½ hours. It leaves from the Big Room near the elevator. At 83 stories deep, the palace is the lowest part of the cave open to the public. By this time, you will have spent four hours in the cave. Take the elevator back up to the top. If you're not yet tuckered out, consider a short hike along the sunny, self-guided ½-mile **Desert Nature Walk** by the visitor center.

To picnic by the birds, bees, and water of **Rattlesnake Springs,** take U.S. 62/180 south from White's City 5½ miles, and turn back west onto Route 418. You'll find old-growth shade trees, grass, picnic tables, restrooms, and water. Many varieties of birds flit from tree to tree. Return to the Carlsbad Caverns entrance road and take the 9½-mile Walnut Canyon Desert Drive loop. Leave yourself enough time to return to the **visitor center** for the evening bat flight.

GETTING HERE AND AROUND

AIR TRAVEL

The nearest full-service airport is in El Paso, 154 miles away. Cavern City Air Terminal, located between Carlsbad and the park, is utilized by smaller, regional carriers.

CAR TRAVEL

Carlsbad Caverns is 27 miles southwest of Carlsbad, New Mexico, and 35 miles north of Guadalupe Mountains National Park via U.S. 62/180. The 7-mile Carlsbad Caverns Highway from White's City is paved with pull-outs, which allow motorists to take in the view. Be alert for wildlife crossing roadways, especially in the early morning and at night.

PARK ESSENTIALS

PARK FEES AND PERMITS

No fee is charged for parking or to enter the aboveground portion of the park. It costs $10 to descend into Carlsbad Caverns either by elevator or through the Natural Entrance. Costs for special tours range from $7 to $20 plus general admission.

Those planning overnight hikes must obtain a free backcountry permit, and all hikers are advised to stop at the visitor center information desk for current information about trails. Trails are poorly defined, but can be followed with a topographic map. Dogs are not allowed in the park, but a kennel is available at the park visitor center for a fee.

PARK HOURS

The park is open year-round, except Christmas Day. From Memorial Day weekend through Labor Day, tours are conducted from 8:30 to 5; the last entry into the cave via the Natural Entrance is at 3:30, and the last entry into the cave via the elevator is at 5. After Labor Day until Memorial Day weekend, tours are conducted from 8:30 to 3:30; the last entry into the cave via the Natural Entrance is at 2, and the last entry into the cave via the elevator is 3:30. Carlsbad Caverns is in the Mountain time zone.

CELL-PHONE RECEPTION

Cell phones only work about 10% of the time in the park. Public telephones are at the visitor center.

RESTAURANTS

Choice isn't an issue inside Carlsbad Caverns National Park because there are just three dining options—the surface-level café, the underground snack bar, and the bring-it-in-yourself option. Luckily, everything is reasonably priced (especially for national park eateries).

Prices in the reviews are the average cost of a main course at dinner, or if dinner is not served, at lunch.

HOTELS

The only overnight option within the arid, rugged park is to make your own campsite in the backcountry, at least half a mile from any trail.

Outside the park, however, options expand. White's City, which is less than 10 miles to the east of the park, has a Rodeway Inn, which is near the boardwalk that connects shopping and entertainment options. In Carlsbad there are even more choices, but many of them aren't as appealing as they once were. The hotels here are aging and not particularly well maintained, so don't expect a mint on your pillow. Still, most are clean if less than opulent.

Prices in the reviews are the lowest cost of a standard double room in high season. For expanded reviews, facilities, and current deals, visit Fodors.com.

VISITOR INFORMATION
PARK CONTACT INFORMATION
Carlsbad Caverns National Park ⊠ *3225 National Parks Hwy., Carlsbad* ☎ *575/785–2232, 877/444–6777 for cave tour reservations* ⊕ *www.nps.gov/cave.*

VISITOR CENTERS
Carlsbad Caverns National Park Visitor Center. Within this user-friendly facility at the top of an escarpment, a 75-seat theater offers engrossing films and ranger programs about the different types of caves. Exhibits offer a primer on bats, geology, wildlife, and the early tribes and settlers that once lived in and passed through the Carlsbad Caverns area. Friendly rangers staff an information desk, where tickets and maps are sold. A gift shop and bookstore also are on the premises. ⊠ *727 Carlsbad Caverns Hwy., 7 miles west of U.S. 62/180* ☎ *575/785–2232* ☉ *Late May–early Sept., daily 8–7; early Sept.–late May, daily 8–5.*

EXPLORING

SCENIC DRIVES

Walnut Canyon Desert Drive. This scenic drive begins ½ mile from the visitor center. It travels 9½ miles along the top of a ridge to the edge of Rattlesnake Canyon and sinks back down through upper Walnut Canyon to the main entrance road. The backcountry scenery on this one-way gravel loop is stunning; go late in the afternoon or early in the morning to enjoy the full spectrum of changing light and dancing colors. Along the way, you'll be able to see Big Hill Seep's trickling water, the tall, flowing ridges of the Guadalupe mountain range, and maybe even some robust mule deer. The scenic road is not for RVs or trailers, and it can occasionally be closed for maintenance.

SCENIC STOPS

FAMILY **The Big Room.** With a floor space equal to about 14 football fields, this
Fodor'sChoice subterranean focal point of Carlsbad Caverns clues visitors in to just
★ how large the caverns really are. The White House could fit in one corner of the Big Room, and wouldn't come close to grazing the 255-foot
ceiling. Entrance can be accessed by elevator or, for the moderately
fit with about an hour to spare, through the Natural Entrance and a
1.25-mile descending trail. Either way, at 750 feet below the surface
you will connect with the self-guided 1.25-mile Big Room loop, a relatively level, paved pathway through the almost hallucinatory wonders
of various formations and decorations. You also get a layman's lesson
on how the cave was carved. An audio guide is available from the visitor center bookstore for a few dollars. Kids under 15 are admitted for
free. ■TIP➜ Even in summer, long pants and long-sleeved shirts are
advised for cave temperatures in the mid-50s. ⊠ *Visitor Center, 727
Carlsbad Caverns Hwy.* 🕮 *$10* ⊘ *Late May–early Sept., daily 8:30–5
(last entry into Natural Entrance at 3:30; last entry into elevator at 5);
early Sept.–late May, daily 8:30–3:30 (last entry into Natural Entrance
at 2; last entry into elevator at 3:30).*

Natural Entrance. As natural daylight recedes, a self-guided, paved trail
leads downward from the yawning mouth of the main cavern, about
100 yards east of the visitor center. The route is winding and sometimes
slick from water seepage above ground. A steep descent of about 750
feet, much of it secured by hand rails, takes you about a mile through
the main corridor and past features such as the Bat Cave and the Boneyard. (Despite its eerie name, the formations here don't look much like
femurs and fibulas; they're more like spongy bone insides.) Iceberg Rock
is a massive boulder that dropped from the cave ceiling millennia ago.
After about a mile, you'll link up underground with the 1.25-mile Big
Room trail and return to the surface via elevator. ■TIP➜ Footware with
a good grip is recommended. ⊠ *7 miles west of U.S. 62/180, 727 Carlsbad Caverns Hwy.* 🕮 *$10* ⊘ *Late May–early Sept., daily 8:30–3:30;
early Sept.–late May, daily 9–2.*

Rattlesnake Springs. Enormous cottonwood trees shade the picnic and
recreation area at this cool, secluded oasis near Black River. The rare
desert wetland harbors butterflies, mammals, and reptiles, as well as
90% of the park's 330 bird species. Don't let the name scare you; there
may be rattlesnakes here, but no more than at any similar site in the
Southwest. Restroom facilities are available, but overnight camping
and parking are not allowed. ⊠ *Hwy. 418* ✛ *Take U.S. 62/180 5½
miles south of White's City and turn west onto Hwy. 418 for 2½ miles.*

EDUCATIONAL OFFERINGS

RANGER PROGRAMS

Fodor'sChoice **Evening Bat Flight Program.** In the amphitheater at the Natural Cave
★ Entrance (off a short trail from main parking lot) a ranger discusses
the park's batty residents before the creatures begin their sundown exo-
dus. The bats aren't on any predictable schedule, so times are a little

CLOSE UP

Plants and Wildlife in Carlsbad Caverns

Without a doubt, the park's most prominent and popular residents are Brazilian free-tailed bats. These bats have bodies that barely span a woman's hand, yet sport wings that would cover a workingman's boot. Female bats give birth to a single pup each year, which usually weighs more than a quarter of what an adult bat does. Their tiny noses and big ears enable them to search for the many tons of bugs they consume over their lifetime. Numbering nearly a third of a million, these tiny creatures are the park's mascot.

Famous bats aside, there is much more wildlife to recommend in the park. One of New Mexico's best birding areas is at Rattlesnake Springs. Summer and fall migrations give you the best chance of spotting the most varieties of the more than 330 species of birds. Lucky visitors may spot a golden eagle, a rare visitor, or get the thrill of glimpsing a brilliant, gray-and-crimson vermilion flycatcher.

Snakes generally appear in summer. ■TIP→ If you're out walking, be wary of different rattlesnake species, such as banded-rocks and diamondbacks. If you see one, don't panic. Rangers say they are more scared of us than we are of them. Just don't make any sudden moves, and slowly walk away or back around the vipers.

This area is also remarkable because of its location in the Chihuahuan Desert, which sprouts unique plant life. There are thick stands of raspy-leaved yuccas, as well as the agave (mescal) plants that were once a food source for early Native-American tribes. The leaves of this leggy plant are still roasted in sand pits by tribal elders during traditional celebrations.

In spring, thick stands of yucca plants unfold white flowers on their tall stalks. Blossoming cacti and desert wildflowers are among the natural wonders of Walnut Canyon. You'll see bright red blossoms adorning reach-for-the-sky ocotillo plants, and sunny yellow blooms sprouting from prickly pear cactus.

---

iffy. Ideally, viewers will first hear the bats preparing to exit, courtesy of an amplified frequency calibrated to human ears, followed by a vortex of black specks swirling out of the cave mouth in search of dinner against the darkening sky. When conditions are favorable, hundreds of thousands of bats will soar off over the span of half an hour or longer. ⊠ *727 Carlsbad Caverns Hwy.* ☎ *575/785–3012* ✉ *Free* ☉ *Mid-May– mid-Oct., nightly at sundown.*

SPORTS AND THE OUTDOORS

BIRD-WATCHING

From redheaded turkey vultures to svelte golden eagles, about 330 species of birds have been identified in Carlsbad Caverns National Park. Ask for a checklist at the visitor center and then start looking for greater roadrunners, red-winged blackbirds, white-throated swifts, northern flickers, and pygmy nuthatches.

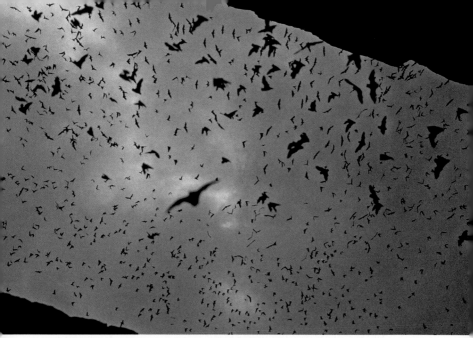

Mexican (sometimes referred to as Brazilian) free-tailed bats swarm out of the caves each evening to hunt for food; they return just before dawn.

FAMILY
Fodor's Choice
★

Rattlesnake Springs. Offering one of the best bird habitats in New Mexico, this is a natural wetland with old-growth cottonwoods. Because southern New Mexico is in the northernmost region of the Chihuahuan Desert, you're likely to see birds that can't be found anywhere else in the United States outside extreme southern Texas and Arizona. If you see a flash of crimson, you might have spotted a vermilion flycatcher. Wild turkeys also flap around this oasis, which also has a shaded picnic area. Potable water and permanent toilets are onsite. As elsewhere in the park, you are expected to keep your footprint small. Do not disturb, and if you pack it in, pack it out. ⊠ *Hwy. 418, 2½ miles west of U.S. 62/180, 5½ miles south of White's City.*

HIKING

Deep, dark, and mysterious, the Carlsbad Caverns are such a park focal point that the 40,000-plus acres of wilderness above them have gone largely undeveloped. This is great news for people who pull on their hiking boots when they're looking for solitude. What you find are rudimentary trails that crisscross the dry, textured terrain and lead up to elevations of 6,000 feet or more. These routes often take a half day or more to travel; at least one, Guadalupe Ridge Trail, is long enough that it calls for an overnight stay. Walkers who just want a little dusty taste of desert flowers and wildlife should try the Desert Nature Walk.

Finding the older, less well-maintained trails can be difficult. Pick up a topographical map at the visitor center bookstore, and be sure to pack a lot of water. There's none out in the desert, and you'll need at least a gallon per person per day. The high elevation coupled with a potent sunshine punch can deliver a nasty sunburn, so pack SPF 30 (or higher) sunblock and a hat, even in winter. You can't bring pets, but you do have to bring a backcountry permit if you're camping. They're free at the visitor center.

EASY

FAMILY **Desert Nature Walk.** While waiting for the night bat-flight program, try taking the 0.5-mile self-guided hike that begins just east of the visitor center. The tagged and identified flowers and plants make this a good place to get acquainted with much of the local desert flora. Part of the trail is an easy stroll even for the littlest ones, and part is wheelchair accessible. The payoff is great for everyone, too: a big, vivid view of the desert basin. *Easy.* ⊠ *Trailhead east of the visitor center.*

FAMILY **Rattlesnake Canyon Overlook Trail.** A 0.25-mile stroll off Walnut Canyon Scenic Drive offers a nice overlook of the green-carpeted Rattlesnake Canyon. *Easy.* ⊠ *Trail begins at mile marker 9 on Walnut Canyon Scenic Dr.*

MODERATE

Juniper Ridge Trail. Climb up in elevation as you head north on this nearly 3-mile trail, which leads to the northern edge of the park and then turns toward Crooked Canyon. While not the most notable trail, it's challenging enough to keep things interesting. Allow yourself half a day, and be sure to bring lots of water, especially when the temperature is high. *Moderate.* ⊠ *Trailhead at mile marker 8.8 of Desert Loop Dr.*

Old Guano Road Trail. Meandering a little more than 3.5 miles one way on mostly flat terrain, the trail dips sharply toward White's City campground, where it ends. Give yourself about half a day to complete the walk. Depending on the temperature, this walk can be taxing, but the high desert sun can be potent any time of the year. Wear a hat and drink lots of water. *Moderate.* ⊠ *Trailhead at the Bat Flight Amphitheater, near the Natural Cave Entrance.*

Rattlesnake Canyon Trail. Rock cairns loom over this trail, which descends from 4,570 to 3,900 feet as it winds into the canyon. Allow half a day to trek down into the canyon and make the somewhat strenuous climb out; the total trip is about 6 miles. *Moderate.* ⊠ *Trail begins at mile marker 9 on Walnut Canyon Desert Dr.*

Fodor's Choice **Yucca Canyon Trail.** Sweeping views of the Guadalupe Mountains and
★ El Capitan give allure to this trail. Drive past Rattlesnake Springs and stop at the park boundary before reaching the Slaughter Canyon Cave parking lot. Turn west along the boundary fence line to the trailhead. The 6-mile round trip begins at the mouth of Yucca Canyon and climbs up to the top of the escarpment. Here you find the panoramic view. Most people turn around at this point; the hearty can continue along a poorly maintained route that follows the top of the ridge. The first part of the hike takes half a day. If you continue on, the hike takes a full day. *Moderate.* ⊠ *Trailhead at Slaughter Canyon Cave parking lot, Hwy. 418, 10 miles west of U.S. 62/180.*

DIFFICULT

Guadalupe Ridge Trail. This long, winding ramble follows an old road all the way to the western edge of the park. Because of its length (about 12 miles), an overnight stay in the backcountry is suggested. The hike may be long, but for serious hikers the up-close-and-personal views into Rattlesnake and Slaughter canyons are more than worth it—not to mention the serenity of being miles and miles away from civilization. *Difficult.* ⊠ *Trailhead 4.8 miles down Desert Loop Dr.*

North Slaughter Canyon Trail. Beginning at the Slaughter Canyon Cave parking lot, the trail traverses a heavily vegetated canyon bottom into a remote part of the park. As you begin hiking, look off to the east (to your right) to see the dun-colored ridges and wrinkles of the Elephant Back formation, the first of many dramatic limestone formations visible from the trail. The route travels 5.5 miles one way, the last 3 miles steeply climbing onto a limestone ridge escarpment. Allow a full day for the round trip. *Difficult.* ⊠ *Trailhead at Slaughter Canyon Cave parking lot, Hwy. 418, 10 miles west of U.S. 62/180.*

CAVING

Carlsbad Caverns is famous for the beauty and breadth of its inky depths, as well as for the accessibility of some of its largest caves. All cave tours, except for the self-guided Natural Entrance and Big Room, are ranger led, so safety is rarely an issue in the caves, no matter how remote. There are no other tour guides in the area, nor is there an equipment retailer other than the Walmart in Carlsbad, 23 miles away. Depending on the difficulty of your cave selection (Spider Cave is the hardest to navigate), you'll need at most knee pads, gloves, flashlight batteries, sturdy pants, hiking boots with ankle support, and some water.

Hall of the White Giant. Plan to squirm through some tight passages for long distances to access a very remote chamber, where you'll see towering, glistening white formations that explain the name. This strenuous, ranger-led tour lasts about four hours. Steep drop-offs might elate you—or make you queasy. Wear sturdy hiking shoes and bring gloves, kneepads, and four AA batteries with you. Visitors must be at least 12 years old. ⊠ *Visitor center, 727 Carlsbad Caverns Hwy.* ☎ *877/444–6777* ⊒ *$20* ⚲ *Reservations essential* ☉ *Tours Sat. at 1.*

Fodor's Choice **King's Palace.** Throughout this regal room, stunningly handsome and
★ indeed fit for a king, you'll see leggy "soda straws" large enough for a giant to sip, plus bizarre formations that defy reality. The tour also winds through the Queen's Chamber, dressed in ladylike, multitiered curtains of stone. The mile-long walk is on a paved trail, but there's one steep hill toward the end. This ranger-guided tour lasts about 1½ hours and gives you a "look" at the natural essence of a cave—a complete blackout, when artificial lights (and sound) are extinguished. While advance reservations are highly recommended, this is the one tour you might be able to sign up for on the spot. Children younger than 4 aren't allowed on this tour. ⊠ *Visitor center, 727 Carlsbad Caverns Hwy.* ☎ *877/444–6777* ⊒ *$8* ☉ *Tours: late May–early Sept., daily 10, 11, noon, 2, and 3; early Sept.–late May, daily 10 and 1.*

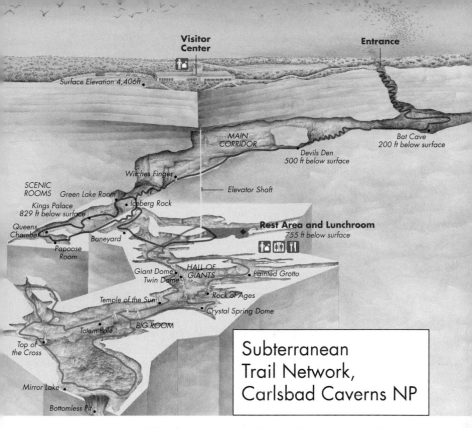

Subterranean Trail Network, Carlsbad Caverns NP

Visitor Center

Entrance

Surface Elevation 4,406 ft

MAIN CORRIDOR

Bat Cave
200 ft below surface

Devils Den
500 ft below surface

Witches Finger

Elevator Shaft

SCENIC ROOMS

Green Lake Room

Iceberg Rock

Kings Palace
829 ft below surface

Queens Chamber

Papoose Room

Boneyard

Rest Area and Lunchroom
755 ft below surface

Giant Dome
Twin Dome

HALL OF GIANTS

Painted Grotto

Temple of the Sun

Rock of Ages

Crystal Spring Dome

Totem Pole

BIG ROOM

Top of the Cross

Mirror Lake

Bottomless Pit

Lower Cave. Fifty-foot vertical ladders and a dirt path lead you into undeveloped portions of Carlsbad Caverns. It takes about half a day to negotiate this moderately strenuous side trip led by a knowledgeable ranger. Visitors must bring gloves and four AA batteries. Children younger than 12 are not allowed on this tour. ⊠ *Visitor center, 727 Carlsbad Caverns Hwy.* ☎ *877/444-6777* ✉ *$20* ⚲ *Reservations essential* ◷ *Tours weekdays at 1.*

Slaughter Canyon Cave. Discovered in the 1930s by a local goatherd, this cave is one of the most popular secondary sites in the park, about 23 miles southwest of the main Carlsbad Caverns and visitor center. Both the hike to the cave mouth and the tour will take about half a day, but it's worth it to view the deep cavern darkness as it's punctuated only by flashlights and, sometimes, headlamps. From the Slaughter Canyon parking area, give yourself 45 minutes to make the steep ½-mile climb up a trail leading to the mouth of the cave. Arrange to be there a quarter of an hour earlier than the appointed time. You'll find that the cave consists primarily of a single corridor, 1,140 feet long, with numerous side passages.

You can take some worthwhile pictures of this cave. Wear hiking shoes with ankle support, and carry plenty of water. You're also expected to bring your own reliable two-D-cell flashlight. Children younger than 6 are not permitted. It's a great adventure if you're in shape and love caving.

✉ *End of Hwy. 418, 10 miles west of U.S. 62/180* ☎ *877/444–6777* ⊕ *www.nps.gov/cave* 💲 *Adults, $15; children and seniors, $7.50* 🔑 *Reservations essential* ⏱ *Memorial Day–mid-Aug., daily at 8:30 am; mid-Aug.–Memorial Day, weekends at 8:30 am.*

Spider Cave. Visitors may not expect to have an adventure in a cavern system as developed and well stocked as Carlsbad Caverns, but serious cavers and energetic types have the chance to crawl on cave floors, clamber up tight tunnels, stoop under overhangs, and climb up steep, rocky pitches. This backcountry cave is listed as "wild," a clue that you might need a similar nature to attempt a visit. Plan to wear your warm, but least-favorite clothes, as they'll probably get streaked with grime. You'll also need soft knee pads, a flashlight (with spare batteries), leather gloves, and water. It will take you half a day to complete this ranger-led tour noted for its adventure and for its continuing role as a living research laboratory. Visitors must be at least 12 years old and absolutely not claustrophobic. ■ **TIP→ The cave is named after the hordes of daddy longlegs that pulsate on the walls of the opening, but they're harmless.** ✉ *Meet at visitor center, 727 Carlsbad Caverns Hwy.* ☎ *877/444–6777* 💲 *$20* 🔑 *Reservations essential* ⏱ *Tours Sun. at 1.*

> **FLYING BLIND**
>
> Bats use a type of sonar system called echolocation to orient themselves and locate their insect dinners at night. About 15 species of bats live in Carlsbad Caverns, although the free-tailed bat is the most prevalent.

TOURS

Cave Resources Office. Those who want to go it alone outside the more established caverns can get permits and information about 10 backcountry caves from the Cave Resources Office in the visitor center. Heed rangers' advice for these remote, undeveloped, nearly unexplored caves. ✉ *727 Carlsbad Caverns Hwy.* ☎ *575/785–2232.*

Ranger-Led Tours. Cavers who wish to explore both developed and wild caves can go on ranger-led tours, some of which require knee pads, gloves, and flashlights. Reservations for the six different tours (Hall of the White Giant, Lower Cave, Slaughter Canyon Cave, Left-Hand Tunnel, King's Palace, and Spider Cave) are required at least a day in advance. Payment is by credit card over the phone or online, or by mailing a check if you're making reservations 21 days or more in advance; confirm first that space is available. ✉ *727 Carlsbad Caverns Hwy.* ☎ *877/444–6777* ⊕ *www.nps.gov/cave.*

WHAT'S NEARBY

NEARBY TOWNS

On the Pecos River, with 2¾ miles of beaches and picturesque riverside pathways, **Carlsbad, New Mexico,** seems suspended between the past and the present. It's part–university town, part–Old West, with a robust Mexican kick. The town square of Mom-and-Pop shops, a block from the river, encircles a Pueblo-style county courthouse designed by New Mexican architect John Gaw Meem. Seven miles east of the caverns is **White's City,** grown from a tiny outpost to a small outpost. This privately owned town is the nearest place to Carlsbad Caverns and contains dining and lodging options, plus the essentials.

VISITOR INFORMATION

Carlsbad Chamber of Commerce ⊠ *302 S. Canal St., Carlsbad* ☎ *575/887–6516* ⊕ *www.carlsbadchamber.com.* **White's City Inc.** ⊠ *17 Carlsbad Caverns Hwy., White's City* ☎ *800/228–3767.*

13

NEARBY ATTRACTIONS

Brantley Lake State Park. In addition to 4,200-acre Brantley Lake and dam, this park 12 miles north of Carlsbad offers primitive camping areas, nature trails, a visitor center, and 51 fully equipped campsites. Half of the campsites are first-come, first-served, while the other half can be reserved. There's also fishing for largemouth bass, bluegill, crappie, carp, catfish, and walleye pike (though authorities recommend practicing catch-and-release due to the high levels of contaminants). There are boat ramps for those with their own vessel. ⊠ *County Rd. 30 (Capitan Reef Rd.), 5 miles off U.S. 285, Carlsbad* ☎ *575/457–2384, 877/664–7787* ⊕ *www.emnrd.state.nm.us* ⊠ *$5 per vehicle for day use; $14 per vehicle for developed campsites; $8 per vehicle for primitive sites* ◎ *Daily, dawn–dusk.*

Carlsbad Museum and Arts Center. Pueblo pottery, American Indian artifacts, and early cowboy and ranch memorabilia are here, along with exhibitions of contemporary art. The real treasure, though, is the McAdoo Collection, with works by painters of the Taos Society of Artists. ⊠ *418 W. Fox St., Carlsbad* ☎ *575/887–0276* ⊕ *www.cityofcarlsbadnm. com/museum.cfm* ⊠ *Free* ◎ *Mon.–Sat. 10–5.*

FAMILY **Living Desert Zoo and Gardens State Park.** More preserve than a traditional zoo, the park contains impressive plants and animals native to the Chihuahuan Desert. The Desert Arboretum has hundreds of exotic cacti and succulents, and the Living Desert Zoo is home to mountain lions, javelinas, deer, elk, bobcats, bison, and a black bear. Nocturnal exhibits let you view the area's nighttime wildlife, too. Though there are shaded rest areas, restrooms, and water fountains, in summer it's more comfortable to visit in the morning, before the desert heats up. ■TIP➜ **Don't have time to tour the park? The expansive view from its perchlike setting is the best in town.** ⊠ *1504 Miehls Dr., off U.S. 285, Carlsbad* ☎ *575/887–5516* ⊕ *www.emnrd.state.nm.us* ⊠ *$5* ◎ *Late May–early Sept., daily 8–5; early Sept.–late May, daily 9–5; last admission at 3:30.*

WHERE TO EAT

IN THE PARK

$ ✕ **Carlsbad Caverns Restaurant.** This comfy, cafeteria-style restaurant—the

AMERICAN   only dining option in the caverns' complex other than an underground snack bar—has the essentials: hamburgers, sandwiches, Mexican fare, and hot roast beef. It opens at 8 and closes at 6:30 between Memorial Day and Labor Day, and at 5 the rest of the year. $ *Average main: $8* ✉ *Visitor center, 7 miles west of U.S. 62/180, 727 Carlsbad Caverns Hwy.* ☎ *575/785–2281* ⌣ *Reservations not accepted.*

$ ✕ **Underground Lunchroom.** At 750 feet underground, near the elevators

FAST FOOD   and entrance to the Big Room, you can grab a snack, soft drink, or club sandwich for a quick break. Service is quick, even when there's a crowd. Closes at 5 Memorial Day to Labor Day, at 3:30 the rest of the year. $ *Average main: $9* ✉ *Visitor center, 7 miles west of U.S. 62/180, 727 Carlsbad Caverns Hwy.* ☎ *575/785–2232* ☉ *No dinner.*

PICNIC AREAS

✕ **Rattlesnake Springs.** Of the several places to picnic in the park, this is the best by far. There are about a dozen picnic tables and grills here, many of them tree-shaded, and drinking water and restrooms are available. The seclusion of the site and the oasis-like draw add to the tranquility. ⚠ Be alert to the presence of wildlife. ✉ *Hwy. 418, 2½ miles west of U.S. 62/180.*

OUTSIDE THE PARK

CARLSBAD

$ ✕ **Bamboo Garden Restaurant.** A popular restaurant with locals, and one

CHINESE   of the few Asian food options in southeastern New Mexico. With a spacious dining room decorated in a rich red and gold Asian style, the Bamboo Garden offers a large buffet and full menu for both lunch and dinner—great for families and groups. $ *Average main: $10* ✉ *1511 S. Canal St., Carlsbad* ☎ *575/887–5145* ⊕ *www.bamboocarlsbad.com* ⌣ *Reservations not accepted* ☉ *Closed Mon.*

$ ✕ **Lucy's Mexicali Restaurant.** "The best margaritas in the world" is the

MEXICAN   motto of this family-owned Mexican food establishment. Hyperbole aside, all the staples are on the menu, plus some not-so-standard items like chicken fajita burritos and enchiladas served the New Mexico way—that is, flat with an egg on top. Try the Tucson-style chimichangas and tasty *carnitas* (beef brisket or chicken sautéed with chili peppers). Be sure to order Adam's Queso, a cheese dish that's a Lucy's original. ■ TIP➜ Lucy's also operates a full bar and weekend entertainment center down the street (✉ *701 S. Canal Street*). $ *Average main: $9* ✉ *710 S. Canal St., Carlsbad* ☎ *575/887–7714* ⊕ *www. lucysmexicalirestaurant.com* ⌣ *Reservations not accepted.*

$ ✕ **No Whiner Diner.** A no-frills eatery that would make Mom and

CAFÉ   Pop proud, the No Whiner Diner offers comfort-food favorites like

FAMILY   meat loaf, chicken-fried steak, and hot and cold sandwiches stacked on homemade bread. It caters to all cravings, from tuna salad to breaded veal, and includes a kids' menu. The owners and the staff will take you in as one of their own, and the prices are reasonable. [$] *Average main: $9* ✉ *1801 S. Canal St., Carlsbad* ☎ *575/234–2815* 🌐 *www.nowhinerdiner.com* ✍ *Reservations not accepted* ⏲ *Closed weekends.*

CAMPING IN CARLSBAD CAVERNS

Backcountry camping is by permit only. No campfires allowed in the park, and all camping is hike-to. Commercial sites can be found in White's City and Carlsbad.

$ CAFÉ 🍴 **Pecos River Cafe.** Stop by for savory breakfast burritos before traveling to Carlsbad Caverns, or swing by for spicy enchiladas after your trek underground. Pecos River Cafe serves Mexican favorites, most with plenty of New Mexico's famous green chilies. There's also a variety of grilled sandwiches, burgers, and other comfort-food staples. The service is fast and accommodating, even during the busy lunch hour. [$] *Average main: $10* ✉ *409 S. Canal St., Carlsbad* ☎ *575/887–8882* ✍ *Reservations not accepted* ⏲ *Closed weekends. No dinner.*

$ BARBECUE 🍴 **Red Chimney.** If you hanker for sweet-and-tangy barbecue, this homey, log-cabin-style spot is the place for you. Sauce from an old family recipe is slathered on chicken, pork, beef, turkey, and ham. Fried catfish and other home-style dishes are also served. If wall-mounted animal heads make you squeamish, you might want to dine elsewhere. [$] *Average main: $10* ✉ *817 N. Canal St., Carlsbad* ☎ *575/885–8744* ✍ *Reservations not accepted* ⏲ *Closed weekends.*

$$ SOUTHWESTERN 🍴 **The Stock Exchange at Old City Hall.** Here you'll find elegance peppered with the unique flavors of New Mexico. Chef and owner Kevin Zink has won competitions for his unique blend of herbs and spices. The menu changes regularly, offering fresh ingredients and a wide variety of chicken, steak, and seafood topped with everything from maple cream sauce to blueberry ketchup. There are several craft beers on tap. The beautifully renovated restaurant is nestled in the bottom of Carlsbad's Old City Hall, hence the name. [$] *Average main: $17* ✉ *220 W. Fox St., Carlsbad* ☎ *575/725–5444* 🌐 *www.thestockexchangenm.com* ⏲ *Closed Sun. and Mon.*

$$ SOUTHWESTERN Fodor's Choice ★ 🍴 **Trinity Hotel.** In a corner bank building dating from 1892, the Trinity Hotel stands elegantly over nearby mundane architecture. With its vaulted ceilings, the hotel's dining room is the perfect place to enjoy pasta, steaks, seafood—most dishes with a distinct New Mexican flavor. Their signature dish is the Chicken Bolloco, essentially fettuccine Alfredo with fresh green chilies added. For an appetizer, the Caliente Goat Cheese (with blackberries and habañero sauce) is a standout. Unwind in the bar, which features wines from across the state, including some from the owner's own vineyards in Deming. Have a sample in the free daily wine tasting from 3 to 7. [$] *Average main: $16* ✉ *201 S. Canal St., Carlsbad* ☎ *575/234–9891* 🌐 *www.thetrinityhotel.com* ✍ *Reservations essential* ⏲ *Closed Sun.*

WHERE TO STAY

OUTSIDE THE PARK

CARLSBAD

$$ HOTEL **Best Western Stevens Inn.** This family-owned hotel has touches of the Southwest culture of the area, like etched glass and carved wooden doors that add some elegance, and prints of Western landscapes that decorate the spacious rooms. **Pros:** established and comfortable; lots of discounts; houses the Blue Cactus Lounge with a full bar and a DJ for dancing. **Cons:** aging property that needs updating. [$] *Rooms from: $146* ✉ *1829 S. Canal St., Carlsbad* ☎ *575/887–2851, 800/730–2851* 🌐 *www.bestwesternnewmexico.com* 🛏 *208 rooms, 12 suites* 🍴 *Breakfast.*

$$$$ HOTEL **Fairfield Inn and Suites.** This Marriott hotel is close to all of Carlsbad's major attractions and on the south end of town, toward the caverns; its stylish, modern rooms feature Wi-Fi and Internet hookups. **Pros:** comfortable beds; building is clean and new. **Cons:** most rooms don't have a refrigerator, although the suites do. [$] *Rooms from: $229* ✉ *2525 S. Canal St., Carlsbad* ☎ *575/887–8000* 🌐 *www.marriott.com* 🛏 *68 rooms, 23 suites* 🍴 *Breakfast.*

$$$$ HOTEL **Hampton Inn and Suites.** On the edge of town leading to the Carlsbad Caverns, the Hampton Inn and Suites is among Carlsbad's newer hotels, within walking distance of a bar and grill, gas station, and Walmart. **Pros:** staff is very friendly and accommodating; clean, new amenities. **Cons:** some rooms need better soundproofing; pricey for the area. [$] *Rooms from: $229* ✉ *120 Esperanza Circle, Carlsbad* ☎ *575/725–5700* 🌐 *www.carlsbadsuites.hamptoninn.com* 🛏 *57 rooms, 28 suites* 🍴 *Breakfast.*

$$$$ HOTEL Fodor's Choice ★ **Holiday Inn Express.** Within walking distance of the only movie theater in Carlsbad, as well as the Carlsbad Mall, the hotel is also close to the Carlsbad hospital and Living Desert Zoo & Gardens State Park. **Pros:** full, hot breakfast; convenient location. **Cons:** a little farther away from the park than other hotels. [$] *Rooms from: $229* ✉ *2210 W. Pierce St., Carlsbad* ☎ *575/234–1252* 🌐 *www.hiexpress.com* 🛏 *56 rooms, 24 suites* 🍴 *Breakfast.*

$$$ B&B/INN Fodor's Choice ★ **Trinity Hotel.** Housed in a gracefully aging building near Carlsbad's historic downtown, the two-story Trinity offers a unique lodging experience in a town known more for its perfunctory motels and motor courts. **Pros:** one-of-a-kind facility with loads of personality; centrally located; less expensive than some other Carlsbad hotels. **Cons:** no elevator or inside access to the lobby. [$] *Rooms from: $190* ✉ *201 S. Canal St., Carlsbad* ☎ *575/234–9891* 🌐 *www.thetrinityhotel.com* 🛏 *7 rooms, 2 suites* 🍴 *Breakfast.*

CHANNEL ISLANDS
NATIONAL PARK

WELCOME TO CHANNEL ISLANDS

TOP REASONS TO GO

★ **Rare flora and fauna:**
The Channel Islands are home to 145 species of terrestrial plants and animals found nowhere else on Earth.

★ **Time travel:** With no cars, phones, or services, these undeveloped islands provide a glimpse of what California was like hundreds of years ago, away from hectic modern life.

★ **Underwater adventures:** The incredibly healthy channel waters rank among the top 10 diving destinations on the planet—but you can also visit the kelp forest virtually via Channel Islands Live, an underwater video program.

★ **Marvelous marine mammals:** More than 30 species of seals, sea lions, whales, and other marine mammals ply the park's waters at various times of year.

★ **Sea-cave kayaking:**
Paddle around otherwise inaccessible portions of the park's 175 miles of gorgeous coastline—including one of the world's largest sea caves.

1 Anacapa. Tiny Anacapa is a 5-mile stretch of three islets, with towering cliffs, caves, natural bridges, and rich kelp forests.

2 San Miguel. Isolated, windswept San Miguel, the park's westernmost island, has an ancient caliche forest and hundreds of archaeological sites chronicling the Native Americans' 13,000-year history on the islands. More than 100,000 pinnipeds (seals and sea lions) hang out on the island's beaches during certain times of year.

3 Santa Barbara. More than 5 miles of scenic trails crisscross this tiny island, known for its excellent wildlife viewing and native plants. It's a favorite destination for diving, snorkeling, and kayaking.

4 Santa Cruz. The park's largest island offers some of the best hikes and kayaking opportunities, one of the world's largest and deepest sea caves, and more species of flora and fauna than any other park island.

Map labels:

Santa Ynez Peak 4,298 ft
101
Harris Point
Point Bennett
Cuyler Harbor
Cabrillo Monument
Lester Ranch site
2
Tyler Bight
San Miguel Island
San Miguel Passage
Sandy Point
Santa Rosa Island
Santa Cruz Channel
West Point
Carrington Point
Vail & Vickers Ranch
Bechers Bay
5
Torrey Pines
Soledad Peak 1,574 ft
East Point
Johnsons Lee
South Point

PACIFIC OCEAN

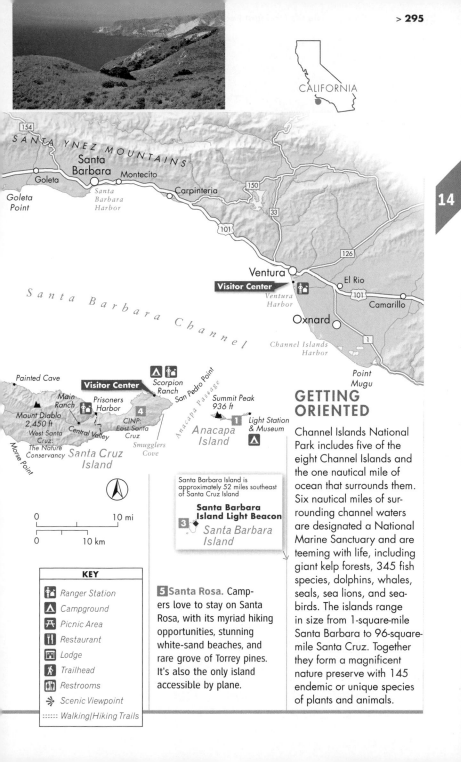

CALIFORNIA

14

Santa Barbara Channel

Ventura

Visitor Center

Ventura Harbor

El Rio

Camarillo

Oxnard

Channel Islands Harbor

Point Mugu

Painted Cave

Visitor Center

Scorpion Ranch

San Pedro Point

Summit Peak 936 ft

Light Station & Museum

Anacapa Island

Main Ranch
Prisoners Harbor

Mount Diablo 2,450 ft

Central Valley

CINP: East Santa Cruz

Smugglers Cove

Anacapa Passage

West Santa Cruz: The Nature Conservancy

Santa Cruz Island

Morse Point

0 _____ 10 mi
0 _____ 10 km

Santa Barbara Island is approximately 52 miles southeast of Santa Cruz Island

Santa Barbara Island Light Beacon

3 Santa Barbara Island

GETTING ORIENTED

Channel Islands National Park includes five of the eight Channel Islands and the one nautical mile of ocean that surrounds them. Six nautical miles of sur-rounding channel waters are designated a National Marine Sanctuary and are teeming with life, including giant kelp forests, 345 fish species, dolphins, whales, seals, sea lions, and sea-birds. The islands range in size from 1-square-mile Santa Barbara to 96-square-mile Santa Cruz. Together they form a magnificent nature preserve with 145 endemic or unique species of plants and animals.

5 **Santa Rosa.** Camp-ers love to stay on Santa Rosa, with its myriad hiking opportunities, stunning white-sand beaches, and rare grove of Torrey pines. It's also the only island accessible by plane.

KEY

🏠	Ranger Station
🔺	Campground
🎋	Picnic Area
🍴	Restaurant
🏨	Lodge
🚶	Trailhead
🚻	Restrooms
⟿	Scenic Viewpoint
⋯⋯	Walking/Hiking Trails

Updated
by Cheryl
Crabtree

On crystal clear days the craggy peaks of Channel Islands are easy to see from the mainland, jutting from the Pacific in such sharp detail it seems you could reach out and touch them. The islands really aren't that far away—a high-speed boat will whisk you to the closest ones in less than an hour—yet very few people ever visit them. Those fearless, adventurous types who do will experience one of the most splendid land-and-sea wilderness areas on the planet.

CHANNEL ISLANDS PLANNER

WHEN TO GO

Channel Islands National Park records about 620,000 visitors each year, but many never venture beyond the visitor center. The busiest times are holidays and summer weekends; if you're going then, make your transportation and accommodation arrangements in advance.

The warm, dry summer and fall months are the best time to go camping. Humpback and blue whales arrive to feed from late June through early fall. The rains usually come December through March—but this is also the best time to spot gray whales and to get discounts at area hotels. In the late spring, thousands of migratory birds descend on the islands to hatch their young, and wildflowers carpet the slopes. The water temperature is nearly always cool, so bring a wet suit if you plan to spend much time in the ocean, even in the summer. Fog, high winds, and rough seas can happen any time of the year.

AVG. HIGH/LOW TEMPS.

JAN.	FEB.	MAR.	APR.	MAY	JUNE
66/44	66/45	66/46	68/48	69/51	71/55

JULY	AUG.	SEPT.	OCT.	NOV.	DEC.
74/57	75/59	75/57	74/53	70/48	66/44

PLANNING YOUR TIME
CHANNEL ISLANDS IN ONE DAY

If you have a few hours or a day to visit the Channel Islands, start with viewing the exhibits at the **Channel Islands National Park Visitor Center** in Ventura. Then cruise over to **East Anacapa** for sweeping views of Santa Cruz Island and the mainland—provided it's not too foggy—and hiking, the primary activity here. Wander through western gull rookeries or peer down from steep cliffs and watch the antics of sea lions and seals. Alternatively, zip out to Scorpion Landing or Prisoner's Harbor on **Santa Cruz Island** on a high-speed catamaran run by Island Packers for more extended hiking, snorkeling, or kayaking.

GETTING HERE AND AROUND
AIR TRAVEL

Channel Islands Aviation flies solely to Santa Rosa Island. You can catch a flight to Santa Rosa Island from the Camarillo Airport, south of Ventura, and the Santa Barbara Airport.

Channel Islands Aviation. This company provides day excursions, surf fishing, and camper transportation year-round, flying from Camarillo Airport, about 10 miles southeast of Ventura, to an airstrip on Santa Rosa (25-minute flight). The operator will also pick up groups of eight or more at Santa Barbara Airport. ✉ *305 Durley Ave., Camarillo* ☎ *805/987–1301* ⊕ *www.flycia.com* ✉ *$160 per person for half day, $220 per person for full day, $300 per person if camping.*

BOAT TRAVEL

The visitor center for Channel Islands National Park is on California's mainland, in the town of Ventura, off U.S. 101. From the harbors at Ventura, Santa Barbara, and Oxnard you can board a boat to one of the islands. If you have your own boat, you can land at any of the islands without a permit, but you should visit the park website for instructions and information on restricted areas. A permit is required to land on the Nature Conservancy property on Santa Cruz Island. Boaters landing at San Miguel must contact the park ranger beforehand.

Island Packers. Sailing on high-speed catamarans from Ventura or a mono-hull vessel from Oxnard, Island Packers goes to Santa Cruz Island daily most of the year, weather permitting. The boats also go to Anacapa several days a week, and to the outer islands from late April through early November. They also cruise along Anacapa's north shore on three-hour wildlife tours (non-landing) several times a week. ✉ *3550 Harbor Blvd., Oxnard* ☎ *805/642–1393* ⊕ *www.islandpackers. com* ✉ *$36–$147* ✉ *1691 Spinnaker Dr., Ventura.*

ISLAND	DISTANCE AND TIME BY BOAT	COST (PER HIKER/CAMPER)
Anacapa Island	14 miles/1 hr from Oxnard	$59/$79
San Miguel Island	58 miles/3 hrs from Ventura	$105/$140
Santa Barbara Island	55 miles/2½–3 hrs from Ventura	$82/$114
Santa Cruz Island	20 miles/1 hr from Ventura	$59/$79
Santa Rosa Island	46 miles/2 hrs from Ventura	$82/$114

TRANSIT TIMES TO THE ISLANDS

CAR TRAVEL

To reach the Ventura harbor, exit U.S. 101 in Ventura at Seaward Boulevard or Victoria Avenue and follow the signs to Ventura Harbor/Spinnaker Drive. To access Channel Islands Harbor in Oxnard, exit U.S. 101 at Victoria Avenue and head south approximately 7 miles to Channel Islands Boulevard. To access dive and whale-watching boats in Santa Barbara, exit U.S. 101 at Castillo Street and head south to Cabrillo Boulevard, then turn right for the harbor entrance. Private vehicles are not permitted on the islands. Pets are also not allowed in the park.

TRAIN TRAVEL

Amtrak makes stops in Santa Barbara, Ventura, and Oxnard; from the Amtrak station, just take a taxi or waterfront shuttle bus to the harbor.

PARK ESSENTIALS

PARK FEES AND PERMITS

There is no fee to enter Channel Islands National Park, but unless you have your own boat, you will pay $36 or more per person for a ride with a boat operator. The cost of taking a boat to the park varies depending on which operator you choose. Also, there is a $15-per-day fee for staying in one of the islands' campgrounds.

If you take your own boat, landing permits are not required to visit islands administered by the National Park Service. However, boaters who want to land on the Nature Conservancy preserve on Santa Cruz Island must have a permit. Visit ⊕ *www.nature.org/cruzpermit* for permit information; allow 10 business days to process and return your permit application. If you anchor in a nearby cove at any island, at least one person should remain aboard the boat at all times. To hike beyond the ranger station on San Miguel you need a reservation and permit; call ☎ *805/658–5711* to be matched up with a ranger, who must accompany you. Anglers must have a state fishing license; for details, call the California Department of Fish and Wildlife at ☎ *916/653–7664* or visit ⊕ *www.wildlife.ca.gov.* More than a dozen Marine Protected Areas (MPAs) with special resource protection regulations surround the islands, so read the guidelines carefully before you depart.

PARK HOURS

The islands are open every day of the year. Channel Islands National Park Visitor Center in Ventura is closed on Thanksgiving and Christmas. Channel Islands National Park is in the Pacific time zone.

CELL-PHONE RECEPTION

In general, cell-phone reception is spotty and varies by location and service provider. Public telephones are available on the mainland near the Channel Islands National Park Visitor Center but not on the islands.

RESTAURANTS

Out on the islands, you won't have any trouble deciding where to dine—there are no restaurants, no snack bars, and in some cases, no potable water. Pack a fancy picnic or a simple sandwich—and don't forget it in your car or hotel. For a quick meal before or after your island trip, each of the harbors has a number of decent eateries nearby.

Back on the mainland, though, it's a dining gold mine. Santa Barbara has a long-standing reputation for culinary excellence, and a "foodie" renaissance in recent years has transformed Ventura into a dining destination—with dozens of new restaurants touting nouvelle cuisine made with organic produce and meats. Fresh seafood is a standout, whether it's prepared simply in wharf-side hangouts or incorporated into sophisticated bistro menus. Dining attire is generally casual, though slightly dressy casual wear is the custom at pricier restaurants.

Prices in the reviews are the average cost of a main course at dinner, or if dinner is not served, at lunch.

HOTELS

It's easy to choose where to stay in the park—your only option is sleeping in your tent in a no-frills campground. If you hanker for more creature comforts, you can splurge on a bunk and meals on a dive boat.

There's a huge range of lodging options on the mainland, from seaside camping to posh international resorts. The most affordable options are in Oxnard, Ventura, and Carpinteria, a small seaside community between Santa Barbara and Ventura. Despite rates that range from pricey to downright shocking, Santa Barbara's numerous hotels and bed-and-breakfasts attract thousands of patrons year-round. Wherever you stay, be sure to make reservations for the summer and holiday weekends (especially Memorial Day, July 4, Labor Day, and Thanksgiving) well ahead of time; it's not unusual for coastal accommodations to fill completely during these busy times. Also be aware that some hotels double their rates during festivals and other events.

Prices in the reviews are the lowest cost of a standard double room in high season. For expanded reviews, facilities, and current deals, visit Fodors.com.

VISITOR INFORMATION

PARK CONTACT INFORMATION

Channel Islands National Park Visitor Center ✉ *1901 Spinnaker Dr., Ventura* ☎ *805/658–5730* ⊕ *www.nps.gov/chis.*

VISITOR CENTERS

Channel Islands National Park Robert J. Lagomarsino Visitor Center. The park's main visitor center has a museum, a bookstore, a three-story observation tower with telescopes, and exhibits about the islands. There's also a marine life exhibit where you can see sea stars clinging to rocks, anemones waving their colorful, spiny tentacles, and a brilliant orange Garibaldi darting around. The center also has full-size reproductions of a male northern elephant seal and the pygmy mammoth skeleton unearthed on Santa Rosa Island in 1994. *Treasure in the Sea,* a 24-minute film narrated by Kevin Costner, shows throughout the day and gives an overview of the islands. Rangers lead various free public programs describing park resources on weekends and holidays at 11 and 3; they can also give you a detailed map and trip-planning packet if you're interested in visiting the actual islands. In summer you can watch live ranger broadcasts of underwater dives and hikes on Anacapa Island, shown at the center Wednesday through Saturday (hike at 11, dive at 2). ✉ *1901 Spinnaker Dr., Ventura* ☎ *805/658–5730* ⊕ *www.nps.gov/chis* ☉ *Daily 8:30–5.*

Outdoors Santa Barbara Visitor Center. The small office in the Santa Barbara Harbor provides maps and other information about Channel Islands National Park and Channel Islands National Marine Sanctuary; the Santa Barbara Maritime Museum is housed in the same building. Call ahead to verify hours. ✉ *113 Harbor Way, Santa Barbara* ☎ *805/884–1475* ⊕ *www.outdoorsb.noaa.gov* ☉ *Daily 11–5.*

EXPLORING

THE ISLANDS

Anacapa Island. Although most people think of it as an island, Anacapa Island actually comprises three narrow islets. The tips of these volcanic formations nearly touch but are inaccessible from one another except by boat. All three islets have towering cliffs, isolated sea caves, and natural bridges; Arch Rock, on East Anacapa, is one of the best-known symbols of Channel Islands National Park. Wildlife viewing is the reason most people come to East Anacapa—particularly in summer when seagull chicks are newly hatched and sea lions and seals lounge on the beaches. Trips to Middle Anacapa Island require a ranger escort.

The compact **museum** on East Anacapa tells the history of the island and houses, among other things, the original lead-crystal Fresnel lens from the island's 1932 lighthouse.

Depending on the season and the number of desirable species lurking about there, a limited number of boats travel to **Frenchy's Cove** at West Anacapa, where you might see anemones, limpets, barnacles, mussel beds, and colorful marine algae in the pristine tide pools. The rest of West Anacapa is closed to protect nesting brown pelicans.

San Miguel Island. The westernmost of the Channel Islands, San Miguel Island is frequently battered by storms sweeping across the North Pacific. The 15-square-mile island's wild, windswept landscape is lush with vegetation. Point Bennett, at the western tip, offers one of the world's most spectacular wildlife displays when more than 100,000 pinnipeds hit its beach. Explorer Juan Rodríguez Cabrillo was the first European to visit this island; he claimed it for Spain in 1542. Legend holds that Cabrillo died on one of the Channel Islands—no one knows where he's buried, but there's a memorial to him on a bluff above Cuyler Harbor.

Plants and Wildlife on the Channel Islands

Channel Islands National Park is home to species found nowhere else on Earth: mammals such as the island fox and the island deer mouse and birds like the island scrub jay live forever on the endangered species list. Thousands of western gulls hatch each summer on Anacapa, then fly off to the mainland where they spend about four years learning all their bad habits. Then they return to the island to roost and have chicks of their own. It all adds up to a living laboratory not unlike the one naturalist Charles Darwin discovered off the coast of South America 200 years ago, which is why the Channel Islands are often called the North American Galápagos.

14

Santa Barbara Island. At about 1 square mile, Santa Barbara Island is the smallest of the Channel Islands and nearly 35 miles south of the others. Triangular in shape, Santa Barbara's steep cliffs—which offer a perfect nesting spot for the Scripps's murrelet, a rare seabird—are topped by twin peaks. In spring, you can enjoy a brilliant display of yellow coreopsis. Learn about the wildlife on and around the islands at the island's small museum.

Santa Cruz Island. Five miles west of Anacapa, 96-square-mile Santa Cruz Island is the largest of the Channel Islands. The National Park Service manages the easternmost 24% of the island; the rest is owned by the Nature Conservancy, which requires a permit to land. When your boat drops you off on the 70 miles of craggy coastline, you see two rugged mountain ranges with peaks soaring to 2,500 feet and deep canyons traversed by streams. This landscape is the habitat of a remarkable variety of flora and fauna—more than 600 types of plants, 140 kinds of land birds, 11 mammal species, five varieties of reptiles, and three amphibian species live here. Bird-watchers may want to look for the endemic island scrub jay, which is found nowhere else in the world.

One of the largest and deepest sea caves in the world, **Painted Cave,** lies along the northwest coast of Santa Cruz. Named for the colorful lichen and algae that cover its walls, Painted Cave is nearly ¼ mile long and 100 feet wide. In spring a waterfall cascades over the entrance. Kayakers may encounter seals or sea lions cruising alongside their boats inside the cave. The Channel Islands hold some of the richest archaeological resources in North America; all artifacts are protected within the park. Remnants of a dozen Chumash villages can be seen on the island. The largest of these villages, at the eastern end of the island, occupied the area now called **Scorpion Ranch.** The Chumash mined extensive chert deposits on the island for tools to produce shell-bead money, which they traded with people on the mainland. You can learn about Chumash history and view artifacts, tools, and exhibits on native plant and wildlife at the interpretive visitor center near the landing dock. Visitors can also explore remnants of the early-1900s ranching era in the restored historic adobe and outbuildings.

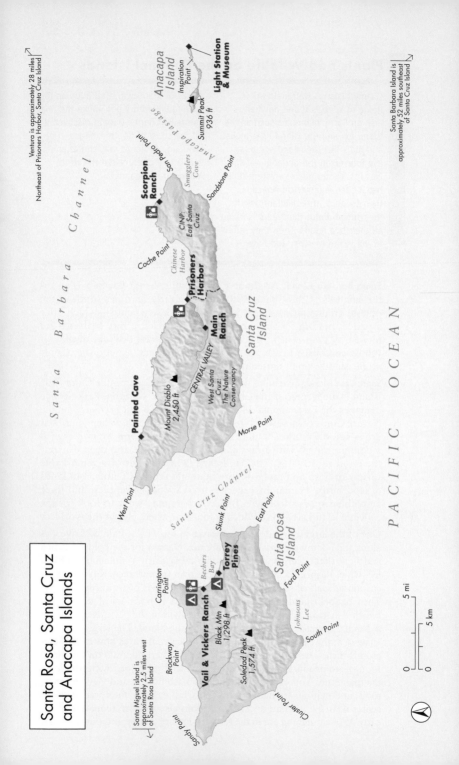

Santa Rosa, Santa Cruz and Anacapa Islands

Ventura is approximately 28 miles Northeast of Prisoners Harbor, Santa Cruz Island

Santa Barbara Island is approximately 52 miles southeast of Santa Cruz Island

Santa Miguel island is approximately 2.5 miles west of Santa Rosa Island

Anacapa Island

Light Station & Museum

Inspiration Point

Summit Peak 936 ft

Anacapa Passage

San Pedro Point

Santa Barbara Channel

Scorpion Point

Scorpion Ranch

Smugglers Cove

Sandstone Point

CINP: East Santa Cruz

Coche Point

Chinese Harbor

Prisoners Harbor

CENTRAL VALLEY

Main Ranch

Santa Cruz Island

Painted Cave

Mount Diablo 2,450 ft

West Santa Cruz: The Nature Conservancy

Morse Point

West Point

Santa Cruz Channel

Skunk Point

East Point

Carrington Point

Brockway Point

Bechers Bay

Torrey Pines

Vail & Vickers Ranch

Black Mtn 1,298 ft

Soledad Peak 1,574 ft

Santa Rosa Island

Ford Point

Johnsons Lee

South Point

Cluster Point

Sandy Point

PACIFIC OCEAN

0   5 mi

0   5 km

Santa Rosa Island. Set between Santa Cruz and San Miguel, Santa Rosa Island is the second largest of the Channel Islands and has a relatively low profile, broken by a central mountain range rising to 1,589 feet. The coastal areas range from broad sandy beaches to sheer cliffs. The island is home to about 500 species of plants, including the rare Torrey pine. Three unusual mammals—the endemic island fox, spotted skunk, and deer mouse—are among those that make their home here. They hardly compare to the mammoths that once roamed the island; a nearly complete skeleton of a 6-foot-tall pygmy mammoth was unearthed here in 1994.

The island was once home to the **Vail & Vickers Ranch,** where cattle were raised from 1901 to 1998. You can catch a glimpse of what the operation was like when you walk from the landing dock to the campground; the route passes by the historic ranch buildings, barns, equipment, and the wooden pier where cattle were brought onto the island.

14

EDUCATIONAL OFFERINGS

RANGER PROGRAMS

Ranger programs are held at the Channel Islands National Park Visitor Center in Ventura.

FAMILY **Channel Islands Live Program.** Can't make the trip to the islands? Experience them virtually through the Channel Islands Live Program, which takes you on interactive tours of the park. In the Live Dive Program, divers armed with video cameras explore the undersea world of the kelp forest off Anacapa Island; images are transmitted to monitors located on the dock at Landing Cove, in the mainland visitor center, and on the Internet. You see bright red sea stars, spiny sea urchins, and brilliant orange Garibaldis. You can even ask the divers questions via interactive lines. The Live Hike Program takes you on a similar interactive virtual tour of Anacapa Island. Live web cams also connect you 24/7 with panoramic views of Anacapa Island, bald eagle nests, and underwater life in a kelp forest. ✉ *Landing Cove* ⊕ *www.nps. gov/chis/planyourvisit/channel-islands-live-nps.htm* 💷 *Free* ☉ *Summer, Wed.–Sat., hike at 11, dive at 2.*

Tidepool Talk. Explore the area's marine habitat without getting your feet wet. Rangers at the Channel Islands Visitor Center demonstrate how animals and plants adapt to the harsh conditions found in tidal pools of the Channel Islands. ✉ *Channel Islands National Park Visitor Center, 1901 Spinnaker Rd., Ventura* ☎ *805/658–5730* 💷 *Free* ☉ *Weekends and holidays at 11:30 (11 in winter) and 3.*

GOOD READS

You can find a handful of books about this little-known gem in the Channel Islands Visitor Center in Ventura. A few good ones are:

■ *The California Channel Islands* by Marla Daily

■ *Channel Islands National Park* by Susan Lamb

■ *Channel Islands National Park* by Tim Hauf

■ *Chumash Ethnobotany: Plant Knowledge Among the Chumash People of Southern California* by Jan Timbrook and Chris Chapman

■ *San Miguel Island: My Childhood Memoir, 1930–1942* by Betsy Lester

■ *Diary of a Sea Captain's Wife: Tales of Santa Cruz Island* by Margaret H. Eaton

Historical Fiction:

■ *Island of the Blue Dolphins* by Scott O'Dell (great for kids)

■ *San Miguel* by T. Coraghessan Boyle

■ *When the Killing's Done* by T. Coraghessan Boyle

SPORTS AND THE OUTDOORS

DIVING

Some of the best snorkeling and diving in the world can be found in the cool waters surrounding the Channel Islands. In the relatively warm water around Anacapa and eastern Santa Cruz, photographers can get great shots of rarely seen giant black bass swimming among the kelp forests. Here you also find a reef covered with red brittle starfish. If you're an experienced diver, you might swim among five species of seals and sea lions, or try your hand at spearing rockfish or halibut near San Miguel and Santa Rosa. The best time to scuba dive is in summer and fall, when the water is often clear up to a 100-foot depth.

TOURS AND OUTFITTERS

Explorer Diving Adventures. The 65-foot *Explorer* ferries passengers out to all the islands for single- and multiday adventures to all the islands. Rates include food, snacks, beverages, and air. ⊠ *1583 Spinnaker Dr., Ventura* ☎ *805/890–1142* ⊕ *www.explorerdiveboat.com* ⊠ *Day trips $125.*

Peace Dive Boat. Ventura Harbor–based Peace Dive Boat runs single and multiday diving adventures near all the Channel Islands. Travelers sleep aboard ship. ⊠ *1691 Spinnaker Dr., Dock G, Ventura* ☎ *805/650–3483* ⊕ *www.peaceboat.com* ⊠ *Day trips from $105.*

Raptor Dive Boat. Ventura Dive & Sport's 46-foot custom boat, the *Raptor,* takes divers on two- and three-tank trips to Anacapa and Santa Cruz islands and is available for private charters. ⊠ *Ventura* ☎ *805/650–7700* ⊕ *www.raptordive.com* ⊠ *Day trips from $110.*

Spectre Dive Boat. This boat runs single-day diving trips to Anacapa and Santa Cruz. Fees include three or four dives, air, and food. ✉ *1575 Spinnaker Dr., Suite 105B-75, Ventura* ☎ *866/225–3483, 805/486–1166* ⊕ *www.calboatdiving.com* 🖃 *$105–$125.*

Truth Aquatics. Trips to the Channel Islands lasting a day or more can be arranged through Santa Barbara–based operator Truth Aquatics. You live aboard the boats on multiday trips; all meals are provided. If you don't want to dive, opt for a one-day adventure and snorkel or kayak while other passengers explore the depths. ✉ *301 W. Cabrillo Blvd., Santa Barbara* ☎ *805/962–1127* ⊕ *www.truthaquatics.com* 🖃 *$90–$835.*

HIKING

The terrain on most of the islands ranges from flat to moderately hilly. There are no services on the islands (and no public phones; cell-phone reception is dicey). You need to bring all your own food, water (except on Santa Cruz and Santa Rosa, where there are water faucets at campgrounds), and supplies.

TOURS AND OUTFITTERS

Truth Aquatics. This outfitter is authorized to land on some of the park's islands for multiday overnight trips that include naturalist-led hikes (you sleep and eat on board the 65-to-90-foot twin-engine vessels). ✉ *301 W. Cabrillo Blvd., Santa Barbara* ☎ *805/962–1127* ⊕ *www. truthaquatics.com* 🖃 *$340–$835.*

EASY

Cuyler Harbor Beach Trail. This easy walk takes you along a 2-mile-long white sand beach on San Miguel. The eastern section is occasionally cut off by high tides. *Easy.* ✉ *Trailhead at San Miguel Campground, San Miguel Island.*

FAMILY **Historic Ranch Trail.** This easy 0.5-mile walk on Santa Cruz Island takes you to a historic ranch where you can visit an interpretive center in an 1800s abode and see remnants of a cattle ranch. *Easy.* ✉ *Trailhead at Scorpion Beach, Santa Cruz Island.*

FAMILY **Inspiration Point Trail.** This 1.5-mile hike along flat terrain takes in most of East Anacapa; there are great views from Inspiration Point and Cathedral Cove. *Easy.* ✉ *Trailhead at Landing Cove, Anacapa Island.*

Water Canyon Trail. Starting at Santa Rosa Campground, this 2-mile walk along a white-sand beach includes some exceptional beachcombing. Frequent strong winds can turn this easy hike into a fairly strenuous excursion, so be prepared. If you extend your walk into Water Canyon, you can follow animal paths to a lush canyon full of native vegetation. *Easy.* ✉ *Trailhead at Santa Rosa Campground, Santa Rosa Island.*

MODERATE

FAMILY **Cavern Point Trail.** This moderate 2-mile hike takes you to the bluffs northwest of Scorpion harbor on Santa Cruz, where there are magnificent coastal views and pods of migrating gray whales from December through March. *Moderate.* ✉ *Trailhead at Scorpion Ranch Campground, Santa Cruz Island.*

Elephant Seal Cove Trail. This moderate-to-strenuous walk takes you across Santa Barbara to a point where you can view magnificent elephant seals from steep cliffs. *Moderate.* ⊠ *Trailhead at Landing Cove, Santa Barbara Island.*

Fodor's Choice   **Prisoners Harbor/Pelican Cove Trail.** Taking in quite a bit of Santa Cruz,
★   this moderate to strenuous 3-mile trail to Pelican Cove is one of the best hikes in the park. Since the hike takes you through Nature Conservancy property, you must be accompanied by an Island Packers naturalist (⇨ *See Island Operators in chapter planner*) or secure a permit (visit ⊕ *www.nature.org/cruzpermit*; allow 10 to 15 business days to process and return your application). *Moderate.* ⊠ *Trailhead at Prisoners Harbor, Santa Cruz Island.*

Torrey Pines Trail. This moderate 5-mile loop climbs up to Santa Rosa's grove of rare Torrey pines and offers stellar views of Becher's Bay and the channel. *Moderate.* ⊠ *Trailhead at Santa Rosa Campground, Santa Rosa Island.*

DIFFICULT

East Point Trail. This strenuous 12-mile hike along beautiful white-sand beaches yields the opportunity to see rare Torrey pines. Some beaches are closed between March and September, so you have to remain on the road for portions of this hike. *Difficult.* ⊠ *Trailhead at Santa Rosa Campground, Santa Rosa Island.*

Lester Ranch Trail. This short but strenuous 2-mile hike leads up a spectacular canyon filled with waterfalls and lush native plants. At the end of a steep climb to the top of a peak, views of the historic Lester Ranch and the Cabrillo Monument await. ■**TIP➜ If you plan to hike beyond the Lester Ranch, you'll need a hiking permit; call or visit the park website for details.** *Difficult.* ⊠ *Trailhead at San Miguel Campground, San Miguel Island* ☎ *805/658–5730.*

Point Bennett Trail. Rangers conduct 15-mile hikes across San Miguel to Point Bennett, where more than 30,000 pinnipeds (three different species) can be seen. *Difficult.* ⊠ *Trailhead at San Miguel Campground, San Miguel Island.*

KAYAKING

The most remote parts of the Channel Islands are accessible only by a sea kayak. Some of the best kayaking in the park can be found on Anacapa, Santa Barbara, and the eastern tip of Santa Cruz. Anacapa has plenty of sea caves, tidal pools, and even natural bridges you can paddle beneath. Santa Cruz has plenty of secluded beaches to explore, as well as seabird nesting sites and seal and sea lion rookeries. One of the world's largest colonies of Scripps's murrelets resides here, and brown pelicans, cormorants, and storm petrels nest in Santa Barbara's steep cliffs.

It's too far to kayak from the mainland out to the islands, but outfitters have tours that take you to the islands. Tours are offered year-round, but high seas may cause trip cancellations between December and March. ⚠ **Channel waters can be unpredictable and challenging.**

Like much of California's central coast, Santa Cruz looks as rugged and undeveloped as it did centuries ago.

Don't venture out alone unless you are an experienced kayaker; guided trips are highly recommended. All kayakers should carry proper safety gear and equipment and be prepared for sudden strong winds and weather changes. Also refrain from disturbing wildlife. Visit the park website for kayaking rules and tips.

The operators listed here hold permits from the National Park Service to conduct kayak tours; if you choose a different company, verify that it holds the proper permits.

TOURS AND OUTFITTERS

Aquasports. This highly regarded company based in Goleta offers guided one-, two-, and three-day trips to Scorpion Cove on Santa Cruz Island for beginner to expert kayakers. They also lead one-day trips to Santa Barbara and Anacapa. Cross-channel passage, instruction, equipment, and guides are included. ■ TIP→ This is a very popular trip—book early. ☎ 800/773–2309, 805/968–7231 ⊕ www.islandkayaking.com ⌨ $155–$455.

Channel Islands Outfitters. You can take a one-day trip to Santa Cruz, Anacapa, and Santa Barbara islands, or overnight multiday excursions to all the islands from this outfitter, authorized by the park to guide kayak, snorkel, hiking, and dive adventures. Trips depart from Ventura, Channel Islands, and Santa Barbara harbors; all include equipment and instruction. Boat transportation is an additional charge. ✉ 117B Harbor Way, Santa Barbara ☎ 805/899–4925 ⊕ www. channelislandso.com ⌨ $75–$1,500.

Santa Barbara Adventure Company. Full-service outfitter Santa Barbara Adventure Company conducts guided single- and multiday kayaking excursions to the Channel Islands. Trips include transportation, equipment, guides, and paddling lessons. ⊠ *301 W. Cabrillo Blvd., Santa Barbara* ☎ *805/884–9283, 877/885–9283* ⊕ *www.sbadventureco.com* ⊠ *$177–$450.*

WHALE-WATCHING

About a third of the world's cetacean species (27 to be exact) can be seen in the Santa Barbara Channel. In July and August, humpback and blue whales feed off the north shore of Santa Rosa. From late December through March, up to 10,000 gray whales pass through the Santa Barbara Channel on their way from Alaska to Mexico and back again, and on a whale-watching trip during this time frame, you should see one or more of them. Other types of whales, but fewer in number, swim the channel June through August.

TOURS

Island Packers. Depending on the season, you can take a three-hour tour or an all-day tour from either Ventura or Channel Islands harbors with Island Packers. From January through March you're almost guaranteed to see gray whales in the channel. ⊠ *1691 Spinnaker Dr., Ventura* ☎ *805/642–1393* ⊕ *www.islandpackers.com* ⊠ *$36–$79.*

WHAT'S NEARBY

NEARBY TOWNS

With a population of more than 100,000, **Ventura** is the main gateway to Channel Islands National Park. It's a classic California beach town filled with interesting restaurants, a wide range of accommodations, and miles of clean, white beaches. South of Ventura is **Oxnard,** a community of 162,000 boasting a busy harbor and uncrowded beaches. Known for its Spanish ambience, **Santa Barbara** has a beautiful waterfront set against a backdrop of towering mountains—plus glistening palm-lined beaches, whitewashed adobe structures with red-tile roofs, and plenty of genteel charm.

VISITOR INFORMATION

Oxnard Convention & Visitors Bureau ⊠ *2786 Seaglass Way, Oxnard* ☎ *805/988–0717* ⊕ *www.visitoxnard.com.* **Santa Barbara Conference & Visitors Bureau and Film Commission** ⊠ *1601 Anacapa St., Santa Barbara* ☎ *805/966–9222, 800/676–1266* ⊕ *www.santabarbaraca.com.* **Ventura Visitors & Convention Bureau** ⊠ *101 S. California St., Ventura* ☎ *805/648–2075, 800/483–6214* ⊕ *www.ventura-usa.com.*

NEARBY ATTRACTIONS

Mission San Buenaventura. The ninth of the 21 California missions, Mission San Buenaventura was established in 1782 but burned to the ground in the 1790s. It was rebuilt and rededicated in 1809. A self-guided tour takes you through a small museum, a quiet courtyard, and a chapel with 250-year-old paintings. ✉ *211 E. Main St., Ventura* ☎ *805/643–4318* ⊕ *www.sanbuenaventuramission.org* ☜ *$2* ◷ *Weekdays 10–5, Sat. 9–5, Sun. 10–4.*

Fodor'sChoice **Mission Santa Barbara.** Widely referred to as the "Queen of Missions,"
★ this is one of the most beautiful and frequently photographed buildings in coastal California. Dating to 1786, the architecture evolved from adobe-brick buildings with thatch roofs to more permanent edifices as the mission's population burgeoned. An earthquake in 1812 destroyed the third church built on the site. Its replacement, the present structure, is still a functioning Catholic church. Mission Santa Barbara has a splendid Spanish/Mexican colonial art collection, as well as Chumash sculptures and the only Native American–made altar and tabernacle left in the California missions. Docents lead 90-minute tours ($8 adult) Thursday and Friday at 11 and Saturday at 10:30. ✉ *2201 Laguna St., at E. Los Olivos St., Santa Barbara* ☎ *805/682– 4713, 805/682–4149 for gift shop* ⊕ *www.santabarbaramission.org* ☜ *$6* ◷ *Daily 9–4:15.*

Fodor'sChoice **Santa Barbara County Courthouse.** Hand-painted tiles and a spiral staircase
★ infuse the courthouse, a national historic landmark, with the grandeur of a Moorish palace. This magnificent building was completed in 1929, part of a rebuilding process after a 1925 earthquake destroyed many downtown structures. At the time, Santa Barbara was also in the midst of a cultural awakening, and the trend was toward an architectural style appropriate to the area's climate and history. The result is the harmonious Mediterranean–Spanish look of much of the downtown area, especially the municipal buildings. An elevator rises to an arched observation area in the courthouse tower that provides a panoramic view of the city. The murals in the ceremonial chambers on the courthouse's second floor were painted by an artist who did backdrops for some of Cecil B. DeMille's films. ✉ *1100 Anacapa St., at E. Anapamu St., Santa Barbara* ☎ *805/962–6464* ⊕ *www.santabarbaracourthouse. org* ◷ *Weekdays 8–4:45, weekends 10–4:30. Free guided tours Mon.– Wed., and Fri. at 10:30, daily at 2.*

FAMILY **Santa Barbara Maritime Museum.** California's seafaring history is the focus here. High-tech, hands-on exhibits, such as a sportfishing activity that lets participants catch a "big one" and a local surfing history retrospective, make this a fun stop for families. On display since fall 2013 is the museum's shining star: an extremely rare, 17-foot-tall First Order Fresnel lens from the historic Point Conception Lighthouse. ✉ *113 Harbor Way, off Shoreline Dr., Santa Barbara* ☎ *805/962–8404* ⊕ *www.sbmm.org* ☜ *$7* ◷ *June–Aug., Thurs.–Tues. 10–6; Sept.–May, Thurs.–Tues. 10–5.*

FAMILY **Santa Barbara Museum of Natural History.** The gigantic skeleton of a blue whale greets you at the entrance of this complex, where major draws include a planetarium, space-related activities and exhibits, a gem and mineral display, and dioramas illustrating Chumash Indian history and culture. Many exhibits have interactive components. ✉ *2559 Puesta del Sol Rd., Santa Barbara* ☎ *805/682–4711* 🌐 *www.sbnature.org* 🎟 *$10* 🕓 *Daily 10–5.*

Stearns Wharf. Built in 1872, historic Stearns Wharf is Santa Barbara's most visited landmark. Expansive views of the mountains, cityscape, and harbor unfold from every vantage point on the three-block-long pier, which has shops and restaurants. ✉ *Cabrillo Blvd. at the foot of State St., Santa Barbara* ☎ *805/897–2683 for info, 805/564–5531 for harbormaster.*

Ventura Oceanfront. The city of San Buenaventura (aka Ventura) edges 4 miles of gorgeous coastline, stretching from the county fairgrounds at the northern border through San Buenaventura State Beach down to Ventura Harbor in the south. The main attraction here is the San Buenaventura City Pier, a historic landmark built in 1872 and restored in 1993. Stroll to the end of the pier and sit on a bench to take in the spectacular ocean, mountain, and island views. Surfers rip the waves just north of the pier, and sunbathers relax on white-sand beaches on either side. The 1-mile-long promenade and the Omer Rains Bike Trail north of the pier attract scores of joggers, surrey cyclers, and bikers throughout the year. ✉ *End of California St. at ocean's edge, Ventura* ☎ *805/648–2075* 🌐 *www.ventura-usa.com* 🎟 *Free (except parking areas at state beaches).*

WHERE TO EAT

IN THE PARK

Picnic Areas. Picnic tables are available on all the islands except San Miguel. You can also picnic on some of the beaches of Santa Cruz, Santa Rosa, and San Miguel; be aware that high winds are always a possibility on Santa Rosa and San Miguel.

OUTSIDE THE PARK

SANTA BARBARA

$$ SEAFOOD 🍴 **Brophy Bros.** The outdoor tables at this casual harborside restaurant in Santa Barbara have perfect views of the marina and mountains. The staff serves enormous, exceptionally fresh fish dishes—don't miss the seafood salad and chowder—and provides you with a pager if there's a long wait for a table. This place is hugely popular, so it can be crowded and loud, especially on weekend evenings. [$] *Average main: $20* ✉ *119 Harbor Way, Santa Barbara* ☎ *805/966–4418* 🌐 *www.brophybros.com* ✍ *Reservations not accepted.*

CLOSE UP

Best Campgrounds on the Channel Islands

Camping is the best way to experience the natural beauty and isolation of Channel Islands National Park. Unrestricted by tour schedules, you have plenty of time to explore mountain trails, snorkel in the kelp forests, or kayak into sea caves. Campsites are primitive, with no water (except on Santa Rosa and Santa Cruz) or electricity. Campfires are not allowed on the islands, though you may use enclosed camp stoves. Use bear boxes for storing your food. You must carry all your gear and pack out all trash. Campers must arrange transportation to the islands before reserving a campsite (and yes, park personnel do check).

National Park Service Reservation System. You can get specifics on each campground and reserve a campsite ($15 per night) by contacting the National Park Service Reservation System up to six months in advance. ☎ 877/444–6777 ⊕ www.recreation.gov.

Del Norte Campground.
This remote campground on Santa Cruz offers backpackers sweeping ocean views from its 1,500-foot perch. It's accessed via a 3.5-mile hike through a series of canyons and ridges. ⊠ Scorpion Beach landing.

East Anacapa Campground.
You need to walk 0.5 mile and ascend more than 150 steps to reach this open, treeless camping area above Cathedral Cove. ⊠ East Anacapa landing.

San Miguel Campground. Accessed by a steep, 1.5-mile hike across the beach and through a lush canyon, this campground is on the site of the Lester Ranch; the Cabrillo Monument is nearby. Be aware that strong winds and thick fog are common here. ⊠ Cuyler Harbor landing.

Santa Barbara Campground.
This seldom-visited campground perched on a cliff above Landing Cove is reached via a challenging 0.5-mile, uphill climb. ⊠ Landing Cove.

Santa Cruz Scorpion Campground.
In a grove of eucalyptus trees, this campground is near the historic buildings of Scorpion Ranch. It's accessed via an easy, 0.5-mile, flat trail from Scorpion Beach landing. ⊠ Scorpion Beach landing.

Santa Rosa Campground.
Backcountry beach camping for kayakers is available on this island; it's a 1.5-mile, flat walk to the campground. There's a spectacular view of Santa Cruz Island across the water and easy access to fantastic hiking trails. ⊠ Bechers Bay landing.

14

$
MEXICAN

✕ **La Super-Rica Taqueria.** Praised by Julia Child, this food stand with a patio on the east side of Santa Barbara serves some of the spiciest and most authentic Mexican dishes between Los Angeles and San Francisco. Fans drive for miles to fill up on the soft tacos served with yummy spicy or mild sauces and legendary beans. Three specials are offered each day. Portions are on the small side; order several dishes to share. $ *Average main: $9* ⊠ *622 N. Milpas, at Alphonse St., Santa Barbara* ☎ *805/963–4940* ⚄ *Reservations not accepted* ▤ *No credit cards* ⊙ *Closed Wed.*

VENTURA

$$ ✕ **Andria's Seafood.** The specialties at this casual, family-oriented restau-
SEAFOOD rant in Ventura Harbor Village are fresh fish-and-chips and homemade
clam chowder. After placing your order at the counter, you can sit out-
side on the patio and enjoy the view of the harbor and marina. $ *Aver-*
age main: $14 ✉ *1449 Spinnaker Dr., Suite A, Ventura* ☎ *805/654–0546*
⊕ *www.andriasseafood.com* ⟲ *Reservations not accepted.*

$$ ✕ **Brophy Bros.** The Ventura outpost of the wildly popular Santa Barbara
SEAFOOD restaurant provides the same fresh seafood-oriented meals in a spacious
second-story setting overlooking the harbor. Feast on everything from
fish-and-chips and crab cakes to chowder and delectable fish—often
straight from the boats moored below. $ *Average main: $18* ✉ *1559*
Spinnaker Dr., in Ventura Harbor Village, Ventura ☎ *805/639–0865*
⊕ *www.brophybros.com* ⟲ *Reservations not accepted.*

$ ✕ **Harbor Cove Café.** Waterfront views next to Channel Islands National
CAFÉ Park visitor center, hearty, cooked-to-order meals, and boxed picnic
lunches make this casual dockside eatery a popular spot for island travelers and beachgoers. Fill up on a breakfast burrito before boarding the
boat, take a boxed deli-sandwich along, and refuel with a hefty Angus
burger, chowder, or fish-and-chips when you return. The café is open for
breakfast and lunch daily, plus dinner Friday and Saturday in summer.
$ *Average main: $10* ✉ *1867 Spinnaker Dr., Ventura* ☎ *805/658–1639*
⊕ *www.harborcovecafe.com* ☾ *No dinner Sun.–Thurs. in summer. No*
dinner rest of year.

$ ✕ **Lure Fish House.** Fresh, sustainably caught seafood charbroiled over a
SEAFOOD mesquite grill, a well-stocked oyster bar, specialty cocktails, and a wine
list heavy on local vintages lure diners into this slick, nautical-theme
space downtown. The menu, which changes daily, centers on the mostly
local catch and organic veggies, and also includes tacos, sandwiches,
and salads. Grilled entrées come with a choice of unusual farm-to-table
sides: quinoa salad, sweet-potato fries, pineapple cole slaw. The regulars
rave about the shrimp-and-chips, cioppino, and citrus crab-cake salad.
$ *Average main: $15* ✉ *60 S. California St., Ventura* ☎ *805/567–4400*
⊕ *www.lurefishhouse.com.*

WHERE TO STAY

OUTSIDE THE PARK

OXNARD

$$$ ⌂ **Embassy Suites Mandalay Beach Resort.** Tropical gardens, small water-
HOTEL falls, and sprawling pool areas surround this Spanish-Mediterranean
FAMILY complex, set on 8 acres of white-sand beach north of Channel Islands
Harbor. **Pros:** on the beach, just a mile to island transportation boats;
family-friendly. **Cons:** 4 miles from island transportation from Ven-
tura Harbor; fee for Wi-Fi; no full kitchens. $ *Rooms from: $199*
✉ *2101 Mandalay Beach Rd., Oxnard* ☎ *805/984–2500* ⊕ *www.*
embassysuitesmandalay.com ⤳ *250 suites* ⦿ *Breakfast.*

SANTA BARBARA

$$$$ RESORT 🏨 **Bacara Resort & Spa.** A luxury resort with four restaurants and a 42,000-square-foot spa and fitness center with 36 treatment rooms, the Bacara provides a gorgeous setting for relaxing retreats. **Pros:** serene natural setting; nature trails; first-rate spa; three zero-edge pools. **Cons:** pricey; not close to downtown; sand on beach not pristine enough for some. [$] *Rooms from: $450* ✉ *8301 Hollister Ave., Goleta* ☎ *805/968–0100, 877/422–4245 toll-free for reservations* 🌐 *www.bacararesort.com* 🛏 *306 rooms, 45 suites* 🍴 *No meals.*

$$$$ RESORT Fodor's Choice ★ 🏨 **Four Seasons: Resort The Biltmore Santa Barbara.** Surrounded by lush, perfectly manicured gardens and across from the beach, Santa Barbara's grande dame has long been a favorite for quiet, California-style luxury. **Pros:** first-class resort; historic Santa Barbara character; personal service; steps from the beach. **Cons:** back rooms are close to train tracks; expensive. [$] *Rooms from: $425* ✉ *1260 Channel Dr., Santa Barbara* ☎ *805/969–2261, 805/332–3442 for reservations* 🌐 *www.fourseasons.com/santabarbara* 🛏 *181 rooms, 26 suites* 🍴 *No meals.*

$$$ HOTEL 🏨 **Franciscan Inn.** Part of this Spanish-Mediterranean motel, a block from the harbor and West Beach, dates back to the 1920s. **Pros:** walking distance from waterfront and harbor; family-friendly; great value. **Cons:** busy lobby; pool can be crowded. [$] *Rooms from: $160* ✉ *109 Bath St., Santa Barbara* ☎ *805/963–8845* 🌐 *www.franciscaninn.com* 🛏 *48 rooms, 5 suites* 🍴 *Breakfast.*

$$$ HOTEL 🏨 **Hotel Indigo.** The closest hotel to the train station, artsy Hotel Indigo (opened in 2012) is a great choice for travelers who appreciate contemporary art and want easy access to dining, nightlife, and the beach. **Pros:** multilingual staff; a block from Stearns Wharf; great value for location. **Cons:** showers only (no bathtubs); train whistles early morning; rooms on small side. [$] *Rooms from: $189* ✉ *121 State St., Santa Barbara* ☎ *805/966–6586, 877/270–1392 toll-free* 🌐 *www.indigosantabarbara.com* 🛏 *41 rooms* 🍴 *No meals.*

$$$$ RESORT Fodor's Choice ★ 🏨 **San Ysidro Ranch.** At this romantic hideaway on a historic property in the Montecito foothills—where John and Jackie Kennedy spent their honeymoon and Oprah sends her out-of-town visitors—guest cottages are scattered among groves of orange trees and flower beds. **Pros:** ultimate privacy; surrounded by nature; celebrity hangout; pet-friendly. **Cons:** very expensive; too remote for some. [$] *Rooms from: $695* ✉ *900 San Ysidro La., Montecito* ☎ *805/565–1700, 800/368–6788* 🌐 *www.sanysidroranch.com* 🛏 *23 rooms, 4 suites, 14 cottages* 🍴 *No meals* ☞ *2-day minimum stay on weekends, 3 days on holiday weekends.*

VENTURA

$$ HOTEL 🏨 **Four Points by Sheraton Ventura Harbor.** The spacious, contemporary rooms here are still gleaming from a total renovation that was completed in 2009. **Pros:** close to island transportation; mostly quiet; short drive or bus ride to historic downtown Ventura. **Cons:** not in the heart of downtown; noisy seagulls sometimes congregate nearby. [$] *Rooms from: $145* ✉ *1050 Schooner Dr., Ventura* ☎ *805/658–1212* 🌐 *www.fourpoints.com/ventura* 🛏 *102 rooms, 4 suites* 🍴 *Breakfast.*

$$ HOTEL 🏨 **Holiday Inn Express Ventura Harbor.** A favorite among Channel Islands visitors, this quiet, comfortable, lodge-inspired property sits right at the Ventura Harbor entrance. **Pros:** quiet at night; easy access to harbor restaurants and activities; five-minute drive to downtown. **Cons:** busy area on weekends; complaints of erratic service. [$] *Rooms from: $130* ✉ *1080 Navigator Dr., Ventura* ☎ *805/856–9533, 800/315–2621* 🌐 *www.holidayinnexpress.com/venturaca* 🛏 *69 rooms* 🍴 *Breakfast.*

$$$$ RESORT Fodor's Choice ★ 🏨 **Ojai Valley Inn & Spa.** This outdoorsy, golf-oriented resort and spa is set on beautifully landscaped grounds, with hillside views in nearly all directions. **Pros:** gorgeous grounds; exceptional outdoor activities; romantic yet kid-friendly. **Cons:** expensive; areas near restaurants can be noisy. [$] *Rooms from: $400* ✉ *905 Country Club Rd., Ojai* ☎ *805/646–1111, 855/697–8780* 🌐 *www.ojairesort.com* 🛏 *231 rooms, 77 suites* 🍴 *No meals.*

$$$ HOTEL 🏨 **Ventura Beach Marriott.** Spacious, contemporary rooms, a peaceful location just steps from San Buenaventura State Beach, and easy access to historic downtown Ventura's arts and culture district make the Marriott a popular choice for travelers who want to explore Ventura. **Pros:** walk to beach and biking/jogging trails; a block from historic pier; great value for location. **Cons:** close to highway; near busy intersection. [$] *Rooms from: $189* ✉ *2055 E. Harbor Blvd., Ventura* ☎ *805/643–6000, 888/236–2427* 🌐 *www.marriottventurabeach.com* 🛏 *272 rooms, 12 suites* 🍴 *Breakfast.*

15

CRATER LAKE
NATIONAL PARK

Visit Fodors.com for advice, updates, and bookings

WELCOME TO CRATER LAKE

TOP REASONS TO GO

★ **The lake:** Cruise inside the caldera basin and gaze into the extraordinary sapphire-blue water of the country's deepest lake.

★ **Native land:** Enjoy the rare luxury of interacting with totally unspoiled terrain.

★ **The night sky:** Billions of stars glisten in the pitch-black darkness of an unpolluted sky.

★ **Splendid hikes:** Accessible trails spool off the main roads and wind past colorful bursts of wildflowers and cascading waterfalls.

★ **Camping at its best:** Pitch a tent or pull up a motor home at Mazama Campground, a beautifully situated, guest-friendly, and well-maintained campground.

1 Crater Lake. The focal point of the park, this non-recreational, scenic destination is known for its deep blue hue.

2 Wizard Island. Visitors can take boat rides to this protruding landmass rising from the western section of Crater Lake; it's a great place for a hike or a picnic.

3 Mazama Village. This is your best bet for stocking up on snacks, beverages, and fuel in the park; it's about 5 miles from Rim Drive.

4 Cleetwood Cove Trail. The only safe, designated trail to hike down the caldera and reach the lake's edge is on the rim's north side off Rim Drive.

GETTING ORIENTED

Crater Lake National Park covers 183,224 acres. Located in southern Oregon less than 100 miles from the California border, it's surrounded by several Cascade Range forests, including the Winema and Rogue River national forests. Of the nearby towns, Klamath Falls is closest at 60 miles south of the park; Ashland and Medford, to the southwest, are approximately 80 miles and 90 miles from the lake, respectively, with Roseburg the farthest away at 110 miles northwest of the park.

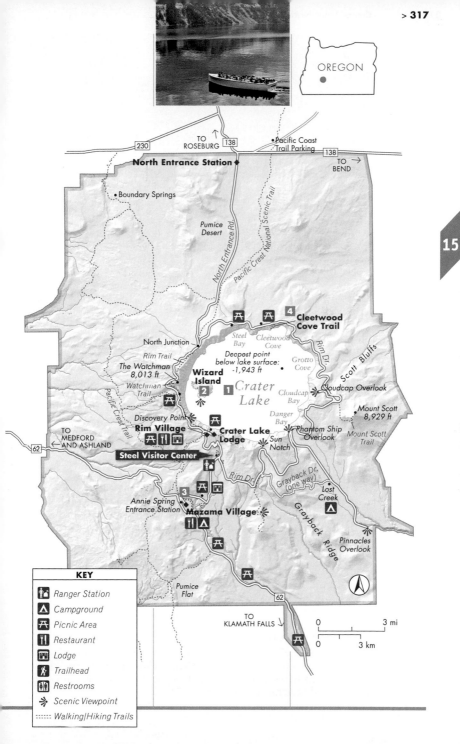

OREGON

TO
ROSEBURG

230 · 138

Pacific Coast
Trail Parking

138

TO →
BEND

North Entrance Station

• Boundary Springs

*Pumice
Desert*

North Entrance Rd.

Pacific Crest National Scenic Trail

15

*Steel
Bay*

*Cleetwood
Cove*

4 · **Cleetwood
Cove Trail**

North Junction

Rim Trail

**Deepest point
below lake surface:
-1,943 ft**

*Grotto
Cove*

Rim Dr.

Scott Bluffs

**The Watchman
8,013 ft**

**Wizard
Island**

2 · **1** · *Crater
Lake*

Cloudcap Overlook

*Watchman
Trail*

*Cloudcap
Bay*

**Mount Scott
8,929 ft**

Pacific Crest Trail

Discovery Point

*Danger
Bay*

*Mount Scott
Trail*

Rim Village

**Crater Lake
Lodge**

*Phantom Ship
Overlook*

TO
MEDFORD
AND ASHLAND

62

*Sun
Notch*

Steel Visitor Center

Rim Dr.

*Grayback Dr.
(one way)*

*Lost
Creek*

3

**Annie Spring
Entrance Station**

Mazama Village

Grayback Ridge

*Pinnacles
Overlook*

KEY

🏠 *Ranger Station*
△ *Campground*
🎋 *Picnic Area*
🍴 *Restaurant*
🏨 *Lodge*
🥾 *Trailhead*
🚻 *Restrooms*
✴ *Scenic Viewpoint*
⋯⋯ *Walking/Hiking Trails*

*Pumice
Flat*

62

TO
KLAMATH FALLS ↓

0 — 3 mi
0 — 3 km

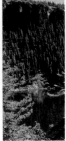

Updated
by Christine
Vovakes

The pure, crystalline blue of Crater Lake astounds visitors at first sight. More than 5 miles wide and ringed by cliffs almost 2,000 feet high, the lake was created approximately 7,700 years ago, following Mt. Mazama's fiery explosion. Days after the eruption, the mountain collapsed on an underground chamber emptied of lava. Rain and snowmelt filled the caldera, creating a sapphire-blue lake so clear that sunlight penetrates to a depth of 400 feet (the lake's depth is 1,943 feet). Today it's both the clearest and deepest lake in the United States—and the ninth deepest in the world.

CRATER LAKE PLANNER

WHEN TO GO

The park's high season is July and August. September and early October tend to draw smaller crowds. From October through June, the entire park virtually closes due to heavy snowfall. The road is kept open just to the rim in winter, except during severe weather.

AVG. HIGH/LOW TEMPS.

JAN.	FEB.	MAR.	APR.	MAY	JUNE
34/18	35/18	37/19	42/23	50/28	58/34

JULY	AUG.	SEPT.	OCT.	NOV.	DEC.
68/41	69/41	63/37	52/31	40/23	34/19

FESTIVALS AND EVENTS

More than 400,000 Bard-loving buffs descend on Ashland (90 miles from Crater Lake) for the annual **Oregon Shakespeare Festival.** Plays run from February to November in three theaters; peak season is July, August, and September ☎ *541/482–4331.*

PLANNING YOUR TIME

CRATER LAKE IN ONE DAY

Begin at **Steel Information Center,** where interpretive displays and a short video introduce you to the story of the lake's formation and its unique characteristics. Then circle the crater's rim by heading northeast on **Rim Drive,** allowing an hour to stop at overlooks—check out the Phantom Ship rock formation in the lake—before you reach **Cleetwood Cove Trail** trailhead, the only safe and legal access to the lake. If you're up to the strenuous challenge, hike down the trail to reach the dock, and hop aboard one of the **tour boats** for a two-hour lake tour with a park ranger as your guide. If you have time, add on a trip to **Wizard Island** for a picnic lunch.

Back on Rim Drive, continue around the lake, stopping at the **Watchman Trail** for a short but steep hike to this peak above the rim, which affords not only a splendid view of the lake, but a broad vista of the surrounding southern Cascades. Wind up your visit at **Crater Lake Lodge**—allow time to wander the lobby of the 1915 structure perched on the rim. Dinner at the lodge restaurant, overlooking the lake and the Cascade sunset, caps the day.

GETTING HERE AND AROUND

Most of the park is accessible only in late June or early July through mid-October. The rest of the year, snow blocks all park roadways and entrances except Highway 62 and the access road to Rim Village from Mazama Village. Rim Drive is typically closed because of heavy snowfall from mid-October to mid-July, and you could encounter icy conditions any month of the year, particularly in early morning.

PARK ESSENTIALS

PARK FEES AND PERMITS

Admission to the park is $10 per vehicle, good for seven days. Backcountry campers and hikers must obtain a free wilderness permit at Rim Visitor Center or Steel Information Center for all overnight trips.

PARK HOURS

Crater Lake National Park is open 24 hours a day year-round; however, snow closes most park roadways October through June. Lodging and dining facilities usually are open from late May to mid-October. The park is in the Pacific time zone.

CELL PHONE RECEPTION

Cell phone reception in the park is unreliable. You'll find public telephones at Crater Lake Lodge and outside the Mazama Village store.

RESTAURANTS

There are a few casual eateries and convenience stores within the park. For fantastic upscale dining on the caldera's rim, head to the Crater Lake Lodge.

Prices in the reviews are the average cost of a main course at dinner, or if dinner is not served, at lunch.

HOTELS

Crater Lake's summer season is relatively brief, and the park's main lodge is generally booked with guest reservations a year in advance. If you don't snag one, check availability as your trip

15

approaches—cancellations are always possible. Outside the park are options in Prospect, Klamath Falls, Roseburg, Medford, and Ashland.

Prices in the reviews are the lowest cost of a standard double room in high season. For expanded reviews, facilities, and current deals, visit Fodors.com.

VISITOR INFORMATION

PARK CONTACT INFORMATION

Crater Lake National Park ☎ 541/594–3000 ⊕ *www.nps.gov/crla.*

VISITOR CENTERS

Rim Visitor Center. In summer you can obtain park information here, take a ranger-led tour, or stop into the nearby Sinnott Memorial, with a small museum and a 900-foot view down to the lake's surface. In winter, snowshoe walks are offered on weekends and holidays. The Rim Village Gift Store and cafeteria are the only services open in winter. ⊠ *Rim Dr. on the south side of the lake, 7 miles north of Annie Spring entrance station* ☎ *541/594–3090* ⊕ *www.nps.gov/crla* ☉ *Late May–late Sept., daily 9:30–5.*

Steel Visitor Center. Open year-round, the information center is part of the park's headquarters; you'll find restrooms and a first-aid station here. There's also a small post office and a shop that sells books, maps, and postcards. In the auditorium, a 22-minute film, *Crater Lake: Into the Deep,* describes the lake's formation and geology, and explores the area's cultural history. ⊠ *Rim Dr., 4 miles north of Annie Spring entrance station* ☎ *541/594–3100* ⊕ *www.nps.gov/crla* ☉ *Early Apr.– early Nov., daily 9–5; mid-Nov.–late Mar., daily 10–4.*

EXPLORING

For most visitors, the star attractions of Crater Lake are the lake itself and the breathtakingly situated Crater Lake Lodge. Other park highlights include the natural, unspoiled beauty of the forest and the geological marvels that you can access along the Rim Drive.

SCENIC DRIVES

Fodors Choice
★

Rim Drive. Take this 33-mile scenic loop for views of the lake and its cliffs from every conceivable angle. The drive alone is at least two hours long; frequent stops at overlooks and short hikes can easily stretch this to a half day. Be aware that Rim Drive is typically closed due to heavy snowfall from mid-October to mid-June, and icy conditions can be encountered any month of the year, particularly in early morning. ⊠ *Drive begins at Rim Village, 7 miles from Annie Spring entrance station along Munson Valley Rd.* ✛ *To get to Rim Dr., access the north entrance road via either Rte. 230 or Hwy. 138, and follow it for about 10 miles.*

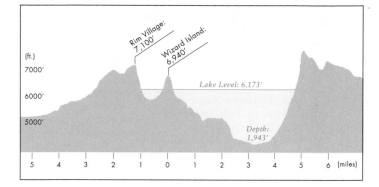

HISTORIC SITES

Fodor's Choice **Crater Lake Lodge.** First built in 1915, this classic log-and-stone struc-
★ ture still boasts the original lodgepole-pine pillars, beams, and stone
fireplaces. The lobby, fondly referred to as the Great Hall, serves as a
warm, welcoming gathering place where you can play games, socialize
with a cocktail, or gaze out of the many windows to view spectacular
sunrises and sunsets by a crackling fire. ⊠ *Rim Village, just east of Rim
Visitor Center* ⊕ *www.craterlakelodges.com.*

SCENIC STOPS

Cloudcap Overlook. The highest road-access overlook on the Crater Lake
rim, Cloudcap has a westward view across the lake to Wizard Island
and an eastward view of Mt. Scott, the volcanic cone that is the park's
highest point, just 2 miles away. ⊠ *2 miles off Rim Dr., 13 miles northeast of Steel Visitor Center* ⊕ *www.nps.gov/crla.*

Discovery Point. This overlook marks the spot at which prospectors first
spied the lake in 1853. Wizard Island is just northeast, close to shore.
⊠ *Rim Dr., 1½ mile north of Rim Village* ⊕ *www.nps.gov/crla.*

Mazama Village. In summer a campground, motor inn, amphitheater,
gas station, post office, and small store are open here. No gasoline is
available in the park from mid-October to mid-May. Snowfall determines when the village and its facilities open and close for the season.
⊠ *Mazama Village Rd., off Hwy. 62, near Annie Spring entrance station* ☎ *541/594–2255, 888/774–2728* ⊕ *www.nps.gov/crla* ☉ *Mid-to-
late May, daily 10–5; June–Aug., daily 7 am–9 pm; Sept.–mid-Oct.,
daily 8–8.*

Phantom Ship Overlook. From this point you can get a close look at
Phantom Ship, a rock formation that resembles a schooner with furled
masts and looks ghostly in fog. ⊠ *Rim Dr., 7 miles northeast of Steel
Information Center* ⊕ *www.nps.gov/crla.*

Pinnacles Overlook. Ascending from the banks of Sand and Wheeler
creeks, unearthly spires of eroded ash resemble the peaks of fairy-tale
castles. Once upon a time, the road continued east to a former entrance.
A path now replaces the old road and follows the rim of Sand Creek

Wildlife in Crater Lake

Two primary types of fish swim beneath the surface of Crater Lake: kokanee salmon and rainbow trout. It's estimated that hundreds of thousands of kokanee inhabit the lake, but because boating and recreational access is so limited they elude many would-be sportsman. Kokanees average about 8 inches in length, but they can grow to nearly 18 inches. Rainbow trout are larger than the kokanee but are less abundant in Crater Lake. Trout—including bull, Eastern brook, rainbow, and German brown—swim in the park's many streams and rivers;

they usually remain elusive because these waterways flow near inaccessibly steep canyons.

Remote canyons shelter the park's elk and deer populations, which can sometimes be seen at dusk and dawn feeding at forest's edge. Black bears and pine martens—cousins of the short-tailed weasel—also call Crater Lake home. Birds such as hairy woodpeckers, California gulls, red-tailed hawks, and great horned owls are more commonly seen in summer in forests below the lake.

(affording more views of pinnacles) to where the entrance arch still stands. ✉ *5 miles northeast of Steel Visitor Center, then 2 miles east on Pinnacles Spur Rd.* ⊕ *www.nps.gov/crla.*

Wizard Island. To get here, hike down the steep Cleetwood Cove Trail (and back up on your return) and board the tour boat *(⇨ See Educational Offerings)* for a two-hour ride ($45). Bring a picnic. If you're in top shape, take the very strenuous 2-mile hike that begins at the boat dock and steeply ascends over rock-strewn terrain to Wizard Summit and a path around the 90-foot-deep crater at the top. A more moderate hike is the 1.8-mile trek on a rocky trail along the shore of the island. ✉ *Via Cleetwood Cove Trail to Wizard Island dock* ☎ *541/594–2255, 888/774–2728* ⊕ *www.craterlakelodges.com* ☉ *Daily late June–mid-Sept.*

EDUCATIONAL OFFERINGS

RANGER PROGRAMS

FAMILY **Boat Tours.** The most extensively used guided tours in Crater Lake are on the water, aboard launches that carry 37 passengers on a two-hour tour accompanied by a ranger. The boats circle the lake; two of the eight daily boats stop at Wizard Island, where you can get off and reboard a minimum of three hours later, or six hours later if you catch the morning boat. The first tour leaves the dock at 9:30 am; the last departs at 3:30 pm. To get to the dock you must hike down Cleetwood Cove Trail, a strenuous 1.1-mile walk that drops 700 feet; only those in excellent physical shape should attempt the hike. Bring adequate water with you. Purchase boat-tour tickets at Crater Lake Lodge, at the top of the trail or through advance reservations. Restrooms are available at the top and bottom of the trail. ✉ *Cleetwood Cove Trail, off Rim Dr., 11 miles north of Rim Village on the north side of the lake* ☎ *541/594–2255, 888/774–2728* ⊕ *www.craterlakelodges.com* 🎫 *$35; $45 with island drop-off* ☉ *Late June–mid-Sept., daily.*

FAMILY **Junior Ranger Program.** Kids ages 6–12 learn about Crater Lake while earning either a Junior Ranger patch or badge in daily sessions during summer months at the Rim Visitor Center, and year-round at the Steel Visitor Center. Pick up free activity booklets at either visitor center. ☎ *541/594–3100* ⊕ *www.nps.gov/crla.*

SPORTS AND THE OUTDOORS

FISHING

Fishing is allowed in the lake, but you may find the experience frustrating—in such a massive body of water, the problem is finding the fish. Try your luck near the Cleetwood Cove boat dock, or take poles on the boat tour and fish off Wizard Island. Rainbow trout and kokanee salmon lurk in Crater Lake's aquamarine depths, and some grow to enormous sizes. You don't need a state fishing license, but to protect the lake's pristine waters, use only artificial bait as opposed to live worms. Private boats are prohibited on the lake.

15

HIKING

EASY

Castle Crest Wildflower Trail. This 1-mile loop that passes through a spring-fed meadow is one of the park's flatter hikes. Wildflowers burst into full bloom here in July. *Easy.* ⊠ *Across the street from Steel Visitor Center parking lot, East Rim Dr.*

Godfrey Glen Trail. This 1-mile loop trail is an easy stroll through an old-growth forest with canyon views. Its dirt path is accessible to wheelchairs with assistance. *Easy.* ⊠ *2.4 miles south of Steel Visitor Center.*

MODERATE

Annie Creek Canyon Trail. This somewhat strenuous 1.7-mile hike loops through a deep stream-cut canyon, providing views of the narrow cleft scarred by volcanic activity. This is a good area to look for flowers and deer. *Moderate.* ⊠ *Mazama Campground, behind ampitheater, between D&E campground loops; Mazama Village Rd., near Annie Spring entrance station.*

Boundary Springs Trail. If you feel like sleuthing, take this moderate 5-mile round-trip hike to the headwaters of the Rogue River. The trail isn't always well marked, so a detailed trail guide is necessary. You'll see streams, forests, and wildflowers along the way before discovering Boundary Springs pouring out of the side of a low ridge. *Moderate.* ⊠ *Pullout on Hwy. 230, near milepost 19, about 5 miles west of the junction with Hwy. 138.*

Watchman Peak Trail. This is one of the best hikes in the park. Though it's less than a mile each way, the trail climbs more than 400 feet—not counting the steps up to the actual lookout, which has great views of Wizard Island and the lake. *Moderate.* ⊠ *Watchman Overlook, 3.8 miles northwest of Rim Village on Rim Dr., west side of the lake.*

DIFFICULT

Cleetwood Cove Trail. This strenuous 2.2-mile round-trip hike descends 700 feet down nearly vertical cliffs along the lake to the boat dock. Be in top shape before you take this one. *Difficult.* ⊠ *Cleetwood Cove trailhead, Rim Dr., 11 miles north of Rim Village, north side of the lake.*

Fodor'sChoice ★ **Mt. Scott Trail.** This strenuous 5-mile round-trip trail takes you to the park's highest point—the top of Mt. Scott, the oldest volcanic cone of Mt. Mazama, at 8,929 feet. The average hiker needs 90 minutes to make the steep uphill trek—and nearly 60 minutes to get down. The trail starts at an elevation of about 7,450 feet, so the climb is not extreme but does get steep in spots. Views of the lake and the broad Klamath Basin are spectacular. *Difficult.* ⊠ *14 miles east of Steel Visitor Center on Rim Dr., east side of the lake, across from the road to Cloudcap Overlook.*

Pacific Crest Trail (PCT). You can hike a portion of the Pacific Crest Trail, which extends from Mexico to Canada and winds through the park for 33 miles. For this prime backcountry experience, catch the trail off Highway 138 about a mile east of the north entrance, where it heads south and then toward the west rim of the lake and circles it for about 6 miles, then descends down Dutton Creek to the Mazama Village area. You'll need a detailed map for this hike; check online or with the PCT association. *Difficult.* ⊠ *Pacific Crest Trail parking lot, north access road off Hwy. 138, 2 miles east of the junction with Hwy. 138.*

> ### SERIOUS SAFETY
>
> There's only one safe way to reach Crater Lake's edge: the Cleetwood Cove Trail from the north rim. The rest of the inner caldera is steep and composed of loose gravel, basalt, and pumice—extremely dangerous, in other words. That's why all hiking and climbing are strictly prohibited inside the rim, and rangers will issue citations for violations.

SKIING

There are no maintained ski trails in the park, although some backcountry trails are marked with blue diamonds or snow poles. Most cross-country skiers park at Rim Village and follow a portion of West Rim Drive toward Wizard Island Overlook (4 miles). The road is plowed to Rim Village, but it may be closed temporarily due to severe storms. Snow tires and chains are essential. The park's online brochure (available at ⊕ *www.nps.gov/crla*) lists additional trails and their length and difficulty.

SWIMMING

Swimming is allowed in the lake, but it's not advised. Made up entirely of snowmelt, Crater Lake is very cold—about 45°F to 56°F in summer. The lagoons on Wizard Island and at Cleetwood Cove are your best choices—but only when the air temperature rises above 80°F, which is rare. If you're able to brave the cold, though, you can say that you've taken a dip in the deepest lake in the United States.

WHAT'S NEARBY

NEARBY TOWNS

Three small cities serve as gateways to Crater Lake—each a 2- to 2½-hour drive to the park. Klamath Lake, the largest freshwater lake in Oregon, is anchored at its south end by the city of **Klamath Falls,** population 21,000. Boasting 300 days of sunshine per year, Klamath Falls is home to acres of parks and marinas from which to enjoy water sports and bird-watching. **Roseburg's** location at the west edge of the southern Cascades led to its status as a timber-industry center—still the heart of the town's economy—but its site along the Umpqua River has drawn fishermen here for years. **Ashland,** one of the premier destinations in the Northwest, is a charming small city set in the foothills of the Siskiyou Mountains. The foundation of the city's appeal is its famed Oregon Shakespeare Festival and its dozens of fine small inns, shops, and restaurants.

VISITOR INFORMATION

Ashland Chamber of Commerce ⊠ *110 E. Main St., Ashland* ☎ *541/482–3486* ⊕ *www.ashlandchamber.com.* **Discover Klamath** ⊠ *205 Riverside Dr., Suite. B, Klamath Falls* ☎ *541/882–1501, 800/445–6728* ⊕ *www.discoverklamath.com.* **Roseburg Visitors & Convention Bureau** ⊠ *410 S.E. Spruce St., Roseburg* ☎ *541/672–9731, 800/444–9584* ⊕ *www.visitroseburg.com.*

15

NEARBY ATTRACTIONS

Fodor'sChoice ★ **Klamath Basin National Wildlife Refuge Complex.** As many as 1,000 bald eagles make Klamath Basin their rest stop, amounting to the largest wintering concentration of these birds in the contiguous United States. Located along the Pacific Flyway bird migration route, the vast acres of freshwater wetlands in the refuge complex serve as a stopover for nearly 1 million waterfowl in the fall. Any time of year is bird-watching season; more than 400 species of birds have been spotted in the Klamath Basin. For a leisurely ramble by car take the tour routes in the Lower Klamath and Tule Lake Refuges. There's a superb bookstore at the visitor center. ⊠ *Visitor Center, 4009 Hill Rd., 20 miles south of Klamath Falls via U.S. 97 or Hwy. 39, Tulelake* ☎ *530/667–2231* ⊕ *www.fws.gov/refuge/Tule_Lake* ☒ *Free* ☉ *Visitor center weekdays 8–4:30, weekends 9–4.*

Fodor'sChoice ★ **Oregon Caves National Monument.** Marble caves, large calcite formations, and huge underground rooms shape this rare adventure in geology. Guided cave tours take place on the hour in late spring and fall, and every half hour June through August. The 90-minute 0.6-mile tour is moderately strenuous with low passageways, twisting turns, and more than 500 stairs; children must be at least 42 inches tall to go on the tour. Cave tours aren't given in winter. Above ground, the surrounding valley holds an old-growth forest with some of the state's largest trees. ⚠ **Park officials say that GPS coordinates for the caves often direct drivers onto a mostly unpaved forest service road meant for four-wheel-drive vehicles. Instead, follow Highway 46 off U.S. 199**

at Cave Junction, which is also narrow and twisty in parts; RVs or trailers over 32 feet not advised. ✉ *19000 Caves Hwy. (Hwy. 46) 20 miles east of U.S. 199, Cave Junction* ☎ *541/592–2100* 🌐 *www.nps.gov/orca* 🎟 *$8.50* 🕒 *Late Mar.–late May, and mid-Oct.–early Nov., daily 10–4; late May–early Sept., daily 9–6; early Sept.–mid-Oct., daily 9–5.*

WHERE TO EAT

IN THE PARK

$$ AMERICAN FAMILY

🍴 **Annie Creek Restaurant.** At this family-friendly dining spot you'll find pizza and pasta along with chicken, beef, and fish entrées. Less expensive sandwich selections are available, plus a breakfast menu. The outdoor seating area is surrounded by towering pine trees. [$] *Average main: $14* ✉ *Mazama Village Rd., near Annie Spring entrance station* ☎ *541/594–2255* 🌐 *www.craterlakelodges.com* 🕒 *Closed mid-Oct.–late May.*

$$$ AMERICAN Fodor's Choice ★

🍴 **Dining Room at Crater Lake Lodge.** Virtually the only place where you can dine well once you're in the park, the lodge emphasizes fresh, regional Northwest cuisine. The dining room is magnificent, with a large stone fireplace and views of Crater Lake's clear-blue waters. Breakfast and lunch are enjoyable here, but the evening menu is the main attraction, with tempting delights such as wild Alaskan salmon, pork loin with apple compote, steak, and vegetarian offerings. An extensive wine list tops off the gourmet experience. No reservations accepted for breakfast and lunch; they're essential for dinner. [$] *Average main: $29* ✉ *Crater Lake Lodge, 1 Lodge Loop Rd., Rim Village* ☎ *541/594–2255* 🌐 *www.craterlakelodges.com* ✍ *Reservations essential* 🕒 *Closed mid-Oct.–late May.*

PICNIC AREAS

Rim Drive. About a half-dozen picnic-area turnouts encircle the lake; all have good views, but they can get very windy. Most have pit toilets, and a few have fire grills, but none have running water. ✉ *Rim Dr.*

Rim Village. This is the only park picnic area with running water. The tables are set behind the visitor center, and most have a view of the lake below. There are flush toilets inside the visitor center. ✉ *Rim Dr. on the south side of the lake, 7 miles north of Annie Spring entrance station.*

Wizard Island. The park's best picnic venue is on Wizard Island; pack a lunch and book yourself on one of the early-morning boat tour departures, reserving space on an afternoon return. There are no formal picnic areas and just pit toilets, but you'll discover plenty of sunny, protected spots where you can have a quiet meal and appreciate the astounding scene that surrounds you. The island is accessible by boat tour only *(⇨ See Educational Offerings).* ✉ *Wizard Island, Crater Lake* 🌐 *www.craterlakelodges.com.*

OUTSIDE THE PARK

$ | **✕ Beckie's Cafe.** You can get break-
AMERICAN | fast, lunch, or dinner at this rustic roadhouse diner 15 miles from Crater Lake's southern entrance, but no one will fault you for skipping your veggies and plunging into dessert. For more than 80 years Beckie's homemade pies have been a must-have treat for travelers on their way to or from the park. Among the year-round selections, very-berry and coconut cream are favorites; savor fresh peach or huckleberry when the fruit is in season—and don't forget to ask for à la mode. $ Average main: $12 ⊠ 56484 Hwy. 62, at Union Creek, Prospect ☎ 541/560–3563 ⊕ www.unioncreekoregon.com/beckies.htm ⌲ Reservations not accepted.

> ### PEST ALERT
>
> Early summer snowmelt often creates watery breeding areas for large groups of mosquitoes. Bring lots of insect repellent in June and July, and expect mosquito swarms in the early morning and at sunset. They can also be a problem later in the summer in campgrounds and on the Cleetwood Cove Trail, so pack repellent if you plan on camping or hiking.

15

$ | **✕ Morning Glory Restaurant.** Stepping inside this sunny converted bunga-
ECLECTIC | low with its Matisse-blue walls, creamy yellow ceiling, and fresh flowers on the table jostles your senses awake even before you've had a whiff of caffeine. Chef-owner Patricia Groth uses organic ingredients whenever possible. You can try dishes like tofu scramble or chorizo eggs with tortillas along with inventive renditions of American classics—one bite of the scrumptious cranberry hazelnut French toast with lemon butter and you'll know why it's so popular. $ Average main: $12 ⊠ 1149 Siskiyou Blvd., Ashland ☎ 541/488–8636 ⊕ www.morninggloryrestaurant.com ⌲ Reservations not accepted ☾ No dinner.

WHERE TO STAY

IN THE PARK

$$ | **⌂ The Cabins at Mazama Village.** In a wooded area 7 miles south of the
HOTEL | lake, this complex is made up of several A-frame buildings and has mostly modest rooms with two queen beds and a private bath. **Pros:** clean and well-kept facility. **Cons:** lots of traffic into adjacent campground. $ Rooms from: $140 ⊠ Mazama Village, near Annie Spring entrance station ☎ 541/594–2255, 888/774–2728 ⊕ www.craterlakelodges.com ⟿ 40 rooms ☾ Closed mid-Oct.–late May ⦿| No meals.

$$$ | **⌂ Crater Lake Lodge.** The period feel of this 1915 lodge on the caldera's
HOTEL | rim is reflected in its lodgepole-pine columns, gleaming wood floors, and stone fireplaces in the common areas. **Pros:** ideal location for watching sunrise and sunset reflected on the lake. **Cons:** very difficult to reserve rooms; some rooms have tubs only, no shower. $ Rooms from: $165 ⊠ 1 Lodge Loop Rd., Rim Village, east of Rim Visitor Center ☎ 541/594–2255, 888/774–2728 ⊕ www.craterlakelodges.com ⟿ 71 rooms ☾ Closed mid-Oct.–late May ⦿| No meals.

CLOSE UP

Best Campgrounds in Crater Lake

Both tent campers and RV enthusiasts will enjoy the heavily wooded and well-equipped setting of Mazama Campground. Drinking water, showers, and laundry facilities help ensure that you don't have to rough it too much. Lost Creek Campground is much smaller, with minimal amenities and a more "rustic" Crater Lake experience.

Lost Creek Campground. The small, remote tent sites here are usually available on a daily basis; in July and August arrive early to secure a spot. ✉ *3 miles south of Rim Rd. on Pinnacles Spur Rd. at Grayback Dr.* ☎ *541/594-3100.*

Mazama Campground. This campground is set well below the lake caldera in the pine and fir forest of the Cascades not far from the main access road (Highway 62). About half the spaces are pull-throughs, some with electricity; no hookups are available. The best tent spots are on some of the outer loops above Annie Creek Canyon. ✉ *Mazama Village, near Annie Spring entrance station* ☎ *541/594-2255, 888/774-2728* 🌐 *www.craterlakelodges.com.*

OUTSIDE THE PARK

$$ B&B/INN 🏨 **Prospect Historic Hotel Bed and Breakfast.** Noted individuals such as Theodore Roosevelt, Zane Grey, Jack London, and William Jennings Bryan have stayed here (in rooms that now bear their names). **Pros:** three waterfalls within walking distance; large property with beautiful grounds and creek; on-site owners. **Cons:** Prospect is a very small town; breakfast is not included with motel units. [$] *Rooms from: $140* ✉ *391 Mill Creek Dr., Prospect* ☎ *541/560–3664, 800/944–6490* 🌐 *www.prospecthotel.com* 🛏 *10 main house rooms, 14 motel rooms* 🍴 *Breakfast.*

$$ RESORT FAMILY 🏨 **Running Y Ranch Resort.** Golfers rave about the Arnold Palmer–designed course at this 3,600-acre Holiday Inn resort situated in a juniper-and-ponderosa-shaded canyon overlooking Upper Klamath Lake. **Pros:** kids enjoy an indoor pool; walkers and joggers have 8 miles of paved trails; property received an ambitious makeover in 2011. **Cons:** may be a bit too far off the beaten path for some. [$] *Rooms from: $149* ✉ *5500 Running Y Rd., 8 miles north of Klamath Falls* ☎ *541/850–5500, 800/569–0029* 🌐 *www.runningy.com* 🛏 *82 rooms, 43 houses* 🍴 *No meals.*

16

DEATH VALLEY
NATIONAL PARK

16

Visit Fodors.com for advice, updates, and bookings

WELCOME TO DEATH VALLEY

TOP REASONS TO GO

★ **Roving rocks:** Death Valley's Racetrack is home to moving boulders, an unexplained phenomenon that has scientists baffled.

★ **Lowest spot on the continent:** Stand on the lowest spot on the continent at Badwater, 282 feet below sea level.

★ **Wildflower explosion:** During the spring, this desert landscape is ablaze with greenery and colorful flowers, especially between Badwater and Ashford Mill.

★ **Ghost towns:** Death Valley is renowned for its Wild West heritage and is home to dozens of crumbling settlements including Ballarat, Cerro Gordo, Chloride City, Greenwater, Harrisburg, Keeler, Leadfield, Panamint City, Rhyolite, and Skidoo.

★ **Naturally amazing:** From canyons to sand dunes to salt flats and dry lake beds, Death Valley serves up plenty of geological treasures.

1 Central Death Valley. Furnace Creek sits in the heart of Death Valley—if you have only a short time in the park, head here. You can visit gorgeous Golden Canyon, Zabriskie Point, the Salt Creek Interpretive Trail, and Artist's Drive, among other popular points of interest.

2 Northern Death Valley. This region is uphill from Furnace Creek, which means marginally cooler temperatures. Be sure to stop by Rhyolite Ghost Town on Highway 374 before entering the park and exploring Moorish Scotty's Castle, colorful Titus Canyon, and jaw-dropping Ubehebe Crater.

3 Southern Death Valley. This is a desolate area, but there are plenty of sights that help convey Death Valley's rich history. Don't miss the Dublin Gulch Caves.

4 Western Death Valley. Panamint Springs Resort is a nice place to grab a meal and get your bearings before moving on to quaint Darwin Falls, smooth rolling sand dunes, beehive-shaped Wildrose Charcoal Kilns, and historic Stovepipe Wells Village.

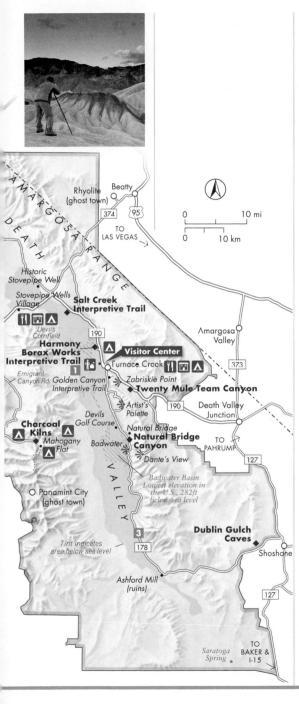

CALIFORNIA

GETTING ORIENTED

Death Valley National Park covers 5,310 square miles, ranges from 6 to 60 miles wide, and measures 140 miles north to south. Within the park, the Panamint Range parallels Death Valley to the west, the Amargosa Range to the east. Nearly the entire park lies in southeastern California, with a small eastern portion crossing over into Nevada.

16

KEY	
🏕	Ranger Station
⛺	Campground
🌲	Picnic Area
🍴	Restaurant
🏨	Lodge
🚶	Trailhead
🚻	Restrooms
✳	Scenic Viewpoint
⋯⋯	Walking/Hiking Trails
= = =	4-Wheel Drive Dirt Road
= = =	2-Wheel Drive Dirt Road

Updated by
Deb Hopewell

The desert is no Disneyland. With its scorching summer heat and vast, sparsely populated tracts of land, it's not often at the top of the list when most people plan their California vacations. But the natural riches of Death Valley—the largest national park outside Alaska—are overwhelming: rolling waves of sand dunes, black cinder cones thrusting up hundreds of feet from a blistered desert floor, riotous sheets of wildflowers, bizarrely shaped Joshua trees basking in the orange glow of a sunset, tiny pupfish that enthrall youngsters, and a silence that is both dramatic and startling.

DEATH VALLEY PLANNER

WHEN TO GO

Most of the park's 1 million annual visitors still come between late fall and early spring, taking advantage of moderate temperatures and the lack of rainfall. During these cooler months you will need to book a room in advance, but don't worry: the park never feels crowded. If you visit in summer, believe everything you've ever heard about desert heat—it can be brutal, with temperatures often topping 120°F. The dry air wicks moisture from the body without causing a sweat, so drink plenty of water. Bring sunglasses, a hat, and sufficient clothing to block the sun's rays and the wind. Flash floods are fairly common; sections of roadway can be flooded or washed away. The wettest month is February, when the park receives an average of 0.3 inch of rain.

AVG. HIGH/LOW TEMPS.

JAN.	FEB.	MAR.	APR.	MAY	JUNE
65/39	73/46	80/54	89/62	99/71	109/80

JULY	AUG.	SEPT.	OCT.	NOV.	DEC.
115/86	113/84	105/75	92/61	76/47	65/38

FESTIVALS AND EVENTS

MARCH FAMILY **Diaz Lake Trout Derby.** The first Saturday of the month, grab your fishing gear and take a shot at the "big one" for a $10 entry fee ($5 for kids 12 and under). ☎ *760/876–4444* ⊕ *www.lonepinechamber.org.*

Annual Art Show & Brunch. Admission is free for this arts-and-crafts show and sale weekend, held inside and on the lawn of the Furnace Creek Ranch and Inn. ☎ *760/852–4420* ⊕ *www.deathvalleychamber.org.*

MAY **Bishop Mule Days.** Entertainment at this five-day festival includes top country-music stars, an arts-and-crafts fair, barbecues, country dances, and the longest-running nonmotorized parade in the U.S. Admission is free. ☎ *760/872–4263* ⊕ *www.muledays.org.*

OCTOBER **Lone Pine Film Festival.** Every Columbus Day weekend, this town pays tribute to its Hollywood history with three days of tours, films, lectures, and celebrity panels. ☎ *760/876–9103* ⊕ *www.lonepinefilmfestival.org.*

NOVEMBER **Death Valley 49er Encampment Days.** Originally a centennial celebration held in 1949 to honor the area's first European visitors, this week-long event draws thousands of people from around the world for art shows, live music, dancing, and even a poker tournament. ⊕ *www.deathvalley49ers.org.*

Shoshone Old West Days. Just outside of Death Valley, this annual festival celebrates Wild West heritage with live performances, arts-and-crafts, and deep-pit barbecue. ☎ *760/852–4335* ⊕ *www.shoshonevillage.com.*

PLANNING YOUR TIME

DEATH VALLEY IN ONE DAY

If you begin the day in Furnace Creek, you can see several sights without doing much driving. Bring plenty of water with you, and some food, too. Get up early and drive the 20 miles on Badwater Road to **Badwater,** which looks out on the lowest point in the Western Hemisphere and is a dramatic place to watch the sunrise. Returning north, stop at **Natural Bridge,** a medium-size conglomerate rock formation that has been hollowed at its base to form a span across the canyon, and then at the **Devil's Golf Course,** so named because of the large pinnacles of salt present here. Detour to the right onto **Artist's Drive,** a 9-mile one-way, northbound route that passes **Artist's Palette.** The reds, yellows, oranges, and greens come from minerals in the rocks and the earth. Four miles north of Artist's Drive you will come to the **Golden Canyon Interpretive Trail,** a 2-mile round trip that winds through a canyon with colorful rock walls. Just before Furnace Creek, take Highway 190 3 miles east to **Zabriskie Point,** overlooking dramatic, furrowed red-brown hills and the **Twenty Mule Team Canyon.** Return to Furnace Creek, where you can grab a meal and visit the museum at the Furnace Creek Visitor Center. Heading north from Furnace Creek, pull off the highway and take a look at the **Harmony Borax Works.**

16

GETTING HERE AND AROUND
CAR TRAVEL

It can take more than three hours to cross from one side of the park to another, so it's important to choose an entrance point that makes sense for what you want to see. If you're driving from Los Angeles, enter through the western portion along Highway 395; if you're coming from Las Vegas, enter from the north at Beatty, Nevada, or via the central entrance at Death Valley Junction. Travelers from Orange County, San Diego, and the Inland Empire should access the park via Interstate 15 North at Baker.

Distances can be deceiving within the park: what seems close can be very far away. Much of the park can be viewed on regularly scheduled bus tours, but these often don't allow time for hikes to sites not seen from the road, such as Salt Creek, Golden Canyon, and Natural Bridge. The best option is to drive to a number of the sites, get out of the car, and walk.

When driving in Death Valley, reliable maps are important, as signage is often limited or, in a few places, nonexistent. Other important accessories include a compass, a mobile phone (though these don't always work in remote areas), and extra food and water (3 gallons per person per day is recommended), plus additional radiator water). If you're able to take a four-wheel-drive vehicle, bring it: many of Death Valley's most spectacular canyons are otherwise inaccessible. Be aware of possible winter closures or driving restrictions due to snow.

Driving Information California Highway Patrol. The California Highway Patrol offers the latest traffic incident information. ☎ *800/427–7623 for recorded info, 760/872–5900 for live dispatcher* ⊕ *cad.chp.ca.gov.* **California State Department of Transportation Hotline.** Call this hotline for updates on Death Valley road conditions. ☎ *800/427–7623* ⊕ *www.dot.ca.gov.*

PARK ESSENTIALS
PARK FEES AND PERMITS

The entrance fee is $20 per vehicle and $10 for those entering on foot, bus, bike, or motorcycle. The payment, valid for seven consecutive days, is collected at the park's entrance stations and at the visitor center at Furnace Creek. (If you enter the park on Highway 190, you won't find an entrance station; remember to stop by the visitor center to pay the fee.) Annual park passes, valid only at Death Valley, are $40.

A permit is not required for groups of 14 or fewer, but if you're planning an overnight visit to the backcountry, complete a registration form at the Furnace Creek Visitor Center. Backcountry camping is allowed in areas that are at least 2 miles from maintained campgrounds and the main paved or unpaved roads and ¼ mile from water sources. Most abandoned mining areas are restricted to day use.

PARK HOURS

Most facilities within the park remain open year-round, daily 8–6.

CELL-PHONE RECEPTION

Results vary, but in general you should be able to get fairly good cell-phone reception on the valley floor. In the surrounding mountains, however, don't count on it.

RESTAURANTS

Inside the park, if you're looking for a special evening out in Death Valley, head to the Inn at Furnace Creek Dining Room, where you'll be spoiled with fine wines and juicy steaks. It's also a great spot to start the day with a hearty gourmet breakfast. Most other eateries within the park are mom-and-pop-type places with basic American fare. Outside the park, dining choices are much the same, with little cafés and homey diners serving up coffee shop–style burgers, chicken, and steaks. If you're vegetarian or vegan, BYOB (bring your own beans).

Prices in the reviews are the average cost of a main course at dinner, or if dinner is not served, at lunch.

HOTELS

It's difficult to find lodging anywhere in Death Valley that doesn't have breathtaking views of the park and surrounding mountains. Most accommodations, aside from the Inn at Furnace Creek, are homey and rustic. Rooms fill up quickly during the fall and spring seasons, and reservations are required about three months in advance for the prime weekends.

Outside the park, head to Beatty or Amargosa Valley in Nevada for a bit of nightlife and casino action. The western side of Death Valley, along the eastern Sierra Nevada, is a gorgeous setting, though it's quite a distance from Furnace Creek. Here, you can stay in the historic Dow Villa Motel, where John Wayne spent many a night, or head farther south to the ghost towns of Randsburg or Cerro Gordo for a true Wild West experience.

Prices in the reviews are the lowest cost of a standard double room in high season. For expanded reviews, facilities, and current deals, visit Fodors.com.

TOURS

Death Valley Adventure Tour (*Adventure Motorcycle [AdMo] Tours*). Motorcycle enthusiasts can sign up for a guided Death Valley Adventure Tour that starts and ends in Las Vegas. The five-day tour ($2,325 with your own bike; rentals start at $700) through Death Valley covers 100–180 miles a day. The tours, which run October through May, include hotel accommodations, gasoline, breakfasts, snacks, a support vehicle, and a professional guide. To join, you'll need a motorcycle driver's license and experience with off-road and all-terrain riding. ⊠ *1300 Highway 2, Wrightwood* ☎ *760/249–1105* ⊕ *www.admotours.com.*

Death Valley & Scotty's Castle Adventure Tour. These 11-hour luxury motor-coach tours of the park pass through its most famous landmarks. Tours include lunch and hotel pickup from designated Las Vegas–area hotels. Tours depart Tuesday and Saturday at 7 am and cost $199 per person. ☎ *800/719–3768 for Death Valley Tours, 800/566–5868, 702/233–1627 for Look Tours.*

Furnace Creek Visitor Center tours. This center has the most tour options, including a weekly 2-mile Harmony Borax Walk and guided hikes to Mosaic Canyon and Golden Canyon. Less strenuous options include wildflower, birding, and geology walks, and a Furnace Creek Inn historical tour. The visitor center also offers orientation programs every half hour daily from 8 to 5. ⊠ *Furnace Creek Visitor Center, Rte. 190, 30 miles northwest of Death Valley Junction* ☎ *760/786–2331.*

16

Plants and Wildlife in Death Valley

There's a general misconception that Death Valley National Park consists of mile upon endless mile of flat desert sands, scattered cacti, and an occasional cow skull. Many people don't realize that across the valley floor from Badwater—the lowest point in the Western Hemisphere—Telescope Peak towers at 11,049 feet above sea level. The extreme topography of Death Valley is a lesson in geology. Two hundred million years ago seas covered the area, depositing layers of sediment and fossils. Between 3.5 million and 5 million years ago faults in the Earth's crust and volcanic activity pushed and folded the ground, causing mountain ranges to rise and the valley floor to drop. The valley was then filled periodically by lakes, which eroded the surrounding rocks into fantastic formations and deposited the salts that now cover the floor of the basin.

Most animal life in Death Valley (51 mammal, 36 reptile, 307 bird, and 3 amphibian species) is found near the limited sources of water. The bighorn sheep spend most of their time in the secluded upper reaches of the park's rugged canyons and ridges. Coyotes often can be seen lazing in the shade next to the golf course and have been known to run onto the fairways to steal a golf ball. The only native fish in the park is the pupfish, which grows to slightly longer than 1 inch. In winter, when the water is cold, the fish lie dormant in the bottom mud, becoming active again in spring. Because they are wary of large moving shapes, you must stand quietly over a pool at Salt Creek to see them.

Botanists say there are more than 1,000 species of plants here (21 exist nowhere else in the world), though many annual plants lie dormant as seeds for all but a few months in spring, when rains trigger a bloom. The rest congregate around the few water sources. Most of the low-elevation vegetation grows around the oases at Furnace Creek and Scotty's Castle, where oleanders, palms, and salt cedar grow. At higher elevations you will find pinyon, juniper, and bristlecone pine.

Pink Jeep Tours Las Vegas. Hop aboard a distinctive, pink four-wheel-drive vehicle with Pink Jeep Tours Las Vegas to visit places—the Charcola Kilns, the Racetrack, and Titus Canyon among them—that your own vehicle might not be able to handle. Pink Jeep tours last 9 to 10 hours from Las Vegas (you also can board at Furnace Creek) and cost up to $239. ✉ *3629 West Hacienda Ave., Las Vegas, Nevada* ☎ *888/900–4480* ⊕ *www.pinkjeep.com*

Gadabout Tours. Take four-day trips (from $899) through Death Valley from Palm Springs, California, in February, March, and November. ✉ *Sheraton Ontario Airport, 428 N. Vineyard Ave., Ontario* ☎ *760/325–5556, 800/952–5068* ⊕ *www.gadabouttours.com.*

VISITOR INFORMATION
PARK CONTACT INFORMATION
Death Valley National Park ☎ *760/786–3200* ⊕ *www.nps.gov/deva.*

VISITOR CENTERS

Furnace Creek Visitor Center and Museum. The exhibits and artifacts here provide a broad overview of how Death Valley formed; you can pick up maps at the bookstore run by the Death Valley Natural History Association. This is also the place to sign up for ranger-led walks (available November through April) or check out a live presentation about the valley's cultural and natural history. The helpful center offers 12-minute slide shows about the park every 30 minutes. Your children are likely to receive plenty of individual attention from the enthusiastic rangers. Ongoing renovations to the center and museum are improving the displays and level of hands-on interactivity. ⊠ *Hwy. 190, 30 miles northwest of Death Valley Junction* ☎ *760/786–3200* ⊕ *www.nps.gov/deva* ⊘ *Daily 8–5.*

Scotty's Castle Visitor Center and Museum. If you visit Death Valley, make sure you make the hour's drive north from Furnace Creek to Scotty's Castle. In addition to living-history tours, you'll find a nice display of exhibits, books, self-guided tour pamphlets, and displays about the castle's creators, Death Valley Scotty and Albert M. Johnson. Fuel up with sandwiches or souvenirs (there's no gasoline sold here anymore) before heading back out to the park. ⊠ *Rte. 267, 53 miles northwest of Furnace Creek and 45 miles northwest of Stovepipe Wells Village* ☎ *760/786–2392* ⊕ *www.nps.gov/deva* ⊘ *Daily 9–4:15 (hrs vary seasonally).*

16

EXPLORING

SCENIC DRIVE

Artist's Drive. This 9-mile, one-way route skirts the foothills of the Black Mountains and provides intimate views of the changing landscape. Once inside the palette, the huge expanses of the valley are replaced by the small-scale natural beauty of pigments created by volcanic deposits. It's a quiet, lonely drive, and shouldn't be rushed. Reach Artist's Palette by heading north off Badwater Road.

HISTORIC SITES

Charcoal Kilns. Ten well-preserved stone kilns, each 25 feet high and 30 feet wide, stand as if on parade. The kilns, built by Chinese laborers for a mining company in 1877, were used to burn wood from pinyon pines to turn it into charcoal. The charcoal was then transported over the mountains into Death Valley, where it was used to extract lead and silver from the ore mined there. If you hike nearby Wildrose Peak, you will be rewarded with terrific views of the kilns. ⊠ *Wildrose Canyon Rd., 37 miles south of Stovepipe Wells.*

Harmony Borax Works. Death Valley's mule teams hauled borax from here to the railroad town of Mojave, 165 miles away. The teams plied the route until 1889, when the railroad finally arrived in Zabriskie. Constructed in 1883, one of the oldest buildings in Death Valley houses the Borax Museum, 2 miles south of the borax works at the Inn at Furnace

Creek (between the restaurants and the post office). Originally a miners' bunkhouse, the building once stood in Twenty Mule Team Canyon. Now it displays mining machinery and historical exhibits. The adjacent structure is the original mule-team barn. ⊠ *Harmony Borax Works Rd., west of Hwy. 190, 2 miles north of Furnace Creek* ⊕ *www.nps.gov/deva/ historyculture/harmony.htm* ⊗ *Daily 9–9.*

Keane Wonder Mine. The tram towers and cables from the old mill used to process gold from Keane Wonder Mine are still here, leading up to the crumbling mine. Due to safety concerns about the crumbling site, the National Park Service banned access to the mine and surrounding area. ⊠ *Access road off Beatty Cutoff Rd., 17½ miles north of Furnace Creek.*

FAMILY **Scotty's Castle.** This Moorish-style mansion, begun in 1924 and never completed, takes its name from Walter Scott, better known as Death Valley Scotty. An ex-cowboy, prospector, and performer in Buffalo Bill's Wild West Show, Scotty always told people the castle was his, financed by gold from a secret mine. In reality, there was no mine, and the house belonged to a Chicago millionaire named Albert Johnson, whom Scott had finagled into investing in the fictitious mine. Despite the con, Johnson and Scott became great friends. The house functioned for a while as a hotel and still contains works of art, imported carpets, handmade European furniture, and a tremendous pipe organ. Costumed rangers, with varying degrees of enthusiasm, re-create life at the castle circa 1939. Check out the Underground Tour, which takes you through a 1/4-mile tunnel in the castle basement. ⊠ *Scotty's Castle Rd. (Hwy. 267), 53 miles north of Salt Creek Interpretive Trail* ☏ *760/786–2392* ⊕ *www.nps.gov/deva* ⊠ *$15* ⊗ *Daily 8:30–4:15, tours daily 9–4 (hrs vary seasonally).*

SCENIC STOPS

Artist's Palette. So called for the contrasting colors of its volcanic deposits, this is one of signature sights of Death Valley. Artist's Drive, the approach to the area, is one way heading north off Badwater Road, so if you're visiting Badwater from Furnace Creek, come here on the way back. The drive winds through foothills of sedimentary and volcanic rocks. About 4 miles into the drive, a short side road veers right to a parking lot that's a few hundred feet before the "palette," whose natural colors include shades of green, gold, and pink. ⊠ *Off Badwater Rd., 11 miles south of Furnace Creek.*

Badwater. At 282 feet below sea level, Badwater is the lowest spot on land in the Western Hemisphere—and also one of the hottest. Stairs and wheelchair ramps descend from the parking lot to a wooden platform that overlooks a sodium chloride pool, a small but remarkably persistent reminder that the valley floor used to contain a lake. You can continue past the platform on a broad, white path that peters out after a half-mile or so. Badwater is one of the most popular and easily accessible sites within the park. From this lowest point, be sure to look across to Telescope Peak, which towers more than 2 miles above the valley floor. ⊠ *Badwater Rd., 19 miles south of Furnace Creek.*

Dante's View. This lookout is more than 5,000 feet up in the Black Mountains. In the dry desert air you can see across most of 110-mile-long Death Valley. The view is astounding. Take a 10-minute, mildly strenuous walk from the parking lot toward a series of rocky overlooks, where with binoculars you can spot some of Death Valley's signature sites. A few interpretive signs point out the highlights below in the valley and across, in the Sierra. Getting here from Furnace Creek takes an hour—time well invested. ⊠ *Dante's View Rd., off Hwy. 190, 35 miles from Badwater, 20 miles south of Twenty Mule Team Canyon.*

Devil's Golf Course. Thousands of miniature salt pinnacles carved into surreal shapes by the desert wind dot this wildly varied landscape. The salt was pushed up to the earth's surface by pressure created as underground salt- and water-bearing gravel crystallized. Get out of your vehicle and take a closer look; you'll see perfectly round holes descending into the ground. ⊠ *Badwater Rd., 13 miles south of Furnace Creek.* ✛ *Turn right onto dirt road and drive 1 mile.*

Golden Canyon. Just South of Furnace Creek, these glimmering mountains are perhaps best known for their role in the original *Star Wars*. The canyon is also a fine hiking spot, with gorgeous views of the Panamint Mountains, ancient dry lake beds, and alluvial fans. If you fork out a quarter for the small trail guide, be forewarned that several of the numbered signs it refers to are missing. ⊠ *Hwy 178* ✛ *From the Furnace Creek Visitor Center, drive 2 miles south on Hwy. 190, then 2 miles south on Hwy. 178 to the parking area. The lot has a kiosk with trail guides.*

16

Racetrack. Getting here involves a 28-mile journey over a rough dirt road, but the reward is well worth the trip. Where else in the world do rocks move on their own? This phenomenon has baffled scientists for years and is perhaps one of the last great natural mysteries. No one has actually seen the rocks in motion, but theory has it that when it rains, the hard-packed lake bed becomes slippery enough that gusty winds push the rocks along—sometimes for several hundred yards. When the mud dries, a telltale trail remains. The trek to the Racetrack can be made in a sedan, but sharp rocks can slash tires; a truck or SUV with thick tires, high clearance, and a spare tire are suggested. ⊠ *27 miles west of Ubehebe Crater via dirt road.*

Sand Dunes at Mesquite Flat. These dunes, made up of minute pieces of quartz and other rock, are ever-changing products of the wind-rippled hills, with curving crests and a sun-bleached hue. The dunes are the most photographed destination in the park, and you can see them at their best at sunrise and sunset. Keep your eyes open for animal tracks—you may even spot a coyote or fox. Bring plenty of water, and note where you parked your car: it's easy to become disoriented in this ocean of sand. If you lose your bearings, climb to the top of a dune and scan the horizon for the parking lot. ⊠ *19 miles north of Hwy. 190, northeast of Stovepipe Wells Village.*

"I loved how soft the dunes in Death Valley National Park looked from a distance in the early morning light. I ventured out far from the road to capture the serene isolation, and found these unexpected print trails.

Stovepipe Wells Village. This tiny 1926 town, the first resort in Death Valley, takes its name from the stovepipe that an early prospector left to indicate where he found water. The area contains a motel, restaurant, grocery store, campgrounds, and landing strip, though first-time park visitors are better off staying in Furnace Creek, which is more central. Off Highway 190, on a 3-mile gravel road immediately southwest, are the multicolor walls of Mosaic Canyon. ⊠ *Hwy. 190, 2 miles from Sand Dunes, 77 miles east of Lone Pine* ⊕ *www. escapetodeathvalley.com.*

Titus Canyon. This is a popular 27-mile drive from Beatty south along Scotty's Castle Road. Along the way you'll pass Leadville Ghost Town, petroglyphs at Klare Spring, and spectacular limestone and dolomite narrows at the end of the canyon. Toward the end, a two-lane gravel road will lead you into the mouth of the canyon. ⊠ *Access road off Scotty's Castle Rd., 33 miles northwest of Furnace Creek.*

Twenty Mule Team Canyon. This canyon was named in honor of the 20-mule teams that, between 1883 and 1889, carried 10-ton loads of borax through the burning desert (though they didn't actually pass through this canyon). Along the 2.7-mile, one-way loop road off Highway 190, you'll find the soft rock walls reach high on both sides, making it seem like you're on an amusement-park ride. Remains of prospectors' tunnels are visible here, along with some brilliant rock formations. ⊠ *20 Mule Team Rd., off Hwy. 190, 4 miles south of Furnace Creek, 20 miles west of Death Valley Junction.*

One from a person along the ridge, and several straight animal prints. The group of tourists in the distance really give us an idea of the enormous vastness of the landscape." —photo by Evan Spiler, Fodors.com member

Ubehebe Crater. At 500 feet deep and ½ mile across, this crater resulted from underground steam and gas explosions about 3,000 years ago. Volcanic ash spreads out over most of the area, and the cinders lie as deep as 150 feet, near the crater's rim. Trek down to the crater's floor or walk around it on a fairly level path. Either way, you need about an hour and will be treated to fantastic views. ⊠ *N. Death Valley Hwy., 8 miles northwest of Scotty's Castle.*

Zabriskie Point. Although only about 710 feet in elevation, this is one of Death Valley National Park's most scenic spots, overlooking a striking panorama of wrinkled, multicolor hills. It's a great place to watch the sunrise, but it can be bustling any time of day. Pair it with a drive out to magnificent Dante's View. ⊠ *Hwy. 190, 5 miles south of Furnace Creek.*

EDUCATIONAL OFFERINGS

RANGER PROGRAMS

FAMILY **Junior Ranger Program.** Children can join this program at any of the three visitor centers, where they can pick up a workbook and complete up to 15 projects (based on their age) to earn souvenir badge.

SPORTS AND THE OUTDOORS

BICYCLING

Mountain biking is permitted on any of the back roads and roadways open to the public (bikes aren't permitted on hiking trails). A free flier with suggested bike routes is at the Furnace Creek Visitor Center; Bicycle Trail, a 4-mile round-trip trek from the visitor center to Mustard Canyon, is a good place to start. Bike rentals are available at the Furnace Creek Resort, by the hour or by the day. ☎ *760/786-3371*

TOURS AND OUTFITTERS

Spirit of the Mojave Mountain Biking Tour (*Escape Adventures*). Mountain bike into the heart of Death Valley during a six-day adventure through the national park. The 110-mile journey (on single-track trails) includes accommodations (both camping and inns). Tours are $1,190 per person; bikes, tents, sleeping bags, helmets, and other gear may be rented for an additional price. Tours are available February–April and October only. ✉ *Death Valley National Park* ☎ *800/596–2953, 702/838–6966* ⊕ *www.escapeadventures.com.*

BIRD-WATCHING

Approximately 350 bird species have been identified in Death Valley. The best place to see the park's birds is along the Salt Creek Interpretive Trail, where you can spot ravens, common snipes, killdeer, spotted sandpipers, and great blue herons. Along the fairways at Furnace Creek Golf Club, you can see kingfishers, peregrine falcons, hawks, Canada geese, yellow warblers, and the occasional golden eagle. Scotty's Castle attracts wintering birds from around the globe that are attracted to its running water, shady trees, and shrubs. Other good spots to find birds are at Saratoga Springs, Mesquite Springs, Travertine Springs, and Grimshaw Lake near Tecopa. You can download a complete park bird checklist, divided by season, at ⊕ *www.nps.gov/deva/naturescience/ birds.htm.* Rangers at Furnace Creek Visitor Center often lead birding walks through Salt Creek between November and March.

FOUR-WHEELING

Maps and SUV guidebooks for four-wheel-drive and other backcountry roads (including the popular Cottonwood/Marble canyons, Racetrack, Eureka Dunes, Saratoga Springs, and Warm Springs Canyon) are offered at the Furnace Creek Visitor Center. Remember: Never travel alone and be sure to pack plenty of water and snacks. Driving off established roads is strictly prohibited in the park.

ROADS

Butte Valley. This 21-mile road in the southwest part of the park climbs from 200 feet below sea level to an elevation of 4,000 feet. The geological formations along the drive reveal the development of Death Valley. ✉ *Trailhead on Warm Spring Canyon Rd., 50 miles south of Furnace Creek Visitor Center.*

Warm Springs Canyon. This route takes you past Warm Springs talc mine and through Butte Valley, over Mengel Pass and toward **Geologists Cabin,** a charming and cheery little cabin where you can spend the night (if nobody else beats you to it!). The cabin, which sits under a cottonwood tree, has a fireplace, table and chairs, and a sink. Farther up the road, the cabins at Mengel's Home and Russell Camp are also open for public use. Keep the historic cabins clean and restock any items that you use. ⊠ *Trailhead on Warm Springs Canyon Rd., off Badwater Rd. (Hwy. 190).*

TOURS

Death Valley SUV Tour (*Death Valley Tours*). The 10-hour Death Valley SUV Tour departs from Las Vegas and takes you on a fully narrated whirl through Death Valley in a four-wheel-drive Jeep. Tours (from $212 per person) depart Monday and Wednesday at 7 am (parties should be minimum of four and maximum of seven people) and include free pickup from designated hotels. Bottled water and snacks are provided, and camera rentals, tripods, and film are available for an additional fee. ⊠ *Death Valley National Park* ☎ *800/719–3768* ⊕ *www.deathvalleytours.net.*

GOLF

16

Furnace Creek Golf Club. Play 9 or 18 holes at the lowest golf course in the world (214 feet below sea level). Its improbably green fairways are lined with date palms and tamarisk trees, and its level of difficulty is rated surprisingly high. The club rents clubs and carts, and there are golf packages available for Furnace Creek Ranch or Furnace Creek Inn guests. In winter, reservations are essential. ⊠ *Hwy. 190, Furnace Creek* ☎ *760/786–2301* ⊕ *www.furnacecreekresort.com* 🖼 *$30–$60* ☉ *Tee times 6–3:30; pro shop 6:30–5.*

HIKING

Plan to hike before or after midday in the spring, summer, or fall, unless you're in the mood for a masochistic baking. Carry plenty of water, wear protective clothing, and keep an eye out for black widows, scorpions, snakes, and other potentially dangerous creatures. Some of the best trails are unmarked; if the opportunity arises, ask for directions.

EASY

FAMILY

Fodor's Choice

★

Darwin Falls. This lovely 2-mile round-trip hike rewards you with a refreshing waterfall surrounded by thick vegetation and a rocky gorge. No swimming or bathing is allowed, but it's a beautiful place for a picnic. Adventurous hikers can scramble higher toward more rewarding views of the falls. *Easy.* ⊠ *Access the 2-mile graded dirt road and parking area off Hwy. 190, 1 mile west of Panamint Springs Resort.*

Natural Bridge Canyon. A 2-mile access road with potholes that could swallow basketballs leads to a parking lot. From there, set off to see interesting geological features in addition to the bridge, which is 0.25 mile away. The one-way trail continues for a few hundred meters, but scenic returns diminish quickly and eventually you're confronted with climbing boulders. *Easy.* ⊠ *Access road off Badwater Rd., 15 miles south of Furnace Creek.*

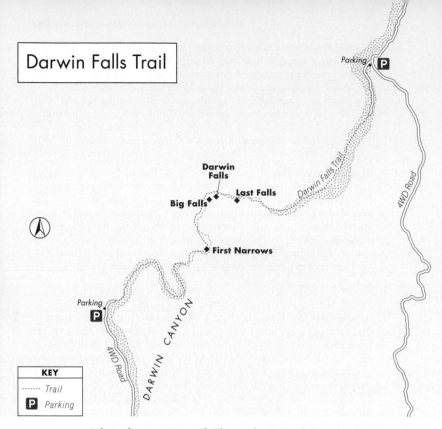

Darwin Falls Trail

Darwin Falls

Last Falls

Big Falls

Darwin Falls Trail

4WD Road

First Narrows

Parking **P**

Parking **P**

DARWIN CANYON

4WD Road

Parking **P**

KEY	
------	Trail
P	Parking

FAMILY **Salt Creek Interpretive Trail.** This trail, a 0.5-mile boardwalk circuit, loops through a spring-fed wash. The nearby hills are brown and gray, but the floor of the wash is alive with aquatic plants such as pickerelweed and salt grass. The stream and ponds here are among the few places in the park to see the rare pupfish, the only native fish species in Death Valley. Animals such as bobcats, fox, coyotes, and snakes visit the spring, and you may also see ravens, common snipes, killdeer, and great blue herons. *Easy.* ⊠ *Off Hwy. 190, 14 miles north of Furnace Creek.*

Titus Canyon. The narrow floor of Titus Canyon is made of hard-packed gravel and dirt, and it's a constant, moderate uphill walk (3-mile roundtrip is the trail's most popular tack). Klare Spring and some petroglyphs are 5.5 miles from the mouth of the canyon, but you can get a feeling for the area on a shorter walk. *Easy.* ⊠ *Death Valley National Park.*

MODERATE

Fall Canyon. This is a 3-mile one-way hike from the Titus canyon parking area. First, walk 0.5 mile north along the base of the mountains to a large wash, then go 2.5 miles up the canyon to a 35-foot dry fall. You can continue by climbing around to the falls on the south side. *Moderate.* ⊠ *Access road off Scotty's Castle Rd., 33 miles northwest of Furnace Creek.*

FAMILY **Mosaic Canyon.** A gradual uphill trail (4 miles round-trip) winds through the smoothly polished walls of this narrow canyon. There are dry falls to climb at the upper end. *Moderate.* ⊠ *Access road off Hwy. 190, ½ mile west of Stovepipe Wells Village.*

DIFFICULT

Fodor'sChoice **Telescope Peak Trail.** The 14-mile round trip begins at Mahogany Flat
★ Campground, which is accessible by a very rough dirt road. The steep and at some points treacherous trail winds through pinyon, juniper, and bristlecone pines, with excellent views of Death Valley and Panamint Valley. Ice axes and crampons may be necessary in winter—check at the Furnace Creek Visitor Center. It takes a minimum of six grueling hours to hike to the top of the 11,049-foot peak and then return. Getting to the peak is a strenuous endeavor; take plenty of water and only attempt it in fall unless you're an experienced hiker. *Difficult.* ⊠ *Off Wildrose Rd., south of Charcoal Kilns.*

HORSEBACK AND CARRIAGE RIDES

TOURS AND OUTFITTERS

Furnace Creek Stables. Set off on a one- or two-hour guided horseback or carriage ride ($45–$70) from Furnace Creek Stables. The rides traverse trails with views of the surrounding mountains, where multicolor volcanic rock and alluvial fans form a background for date palms and other vegetation. Evening carriage rides take passengers around the golf course and Furnace Creek Ranch. Cocktail rides, with champagne, margaritas, and hot spiced wine, are available. The stables are open October–May only. ⊠ *Hwy. 190, Furnace Creek* ☎ *760/614–1018* ⊕ *www.furnacecreekstables.net.*

16

ARTS AND ENTERTAINMENT

Marta Becket's Amargosa Opera House. An artist and dancer from New York, Becket first visited the former railway town of Amargosa while on tour in 1964. Three years later she returned to town and bought a boarded-up theater that sat amid a group of rundown mock–Spanish Colonial buildings. To compensate for the sparse audiences in the early days, Becket painted a Renaissance-era Spanish crowd on the walls and ceiling, turning the theater into a trompe l'oeil masterpiece. Now in her late 80s, Becket occasionally still takes the stage. After the show you can meet her in the adjacent gallery, where she sells her paintings and autographs her books. There are no performances mid-May through September. Reservations are required. ⊠ *Rte. 127, Death Valley Junction* ☎ *760/852–4441* ⊕ *www.amargosa-opera-house.com* ⊠ *$20* ☉ *Oct.–May (through Mother's Day weekend).*

SHOPPING

Experienced desert travelers carry an ice chest stocked with food and beverages. You're best off replenishing your food stash in Ridgecrest, Barstow, or Pahrump, larger towns that have a better selection and nontourist prices.

Furnace Ranch General Store. This convenience store carries groceries, souvenirs, camping supplies, and other basics. ☒ *Hwy. 190, Furnace Creek* ☎ *760/786–2345* ⊕ *www.furnacecreekresort.com/activities/shopping* ☉ *Daily 7 am–11 pm.*

WHAT'S NEARBY

NEARBY TOWNS

Founded at the turn of the 20th century, **Beatty** sits 16 miles east of the California-Nevada border on Death Valley's northern side. Named for a single pine tree found at the bottom of the canyon of the same name, **Lone Pine,** on the park's west side, is where you'll find Mt. Whitney, the highest peak in the continental United States, at 14,496 feet. The nearby Alabama Hills have been used in many movies and TV scenes, including segments in *The Lone Ranger.* Down south, unincorporated **Shoshone,** a very small town at the edge of Death Valley, started out as a mining town. The area, dotted with tamarisk trees and date palms, is home to a natural warm-springs pool fed by an underwater river.

VISITOR INFORMATION

Beatty Chamber of Commerce ☒ *119 E. Main St., Beatty, Nevada* ☎ *775/553–2424* ⊕ *www.beattynevada.org.* **Death Valley Chamber of Commerce** ☒ *860 Tecopa Hot Springs Rd., Tecopa* ☎ *760/852–4420* ⊕ *www.deathvalleychamber.org.* **Lone Pine Chamber of Commerce** ☒ *120 S. Main St., Lone Pine* ☎ *760/876–4444* ⊕ *www.lonepinechamber.org.*

NEARBY ATTRACTIONS

Air Flight Test Center Museum at Edwards Air Force Base. The museum at what many consider to be the birthplace of supersonic flight chronicles the rich history of flight testing. A dozen airplanes are on exhibit, from the first F-16B to the giant B-52D bomber. To visit, you must pass a security screening by providing your full name, Social Security number or driver's license number, and date and place of birth at least one week in advance. The 90-minute walking tours are open to the public on two Fridays of each month. ☒ *405 S. Rosamond Blvd., off Yeager Blvd., Edwards* ☎ *661/277–3517* ⊕ *www.afftcmuseum.org* ☑ *Free* ☉ *Two Fridays of each month, tours every 90 mins 9:30–3.*

FAMILY **Ancient Bristlecone Pine Forest.** About an hour's drive from Bishop you can view some of the oldest living trees on earth, some of which date back more than 40 centuries. The world's largest bristlecone pine can be found in Patriarch Grove. ☒ *Schulman Grove Visitor Center,*

"I'd always wanted to photograph this remote location, and on my drive into Death Valley I was rewarded at Zabriskie Point with this amazing view." —photo by Rodney Ee, Fodors.com member

White Mountain Rd. (⊕ from U.S. 395, turn east onto Hwy. 168 and follow signs for 23 miles), Bishop ⊠ $3 ⊙ Mid-May–Nov., as weather permits.

Ballarat Ghost Town. This crusty, dusty town saw its heyday between 1897 and 1917. There's a store-museum where you can grab a cold soda before venturing out to explore the crumbling landscape. Ballarat's more infamous draw is **Barker Ranch,** accessible with four-wheel drive, where convicted murderer Charles Manson and his "family" were captured after the 1969 Sharon Tate murder spree. *⊠ From Hwy. 395, exit SR-178 and travel 45 miles to the historic marker; Ballarat is 3½ miles from the pavement.*

Manzanar National Historic Site. A reminder of an ugly episode in U.S. history, the former Manzanar War Relocation Center is where some 10,000 Japanese-Americans were confined behind barbed-wire fences between 1942 and 1945. Today not much remains of Manzanar but a guard post, the auditorium, and some concrete foundations. But you can drive the one-way dirt road past the ruins to a small cemetery, where a monument stands. Signs mark where the barracks, a hospital, a school, and the fire station once stood. An outstanding 8,000-square-foot interpretive center has exhibits and screens a short film. ■TIP→ **This place has great bathrooms.** *⊠ U.S. 395, 11 miles north of Lone Pine ☎ 760/878–2932 ⊕ www.nps.gov/manz ⊠ Free ⊙ Park: daily dawn–dusk. Center: Apr.–Nov., daily 9–5:30; Nov.–Apr., daily 9–4:30.*

Mt. Whitney Fish Hatchery. Here's a delightful place for a family picnic. Bring some change for the fish-food machines; the lakes are full of hefty, always-hungry breeder trout. Built in 1915, the hatchery was one of the first trout farms in California, and today it produces fish that stock lakes throughout the state. ⊠ *Fish Hatchery Rd., 2 miles north of town, Independence* ☏ *760/876–4128* ⊕ *mtwhitneyfishhatchery.org* ☞ *Free* ☉ *Thurs.–Mon. 9–4.*

Fodor's Choice   **Petroglyph Canyons.** The two canyons, commonly called Big Petroglyph
★   and Little Petroglyph, are in the Coso Mountain range on the million-acre U.S. Naval Weapons Center at China Lake. Each of the canyons holds a superlative concentration of ancient rock art, the largest of its kind in the Northern Hemisphere. Thousands of well-preserved images of animals and humans are scratched or pecked into dark basaltic rocks. The military requires everyone to produce a valid driver's license, Social Security number, passport, and vehicle registration before the trip (nondrivers must provide a birth certificate). ⊠ *Ridgecrest* ⊕ *www. maturango.org* ☞ *$40; tours booked through Maturango Museum.*

Maturango Museum. The only way to see the amazing Coso petroglyphs is on a guided tour conducted by the Maturango Museum. Tours ($40) depart from the museum February–June, and September or October–early December; call for tour times. Children under 10 are not allowed on the tour. The museum's interesting exhibits survey the area's art, history, and geology. ⊠ *100 E. Las Flores Ave., at Hwy. 178, Ridgecrest* ☏ *760/375–6900* ⊕ *www.maturango.org* ☞ *$5* ☉ *Daily 10–5.*

FAMILY   **Randsburg.** The Rand Mining District first boomed when gold was dis-
Fodor's Choice   covered in the Rand Mountains in 1895. Along with neighboring settle-
★   ments, it grew further due to the success of the Yellow Aster Mine, which yielded $3 million worth of gold before 1900. Rich tungsten ore, used in World War I to make steel alloy, was discovered in 1907, and silver was found in 1919. Randsburg is one of the few gold-rush communities not to have become a ghost town; the tiny city jail is among the original buildings still standing in this town with a population under 100. In nearby Johannesburg, 1 mile south of Randsburg, spirits are said to dwell in the stunning Old West cemetery in the hills above town. ⊠ *Hwy. 395, near the junction with Rte. 14.*

FAMILY   **Rhyolite.** Though it's not within the boundary of Death Valley National Park, this Nevada ghost town, named for the silica volcanic rock nearby, is still a big draw. Around 1904, Rhyolite's Montgomery Shoshone Mine caused a financial boom, and fancy buildings sprung up all over town. Today you can still explore many of the crumbling edifices. The Bottle House, built by miner Tom Kelly out of almost 50,000 Adolphus Busch beer bottles, is a must-see. ⊠ *Hwy. 374, 35 miles north of Furnace Creek Visitor Center and 5 miles west of Beatty, Nevada.*

Shoshone Museum. This museum chronicles the local history of Death Valley and houses a unique collection of period items, and minerals and rocks from the area. ⊠ *Rte. 127, Shoshone* ☏ *760/852–4524* ⊕ *www. shoshonevillage.com/shoshone-museum.html* ☞ *Free* ☉ *Wed.–Mon. 9–3.*

Trona Pinnacles National Natural Landmark. Fantastic-looking formations of calcium carbonate, known as tufa, were formed underwater along fault lines in the bed of what is now Searles Dry Lake. Some of the more than 500 spires stand as tall as 140 feet, creating a landscape so surreal that it doubled for outer-space terrain in the film *Star Trek V.*

An easy-to-walk 0.5-mile trail allows you to see the tufa up close, but wear sturdy shoes—tufa cuts like coral. The best road to the area can be impassable after a rainstorm. ✉ *Pinnacle Rd., 5 miles south of Hwy. 178, 18 miles east of Ridgecrest* ☎ *760/384–5400 for Ridgecrest BLM office* 🌐 *www.blm.gov/ca/st/en/fo/ridgecrest/trona.3.html.*

SCENIC DRIVES

Highway 395. For a gorgeous view of the eastern Sierra, travel north of Death Valley along Highway 395 where you'll discover wandering elk herds, trout hatcheries, and breathtaking views of Mt. Whitney, the highest mountain (14,496 feet) in the continental United States. Drive south on Highway 395, between Olancha and Big Pine, and you'll notice the massive salt-crusted **Owens Lake,** which was drained between 1900 and 1920 as water from the Sierra was diverted to Los Angeles. Today, up to one-fourth of the water flow is being reintroduced to the lake, in part because of the toxic dust storms that have interrupted operations at China Lake Naval Weapons Base and caused the largest stationary source of air pollution in the country. If you drive to the northwest end of the lake, near the abandoned Pittsburg Plate Glass Soda Ash Plant, you can see brilliant red salt flats, caused by billions of microscopic halobacteria that survive there. Revered by the National Audubon Society, the lake is home to more than 241 migrating birds, including the snowy plover, American white pelican, golden eagle, and countless grebes, bitterns, blue herons, and cranes.

WHERE TO EAT

IN THE PARK

$ AMERICAN 🍴 **19th Hole.** Next to the clubhouse of the world's lowest golf course, this open-air spot serves hamburgers, hot dogs, chicken, and sandwiches. The full-service bar has a drive-through service for golfers in carts. [$] *Average main: $8* ✉ *Furnace Creek Golf Club, Hwy. 190, Furnace Creek* ☎ *760/786–2345* 🌐 *www.furnacecreekresort.com/activities/dining* ⏲ *Closed Jun.–Sept. No dinner.*

$$ CAFÉ FAMILY 🍴 **Forty-Niner Cafe.** This casual coffee shop serves basic American fare for breakfast (except in the summer), lunch, and dinner. It's done up in a rustic mining style with whitewashed pine walls, vintage map–covered tables, and prospector-branded chairs. Past menus and old photographs decorate the walls. [$] *Average main: $15* ✉ *Furnace Creek Ranch, Hwy. 190, Furnace Creek* ☎ *760/786–2345* 🌐 *www.furnacecreekresort.com.*

CLOSE UP

Best Campgrounds in Death Valley

You'll need a high-clearance or 4X4 vehicle to reach these locations. To find out where you can camp in the backcountry, pick up a copy of the backcountry map at the visitor center, or check the website 🌐 *www.nps.gov/deva/planyourvisit/camping.htm.*

You can only build fires in the metal fire grates that are available at most campgrounds, though fires may be restricted in summer (check with rangers about current conditions). Wood gathering is prohibited at all campgrounds. A limited supply of firewood is available at general stores in Furnace Creek and Stovepipe Wells, but because prices are high and supplies limited, you're better off bringing your own if you intend to camp. Camping is prohibited in the historic Inyo, Los Burro, and Ubehebe Crater areas, as well as all day-use spots, including Aguerberry Point Road, Cottonwood Canyon Road, Racetrack Road, Skidoo Road, Titus Canyon Road, Wildrose Road, and West Side Road.

Furnace Creek. This campground, 196 feet below sea level, has some shaded tent sites and is open all year. ✉ *Hwy. 190, Furnace Creek* ☎ *800/365–2267.*

Mahogany Flat. If you have a four-wheel-drive vehicle and want to scale Telescope Peak, the park's highest mountain, you might want to sleep at one of the few shaded spots in Death Valley, at a cool 8,133 feet. ✉ *Off Wildrose Rd., south of Charcoal Kilns* ☎ *No phone.*

Panamint Springs Resort. Part of a complex that includes a motel and cabin, this campground is surrounded by cottonwoods. The daily fee includes use of the showers and restrooms. ✉ *Hwy. 190, 28 miles west of Stovepipe Wells* ☎ *775/482–7680.*

Sunset Campground. This first-come, first-served campground is a gravel-and-asphalt RV city. ✉ *Sunset Campground Rd., 1 mile north of Furnace Creek* ☎ *800/365–2267.*

Texas Spring. This campsite south of the Furnace Creek Visitor Center has good views and facilities and is a few dollars cheaper than Furnace Creek. ✉ *Off Badwater Rd., south of Furnace Creek Visitor Center* ☎ *800/365–2267.*

$$$ AMERICAN Fodor's Choice ★

🍴 **Furnace Creek Inn Dining Room.** Fireplaces, beamed ceilings, and spectacular views provide a visual feast to match the inn's ambitious menu. Dishes may include such desert-theme items as crispy cactus fritters, and simpler fare such as salmon and free-range chicken and filet mignon all pair well with the signature prickly-pear margarita. There's a seasonal menu of vegetarian dishes, too. There's a minimal evening dress code (no T-shirts or shorts). Lunch is served, too, and you can always have afternoon tea in the lobby, an inn tradition since 1927. Breakfast and Sunday brunch are also served. Reservations are essential for dinner only. [$] *Average main: $28* ✉ *Furnace Creek Inn Resort, Hwy. 190, Furnace Creek* ☎ *760/786–3385* 🌐 *www.furnacecreekresort.com* ✍ *Reservations essential* ⏲ *Closed Jun.–Sept.*

$$ AMERICAN 🍴 **Panamint Springs Resort Restaurant.** This is a great place for steak and a beer —choose from more than 150 different beers and ales—or pasta and a salad. In summer, evening meals are served outdoors on the porch, which has spectacular views of Panamint Valley. Breakfast and lunch are also served. Reservations are suggested for dinner. [$] *Average main: $20* ✉ *Hwy. 190, 31 miles west of Stovepipe Wells* ☎ *775/482–7680* 🌐 *www.panamintsprings.com/services/dining-bar.*

$$ AMERICAN 🍴 **Toll Road Restaurant.** There are wagon wheels in the yard and Old West artifacts on the interior walls at this restaurant in the Stovepipe Wells Village hotel. A stone fireplace heats the dining room. A full menu, with steaks, chicken, fish, and pasta, is served October through mid-May; breakfast and dinner buffets are laid out during summer. Quench your thirst in the full-service saloon. [$] *Average main: $18* ✉ *Hwy. 190, Stovepipe Wells* ☎ *760/786–2387* 🌐 *www.escapetodeathvalley.com/our-restaurants* ⏲ *No lunch mid-May–Oct.*

$$$$ STEAKHOUSE FAMILY 🍴 **Wrangler Buffet and Steakhouse.** This casual, family-style restaurant has a buffet for breakfast and lunch, and steakhouse favorites (chicken, fish, barbecue platter) for dinner. It's slightly more formal than the other restaurant at the Ranch at Furnace Creek, the Forty-Niner Cafe. Still, there's no dress code and reservations aren't required. [$] *Average main: $31* ✉ *Furnace Creek Ranch, Hwy. 190, Furnace Creek* ☎ *760/786–2345* 🌐 *www.furnacecreekresort.com.*

OUTSIDE THE PARK

$$ AMERICAN 🍴 **Crowbar Caf and Saloon.** In an old wooden building where antique photos adorn the walls and mining equipment stands in the corners, the Crowbar serves enormous helpings of regional dishes such as steak and taco salads. Home-baked fruit pies make fine desserts, and frosty beers are surefire thirst quenchers. [$] *Average main: $15* ✉ *Rte. 127, Shoshone* ☎ *760/852–4123* 🌐 *www.shoshonevillage.com/shoshone-crowbar-cafe-saloon.html.*

$ AMERICAN FAMILY 🍴 **Randsburg General Store.** Built as Randsburg's Drug Store in 1896, this popular biker and family spot is one of the area's few surviving ghost-town buildings with original furnishings intact, such as tin ceiling, light fixtures, and a 1904 marble-and-stained-glass soda fountain. You can still enjoy a phosphate soda from that same fountain, or lunch on slow-roasted BBQ sandwiches and blueberry milkshakes along with chili, hamburgers, and breakfast. [$] *Average main: $10* ✉ *35 Butte Ave., Randsburg* ☎ *760/374–2143* ⏲ *Closed Wed.*

$ AMERICAN 🍴 **Mt. Whitney Restaurant.** A boisterous family-friendly restaurant with four flat-screen televisions, this place serves the best burgers in town—but in addition to the usual beef variety, you can choose from ostrich, elk, venison, and buffalo burgers. [$] *Average main: $10* ✉ *227 S. Main St., Lone Pine* ☎ *760/876–5751.*

WHERE TO STAY

IN THE PARK

During the busy season (November–March) you should make reservations for lodgings within the park several months in advance.

$$$$
HOTEL
Fodor'sChoice
★

Furnace Creek Inn. This is Death Valley's most luxurious accommodation, going so far as to have valet parking. **Pros:** refined; comfortable; great views. **Cons:** a far cry from roughing it; expensive. $ *Rooms from: $375 ⊠ Furnace Creek Village, near intersection of Hwy. 190 and Badwater Rd. ☎ 760/786–2345 ⊕ www.furnacecreekresort.com ⊗ 66 rooms ⊗ Closed mid-May–mid-Oct.* ⦿ *Breakfast.*

$
B&B/INN

Panamint Springs Resort. Ten miles inside the west entrance of the park, this low-key resort overlooks the sand dunes and peculiar geological formations of the Panamint Valley. **Pros:** slow-paced; friendly; there's a glorious amount of peace and quiet after sundown. **Cons:** far from the park's main attractions. $ *Rooms from: $79 ⊠ Hwy. 190, 28 miles west of Stovepipe Wells ☎ 775/482–7680 ⊕ www.deathvalley.com/psr ⊗ 14 rooms, 1 cabin* ⦿ *No meals.*

$$
RESORT
FAMILY

The Ranch at Furnace Creek. Originally crew headquarters for the Pacific Coast Borax Company, the four buildings here have motel-style rooms that are good for families. **Pros:** good family atmosphere; central location. **Cons:** rooms can get hot despite air-conditioning; parking near your room can be problematic. $ *Rooms from: $175 ⊠ Hwy. 190, Furnace Creek ☎ 760/786–2345, 800/236–7916 ⊕ www. furnacecreekresort.com ⊗ 224 rooms* ⦿ *No meals.*

$$
HOTEL

Stovepipe Wells Village. If you prefer quiet nights and an unfettered view of the night sky and nearby sand dunes, this property is for you. **Pros:** intimate, relaxed; no big-time partying; authentic desert-community ambience. **Cons:** isolated; a bit dated. $ *Rooms from: $120 ⊠ Hwy. 190, Stovepipe Wells ☎ 760/786–2387 ⊕ www.escapetodeathvalley. com ⊗ 83 rooms* ⦿ *No meals.*

OUTSIDE THE PARK

$
HOTEL

Dow Villa Motel and Hotel. Built in 1923 to cater to the film industry, Dow Villa is in the center of Lone Pine. **Pros:** clean rooms; great mountain views; in-room whirlpool tubs. **Cons:** somewhat dated decor; some rooms share bathrooms. $ *Rooms from: $105 ⊠ 310 S. Main St., Lone Pine ☎ 760/876–5521, 800/824–9317 ⊕ www.dowvillamotel. com ⊗ 91 rooms* ⦿ *No meals.*

GLACIER AND WATERTON LAKES NATIONAL PARKS

WELCOME TO GLACIER AND WATERTON LAKES

TOP REASONS TO GO

★ **Witness the Divide:** The rugged mountains that weave their way through Glacier and Waterton along the Continental Divide seem to have glaciers in every hollow melting into tiny streams, raging rivers, and icy-cold mountain lakes.

★ **Just hike it:** There are hundreds of miles of trails that cater to hikers of all levels—from all-day hikes to short strolls.

★ **Go to the sun:** Crossing the Continental Divide at the 6,646-foot-high Logan Pass, Glacier's Going-to-the-Sun Road is a spectacular drive.

★ **View the wildlife:** This is one of the few places in North America where all native carnivores, including grizzlies, black bears, coyotes, and wolves, still survive.

★ **See the glaciers:** Approximately 150 glaciers were present in Glacier National Park in 1850; by 2010, there were only 25 left. Some climate models predict that some of the largest glaciers in the park will vanish by 2030.

1 West Glacier. Known to the Kootenai people as "sacred dancing lake," Lake McDonald is the largest glacial water basin lake in Glacier National Park.

2 Logan Pass. At 6,646 feet, this is the highest point on the Going-to-the-Sun Road. From mid-June to mid-October, a 1½-mile boardwalk leads to an overlook that crosses an area filled with lush meadows and wildflowers.

3 East Glacier. St. Mary Lake and Many Glacier are the major highlights of the eastern side of Glacier. Services and amenities are located at both sites.

4 Backcountry. This is some of the most incredible terrain in North America and provides the right combination of beautiful scenery and isolation. Although Waterton is a much smaller park, its backcountry trails connect with hiking trails in both Glacier and British Columbia's Akamina-Kishinena Provincial Park.

5 Waterton Lakes. The Canadian national park is the meeting of two worlds: the flatlands of the prairie and the abrupt upthrust of the mountains.

MONTANA

Polebridge

GETTING ORIENTED

In the rocky northwest corner of Montana, Glacier National Park encompasses 1.2 million acres (1,563 square miles) of untrammeled wilds. Within the park, there are 25 named glaciers (which are ever-so-slowly diminishing), 200 lakes, and 1,000 miles of streams. Neighboring Waterton Lakes National Park, across the border in Alberta, Canada, covers another 130,000 acres. In 1932, the parks were unified to form the Waterton-Glacier International Peace Park—the first international peace park in the world—in recognition of the two nations' friendship and dedication to peace.

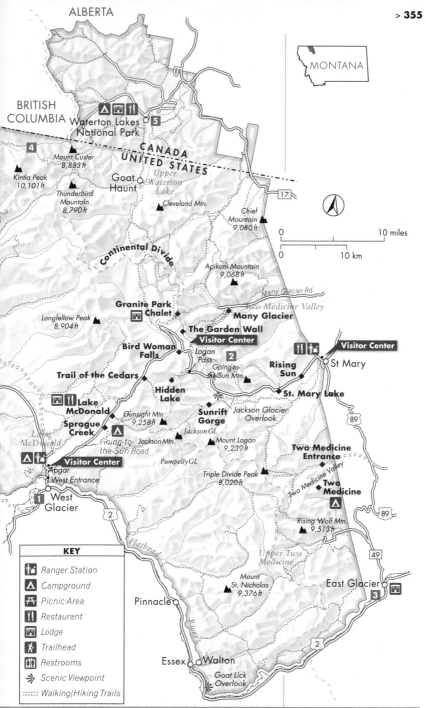

MONTANA

ALBERTA

BRITISH
COLUMBIA

Waterton Lakes
National Park

5

CANADA
UNITED STATES

4

Mount Custer
8,883 ft

Kintla Peak
10,101 ft

Thunderbird
Mountain
8,790 ft

Goat
Haunt

Upper
Waterton
Lake

Cleveland Mtn.

Chief
Mountain
9,080 ft

17

Continental Divide

Apikuni Mountain
9,068 ft

Many Glacier Rd.

Longfellow Peak
8,904 ft

Granite Park
Chalet

Many Glacier

Two Medicine Valley

The Garden Wall
Visitor Center

Bird Woman
Falls

Logan
Pass

2

Going-to-
the Sun Mtn.

Rising
Sun

Visitor Center

St Mary

Trail of the Cedars

Hidden
Lake

St. Mary Lake

89

Lake
McDonald

Sprague
Creek

Gunsight Mtn.
9,258 ft

Going-to-
the-Sun Road

Jackson Mtn.

Sunrift
Gorge

Jackson Gl.

Jackson Glacier
Overlook

Mount Logan
9,239 ft

Lake
McDonald

Visitor Center

Pumpelly Gl.

Two Medicine
Entrance

Apgar
West Entrance

West
Glacier

1

2

Triple Divide Peak
8,020 ft

Two Medicine Valley

Two
Medicine

89

Rising Wolf Mtn.
9,513 ft

49

Flathead

Upper Two
Medicine

KEY

Mount
St. Nicholas
9,376 ft

East Glacier

3

Ranger Station

Campground

Picnic Area

Restaurant

Lodge

Trailhead

Restrooms

Scenic Viewpoint

Walking/Hiking Trails

Pinnacle

River

Essex

Walton

Goat Lick
Overlook

2

0   10 miles

0   10 km

17

Updated by
Debbie Olsen

The massive peaks of the Continental Divide in northwest Montana are the backbone of Glacier National Park and its sister park in Canada, Waterton Lakes, which together make up the International Peace Park. From their slopes, melting snow and alpine glaciers yield the headwaters of rivers that flow west to the Pacific Ocean, north to the Arctic Ocean, and southeast to the Atlantic Ocean via the Gulf of Mexico. Coniferous forests, thickly vegetated stream bottoms, and green-carpeted meadows provide homes and sustenance for all kinds of wildlife.

GLACIER AND WATERTON PLANNER

WHEN TO GO

Of the 2 million annual visitors to Glacier and 400,000 to Waterton, most come between July 1 and September 15, when the streams are flowing, wildlife is roaming, and naturalist programs are fully underway. Snow removal on the alpine portion of Going-to-the-Sun Road is usually completed by mid-June; the opening of Logan Pass at the road's summit marks the summer opening of Glacier. Canada's Victoria Day in late May marks the beginning of the season in Waterton. Spring and fall are quieter. By October, snow forces the closing of most park roads.

AVG. HIGH/LOW TEMPS.

Glacier

JAN.	FEB.	MAR.	APR.	MAY	JUNE
28/15	35/19	42/23	53/30	64/37	71/44

JULY	AUG.	SEPT.	OCT.	NOV.	DEC.
79/47	78/46	67/39	53/32	37/25	30/18

Waterton Lakes

JAN.	FEB.	MAR.	APR.	MAY	JUNE
32/12	34/14	42/22	50/29	59/37	66/43

JULY	AUG.	SEPT.	OCT.	NOV.	DEC.
73/46	72/44	63/38	53/33	38/22	33/15

FESTIVALS AND EVENTS

WINTER **Ski Fest.** This annual celebration of cross-country skiing is a great way to introduce newcomers to kick-and-glide skiing. Equipment demonstrations, free ski lessons, free trail passes, and family activities are scheduled at the Izaak Walton Inn in Essex, Montana. ☎ *406/888–5700* ⊕ *www.izaakwaltoninn.com.*

Whitefish Winter Carnival. For more than 40 years this winter carnival has been the scene of lively festivities, including a grand parade with more than 100 entries, a torchlight parade on skis, a penguin dip, and other family-friendly activities. ☎ *406/862–3501* ⊕ *www. whitefishwintercarnival.com.*

SUMMER **Canada Day.** On July 1, all guests get into the national parks free of charge in honor of Canada's birthday. Waterton also has special activities for families such as treasure hunts and street-theater performances. ☎ *403/859–5133.*

Montana Dragon Boat Festival. Held on Flathead Lake, this lively festival features 95 teams of 20 paddlers each racing 46-foot-long Hong Kong–style boats. The festival also has great children's activities, live music, and goods made in Montana. ☎ *888/888–2308, 406/758–2820* ⊕ *montana.racedragonboats.com.*

Summer Concert Series. Running each Thursday from mid-June to early August, the series is held in the Don Lawrence Amphitheater at Marantette Park in Columbia Falls. Types of music vary, but the Don Lawrence Big Band performs every year. ☎ *406/892–2072.*

Waterton Wildflower Festival. Wildflower walks, horseback rides, hikes, watercolor workshops, photography classes, and family events help visitors and locals celebrate the annual blooming of Waterton's bountiful wildflowers. ☎ *403/859–2663, 800/215–2395* ⊕ *www. watertonwildflowers.com.*

FALL **NW Montana Antique Threshing Bee.** Steam threshing machines, steam plows, antique tractors, and engines flex muscles in the Parade of Power, organized by the Northwest Montana Antique Power Association in Columbia Falls. Participants challenge friends and neighbors to tractor barrel races and shingle-making events, while children of all ages enjoy miniature steam-train rides, music, food, and entertainment. ☎ *406/756–5577, 406/862–2675, 866/592–9608.*

Waterton Wildlife Weekend. Wildlife viewing is at its best in Waterton during the fall. This weekend features wildlife events including viewing on foot, on horseback, and by boat. There are also photography, drawing, and sketching courses. ☎ *800/215–2395, 403/859–2663* ⊕ *www. watertonwildlife.com.*

17

PLANNING YOUR TIME
GLACIER IN ONE DAY
It's hard to beat the **Going-to-the-Sun Road** for a one-day trip in Glacier National Park. This itinerary takes you from west to east—if you're starting from St. Mary, take the tour backward. First, however, call the Glacier Park Boat Company (☎ *406/257–2426*) to make a reservation for the **St. Mary Lake** or **Lake McDonald boat tour,** depending on where you end up. Then drive up Going-to-the-Sun Road to **Avalanche Creek Campground,** and take a 30-minute stroll along the fragrant **Trail of the Cedars.** Afterward, continue driving up—you can see views of waterfalls and wildlife to the left and an awe-inspiring, precipitous drop to the right. At the summit, **Logan Pass,** your arduous climb is rewarded with a gorgeous view of immense peaks, sometimes complemented by a herd of mountain goats. Stop in at the **Logan Pass Visitor Center,** then take the 1.5-mile **Hidden Lake Nature Trail** up to prime wildlife-viewing spots. Picnic at the overlook above Hidden Lake. In the afternoon, continue driving east over the mountains. Stop at the **Jackson Glacier Overlook** to view one of the park's largest glaciers. Continue down; eventually the forest thins, the vistas grow broader, and a gradual transition to the high plains begins. When you reach **Rising Sun Campground,** take the one-hour St. Mary Lake boat tour to St. Mary Falls. If you'd rather hike, the 1.2-mile **Sun Point Nature Trail** also leads to the falls. (Take the boat tour if you're driving from east to west.) The Going-to-the-Sun Road is generally closed from mid-September to mid-June.

WATERTON IN ONE DAY
Begin your day with a stop at the **Waterton Information Centre** to pick up free maps and information about interpretive programs and schedules.

Behind the reception center is the **Bear's Hump Trailhead,** where you can enjoy a relatively easy 1.4-km (0.9-mile) hike to a beautiful scenic overlook. After the hike, drive up the hill to the historic **Prince of Wales Hotel** to enjoy the view.

Next, visit **Waterton Townsite** for an early lunch. Afterward, walk the easy 3-km (2-mile) **Townsite Loop Trail,** stopping to view **Cameron Falls** and explore the trail behind the falls.

End the day with a scenic, two-hour **Waterton Inter-Nation Shoreline Cruise** across the border to **Goat Haunt Ranger Station** and back.

GETTING HERE AND AROUND
AIR TRAVEL
The nearest airports to Glacier are in Great Falls and Kalispell, Montana. The nearest airport to Waterton Lakes is in Calgary.

BUS TRAVEL
Glacier National Park operates a free shuttle along the Going-to-the-Sun Road from July 1 through early September. The shuttle runs from Apgar to St. Mary Visitor Center, and park info centers have information on departure times. Parks Canada also operates a free shuttle along the Red Rock Canyon Parkway in Waterton during the summer months.

CAR TRAVEL

On the east, U.S. 89 accesses Many Glacier and St. Mary, while Route 49 reaches Two Medicine. On the west, U.S. 2 goes to West Glacier. At the northwestern edge of Glacier, North Fork Road connects to Polebridge. Take the Chief Mountain Highway to access Waterton Lakes during the summer or Highway 89 to Alberta Highway 2 through Cardston and then west to the park via Highway 5 any time of the year.

The roads in both parks are either paved or gravel and become deteriorated from freezing and thawing. Drive slowly and anticipate that rocks and wildlife may be around the corner. Road reconstruction is part of the park experience as there are only a few warm months in which road crews can complete projects. Gasoline is available along most paved roads. Scenic pull-outs are frequent; watch for other vehicles pulling in or out, and watch for children in parking areas. Most development and services center on St. Mary Lake in the east and Lake McDonald in the west.

BORDER
CROSSINGS
A passport is required of everyone crossing the Canadian/U.S. border. When you arrive at the border crossing, customs officers will ask you a series of questions about where you are going, where you are from, and the like. You and your vehicle are subject to random search. Firearms are prohibited, except hunting rifles, which require special advance permission. Soil, seeds, meat, and many fruits are also prohibited. Kids traveling with only one parent need a notarized letter from the other parent giving permission to enter Canada or the United States. If you are traveling with pets, you need proof of up-to-date immunizations to cross the border in either direction. Citizens from most countries (Canada, Mexico, and Bermuda are exceptions) entering the United States from Canada must pay $6 (cash only) at the border for a required I–94 or I–94W Arrival-Departure Record form, to be returned to border officials when leaving the U.S. Contact United States Customs (☎ *406/335–2611* ⊕ *www.cbp. gov*) or the Canada Border Services Agency (☎ *403/344–3767* ⊕ *www. cbsa-asfc.gc.ca*) for more information.

PARK ESSENTIALS

PARK FEES AND PERMITS

Entrance fees for Glacier are $25 per vehicle or $12 for one person on foot or bike in summer (May–October). In winter (November–April), entrance fees drop to $15 per vehicle or $10 per person. Entrance fees are good for seven days or you can purchase an annual pass for $35. A day pass to Waterton Lakes costs C$7.80 for an individual or C$14.70 for a family, and an annual pass costs C$39 for an individual or C$98.10 for a family. *Passes to Glacier and Waterton must be paid separately.*

At Glacier the required backcountry permit is $5 per person per day or $60 per year from the Apgar Backcountry Permit Center after mid-April for the upcoming summer. Advance reservations cost $30. You can find the latest backcountry information and a form that can be faxed to the backcountry office on the park's official website, ⊕ *www.nps.gov/glac/ planyourvisit/backcountry.htm.*

Waterton requires backcountry camping permits for use of its 13 backcountry camp spots, with reservations available up to 90 days in advance. Buy the permit for C$9.80 per adult per night—reserve for an additional C$11.70—at the visitor reception center (☎ *403/859–5133*).

17

PARK HOURS

The parks are open year-round, but most roads and facilities close October through May. The parks are in the Mountain time zone.

CELL-PHONE RECEPTION

Cell-phone coverage is improving, but in mountainous terrain it is common to have poor reception. Depending on your cell phone carrier, cell service is best available in West Glacier and St. Mary in Glacier National Park and in the Waterton Townsite in Waterton Lakes National Park. Find pay phones at Avalanche Campground, Glacier Highland Motel and Store, Apgar, St. Mary Visitor Center, Two Medicine Campstore, and all lodges except Granite Park Chalet and Sperry Chalet. Several pay phones are also available in the townsite of Waterton Lakes National Park.

RESTAURANTS

Steakhouses featuring certified Angus beef are typical of the region; in recent years, resort communities have diversified their menus to include bison meat, fresh fish, and savory vegetarian options. Small cafés offer hearty, inexpensive meals, and you can pick up on local history through conversation with the local denizens. Trout, venison, elk, moose, and bison appear on the menus inside the park. Attire everywhere is decidedly casual.

Prices in the reviews are the average cost of a main course at dinner, or if dinner is not served, at lunch.

HOTELS

Lodgings in the parks tend to be fairly rustic and simple, though there are a few grand lodges and some modern accommodations. Some modern hotels offer facilities such as swimming pools, hot tubs, boat rentals, guided excursions, or fine dining. Although there is a limited supply of rooms within both parks, the prices are relatively reasonable. It's best to reserve well in advance, especially for July and August.

Hotel prices are per night for two people in a standard double Prices in the reviews are the lowest cost of a standard double room in high season. For expanded reviews, facilities, and current deals, visit Fodors.com.

TOURS

Red Jammer Bus Tours. These scheduled, driver-narrated bus tours cover most of the park accessible by road. The tour of Going-to-the-Sun Road is a favorite, as it is conducted in "jammers," vintage 1936 red buses with roll-back tops, and provides plenty of photo opportunities at roadside pull-outs. Short trips and full-day trips are available, and you can arrange packages that include activities as well as accommodations. Reservations are essential. ☎ *406/892–2525, 403/236–3400* ⊕ *www.glaciernationalparklodges.com* ✉ *$40–$80* ☾ *June–Sept.*

Sun Tours. Tour the park and learn the Blackfeet perspective with these native guides who concentrate on how Glacier's features are relevant to the Blackfeet Nation, past and present. June–September, tours depart daily from East Glacier at 29 Glacier Avenue at 8 am and the St. Mary Visitor Center at 9:15 am in air-conditioned coaches. ⊠ *29 Glacier Ave., East Glacier* ☎ *406/226–9220, 800/786–9220* ⊕ *www.glaciersuntours.com* ✉ *$35–$75.*

VISITOR INFORMATION
PARK CONTACT INFORMATION
Glacier National Park ☎ *406/888–7800* ⊕ *www.nps.gov/glac.*

Waterton Lakes National Park ☎ *403/859–5133, 403/859–2224 year-round* ⊕ *www.pc.gc.ca/waterton.*

GLACIER VISITOR CENTERS
FAMILY **Apgar Visitor Center.** This is a great first stop if you're entering the park from the west. Here you can get all kinds of information, including maps, permits, books, and the *Junior Ranger* newspaper. You can plan your route on a large relief map to get a glimpse of where you're going. In winter, the rangers offer free snowshoe walks. Snowshoes can be rented for $2 at the visitor center. ⊠ *2 miles north of West Glacier in Apgar Village* ☎ *406/888–7800* ☉ *Mid-May–mid-June, daily 9–4:30; mid-June–Aug., daily 8–5:30; Sept.–mid-Oct., daily 8:30–5; mid-Oct.–mid-May, weekends 9–4:30.*

Logan Pass Visitor Center. Built of stone, this center stands sturdy against the severe weather that forces it to close in winter. Books, maps, and more are stocked inside. Rangers staff the center and give 10-minute talks on the alpine environment. ⊠ *34 miles east of West Glacier, 18 miles west of St. Mary* ☎ *406/888–7800* ☉ *Mid-June–Aug., daily 9–7; Sept., daily 9:30–4.*

St. Mary Visitor Center. The park's largest visitor complex has a huge relief map of the park's peaks and valleys and provides a 15-minute orientation video. Exhibits are designed to help visitors understand the park from the perspective of its original inhabitants—the Blackfeet, Salish, Kootenai, and Pend d'Orielle tribes. Rangers host evening presentations during the peak summer months. The center has books and maps for sale, backcountry camping permits, and large viewing windows facing the 10-mile-long St. Mary Lake. ⊠ *Going-to-the-Sun Rd., off U.S. 89* ☎ *406/732–7750* ☉ *Mid-May–mid-Sept., daily 8–5, with extended hours during summer.*

WATERTON VISITOR CENTERS
Waterton Information Centre. Stop here on the eastern edge of Waterton Townsite to pick up brochures, maps, and books. The park runs a free Waterton Xplorers program for kids ages 6–11, and you can pick up program booklets at this site. Park interpreters are on hand to answer questions and give directions. ⊠ *Waterton Rd., before you reach townsite* ☎ *403/859–5133, 403/859–2224* ☉ *Mid-May–mid-June, daily 8–6; mid-June–early Sept., daily 8–8; early Sept.–early Oct., daily 9–6.*

17

GLACIER NATIONAL PARK

EXPLORING

SCENIC DRIVES

Fodor'sChoice
★
Going-to-the-Sun Road. This magnificent, 50-mile highway—the only American roadway designated both a National Historic Landmark and a National Civil Engineering Landmark—crosses the crest of the Continental Divide at Logan Pass and traverses the towering Garden Wall. Open from mid-June to mid-September only (due to heavy snow-falls), this is one of the most stunning drives in Glacier National Park. A multiyear Sun Road rehabilitation project will result in some driving delays due to reconstruction. ■TIP➔ **The drive is susceptible to frequent delays in summer. To avoid traffic jams and parking problems, take the road early in the morning or late in the evening (when the lighting is ideal for photography and wildlife is most likely to appear).** Vehicle size is restricted to under 21 feet long, 10 feet high, and 8 feet wide, including mirrors, between Avalanche Creek Campground and Sun Point. Cyclists enjoy traveling the open part of the road in early June before it is open to vehicular traffic.

Many Glacier Road. This 12-mile drive enters Glacier on the northeast side of the park, west of Babb, and travels along Sherburne Lake for almost 5 miles, penetrating a glacially carved valley surrounded by mountains. It passes through meadows and a scrubby forest of lodge-pole pines, aspen, and cottonwood. The farther you travel up the valley, the more clearly you'll be able to see Grinnell and Salamander glaciers. The road passes Many Glacier Hotel and ends at the Swiftcurrent Campground. It's usually closed from October to May.

HISTORIC SITES

FAMILY
Apgar. On the southwest end of Lake McDonald, this tiny hamlet has a few stores, an ice-cream shop, motels, ranger buildings, a campground, and a historic schoolhouse. A store called the Montana House is open year-round in the village, but no other services remain open from November to mid-May, except the weekend-only visitor center. Across the street from the Apgar visitor center, **Apgar Discovery Cabin** is filled with animal posters, kids' activities, and maps. ⊠ *2 miles north of west entrance* ☎ *406/888–7939* ⊙ *Cabin: mid-June–Labor Day, daily 1:30–3.*

SCENIC STOPS

ALONG THE GOING-TO-THE-SUN ROAD

The Going-to-the-Sun Road, arguably the most beautiful drive in the country, connects Lake McDonald on the west side of Glacier with St. Mary Lake on the east. Turnoffs provide views of the high country and glacier-carved valleys. The sights here are listed in order from west to east. If you don't want to drive the Going-to-the-Sun Road, consider making the ride in a "jammer," an antique red bus operated by Xanterra (⊕ *www.glacierparklodges.com*). The drivers double as guides, and they can roll back the tops of the vehicles to give you improved views.

Plants and Wildlife in Glacier and Waterton

In summer, a profusion of new flowers, grasses, and budding trees covers the landscape high and low. Spring attracts countless birds, from golden eagles riding thermals north to Canada and Alaska to rare harlequin ducks dipping in creeks. Snow-white mountain goats, with their wispy white beards and curious stares, are seen in alpine areas, and sure-footed bighorn sheep graze the high meadows in the short summers. The largest population of grizzly bears in the lower 48 states lives in the wild in and around the park. Feeding the animals is illegal.

Visiting Glacier in winter makes for easy tracking of many large animals like moose, elk, deer, mountain lions, wolf, lynx, and their smaller neighbors—the snowshoe hare, pine marten, beaver, and muskrat.

In park lakes, sportfishing species include burbot (ling), northern pike, whitefish, grayling, cutthroat, rainbow, lake (Mackinaw), kokanee salmon, and brook trout.

The Garden Wall. An abrupt and jagged wall of rock juts above the road and is visible for about 10 miles as it follows Logan Creek from just past Avalanche Creek Campground to Logan Pass. ⊠ *24–34 miles northeast of West Glacier.*

Hidden Lake Overlook. Take a walk from Logan Pass up to see the crystalline Hidden Lake, which often still has ice clinging to it in early July. It's a 1.5-mile hike on an uphill grade, partially on a boardwalk that protects the abundant wildflowers. ⊠ *Trailhead behind Logan Pass Visitor's Center.*

Jackson Glacier Overlook. On the east side of the Continental Divide, you come into view of Jackson Glacier looming in a rocky pass across the upper St. Mary River valley. If it isn't covered with snow, you'll see sharp peaks of ice. The glacier is shrinking and may disappear in another 100 years. ⊠ *5 miles east of Logan Pass.*

Logan Pass. At 6,646 feet, this is the highest point in the park accessible by motor vehicle. It presents unparalleled views of both sides of the Continental Divide and is frequented by mountain goats, bighorn sheep, and grizzly bears. It is extremely crowded in July and August. The Logan Pass Visitor Center is located just east of the pass. ⊠ *34 miles east of West Glacier, 18 miles west of St. Mary.*

St. Mary Lake. When the breezes calm, the second largest lake in Glacier National Park mirrors the snowcapped granite peaks that line the St. Mary Valley. To get a good look at the beautiful scenery, follow the Sun Point Nature Trail along the lake's shore. The hike is 1 mile each way. ⊠ *1 mile west of St. Mary.*

OTHER SCENIC STOPS

Goat Lick Overlook. Mountain goats frequent this natural salt lick on a cliff above the Middle Fork of the Flathead River. You can watch the wildlife from an observation stand. ⊠ *2½ miles east of Walton Ranger Station on U.S. 2.*

17

Grinnell and Salamander Glaciers. These glaciers formed as one ice mass, but in 1926 they broke apart and have been shrinking ever since. The best viewpoint is reached by the 5.5-mile Grinnell Glacier Trail from Many Glacier. The trailhead is at the far northwestern end of Lake Josephine. You can get there by boat, or by foot via the trail behind the Many Glacier Hotel.

To learn more about the geology of the area, take a daily ranger-led hike to Grinnell Valley that departs each morning from the Many Glacier Picnic Area and takes about six hours. Ranger-led programs run from the third week in June through Labor Day.

Lake McDonald. This beautiful 10-mile-long lake is the largest lake in the park and is accessible year-round on Going-to-the-Sun Road. Take a boat ride to the middle for a view of the surrounding glacier-clad mountains. You can go fishing and horseback riding at either end, and in winter, snowshoe and cross-country ski. ⊠ *2 miles north of west entrance.*

Running Eagle Falls (Trick Falls). Cascading near Two Medicine, these are actually two different waterfalls from two different sources. In spring, when the water level is high, the upper falls join the lower falls for a 40-foot drop into Two Medicine River; in summer, the upper falls dry up, revealing the lower 20-foot falls that start midway down the precipice. ⊠ *2 miles east of Two Medicine entrance.*

Two Medicine Valley. Rugged, often windy, and always beautiful, the valley is a remote 9-mile drive from Route 49 and is surrounded by some of the park's most stark, rocky peaks. On and around the valley's lake you can rent a canoe, take a narrated boat tour, camp, and hike. Be aware that bears frequent the area. The road is closed from late October through late May. ⊠ *Two Medicine entrance, 9 miles east of Rte. 49* ☎ *406/888–7800, 406/257–2426 for boat tours.*

EDUCATIONAL OFFERINGS
CLASSES AND SEMINARS

FAMILY **Glacier Institute.** Based near West Glacier at the Field Camp and on the remote western boundary at the Big Creek Outdoor Education Center, this learning institute offers more than 75 field courses for kids and adults. Year-round, experts in wildlife biology, native plants, and river ecology lead treks into Glacier's backcountry on daylong and multiday programs. ⊠ *137 Main St., Kalispell* ☎ *406/755–1211* ⊕ *www.glacierinstitute.org.*

KIDS' CAMPS

FAMILY **Adventure Camps.** Youngsters ages 6 to 8 can partake of one-day naturalist courses, while kids 11 to 13 can take weeklong hiking and rafting trips. Some camps involve backcountry camping while others are based out of the Big Creek or Glacier Park field camps. Subjects range from ecology and birding to wildflowers, predators and prey, and backcountry medicine. Three-day family camps for ages 7 and up are also on offer. ⊠ *137 Main St., Kalispell* ☎ *406/755–1211* ⊕ *www. glacierinstitute.org* 🖃 *$50–$325* ☉ *June–Aug.*

The scenic, 50-mile Going-to-the-Sun Road takes about two hours to drive, depending on how often you stop.

RANGER PROGRAMS

These programs are free to visitors. Most run daily, July through Labor Day and include experiences such as guided hikes, historical tours, and naturalist discussions. Native America Speaks is a unique program that allows tribal members to share their knowledge of the history and culture of Native America through storytelling, poetry, music, and dancing. For information on ranger programs, call ☎ 406/888–7800.

FAMILY **Children's Programs.** Ranger-led activities take place in many locations throughout the park. Kids learn about bears, wolves, geology, and more via hands-on activities, such as role-playing skits and short hikes. Check the Apgar Education Cabin located near the Apgar Visitor Center for schedules and locations.

FAMILY **Evening Campfire Programs.** Rangers lead evening discussions on the park's wildlife, geology, and history. The programs occur at park campgrounds, beginning at 8 or 9. Topics and dates are posted at campgrounds, lodges, and the St. Mary Visitor Center.

FAMILY **Junior Ranger Program.** Year-round, children ages 6–12 can become Junior Rangers by completing activities in the *Junior Ranger* newspaper available at the park visitor centers.

FAMILY **Naturalist Activities.** Evening slide programs, guided hikes, and boat tours are among the ranger-led activities held at various sites in the park. A complete schedule of programs is listed in *Glacier Explorer,* a national park service publication distributed at the visitor centers. A list of ranger-led activities is also posted at the Apgar Visitor Center and at many of the campgrounds and lodges in the park.

DID YOU KNOW?

Grizzly bears can run up to 40 mph and live 30 years in the wild. These 350- to 800-pound omnivores can stretch to 8 feet tall. Here a young grizzly stands on two feet just off the Grinnell Glacier Trail.

SPORTS AND THE OUTDOORS

MULTISPORT OUTFITTERS

Glacier Guides and Montana Raft Company. Take a raft trip through the stomach-churning white water of the Middle Fork of the Flathead and combine it with a hike, horseback ride, or a barbecue. Guided hikes, fly-fishing trips, and multiday adventures can also be arranged. ✉ *11970 U.S. 2 E, 1 mile west of West Glacier* ☎ *406/387–5555, 800/521–7238* ⊕ *www.glacierguides.com* ☾ *May–Oct.*

Glacier Raft Company and Outdoor Center. In addition to running fishing trips, family float rides, saddle and paddle adventures, and high-adrenaline white-water adventure rafting (including multiday excursions), this outfitter will set you up with camping, backpacking, and fishing gear. There's a full-service fly-fishing shop and outdoor store. You can stay in one of 12 log cabins that sleep 6 to 14 people. ✉ *11957 U.S. 2 E, West Glacier* ☎ *406/888–5454, 800/235–6781* ⊕ *www.glacierraftco. com* ☾ *Year-round; rafting mid-May–Sept.*

Great Northern Whitewater. Sign up for daily white-water, kayaking, and fishing trips. Multiday trips can also be arranged. This outfitter also rents Swiss-style chalets with views of Glacier's peaks. ✉ *12127 U.S. 2 E, 1 mile south of West Glacier* ☎ *406/387–5340, 800/735–7897* ⊕ *www.greatnorthernresort.com* ☾ *May–Oct.*

Wild River Adventures. Brave the whitewater in an inflatable kayak or a traditional raft or enjoy a scenic float with these guys, who will paddle you over the Middle Fork of the Flathead, and peddle you tall tales all the while. They also provide trail rides and scenic fishing trips on rivers around Glacier Park. ✉ *11900 U.S. 2 E, 1 mile west of West Glacier* ☎ *406/387–9453, 800/700–7056* ⊕ *www.riverwild.com* ☾ *Mid-May–Sept.*

BICYCLING

Cyclists in Glacier must stay on roads or bike routes and are not permitted on hiking trails or in the backcountry. The one-lane, unpaved Inside North Fork Road from Apgar to Polebridge is well suited to mountain bikers. Two Medicine Road is an intermediate paved route, with a mild grade at the beginning, becoming steeper as you approach Two Medicine Campground. Much of the western half of Going-to-the-Sun Road is closed to bikes from 11 to 4. Other restrictions apply during peak traffic periods and road construction. Many cyclists enjoy the Going-to-the-Sun Road prior to its opening to vehicular traffic in mid-June. You cannot cycle all the way over the pass in early June, but you can cycle as far as the road is plowed and ride back down without encountering much traffic besides a few snowplows and construction vehicles. You can find thrilling off-road trails just outside the park near Whitefish. There are no bike rental shops inside the park, but there are two in the nearby town of Whitefish.

OUTFITTERS

Glacier Cyclery. Daily and weekly bike rentals of touring, road, and mountain bikes for all ages and skill levels are available here. The shop also sells bikes, equipment, and attire and does repairs. Information on local trails is available on its website and in the store. ✉ *326 E. 2nd St., Whitefish* ☎ *406/862–6446* ⊕ *www.glaciercyclery.com.*

17

Great Northern Cycles. You can rent road bikes and mountain bikes from this Whitefish outfitter. They also service and repair bikes and sell cycling attire and gear. Information about area trails and rides can be found on its website. Rentals cost $39 per day for road bikes or $49 per day for mountain bikes. Save $10 per day by renting for three or more days. ⊠ *328 Central Ave., Whitefish* ☎ *406/862–5231* ⊕ *www. greatnortherncycles.com.*

BOATING AND RAFTING

Glacier has many stunning lakes and rivers, and boating is a popular park activity. Many rafting companies provide adventures along the border of the park on the Middle and North Forks of the Flathead River. The Middle Fork has some excellent white water, while the North Fork has both slow-moving and fast-moving sections. If you bring your own raft or kayak—watercraft such as Sea-Doos or Jet Skis are not allowed in the park—stop at the Hungry Horse Ranger Station in the Flathead National Forest near West Glacier to obtain a permit. Consider starting at Ousel Creek and floating to West Glacier on the Middle Fork of the Flathead River.

TOURS AND OUTFITTERS

Glacier Park Boat Company. This company gives tours on five lakes. A **Lake McDonald cruise** takes you from the dock at Lake McDonald Lodge to the middle of the lake for an unparalleled view of the Continental Divide's Garden Wall. **Many Glacier tours** on Swiftcurrent Lake and Lake Josephine depart from Many Glacier Hotel and provide views of the Continental Divide. **Two Medicine Lake cruises** leave from the dock near the ranger station and lead to several trails. **St. Mary Lake cruises** leave from the launch near Rising Sun Campground and head to Red Eagle Mountain and other spots. The tours last 45–90 minutes. You can rent kayaks ($15 per hour), canoes ($18 per hour), rowboats ($18 per hour), and small motorboats ($25 per hour) at Apgar, Two Medicine, and Many Glacier. ☎ *406/257–2426* ⊕ *www.glacierparkboats. com* ⊠ *Tours $12–$24, rentals $18–$25 per hr* ☉ *May–Sept.*

FISHING

Within Glacier there's an almost unlimited range of fishing possibilities, with a catch-and-release policy encouraged. You can fish in most waters of the park, but the best fishing is generally in the least accessible spots. A fishing license is not required inside the park boundary, but you must stop by a park office to pick up a copy of the regulations. The fishing season runs from the third Saturday in May to November 30. There are several companies that offer guided fishing trips in the area. ■TIP➔ **Fishing on both the North Fork and the Middle Fork of the Flathead River requires a Montana conservation license ($10) plus a Montana fishing license ($15 for two consecutive days or $60 for a season). They are available at most convenience stores, sports shops, and from the Montana Department of Fish, Wildlife, and Parks** (☎ *406/752–5501* ⊕ *www.fwp.mt.gov*).

HIKING

With 730 miles of marked trails, Glacier is a hiker's paradise. Trail maps are available at all visitor centers and entrance stations. Before hiking, ask about trail closures due to bear or mountain lion activity. Never hike alone. For backcountry hiking, pick up a permit from park headquarters or the Apgar Backcountry Permit Center (☎ 406/888–7939) near Glacier's west entrance.

TOURS

Glacier Guides. The exclusive backpacking guide service in Glacier National Park can arrange guided day hikes or multiday hikes. Guided hiking tours are customized to match the skill level of the hikers with plenty of stops to identify plants, animals, and habitats. ☎ 406/891–2173, 800/735–9514 ⊕ *www.glacierguides.com.*

EASY

Avalanche Lake Trail. From Avalanche Creek Campground, take this 3-mile trail leading to mountain-ringed Avalanche Lake. The walk is relatively easy (it ascends 500 feet), making this one of the most accessible backcountry lakes in the park. Crowds fill the parking area and trail during July and August and on sunny weekends in May and June. *Easy.* ✉ *Trailhead across from Avalanche Creek Campground, 15 miles north of Apgar on Going-to-the-Sun Rd.*

FAMILY **Baring Falls.** For a nice family hike, try the 1.3-mile path from the Sun Point parking area. It leads to a spruce and Douglas fir wood; cross a log bridge over Baring Creek and you arrive at the base of gushing Baring Falls. *Easy.* ✉ *Trailhead 11 miles east of Logan Pass on Going-to-the-Sun Rd. at the Sun Point parking area.*

Hidden Lake Nature Trail. This uphill, 1.5-mile trail runs from Logan Pass southwest to Hidden Lake Overlook, from which you get a beautiful view of the lake and McDonald Valley. In spring, ribbons of water pour off the rocks surrounding the lake. *Easy.* ✉ *Trailhead directly behind Logan Pass Visitor Center.*

Sun Point Nature Trail. This short, well-groomed, 1.3-mile trail allows you to walk along the cliffs and shores of picturesque St. Mary Lake. There is a stunning waterfall at the end of the hike. You may choose to hike one-way and take a boat transfer back. *Easy.* ✉ *Trailhead 11 miles east of Logan Pass on Going-to-the-Sun Rd. at Sun Point parking area.*

FAMILY **Trail of the Cedars.** This wheelchair-accessible, 0.5-mile boardwalk loop through an ancient cedar and hemlock forest is a favorite of families with small children and people with disabilities. Interpretive signs describe the habitat and natural history of the rain forest. *Easy.* ✉ *Trailhead across from Avalanche Creek Campground, 15 miles north of Apgar on Going-to-the-Sun Rd.*

17

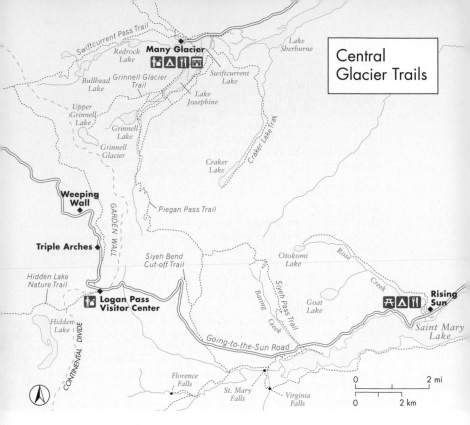

MODERATE

Fodor's Choice **Highline Trail.** From the Logan Pass parking lot, hike north along the Garden Wall and just below the craggy Continental Divide. Wildflowers dominate the 7.6 miles to Granite Park Chalet, a National Historic Landmark, where hikers with reservations can overnight. Return to Logan Pass along the same trail or hike down 4.5 miles (a 2,500-foot descent) on the Loop Trail. *Moderate.* ⊠ *Trailhead at the Logan Pass Visitor Center.*

Iceberg Lake Trail. This moderately strenuous 9-mile round-trip hike passes the gushing Ptarmigan Falls, then climbs to its namesake, where icebergs bob in the chilly mountain loch. Mountain goats hang out on sheer cliffs above, bighorn sheep graze in the high mountain meadows, and grizzly bears dig for glacier lily bulbs, grubs, and other delicacies. Rangers lead hikes here almost daily in summer, leaving at 8:30 am. *Moderate.* ⊠ *Trailhead at the Swiftcurrent Inn parking lot off Many Glacier Rd.*

DIFFICULT

Grinnell Glacier Trail. The strenuous 5.5-mile hike to Grinnell Glacier, the park's largest and most accessible glacier, is marked by several spectacular viewpoints. You start at Swiftcurrent Lake's picnic area, climb a moraine to Lake Josephine, then climb to the Grinnell Glacier overlook. Halfway up, turn around to see the prairie land to the northeast. You can shortcut the trail by 2 miles each way by taking two scenic boat rides across Swiftcurrent Lake and Lake Josephine. From July to mid-September, a ranger-led hike departs from the Many Glacier Hotel boat dock most mornings at 8:30. *Difficult.* ⊠ *Trail begins at Lake Josephine boat dock.*

Two Medicine Valley Trails. One of the least-developed areas of Glacier, the lovely southeast corner of the park is a good place for a quiet day hike,

although you should look out for signs of bears. The trailhead to Upper Two Medicine Lake and Cobalt Lake begins west of the boat dock and camp supply store where you can make arrangements for a boat pick-up or drop-off across the lake. *Difficult.* ⊠ *Trailhead is west of the boat dock and camp supply store at Two Medicine Campground, 9 miles west of Rte. 49.*

HORSEBACK RIDING

Horses are permitted on many trails within the parks; check for seasonal exceptions. Horseback riding is prohibited on paved roads. You can pick up a brochure about suggested routes and outfitters from any visitor center or entrance station. The Sperry Chalet Trail to the view of Sperry Glacier above Lake McDonald is a tough 7-mile climb.

17

TOURS AND OUTFITTERS

Glacier Gateway Outfitters. At this outfitter in East Glacier, a Blackfoot cowboy guides riders on Blackfeet Nation land adjacent to the Two Medicine area of Glacier National Park. Rides, which are one hour or one day, climb through aspen groves to high-country views of Dancing Lady and Bison mountains. Riders must be 7 or older and reservations are essential. ⊠ *East Glacier* ☎ *406/226–4408, 406/338–5560* ⊠ *$30–$180* ⊗ *May–Sept.*

Swan Mountain Outfitters. The only outfitter that offers horseback riding inside the park, Swan Mountain Outfitters begins its rides at Apgar, Lake McDonald, and Many Glacier. Trips for beginning to advanced riders cover both flat and mountainous territory. Fishing can also be included. Riders must be 7 or older and weigh less than 250 pounds. Reservations are essential. ⊠ *Coram* ☎ *877/888–5557 for central reservation line, 406/888–5010 for Apgar Corral, 406/888–5121 for Lake McDonald Corral, 406/732–4203 for Many Glacier Corral* ⊕ *www. swanmountainoutfitters.com/glacier* ⊠ *$40 for 1 hr, $65 for 2 hrs, $115 for ½ day, $170 for full day, $295 for overnight trip* ⊗ *Late May–mid-Sept.*

SKIING AND SNOWSHOEING

Cross-country skiing and snowshoeing are increasingly popular in the park. Glacier distributes a free pamphlet entitled *Ski Trails of Glacier National Park,* with 16 noted trails. You can start at Lake McDonald Lodge and ski cross-country up Going-to-the-Sun Road. The 2.5-mile Apgar Natural Trail is popular with snowshoers. No restaurants or stores are open in winter in Glacier.

The History of Glacier National Park

The history of Glacier National Park started long before Congress named the spectacular wilderness a national park. American Indians, including the Blackfeet, Kootenai, and Salish, regularly traversed the area's valleys for centuries before white immigrants arrived. For the most part, these migratory people crossed the Rocky Mountains in search of sustenance in the form of roots, grasses, berries, and game. Many tribes felt that the mountains, with their unusual glacier-carved horns, cirques, and aretes, were spiritually charged. Later, white people would be similarly inspired by Glacier's beauty and would nickname the area atop the Continental Divide the "Crown of the Continent."

White trappers arrived in the area as early as the 1780s. Then, in 1805, Lewis and Clark passed south of what is now Glacier National Park. Attracted by the expedition's reports of abundant beaver, many more trappers, primarily British, French, and Spanish, migrated to the region. For most of the early to mid-1800s, human activity in the area was limited to lone trappers and migrating Indians.

On their journey west, Lewis and Clark sought but did not find the elusive pass over the Rockies, now known as Marias Pass, on the southern edge of the park. Whether their scouts were unaware of the relatively low elevation—5,200 feet—of the pass, or whether they feared the Blackfeet that controlled the region, is unknown. The pass went undiscovered until 1889, when surveyors for the Great Northern Railway found it in the dead of winter. By 1891 the Great Northern Railway's tracks had crossed Marias Pass, and by 1895 the railroad had completed its westward expansion.

As homesteaders, miners, and trappers poured into the Glacier area in the late 1800s, the American Indian population seriously declined. The Blackfeet were devastated by small-pox epidemics—a disease previously unknown in North America—from the mid-1800s until the early 1900s. The disease, and a reduced food supply due to the overhunting of buffalo, stripped the Blackfeet of their power and, eventually, their land. In 1895, the tribe sold the area now within the park to the U.S. government, which opened it to miners. Returns on the mines were never very substantial, and most were abandoned by 1905.

Between the late 1880s and 1900, *Forest and Stream* magazine editor George Grinnell made several trips to the mountains of northwestern Montana. He was awed by the beauty of the area and urged the U.S. government to give it park status, thus protecting it from mining interests and homesteaders. At the same time, the Great Northern Railway company was spreading the word about the area's recreational opportunities. The company built seven backcountry chalets to house guests, and promised tourists from the East a back-to-nature experience with daylong hikes and horseback rides between the chalets. Visitors arrived by train at West Glacier, took a stagecoach to Lake McDonald, a boat to the lakeside Snyder Hotel, and began their nature adventures from there. Between Grinnell's political influence and the Great Northern's financial interests, Congress found reason enough to establish Glacier National Park; the bill was signed by President William Howard Taft in 1910.

TOURS AND OUTFITTERS

Glacier Adventure Guides. This organization leads one-day or multiday guided snowshoe trips on the park's scenic winter trails. On overnight trips, you stay in igloos and snow caves. During the summer months, they offer guided hiking and rock climbing adventures outside the park. ☎ *877/735–9514, 406/892–2173* ⊕ *www.glacieradventureguides.com* ✉ *$35–$150* ⊙ *Mid-Nov.–May.*

Izaak Walton Inn. Just outside the southern edge of the park, the Izaak Walton Inn has more than 20 miles of groomed cross-country ski trails on the property and offers lessons as well as guided ski and snowshoe tours inside the park. The hotel is one of the few places in the area that is both open during the winter months and accessible by Amtrak train—a nice perk, because then you don't have to worry about driving on icy mountain roads. ✉ *290 Izaak Walton Inn Rd., off U.S. 2, Essex* ☎ *406/888–5700* ⊕ *www.izaakwaltoninn.com* ⊙ *Mid-Nov.–May.*

WATERTON LAKES NATIONAL PARK

EXPLORING

SCENIC DRIVES

Akamina Parkway. Take this winding 16-km (10-mile) road up to Cameron Lake, but drive slowly and watch for wildlife. It's common to see bears along the way. At the lake you will find a relatively flat, paved, 1.6-km (1-mile) trail that hugs the western shore and makes a nice walk. Bring your binoculars, because it's common to see grizzly bears on the lower slopes of the mountains at the far end of the lake. ⚠ **Severe flooding washed out parts of this road in spring 2013, and at this writing it was being reconstructed. The road is expected to reopen for the 2014 season, but call the park to be sure.**

Red Rock Parkway. The 15-km (9-mile) route takes you from the prairie up the Blakiston Valley to Red Rock Canyon, where water has cut through the earth, exposing red sedimentary rock. Watch for wildlife—it's common to see bears just off the road—especially in the autumn months when the berries are ripe. Parks Canada offers a free shuttle service to Red Rock Canyon. Check at the information center for departure and return times.

HISTORIC SITES

First Oil Well in Western Canada. Alberta is known worldwide for its oil and gas production, and the first oil well in western Canada was established in 1902 in what is now the park. Stop at this National Historic Site to explore the wellheads, drilling equipment, and remains of the Oil City boomtown. ✉ *Watch for sign 7.7 km (4.8 miles) up the Akamina Pkwy.*

Prince of Wales Hotel. Named for the prince who later became King Edward VIII, this lovely hotel was constructed between 1926 and 1927 and was designated a National Historic Site in 1995. Stand on the ridge outside the hotel and take in the magnificent view or pop inside and enjoy it from the comfort of the expansive lobby. Tea is served in the lobby during the afternoons. ✉ *Off Hwy. 5* ☎ *406/756–2444, 403/859–2231 mid-May–late Sept.* ⊕ *www.glacierparkinc.com* ⊙ *Mid-May–late Sept.*

17

SCENIC STOPS

Cameron Lake. The jewel of Waterton, Cameron Lake sits in a land of glacially carved cirques (steep-walled basins). In summer, hundreds of varieties of alpine wildflowers fill the area, including 22 kinds of wild orchids. Canoes, rowboats, kayaks, and fishing gear can be rented here. ⊠ *Akamina Pkwy., 13 km (8 miles) southwest of Waterton Park Townsite.*

Goat Haunt Ranger Station. Reached only by foot trail or tour boat from Waterton Townsite, this spot on the U.S. end of Waterton Lake is the stomping ground for mountain goats, moose, grizzlies, and black bears. The ranger posted at this remote station gives thrice-daily 10-minute overviews of Waterton Valley history. ⊠ *South end of Waterton Lake* ☎ *406/888–7800, 403/859–2362* ⊕ *www.watertoncruise.com* ✉ *Tour boat $40* ☾ *Mid-May–Oct.*

Waterton Townsite. This is a decidedly low-key community, roughly in the geographical center of the park. In summer it swells with tourists, and local restaurants and shops open to serve them. In winter only a few motels are open, and services are limited.

EDUCATIONAL OFFERINGS

Evening interpretive programs are offered from late June until Labor Day at the Falls Theatre, near Cameron Falls, and the townsite campground. These one-hour sessions begin at 8. A guided International Peace Park hike is held every Wednesday and Saturday in July and August. The 14-km (9-mile) hike begins at the Bertha trailhead, and is led by Canadian and American park interpreters. You take lunch at the International Border before continuing on to Goat Haunt in Glacier National Park, Montana, and returning to Waterton via boat. A fee is charged for the return boat trip. You must preregister for this hike at the Waterton Information Centre.

SPORTS AND THE OUTDOORS

The park contains numerous short hikes for day-trippers and some longer treks for backpackers. Upper and Middle Waterton and Cameron lakes provide peaceful havens for boaters. A tour boat cruises across Upper Waterton Lake, crossing the U.S.–Canada border, and the winds that rake across that lake create an exciting ride for windsurfers—bring a wet suit, though; the water remains numbingly cold throughout summer.

BICYCLING

Bikes are allowed on some trails, such as the 3-km (2-mile) Townsite Loop Trail. A great family bike trail is the 4.3-mile (one-way) paved Kootenai Brown Trail, which leads from the townsite to the park gates along the edge of the lakes. A ride on mildly sloping Red Rock Canyon Road isn't too difficult (once you get past the first hill). Cameron Lake Road is an intermediate-to-advanced paved route.

OUTFITTERS

FAMILY **Pat's Waterton.** Choose from surrey bikes, mountain bikes, or motorized scooters. Pat's also rents tennis rackets, strollers, and binoculars. ⌂ *Corner of Mt. View Rd., Waterton Townsite* ☎ *403/859–2266* ⊕ *www.watertoninfo.com/m/pats.html.*

BOATING

Nonmotorized boats can be rented at Cameron Lake in summer; private craft can be used on Upper and Middle Waterton lakes.

TOURS AND OUTFITTERS

Waterton Inter-Nation Shoreline Cruise Co. This company's two-hour round-trip boat tour along Upper Waterton Lake from Waterton Townsite to Goat Haunt Ranger Station is one of the most popular activities in Waterton. (Note that because Goat Haunt is in the United States, you must clear customs if you want to stay at Goat Haunt and hike into Glacier from there.) The narrated tour passes scenic bays, sheer cliffs, and snow-clad peaks. ⌂ *Waterton Townsite Marina, on the northwest corner of Waterton Lake near the Bayshore Inn* ☎ *403/859–2362* ⊕ *www.watertoncruise.com* ⌂ *C$40* ⊙ *May–early Oct., multiple cruises daily.*

HIKING

There are 225 km (191 miles) of trails in Waterton Lakes that range in difficulty from short strolls to strenuous treks. Some trails connect with the trail systems of Glacier and British Columbia's Akamina-Kishenina Provincial Park. The wildflowers in June are particularly stunning along most trails. *Hiking Glacier and Waterton National Parks,* by Erik Molvar, has detailed information including pictures and GPS-compatible maps for 60 of the best hiking trails in both parks.

17

TOURS

Waterton Outdoor Adventures. This is the headquarters for hiker shuttle services that run throughout Waterton to most of the major trailheads; they can also arrange certified hiking guides for groups. You can reserve shuttles two months in advance. ⌂ *Tamarack Village Sq.* ☎ *403/859–2378* ⊕ *www.hikewaterton.com* ⊙ *May–Sept.*

EASY

FAMILY **Bear's Hump Trail.** This steep 2.7-km (1.7-mile) trail climbs up the mountainside to an overlook with a great view of Upper Waterton Lake and the townsite. *Easy.* ⌂ *Trailhead directly behind the Waterton Information Centre bldg.*

FAMILY **Cameron Lake Shore Trail.** This relatively flat, paved, 1.5-km (1-mile) trail is a peaceful place for a walk. Look for wildflowers along the shoreline and grizzlies on the lower slopes of the mountains at the far end of the lake. *Easy.* ⌂ *Trailhead at the lakeshore in front of the parking lot, 13 km (8 miles) southwest of Waterton Townsite.*

Crandell Lake Trail. This easy 2.5-km (1.5-mile) trail follows an old wagon road to lead to Oil City. *Easy.* ⌂ *Trail begins about halfway up the Akamina Pkwy.*

BEST BETS FOR FAMILIES

Bicycle Built for Three. Rent a surrey bike at Pat's Waterton store and enjoy peddling around the townsite. A surrey bike has a flat seat and a canopy and can hold up to three people, so it is great for families.

Climb Bear's Hump. This 2.7-km (1.7-mile) trail takes you from the Waterton Information Centre up the mountainside to an overlook with a great view of Upper Waterton Lake and the townsite.

Family Adventure Camp. Experience an educational and fun family adventure program with the Glacier Institute. Programs range in length from one day to one week.

Hidden Lake Nature Trail. This uphill, 2.4-km (1.5-mile), self-guided trail runs from Logan Pass southwest to Hidden Lake Overlook, from which you get a beautiful view of the lake and McDonald Valley. In spring, ribbons of water pour off the rocks surrounding the lake. A boardwalk protects the abundant wildflowers and spongy tundra on the way.

Lake McDonald. Rent a canoe and enjoy paddling around the lake. If you work up a sweat, you can go for a swim in the lake afterward.

MODERATE

Bertha Lake Trail. This 13-km (8-mile) trail leads from the Waterton Townsite through a Douglas fir forest to a beautiful overlook of Upper Waterton Lake, then on to Lower Bertha Falls. If you continue on, a steeper climb will take you past Upper Bertha Falls to Bertha Lake. The wildflowers are particularly stunning along this trail in June. *Moderate.* ⊠ *Trailhead on south end of Waterton Townsite; head toward the lake and you will find a parking lot on the west side of the road.*

DIFFICULT

Fodor's Choice **Crypt Lake Trail.** This awe-inspiring, strenuous, 9-km (5.5-mile) trail ★ is proclaimed by some to be one of the most stunning hikes in the Canadian Rockies. Conquering the trail involves a boat taxi across Waterton Lake, a climb of 2,300 feet, a crawl through a tunnel that measures almost 100 feet, and a climb along a sheer rock face. The reward is a 600-foot-tall cascading waterfall and the turquoise waters of Crypt Lake. *Difficult.* ⊠ *Trailhead at Crypt Landing accessed by ferry from Waterton Townsite.*

HORSEBACK RIDING

Rolling hills, grasslands, and rugged mountains make riding in Waterton Lakes a real pleasure. Scenery, wildlife, and wildflowers are easily viewed from the saddle and many of the park trails allow horses.

TOURS AND OUTFITTERS

Alpine Stables. At these stables you can arrange hourlong trail rides and all-day guided excursions within the park as well as multiday pack trips through the foothills of the Rockies. ☎ *403/859–2462 May–Sept., 403/653–2449 Oct.–Apr.* ⊕ *www.alpinestables.com* ✎ *C$38 to C$150* ☾ *May–Sept.*

SWIMMING

FAMILY **Waterton Health Club.** This club, at the Waterton Lakes Lodge Resort, has an 18-meter (56-foot) saltwater pool, a hot tub, a sauna, and a gym. Guests of the lodge can use the facilities for free, but if you are staying elsewhere in the park you can purchase a pass. A one-week membership to the facility will cost C$18.90. The facilities are open daily 9 to 9, and towels are provided. ⊠ *101 Clematis Ave., Waterton Townsite* ☏ *403/859–2150, 888/985–6343* ⊕ *watertonlakeslodge.com.*

FAMILY **Waterton Lakes.** These lakes are chilly year-round, but they are still a great place to cool off after a long hot day of hiking. Most visitors can only handle dipping a toe or two, some wade, and a few brave souls join the "polar bear club" and submerge themselves completely. ⊠ *Waterton Townsite.*

WHAT'S NEARBY

You can easily spend a week exploring Waterton and Glacier, but you may wish to take in some nearby sights as well. The Canadian town of Cardston is about 30 minutes east of Waterton Lakes National Park and is the site of the Remington Carriage Museum, containing North America's largest collection of horse-drawn vehicles. Cardston also has an excellent live theater program in summer. About 90 minutes northeast you can visit Head-Smashed-In Buffalo Jump, a UNESCO World Heritage Site, outside the town of Fort Macleod. Outside Glacier National Park are the gateway towns of East Glacier, West Glacier, and Columbia Falls, where you can find tour operators, accommodations, restaurants, and stores. Not far from Glacier Park are the towns of Essex, Kalispell, Whitefish, Browning, and Bigfork. Here you will find some excellent golf courses, world-class cross-country and downhill skiing, summer and winter festivals, diverse recreational opportunities, accommodations, and restaurants.

17

NEARBY TOWNS

Bigfork. About 45 minutes from Glacier's west entrance on Flathead Lake's pristine northeast shore, Bigfork twinkles with decorative lights that adorn its boutique shops and fine restaurants. Bigfork is a wonderful art community with excellent galleries and one of the finest repertory theaters in the northwest. ⊠ *Bigfork* ⊕ *www.bigfork.org.*

Browning. Thirty-five miles to the east of Glacier, Browning is the center of the Blackfeet Nation, whose name is thought to have been derived from the color of their painted or dyed black moccasins; there are about 13,000 enrolled tribal members. The city's main attractions are the Museum of the Plains Indian and the Blackfeet Heritage Center and Art Gallery. ⊠ *Browning* ⊕ *www.browningmontana.com.*

Cardston. Just 28 miles east of Waterton, Cardston is home to the Alberta Temple, built by the Mormon pioneers who established the town. The Remington Carriage Museum contains North America's largest collection of horse-drawn vehicles. The Carriage House Theatre (⊕ *www.carriagehousetheatre.com*) features entertaining live theatrical performances most summer evenings. ⊠ *Cardston.*

Columbia Falls. This small town only 15 miles west of Glacier National Park has restaurants, services, and accommodations. Near the town are two excellent golf courses, a waterpark, and more than 80 miles of groomed snowmobile trails in winter. ⊠ *Columbia Falls* ⊕ *www. columbiafallschamber.org.*

East Glacier. Early tourists to Glacier National Park first stopped in East Glacier, where the Great Northern Railway had established a station. Although most people coming from the east now enter by car through St. Mary, East Glacier, population about 400, attracts visitors with its quiet, secluded surroundings and lovely Glacier Park Lodge. ⊠ *East Glacier* ⊕ *www.eastglacierpark.info.*

Essex. The village of Essex borders the southern tip of the park and is the site of the main rail and bus terminals for visitors coming to the park. ⊠ *Essex.*

West Glacier. The green waters of the Flathead River's Middle Fork and several top-notch outfitters make West Glacier an ideal base for river sports such as rafting and fishing. There are several good accommodations and restaurants here. ⊠ *West Glacier* ⊕ *westglacier.com.*

Whitefish. The best base for the park is Whitefish, 25 miles west of Glacier. With a population of 6,000, the town has a well-developed nightlife scene and good restaurants, galleries, and shops. ⊠ *Whitefish* ⊕ *www.explorewhitefish.com.*

VISITOR INFORMATION

Bigfork Area Chamber of Commerce ⊠ *8155 Hwy. 35, Bigfork* ☎ *406/837–5888* ⊕ *www.bigfork.org.* **East Glacier Chamber of Commerce** ⊠ *909 Montana Rte. 49 N, East Glacier* ☎ *406/226–4403.* **Glacier Country Tourism** ⊠ *140 N. Higgens Ave., Suite 204, Missoula* ☎ *800/338–5072* ⊕ *www.glaciermt.com.* **Town of Cardston** ☎ *403/653–3366, 888/434–3366* ⊕ *www.cardston.ca.* **Waterton Chamber of Commerce and Visitors Association** ☎ *403/859–2224* ⊕ *www.mywaterton.ca.* **Whitefish Chamber of Commerce** ⊠ *307 Spokane Ave., Suite 103, Whitefish* ☎ *403/862–3501, 877/862–3548* ⊕ *www.whitefishchamber.org.*

NEARBY ATTRACTIONS

FAMILY **Big Sky Waterpark.** During summer, the most popular place between the hardworking lumber town of Columbia Falls and Glacier National Park is the Big Sky Waterpark. Besides the 10 waterslides and a golf course, there are arcade games, bumper cars, a carousel, barbecue grills, a picnic area, and food service. ⊠ *7211 U.S. 2 E, junction of U.S. 2 and Hwy. 206, Columbia Falls* ☎ *406/892–5026, 406/892–1908* ⊕ *www. bigskywp.com* 🎟 *$24.99* ☉ *Memorial Day–Labor Day, daily 10–8.*

Museum of the Plains Indian. The impressive collection of artifacts from the Blackfeet at this museum includes clothing, saddlebags, and artwork. ⊠ *19 Museum Loop, Browning* ☎ *406/338–2230* ⊕ *www. browningmontana.com* 🎟 *$4 June–Sept., free Oct.–May* ☉ *June–Sept., daily 9–4:45; Oct.–May, weekdays 10–4:30.*

AREA ACTIVITIES

SPORTS AND THE OUTDOORS

DOGSLEDDING

Dog Sled Adventures. The dogs are raring to run late November to mid-April at Dog Sled Adventures. Your friendly musher will gear the ride to the passengers, from kids to senior citizens; bundled up in a sled, you'll be whisked through Stillwater State Forest on a 1½-hour ride over a 12-mile trail. Reservations are essential. ⊠ *U.S. 93, 20 miles north of Whitefish, 2 miles north of Olney* ☎ *406/881–2275* ⊕ *www. dogsledadventuresmt.com.*

SKIING AND SNOWBOARDING

Whitefish Mountain Resort. Eight miles from Whitefish, this has been one of Montana's top ski areas since the 1930s, yet it remains comfortably small. The resort is popular among train travelers from the Pacific Northwest and the upper Midwest. Whitefish mountain has good powder skiing, nice glades, and groomed trails for all ski levels. In summer there are bike trails, an alpine slide, an aerial adventure park, and a zip line. The mountain's stats include a 2,500-foot vertical drop; 3,000 skiable acres; terrain that is 25% beginner, 50% intermediate, and 25% advanced; two high-speed quad chairs, one quad chair, four triple chairs, one double chair, and three surface lifts. ☎ *406/862–2900 or 800/858–3930 for information, 406/862–7669 for snow report* ⊕ *www. skiwhitefish.com* 🎿 *One-day lift ticket $75* ☉ *Thanksgiving–early Apr. and mid-June–mid-Sept., daily 9–4:30.*

17

WHERE TO EAT

IN THE PARKS

GLACIER

$$ ╳ **Lake McDonald Lodge Restaurants.** In Russell's Fireside Dining Room,
AMERICAN take in a great view while choosing between standards such as pasta, steak, wild game, and salmon. There are also some delicious salads and other local favorites on the menu such as five-spice Peking duck breast. Make sure to check out the pastry chef's daily dessert special, which has included such items as strawberry shortcake and apple bread pudding with caramel-cinnamon sauce. The restaurant has an excellent breakfast buffet, a children's menu, and box lunches on request. Across the parking lot is a cheaper alternative, **Jammer Joe's Grill & Pizzeria**, which serves burgers and pasta for lunch and dinner. 🄢 *Average main: $20* ⊠ *10 miles north of Apgar on Going-to-the-Sun Rd.* ☎ *406/888–5431, 406/892–2525* ⊕ *www.glaciernationalparklodges.com* ☉ *Closed early Oct.–early June.*

$$ ╳ **Ptarmigan Dining Room.** This newly remodeled dining room is one of
AMERICAN the most picturesque dining spots in the park—with stunning views of Grinnell Point over Swiftcurrent Lake to be enjoyed through its massive windows. French-American cuisine is served amid Swiss-style decor. Signature dishes include the wild game sausage sampler, buffalo Stroganoff, and Rocky Mountain trout. Each night there's a chef's special such

as fresh fish or pork prime rib with a huckleberry demi-glace. Pop into the adjacent Swiss Lounge to enjoy a Montana microbrew or a huckleberry daiquiri before or after dinner. [$] *Average main: $20* ✉ *Many Glacier Rd.* ☎ *406/732–4411* 🌐 *www.glaciernationalparklodges.com* ⏲ *Closed late Sept.–early June.*

PICNIC AREAS

There are picnic spots at most campgrounds and visitor centers. Each has tables, grills, and drinking water in summer.

Sun Point. On the north side of St. Mary Lake, this is one of the most beautiful places in the park for a picnic. ✉ *Sun Point Trailhead.*

WATERTON LAKES

$$$ STEAKHOUSE 🍴 **Lakeside Chophouse.** At Waterton's only lakefront restaurant, large windows provide spectacular views of Waterton Lakes and Mount Vimi and a window seat or patio table provide the best views. This is the spot in the park for a steak dinner—locally raised Alberta beef is a staple menu item. The petite filet mignon with garlic butter, the ribeye with chimichurri sauce, or the Cajun-blackened New York steak are all good bets. Other menu highlights are miso-glazed Atlantic salmon, Mumbai butter chicken, and rosemary-crusted Alberta lamb chops. The restaurant has a breakfast buffet, lunch, and dinner service. [$] *Average main: C$28* ✉ *111 Waterton Ave., Waterton Townsite* ☎ *888/527–9555, 403/859–2211* 🌐 *www.bayshoreinn.com* ⏲ *Closed mid-Oct.–Apr.*

$ HOT DOG FAMILY 🍴 **Wieners of Waterton.** If there is such a thing as a gourmet hot dog, then this is the place to find it. Wieners of Waterton bakes their buns fresh daily and sources their all-beef weiners and smokies locally—except for the genuine Nathan's dogs, which are shipped from New York City. They even have an antidog made with falafel and topped with hummus, tzatziki sauce, and fresh veggies for those looking for a vegeterian meal. There are plenty of homemade sauces and tons of interesting toppings to choose from. Sides include sweet potato fries, fried pickles, kettle chips, or classic Canadian *poutine* (fries served with gravy and cheese curds). [$] *Average main: C$7* ✉ *301 Wildflower Ave., Waterton Townsite* ☎ *403/859–0007* 🌐 *www.wienersofwaterton.com* ✍ *Reservations not accepted* ⏲ *Closed Oct.–Apr.*

OUTSIDE THE PARKS

$$$ AMERICAN 🍴 **Belton Chalet Grill Dining Room.** This is a lovely dining room with original wainscoting and leaded-glass windows, but if the weather is nice you should ask for a table on the deck where you can see the sunset behind the mountains or watch the trains roll by. Menu specialties include buffalo meatloaf, wild salmon with fennel and coriander, and the bacon-wrapped beef fillet. The restaurant remains open most of the year (weekends only in the winter months). For a quick bite, sit in the lounge and enjoy the taproom menu that features casual items like Thai salad and steak tacos. [$] *Average main: $27* ✉ *Rte. 49, next to railroad station, 12575 U.S. 2 E, West Glacier* ☎ *406/888–5000, 888/235–8665* ⏲ *Closed early Oct.–early Dec. and late Mar.–late May. Closed Mon.–Thurs. early Dec.–late Mar. (brunch only Sun. Dec.–Mar.). No lunch.*

CLOSE UP

Best Campgrounds in Glacier and Waterton

There are 10 major campgrounds in Glacier National Park and excellent backcountry sites for backpackers. Reservations for Fish Creek and St. Mary Campgrounds are available through the National Park Reservation Service (☎ 877/444–6777 or 518/885–3639 ⊕ www.recreation. gov). Reservations may be made up to five months in advance. Parks Canada operates four campgrounds in Waterton Lakes that range from fully serviced to unserviced sites. There are also some backcountry campsites. Visitors can prebook campsites for a fee of C$11 online or C$13.50 by phone. The reservation service is available at ⊕ www.reservation.parkscanada.gc.ca or by phone at ☎ 877/737–3783.

BEST OPTIONS IN GLACIER
Apgar Campground. This popular and large campground on the southern shore of Lake McDonald has many activities and services. ⊠ Apgar Rd. ☎ 406/888–7800.

Avalanche Creek Campground. This peaceful campground on Going-to-the-Sun Road is shaded by huge red cedars and bordered by Avalanche Creek. ⊠ 25 km (15.7 miles) from West entrance on Going-to-the-Sun Rd. ☎ 406/888–7800.

Kintla Lake Campground. Beautiful and remote, this is a trout fisherman's dream. ⊠ 23 1/2 km (14 miles) north of Polebridge Ranger Station on Inside North Fork Rd.

Many Glacier Campground.
One of the most beautiful spots in the park is also a favorite for bears. ⊠ Next to Swiftcurrent Motor Inn on Many Glacier Rd.

Sprague Creek Campground.
This sometimes noisy roadside campground for tents, RVs, and truck campers (no towed units) offers spectacular views of the lake and sunsets and fishing from shore. ⊠ Going-to-the-Sun Rd., 1.6 km (1 mile) south of Lake McDonald Lodge ☎ 406/888–7800.

St. Mary Campground. This large, grassy spot alongside the lake and stream has mountain views and cool breezes. ⊠ 1.4 km (0.9 mile) from St. Mary entrance to Going-to-the-Sun Rd. ☎ 406/888–7800.

BEST OPTIONS IN WATERTON
Crandell Campground. Located along the Red Rock Parkway a short hike from Crandell Lake, this campground is surrounded by montane forest. ⊠ On Red Rock Pkwy., 2 km (1.2 miles) before Cradell Lake ☎ 403/859–5133.

Waterton Townsite Campground.
Though the campground is busy, noisy, and windy, sites here are grassy and flat with access to kitchen shelters and have views down the lake into the U.S. part of the Peace Park. ⊠ Waterton and Vimy Aves. ☎ 905/426–4648, 877/737–3783.

17

$$ MEXICAN ✗**Serrano's.** Mexican food in Montana! After a day on the dusty trail, Serrano's is a real treat whether dining inside or on the back patio. Try a taco salad, a beef burrito, or a chicken enchilada with one of the restaurant's famous margaritas; dinners are served with complimentary chips and homemade salsa. The Mexican flan is delicious, but you may want to try the less traditional huckleberry carrot cake for dessert. Don't be surprised if there's a line during July, August, and

early September—the restaurant is a favorite with locals and visitors alike and it doesn't take reservations. $ *Average main: $14* ✉ *29 Dawson Ave., East Glacier* ☎ *406/226–9392* ⊕ *www.serranosmexican.com* ⚭ *Reservations not accepted* ⊘ *Closed Oct.–Apr.*

$$ ✕ **Three Forks Grille.** You'll find Italian-influenced classic mountain
AMERICAN cuisine with an emphasis on fresh, local ingredients at this restaurant near the Main Street area of Columbia Falls. It has hardwood floors, an open-beam ceiling, and dining on two levels, with local artwork adorning the walls. The menu changes regularly, but always features local hand-cut steaks, wild game, and fresh seafood. Grilled Montana rainbow trout marinated in lime, herbs, and virgin olive oil served with chickpea and farro salad is a recurring menu item. For something casual and inexpensive, try the Three Forks burger with garlic confit and gorgonzola cheese or the Three Forks Caesar salad with grilled lemon and house-smoked rainbow trout. $ *Average main: $19* ✉ *729 Nucleas Ave., Columbia Falls* ☎ *406/892–2900* ⊕ *threeforksgrille.com.*

WHERE TO STAY

IN THE PARKS

GLACIER

$$ 🖼 **Lake McDonald Lodge.** On the shores of Lake McDonald not far
HOTEL from Apgar and West Glacier, this lodge is an ideal base for exploring the western side of the park and is one of the great historic lodges of the West. **Pros:** lovely lakeside setting; historic property; close to Apgar, West Glacier, and Going-to-the-Sun Road. **Cons:** rustic; no TV (except for in the suites); small bathrooms. $ *Rooms from: $137* ✉ *Going-to-the-Sun Rd.* ☎ *406/892–2525, 406/888–5431* ⊕ *www.glaciernationalparklodges.com* ⇜ *74 rooms, 38 cabins* ⦿⦿ *No meals.*

$$$ 🖼 **Many Glacier Hotel.** The most isolated of the grand hotels—it's on
HOTEL Swiftcurrent Lake on the northeast side of the park—this is also one of the most scenic, especially if you nab one of the lake-view balcony rooms. **Pros:** stunning views from lodge; secluded; good hiking trails nearby. **Cons:** rustic rooms; no TV; no Internet. $ *Rooms from: $179* ✉ *Many Glacier Rd., 12 miles west of Babb* ☎ *406/892–2525, 406/732–4411* ⊕ *www.glaciernationalparklodges.com* ⇜ *206 rooms, 6 family rooms, 2 suites* ⦿⦿ *No meals.*

$$ 🖼 **Village Inn.** Situated on the shores of beautiful Lake McDonald, this
HOTEL motel is listed on the national register of historic places; although the property shows it age, it's clean and well cared-for. **Pros:** great views; nice location in Apgar Village; some kitchenettes. **Cons:** rustic motel; smaller property; few amenities. $ *Rooms from: $146* ✉ *Apgar Village* ☎ *406/756–2444* ⊕ *www.glaciernationalparklodges.com* ⇜ *36 rooms* ⦿⦿ *No meals.*

WATERTON

$$$ HOTEL 🏨 **Bayshore Inn.** On the shores of Waterton Lake, this inn has lovely views and the only on-site spa in Waterton, and as it's right in town with multiple eating establishments on the property, you don't have to walk far to find most services. **Pros:** lakefront views; on-site spa; located right in Waterton Townsite. **Cons:** older style rooms; motor inn. [$] *Rooms from: C$199* ✉ *111 Waterton Ave., Waterton Townsite* ☎ *888/527–9555, 403/859–2211* 🌐 *www.bayshoreinn.com* 🛏 *66 rooms, 4 suites* 🕒 *Closed mid-Oct.–Apr.* 🍴 *No meals.*

$$$ HOTEL FAMILY 🏨 **Waterton Lakes Lodge.** Located in the heart of Waterton Townsite, this hotel has the only indoor swimming pool in Waterton, a hot tub, a games room, an extensive fitness center, and an on-site restaurant. **Pros:** on-site swimming pool; rooms for larger groups; good location in townsite. **Cons:** dated decor; some rooms are small. [$] *Rooms from: C$199* ✉ *101 Clematis Ave., Waterton Townsite* ☎ *888/985–6343, 403/859–2150* 🌐 *www.watertonlakeslodge.com* 🛏 *81 rooms* 🍴 *No meals.*

OUTSIDE THE PARKS

$$$ HOTEL 🏨 **Belton Chalet.** This carefully restored 1910 railroad hotel, the original winter headquarters for the park, has a great location just outside the West Glacier entrance and cozy, bright rooms with original woodwork around the windows and period furnishings. **Pros:** excellent restaurant on site; wraparound decks with lovely views; historic property. **Cons:** train noise; rustic; no a/c or TV. [$] *Rooms from: $155* ✉ *12575 U.S. 2 E, West Glacier* ☎ *406/888–5000, 888/235–8665* 🌐 *www.beltonchalet.com* 🛏 *25 rooms, 2 cottages* 🍴 *Breakfast.*

$$$$ RENTAL FAMILY 🏨 **Glacier Outdoor Center Cabins.** Five minutes from the entrance to West Glacier, these cozy cabins with fully equipped kitchens, living rooms, barbecues, and private decks are ideal for families. **Pros:** great for families; can accommodate large groups; kitchens in cabins. **Cons:** outside the townsite; no on-site restaurant. [$] *Rooms from: $299* ✉ *12400 U.S. 2 E, West Glacier* ☎ *800/235–6781, 406/888–5454* 🌐 *www.glacierraftco.com* 🛏 *12 rooms* 🍴 *No meals.*

$$$ HOTEL 🏨 **Glacier Park Lodge.** Just outside the east side of the park, across from the Amtrak station, this beautiful full-service hotel built in 1913 is supported by 500- to 800-year-old fir and 3-foot-thick cedar logs. **Pros:** on-site golf course; scenic location; lots of activities. **Cons:** small bathrooms; no elevator; no a/c. [$] *Rooms from: $152* ✉ *Off U.S. 2, East Glacier* ☎ *406/892–2525, 406/226–9311* 🌐 *www.glacierparkinc.com* 🛏 *161 rooms* 🍴 *No meals.*

$$$$ B&B/INN 🏨 **Great Bear Inn.** A stay at this cozy inn—a large log structure with a wraparound deck that provides wonderful mountain views and a comfortable lounge area where guests can relax and visit—includes a gourmet multicourse dinner and a simple continental breakfast. **Pros:** gourmet dinner included; intimate lodge; close to West Glacier. **Cons:** tricky to find; isolated; must drive to reach other amenities. [$] *Rooms from: $375* ✉ *5672 Blankenship Rd., West Glacier* ☎ *406/250–4577* 🌐 *www.thegreatbearinn.com* 🛏 *9 rooms, 2 cabins* 🍴 *Some meals.*

$$$ HOTEL 🏛 **Izaak Walton Inn.** This historic railway lodge just outside the southern edge of Glacier National Park under the shadow of the Great Bear Wilderness is popular with railway buffs: it was originally built to house railway workers and is decorated with railroad memorabilia. **Pros:** good location in the middle between East and West Glacier; open year-round; fun railway theme. **Cons:** train noise can be a problem; no phones or TVs in rooms; no cell-phone access. [$] *Rooms from: $159* ✉ *290 Izaak Walton Inn Rd., off U.S. 2, Essex* ☎ *406/888–5700* 🌐 *www.izaakwaltoninn.com* 🛏 *33 rooms, 6 cottages, 6 cabins* 🍴 *No meals.*

GRAND CANYON
NATIONAL PARK

Visit Fodors.com for advice, updates, and bookings

WELCOME TO GRAND CANYON

TOP REASONS TO GO

★ **Its iconic status:** This is one of those places where you really want to say, "Been there, done that!"

★ **Awesome vistas:** Painted Desert, sandstone canyon walls, pine and fir forests, mesas, plateaus, volcanic features, the Colorado River, streams, and waterfalls make for some jaw-dropping moments.

★ **Year-round adventure:** Outdoor junkies can bike, boat, camp, fish, hike, ride mules, whitewater raft, watch birds and wildlife, cross-country ski, and snowshoe.

★ **Continuing education:** Adults and kids can have fun learning, thanks to free park-sponsored nature walks and interpretive programs.

★ **Sky-high and river-low experiences:** Experience the canyon via plane, train, and automobile, as well as by helicopter, row- or motorboat, bike, mule, or foot.

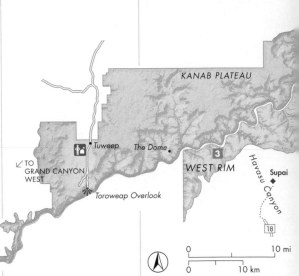

1 South Rim. The South Rim is where the action is: Grand Canyon Village's lodging, camping, eateries, stores, and museums, plus plenty of trailheads into the canyon. Visitor services and facilities are open and available daily, including holidays. Four free shuttle routes cover more than 35 stops, and visitors who'd rather relax than rough it can treat themselves to comfy hotel rooms and elegant restaurant meals (lodging and camping reservations are essential).

2 North Rim. Of the nearly 5 million people who visit the park annually, 90% enter at the South Rim, but many consider the North Rim even more gorgeous—and worth the extra effort. Open only from mid-May to the end of October (or the first good snowfall), the North Rim has legitimate bragging rights: at more than 8,000 feet above sea level (1,000 feet higher than the South Rim), it has precious solitude and seven developed viewpoints. Rather than staring into the canyon's depths, you get a true sense of its expanse.

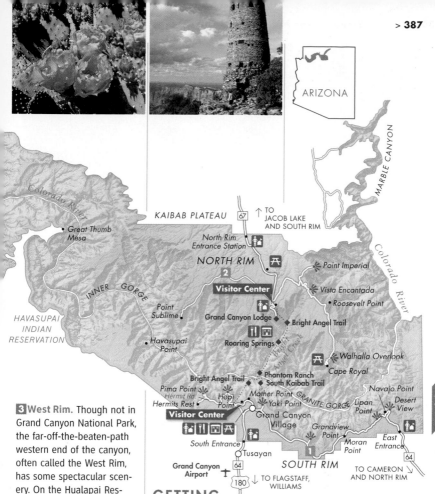

ARIZONA

KAIBAB PLATEAU · 67 ↑ TO JACOB LAKE AND SOUTH RIM

MARBLE CANYON

Colorado River

Great Thumb Mesa

North Rim Entrance Station

NORTH RIM · 2

Visitor Center

Point Imperial

Vista Encantada

Roosevelt Point

Point Sublime

INNER GORGE

Grand Canyon Lodge

Bright Angel Trail

HAVASUPAI INDIAN RESERVATION

Havasupai Point

Roaring Springs

Walhalla Overlook

Cape Royal

Bright Angel Trail

Phantom Ranch
South Kaibab Trail

Pima Point

Hermit Rd.
Hermits Rest

Hopi Point

Mather Point GRANITE GORGE
Yaki Point

Navajo Point

Lipan Point

Desert View

Visitor Center

Grand Canyon Village

Grandview Point

South Entrance

Tusayan

SOUTH RIM

East Entrance

Grand Canyon Airport

Moran Point

TO CAMERON AND NORTH RIM

180 ↓ TO FLAGSTAFF, WILLIAMS

18

3 West Rim. Though not in Grand Canyon National Park, the far-off-the-beaten-path western end of the canyon, often called the West Rim, has some spectacular scenery. On the Hualapai Reservation, the Skywalk has become a major draw. This U-shape glass-floored deck juts out 3,600 feet above the Colorado River and isn't for the faint of heart.

GETTING ORIENTED

Grand Canyon National Park is a superstar—biologically, historically, and recreationally. One of the world's best examples of arid-land erosion, the canyon provides a record of three of the four eras of geological time. Almost 2 billion years' worth of Earth's history is written in the colored layers of rock stacked from the river bottom to the top of the plateau. In addition to its diverse fossil record, the park reveals long-ago traces of human adaptation to an unforgiving environment. It's also home to several major ecosystems, five of the world's seven life zones, three of North America's four desert types, and all kinds of rare, endemic, and protected plant and animal species.

KEY

🧍	Ranger Station
⛺	Campground
⛱	Picnic Area
🍴	Restaurant
🏨	Lodge
🥾	Trailhead
🚻	Restrooms
⚜	Scenic Viewpoint
⋯⋯	Walking/Hiking Trails

Updated by
Mara Levin
and Elise Riley
When it comes to the Grand Canyon, there are statistics and there are sensations. While the former are impressive—the canyon measures in at an average width of 10 miles, length of 277 river miles, and depth of 1 mile—they don't truly prepare you for that first impression. Seeing the canyon for the first time is an astounding experience—one that's hard to wrap your head around. In fact, it's more than an experience, it's an emotion, one that's only just beginning to be captured with the superlative "Grand."

Roughly 5 million visitors come to the park each year. They can access the canyon via two main points: the South Rim and the North Rim. The width from the North Rim to the South Rim varies from 600 feet to 18 miles, but traveling between rims by road requires a 215-mile drive. Hiking arduous trails from rim to rim is a steep and strenuous trek of at least 21 miles, but it's well worth the effort. You'll travel through five of North America's seven life zones. (To do this any other way, you'd have to journey from the Mexican desert to the Canadian woods.) In total, more than 600 miles of mostly very primitive trails traverse the canyon, with about 51 of those miles maintained. West of Grand Canyon National Park, the tribal lands of the Hualapai and the Havasupai lie along the so-called West Rim of the canyon.

GRAND CANYON PLANNER

WHEN TO GO
There's no bad time to visit the canyon, though the busiest times of year are summer and spring break. Visiting during these peak seasons, as well as holidays, requires patience and a tolerance for crowds. Note that weather changes on a whim in this exposed high-desert region. The North Rim shuts down from the end of October through mid-May due to weather conditions and related road closures.

AVG. HIGH/LOW TEMPS.
South Rim

JAN.	FEB.	MAR.	APR.	MAY	JUNE
41/18	45/21	51/25	60/32	70/39	81/47

JULY	AUG.	SEPT.	OCT.	NOV.	DEC.
84/54	82/53	76/47	65/36	52/27	43/20

North Rim

JAN.	FEB.	MAR.	APR.	MAY	JUNE
37/16	39/18	44/21	53/29	62/34	73/40

JULY	AUG.	SEPT.	OCT.	NOV.	DEC.
77/46	75/45	69/39	59/31	46/24	40/20

Inner Canyon

JAN.	FEB.	MAR.	APR.	MAY	JUNE
56/36	62/42	71/48	82/56	92/63	101/72

JULY	AUG.	SEPT.	OCT.	NOV.	DEC.
106/78	103/75	97/69	84/58	68/46	57/37

FESTIVALS AND EVENTS

MAY **Williams Rendezvous Days.** A black-powder shooting competition, 1800s-era crafts, horse-barrel racing, and a parade fire up Memorial Day weekend in honor of Bill Williams, the town's namesake mountain man. ☎ *928/635–4061* ⊕ *www.experiencewilliams.com.*

AUGUST **Grand Canyon Music Festival.** For three weekends in late August–early September, this festival brings mostly chamber music to the Shrine of Ages amphitheater at Grand Canyon Village. In the early 1980s, music aficionados Robert Bonfiglio and Clare Hoffman hiked through the Grand Canyon and decided the stunning spectacle should be accompanied by the strains of a symphony. One of the park rangers agreed, and the wandering musicians performed an impromptu concert. Encouraged by the experience, Bonfiglio and Hoffman started the festival. ☎ *928/638–9215, 800/997–8285* ⊕ *www.grandcanyonmusicfest.org.*

DECEMBER **Mountain Village Holiday.** Williams hails the holidays with a parade of lights, ice-skating rink, and live entertainment in December–early January. ☎ *928/635–4061* ⊕ *www.experiencewilliams.com.*

PLANNING YOUR TIME

Plan ahead: Mule rides require at least a six-month advance reservation, and longer for the busy season (most can be reserved up to 13 months in advance). Multiday rafting trips should be reserved at least a year in advance.

Grand Canyon National Park. Before you go, get the complimentary *Trip Planner,* updated regularly, from the Grand Canyon National Park. ☎ *928/638–7888* ⊕ *www.nps.gov/grca.*

Once you arrive, pick up the free detailed map and the *Guide,* a newspaper with a schedule of free programs.

The park is most crowded on the South Rim, especially near the south entrance and in Grand Canyon Village, as well as on the scenic drives, particularly the 23-mile Desert View Drive.

THE SOUTH RIM IN ONE DAY

Start early, pack a picnic lunch, and drive to the South Rim's **Grand Canyon Visitor Center** just north of the south entrance, to pick up info and see your first incredible view at **Mather Point.** Continue east along **Desert View Drive** for about 2 miles to **Yaki Point.** Next, continue driving 7 miles east to **Grandview Point** for a good view of the buttes Krishna Shrine and Vishnu Temple. Go 4 miles east and catch the view at **Moran Point,** then 3 miles to the **Tusayan Ruin and Museum,** where a small display is devoted to the history of the Ancestral Puebloans. Continue another mile east to **Lipan Point** to view the Colorado River. In less than a mile, you'll arrive at **Navajo Point,** the highest elevation on the South Rim. **Desert View and Watchtower** is the final attraction along Desert View Drive.

On your return drive, stop off at any of the picnic areas for lunch. Once back at Grand Canyon Village, walk the paved **Rim Trail** to **Maricopa Point.** Along the way, pick up souvenirs in the village and stop at historic **El Tovar Hotel** for dinner (be sure to make reservations well in advance). If you have time, take the shuttle on **Hermit Road** to **Hermits Rest,** 7 miles away. Along that route, Hopi Point and Powell Point are excellent spots to watch the sunset.

THE NORTH RIM IN ONE DAY

For your day at the North Rim, we suggest a hike and a drive. The most popular trails on the North Rim are **Transept Trail,** which starts near the Grand Canyon Lodge and has little elevation change, making it good for children; and **Cliff Springs Trail,** which starts near Cape Royal and leads to good views of the canyon.

For your drive, travel up the two-lane Cape Royal Road through the Kaibab National Forest to **Point Imperial**—at 8,803 feet, it's the highest vista on either rim and has views of the Vermilion Cliffs, the Painted Desert, Navajo Mountain, and more. If you have more time, you can take a **mule ride** into the canyon. The trails for the mules are a bit easier on this side of the canyon. Riders must be at least age 7. Or listen to a **ranger-led talk.** Schedules are posted at the Grand Canyon Lodge near the North Rim Visitor Center.

GETTING HERE AND AROUND

Roughly 5 million visitors come to the Grand Canyon each year. They can access the canyon via two main points: the South Rim and the North Rim. A third option, though not within the national park, are the tribal lands of the Hualapai and the Havasupai along the so-called West Rim of the canyon.

AIR TRAVEL

North Las Vegas Airport in Las Vegas is the primary air hub for charter flights to **Grand Canyon National Parks Airport** (*GCN* ☎ *928/638–2446*). The nearest airport to the North Rim is **St. George Municipal Airport** (☎ *435/627–4080* ⊕ *www.flysgu.com*) in Utah, 164 miles north, with regular service provided by both Delta and United Airlines.

Tips for Avoiding Grand Canyon Crowds

It's hard to commune with nature while you're searching for a parking place, dodging video cameras, and stepping away from strollers. However, this scenario is likely only during the peak summer months. One option is to bypass Grand Canyon National Park altogether and head to the West Rim of the canyon, tribal land of the Hualapai and Havasupai. If only the park itself will do, the following tips will help you to keep your distance and your cool.

TAKE ANOTHER ROUTE
Avoid road rage by choosing a different route to the South Rim, forgoing traditional Highway 64 and U.S. 180 from Flagstaff. Take U.S. 89 north from Flagstaff instead, passing near Sunset Crater and Wupatki national monuments. When you reach the junction with Highway 64, take a break at Cameron Trading Post (1 mile north of the junction)—or stay overnight. This is a good place to shop for Native American artifacts, souvenirs, and the usual postcards, dream-catchers, recordings, and T-shirts. There are also high-quality Navajo rugs, jewelry, and other authentic handicrafts, and you can sample Navajo tacos. U.S.

64 to the west takes you directly to the park's east entrance; the scenery along the Little Colorado River gorge en route is eye-popping. It's 23 miles from the east entrance to the visitor center at Grand Canyon Visitor Center.

EXPLORE THE NORTH RIM
Although the North Rim is just 10 miles across from the South Rim, the trip to get there by car is a five-hour drive of 215 miles. At first it might not sound like the trip would be worth it, but the payoff is huge. Along the way, you'll travel through some of the prettiest parts of the state and be granted even more stunning views than those on the more easily accessible South Rim. Those who make the North Rim trip often insist it has the canyon's most beautiful views and best hiking. To get to the North Rim from Flagstaff, take U.S. 89 north past Cameron, turning left onto U.S. 89A at Bitter Springs. En route you'll pass the area known as Vermilion Cliffs. At Jacob Lake, take Highway 67 directly to the Grand Canyon North Rim. North Rim services are closed from November through mid-May because of heavy snow, but in summer months and early fall, it's a wonderful way to beat the crowds at the South Rim.

18

CAR TRAVEL
The best route into the park from the east or south is from Flagstaff. Take U.S. 180 northwest to the park's southern entrance and Grand Canyon Village. From the west on Interstate 40, the most direct route to the South Rim is on U.S. 180 and Highway 64.

To reach the North Rim by car, take U.S. 89 north from Flagstaff past Cameron, turning left onto U.S. 89A at Bitter Springs. At Jacob Lake, take Highway 67 directly to the Grand Canyon North Rim. You can drive yourself to the scenic viewpoints and trailheads; the only transportation offered in the Park is a shuttle twice each morning that brings eager hikers from Grand Canyon Lodge to the North Kaibab Trailhead (a 2-mile trip). Note that the North Rim shuts down in winter following the first major snowfall (usually the end of October); Highway 67 south of Jacob Lake is closed.

■ TIP➔ When driving off major highways in low-lying areas, watch for rain clouds. Flash floods from sudden summer rains can be deadly. To check on road conditions, call the Arizona Department of Transportation's recorded hotline (☎ 888/411–7623 or 511 from any phone).

The park is most crowded near the east and south entrances and in Grand Canyon Village, as well as on the 23-mile Desert View Drive. After you enter the park's South Rim you can drive on the roads that are open to traffic (Hermits Rest is open only to shuttles March through November), or you can try to avoid the congestion by parking your car in the village parking lot and taking advantage of the free shuttles. By car, traveling between the South Rim and the North Rim requires a 215-mile drive via Highways 64, 89, and 67. By foot, it's a steep and strenuous trek of at least 21 miles on arduous hiking trails down the canyon to Phantom Ranch and then up the other side via the North and South Kaibab trails. At the West Rim, visitors aren't allowed to travel in their own vehicles to the viewpoints once they reach the rim; they must purchase a tour package from Hualapai Tourism.

SHUTTLE TRAVEL

The South Rim is open to car traffic year-round, though access to Hermits Rest is limited to shuttle buses part of the year. There are four free shuttle routes: The **Hermits Rest Route** operates March through November, between Grand Canyon Village and Hermits Rest. The **Village Route** operates year-round in the village area near the Grand Canyon Visitor Center. The **Kaibab Rim Route** goes from the visitor center to Yaki Point, including a stop at the South Kaibab Trailhead. The **Tusayan Route** operates summer only and runs from Grand Canyon Visitor Center to the town of Tusayan. ■ TIP➔ In summer, South Rim roads are congested, and it's easier, and sometimes required, to park your car and take the free shuttle. Running from one hour before sunrise until one hour after sunset, shuttles arrive every 15 to 30 minutes at 30 clearly marked stops.

From mid-May to mid-October, the **Trans Canyon Shuttle** (☎ 928/638–2820 ⊕ *www.trans-canyonshuttle.com*) travels daily between the South and North rims—the ride takes 4½ hours each way. One-way fare is $85, round-trip $160. Reservations are required.

TRAIN TRAVEL

Grand Canyon Railway. There is no need to deal with all of the other drivers racing to the South Rim. Sit back and relax in the comfy train cars of the Grand Canyon Railway. Live music and storytelling enliven the trip as you journey past the landscape through prairie, ranch, and national park land to the log-cabin train station in Grand Canyon Village. You won't see the Grand Canyon from the train, but you can walk or catch the shuttle at the restored, historic Grand Canyon Railway Station. The vintage train departs from the Williams Depot every morning, and makes the 65-mile journey in 2¼ hours. You can do the round trip in a single day; however, it's a more relaxing and enjoyable strategy to stay for a night or two at the South Rim before returning to Williams. ⇨ *See Grand Canyon Railway Hotel in Where to Stay.* ☎ *800/843–8724* ⊕ *www.thetrain.com* ✉ *$75–$190 round-trip.*

PARK ESSENTIALS
PARK FEES AND PERMITS

A fee of $25 per vehicle or $12 per person for pedestrians and cyclists is good for one week's access at both rims.

The $50 Grand Canyon Pass gives unlimited access to the park for 12 months.

No permits are needed for day hikers; but **backcountry permits** (☎ *928/638–7875* ⊕ *www.nps.gov/grca* ✉ *$10, plus $5 per person per night*) are necessary for overnight hikers camping below the rim. Permits are limited, so make your reservation as far in advance as possible—they're taken by fax (📠 *928/638–2125*) or mail only, up to four months ahead of arrival. **Camping** in the park is restricted to designated campgrounds (☎ *877/444–6777* ⊕ *www.recreation.gov*).

PARK HOURS

The South Rim is open continuously every day of the year (weather permitting), while the North Rim is open from May through the end of October. The park is in the Mountain time zone year-round. Daylight savings time isn't observed.

CELL-PHONE RECEPTION

Cell phone coverage can be spotty at both the South Rim and North Rim—though Verizon customers report better reception at the South Rim. Don't expect a strong signal anywhere in the park.

RESTAURANTS

Within the park on the South Rim, you can find everything from cafeteria food to casual café fare to creatively prepared, Western- and Southwestern-inspired American cuisine. There's even a coffeehouse with organic joe. Reservations are accepted (and recommended) only for dinner at El Tovar Dining Room; they can be made up to six months in advance with El Tovar room reservations, 30 days in advance without. You should also make dinner reservations at the Grand Canyon Lodge Dining Room on the North Rim—as the only "upscale" dining option, the restaurant fills up quickly at dinner throughout the season (the two other choices on the North Rim are a cafeteria and a chuck-wagon-style Grand Cookout experience). The dress code is casual across the board, but El Tovar is your best option if you're looking to dress up a bit and thumb through an extensive wine list. Drinking water and restrooms aren't available at most picnic spots.

Eateries outside the park generally range from mediocre to terrible—you didn't come all the way to the Grand Canyon for the food, did you? Our selections highlight your best options. Of towns near the park, Williams definitely has the leg up on culinary variety and quality, with Tusayan (near the South Rim) and Jacob Lake (to the north) offering mostly either fast food or merely adequate sit-down restaurants. Near the park, even the priciest places welcome casual dress. On the Hualapai and Havasupai reservations in Havasu Canyon and on the West Rim, dining is limited and basic.

Prices in the reviews are the average cost of a main course at dinner or, if dinner isn't served, at lunch.

18

HOTELS

The park's accommodations include three "historic-rustic" facilities and four motel-style lodges, all of which have undergone significant upgrades over the past decade. Of the 922 rooms, cabins, and suites, only 203, all at the Grand Canyon Lodge, are at the North Rim. Outside El Tovar Hotel, the canyon's architectural highlight, accommodations are relatively basic but comfortable, and the most sought-after rooms have canyon views. Rates vary widely, but most rooms fall in the $100 to $180 range, though the most basic units at the South Rim go for just $83.

Reservations are a must, especially during the busy summer season. ■TIP→ If you want to get your first choice (especially Bright Angel Lodge or El Tovar), make reservations as far in advance as possible; they're taken up to 13 months ahead. You might find a last-minute cancellation, but you shouldn't count on it. Although lodging at the South Rim will keep you close to the action, the frenetic activity and crowded facilities are off-putting to some. With short notice, the best time to find a room on the South Rim is in winter. And though the North Rim is less crowded than the South Rim, the only lodging available is at Grand Canyon Lodge.

Just south of the South Rim park boundary, Tusayan's hotels are in a convenient location but without bargains, while Williams (about an hour's drive) can provide price breaks on food and lodging, as well as a respite from the crowds. Extra amenities (e.g., swimming pools and gyms) are also more abundant. Reservations are always a good idea. At the West Rim, lodging options are extremely limited; you can purchase a "package," which includes lodging and a visitation permit, through Hualapai Tourism.

Prices in the reviews are the lowest cost of a standard double room in high season. For reviews, facilities, and current deals, visit Fodors.com.

Xanterra Parks & Resorts. Xanterra Parks & Resorts operates all lodging and dining services at the South Rim as well as Phantom Ranch, deep inside the canyon. ☎ *888/297–2757* ⊕ *www.grandcanyonlodges.com.*

TOURS

Transportation-services desks are maintained at Bright Angel, Maswik Lodge, and Yavapai Lodge (closed in winter) in Grand Canyon Village. The desks provide information and handle bookings for sightseeing tours, taxi and bus services, and mule rides (but don't count on last-minute availability). There's also a concierge at El Tovar that can arrange most tours, with the exception of mule rides. On the North Rim, Grand Canyon Lodge has general information about local services.

Xanterra Motorcoach Tours. Narrated by knowledgeable guides, tours include the Hermits Rest Tour, which travels along the old wagon road built by the Santa Fe Railway; the Desert View Tour, which glimpses the Colorado River's rapids and stops at Lipan Point; Sunrise and Sunset Tours; and combination tours. Children 16 and younger are free when accompanied by a paying adult. ☎ *303/297–2757, 888/297–2757* ⊕ *www.grandcanyonlodges.com* ✉ *$21–$60.*

VISITOR INFORMATION

PARK CONTACT INFORMATION

Grand Canyon West ☎ 888/868–9378, 928/769–2636 ⊕ *www. hualapaitourism.com.*

SOUTH RIM VISITOR CENTERS

Desert View Information Center. Near the watchtower, at Desert View Point, the nonprofit Grand Canyon Association store and information center has a nice selection of books, park pamphlets, gifts, and educational materials. All sales from the Association stores go to support the park programs. ✉ *East entrance* ☎ *800/858–2808, 928/638–7888* ⊙ *Daily 9–5; hrs vary in winter.*

Grand Canyon Verkamp's Visitor Center. After 102 years of selling memorabilia and knickknacks on the South Rim across from El Tovar Hotel, Verkamp's Curios moved into the park's newest visitor center in 2008. The building now serves as a bookstore, ranger station, and museum with exhibits on the Verkamp family and the pioneer history of the region. ✉ *Desert View Dr. across from El Tovar Hotel, Grand Canyon Village* ☎ *928/638–7146* ⊙ *Daily 8–7; ranger station 8–5.*

Grand Canyon Visitor Center. The park's main orientation center, known formerly as Canyon View Information Plaza, near Mather Point, provides pamphlets and resources to help plan your sightseeing as well as engaging interpretive exhibits on the park. Rangers are on hand to answer questions and aid in planning canyon excursions. A bookstore is stocked with books covering all topics on the Grand Canyon, and a daily schedule of ranger-led hikes and evening lectures is posted on a bulletin board inside. A 20-minute film about the history, geology, and wildlife of the canyon plays every 30 minutes in the theater. There's ample parking by the information center, though it is also accessible via a short walk from Mather Point, a short ride on the shuttle bus Village Route, or a leisurely 1-mile walk on the Greenway Trail—a paved pathway that meanders through the forest. ✉ *450 State Rte. 64east side of Grand Canyon Village* ☎ *928/638–7888* ⊕ *www.explorethecanyon. com* ⊙ *Daily 8–5, outdoor exhibits may be viewed anytime.*

Yavapai Geology Museum. Learn about the geology of the canyon at this museum and bookstore run by the Grand Canyon Association. You can also catch the park shuttle bus or pick up information for the Rim Trail here. The views of the canyon and Phantom Ranch from inside this historic building are stupendous. ✉ *1 mile east of Market Plaza, Grand Canyon Village* ☎ *928/638–7888* ⊙ *Daily 8–8; hrs vary in winter.*

NORTH RIM VISITOR CENTER

North Rim Visitor Center. View exhibits, peruse the bookstore, and pick up useful maps and brochures at this visitor center. Interpretive programs are often scheduled in summer. If you're craving coffee, it's a short walk from here to the Roughrider Saloon at the Grand Canyon Lodge. ✉ *Near the parking lot on Bright Angel Peninsula* ☎ *928/638–7864* ⊕ *www.nps.gov/grca* ⊙ *Mid-May–mid-Oct., daily 8–6; mid-Oct.–Nov., daily 9–4.*

18

GRAND CANYON SOUTH RIM

EXPLORING

Visitors to the canyon converge mostly on the South Rim, and mostly in summer. Grand Canyon Village is here, with most of the park's lodging and camping, trailheads, restaurants, stores, and museums, along with a nearby airport and railroad depot. Believe it or not, the average stay in the park is a mere half day or so; this is not advised! You need to spend several days to truly appreciate this marvelous place, but at the very least, give it a full day. Hike down into the canyon, or along the rim, to get away from the crowds and experience nature at its finest.

SCENIC DRIVES

Hermit Road. The Santa Fe Company built Hermit Road, formerly known as West Rim Drive, in 1912 as a scenic tour route. Nine overlooks dot this 7-mile stretch, each worth a visit. The road is filled with hairpin turns, so make sure you adhere to posted speed limits. A 1.5-mile Greenway trail offers easy access to cyclists looking to enjoy the original 1912 Hermit Rim Road. From March through November, Hermit Road is closed to private auto traffic because of congestion; during this period, a free shuttle bus carries visitors to all the overlooks. Riding the bus round-trip without getting off at any of the viewpoints takes 75 minutes; the return trip stops only at Pima, Mohave, and Powell points.

HISTORIC SITES

Tusayan Ruin and Museum. Completed in 1932, this museum offers a quick orientation to the lifestyles of the prehistoric and modern Indian populations associated with the Grand Canyon and the Colorado Plateau. Adjacent, an excavation of an 800-year-old dwelling gives a glimpse of the lives of some of the area's earliest residents. Of special interest are split-twig figurines dating back 2,000 to 4,000 years, a replica of a 10,000-year-old spear point, and other artifacts left behind from by ancient cultures. Twice daily, a ranger leads an interpretive tour of the Ancestral Puebloan village along a 0.1-mile, paved loop trail. ⊠ *Desert View Dr., about 20 miles east of Grand Canyon Village* ☎ *928/638–7888* 🎫 *Free* ☉ *Daily 9–5.*

SCENIC STOPS

The Abyss. At an elevation of 6,720 feet, the Abyss is one of the most awesome stops on Hermit Road, revealing a sheer drop of 3,000 feet to the Tonto Platform, a wide terrace of Tapeats sandstone about two-thirds of the way down the canyon. From the Abyss you'll also see several isolated sandstone columns, the largest of which is called the Monument. ⊠ *Hermit Rd., about 5 miles west of Hermit Rd. Junction*

Desert View and Watchtower. From the top of the 70-foot stone-and-mortar watchtower, even the muted hues of the distant Painted Desert to the east and the Vermilion Cliffs rising from a high plateau near the Utah border are visible. In the chasm below, angling to the north toward Marble Canyon, an imposing stretch of the Colorado River reveals

Plants and Wildlife in the Grand Canyon

Eighty-nine mammal species inhabit Grand Canyon National Park, as well as 355 species of birds, 56 kinds of reptiles and amphibians, and 17 kinds of fish. The rare Kaibab squirrel is found only on the North Rim—you can recognize them by their all-white tails and black undersides. The pink Grand Canyon rattlesnake lives at lower elevations within the canyon. Hawks and ravens are visible year-round. The endangered California condor has been reintroduced to the canyon region. Park rangers give daily talks on the magnificent birds, whose wingspan measures 9 feet. In spring, summer, and fall, mule deer, recognizable by their large ears, are abundant at the South Rim. Don't be fooled by gentle appearances; these guys can be aggressive. It's illegal to feed them, as it'll disrupt their natural habitats, and increase your risk of getting bitten or kicked.

The best times to see wildlife are early in the morning and late in the afternoon. Look for out-of-place shapes and motions, keeping in mind that animals occupy all layers in a natural habitat and not just at your eye level. Use binoculars for close-up views. While out and about try to fade into the woodwork by keeping your movements limited and noise at a minimum.

More than 1,700 species of plants color the park. The South Rim's Coconino Plateau is fairly flat, at an elevation of about 7,000 feet, and covered with stands of pinyon and ponderosa pines, junipers, and Gambel's oak trees. On the Kaibab Plateau on the North Rim, Douglas fir, spruce, quaking aspen, and more ponderosas prevail. In spring you're likely to see asters, sunflowers, and lupine in bloom at both rims.

18

itself. Up several flights of stairs, the watchtower houses a glass-enclosed observatory with powerful telescopes. ⊠ *Desert View Dr., about 23 miles east of Grand Canyon Village* ☎ *928/638–2736* ⊙ *Daily 8–8; hrs vary in winter.*

Hermits Rest. This westernmost viewpoint and Hermit Trail, which descends from it, were named for "hermit" Louis Boucher, a 19th-century French-Canadian prospector who had a number of mining claims and a roughly built home down in the canyon. Views from here include Hermit Rapids and the towering cliffs of the Supai and Redwall formations. In the stone building at Hermits Rest you can buy curios and snacks. ⊠ *Hermit Rd., about 8 miles west of Hermit Rd. Junction*

Hopi Point. From this elevation of 6,800 feet, you can see a large section of the Colorado River; although it appears as a thin line, the river is nearly 350 feet wide below this overlook. The overlook extends farther into the canyon than any other point on Hermit Road. The unobstructed views make this a popular place to watch the sunset.

Across the canyon to the north is Shiva Temple, which remained an unexplored section of the Kaibab Plateau until 1937. That year, Harold Anthony of the American Museum of Natural History led an expedition to the rock formation in the belief that it supported life that had

BEST GRAND CANYON VIEWS

The best time of day to see the canyon is before 10 am and after 4 pm, when the angle of the sun brings out the colors of the rock, and clouds and shadows add dimension. Colors deepen dramatically among the contrasting layers of the canyon walls just before and during sunrise and sunset.

Hopi Point is the top spot on the South Rim to watch the sun set; **Yaki** and **Pima** points also offer vivid views. For a grand sunrise, try **Mather** or **Yaki** points.

■TIP➔ Arrive at least 30 minutes early for sunrise views and as much as 90 minutes for sunset views at these points. For another point of view, take a leisurely stroll along the Rim Trail and watch the color change along with the views. Timetables are listed in the *Guide* and are posted at park visitor centers.

been cut off from the rest of the canyon. Imagine the expedition members' surprise when they found an empty Kodak film box on top of the temple—it had been left behind by Emery Kolb, who felt slighted for not having been invited to partake of Anthony's tour.

Directly below Hopi Point lies Dana Butte, named for a prominent 19th-century geologist. In 1919, an entrepreneur proposed connecting Hopi Point, Dana Butte, and the Tower of Set across the river with an aerial tramway, a technically feasible plan that fortunately has not been realized. ⊠ *Hermit Rd., about 4 miles west of Hermit Rd. Junction.*

Lipan Point. Here, at the canyon's widest point, you can get an astonishing visual profile of the gorge's geologic history, with a view of every eroded layer of the canyon—you can also observe one of the longest stretches of visible Colorado River. The spacious panorama stretches to the Vermilion Cliffs on the northeastern horizon and features a multitude of imaginatively named spires, buttes, and temples—intriguing rock formations named after their resemblance to ancient pyramids. You can also see Unkar Delta, where a creek joins the Colorado to form powerful rapids and a broad beach. Ancestral Puebloan farmers worked the Unkar Delta for hundreds of years, growing corn, beans, and melons. ⊠ *Desert View Dr., about 25 miles east of Grand Canyon Village.*

Mather Point. You'll likely get your first glimpse of the canyon from this viewpoint, one of the most impressive and accessible (and most crowded) on the South Rim. Named for the National Park Service's first director, Stephen Mather, this spot yields extraordinary views of the Grand Canyon, including deep into the inner gorge and numerous buttes: Wotans Throne, Brahma Temple, and Zoroaster Temple, among others. The Grand Canyon Lodge, on the North Rim, is almost directly north from Mather Point and only 10 miles away—yet you have to drive 215 miles to get from one spot to the other. ⊠ *Near Grand Canyon Visitor Center* ☎ *928/638–7888* ⊕ *www.nps.gov/grca.*

Moran Point. This point was named for American landscape artist Thomas Moran, who was especially fond of the play of light and shadows from this location. He first visited the canyon with John Wesley

Powell in 1873. "Thomas Moran's name, more than any other, with the possible exception of Major Powell's, is to be associated with the Grand Canyon," wrote noted canyon photographer Ellsworth Kolb. It's fitting that Moran Point is a favorite spot of photographers and painters. ⊠ *Desert View Dr., about 17 miles east of Grand Canyon Village.*

Trailview Overlook. Look down on a dramatic view of the Bright Angel and Plateau Point trails as they zigzag down the canyon. In the deep gorge to the north flows Bright Angel Creek, one of the region's few permanent tributary streams of the Colorado River. Toward the south is an unobstructed view of the distant San Francisco Peaks, as well as Bill Williams Mountain (on the horizon) and Red Butte (about 15 miles south of the canyon rim). ⊠ *Hermit Rd., about 2 miles west of Hermit Rd. Junction.*

Yaki Point. Stop here for an exceptional view of Wotan's Throne, a flat-top butte named by François Matthes, a U.S. Geological Survey scientist who developed the first topographical map of the Grand Canyon. The overlook juts out over the canyon, providing unobstructed views of inner-canyon rock formations, South Rim cliffs, and Clear Creek canyon. About a mile south of Yaki Point, you'll come to the trailhead for the South Kaibab Trail. The point is one of the best places on the South Rim to watch the sunset. ⊠ *Desert View Dr., 2 miles east of Grand Canyon Village.*

Fodor's Choice **Yavapai Point.** This is also one of the best locations on the South Rim
★ to watch the sunset. Dominated by the Yavapai Geology Museum and Observation Station, this point displays panoramic views of the mighty gorge through a wall of windows. Exhibits at the museum include videos of the canyon floor and the Colorado River, a scaled diorama of the canyon with national park boundaries, fossils and rock fragments used to re-create the complex layers of the canyon walls, and a display on the natural forces used to carve the chasm. Rangers dig even deeper into Grand Canyon geology with free ranger programs daily. Check ahead for special events, guided walks, and program schedules. There's also a bookstore. ⊠ *Adjacent to Grand Canyon Village* 🖃 *Free* ⊙ *Daily 8–8; hrs vary in winter.*

EDUCATIONAL OFFERINGS

Grand Canyon Field Institute. Instructors lead guided educational tours, hikes around the canyon, and weekend programs at the South Rim. With more than 200 classes a year, tour topics include everything from archaeology and backcountry medicine to photography and natural history. Contact GCFI for a schedule and price list. Private hikes can be arranged. Discounted classes are available for members; annual dues are $35. ☎ *928/638–2485, 866/471–4435* ⊕ *www.grandcanyon.org/ fieldinstitute* 🖃 *$475–$850 for most classes.*

RANGER PROGRAMS

Interpretive Ranger Programs. The National Park Service sponsors all sorts of orientation activities, such as daily guided hikes and talks, which change with the seasons. The focus may be on any aspect of the canyon—from geology and flora and fauna to history and early inhabitants. For schedules on the South Rim, go to Grand Canyon Visitor Center, pick up a free copy of the *Guide,* or check online. ☎ *928/638–7888* ⊕ *www.nps.gov/grca* 🖃 *Free.*

18

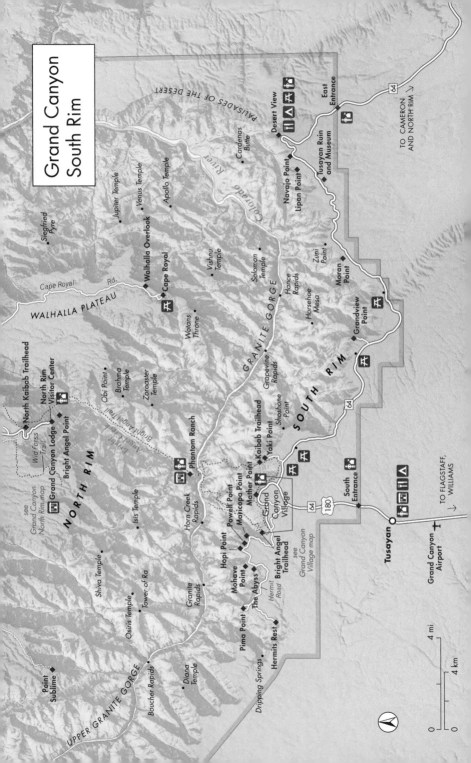

Grand Canyon South Rim

PALISADES OF THE DESERT

Colorado River

GRANITE GORGE

UPPER GRANITE GORGE

WALHALLA PLATEAU

Cape Royal Rd.

NORTH RIM

SOUTH RIM

Siegfried Pyre

Jupiter Temple

Venus Temple

Apollo Temple

Cardenas Butte

Walhalla Overlook

Cape Royal

Vishnu Temple

Wotans Throne

Solomon Temple

Hance Rapids

Horseshoe Mesa

Zuni Point

Moran Point

Navajo Point

Lipan Point

Desert View

Tusayan Ruin and Museum

East Entrance

TO CAMERON AND NORTH RIM

Obi Point

Brahma Temple

Zoroaster Temple

North Kaibab Trailhead

North Rim Visitor Center

Wid Forks Trail

Bright Angel Point

Grand Canyon Lodge

see Grand Canyon North Rim map

Bright Angel Trail

North Kaibab Trail

Phantom Ranch

Grapevine Rapids

Shoshone Point

Kaibab Trailhead

Yaki Point

Grandview Point

Isis Temple

Horn Creek Rapids

Powell Point

Maricopa Point

Mother Point

Grand Canyon Village

see Grand Canyon Village map

South Entrance

TO FLAGSTAFF, WILLIAMS

Shiva Temple

Tower of Ra

Hopi Point

Mohave Point

The Abyss

Bright Angel Trailhead

Hermit Road

Tusayan

Grand Canyon Airport

Osiris Temple

Granite Rapids

Pima Point

Hermits Rest

Diana Temple

Dripping Springs

Boucher Rapids

Point Sublime

4 mi

4 km

0

0

FAMILY **Junior Ranger Program for Families.** The Junior Ranger Program provides a free, fun way to look at the cultural and natural history of this sublime destination. These hands-on educational programs for children ages 4 and up include guided adventure hikes, ranger-led "discovery" activities, and book readings. ☎ 928/638–7888 ⊕ *www.nps.gov/grca/forkids/ beajuniorranger.htm* ✉ *Free.*

SPORTS AND THE OUTDOORS

AIR TOURS
Flights by plane and helicopter over the canyon are offered by a number of companies, departing for the Grand Canyon Airport at the south end of Tusayan. Though the noise and disruption of so many aircraft buzzing the canyon is controversial, flightseeing remains a popular, if expensive, option. You'll have more visibility from a helicopter but they're louder and more expensive than the fixed-wing planes. Prices and lengths of tours vary, but you can expect to pay about $149 per adult for short plane trips and approximately $179–$250 for brief helicopter tours (and about $450 for tours leaving from Vegas). These companies often have significant discounts in winter—check the company websites to find the best deals.

Grand Canyon Airlines. Grand Canyon Airlines fly fixed-wing aircraft on a 50-minute tour of the eastern edge of the Grand Canyon, the North Rim, and the Kaibab Plateau. All-day combination tours combine flightseeing with four-wheel-drive tours and float trips on the Colorado River. The company also schedules helicopter tours that leave from Las Vegas (plane flight from Las Vegas to Grand Canyon Airport, then helicopter flight into the canyon). ✉ *Grand Canyon Airport, Tusayan* ☎ 928/638–2359, 866/235–9422 ⊕ *www.grandcanyonairlines.com.*

Maverick Helicopters. Maverick Helicopters offers 25- and 45-minute tours of the South Rim, North Rim, and Dragon Corridor of the Grand Canyon. A landing tour option for those leaving from Las Vegas sets you down in the canyon for a short snack below the rim. ✉ *Grand Canyon Airport, 6075 South Las Vegas Blvd., Grand Canyon* ☎ 928/638–2622, 800/962–3869 ⊕ *www.flymaverick.com.*

Papillon Grand Canyon Helicopters. Papillon Grand Canyon Helicopters offers a variety of fixed-wing and helicopter tours, leaving both from Grand Canyon Airport and Vegas, of the canyon. Combination tour options include off-road jeep tours and smooth-water rafting trips. ✉ *Grand Canyon Airport, Tusayan* ☎ 928/638–2764, 888/635–7272 ⊕ *www.papillon.com.*

HIKING
Although permits are not required for day hikes, you must have a backcountry permit for longer trips *(⇨ See Park Fees and Permits at the start of this chapter).* Some of the more popular trails are listed here; more detailed information and maps can be obtained from the Backcountry Information Centers. Also, rangers can help design a trip to suit your abilities.

18

Remember that the canyon has significant elevation changes and, in summer, extreme temperature ranges, which can pose problems for people who aren't in good shape or who have heart or respiratory problems. ■TIP➔ **Carry plenty of water and energy foods.** The majority of each year's 400 search-and-rescue incidents result from hikers underestimating the size of the canyon, hiking beyond their abilities, or not packing sufficient food and water.

⚠ **Under no circumstances should you attempt a day hike from the rim to the river and back.** Remember that when it's 80°F on the South Rim, it's 110°F on the canyon floor. Allow two to four days if you want to hike rim to rim (it's easier to descend from the North Rim, as it's more than 1,000 feet higher than the South Rim). Hiking steep trails from rim to rim is a strenuous trek of at least 21 miles and should only be attempted by experienced canyon hikers.

EASY

Fodor'sChoice **Rim Trail.** The South Rim's most popular walking path is the 12-mile
★ (one-way) Rim Trail, which runs along the edge of the canyon from Pipe Creek Vista (the first overlook on Desert View Drive) to Hermits Rest. This walk, which is paved to Maricopa Point and for the last 1.5 miles to Hermits Rest, visits several of the South Rim's historic landmarks. Allow anywhere from 15 minutes to a full day, depending on how much of the trail you want to cover; the Rim Trail is an ideal day hike, as it varies only a few hundred feet in elevation from Mather Point (7,120 feet) to the trailhead at Hermits Rest (6,650 feet). The trail also can be accessed from several spots in Grand Canyon Village and from the major viewpoints along Hermit Road, which are serviced by shuttle buses during the busy summer months. *Easy.* ■TIP➔ **On the Rim Trail, water is only available in the Grand Canyon Village area and at Hermits Rest.**

MODERATE

Bright Angel Trail. This well-maintained trail is one of the most scenic hiking paths from the South Rim to the bottom of the canyon (9.6 miles each way). Rest houses are equipped with water at the 1.5- and 3-mile points from May through September and at Indian Garden (4 miles) year-round. Water is also available at Bright Angel Campground, 9.25 miles below the trailhead. Plateau Point, on a spur trail about 1.5 miles below Indian Garden, is as far as you should attempt to go on a day hike; the round trip will take six to nine hours.

Bright Angel Trail is the easiest of all the footpaths into the canyon, but because the climb out from the bottom is an ascent of 5,510 feet, the trip should be attempted only by those in good physical condition and should be avoided in midsummer due to extreme heat. The top of the trail can be icy in winter. Originally a bighorn sheep path and later used by the Havasupai, the trail was widened late in the 19th century for prospectors and is now used for both mule and foot traffic. Also note that mule trains have the right-of-way—and sometimes leave unpleasant surprises in your path. *Moderate.* ⊠ *Trailhead at Kolb Studio, Hermits Rd.*

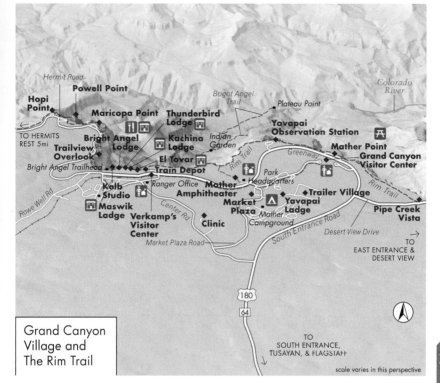

Grand Canyon
Village and
The Rim Trail

scale varies in this perspective

18

DIFFICULT

South Kaibab Trail. This trail starts near Yaki Point, 4 miles east of Grand Canyon Village and is accessible via the free shuttle bus. Because the route is so steep (and sometimes icy in winter)—descending from the trailhead at 7,260 feet down to 2,480 feet at the Colorado River—and has no water, many hikers take this trail down, then ascend via the less-demanding Bright Angel Trail. Allow four to six hours to reach the Colorado River on this 6.4-mile trek. At the river, the trail crosses a suspension bridge and runs on to Phantom Ranch. Along the trail there is no water and very little shade. There are no campgrounds, though there are portable toilets at Cedar Ridge (6,320 feet), 1.5 miles from the trailhead. Toilets and an emergency phone are also available at the Tipoff, 4.6 miles down the trail (3 miles past Cedar Ridge). The trail corkscrews down through some spectacular geology. Look for (but don't remove) fossils in the limestone when taking water breaks. ■ TIP➔ Even though an immense network of trails winds through the Grand Canyon, the popular corridor trails (Bright Angel and South Kaibab) are recommended for hikers new to the region. *Difficult.* ⊠ *Trailhead at Yaki Point, Desert View Dr.*

MULE RIDES

Mule rides provide an intimate glimpse into the canyon for those who have the time, but not the stamina, to see the canyon on foot. ■TIP→ Reservations are essential and are accepted up to 13 months in advance.

These trips have been conducted since the early 1900s. A comforting fact as you ride the narrow trail: no one's ever been killed while riding a mule that fell off a cliff. (Nevertheless, the treks are not for the faint of heart or people in questionable health.)

TOURS AND OUTFITTERS

Xanterra Parks & Resorts Mule Rides. These trips delve into the canyon from the South Rim to Phantom Ranch, or east along the canyon's edge (the Plateau Point rides were discontinued in 2009). Riders must be at least 55 inches tall, weigh less than 200 pounds, and understand English. Children under 15 must be accompanied by an adult. Riders must be in fairly good physical condition, and pregnant women are advised not to take these trips.

The three-hour ride along the rim costs $125 (water and snack included). An overnight with a stay at Phantom Ranch at the bottom of the canyon is $507 ($895 for two riders). Two nights at Phantom Ranch, an option available from November through March, will set you back $714 ($1,192 for two). Meals are included. Reservations (by phone), especially during the busy summer months, are a must, but you can check at the Bright Angel Transportation Desk to see if there's last-minute availability. ☎ 888/297–2757 ⊕ www.grandcanyonlodges. com ⌨ Reservations essential ⊗ Phantom Ranch rides daily; Rim rides mid-Mar.–Oct., twice daily; Nov.–mid-Mar., once daily.

GRAND CANYON NORTH RIM

The North Rim stands 1,000 feet higher than the South Rim and has a more alpine climate, with twice as much annual precipitation. Here, in the deep forests of the Kaibab Plateau, the crowds are thinner, the facilities fewer, and the views even more spectacular. Due to snow, the North Rim is off-limits in winter. The buildings and concessions are closed November through mid-May. The road and entrance gate close when the snow makes them impassable—usually by the end of November.

Lodgings are limited in this more remote park, with only one historic lodge (with cabins and hotel-type rooms as well as a restaurant) and a single campground. Dining options have opened up a little with the addition of the Grand Cookout, offered nightly with live entertainment under the stars. Your best bet may be to pack your camping gear and hiking boots and take several days to explore the lush Kaibab Forest. The canyon's highest, most dramatic rim views also can be enjoyed on two wheels (via primitive dirt access roads) and on four legs (courtesy of a trusty mule).

EXPLORING

SCENIC DRIVE

Highway 67. Open mid-May to roughly mid-November (or the first big snowfall), the two-lane paved road climbs 1,400 feet in elevation as it passes through the Kaibab National Forest. Also called the "North Rim Parkway," this scenic route crosses the limestone-capped Kaibab Plateau—passing broad meadows, sun-dappled forests, and small lakes and springs—before abruptly falling away at the abyss of the Grand Canyon. Wildlife abounds in the thick ponderosa pine forests and lush mountain meadows. It's common to see deer, turkeys, and coyotes as you drive through this remote region. Point Imperial and Cape Royal branch off this scenic drive, which runs from Jacob Lake to Bright Angel Point.

HISTORIC SITE

Grand Canyon Lodge. Built in 1937 by the Union Pacific Railroad (replacing the original 1928 building, which burned in a fire), the massive stone structure is listed on the National Register of Historic Places. Its huge sunroom has hardwood floors, high-beam ceilings, and a marvelous view of the canyon through plate-glass windows. On warm days, visitors sit in the sun and drink in the surrounding beauty on an outdoor viewing deck, where National Park Service employees deliver free lectures on geology and history. ⊠ *10 Albright St., off Hwy. 67 near Bright Angel Point* ☎ *928/638–2631* ⊕ *www.grandcanyonlodges.com.*

SCENIC STOPS

Bright Angel Point. This trail, which leads to one of the most awe-inspiring overlooks on either rim, starts on the grounds of the Grand Canyon Lodge and runs along the crest of a point of rocks that juts into the canyon for several hundred yards. The walk is only 0.5 mile round-trip, but it's an exciting trek accented by sheer drops on each side of the trail. In a few spots where the route is extremely narrow, metal railings ensure visitors' safety. The temptation to clamber out to precarious perches to have your picture taken could get you killed—every year several people die from falls at the Grand Canyon. ⊠ *North Rim Dr.*

Cape Royal. A popular sunset destination, Cape Royal showcases the canyon's jagged landscape; you'll also get a glimpse of the Colorado River, framed by a natural stone arch called Angels Window. In autumn, the aspens turn a beautiful gold, adding even more color to an already magnificent scene of the forested surroundings. The easy and rewarding 1-mile round-trip hike along **Cliff Springs Trail** starts here; it takes you through a forested ravine and terminates at Cliff Springs, where the forest opens to another impressive view of the canyon walls. ⊠ *Cape Royal Scenic Dr., 23 miles southeast of Grand Canyon Lodge.*

Point Imperial. At 8,803 feet, Point Imperial has the highest vista point at either rim. It offers magnificent views of both the canyon and the distant country: the Vermilion Cliffs to the north, the 10,000-foot Navajo Mountain in Utah to the northeast, the Painted Desert to the east, and the Little Colorado River canyon to the southeast. Other prominent points of interest include views of Mount Hayden, Saddle Mountain, and Marble Canyon. ⊠ *Point Imperial Rd., 2.7 miles off Cape Royal Rd., 11 miles northeast of Grand Canyon Lodge.*

Fodor's Choice
★

Point Sublime. You can camp within feet of the canyon's edge at this awe-inspiring site. Sunrises and sunsets are spectacular. The winding road, through gorgeous high country, is only 17 miles, but it will take you at least two hours, one-way. The road is intended only for vehicles with high-road clearance (pickups and four-wheel-drive vehicles). It is also necessary to be properly equipped for wilderness road travel. Check with a park ranger or at the information desk at Grand Canyon Lodge before taking this journey. You may camp here only with a permit from the Backcountry Information Center. ⊠ *North Rim Dr., about 20 miles west of North Rim Visitor Center.*

Roosevelt Point. Named after the president who gave the Grand Canyon its national monument status in 1908 (it was upgraded to national park status in 1919), Roosevelt Point is the best place to see the confluence of the Little Colorado River and the Grand Canyon. The cliffs above the Colorado River south of the junction are known as the Palisades of the Desert. A short woodland loop trail leads to this eastern viewpoint. ⊠ *Cape Royal Rd., 18 miles east of Grand Canyon Lodge.*

EDUCATIONAL OFFERINGS
RANGER PROGRAMS

FAMILY **Discovery Pack Junior Ranger Program.** In summer, children ages 6 to 14 can take part in these hands-on educational programs and earn a Junior Ranger certificate and badge. Children meet at park headquarters to attend a 1½-hour ranger-led session first. ☎ *928/638–7967* ⊕ *www.nps.gov/grca* ⊠ *Free* ☉ *Mid-June to Labor Day, meets daily at 9.*

Interpretive Ranger Programs. Daily guided hikes and talks during one of the programs offered may focus on any aspect of the canyon—from geology and flora and fauna to history and the canyon's early inhabitants. For schedules, go to the Grand Canyon Lodge or download a free copy of the *Guide* to the North Rim from the park website. ☎ *928/638–7967* ⊕ *www.nps.gov/grca* ⊠ *Free.*

18

SPORTS AND THE OUTDOORS

HIKING
EASY

Cape Final Trail. This 2-mile gravel path follows an old jeep trail through a ponderosa pine forest to the canyon overlook at Cape Final with panoramic views of the northern canyon, the Palisades of the Desert, and the impressive spectacle of Juno Temple. *Easy.* ⊠ *Trailhead at dirt parking lot on Cape Royal Rd., 5 miles south of Roosevelt Point.*

Grand Canyon
North Rim

0 5 mi
0 5 km

SOUTH CANYON

MARBLE CANYON

445

TO
JACOB LAKE,
MARBLE CANYON
AND SOUTH RIM

67

KAIBAB PLATEAU

North Rim
Entrance Station

Tatahatso
Point

Point
Hansbrough

PAINTED DESERT

NAVAJO
INDIAN
RESERVATION

Nankoweap
Rapids

TO
POINT SUBLIME

Point Imperial

Bourke Point

Nankoweap
Mesa

Point Imperial Road

Kwagunt Butte

NORTH RIM

Ken Patrick
Trail

Vista Encantada

Tritle Peak

Roosevelt Point

Atoko Point

Wildforss Trail

North Rim
Visitor Center

WALHALLA PLATEAU

Siegfried Pyre

Chuar Butte

Grand Canyon Lodge
Bright Angel Point

Shiva Temple

Cottonwood
Campground

Bright Angel Creek

North Kaibab Trail

Obi Point

Cape Royal Road

Temple Butte

Cape Final
Trail

Walhalla
Ruins

Jupiter Temple

Osiris Temple

Isis Temple

Brahma
Temple

Venus Temple

Granite
Rapids

Zoroaster
Temple

Cliff Springs
Trail

Cape Royal

Apollo Temple

Horn Creek
Rapids

Phantom Ranch

Cape Royal
Trail

Wotans
Throne

Vishnu
Temple

Cardenas
Butte

Bright Angel Trail

Hopi
Point

SOUTH RIM

GRANITE GORGE

Solomon
Temple

PALISADES OF THE DESERT

The
Abyss

Mather
Point

South Kaibab
Trail

Grapevine
Rapids

Desert View

Hermit
Road

Yaki Point

64

Grand Canyon Village

Hance
Rapids

Navajo Point

Lipan Point

TO FLAGSTAFF,
WILLIAMS

Colorado River

FAMILY **Roosevelt Point Trail.** This easy 0.2-mile round-trip trail loops through the forest to the scenic viewpoint. Allow 20 minutes for this short, secluded hike. *Easy.* ⊠ *Trailhead at Cape Royal Rd.* ⊕ *www.nps.gov/grca.*

FAMILY **Transept Trail.** This 3-mile (round-trip), 1½-hour trail begins near the Grand Canyon Lodge at 8,255 feet. Well maintained and well marked, it has little elevation change, sticking near the rim before reaching a dramatic view of a large stream through Bright Angel Canyon. The route leads to a side canyon called Transept Canyon, which geologist Clarence Dutton named in 1882, declaring it "far grander than Yosemite." Check the posted schedule to find a ranger talk along this trail; it's also a great place to view fall foliage. Flash floods can occur any time of the year, especially June through September when thunderstorms develop rapidly. *Easy.* ⊠ *Trailhead at near the Grand Canyon Lodge's east patio.*

MODERATE

Uncle Jim Trail. This 5-mile, three-hour loop starts at 8,300 feet and winds south through the forest, past Roaring Springs and Bright Angel canyons. The highlight of this rim hike is Uncle Jim Point, which, at 8,244 feet, overlooks the upper sections of the North Kaibab Trail. *Moderate.* ⊠ *Trailhead at North Kaibab Trail parking lot.*

Widforss Trail. Round-trip, Widforss Trail is 9.8 miles, with an elevation change of only 200 feet. Allow five to six hours for the hike, which starts at 8,080 feet and passes through shady forests of pine, spruce, fir, and aspen on its way to Widforss Point, at 7,900 feet. Here you'll have good views of five temples: Zoroaster, Brahma, and Deva to the southeast and Buddha and Manu to the southwest. You are likely to see wildflowers in summer, and this is a good trail for viewing fall foliage. It's named in honor of artist Gunnar M. Widforss, renowned for his paintings of national park landscapes. *Moderate.* ⊠ *Trailhead at Point Sublime Rd.*

DIFFICULT

North Kaibab Trail. At 8,241 feet, this trail, like the roads leading to the North Rim, is open only from May through late October or early November (depending on the weather). It is recommended for experienced hikers only, who should allow four days for the full hike. The long, steep path drops 5,840 feet over a distance of 14.5 miles to Phantom Ranch and the Colorado River, so the National Park Service suggests that day hikers not go farther than Roaring Springs (5,020 feet) before turning to hike back up out of the canyon. After about 7 miles, Cottonwood Campground (4,080 feet) has drinking water in summer, restrooms, shade trees, and a ranger. *Difficult.* ■TIP➔ A free shuttle takes hikers to the North Kaibab trailhead twice daily from Grand Canyon Lodge; reserve a spot the day before. ⊠ *Trailhead is 2 miles north of the Grand Canyon Lodge.*

MULE RIDES

TOURS AND OUTFITTERS

FAMILY **Canyon Trail Rides.** This company leads mule rides on the easier trails of the North Rim. A one-hour ride (minimum age seven) runs $40. Half-day trips on the rim or into the canyon (minimum age 10) cost $80. Weight limits are 200 pounds for canyon rides and 220 pounds for the rim rides. Available daily from May 15 to October 15, these excursions are popular, so make reservations in advance. ☎ *435/679–8665* ⊕ *www.canyonrides.com.*

18

GRAND CANYON WEST RIM

The West Rim is a 5-hour drive from the South Rim of Grand Canyon National Park or a 2½-hour drive from Las Vegas. From Kingman, drive north 30 miles on U.S. 93, and then turn right onto Pierce Ferry Road and follow it for 28 miles. (A more scenic alternative is to drive 42 miles north on Stockton Hill Road, turning right onto Pierce Ferry Road for 7 miles, but this takes a bit longer because Stockton Hill Road has a lower speed limit than the wide, divided U.S. 93 highway.) Turn right (east) on to Diamond Bar Road and follow for 21 miles to Grand Canyon West entrance.

The dusty, bumpy 9-mile stretch of unpaved road leading to Grand Canyon West isn't recommended for RVs and low-clearance vehicles; however, this road is scheduled to be paved by early 2014. For a gentler approach to the West Rim, visitors can park at the Grand Canyon West Park & Ride Station on Pierce Ferry Road and take a shuttle to the West Rim ($16 per person); reservations are recommended.

Visitors aren't allowed to travel in their own vehicles to the viewpoints once they reach the West Rim, and must purchase a tour package—which can range from day use to horseback or helicopter rides to lodging and meals—from Hualapai Tourism.

EXPLORING

Hualapai Tourism. At the Welcome Center, Hualapai Tourism, run by the Hualapai tribe, offers the basic Hualapai Legacy tour package ($44 per person, including taxes and fees), which includes a Hualapai visitation permit and "hop-on, hop-off" shuttle transportation to three sites. The shuttle will take you to Eagle Point, where the Indian Village walking tour visits authentic dwellings. Educational displays there uncover the culture of five different American Indian tribes (Havasupai, Plains, Hopi, Hualapai, and Navajo), and intertribal, powwow-style dance performances entertain visitors at the nearby amphitheater. The shuttle also goes to Hualapai Ranch, site of Western performances, cookouts, horseback and wagon rides, and the only lodging on the West Rim; and Guano Point, where the "High Point Hike" offers panoramic views of the Colorado River. At all three areas, local Hualapai guides and roaming "ambassadors" add a American Indian perspective to a canyon trip that you won't find on North and South Rim tours.

For extra fees, you can add meals (there are cafés at each of the three stops), overnight lodging at Hualapai Ranch, a helicopter trip into the canyon, a pontoon boat trip on the Colorado, a horseback ride along the canyon rim, or a walk on the Skywalk.

At this writing, a three-level, 6,000-square-foot visitor center is planned. The date of completion is currently uncertain, but eventually this complex is expected to include a museum, movie theater, gift shop, and at least two restaurants. ✉ *Grand Canyon West* ☎ *928/769–2636, 888/868–9378* ⊕ *www.hualapaitourism.com* 🖼 *$44* ☉ *Daily.*

Grand Canyon Skywalk. The Skywalk, which opened in 2007, is a cantilevered glass terrace suspended nearly 4,000 feet above the Colorado River and extends 70 feet from the edge of the Grand Canyon. Approximately 10 feet wide, the bridge's deck, made of tempered glass several inches thick, has 5-foot glass railings on each side creating an unobstructed open-air platform. Admission to the skywalk is a separate add-on to the basic Grand Canyon West admission. Visitors must store personal items, including cameras, cell phones, and video cameras, in lockers before entering. A professional photographer takes photographs of visitors, which can be purchased from the gift shop. ⊕ *www. hualapaitourism.com* ✉ *$29.95*

> **EXPLORING AMERICAN INDIAN COUNTRY**
>
> When visiting Native American reservations, respect tribal laws and customs. Remember you are a guest in a sovereign nation. Do not wander into residential areas or take photographs of residents without first asking permission. Possessing or consuming alcohol is illegal on tribal lands. In general, the Hualapai and Havasupai are quiet, private people. Offer respect and do not pursue conversations or personal interactions unless invited to do so.

WHAT'S NEARBY

The northwest section of Arizona is geographically fascinating. In addition to the Grand Canyon, it's home to national forests, national monuments, and national recreation areas. Towns, however, are small and scattered. Many of them cater to visiting adventurers, and Native American reservations dot the map.

18

NEARBY TOWNS

Towns near the canyon's South Rim include the tiny town of Tusayan, 1 mile south of the entrance station, and Williams, the "Gateway to the Grand Canyon," 58 miles south.

Tusayan has basic amenities and an airport that serves as a starting point for airplane and helicopter tours of the canyon. The cozy mountain town of **Williams,** founded in 1882 when the railroad passed through, was once a rough-and-tumble joint, replete with saloons and bordellos. Today it reflects a much milder side of the Wild West, with 3,300 residents and more than 25 motels and hotels. Wander along the main street—part of historic Route 66, but locally named, like the town, after trapper Bill Williams—and indulge in Route 66 nostalgia inside antiques shops or souvenir and T-shirt stores.

The communities closest to the North Rim—all of them tiny and with limited services—include Fredonia, 76 miles north; Marble Canyon, 80 miles northeast; Lees Ferry, 85 miles east; and Jacob Lake, 45 miles north.

Fredonia, a small community of about 1,050, approximately an hour's drive north of the Grand Canyon, is often referred to as the gateway to the North Rim; it's also relatively close to Zion and Bryce Canyon national parks in Utah. **Marble Canyon** marks the geographical beginning of the Grand Canyon at its northeastern tip. It's a good stopping point if you're driving U.S. 89 to the North Rim. En route from the South Rim to the North Rim is **Lees Ferry,** where most of the area's river rafts start their journey. The tiny town of **Jacob Lake,** nestled high in pine country at an elevation of 7,925 feet, was named after Mormon explorer Jacob Hamblin, also known as the "Buckskin Missionary." It has a hotel, café, campground, and lush mountain countryside.

VISITOR INFORMATION

Kaibab National Forest, North District ⊠ *430 S. Main St., Fredonia* ☎ *928/643–7395* ⊕ *www.fs.usda.gov/kaibab.* **Kaibab National Forest, Tusayan Ranger District** ⊠ *176 Lincoln Log Loop, Grand Canyon* ☎ *928/638–2443* ⊕ *www.fs.usda.gov/kaibab.* **Kaibab Plateau Visitor Center** ⊠ *Hwy. 89A/AZ 67, HC 64, Jacob Lake* ☎ *928/643–7298* ⊕ *www.fs.usda.gov/kaibab* ☉ *Closed Dec.–mid-May.* **Williams Visitor Center** ⊠ *200 W. Railroad Ave., at Grand Canyon Blvd., Williams* ☎ *928/635–1418, 800/863–0546* ⊕ *www.experiencewilliams.com* ☉ *Daily 8–5.*

NEARBY ATTRACTIONS

National Geographic Visitor Center Grand Canyon. Here you can schedule and purchase tickets for air tours, buy a national park pass, and access the park by special entry lanes. However, the biggest draw at the visitor center is the six-story IMAX screen that features the 34-minute movie, *Grand Canyon: The Hidden Secrets.* You can learn about the geologic and natural history of the canyon, soar above stunning rock formations, and ride the rapids through the rocky gorge. The film is shown every hour on the half-hour. ⊠ *Hwy. 64/U.S. 180, 2 miles south of the Grand Canyon's south entrance, 450 Hwy. 64, Tusayan* ☎ *928/638–2203, 928/638–2468* ⊕ *www.explorethecanyon.com* 🎟 *$13.72 for IMAX movies* ☉ *Mar.–Oct., daily 8 am–10 pm; Nov.–Feb., daily 10:30–6:30.*

Vermilion Cliffs National Monument. West from the town of Marble Canyon are these spectacular cliffs, more than 3,000 feet high in many places. Keep an eye out for condors; the giant endangered birds were reintroduced into the area in 1996. Reports suggest that the birds, once in captivity, are surviving well in the wilderness. ☎ *435/688–3200* ⊕ *www.blm.gov/az.*

AREA ACTIVITIES

SPORTS AND THE OUTDOORS
FISHING
The stretch of ice-cold, crystal clear water at Lees Ferry off the North Rim provides arguably the best trout fishing in the Southwest. Many rafters and anglers stay the night in a campground near the river or in nearby Marble Canyon before hitting the river at dawn.

Arizona Game and Fish Department. Fish for trout, crappie, catfish, and smallmouth bass at a number of lakes surrounding Williams. To fish on public land, anglers ages 14 and older are required to obtain a fishing license from the Arizona Game and Fish Department. ☎ *928/774–5045* ⊕ *www.azgfd.gov.*

RAFTING

Fodor's Choice
★

The National Park Service authorizes 16 concessionaires to run rafting trips through the canyon—you can view a full list at the park's website (⊕ *www.nps.gov/grca/planyourvisit/river-concessioners.htm*). Trips run from 3 to 16 days, depending on whether you opt for the upper canyon, lower canyon, or full canyon. You can also experience a one-day rafting trip, running a few rapids in Grand Canyon West with the Hualapai tribe.

TOURS AND
OUTFITTERS

Arizona Raft Adventures. Arizona Raft Adventures organizes 6- to 16-day paddle and/or motor trips through the upper, lower, or "full" canyon, for all skill levels. Trips, which run $1,985 to $4,040 (all fees and taxes included), depart April through October. ⊠ *4050 East Huntington Dr., Flagstaff* ☎ *928/526–8200, 800/786–7238* ⊕ *www.azraft.com.*

Canyoneers. With a reputation for high quality and a roster of 3- to 14-day trips, Canyoneers is popular with those who want to do some hiking as well. The five-day "Best of the Grand" trip includes a hike down to Phantom Ranch. The motorized and oar trips, available April through September, cost between $1,056 and $3,650. ⊠ *Flagstaff* ☎ *928/526–0924, 800/525–0924* ⊕ *www.canyoneers.com.*

Grand Canyon Expeditions. You can count on Grand Canyon Expeditions to take you down the Colorado River safely and in style: it limits the number of people on each boat to 14, and evening meals might include filet mignon, pork chops, or shrimp. The mid-April through mid-September trips cost $2,650 to $4,199 for 8 to 16 days. ☎ *435/644–2691, 800/544–2691* ⊕ *www.gcex.com.*

Wilderness River Adventures. One of the canyon's larger rafting outfitters, Wilderness River Adventures runs a wide variety of trips from 3 to 16 days, oar or motorized, from April to October. Their most popular trip is the seven-day motor trip. ⊠ *Page* ☎ *928/645–3296, 800/992–8022* ⊕ *www.riveradventures.com.*

18

WHERE TO EAT

IN THE PARK

SOUTH RIM

$$$
STEAKHOUSE

✕ **Arizona Room.** The canyon views from this casual Southwestern-style steakhouse are the best of any restaurant at the South Rim. The menu includes such delicacies as chili-crusted pan-seared wild salmon, chipotle barbecue baby back ribs, and half-pound buffalo burgers with Gorgonzola aioli. For dessert, try the cheesecake with prickly-pear syrup paired with one of the house's specialty coffee drinks. Seating is first-come, first served, so arrive early to avoid the crowds. $ *Average main: $22* ⊠ *Bright Angel Lodge, Desert View Dr., Grand Canyon Village* ☎ *928/638–2631* ⊕ *www.grandcanyonlodges.com* ⚱ *Reservations not accepted* ⊗ *Closed Jan. and Feb. No lunch Nov. and Dec.*

Continued on page 422

EXPLORING THE
COLORADO RIVER

By Carrie Frasure

High in Colorado's Rocky Mountains, the Colorado River begins as a catch-all for the snowmelt off the mountains west of the Continental Divide. By the time it reaches the Grand Canyon, the Colorado has been joined by multiple tributaries to become a raging river, red with silt as it sculpts spectacular landscapes. A network of dams can only partially tame this mighty river.

Snaking its way through five states, the Colorado River is an essential water source to the arid Southwest. Its natural course runs 1,450 miles from its origin in Colorado's La Poudre Pass Lake in Rocky Mountain National Park to its final destination in the Gulf of California, also called the Sea of Cortez. In northern Arizona, the Colorado River has been a powerful force in shaping the Grand Canyon, where it flows 4,000 to 6,000 feet below the rim. Beyond the canyon, the red river takes a lazy turn at the Arizona–Nevada border, where Hoover Dam creates the reservoir at Lake Mead. The Colorado continues at a relaxed pace along the Arizona–California border, providing energy and irrigation in Arizona, California, and Nevada before draining into northwestern Mexico.

A RIVER RUNS THROUGH IT

Stretching along 277 miles of the Colorado River is one of the seven natural wonders of the world, the Grand Canyon ranges in width from 4 to 18 miles, while the walls around it soar up to a mile high. Nearly 2 billion years of geologic history and majesty are revealed in exposed tiers of rock cut deep in the Colorado Plateau. What caused this incredible marvel of nature? Erosion by water coupled with driving wind are most likely the major culprits: under the sculpting power of wind and water, the shale layers eroded into slopes and the harder sandstone and limestone layers created terraced cliffs. Other forces that may have helped shape the canyon include ice, volcanic activity, continental drift, and earthquakes.

WHO LIVES HERE
Native tribes have lived in the canyon for thousands of years and continue to do so, looking to the river for subsistence. The plateau-dwelling Hualapai ("people of the tall pines") live on a million acres along 108 miles of the Colorado River in the West Rim. The Havasupai ("people of the blue green water") live deep within the walls of the 12-mile-long Havasu Canyon—a major side canyon connected to the Grand Canyon.

ENVIRONMENTAL CONCERNS
When the Grand Canyon achieved national park status in 1919, only 44,173 people made the grueling overland trip to see it—quite a contrast from today's nearly 5 million annual visitors. The tremendous increase in visitation has greatly impacted the fragile ecosystems, as has Lake Powell's Glen Canyon Dam, which was constructed in the 1950s and '60s. The dam has changed the composition of the Colorado River, replacing warm water rich in sediments (nature's way of nourishing the riverbed and banks) with mostly cool, much clearer water. This has introduced nonnative plants and animals that threaten the extinction of several native species. Air pollution has also affected visibility and the constant buzz of aerial tours has disturbed the natural solitude.

Above and right, views of Colorado River in the Grand Canyon from Toroweap.

DID YOU KNOW?

The North Rim's isolated Toroweap overlook (also called Tuweep) is perched 3,000 feet above the canyon floor: a height equal to stacking the Sears Tower and Empire State Building on top of each other.

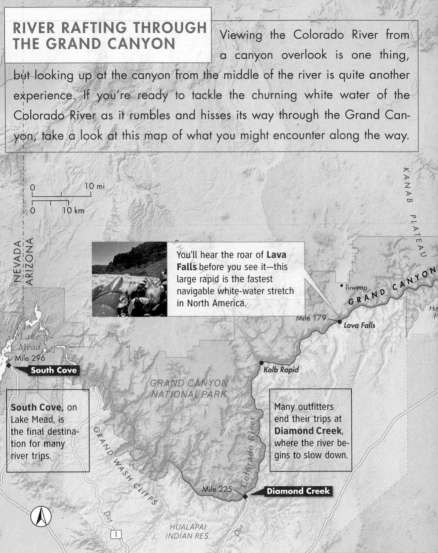

RIVER RAFTING THROUGH THE GRAND CANYON

Viewing the Colorado River from a canyon overlook is one thing, but looking up at the canyon from the middle of the river is quite another experience. If you're ready to tackle the churning white water of the Colorado River as it rumbles and hisses its way through the Grand Canyon, take a look at this map of what you might encounter along the way.

0   10 mi

0   10 km

KANAB PLATEAU

NEVADA
ARIZONA

Tuweep

GRAND CANYON

You'll hear the roar of **Lava Falls** before you see it—this large rapid is the fastest navigable white-water stretch in North America.

Mile 179

Lava Falls

Lake Mead
Mile 296

South Cove

GRAND CANYON NATIONAL PARK

Kolb Rapid

South Cove, on Lake Mead, is the final destination for many river trips.

Many outfitters end their trips at **Diamond Creek**, where the river begins to slow down.

GRAND WASH CLIFFS

Colorado River

Mile 225

Diamond Creek

Dirt

Dirt

HUALAPAI INDIAN RES.

Peach Springs

1

COLORADO RIVER TRIPS

Time and Length	Entry and Exit points	Cost/person
1 day Float trip	Glen Canyon Dam to Lees Ferry (no rapids)	$75–$89
1 day Combo trip	Diamond Creek, then helicopter to West Rim	$381
3–4 days	Lees Ferry to Phantom Ranch	*$700–$1,300
6 days, 89 mi	Phantom Ranch to Diamond Creek	$1,850–$2,300
9–10 days, 136 mi	Lees Ferry to Diamond Creek	$2,300–$3,100
14–16 days, 225 mi	Lees Ferry to South Cove	$3,300–$4,000

*Trips either begin or end at Phantom Ranch/Bright Angel Beach at the bottom of the Grand Canyon, at river mile 87

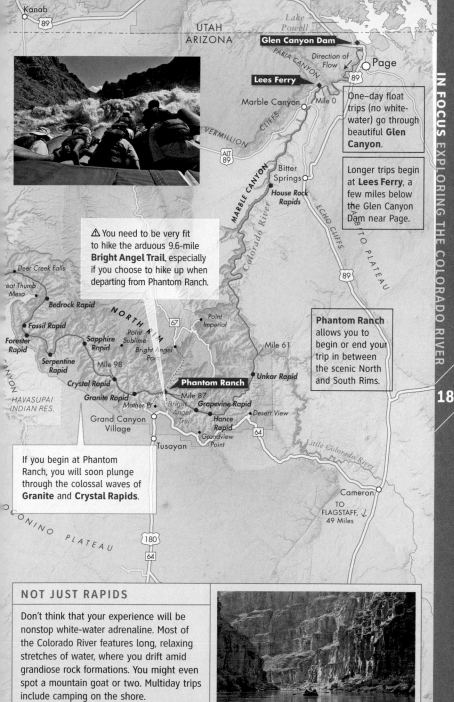

Kanab
89

UTAH
ARIZONA

Lake Powell

Glen Canyon Dam

Direction of Flow

Page
89

PARIA CANYON

Lees Ferry

Marble Canyon

Mile 0

VERMILLION CLIFFS

ALT 89

MARBLE CANYON

Bitter Springs

House Rock Rapids

ECHO CLIFFS

Colorado River

89

TO PLATEAU

One-day float trips (no white-water) go through beautiful **Glen Canyon**.

Longer trips begin at **Lees Ferry**, a few miles below the Glen Canyon Dam near Page.

Deer Creek Falls

eat Thumb Mesa

Bedrock Rapid

NORTH RIM

Fossil Rapid

Forester Rapid

Sapphire Rapid

Serpentine Rapid

Mile 98

Crystal Rapid

Granite Rapid

Mather Pt.

HAVASUPAI INDIAN RES.

CANYON

Point Sublime

Bright Angel Point

67

Point Imperial

Mile 61

⚠ You need to be very fit to hike the arduous 9.6-mile **Bright Angel Trail**, especially if you choose to hike up when departing from Phantom Ranch.

Phantom Ranch

Mile 87

Bright Angel Trail

Unkar Rapid

Grapevine Rapid

Hance Rapid

Desert View

Grandview Point

64

Grand Canyon Village

Tusayan

Little Colorado River

Phantom Ranch allows you to begin or end your trip in between the scenic North and South Rims.

If you begin at Phantom Ranch, you will soon plunge through the colossal waves of **Granite** and **Crystal Rapids**.

OCONINO PLATEAU

180

64

Cameron

TO FLAGSTAFF, ↓ 49 Miles

NOT JUST RAPIDS

Don't think that your experience will be nonstop white-water adrenaline. Most of the Colorado River features long, relaxing stretches of water, where you drift amid grandiose rock formations. You might even spot a mountain goat or two. Multiday trips include camping on the shore.

PLANNING YOUR RIVER RAFTING TRIP

OAR, MOTOR, OR HYBRID?

Base the type of trip you choose on the amount of effort you want to put in. Motor rafts, which are the roomiest of the choices, cover the most miles in less time and are the most comfortable. Guides do the rowing on oar boats and these smaller rafts offer a wilder ride. All-paddle trips are the most active and require the most involvement from guests. Hybrid trips are popular because they offer both the opportunity to paddle and to relax.

THE GEAR

Life jackets, beverages, tents, sheets, tarps, sleeping bags, dry bags, first aid, and food are provided—but you'll still need to plan ahead by packing clothing, hats, sunscreen, toiletries, and other sundries. Commercial outfitters allow each river runner two waterproof bags to store items during the day—just keep in mind that one of these will be filled up with the provided sleeping bag and tarp. ■TIP➔ Bring a rain suit: summer thunderstorms are frequent and chilly.

WHEN TO GO

Lots of people book trips for summer's peak period: June through August. If you're flexible, take advantage of the Arizona weather and go from May to early June or in September. ■TIP➔ Seats fill up quickly; make reservations for multiday trips a year or two in advance.

TOUR OPERATORS

Arizona Raft Adventures ☎ 928/526–8200 or 800/786–7238 ⊕ www.azraft.com

Canyoneers ☎ 928/526–0924 or 800/525–0924 ⊕ www.canyoneers.com

Grand Canyon Expeditions ☎ 435/644–2691 or 800/544–2691 ⊕ www.gcex.com

Hualapai River Runners
☎ 928/769–2636 or 888/868–9378
⊕ www.hualapaitourism.com

Wilderness River Adventures ☎ 928/645–3296 or 800/992–8022 ⊕ www.river adventures.com

⇨ *See "Rafting" in the Sports and the Outdoors section of What's Nearby the Grand Canyon? for more information.*

DID YOU KNOW?

As you're hanging on for dear life, consider this: Civil War veteran John Wesley Powell chartered these treacherous rapids in 1869—not only were conditions more dangerous then, but he had only one arm.

$$ ✕ Bright Angel Restaurant. The draw here is casual and affordable. No-
SOUTHWESTERN   surprises dishes will fill your belly at breakfast, lunch, or dinner. Entrées
include such basics as salads, steaks, lasagna, burgers, fajitas, and fish
tacos (sandwiches are options at lunch). Or you can step it up a notch
and order some of the same selections straight from the Arizona Room
menu including prime rib, baby back ribs, and wild salmon. For des-
sert try the warm apple grunt cake topped with vanilla ice cream. Be
prepared to wait for a table: the dining room bustles all day long. The
plain decor is broken up with large-pane windows and original art-
work. ⓢ *Average main: $12* ⊠ *Bright Angel Lodge, Desert View Dr.,
Grand Canyon Village* ☎ *928/638–2631* ⊕ *www.grandcanyonlodges.
com* ⚎ *Reservations not accepted.*

$ ✕ Canyon Café at Yavapai Lodge. Open for breakfast, lunch, and dinner,
AMERICAN   this cafeteria in the Market Plaza also serves specials such as chicken
potpie, fried catfish, and fried chicken. Fast-food favorites here include
pastries, burgers, and pizza. There isn't a fancy bar here, but you can
order beer and wine with your meal. Resembling an old-fashioned diner,
this cafeteria seats 345 guests and has easy-to-read signs that point the
way to your favorite foods. Hours are limited in winter—it's best to call
ahead then. ⓢ *Average main: $6* ⊠ *Yavapai Lodge, Desert View Dr.,
Grand Canyon Village* ☎ *928/638–2631* ⊕ *www.grandcanyonlodges.
com/canyon-cafe-423.html* ⚎ *Reservations not accepted.*

$$$ ✕ El Tovar Dining Room. No doubt about it—this is the best restaurant for
SOUTHWESTERN   miles. Modeled after a European hunting lodge, this rustic 19th-cen-
Fodor's Choice   tury dining room built of hand-hewn logs is worth a visit. The cuisine
★   is modern Southwestern with an exotic flair. Start with the smoked-
salmon-and-goat-cheese crostini or the acclaimed black bean soup.
The dinner menu includes such hearty yet creative dishes as cherry-
merlot-glazed duck with roasted poblano black bean rice, grilled New
York strip steak with cornmeal-battered onion rings, and a wild salmon
tostada topped with organic greens and tequila vinaigrette. The dining
room also has an extensive wine list. ■**TIP→ Dinner reservations can
be made up to six months in advance with room reservations and 30
days in advance for all other visitors.** If you can't get a dinner table,
consider lunch or breakfast—the best in the region with dishes like
polenta corncakes with prickly pear–pistachio butter, and blackened
breakfast trout and eggs. ⓢ *Average main: $27* ⊠ *El Tovar Hotel, Des-
ert View Dr., Grand Canyon Village* ☎ *303/297–2757, 888/297–2757
for reservations only, 928/638–2631* ⊕ *www.grandcanyonlodges.com/
el-tovar-421.html* ⚎ *Reservations essential.*

$ ✕ Maswik Cafeteria. You can get a burger, hot sandwich, pasta, or Mexi-
AMERICAN   can fare at this food court, as well as pizza by the slice and wine and beer
in the adjacent Maswik Pizza Pub. This casual eatery is 0.25 mile from
the rim. Lines can be long during high-season lunch and dinner, but
everything moves fairly quickly. ⓢ *Average main: $7* ⊠ *Maswik Lodge,
Desert View Dr., Grand Canyon Village* ⊕ *www.grandcanyonlodges.
com* ⚎ *Reservations not accepted.*

TOP PICNIC SPOTS

Bring your picnic basket and enjoy dining alfresco surrounded by some of the most beautiful backdrops in the country. Be sure to bring water, as it's unavailable at many of these spots, as are restrooms.

■ **Buggeln,** 15 miles east of Grand Canyon Village on Desert View Drive, has some secluded, shady spots.

■ **Cape Royal,** 23 miles south of the North Rim Visitor Center, is the most popular designated picnic area on the North Rim due to its panoramic views.

■ **Grandview Point** has, as the name implies, grand vistas; it's 12 miles east of the village on Desert View Drive.

■ **Point Imperial,** 11 miles northeast of the North Rim Visitor Center, has shade and some privacy.

NORTH RIM

$ AMERICAN

🍴 **Deli in the Pines.** Dining choices are very limited on the North Rim, but this is your best bet for a meal on a budget. Selections include pizza, salads, deli sandwiches, hot dogs, homemade breakfast pastries and burritos, and soft-serve ice cream. Best of all, there is an outdoor seating area for dining alfresco. It's open for breakfast, lunch, and dinner. [$] *Average main: $6* ✉ *Grand Canyon Lodge, Bright Angel Point, North Rim* ☎ *928/638–2611* 🌐 *www.grandcanyonforever.com* ✍ *Reservations not accepted* 🕒 *Closed mid-Oct.–mid-May.*

$$$ AMERICAN Fodor's Choice ★

🍴 **Grand Canyon Lodge Dining Room.** The historic lodge has a huge, high-ceilinged dining room with spectacular views and decent food, though the draw here is definitely the setting. You might find pecan-glazed pork chop, bison flank steak, and grilled ruby trout for dinner. The filling, simply prepared food here takes a flavorful turn with Southwestern spices and organic selections. It's also open for breakfast and lunch. A full-service bar and an impressive wine list add to the relaxed atmosphere of the only full-service, sit-down restaurant on the North Rim. Dinner reservations are essential in summer and on spring and fall weekends. [$] *Average main: $24* ✉ *Grand Canyon Lodge, Bright Angel Point, North Rim* ☎ *928/638–2611* 🌐 *www.grandcanyonforever.com* 🕒 *Closed mid-Oct.–mid-May.*

$$$ AMERICAN FAMILY

🍴 **Grand Cookout.** Dine under the stars and enjoy live entertainment at this chuck-wagon-style dining experience—a popular family-friendly choice among the North Rim's limited dining options. Fill up on Western favorites including barbecue beef brisket, roasted chicken, baked beans, and cowboy biscuits. The food is basic and tasty, but the real draw is the nightly performance of Western music and tall tales. Transportation from the Grand Canyon Lodge to the cookout (1 mile away) is included in the price. Be sure to call before 4 pm for dinner reservations. Advance reservations are taken by phone (during winter months) or at the Grand Canyon Lodge registration desk. [$] *Average main: $30* ✉ *Grand Canyon Lodge, North Rim* ☎ *928/638–2611, 928/645–6865 in winter* 🌐 *www.grandcanyonforever.com* ✍ *Reservations essential* 🕒 *Closed Oct.–May.*

OUTSIDE THE PARK

TUSAYAN

$$
AMERICAN
FAMILY

✕ **Canyon Star Restaurant and Saloon.** Relax in the rustic timber-and-stone dining room at the Grand Hotel for reliable if uninspired American food, with an emphasis at dinner on steaks and barbecue. Other popular options include barbecue chicken and ribs, and Mexican fare. Most nights there's entertainment: live guitar or banjo music year-round, and American Indian dancers in summer—all great for families. There's a kids' menu, and the Canyon Star also serves breakfast and lunch daily. In summer, be sure to reserve a table at dinner. There's also a coffee bar in the hotel lobby. $ *Average main: $18* ⊠ *Hwy. 64/U.S. 180, Tusayan* ☎ *928/638–3333* ⊕ *www.grandcanyongrandhotel.com* ⊗ *No lunch during winter.*

$$$
AMERICAN

✕ **The Coronado Room.** Inside the Best Western Grand Canyon Squire Inn is the most sophisticated cuisine in Tusayan in an upscale dining room with attentive service. The menu includes well-prepared, hearty American food, with an emphasis on game (elk, venison, buffalo), plus grilled seafood, escargot, and oversize desserts. There's a good-size wine list, too. Although classier than most eateries in these parts, dress is still casual and the vibe relaxed. Reservations are a good idea, particularly in the busy season. $ *Average main: $22* ⊠ *Hwy 64/U.S. 180, 100 Hwy 64, Tusayan* ☎ *928/638–2681* ⊕ *www.grandcanyonsquire.com* ⊗ *No lunch.*

WILLIAMS

$$
AMERICAN
FAMILY

✕ **Cruisers Café 66.** A festive spot for a nostalgic meal, this diner patterned after a classic '50s-style, high-school hangout (but with cocktail service) pleases kids and adults with a large menu of family-priced American classics—good burgers and fries, barbecue pork sandwiches, salads, and thick malts, plus a choice steak that'll set you back about $20. The Grand Canyon Brewery, accessed by a side entrance, adds to the casual fun—just saddle up to a hand-carved log bar stool and order one of five microbrews on tap. A large mural of the town's heyday along the "Mother Road" and historic cars out front make this a Route 66 favorite. Kids enjoy the relaxed atmosphere and jukebox tunes. $ *Average main: $15* ⊠ *233 W. Rte. 66, Williams* ☎ *928/635–2445* ⊕ *www.cruisers66.com.*

$$$
ECLECTIC
Fodor's Choice
★

✕ **Red Raven Restaurant.** Chef-owned David Haines cultivates a devoted foodie following with this dapper storefront bistro in the heart of downtown Williams that features warm lighting and romantic booth seating. Creatively presented fare blends American, Italian, and Asian ingredients—specialties include a starter of crisp tempura shrimp salad with a ginger-sesame dressing, and mains like charbroiled salmon with basil butter over cranberry–pine nut couscous, and pork tenderloin with cilantro pesto, served with mashed potatoes and sautéed local vegetables. The well-selected wine and beer list is one of the most extensive in the region. $ *Average main: $21* ⊠ *135 W. Rte. 66, Williams* ☎ *928/635–4980* ⊕ *www.redravenrestaurant.com.*

WHERE TO STAY

IN THE PARK

SOUTH RIM

$ **Bright Angel Lodge.** Famed architect Mary Jane Colter designed this
HOTEL 1935 log-and-stone structure, which sits within a few yards of the
FAMILY canyon rim and blends superbly with the canyon walls. **Pros:** some
rooms have canyon vistas; all are steps away from the rim; Internet
kiosks and transportation desk for the mule ride check-in are in the
lobby; good value for the amazing location. **Cons:** the popular lobby
is always packed; parking is a bit of a hike; lack of elevators make
accessibility an issue for lodge rooms. $ *Rooms from: $83* ✉ *Desert
View Dr., Grand Canyon Village* ☎ *888/297–2757 for reservations
only, 928/638–2631* ⊕ *www.grandcanyonlodges.com* ↬ *37 rooms, 18
with bath; 50 cabins* ⦿ *No meals.*

$$$ **El Tovar Hotel.** The hotel's proximity to all of the canyon's facilities,
HOTEL European hunting-lodge atmosphere, attractively updated rooms and tile
Fodor's Choice baths, and renowned dining room make it the best place to stay on the
★ South Rim. **Pros:** historic lodging just steps from the South Rim; fabulous
lounge with outdoor seating and canyon views; best in-park dining on site.
Cons: books up quickly. $ *Rooms from: $183* ✉ *Desert View Dr., Grand
Canyon Village* ☎ *888/297–2757 for reservations only, 928/638–2631*
⊕ *www.grandcanyonlodges.com* ↬ *66 rooms, 12 suites* ⦿ *No meals.*

$$$ **Kachina Lodge.** On the rim halfway between El Tovar and Bright
HOTEL Angel Lodge, this motel-style lodge has many rooms with partial can-
yon views ($11 extra). **Pros:** partial canyon views in half the rooms;
family-friendly; steps from the best restaurants in the park. **Cons:** check-
in takes place at El Tovar Hotel; limited parking; pleasant but bland
furnishings. $ *Rooms from: $180* ✉ *Desert View Dr., Grand Canyon
Village* ☎ *888/297–2757 for reservations only, 928/638–2631* ⊕ *www.
grandcanyonlodges.com* ↬ *49 rooms* ⦿ *No meals.*

$ **Maswik Lodge.** Accommodations are far from crowds and noise and
HOTEL nestled in a shady ponderosa pine forest, with options ranging from
FAMILY rustic cabins to more modern motel-style rooms. **Pros:** larger rooms
here than in older lodgings; good for families; affordable dining options.
Cons: rooms lack historic charm and cabins as well as rooms in the
South Section are quite plain; tucked away from the rim in the forest.
$ *Rooms from: $92* ✉ *Grand Canyon Village* ☎ *888/297–2757 for reservations only, 928/638–2631* ⊕ *www.grandcanyonlodges.com* ↬ *278
rooms* ⦿ *No meals.*

$ **Phantom Ranch.** In a grove of cottonwood trees on the canyon floor,
B&B/INN Phantom Ranch is accessible only to hikers and mule trekkers; there are
40 dormitory beds and 14 beds in cabins, all with shared baths. **Pros:** only
inner-canyon lodging option; fabulous canyon views; remote access limits
crowds. **Cons:** accessible only by foot or mule; few amenities or means of
outside communication. $ *Rooms from: $46* ✉ *On canyon floor, at intersection of Bright Angel and Kaibab trails* ☎ *303/297–2757, 888/297–2757*
⊕ *www.grandcanyonlodges.com* ↬ *4 dormitories and 9 cabins (some cabins with outside showers reserved for mule riders)* ⦿ *Some meals.*

18

$$$ HOTEL 🏨 **Thunderbird Lodge.** This motel with comfortable, simple rooms with the modern amenities you'd expect at a typical mid-price chain hotel is next to Bright Angel Lodge in Grand Canyon Village. **Pros:** partial canyon views in some rooms; family-friendly. **Cons:** rooms lack personality; check-in takes place at Bright Angel Lodge; limited parking. [$] *Rooms from: $180* ✉ *Desert View Dr., Grand Canyon Village* ☎ *888/297–2757 for reservations only, 928/638–2631* 🌐 *www.grandcanyonlodges.com* 🛏 *55 rooms* 🍴 *No meals.*

DUFFEL SERVICE: LIGHTEN YOUR LOAD

Hikers staying at either Phantom Ranch or Bright Angel Campground can also take advantage of the ranch's duffel service: bags or packs weighing 30 pounds or less can be transported to the ranch by mule for a fee of $64.64 each way. As is true for many desirable things at the canyon, reservations are a must.

$$ HOTEL 🏨 **Yavapai Lodge.** The largest motel-style lodge in the park is tucked in a pinyon and juniper forest at the eastern end of Grand Canyon Village, near the RV park. **Pros:** transportation-activities desk on site in the lobby; near Market Plaza in Grand Canyon Village; forested grounds. **Cons:** farthest in-park lodging from the rim. [$] *Rooms from: $125* ✉ *Grand Canyon Village* ☎ *888/297–2757 for reservations only, 928/638–2961* 🌐 *www.grandcanyonlodges.com* 🛏 *358 rooms* ⏲ *Closed Jan. and Feb.* 🍴 *No meals.*

NORTH RIM

$$ HOTEL Fodor's Choice ★ 🏨 **Grand Canyon Lodge.** This historic property, constructed mainly in the 1920s and '30s, is the premier lodging facility in the North Rim area. **Pros:** steps away from gorgeous North Rim views; close to several easy hiking trails. **Cons:** as the only in-park North Rim lodging option, this lodge fills up fast; few amenities and very limited Internet access. [$] *Rooms from: $124* ✉ *Grand Canyon National Park, Hwy. 67, North Rim* ☎ *877/386–4383, 928/638–2611 May–Oct., 928/645–6865 Nov.–Apr.* 🌐 *www.grandcanyonforever.com* 🛏 *40 rooms, 178 cabins* ⏲ *Closed mid-Oct.–mid-May* 🍴 *No meals.*

OUTSIDE THE PARK

TUSAYAN

$$$ HOTEL FAMILY 🏨 **Best Western Grand Canyon Squire Inn.** About 1 mile from the park's south entrance, this motel lacks the historic charm of the older lodges at the canyon rim, but has more amenities, including a small cowboy museum in the lobby, an upscale gift shop, and one of the better restaurants in the region. **Pros:** a cool pool in summer and a hot tub for cold winter nights; children's activities at the Family Fun Center; close to South Rim. **Cons:** hall noise can be an issue with all of the in-hotel activities. [$] *Rooms from: $229* ✉ *100 Hwy. 64* ☎ *928/638–2681, 800/622–6966* 🌐 *www.grandcanyonsquire.com* 🛏 *250 rooms, 4 suites* 🍴 *Breakfast.*

$$$ HOTEL 🏨 **The Grand Hotel.** At the south end of Tusayan, this popular hotel has bright, clean rooms decorated in Southwestern colors, a cozy stone-and-timber lobby, and free Wi-Fi. **Pros:** coffee stand for a quick

Best Campgrounds in the Grand Canyon

Within the national park, camping is permitted only in designated campsites. Some campgrounds charge nightly camping fees in addition to entrance fees, and some accept reservations up to five months in advance through ⊕ *www.recreation.gov*. Others are first-come, first-served.

In-park camping in a spot other than a developed rim campground requires a permit from the Backcountry Information Center, which also serves as your reservation. Permits can be requested by mail or fax only; applying well in advance is recommended. Call ☎ *928/638–7875* between 1 pm and 5 pm Monday through Friday for information.

Outside the park boundaries, there are campgrounds near the South and North rims, and in Havasu Canyon and the Kaibab National Forest. There's no camping on the West Rim, but you can pitch a tent on the beach near the Colorado River.

SOUTH RIM
Bright Angel Campground.
This backcountry campground is near Phantom Ranch, at the bottom of the canyon. There are toilet facilities and running water, but no showers. ⊠ *Intersection of South and North Kaibab trails* ☎ *928/638–7875.*

Desert View Campground.
Popular for spectacular views of the canyon from the nearby watchtower, this campground doesn't take reservations; show up before noon, as it fills up fast in summer. ⊠ *Desert View Dr., 23 miles east of Grand Canyon Village off Hwy. 64.*

Indian Garden.
Halfway down the canyon is this backcountry campground, en route to Phantom Ranch on the Bright Angel Trail. Running water and toilet facilities are available, but not showers. ⊠ *Bright Angel Trail* ☎ *928/638–7875.*

NORTH RIM
North Rim Campground.
The only designated campground at the North Rim of Grand Canyon National Park sits 3 miles north of the rim, near the general store, and has 84 RV and tent sites (no hookups). ⊠ *Hwy. 67* ☎ *928/638–7888* ⊕ *www.recreation.gov.*

OUTSIDE THE PARK
Diamond Creek.
You can camp on the banks of the Colorado River, but your peace might be interrupted by the fact that this smooth beach is a launch point for river runners. The Hualapai permit camping on their tribal lands here, with an overnight camping permit of $32.10 per person per night, which can be purchased at the Hualapai Lodge. ☎ *928/769–2210 or 888/255–9550* ⊕ *www.hualapaitourism.com.*

Kaibab National Forest.
Both developed and undeveloped campsites are available on a first-come, first-served basis May through September at this forest that surrounds Williams and extends to the Grand Canyon. ☎ *928/699–1239 or 928/638–2443* ⊕ *www.fs.usda.gov/kaibab.*

18

morning pick-me-up; gift shop stocked with outdoor gear and regional books. **Cons:** 15-minute drive to the Grand Canyon. [$] *Rooms from: $209* ✉ *149 State Hwy. 64* ☎ *928/638–3333, 888/634–7263* 🌐 *www.grandcanyongrandhotel.com* 🛏 *121 rooms* 🍴 *No meals.*

WILLIAMS

$ HOTEL FAMILY 🏨 **Canyon Motel and RV Park.** Railcars, cabooses, and cottages make up this 13-acre property on the outskirts of Williams, about a one-hour drive to the park. **Pros:** family-friendly property with hiking, horseshoes, playground, and indoor swimming pool; general store; owners are friendly and helpful. **Cons:** a few miles from Williams dining options; RV park traffic. [$] *Rooms from: $75* ✉ *1900 E. Rodeo Rd., Rte. 66, Williams* ☎ *928/635–9371, 800/482–3955* 🌐 *www.thecanyonmotel.com* 🛏 *18 rooms, 5 railcar suites* 🍴 *No meals.*

$$ HOTEL 🏨 **Grand Canyon Railway Hotel.** Designed to resemble the train depot's original Fray Marcos lodge, this hotel features attractive Southwestern-style accommodations with large bathrooms and comfy beds with upscale linens. **Pros:** railway package options; game room and outdoor playground; short walk from historic downtown restaurants and bars. **Cons:** railroad noise. [$] *Rooms from: $169* ✉ *233 North Grand Canyon Blvd., Williams* ☎ *928/635–4010, 800/843–8724* 🌐 *www.thetrain.com* 🛏 *287 rooms, 11 suites* 🍴 *No meals.*

NORTH RIM

$$ HOTEL 🏨 **Jacob Lake Inn.** The bustling lodge at Jacob Lake Inn is a popular stop for those heading to the North Rim, 45 miles south. **Pros:** grocery store, coffee shop, and restaurant; quiet rooms. **Cons:** small bathroom in cabins; worn furnishings; old-fashioned key locks. [$] *Rooms from: $139* ✉ *Hwy. 89A & AZ-67, Jacob Lake* ☎ *928/643–7232* 🌐 *www.jacoblake.com* 🛏 *32 rooms, 26 cabins* 🍴 *No meals.*

$ HOTEL 🏨 **Marble Canyon Lodge.** This Arizona Strip lodge popular with anglers and rafters opened in 1929 on the same day the Navajo Bridge was dedicated; a 2010 renovation updated all rooms and bathrooms. **Pros:** convenience store, restaurant, and trading post; great fishing on the Colorado River. **Cons:** no-frills rustic lodging; more than 70 miles to the Grand Canyon North Rim. [$] *Rooms from: $80* ✉ *¼ mile west of Navajo Bridge on U.S. 89A, Marble Canyon* ☎ *928/355–2225, 800/726–1789* 🌐 *www.marblecanyoncompany.com* 🛏 *46 rooms, 8 apartments* 🍴 *No meals.*

GRAND TETON NATIONAL PARK

WELCOME TO GRAND TETON

TOP REASONS TO GO

★ **Heavenward hikes:** Trek where grizzled frontiersmen roamed. Jackson Hole got its name from mountain man Davey Jackson; now there are hundreds of trails for you to explore.

★ **Wildlife big and small:** Keep an eye out for little fellows like short-tailed weasels and beaver, as well as bison, elk, wolves, and both black and grizzly bears.

★ **Waves to make:** Float the Snake River or take a canoe onto Jackson Lake or Jenny Lake.

★ **Homesteader history:** Visit the 1890s barns and ranch buildings of Mormon Row or Menor's Ferry.

★ **Cycling paradise:** Take to two wheels for safe, speedy transport to and through Grand Teton on miles of pathways and rural roads, then get off the beaten path for spectacular singletrack.

★ **Trout trophies:** Grab your rod and slither over to the Snake River, where cutthroat trout are an angler's delight.

1 Antelope Flats. Buffalo and antelope frequently roam across this sagebrush-covered area of the park northeast of Moose, and it is also where homesteader barns along Mormon Row dot the landscape. It's a popular place for wildflower viewing and bicycle rides.

2 Jenny Lake. In this developed area, you can go to the visitor center, purchase supplies, or talk to a ranger—plus ride a boat across the lake, hike around it, have a picnic, or camp nearby.

3 Moose. Just north of Craig Thomas Discovery and Visitor Center, this historical area is home to the tranquil Chapel of the Transfiguration and Menor's Ferry, the only way across the Snake until a bridge was built in 1927.

4 Oxbow Bend. At this famously scenic spot, the Snake River, its inhabitants, and the Tetons all converge, especially in early morning or near dusk. You're likely to see moose feeding in willows, elk grazing in aspen stands, and birds such as bald eagles, osprey, sandhill cranes, ducks, and American white pelicans.

GETTING ORIENTED

Grand Teton's rugged peaks jut more than a mile above the valley floor in Jackson Hole. Without any foothills to soften the blow, the sight of these glacier-scoured crags is truly striking. Several piedmont lakes reflect the mountains, and the winding Snake River cuts south through the expansive sagebrush flats in the heart of the park. The northern portion of the park is outstanding wildlife-watching territory—you can see everything from rare birds to lumbering moose to the big predators (wolves and black and grizzly bears). Two main roads run through the 310,000-acre park; Highway 26/89/191 curves along the eastern or outer side, and Teton Park Road (closed during winter) runs close to the foot of the mountain range.

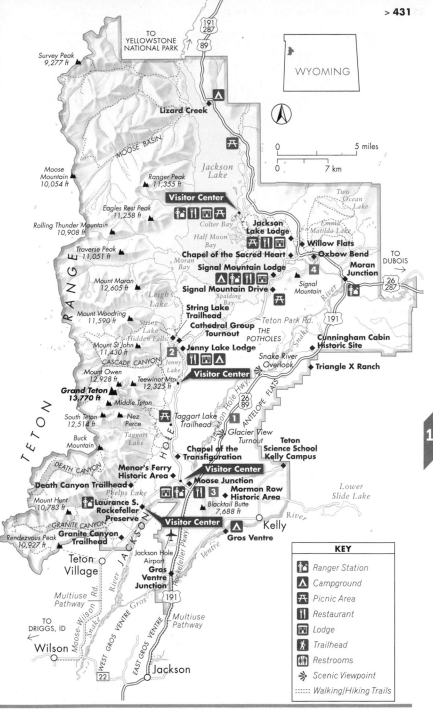

TO
YELLOWSTONE
NATIONAL PARK

191
287
89

WYOMING

Survey Peak
9,277 ft

Lizard Creek

MOOSE BASIN

*Jackson
Lake*

*Moose
Mountain
10,054 ft*

*Ranger Peak
11,355 ft*

0   5 miles

0   7 km

*Two
Ocean
Lake*

Visitor Center

*Eagles Rest Peak
11,258 ft*

*Rolling Thunder Mountain
10,908 ft*

Colter Bay

*Half Moon
Bay*

**Jackson
Lake Lodge**

*Emma
Matilda Lake*

Willow Flats

Oxbow Bend

TO
DUBOIS

*Traverse Peak
11,051 ft*

*Moran
Bay*

Chapel of the Sacred Heart

Signal Mountain Lodge

**Moran
Junction**

26
287

*Mount Moran
12,605 ft*

Signal Mountain Drive

*Signal
Mountain*

*Leigh
Lake*

*Spalding
Bay*

*Snake
River*

*Mount Woodring
11,590 ft*

**String Lake
Trailhead**

Teton Park Rd.

*String
Lake*

Hidden Falls

**Cathedral Group
Tournout**

*THE
POTHOLES*

**Cunningham Cabin
Historic Site**

*Mount St John
11,430 ft*

2

CASCADE CANYON

Jenny Lake Lodge

*Jenny
Lake*

191

*Snake River
Overlook*

Triangle X Ranch

*Mount Owen
12,928 ft*

*Teewinot Mtn
12,325 ft*

Visitor Center

**Grand Teton
13,770 ft**

Middle Teton

26
89

*South Teton
12,514 ft*

*Nez
Perce*

**Taggart Lake
Trailhead**

1

ANTELOPE FLATS

*Buck
Mountain*

*Taggart
Lake*

*Glacier View
Turnout*

**Teton
Science School
Kelly Campus**

19

DEATH CANYON

**Chapel of the
Transfiguration**

*Lower
Slide Lake*

**Menor's Ferry
Historic Area**

Visitor Center

*Mount Hunt
10,783 ft*

Death Canyon Trailhead

Phelps Lake

Moose Junction

**Mormon Row
Historic Area**

**Laurance S.
Rockefeller
Preserve**

3

*Blacktail Butte
7,688 ft*

River

GRANITE CANYON

Visitor Center

Kelly

*Rendezvous Peak
10,927 ft*

**Granite Canyon
Trailhead**

Gros Ventre

**Teton
Village**

*Jackson Hole
Airport*

Ventre

*Multiuse
Pathway*

**Gros
Ventre
Junction**

191

TO
DRIGGS, ID

*Multiuse
Pathway*

Wilson

22

Jackson

WEST GROS VENTRE

EAST GROS VENTRE

KEY	
🏠	*Ranger Station*
▲	*Campground*
⊼	*Picnic Area*
🍴	*Restaurant*
▣	*Lodge*
🏃	*Trailhead*
🚻	*Restrooms*
✷	*Scenic Viewpoint*
⋯⋯	*Walking/Hiking Trails*

Updated by
Johanna Love

Your jaw might drop the first time you see the Teton Range rising above the Jackson Hole valley floor. With no foothills to get in the way, you'll have a close-up, unimpeded view of magnificent, jagged, snowcapped peaks. This massif is long on natural beauty, dominated by the 13,770-foot Grand Teton. Before your eyes, mountain glaciers creep down 12,605-foot Mt. Moran. Large and small lakes gleam along the range's base. Many of the West's iconic animals (elk, bears, bald eagles) call this park home.

GRAND TETON PLANNER

WHEN TO GO

In July and August all the roads, trails, and visitor centers are open, and the Snake River's float season is in full swing. ■ TIP→ **To have access to most services without the crowds, plan a trip in late May, June, or September.** Lower rates and smaller crowds can be found in spring and fall, but some services and roads are limited. Grand Teton Lodge Company, the park's major concessionaire, winds down its activities in late September, and most of Teton Park Road closes from November through April. In spring and fall, the road is open to pedestrians, cyclists, and in-line skaters; in winter, it's transformed into a cross-country ski trail.

Towns outside the park rev up in winter. Teton Village and Jackson both buzz with the energy of Snow King Resort and Jackson Hole Mountain Resort, the former conveniently in town, the latter an international skiing hot spot 13 miles from Jackson. (Prices rise for the peak winter season.) U.S. Highway 26/191/89 stays open all winter.

AVG. HIGH/LOW TEMPS.

JAN.	FEB.	MAR.	APR.	MAY	JUNE
28/5	33/8	43/17	53/24	63/31	74/37

JULY	AUG.	SEPT.	OCT.	NOV.	DEC.
82/41	81/39	71/31	59/23	40/16	28/6

FESTIVALS AND EVENTS

YEAR-ROUND **Grand Teton Music Festival.** Since 1962, this summer symphony has been wowing audiences in the world-reknowned Walk Festival Hall in Teton Village. Under the direction of Maestro Donald Runnicles, the festival presents full orchestra concerts Friday and Saturday in July and the first half of August, and smaller ensembles Tuesday to Thursday. In winter, live concerts are presented at least monthly. Tickets cost $20–$50, but many free performances are offered. ☎ *307/733–1128* ⊕ *www.gtmf.org.*

MARCH **Pole-Pedal-Paddle.** This event is a minimarathon, ski-cycle-boat relay race, usually held the last Saturday of March, starting at Jackson Hole Mountain Resort and finishing in Snake River Canyon. ☎ *307/733–6433* ⊕ *www.polepedalpaddle.com.*

MAY **ElkFest.** The third weekend of May features a free, two-day festival centered on the Jackson Hole Boy Scout Elk Antler Auction, where thousands of pounds of naturally shed antlers are sold to the highest bidder. Pick up some horns for your own decor, get a taste of the High Noon Chili Cookoff, or just enjoy the spectacle of khaki-clad lads hauling around massive racks. ⊠ *Jackson* ☎ *307/733–3316* ⊕ *www.elkfest.org.*

Old West Days. Memorial Day weekend festivities include a rodeo, parade, brew fest, Mountain Man Rendezvous (atlatal competition, anyone?), and cowboy music, plus the start of the Jackson Hole Shootout's summer performances. ⊠ *Town Square, Jackson* ☎ *307/733–3316* ⊕ *www.jacksonholewy.net/events/old_west_days.php.*

MAY– **The Shootout.** Gunslingers stage the Shootout in the summer at 6 pm daily
SEPTEMBER (except Sunday) on the northeast corner of the Jackson Town Square. Don't worry, the bullets aren't real. ☎ *307/733–3316.*

SEPTEMBER **Fall Arts Festival.** More than 50 events celebrate art, music, food, and wine throughout Jackson Hole during the 11-day annual festival, which runs from the first to second weekend of September. The 2014 gathering will be the 30th annual. ⊠ *Town Square, Jackson* ☎ *307/733–3316* ⊕ *www.jacksonholechamber.com/fall_arts_festival.*

PLANNING YOUR TIME
GRAND TETON IN ONE DAY

Begin the day by packing a picnic lunch or picking one up at a Jackson eatery. Arrive at **Craig Thomas Discovery and Visitor Center** in time for a 9 am, two-hour, guided Snake River scenic float trip (make reservations in advance with one of the half-dozen outfitters that offer the trip). When you're back on dry ground, drive north on Teton Park Road, stopping at scenic turnouts—don't miss Teton Glacier—until you reach South Jenny Lake Junction.

19

Park at the Jenny Lake ranger station and take the 20-minute boat ride to the **west shore boat dock** for a short but breathtaking hike to **Hidden Falls** or **Inspiration Point.** Return to your car by midafternoon, drive back to Teton Park Road, and head north to Signal Mountain Road to catch an elevated view of the Tetons. In late afternoon descend the mountain and continue north on Teton Park Road.

At Jackson Lake Junction, you can go east to **Oxbow Bend** or north to **Willow Flats,** both excellent spots for wildlife viewing before you head to **Jackson Lake Lodge** for dinner and an evening watching the sun set over the Tetons. Or if you'd like to get back on the water, drive to **Colter Bay Marina,** where you can board a 1½-hour sunset cruise across Jackson Lake to Elk Island. You can reverse this route if you're heading south from Yellowstone: start the day with a 7:30 breakfast cruise from Colter Bay and end it with a sunset float down the Snake River.

GETTING HERE AND AROUND

AIR TRAVEL

Jackson Hole Airport (JAC), the only commercial airport inside a national park, was established before the park opened. Five airlines service the modern airport.

BUS TRAVEL

Grand Teton Lodge Company has shuttle service that makes six trips a day between Colter Bay and Jackson, with several stops in between. It's free for guests of the lodge and $12 for everyone else.

CAR TRAVEL

The best way to see Grand Teton National Park is by car. Unlike Yellowstone's Grand Loop, Grand Teton's road system doesn't allow for easy tour-bus access to the major sights. Only a car will get you close to Jenny Lake, into the remote Gros Ventre Range on the east side of the valley, and to the top of Signal Mountain. You can stop at many points along the roads within the park for a hike or a view. Be extremely cautious in winter when whiteouts and ice are not uncommon. There are adequate road signs throughout the park, but a map is handy to have in the vehicle.

Jackson Hole's main highway (U.S. 89/191) runs the entire length of the park, from Jackson to Yellowstone National Park's south entrance. (This highway is also called Route 26 south of Moran Junction and U.S. 287 north of Moran Junction.) This road is open all year from Jackson to Moran Junction and north to Flagg Ranch, 2 miles south of Yellowstone. Depending on traffic, the southern (Moose) entrance to Grand Teton is about 15 minutes from downtown Jackson via the highway. Coming from the opposite direction on the same road, the northern boundary of the park is about 15 minutes south of Yellowstone National Park. Also open year-round, U.S. 26/287 runs east from Dubois over Togwotee Pass to the Moran entrance station, a drive of about one hour.

Two back-road entrances to Grand Teton require high-clearance vehicles. Both are closed by snow from November through mid-May and can be heavily rutted through June. Moose-Wilson Road (Wyoming Highway 390) starts at Route 22 in Wilson (5 miles west of Jackson) and travels 7 miles north past Teton Village to the Granite Canyon entrance station. Of the 9 miles from here to Moose, 1½ are gravel. It's closed to large trucks, trailers, and RVs. Even rougher is 60-mile Grassy Lake Road, which heads east from Route 32 in Ashton, Idaho, through Targhee National Forest. It connects with U.S. 89/287 in the John D. Rockefeller Jr. Memorial Parkway, sandwiched between Grand Teton and Yellowstone.

PARK ESSENTIALS
PARK FEES AND PERMITS
Park entrance fees cost $25 per car, truck, or RV; $20 per motorcycle; and $12 per person on foot or bicycle, good for seven days in both Grand Teton and Yellowstone parks. Annual park passes are $50. A winter day-use fee is $5.

Backcountry permits, which must be retrieved in person at the Craig Thomas Visitor Center, Colter Bay Visitor Center, or Jenny Lake Ranger Station, are $25, with an additional $10 fee for advance reservations. Permits are required for all overnight stays outside designated campgrounds.

For those bringing boats into the park, seven-day boat permits are available year-round at Craig Thomas Discovery and Visitor Center and in summer at Colter Bay and Signal Mountain ranger stations. They cost $20 for motorized craft and $10 for nonmotorized craft and are good for seven days. Annual permits are $40 for motorized craft and $20 for nonmotorized craft. State law also requires a special Aquatic Invasive Species decal. Wyoming residents pay $10 for motorized watercraft and $5 for nonmotorized craft; out-of-state visitors pay $30 and $15, respectively.

PARK HOURS
The park is open 24/7 year-round. It's in the Mountain time zone.

CELL-PHONE RECEPTION
Cell phones work in most developed areas and occasionally on trails. Public phones are at Dornan's, south Jenny Lake, Signal Mountain Lodge, Moran Entrance Station, Jackson Lake Lodge, Colter Bay Village, Leeks Marina, and Flagg Ranch.

RESTAURANTS
Though the park itself has some excellent restaurants, don't miss dining in Jackson, where restaurants combine game, fowl, and fish with the enticing spices and sauces of European cuisine and the lean ingredients, vegetarian entrées, and meat cuts that reflect the desires of health-conscious diners. Steaks are usually cut from grass-fed Wyoming or Montana beef, but you'll also find buffalo and elk on the menu; poultry and pasta are offered by most restaurants, as are fresh salads and fish (trout, tilapia, and salmon are most common). Just about everywhere, you can order a burger or a bowl of homemade soup. Casual is the word for most dining both within and outside the park. An exception is Jenny Lake Lodge, where jackets and ties are recommended for dinner. Breakfast is big: steak and eggs, pancakes, biscuits and gravy; lunches are lighter, often taken in a sack to enjoy on the trail.

Prices in the reviews are the average cost of a main course at dinner, or if dinner is not served, at lunch.

19

HOTELS

The choice of lodging properties within the park is as diverse as the landscape itself. Here you'll find simple campgrounds, cabins, and standard motel rooms. You can also settle into a homey bed-and-breakfast or a luxurious suite in a full-service resort. Between June and August, rates go up and rooms are harder to get without advanced reservations. Nonetheless, if you're looking to stay in a national park that's tailored to individual pursuits, this is it. Although this park is becoming more popular and crowded each year, it still resembles the haven its founders envisioned in 1929 and when it was expanded in 1950, a place where people can contemplate and interact with nature.

For information on lodging and dining in the park, contact the park's largest concessionaire, Grand Teton Lodge Company. ☎ *307/543–2811* ⊕ *www.gtlc.com.*

Prices in the reviews are the lowest cost of a standard double room in high season. For expanded reviews, facilities, and current deals, visit Fodors.com.

TOURS

Grand Teton Lodge Company Bus Tours. Half-day tours depart from Jackson Lake Lodge and include visits to scenic viewpoints, visitor centers, and other park sites. Guides provide information about park geology, history, wildlife, and ecosystems. Buy tickets in advance at Colter Bay or Jackson Lake Lodge activities desks. Full-day tours continue into Yellowstone. ✉ *Jackson Lake Lodge* ☎ *307/543–2811, 800/628–9988* ⊕ *www.gtlc.com* ⊠ *$50–$110* ☉ *Mid-May–early Oct., Mon.–Sat.*

Gray Line Bus Tours. Full-day bus tours from Jackson provide an overview of Grand Teton National Park. You'll learn about the park's geology, history, birds, plants, and wildlife. ✉ *1580 W. Martin La., Jackson* ☎ *307/733–3135, 800/443–6133* ⊕ *www.graylinejh.com* ⊠ *$115* ☉ *June–Sept., Mon., Wed., and Fri.*

Jackson Lake Cruises. Grand Teton Lodge Company runs 1½-hour Jackson Lake cruises from Colter Bay Marina throughout the day, as well as three-hour breakfast cruises and sunset cruises. Guides explain how forest fires and glaciers have shaped the Grand Teton landscape. ✉ *2 miles off U.S. 89/191/287, 5 miles north of Jackson Lake Junction* ☎ *307/543–3100, 800/628–9988* ⊕ *www.gtlc.com* ⊠ *$30–$60* ☉ *Late May–mid-Sept.*

VISITOR INFORMATION

PARK CONTACT INFORMATION

Grand Teton National Park ☎ *307/739–3300* ⊕ *www.nps.gov/grte.*

VISITOR CENTERS

Colter Bay Visitor Center. A small display shows off a few items from the park's collection of American Indian artifacts. (Hundreds more are being cleaned and restored for future displays.) In summer, rangers lead daily 15-minute chats about the park's history and climate on the back deck. ✉ *U.S. 89/191/287, ½ mile west of Colter Bay Junction, Oxbow Bend* ☎ *307/739–3594* ☉ *June–early Sept., daily 8–7; rest of Sept., daily 8–5.*

Craig Thomas Discovery and Visitor Center. This sleek center has interactive and interpretive exhibits dedicated to themes of preservation, mountaineering, and local wildlife. There's also a 3-D map of the park and streaming video along a footpath showing the area's intricate natural features. Dozens of Native American artifacts from the David T. Vernon Collection are housed here. A plush, 155-seat theater occasionally screens nature documentaries. ⊠ *½ mile west of Moose Junction, Moose* ☎ *307/739–3399* ⊙ *Early June–early Sept., daily 8–7; call for fall and spring hrs.*

Jenny Lake Visitor Center. This historic log cabin was used as a studio by the first and only official park photographer, Harrison Crandall. Geology exhibits explain how the mountains ended up where they are. ⊠ *S. Jenny Lake Junction, 8 miles north of Moose Junction on Teton Park Rd., Jenny Lake* ☎ *307/739–3392* ⊙ *June–early Sept., daily 8–7; call for spring and fall hrs.*

Laurance S. Rockefeller Preserve Interpretive Center. This contemporary structure feels more like an art gallery than an interpretive facility. The elegant, eco-friendly building is more than just eye candy—you can experience the sounds of the park in a cylindrical audio chamber, and laminated maps in the reading room are great for trip planning. ⊠ *East side of Moose-Wilson Rd., about 4 miles south of Moose and 3 miles north of Granite Canyon Entrance Station* ☎ *307/739–3654* ⊙ *Late May–early Sept., daily 8–6; call for off-season hrs.*

EXPLORING

SCENIC DRIVES

FAMILY **Antelope Flats Road.** Off U.S. 191/26/89, about 2 miles north of Moose Junction, this narrow road wanders eastward over sagebrush flats. The road intersects the gravel Mormon Row, where you can turn off to see abandoned homesteaders' barns and houses from the turn of the 20th century. Less than 2 miles past Mormon Row is a three-way intersection where you can turn right to loop around past the town of Kelly and Gros Ventre campground and rejoin U.S. 191/26/89 at Gros Ventre Junction. Keep an eye out for pronghorn, bison, moose, raptors, and cyclists.

Fodor's Choice ★ **Jenny Lake Scenic Drive.** This 4-mile, one-way loop provides the park's best roadside close-ups of the Tetons as it winds south through groves of lodgepole-pine and open meadows. Roughly 1.5 miles off Teton Park Road, the Cathedral Group Turnout faces 13,770-foot Grand Teton (the range's highest peak), flanked by 12,928-foot Mt. Owen and 12,325-foot Mt. Teewinot.

FAMILY **Signal Mountain Road.** This exciting drive climbs 700 feet along a 4-mile stretch of switchbacks. As you travel through forest you can catch glimpses of Jackson Lake and Mt. Moran. At the top of the winding road, park and follow the well-marked dirt path to one of the best panoramas in the park. From 7,593 feet above sea level your gaze can sweep over all of Jackson Hole and the 40-mile Teton Range. The views are particularly dramatic at sunset. The road is not appropriate for long trailers and is closed in winter. ⊠ *Off Teton Park Rd., south of Jackson Lake Junction.*

19

HISTORIC SITES

Cunningham Cabin Historic Site. At the end of a gravel spur road, an easy 0.75-mile trail runs through sagebrush around Pierce Cunningham's 1890 log-cabin homestead. Although you can peer inside, the building has no furnishings or displays. Watch for badgers, coyotes, and Uinta ground squirrels in the area. ⊠ *½ mile off Jackson Hole Hwy., 5 miles south of Moran Junction, Antelope Flats.*

Menor's Ferry Historic Area. Down a path from the Chapel of the Transfiguration, the ferry on display here is not the original, but it's an accurate re-creation of the double-pontoon craft built by Bill Menor in 1894. It demonstrates how people crossed the Snake River before bridges were built. In the cluster of turn-of-the-20th-century buildings there are historical displays. Pick up a pamphlet for a self-guided tour, and check out the nearby general store, where candy and soda are sold in the summer. The ferry typically runs after spring runoff, between June and August, and only when a park ranger is available to operate it. ⊠ *½ mile off Teton Park Rd., 1 mile north of Moose Junction* ⊙ *Daily dawn–dusk.*

Mormon Row Historic Area. Settled by homesteaders between 1896 and 1907, this area received its name because many of them were members of the Church of Jesus Christ of Latter-day Saints, also known as Mormons. The remaining barns, homes, and outbuildings are representative of early homesteading in the West. You can wander around, hike the row, and take photographs. The T. A. Moulton Barn turned 100 in 2013 and is said to be the most-photographed barn in the state. ⊠ *Just off Antelope Flats Rd., 2 miles north of Moose Junction* ⊙ *Daily.*

SCENIC STOPS

Chapel of the Sacred Heart. This small log Catholic chapel sits in the pine forest with a view of Jackson Lake. It's open only for services, but you can enjoy the view anytime. ⊠ *½ mile north of Signal Mountain Lodge, off Teton Park Rd.* ☎ *307/733–2516* ⊙ *Services June–Sept., weekends at 5.*

Chapel of the Transfiguration. This tiny chapel built in 1925 on land donated by Maud Noble is still a functioning Episcopal church. Couples come here to exchange vows with the Tetons as a backdrop, and tourists snap photos of the small church with its awe-inspiring view. ⊠ *Chapel of the Transfiguration Rd., ½ mile off Teton Park Rd., Moose* ☎ *307/733–2603* ⊕ *www.stjohnsjackson.org* ⊙ *Services late May–late Sept., Sun. at 8 and 10.*

Jackson Lake. The biggest of Grand Teton's glacier-carved lakes, this body of water in the northern reaches of the park was enlarged by construction of the Jackson Lake Dam in 1906. You can fish, sail, and windsurf here. Three marinas (Colter Bay, Leeks, and Signal Mountain) provide access for boaters, and several picnic areas, campgrounds, and lodges overlook the lake. ⊠ *U.S. 89/191/287 from Lizard Creek to Jackson Lake Junction, and Teton Park Rd. from Jackson Lake Junction to Signal Mountain Lodge.*

CLOSE UP

Plants and Wildlife in Grand Teton

Grand Teton's short growing season and arid climate create a complex ecosystem and hardy plant species. The dominant elements are big sagebrush, which gives a gray-green cast to the valley, lodgepole pine trees, quaking aspen, and ground-covering wildflowers such as bluish-purple lupine. In spring and early summer you will see the vibrant yellow arrowleaf balsamroot and low larkspur. Jackson Hole's short growing season gives rise to spectacular if short-lived displays of wildflowers, best seen mid-June to early July. The changing of the aspen and cottonwood leaves in early fall can be equally spectacular.

On almost any trip to Grand Teton, you will see bison, pronghorn antelope, and moose. More rarely you will see a black or grizzly bear, fox, or wolf. Watch for elk along the forest edge, and, in the summer, on Teton Park Road. Oxbow Bend and Willow Flats are good places to look for moose, beaver, and otter in twilight hours any time of year. Pronghorn and bison appear in summer along the highway and Antelope Flats Road.

The park's smaller animals—yellow-bellied marmots, pikas, and Uinta ground squirrels, as well as a variety of birds and waterfowl—are commonly seen along park trails and waterways. Seek out water sources—the Snake River, the glacial lakes, and marshy areas—to see birds such as bald eagles, ospreys, ducks, and trumpeter swans. Your best chance to see wildlife is at dawn or dusk.

Jenny Lake. Named for the Shoshone wife of mountain man Beaver Dick Leigh, this glacier-carved lake south of Jackson Lake draws paddlesports enthusiasts to its pristine waters and hikers to its tree-shaded trails. ⊠ *Off Teton Park Rd. midway between Moose and Jackson Lake.*

Oxbow Bend. This peaceful spot overlooks a quiet backwater left by the Snake River when it cut a new southern channel. White pelicans stop here on their spring migration (many stay on through summer), sandhill cranes and trumpeter swans visit frequently, and great blue herons nest amid the cottonwoods along the river. Use binoculars to search for bald eagles, osprey, moose, beaver, and otter. The Oxbow is known for the reflection of Mt. Moran that marks its calm waters in early morning. ⊠ *U.S. 89/191/287, 2½ miles east of Jackson Lake Junction.*

Willow Flats. You will almost always see moose grazing in this marshy area, in part because of its good growth of willow bushes, where moose both eat and hide. This is also a good place to see birds and waterfowl. ⊠ *U.S. 89/191/287, 1 mile north of Jackson Lake Junction.*

EDUCATIONAL OFFERINGS

CLASSES AND SEMINARS

FAMILY **Teton Science School.** Adults, teenagers, and families can join one of the school's wildlife expeditions in Grand Teton, Yellowstone, and surrounding forests to see and learn about wolves, bears, bighorn sheep, and other animals. Summer weekday programs like Tracking Thursdays

19

and Feathered Fridays usually include a picnic. Junior high and high school students can take multiday (and sometimes multiweek) field adventures. ✉ *700 Coyote Canyon Rd., Jackson* ☎ *307/733–1313* ⊕ *www.tetonscience.org* ✉ *Half-day tours $125; weeknight programs $15–$30; multiday programs $225–$3,800.*

RANGER PROGRAMS

Campfire Programs. Park rangers lead free nightly slide shows from June through September at the Colter Bay, Gros Ventre, and Signal Mountain amphitheaters. For schedules of topics, check at visitor centers or in the *Grand Teton Guide* park newspaper. ✉ *Colter Bay Amphitheater, 2 miles off U.S. 89/191/287, 5 miles north of Jackson Lake Junction* ☎ *307/739–3399, 307/739–3594* ⊙ *June and July, daily at 9:30 pm; Aug. and Sept., daily at 9 pm* ✉ *Gros Ventre Amphitheater, 4 miles off U.S. 26/89/191 and 2½ miles west of Kelly on Gros Ventre River Rd., 6 miles south of Moose Junction* ✉ *Signal Mountain Amphitheater, Teton Park Rd., 4 miles south of Jackson Lake Junction.*

FAMILY **Junior Ranger Program.** Children and even adults can earn a Junior Ranger badge or patch by attending a program and filling out a pamphlet. Learn about the natural world of the park on an easy 2-mile hike with a ranger. Kids should wear old clothes and bring water, rain gear, and insect repellent. The 2½-hour Inspiration Point hike departs daily at 8:30; round-trip boat fare is $12. ✉ *Meet outside Jenny Lake Visitor Center* ☎ *307/739–3399, 307/739–3594.*

FAMILY **Nature Explorer's Backpack Program.** Rangers lend a nature journal and a backpack full of activities to children ages 6 through 12 before sending them out along the trails at the Rockefeller Preserve. ✉ *Laurance S. Rockefeller Preserve Interpretive Center, east side of Moose-Wilson Rd., 4 miles south of Moose and 3 miles north of Granite Canyon Entrance Station* ☎ *307/739–3654* ⊙ *Late May–early Sept., daily 8–6.*

FAMILY **Ranger Walks.** Rangers lead free walks throughout the park in summer, from a two-hour hike to Taggart Lake to a three-hour forest stroll at Colter Bay. The talks focus on a variety of subjects from wildlife to birds and flower species to geology. ☎ *307/739–3300* ⊙ *Early June– early Sept.*

SPORTS AND THE OUTDOORS

BICYCLING

Since the first paved pathways were completed in Jackson Hole in 1996, the valley has become a cyclist's paradise. Almost 60 miles of paved pathways thread through Jackson Hole, with more in the works. Those on two wheels can access Grand Teton on a path that begins at the north end of town and travels 21 miles to South Jenny Lake Junction. A bike lane permits two-way bike traffic along the one-way Jenny Lake Loop Road, a one-hour ride. The River Road, 4 miles north of Moose, is an easy four-hour mountain-bike ride along a ridge above the Snake River on a gravel road. Bicycles are not allowed on trails or in the backcountry in the park.

On the Bridger-Teton National Forest that surrounds Jackson, the Snow King Mountain trail system offers miles of singletrack, from easy to challenging. The Cache Creek to Game Creek loop is a 25-mile ride on dirt roads, trails, and a paved pathway. Roadies can enjoy the rural Fish Creek or Fall Creek roads, and downhillers revel in the Bike Park at Jackson Hole Mountain Resort. Maps can be obtained at the Jackson Hole and Greater Yellowstone Visitor Center at the north end of town on Cache Street.

OUTFITTERS

Hoback Sports. Get your own bike tuned up or rent one: road, mountain, hybrid, kids, and trailers. The shop also sells bikes, clothing, and accessories, and offers daily mountain bike tours. ⊠ *520 W. Broadway, #3, Jackson* ☎ *307/733–5335* ⊕ *www.hobacksports.com* ☉ *Daily 10–6.*

Teton Mountain Bike Tours. Mountain bikers of all skill levels can take guided half-, full-, or multiday tours with Teton Mountain Bike Tours into both Grand Teton and Yellowstone national parks, as well as winter tours of Jackson Hole on snow bikes with fat, studded tires. The store has rentals and is right across from the pathway leading to Grand Teton. ⊠ *545 N. Cache St., Jackson* ☎ *307/733–0712, 800/733–0788* ⊕ *www.tetonmtbike.com* ✉ *Half- to full-day trips $65–$110, 4-day Teton/Yellowstone tour $1,995* ☉ *May–Sept.*

BIRD-WATCHING

With more than 300 species of birds in the park, the Tetons make excellent bird-watching country. Here you might spot both the calliope hummingbird (the smallest North American hummingbird) and the trumpeter swan (the world's largest waterfowl). The two riparian habitats described here draw lots of attention, but there are many other bird-busy areas as well. Birds of prey circle around Antelope Flats Road, for instance—the surrounding fields are good hunting turf for red-tailed hawks and prairie falcons. At Taggart Lake you might see woodpeckers, bluebirds, and hummingbirds. Look for songbirds, such as pine and evening grosbeaks and Cassin's finches, in surrounding open pine and aspen forests.

Oxbow Bend. Some seriously impressive birds congregate at this quiet spot. In spring, white pelicans stop by during their northerly migration; in summer, bald eagles, great blue herons, and osprey nest nearby. Year-round, you'll have a good chance of seeing trumpeter swans. Nearby Willow Flats has similar bird life, plus sandhill cranes. ⊠ *U.S. 89/191/287, 2 miles east of Jackson Lake Junction.*

Phelps Lake. The moderate, 1.8-mile round-trip Phelps Lake Overlook Trail takes you from the Death Canyon trailhead up conifer- and aspen-lined glacial moraine to a view that's accessible only by foot. Expect abundant bird life: Western tanagers, Northern flickers, and ruby-crowned kinglets thrive in the bordering woods, and hummingbirds feed on scarlet gilia beneath the overlook. Don't neglect the Phelps Lake Trail, which circles the lake and is accessible from either Death Canyon or the Rockefeller Preserve. ⊠ *Moose-Wilson Rd., about 3 miles off Teton Park Rd.*

19

BOATING AND WATER SPORTS

Water sports in Grand Teton are diverse. You can float the Snake River, which runs high and fast early in the season (May and June) and more slowly during the latter part of the summer. Canoes, kayaks, and stand-up paddleboards dominate the smaller lakes and share the water with motorboats on impressively large Jackson Lake. Motorboats also are allowed on Jenny Lake, but there's an engine limit of 10 horsepower. You can launch your boat at Colter Bay, Leek's Marina, Signal Mountain, and Spalding Bay on Jackson Lake.

If you're floating the Snake River on your own, you are required to purchase a permit ($20 per boat for the entire season, or $10 per raft for seven days). Permits are available year-round at Craig Thomas Discovery and Visitor Center and in summer at Colter Bay. Before you set out, check with park rangers for current conditions.

You may prefer to take one of the many guided float trips through calm-water sections of the Snake; outfitters pick you up at the float-trip parking area near Craig Thomas Discovery and Visitor Center for a 15-minute drive to upriver launch sites. Ponchos and life preservers are provided. Early morning and evening floats are your best bets for wildlife viewing, but be sure to carry a jacket or sweater. Float season runs mid-April to December 15.

Colter Bay Marina. All types of services are available to boaters, including free parking for boat trailers and vehicles, free mooring, guided fishing trips, boat rentals, and fuel. ⊠ *On Jackson Lake* ☎ *307/543–3100, 800/628–9988.*

Leek's Marina. Parking for boat trailers and other vehicles is available for up to three nights. There are no boat rentals, but you can get fuel, and there's free short-term docking plus a superb pizza restaurant. This marina is operated by park concessionaire Signal Mountain Lodge. ⊠ *U.S. 89/191/287, 6 miles north of Jackson Lake Junction* ☎ *307/543–2831* ☉ *Mid-May–late Sept.*

Signal Mountain Lodge Marina. The marina rents pontoon boats, deck cruisers, motorboats, kayaks, and canoes by the hour or all day; rates start at $16 an hour for a kayak to $117 an hour for a deck cruiser. ⊠ *Teton Park Rd., 3 miles south of Jackson Lake Junction* ☎ *307/543–2831* ☉ *Mid-May–late Sept.*

TOURS AND OUTFITTERS

Barker-Ewing Float Trips. Travel the peaceful parts of the Snake River looking for wildlife as knowledgeable guides talk about area history, plants, and animals. ⊠ *Moose* ☎ *307/733–1800, 800/365–1800* ⊕ *www.barkerewing.com* ☞ *$70* ☉ *May–Sept.*

Grand Teton Lodge Company. Rent motorboats, kayaks, and canoes at Colter Bay from Grand Teton Lodge Company. The company also offers scenic raft trips on the Snake River. ⊠ *2 miles off U.S. 89/191/287, 5 miles north of Jackson Lake Junction* ☎ *307/543–3100, 800/628–9988* ⊕ *www.gtlc.com* ☞ *Kayaks and canoes $17 per hr, motorboats $40 per hr* ☉ *Late May–late Sept.*

Mad River Boat Trips. Mad River leads a variety of white-water and scenic float trips, some combined with breakfast, lunch, or dinner. ⊠ *Jackson* ☎ *307/733–6203, 800/458–7238* ⊕ *www.mad-river.com* ⊠ *$72–$124* ⊙ *Mid-May–Sept.*

Rendezvous River Sports. Join the stand-up paddleboard craze with help from the river rats at Rendezvous. Kayaking instruction and guided trips on area rivers and lakes are also available. The shop rents kayaks, canoes, rafts, and paddleboards. ⊠ *Jackson* ☎ *307/733–2471* ⊕ *www.jacksonholekayak. com* ⊠ *Half-day clinic $110–$250, full-day $145–$340* ⊙ *Apr.–Oct.*

Triangle X National Park Float Trips. Knowlegeable and charismatic guides row you down 10 miles of the Snake River through pristine riparian habitat in Grand Teton National Park. Try dawn or sunset supper floats for best wildlife viewing. ⊠ *Moose* ☎ *307/733–5500, 888/860–0005* ⊕ *nationalparkfloattrips.com* ⊠ *$70* ⊙ *Mid-May–Sept.*

CLIMBING

The Teton Range has some of the nation's most diverse mountaineering. Excellent rock, snow, and ice routes abound. Unless you're already a pro, it's recommended that you take a course from one of the park's concessionaire climbing schools before tackling the tough terrain. Practice your moves at Teton Boulder Park, a free outdoor artificial climbing wall in Phil Baux Park at the base of Snow King Mountain.

TOURS

Exum Mountain Guides. The oldest guide service in North America leads a variety of climbing experiences, including one-day mountain climbs, weeklong clinics culminating with a two-day ascent of the Grand Teton, and backcountry adventures on skis and snowboards. ☎ *307/733–2297* ⊕ *www.exumguides.com* ⊠ *One-day climbs $255–$395.*

Jackson Hole Mountain Guides. Beginning to advanced climbers can get instruction or explore classic granite routes in the Tetons and beyond. ⊠ *1325 S. Hwy. 89, Suite 104, Jackson* ☎ *307/733–4979, 800/239–7642* ⊕ *www.jhmg.com* ⊠ *Basic group class $160; one-day guided climbs $295–$500.*

19

FISHING

Rainbow, brook, lake, and native cutthroat trout inhabit the park's waters. The Snake's 75 miles of river and tributary are world-renowned for their fishing. To fish in Grand Teton National Park, you need a Wyoming fishing license. A day permit for nonresidents is $14, and an annual permit is $92 plus a $12.50 conservation stamp; for state residents a license costs $24 per season plus $12.50 for a conservation stamp. Children under age 14 can fish free with an adult who has a license.

Wyoming Game and Fish Department. Buy a fishing license at Colter Bay Marina, Dornan's, Signal Mountain Lodge, and at area sporting-goods stores, where you also can get solid information on good fishing spots and the best flies or lures to use. Or get one directly from the Wyoming Game and Fish Department. ⊠ *420 N. Cache St., Jackson* ☎ *307/733–2321* ⊕ *gf.state.wy.us.*

TOURS

Grand Teton Lodge Company. The park's major concessionaire, Grand Teton Lodge Company, operates guided fishing trips on Jackson Lake and guided fly-fishing trips on the Snake River. Make reservations at the activities desks at Colter Bay Village or Jackson Lake Lodge, where trips originate. ✉ *Colter Bay Marina or Jackson Lake Lodge* ☎ *307/543–3100, 800/628–9988* ⊕ *www.gtlc.com* ✎ *$176–$525* ⊗ *June–Sept.*

Signal Mountain Lodge. Half-day Jackson Lake guided fishing trips depart from the marina at Signal Mountain Lodge. Equipment and tackle are included in the price. ✉ *Teton Park Rd., 3 miles south of Jackson Lake Junction* ☎ *307/543–2831* ⊕ *www.signalmountainlodge.com* ✎ *$280* ⊗ *Mid-May–late Sept.*

HIKING

Most of Grand Teton's trails are unpaved, with just a few short paved sections in the vicinity of developed areas. You can get trail maps and information about hiking conditions from rangers at the park visitor centers at Moose, Jenny Lake, or Colter Bay, where you will also find bathrooms or outhouses; there are no facilities along trails themselves. Of the more than 250 miles of maintained trails, the most popular are those around Jenny Lake, the Leigh and String lakes area, and Taggart Lake Trail, with views of Avalanche Canyon.

Frontcountry or backcountry you may see moose and bears—keep your distance. Pets are not permitted on trails or in the backcountry, but you can take them along roadsides as long as they are on a leash no more than 6 feet long. Always let someone know where you are going and when you expect to return, and carry plenty of water, snacks, rain gear, warm clothes, bear spray, and a cell phone.

EASY

Cascade Canyon Trail. Take the 20-minute boat ride ($12) from the Jenny Lake dock to the start of a gentle, 0.5-mile climb to 200-foot Hidden Falls, the park's most popular and crowded trail destination. With the boat ride, plan on a couple of hours to experience this trail. Listen here for the distinctive bleating of the rabbitlike pikas among the glacial boulders and pines. The trail continues 0.5 mile to Inspiration Point over a rocky path that is moderately steep. There are two points on the climb that afford good views of Jenny Lake and the surrounding area, but keep climbing; after passing a rock wall you'll finally reach the true Inspiration Point, with the best views. *Easy.* ✉ *Trailhead at Jenny Lake Visitor Center, ¼ mile off Teton Park Rd., 8 miles north of Moose Junction.*

Colter Bay Nature Trail Loop. This very easy, 1.75-mile round-trip excursion treats you to views of Jackson Lake and the Tetons. As you follow the level trail from Colter Bay Visitor Center and along the forest's edge, you may see moose and bald eagles. Allow yourself two hours to complete the walk. *Easy.* ✉ *Trailhead at Colter Bay Visitor Center, 1 mile off U.S. 89/191/287, 5 miles north of Jackson Lake Junction.*

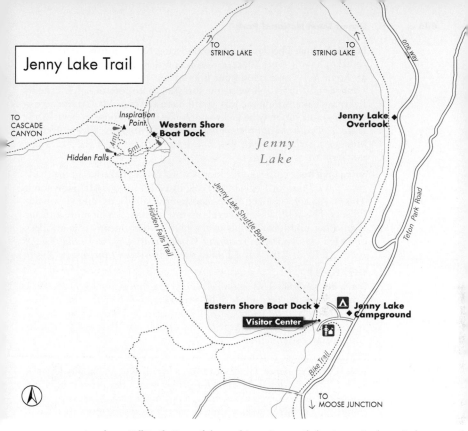

Jenny Lake Trail

TO STRING LAKE

TO STRING LAKE

one way

TO CASCADE CANYON

Inspiration Point

.4mi.

.5mi.

Hidden Falls

Western Shore Boat Dock

Jenny Lake Overlook

Jenny Lake

Hidden Falls Trail

Jenny Lake Shuttle Boat

Teton Park Road

Eastern Shore Boat Dock

Jenny Lake Campground

Visitor Center

Bike Trail

TO
↓ MOOSE JUNCTION

Lunchtree Hill Trail. One of the park's easiest trails begins at Jackson Lake Lodge and leads 0.5 mile to the top of a hill above Willow Flats. The area's willow thickets, beaver ponds, and wet, grassy meadows make it a birder's paradise. Look for sandhill cranes, hummingbirds, and the many types of songbirds described in the free bird guide available at visitor centers. You might also see moose. The round-trip walk takes no more than half an hour. *Easy.* ⊠ *Trailhead at Jackson Lake Lodge, U.S. 89/191/287, ½ mile north of Jackson Lake Junction.*

MODERATE

FAMILY **Jenny Lake Trail.** You can walk to Hidden Falls from Jenny Lake ranger station by following the mostly level trail around the south shore of the lake to Cascade Canyon Trail. Jenny Lake Trail continues around the lake for 6.5 miles. It's an easy trail—classed here as moderate because of its length—that will take you two to three hours. You'll walk through a lodgepole-pine forest, have expansive views of the lake and the land to the east, and hug the shoulder of the massive Teton range itself. Along the way you are likely to see elk, pikas, golden-mantled ground squirrels, a variety of ducks and water birds, plus you may hear elk bugling, birdsong, and the chatter of squirrels. *Moderate.* ⊠ *Trailhead at Jenny Lake Visitor Center, S. Jenny Lake Junction, ½ mile off Teton Park Rd., 8 miles north of Moose Junction.*

Leigh Lake Trail. The flat trail follows String Lake's northeastern shore to Leigh Lake's south shore, covering 2 miles in a round-trip of about an hour. You can extend your hike into a moderate 7.5-mile, four-hour round trip by following the forested east shore of Leigh Lake to Bearpaw Lake. Along the way you'll have views of Mt. Moran across the lake, and you may be lucky enough to spot a moose or bear. *Moderate.* ⊠ *Trailhead at northwest corner of String Lake Picnic Area, ½ mile west of Jenny Lake Rd., 2 miles off Teton Park Rd., 12 miles north of Moose Junction.*

String Lake Trail. This 3.5-mile loop around String Lake lies in the shadows of 11,144-foot Rockchuck Peak and 11,430-foot Mt. Saint John. This is also a good place to see moose, hear songbirds, and view wildflowers. This trail, which takes about three hours, is a bit more difficult than other mid-length trails in the park, which means it is also less crowded. *Moderate.* ⊠ *Trailhead ¼ mile west of Jenny Lake Rd., 2 miles off Teton Park Rd., 12 miles north of Moose Junction.*

DIFFICULT

Death Canyon Trail. This 7.6-mile trail to the junction with Static Peak Trail is strenuous, with lots of hills to traverse before the final 1,061-foot climb up into Death Canyon. Plan to spend most of the day on this steep trail. *Difficult.* ⊠ *Trailhead off Moose-Wilson Rd., 4 miles south of Moose Junction.*

TOURS

Hole Hiking Experience. Guides lead hikes for all ages and ability levels in Grand Teton National Park and forests beyond. They provide information about the history, geology, and ecology of the area. Many trips incorporate yoga or have a holistic bent. In winter, snowshoe tours are offered. ⊠ *Jackson* ☎ *307/690–4453, 866/733–4453* ⊕ *www.holehike.com.*

HORSEBACK RIDING

You can arrange a guided horseback tour at Colter Bay Village and Jackson Lake Lodge corrals or with a number of private outfitters. Most offer rides of an hour or two up to all-day excursions. If you want to spend even more time riding in Grand Teton and the surrounding mountains, consider a stay at a dude ranch. Shorter rides are almost all appropriate for novice riders, while more experienced cowboys and cowgirls will enjoy the longer journeys where the terrain gets steeper and you may wind through deep forests. For any ride be sure to wear long pants and boots (cowboy boots or hiking boots). Because you may ride through trees, a long-sleeve shirt is also a good idea and a hat is always appropriate, but it should have a stampede string to make sure it stays on your head if the wind comes up.

TOURS

Colter Bay Village Corral. One- and two-hour rides leave Colter Bay Village Corral for a variety of destinations. Short jaunts head around several secluded ponds on Hermitage Point. ⊠ *2 miles off U.S. 89/191/287, 5 miles north of Jackson Lake Junction* ☎ *307/543–3100, 800/628–9988* ⊕ *www.gtlc.com* ⌂ *$40–$60* ☉ *June–Sept.*

Jackson Lake Lodge Corral. Two-hour trail rides follow secluded paths to peaceful Emma Matilda Lake and Oxbow Bend. ⊠ *U.S. 89/191/287, ½ mile north of Jackson Lake Junction* ☎ *307/543–3100, 800/628–9988* ⊕ *www.gtlc.com* ☜ *$75* ⊙ *June–Sept.*

WINTER SPORTS

Grand Teton has some of North America's finest and most varied cross-country skiing. Ski the gentle 3-mile Swan Lake–Heron Pond Loop near Colter Bay, the mostly level 10-mile Jenny Lake Trail, or the moderate 4-mile Taggart Lake–Beaver Creek Loop and 5-mile Phelps Lake Overlook Trail. Teton Park Road is groomed for classic and skate-skiing from early January to mid-March. In winter, overnight backcountry travelers must register or make a reservation at the Craig Thomas Discovery and Visitor Center.

Snowmobiling is permitted on Jackson Lake only for ice fishing. Since snowmobiles must be towed into the park, sledders pay only the regular park entrance fees. Snowmobilers wishing to proceed north from Flagg Ranch into Yellowstone National Park must be with a commercial tour guide.

The Flagg Ranch Information Station is closed in winter but ski and snowshoe trails are open and marked with flagging tape. Pick up a map at the Flagg Ranch convenience store. For information about a free, ranger-guided snowshoe walk, call the Craig Thomas Discovery and Visitor Center.

TOURS AND OUTFITTERS

Pepi Stiegler Sports. Buy or rent skis or snowboards at Pepi's, conveniently located at the base of Jackson Hole Mountain Resort. The array of clothing and accessories is the largest in the valley. ⊠ *3395 W. Village Dr., Teton Village* ☎ *307/733–4505* ⊕ *www.pepistieglers.com* ☜ *Ski or snowboard rental $28–$52* ⊙ *Closed May–Oct.* ⊠ *3255 W. Village Dr., Teton Village* ☎ *307/733–6838*

Skinny Skis. The hub for nordic skiing in the valley sells and rents equipment for snowshoeing, skate-skiing, and classic cross-country skiing. It's also the place to find down jackets, wool base layers, and advice on what trails to explore. ⊠ *65 W. Deloney Ave., Jackson* ☎ *307/733–6094* ⊕ *www.skinnyskis.com* ⊙ *Mon.–Sat. 9–6, Sun. 10–5.*

Togwotee Mountain Lodge. Rent a snowmobile and explore 600-plus miles of groomed trails and endless powder-filled meadows along the Continental Divide. ⊠ *27655 Rte. 26/U.S. 287, Moran* ☎ *307/543–2847, 866/278–4245* ⊕ *www.togwoteelodge.com* ☜ *Snowmobile rental $164–$209* ⊙ *Closed May–Oct.*

19

WHAT'S NEARBY

NEARBY TOWNS

The major gateway to Grand Teton National Park is **Jackson**—but don't confuse this with Jackson Hole. Jackson Hole is the mountain-ringed valley that houses Jackson and much of Grand Teton National Park. The town of Jackson, located south of the park, is a small community (roughly 9,700 residents) that gets flooded with 3 to 4 million visitors annually. Expensive homes and fashionable shops have sprung up all over, but Jackson manages to maintain its character. With its wooden boardwalks and old-fashioned storefronts, the town center still looks a bit like a Western movie set. There's a lot to do here, both downtown and in the surrounding countryside.

If it's skiing you're after, **Snow King Resort** is the oldest resort in the valley, and its 7,808-foot mountain overlooks the town of Jackson and the National Elk Refuge. It's at the end of Snow King Avenue. **Teton Village,** on the southwestern side of the park, is a cluster of businesses centered around the facilities of the Jackson Hole Mountain Resort. This ski and snowboard area has the longest continuous vertical rise in the U.S. at 4,139 feet, accessed by an aerial tram to the top of Rendezvous Mountain (10,450 feet). A gondola and various other lifts take skiers to other sections of the mountain. There are plenty of places to eat, stay, and shop here.

On the "back side of the Tetons," as eastern Idaho is known, is **Driggs,** the western gateway to Yellowstone and Grand Teton. Easygoing and rural, Driggs resembles the Jackson of a few decades ago. To reach the park from here you have to cross a major mountain pass that is sometimes closed in winter by avalanches. **Dubois,** about 85 miles east of Jackson, is the least known of the gateway communities to Grand Teton and Yellowstone, but this town of 1,000 has all the services of the bigger towns. You can still get a room for the night here during the peak summer travel period without making a reservation weeks or months in advance (though it's a good idea to call a week or so before you intend to arrive).

About an hour to the south is **Pinedale,** another small Wyoming town with lodging, restaurants, and attractions. Energy development has made the area a hopping place these days, so be sure to plan ahead if you want to stay in town.

VISITOR INFORMATION

Colter Bay Visitor Center ⊠ *6 miles north of Jackson Lake Junction on U.S. 89/191/287, Moran* ☎ *307/739-3594* ⊕ *www.nps.gov/grte/planyourvisit/ cbvc.htm* ⊗ *Memorial Day–Sept., daily 8–7; Oct.–May, daily 9–5.* **Dubois Chamber of Commerce** ⊠ *616 W. Ramshorn St., Dubois* ☎ *888/455-2556* ⊕ *www.duboiswyomingchamber.org.* **Eastern Idaho Visitor Information Center** ⊠ *425 N. Capitol Ave., Idaho Falls, Idaho* ☎ *208/523-1010, 866/365-6943* ⊕ *www.visitidaho.org/regions/eastern.* **Jackson Chamber of Commerce** ☎ *307/733-3316* ⊕ *www.jacksonholechamber.com.*

Granite Hot Springs

Soothing thermal baths in pristine outback country await in the heart of the Bridger-Teton National Forest, just a short drive south of Jackson. Concerted local and federal efforts have preserved the wild lands in this hunter and fisherman's paradise where ranches dot the valley floor. The Snake River turns west, and the contours sheer into steep vertical faces. At Hoback Junction, about 11 miles south of Jackson, head east (toward Pinedale) on U.S. Highway 189/191 and follow the Hoback River east through its beautiful canyon. Keep an eye out for life-jacketed rafters and kayakers who float through Hoback Canyon.

A tributary canyon 10 miles east of the junction is followed by a well-maintained and -marked gravel road to Granite Hot Springs (☎ 307/734–7400), in the Bridger-Teton National Forest. Drive 9 miles off U.S. 189/191 (northeast) on Granite Creek Road to reach the hot springs. People also come for the shady, creekside campground and moderate hikes up Granite Canyon to passes with panoramic views. You'll want to drive with some caution, as there are elevated turns, the possibility of a felled tree, and wandering livestock that can own the road ahead on blind curves. In winter the hot springs are accessed only by skis, snowmobile, or dogsled from the highway. The 93°F to 112°F thermal bath at the end of the road is pure bliss, but it's closed from November through December 10 and from April to May 20. Admission costs $6 per person, cash or check only. Call for hours, which vary by season.

Jackson Hole and Greater Yellowstone Visitor Center. Stop at the Jackson Hole and Greater Yellowstone Visitor Center to get information about area attractions and to see wildlife displays that include bronze elk sculptures outside and a herd of stuffed elk in the lobby. The center is jointly operated by several organizations and governmental agencies—including the U.S. Forest Service, U.S. Fish and Wildlife Service, U.S. Department of the Interior, and Wyoming Game and Fish Department—so you can get information about the entire region. ■TIP→ From early December to late March, buses depart every 15 minutes to take visitors 2½ miles north for sleigh rides that glide close to grazing elk on the refuge. ⊠ *532 N. Cache St., Jackson* ☎ *307/733–3316* ⊕ *www.fs.fed.us/jhgyvc* ☉ *Late May–Sept., daily 8–7; Oct.–late May, daily 9–5.*

Sublette County Chamber of Commerce ⊠ *19 E. Pine St., Pinedale* ☎ *307/367–2242* ⊕ *www.sublettechamber.com.* **Teton Valley Chamber of Commerce** ⊠ *57 S. Main St., Driggs, Idaho* ☎ *208/354–2500* ⊕ *www.tetonvalleychamber.com.*

19

NEARBY ATTRACTIONS

DUBOIS

FAMILY **National Bighorn Sheep Interpretive Center.** The local variety is known as the Rocky Mountain bighorn, but you can learn about all kinds of bighorn sheep here. Among the exhibits of mounted specimens here are the Super Slam diorama, with one of each type of wild sheep in the world, and two bighorn rams fighting during the rut. Hands-on exhibits illustrate a bighorn's body language, characteristics, and habitat. Reserve ahead for winter wildlife-viewing tours ($50) to Whiskey Mountain. ⊠ *907 W. Ramshorn Ave.* ☎ *307/455–3429* ⊕ *www. bighorn.org* ▨ *$2.50* ⊙ *Memorial Day–Labor Day, Mon.–Sat. 9–6, Sun. 9–5; early Sept.–late May, Mon.–Sat. 9–5.*

JACKSON

Bridger-Teton National Forest. This 3.4-million-acre forest has something for everyone: history, hiking, camping, and wildlife. It encompasses the Teton Wilderness east of Grand Teton National Park and south of Yellowstone National Park, the Gros Ventre Wilderness southeast of Jackson, and the Bridger Wilderness farther south and east. No motor vehicles are allowed in the wilderness, but there are many scenic drives, natural springs where you can swim or soak throughout the year, and cultural sights like abandoned lumber camps in the forest between the wildernesses. The peaks reach higher than 13,000 feet, and the area is liberally sprinkled with more than a thousand high-mountain lakes, where fishing is generally excellent. ⊠ *Forest headquarters, 340 N. Cache St.* ☎ *307/739–5500* ⊕ *www.fs.fed.us/r4/btnf* ▨ *Free.*

FAMILY **Jackson Hole Museum.** A much-expanded and year-round museum debuted in 2011. See exhibits about area homesteaders and find out how Dead Man's Bar got its name. You can also learn about Jackson's all-female town government, not to mention a lady sheriff who claimed to have killed three men before hanging up her spurs. Among the exhibits are American Indian, ranching, and cowboy artifacts. ⊠ *225 N. Cache St.* ☎ *307/733–2414* ⊕ *www.jacksonholehistory.org* ▨ *$6* ⊙ *Mon.–Sat. 10–6, Sun. noon–5.*

FAMILY **National Elk Refuge.** Wildlife abounds on this 25,000-acre refuge throughout the year. From late November to March, the highlight is the more than 7,000 elk, many with enormous antler racks, that winter here. Elk can be observed from various pullouts along U.S. 191 or by slowly driving your car on the refuge's winding, unpaved roads. You can take a horse-drawn sleigh ride for the chance to see the elk up close. Among the other animals that make their home here are buffalo, bighorn sheep, and coyotes, as well as trumpeter swans and other waterfowl. In summer, the range is light on big game, but you can tour a historic homestead from June to September. From mid-December to early April, sleigh rides depart every 15 minutes or so from the Jackson Hole and Greater Yellowstone Visitor Center. Wear warm clothing, including hats, gloves, boots, long johns, and coats. ⊠ *Northeast of Jackson along Refuge Rd.* ☎ *307/733–9212 for refuge, 307/734–9378 for visitor center* ⊕ *www.fws.gov/refuge/national_elk_refuge* ▨ *Sleigh rides $19* ⊙ *Daily dawn–dusk.*

National Museum of Wildlife Art. See an impressive collection of wildlife art—most of it devoted to North American species—in 14 galleries displaying the work of artists Karl Bodmer, Albert Bierstadt, Charles Russell, John Clymer, Robert Bateman, Carl Rungius, and others. A deck here affords views across the National Elk Refuge, where, particularly in winter, you can see wildlife in a natural habitat. An elaborate 0.75-mile outdoor sculpture trail includes a monumental herd of bronze bison by Richard Loffler trudging across the butte. ⊠ *2820 Rungius Rd.* ☎ *307/733–5771* ⊕ *www.wildlifeart.org* ⊡ *$12* ⊙ *Mid-May–mid-Oct., daily 9–5; mid-Oct.–mid-May, Mon.–Sat. 9–5, Sun. 11–5.*

PINEDALE

FAMILY **Museum of the Mountain Man.** Preserving the history of the area's trapper heritage, this museum displays 19th-century guns, traps, clothing, and beaver pelts. There's also an interpretive exhibit devoted to the pioneer and ranch history of Sublette County as well as an overview of the Western fur trade. In summer the museum hosts living-history demonstrations, children's events, a reenactment of the early 19th-century Green River Rendezvous, and lectures. ⊠ *700 E. Hennick Rd.* ☎ *307/367–4101, 877/686–6266* ⊕ *www.museumofthemountainman. com* ⊡ *$5* ⊙ *May–Sept., daily 9–5; Oct., Mon.–Sat. 9–4.*

AREA ACTIVITIES

BOATING

The companies that operate in Grand Teton also generally have trips on other area waters. The Snake River outside the park has spectacular white-water stretches. The rafting season runs from late May through August, with the wildest water during June.

GOLF

Jackson Hole Golf and Tennis Club. This 18-hole course redesigned by Robert Trent Jones has views of the Teton Range and an eco-friendly and elegant clubhouse. It has been ranked among Wyoming's top courses. ⊠ *5000 Spring Gulch Rd., 9 miles north of Jackson on U.S. 189, then 2 miles west at Gros Ventre Junction* ☎ *307/733–3111* ⊕ *www.jhgtc. com* ⚑ *18 holes. 7409 yards. Par 72. Green Fee: $65–$185* ⊙ *Late Apr.–mid-Oct.* ☞ *Facilities: Driving range, putting green, pitching area, golf carts, pull carts, rental clubs, pro-shop, golf academy/lessons, restaurant, bar.*

Teton Pines Resort and Country Tennis Club. Arnold Palmer and Ed Seay designed this relatively flat 18-hole course near Teton Village. It has views of the Tetons, abundant wildlife, and is certified as an Audubon course. In winter it becomes a well-groomed cross-country ski track with a full-service shop. The restaurant is excellent. ⊠ *3450 N. Clubhouse Dr., Wilson* ☎ *307/733–1005, 800/238–2223* ⊕ *www. tetonpines.com* ⚑ *18 holes. 7412 yards. 72 par. Green Fee: $120–$160* ⊙ *May–mid-Oct.* ☞ *Facilities: driving range, putting green, pitching area, golf carts, pull carts, caddies, rental clubs, pro-shop, lessons, restaurant, bar.*

19

WINTER SPORTS

Jackson Hole Mountain Resort. Skiers and snowboarders love Jackson Hole, one of the great skiing experiences in America on 2,500 acres. There are literally thousands of routes up and down the mountain, and not all of them are hellishly steep, despite Jackson's reputation. In the summer, a mountain-bike park takes advantage of the legendary terrain. ⊠ *Jackson Hole* ☎ *307/733–2292, 800/333–7766* ⊕ *www. jacksonhole.com.*

ARTS AND ENTERTAINMENT

ART GALLERIES

Tayloe Piggott Gallery. A hot spot for contemporary work, Tayloe Piggott Gallery leaves wildlife and landscape art behind in favor of hip and often playful painting, sculpture, and jewelry. It's a bit of SoHo nestled in the Rockies. ⊠ *62 S. Glenwood St., Jackson* ☎ *307/733–0555* ⊕ *www.tayloepiggottgallery.com.*

Trailside Galleries. Trailside Galleries has traditional western art, including paintings by the biggest names—Charles M. Russell, John Clymer, and Howard Terpning—along with today's most talented western painters, such as Z. S. Liang, Nancy Glazier, and Bill Anton. ⊠ *130 E. Broadway, Jackson* ☎ *307/733–3186* ⊕ *www.trailsidegalleries.com.*

Under the Willow Photo Gallery. Abi Garaman has been capturing images of Jackson Hole and Grand Teton National Park on film for more than 50 years. Many of his wide selection of images of wildlife, mountains, barns, and more are displayed at Under the Willow Photo Gallery. ⊠ *50 S. Cache St., Jackson* ☎ *307/733–6633* ⊕ *www.underthewillow.com.*

Fodor's Choice   **Wild by Nature Gallery.** Here you'll find wildlife and landscape photography by Henry W. Holdsworth, plus note cards and gifts. The artist has several coffee-table books for sale with some of the Tetons' most striking and classic imagery. ⊠ *95 W. Deloney Ave., Jackson* ☎ *307/733–8877* ⊕ *www.wildbynaturegallery.com.*
★

MUSIC

FAMILY   **Bar J Chuckwagon.** This may be the best value in Jackson Hole. You get
Fodor's Choice   a complete ranch-style meal plus a rollicking Western show. Served on
★   a tin plate, the food is barbecued beef, chicken, or ribeye steak with potatoes, beans, biscuits, applesauce, and spice cake, along with lemonade or ranch coffee. The talented Bar J Wranglers croon, play instruments, share cowboy stories, and even yodel. The dinner and show take place inside, so don't let the weather keep you away. The doors open at 5:30, so you can explore the Bar J's Western village—including a saloon and several shops—before the dinner bell rings at 7. Reservations are a good idea. ⊠ *Off Moose-Wilson Rd., 1 mile north of Hwy. 22, Wilson* ☎ *307/733–3370* ⊕ *www.barjchuckwagon.com* ☉ *Closed Oct.–Memorial Day.*

SHOPPING

Cowboy Shop. From silk scarves to big shiny buckles, if cowboys wear it, here's the place to get it. Western-style clothing includes hats, boots, and leather goods for all ages. ⊠ *129 W. Pine St., Pinedale* ☎ *307/367–4300* ⊕ *www.cowboyshop.com.*

Hide Out Leathers. Men's and women's clothing, including coats and vests made with local designs, are the specialty here. You'll also find home decor such as pillows and throws. ⊠ *40 N. Center St., Jackson* ☎ *307/733–2422* ⊕ *www.hideoutleathers.com.*

JD High Country Outfitters. Well stocked with the best in outdoor equipment for winter and summer, the shop formerly known as Jack Dennis is known internationally as a fishing and sporting headquarters. You can get everything from a backpack to skis and hunting rifles, as well as clothing and other supplies. Fishing equipment can be rented. ⊠ *50 E. Broadway, Jackson* ☎ *307/733–3270* ⊕ *www.jdhcoutfitters.com.*

SPAS

Bear and Doe Banya Spa. The only Russian-style banya in Wyoming has been a local's favorite massage spot for a decade. Remodeled in 2011 to include a propane-fired cedar sauna, infrared sauna, steam room and cold plunge, it's the perfect place to soothe overworked muscles, relax with friends, and even get thwacked with birch branches to improve circulation. ⊠ *35 E. Simpson Ave., Jackson* ☎ *307/732–0863* ⊕ *www.bearanddoebanya.com.*

WHERE TO EAT

IN THE PARK

19

$$ ✕ **Dornan's Chuck Wagon.** Hearty portions of beef, beans, potatoes,
AMERICAN short ribs, stew, and lemonade or hot coffee are the dinner standbys
FAMILY at Dornan's. Locals know this spot for the barbecue cooked over wood fires. At breakfast, count on old-fashioned staples such as sourdough pancakes or biscuits and gravy. You can eat your chuck-wagon meal inside one of the restaurant's teepees if it happens to be raining or windy; otherwise, sit at outdoor picnic tables with views of the Snake River and the Tetons. The quick service and inexpensive prices make this a good choice for families. $ *Average main: $20* ⊠ *10 Moose Rd., off Teton Park Rd.* ☎ *307/733–2415* ⊕ *www.dornans.com* ⊗ *Closed early Sept.–mid-June.*

$$ ✕ **Dornan's Pizza & Pasta Company.** Tasty Italian fare is the draw at
PIZZA (this) Dornan's, but you'll also find generous margaritas, a surprisingly diverse wine list, and occasional live music. Place your order at the front counter, then head to a table inside, on the side deck, or upstairs on the roof with stunning mountain views. This extremely popular eatery also serves steak and salads. The long inside bar has stellar views and friendly barkeeps. Check Dornan's schedule for live music and be sure to explore the wine shop next door: it's one of the most varied and

well-stocked in the state, and there's no corkage fee when you buy wine for your meal. [$] *Average main: $14* ✉ *10 Moose Rd., off Teton Park Rd.* ☎ *307/733–2415* 🌐 *www.dornans.com.*

$$$ AMERICAN 🍴 **Jackson Lake Lodge Mural Room.** One of the park's best restaurants gets its name from a 700-square-foot mural painted by Western artist Carl Roters. The mural details an 1837 Wyoming mountain man rendezvous and covers two walls of the dining room. Select from a menu that includes trout, elk, beef, and chicken. The plantain-crusted trout is a great choice, or try the bison prime rib. The tables face tall windows with panoramic views of Willow Flats and Jackson Lake to the northern Tetons. [$] *Average main: $28* ✉ *U.S. 89/191/287, ½ mile north of Jackson Lake Junction* ☎ *307/543–3463, 800/628–9988* 🌐 *www.gtlc.com* 🕐 *Closed mid-Oct.–late May.*

$$ AMERICAN 🍴 **Jackson Lake Lodge Pioneer Grill.** With an old-fashioned soda fountain, friendly service, and seats along a winding counter, this eatery recalls a 1950s-era luncheonette. Tuck into burgers, sundaes, and other classic American fare. [$] *Average main: $15* ✉ *U.S. 89/191/287, ½ mile north of Jackson Lake Junction* ☎ *307/543–2811* 🌐 *www.gtlc.com* 🕐 *Closed early Oct.–late May.*

$$$$ AMERICAN 🍴 **Jenny Lake Lodge Dining Room.** Elegant yet rustic, Grand Teton's finest restaurant has one of the most ambitious menus in any national park. The menu is always changing and includes dishes like tempura squash blossoms and pinot-glazed veal cheeks. The wine list is equally extensive. Breakfast and dinner are prix-fixe, and though lunch is à la carte, the inventive soups and panini are no less decadent. Jackets are strongly encouraged for men at dinner. [$] *Average main: $77* ✉ *Jenny Lake Rd., 2 miles off Teton Park Rd., 12 miles north of Moose Junction* ☎ *307/733–4647, 800/628–9988* 🌐 *www.gtlc.com* ✍ *Reservations essential* 🕐 *Closed early Oct.–late May.*

$ AMERICAN 🍴 **John Colter Cafe Court.** Quick and cheap is the name of the game at this no-frills cafeteria, with a menu of simple sandwiches and salads, plus a few bottled beers. [$] *Average main: $8* ✉ *5 miles north of Jackson Lake Lodge* ☎ *307/543–2811* 🌐 *www.gtlc.com* 🕐 *Closed early Sept.–early June.*

$$ AMERICAN 🍴 **The Peaks.** At Signal Mountain Lodge, this casual Western-style bistro has exposed ceiling beams and expansive windows overlooking Jackson Lake and the Tetons. Fish is the kitchen's specialty. Wild-caught salmon is served in a sauce of lemon, capers, and parsley, and the trout cakes are a superb appetizer. The Trapper Grill next door also serves lunch, and in the adjacent Deadman's Bar, the mountain of nachos and huckleberry margaritas are crowd favorites. [$] *Average main: $19* ✉ *Teton Park Rd., 4 miles south of Jackson Lake Junction* ☎ *307/543–2831* 🌐 *www.signalmountainlodge.com* 🕐 *Closed mid-Oct.–mid-May.*

$$ AMERICAN 🍴 **Ranch House at Colter Bay Village.** The Ranch House offers friendly service and inexpensive prices, making it a good choice for travelers on a budget or families who can't take another cafeteria meal. Western-style meals—thick steaks, barbecued ribs, chicken with chili sauce—dominate the menu. ■ **TIP→ The kitchen will prep your day's catch if you deliver it by 4 pm.** [$] *Average main: $17* ✉ *2 miles off U.S. 89/191/287, 5 miles north of Jackson Lake Junction, Colter Bay* ☎ *307/543–2811* 🌐 *www.gtlc.com* 🕐 *Closed late Sept.–late May.*

PICNIC AREAS

The park has 11 designated picnic areas, each with tables and grills, and most with pit toilets and water pumps or faucets. In addition to those listed here you can find picnic areas at Colter Bay Village Campground, Cottonwood Creek, the east shore of Jackson Lake, and South Jenny Lake and String Lake trailhead.

Chapel of the Sacred Heart. From this intimate lakeside picnic area you can look across southern Jackson Lake to Mt. Moran. ✉ *¼ mile east of Signal Mountain Lodge, off Teton Park Rd.*

Colter Bay. This big picnic area, spectacularly located right on the beach at Jackson Lake, gets crowded in July and August. It's conveniently close to flush toilets and stores. ✉ *2 miles off U.S. 89/191/287, 5 miles north of Jackson Lake Junction.*

Jenny Lake. Adjacent to the Jenny Lake shuttle boat dock is this shaded, pine-scented picnic site. After lunch, take the shuttle boat across the lake and enjoy a half-mile hike to Hidden Falls. ✉ *Near Jenny Lake Visitor Center.*

OUTSIDE THE PARK

$ AMERICAN

🍴 **The Bunnery.** Lunch is served year-round and dinner is served in summer, but it's the breakfasts of savory omelets and home-baked pastries that are irresistible. Try a giant almond stick, sticky bun, or a slice of raspberry, strawberry, or blueberry pie. There's also a decent vegetarian selection. All the breads are house made, most from flour that includes oats, sunflower, and millet; the OSM waffle is dense and delectable. It's elbow to elbow inside, so you may have to wait to be seated on busy mornings, but any inconvenience is well worth it. In summer there's outdoor seating. [$] *Average main: $9* ✉ *Hole-in-the-Wall Mall, 130 N. Cache St., Jackson* ☎ *307/734–0075* 🌐 *www.bunnery.com* ⏲ *No dinner Sept.–May.*

19

$$$$ AMERICAN Fodor's Choice ★

🍴 **Couloir.** The gondola at Teton Village whisks you to this stylish dining room at 9,095 feet. Gaze down on Jackson Hole while lingering over signature cocktails and a smart, contemporary prix-fixe dinner menu. Entrées might include house-smoked bison cuts or fork-ready Kurobuta pork, along with clever sides like chickpea pancakes and fried-green "Wyomatoes," locally grown tomatoes. Faux cowhide upholstery and a towering bar give the room a fun, modern feel. Days and hours can change with the seasons, so call for reservations. ■ **TIP→ For the same view with a smaller price tag, enjoy live music and huge portions of upscale bar food outside on the Deck from 4:30 to sunset in summer.** [$] *Average main: $85* ✉ *Atop Bridger Gondola at Jackson Hole Mountain Resort, Teton Village* ☎ *307/739–2675* 🌐 *www.jacksonhole.com/couloir-restaurant.html* ✍ *Reservations essential* ⏲ *Closed late Sept.–late Nov. and Apr.–mid-June. Lunch in winter only.*

$$$ MODERN ITALIAN

🍴 **Il Villaggio Osteria.** Underneath rustic barnwood timbers and columns or on an open-air patio, diners enjoy the flavors of Italy fused with fresh, inventive touches. Try the apple and Saint André triple-cream bruschetta, house-pulled mozzarella wrapped in smoked pancetta, or a generous slice of gooey lasagna. On the lower floor of the eco-chic Hotel

Terra, the restaurant has an extensive wine list that includes bottles from Spain, Portugal, and Germany, as well as Italy and the U.S. $ *Average main: $26* ⊠ *3335 W. Village Dr., Teton Village* ☎ *307/739–4100* ⊕ *www.jhosteria.com* ⊗ *No lunch.*

$$$
ITALIAN
✕ **Nani's Ristorante and Bar.** The ever-changing menu at this cozy restaurant—a longtime favorite among the locals—may include braised veal shanks with saffron risotto, lasagna, and other Italian specialties. The knowledgeable staff will help you through the rotating menu, which focuses on a different region each month. The grandly presented Teton Tiramisu is a must for dessert. Almost hidden behind a motel, this place attracts gourmets who appreciate the fine cuisine. The wine list features a wide range of sparkling wines, regional Italian and non-Italian wines, and wines by the glass. Vegan and gluten-free choices are offered. $ *Average main: $28* ⊠ *242 N. Glenwood St., Jackson* ☎ *307/733–3888* ⊕ *www.nanis.com* ⊗ *No lunch.*

$
MEXICAN
FAMILY
✕ **Pica's Taqueria.** A favorite among locals, Pica's serves authentic Mexican dishes at an affordable price. From fish tacos and huge wet burritos to delectable chopped salads, the food is consistently fresh and delicious, and the margaritas are strong. Located a mile from the bustle of town square, basic counters and tables are surrounded by bright folk art. In summer, the sunny patio tables are dog-friendly. $ *Average main: $10* ⊠ *1160 Alpine La., Jackson* ☎ *307/734–4457* ⊕ *www.picastaqueria.com.*

$$$
AMERICAN
Fodor's Choice
★
✕ **Snake River Grill.** One of Jackson's best dining options, this sophisticated dining room offers creatively prepared dishes like free-range veal chops, grilled venison, buffalo strip steak, elk chops, and grilled Idaho trout. The menu changes seasonally and reflects what is available in the market. The extensive wine list seems to pick up another award every year or so. $ *Average main: $28* ⊠ *84 E. Broadway Ave., Jackson* ☎ *307/733–0557* ⊕ *www.snakerivergrill.com* ⊗ *Closed Apr. and Nov. No lunch.*

$$
THAI
Fodor's Choice
★
✕ **Teton Thai.** Right by the Ranch Lot at the base of Jackson Hole Mountain Resort in Teton Village, the restaurant is owned by people of Thai heritage, and the cuisine reflects it. Try *gang khio wan* (green curry), *tom yum gai* (hot and sour soup with chicken), or Crying Tiger (wine-soaked beef with tangy dipping sauce). The pad thai is the best in the state. There's a full bar, and on the other side of Teton Pass, a second location in Driggs, Idaho, serves an identical menu. $ *Average main: $15* ⊠ *7342 Granite Loop Rd., Teton Village* ☎ *307/733–0022* ⊕ *www.tetonthai.com* $ *Average main: $15* ⊠ *18 N. Main St., Driggs, Idaho* ☎ *208/787–8424* ⊕ *www.tetonthai.com* ⊗ *Closed Sun. No lunch Sat.*

WHERE TO STAY

IN THE PARK

$$
HOTEL
🏠 **Colter Bay Village.** Near Jackson Lake, this cluster of Western-style cabins—some with one room, others with two or more—is within walking distance of the lake. **Pros:** prices are good for what you get; many nearby facilities. **Cons:** little sense of privacy; not all cabins have bathrooms. $ *Rooms from: $150* ⊠ *2 miles off U.S. 89/191/287, 10*

miles north of Jackson Lake Junction, Colter Bay ☎ 307/543–3100, 800/628–9988 🌐 www.gtlc.com 🛏 166 cabins (9 with shared baths), 66 tent cabins ⏲ Closed late Sept.–late May 🍴 No meals.

$$$ RESORT 🏨 **Dornan's Spur Ranch Cabins.** Part of Dornan's shopping-dining-recreation development at Moose, this clutch of one- and two-bedroom cabins has great views of the Tetons and the Snake River. **Pros:** cabins are simple but clean; full kitchens can save you money. **Cons:** not much privacy; little atmosphere; no fireplaces. [$] *Rooms from: $185 ✉ 10 Moose Rd., off Teton Park Rd. at Moose Junction, Moose ☎ 307/733–2522 🌐 www.dornans.com 🛏 8 1-bedroom cabins, 4 2-bedroom cabins 🍴 No meals.*

$$$$ HOTEL 🏨 **Jackson Lake Lodge.** This sprawling resort stands on a bluff with spectacular views across Jackson Lake to the Tetons. **Pros:** central location for visiting Grand Teton and Yellowstone; heated outdoor pool. **Cons:** rooms without views are pricey for what you get; the hotel hosts a lot of large meetings. [$] *Rooms from: $229 ✉ U.S. 89/191/287, ½ mile north of Jackson Lake Junction ☎ 307/543–3100, 800/628–9988 🌐 www.gtlc.com 🛏 385 rooms ⏲ Closed early Oct.–mid-May 🍴 No meals.*

$$$$ RESORT Fodor'sChoice ★ 🏨 **Jenny Lake Lodge.** This lodge, the most expensive and arguably the most elegant in any national park, has been serving travelers since the 1920s. **Pros:** maximum comfort in a pristine setting; perhaps the best hotel in the national park system. **Cons:** very expensive; not suitable for kids under 17; pretty formal for a national-park property. [$] *Rooms from: $689 ✉ Jenny Lake Rd., 2 miles off Teton Park Rd., 12 miles north of Moose Junction ☎ 307/733–4647, 800/628–9988 🌐 www.gtlc.com 🛏 37 cabins ⏲ Closed early Oct.–late May 🍴 Some meals.*

$ B&B/INN 🏨 **Moulton Ranch Cabins.** Along Mormon Row, these cabins stand a few dozen yards south of the famous Moulton Barn seen on brochures for the park. **Pros:** quiet and secluded; picturesque setting. **Cons:** fairly basic accommodations; little nightlife nearby. [$] *Rooms from: $100 ✉ Off Antelope Flats Rd., off U.S. 26/89/191, 2 miles north of Moose Junction ☎ 307/733–3749 🌐 www.moultonranchcabins.com 🛏 5 cabins ⏲ Closed Oct.–May. 🍴 No meals.*

$$$ HOTEL 🏨 **Signal Mountain Lodge.** On Jackson Lake's southern shoreline, the lodge's main building has a cozy lounge and a grand pine deck overlooking the lake, while some of the pine-shaded cabins are equipped with sleek kitchens. **Pros:** restaurants and bar are popular hot spots; on-site gas station; general store sells ice. **Cons:** rooms are motel-basic; fireplaces are gas. [$] *Rooms from: $174 ✉ Teton Park Rd., 3 miles south of Jackson Lake Junction ☎ 307/543–2831 🌐 www.signalmountainlodge.com 🛏 47 rooms, 32 cabins ⏲ Closed mid-Oct.–mid-May 🍴 No meals.*

OUTSIDE THE PARK

$$$$ HOTEL 🏨 **Alpenhof Lodge.** With more atmosphere than anything else in Teton Village, this Austrian-style hotel sits next to the tram in the heart of Jackson Hole Mountain Resort. **Pros:** quaint feel; cozy surroundings; spa treatments available. **Cons:** some rooms are small, especially for the price. [$] *Rooms from: $204 ✉ 3255 West Village Dr., Teton Village ☎ 307/733–3242, 800/732–3244 🌐 www.alpenhoflodge.com 🛏 42 rooms ⏲ Closed early Apr.–May 1; restaurants closed Nov. 🍴 Breakfast.*

$$$$ RESORT **Amangani.** This exclusive resort built of sandstone and redwood blends into the landscape of Gros Ventre Butte, affording beautiful views of Spring Creek Gulch from its cliff-top location. **Pros:** extremely luxurious; impeccable service; excellent views of the Tetons; extensive amenities. **Cons:** very expensive; too detached from the mundane world below (even by Jackson standards). *$ Rooms from: $825 ⊠ 1535 N.E. Butte Rd., Jackson ☎ 307/734–7333, 877/734–7333 ⊕ www.amangani. com ⇗ 40 suites* ⦿ *Some meals.*

$$ HOTEL **Antler Inn.** No motel in Jackson has a better location than the Antler, a block south of Town Square. **Pros:** restaurants nearby; family-run operation; good prices in the off-season. **Cons:** frequently booked in summer. *$ Rooms from: $145 ⊠ 43 W. Pearl St., Jackson ☎ 307/733– 2535, 800/522–2406 ⊕ www.townsquareinns.com/antler-inn ⇗ 110 rooms* ⦿ *No meals.*

$$$$ HOTEL **Hotel Terra.** Other properties talk the eco-talk, but opulent Hotel Terra takes green hospitality to the next level. It's also luxe to the core, with a hip, urban feel and all the amenities the price tag suggests. **Pros:** greenest hotel ever; expert staff; organic spa. **Cons:** not for budget-conscious; located in a crowded corner of Teton Village. *$ Rooms from: $329 ⊠ Teton Village, just west of Mangy Moose ☎ 307/379–4000, 800/631–6281 ⊕ www.hotelterrajacksonhole.com ⇗ 132 rooms* ⦿ *Some meals.*

$$$$ HOTEL **The Lexington at Jackson Hole.** Within walking distance of Town Square, this lodging has some of the town's best appointed rooms for people with disabilities. **Pros:** walking distance to town; small pool and Jacuzzi. **Cons:** limited views; must drive to mountains. *$ Rooms from: $289 ⊠ 285 N. Cache St., Jackson ☎ 307/733–2648, 888/771–2648 ⊕ www. lexingtonhoteljacksonhole.com ⇗ 91 rooms, 53 suites* ⦿ *Breakfast.*

$$$$ RESORT FAMILY **R Lazy S Ranch.** Jackson Hole, with the spectacle of the Tetons in the background, is true dude-ranch country, and the R Lazy S is one of the finest in the area. **Pros:** authentic all-inclusive dude ranch experience; very popular with older kids; absolutely beautiful setting. **Cons:** few modern trappings; not for the high-maintenance traveler. *$ Rooms from: $269 ⊠ 1 mile north of Teton Village on the outskirts of Grand Teton National Park, Teton Village ☎ 307/733–2655 ⊕ www.rlazys. com ⇗ 14 cabins* ▤ *No credit cards* ☉ *Closed Oct.–mid-June* ⦿ *All meals* ⟲ *1-week minimum.*

$$$$ HOTEL **Snake River Lodge & Spa.** Anchored by Wyoming's largest spa, Snake River pulls off a nice of blend of genteel resort and faux-folksy lodge. **Pros:** Cool public spaces; vast menu in the spa. **Cons:** Labyrinthine hallways, most rooms have no real view. *$ Rooms from: $339 ⊠ 7710 Granite Loop Rd., Teton Village ☎ 307/732–6000, 866/975–7625 ⊕ www.snakeriverlodge.com ⇗ 153 rooms* ⦿ *No meals.*

$$$$ HOTEL FAMILY **Snow King Hotel.** Completely renovated in 2013, this hotel has a modern Western feel, outdoor firepits near the pool, and one of the hottest new restaurants in town. **Pros:** central location; ski-in, ski-out; new on-site cycling and ski shop. **Cons:** large groups often dominate the property; somewhat expensive for level of luxury. *$ Rooms from: $295 ⊠ 400 E. Snow King Ave., Jackson ☎ 307/733–5200 ⊕ www.snowking. com ⇗ 202 rooms* ⦿ *No meals.*

Best Campgrounds in Grand Teton

You'll find a variety of campgrounds, from small areas where only tents are allowed to full RV parks with all services. If you don't have a tent but want to bring your sleeping bags, you can take advantage of the tent cabins at Colter Bay, where you have a hard floor, cots, and canvas walls for shelter. Standard campsites include a place to pitch your tent or park your trailer/camper, a fire pit for cooking, and a picnic table. All developed campgrounds have toilets and water; plan to bring your own firewood. Check in at National Park Service campsites as early as possible—sites are assigned on a first-come, first-served basis.

GTNP-Backcountry Permits. You can reserve a backcountry campsite between January 5 and May 15 for a $35 nonrefundable fee using the online reservation system. Two-thirds of all sites are set aside for in-person, day-before permits, so you can also take a chance that the site you want will be open when you arrive in the park. In that case the fee is $25, but a trip to Craig Thomas Visitor and Discovery Center or Jenny Lake Ranger Station is still required for a permit and mandatory bear-proof food storage canister. Jackson Hole Mountain Resort tram provides quick access to the park's backcountry, which can also be reached on foot from trailheads throughout the park. 🖥 *307/739–3443* ⊕ *www.nps. gov/grte/planyourvisit/bcres.htm.*

Colter Bay Campground. Busy, noisy, and filled by noon, this campground has both tent and trailer or RV sites. And one great advantage: it's centrally located. ⊠ *2 miles off U.S. 89/191/287, 5 miles north of Jackson Lake Junction, Colter Bay* ☎ *307/543–3100, 800/628–9988.*

Flagg Ranch. Situated in a shady pine grove overlooking the headwaters of the Snake River, these sites provide a great base for exploring Grand Teton or Yellowstone. Showers and laundry facilities are a bonus, and camper cabins are available. ⊠ *U.S. 89/191/287, 20 miles north of Jackson Lake Junction* ☎ *307/543–2861, 800/443–2311.*

Gros Ventre. The park's biggest campground is set in an open, grassy area on the bank of the Gros Ventre River, away from the mountains and 2½ miles west of Kelly, Wyoming. ⊠ *4½ miles off U.S. 26/89/191, 2½ miles west of Kelly on Gros Ventre Rd., 6 miles south of Moose Junction* ☎ *307/543–3100, 800/628–9988.*

Jenny Lake. Wooded sites and Teton views make this tent-only site the most desirable campground in the park, and it fills early. ⊠ *Jenny Lake, ½ mile off Teton Park Rd., 8 miles north of Moose Junction* ☎ *307/543–3100, 800/628–9988.*

Lizard Creek. Views of Jackson Lake, wooded sites, and the relative isolation of this campground make it a relaxing choice. ⊠ *U.S. 89/191/287, 13 miles north of Jackson Lake Junction* ☎ *307/543–2831, 800/672–6012.*

Signal Mountain. This campground in a hilly setting on Jackson Lake has boat access to the lake. ⊠ *Teton Park Rd., 3 miles south of Jackson Lake Junction* ☎ *307/543–2831, 800/672–6012.*

19

$$$$ B&B/INN 🏨 **Teton Tree House.** On a steep hillside and surrounded by trees, this cozy lodgepole-pine B&B is a real retreat. **Pros:** scenic locale; good breakfast; knowledgeable hosts. **Cons:** not open in winter; must drive to town; small climb up to the B&B; no kids under 5. [$] *Rooms from: $225* ✉ *6175 Heck of a Hill Rd., Wilson* ☎ *307/733–3233* 🌐 *www.atetontreehouse-jacksonhole.com* 🛏 *6 rooms* 🕒 *Closed Oct.–May* 🍴 *Breakfast.*

$$$$ B&B/INN Fodor's Choice ★ 🏨 **The Wildflower Inn.** You'll enjoy great gourmet breakfasts at this cozy, clean, and comfortable country inn just down the road from Jackson Hole Mountain Resort and Teton Village, surrounded by 3 acres of aspen and pine trees frequented by moose, deer, and other native wildlife. **Pros:** excellent views; frequent wildlife sightings; plenty of loaner gear available. **Cons:** fills up far in advance; 12 miles from Jackson. [$] *Rooms from: $360* ✉ *3725 Moose-Wilson Rd., Jackson* ☎ *307/733–4710, 800/893–7910* 🌐 *www.jacksonholewildflower.com* 🛏 *5 rooms* 🍴 *Breakfast.*

$$$$ HOTEL Fodor's Choice ★ 🏨 **The Wort Hotel.** Built in 1941, this brick Victorian hotel a block from Town Square seems to have been around as long as the Tetons, but it feels up-to-date inside. **Pros:** charming old building with lots of history; convenient downtown location; some good-value package deals. **Cons:** limited views; must drive to parks and mountains. [$] *Rooms from: $389* ✉ *50 N. Glenwood St., Jackson* ☎ *307/733–2190, 800/322–2727* 🌐 *www.worthotel.com* 🛏 *59 rooms, 5 suites* 🍴 *Breakfast.*

GREAT BASIN
NATIONAL PARK

WELCOME TO GREAT BASIN

TOP REASONS TO GO

★ **Ancient tree spottings:** The bristlecone pines in Great Basin are thousands of years old.

★ **Desert skyscraper:** Wheeler Peak rises out of the vast desert basin with summit temperatures often 20–30 degrees below that of the visitor center.

★ **Rare shields:** Look for hundreds of these unique disk-shape formations inside Lehman Caves.

★ **Gather your pine nuts while you may:** Come in the fall and go a little nutty, as you can gather up to three gunnysacks of pinyon pine nuts, found in abundance throughout the park and tasting oh-so-yummy—they're great on salads.

1 Lehman Caves. Highlighted by the limestone cavern, this is the primary destination of most Great Basin visitors. It includes a popular visitor center and two campgrounds (both accessible for RVers). Nearby is the start of the Wheeler Peak Scenic Drive.

2 Wheeler Peak. Rarely is a crown jewel truly so—but just look at this 13,063-footer when it's capped with snow. Hikers can climb the mountain via day-use-only trails, which also lead to three small alpine lakes, a glacier, and some ancient bristlecone pines.

3 Granite Basin. This is the less crowded part of an already sparsely visited park. Trails follow a handful of creeks around Pyramid Peak, and six primitive campgrounds line Snake Creek. A bristlecone pine grove is nearby, though far off any beaten path.

4 Arch Canyon. A high-clearance, four-wheel-drive vehicle is recommended, and stout boots are critical if you want to get to Lexington Arch, which is unusual in that it is formed of limestone, not sandstone as most arches are. This is a day-use-only area.

GETTING ORIENTED

One of the smallest (77,180 acres) and least visited national parks in the lower 48 states, Great Basin National Park, on the Nevada–Utah border, occupies only a minute fraction of the almost 200,000 square miles of the Great Basin desert—yet it exemplifies the landscape and ecology of the region. The surrounding high desert (4,500–6,200 feet in elevation) is the largest desert in the United States, bordered by the Sierra Nevada range, the Rocky Mountains, the Columbia Plateau, and the Mojave and Sonoran deserts. It covers 75% of the state of Nevada and extends into California, Utah, and Idaho.

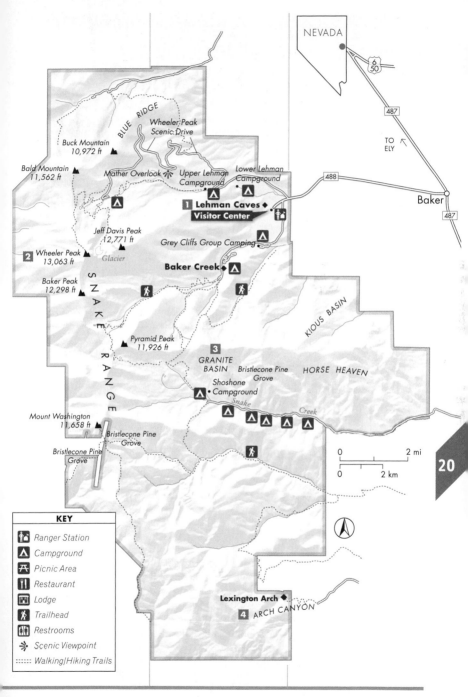

NEVADA

TO ELY

Baker

BLUE RIDGE

Wheeler Peak Scenic Drive

Buck Mountain 10,972 ft

Bald Mountain 11,562 ft

Mather Overlook

Upper Lehman Campground

Lower Lehman Campground

1 Lehman Caves ◆
Visitor Center

Jeff Davis Peak 12,771 ft

Grey Cliffs Group Camping

2 Wheeler Peak 13,063 ft

Glacier

Baker Creek ◆

Baker Peak 12,298 ft

S N A K E   R A N G E

Pyramid Peak 11,926 ft

KIOUS BASIN

3
GRANITE BASIN

Bristlecone Pine Grove

HORSE HEAVEN

Shoshone Campground

Snake Creek

Mount Washington 11,658 ft

Bristlecone Pine Grove

Bristlecone Pine Grove

0   2 mi
0   2 km

20

Lexington Arch ◆

4 ARCH CANYON

KEY	
🏚	*Ranger Station*
🔺	*Campground*
🏕	*Picnic Area*
🍴	*Restaurant*
🏨	*Lodge*
🚶	*Trailhead*
🚻	*Restrooms*
➷	*Scenic Viewpoint*
⋯⋯	*Walking/Hiking Trails*

Updated by
Steve Pastorino

Rising 13,063 feet out of a massive 200,000-square-mile basin, Wheeler Peak beckons visitors with an entirely unique ecosystem. High desert meets alpine forest here, with a limestone cave to boot. Fewer than 100,000 visitors (compared to 3 million at Utah's Zion National Park) will find their way to this off-the-beaten-path park annually, but for them, the rewards will be ample. Surface water in the Great Basin has no outlet to the sea, so it pools in more than 200 small basins throughout the steep mountain ranges. Along with these alpine lakes, the dramatic mountains shelter lush meadows, limestone formations, and ancient bristlecone pines. Within the park is the southernmost permanent glacier on the continent.

GREAT BASIN PLANNER

WHEN TO GO

As one of the least-visited national parks in the country, Great Basin National Park is never crowded. The small number of visitors ensures that most any time is a fine time to visit this park, though of course much of that number will pass through the entry gates during the warmer months. In summer the high-desert weather here is typically mild, so you'll be comfortable in shorts and T-shirts during the day—though temperatures drop at night, so bring light jackets and pants.

A winter visit can be sublime in its solitude, but the hardy visitor must be prepared for the elements, especially if the backcountry is a destination. With temperatures hovering in the low teens, heavy coats, jeans, and sweaters are recommended. Some roads might be impassable in inclement weather; check ahead with a park ranger.

AVG. HIGH/LOW TEMPS.

JAN.	FEB.	MAR.	APR.	MAY	JUNE
41/18	44/21	48/24	56/31	66/40	76/48

JULY	AUG.	SEPT.	OCT.	NOV.	DEC.
86/57	83/56	75/47	62/47	49/26	42/20

FESTIVALS AND EVENTS

SUMMER **Silver State Classic Challenge.** Twice a year, muscle car enthusiasts close Route 318 for the country's largest (and most venerable) open-road race for amateur fast-car drivers. The event occurs south of Ely on Route 318, from Lund to Hiko. ☎ *702/631–6166* ⊕ *www.silverstateclassic.com.*

White Pine County Fair. Livestock, flower, and vegetable competitions, plus a hay contest, carnival rides, food booths, dancing, and a buckaroo breakfast make this fair, held at the White Pine County Fairgrounds in Ely, the real thing. ☎ *775/289–4691* ⊕ *www.wpcfair.com.*

PLANNING YOUR TIME

GREAT BASIN IN ONE DAY

Start your visit with the 90-minute tour of the fascinating limestone caverns of **Lehman Caves,** the park's most famous attraction. If you have time before or after the tour, hike the short and family-friendly **Mountain View Nature Trail,** near the Lehman Caves Visitor Center, to get your first taste of the area's pinyon-juniper forests. Stop for lunch at the Lehman Caves Cafe or at least plan on a hand-scooped ice-cream treat—or have a picnic near the visitor center.

In the afternoon, take a leisurely drive up to **Wheeler Peak,** the park's tallest mountain at just over 13,000 feet. You can stop about halfway along your drive to hike the short **Osceola Ditch Trail,** a remnant of the park's gold-mining day, or, alternatively, just enjoy the fantastic views from the two overlooks. If you're feeling energetic when you reach Wheeler Peak, hike some of the trails there.

GETTING HERE AND AROUND

CAR TRAVEL

The entrance to Great Basin is on Route 488, 5 miles west of its junction with Route 487. From Ely, take U.S. 6/50 to Route 487. From Salt Lake City or Cedar City, Utah, take I–15 South to U.S. 6/50 West; from Las Vegas, drive north on I–15 and then north on Route 93 to access U.S. 6/50. The nearest airports are in Cedar City (120 miles), Salt Lake City (240 miles), and Las Vegas (287 miles).

In the park, Baker Creek Road and portions of Wheeler Peak Scenic Drive, above Upper Lehman Creek, are closed from November to June. The road to the visitor center and the roads to the developed campgrounds are paved, but the going is tough in winter and two-wheel-drive cars don't do well. RVs and trailers aren't allowed above Lower Lehman Creek. With an 8% grade, the road to Wheeler Peak is steep and curvy, but not dangerous if you take it slow. Motorcyclists should watch for gravel on the road's surface.

20

PARK ESSENTIALS
PARK FEES AND PERMITS
Admission to the park is free, but if you want to tour Lehman Caves there's a fee ($4–$10, depending on age and tour length). To fish in Great Basin National Park, those 12 and older need a state fishing license from the Nevada Department of Wildlife (⊕ *www.ndow.org*). The resident license costs $13 for kids 12–15 and $29 for those 16 and older; the one-day nonresident license is $18, plus $7 for each additional day at time of purchase. Backcountry hikers do not need permits, but for your own safety you should fill out a form at the visitor center before setting out.

PARK HOURS
The park is open 24/7 year-round. It's in the Pacific time zone.

CELL-PHONE RECEPTION
The only public phone in the park is at the visitor center. There is no reliable cell-phone reception.

RESTAURANTS
Dining in the park itself is limited to the basic lunch fare at the Lehman Caves Cafe and Gift Shop. Nearby Baker, a town of less than 100 people, has an option or two.

Prices in the reviews are the average cost of a main course at dinner, or if dinner is not served, at lunch.

HOTELS
There is no lodging in the park, so unless you're willing and able to snag one of the park's first-come, first-served campsites, or expect to camp in the backcountry, plan on lodging in nearby Baker or in Ely.

Prices in the reviews are the lowest cost of a standard double room in high season. For expanded reviews, facilities, and current deals, visit Fodors.com.

VISITOR INFORMATION
PARK CONTACT INFORMATION
Great Basin National Park ⊠ *Rte. 488, Baker* ☎ *775/234–7331* ⊕ *www. nps.gov/grba.*

VISITOR CENTERS
Great Basin Visitor Center. Here you can see exhibits on the flora, fauna, and geology of the park, or ask a ranger to suggest a favorite hike. Books, videos, and souvenirs are for sale; water is available, but for snacks continue up the road to the Lehman Caves Visitor Center. ⊠ *Rte. 487, just north of Baker* ☎ *775/234–7331* ⊙ *Oct.–mid-May, daily 8–4:30; mid-May–Sept., daily 8–5:30.*

Lehman Caves Visitor Center. Regularly scheduled cave tours lasting 60 or 90 minutes depart from here. Mountain View Nature Trail encircles the visitor center and includes Rhodes Cabin and the historic cave entrance. Exhibits highlight the gnarled and ancient bristlecone pine and other park flora, plus cave formations. Buy gifts for friends and family back home at the bookstore. ⊠ *Rte. 488, ½ mile inside park* ☎ *775/234–7331* ⊙ *Daily 8–4:30.*

Lehman Caves: It's amazing what a little water and air can do to a room.

EXPLORING

SCENIC DRIVES

Baker Creek Road. Though less popular than the Wheeler Peak Scenic Drive, this gravel road affords gorgeous views of Wheeler Peak, the Baker Creek Drainage, and Snake Valley. The road is closed in the winter, and there are no pull-outs or scenic overlooks. ⊠ *Off Rte. 488, ½ mile inside the park boundary.*

Wheeler Peak Scenic Drive. Less than a mile from the visitor center off Route 488, turn onto this paved road that winds its way up to elevations of 10,000 feet. The road takes you through pygmy forest in lower elevations; as you climb, the air cools as much as 20–30 degrees. Along the way, overlooks offer awe-inspiring views of the Snake Range mountains, and a short hiking trail leads to views of the Osceola mining site. Turn off at Mather Overlook, elevation 9,000 feet, for the best photo ops. Allow 1½ hours for the 24-mile round-trip, not including hikes. ⊠ *Off Rte. 488, just inside park, about 5 miles west of Baker.*

SCENIC STOPS

Lehman Caves. In 1885, rancher and miner Absalom Lehman discovered this underground wonder—a single limestone and marble cavern ¼-mile long. Inside, stalactites, stalagmites, helictites, flowstone, popcorn, and other bizarre mineral formations cover almost every surface.

Lehman Caves is one of the best places to see rare shield formations, created when calcite-rich water is forced from tiny cracks in a cave wall, ceiling, or floor. Year-round the cave maintains a constant, damp temperature of 50°F, so wear a light jacket and nonskid shoes when you take the tour. Go for the full 90-minute tour if you have time; it's offered four or five times per day, as is the 60-minute tour. Children under age 5 are not allowed on the 90-minute tours; those under 16 must be accompanied by an adult. Take the 0.3-mile Mountain View Nature Trail beforehand to see the original cave entrance and **Rhodes Cabin,** where black-and-white photographs of the park's earlier days line the walls. ⊠ *Lehman Caves Visitor Center* ☎ *775/234-7331* 💲 *$4–$10* 🕐 *Daily 8–4:30.*

EDUCATIONAL OFFERINGS

RANGER PROGRAMS

Campfire Programs. On summer evenings the park offers these programs at two of its campgrounds, Upper Lehman Creek and Wheeler Peak. The 30- to 45-minute programs cover a range of subjects related to Great Basin's cultural and natural history and resources. Dress warmly and bring a flashlight. Program times vary, so call for information. ⊠ *Wheeler Peak Scenic Dr., 4 miles (Upper Lehman Creek) and 12 miles (Wheeler Peak) from the Lehman Caves Visitor Center* ☎ *775/234-7331* 💲 *Free* 🕐 *Mid-June–Labor Day.*

FAMILY **Junior Ranger Program.** Youngsters answer questions and complete activities related to the park and then are sworn in as Junior Rangers and receive a Great Basin Bristlecone badge. ☎ *775/234-7331* ⊕ *www.nps.gov/grba.*

SPORTS AND THE OUTDOORS

Great Basin National Park is a great place for experienced outdoor enthusiasts. There are no outfitters to guide you, and there are no nearby shops that rent or sell sporting equipment, so bring everything you might need and be prepared to go it alone. Permits are not required to go off the beaten path, but such adventurers are encouraged to register with a ranger just in case. The effort is worth it, for the backcountry is wide open and not at all crowded no matter the time of year (just keep an eye on the weather). As is the case in all national parks, bicycling is restricted to existing roads, but as the park sees fewer visitors than other national parks, road cyclists will find few cars to trouble them.

BIRD-WATCHING

Great Basin National Park might not be crowded with people, but it sports an impressive list of bird species sighted—238, according to the National Park Service checklist. Some species, such as the common raven and American robin, can be seen at most locations. Others, such as the red-naped sapsucker, are more commonly seen near Lehman Creek.

Plants and Wildlife in Great Basin

Despite the cold, dry conditions in Great Basin, 411 plant species thrive; 13 are considered sensitive species. The region gets less than 10 inches of rain a year, so plants have developed some ingenious methods of dealing with the desert's harshness. For instance, many flowering plants will only grow and produce seeds in a year when there is enough water. Spruces, pines, and junipers have set down roots here, and the bristlecone pine has been doing so for thousands of years.

The park's plants provide a variety of habitats for animals and for more than 230 bird species. In the sagebrush are jackrabbits, ground squirrels, chipmunks, and pronghorns. Mule deer and striped skunks abound in the pygmy forest of pinyon pine and juniper trees. Shrews, ringtail cats, and weasels make their homes around the springs and streams. Mountain lions, bobcats, and sheep live on the rugged slopes and in valleys. The park is also home to coyotes, kit fox, and badgers. Treat the Great Basin rattlesnake with respect. Bites are uncommon and rarely fatal, but if you're bitten, remain calm and contact a ranger immediately.

CROSS-COUNTRY SKIING

Lehman Creek Trail. In summer, descend 2,050 feet by hiking Lehman Creek Trail one-way (downhill) from Wheeler Peak campground to Upper Lehman Creek campground. In winter, it is the most popular cross-country skiing trail in the park. It's marked with orange flags, making it easy to find. You may need snowshoes to reach the skiable upper section.

HIKING

You'll witness beautiful views by driving along the Wheeler Peak Scenic Drive and other park roads, but hiking allows an in-depth experience that just can't be matched. Trails at Great Basin run the gamut from relaxing ¼-mile trails to multiday backpacking specials, so everyone can find a path that matches personal ability, fitness level, and desired destination, be it mountain peak, flowered meadow, or evergreen forest. When you pick up a trail map at the visitor center, ask about trail conditions (many are unpaved, and some are maintained less than others) and bring appropriate clothing when you set out from any trailhead. No matter the trail length, always carry water, and remember that the trails are at high elevations, so pace yourself accordingly. Do not enter abandoned mineshafts or tunnels, for they are unstable and potentially dangerous. Those who head out for the backcountry need not obtain a permit, but are encouraged to register at either of the two visitor centers. Though Great Basin is a high desert, winters can be harsh, so always inquire about the weather ahead of time at the visitor center.

20

EASY

FAMILY **Mountain View Nature Trail.** Just past the Rhodes Cabin on the right side of the visitor center, this short and easy trail (0.3 miles) through pinyon pine and juniper trees is marked with signs describing the plants. The path passes the original entrance to Lehman Caves and loops back to the visitor center. It's a great way to spend a half hour or so while you wait for your cave tour to start. *Easy.* ⊠ *Trailhead at Lehman Caves Visitor Center.*

Osceola Ditch Trail. In 1890, at a cost of $108,223, the Osceola Gravel Mining Company constructed an 18-mile-long trench. The ditch was part of an attempt to glean gold from the South Snake Range, but water shortages and the company's failure to find much gold forced the mining operation to shut down in 1905. You can reach portions of the eastern section of the ditch on foot via the Osceola Ditch Trail, which passes through pine and fir trees. Allow 30 minutes for this easy 0.3-mile round-trip hike. *Easy.* ⊠ *Trailhead off Wheeler Peak Scenic Dr.*

MODERATE

Alpine Lakes Trail. This moderate, 2.7-mile trek loops past the beautiful Stella and Teresa lakes from the trailhead at the top of the Wheeler Park Scenic Drive. You'll rise and fall about 600 feet in elevation as you pass through subalpine and alpine forest. The views of Wheeler Peak, amid wildflowers (in summer), white fir, twisted aspens, and gnarled ponderosa pines, make this a memorable hike. ■TIP→ The trailhead is at nearly 10,000 feet, so make sure you're adjusted to the altitude and prepared for changing weather. Allow three hours. *Moderate.* ⊠ *Trailhead at Bristlecone parking area, near end of Wheeler Peak Scenic Dr.*

Fodor's Choice ★ **Bristlecone Pine Trail.** Though the park has several bristlecone pine groves, the only way to see the ancient trees up close is to hike this trail. From the parking area to the grove, it's a moderate 1.4-mile hike that takes about an hour each way. Rangers offer informative talks daily in season; inquire at the visitor center. The Bristlecone Pine Trail also leads to the **Glacier Trail,** which skirts the southernmost permanent ice field on the continent and ends with a view of a small alpine glacier, the only one in Nevada. From there it's less than 3 miles back to the parking lot. Allow three hours for the moderate hike and remember the trailhead is at 9,800 feet above sea level. *Moderate.* ⊠ *Trailhead at Summit Trail parking area, Wheeler Peak Scenic Dr., 12 miles from Lehman Caves Visitor Center.*

GOOD READS

■ *Hiking Great Basin National Park,* by Bruce Grubbs, will get your Great Basin trip off on the right foot.

■ *Trails to Explore in Great Basin National Park,* by Rose Houk, is all about hiking in the park.

■ *Geology of the Great Basin,* by Bill Fiero, and *Basin and Range,* by John McPhee, present geological tours of the Great Basin.

DIFFICULT

Baker Lake Trail. This full-day, 12-mile hike can easily be made into a two-day backpacking trip. You'll gain a total of 2,620 feet in elevation on the way to Baker Lake, a jewel-like alpine lake with a backdrop of mountainous cliffs. *Difficult.* ⊠ *Trailhead off Baker Creek Rd., going south from just east of the Lehman Caves Visitor Center.*

Fodor's Choice **Wheeler Peak Summit Trail.** Begin this full-day, 8.6-mile hike early in the ★ day so as to minimize exposure to afternoon storms. Depart and return to Summit Trailhead near the top of Wheeler Peak Scenic Drive. Most of the route follows a ridge up the mountain to the summit. ⚠ Elevation gain is 2,900 feet to 13,083 feet above sea level, so hikers should have good stamina and be prepared for altitude sickness and/or hypothermia due to drastic temperature and weather changes. *Difficult.* ⊠ *Trailhead at Summit Trail parking area, off Wheeler Peak Scenic Dr.*

WHAT'S NEARBY

NEARBY TOWNS

An hour's drive west of the park, at the intersection of three U.S. highways, **Ely** (population 4,008) is the biggest town in the area. It grew up in the second wave of the early Nevada mining boom, right at the optimistic turn of the 20th century. For 70 years copper kept the town in business, but when it ran out in the early 1980s Ely declined fast. Then, in 1986, the National Park Service designated Great Basin National Park 68 miles to the east and the town got a boost. Ely has since been rebuilt and revitalized and is now home to a railroad museum, the county seat, and a great old hotel-casino (Hotel Nevada), as well as plenty of hotels and tourist amenities. If you want to get closer to the park, you can stay in tiny **Baker** (population roughly 75), which sits at the main park entrance. Little more than a cluster of small businesses a few miles south of U.S. 6/50 on Route 487, the desert oasis is 5 miles from the visitor center.

VISITOR INFORMATION

White Pine County Tourism and Recreation Board ⊠ *Bristlecone Convention Center, 150 6th St., Ely* ☎ *800/496–9350, 775/289–3720* ⊕ *www.elynevada.net.* **Great Basin Business and Tourism Council** ⊠ *10 Main St., Baker* ⊕ *www.greatbasinpark.com.*

20

NEARBY ATTRACTIONS

Cave Lake State Park. At 7,300 feet above sea level in the pine and juniper forest of the big Schell Creek Range that borders Ely on the east, this is an idyllic spot. You can spend a day fishing for rainbow and brown trout in the reservoir, and a night sleeping under the stars. Arrive early; it gets crowded. Access may be restricted in winter. ⊠ *15 miles southeast of Ely via U.S. 50/6/93* ⊕ *www.parks.nv.gov/cl.htm* 💲 *$7* ⊙ *Daily 24 hrs.*

FAMILY **Nevada Northern Railway Museum.** During the mining boom the Nevada Northern Railroad connected East Ely, Ruth, and McGill to the transcontinental rail line in the northeast corner of Nevada. The whole operation is now a museum. You can tour the depot, offices, warehouses, yard, roundhouses, and repair shops, and catch a ride on one of the trains daily in summer. You can even stay overnight in a caboose or bunkhouse. ✉ *1100 Ave. A, Ely* ☎ *866/407–8326* 🌐 *www.nnry.com* 🎟 *$5* 🕒 *July and Aug., daily 8–5; Sept.–June, Wed.–Mon. 8–5.*

U.S. 93 Scenic Byway. The 68 miles between the park and Ely make a beautiful drive with diverse views of Nevada's paradoxical geography: dry deserts and lush mountains. You'll catch an occasional glimpse of a snake, perhaps a rattler, slithering on the road's shoulder, or a lizard sunning on a rock. Watch for deer. A straight drive to Ely takes a little more than an hour; if you have the time to take a dirt-road adventure, don't miss the Ward Charcoal Ovens or a peek at Cave Lake.

Ward Charcoal Ovens State Historic Park. In the desert south of Ely is this row of six beehive-shaped, 30-foot-tall ovens that could burn 35 cords of wood at once. From 1876–1879, the ovens turned pinyon, juniper, and mountain mahogany into charcoal, which was used for refining local silver and copper ore. It's a well-preserved piece of unique mining history. ✉ *U.S. 50/6/93, 7 miles south of Ely, 11 miles southwest on Cave Valley Rd.* ☎ *775/289–1693* 🌐 *www.parks.nv.gov/ww.htm* 🎟 *$7* 🕒 *Daily, 24 hrs.*

BEST BETS FOR FAMILIES

- **Bristlecone Pine Hike.** Enjoy this hike (2 miles long and almost 2 miles high) to see the park's signature trees in the Wheeler Peak cirque. Bristlecone pines are ancient, often thousands of years old, and gnarled—in other words, pretty cool for kids.
- **Lehman Caves.** The consistently cool cave air will give you goose bumps, as will the array of stalactites, stalagmites, and fantasylike chambers.
- **Nevada Northern Railway Museum.** Ride the rails year-round at this attraction in Ely.

WHERE TO EAT

IN THE PARK

$ AMERICAN FAMILY 🍴 **Lehman Caves Cafe and Gift Shop.** The menu here includes light breakfasts, soup-and-sandwich lunches, and freshly baked desserts. Beat the heat on the long porch with large ice-cream sandwiches made by hand. [$] *Average main: $5* ✉ *Next to visitor center* ☎ *775/234–7221* 🌐 *www.greatbasinpark.com/lehmangifts.htm* 🕒 *Closed Nov.–Mar. No dinner.*

PICNIC AREAS

Lehman Caves Visitor Center Picnic Area. This full-service picnic site, with tables, fire grills, water, and restrooms (the latter two available during the summer) is a short walk from the visitor center. Summer hours are often extended beyond the standard 8–4:30. ✉ *Just north of Lehman Caves Visitor Center.*

CLOSE UP

Best Campgrounds in Great Basin

Great Basin has four developed campgrounds, all easily accessible by car, but only the Lower Lehman Creek Campground is open year-round.

Primitive campsites around Snake and Strawberry creeks are open year-round and are free; however, snow and rain can make access to the sites difficult. None have RV hookups (but RVers can stay at Whispering Elms in nearby Baker).

Baker Creek Campground. The turnoff is just past the park entrance, on the left as you approach the Lehman Caves Visitor Center. ✉ *2½ miles south of Rte. 488, 3 miles from visitor center* ☎ *No phone.*

Lower Lehman Creek Campground. Other than Great Basin's primitive sites, this is the only campground in the park that is open year-round. It's the first turnoff past the Lehman Caves Visitor Center. ✉ *2½ miles from visitor center on Wheeler Peak Scenic Dr.* ☎ *No phone.*

Upper Lehman Creek Campground. About a mile past the Lower Lehman Creek turnoff, this camp fills up quickly in the summer. ✉ *4 miles from visitor center on Wheeler Peak Scenic Dr.* ☎ *No phone.*

Wheeler Park Campground. This cool campground at the end of Wheeler Peak Scenic Drive has stunning views and is near trailheads. ✉ *12 miles from Lehman Caves Visitor Center on Wheeler Peak Scenic Dr.* ☎ *No phone.*

Whispering Elms Campground. The largest camping facility close to but not inside the park is also the nearest to offer hookups for RVs. It is open year-round. ✉ *Rte. 487, behind Great Basin Lodge, Baker* ☎ *775/234-9900.*

Pole Canyon Trailhead Picnic Area. Inaccessible when Baker Creek Road is closed in the winter, this picnic area at the mouth of a canyon has a handful of tables and fire grills but no water. It does have a restroom. Access is via an unimproved road. ✉ *East of entrance to Grey Cliffs Group Camping site, at the mouth of Pole Canyon.*

Upper Lehman Creek Campground. There are a handful of places here where you can sit down for a bite and a breather. A group picnic site requires advance reservations, but areas near the host site and amphitheater are first-come, first-served. Water is available. ✉ *4 miles from the Lehman Caves Visitor Center on Wheeler Peak Scenic Dr.*

OUTSIDE THE PARK

$ AMERICAN 🍴 **The Border Inn.** The Snake Valley is ranch country, so it's no surprise that meat and potatoes dominate the menu at the Border Inn. You'll find hearty fare like hamburgers, chicken-fried steak, sandwiches, and steaks. There is also a full bar and a few slot machines in an adjacent room. The green-chili-and-cheese omelet is the highlight of the daily breakfast menu. [$] *Average main: $10* ✉ *U.S. 6/50, 13 miles east of Great Basin National Park, Baker* ☎ *775/234–7300* 🌐 *www.borderinncasino.com.*

$$ MEDITERRANEAN FAMILY 🍴 **Lectrolux Cafe.** "Stick to Mama Rose's Pasta Bolognese and no one gets hurt," is the quirky Lectrolux Cafe's mantra, but there's more to this menu than pasta. The offerings lean Mediterranean but the accommodating owners serve salmon, burgers, steaks, and more. The brightly painted dining room is equal parts deli, gift shop, and hotel lobby, and also boasts the best-stocked bar in the Great Basin, with eight single-malt scotches, a variety of grappas, and dozens of wines and beers to choose from. [$] *Average main: $15* ✉ *Silver Jack Inn, Rte. 487, 5 miles south of U.S. 50 near park entrance, Baker* ☎ *775/234–7323* 🌐 *www.silverjackinn.com* 🕒 *Closed Nov.–Feb.*

WHERE TO STAY

OUTSIDE THE PARK

$ B&B/INN 🏨 **All Aboard Bed and Bistro.** After a dusty journey to hardscrabble Ely, there may be no better spot to bed down than this dignified, early 20th-century house just a block from the historic train station. **Pros:** inviting front porch; huge trees shade a grassy yard; clean rooms; café serves breakfast and lunch. **Cons:** no elevator to second floor. [$] *Rooms from: $90* ✉ *200 E. 11th St., Ely* ☎ *775/289–5221* 🌐 *www.allaboardcafeandinn.com* 🛏 *5 rooms* 🍽 *Breakfast.*

$ HOTEL 🏨 **The Border Inn.** Located on the Nevada side of the border with Utah on Route 50, the Border Inn has all the basics: clean rooms with air-conditioning including five with kitchenettes, the area's only gas station, a full-service restaurant, free Wi-Fi, and a casino to boot. **Pros:** restaurant, gas, and groceries all here. **Cons:** gravel parking lot is dusty. [$] *Rooms from: $49* ✉ *U.S. 6/50, 13 miles east of Great Basin National Park, Baker* ☎ *775/234–7300* 🌐 *www.borderinncasino.com* 🛏 *29 rooms* 🍽 *No meals.*

$$ HOTEL 🏨 **La Quinta Inn & Suites.** The newest and largest hotel in Ely, the La Quinta Inn & Suites is a clean, fresh, comfortable stay in an otherwise dusty desert town. **Pros:** complimentary hot breakfast; pool; full grocery store next door. **Cons:** on an unattractive strip of motels; too far to walk to Main Street. [$] *Rooms from: $120* ✉ *1591 Great Basin Blvd., Ely* ☎ *775/289–8833* 🌐 *www.lq.com* 🛏 *100* 🍽 *Breakfast.*

$$ HOTEL 🏨 **Ramada Inn and Copper Queen Casino.** Some of the friendliest staff in Ely work at the Copper Queen, where the rooms have king or queen beds, and every one has a coffeepot. **Pros:** on-site Italian restaurant, pub, and casino. **Cons:** entire property absorbs smoky odor from the casino; not for nonsmokers. [$] *Rooms from: $120* ✉ *805 Great Basin Blvd., Ely* ☎ *775/289–4884, 800/851–9526* 🌐 *www.elyramada.com* 🛏 *65 rooms* 🍽 *Breakfast.*

$ HOTEL 🏨 **Silver Jack Inn.** For being about as far off the beaten track as you can get in the Nevada desert, this tiny motel is a cozy oasis of rooms surrounding a tree-filled lawn and a relaxing patio. **Pros:** funky artistic decor; eclectic menu. **Cons:** Baker is a no-stoplight town with no more than about 20 structures. [$] *Rooms from: $69* ✉ *10 Main St., Baker* ☎ *775/234–7323* 🌐 *www.silverjackinn.com* 🛏 *10 rooms* 🍽 *No meals.*

GREAT SAND DUNES NATIONAL PARK

WELCOME TO GREAT SAND DUNES

TOP REASONS TO GO

★ **Dune climbing:** Trek through the 30 square miles of main dunes in this landlocked dune field.

★ **Unrivaled diversity:** You can see eight completely different life zones in this park, ranging from salty wetlands and lush forests to parched sand sheet and frozen alpine peaks, all in a single day.

★ **Bounty of bison:** Take a ride around the west end of the park, where more than 2,000 bison roam in the grasslands and wetlands.

★ **Aspens in autumn:** Take a hike—or, if you've got a high-clearance four-wheel-drive vehicle and good driving skills, take the rough road—up to Medano Pass during fall foliage season when the aspens turn gold.

★ **Vigorous hikes:** Pack a picnic lunch and climb up to High Dune, followed by the more strenuous stretch over to Star Dune. Or tackle the dramatic Music Pass Trail, which takes you to the tree line and covers 3.5 miles (and 2,000 feet in elevation change) each way.

1 Sand dunes. The 30-square-mile field of sand has no designated trails. The highest dune in the park—and, in fact, in North America—is 750-foot-high Star Dune.

2 Sangre de Cristo Mountains. Named the "Blood of Christ" Mountains by Spanish explorers because of their ruddy color—especially at sunrise and sunset—the range contains 10 of Colorado's 54 Fourteeners (mountains taller than 14,000 feet). Six that are more than 13,000 feet tall are within the preserve itself.

3 Forest. Ponderosa pines populate the forested areas around the Sangre de Cristo Mountains in the preserve and park's eastern boundaries.

4 Grasslands. Wildlife, such as elk and bison, feed on the park's grassy areas, primarily found in the park's southern area and the Great Sand Dunes National Preserve.

5 Wetlands. Popular with a variety of birds and amphibians, these seasonal wetlands form in the area around Medano Creek, where cottonwood and willow trees also thrive.

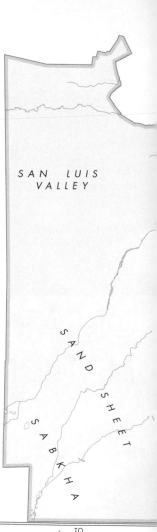

SAN LUIS VALLEY

SAND SHEET

SABKHA

← TO MOSCA

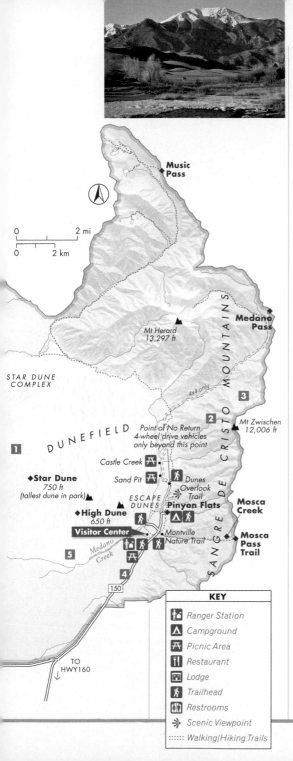

COLORADO

GETTING ORIENTED

The Great Sand Dunes National Park and Preserve encompasses 150,000 acres (about 234 square miles) of land and mountains surrounding the dunes. Looking at the dunes from the west, your eye sweeps over the grassland and sand sheet, a vast expanse of smaller dunes and flatter sections of sand and knee-high brush. The Sangre de Cristo Mountains rear up in the east behind the dunes, forming a dramatic backdrop and creating a stunning juxtaposition of color and form. Depending on the time of year, you'll hear a quiet gurgle or a real rush from Medano Creek, which flows along the eastern edge of the dunes (*medano* is Spanish for "sand dune," pronounced *meh*-dah-noh). Hiking trails thread these mountains—the "preserve" area—where you can walk quietly through aspens and evergreens.

Map labels

Music Pass

Medano Pass

Mt Herard 13,297 ft

STAR DUNE COMPLEX

Mt Zwischen 12,006 ft

4x4 only

3

2

DUNEFIELD

Point of No Return 4-wheel drive vehicles only beyond this point

Castle Creek

Sand Pit

Dunes Overlook Trail

1

◆Star Dune 750 ft (tallest dune in park)

ESCAPE DUNES

Pinyon Flats

Mosca Creek

◆High Dune 650 ft

Visitor Center

Montville Nature Trail

Mosca Pass Trail

Medano Creek

5

4

150

SANGRE DE CRISTO MOUNTAINS

TO HWY160

0   2 mi
0   2 km

KEY

- 🏠 Ranger Station
- ▲ Campground
- 🌲 Picnic Area
- 🍴 Restaurant
- 🏠 Lodge
- 🏃 Trailhead
- 🚻 Restrooms
- ⚡ Scenic Viewpoint
- ⋯⋯ Walking/Hiking Trails

Updated by
Ricardo Baca

Created by winds that sweep the San Luis Valley floor, the enormous sand dunes that form the heart of Great Sand Dunes National Park and Preserve are an improbable, unforgettable sight. The dunes, as curvaceous as Rubens' nudes, stretch for more than 30 square miles. Because they're made of sand, the dunes' very existence seem tenuous, as if they might blow away before your eyes, yet they're solid enough to withstand 440,000 years of Mother Nature—and the modern stress of hikers and saucer-riding thrill seekers.

GREAT SAND DUNES PLANNER

WHEN TO GO

About 300,000 visitors come to the park each year, most on summer weekends; they tend to congregate around the main parking area and Medano Creek. To avoid the crowds, hike away from the main area up to the High Dune. Or come in the winter, when the park is a place for contemplation and repose—as well as skiing and sledding.

Fall and spring are the prettiest times to visit, with the surrounding mountains still capped with snow in May, and leaves on the aspen trees turning gold in September and early October. In summer, the surface temperature of the sand can climb to 140°F in the afternoon, so climbing the dunes is best in the morning or late afternoon. Since you're at a high altitude—about 8,200 feet at the visitor center—the air temperatures in the park itself remain in the 70s most of the summer.

AVG. HIGH/LOW TEMPS.

JAN.	FEB.	MAR.	APR.	MAY	JUNE
35/10	39/14	47/21	56/28	66/37	77/45

JULY	AUG.	SEPT.	OCT.	NOV.	DEC.
81/51	78/49	71/42	60/32	46/20	36/11

FESTIVALS AND EVENTS

FAMILY **Alamosa Round-Up Rodeo.** The last week in June marks the annual rodeo competition in Alamosa, a genuine Wild West event including barrel racers, bulls, broncos, and bareback riding. ⊕ *www.alamosaroundup. com* ✉ *$12.*

PLANNING YOUR TIME

GREAT SAND DUNES IN ONE DAY

Arrive early in the day during the summer so you can hike up to **High Dune** and get a view of the entire dune field. Round-trip, the walk itself should take about 1½ to 2 hours (plus time to jump off or slide down the dunes). In the afternoon, hop into the car and head to Zapata Falls, hike on the short-and-shady Montville Nature Trail, or head for the longer Mosca Pass Trail, which follows a small creek through cool aspens and evergreens to one of the lower mountain passes.

In the spring and early summer or fall, when the temperatures are cooler, first walk up to the High Dune to enjoy the view. If you're game to hike farther, head to **Star Dune** for a picnic lunch. Hike down the eastern ridge to Medano Creek, then head to the western end of the park to explore the sand sheet, grasslands, and wetlands. If you're here on a morning when there's a hayride (or four-wheel-drive) tour to see the bison, take it and then head off on your hikes.

GETTING HERE AND AROUND

CAR TRAVEL

Great Sand Dunes National Park and Preserve is about 240 miles from both Denver and Albuquerque, and roughly 180 miles from Colorado Springs and Santa Fe. The fastest route from Denver is I–25 south to U.S. 160, heading west to just past Blanca, to Highway 150 north, which goes right to the park's main entrance. For a more scenic route, take U.S. 285 over Kenosha, Red Hill, and Poncha Passes, turn onto Highway 17 just south of Villa Grove, then take County Lane 6 to the park (watch for signs just south of Hooper). From Albuquerque, go north on I–25 to Santa Fe, then north on U.S. 285 to Alamosa, then U.S. 160 east to Highway 150. From the west, Highway 17 and County Lane 6 take you to the park. The park entrance station is about 3 miles from the park boundary, and it's about a mile from there to the visitor center; the main parking lot is about a mile farther.

PARK ESSENTIALS

PARK FEES AND PERMITS

Entrance fees are $3 per adult above age 15 and are valid for one week from date of purchase. Children are admitted free at all times. Pick up camping permits ($20 per night per site at Pinyon Flats Campground) and backpacking permits (free) at the visitor center.

Plants and Wildlife in Great Sand Dunes

The salty wetlands are dotted with sedges, rushes, and other plants that are tolerant of changes in water salinity and levels, while the sand sheet and grasslands have prickly pear, rabbit brush, and yucca. The dune field looks barren from afar, but up close you see various grasses have rooted in swales among the dunes. Juniper, pinyon, and ponderosa pine trees grow on the lower portions of the mountain, hardy spruce and fir trees survive in the subalpine forest zone, and lichens and tiny flowers cling to the rock at the top.

Birds inhabit the wetlands; short-horned lizards, elk, and pronghorns live in the sand sheet and grassland; and Great Sand Dunes tiger beetles and Ord's kangaroo rats breed in the dune field. In the forests and on the mountainsides, raptors fly overhead, while mule deer and Rocky Mountain bighorn sheep graze.

■TIP➔ Be cautious around wild animals and never approach them. (If you're taking pictures, this is a good time to use a telephoto lens.) Campers should check with rangers about precautions to avoid bear problems.

PARK HOURS
The park is open 24/7. It is in the Mountain time zone.

CELL-PHONE RECEPTION
Cell-phone reception in the park is sporadic. Public telephones are at the visitor center, dunes parking lot, and at the Pinyon Flats campground—you need a calling card (these aren't coin-operated phones).

RESTAURANTS
There are no dining establishments in the park. In the visitor center and at the campground there are vending machines with drinks that are stocked mid-spring through mid-fall. There is one picnic area in the park.

Prices in the reviews are the average cost of a main course at dinner or, if dinner is not served, at lunch.

HOTELS
There are no hotels, motels, or lodges in the park. The nearest lodge is right outside the park entrance, and there are many hotels in Alamosa and a handful of them in other surrounding towns including Salida, Walsenburg, and Monte Vista.

Prices in the reviews are the lowest cost of a standard double room in high season. For expanded reviews, facilities, and current deals, visit Fodors.com.

VISITOR INFORMATION
PARK CONTACT INFORMATION
Great Sand Dunes National Park and Preserve ⊠ *11999 Hwy. 150, Mosca* ☎ *719/378–6399* ⊕ *www.nps.gov/grsa.*

VISITOR CENTERS

Great Sand Dunes Visitor Center. View exhibits and artwork, browse in the bookstore, and watch a 20-minute film with an overview of the dunes. Rangers are on hand to answer questions. Facilities include restrooms and a vending machine stocked with soft drinks and snacks, but no other food. (The Great Sand Dunes Oasis, just outside the park boundary, has a café that is open generally late April through early October.) ⊠ *Near park entrance* ☎ *719/378–6399* ⊘ *Late May–early Sept., daily 8:30–6:30; early Sept.–late May, 9–4:30.*

EXPLORING

SCENIC DRIVES

Medano Pass Primitive Road. This 22-mile road connects Great Sand Dunes with the Wet Mountain Valley and Highway 69 on the east side of the Sangre de Cristo Mountains via a climb to Medano Pass (about 10,000 feet above sea level) and affords stunning views, especially in late September when the aspen trees change color. It also provides access to campsites in the national preserve. It is a four-wheel-drive-only road that is best driven by someone who already has good driving skills on rough, unpaved roads. (Your four-wheel-drive vehicle must have high clearance and be engineered to go over rough roads, and you may need to drop your tires' air pressure.) The road has sections of deep, loose sand, and it crosses Medano Creek nine times. Before you go, stop at the visitor center for a map and ask about current road conditions. Drive time pavement to pavement is 2½ to 3 hours.

SCENIC STOPS

Dune Field. The more than 30 square miles of big dunes in the heart of the park is the main attraction, although the surrounding sand sheet does have some smaller dunes. You can start putting your feet in the sand three miles past the main park entrance.

High Dune. This isn't the park's highest dune, but it's high enough in the dune field to provide a view of all the dunes from its summit. It's on the first ridge of dunes you see from the main parking area.

EDUCATIONAL OFFERINGS

RANGER PROGRAMS

Interpretive Programs. Terrace talks and nature walks designed to help visitors learn more about the Great Sand Dunes National Park are scheduled most days from late May through September, and sporadically in April and October. ⊠ *Visitor center* ☎ *719/378–6399* 🎬 *Free.*

FAMILY **Junior Ranger Programs.** In summer, children ages 3 through 12 can join age-appropriate activities to learn about plants, animals, and the park's ecology, and they can become Junior Rangers by working successfully through an activity booklet available at the visitor center. Youngsters can learn about the park prior to their trip via an interactive online program for kids at ⊕ *www.nps.gov/grsa/forkids/beajuniorranger.htm*. If they complete the self-led program, they'll recieve a patch or a badge. ☎ *719/378–6399*.

TOURS

FAMILY **Bison Tour.** The Nature Conservancy, an international nonprofit conservation organization, owns a 103,000-acre ranch that includes a herd of roughly 2,500 bison in the

DID YOU KNOW?

American Indians used to peel ponderosa pines in order to eat the inner bark (which is rich in calcium) and use the pine gum for medicinal purposes. You can view many of these "culturally modified" trees at Great Sand Dunes.

50,000-acre Medano Ranch section, in the southwest corner of the park. The conservancy offers a two-hour tour focused on the "Wild West" section of the park, where bison—along with coyotes, elk, deer, pronghorns, porcupines, and birds such as great horned owls and red-tailed hawks—roam in the grasslands and wetlands. Depending on the season, the tour will be led either as a hayride or as a four-wheel-drive-vehicle excursion. On Tuesday, Friday, and Saturday, tours are $50 for adults 12 and older, $25 for children, and free for kids 5 and younger. ✉ *Tours begin at the Nature Conservancy's Zapata Ranch Headquarters, 5303 Hwy. 150, Mosca* ☎ *888/592–7282, 719/378–2356* ⊕ *www.zranch.org* 🎫 *$50.*

SPORTS AND THE OUTDOORS

BIRD-WATCHING

The San Luis Valley is famous for its migratory birds, many of which stop in the park. Great Sand Dunes also has many permanent feathered residents. In the wetlands, you might see American white pelicans and the American avocet. On the forested sections of the mountains there are goshawks, northern harriers, gray jays, and Steller's jays. And in the alpine tundra there are golden eagles, hawks, horned larks, and white-tailed ptarmigan.

FISHING

Fly fishermen can angle for Rio Grande cutthroat trout in the upper reaches of Medano Creek, which is accessible by four-wheel-drive vehicle. It's catch-and-release only, and a Colorado license is required (☎ *800/244–5613*). There's also fishing in Upper and Lower Sand Creek Lakes, but it's a very long hike (3 or 4 miles from the Music Pass trailhead, located on the far side of the park in the San Isabel National Forest).

HIKING

Visitors can walk just about anywhere on the sand dunes in the heart of the park. The best view of all the dunes is from the top of High Dune. There are no formal trails because the sand keeps shifting, but you don't really need them: It's extremely difficult to get lost out here.

■TIP➜ Before taking any of the trails in the preserve, rangers recommend stopping at the visitor center and picking up the handout that lists the trails, including their degree of difficulty. The dunes can get very hot in the summer, reaching up to 140°F in the afternoon. If you're hiking, carry plenty of water; if you're going into the backcountry to camp overnight, carry even more water and a water filtration system. A free permit is required to backpack in the park. Also, watch for weather changes. If there's a thunderstorm and lightning, get off the dunes or trail immediately, and seek shelter. Before hiking, leave word with someone indicating where you're going to hike and when you expect to be back. Tell that contact to call 911 if you don't show up when expected.

> ### GOOD READS
>
> ■ *Great Sand Dunes: The Shape of the Wind,* by Stephen Trimble, covers dune history, ecology, scenery, and wildlife.
>
> ■ *The Essential Guide to Great Sand Dunes National Park and Preserve,* by Charlie and Diane Winger, is a must-have for trip planning.

EASY

FAMILY **Hike to High Dune.** Get a panoramic view of all the surrounding dunes from the top of High Dune. Since there's no formal path, the smartest approach is to zigzag up the dune ridgelines. High Dune is 650 feet high, and to get there and back takes about 1½ to 2 hours. It's 1.2 miles each way, but it can feel like a lot longer if there's been no rain for some time and the sand is soft. If you add on the walk to Star Dune, which is another 1.5 miles there and back, plan on another two hours and a strenuous workout up and down the dunes. *Easy.* ⊠ *Start from main dune field.*

MODERATE

Fodor'sChoice **Mosca Pass Trail.** This moderately challenging trail follows the route laid
★ out centuries ago by Native Americans, which became the Mosca Pass toll road used in the late 1800s and early 1900s. This is a good afternoon hike, because the trail rises through the trees and subalpine meadows, often following Mosca Creek. It is 3.5 miles one-way, with a 1,500-foot gain in elevation. Hiking time is two to three hours each way. *Moderate.* ⊠ *Shares Montville Trailhead, just north of the visitor center.*

DIFFICULT

Music Pass Trail. This steep trail offers superb views of the glacially carved Upper Sand Creek Basin, ringed by several 13,000-foot peaks and the Wet Mountain Valley to the east. At the top of the pass you are about 11,000 feet above sea level and surrounded by yet higher mountain peaks. It's 3.5 miles and a 2,000-foot elevation gain one way from the lower parking lot on the east side of the preserve, off Forest Service

Road 119, and 1 mile from the upper parking lot (reachable only by four-wheel-drive). Depending on how fit you are and how often you stop, it can take six hours round-trip from the lower lot. *Difficult.* ⊠ *Trailhead at eastern side of park, off Hwy. 69, 4½ miles south of Westcliffe.* ⊕ *Turn off Hwy. 69 to the west at the sign for Music Pass and South Colony Lakes Trails. At the "T" junction, turn left onto South Colony Rd. At the end of the ranch fence on the right you'll see another sign for Music Pass.*

WHAT'S NEARBY

The vast expanse one sees from the dunes is the San Luis Valley. Covering 8,000 square miles (and with an average altitude of 7,500 feet), the San Luis Valley is the world's largest alpine valley, sprawling on a broad, flat, dry plain between the San Juan Mountains to the west and the Sangre de Cristo range to the east, and extending south into northern New Mexico. The area is one of the state's major agricultural producers.

NEARBY TOWNS

Alamosa, the San Luis Valley's major city, is 35 miles southwest of Great Sand Dunes via U.S. 160 and Highway 150. It's a casual, central base for exploring the park and the surrounding region. The rest of the area is dotted with tiny towns, including **Mosca, Blanca, Antonito,** and **Fort Garland,** to the south of the park, and **Monte Vista, Del Norte,** and **Hooper** to the west. They are all within an hour's drive from the park.

VISITOR INFORMATION
Alamosa Convention & Visitors Bureau ⊠ *610 State Ave., Alamosa* ☎ *800/258-7597, 719/589-3681* ⊕ *www.alamosa.org.* **Del Norte Chamber of Commerce** ⊠ *505 Grand Ave., Del Norte* ⊕ *www.delnortechamber.org.* **Monte Vista Chamber of Commerce** ⊠ *947 1st Ave., Monte Vista* ☎ *719/852-2731* ⊕ *www.monte-vista.org.*

NEARBY ATTRACTIONS

Fort Garland Museum. Colorado's first military post was established here in 1858 to protect settlers in the San Luis Valley, which was then part of the Territory of New Mexico. The legendary Kit Carson once served here, and the six original adobe structures are still standing. The fort features a re-creation of the commandant's quarters from Carson's era, as well as period military displays, and a rotating local folk-art exhibit. ⊠ *29477 Hwy. 159, Fort Garland* ☎ *719/379-3512* ⊕ *museumtrail. org/fortgarlandmuseum.asp* ⊟ *$5* ⊙ *Apr.–Oct., daily 9–5; Nov.–Mar., Thurs.–Mon. 10–4.*

FAMILY **Zapata Falls Recreation Area.** If it's a hot day, take a drive to the falls section of the Zapata Falls Recreation Area, about 7 miles south of Great Sand Dunes National Park (and about 10 miles north of Alamosa). From the trailhead, it's a 0.5-mile hike to the 40-foot waterfall and a mildly steep trail, which can include wading in a stream and walking

Near water in the park's grasslands area is where you might see elk, mule deer, and lizards.

through a narrow gorge to view the falls (depending on water levels). Air temperatures in the gorge are always cool and inviting, and the falls are beautiful, but be careful of the current (and slippery rocks) here. A picnic area and restrooms are at the entrance. The trailhead is 3½ miles off Highway 150, between mile markers 10 and 11. ✉ *Rio Grande National Forest Supervisor's Office, 1803 W. U.S. 160, Monte Vista* ☎ *719/852–5941* ⊕ *fs.usda.gov/riogrande* 💲 *Free* ☉ *Daily.*

AREA ACTIVITIES

SPORTS AND THE OUTDOORS
FISHING
Colorado fishing license. There are plenty of fisheries in the area where you can catch trout, pike, and perch, including the Rio Grande, the Conejos River, and Sanchez, Smith, and Platoro reservoirs. A Colorado fishing license is required ($9 for one day, $21 for five days). ✉ *Colorado Division of Wildlife, SE Region Service Center, 4255 Sinton Rd., Colorado Springs* ☎ *800/244–5613* ⊕ *wildlife.state.co.us/fishing.*

EDUCATIONAL OFFERINGS
Colorado Field Institute. This nonprofit teams up with the experts at the park and other area organizations, such as the Rio Grande National Forest, San Luis Valley National Wildlife Refuges Complex, and the Nature Conservancy's Medano/Zapata Ranch to conduct in-depth outdoor educational programs on the natural and cultural resources of the area. Check its website for the lecture and field trip schedule. ⊕ *www. coloradofieldinstitute.org* ☉ *Hrs and locations vary; call ahead.*

ARTS AND ENTERTAINMENT

ART GALLERIES

Luther Bean Museum and Art Gallery. This Adams State College museum displays American Indian pottery and textiles, European porcelain, photography, and furniture collections in a handsome, wood-paneled 19th-century drawing room, as well as changing exhibits of regional arts and crafts. ✉ *Richardson Hall, Room 256, 208 Edgemont Blvd., Alamosa* ☎ *719/587–7827* 🌐 *www.adams.edu/lutherbean* 🎟 *Free* 🕒 *Weekdays 10–2.*

SCENIC DRIVES

Manassa, San Luis, and Fort Garland Loop. To get a real feel for this area, take an easy driving loop from Alamosa through much of the San Luis Valley (the whole trip is about 95 miles). Head east on U.S 160 to Fort Garland, south on Highway 159 to San Luis, west on Highways 159 and 142 to Manassa, then north on U.S. 285 back to Alamosa. More than half of the route is part the Los Caminos Antiguos Drive, one of Colorado's Scenic Byways.

WHERE TO EAT

IN THE PARK

PICNIC AREAS

Mosca Creek. Great Sand Dunes National Park's only picnic area is shaded by cottonwood trees. It has a dozen places where visitors can park a car or small RV near a picnic table and a grill. ✉ *South of the dunes parking lot.*

OUTSIDE THE PARK

$ ASIAN 🍴 **East West Grill.** Noodles and teriyaki top the menu at this casual, almost fast-food-style place with dine-in or carry-out options. The salads and bento boxes are great. [$] *Average main: $6* ✉ *408 4th St., Alamosa* ☎ *719/589–4600* 🌐 *www.east-westgrill.com.*

$ CAFÉ 🍴 **Milagros Coffeehouse.** The coffee is full-bodied at this combination coffeehouse, Internet café, and used-book store, where all profits go to local charities. The breakfast bagels are especially tasty. [$] *Average main: $4* ✉ *529 Main St., Alamosa* ☎ *719/589–9299* 🌐 *www.milagrosalamosa.com* 🕒 *No dinner Sun.*

$ AMERICAN 🍴 **The Oasis Cafe.** The no-frills restaurant in the Great Sand Dunes Oasis (which includes a grocery store and gas station as well as motel rooms and campsites), just outside the park entrance, is open for breakfast, lunch, and dinner. The Navajo taco (served on fry bread) and beef or chicken burritos are among the most popular items, although the menu ranges from grilled-cheese sandwiches to steaks. [$] *Average main: $11* ✉ *5400 Hwy. 150, Mosca* ☎ *719/378–2222* 🌐 *www.greatdunes.com* 🕒 *Closed mid-Sept.–late Apr.*

CLOSE UP

Best Campgrounds in Great Sand Dunes

Great Sand Dunes has one campground, open year-round. During weekends in the summer, it can fill up with RVs and tents by midafternoon. Black bears live in the preserve, so when camping there, keep your food, trash, and toiletries in the trunk of your car (or use bear-proof containers). There is one campground and RV park near the entrance to Great Sand Dunes, and several others in the area.

Pinyon Flats Campground. Set in a pine forest about a mile past the visitor center, this campground has a trail leading to the dunes. Sites are available on a first-come, first-served basis; RVs are allowed, but there are no hookups. ✉ *On the main park road, near the visitor center* ☎ *719/378–6399.*

WHERE TO STAY

OUTSIDE THE PARK

$ HOTEL 🏨 **Best Western Alamosa Inn.** This sprawling, well-maintained complex is your best bet for reasonably priced lodgings. **Pros:** reliable basic accommodations; easy to find. **Cons:** noisy street; nothing but fast food nearby. [$] *Rooms from: $93* ✉ *2005 Main St., Alamosa* ☎ *719/589–2567, 800/459–5123* 🌐 *www.bestwestern.com/alamosainn* 🛏 *52 rooms, 1 suite* 🍴 *Breakfast.*

$ HOTEL FAMILY 🏨 **Conejos Canyon River Ranch.** Located within the Rio Grande National Forest on the Conejos River, 42 miles southwest of Alamosa, this peaceful, family-friendly retreat is an excellent base for fishing. **Pros:** gorgeous riverfront setting; access to national forest; plenty of activities for adults and kids; on-site gift shop. **Cons:** no amenities nearby; more than an hour from the Great Sand Dunes. [$] *Rooms from: $98* ✉ *25390 Hwy. 17, Antonito* ☎ *719/376–2464* 🌐 *www.conejosranch.com* 🛏 *8 rooms, 8 cabins* 🕒 *Limited rooms and cabins available Dec.–Apr.* 🍴 *Breakfast.*

$ HOTEL 🏨 **Ft. Garland Motor Inn.** This cheerful, squeaky-clean motel is just a few miles south of the Great Sand Dunes, in the tiny town of Ft. **Pros:** spotless, comfortable rooms; 20 minutes from park. **Cons:** no pool or other recreational amenities in hotel; no great eating options nearby. [$] *Rooms from: $94* ✉ *411 U.S. 160, Fort Garland* ☎ *719/379–2993* 🌐 *www.garlandmotorinn.com* 🛏 *15 rooms.*

$ HOTEL 🏨 **Great Sand Dunes Lodge.** Located right at the entrance of the park, behind the Oasis, this simple lodge offers clean, comfortable rooms with private balconies (and great views of the dunes and mountains). **Pros:** closest hotel rooms to the dunes; great views. **Cons:** with the exception of the nearby Oasis Cafe, the nearest restaurants are more than 20 miles away. [$] *Rooms from: $95* ✉ *7900 Hwy. 150 N, Mosca* ☎ *719/378–2900* 🌐 *www.gsdlodge.com* 🛏 *12 rooms* 🕒 *Closed mid-Oct.–mid-Mar.*

$$$$ ALL-INCLUSIVE

Zapata Ranch. Part of a 103,000-acre working cattle and bison ranch owned by the Nature Conservancy, the Zapata Ranch is focused mainly on all-inclusive, weeklong stays, during which guests learn about bison, land conservation, and renewable ranching practices, and participate in ranch activities (including branding cattle and mending fences). **Pros:** beautiful setting among mature cottonwoods; historic lodge buildings; terrific restaurant with indoor and outdoor seating. **Cons:** much pricier than other area accommodations; limited capacity (the ranch rents only those rooms that aren't reserved for guest ranch visitors). [$] *Rooms from: $285* ✉ *5305 Hwy. 150* ☎ *888/592–7282, 719/378–2356* 🌐 *www.zranch.org* 🛏 *15 rooms* 🍴 *All-inclusive.*

GUADALUPE MOUNTAINS NATIONAL PARK

WELCOME TO GUADALUPE MOUNTAINS

TOP REASONS TO GO

★ **Tower over Texas:** The park is home to 8,749-foot Guadalupe Peak, the highest point in the state.

★ **Fall for fiery foliage:** Though surrounded by arid desert and rocky soil, the park has miles of beautiful foliage in McKittrick Canyon. In late October you can watch it burst into flaming colors.

★ **Hike unhindered:** The main activity at the park is hiking its rugged, remote, and often challenging trails: 80 miles worth will keep you captivated and spry—and far away from civilization.

★ **Eat with elk, loll with lions:** Despite the surrounding arid region, a variety of wildlife—including shaggy brown elk, furtive mountain lions, and shy black bears—traipse the mountains, woods, and desert here.

1 Guadalupe Peak. This crude, rocky pinnacle tops 8,700 feet and towers over the rest of the park's peaks. Those who brave the seven-hour-plus round trip to the summit are rewarded with breathtaking views of New Mexico and southwestern Texas.

2 McKittrick Canyon. In late October and early November, the lush green foliage along McKittrick Canyon's trout-filled desert stream bursts into russet, amber, and gold hues. An easy, wheelchair-accessible ramble takes visitors through this geological wonder.

3 El Capitan. Not to be confused with equally impressive El Capitan in Yosemite National Park, this 3,000-foot cliff dominates the southern skyline of the Guadalupe Range. It has visitors talking and hikers walking: a 6- to 11-mile-plus trail winds around the base of this massive limestone formation.

4 Manzanita Spring. The area around this idyllic stream and picnic spot has a little bit of everything: a spring feeds lush grasses and trees, giving life to hundreds of wildflowers. Birds hang out here to enjoy the tasty seeds and insects

that the water, shade, and vegetation provide. Plus, it's only a 0.2-mile stroll from here to the Frijole Ranch History Museum.

5 Frijole Ranch History Museum. This easily accessible former ranch home is the oldest intact structure in the park, set amid several rock-walled outbuildings and a landscaped yard. The museum injects a bit of man-made history into the natural surroundings, which include two nearby springs.

NEW MEXICO
TEXAS
Cutoff Mountain 6,933 ft

Butterfield Route

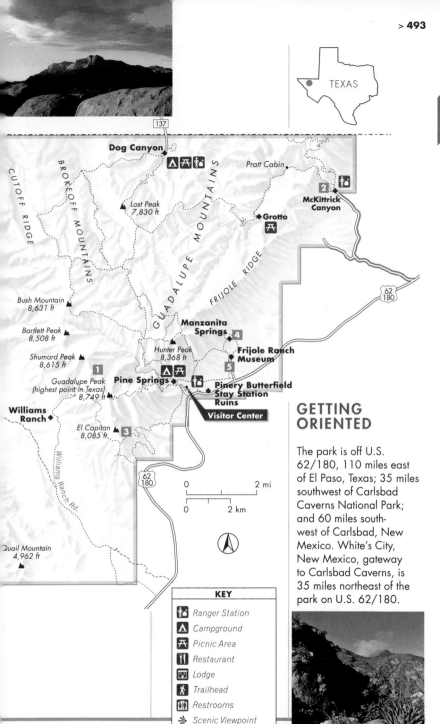

TEXAS

22

137

Dog Canyon 🔺⛱🚻

Pratt Cabin •

🚻 **2**

McKittrick Canyon

Lost Peak 7,830 ft ▲

C U T O F F   R I D G E

B R O K E O F F   M O U N T A I N S

G U A D A L U P E   M O U N T A I N S

F R I J O L E   R I D G E

♦ **Grotto** ⛱

Bush Mountain 8,631 ft ▲

62 180

Bartlett Peak 8,508 ft ▲

Manzanita Springs ♦ **4**

Hunter Peak 8,368 ft ▲

♦ **Frijole Ranch Museum**

5

Shumard Peak 8,615 ft ▲

Guadalupe Peak (highest point in Texas) 8,749 ft ▲

1

Pine Springs 🔺⛱ 🚻

♦ **Pinery Butterfield Stay Station Ruins**

Williams Ranch ♦

El Capitan 8,085 ft ▲ **3**

Visitor Center

W i l l i a m s   R a n c h   R d .

62 180

0 ——— 2 mi

0 ——— 2 km

Quail Mountain 4,962 ft ▲

🔼

GETTING ORIENTED

The park is off U.S. 62/180, 110 miles east of El Paso, Texas; 35 miles southwest of Carlsbad Caverns National Park; and 60 miles southwest of Carlsbad, New Mexico. White's City, New Mexico, gateway to Carlsbad Caverns, is 35 miles northeast of the park on U.S. 62/180.

	KEY
🚻	Ranger Station
🔺	Campground
⛱	Picnic Area
🍴	Restaurant
🏠	Lodge
🚶	Trailhead
🚻	Restrooms
🔼	Scenic Viewpoint
⋯⋯	Walking/Hiking Trails

Updated by
Marty Racine

Guadalupe Mountains National Park is a study in extremes: it has mountaintop forests but also rocky canyons, arid deserts, and a stream that winds through verdant woods. The park is home to the Texas madrone tree, found commonly only here and in Big Bend National Park. Guadalupe Mountains National Park also has the distinction of hosting the loftiest spot in Texas: 8,749-foot Guadalupe Peak. The mountain dominates the view from every approach, but it's just one member of a rugged range carved by wind, water, and time.

GUADALUPE MOUNTAINS PLANNER

WHEN TO GO

Trails here are rarely crowded, except in fall, when foliage changes colors in McKittrick Canyon, and during spring break in March. Still, this is a very remote area, and you probably won't find too much congestion at any time. Hikers are more apt to explore backcountry trails in spring and fall, when it's cooler but not too cold. Snow, not uncommon in the winter months, can linger in the higher elevations. The windy season is March through May, and the rainy months are July and August.

AVG. HIGH/LOW TEMPS.

JAN.	FEB.	MAR.	APR.	MAY	JUNE
53/30	58/35	63/38	71/46	78/55	88/63

JULY	AUG.	SEPT.	OCT.	NOV.	DEC.
87/63	84/62	78/57	71/49	61/38	57/33

PLANNING YOUR TIME
GUADALUPE IN ONE DAY

Start your tour at **Headquarters Visitor Center,** also known as the Pine Springs Ranger Station, where an exhibit and slide show introduce the park's wildlife and geology. Nearby is the 0.75-mile, round-trip, wheelchair-accessible **Pinery Trail,** which rambles to the Pinery Butterfield Stage Station ruins. As you take in the sights, do not touch the ruins' fragile walls; the site is quite vulnerable. Next, head to the **Frijole Ranch History Museum,** housed in a vacated yet well-preserved ranch home built in 1876.

Once you're done exploring the shaded grounds and admiring the labor that built the compound, turn onto the trailhead behind the ranch house for the 0.2-mile stroll to the calming waters of **Manzanita Spring,** one of two watering holes that gurgle within a couple of miles of the museum. Park staff call such areas riparian zones. These oases supply the fragile wildlife here, and can sometimes look like Pre-Raphaelite paintings, with mirrored-surface ponds and delicate flowers and greenery.

Afterward, pay a visit to the famed **McKittrick Canyon.** Regardless of the season, the dense foliage and basin stream are worth the hike—though it's best to visit it in late October and early November when the trees burst into color. There isn't a direct route, but you can get here quickly by driving northeast from the visitor center on U.S. 62/180. Follow it to the gate at the western turnoff, which is locked at sunset. Head northwest through the gate (ignoring the service road) in your car, and you'll arrive at the canyon.

Take your time walking the **McKittrick Canyon Trail,** which leads to Pratt Lodge, or the strenuous but rewarding 8.4-mile **Permian Reef Trail,** which takes you up thousands of feet, past monumental geological formations. Or traverse the easy, short (less than 1 mile) **McKittrick Canyon Nature Loop.**

GETTING HERE AND AROUND
CAR TRAVEL

About half of the Guadalupe Mountains is a designated wilderness, so few roadways penetrate the park. Most sites are accessible off U.S. 62/180. Dog Canyon Campground, on the north end of the park, can be reached via Route 137 from New Mexico.

PARK ESSENTIALS
PARK FEES AND PERMITS

An admission fee of $5 for everyone 16 and older is collected at the visitor center, and is good for one week. Camping is $8 a night per site; pay at the visitor center or at self-registration boards in campgrounds. For overnight backpacking trips, you must get a free permit from either Headquarters Visitor Center or Dog Canyon Ranger Station.

PARK HOURS

The park is open 24/7, year-round. It's in the Mountain time zone.

CELL-PHONE RECEPTION

Cell phones with far-reaching service can pick up signals at key points along trails. Alternatively, public phones are located at Dog Canyon Ranger Station, Headquarters Visitor Center, McKittrick Contact Station, and Pine Springs Campground.

RESTAURANTS

Dining in the park is a do-it-yourself affair. Ranger stations don't serve meals or sell picnic items, though nearby White's City offers some basics—sodas, snacks, and the like.

Prices in the reviews are the average cost of a main course at dinner, or if dinner is not served, at lunch.

HOTELS

There are no hotels within the park. Your best options are in White's City or Carlsbad.

Prices in the reviews are the lowest cost of a standard double room in high season. For expanded reviews, facilities, and current deals, visit Fodors.com.

VISITOR INFORMATION

VISITOR CENTERS

Fodors Choice
★

Headquarters Visitor Center. You can pick up maps, brochures, and other information at the Headquarters Visitor Center, aka Pine Springs Ranger Station, with easy access off the highway. A slide show and a 12-minute movie provide a quick introduction to the park, half of which is protected as a designated wilderness area. Some nicely crafted exhibits depict typical wildlife and plant scenes ranging from lowland desert to forested mountaintop, while outside the entrance native flora are marked for identification. ⊠ *400 Pine Canyon Dr., off U.S. 62/180, 55 miles southwest of Carlsbad, 110 mile east of El Paso* ☎ *915/828–3251* 🖨 *915/828–3269* ⊕ *www.nps.gov/gumo* ☉ *Daily 8–4:30.*

McKittrick Contact Station. Poster-size illustrations in a shaded, outdoor patio area tell the geological story of the Guadalupe Mountains, believed to have been carved from an ancient sea. You can also hear the recorded memoirs of oilman Wallace Pratt, who donated his ranch and surrounding area to the federal government for preservation. Nearby trailheads access a 0.9-mile nature loop and lengthier hikes. ⊠ *4 miles off U.S. 62/180, 7 miles northeast of Headquarters Visitor Center* ☎ *915/828–3251* ☉ *June–Aug., daily 8–6; Sept.–May, daily 8–4:30.*

EXPLORING

SCENIC DRIVES

Williams Ranch Road. Take in panoramic views and see limestone cliffs up close on this 7¼-mile, one-way drive over what was once the Butterfield Overland Mail Stage Line. The closest highway, U.S. 62/180, parallels a segment of the old trail. The route is rough—you need a high-clearance, four-wheel-drive vehicle—but enjoyable. It takes about an hour. The road leads to an old ranch house at the base of a 3,000-foot cliff, where James "Dolph" Williams worked with his partner, an Indian named Geronimo (no relation to the historical figure). This is a day-trip only; overnight parking prohibited. ■ TIP→ **The drive is locked, so pick up a gate key at Headquarters Visitor Center.** ⊠ *¾ mile off U.S. 62/180, 8.3 mile southwest of Pine Springs* ✛ *Drive west on U.S. 62/180 from Headquarters Visitor Center for 8¼ mile until you see brown metal gate on north side with National Park Service sign. Continue through 2 locked gates (lock them behind you).* ⊙ *Daily dawn–dusk.*

HISTORIC SITES

FAMILY

Fodor's Choice

★

Frijole Ranch History Museum. Displays and photographs depict ranch life and early park history inside this old ranch-house museum, occupying what is believed to be the region's oldest intact structure. Hiking trails, which are easy to travel and great for kids, spoke off from the shady, tree-lined grounds; one leads to wildlife oases Manzanita Spring and Smith Spring. ■ TIP→ **Due to staffing shortages, the museum might be closed, especially in summer "low" season, so call ahead.** Still, this is a worthwhile (and accessible) destination, as you can explore the ranch grounds replete with outbuildings, an orchard and still-functioning irrigation system. It is also a peaceful setting reflecting echoes of the past. ⊠ *Access road 1 mile northeast of Headquarters Visitors Center, Frijole Ranch Rd. north of U.S. 62/180* ☎ *915/828–3251* ⊕ *www.nps.gov/ gumo* ⊠ *Free* ⊙ *Grounds open daily; museum daily 8–4:30.*

Pinery Butterfield Stage Station Ruins. In the mid-1800s passengers en route from St. Louis or San Francisco on the old Butterfield Overland Mail stagecoach route would stop here for rest and refreshment. At more than a mile elevation, the station was the highest on the route, but it operated for only about a year. The ruins provide a reasonable peek into the past: several buildings with rock walls (but no roofs) layered on the desert floor. Please do not touch. You can drive here from U.S. 62/180 or take a paved 0.75-mile round-trip trail from Headquarters Visitor Center. ⊠ *½ mile east of Headquarters Visitors Center.*

SCENIC STOPS

Fodor's Choice

★

McKittrick Canyon. A desert creek flows through this canyon, considered one of the wondrous sights in Texas, lined with walnut, maple, and other trees that explode into brilliant hues each autumn. Call the visitor center to chart the progress of the colorful fall foliage; the spectacular changing of the leaves often extends into November, depending on the weather. You're likely to spot mule deer heading for the water here. The canyon is ground zero for several hiking trails, including Pratt Cabin (two to three hours) and the Grotto (four hours). ⊠ *4 miles off U.S. 62/180, about 7 miles northeast of Headquarters Visitor Center.*

EDUCATIONAL OFFERINGS

RANGER PROGRAMS

FAMILY **Junior Ranger Program.** The park offers a self-guided Junior Program: kids choose activities from a workbook—including taking nature hikes and answering questions based on park exhibits—and earn a patch and certificate once they've completed three. If they complete six, they earn an additional patch. ⊠ *Headquarters Visitors Center, about 1 mile north of U.S. 62/180* 📞 *915/828–3251* 📧 *Free.*

SPORTS AND THE OUTDOORS

BIRD-WATCHING

More than 300 species of birds have been spotted in the park, including the ladder-backed woodpecker, Scott's oriole, Say's phoebe, and white-throated swift. Many migratory birds—such as fleeting hummingbirds and larger but less graceful turkey vultures—stop at Guadalupe during spring and fall migrations. **Manzanita Springs,** near the Frijole Ranch History Museum, is an excellent birding spot. As with hiking, there aren't any local guides, but rangers at the Dog Canyon and Pine Springs ranger stations can help you spot some native species. Books on birding are available at the Pine Springs Ranger Station; visitors might find the Natural History Association's birding checklist for Guadalupe Mountains National Park especially helpful. It will be easy to spot the larger birds of prey circling overhead, such as keen-beaked golden eagles and swift, red-tailed hawks. Be on the lookout for owls in the **Bowl** area, and watch for swift-footed roadrunners in the desert areas (they're quick, but not as speedy as their cartoon counterpart).

HIKING

No matter which trail you select, be sure to pack wisely—the park doesn't sell anything. This includes the recommended gallon of water per day per person, as well as sunscreen, sturdy footwear, and hats. (Bring $5, too—that's the additional cost to use the trails, payable at the visitor centers.) The area has a triple-whammy regarding sun ailments: it's very open, very sunny, and has a high altitude (which makes sunburns more likely). Slather up. And be sure to leave Fido at home—few of the park's trails allow pets.

HIKING RESOURCES

Dog Canyon Ranger Station. The staff at the Dog Canyon Ranger Station can help plan your day hike, horseback ride, or overnight backpacking trip. Dog Canyon is an excellent gateway to the high country of the park's northern boundary mere miles from the New Mexico state line. The ranger station can be accessed from New Mexico by Route 137 off U.S. 285 (12 miles north of Carlsbad) or by County Road 408 off U.S. 62/180 (9 miles south of Carlsbad), which links to 137. ⊠ *Rte. 137* 📞 *575/981–2418.*

CLOSE UP

Plants and Wildlife in Guadalupe Mountains

22

Despite the constant wind and the arid conditions, more than a thousand species of plants populate the mountains, chasms, and salt dunes that comprise the park's different geologic zones. Some grow many feet in a single night; others bloom so infrequently they're called "century plants." In fall, McKittrick Canyon's oaks, bigtooth maples, and velvet ashes go Technicolor above the little stream that traverses it. Barren-looking cacti burst into yellow, red, and purple bloom in spring, and wildflowers can carpet the park for thousands of acres after unusually heavy rains.

More than 86,000 acres of mountains, chasms, canyons, woods, and deserts house an incredible diversity of wildlife, including hallmark Southwestern species like roadrunners and long-limbed jackrabbits, which run so fast they appear to float on their enormous, black-tipped ears. Other furry residents include coyotes, black bears, mountain lions, fox, deer, elk, and badgers. You may also spot numerous winged creatures: 300 different bird species, 90 types of butterflies, and 16 species of bats.

Plenty of reptiles and insects make their homes here, too: coachwhip snakes, diamondback rattlers, whiptail lizards, scorpions, and lovelorn tarantulas (the only time you might spy them is in the fall, when they search for mates), to name a few. Texas's famous (and threatened) horned lizards—affectionately called "horny toads"—can also be seen waddling across the soil in search of ants and other insects. Rangers caution parents not to let little ones run too far ahead on the trails. ■**TIP→** Rattlesnakes are common here. They're not aggressive, so try to remain calm and give a wide berth to any you spot.

The bookstore at the **Pine Springs Ranger Station** also sells hiking guides. These and other guides can also be found at ⊕ *www.ccgma.org.*

EASY

FAMILY **Indian Meadows Nature Trail.** A mostly level trail in Dog Canyon, this 0.5-mile hike crosses an arroyo into meadowlands. It's a good way to spend about 45 minutes savoring the countryside. *Easy.* ⊠ *Trailhead across from Dog Canyon Ranger Station.*

FAMILY **McKittrick Nature Loop.** Signs along this mile-long loop explain the geological and botanical history of the area, and the views, while not spectacular, are engaging enough to hold your interest. The trail is not wheelchair or stroller accessible due to the narrow pathway and rocky terrain. ■**TIP→** You can take the loop in either of two directions when you come to a fork in the trail. *Easy.* ⊠ *Shares McKittrick Canyon Trailhead at northeast corner of park.*

MODERATE

Devil's Hall Trail. Wind through Chihuahua Desert habitat thick with spiked agave plants, prickly pear cacti, and giant boulders, and Devil's Hall, a narrow canyon about 10 feet wide and 100 feet deep. If you travel at a leisurely pace, this 4-mile trail will take about half a day. *Moderate.* ⊠ *Shares Pine Springs Trailhead, in the RV section of Pine Springs Campground.*

The sun sets over the desert landscape of west Texas at Guadalupe Mountains National Park.

El Capitan/Salt Basin Overlook Trails. Several trails combine to form a popular loop through the low desert. El Capitan skirts the base of El Capitan peak for about 3.5 miles, leading to a junction with Salt Basin Overlook. The 4.5-mile Salt Basin Overlook trail begins at the Pine Springs Trailhead and has views of the stark, white salt flat below and loops back onto the El Capitan Trail. The 11.3-mile round trip is not recommended during the intense heat of summer, since there is absolutely no shade. *Moderate.* ⊠ *El Capitan shares Pine Springs Trailhead.*

Marcus Overlook. A 4.5-mile round-trip rewards you with a panoramic view of West Dog Canyon. Set aside about half a day for it. *Moderate.* ⊠ *Trail accessed at Rte. 137, 60 miles southwest of U.S. 285.*

Fodor's Choice ★ **Pratt Lodge Trail.** View stream and canyon woodlands along a 4.5-mile round-trip excursion that leads to the vacant Pratt Lodge, a stone cabin built during the Great Depression in the "most beautiful spot in Texas," according to its original owner, Wallace Pratt. Perhaps he was enthralled by an oasis of running water carving through the canyon floor or a colorful riot of autumn foliage. Plan on at least two hours if you walk at a fast pace, but give yourself another hour or two if you want to take your time. *Moderate.* ⊠ *Trailhead at McKittrick Canyon Ranger Station, 4 miles off U.S. 62/180, about 7 miles northeast of Headquarters Visitors Center.*

FAMILY Fodor's Choice ★ **Smith Spring Trail.** Departing from the Frijole Ranch, the trail heads for a shady oasis where you're likely to spot mule deer and elk drawn to the miracle of water in the desert. As a bonus, the route passes Manzanita Spring, another wildlife refuge only 0.2 mile past Frijole Ranch. Allow 1½ hours to complete the 2.2-mile round-trip walk. This is a good hike for older kids whose legs won't tire as easily, but it is not wheelchair accessible past Manzanita Spring. *Moderate.* ⊠ *Trailhead off access road 1 mile northeast of Headquarters Visitor Center.*

DIFFICULT

Fodor'sChoice
★ **The Bowl.** Cutting through forests of pine and Douglas fir, this trail to an aptly named mountaintop valley is considered one of the most gorgeous in the park. The strenuous 9-mile round trip—which can take up to 10 hours, depending on your pace—is where rangers go when they want to enjoy themselves. ■ **TIP→ Don't forget to bring (and drink) lots of water.** *Difficult.* ⊠ *Shares Pine Springs Trailhead.* ⊹ *From Pine Springs Campground, follow Frijole/Foothills Trail, and Bear Canyon Trail to top; then turn left onto Bowl Trail.*

Fodor'sChoice
★ **Guadalupe Peak Trail.** An 8.5-mile workout over a steep grade to the top of Texas pays off with a passage through various ecosystems and some great views. The round-trip hike can take up to eight hours to complete, but the trail is clearly defined and does not require undue athleticism. The steepest climbs are in the beginning, when you are likely to be freshest. In summer, start this hike in early morning to allow a descent before afternoon thunderstorms flare up. ⚠ **Lightning targets high peaks. Be alert to changing weather and head for lower ground if conditions worsen.** Also, Guadalupe Peak is considered one of the windiest points in the U.S. *Difficult.* ⊠ *Trail accessed via Pine Springs Trail, in RV section of Pine Springs Campground.*

Permian Reef Geology Trail. If you're in shape and have a serious geological bent, you may want to hike this approximately 8.5-mile round-trip climb. It heads through open, expansive desert country to a forested ridge with Douglas fir and ponderosa pines. Panoramic views of McKittrick Canyon and the surrounding mountain ranges allow you to observe many rock layers. A geology guidebook coordinated to trail makers is available at the visitor center. Set aside at least eight hours for this trek. *Difficult.* ⊠ *Shares McKittrick Canyon Trailhead at the northeast corner of the park.*

WHERE TO EAT

IN THE PARK

The park has no snack bars or restaurants, but several picnic areas are available. Wood and charcoal fires are not allowed anywhere in the park. If you want to cook a hot meal, bring a camp stove.

PICNIC AREAS

Fodor'sChoice
★ **Dog Canyon Campground.** Thirteen campsites have picnic tables, which you can use during the day for free. This is a lovely shaded area where you're very likely to see mule deer. Drinking water and restrooms are available at the site. This area is about a two-hour drive from the Headquarters Visitor Center. ⊠ *Off Rte. 137, 65 miles southwest of Carlsbad.*

Frijole Ranch Campground. Not very secluded but cooler than nearby Pine Springs Campground, Frijole sports newly constructed picnic shelters that can accommodate large groups near the parking area. Two picnic

Best Campgrounds in Guadalupe Mountains

The park has two developed campgrounds that charge fees, and 10 designated primitive, backcountry sites where you can camp for free. First, obtain a permit at Headquarters Visitor Center or Dog Canyon Ranger Station. Visitors haul their supplies for miles to stretch out on the unspoiled land of these backcountry sites. In the backcountry, no restrooms are provided; visitors may dig their own privies, but toilet paper and other paper waste should be packed out. Wood and charcoal fires are prohibited throughout the park, but you can use your camp stove at both the developed and backcountry sites.

Dog Canyon Campground.
This campground is remote and a little tricky to find, but well worth the effort. The very well-maintained camping area is in a coniferous forest. ⊠ *Rte. 137, just within park northern entrance* ☎ *575/981–2418.*

Pine Springs Campground.
You'll be snuggled amid pinyon and juniper trees at the base of a tall mountain peak at this site behind the Headquarters Visitor Center. ⊠ *At park east entrance, off U.S. 62/180* ☎ *915/828–3251.*

---

tables are also set up under tall trees. Restrooms are available nearby and at the Frijole Ranch History Museum, but hours of operation there can be inconsistent. ⊠ *Access road 1 mile northeast of Headquarters Visitors Center.*

Pine Springs Campground. Drinking water, restrooms, and a picnic area are available at this site near the Headquarters Visitor Center. Shade, however, can be a bit sparse in the intense summer heat. A network of hiking trails will help you walk off that hearty lunch. ⊠ *Behind Headquarters Visitors Center.*

OUTSIDE THE PARK

Tiny **White's City, New Mexico,** 35 miles to the northeast off U.S. 62/180, is more a crossroads than a town, but it does have the Cactus Café and J.J.'s Steakhouse. The town of **Carlsbad, New Mexico,** 55–60 miles northeast of the park, has more amenities. ⇨ *For dining options near the park, see Where to Eat in Carlsbad Caverns National Park (Chapter 13).*

WHERE TO STAY

OUTSIDE THE PARK

⇨ *For lodging options near the park, see Where to Stay in Carlsbad Caverns National Park (Chapter 13).*

JASPER
NATIONAL PARK

WELCOME TO
JASPER NATIONAL PARK

TOP REASONS TO GO

★ **Larger than life:** Almost as large as the entire state of Connecticut, Jasper is the largest of the Canadian Rocky Mountain national parks, and one of the world's largest protected mountain ecosystems.

★ **Spectacular scenery:** Jasper's scenery is rugged and mountainous. Within its boundaries are crystal clear mountain lakes, thundering waterfalls, jagged mountain peaks, and ancient glaciers.

★ **Wonderful wildlife:** The Canadian Rockies provide a diverse habitat for 277 bird species and 69 species of mammals, including deer, elk, moose, sheep, goats, and bears.

★ **Columbia Icefield:** The largest icefield south of Alaska, the Columbia Icefield is also the hydrographic apex of North America, with water flowing to three different oceans from one point.

1 Yellowhead Corridor. Trans-Canada Highway 16 (Yellowhead Highway) travels through the foothills and main ranges of the Canadian Rockies. Highlights are views of the Jasper Lake sand dunes (Km 27), Disaster Point Animal Lick (Km 39.5), Pocahontas Townsite (Km 39.5), the Coal Mine Interpretive Trail (Km 39.5), and Miette Hot Springs (Km 43).

2 Jasper Townsite. Shops, restaurants, nightclubs, and the main park information center are here. Just outside town are Lac Beauvert, Lake Annette, and Lake Edith, plus Old Fort Point, and Whistlers Tramway.

3 Maligne Valley. Highlights of this region include the Athabasca Valley Lookout (Km 5.8), Maligne Canyon (Km 7), Medicine Lake (Km 20.7), and Maligne Lake (Km 45), where the paved road ends.

BRITISH COLUMBIA

4 Cavell Road. The road is just past the Astoria River bridge (Km 11.7) on Highway 93A, south of Jasper Townsite. Depending on weather conditions, it's open from early June to mid-October. Highlights include Astoria Valley Viewpoint, Mt. Edith Cavell, and Cavell Meadows.

5 Icefield Parkway. Highway 93 spans 210 km (130 miles) between Jasper Townsite and Lake Louise and is one of the world's most spectacular drives. Highlights include Athabasca Falls (Km 31), Sunwapta Falls (Km 55), Columbia Icefield (Km 103), Sunwapta Pass (Km 108), and the Weeping Wall (Km 125).

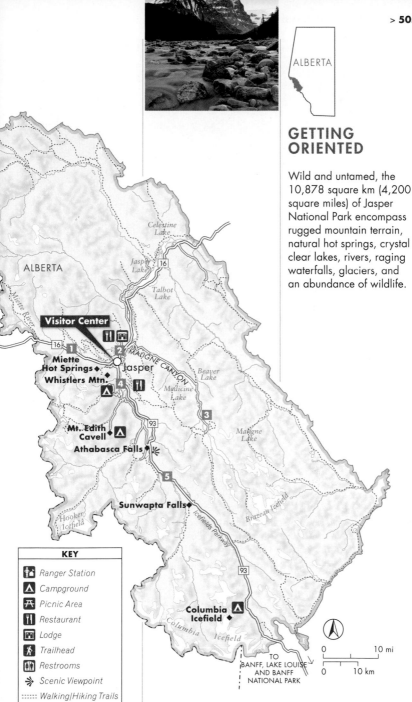

23

GETTING ORIENTED

Wild and untamed, the 10,878 square km (4,200 square miles) of Jasper National Park encompass rugged mountain terrain, natural hot springs, crystal clear lakes, rivers, raging waterfalls, glaciers, and an abundance of wildlife.

ALBERTA

Celestine Lake

Jasper Lake

16

Talbot Lake

Miette River

ALBERTA

Visitor Center

16 **1**

2

MALIGNE CANYON

Jasper

Beaver Lake

Miette Hot Springs◆

Whistlers Mtn.◆

4

Medicine Lake

Mt. Edith Cavell◆

93

Maligne Lake

3

Athabasca Falls◆

5

Sunwapta Falls◆

Icefields Parkway

Brazeau Icefield

Hooker Icefield

93

KEY

🏕	Ranger Station
▲	Campground
🛖	Picnic Area
🍴	Restaurant
🖼	Lodge
🚶	Trailhead
🚻	Restrooms
⚡	Scenic Viewpoint
⋯	Walking/Hiking Trails

Columbia Icefield◆ ▲

Columbia Icefield

TO BANFF, LAKE LOUISE AND BANFF NATIONAL PARK

0   10 mi

0   10 km

Updated by
Debbie Olsen

Jagged mountain peaks, shimmering glaciers, and crystal clear lakes are just part of the incredible scenery that makes up the largest and wildest of Canada's Rocky Mountain parks. Situated along the eastern slopes of the Rockies in west-central Alberta, Jasper National Park encompasses 10,878 square km (4,200 square miles) of land and is home to an astonishing variety of wildlife.

JASPER PLANNER

WHEN TO GO

An old saying in the Canadian Rockies states, "If you don't like the weather, just wait a minute." The weather in Jasper National Park is unpredictable and ever changing, so you need to prepare for all weather conditions, especially when hiking. The summer months can be hot enough for swimming in Lake Edith one day and icy cold the next. Temperatures in winter are usually well below freezing, but occasionally warm Chinook winds blow in and begin to melt the snow.

July and August are the peak travel months for visitors—and the best time for hiking and viewing wildflowers. If you are traveling then, book accommodations well in advance and expect to pay a bit more.

Temporary road closures may occur due to adverse weather conditions.

AVG. HIGH/LOW TEMPS.

JAN.	FEB.	MAR.	APR.	MAY	JUNE
24/5	38/12	42/23	55/24	66/34	66/43
JULY	AUG.	SEPT.	OCT.	NOV.	DEC.
70/44	70/40	58/35	52/29	38/21	29/10

FESTIVALS AND EVENTS

WINTER **Canadian Rockies Snow Battle.** Think of it as a snowball fight with rules. Teams of seven to nine players compete for the Canadian National Championship in the Japanese sport of Yukigassen. This event typically takes place over a weekend in late November, and it's fun to watch and fun to play. ⊠ *500 Cannaught Dr., Jasper* ☎ *780/852–6236* ⊕ *www. jasper.travel/snowbattle.*

Jasper in January. Jasper's biggest winter celebration includes an ice-sculpting contest, wine tastings, great live music, a chili cook-off, and more over more than two weeks. ⊠ *500 Connaught Dr., Jasper* ☎ *780/852–6236* ⊕ *jasperinjanuary.com.*

Jasper Welcomes Winter. This annual four-day festival in early December celebrates the arrival of winter. Special activities for the entire family include the Santa Claus Parade, skating parties, and a Christmas Craft Fair. ⊠ *500 Connaught Dr., Jasper* ☎ *780/852–3858.*

SUMMER **Canada Day.** July 1, Canada's birthday, is celebrated with a parade, a full day of activities, and fireworks at dusk. ☎ *780/852–6176* ⊕ *www. jaspercanadaday.com.*

Parks Day. Celebrating the country's natural wonders, this annual event takes place in mid-July. There are activities for the whole family, a fair on the lawn in the middle of town, and free guided hikes to some of Jasper National Park's most interesting spots. ⊠ *500 Connaught Dr., Jasper* ☎ *780/852–6176* ⊕ *www.friendsofjasper.com.*

PLANNING YOUR TIME
JASPER IN ONE DAY
Make a stop at the **Jasper Information Centre** to get maps of the park and information about any special activities before driving up to **Mt. Edith Cavell.** The 1 km (0.5-mile) trail from the parking lot leads to the base of an imposing cliff where you can see the stunning Angel Glacier. If you are feeling energetic, take the steep 3-km (2-mile) trail that climbs up the valley to **Cavell Meadows,** which are carpeted with wildflowers from mid-July to mid-August. Return to Jasper Townsite for lunch. In the afternoon, take the 45-minute drive southeast of the townsite to beautiful **Maligne Lake,** the second-largest glacier-fed lake in the world. Explore the lake and make a stop at **Spirit Island** on a 1½-hour guided boat tour with **Maligne Lake Scenic Cruises.** Return to the townsite for supper and end your day by participating in a free ranger-led evening interpretive program at **Whistlers Outdoor Theatre,** south of Jasper Townsite at Whistlers Campground.

GETTING HERE AND AROUND
Jasper National Park is in central Alberta in the Canadian Rockies. It is 178 km (111 miles) north of Banff Townsite and 50 km (31 miles) east of Jasper Townsite.

AIR TRAVEL
The closest international airports are in Edmonton, 362 km (225 miles) to the east, and Calgary, 480 km (298 miles) to the southeast.

23

BUS TRAVEL

Greyhound Canada (☎ *800/661–8747, 800/231–2222 in U.S.* ⊕ *www. greyhound.ca*) provides regular service to Jasper from Calgary, Edmonton, and Vancouver; and **Brewster Sightseeing Excurions** (☎ *800/760–6934* ⊕ *www.explorerockies.com*) provides transportation between Calgary and Edmonton international airports and Jasper.

CAR TRAVEL

Car-rental agencies are available at both airports, as well as in Jasper. The Edmonton airport is closer to Jasper than the Calgary one and driving is the easiest way to get from either city to Jasper.

TRAIN TRAVEL

Train service is available three times per week (Tuesday, Friday, and Sunday) from Edmonton to Jasper with **VIA Rail Canada** (☎ *888/842– 7245* ⊕ *www.viarail.ca*).

PARK ESSENTIALS

PARK FEES AND PERMITS

A park entrance pass is C$9.80 per person or C$19.60 maximum per vehicle per day. Larger buses and vans pay a group rate. An annual pass costs C$67.70 per adult or C$136.40 per family or group.

Permits, obtained from the park's information center (☎ *780/852–6177*) are required for backcountry camping (C$9.80 per day), campfires (C$8.80 per day), using dumping stations (C$8.80 per day), and fishing (C$9.80 per day).

PARK HOURS

The park is open 24/7 year-round. It is in the Mountain time zone.

CELL-PHONE RECEPTION

Cell phones generally work only in and around the town of Jasper.

RESTAURANTS

Jasper's casual restaurants offer a wide variety of cuisines, including Greek, Italian, Japanese, French, and North American. Regional specialties include Alberta beef, lamb, pheasant, venison, elk, bison, trout, and BC (British Columbia) salmon. For the best views in town, try the cafeteria-style Treeline Restaurant at the top of the Jasper Tramway, 7,500 feet above sea level. Just know that people go to Treeline for the view, not the food.

Prices in the reviews are the average cost of a main course at dinner, or if dinner is not served, at lunch. Note that all prices in this chapter are in Canadian dollars, unless stated otherwise.

HOTELS

Accommodations in this area include luxury resorts, fine hotels, reasonably priced motels, rustic cabins, and backcountry lodges. Reserve your accommodations in advance if you are traveling during the peak summer season.

Prices in the reviews are the lowest cost of a standard double room in high season. Note that all prices in this chapter are in Canadian dollars, unless stated otherwise. For expanded reviews, facilities, and current deals, visit Fodors.com.

TOURS

FAMILY **Jasper Adventure Centre.** Guided tours, birding trips, ice walks, and snow-shoeing tours are all available here. Rates start at C$69 per person, with most tours lasting three hours. The center also handles bookings for canoeing, rafting, and other types of excursions. ⊠ *611 Patricia St.* ☎ *780/852–5595* ⊕ *www.jasperadventurecentre.com.*

Maligne Adventures. This outfitter offers everything from day treks to overnight backpacking trips and heli-hiking excursions. They also have porters who can carry some of the heavy gear. The Maligne Canyon Icewalk is a popular tour during the winter months. Rates start at C$55 per person. ⊠ *616 Patricia St.* ☎ *780/852–0167, 866/625–4463* ⊕ *www.maligneadventures.com.*

Walks and Talks Jasper. Birding trips, nature walks, guided hiking, cross-country ski tours, and ice-field tours are some of this company's offerings. Rates start at C$55 per person, with most tours lasting about three hours. ⊠ *626 Connaught Dr.* ☎ *780/852–4994, 888/242–3343* ⊕ *www.walksntalks.com.*

VISITOR INFORMATION
PARK CONTACT INFORMATION
Jasper National Park ☎ *780/852–6176* ⊕ *www.pc.gc.ca/jasper.*

VISITOR CENTERS
Jasper Information Centre. A registered National Historic Site, this information center is in Jasper Townsite and is worth a stop even if you don't need advice. Completed in 1914, this building is constructed of cobblestone and timber and is one of the finest examples of rustic architecture in Canada's national parks. Inside you will find Tourism Jasper travel counselors as well as Parks Canada staff. You can pick up maps, informative brochures, and other materials to help you explore the parks and its trails. Tourism Jasper can provide advice and assistance with tour operators, restaurants, and accommodations. A small gift shop and restroom facilities are also inside the building. Parks Canada also operates an information desk at the Icefields Centre, 103 km (64 miles) south of Jasper Townsite. ⊠ *500 Connaught Dr.* ☎ *780/852–6176* ⊕ *www. jasper.travel* ⊙ *Apr.–June 14 and Oct., daily 9–5; June 15–Sept. 4, daily 8:30–7; Sept. 5–30, daily 9–6; Nov.–Mar., daily 9–4.*

EXPLORING

SCENIC DRIVES

Scenic drives skirt the base of glaciers, stunning lakes, and exceptional wildlife-viewing areas. The 230-km (143-mile) **Icefields Parkway** that connects Jasper with Banff provides access to the largest ice field south of Alaska and takes you to the very edge of the treeless alpine tundra. ⇨ *For more details on parkway, see Banff National Park, Chapter 7.*

Within Jasper, **Maligne Lake Road,** and **Pyramid Lake Road** are good scenic drives, south and north of the townsite, respectively.

SCENIC STOPS

Athabasca Falls. At Athabasca Falls, the Athabasca River is compressed through a narrow gorge, producing a violent torrent of water. Trails and overlooks provide good viewpoints. ⊠ *Icefields Pkwy. and Hwy. 93A, 31 km (19 miles) south of Jasper.*

Disaster Point Animal Lick. Disaster Point Animal Lick, less than 5 km (3 miles) before Highway 16 from Jasper reaches the turn for Miette Hot Springs, is the most easily accessible spot in the park for encountering bighorn sheep. It's a rare summer moment when the sheep haven't descended from the adjacent steep slopes to lick up the mineral-rich mud, wandering back and forth across the road. You're likely to see numerous cars stopped by the side of the road. ⊠ *Hwy. 16, 53 km (33 miles) northeast of Jasper.*

FAMILY **Jasper Tramway.** The Jasper Tramway whisks you 3,191 vertical feet up the steep flank of Whistlers Mountain to an impressive overlook of the townsite and the surrounding mountains. The seven-minute ride takes you to the upper station, above the tree line (be sure to bring warm clothes). A 30- to 45-minute hike from here leads to the summit, which is 8,085 feet above sea level. Several unmarked trails lead through the alpine meadows beyond. ⊠ *Whistlers Mountain Rd., off Hwy. 93, 3 km (2 miles) south of Jasper* ☎ *780/852–3093* ⊕ *www.jaspertramway. com* ☎ *C$32 round-trip* ☉ *June–early Sept., daily 9–8; Apr., May, and early Sept.–Oct., daily 10–5.*

Maligne Canyon. The Maligne River cuts a 165-foot-deep gorge through limestone bedrock at Maligne Canyon. An interpretive trail winds its way along the river, switching from side to side over six bridges as the canyon progressively deepens. The 4-km (2½-mile) trail along the canyon can be crowded, especially near the trailhead. Just off the path, at the Maligne Canyon teahouse, are a restaurant and a good Native American crafts store. If you visit in winter, a Maligne Canyon ice walk offers spectacular scenery from the bottom of the frozen canyon. ⊠ *Maligne Lake Rd., 11 km (7 miles) south of Jasper.*

Maligne Lake. The remarkably blue, 22-km-long (14-mile-long) Maligne Lake is one of the largest glacier-fed lakes in the world. The first outsider known to visit the lake was Henry MacLeod, a surveyor looking for a possible route for the Canadian Pacific Railway, in 1875. A couple of day hikes (approximately four hours round-trip), with some steep sections, lead to alpine meadows that have panoramic views of the lake and the surrounding mountain ranges. You can also take horseback-riding and fishing trips, and there's an excellent cafeteria. ⊠ *Maligne Lake Rd., 44 km (27 miles) southeast of Jasper* ⊕ *www.malignelake.com.*

   Maligne Tours. You can explore Maligne Lake in a rented canoe or on a 1½-hour **scenic cruise** with Maligne Tours. The Family of Explorers Cruise includes special onboard activities for kids, snacks, and a nature-based scavenger hunt at the island. Afternoon tea can be enjoyed at the historic Maligne Lake Chalet. ⊠ *627 Patricia St., Jasper* ☎ *780/852–3370, 780/852–4803* ⊕ *www.malignelake.com* ☎ *C$62* ☉ *June and Sept.–early Oct., daily 10–4; July and Aug., daily 10–5.*

Plants and Wildlife in Jasper

In Jasper it is possible to stand in a field of wildflowers, hike through a thick subalpine forest, stand on a glacier, and revel in the solitude of the fragile alpine zone all in one day. A wide array of plants occupies the parks' three life zones of montane, alpine, and subalpine. In fact, about 1,300 species of plants and 20,000 types of insects and spiders are part of the complex web of life in the Canadian Rockies.

Jasper's vast wilderness is one of the few remaining places with a full range of carnivores, such as grizzly bears, black bears, wolves, coyotes, cougars, and wolverines. There are also large populations of elk, deer, bighorn sheep, and mountain goats among the park's nearly 53 species of mammals—which are often seen right from the roadsides. Each year hundreds of animals are killed along Jasper's highways, so it is vital to observe all speed limits and especially to slow down in special animal-sighting speed-zone areas. When hiking, keep your distance from wild animals and make a lot of noise as a means of avoiding contact with large mammals, especially bears.

Miette Hot Springs. The naturally heated mineral waters of Miette Hot Springs originate from three springs and are cooled to 104°F to allow bathing in the two hot pools. There's also an adjacent cold pool—especially popular with the younger crowd—which is definitely on the cool side, at about 59°F. A short walk leads to the remnants of the original hot-springs facility, where several springs still pour hot sulfurous water into the adjacent creek. Day passes and bathing suit, locker, and towel rentals are available. ⊠ *Miette Hot Springs Rd., off Hwy. 16, 58 km (36 miles) northeast of Jasper* ☎ *780/866–3939* ⊕ *www.parkscanada.gc.ca/hotsprings* ⊠ *C$6.05* ☉ *Mid-May–late June and early Sept.–early Oct., daily 10:30–9; late June–early Sept., daily 8:30 am–10:30 pm.*

Fodor's Choice
★
Mt. Edith Cavell. The highest mountain in the vicinity of Jasper, Mt. Edith Cavell towers at 11,033 feet and shows its permanently snow-clad north face to the town. It's named after a World War I British nurse who stayed in Belgium to treat wounded Allied soldiers after Brussels fell to the Germans; she was executed for helping prisoners of war escape. ■ **TIP→ The mountain is arguably the most spectacular site in the park reachable by car.** From Highway 93A, a narrow, winding 14½-km (9-mile) road (often closed until the beginning of June) leads to a parking lot at the base of the mountain. Trailers are not permitted on this road, but they can be left at a separate parking lot near the junction with 93A. Several scenic lookouts along the route offer access to trails leading up the **Tonquin Valley,** one of the premier hiking areas. ⊠ *Off Hwy. 93A, 27 km (17 miles) south of Jasper.*

EDUCATIONAL OFFERINGS

INTERPRETIVE PROGRAMS

FAMILY   **Friends of Jasper National Park.** A group of enthusiastic volunteers runs a number of excellent programs during the summer months. The offerings include a junior naturalist program, birding tours, hiking tours, and historical walks. The group also loans out hiking kits with binoculars, maps, first-aid materials, and other useful items. Kits can be picked up at the shop in the information center. ⊠ *Jasper Information Centre, 500 Connaught Dr.* ☎ *780/852–4341* ⊕ *www.friendsofjasper.com.*

FAMILY   **Whistlers Outdoor Theatre.** Interpretive programs are offered daily during the summer months at the theater at Whistlers Campground. Programs are appropriate for both children and adults, and a schedule of seminars and activities is available at the information center. Parks Canada interpreters use theater, singing, dancing, and storytelling to help visitors young and old learn more about the flora and fauna in the park. ⊠ *Whistlers Campground, Hwy. 93* ☞ *Free* ☉ *Late June– early Sept.*

SPORTS AND THE OUTDOORS

In the northern half of the park, backpacking and horse-packing trips offer wilderness seclusion, while the park's southern half rewards trekkers with dramatic glacial scenery. Day hikes are popular around Mt. Edith Cavell, Miette Hot Springs, and Maligne Lake; Pyramid Lake and the Fairmont Jasper Park Lodge are destinations for horseback riding.

MULTISPORT OUTFITTERS

Alpine Club of Canada. Reservations for backcountry huts can be made through the Alpine Club of Canada. ☎ *403/678–3200* ⊕ *www. alpineclubofcanada.ca.*

Alternative Adventures. This outfitter operates out of a camping resort 10 km (6.2 miles) west of Hinton on Hwy 16—about a 35-minute drive from Jasper. A variety of adventures including ziplining, hang-gliding instruction, paragliding instruction, power-kiting instruction, and eco-adventures are on offer. ⊠ *On Hwy. 16, 10 km (6.2 miles) east of the east Jasper National Park Gate* ☎ *780/817–9696* ⊕ *www. alternativeadventures.ca.*

Boat House. Kayaks, paddleboats, and canoes are available at the Boat House from C$30 an hour to C$120 a day. ⊠ *Fairmont Jasper Park Lodge, Hwy. 16* ☎ *780/852–5708* ⊕ *www.fairmont.com/jasper.*

Canadian Skyline Adventures. Hire an experienced guide to take you to the most scenic places in Jasper National Park—including the world-famous Skyline Trail. Guides can also take you on an epic backcountry canoe trip or a two-day trip to Spirit Island on beautiful Maligne Lake. ⊠ *Jasper* ☎ *780/820–0772* ⊕ *www.canadianskylineadventures.com.*

Gravity Gear. Ice climbing, backcountry skiing, and mountaineering trips led by certified guides are offered by Gravity Gear. ⊠ *618 Patricia St.* ☎ *780/852–3155, 888/852–3155* ⊕ *www.gravitygearjasper.com.*

Jasper Adventure Centre. A variety of tours and adventures inside Jasper and Banff can be organized by Jasper Adventure Centre, including guided hiking adventures, icewalks on the Athabasca Glacier, tours of the Icefield Parkway, and train excursions. ✉ *414 Connaught Dr.* ☎ *780/852–5595, 800/565–7547* ⊕ *www.jasperadventurecentre.com.*

Jasper Dive Adventures. During World War II, a top-secret British mission known as Project Habbakuk took place in Jasper National Park. The goal was to produce an unsinkable aircraft carrier from pykrete (a mixture of wood pulp and ice). When the project was canceled, the unfinished ship was sunk in Patricia Lake. This company offers guided diving tours of the remains along with equipment rentals and scuba certification courses. ✉ *Jasper* ☎ *780/852–3560* ⊕ *www.jasperdiveadventures.com.*

Jasper Motorcycle Tours. Experience the Canadian Rockies in comfort on a thrilling, chauffeured motorcycle tour. A professional driver can carry up to two guests per sidecar-style motorcycle. Rentals of Harley David-son Heritage Classic and Harley Fatboy motorcycles are also available to licensed drivers. ✉ *610 Patricia St.* ☎ *780/931–6100* ⊕ *www.jaspermotorcycletours.com.*

Jasper Source for Sports. At Jasper Source for Sports you can rent bikes, fishing and camping supplies, and ski and snowboard equipment. ✉ *406 Patricia St.* ☎ *780/852–3654* ⊕ *www.jaspersports.com.*

Pyramid Lake Boat House. Canoes, rowboats, kayaks, paddleboats (all $20 per half hour), and electric boats ($89 per hour) are available at the Pyramid Lake Boat House at Pyramid Lake Resort. The company also sells fishing licenses and has rod and reel rentals. ✉ *Pyramid Lake Resort, 5.5 km north of Jasper Townsite on Pyramid Lake Rd.* ☎ *780/852–4900, 888/717–1277* ⊕ *www.mpljasper.com.*

Tonquin Valley Adventures. Hiking, skiing, and horseback trips into the Tonquin Valley are offered by Tonquin Valley Adventures. In winter there's a private cabin with cooking equipment provided; in the summer there's a cook at the cabin. Bring your fishing gear—there are boats at the cabin and a lake with wild rainbow trout. ☎ *780/852–1188* ⊕ *www.tonquinadventures.com.*

Tonquin Valley Backcountry Lodge. Here you can sample hiking, skiing, fishing, and horseback trips into the Tonquin Valley. Guests stay at a backcountry lodge with meals included. ☎ *780/852–3909* ⊕ *www.tonquinvalley.com.*

Totem Ski Shop. Summer and winter sports equipment and clothing are available at Totem Ski Shop. ✉ *408 Connaught Dr.* ☎ *780/852–3078* ⊕ *www.totemskishop.com.*

AIR TOURS

OUTFITTERS

High Country Helicopter Tours. Call to arrange a helicopter tour of the park, heli-hiking, or snowshoeing. Flights take off from Jasper Hinton Airport, just outside the park. ☎ *877/777–4354, 780/852–0125* ⊕ *www.hcheli.com* ✉ *$165–$849.*

Icefield Helicopter Tours. This outfitter offers a bird's-eye view of the Columbia Icefields. They also have heli-yoga, heli-horseback riding, heli-hiking, heli-fishing, romance tours, and other helicopter tours outside the park. Flights take off from their Icefield heli-base. ☎ *888/844–3514, 403/721–2100* ⊕ *www.icefieldheli.com* ✉ *$189–$695.*

BIRD-WATCHING

An astonishing 277 species of birds make their home in the Canadian Rockies. The golden eagle migration, which occurs in the spring and fall, is the biggest birding event in the park. In late September and early October, you may be able to see more than 200 eagles in one day at the east end of the park (Pocahontas area). At other times of year, the best place to observe birds is at **Cottonwood Slough** along Pyramid Lake Road. This spot is a good place to find Barrow's goldeneye, warblers, snipes, soras and hummingbirds, and red-necked grebe.

BOATING AND RAFTING

Boating in rowboats and canoes is allowed on most of the ponds and lakes in the park. Boats with electric motors without on-board generators are allowed on most road-accessible lakes, but the use of gas-powered motors is restricted. It's always wise to ask park staff about restrictions before launching your boat.

The rafting season runs from May through September and children as young as 6 years of age can participate on some of the float trips. The Athabasca River has Class II white-water rapids; the Sunwapta and Fraser rivers have Class III rapids.

TOURS AND OUTFITTERS

Jasper Raft Tours. Take a half-day float trip on the Athabasca with Jasper Raft Tours. ☎ *780/852–2665, 888/553–5628* ⊕ *www.jasperrafttours.com.*

Jasper Whitewater Rafting. A well-regarded local company, Jasper Whitewater Rafting runs a variety of rafting adventures on the Athabasca and Sunwapta rivers. ⊠ *Picks up at Sunwapta Falls parking lot, Jasper* ☎ *780/852–7238, 800/557–7238* ⊕ *www.whitewaterraftingjasper.com.*

Maligne Rafting Adventures. This tour operator offers rafting on the Athabasca, Sunwapta, and Fraser rivers as well as inflatable kayak trips. Overnight and day trips are available on Class II, III, or IV rapids. ⊠ *616 Patricia St., Jasper* ☎ *780/852–3370, 866/625–4463* ⊕ *www. raftjasper.com.*

Mount Robson Whitewater Rafting. This outfitter offers rafting excursions on the Fraser River near Mount Robson Provincial Park, 89 km (55 miles) west of Jasper. Rafters can choose between a two-hour scenic float trip, a three-hour whitewater excursion, or a full-day rafting adventure on Class I and Class III rapids. Free overnight camping is available with the purchase of any rafting trip. ⊠ *Mount Robson Lodge, on Hwy. 16, 5 km (3 miles) west of Mt. Robson Provincial Park* ☎ *250/852–4566, 888/566–7238* ⊕ *www.mountrobsonwhitewater.com* ✉ *$59–$139.*

Rocky Mountain River Guides. You can experience a variety of rafting trips for different levels of rafters with Rocky Mountain River Guides. ⊠ *626 Connaught Dr., Jasper* ☎ *780/852–3777* ⊕ *www.rmriverguides.com.*

Whitewater Rafting (Jasper) Ltd. Whitewater Rafting (Jasper) Ltd. offers half-day trips on the Athabasca and Sunwapta rivers. ☎ *780/852– 7238, 800/557–7238.*

GOLF

23

Fairmont Jasper Park Lodge. This award-winning golf resort features a championship 18-hole, par-71, Stanley Thompson–designed course. Packages that include accommodations and golf can be found on the website. ⊠ *1 Lodge Rd.* ☎ *780/852–6090* ⊕ *www.fairmont.com/jasper/ activities-services/golf* ⚘. *18 holes. 6663 yds. Par 71. Slope 130. Green Fee: C$180* ☞ *Facilities: Driving range, putting green, pitching area, golf carts, pull carts, rental clubs, pro-shop, lessons, restaurant, bar.*

HIKING

Long before Jasper was established as a national park, a vast network of trails provided an essential passageway for wildlife, First Nations people, explorers, and fur traders. More than 1,200 km (746 miles) of hiking trails in Jasper provide an opportunity to truly experience wilderness, and hardcore backpackers will find multiday loops of more than 160 km (100 miles). The trails at Mt. Edith Cavell and Maligne Canyon should not be missed.

A few of these trails are restricted to pedestrians, but hikers, mountain bikers, and equestrian users may share most of them. There are several paved trails that are suitable for wheelchairs, while others are rugged backcountry trails designed for backpacking trips. Bathrooms are found along the most used day-use trails. You may see elk, bighorn sheep, moose, and mountain goats along the way. It is never a good idea to surprise a large animal such as an elk or bear, so make plenty of noise as you go along, avoid hiking alone, carry bear spray, and stick to designated trails.

EASY

FAMILY **Lake Annette Loop.** This short loop trail with interpretive signage is paved and mostly level and was designed especially for wheelchair use. Toilets are at two locations, and there is a shelter halfway around. The kid-friendly 2.4-km (1.5-mile) loop will take an hour to complete. *Easy.* ⊠ *Trailhead on the right side of the Lake Annette picnic area's western parking lot.*

FAMILY **Maligne Canyon.** This 2.1-km (1.3-mile), one-way trail 8 km (5 miles) east of Jasper Townsite leads to views of Jasper's famous limestone gorge and will take one to two hours to complete. Six bridges stretch across the canyon, and a winding trail gains about 330 feet in elevation. Signage lines the trail that leads to a waterfall at the head of the canyon. *Easy.* ⊠ *Trailhead at Fifth Bridge, 8 km (5 miles) east of Jasper via Hwy. 16 and the Maligne Rd.*

Old Fort Point Loop. Shaped by glaciers, Old Fort Point is a bedrock knob that provides an excellent view of Jasper. It will take one to two hours to complete the 3.5-km (2.2-mile) loop trail. There is a wide, easy path

that begins behind the information kiosk and leads to a section of trail that is very steep. It's common to see Rocky Mountain bighorn sheep, the provincial mammal of Alberta, from this trail. You pass the oldest rock in Jasper National Park, but the real highlight is the view from the top. *Easy.* ⊠ *Trailhead 1.6 km (1 mile) from Jasper Townsite* ⊹ *Follow Hwy. 93A to the Old Fort Point/Lac Beauvert access road. Turn left, cross the Athabasca River, then park in the lot on the right.*

FAMILY **Path of the Glacier Loop.** This must-do 1.6-km (1-mile) trail only takes about an hour. The start of the kid-friendly trail is paved and runs across a rocky landscape that was once covered in glacial ice. Eventually you come to Cavell Pond, which is fed by Cavell Glacier. Small icebergs often float in the water. Across the valley, you will have a good view of the Angel Glacier resting her wings between Mt. Edith Cavell and Sorrow Peak. *Easy.* ⊠ *Trailhead at parking lot at the end of Cavell Rd.* ⊹ *Heading south on Icefields Pkwy., turn right on Hwy. 93A. Follow 93A for 5.5 km (3.4 miles), turn right on Cavell Rd., and drive 15 km (9.3 miles) to the end.*

FAMILY **Valley of the Five Lakes.** It takes two to three hours to complete this family-friendly 4.2-km (2.3-mile) hike. Five small lakes are the highlight of the trip, which takes you through a lodgepole pine forest, across the Wabasso Creek wetlands, and through a flowery meadow. Watch for birds, beavers, and other wildlife along the way. Turn this into a moderately difficult hike by continuing another 10 km (6.2 miles) to Old Fort Point. *Easy.* ⊠ *Trailhead on Hwy. 93, 9 km (5.6 miles) south of Jasper townsite.*

MODERATE

Fodor's Choice **Cavell Meadows Loop.** This moderately steep 8-km (5-mile) trail will take ★ four to six hours. Into early summer the upper section is still covered in snow and not recommended, but from mid-July to mid-August you can enjoy the carpet of wildflowers. There's also an excellent view of the Angel Glacier. *Moderate.* ⊠ *Trailhead at parking lot at the end of Cavell Rd.* ⊹ *Heading south on Icefields Pkwy., turn right on Hwy. 93A. Follow 93A for 5.5 km (3.4 miles), turn right on Cavell Rd., and drive 15 km (9.3 miles) to the end.*

DIFFICULT

Wilcox Pass. Excellent views of the Athabasca Glacier are the highlight of this strenuous, 8-km (5-mile) hike near the Icefield Centre. This pass was originally used by explorers and First Nations people and is fairly steep. Keep an eye out for wildflowers and bighorn sheep. Be sure to dress in warm layers, because this pass can be snowy until late July. *Difficult.* ⊠ *Trailhead at parking area on left-hand side of the Wilcox Creek Campground entrance road, 3.1 km (1.9 miles) south of Icefield Centre.*

WILDERNESS HIKING

Jasper's backcountry is some of the wildest and most pristine of any mountain park in the world. For information on overnight camping quotas on the Skyline and Tonquin Valley trails or on any of the hundreds of hiking and mountain-biking trails in the area, contact the park information center.

Skyline Trail. The trail meanders for 44 km (27 miles) past some of the park's best scenery, at or above the tree line. Reservations recommended. ☎ *780/852–6177.*

Tonquin Valley. Near Mt. Edith Cavell, Tonquin Valley is one of Canada's classic backpacking areas. Its high mountain lakes, bounded by a series of steep rocky peaks known as the Ramparts, attract many hikers in high summer.

HORSEBACK RIDING

Several outfitters offer one-hour, half-day, full-day, and multiday guided trips within the park. Participants must be at least age 6 to participate in a riding trip, but pony rides are available for younger children. It's wise to make your reservations well in advance, especially during the peak summer months and for multiday journeys. Horses can be boarded at the commercial holding facilities available through the Cottonwood Corral Association at Pyramid Riding Stables.

TOURS AND OUTFITTERS

Jasper Park Stables. These stables offer rides and full-day excursions into the hills overlooking Jasper; there are also carriage rides and winter sleigh rides. ⊠ *Pyramid Resort, Pyramid Lake Rd.* ☎ *780/852–3562* ⊕ *www.jasperparkstables.com.*

Skyline Trail Rides. The company offers lessons and one-hour to half-day rides. Multiday trips into the backcountry are also available. ⊠ *Fairmont Jasper Park Lodge, Hwy. 16* ☎ *780/852–4215, 888/852–7787* ⊕ *www.skylinetrail.com.*

Tonquin Valley Adventures. All-inclusive three, four, or five-day pack trip into the Tonquin Valley are the specialty of Tonquin Valley Pack Trips. You stay at a lakefront backcountry lodge. They also offer a self-guided hiker's package for those who prefer to get to the lodge on foot and a self-guided ski package in winter. ☎ *780/852–3909* ⊕ *www.tonquinadventures.com.*

SWIMMING

FAMILY   **Annette Lake and Edith Lake.** These two lakes with women's names have sandy beaches and water that reaches the low 70s°F during warm spells. ⊠ *Near Fairmont Jasper Park Lodge, Hwy. 16.*

Horseshoe Lake. As the name implies, Horseshoe Lake is shaped like a horseshoe and is surrounded by cliffs. Although the water can be cold, locals like to swim and jump from the rocks and cliffs into the lake. ⊠ *Approximately 25 km (15½ mile) south of Jasper Townsite, Hwy. 93.*

FAMILY   **Jasper Aquatic Center.** This recreation facilty has a 180-foot indoor waterslide, a 25-meter swimming pool, and a kiddie pool. A steam room and a hot tub are also on site, and towel and suit rentals are available. The center closes for two weeks in the fall. ⊠ *305 Bonhomme St.* ☎ *780/852–3663* 🎟 *C$7* ☉ *Daily 2–9.*

WINTER SPORTS

With more than 300 km (186 miles) of trails, Jasper is one of the largest cross-country ski areas in Canada. There is a wide choice of groomed and natural trails for skiing and snowshoeing, and equipment and local guides can be arranged through local ski shops. Current cross-country ski information is available at the park visitor center. Downhill skiers will enjoy Marmot Basin, a 20-minute drive from town.

Marmot Basin. Near Jasper, Marmot Basin has the longest high-speed quad chair in the Alberta Canadian Rockies. The resort inludes a wide mix of downhill skiing terrain (75 runs, nine lifts, and a terrain park with all the toys), and the slopes are a little less crowded than those around Banff, especially on weekdays. There are three day lodges, two of which are at mid-mountain. Discounted lift tickets are available during the Jasper in January winter festival. ⊠ *Hwy. 93A* ☎ *780/852–3816, 866/952–3816* ⊕ *www.skimarmot.com* 🎫 *C$82.50.*

Pyramid Lake and Patricia Lake. This pair of pretty lakes has excellent, groomed cross-country trails. ⊠ *Pyramid Lake Rd.*

WHAT'S NEARBY

Jasper National Park is 287 km (178 miles) north of Banff National Park, 400 km (249 miles) northwest of the city of **Calgary,** 360 km (224 miles) west of the city of **Edmonton,** and 55 km (34 miles) west of the town of **Hinton** and the Jasper/Hinton Airport. Most visitors arrive through either Calgary or Edmonton—both near the major highway—where the two international airports are located.

VISITOR INFORMATION
Tourism Jasper ☎ *780/852–3858* ⊕ *www.jasper.travel.*

WHERE TO EAT

IN THE PARK

PICNIC AREAS

Airport. This large area has a shelter and is ideal for family reunions because it can be reserved in advance for a fee of C$50. It's 15 km (9 miles) from Jasper. ⊠ *Off Hwy. 16 E* ☎ *780/852–6176.*

Athabasca Falls. Dine beside the stunning Athabasca Falls. The picnic area is 30 km (19 miles) from Jasper. ⊠ *Off Icefields Pkwy.*

FAMILY **Lake Annette.** Beside Lake Annette, this picnic area has shelters and tables and is a favorite with families who come to the lake to swim. ⊠ *Near junction of Maligne Lake Rd. and Hwy. 16.*

Sixth Bridge. This picnic area sits beside the Maligne River near where it flows into the Athabasca River. There are no shelters, but it's a favorite with locals because of the scenic location. ⊠ *Off Maligne Lake Rd., 2.2 km (1.3 miles) from Hwy. 16 junction.*

23

OUTSIDE THE PARK

$ BAKERY 🍴 **Bear's Paw Bakery.** This cozy little downtown bakery is a great stop for breakfast or lunch. The staff here makes yummy muffins, scones, and fresh cinnamon buns for breakfast and sandwiches and wraps for lunch. Fresh-baked cookies, cakes, and artisan breads are also available, along with a wide variety of coffees and teas. There are a few tables for dining inside. Popular with locals and visitors, it can be packed during peak times. The owners also run the Other Paw, two blocks away. [$] *Average main: C$8* ✉ *4 Cedar Ave., near Connaught Dr., Jasper* ☎ *780/852–3233* 🌐 *www.bearspawbakery.com* ✍ *Reservations not accepted* ⏲ *No dinner.*

$$$ CANADIAN 🍴 **Evil Dave's.** A funky atmosphere and creative menu make this downtown restaurant a fun place to dine. Although the original owner, Dave, is no longer running the place, the current chef is the only female Red Seal chef in Jasper. Evil entrees include such specialties as Malicious Salmon (blackened salmon with sweet curry yogurt), Malevolent Meatloaf (Alberta bison wrapped in wild boar bacon), Nefarious Chicken (Parmesan crusted with salsa), and the Glad Cow (vegetarian lasagna). Lucious lollipop shrimp make a deliciously sinful starter. There's a creative kids' menu and an extensive selection of gluten-free dishes. [$] *Average main: C$25* ✉ *622 Patricia St., Jasper* ☎ *780/852–3323* 🌐 *www.evildavesgrill.com* ⏲ *No lunch.*

$$ PIZZA 🍴 **Famoso.** Authentic fire-roasted Neapolitan-style pizzas made in a real bell oven are the specialty at this small pizzeria in the upper lever of a downtown building. The atmosphere is casual, and though you seat yourself and order over a counter, servers bring the food and drinks to your table. A wide variety of pizzas are on the menu, ranging from classic pizza margherita to interesting combinations like cavoletti (brussels sprouts, prosciutto crisps, gorgonzola cheese, dates, and walnuts) and prosciutto with arugula. Enjoy a gelato for dessert. [$] *Average main: C$15* ✉ *607 Patricia St., Jasper* ☎ *780/852–5577* 🌐 *www.famoso.ca.*

$$$ CANADIAN 🍴 **Fiddle River.** This pine-finished, second-floor dining room has great views of the railway station, downtown Jasper, and the mountains, and the Canadian seafood, wild game, and Alberta AAA beef dishes are classic and delicious. Daily specials are featured on a chalkboard menu that is moved from table to table. Appetizers are creative; the feta-and-shrimp-stuffed Moroccan dates are wonderful. You can't go wrong with the pistachio-and-pumpkin-seed-crusted panfried rainbow trout or the rack of lamb with sweet cherries and fresh mint for the main course. A great selection of Canadian wines complement the menu offerings. [$] *Average main: C$30* ✉ *620 Connaught Dr., Jasper* ☎ *780/852–3032* 🌐 *www.fiddleriverrestaurant.com* ⏲ *No lunch.*

$$$$ CANADIAN 🍴 **Moose's Nook Northern Grill.** Contemporary Canadian cuisine is made with fresh local ingredients from the Rockies and the prairies at this rustic and casual restaurant in the upscale Fairmont Jasper Park Lodge. Live music plays every night in summer. The Vancouver Island Dungeness crab cake is a signature appetizer, and you can never go wrong with the Alberta beef tenderloin served with butter-whipped horseradish potatoes and wild mushroom ragout. For a unique culinary experience, ask to dine at the chef's table and enjoy a private five-course

CLOSE UP

Best Campgrounds in Jasper

Parks Canada operates campgrounds in Jasper National Park that have a total of 1,772 available sites during the peak season. There is winter camping only at Wapiti campground. Hookup sites are available at Whistlers and Wapiti campgrounds only, so reserve a site in advance if you are traveling during the peak summer season. In addition to standard camping sites, Parks Canada operates Cottage Tents and new oTENTiks at Whistler's Campground. These accommodations are a cross between a cabin and a tent and sleep up to six people on foam mattresses, a good choice for novice campers. Call ☎ *780/852–6176 or 877/737–3783* or go online at 🌐 *www.pccamping.ca* for reservations.

Columbia Icefield Campground. This rustic campground is near a creek and has great views of the Columbia Icefield. ✉ *Hwy. 93, 106 km (66 miles) south of Jasper Townsite.*

Jonas Creek Campground. This small, primitive campground is in a quiet spot along a creek off the Icefields Parkway. Sites are first-come, first-served. ✉ *Just off Icefields Pkwy., 75 km (47 miles) south of Jasper Townsite.*

Mt. Kerkeslin Campground. This is a very basic campground with few facilities. Tent camping is available, and there are fire pits for cooking. ✉ *Hwy. 93, 35 km (22 miles) south of Jasper Townsite.*

Wabasso Campground. Families flock to this campground because of its playground and many amenities. ✉ *Hwy. 93A, 16 km (10 miles) south of Jasper Townsite.*

Wapiti Campground. Close to Jasper, this campground is near a number of good hiking trails. There are 53 unserviced sites that are open during the winter season. ✉ *Hwy. 93, 5 km (3 miles) south of Jasper Townsite.*

Whistlers Campground. This campground is the largest and has the most amenities and the greatest variety of camping options. It's the number-one choice for families because of the on-site interpretive programs at Whistlers Outdoor Theatre. ✉ *Hwy. 93, 3 km (2 miles) south of Jasper Townsite.*

23

tasting menu. Children under 5 eat free and children under 12 enjoy a special menu. [$] *Average main: C$40* ✉ *Fairmont Jasper Park Lodge, off Hwy. 16, Jasper* ☎ *780/852–3301, 800/441–1414* 🌐 *www.fairmont.com/jasper* ⏲ *Closed Nov.–Apr. No lunch.*

$$$ JAPANESE ✕ **Oka Sushi.** This is slow food at its best, with just one chef and one server and patrons sitting either at tables along the perimeter or at the small bar, watching the sushi as it's prepared à la minute. Tatsuhiko Okaki, the owner and chef, is famous for using the freshest ingredients and creating a variety of tantalizing combinations. Try the Jasper Roll, made with crabmeat and shrimp and served with a spicy sauce. Sapporo beer and sake provide a nice complement to the meal. Only about a dozen people can fit in this sushi bar at once, and reservations—only possible for the earliest seatings at 6 and 6:30—should be made well in advance. [$] *Average main: C$27* ✉ *Fairmont Jasper Park Lodge, off Hwy. 16, Jasper* ☎ *780/852–1114* 🌐 *www.fairmont.com/jasper/dining/okasushi* ✍ *Reservations essential* ⏲ *Closed Sun. No lunch.*

$$$$ CANADIAN Fodor's Choice ★ 🍴 **Tekarra.** In a log cabin near the confluence of the Athabasca and Miette rivers, this restaurant has a charming rustic feel, but don't let the simple architecture fool you—the cuisine is some of the finest in the Canadian Rockies. Chef David Husereau sources local ingredients and does his own baking, smoking, and curing. Try the trio of wild sockeye salmon appetizer and you'll be able to taste the difference and see it—the presentation is wonderful. Other specialties include the peppered beef tenderloin with forest mushrooms and angel hair pasta, macadamia-crusted rack of lamb with crispy truffle mashed potato, and the duck prepared two ways. An excellent gluten-free menu is available. Hot chocolate soufflé with homemade vanilla ice cream is the house specialty, but if you have trouble selecting a dessert, try sharing the sampler plate. They also have an extensive martini list. [$] *Average main: C$35* ✉ *Tekarra Lodge Resort, Hwy. 93A, Jasper* ☎ *780/852–4624* 🌐 *www.tekarrarestaurant.com* 🕒 *Closed early Oct.–mid-May.*

WHERE TO STAY

IN THE PARK

$$$ HOTEL FAMILY 🏨 **Alpine Village.** Facing the Athabasca River, this cabin resort feels like it's miles away from civilization even though it's a three-minute drive from Jasper. **Pros:** well-kept property; kitchen suites; lovely location across from the Athabasca River. **Cons:** outside the town; closed in winter; limited Wi-Fi access. [$] *Rooms from: C$180* ✉ *Hwy. 93A N, 2.5 km southeast of Jasper Townsite* ☎ *780/852–3285* 🌐 *www.alpinevillagejasper.com* 🛏 *49 rooms* 🍽 *No meals.*

$$$$ RESORT FAMILY Fodor's Choice ★ 🏨 **Fairmont Jasper Park Lodge.** On the shores of magnificent Lac Beauvert about 7 km (4.5 miles) northeast of the Jasper Townsite, the Jasper Park Lodge is a mix of civilized luxury and rustic Canadian charm that is a destination in itself. **Pros:** many amenities; beautiful setting; top-notch dining. **Cons:** 10-minute drive to townsite; on-site dining can be pricey. [$] *Rooms from: C$329* ✉ *1 Old Lodge Rd.* ☎ *780/852–3301, 866/441–1414* 🌐 *www.fairmont.com/jasper* 🛏 *446 rooms, 100 suites* 🍽 *No meals.*

$$$ HOTEL FAMILY 🏨 **Patricia Lake Bungalows.** Lakefront solitude is the highlight of these comfortable lodgings, which are on the shores of one of the most tranquil lakes in the park. **Pros:** good value; quiet location; lovely property and grounds. **Cons:** five-minute drive from town, limited Wi-Fi access. [$] *Rooms from: C$189* ✉ *Pyramid Lake Rd.* ☎ *780/852–3560* 🌐 *www.patricialakebungalows.com* 🛏 *10 rooms, 18 suites, 22 cabins* 🕒 *Closed mid-Oct.–Apr.* 🍽 *No meals*

$$$ HOTEL FAMILY 🏨 **Sawridge Inn and Conference Centre.** Located on the edge of Jasper, this three-story hotel is built around a spacious and impressive atrium filled with lush plants, a three-story fireplace, a swimming pool, a spa, a restaurant, and two lounges. **Pros:** lots of amenities; free Wi-Fi; refrigerator in room. **Cons:** restaurant in atrium can be noisy; popular with tour buses; 15-minute walk to downtown. [$] *Rooms from: C$175* ✉ *82 Connaught Dr., Jasper* ☎ *780/852–5111, 888/729–7343* 🌐 *www.sawridgejasper.com* 🛏 *153 rooms, 4 suites* 🍽 *No meals.*

JOSHUA TREE NATIONAL PARK

WELCOME TO JOSHUA TREE

TOP REASONS TO GO

★ **Rock climbing:** Joshua Tree is a world-class site with challenges for climbers of just about every skill level.

★ **Peace and quiet:** Savor the solitude of one of the last great wildernesses in America.

★ **Stargazing:** You'll be mesmerized by the Milky Way flowing across the summer sky. For spectacular natural fireworks, visit in mid-August during the Perseid meteor shower and watch shooting stars streak overhead.

★ **Wildflowers:** In spring, the hillsides explode in a patchwork of yellow, blue, pink, and white.

★ **Sunsets:** Twilight is a magical time here, especially during the winter, when the setting sun casts a golden glow on the mountains.

1 Keys View. This is the most dramatic overlook in the park—on clear days you can see Signal Mountain in Mexico.

2 Hidden Valley. Crawl between the big rocks and you'll understand why this boulder-strewn area was once a cattle rustlers' hideout.

3 Cholla Cactus Garden. Come here in the late afternoon, when the spiky stalks of the bigelow (jumping) cholla cactus are backlit against an intense blue sky.

4 Oasis of Mara. Walk the nature trail around this desert oasis, which the first settlers, the Serrano, dubbed "the place of little springs and much grass."

CALIFORNIA

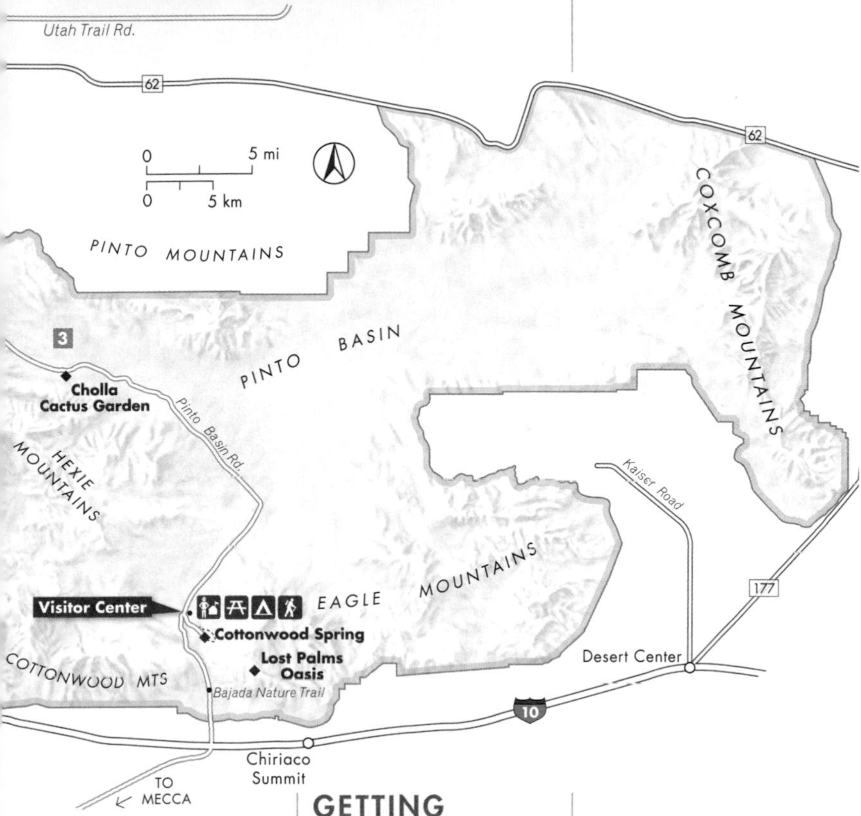

24

Utah Trail Rd.

62

0 _____ 5 mi
0 _____ 5 km

62

PINTO MOUNTAINS

COXCOMB MOUNTAINS

3

PINTO BASIN

♦ **Cholla Cactus Garden**

Pinto Basin Rd.

HEXIE MOUNTAINS

Kaiser Road

177

Visitor Center 🏕️🏕️⛺🚶 EAGLE MOUNTAINS

♦ **Cottonwood Spring**

Lost Palms Oasis ♦

COTTONWOOD MTS

Bajada Nature Trail

Desert Center

10

Chiriaco Summit

TO MECCA ←

KEY
🏕️ Ranger Station / Information
⛺ Campground
🌲 Picnic Area
🚶 Trailhead
🚻 Restrooms
➹ Scenic Viewpoint
⋯⋯ Walking/Hiking Trails
═══ 4-Wheel Drive Dirt Road

GETTING ORIENTED

Daggerlike tufts grace the branches of the namesake of Joshua Tree National Park in southeastern California, where the arid Mojave Desert meets the sparsely vegetated Colorado Desert (part of the Sonoran Desert, which lies across California, Arizona, and Northern Mexico). Passenger cars are fine for paved areas, but you'll need four-wheel drive for many of the rugged backcountry roadways. At the park's most popular sites, parking is limited. Joshua Tree does not have public transportation.

Updated by
John Blodgett

Ruggedly beautiful desert scenery attracts more than a million visitors each year to Joshua Tree National Park, one of the last great wildernesses in the continental United States. Its mountains support mounds of enormous boulders and jagged rock; natural cactus gardens and lush oases shaded by tall fan palms mark the meeting place of the Mojave (high) and Sonora (low) deserts. Extensive stands of Joshua trees gave the park its name; the plants (members of the yucca family of shrubs) reminded Mormon pioneers of the biblical Joshua, with their thick, stubby branches representing the prophet raising his arms toward heaven.

JOSHUA TREE PLANNER

WHEN TO GO

October through May, when the desert is cooler, is when most visitors arrive. Daytime temperatures range from the mid-70s in December and January to mid-90s in October and May. Lows can dip to near freezing in midwinter, and you may even encounter snow at the higher elevations. Summers can be torrid, with daytime temperatures reaching 110°F.

AVG. HIGH/LOW TEMPS.

JAN.	FEB.	MAR.	APR.	MAY	JUNE
62/32	65/37	72/40	80/50	90/55	100/65

JULY	AUG.	SEPT.	OCT.	NOV.	DEC.
105/70	101/78	96/62	85/55	72/40	62/31

FESTIVALS AND EVENTS

FEBRUARY **Riverside County Fair & National Date Festival.** Head to Indio for camel and ostrich races. ☎ *800/811–3247* ⊕ *www.datefest.org.*

OCTOBER **Pioneer Days.** Outhouse races, beard contests, and arm wrestling mark this annual mid-October celebration in Twentynine Palms. The event also features a parade, carnival, gunfighters, and a blacksmith demonstration. ☎ *760/367–3445.*

PLANNING YOUR TIME
JOSHUA TREE IN ONE DAY

After stocking up on water, snacks, and lunch in Yucca Valley or Joshua Tree (you won't find any supplies inside the park), begin your visit at the **Joshua Tree Visitor Center,** where you can pick up maps and peruse exhibits to get acquainted with what awaits you. Enter the park itself at the nearby **West Entrance Station** and continue driving along the highly scenic and well-maintained **Park Boulevard.** Stop first at **Hidden Valley,** where you can relax at the picnic area or hike the easy 1-mile loop trail. After a few more miles turn left onto the spur road that takes you to the trailhead for the **Barker Dam Nature Trail.** Walk the easy 1.3-mile loop to view a water tank ranchers built to quench their cattle's thirst; along the way you'll spot birds and a handful of cactus varieties. Return to Park Boulevard and head south; you'll soon leave the main road again for the drive to **Keys View.** The easy loop trail here is only 0.25 miles, but the views extend for miles in every direction—look for the San Andreas Fault, the Salton Sea, and nearby mountains. Return to Park Boulevard, where you'll find **Cap Rock,** another short loop trail winding amid rock formations and Joshua trees.

Continuing along Park Boulevard, the start of the 18-mile self-guided **Geology Tour Road** will soon appear on your right. A brochure outlining its 16 stops is available here; note that the round trip will take about two hours, and high-clearance vehicles are recommended after stop 9. ⚠ Do not attempt if it has recently rained. Back on Park Boulevard, you'll soon arrive at the aptly named **Skull Rock.** This downright spooky formation is next to the parking lot; a nearby trailhead marks the beginning of a 1.7-mile nature trail. End your day with a stop at the **Oasis Visitor Center** in Twentynine Palms, where you can stroll through the historic **Oasis of Mara,** popular with area settlers.

GETTING HERE AND AROUND
CAR TRAVEL

An isolated island of pristine wilderness—a rarity these days—Joshua Tree National Park is within a short drive of 11 million Southern California residents. Most visitors, in fact, make the two-hour drive from the Los Angeles area to enjoy a weekend of solitude in 792,726 acres of untouched desert. The urban sprawl of Palm Springs (home to the nearest airport) is 45 miles away, but gateway towns Joshua Tree, Yucca Valley, and Twentynine Palms are just north of the park. If you're staying in the Palm Springs area, you can enjoy the highlights of the park in one day, including a stop for a picnic at a scenic spot.

■TIP→ If you'd prefer not to drive, most Palm Springs area hotels can arrange a half- or full-day tour that hits the highlights of Joshua Tree National Park. But you'll need to spend two or three days camping here to truly experience the quiet beauty of the desert.

PARK ESSENTIALS

PARK FEES AND PERMITS

Park admission is $15 per car, $5 per person on foot, bicycle, motorcycle, or horse. The Joshua Tree Pass, good for one year, is $30. Free permits—available at all visitor centers—are required for rock climbing.

PARK HOURS

The park is open every day, around the clock. The park is in the Pacific time zone.

CELL-PHONE RECEPTION

Cell phones don't work in most areas of the park. Pay phones are at Oasis Visitor Center and Black Rock Canyon Campground; there are no telephones in the interior of the park.

RESTAURANTS

Dining options in the gateway towns around Joshua Tree National Park are extremely limited—you'll mostly find fast-food outlets and a few casual cafés in Yucca Valley and Twentynine Palms. The exception is the restaurant at 29 Palms Inn, which has an interesting California-cuisine menu that features lots of veggies. Still, you'll have to travel to the Palm Springs desert resort area for a fine-dining experience.

Prices in the reviews are the average cost of a main course at dinner, or if dinner is not served, at lunch.

HOTELS

Lodging choices in the Joshua Tree National Park area are limited to a few motels, chain hotels, and a luxury bed-and-breakfast establishment in the gateway towns. In general, most offer few amenities and are modestly priced. Book ahead for the spring wildflower season—reservations may be difficult to obtain then.

For a more extensive range of lodging options, you'll need to head to Palm Springs and the surrounding desert resort communities.

Prices in the reviews are the lowest cost of a standard double room in high season. For expanded reviews, facilities, and current deals, visit Fodors.com.

TOURS

Big Wheel Tours. Based in Palm Desert, Big Wheel Tours offers van excursions, jeep tours, and hiking trips through the park. Pickups are available at Palm Springs area hotels. ☎ *760/779–1837* ⊕ *www.bwbtours. com* ✉ *$99–$159.*

Elite Land Tours. Elite Land Tours offer luxurious four-hour exursions to remote areas of the park where you're likely to see wildlife. Transportation from area hotels is available. ✉ *185 S. Indian Canyon Dr.* ☎ *760/318–1200* ✉ *$129–$159.*

Trail Discovery. You can get a full day of exploring Joshua Tree with Trail Discovery. Park admission, bottled water, hip-packs, snacks, and fruit are included. Transportation is available from Palm Springs and Cathedral City. ☎ *760/861–6292* ⊕ *www.palmspringshiking.com* 🚐 *$95–$135.*

VISITOR INFORMATION
PARK CONTACT INFORMATION
Joshua Tree National Park ✉ *74485 National Park Dr., Twentynine Palms* ☎ *760/367–5500* ⊕ *www. nps.gov/jotr.*

VISITOR CENTERS
Cottonwood Visitor Center. Exhibits in this small center, staffed by rangers and volunteers, illustrate the region's natural history. The center also has restrooms. ✉ *Cottonwood Spring, Pinto Basin Rd.* ⊕ *www. nps.gov/jotr* ⊗ *Daily 8–4.*

> ## PLANTS AND WILDLIFE IN JOSHUA TREE
>
> Joshua Tree will shatter your notions of the desert as a wasteland. Life flourishes here, as flora and fauna have adapted to heat and drought. In most areas you'll be walking among native Joshua trees, ocotillos, and yuccas. One of the best spring desert wildflower displays in Southern California blooms here. You'll see plenty of animals—reptiles such as nocturnal sidewinders, birds like golden eagles or burrowing owls, and occasionally mammals like coyotes and bobcats.

24

Joshua Tree Visitor Center. This visitor center has interesting exhibits illustrating park geology, cultural and historic sites, and hiking and rock-climbing activities. There's also a small bookstore. Restrooms with flush toilets are on the premises, and showers are nearby. ✉ *6554 Park Blvd., Joshua Tree* ☎ *760/366–1855* ⊕ *www.nps.gov/jotr* ⊗ *Daily 8–5.*

Oasis Visitor Center. Exhibits here illustrate how Joshua Tree was formed, reveal the differences between the park's two types of desert, and demonstrate how plants and animals eke out an existence in this arid climate. Take the 0.5-mile nature walk through the nearby Oasis of Mara, which is alive with cottonwood trees, palm trees, and mesquite shrubs. Facililies include picnic tables, restrooms, and a bookstore. ✉ *74485 National Park Dr., Twentynine Palms* ☎ *760/367–5500* ⊕ *www.nps. gov/jotr* ⊗ *Daily 8–5.*

EXPLORING

You can experience Joshua Tree National Park on several levels. Even on a short excursion along Park Boulevard between the Joshua Tree entrance station and Oasis of Mara, you'll see some of the best desert scenery in North America—including a staggering abundance of flora visible along a dozen self-guided nature trails. You'll also see remnants of homesteads from a century ago, now mostly abandoned and wind-worn. If rock climbing is your passion, this is the place for you; boulder-strewn mountaintops and slopes beckon. But in the end, Joshua Tree National Park is a pristine wilderness where you can enjoy a solitary stroll along an animal trail and commune with nature. The sites listed below include most of the highlights, each appealing in its own way. Be sure to take some time to explore on your own and enjoy the peace and quiet.

SCENIC DRIVES

Geology Motor Tour. Some of the park's most fascinating landscapes can be observed from this 18-mile dirt road. Parts of the journey are rough, so make sure you have a 4X4. Sights to see include a 100-year-old stone dam called Squaw Tank, defunct mines, and a large plain with an abundance of Joshua trees. There are 16 stops along the way, so give yourself about two hours to make the round trip. ⊠ *South of Park Blvd., west of Jumbo Rocks.*

Park Boulevard. If you have time only for a short visit, driving Park Boulevard is your best choice. Traversing the most scenic portions of Joshua Tree, this well-paved road connects the north and west entrances in the park's high desert section. Along with some sweeping desert views, you'll see jumbles of splendid boulder formations, stands of Joshua trees, and Hidden Valley and Barker Dam, remnants of the area's wild and woolly past. From the Oasis Visitor Center, drive south. After about 5 miles, the road forks; turn right and head west toward Jumbo Rocks (clearly marked with a road sign).

Pinto Basin Road. This paved road takes you from high Mojave desert to low Colorado desert. A long, slow drive, the route runs from the main part of the park to I–10; it can add as much as an hour to and from Palm Springs (round-trip), but the views and roadside exhibits make it worth the extra time. From the Oasis Visitor Center, drive south. After about 5 miles, the road forks; take a left and continue another 9 miles to the Cholla Cactus Garden, where the sun fills the cactus needles with light. Past that is the Ocotillo Patch, filled with spindly plants bearing razor-sharp thorns and brilliant red flowers. Side trips from this route require a 4X4.

HISTORIC SITES

FAMILY **Hidden Valley.** This legendary cattle-rustlers hideout is set among big boulders, which kids love to scramble over and around. There are shaded picnic tables here. ⊠ *Park Blvd., 14 miles south of West Entrance.*

Fodor'sChoice **Keys Ranch.** This 150-acre ranch, which once belonged to William and
★ Frances Keys and is now on the National Historic Register, illustrates one of the area's most successful attempts at homesteading. The couple raised five children under extreme desert conditions. Most of the original buildings, including the house, school, store, and workshop, have been restored to the way they were when William died in 1969. The only way to see the ranch is on one of the 90-minute walking tours usually offered daily October to May; call ahead to confirm. ⊠ *2 miles north of Barker Dam Rd.* ☎ *760/367–5555* ⊕ *www.nps.gov* ☛ *Tour $5, available at visitor centers* ⊗ *Oct.–May, daily at 10 and 1.*

Lost Horse Mine. This historic mine, which produced 10,000 ounces of gold and 16,000 ounces of silver between 1894 and 1931, was among Southern California's most productive mines. The 10-stamp mill is considered one of the best preserved of its type in the park system. The site is accessed via a fairly strenuous 2-mile hike. ⊠ *Keys View Rd., about 15 miles south of West Entrance.*

SCENIC STOPS

Barker Dam. Built in 1905 by ranchers and miners to hold water for cattle and mining operations, the dam now collects rainwater and is a good place to spot wildlife such as the elusive bighorn sheep. ⊠ *Barker Dam Rd., off Park Blvd., 14 miles south of West Entrance.*

Cholla Cactus Garden. This stand of bigelow cholla (sometimes called jumping cholla, since its hooked spines seem to jump at you) is best seen and photographed in late afternoon, when the backlit spiky stalks stand out against a colorful sky. ⊠ *Pinto Basin Rd., 20 miles north of Cottonwood Visitor Center.*

Cottonwood Spring. Home to the native Cahuilla people for centuries, this spring provided water for travelers and early prospectors. The area, which supports a large stand of fan palms, is a stop for migrating birds and a winter water source for bighorn sheep. A number of gold mines were located here, and the area still has some remains, including an *arrastra* (a gold ore–grinding tool) and concrete pillars. ⊠ *Cottonwood Visitor Center.*

Fortynine Palms Oasis. A short drive off Highway 62, this site is a bit of a preview of what the park's interior has to offer: stands of fan palms, interesting petroglyphs, and evidence of fires built by early American Indians. Since animals frequent this area, you may spot a coyote, bobcat, or roadrunner. ⊠ *End of Canyon Rd., 4 miles west of Twentynine Palms.*

Fodor$Choice **Keys View.** At 5,185 feet, this point affords a sweeping view of the Santa
★ Rosa Mountains and Coachella Valley, the San Andreas Fault, the peak of 11,500-foot Mount San Gorgonio, the shimmering surface of Salton Sea, and—on a rare clear day—Signal Mountain in Mexico. Sunrise and sunset are magical times, when the light throws rocks and trees into high relief before bathing the hills in brilliant shades of red, orange, and gold. ⊠ *Keys View Rd., 21 miles south of park's west entrance.*

Lost Palms Oasis. More than 100 fan palms comprise the largest group of the exotic plants in the park. A spring bubbles from between the rocks, but disappears into the sandy, boulder-strewn canyon. If you hike along the 4-mile trail, you might spot bighorn sheep. ⊠ *Cottonwood Visitor Center.*

Ocotillo Patch. Stop here for a roadside exhibit on the dramatic display made by the red-tipped succulent after even the shortest rain shower. ⊠ *Pinto Basin Rd., about 3 miles east of Cholla Cactus Gardens.*

EDUCATIONAL OFFERINGS

LECTURES

The Desert Institute at Joshua Tree National Park. This organization offers a full schedule of educational lectures on topics such as the birds of Joshua Tree National Park, hiking, gourmet campfire cuisine, and photography. Classes meet at various locations; many include field trips within the park. ⊠ *74485 National Park Dr., Twentynine Palms* ☎ *760/367–5535* ⊕ *www.joshuatree.org.*

Stargazing. At Joshua Tree National Park you can tour the Milky Way on summer evenings using binoculars. Rangers also offer programs on Saturday evenings when the moon isn't visible. Pick up a schedule at a visitor center. ⊠ *Cottonwood Campground Amphitheater and Oasis Visitor Center.*

> ### LOOK, DON'T TOUCH—REALLY
>
> Some cactus needles, like those on the cholla, can become embedded in your skin with just the slightest touch. If you do get zapped, use tweezers to gently pull it out.

RANGER PROGRAMS

Rangers offer a full schedule of hour-long programs to help you explore the park fall through spring; the schedule is limited in the hot summer months. Refer to the guide available at visitor centers for specific schedules, as times and destinations vary.

Evening Programs. Rangers present hourlong Saturday evening lectures at Black Rock Canyon Nature Center, Cottonwood Amphitheater, Indian Cove Amphitheater, and Jumbo Rocks Campground. Topics range from natural history to local lore. The schedule is posted at the visitor centers. ▭ *Free* ◷ *Oct.–Apr., Sat. at 7; May, Sat. at 8.*

SPORTS AND THE OUTDOORS

BICYCLING

Mountain biking is a great way to see Joshua Tree. Bikers are restricted to roads that are used by motorized vehicles, including the main park roads and a few four-wheel-drive trails. Most scenic stops and picnic areas, and the Wallstreet trailhead, have bike racks.

Black Eagle Mine Road. This 9-mile dead-end road is peppered with defunct mines. It runs along the edge of a former lake bed, then crosses a number of dry washes before navigating several of Eagle Mountain's canyons. ⊠ *Trailhead off Pinto Basin Rd., 6½ miles north of Cottonwood Visitor Center.*

Covington Flats. This 4-mile route takes you past impressive Joshua trees as well as pinyon pines, junipers, and areas of lush desert vegetation. It's tough going toward the end, but once you reach 5,516-foot Eureka Peak you'll have great views of Palm Springs, the Morongo Basin, and the surrounding mountains. ⊠ *Trailhead at Covington Flats picnic area, La Contenta Rd., 10 miles south of Rte. 62.*

Pinkham Canyon and Thermal Canyon Roads. This challenging 20-mile route begins at the Cottonwood Visitor Center and loops through the Cottonwood Mountains. The unpaved trail follows Smoke Tree Wash through Pinkham Canyon, rounds Thermal Canyon, and loops back to the beginning. Rough in places, the road travels through soft sand and rocky flood plains. ⊠ *Trailhead at Cottonwood Visitor Center.*

Queen Valley. This 13.4-mile network of mostly level roads winds through one of the park's most impressive groves of Joshua trees. ⊠ *Trailhead at Hidden Valley Campground.*

DID YOU KNOW?

Found only in Arizona, California, Nevada, and Utah, the Joshua tree (*Yucca brevifolia*) is actually a member of the agave family. American Indians used the Joshua tree's hearty foliage like leather, forming it into everyday items like baskets and shoes. Later, early settlers used its core and limbs for building fences to contain their livestock.

BIRD-WATCHING

Joshua Tree, located on the inland portion of the Pacific Flyway, hosts about 240 species of birds, and the park is a popular seasonal location for bird-watching. During the fall migration, which runs mid-September through mid-October, there are several reliable sighting areas. At Barker Dam you might spot white-throated swifts, several types of swallows, or red-tailed hawks. Lucy's warbler, lesser goldfinches, and Anna's hummingbirds cruise around Cottonwood Spring, a serene palm-shaded setting where you'll likely see the largest concentrations of birds in the park. At Black Rock Canyon and Covington Flats, you're likely to see La Conte's thrashers, ruby-crowned kinglets, and warbling vireos. Rufus hummingbirds, Pacific slope flycatchers, and various warblers are frequent visitors to Indian Cove. Lists of birds found in the park, as well as information on recent sightings, are available at visitor centers.

HIKING

There are more than 190 miles of hiking trails in Joshua Tree, ranging from quarter-mile nature trails to 35-mile treks. Some connect with each other, so you can design your own desert maze. Remember that drinking water is hard to come by—you won't find water in the park except at the entrances. Bring along at least a gallon per person for all but the shortest hikes, more if the weather is hot. Before striking out on a hike or apparent nature trail, check out the signage. Roadside signage identifies hiking- and rock-climbing routes.

EASY

Cap Rock. This 0.5-mile wheelchair-accessible loop—named after a boulder that sits atop a huge rock formation like a cap—winds through fascinating rock formations and has signs that explain the geology of the Mojave Desert. *Easy.* ⊠ *Trailhead at junction of Park Blvd. and Keys View Rd.*

FAMILY **Hidden Valley.** Crawl through the rocks surrounding Hidden Valley to see where cattle rustlers supposedly hung out on this 1-mile loop. *Easy.* ⊠ *Trailhead at Hidden Valley Picnic Area.*

Indian Cove Trail. Look for lizards and roadrunners along this 0.5-mile loop that follows a desert wash. A walk along this well-signed trail reveals signs of Indian habitation, animals, and flora such as desert willow and yucca. *Easy.* ⊠ *Trailhead at west end of Indian Cove Campground.*

Oasis of Mara. A stroll along this short, wheelchair-accessible trail, located just outside the visitor center, reveals how early settlers took advantage of this oasis, which was first settled by the Serrano Indians. *Mara* means "place of little springs and much grass" in their language. The Serrano, who farmed the oasis until the mid-1850s, planted one palm tree for each male baby born during the first year of the settlement. *Easy.* ⊠ *Trailhead at Oasis Visitor Center.*

Skull Rock Trail. The 1.7-mile loop guides hikers through boulder piles, desert washes, and a rocky alley. It's named for what is perhaps the park's most famous rock formation, which resembles a human head. Access is across the highway from Jumbo Rocks Campground. *Easy.* ⊠ *Trailhead at Jumbo Rocks Campground.*

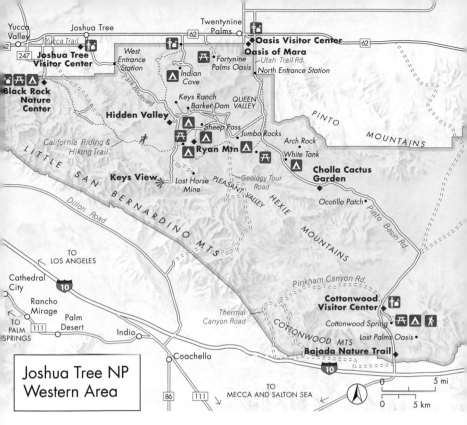

Joshua Tree NP
Western Area

MODERATE

California Riding and Hiking Trail. This well-traveled route stretches for 35 miles between the Black Rock Canyon Entrance and the North Entrance. You can access the trail for a short or long hike at several points. The visitor centers have trail maps. *Moderate.* ⊠ *Trailheads at Upper Covington Flats, Ryan Campground, Twin Tanks, south of north park entrance, and Black Rock Canyon.*

Hi-View Nature Trail. This 1.3-mile loop climbs nearly to the top of 4,500-foot Summit Peak. The views of nearby Mt. San Gorgonio (snow-capped in winter) make the moderately steep journey worth the effort. You can pick up a pamphlet describing the vegetation you'll see along the way at any visitor center. *Moderate.* ⊠ *Trailhead ½ mile west of Black Rock Canyon Campground.*

Fodor's Choice ★ **Ryan Mountain Trail.** The payoff for hiking to the top of 5,461-foot Ryan Mountain is one of the best panoramic views of Joshua Tree. From here you can see Mt. San Jacinto, Mt. San Gorgonio, Lost Horse Valley, and the Pinto Basin. You'll need two to three hours to complete the 3-mile round trip. *Moderate.* ⊠ *Trailhead at Ryan Mountain parking area, 16 miles southeast of park's west entrance, or at Sheep Pass, 16 miles southwest of Oasis Visitor Center.*

DIFFICULT

Boy Scout Trail. The moderately strenuous 8-mile trail, suitable for back-packers, extends from Indian Cove to Park Boulevard. It runs through the westernmost edge of the Wonderland of Rocks (where you're likely to see climbers on the outcroppings), passing through a forest of Joshua trees, past granite towers, and around willow-lined pools. Completing the round-trip journey requires camping along the way, so you may want to hike only part of the trail or have a car waiting at the other end. *Difficult.* ⊠ *Trail-head between Quail Springs Picnic Area and Indian Cove Campground.*

Lost Palms Oasis Trail. Allow four to six hours for the moderately strenu-ous, 7.5-mile round trip, which leads to the most impressive oasis in the park. You'll find more than 100 fan palms and an abundance of wildflowers here. *Difficult.* ⊠ *Trailhead at Cottonwood Spring Oasis.*

Mastodon Peak Trail. Some boulder scrambling is required on this 3-mile hike up 3,371-foot Mastodon Peak, but the journey rewards you with stunning views of the Salton Sea. The trail passes through a region where gold was mined from 1919 to 1932, so be on the lookout for open mines. The peak draws its name from a large rock formation that early miners believed looked like the head of a prehistoric behemoth. *Difficult.* ⊠ *Trailhead at Cottonwood Spring Oasis.*

24

HORSEBACK RIDING

More than 200 miles of equestrian trails are gradually being added as part of a backcountry and wilderness management plan at Joshua Tree, and vis-itors are welcome to bring their own animals. Trail maps are available at visitor centers. Ryan and Black Rock campgrounds have designated areas for horses and mules, including a section near the park's west entrance.

ROCK CLIMBING

Fodor'sChoice ★ With an abundance of weathered igneous boulder outcroppings, Joshua Tree is one of the nation's top winter-climbing destinations. There are more than 4,500 established routes offering a full menu of climbing experiences—from bouldering for beginners in the Wonderland of Rocks to multiple-pitch climbs at Echo Rock and Saddle Rock. The best-known climb in the park is Hidden Valley's Sports Challenge Rock. A map inside the *Joshua Tree Guide* shows locations of selected wilder-ness and nonwilderness climbs.

TOURS AND OUTFITTERS

Joshua Tree Rock Climbing School. The school offers several programs, from one-day introductory classes to multiday programs for experienced climb-ers, and provides all needed equipment. Beginning classes ($150), offered year-round on most weekends, are limited to six people age eight or older. ☎ 760/366–4745, 800/890–4745 ⊕ *www.joshuatreerockclimbing.com.*

Vertical Adventures Rock Climbing School. About 1,000 climbers each year learn the sport in Joshua Tree National Park through this school. Classes, offered September–May, meet at a designated location in the park, and all equipment is provided. A one-day class costs $145. ☎ 800/514–8785 ⊕ *www.verticaladventures.com.*

WHAT'S NEARBY

NEARBY TOWNS

Palm Springs, about a 45-minute drive from the North Entrance Station at Joshua Tree, serves as the home base for most park visitors. This city of 48,000 has 95 golf courses, 600 tennis courts, and 50,000 swimming pools. A hideout for Hollywood stars since the 1920s, Palm Springs offers a glittering array of shops, restaurants, and hotels. Stroll down Palm Canyon Drive and you're sure to run into a celebrity or two. About 9 miles north of Palm Springs and closer to the park is **Desert Hot Springs,** which has more than 1,000 natural hot mineral pools and 40 health spas ranging from low-key to luxurious. **Yucca Valley** is the largest and fastest growing of the communities straddling the park's northern border. The town boasts a handful of motels, supermarkets, and a Walmart. Tiny **Joshua Tree,** the closest community to the park's West Entrance, is where the serious rock climbers make their headquarters. **Twentynine Palms,** known as "two-nine" by locals, is sandwiched between the Marine Corps Air Ground Task Force Center to the north and Joshua Tree National Park to the south. Here you'll find a smattering of coffeehouses, antiques shops, and cafés.

VISITOR INFORMATION

California Welcome Center Yucca Valley ⊠ *56711 Twentynine Palms Hwy., Yucca Valley* ☎ *760/365–5464* ⊕ *www.visitcwc.com.* **Joshua Tree Chamber of Commerce** ⊠ *6448 Hallee Rd., Joshua Tree* ☎ *760/366–3723* ⊕ *www.joshuatreechamber.org.* **Palm Springs Bureau of Tourism** ⊠ *2109 N. Palm Canyon Dr., Palm Springs* ☎ *760/778–8415, 800/348–7746* ⊕ *www.visitpalmsprings.com.* **Twentynine Palms Chamber of Commerce** ⊠ *73484 Twentynine Palms Hwy., Twentynine Palms* ☎ *760/367–3445* ⊕ *www.29chamber.org.* **Yucca Valley Chamber of Commerce** ⊠ *56711 Twentynine Palms Hwy., Yucca Valley* ☎ *760/365–6323* ⊕ *www.yuccavalley.org.*

NEARBY ATTRACTIONS

FAMILY **Coachella Valley History Museum.** Make a date to learn about dates at this museum inside a former farmhouse. The exhibits here provide an intriguing glimpse into irrigation, harvesting, and other farming practices; a timeline and other displays chronicle how the industry emerged in the desert a century ago. ⊠ *82616 Miles Ave., Indio* ☎ *760/342–6651* ⊕ *www.cvhm.org* ☑ *$10* ⊙ *Oct.–May, Thurs.–Sat. 10–4, Sun. 1–4.*

FAMILY **Hi-Desert Nature Museum.** Creatures that make their homes in Joshua Tree National Park are the focus here. A small live-animal display includes scorpions, snakes, ground squirrels, and chuckwallas (a type of lizard). You'll also find rocks, minerals, and fossils from the Paleozoic era and Native American artifacts, and there's a children's room. ⊠ *Yucca Valley Community Center, 57116 Twentynine Palms Hwy., Yucca Valley* ☎ *760/369–7212* ⊕ *hidesertnaturemuseum.org* ☑ *Free* ⊙ *Tues.–Sat. 10–5.*

Learn about the park's flora and fauna by attending the ranger programs.

Oasis of Murals. The history and current life of Twentynine Palms is depicted in this collection of 20 murals painted on the sides of buildings. If you drive around town, you can't miss the murals, but you can also pick up a free map from the Twentynine Palms Chamber of Commerce.

Pioneertown. In 1946 Roy Rogers, Gene Autry, the Sons of the Pioneers (the music group for whom the town is named), and Russ Hayden built Pioneertown, an 1880s-style Wild West movie set complete with hitching posts, saloon, and an OK Corral. You can stroll past wooden and adobe storefronts and feel like you're back in the Old West. Or not: Pappy and Harriet's Pioneertown Palace, now the town's top draw, has evolved into a hip venue for indie and other bands. ⊠ *53688 Pioneertown Rd., 4 miles north of Yucca Valley, Pioneertown* ⊕ *pappyandharriets.com.*

WHERE TO EAT

IN THE PARK

PICNIC AREAS

Black Rock Canyon. Set among Joshua trees, pinyon pines, and junipers, this popular picnic area has barbecue grills and drinking water. It's one of the few with flush toilets. ⊠ *End of Joshua La. at the Black Rock Canyon Campground.*

Best Campgrounds in Joshua Tree

Camping is the best way to experience the stark, exquisite beauty of Joshua Tree. You'll also have a rare opportunity to sleep outside in a semi-wilderness setting. The campgrounds, set at elevations from 3,000 to 4,500 feet, have only primitive facilities; few have drinking water. Black Rock and Indian Cove campgrounds, on the northern edge of the park, accept reservations up to six months in advance, and only for October through Memorial Day. Campsites elsewhere are on a first-come, first-served basis. Belle and White Tank campgrounds, and parts of Black Rock Canyon, Cottonwood, and Indian Cove campgrounds, are closed from the day after Memorial Day to September.

Belle Campground. This small campground is popular with families, as there are a number of boulders kids can scramble over and around. ⊠ *9 miles south of Oasis of Mara* ☎ *760/367–5500* ⊕ *www.nps.gov/jotr.*

Black Rock Canyon Campground. Set among juniper bushes, cholla cacti, and other desert shrubs, Black Rock Canyon is one of the prettiest campgrounds in Joshua Tree. ⊠ *Joshua La., south of Hwy. 62 and Hwy. 247* ☎ *760/367–5500* ⊕ *www.recreation.gov.*

Cottonwood Campground. In spring this campground, the southernmost

one in the park (and therefore often the last to fill up), is surrounded by some of the desert's finest wildflowers. ⊠ *Pinto Basin Rd., 32 miles south of North Entrance Station* ☎ *760/367–5500* ⊕ *www.nps.gov/jotr.*

Hidden Valley Campground. This campground is a favorite with rock climbers, who make their way up valley formations that have names like the Blob, Old Woman, and Chimney Rock. ⊠ *Off Park Blvd., 20 miles southwest of Oasis of Mara* ☎ *760/367–5500* ⊕ *www.nps.gov/jotr.*

Indian Cove Campground. This is a sought-after spot for rock climbers, primarily because it lies among the 50 square miles of rugged terrain at the Wonderland of Rocks. ⊠ *Indian Cove Rd., south of Hwy. 62* ☎ *760/367–5500* ⊕ *www.nps.gov/jotr.*

Jumbo Rocks. Each campsite at this well-regarded campground tucked among giant boulders has a bit of privacy. It's a good home base for visiting many of Joshua Tree's attractions. ⊠ *Park Blvd., 11 miles from Oasis of Mara* ☎ *760/367–5500* ⊕ *www.nps.gov/jotr.*

White Tank. This small, quiet campground is popular with families because a nearby trail leads to a natural arch. ⊠ *Pinto Basin Rd., 11 miles south of Oasis of Mara* ☎ *760/367–5500* ⊕ *www.nps.gov/jotr.*

Covington Flats. This is a great place to get away from crowds. There's just one table, and it's surrounded by flat, open desert dotted here and there by Joshua trees. ⊠ *La Contenta Rd., 10 miles from Rte. 62.*

Hidden Valley. Set among huge rock formations, with picnic tables shaded by dense trees, this is one of the most pleasant places in the park to stop for lunch. ⊠ *Park Blvd., 14 miles south of the west entrance.*

OUTSIDE THE PARK

$ AMERICAN 🍴 **C&S Coffee Shop.** If you're yearning for pork chops and gravy for breakfast or eggs over easy for dinner, head to this tidy diner, which has been a local hangout since 1946. The typical diner menu also features soups, salads, and sandwiches, all cooked to order and presented in heaping portions. Don't miss the perfectly cooked fries. Expect a cheery welcome and prompt service. [$] *Average main: $8* ✉ *55795 Twentynine Palms Hwy., Yucca Valley* ☎ *760/365–9946.*

$ MEXICAN 🍴 **Edchada's.** Rock climbers who spend their days in Joshua Tree swear by the margaritas at this Mexican eatery. Specialties include prodigious portions of fajitas, carnitas, seafood enchiladas, and fish tacos. [$] *Average main: $12* ✉ *73502 Twentynine Palms Hwy., Twentynine Palms* ☎ *760/367–2131.*

$$$ AMERICAN 🍴 **Pappy & Harriet's Pioneertown Palace.** Smack in the middle of a Western-movie-set town is this Western-movie-set saloon where you can have dinner, relax over a drink at the bar, or check out some great indie bands and other acts—Leon Russell, Sonic Youth, the Get Up Kids, and Robert Plant have all played here, as have many Cali groups. The food ranges from Tex-Mex to Santa Maria–style barbecue to steak and burgers. No surprises but plenty of fun. ■ **TIP→ Pappy & Harriet's may be in the middle of nowhere, but you'll need reservations for dinner on weekends.** [$] *Average main: $24* ✉ *53688 Pioneertown Rd., Pioneertown* ☎ *760/365–5956* 🌐 *www.pappyandharriets.com* ✍ *Reservations essential* ⏲ *Closed Tues. and Wed.*

$ CAFÉ 🍴 **Park Rock Café.** If you're on your way to the national park on Highway 62, stop in the town of Joshua Tree to grab a hearty breakfast bagel sandwich and order a box lunch to take with you. The café creates some interesting sandwiches, including a healthy concoction with avocado and nuts on squaw bread (a dense, multigrain bread made with molasses). The lentil barley soup is a favorite. Outside dining is pleasant here. [$] *Average main: $9* ✉ *6554 Park Blvd., Joshua Tree* ☎ *760/366–8200* 🌐 *jtparkrockcafe.com* ⏲ *No dinner.*

WHERE TO STAY

OUTSIDE THE PARK

$$$ B&B/INN 🏨 **29 Palms Inn.** The closest lodging to the entrance to Joshua Tree National Park, the funky 29 Palms Inn scatters a collection of adobe and wood-frame cottages, some dating back to the 1920s and 1930s, over 70 acres of grounds that include the ancient Oasis of Mara and are popular with birds and bird-watchers year-round. **Pros:** gracious hospitality; exceptional bird-watching; popular with artists. **Cons:** rustic accommodations; limited amenities. [$] *Rooms from: $168* ✉ *73950 Inn Ave., Twentynine Palms* ☎ *760/367–3505* 🌐 *www.29palmsinn.com* 🛏 *18 rooms, 5 suites* 🍽 *Breakfast.*

$ B&B/INN 🏨 **Casa Cody.** The service is personal and gracious at this historic B&B near the Palm Springs Art Museum; spacious studios and one- and two-bedroom suites hold Santa Fe–style rustic furnishings. **Pros:**

family-size digs; friendly ambience; good value. **Cons:** old buildings; limited amenities. $ *Rooms from: $99* ✉ *175 S. Cahuilla Rd., Palm Springs* ☎ *760/320–9346, 800/231–2639* 🌐 *www.casacody.com* 🛏 *18 rooms, 8 suites, 1 cottage* 🍴 *Breakfast.*

$$ B&B/INN 🏨 **Movie Colony Hotel.** Designed in 1935 by Albert Frey, this intimate hotel evokes mid-century minimalist ambience. Its gleaming white, two-story buildings, flanked with balconies and porthole windows, bring to mind a luxury yacht. **Pros:** architectural icon; happy hour; cruiser bikes. **Cons:** close quarters; off the beaten path; staff not available 24 hours. $ *Rooms from: $124* ✉ *726 N. Indian Canyon Dr., Palm Springs* ☎ *760/320–6340, 888/953–5700* 🌐 *www.moviecolonyhotel.com* 🛏 *13 rooms, 3 suites* 🍴 *Breakfast.*

$$ B&B/INN 🏨 **Orbit In Hotel.** Step back to 1957 at this hip inn on a quiet backstreet downtown: the architectural roots here date back to the late 1940s and '50s—nearly flat roofs, wide overhangs, glass everywhere—with the ambience to match. **Pros:** saltwater pool; in-room spa services; Orbitini cocktail hour. **Cons:** best for couples; style not to everyone's taste; staff not available 24 hours. $ *Rooms from: $149* ✉ *562 W. Arenas Rd., Palm Springs* ☎ *760/323–3585, 877/996–7248* 🌐 *www.orbitin.com* 🛏 *9 rooms* 🍴 *Breakfast.*

$$ B&B/INN 🏨 **Roughley Manor.** To the wealthy pioneer who erected the stone mansion now occupied by this B&B, expense was no object, which is evident in the 50-foot-long planked maple floor in the great room, the intricate carpentry on the walls, and the huge stone fireplaces that warm the house on the rare cold night. **Pros:** elegant rooms and public spaces; good stargazing in the gazebo; great horned owls on property. **Cons:** somewhat isolated location; three-story main building doesn't have an elevator. $ *Rooms from: $135* ✉ *74744 Joe Davis Dr., Twentynine Palms* ☎ *760/367–3238* 🌐 *www.roughleymanor.com* 🛏 *2 suites, 7 cottages* 🍴 *Breakfast.*

LASSEN VOLCANIC NATIONAL PARK

WELCOME TO
LASSEN VOLCANIC

TOP REASONS TO GO

★ **Hike a volcano:**
The 2½-mile trek up Lassen Peak rewards you with a spectacular view of far northern California.

★ **Spot a rare bloom:**
The Lassen Smelowskia, a small white-to-pinkish flower, grows only in Lassen Volcanic National Park, mainly on Lassen Peak.

★ **View volcano varieties:**
All four types of volcanoes found in the world—shield, plug dome, cinder cone, and composite—are represented in Lassen Volcanic National Park.

★ **Listen to the earth:**
The park's thumping mud pots and venting fumaroles roil, gurgle, and belch a raucous symphony from beneath the earth's crust.

★ **Escape the crowds:**
Lassen, in sparsely populated far northern California, is one of the least-visited national parks.

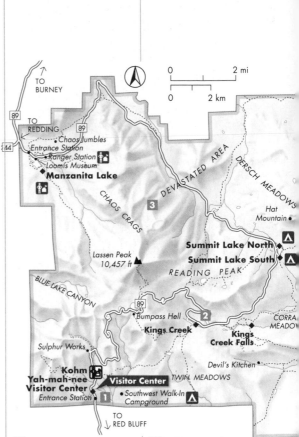

1 Southwest. Geothermal activity is greatest in the southwest area; you'll see evidence on hikes to Bumpass Hell and Devil's Kitchen. Walkways beside the former Sulphur Works on Lassen Park Road, just past the Kohm Yah-mah-nee Visitor Center, provide easy access to smelly, belching fumaroles.

2 Middle. Marsh meadows and stunning falls highlight the Kings Creek area in the park's southern midsection. Farther north, Summit Lake—in the midst of a red fir forest at an elevation of about 6,700 feet—has two campgrounds and a trail leading to several smaller lakes.

3 **Northwest.** Lassen Park Road winds past the barren rubble of Devastated Area, providing stunning views of Lassen Peak and passing Chaos Jumbles before reaching lush, wooded Manzanita Lake.

4 **Eastern.** Among the delights found in the least accessible and least visited part of the park are Cinder Cone and Ash Butte, lava beds, and meadows, plus beautiful Snag and Juniper lakes and the many creeks that flow out of them.

CALIFORNIA

GETTING ORIENTED

From gurgling mud pots and hissing steam vents, to tranquil lakes and lily-covered ponds, to jagged mountain peaks bordered by flowering meadows, Lassen Volcanic National Park's varied landscapes are certain to soothe, awe, and intrigue. Whether you want to climb to the top of a dormant volcano or simply loll at the water's edge as birdsong drifts down from tall pines, you'll find unexpected pleasures in this park formed by molten lava.

25

KEY
👫 Ranger Station
🔺 Campground
🛆 Picnic Area
🍴 Restaurant
🖼 Lodge
🏃 Trailhead
👫 Restrooms
⇲ Scenic Viewpoint
⋯⋯ Walking/Hiking Trails

Updated by Christine Vovakes

A dormant plug dome, Lassen Peak is the focus of Lassen Volcanic National Park. The peak began erupting in May 1914, sending pumice, rock, and snow thundering down the mountain, and gas and hot ash billowing into the atmosphere. Lassen's most spectacular outburst was in 1915 when it blew a cloud of ash almost 6 miles high. The resulting mudflow destroyed vegetation for miles in some directions; the evidence is still visible today, especially in Devastated Area. The volcano finally came to rest in 1921.

LASSEN VOLCANIC PLANNER

WHEN TO GO
The park is open year-round, though most roads are closed from late October to mid-June due to snow.

AVG. HIGH/LOW TEMPS.

JAN.	FEB.	MAR.	APR.	MAY	JUNE
50/13	51/13	53/16	61/23	70/29	79/34
JULY	AUG.	SEPT.	OCT.	NOV.	DEC.
84/40	85/40	78/36	69/30	56/21	50/14

PLANNING YOUR TIME
LASSEN VOLCANIC IN ONE DAY
Start your day early at the park's northwest entrance, accessible via Highway 44 from Redding. Make a stop at the **Loomis Museum,** where you can view exhibits before taking the easy, 1-mile round-trip **Lily Pond Nature Trail.** Back at the museum, drive down to **Manzanita Lake;** take a mid-morning break and pick up supplies for a picnic lunch at the **Camper**

Store before taking the main road toward **Lassen Peak.** As you circle the peak on its northern flank, you come on **Devastated Area,** testimony to the damage done by the 1915 eruptions. Continue to **Summit Lake,** where you can picnic and swim, or to **Kings Creek,** an area of lush meadows where you can hike to **Kings Creek Falls.** Allow at least two hours to make the 3-mile round-trip hike, which ends in a 700-foot descent to the falls. If time permits, continue to the **Sulphur Works** to stroll sidewalks that skirt sulfur-emitting steam vents.

GETTING HERE AND AROUND

CAR TRAVEL

From the north, take the Highway 44 exit off Interstate 5 and travel east about 48 miles to Highway 89. Turn right and drive 1 mile to the northwest entrance station. From the south, take the second Red Bluff exit off I–5, head east, and turn left onto Highway 36. Drive approximately 45 miles, and turn left onto Highway 89. From there it's about 8 miles to the southwest entrance ranger station. The 30-mile main park road, Lassen Park Road/Highway 89, starts at the southwest entrance, skirts around three sides of Lassen Peak, and exits the park on the northwest side.

25

PARK ESSENTIALS

PARK FEES AND PERMITS

The $10 fee per car covers seven days. Those entering by bus, bicycle, horse, motorcycle, or on foot pay $5. There's a $25 annual park pass that also covers Whiskeytown NRA. For backcountry camping, pick up a free wilderness permit at the Loomis Museum or at the north and south entrance ranger stations, or download one at ⊕ *www.nps.gov/lavo.*

PARK HOURS

The park is open 24/7 year-round. It is in the Pacific time zone.

CELL-PHONE RECEPTION

Cell phones don't work in many parts of the park. There are pay telephones outside the Manzanita Camper Store and the Loomis Museum.

RESTAURANTS

The best dining in the park might be the fresh catch any anglers in your group snag. Otherwise, you'll find simple fare at Lassen Café and Gifts and at the Manzanita Lake Camper Store. Those hiking or camping near Drakesbad Guest Ranch can call ahead and reserve a place at their table (☎ 866/999–0914). Enjoy a variety of dining choices, ranging from grilled steaks to ethnic specialties, in Red Bluff, Redding, and Chester.

Prices in the reviews are the average cost of a main course at dinner, or if dinner is not served, at lunch.

HOTELS

Drakesbad Guest Ranch is the only lodging available inside Lassen. It's rustic—no electricity, just old-fashioned kerosene lamps—and expensive, but reservations are often fully booked a year or more in advance. In towns surrounding the park there's everything from elegant bed-and-breakfasts to chain hotels to simple, inexpensive rooms.

Prices in the reviews are the lowest cost of a standard double room in high season. For expanded reviews, facilities, and current deals, visit Fodors.com.

VISITOR INFORMATION

PARK CONTACT INFORMATION

Lassen Volcanic National Park Headquarters ✉ *38050 Hwy. 36 E, Mineral* ☎ *530/595–4444* ⊕ *www.nps.gov/lavo.*

VISITOR CENTERS

Kohm Yah-mah-nee Visitor Center. Pick up maps, trail and road guides, and inquire about children's activities and ranger-led programs here. Completed in 2008, this center at the park's southwest entrance screens a film about the park and has interactive exhibits that will wow the kids. Restrooms and first-aid facilities make this a handy stop. Food, beverages, and books are available at Lassen Café and Gifts. ✉ *Hwy. 89, north of Mineral* ☎ *530/595–4480* ⊕ *www.nps.gov/lavo* ۞ *Visitor center daily 9–5; café closed weekdays mid-Oct.–late May.*

EXPLORING

SCENIC DRIVES

Fodor'sChoice **Lassen Scenic Byway.** This 185-mile scenic drive begins in Chester and
★ loops through the forests, volcanic peaks, geothermal springs, and lava fields of Lassen National Forest and Lassen Volcanic National Park, providing for an all-day excursion into dramatic wilderness. From Chester, take Highway 36 west to Highway 89 north through the park, then Highway 44 east to Highway 36 west back to Chester. Parts of the road are inaccessible in winter. ☎ *800/427–7623 for CA Highway info service, 530/595-4480 for Lassen Park visitor center* ⊕ *www.nps.gov/lavo.*

HISTORIC SITES

Loomis Museum. Here you can view artifacts from the park's 1914 and 1915 eruptions, including dramatic original photographs taken by Benjamin Loomis, who was instrumental in the park's establishment. The museum also has a bookstore, films about the park's history, and excellent exhibits on the area's American Indian heritage. ✉ *Lassen Park Rd. at Manzanita Lake* ☎ *530/595–6140* ⊕ *www.nps.gov/lavo* ⧰ *Free* ۞ *Memorial Day–late Oct., daily 9–5.*

SCENIC STOPS

Boiling Springs Lake. A worthwhile, if occasionally muddy, 3-mile hike from the Drakesbad Guest Ranch, Boiling Springs Lake is surrounded by steep cliffs topped with trees. Constant bubbles release sulfuric steam into the air. ✉ *Trailhead parking near the end of Warner Valley Rd., near Drakesbad Guest Ranch.*

Bumpass Hell. This site's quirky name came about when a man with the last name of Bumpass was severely burned after falling into the boiling springs. A scenic but strenuous 3-mile round-trip hike brings you close to hot springs, hissing steam vents, and roiling mudpots. ✉ *Trailhead at end of paved parking area off Lassen Park Rd., 6 miles from the southwest entrance ranger station.*

Plants and Wildlife in Lassen Volcanic

Because of its varying elevations, Lassen has several different ecological habitats. Below 6,500 feet you can find ponderosa pine, Jeffrey pine, sugar pine, white fir, and several species of manzanita, gooseberry, and Ceanothus. Wildflowers—wild iris, spotted coralroot, pyrola, violets, and lupine—surround the hiking trails in spring and early summer.

The Manzanita Lake area has the best bird-watching opportunities, with yellow warblers, pied-billed grebes, white-headed and hairy woodpeckers, golden-crowned kinglets, and Steller's jays. The area is also home to rubber boas, garter snakes, brush rabbits, Sierra Nevada red foxes, black-tailed deer, coyotes, and the occasional mountain lion.

At elevations of 6,500–8,000 feet are red fir forests populated by many of the same wildlife as the lower regions, with the addition of black-backed three-toed woodpeckers, blue grouse, snowshoe hare, pine martens, and the hermit thrush.

Above 8,000 feet the environment is harsher, with bare patches of land between subalpine forests. You'll find whitebark pine, groves of mountain hemlock, small pikas, yellow-bellied marmots, and the occasional black bear. Bird-watchers should look for gray-crowned rosy finches, rock wrens, golden eagles, falcons, and hawks. California tortoiseshell butterflies are found on the highest peaks. If you can visit in winter, you'll see one of the park's most magnificent seasonal sights: massive snowdrifts up to 30 and 40 feet high.

25

Chaos Jumbles. More than 350 years ago, an avalanche from the Chaos Crags lava domes scattered hundreds of thousands of rocks—many of them 2–3 feet in diameter—over a couple of square miles. ⊠ *Lassen Park Rd., 2 miles northeast of the northwest entrance ranger station.*

Devastated Area. Lassen Peak's 1915 eruptions cleared the area of all vegetation, though there are a few signs of life after all these years. An easy interpretive trail loop, less than 0.5 mile total, is paved and wheelchair accessible. ⊠ *Lassen Park Rd., 2½ miles north of Summit Lake.*

Devils Kitchen. One of the park's three main geothermal areas, this is a great place to view mud pots, steam vents, and boiling pools. It's much less frequented than Bumpass Hell, so you can expect more wildlife during your moderately difficult 4.2-mile round-trip hike. You need to drive on a partially paved road to reach the trailhead. ⊠ *Trailhead parking near the end of Warner Valley Rd., near Drakesbad Guest Ranch.*

Fodor'sChoice ★ **Lassen Peak.** When this now-dormant plug dome volcano erupted in 1915, it spewed a huge mushroom cloud of debris almost 6 miles into the air. A fabulous panoramic view makes the strenuous 2.5-mile hike to the 10,457-foot summit worth the effort. ■TIP➔ A multiyear restoration project means all or part of the trail will be closed at certain times, so call ahead. At this writing trail work was expected to be completed in 2015. ⊠ *Lassen Park Rd., 7 miles from southwest entrance ranger station* ☎ *530/595–4480.*

Manzanita Lake. Lassen Peak is reflected in the waters of Manzanita Lake, which has good catch-and-release trout fishing, as well as a pleasant trail for exploring the area's abundant wildlife. ⊠ *Lassen Park Rd. at northwest entrance ranger station.*

FAMILY **Sulphur Works Thermal Area.** Proof of Lassen Peak's volatility becomes evident shortly after you enter the park at the southwest entrance. Sidewalks skirt boiling springs and sulphur-emitting steam vents. This area is usually the last site to close because of snow. ⊠ *Lassen Park Rd., 1 mile from the southwest entrance ranger station.*

> ## LASSEN'S VOLCANOES
>
> The four types of volcanoes in the world—cinder cone, composite, plug dome, and shield—are all represented in the park. These, along with fumaroles, mud pots, lakes, and bubbling hot springs, create a fascinating, but dangerous, landscape. ⚠ Stay on the trails and railed boardwalks to avoid falling into boiling water or through thin-crusted areas.

Summit Lake. The midpoint between the northern and southern entrances, Summit Lake is a good place to take an afternoon swim. A trail leads around the lakeshore, and several other trails diverge toward a cluster of smaller lakes in the more remote eastern section of the park. ⊠ *Lassen Park Rd., 17½ miles from southwest entrance ranger station.*

EDUCATIONAL OFFERINGS

If you're wondering why fumaroles fume, how lava tubes are formed, or which critter left those tracks beside the creek, check out the array of ranger-led programs. Most groups meet outside Loomis Museum or near Manzanita Lake. To learn what's available, see park bulletin boards.

RANGER PROGRAMS

Bear Necessities. Learn about black bears in this under-an-hour ranger-led talk. ⊠ *Outside Loomis Museum, north entrance to the park* ☎ *530/595–4480* ⊕ *www.nps.gov/lavo* ⊗ *Mid-June–mid-Aug., Wed. at 2.*

Early Birds. Take a morning stroll and learn about the birds of Manzanita Lake. ⊠ *Meet outside the Manzanita Lake Camp Store* ☎ *530/595–4480* ⊕ *www.nps.gov/lavo* ⊗ *Sat. at 8.*

FAMILY **Kids Program.** Junior Rangers, ages 7 to 12, meet for 45 minutes three times a week with rangers. Junior Firefighters gather on Thursday mornings to learn about the role wildfires have in shaping our national parks. Youngsters unable to attend the sessions can earn patches by completing certain requirements. Those under 7 can join the Chipmunk Club and get a sticker after filling out a nature sheet. ⊠ *Outside Loomis Museum, Manzanita Lake Amphitheater, and Kohm Yah-mah-nee Ampitheater* ☎ *530/595–4480* ⊕ *www.nps.gov/lavo.*

Starry Nights. Rangers discuss myths and contemporary theories about galaxies, stars, and planets beneath the night sky in a 45-minute program. ⊠ *Devastated Area parking lot, Lassen Park Rd., 2½ miles north of Summit Lake* ☎ *530/595–4480* ⊕ *www.nps.gov/lavo* ⊗ *Wed. at 9.*

Volcanoes!. Explore the park's geology and volcanic history. ⊠ *Meet outside Loomis Museum* ☎ *530/595–4480* ⊕ *www.nps.gov/lavo* ⊗ *Thurs. and Sun. at 1:30.*

SPORTS AND THE OUTDOORS

Lassen is a rugged adventurer's paradise, but be prepared for sudden changes in the weather: in summer, hot temperatures can make high-altitude hikers woozy and fierce thunderstorms drench the mountains; in winter, blizzard conditions can develop quickly.

A GOOD READ

Lassen Volcanic National Park & Vicinity, by Jeffrey P. Schaffer, is one of the most comprehensive books about the park.

BICYCLING

Biking is allowed on park roads but not park trails. Cyclists under 18 must wear a helmet. Skateboarding and rollerblading are prohibited.

OUTFITTERS

Bikes, Etc. A one-day rental at Bikes, Etc. is $20. ⊠ *2400 Athens Ave., Redding* ☎ *530/246–2453* ⊘ *Mon.–Sat. 9:30–6.*

Bodfish Bicycles & Quiet Mountain Sports. Rent mountain bikes at Bodfish Bicycles & Quiet Mountain Sports for $10 an hour or $33 a day. ⊠ *149 Main St., Chester* ☎ *530/258–2338* ⊕ *www.bodfishbicycles.com* ⊘ *Tues.–Sat. 10–5, Sun. 2–4.*

Redding Sports Ltd. Bike rentals at Redding Sports Ltd. run $40 for 24 hours. ⊠ *950 Hilltop Dr., Redding* ☎ *530/221–7333* ⊕ *www. reddingsportsltd.com* ⊘ *Mon.–Sat. 9–7, Sun. 10–6.*

FISHING

The best place to fish is in Manzanita Lake—but here it's catch and release only. Butte, Snag, and Horseshoe lakes, along with several creeks and streams, are popular fishing destinations within the park. Anglers will need a California freshwater fishing license; you can pick up an application at most sporting-goods stores or download it from the California Department of Fish and Game's Web site (⊕ *www.dfg.ca.gov*). Ask about fishing conditions at bait-and-tackle shops.

OUTFITTERS

Ayoobs Hardware. Stop by Ayoobs Hardware for tackle, bait, and local yore. ⊠ *201 Main St., Chester* ☎ *530/258–2611* ⊘ *Mon.–Sat. 7:30–5, Sun. 8–1.*

The Fishen Hole. The Fishen Hole, a few miles from Shasta Lake, sells bait, tackle, and fishing licenses. You can inquire here about fishing conditions. ⊠ *3844 Shasta Dam Blvd., Shasta Lake* ☎ *530/275–4123* ⊘ *Weekdays 7–5, weekends 6–5.*

The Fly Shop. Famous among fly fishers, the Fly Shop carries tackle and equipment and offers guide services. ⊠ *4140 Churn Creek Rd., Redding* ☎ *530/222–3555* ⊕ *www.flyshop.com* ⊘ *Daily 7:30–6.*

The Sports Nut. Buy fishing and camping gear at the Sports Nut. ⊠ *208 Main St., Chester* ☎ *530/258–3327* ⊘ *May–Dec., Mon.–Sat. 8–5 and Sun. 8–2.*

HIKING

Of the 150 miles of hiking trails within the park, 18 miles are part of the Pacific Crest Trail. Trails vary greatly, some winding through coniferous forest and others across alpine tundra or along waterways.

EASY

FAMILY **Lily Pond Nature Trail.** This 1-mile jaunt loops past a small lake and through a wooded area, ending at a pond that is filled with yellow water lilies in summer. Marked with interpretive signs, this easy trail is a good choice for families with kids. *Easy.* ⊠ *Trailhead across the road from Loomis Museum, Lassen Park Rd., near the northwest entrance ranger station.*

MODERATE

Fodor's Choice **Bumpass Hell Trail.** Boiling springs, steam vents, and mud pots highlight
★ this 3-mile round-trip hike. Expect the loop to take about two hours. During the first mile of the hike there's a gradual climb of 500 feet before a steep 300-foot descent to the basin. You'll encounter rocky patches, so wear hiking boots. ⚠ **Stay on trails and boardwalks near the thermal areas, as what appears to be firm ground may be only a thin crust over scalding mud.** *Moderate.* ⊠ *Trailhead at end of paved parking area off Lassen Park Rd., 6 miles from the southwest entrance ranger station.*

Crumbaugh Lake Hike. A 2.6-mile round-trip hike through meadows and forests to Cold Boiling and Crumbaugh lakes, this excursion is an excellent way to view spring wildflowers. *Moderate.* ⊠ *Trailhead off access road 0.1 mile from Kings Creek picnic area, Lassen Park Rd., 13 miles north of the southwest entrance ranger station.*

Kings Creek Falls Hike. Nature photographers love this 3-mile round-trip hike through forests dotted with wildflowers. A steep 700-foot descent leads to the spectacular falls. It can be slippery in spots, so watch your step. Be in top shape for this hike. *Moderate.* ⊠ *Trailhead on southeast side of Lassen Park Rd., 12 miles from the southwest entrance ranger station.*

Mill Creek Falls. This 2½-hour 3.8-mile round-trip hike through forests and wildflowers takes you to where East Sulphur and Bumpass creeks merge to create the park's highest waterfall. *Moderate.* ⊠ *Trailhead on the east side of the parking lot for the Southwest Walk-In Campground, near amphitheater east of Kohm Yah-mah-nee Visitor Center.*

DIFFICULT

Cinder Cone Trail. Though a little out of the way, this is one of Lassen's most fascinating—and strenuous—trails. It's for more experienced hikers, since the 4-mile round-trip hike to the cone summit includes a steep 800-foot climb over ground that's slippery in parts with loose cinders. Pick up the trail brochure at Loomis Museum or Kohm Yah-mah-nee Visitor Center. *Difficult.* ⊠ *Trailhead at the southwest side of Butte Lake boat ramp; off Hwy. 44, 24 miles east of Manzanita Lake.*

25

Fodor's Choice **Lassen Peak Hike.** This trail winds 2.5 miles to the mountaintop. It's
★ a tough climb—2,000 feet uphill on a steady, steep grade—but the
reward is a spectacular view. At the peak you can see into the rim
and view the entire park (and much of California's far north). Bring
sunscreen, water, and a jacket since it's often windy and much cooler
at the summit. ■ TIP→ A multiyear restoration project means that all
or part of the trail will be open only a few times during the year, so call
ahead. Depending on funding, trail work is expected to be completed
in 2015. *Difficult.* ✉ *Trailhead past a paved parking area off Lassen
Park Rd., 7 miles north of the southwest entrance ranger station.*

HORSEBACK RIDING

Drakesbad Guest Ranch. This in-park property offers guided rides to nonguests who make reservations in advance. Among the options is a two-
hour lope to Devils Kitchen. There's also a five-lake loop for advanced
riders. ✉ *End of Warner Valley Rd., Chester* ☎ *866/999–0914* ⊕ *www.
drakesbad.com* 💲 *$50–$190* ⊙ *Early June–mid-Oct.*

SNOWSHOEING

You can try snowshoeing anywhere in the park. The gentlest places are
in the northern district, while more challenging terrain is in the south.

■ TIP→ Beware of hidden cavities in the snow. Park officials warn that
heated sulphur emissions, especially in the Sulphur Works Area, can
melt out dangerous snow caverns, which may be camouflaged by thin
layers of fresh snow that skiers and snowshoers can easily fall through.

TOURS AND OUTFITTERS

Lassen Mineral Lodge. At Lassen Mineral Lodge snowshoes are $12 a day;
skis and poles are $16. ✉ *Hwy. 36, Mineral* ☎ *530/595–4422* ⊕ *www.
minerallodge.com.*

Redding Sports, Ltd. At this shop snowshoes are $15 per pair per day;
skis, boots, and poles are $20 per day. ✉ *950 Hilltop Dr., Redding*
☎ *530/221–7333* ⊕ *www.reddingsportsltd.com* ⊙ *Mon.–Sat. 9–7,
Sun. 10–6.*

Snowshoe Walks. On weekends from late December through early April,
park rangers lead 2-hour snowshoe walks that explore the park's geology and winter ecology. The hikes require moderate exertion at an
elevation of 7,000 feet; children under 8 are not allowed. If you don't
have snowshoes you can borrow a pair; $1 donation suggested. Walks
are first-come, first-served; meet outside the Kohm Yah-mah-nee Visitor
Center. ✉ *Lassen Park Rd. near the southwest entrance ranger station*
☎ *530/595–4480* ⊕ *www.nps.gov/lavo* 💲 *Free* ⊙ *Late Dec.–early Apr.,
weekends at 1:30.*

WHAT'S NEARBY

NEARBY TOWNS

The tiny logging town of **Chester,** on Highway 36, 30 miles from the southwest park entrance, serves as the commercial center for the entire Lake Almanor area. It's one of the best kicking-off points for the park, but the accommodations and services are limited. **Susanville,** 35 miles east of Chester, is a high-desert town named after a pioneer's daughter. **Red Bluff** maintains a mix of Old West toughness and late 1800s gentility: restored Victorians line the streets west of Main Street, while the downtown looks like a stage set for a Western. This small town is a good place to stock up before heading into the park; it's 52 miles from Lassen's southwest entrance via Highway 36. With a population of 90,755, **Redding** is the largest city in the far northern portion of California; it's the area's main commercial center. Redding is 32 miles north of Red Bluff via Interstate 5 and 50 miles west of the park's northwest entrance via Highway 44. Both Red Bluff and Redding offer the most accommodations and services in the area; each is an hour's drive from the park.

VISITOR INFORMATION

Lake Almanor Area Chamber of Commerce ✉ *289 Main St., Chester* ☎ *530/258-2426* ⊕ *www.lakealmanorarea.com.* **Lassen County Chamber of Commerce** ✉ *75 N. Weatherlow St., Susanville* ☎ *530/257-4323* ⊕ *www.lassencountychamber.org.* **Red Bluff–Tehama County Chamber of Commerce** ✉ *100 Main St., Red Bluff* ☎ *530/527-6220* ⊕ *www.redbluffchamber.com.* **Redding Convention and Visitors Bureau** ✉ *844 Sundial Bridge Dr., Redding* ☎ *800/874-7562, 530/225-4100* ⊕ *www.visitredding.com.*

NEARBY ATTRACTIONS

Fodor's Choice ★ **Lake Shasta Caverns.** Stalagmites, stalactites, flowstone deposits, and crystals entice visitors to the Lake Shasta Caverns. To see this impressive spectacle, you must take the two-hour tour, which includes a catamaran ride across the McCloud arm of Lake Shasta and a bus ride up North Grey Rocks Mountain to the cavern entrance. The caverns are 58°F year-round, making them a cool retreat on a hot summer day. The most awe-inspiring of the limestone rock formations is the glistening Cathedral Room, which appears to be gilded. During peak summer months (June through August), tours depart every half hour; in April, May, and September it's every hour. A gift shop is open from 8 to 4:30. ✉ *20359 Shasta Caverns Rd., off I–5, 17 miles north of Redding, Lakehead* ☎ *530/238-2341, 800/795-2283* ⊕ *lakeshastacaverns.com* 🖅 *$24* ⊙ *June–Aug., tours on the half hour, daily 9–4; Apr., May, and Sept., tours on the hour, daily 9–3; Oct.–Mar., tours at 10, noon, and 2.*

FAMILY
Fodor's Choice ★ **Turtle Bay Exploration Park.** This park features walking trails, an arboretum and botanical gardens, and lots of interactive exhibits for kids, including a gold-panning area and the seasonal butterfly exhibit. The main draw is the stunning **Sundial Bridge,** which links the Sacramento

25

River Trail and the park's arboretum and gardens. Access to the bridge and arboretum is free, but there's a fee for the museum. ✉ *844 Sundial Bridge Dr., off Hwy. 44, Redding* ☎ *530/243–8850* 🌐 *www.turtlebay.org* 🎟 *Museum $14* 🕒 *May.–early Sept., Mon.–Sat. 9–5, Sun. 10–5; early Sept.–Apr., Wed.–Sat. 9–4, Sun. 10–4.*

AREA ACTIVITIES

Whether you want to camp in national forests, wade in creeks, watch dragonflies dip over meadows thick with wildflowers, or stargaze while listening to a chorus of crickets, the great outdoors is the draw here. When you're ready to merge with civilization, the towns near Lassen Volcanic offer shopping, movies, dining, and the ever-popular activity, people-watching.

SPORTS AND THE OUTDOORS

BOATING AND FISHING

Twenty-one types of fish, including rainbow trout and salmon, inhabit Lake Shasta. The lake area also has one of the state's largest nesting populations of bald eagles. Rent boats, Jet Skis, and windsurfing boards at marinas and resorts along the 370-mile shoreline. The Sacramento River and its numerous creeks and tributaries also attract fishing enthusiasts from across the country.

WHERE TO EAT

IN THE PARK

$ CAFÉ 🍴 **Lassen Café & Gifts.** Coffee and hot cocoa, wine and beer, and sandwiches, soup, salad, hot dogs, and chili are on the menu here. [$] *Average main: $9* ✉ *Lassen Park Rd., inside Kohm Yah-mah-nee Visitor Center* ☎ *530/595–4480, 530/529–1512* 🌐 *www.lassenrecreation.com* 🕒 *Closed weekdays mid-Oct.–late May.*

$ CAFÉ 🍴 **Manzanita Lake Camper Store.** Pick up simple prepared foods, groceries, and beverages here. An ATM and pay phone are also available. [$] *Average main: $9* ✉ *Lassen Park Rd., at Manzanita Lake Campground* ☎ *530/335–7557* 🌐 *www.lassenrecreation.com* 🕒 *Closed mid-Oct.–mid May.*

PICNIC AREAS

Kings Creek. Picnic tables are beside a creek in a shady area. There are no amenities except vault toilets. ✉ *Off Lassen Park Rd., 11½ miles north of the southwest entrance ranger station.*

Lake Helen. This site, with picnic tables and vault toilets, has views of several peaks, including Lassen Peak. ✉ *Lassen Park Rd., 6 miles north of southwest entrance ranger station near Bumpass Hell trailhead.*

Manzanita Lake. In addition to the Camper Store, there are picnic tables, a campground, simple cabins, and potable water here and restrooms nearby. ✉ *Lassen Park Rd., near northwest entrance ranger station* 🕒 *Closed mid-Oct.–late May.*

CLOSE UP

Best Campgrounds in Lassen Volcanic

Sites at Lassen's eight campgrounds have wide appeal, from large groups singing around the campfire to solitary hikers seeking a quiet place under the stars. You can drive a vehicle to all campgrounds except the Southwest Walk-In. This is the only campground open year-round; the others usually open in June and close in early fall. Campfires are restricted to fire rings. Lassen has black bears, so be sure to secure your food and garbage properly by using the bear boxes provided at the park's campsites. For more camping information, go to 🌐 *www.recreation.gov.*

Juniper Lake. On the east shore of the park's largest lake, campsites are close to the water in a wooded area. To reach the campgrounds, you have to take a rough gravel road that leads 13 miles north of Chester and enters at the park's southeast corner; trailers not advised. No potable water. ✉ *Chester Juniper Lake Rd, approximately 13 miles north of Hwy. 36. No reservations.*

Manzanita Lake. The largest of Lassen campgrounds accommodates RVs up to 35 feet, and also has a few rustic cabins. Many ranger programs begin here, and a trail nearby leads to a crater that holds Crags Lake. ✉ *Off Lassen Park Rd., 2 miles east of junction of hwys. 44 and 89* ☎ *877/444–6777.*

Southwest Walk-In. This relatively small campground lies within a red fir forest and has views of Brokeoff Peak. Snow camping is allowed in this site, the only park campground open year-round, but from October to June no drinking water is available. ✉ *Near southwest entrance, beside* Kohm Yah-mah-nee Visitor Center. No reservations; open year-round.

Summit Lake North. This completely forested campground has easy access to backcountry trails. You'll likely observe deer grazing. ✉ *Lassen Park Rd., 12 miles south of Manzanita Lake and 17½ miles north of southwest entrance* ☎ *877/444–6777.*

Summit Lake South. Less crowded than its neighbor to the north, this campground has wet meadows where wildflowers grow in the spring. No potable water after mid-September. ✉ *Lassen Park Rd., 12 miles south of Manzanita Lake and 17½ miles north of southwest entrance* ☎ *877/444–6777.*

25

OUTSIDE THE PARK

$$ STEAKHOUSE 🍴 **Green Barn Steakhouse.** You're likely to find cowboys sporting Stetsons and spurs feasting on sizzling porterhouse, baby back ribs, and prime rib at Red Bluff's premier steakhouse. For lighter fare, there's rainbow trout or clam fettuccine. Don't miss the bread pudding with rum sauce. The lounge is usually hopping, especially when there's an event at the nearby rodeo grounds. [$] *Average main: $19* ✉ *5 Chestnut Ave., at Antelope Blvd., Red Bluff* ☎ *530/527–3161* ✍ *Reservations not accepted* 🕒 *Closed Sun.*

$ AMERICAN 🍴 **Kopper Kettle Cafe.** Locals return again and again to this tidy restaurant that serves home-cooked lunches and dinners. Head here for breakfast whenever you've got a hankering for scrambled eggs or biscuits and gravy. [$] *Average main: $14* ✉ *243 Main St., at Myrtle St., Chester* ☎ *530/258–2698.*

$ ✕ **Maria's Mexican Restaurant.** A festive atmosphere prevails at this fam-
MEXICAN   ily-friendly restaurant serving traditional south-of-the-border fare.
FAMILY   This is one of the few restaurants in the area with a full bar, and it's
the perfect place to enjoy a margarita at the end of a long day of
hiking. Lunch specials are a good deal. $ *Average main: $11* ⊠ *159
Main St., Chester* ☎ *530/258–2262* ≋ *Reservations not accepted*
⊘ *Closed Sun.*

WHERE TO STAY

IN THE PARK

$$$$ ⛺ **Drakesbad Guest Ranch.** With propane furnaces and kerosene lamps,
B&B/INN   everything about this century-old property harkens back to a simpler
time. **Pros:** a true back-to-nature experience; great for family adventures. **Cons:** accessible only via a partially paved road leading out of
Chester. $ *Rooms from: $338* ⊠ *End of Warner Valley Rd., Chester*
☎ *866/999–0914* ⊕ *www.drakesbad.com* ⤵ *19 rooms* ⊘ *Closed mid-
Oct.–early June* ⑩ *All meals.*

OUTSIDE THE PARK

$$ ⛺ **Best Western Rose Quartz Inn.** Down the road from Lake Almanor
HOTEL   and close to Lassen Volcanic National Park, this small-town inn bal-
ances traditional decor and up-to-the-minute amenities like Wi-Fi. **Pros:**
near national park; within easy walking distance of town's restau-
rants. **Cons:** standard rooms on the pricey side. $ *Rooms from: $120*
⊠ *306 Main St., Chester* ☎ *530/258–2002, 888/571–4885* ⊕ *www.
bestwesterncalifornia.com/chester-hotels* ⤵ *51 rooms* ⑩ *Breakfast.*

$$ ⛺ **Bidwell House.** Some guest rooms at this 1901 ranch house have
B&B/INN   wood-burning stoves, claw-foot tubs, and antique furnishings; a sepa-
Fodor's Choice   rate cottage with a kitchen sleeps six. **Pros:** unique decor in each room;
★   beautiful wooded setting; near Lake Almanor. **Cons:** not ideal for kids.
$ *Rooms from: $125* ⊠ *1 Main St., Chester* ☎ *530/258–3338* ⊕ *www.
bidwellhouse.com* ⤵ *14 rooms, 2 with shared bath* ⑩ *Breakfast.*

$ ⛺ **High Country Inn.** Rooms are spacious in this colonial-style motel on
HOTEL   the eastern edge of town. **Pros:** great mountain views; heated pool.
Cons: lots of traffic in the area. $ *Rooms from: $84* ⊠ *3015 Riverside
Dr., at Main St., Susanville* ☎ *530/257–3450, 866/454–4566* ⊕ *www.
high-country-inn.com* ⤵ *66 rooms* ⑩ *Breakfast.*

MESA VERDE
NATIONAL PARK

WELCOME TO MESA VERDE

TOP REASONS TO GO

★ **Ancient artifacts:** Mesa Verde is a time capsule for the Ancestral Puebloan culture, which flourished between 700 and 1,400 years ago; more than 4,000 archaeological sites and 3 million objects have been unearthed here.

★ **Bright nights:** Mesa Verde's lack of light and air pollution, along with its high elevation make for spectacular views of the heavens, punctuated by shooting stars, passing satellites, and—if the conditions are right—the Milky Way.

★ **Cliff dwellings:** Built atop the pinyon-covered mesa tops and hidden in the park's valleys is a wondrous collection of 600 ancient dwellings, some carved directly into the sandstone cliff faces.

★ **Geological marvels:** View the unique geology that drew the Ancient Puebloan people to the area: protected desert canyons, massive alcoves in the cliff walls, thick bands of sandstone, continuous seep springs, and soils that could be used for both agriculture and architecture.

1 **Morefield Campground.** Near the park entrance, this large campground (the only one in Mesa Verde) includes a village area with a gas station and store. The best-known sites are farther in, but this one is close to some of the best hiking trails in the park.

2 **Visitor and Research Center.** Turn left at the entrance for the park's new visitor's center. Buy tickets for the popular ranger-led tours here and learn everything you need to know to plan a great trip.

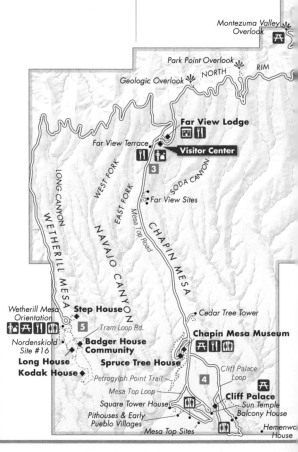

COLORADO

3 **Far View.** Almost an hour's drive (but just 18 miles) from Mesa Verde's entrance, Far View is the park's epicenter, with several restaurants and the park's only overnight lodge. The fork in the road here takes you west toward the sites at Wetherill Mesa or south toward Chapin Mesa.

4 **Chapin Mesa.** Home to the park's most famous cliff dwellings and archaeological sites, the Chapin Mesa area includes the famous 150-room Cliff House dwelling and other man-made and natural wonders. It's also home to the Chapin Mesa Archeological Museum, where you can take a free tour of nearby Spruce Tree House.

GETTING ORIENTED

Perhaps no other area offers as much evidence into the Ancestral Puebloan culture as Mesa Verde National Park. Several thousand archaeological sites have been found, and research is ongoing to discover more. The carved-out homes and assorted artifacts, many of which are displayed at the park's Chapin Mesa Archeological Museum, belonged to ancestors of today's Hopi, Zuni, and Pueblo tribes, among others. Due to the sensitive nature of these sites, hiking in the park is restricted to designated trails, and certain cliff dwellings may be accessed only on ranger-led tours during the peak summer season.

26

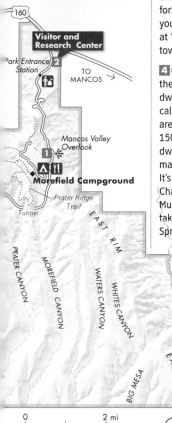

160

Visitor and Research Center

Park Entrance Station **2**

TO MANCOS →

Mancos Valley Overlook

1

Morefield Campground

Prater Ridge Trail

Tunnel

PRATER CANYON

MOREFIELD CANYON

WATERS CANYON

WHITES CANYON

EAST RIM

MANCOS CANYON

BIG MESA

EAST RIM

0 ————— 2 mi
0 ————— 2 km

5 **Wetherill Mesa.** It's less visited than Chapin Mesa, but just as rewarding for visitors. Take the park tram and see Long House, Two Raven House, Kodak House, and Badger House Community.

KEY	
🏠	Ranger Station
▲	Campground
🌲	Picnic Area
🍴	Restaurant
🏨	Lodge
🚶	Trailhead
🚻	Restrooms
⋇	Scenic Viewpoint
⋯⋯	Walking/Hiking Trails

Updated by
Aimee Heckel

Unlike the other national parks, Mesa Verde earned its status from its ancient cultural history rather than its geological treasures. President Theodore Roosevelt established it in 1906 as the first national park to "preserve the works of man," in this case that of the Ancestral Puebloans, also known as the Anasazi. They lived in the region from roughly 550 to 1300; they left behind more than 4,000 archaeological sites spread out over 80 square miles. Their ancient dwellings, set high into the sandstone cliffs, are the heart of the park.

Mesa Verde (which in Spanish means, literally, "Green Table," but translates more accurately to something like "green flat-topped plateau") is much more than an archaeologist's dreamland, however. It's one of those windswept places where man's footprints and nature's paintbrush—some would say chisel—meet. Rising dramatically from the San Juan Basin, the jutting cliffs are cut by a series of complex canyons and covered in several shades of green, from pines in the higher elevations down to sage and other mountain brush on the desert floor. From the tops of the smaller mesas, you can look across to the cliff dwellings in the opposite rock faces. Dwarfed by the towering cliffs, the sand-color dwellings look almost like a natural occurrence in the midst of the desert's harsh beauty.

MESA VERDE PLANNER

WHEN TO GO

The best times to visit the park are late May, early June, and most of September, when the weather is fine but the summer crowds have thinned. Mid-June through August is Mesa Verde's most crowded time. In July and August, lines at the museum and visitor center may last half an hour. Afternoon thunderstorms are common in July and August.

The park gets as much as 100 inches of snow in winter. Snow may fall as late as May and as early as October, but there's rarely enough to hamper travel. In winter, the Wetherill Mesa Road is closed, but you can still get a glimpse of some of the Wetherill Mesa sandstone dwellings, sheltered from the snow in their cliff coves, from the Chapin Mesa area.

AVG. HIGH/LOW TEMPS.

JAN.	FEB.	MAR.	APR.	MAY	JUNE
40/18	44/22	50/26	60/33	70/42	81/51

JULY	AUG.	SEPT.	OCT.	NOV.	DEC.
86/57	84/55	77/49	65/38	50/27	41/20

FESTIVALS AND EVENTS

JUNE **Mountain Ute Bear Dance.** This traditional dance, the local version of a Sadie Hawkins (in which the women choose their dance partners—and the selected men can't refuse), is held in June on the Tawaoc Ute reservation south of Cortez. The event celebrates spring and the legacy of a mythical bear who taught the Ute people her secrets. It's part of a multiday festival that includes music, races, and softball games, and culminates with an hourlong dance that's over when only one couple remains. ☎ 970/565–3751 ⊕ *www.utemountainute.com.*

JULY **Durango Fiesta Days.** A parade, rodeo, barbecue, street dance, cook-offs, and more come to the Durango Fairgrounds on the last weekend of July. ☎ 970/247–8835 ⊕ *www.durangofiestadays.com.*

OCTOBER **Durango Cowboy Poetry Gathering.** A parade and dance accompany art
FAMILY exhibitions, poetry readings, music, and storytelling in this four-day event run by the Durango Cowboy Poetry Gathering, a nonprofit set up to preserve the traditions of the American West. It's held the first weekend in October. ☎ 970/749–2995 ⊕ *www.durangocowboypoetrygathering.org.*

PLANNING YOUR TIME

MESA VERDE IN ONE DAY

For a full experience, take at least one ranger-led tour of a major cliff dwelling site, as well as a few self-guided walks. Arrive early and stop first at the new Visitor and Research Center, where you can purchase tickets for Cliff Palace and Balcony House tours on Chapin Mesa. If it's going to be a hot day, you might want to take an early-morning or late-afternoon bus tour. Drive to the **Chapin Mesa Museum** to watch a 25-minute film introducing you to the area and its history. Just behind the museum is the trailhead for the 0.5-mile-long **Spruce Tree House Trail**, which leads to the best-preserved cliff dwelling in the park. Then drive to **Balcony House** for an hourlong, ranger-led tour.

Have lunch at the Spruce Tree House cafeteria or the Cliff Palace picnic area. Afterward take the ranger-led tour of **Cliff Palace** (one hour). Use the rest of the day to explore the overlooks and trails off the 6-mile loop of **Mesa Top Loop Road.** Or head back to the museum and take **Petroglyph Point Trail** to see a great example of Ancestral Puebloan rock carvings. A leisurely walk along the Mesa Top's **Soda Canyon Overlook Trail** (off Cliff Palace Loop Road) gives you a beautiful bird's-eye view of the canyon below. On the drive back toward the park entrance, be sure to check out the view from **Park Point.**

26

GETTING HERE AND AROUND
AIR TRAVEL
The cities of Durango (36 miles east of the park entrance) and Cortez (11 miles to the west) have airports.

CAR TRAVEL
The park has just one entrance, off U.S. 160, between Cortez and Durango in what's known as the Four Corners area (which spans the intersection of Colorado, New Mexico, Arizona, and Utah). Most of the roads at Mesa Verde involve steep grades and hairpin turns, particularly on Wetherill Mesa. Vehicles over 8,000 pounds or 25 feet are prohibited on this road. Trailers and towed vehicles are prohibited past Morefield Campground. Check the condition of your vehicle's brakes before driving the road to Wetherill Mesa. For the latest road information, tune to 1610 AM, or call ☎ 970/529–4461. Off-road vehicles are prohibited in the park. At less-visited Wetherill Mesa, you must leave you car behind and hike or ride the tram to Long House, Kodak House, and Badger House Community.

PARK ESSENTIALS
PARK FEES AND PERMITS
Admission is $15 per vehicle for a seven-day permit. An annual pass is $30. Ranger-led tours of Cliff Palace, Long House, and Balcony House are $3 per person. You can also take ranger-guided bus tours from the Far View Lodge, which last between 3½ and 4 hours and cost $42–$48 ($37 for kids; under 5 free). Backcountry hiking and fishing are not permitted at Mesa Verde.

PARK HOURS
Mesa Verde's facilities each operate on their own schedule, but most are open daily, from Memorial Day through Labor Day, between about 8 am and sunset. The rest of the year, they open at 9. In winter, the Spruce Tree House is open only to offer a few scheduled tours each day. Wetherill Mesa (and all of the sites it services) is open only from Memorial Day through Labor Day. Far View Visitor Center, Far View Terrace, and Far View Lodge are open between April and October. Morefield Campground and the sites nearby are open from mid-May through mid-October.

CELL-PHONE RECEPTION AND INTERNET
Officially, there is no cell service in the park, although you might get a signal at the Morefield Campground area, which is the closest to the neighboring towns of Cortez and Mancos. Public telephones can be found at all the major visitor areas (Morefield, Far View, and Spruce Tree). You can get free Wi-Fi in the lobby of Far View Lodge and at the Morefield Campground store.

RESTAURANTS
Dining options in Mesa Verde are limited inside the park, but comparatively plentiful and varied if you're staying in Cortez or Durango. In surrounding communities, Southwestern restaurants and steakhouses are common options.

Prices in the reviews are the average cost of a main course at dinner or, if dinner isn't served, at lunch.

The Cliff Palace at Mesa Verde National Park is lit up for Christmas.

HOTELS

All 150 rooms of the park's Far View Lodge, open April through October, fill up quickly—so reservations are recommended, especially if you plan to visit on a weekend in summer. Options in the surrounding area include chain hotels, cabins, and bed-and-breakfast inns. Durango in particular has a number of hotels in fine old buildings reminiscent of the Old West.

Prices in the reviews are the lowest cost of a standard double room in high season. For expanded hotel reviews, facilities, and current deals, visit Fodors.com.

TOURS

BUS TOURS

FAMILY **ARAMARK Tours.** If you want a well-rounded visit to Mesa Verde's most popular sites, consider a group tour. The park concessionaire provides all-day and half-day guided tours of the Chapin Mesa and Far View sites, departing in buses from either Morefield Campground or Far View Lodge. Tours are led by Aramark guides or park rangers, who share information about the park's history, geology, and excavation processes. Cold water is provided, but you'll need to bring your own snacks. Buy tickets at Far View Lodge, Far View Terrace, the Morefield Campground, or online. Tours sell out, so reserve in advance. ☒ *1 Navajo Hill* ☎ *970/529–4422, 800/449–2288* ⊕ *www.visitmesaverde. com* ✉ *$42–$48* ⊙ *Mid-Apr.–mid-Oct., daily, departs at 8 and 1.*

VISITOR INFORMATION

PARK CONTACT INFORMATION

Mesa Verde National Park ☏ 970/529–4465 ⊕ *www.nps.gov/meve.*

VISITOR CENTERS

The Visitor and Research Center and the Chapin Mesa Archeological Museum are both open from late May to early November.

Chapin Mesa Archeological Museum. This is an excellent first stop for an introduction to Ancestral Puebloan culture, as well as the area's development into a national park. Exhibits showcase original textiles and other artifacts, and a theater plays an informative film every 30 minutes. Rangers are available to answer your questions, and there's also a sign-in sheet for hiking trails. The museum sits at the south end of the park entrance road and overlooks Spruce Tree House. Nearby, you'll find park headquarters, a gift shop, a post office, a snack bar, and bathrooms. ⊠ *Park entrance road, 5 miles south of Far View Visitor Center, 20 miles from park entrance* ☏ *970/529–4465* ⊕ *www.nps.gov/meve/ planyourvisit/museum.htm* ☐ *Free* ☉ *Jan.–early Mar., daily 9–4:30; early Mar.–early Apr., daily 9-5; early Apr.–mid-Oct., daily 8–6:30; mid-Oct.–early Nov., daily 8–5; and early Nov.–late Dec., daily 9–5.*

Mesa Verde Visitor and Research Center. Mesa Verde's new visitor center is the place to go to sign up for tours and get the information you need to plan a successful trip. ■TIP➔ **This is the only place in the park to buy tickets for the Cliff Palace, Balcony House, and Long House ranger-led tours.** The sleek, energy-efficient research center is filled with more than 3 million artifacts and archives. The center features indoor and outdoor exhibits, a gift shop, picnic tables, and a museum. A selection of books, maps, and videos on the history of the park are available, and rangers are on hand to answer questions and explain the history of the Ancestral Puebloans. ⊠ *Park entrance on the left* ☏ *970/529–4465* ⊕ *www.nps. gov/meve/planyourvisit/meve_vc.htm* ☉ *Jan.–early Apr., daily 8:30–4:30; early Apr.–late May, daily 8–5; late May–early Sept., daily 7:30–7; early Sept.–early Nov., daily 8–5; early Nov.–late Dec., daily 8:30–4:30.*

EXPLORING

SCENIC DRIVES

Mesa Top Loop Road. This 6-mile drive skirts the scenic rim of Chapin Mesa and takes you to several overlooks and short, paved trails. You'll get great views of Sun Temple and Square Tower, as well as Cliff Palace, Sunset House, and several other cliff dwellings visible from the Sun Point Overlook. ☉ *Daily 8 am–sunset.*

Park Entrance Road. The main park road, also known as SH 10, leads you from the entrance off U.S. 160 to the Far View complex, 15 miles from the park entrance. As a break from the switchbacks, you can stop at a couple of pretty overlooks along the way, but hold out for Park Point, which, at the mesa's highest elevation (8,572 feet), gives you unobstructed 360-degree views. Note that trailers and towed vehicles are not permitted beyond Morefield Campground.

Plants and Wildlife in Mesa Verde

Mesa Verde is home to 640 species of plants, including a number of native plants found nowhere else. Its lower elevations feature many varieties of shrubs, including rabbitbrush and sagebrush. Higher up, you'll find mountain mahogany, yucca, pinyon, juniper, and Douglas fir. During warmer months, brightly colored blossoms, like the yellow perky Sue, blue lupines, and bright-red Indian paintbrushes, are scattered throughout the park.

The park is also home to a variety of migratory and resident animals, including 74 species of mammals. Drive slowly along the park's roads; mule deer are everywhere. You may spot wild turkeys, and black bear encounters are not unheard of on the hiking trails. Bobcats, coyotes, and mountain lions are also around, but they are seen less frequently. About 200 species of birds, including threatened Mexican spotted owls,

red-tailed hawks, golden eagles, and noisy ravens, also live here. On the ground, you should keep your eyes and ears open for lizards and snakes, including the poisonous—but shy— prairie rattlesnake. As a general rule, animals are most active in the early morning and at dusk.

Many areas of the park have had extensive fire damage over the years. In fact, wildfires here have been so destructive they are given names, just like hurricanes. For example, the Bircher Fire in 2000 consumed nearly 20,000 acres of brush and forest, much of it covering the eastern half of the park. It will take several centuries for the woodland there to look as verdant as the area atop Chapin Mesa, which escaped the fire. But in the meantime, you'll have a chance to glimpse nature's powerful rejuvenating processes in action; the landscape in the fire-ravaged sections of the park is already filling in with vegetation.

26

Wetherill Mesa Road. This 12-mile mountain road, stretching from the Far View Visitor Center to the Wetherill Mesa, has sharp curves and steep grades (and is restricted to vehicles less than 25 feet long and 8,000 pounds). It's open from Memorial Day to Labor Day. Roadside pull-outs offer unobstructed views of the Four Corners region. At the end of the road, you can access Step House and Long House, plus the park's free tram service, which takes you to the Badger House. ⊙ *Memorial Day to Labor Day, daily 8–4:30.*

HISTORIC SITES

Badger House Community. A self-guided walk along paved and gravel trails takes you through a group of four mesa-top dwellings. The community, which covers nearly 7 acres, dates back to the year 650, the Basketmaker Period, and includes a primitive, semi-subterranean pit house and what's left of a multistoried stone pueblo. Allow about 45 minutes to see the sites. The trail is 2.4 miles round-trip; if you take the free tram from the Wetherill kiosk, you'll save a mile of walking. ⊠ *Wetherill Mesa Rd., 12 miles from Far View Visitor Center* ⊕ *www. nps.gov/meve/historyculture/mt_badger_house.htm* ⊠ *Free* ⊙ *Memorial Day–Labor Day, daily 9:30–4:30.*

Balcony House. The stonework of this 40-room cliff dwelling, which housed about 40 or 50 people, is impressive, but you're likely to be even more awed by the skill it must have taken to reach this place. Perched in a sandstone cove 600 feet above the floor of Soda Canyon, Balcony House seems almost suspended in space. Even with the aid of modern passageways and a partially paved trail, today's visitors must climb a 32-foot ladder and crawl through a 12-foot-long tunnel to enter. Surrounding the house is a courtyard with a parapet wall and the intact balcony for which the house is named. A favorite with kids, the dwelling is accessible only on a ranger-led tour. Purchase ticket at the Visitor and Research Center, Morefield Ranger Station, or the Colorado Welcome Center in Cortez. ⊠ *Cliff Palace/Balcony House Rd., 10 miles south of Far View Visitor Center, Cliff Palace Loop* ▦ *$3* ☉ *Apr.–mid-Oct., daily 9–5.*

> **GOOD READS**
>
> ■ *Mesa Verde National Park: Shadows of the Centuries,* by Duane A. Smith, discusses the history and current issues facing the park.
>
> ■ *Ancient Peoples of the American Southwest,* by Stephen Plog, is an archaeologist's account of the Ancestral Puebloans (also known as the Anasazi) and two other cultures.
>
> ■ *Mesa Verde: Ancient Architecture,* by Jesse Walter Fewkes, tells the stories behind the park's dwellings.

Fodor's Choice ★ **Cliff Palace.** This was the first major Mesa Verde dwelling seen by cowboys Charlie Mason and Richard Wetherill in 1888. It is also the largest, containing about 150 rooms and 23 kivas on three levels. Getting there involves a steep downhill hike and three ladders. Purchase tickets at the Visitor and Research Center, Morefield Ranger Station, and at the Colorado Welcome Center in Cortez. From Memorial Day through Labor Day, rangers in historical costumes lead a 90-minute Twilight Tour of the site. These tours run daily just before twilight; tickets are available only at the Visitor and Research Center. ⊠ *Cliff Palace Overlook, about 2½ miles south of Chapin Mesa Archeological Museum* ▦ *Basic tour $3; Twilight tour $10* ☉ *Late May–early Sept., daily 9–6; early Sept.–mid-Oct., daily 9–5; late Oct.–early Nov., daily 9–4.*

FAMILY **Far View Sites Complex.** This was probably one of the most densely populated areas in Mesa Verde, comprising as many as 50 villages in a ½-square-mile area at the top of Chapin Mesa. Most of the sites here were built between 900 and 1300. Begin the self-guided tour at the interpretive panels in the parking lot, then proceed down a 0.5-mile, level trail. ⊠ *Park entrance road, near the Chapin Mesa area* ▦ *Free* ☉ *Daily 8 am–sunset.*

Long House. This Wetherill Mesa cliff dwelling is the second largest in Mesa Verde. It is believed that about 150 people lived in Long House, so named because of the size of its cliff alcove. The spring at the back of the cave is still active today. The in-depth, ranger-led tour begins a short distance from the parking lot and takes about 90 minutes. Even though you will hike less than a mile, be prepared to climb two 15-foot ladders. Buy your ticket at the Visitor and Research Center, Morefield Ranger Station, or at the Colorado Welcome Center in Cortez. ⊠ *On Wetherill Mesa, 29 miles past the Visitor Center, near mile marker 15, Tram Route* ⧁ *Tours $3* ⊙ *Memorial Day–Labor Day, daily 10–4.*

FAMILY **Spruce Tree House.** This 138-room complex is the best-preserved site in the park, and the rooms and ceremonial chambers are more accessible to visitors than those in other sites. Here you can actually enter a kiva, via a short ladder that goes underground, just as the original inhabitants did. It's a great place for kids to explore, but because of its location in the heart of the Chapin Mesa area, Spruce Tree House can resemble a crowded playground during busy periods. Tours are self-guided from spring to fall (allow 45 minutes to an hour), but a park ranger is on site to answer questions. Sign up for ranger-guided tours in the winter. The trail leading to Spruce Tree House starts behind the museum and leads you 100 feet down into the canyon. You may find yourself breathing hard by the time you make it back up to the parking lot. ⊠ *At the Chapin Mesa Archeological Museum, 5 miles south of Far View Visitor Center* ⧁ *Free* ⊙ *Memorial Day–Labor Day, daily 8:30–6:30; early Sept.–mid-Oct., daily 9–6:30; mid-Oct.–early Nov., daily 9–5; early Nov.–Memorial day, open only during free guided tours at 10, 1, and 3:30.*

Step House. So named because of a crumbling prehistoric stairway leading up from the dwelling, Step House is reached via a paved (but steep) trail that's 0.75 mile long. The house is unique in that it shows clear evidence of two separate occupations: the first around 626, the second a full 600 years later. The self-guided tour takes about 45 minutes. ⊠ *Wetherill Mesa Rd., 12 miles from Far View Visitor Center* ⊕ *www. nps.gov/meve/historyculture/cd_step_house.htm* ⧁ *Free* ⊙ *Memorial Day–Labor Day, daily 10–5.*

Sun Temple. Although researchers assume it was probably a ceremonial structure, they're unsure of the exact purpose of this complex, which has no doors or windows in most of its chambers. Because the building was not quite half-finished when it was left in 1276, some researchers surmise it might have been constructed to stave off whatever disaster caused its builders—and the other inhabitants of Mesa Verde—to leave. ⊠ *Mesa Top Loop Rd., about 2 miles south of Chapin Mesa Archeological Museum* ⊕ *www.nps.gov/meve/historyculture/mt_sun_temple.htm* ⧁ *Free* ⊙ *Daily 8–sunset.*

Pit Houses and Early Pueblo Villages. Three dwellings, built on top of each other from 700 to 950, at first look like a mass of jumbled walls, but an informational panel helps identify the dwellings—and the stories behind them are fascinating. The 325-foot trail from the walking area is paved, wheelchair accessible, and near a restroom. ⊠ *Mesa Top Loop Rd., about 2½ miles south of Chapin Mesa Archeological Museum* ⧁ *Free* ⊙ *Daily 8 am–sunset.*

26

SCENIC STOPS

Cedar Tree Tower. A self-guided tour takes you to, but not through, a tower and kiva built between AD 1100 and 1300 and connected by a tunnel. The tower-and-kiva combinations in the park are thought to have been either religious structures or signal towers. ⊠ *Near the four-way intersection on Chapin Mesa; park entrance road, 1½ miles north of Chapin Mesa Archeological Museum* 🖃 *Free.*

Kodak House Overlook. Get an impressive view into the 60-room Kodak House and its several small kivas from here, only accessible via the tram. The house, closed to the public, was named for a Swedish researcher who absentmindedly left his Kodak camera behind here in 1891. ⊠ *Wetherill Mesa Rd., about 0.2 mile south of kiosk (tram stop)* ☉ *Memorial Day–Labor Day, daily 10–5.*

Soda Canyon Overlook. Get your best view of Balcony House here. You can also read interpretive panels about the site and the surrounding canyon geology. ⊠ *Cliff Palace Loop Rd., about 1 mile north of Balcony House parking area.*

EDUCATIONAL OFFERINGS

RANGER PROGRAMS

FAMILY **Evening Ranger Campfire Program.** Every night in summer at the Morefield Campground Amphitheater, park rangers present a different 45- to 60-minute program on topics such as stargazing, history, wildlife, and archaeology. Several evenings a week, you can also find free, hourlong ranger talks in the Far View Lodge library. ⊠ *Morefield Campground Amphitheater, 4 miles south of park entrance* 🕿 *970/529–4465* 🖃 *Free* ☉ *Memorial Day–Labor Day, daily at 9. Lodge programs start at 7.*

Far View Sites Walk. This one-hour, self-guided walk winds through the mesa top sites in the Far View area. ⊠ *Far View House, 1 mile south of Far View Visitor Center* 🕿 *970/529–4465* 🖃 *Free* ☉ *Memorial Day–Labor Day, weekdays at 4; Labor Day–mid-Oct., Mon. at 4.*

FAMILY **Junior Ranger Program.** Children ages 4 through 12 can earn a certificate and badge for successfully completing at least four activities in the park's Junior Ranger booklet (available at the park or online). ⊠ *Mesa Verde Visitor and Research Center or Chapin Mesa Archeological Museum* 🕿 *970/529–4465* ⊕ *www.nps.gov/meve/forkids/beajuniorranger.htm.*

Ranger-Led Tours. The cliff dwellings known as Balcony House, Cliff Palace, and Long House can be explored only on ranger-led tours; the first two last about an hour, the third is 90 minutes. Buy tickets at the Visitor and Research Center. These are active tours and may not be suitable for children; each requires climbing ladders without handrails and squeezing through tight spaces. Be sure to bring water and sunscreen. 🕿 *970/529–4465* ⊕ *www.nps.gov/meve/planyourvisit/visitcliffdwelling.htm* 🖃 *$3* ☉ *Cliff Palace: early Apr.–early Nov. Balcony House: late Apr.–early Oct. Long House: Memorial Day–Labor Day. See website for dates and times.*

SPORTS AND THE OUTDOORS

At Mesa Verde, outdoor activities are restricted, due to the fragile nature of the archaeological treasures here. Hiking (allowed on marked trails only) is the best option, especially as a way to view some of the Ancestral Puebloan dwellings.

BIRD-WATCHING

Turkey vultures soar between April and October, and large flocks of ravens hang around all summer. Among the park's other large birds are red-tailed hawks, great horned owls, and a few golden eagles. The Steller's jay (the male looks like a blue jay with a dark hat on) frequently pierces the pinyon-juniper forest with its cries, and hummingbirds dart from flower to flower in the summer and fall. Any visit to cliff dwellings late in the day will include frolicking white-throated swifts, which make their home in rock crevices overhead. Pick up a copy of the park's "Checklist of the Birds" brochure or visit the National Park Service's website (⊕ *www.nps.gov/meve/planyourvisit/birdwatching.htm*) for a detailed listing of the feathered inhabitants here.

HIKING

A handful of trails lead beyond Mesa Verde's most visited sites and offer more solitude than the often-crowded cliff dwellings. The best canyon vistas can be reached if you're willing to huff and puff your way through elevation changes and switchbacks. Carry more water than you think you'll need, wear sunscreen, and bring rain gear—cloudbursts can come seemingly out of nowhere. Certain trails are open seasonally, so check with a ranger before heading out. No backcountry hiking is permitted in Mesa Verde, and pets are prohibited.

EASY

FAMILY **Farming Terrace Trail.** This 30-minute, 0.5-mile loop begins and ends on the spur road to Cedar Tree Tower, about 1 mile north of the Chapin Mesa area. It meanders through a series of check dams, which the Ancestral Puebloans built to create farming terraces. *Easy.* ⊠ *Park entrance road, 4 miles south of Far View Visitor Center.*

Knife Edge Trail. Perfect for a sunset stroll, this easy 2-mile, round-trip walk around the north rim of the park leads to an overlook of the Montezuma Valley. If you stop at all the flora identification points that the trail guide pamphlet suggests, the hike should take about 1½ to 2 hours. The patches of asphalt you're likely to spot along the way are leftovers from old Knife Edge Road, built in 1914 as the main entryway into the park. *Easy.* ⊠ *Morefield Campground, 4 miles from park entrance.*

FAMILY **Soda Canyon Overlook Trail.** One of the easiest and most rewarding hikes in the park, this little trail travels 1.5 miles round-trip through the forest on almost completely level ground. The overlook is an excellent point from which to photograph the Chapin Mesa–area cliff dwellings. *Easy.* ⊠ *Cliff Palace Loop Rd., about 1 mile north of Balcony House parking area.*

MODERATE

Petroglyph Point Trail. Scramble along a narrow canyon wall to reach the largest and best-known petroglyphs in Mesa Verde. Older literature occasionally refers to the destination of this 2.4-mile loop hike as "Pictograph Point," but that's a misnomer. Pictographs are painted onto the rock, and petroglyphs are carved into it. If you pose for a photo just right, you can manage to block out the gigantic "don't touch" sign next to the rock art. A map—available at any ranger station—points out three dozen points of interest along the trail. The trail is open only when Spruce Tree House is open; check with a ranger to verify times. *Moderate.* ⊠ *Spruce Tree House, next to Chapin Mesa Archeological Museum* ⊙ *Contact ranger for hours.*

Spruce Canyon Trail. While Petroglyph Point Trail takes you along the side of the canyon, this trail ventures down into its depths. It's only 2.4 miles long, but you descend about 600 feet in elevation. Remember to save your strength; what goes down must come up again. Access to the trail is limited to times when Spruce Tree House is open; check with a ranger beforehand. *Moderate.* ⊠ *Spruce Tree House, next to Chapin Mesa Archeological Museum* ⊙ *Check with ranger for times; registration required.*

DIFFICULT

Prater Ridge Trail. This 7.8-mile round-trip loop, which starts and finishes at Morefield Campground, is the longest hike you can take inside the park. It provides fine views of Morefield Canyon to the south and the San Juan Mountains to the north. About halfway through the hike, you'll see a cut-off trail that you can take, which shortens the trip to 5 miles. *Difficult.* ⊠ *West end of Morefield Campground, 4 miles from park entrance.*

STARGAZING

There are no large cities in the Four Corners area, so there is little artificial light to detract from the stars in the night sky. Far View Lodge and Morefield Campground are great for sky watching.

SHOPPING

Chapin Mesa Archeological Museum Shop. Books and videos are the primary offering here, with more than 400 titles on Ancestral Puebloan and southwestern topics. You can also find a selection of touristy T-shirts and hats. ⊠ *Spruce Tree Terrace, near Chapin Mesa Archeological Museum, 5 miles from Far View Visitor Center* ☎ *970/529–4445.*

Far View Terrace Shop. In the same building as the Far View Terrace Cafe, this is the largest gift shop in the park, with gifts, souvenirs, American Indian art, toys, and T-shirts galore. ⊠ *Mesa Top Loop Rd., 15 miles south of park entrance* ☎ *970/529–4421, 800/449–2288.*

WHAT'S NEARBY

NEARBY TOWNS

A onetime market center for cattle and crops, **Cortez,** 11 miles west of the park, is now the largest gateway town to Mesa Verde and a base for tourists visiting the Four Corners region. You can still see a rodeo here at least once a year. **Dolores,** steeped in a rich railroad history, is on the Dolores River, 19 miles north of Mesa Verde. Near both the San Juan National Forest and McPhee Reservoir, Dolores is a favorite of outdoor enthusiasts. East of Mesa Verde by 36 miles, **Durango,** the region's main hub, comes complete with a variety of restaurants and hotels, shopping, and outdoor equipment shops. Durango became a town in 1881 when the Denver and Rio Grande Railroad pushed its tracks across the neighboring San Juan Mountains.

VISITOR INFORMATION

Dolores Chamber of Commerce ⊠ *201 Railroad Ave., Dolores* ☎ *970/882–4018, 800/807–4712* ⊕ *www.doloreschamber.com* ☉ *May–late Oct., daily 9–4; Nov.–May, daily noon–4.* **Durango Welcome Center** ⊠ *802 Main Ave., Durango* ☎ *970/247–3500, 888/631–7011* ⊕ *www.durango.org.* **Mesa Verde Visitor Information Bureau** ⊠ *928 E. Main St., Cortez* ☎ *970/565–8227, 800/253–1616* ⊕ *www.swcolo.org.*

NEARBY ATTRACTIONS

FAMILY **Anasazi Heritage Center.** Operated by the Federal Bureau of Land Management, this museum houses artifacts culled from more than 1,500 excavations in the region. The Anasazi Heritage Center has permanent exhibits showcasing the archaeology, history, and culture of the Ancestral Puebloans and other indigenous peoples. There are also two 12th-century pueblos, named after the Spanish friars Dominguez and Escalante, within walking distance. A full-scale replica of an ancient pit-house dwelling illustrates how the people lived around AD 850. It also houses the visitors center and jumping-off point for the **Canyons of the Ancients National Monument.** ⊠ *27501 State Hwy. 184, 3 miles west of Dolores* ☎ *970/882–5600* ⊕ *www.blm.gov/co/st/en/fo/ahc.html* ⊡ *$3* ☉ *Mar.–Oct., daily 9–5; Nov.–Feb., daily 10–4.*

Crow Canyon Archaeological Center. Professionals, students, and any would-be Indiana Joneses come here to learn about ancient relics. Among the more popular offerings of the center's educational programs are weeklong "Archaeology Adventures," which allow visitors to work alongside professional archaeologists as they search for pottery, stone tools, and other artifacts at excavation sites throughout the area, then clean and catalog their finds in the lab. The program includes a special guided tour of Mesa Verde National Park. ⊠ *23390 County Rd. K, Cortez* ☎ *970/565–8975, 800/422–8975* ⊕ *www.crowcanyon.org.*

Ute Mountain Tribal Park. The only way to see this spectacular 125,000-acre park, located inside the Ute reservation, is by taking a guided tour. Expert tribal guides lead strenuous day-long hikes into this dazzling

Marketing the Four Corners Monument

There's no view to speak of at Four Corners Monument, but it's a popular photo op nonetheless. Set on Navajo land, about one usually dusty mile off U.S. 60, the monument is the only place in the nation where the borders of four states meet. The first permanent marker, a simple "look-what's-here," was erected at the intersection of Colorado, Utah, New Mexico, and Arizona in 1912. As long as there have been cameras, people have gone out of their way just to stand in such a way as to be in four states at once.

The monument was refurbished in 1992, and a larger marker, consisting of a bronze disk embedded in granite, was put in place. Though bigger and more ornate than the first marker, it still seems far too unassuming to have attracted the bazaar that surrounds it. In response to a ready market of tourists and trinket hounds, the main drive is rimmed with plywood booths hawking Ute, Navajo, Apache, and other American Indian artwork, crafts, artifacts, and rugs. You can also buy fry bread and corn on the cob. It's all genuine, but the opportunistic nature of the site—it costs $3 per person just to enter (cash only; kids 6 and under are free)—detracts from what began as the simple fascination of standing at the very point where four southwestern states meet.

No major cities are nearby. Cortez, Colorado, is 40 miles away on U.S. 60; tiny Teec Nos Pos, Arizona, is 6 miles away; Shiprock, New Mexico, is about 27 miles to the east; and Bluff, Utah, is 53 miles distant.

The Navajo Nation Parks and Recreation Department administers the Four Corners Monument, along with numerous natural sites and thousands of square miles of pristine wilderness. The site is open 8–7 May through September and 8–5 October through April. For more information, email ✑ *nslim@navajonationparks.org.*

26

repository of Ancestral Puebloan ruins, including beautifully preserved cliff dwellings, pictographs, and petroglyphs. There are also less-demanding half-day tours, as well as private and custom tour options. Tours start at the park's visitor center, off U.S. 160. ⊠ *U.S. 160/491* ☎ *970/565–3751, 800/847–5485.*

AREA ACTIVITIES

SPORTS AND THE OUTDOORS
FISHING
McPhee Reservoir. In 1968, state officials approved the construction of an irrigation dam across the Dolores River, forming the McPhee Reservoir, the second largest in the state. It draws anglers looking to bag a variety of warm- and cold-water fish along its 50 miles of shoreline, which is surrounded by spectacular specimens of juniper and sage as well as large stands of pinyon pine. There's a boat ramp and a generous fish-cleaning station. The area also has camping, hiking, and a relatively easy mountain-bike trail, and the mesa offers panoramic views of the surrounding San Juan National Forest. ⊠ *Forest Service Rd. 271, off State Hwy. 184, about 9 miles northwest of Dolores.*

Duranglers. In business since 1983, Duranglers sells rods, reels, flies, and other equipment, gives fly-fishing lessons, and runs guided trips to top trout-fishing spots in the area, including the San Juan, Animas, Dolores, Piedras, and Los Pinos rivers. ⊠ *923 Main Ave., Durango* ☎ *970/385–4081* ⊕ *www.duranglers.com.*

RAFTING

Beginning in the San Juan Mountains of southwestern Colorado, the Dolores River runs north for more than 150 miles before joining the Colorado River near Moab, Utah. This is one of those rivers that tends to flow madly in spring and diminish considerably by midsummer, and for that reason rafting trips are usually run in April and May, and occasionally early June.

Durango Rivertrippers. This outfitter runs two- and four-hour trips down the Animas River. You can up your adrenaline output by swapping the raft for an inflatable kayak on any of the Animas River trips. Or ask about zipline and rafting packages, tube rentals, and ATV tours. ⊠ *720 Main Ave., Durango* ☎ *970/259–0289* ⊕ *www. durangorivertrippers.com.*

HIKING

Animas View Overlook Trail. If you're pressed for time (but still want spectacular views), try the 0.7-mile Animas View Overlook Trail. It takes you past signs explaining local geology, flora, and fauna before bringing you to a precipice with an unparallelled view of the valley and the surrounding Needle Mountains. It's the only wheelchair-accessible trail in the area. ⊠ *Trailhead at Forest Rd. 171, milepost 8, Durango.*

Fodor's Choice
★ **Colorado Trail.** Starting a few miles northwest of Durango, the Colorado Trail covers about 500 miles on its way to Denver. You're not obliged to go that far, of course. Just a few miles in and out will give you a taste of this epic trail, which winds through mountain ranges and high passes and some of the most amazing mountain scenery around. ⊠ *Trailhead off County Rd. 204, Durango* ⊕ *www.coloradotrail.org.*

ARTS AND ENTERTAINMENT

Cortez Cultural Center. The Cortez Cultural Center has exhibits on regional artists and Ancestral Puebloan culture, as well as events and fairs. Summer evening programs include Native American dances, sand painting, rug weaving, pottery-making demonstrations, theater, and storytelling. ⊠ *25 N. Market St., Cortez* ☎ *970/565–1151* ⊕ *www. cortezculturalcenter.org* ⊠ *Free* ☉ *May–Sept., daily 10–10; Sept. and May, daily 10–6; Oct.–Apr., daily 10–5.*

ART GALLERIES

Toh-Atin Gallery. Recognized as one of the region's best Native American galleries, Toh-Atin specializes in Navajo rugs and weavings. There's also a wide range of paintings and prints, pottery, baskets, and jewelry made by the artisans of many Southwestern tribes. ⊠ *145 W. 9th St., Durango* ☎ *970/247–8277, 800/525–0384* ⊕ *www.toh-atin.com.*

NIGHTLIFE

Diamond Belle Saloon. Awash in flocked wallpaper and lace, the Diamond Belle Saloon is dominated by a gilt-and-mahogany bar. With its primo location—on the ground floor of the historic Strater Hotel—and a staff of ragtime piano players and waitresses dressed as saloon girls, the Diamond Belle can really pack them in. Be sure to try the espresso martini; if you're hungry, try the much-hailed Diamond burger. ✉ *699 Main Ave., Durango* ☎ *970/247–4431* 🌐 *www.diamondbelle.com.*

SHOPPING

Notah Dineh Trading Company and Museum. This store specializing in Navajo rugs has the largest collection in the area. There are also handmade baskets, beadwork, pottery, and jewelry. If you stop in the free museum you can see relics of the Old West. ✉ *345 W. Main St.* ☎ *800/444–2024* 🌐 *www.notahdineh.com.*

SCENIC DRIVES

TRAIN RIDE

FAMILY Fodor's Choice ★ **Durango & Silverton Narrow Gauge Railroad.** The most entertaining way to relive the halcyon days of the Old West is to take a ride on the Durango & Silverton Narrow Gauge Railroad, a nine-hour round-trip journey along the 45-mile railway to Silverton. You'll travel in comfort in lovingly restored coaches or in the open-air cars called gondolas as you listen to the train's shrill whistle as it chugs along. On the way, you get a good look at the Animas Valley, which in some parts is broad and green and in others narrow and rimmed with rock. The train runs daily from early May to late October. A shorter excursion—to Cascade Canyon, 26 miles away—in heated coaches is available in winter. The train departs from the Durango Depot, constructed in 1882 and beautifully restored. Next door is the Durango & Silverton Narrow Gauge Railroad Museum. ✉ *479 Main Ave., Durango* ☎ *970/247–2733, 888/872–4607* 🌐 *www.durangotrain.com* 🎫 *$85–$189.*

WHERE TO EAT

IN THE PARK

$ AMERICAN 🍴 **Far View Terrace Cafe.** This full-service cafeteria offers great views, but it's nothing fancy. Grab a simple coffee here or head across the dining room to Mesa Mocha for a latte. Order an omelet cooked to order as you watch, or select from four different types of berries and three types of yogurts at the yogurt bar. If you're in a hurry to hit the park trails, you can take away a Grab & Go lunch. Dinner options include a Navajo taco piled high with all the fixings. [$] *Average main: $8* ✉ *Across from Far View Visitor Center* ☎ *970/529–4444* 🌐 *www.visitmesaverde.com/dining/far-view-terrace-cafe.aspx* 🕒 *Closed late Oct.–late Apr.*

26

$ ✕ **Knife's Edge Cafe.** Located in the Morefield Campground, this simple
CAFÉ   restaurant in a covered outdoor terrace with picnic tables serves a hearty
FAMILY   all-you-can-eat pancake breakfast with sausage every morning. Coffee
and beverages are also available. $ *Average main: $6 ⊠ 4 miles south
of park entrance ☎ 970/565–2133 ⊙ Closed mid–Oct.–early May. No
lunch or dinner.*

$$$ ✕ **Metate Room.** The park's rugged terrain contrasts with this relaxing
AMERICAN   space just off the lobby of the Far View Lodge. The well-regarded
Fodor's Choice   dining room is candlelighted, but the atmosphere remains casual. A
★   wall of windows affords wonderful Mesa Verde vistas. The menu is
based on regional heritage foods, including corn, beans, and squash
(all staples for the Ancestral Puebloans). Many entrées are unique, such
as cinnamon-chili pork tenderloin or regional quail with prickly-pear
red-pepper jam. Every table gets mesa bread and black bean hummus
for starters. There's an array of local wines (try Cortez's own Guy
Drew) and cocktails with kitschy names, like the "Long House Lem-
onade." Gluten-free and vegan options are available. $ *Average main:
$25 ⊠ Far View Lodge, across from Far View Visitor Center, 15 miles
southwest of park entrance ☎ 970/529–4421 ⊕ www.visitmesaverde.
com/dining/metate-room.aspx ⌲ Reservations not accepted ⊙ Closed
late Oct.–late Apr. No lunch.*

$ ✕ **Spruce Tree Terrace Cafe.** This small cafeteria has a limited selection
AMERICAN   of hot food, salads, and sandwiches. The patio is pleasant, and it's
conveniently located across the street from the museum. The Spruce
Tree Terrace is also the only food concession in the park that's open
year-round for lunch. Try the popular Navajo tacos. $ *Average main:
$8 ⊠ Near Chapin Mesa Archeological Museum, 5 miles south of the
Far View Visitor Center ☎ 970/529–4521 ⊕ www.visitmesaverde.com/
dining/spruce-tree-terrace-cafe.aspx ⊙ No dinner Nov.–mid-Mar.*

PICNIC AREAS

FAMILY   **Chapin Mesa.** This is the nicest and largest picnic area in the park. It has
about 40 tables under shade trees and a great view into Spruce Canyon,
as well as flushing toilets. ⊠ *Near Chapin Mesa Archeological Museum,
5 miles south of Far View Visitor Center.*

Wetherill Mesa. Ten tables placed under lush shade trees, along with
nearby drinking water and restrooms, make this a pleasant spot for
lunch. ⊠ *12 miles southwest of Far View Visitor Center.*

OUTSIDE THE PARK

$$ ✕ **Ken & Sue's.** Plates are big and the prices are reasonable at Ken &
MODERN   Sue's, one of Durango's favorite restaurants. Locals are wild for the
AMERICAN   artfully prepared contemporary cuisine, served in an open and airy
space. Try the pistachio-crusted grouper with vanilla-rum butter, or
Aunt Lydia's meatloaf with red-wine gravy and mashed potatoes. Enjoy
your meal in the pleasant, brick-walled dining room or ask for a table
on the large, pretty patio in the back. $ *Average main: $18 ⊠ 636
Main Ave., Durango ☎ 970/385–1810 ⊕ www.kenandsues.com ⊙ No
lunch weekends.*

CLOSE UP

Best Campgrounds in Mesa Verde

Morefield Campground is the only option within the park, and it's an excellent one. Reservations are accepted; it's open late May through early September. In nearby Mancos, just across the highway from the park entrance, there's a campground with full amenities (but no electrical hookups), while the San Juan National Forest offers backcountry camping.

Morefield Campground. With 267 campsites, including 15 full-hookup RV sites, access to trailheads, and plenty of amenities, the only campground in the park is an appealing mini-city for campers. It's a 40-minute drive to reach the park's most popular sites. Reservations are accepted. ✉ *4 miles south of park entrance,* ☎ *970/564–4300, 800/449–2288* ⊕ *www.visitmesaverde.com.*

$ | AMERICAN

✕ **Olde Tymer's Cafe.** If you're looking for the locals, look no further than Olde Tymer's Cafe—known in these parts as OTC—a bustling café and bar in a beautiful old building on Main Avenue with an inviting patio in the back. The hamburger is a huge specimen on a fat, fresh bun, and the salads and sandwiches are piled high. There's a different special every night—including $5 burgers on Mondays—and a respectable roster of beers on tap, including local Durango brews. Ⓢ *Average main: $9* ✉ *1000 Main Ave., Durango* ☎ *970/259–2990* ⊕ *www.otcdgo.com.*

26

$$$$ | STEAKHOUSE

✕ **Ore House.** Durango is a meat-and-potatoes kind of town, and the Ore House is Durango's idea of a steakhouse. The aroma of beef smacks you in the face as you walk past, but there are also organic chicken and wild-caught seafood dishes available. This local favorite serves enormous slabs of aged Angus that are hand cut daily. For a special occasion try the chateaubriand for two ($68). Ⓢ *Average main: $32* ✉ *147 E. College Dr., Durango* ☎ *970/247–5707* ⊕ *www.orehouserestaurant.com.*

WHERE TO STAY

IN THE PARK

$$ | HOTEL

🏨 **Far View Lodge.** Talk about a view—all rooms have a private balcony, from which you can admire views of the neighboring states of Arizona, Utah, and New Mexico up to 100 miles in the distance. **Pros:** close to the key sites; views are spectacular. **Cons:** simple rooms and amenities, with no TV; walls are thin and less than soundproof; limited cell phone service. Ⓢ *Rooms from: $135* ✉ *Across from Far View Visitor Center, 15 miles southwest of park entrance* ☎ *602/331–5210, 800/449–2288* ⊕ *www.visitmesaverde.com* ⇔ *150 rooms* ⊙ *Closed Nov.–Mar.* ⊘ *No meals.*

OUTSIDE THE PARK

$ HOTEL **American Holiday Mesa Verde Inn.** This is arguably the nicest motel on the strip, mostly because its air-conditioned rooms are spacious and pleasantly decorated. **Pros:** reasonably priced; near the national park; outdoor pool. **Cons:** can get noisy; nothing fancy. [$] *Rooms from: $65* ✉ *640 S. Broadway* ☎ *970/565–3773* 🌐 *www.cortezmesaverdeinn.com* 🛏 *84 rooms* 🍴 *No meals.*

$$$ B&B/INN **Rochester Hotel.** The recently renovated Rochester Hotel is funky yet chic, with marquee-lighted movie posters from Hollywood Westerns filmed nearby lining the airy hallways. **Pros:** free guest parking; large rooms; free use of cruiser bikes in town. **Cons:** can be noisy, no counter space in bathrooms. [$] *Rooms from: $169* ✉ *726 E. 2nd Ave., Durango* ☎ *970/385–1920* 🌐 *www.rochesterhotel.com* 🛏 *27 rooms* 🍴 *Breakfast.*

$$$ HOTEL Fodor's Choice ★ **Strater Hotel.** Still the hottest spot in town, this Western grande dame opened for business in 1887 and has been visited by Butch Cassidy, Louis L'Amour (he wrote *The Sacketts* here), Francis Ford Coppola, John Kennedy, and Marilyn Monroe (the latter two stayed here at separate times). **Pros:** right in the thick of things; genuine Old West feel. **Cons:** no off-street parking; when the bar gets going, rooms above it get no peace. [$] *Rooms from: $184* ✉ *699 Main Ave., Durango* ☎ *970/247–4431, 800/247–4431* 🌐 *www.strater.com* 🛏 *93 rooms* 🍴 *Breakfast.*

MOUNT RAINIER
NATIONAL PARK

WELCOME TO MOUNT RAINIER

TOP REASONS TO GO

★ **The mountain:** Some say Mt. Rainier is the most magical mountain in America. At 14,411 feet, it is a popular peak for climbing, with more than 10,000 attempts per year—half of which are successful.

★ **The glaciers:** About 35 square miles of glaciers and snowfields encircle Mt. Rainier, including Carbon Glacier and Emmons Glacier, the largest glaciers by volume and area, respectively, in the continental United States.

★ **The wildflowers:** More than 100 species of wildflowers bloom in the park's high meadows; the display dazzles from midsummer until the snow flies.

★ **Fabulous hiking:** More than 240 miles of maintained trails provide access to old-growth forest, river valleys, lakes, and rugged ridges.

★ **Unencumbered wilderness:** Under the provisions of the 1964 Wilderness Act and the National Wilderness Preservation System, 97% of the park is preserved as wilderness.

1 Longmire. Inside the Nisqually Gate explore Longmire historic district's museum and visitor center, ruins of the park's first hotel, or the nature loop. Nearby, delicate footbridges span the thundering Christine and Narada falls.

2 Paradise. The park's most popular destination is famous for wildflowers in summer and skiing in winter. Skyline Trail is one of many hiking routes that crisscross the base of the mountain; the larger of the two park lodges is also here.

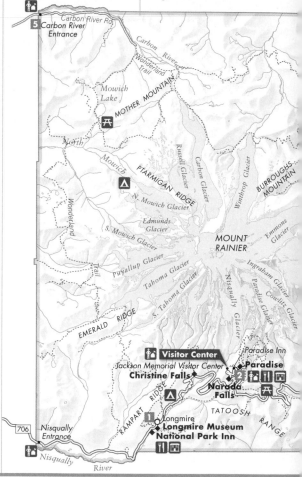

3 Ohanapecosh. Closest to the southeast entrance and the town of Packwood, the old-growth trees of the Grove of the Patriarchs are a must-see. Another short trail around nearby Tipsoo Lake has great views.

4 Sunrise and White River. This side of the park is easy to visit in summer if you enter from the east side, but it's a long drive from the southwest entrance. Sunrise is the highest stretch of road in the park and a great place to take in the alpenglow—reddish light on the peak of the mountain near sunrise and sunset. Mount Rainier's premier mountain-biking area, White River, is also the gateway to more than a dozen hiking trails.

5 Carbon River and Mowich Lake. Near the Carbon River Entrance Station is a swath of temperate forest, but to really get away from it all, follow the windy gravel roads to remote Mowich Lake.

GETTING ORIENTED

The jagged white crown of Mt. Rainier is the showpiece of the Cascades and the focal point of this 337-square-mile national park. The most popular destination in the park, Paradise, is in the southern region; Ohanapecosh, the Grove of the Patriarchs, and Tipsoo Lake are in the southeastern corner. Mount Rainier National Park's eastern and northern areas are dominated by wilderness. The snowy folds of the Cascade mountain range stretch out from this Washington park; Seattle is roughly 50 miles north and the volcanic ruins of Mt. St. Helens 100 miles south.

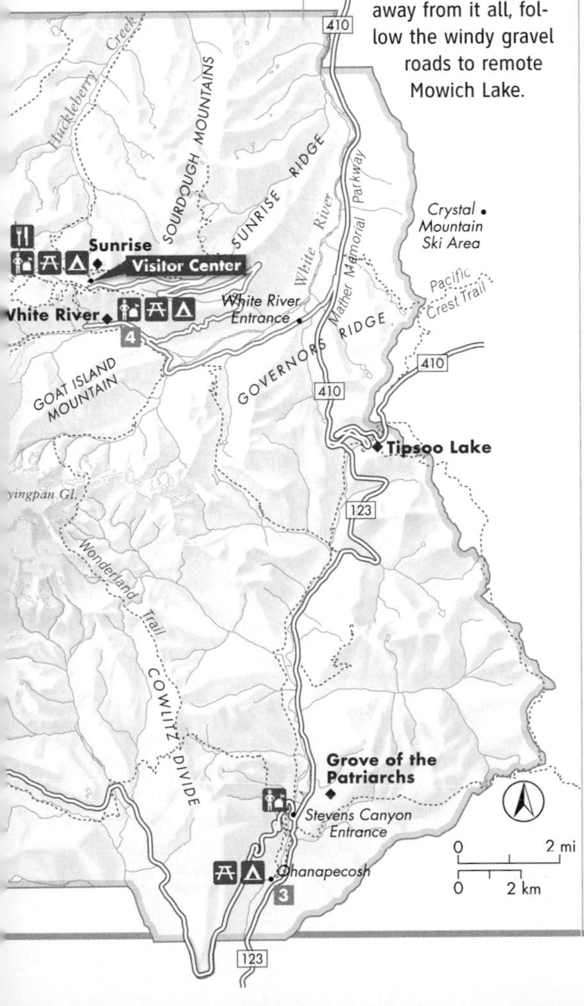

KEY

- Ranger Station
- Campground
- Picnic Area
- Restaurant
- Lodge
- Trailhead
- Restrooms
- Scenic Viewpoint
- Walking/Hiking Trails

Updated by
Shelley Arenas

Like a mysterious, white-clad chanteuse, veiled in clouds even when the surrounding forests and fields are bathed in sunlight, Mt. Rainier is the centerpiece of its namesake park. The impressive volcanic peak stands at an elevation of 14,411 feet, making it the fifth-highest peak in the lower 48 states. Nearly 2 million visitors a year enjoy spectacular views of the mountain and return home with a lifelong memory of its image.

The mountain holds the largest glacial system in the contiguous United States, with more than two-dozen major glaciers. On the lower slopes you find silent forests made up of cathedral-like groves of Douglas fir, western hemlock, and western red cedar, some more than 1,000 years old. Water and lush greenery are everywhere in the park, and dozens of thundering waterfalls, accessible from the road or by a short hike, fill the air with mist.

MOUNT RAINIER PLANNER

WHEN TO GO

Rainier is the Puget Sound's weather vane: if you can see it, skies will be clear. Visitors are most likely to see the summit July through September. Crowds are heaviest in summer, too, meaning the parking lots at Paradise and Sunrise often fill before noon, campsites are reserved months in advance, and other lodgings are reserved as much as a year ahead.

True to its name, Paradise is often sunny during periods when the lowlands are under a cloud layer. The rest of the year, Rainier's summit gathers lenticular clouds whenever a Pacific storm approaches; once the peak vanishes from view, it's time to haul out rain gear. The rare periods of clear winter weather bring residents up to Paradise for cross-country skiing.

AVG. HIGH/LOW TEMPS.

JAN.	FEB.	MAR.	APR.	MAY	JUNE
36/24	40/26	44/28	53/32	62/37	66/43

JULY	AUG.	SEPT.	OCT.	NOV.	DEC.
75/47	74/47	68/43	57/38	45/31	39/28

PLANNING YOUR TIME

MOUNT RAINIER IN ONE DAY

The best way to get a complete overview of Mount Rainier in a day is to enter via Nisqually and begin your tour by browsing in **Longmire Museum.** When you're done, get to know the environment in and around Longmire Meadow and the overgrown ruins of Longmire Springs Hotel on the 0.5-mile **Trail of the Shadows** nature loop.

From Longmire, Highway 706 East climbs northeast into the mountains toward Paradise. Take a moment to explore gorgeous **Christine Falls,** just north of the road 1½ miles past Cougar Rock Campground, and **Narada Falls,** 3 miles farther on; both are spanned by graceful stone footbridges. Fantastic mountain views, alpine meadows crosshatched with nature trails, a welcoming lodge and restaurant, and the excellent **Jackson Memorial Visitor Center** combine to make lofty Paradise the primary goal of most park visitors. One outstanding (but challenging) way to explore the high country is to hike the 5-mile round-trip **Skyline Trail** to Panorama Point, which rewards you with stunning 360-degree views.

Continue eastward on Highway 706 East for 21 miles and leave your car to explore the incomparable, thousand-year-old **Grove of the Patriarchs.** Afterward, turn your car north toward White River and **Sunrise Visitor Center,** where you can watch the alpenglow fade from Mt. Rainier's domed summit.

GETTING HERE AND AROUND

CAR TRAVEL

The Nisqually entrance is on Highway 706, 14 miles east of Route 7; the Ohanapecosh entrance is on Route 123, 5 miles north of U.S. 12; and the White River entrance is on Route 410, 3 miles north of the Chinook and Cayuse passes. These highways become mountain roads as they reach Rainier, winding up and down many steep slopes, so cautious driving is essential: use a lower gear, especially on downhill sections, and take care not to overheat brakes by constant use. These roads are subject to storms any time of year and are repaired in the summer from winter damage and washouts.

Side roads into the park's western slope are narrower, unpaved, and subject to flooding and washouts. All are closed by snow in winter except Highway 706 to Paradise and Carbon River Road, though the latter tends to flood near the park boundary. (Route 410 is open to the Crystal Mountain access road entrance.)

Park roads have a maximum speed of 35 mph in most places, and you have to watch for pedestrians, cyclists, and wildlife. Parking can be difficult during peak summer season, especially at Paradise, Sunrise,

27

Grove of the Patriarchs, and at the trailheads between Longmire and Paradise; arrive early if you plan to visit these sites. All off-road-vehicle use—4X4 vehicles, ATVs, motorcycles, snowmobiles—is prohibited in Mount Rainier National Park.

PARK ESSENTIALS
PARK FEES AND PERMITS

The entrance fee of $15 per vehicle and $5 for those on foot, motorcycle, or bicycle is good for seven days. Annual passes are $30. Climbing permits are $44 per person per climb or glacier trek. Wilderness camping permits must be obtained for all backcountry trips, and advance reservations are highly recommended.

PARK HOURS

Mount Rainier National Park is open 24/7 year-round, but with limited access in winter. Gates at Nisqually (Longmire) are staffed year-round during the day; facilities at Paradise are open daily from late May to mid-October; and Sunrise is open daily July to early September. During off-hours you can buy passes at the gates from machines that accept credit and debit cards. Winter access to the park is limited to the Nisqually entrance, and the Jackson Memorial Visitor Center at Paradise is open on weekends and holidays in winter. The road from Longmire to Paradise is closed Tuesdays and Wednesdays during the winter; the Paradise snow-play area is open Thursday to Monday when there is sufficient snow.

CELL-PHONE RECEPTION

Cell-phone reception is unreliable throughout much of the park, although access is clear at Paradise, Sunrise, and Crystal Mountain. Public telephones are at all park visitor centers, at the National Park Inn at Longmire, and at Paradise Inn at Paradise.

RESTAURANTS

A limited number of restaurants are inside the park, and a few worth checking out lie beyond its borders. Mount Rainier's picnic areas are justly famous, especially in summer, when wildflowers fill the meadows. Resist the urge to feed the yellow pine chipmunks darting about.

Prices in the reviews are the average cost of a main course at dinner, or if dinner is not served, at lunch.

HOTELS

The Mount Rainier area is remarkably bereft of quality lodging. Rainier's two national park lodges, at Longmire and Paradise, are attractive and well maintained. They exude considerable history and charm, especially Paradise Inn, but unless you've made summer

PLANTS AND WILDLIFE IN MOUNT RAINIER

Wildflower season in the meadows at and above timberline is mid-July through August. Large mammals like deer, elk, black bears, and cougars tend to occupy the less accessible wilderness areas of the park and thus elude the average visitor; smaller animals like squirrels and marmots are easier to spot. The best times to see wildlife are at dawn and dusk at the forest's edge. Fawns are born in May, and the bugling of bull elk on the high ridges can be heard in late September and October, especially on the park's eastern side.

reservations a year in advance, getting a room can be a challenge. Dozens of motels, cabin complexes, and private vacation home rentals are near the park entrances; while they can be pricey, the latter are convenient for longer stays.

Prices in the reviews are the lowest cost of a standard double room in high season. For expanded reviews, facilities, and current deals, visit Fodors.com.

VISITOR INFORMATION

PARK CONTACT INFORMATION

Mount Rainier National Park ✉ *55210 238th Ave. E, Ashford* ☎ *360/569–2211, 360/569–6575* ⊕ *www.nps.gov/mora.*

VISITOR CENTERS

Jackson Memorial Visitor Center. High on the mountain's southern flank, this center houses exhibits on geology, mountaineering, glaciology, and alpine ecology. Multimedia programs are staged in the theater; there's also a snack bar and gift shop. This is the park's most popular visitor destination, and it can be quite crowded in summer. ✉ *Hwy. 706 E, 19 miles east of Nisqually park entrance* ☎ *360/569–6571* ⊕ *www.nps.gov/mora/planyourvisit/paradise.htm* ☉ *June 15–Sept. 1, daily 10–7; Sept. 2–8, daily 10–6; Sept. 9–Oct. 14, daily 10–5; Oct. 19–31, weekends 10–5.*

Longmire Museum and Visitor Center. Glass cases inside this museum preserve the park's plants and animals, including a stuffed cougar. Historical photographs and geographical displays provide a worthwhile overview of the park's history. The adjacent visitor center has some perfunctory exhibits on the surrounding forest and its inhabitants, as well as pamphlets and information about park activities. ✉ *Hwy. 706, 10 miles east of Ashford, Longmire* ☎ *360/569–6575* ⊕ *www.nps.gov/mora/planyourvisit/longmire.htm* ▱ *Free* ☉ *July–mid-Oct., daily 9–5; mid-Oct.–June, daily 9–4:30.*

Sunrise Visitor Center. Exhibits at this center explain the region's sparser alpine and subalpine ecology. A network of nearby loop trails leads you through alpine meadows and forest to overlooks that have broad views of the Cascades and Rainier. The visitor center has a snack bar and gift shop. ✉ *Sunrise Rd., 15 miles from the White River park entrance* ☎ *360/663–2425* ⊕ *www.nps.gov/mora/planyourvisit/sunrise.htm* ☉ *Early July–early Sept, daily 9–6.*

EXPLORING

SCENIC DRIVES

Chinook Pass Road. Route 410, the highway to Yakima, follows the eastern edge of the park to Chinook Pass, where it climbs the steep, 5,432-foot pass via a series of switchbacks. At its top, take in broad views of Rainier and the east slope of the Cascades. The pass usually closes for the winter in November. ⊕ *www.wsdot.wa.gov/traffic/passes/chinook.*

27

Mowich Lake Road. In the northwest corner of the park, this 24-mile mountain road begins in Wilkeson and heads up the Rainier foothills to Mowich Lake, traversing beautiful mountain meadows along the way. Mowich Lake is a pleasant spot for a picnic. The road is open mid-July to mid-October. ⊕ *www. nps.gov/mora/planyourvisit/ carbon-and-mowich.htm.*

Paradise Road. This 9-mile stretch of Highway 706 winds its way up the mountain's southwest flank from Longmire to Paradise, taking you from lowland forest to the

> ### FLOOD DAMAGE
>
> Harsh winter weather and heavy spring rains cause road damage and closings every year. Those with the most snow and storm debris usually include Carbon River Road, Stevens Canyon Road, Westside Road to Dry Creek, and Highway 706 from Longmire to Paradise. ■ TIP➜ Before your trip, confirm site and road openings with one of the park's visitor centers.

ever-expanding vistas of the mountain above. Visit on a weekday if possible, especially in peak summer months, when the road is packed with cars. The route is open year-round though there may be some weekday closures in winter. From November through April, all vehicles must carry chains.

Sunrise Road. This popular (and often crowded) scenic road carves its way 11 miles up Sunrise Ridge from the White River Valley on the northeast side of the park. As you top the ridge there are sweeping views of the surrounding lowlands. The road is open late June to October.

HISTORIC SITES

National Park Inn. Even if you don't plan to stay overnight, you can stop by year-round to view the architecture of this inn, built in 1917 and on the National Register of Historic Places. While you're here, relax in front of the fireplace in the lounge, stop at the gift shop, or dine at the restaurant. ✉ *Longmire Visitor Complex, Hwy. 706, 10 miles east of Nisqually entrance, Longmire* ☎ *360/569–2411* ⊕ *www. mtrainierguestservices.com/accommodations/national-park-inn.*

SCENIC STOPS

Christine Falls. These two-tiered falls were named in honor of Christine Louise Van Trump, who climbed to the 10,000-foot level on Mt. Rainier in 1889 at the age of 9, despite having a crippling nervous-system disorder. ✉ *Next to Hwy. 706, about 2½ miles east of Cougar Rock Campground.*

Fodor's Choice
★
Grove of the Patriarchs. Protected from the periodic fires that swept through the surrounding areas, this small island of 1,000-year-old trees is one of Mount Rainier National Park's most memorable features. A 1.5-mile loop trail heads through the old-growth forest of Douglas fir, cedar, and hemlock. ✉ *Rte. 123, west of the Stevens Canyon entrance* ⊕ *www.nps.gov/mora/planyourvisit/ohanapecosh.htm.*

Narada Falls. A steep but short trail leads to the viewing area for these spectacular 168-foot falls, which expand to a width of 75 feet during peak flow times. In winter the frozen falls are popular with ice climbers. ⊠ *Along Hwy. 706, 1 mile west of the turnoff for Paradise, 6 miles east of Cougar Rock Campground* ⊕ *www.nps.gov/mora.*

FAMILY **Tipsoo Lake.** The short, pleasant trail that circles the lake—ideal for families—provides breathtaking views. Enjoy the subalpine wildflower meadows during the summer months; in early fall there is an abundant supply of huckleberries. ⊠ *Off Cayuse Pass east on Rte. 410* ⊕ *www. nps.gov/mora/planyourvisit/sunrise.htm.*

EDUCATIONAL OFFERINGS

RANGER PROGRAMS

FAMILY **Junior Ranger Program.** Youngsters ages 6 to 11 can pick up an activity booklet at a visitor center and fill it out as they explore the park. When they complete it, they can show it to a ranger and receive a Mount Rainier Junior Ranger badge. ⊠ *Visitor centers* ☎ *360/569–2211* ⊕ *www. nps.gov/mora/forkids/index.htm* 🎫 *Free.*

Ranger Programs. Park ranger-led activities include **guided snowshoe walks** in the winter (suitable for those older than 8) as well as **evening programs** during the summer at Cougar Rock, Ohanapecosh, and White River campgrounds, and at the Paradise Inn. Evening talks may cover subjects such as park history, its flora and fauna, or interesting facts on climbing Mt. Rainier. There are also daily guided programs that start at the Jackson Visitor Center, including meadow and vista walks, tours of the Paradise Inn, and a morning ranger chat. ⊠ *Visitor centers* ☎ *360/569–2211* ⊕ *www.nps.gov/mora/planyourvisit/ rangerprograms.htm* 🎫 *Free.*

SPORTS AND THE OUTDOORS

MULTISPORT OUTFITTERS

RMI Expeditions. Reserve a private hiking guide through this highly regarded outfitter, or take part in its one-day mountaineering classes (mid-May through late September), where participants are evaluated on their fitness for the climb and must be able to withstand a 16-mile round-trip hike with a 9,000-foot gain in elevation. The company also arranges private cross-country skiing and snowshoeing guides. ⊠ *30027 Hwy. 706 E, Ashford* ☎ *888/892–5462, 360/569–2227* ⊕ *www. rmiguides.com* 🎫 *$991 for four-day package.*

Whittaker Mountaineering. You can rent hiking and climbing gear, skis, snowshoes, snowboards, and other outdoor equipment at this all-purpose Rainier Base Camp outfitter, which also arranges for private cross-country skiing and hiking guides. ⊠ *30027 Hwy. 706 E, Ashford* ☎ *800/238–5756* ⊕ *www.whittakermountaineering.com.*

27

Mount Rainier,
Looking North

MOUNT RAINIER

Columbia Crest
14,411 ft

Liberty Cap
14,122 ft

Point Success
14,153 ft

Little Tahoma Peak
11,138 ft

Disappointment Cleaver

CATHEDRAL ROCKS

Anvil Rock
9,584 ft

McClure Rock
7,385 ft

Unicorn Peak
6,917 ft

Paradise Glaciers

Camp Muir
10,188 ft

Muir Snowfield

Ingraham Glacier

Gibraltar Rock
12,660 ft

Nisqually Glacier

Panorama Point
6,800 ft

Paradise

Alta Vista

Louise Lake

The Castle

Reflection Lakes

Pinnacle Peak
6,562 ft

Wilson Glacier

Skyline Trail

Jackson Memorial
Visitor Center

SUNSET AMPHITHEATER

St. Andrews Rock
10,992 ft

SUCCESS CLEAVER

Van Trump Glaciers

WAPOWETY CLEAVER

Kautz Glacier

Success Glacier

Plummer Peak
6,370 ft

CUSHMAN CREST

Lane Peak
6,012 ft

TATOOSH RANGE

PUYALLUP CLEAVER

Tahoma Glacier

Tahoma Glacier

GLACIER ISLAND

South Tahoma Glacier

SUCCESS DIVIDE

Pyramid Glaciers

Mildred Point

VAN TRUMP PARK

Wahpenayo Peak
6,231 ft

Chutla Peak

Tokaloo Rock
7,684 ft

Iron Mountain
6,283 ft

EMERALD RIDGE

Pyramid Peak
6,937 ft

PYRAMID PARK

Eagle Peak
5,958 ft

Creek

Pyramid

Rampart Ridge Trail

RAMPART RIDGE

THE RAMPARTS

Cougar Rock

Longmire

KEY

Paved Roads

Hiking Trails

Climbing Routes

BIRD-WATCHING

Be alert for kestrels, red-tailed hawks, and, occasionally, golden eagles on snags in the lowland forests. Also present at Rainier, but rarely seen, are great horned owls, spotted owls, and screech owls. Iridescent rufous hummingbirds flit from blossom to blossom in the drowsy summer lowlands, and sprightly water ouzels flutter in the many forest creeks. Raucous Steller's jays and gray jays scold passersby from trees, often darting boldly down to steal morsels from unguarded picnic tables. At higher elevations, look for the pure white plumage of the white-tailed ptarmigan as it hunts for seeds and insects in winter. Waxwings, vireos, nuthatches, sapsuckers, warblers, flycatchers, larks, thrushes, siskins, tanagers, and finches are common throughout the park.

HIKING

Although the mountain can seem remarkably benign on calm summer days, hiking Rainier is not a city-park stroll. Dozens of hikers and trekkers annually lose their way and must be rescued—and lives are lost on the mountain each year. Weather that approaches cyclonic levels can appear quite suddenly, any month of the year. All visitors venturing far from vehicle access points, with the possible exception of the short loop hikes listed here, should carry day packs with warm clothing, food, and other emergency supplies.

27

EASY

Nisqually Vista Trail. Equally popular in summer and winter, this trail is a 1.25-mile round trip through subalpine meadows to an overlook point for Nisqually Glacier. The gradually sloping path is a favorite venue for cross-country skiers in winter; in summer, listen for the shrill alarm calls of the area's marmots. *Easy.* ⊠ *Trailhead at Jackson Memorial Visitor Center, Rte. 123, 1 mile north of Ohanapecosh, at the high point of Hwy. 706* ⊕ *www.nps.gov/mora/planyourvisit/nisqually-vista.htm.*

Sourdough Ridge Trail. The mile-long loop of this self-guided trail takes you through the delicate subalpine meadows near the Sunrise Visitor Center. A gradual climb to the ridgetop yields magnificent views of Mt. Rainier and the more distant volcanic cones of Mt. Baker, Mt. Adams, and Glacier Peak. *Easy.* ⊠ *Trailhead at Sunrise Visitor Center, Sunrise Rd., 15 miles from the White River park entrance* ⊕ *www.nps.gov/ mora/planyourvisit/day-hiking-at-mount-rainier.htm.*

Trail of the Shadows. This 0.75-mile loop is notable for its glimpses of meadowland ecology, its colorful soda springs (don't drink the water), James Longmire's old homestead cabin, and the foundation of the old Longmire Springs Hotel, which was destroyed by fire around 1900. *Easy.* ⊠ *Trailhead at Hwy. 706, 10 miles east of Nisqually entrance* ⊕ *www.nps.gov/mora/planyourvisit/day-hiking-at-mount-rainier.htm.*

MODERATE

Fodor's Choice
★

Skyline Trail. This 5-mile loop, one of the highest trails in the park, beckons day-trippers with a vista of alpine ridges and, in summer, meadows filled with brilliant flowers and birds. At 6,800 feet, Panorama Point, the spine of the Cascade Range, spreads away to the east, and Nisqually Glacier tumbles downslope. *Moderate.* ✉ *Trailhead at Jackson Memorial Visitor Center, Rte. 123, 1 mile north of Ohanapecosh at the high point of Hwy. 706* ⊕ *www.nps.gov/mora/planyourvisit/skyline-trail.htm.*

Van Trump Park Trail. You gain an exhilarating 2,200 feet on this route while hiking through a vast expanse of meadow with views of the southern Puget Sound. The 5.8-mile track provides good footing, and the average hiker can make it up in three to four hours. *Moderate.* ✉ *Trailhead off Hwy. 706 at Christine Falls, 4.4 miles east of Longmire* ⊕ *www.nps.gov/mora/planyourvisit/van-trump-trail.htm.*

DIFFICULT

Fodor'sChoice
★

Wonderland Trail. All other Mt. Rainier hikes pale in comparison to this stunning 93-mile trek, which completely encircles the mountain. The trail passes through all the major life zones of the park, from the old-growth forests of the lowlands to the alpine meadows and goat-haunted glaciers of the highlands—pick up a mountain-goat sighting card from a ranger station or visitor center if you want to help in the park's effort to learn more about these elusive animals. Wonderland is a rugged trail; elevation gains and losses totaling 3,500 feet are common in a day's hike, which averages 8 miles. Most hikers start out from Longmire or Sunrise and take 10–14 days to cover the 93-mile route. Snow lingers on the high passes well into June (sometimes July); count on rain any time of the year. Campsites are wilderness areas with pit toilets and water that must be purified before drinking. Only hardy, well-equipped, and experienced wilderness trekkers should attempt this trip, but those who do will be amply rewarded. Wilderness permits are required, and reservations are strongly recommended. *Difficult.* ✉ *Trailhead at Longmire Visitor Center, Hwy. 706, 17 miles east of Ashford; or at Sunrise Visitor Center, Sunrise Rd., 15 miles west of the White River park entrance* ⊕ *www.nps.gov/mora/planyourvisit/the-wonderland-trail.htm.*

MOUNTAIN CLIMBING

Climbing Mt. Rainier is not for amateurs; each year, adventurers die on the mountain, and many become lost and must be rescued. Near-catastrophic weather can appear quite suddenly, any month of the year. If you're experienced in technical, high-elevation snow, rock, and ice-field adventuring, Mt. Rainier can be a memorable adventure. Climbers can fill out a climbing card at the Paradise, White River, or Carbon River ranger stations and lead their own groups of two or more. Climbers must register with a ranger before leaving and check out on return. A $44 annual climbing fee applies to anyone heading above 10,000 feet or onto one of Rainier's glaciers. During peak season it is recommended that climbers make their camping reservations ($20 per site) in advance; reservations are taken by fax and mail beginning in mid-March on a first-come, first-served basis (find the reservation form at ⊕ *www.nps.gov/mora/planyourvisit/climbing.htm*).

SKIING AND SNOWSHOEING

Mount Rainier is a major Nordic ski center for cross-country and telemark skiing. Although trails are not groomed, those around Paradise are extremely popular. If you want to ski with fewer people, try the trails in and around the Ohanapecosh–Stevens Canyon area, which are just as beautiful and, because of their more easterly exposure, slightly less subject to the rains that can douse the Longmire side, even in the dead of winter. Never ski on plowed main roads, especially around Paradise—the snowplow operator can't see you. Rentals aren't available on the eastern side of the park.

Deep snows make Mount Rainier a snowshoeing pleasure. The Paradise area, with its network of trails, is the best choice. The park's east side roads, Routes 123 and 410, are unplowed and provide other good snowshoeing venues, although you must share the main routes with snowmobilers.

GOOD READS

■ An excellent general guide to the park, *Mount Rainier: A Visitor's Companion,* by Wuerthner and Moore, is now out of print but often available through used booksellers.

■ For day hikers, a comprehensive guide to 70 trails in the park is *Day Hiking: Mount Rainier National Park Trails,* by Dan A. Nelson.

■ *Mount Rainier: Notes and Images from Our Iconic Mountain* provides a visual tour of the mountain, with photos by James Martin and essays by John Harlin III.

27

Paradise Snowplay Area and Nordic Ski Route. Sledding on flexible sleds (no toboggans or runners), inner tubes, and plastic saucers is allowed only in the Paradise snow-play area adjacent to the Jackson Visitor Center. The area is open when there is sufficient snow, usually Thursdays through Mondays from late December through mid-March. The easy, 3½-mile Paradise Valley Road Nordic ski route begins at the Paradise parking lot and follows Paradise Valley/Stevens Canyon Road to Reflection Lakes. Equipment rentals are available at Whittaker Mountaineering in Ashford or at the National Park Inn's General Store in Longmire. ⊠ *Adjacent to the Jackson Visitor Center at Paradise* ☎ *360/569–2211* ⊕ *www.nps.gov/mora/planyourvisit/winter-recreation.htm.*

TOURS AND OUTFITTERS

General Store at the National Park Inn. The store at the National Park Inn in Longmire rents cross-country ski equipment and snowshoes. It's open daily in winter, depending on snow conditions. ⊠ *National Park Inn, Longmire* ☎ *360/569–2411* ⊕ *www.mtrainierguestservices.com/activities-and-events/winter-activities/cross-country-skiing.*

DID YOU KNOW?

Named after British admiral Peter Rainier in the late 18th century, Mt. Rainier had an earlier name. Tahoma (also Takhoma), its American Indian name, means "the mountain that was God." Various unsuccessful attempts have been made to restore the aboriginal name to the peak. Of course, to most Puget Sound residents, Rainier is simply "the mountain."

WHAT'S NEARBY

NEARBY TOWNS

Ashford sits astride an ancient trail across the Cascades used by the Yakama Indians to trade with the coastal tribes of western Washington. The town began as a logging railway terminal; today it's the main gateway to Mt. Rainier—and the only year-round access point to the park—with lodges, restaurants, grocery stores, and gift shops. Surrounded by Cascade peaks, **Packwood** is a pretty mountain village on U.S. 12, below White Pass. Between Mt. Rainier and Mt. St. Helens, it's a perfect jumping-off point for exploring local wilderness areas.

VISITOR INFORMATION

Destination Packwood Association ⊠ *103 Main St. E, Packwood* ☎ *360/494–2223, 800/963–7898* ⊕ *www.destinationpackwood.com.*

NEARBY ATTRACTIONS

Goat Rocks Wilderness. The crags in Gifford Pinchot National Forest, south of Mt. Rainier, are aptly named. You often see mountain goats here, especially when you hike into the backcountry. Goat Lake is a particularly good spot for viewing these elusive creatures. See the goats without backpacking by taking Forest Road 2140 south from U.S. 12. The goats will be on Stonewall Ridge looming up ahead of you. ⊠ *Gifford Pinchot National Forest Headquarters, 10600 N.E. 51st St. Circle, Vancouver* ☎ *360/891–5000* ⊕ *www.fs.fed.us/gpnf/recreation/wilderness.*

Johnston Ridge Observatory. With the most spectacular views of the crater and lava dome of Mt. St. Helens, this observatory also has exhibits that interpret the geology of the mountain and explain how scientists monitor an active volcano. ⊠ *Rte. 504, 53 miles east of I–5, Castle Rock* ☎ *360/274–2140* ⊕ *www.fs.usda.gov/recarea/mountsthelens/recarea/?recid=31562* ⊠ *$8* ⊗ *May–Oct., daily 10–6.*

FAMILY **Mount Rainier Scenic Railroad.** This train takes you through lush forests and across scenic bridges, covering 14 miles of incomparable beauty. Seasonal theme trips, such as the Great Pumpkin Express and the Snowball Express, are also available. The trains depart from Elbe, 11 miles west of Ashford, then bring passengers to a lovely picnic area near Mineral Lake before returning. ⊠ *54124 Mountain Hwy. E, Mineral* ☎ *360/569–2588, 888/783–2611* ⊕ *www.mrsr.com* ⊠ *$26–$29* ⊗ *Mid-May–Oct., weekends (also Thurs. and Fri. in summer); some seasonal trips in Dec. and Mar.*

Mount St. Helens Science and Learning Center. Exhibits at this multimillion-dollar facility document the great 1980 blast of Mt. St. Helens and its effects on the surrounding 150,000 acres, which were devastated but are in the process of a remarkable recovery. A 0.25-mile trail leads from the visitor center to Coldwater Lake, which has a recreation area. ⊠ *19000 Spirit Lake Hwy. (Rte. 504), 43 miles east of I–5, Toutle* ☎ *360/274–2131* ⊕ *www.mshslc.org* ⊠ *Free* ⊗ *May–Oct., daily 10–6.*

Mount St. Helens Visitor Center. This facility, one of three visitor centers along Route 504 on the west side of the mountain, has exhibits documenting the eruption, plus a walk-through volcano. ⊠ *Rte. 504, 5 miles east of I–5, Silver Lake* ☎ *360/274–2131* ⊕ *www.parks.wa.gov/ stewardship/mountsthelens* ⌫ *$5* ⊗ *May 16–Sept. 15, daily 9–5; Sept. 16–May 15, daily 9–4.*

Northwest Trek Wildlife Park. One of the pioneers in modern zoo operation, this park consists of large, natural enclosures where native animals such as elk, caribou, moose, and deer roam free. Five miles of nature trails meander near the enclosures, and the hands-on Cheney Discovery Center provides an up-close wildlife experience. Hop on a tram for a narrated tour of the park; another tour lets you accompany keepers while they feed the wildlife. ⊠ *Rte. 161, about 35 miles west of Mt. Rainier National Park, Eatonville* ☎ *360/832–6122* ⊕ *www.nwtrek. org* ⌫ *$17* ⊗ *Late June–early Sept., daily 9:30–6; late Sept., weekdays 9:30–4, weekends 9:30–5; Oct., weekdays 9:30–3, weekends 9:30–4; Nov.–Feb., weekends 9:30–3; Mar., weekdays 9:30–3, weekends 9:30– 4; Apr., weekdays 9:30–4, weekends 9:30–5.*

AREA ACTIVITIES

SPORTS AND THE OUTDOORS

SKIING

27

Crystal Mountain Ski Area. Washington State's biggest and best-known ski area has a 3,100-foot vertical drop, 10 lifts (plus a children's lift), and 57 runs. In summer, it's open for hiking, rides on the Mt. Rainier Gondola, and meals at the Summit House, all providing sensational views of Rainier and the Cascades. ⊠ *Crystal Mountain Blvd., off Rte. 410, Crystal Mountain* ☎ *360/663–2265* ⊕ *www.crystalmountainresort.com* ⌫ *$65 winter lift ticket, $20 gondola ticket* ⊗ *Mid.-Nov.–mid.-Apr., daily 9–4; June–Aug., weekends and holidays 10–4.*

WHERE TO EAT

IN THE PARK

$$$ ✕ **National Park Inn Dining Room.** Photos of Mt. Rainier taken by top
ECLECTIC photographers adorn the walls of this inn's large dining room, a bonus on the many days the mountain refuses to show itself. Meals are simple but tasty: pot roast with yukon gold mashed potatoes, rainbow trout, and blackberry cobbler à la mode. For a hearty start to the day, try the country breakfast or oatmeal brûlée. Ⓢ *Average main: $21* ⊠ *Hwy. 706, Longmire* ☎ *360/569–2411* ⊕ *www.mtrainierguestservices.com* ⌫ *Reservations not accepted.*

$ ✕ **Paradise Camp Deli.** Grilled meats, sandwiches, salads, and soft drinks
AMERICAN are served daily from May through early October and on weekends
FAMILY and holidays during the rest of the year. Ⓢ *Average main: $8* ⊠ *Jackson Visitor Center, Paradise Rd. E, Paradise* ☎ *360/569–2400* ⊕ *www. mtrainierguestservices.com* ⊗ *Closed weekdays early Oct.–Apr.*

CLOSE UP

Best Campgrounds in Mount Rainier

Three drive-in campgrounds are in the park—Cougar Rock, Ohanapecosh, and White River—with almost 500 sites for tents and RVs. None has hot water or RV hookups. The more primitive Mowich Lake Campground has 10 walk-in sites for tents only. For backcountry camping, get a free wilderness permit at a visitor center. Primitive sites are spaced at 7- to 8-mile intervals along the Wonderland Trail.

Cougar Rock Campground. A secluded, heavily wooded campground with an amphitheater, Cougar Rock is one of the first to fill up. Reservations are accepted for summer only. ✉ *2½ miles north of Longmire* ☎ 877/444–6777.

Mowich Lake Campground. This is Rainier's only lakeside campground. At 4,959 feet, it's also peaceful and secluded. ✉ *Mowich Lake Rd., 6 miles east of park boundary* ☎ *360/569–2211*.

Ohanapecosh Campground. This lush, green campground in the park's southeast corner has an amphitheater and self-guided trail. It's one of the first campgrounds to open for the season. ✉ *Rte. 123, 1½ miles north of park boundary* ☎ 877/444–6777.

White River Campground. At an elevation of 4,400 feet, White River is one of the park's highest and least wooded campgrounds. Here you can enjoy campfire programs, self-guided trails, and partial views of Mt. Rainier's summit. ✉ *5 miles west of White River entrance* ☎ *360/569–2211*.

$$$ AMERICAN

🍴 **Paradise Inn.** Where else can you enjoy Sunday brunch in a historic, heavy-timbered lodge halfway up a mountain? Tall windows provide terrific views of Rainier, and the warm glow of native wood permeates the large dining room. The lunch menu is simple and healthy—four kinds of burgers (black bean, chicken, bison, and beef), salads, and the like. For dinner, there's nothing like a hearty plate of the inn's signature bourbon buffalo meat loaf. [$] *Average main: $22* ✉ *E. Paradise Rd., near Jackson Visitor Center, Paradise* ☎ *360/569–2275* 🌐 *www.mtrainierguestservices.com* ✍ *Reservations not accepted* ⏲ *Closed Oct.–late May.*

$ AMERICAN FAMILY

🍴 **Sunrise Day Lodge Food Service.** A cafeteria and grill serve inexpensive hamburgers, chili, and hot dogs from late June to early September. [$] *Average main: $8* ✉ *Sunrise Rd., 15 miles from the White River park entrance* ☎ *360/663–2425* 🌐 *www.mtrainierguestservices.com* ⏲ *Closed early Sept.–early July.*

PICNIC AREAS

Park picnic areas are open July through September only.

Paradise. This site has great views on clear days. After picnicking at Paradise, you can take an easy hike to one of the many waterfalls in the area—Sluiskin, Myrtle, or Narada, to name a few. ✉ *Hwy. 706, 11 miles east of Longmire.*

Sunrise. Set in an alpine meadow that's filled with wildflowers in July and August, this picnic area provides expansive views of the mountain and surrounding ranges in good weather. ✉ *Sunrise Rd., 11 miles west of the White River entrance.*

OUTSIDE THE PARK

$$$ AMERICAN
🍴 **Alexander's Country Inn & Restaurant.** This woodsy country inn serves some of the best food in the area. Ceiling fans and wooden booths lining the walls add a touch of whimsy to the 1912 building. Try the steak or trout—freshly caught from the pond on the grounds. The homemade bread is fantastic, and the blackberry pie is a must for dessert. Dine inside or outside on a patio overlooking a waterfall. Box lunches for adventurers are available. [$] *Average main: $23* ✉ *37515 Hwy. 706 E, Ashford* ☎ *360/569–2323, 800/654–7615* 🌐 *www.alexanderscountryinn.com* 🕒 *No lunch Mon.–Thurs.*

$ AMERICAN FAMILY
🍴 **Scaleburgers.** Once a 1939 logging-truck weigh station, the building is now a popular restaurant serving homemade hamburgers, fries, and shakes. Eat outside on tables overlooking the hills and scenic railroad. [$] *Average main: $6* ✉ *54109 Mountain Hwy. E, 11 miles west of Ashford, Elbe* ☎ *360/569–2247* 💳 *No credit cards* 🕒 *Limited hrs in winter; call ahead.*

$$$ PACIFIC NORTHWEST
🍴 **Summit House.** On top of Crystal Mountain at 6,872 feet is Washington's highest-elevation restaurant. The menu features northwest cuisine, including Dungeness crab cakes, elk medallions, coho salmon, and huckleberry ice cream. With stunning views of Mt. Rainier, the restaurant is a popular stop for skiers, hikers, and summer tourists, too. Sit inside to stay warm by the fireplace, or sit outside on the patio and watch chipmunks run along the nearby rocks. The restaurant is reached by riding the scenic Mt. Rainier Gondola from the base of Crystal Mountain; note that gondola tickets ($20/adults) must be purchased separately. As the only restaurant at the summit, reservations are strongly advised, though walk-ins are accepted when space is available. [$] *Average main: $23* ✉ *33914 Crystal Mountain Blvd., Crystal Mountain* ☎ *360/663–3085* 🌐 *crystalmountainresort.com* 🕒 *Open seasonally during summer and ski season; check website or call for current hrs.*

27

WHERE TO STAY

IN THE PARK

$$$ HOTEL
🏨 **National Park Inn.** A large stone fireplace warms the common room of this country inn, the only one of the park's two inns that's open year-round. **Pros:** classic ambience; open all year. **Cons:** jam-packed in summer; must book far in advance; some rooms have shared bath. [$] *Rooms from: $152* ✉ *Longmire Visitor Complex, Hwy. 706, 6 miles east of Nisqually entrance, Longmire* ☎ *360/569–2275* 🌐 *www.mtrainierguestservices.com* 🛏 *25 rooms, 18 with bath* 🍽 *No meals.*

$$$ HOTEL
Fodor's Choice ★
🏨 **Paradise Inn.** With its hand-carved Alaskan cedar logs, burnished parquet floors, stone fireplaces, Indian rugs, and glorious mountain views, this 1917 inn is a classic example of a national park lodge. **Pros:** central to trails; pristine vistas; nature-inspired details. **Cons:** noisy in high season. [$] *Rooms from: $150* ✉ *E. Paradise Rd., near Jackson Visitor Center, Paradise* ☎ *360/569–2275* 🌐 *www.mtrainierguestservices.com* 🛏 *121 rooms* 🕒 *Closed Oct.–mid-May* 🍽 *No meals.*

OUTSIDE THE PARK

$$ B&B/INN 🏨 **Alexander's Country Inn.** Serving guests since 1912, this top-notch lodging sits just a mile from Mt. Rainier's Nisqually Entrance. **Pros:** luxurious amenities, especially considering moderate rates; on-site day spa. **Cons:** lots of breakables means it's not great for children. $ *Rooms from: $130* ✉ *37515 Hwy. 706 E, 4 miles east of Ashford, Ashford* ☎ *360/569–2323, 800/654–7615* 🌐 *www.alexanderscountryinn.com* 🛏 *12 rooms, 2 3-bedroom houses* 🍴 *Breakfast.*

$$$$ B&B/INN FAMILY 🏨 **Alta Crystal Resort.** In the national forest, this small resort with family-friendly amenities feels remote yet is close to Mt. Rainier's Sunrise entrance and Crystal Mountain Ski Resort. **Pros:** very family-friendly; easy access to trails; owners are knowledgeable about the area. **Cons:** not close to restaurants or grocery store; limited cell-phone reception. $ *Rooms from: $260* ✉ *68317 Rte. 410 E, Greenwater* ☎ *360/663–2500, 800/277–6475* 🌐 *www.altacrystalresort.com* 🛏 *23 suites, 1 cabin* 🍴 *No meals.*

$$$$ RENTAL 🏨 **Silver Skis Condominiums.** With rooms overlooking Crystal Mountain Resort, Silver Skis Condominiums provide convenient slopeside family-friendly lodging. **Pros:** each unit uniquely decorated by its owner; lots of amenities for families; off-season rates make this a good base for summer recreation, too. **Cons:** many of the condos have loft or bunk beds and may not be accessible for all; condos fill up quickly during the ski season. $ *Rooms from: $310* ✉ *33000 Crystal Mountain Blvd., Crystal Mountain* ☎ *360/663–2558, 888/668–4368* 🌐 *www.crystalmountainlodging.com* 🛏 *96 condos* 🍴 *No meals.*

$$$ B&B/INN 🏨 **Stormking Spa and Cabins.** In a forest setting a mile from the Nisqually entrance of Mount Rainier National Park, Stormking features five luxury cabins for adults: four are shaped like yurts, and all have cozy gas fireplaces, hot tubs, private outdoor seating areas, and natural finishes of wood and stone. **Pros:** very romantic and secluded; reasonably priced for special occasion getaways; deer and other wildlife frequent the property. **Cons:** no full kitchens; Wi-Fi available at spa but not in cabins. $ *Rooms from: $190* ✉ *37311 Hwy. 706 E, Ashford* ☎ *360/569–2964* 🌐 *www.stormkingspa.com* 🛏 *5 cabins* 🍴 *Breakfast.*

$ B&B/INN 🏨 **Wellspring.** In the woods outside Ashford, the accommodations here include tastefully designed log cabins, tent cabins, a tree house, and a room in a greenhouse. **Pros:** unique lodging with a wide range of prices, depending on the room; some options good for groups; relaxing spa and hot soaking tubs. **Cons:** limited amenities. $ *Rooms from: $95* ✉ *54922 Kernehan Rd., Ashford* ☎ *360/569–2514* 🌐 *www.wellspringspa.com* 🛏 *5 rooms, 6 cabins, 3 tent cabins, 1 cottage, 1 treehouse, 1 lodge* 🍴 *Breakfast.*

NORTH CASCADES
NATIONAL PARK

28

Visit Fodors.com for advice, updates, and bookings

WELCOME TO NORTH CASCADES

TOP REASONS TO GO

★ **Pure wilderness:** Nearly 400 miles of mountain and meadow trails immerse hikers in pristine natural panoramas, with sure sightings of bald eagles, deer, elk, and other wildlife.

★ **Majestic glaciers:** The North Cascades are home to several hundred moving ice masses, more than half of the glaciers in the United States.

★ **Splendid flora:** A bright palette of flowers blankets the hillsides in midsummer, while October's colors paint the landscape in vibrant autumn hues.

★ **Thrilling boat rides:** Lake Chelan, Lake Ross, and the Stehekin River are the starting points for kayaking, white-water rafting, and ferry trips.

★ **19th-century history:** Delve into the state's farming, lumber, and logging pasts in clapboard towns and homesteads around the park.

1 North Unit. The park's creek-cut northern wilderness, centered on snowy Mount Challenger, stretches north from Highway 20 over the Picket Range toward the Canadian border. It's an endless landscape of pine-topped peaks and ridges.

2 South Unit. Hike lake-filled mountain foothills in summer to take in vistas of blue skies and flower-filled meadows. Waterfalls and wildlife are abundant here.

3 Ross Lake National Recreation Area. Drawing a thick line from British Columbia all the way down to the North Cascades Scenic Highway, placid Ross Lake is edged with pretty bays that draw swimmers and boaters.

4 Lake Chelan National Recreation Area. Ferries steam between small waterfront towns along this pristine waterway, while kayakers and hikers follow quiet trails along its edges. This is one of the Northwest's most popular summer escapes, with nature-bound activities and rustic accommodations.

WASHINGTON

GETTING ORIENTED

The park rises upward from the massive Cascade ranges seen northeast of Seattle, widening in a swath of snow-covered peaks all the way to the Canadian border. The broad Skagit River and many large creeks cut through the valleys; most end in the long arm of Lake Chelan in the south or in the snakelike expanse of Ross Lake at the park's northern edge. Even in summer, valleys can start the day shrouded in fog; it's best to drive the highway west to east in afternoon. A morning start is a good choice coming the other way. The most sensational scenery, however, is reached by hiking to one of the high park passes or mountain lookouts.

28

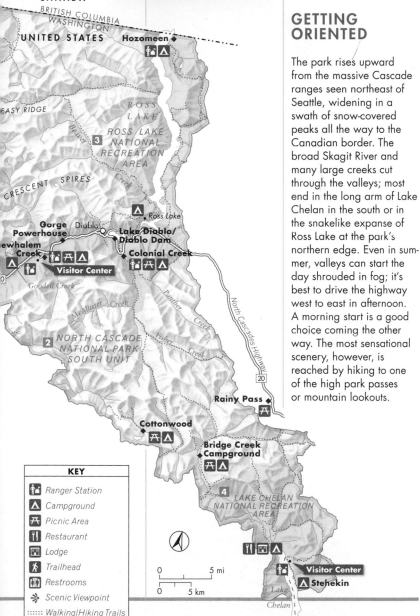

CANADA

BRITISH COLUMBIA
WASHINGTON

UNITED STATES   Hozomeen ◆

EASY RIDGE

ROSS LAKE

3   ROSS LAKE NATIONAL RECREATION AREA

Beaver Creek

CRESCENT SPIRES

Ross Lake ◆

Gorge   Diablo
Powerhouse   ◆
ewhalem Creek   Lake Diablo/
    Diablo Dam
    Colonial Creek

Visitor Center

Goodell Creek

McAllister Creek

Panther Creek

North Cascades Highway

2   NORTH CASCADE NATIONAL PARK SOUTH UNIT

Fisher Creek

20

Rainy Pass ◆

Cottonwood ◆

Bridge Creek Campground ◆

4   LAKE CHELAN NATIONAL RECREATION AREA

KEY

- 👫 Ranger Station
- ▲ Campground
- 🎪 Picnic Area
- 🍴 Restaurant
- 🏨 Lodge
- 🚶 Trailhead
- 🚻 Restrooms
- ✷ Scenic Viewpoint
- ⋯⋯ Walking/Hiking Trails

0   5 mi
0   5 km

Visitor Center
▲ Stehekin

Lake Chelan

Updated by
Shelley Arenas

Countless snow-clad mountain spires dwarf narrow glacial valleys in this 505,000-acre expanse of the North Cascades, which encompasses three diverse natural areas. North Cascades National Park is the core of the region, flanked by Lake Chelan National Recreation Area to the south and Ross Lake National Recreation Area to the north; all are part of the Stephen T. Mather Wilderness Area. It's a spectacular gathering of snowy peaks, glacial meadows, plunging canyons, and cold, deep-blue lakes. Traditionally the lands of several American Indian tribes, it's fitting that it's still completely wild—and wildlife-filled.

NORTH CASCADES PLANNER

WHEN TO GO

The spectacular, craggy peaks of the North Cascades—often likened to the Alps—are breathtaking anytime. Summer is peak season, especially along the alpine stretches of Highway 20; weekends and holidays can be crowded. Summer is short and glorious in the high country, extending from snowmelt (late May to July, depending on the elevation and the amount of snow) to early September.

The North Cascades Highway is a popular autumn drive in September and October, when the changing leaves put on a colorful show. The lowland forest areas, such as the complex around Newhalem, can be visited almost any time of year. These are wonderfully quiet in early spring or late autumn on mild, rainy days. Snow closes the North Cascades Highway from November through mid-April.

AVG. HIGH/LOW TEMPS.

JAN.	FEB.	MAR.	APR.	MAY	JUNE
39/30	43/32	49/34	56/38	64/43	70/49

JULY	AUG.	SEPT.	OCT.	NOV.	DEC.
76/52	76/53	69/49	57/42	45/36	39/31

PLANNING YOUR TIME
NORTH CASCADES IN ONE DAY

The **North Cascades Highway,** with its breathtaking mountain and meadow scenery, is one of the most memorable drives in the United States. Although many travelers first head northeast from Seattle into the park and make this their grand finale, if you start from Winthrop, at the south end of the route, traffic is lighter and there's less morning fog. Either way, the main highlight is **Washington Pass,** the road's highest point, where an overlook affords a sensational panorama of snow-covered peaks.

Rainy Pass, where the road heading north drops into the west slope valleys, is another good vantage point. Old-growth forest begins to appear, and after about an hour you reach **Gorge Creek Falls overlook** with its 242-foot cascade. Continue west to Newhalem and stop for lunch, then take a half-hour stroll along the **Trail of the Cedars.** Later, stop at the **North Cascades Visitor Center** and take another short hike. It's an hour drive down the Skagit Valley to Sedro-Woolley, where bald eagles are often seen along the river in winter.

GETTING HERE AND AROUND
CAR TRAVEL

Highway 20, the North Cascades Highway, splits the park's north and south sections. The gravel Cascade River Road, which runs southeast from Marblemount, peels off Highway 20; Sibley Creek/Hidden Lake Road (USFS 1540) turns off Cascade River Road to the Cascade Pass trailhead. Thornton Creek Road is another rough four-wheel-drive track. For the Ross Lake area in the north, the unpaved Hozomeen Road (Silver–Skagit Road) provides access between Hope, British Columbia, and Silver Lake and Skagit Valley provincial parks. From Stehekin, the Stehekin Valley Road continues to High Bridge, Car Wash Falls, Bridge Creek, and Cottonwood campgrounds—although seasonal floods may cause washouts. Note that roads are narrow and closed from October to June, many sights are off the beaten path, and the scenery is so spectacular that, once you're in it, you'll want to make more than a day trip.

PARK ESSENTIALS
PARK FEES AND PERMITS

There are no entrance fees to the national park and no parking fees at trailheads on park land. A Northwest Forest Pass, required for parking at Forest Service trailheads, is $5 per vehicle for one calendar day or $30 for one year. A free wilderness permit is required for all overnight stays in the backcountry; these are available in person only. Dock permits for boat-in campgrounds are also $5 per day. Passes and permits are sold at visitor centers and ranger stations around the park area.

28

PARK HOURS

The park never closes, but access is limited by snow in winter. Highway 20 (North Cascades Highway), the major access to the park, is partially closed from mid-November to mid-April.

CELL-PHONE RECEPTION

Cell-phone reception in the park is unreliable. Public telephones are found at the North Cascades Visitor Center and Skagit Information Center in Newhalem, and the Golden West Visitor Center and North Cascades Stehekin Lodge in Stehekin.

RESTAURANTS

There are no formal restaurants in North Cascades National Park, just a lakeside café at the North Cascades Environmental Learning Center. The only other place to eat out is in Stehekin, at the Stehekin Valley Ranch dining room, North Cascades Lodge, or the Stehekin Pastry Company; all serve simple, hearty, country-style meals and sweets. Towns within a few hours of the park on either side have a few small eateries, and a few lodgings have small dining rooms with skilled chefs who craft high-end meals of locally grown products, matched with extensive wine lists. Otherwise, don't expect fancy decor or gourmet frills—just friendly service and generally delicious homemade stews, roasts, grilled fare, soups, salads, and baked goods.

Prices in the reviews are the average cost of a main course at dinner, or if dinner is not served, at lunch.

HOTELS

Accommodations in North Cascades National Park are rustic, cozy, and comfortable. Options range from plush Stehekin lodges and homey cabin rentals to spartan Learning Center bunks and campgrounds. Expect to pay roughly $50 to $200 per night, depending on the rental size and the season. Book at least three months in advance, or even a year for popular accommodations in summer. Outside the park are numerous resorts, motels, bed-and-breakfasts, and even overnight boat rentals in Chelan, Concrete, Glacier, Marblemount, Sedro-Woolley, Twisp, and Winthrop.

Prices in the reviews are the lowest cost of a standard double room in high season. For expanded reviews, facilities, and current deals, visit Fodors.com.

TOURS

North Cascades Institute (NCI). Come here for information on park hiking, wildlife watching, horseback riding, climbing, boat rentals, and fishing, as well as classroom education and hands-on nature experiences. Guided tours staged from the center include mountain climbs, pack-train excursions, and float trips on the Skagit and Stehekin rivers. Choices range from forest ecology and backpacking trips to explorations of the Cascades hot springs. There's even a research library, a dock on Diablo Lake, an amphitheater, and overnight lodging. ⊠ *1940 Diablo Dam Rd., Diablo* 🕿 *360/854–2599 for headquarters, 206/526–2599 for Environmental Learning Center* ⊕ *www.ncascades.org.*

VISITOR INFORMATION

PARK CONTACT INFORMATION

North Cascades National Park ✉ *810 Hwy. 20, Sedro-Woolley* ☎ *360/854–7200* ⊕ *www.nps.gov/noca.*

VISITOR CENTERS

Chelan Ranger Station. The base for the Chelan National Recreation Area and Wenatchee National Forest has an information desk and a shop selling regional maps and books. ✉ *428 W. Woodin Ave., Chelan* ☎ *509/682–4900* ⊕ *www.nps.gov/noca/planyourvisit/visitorcenters.htm* ⊗ *Weekdays 7:45–4:30.*

Glacier Public Service Center. This office doubles as a headquarters for the Mt. Baker–Snoqualmie National Forest; it has maps, a book and souvenir shop, and a permits desk. The center is also right on the way to some of the park's main trailheads. ✉ *10091 Mt. Baker Hwy., Glacier* ☎ *360/599–2714* ⊕ *www.nps.gov/noca/planyourvisit/visitorcenters.htm* ⊗ *Early June, Fri.–Tues. 8–4:30; mid-June–mid-Oct., daily 8–4:30; mid-Oct.–early June, weekends 9–3.*

Golden West Visitor Center. Rangers here offer guidance on hiking, camping, and other activities, as well as audiovisual and children's programs and bike tours. There's also an arts-and-crafts gallery. Maps and concise displays explain the layered ecology of the valley, which encompasses in its length virtually every ecosystem in the Northwest. Campers can pick up free backcountry permits. Note that access is by floatplane, ferry, or trail only. ✉ *Stehekin Valley Rd., ¼ mile north of Stehekin Landing, Stehekin* ☎ *360/854–7365* ⊕ *www.nps.gov/noca/planyourvisit/visitorcenters.htm* ⊗ *Mid-Oct.–Mar., Mon., Wed., and Fri. 12:30–1:30; Apr.–mid-May, weekdays 12:30–2, weekends 10–2; Memorial Day–Sept., daily 8:30–5; early Oct.–mid-Oct., daily 10–2.*

North Cascades Park & Forest Information Center. This is the park's major administrative center and the place to pick up passes, permits, and information about current conditions. ✉ *810 Hwy. 20, Sedro-Woolley* ☎ *360/856–7200, 360/854–7200* ⊕ *www.nps.gov/noca/planyourvisit/visitorcenters.htm* ⊗ *Mid-Oct.–mid-May, weekdays 8–4:30; mid-May–mid-Oct., daily 8–4:30.*

North Cascades Visitor Center. The main visitor facility for the park complex has extensive displays on surrounding landscape. Learn about the history and value of old-growth trees, the many creatures that depend on the rain-forest ecology, and the effects of human activity on the ecosystem. Park rangers frequently conduct programs; check bulletin boards for schedules. ✉ *Milepost 120, North Cascades Hwy. (Hwy. 20), Newhalem* ☎ *206/386–4495* ⊕ *www.nps.gov/noca/planyourvisit/*

PLANTS AND WILDLIFE IN NORTH CASCADES

Bald eagles are present year-round along the Skagit River and the lakes—in December, hundreds flock to the Skagit to feed on a rare winter salmon run, and remain through January. Spring and early summer bring black bears to the roadsides in the high country. Deer and elk can often be seen in early morning and late evening, grazing and browsing at the forest's edge. Other mountain residents include beaver, marmots, pika, otters, skunks, opossums, and smaller mammals, as well as forest and field birds.

28

visitorcenters.htm ⊙ *May and June, daily 9–5; July and Aug., daily 9–6; Sept. and Oct., daily 9–5. Closed Nov.–Apr.*

Wilderness Information Center. The main stop to secure backcountry and climbing permits for North Cascades National Park and the Lake Chelan and Ross Lake recreational areas, this office has maps, a bookshop, and nature exhibits. If you arrive after hours, there's a self-register permit stop outside. ⊠ *Off milepost 105.9, N. Cascades Hwy., 7280 Ranger Station Rd., Marblemount* ☎ *360/854–7245* ⊕ *www.nps.gov/ noca/planyourvisit/visitorcenters.htm* ⊙ *May–June and Sept.–mid-Oct., Sun.–Thurs. 8–4:30, Fri. and Sat. 7–6; July–Aug., Sun.–Thurs. 7–6, Fri. and Sat. 7–8. Closed Nov.–Apr.*

EXPLORING

SCENIC DRIVES

North Cascades Highway. Also known as Highway 20, this classic scenic route first winds through the green pastures and woods of the upper Skagit Valley, the mountains looming in the distance. Beyond Concrete, a former cement-manufacturing town, the highway climbs into the mountains, passes the Ross and Diablo dams, and traverses Ross Lake National Recreation Area. Here several pullouts offer great views of the lake and the surrounding snowcapped peaks. From June to September, the meadows are covered with wildflowers, and from late September through October, the mountain slopes flame with fall foliage. The pinnacle point of this stretch is 5,477-foot-high Washington Pass: look east, to where the road descends quickly into a series of hairpin curves between Early Winters Creek and the Methow Valley. Remember, this section of the highway is closed from roughly November to April, depending on snowfall, and sometimes closes temporarily during the busy summer season due to mudslides from storms. From the Methow Valley, Highway 153 takes the scenic route along the Methow River's apple, nectarine, and peach orchards to Pateros, on the Columbia River; from here, you can continue east to Grand Coulee or south to Lake Chelan. ⊕ *www.cascadeloop.com.*

HISTORIC SITES

Buckner Homestead. Dating from 1889, this restored pioneer farm includes an apple orchard, farmhouse, barn, and many ranch buildings. One-hour ranger-guided tours of the property are offered on weekends in July and August; otherwise, you can pick up a self-guided tour booklet from the drop box. ⊠ *Stehekin Valley Rd., 3½ miles north of Stehekin Landing, Stehekin* ⊕ *www.bucknerhomestead.org* ⊙ *June–Sept., daily 9–5.*

SCENIC STOPS

Gorge Powerhouse/Ladder Creek Falls and Rock Gardens. A powerhouse is a powerhouse, but the rock gardens overlooking Ladder Creek Falls, 7 miles west of Diablo, are beautiful and inspiring. ⊠ *North Cascades Hwy. (Hwy. 20), 2 miles east of North Cascades Visitor Center, Newhalem* ☎ *360/854–2589* ⊕ *www.seattle.gov/light/tours/skagit* ⬚ *Free* ⊙ *May–Sept., daily dawn to dusk.*

Fodor'sChoice **Stehekin.** One of the most beautiful and secluded valleys in the Pacific
★ Northwest, Stehekin was homesteaded by hardy souls in the late 19th century. It's actually not a town, but rather a small community set at the northwest end of Lake Chelan, and it's accessible only by boat, floatplane, or trail. Year-round residents—who have intermittent outside communications, boat-delivered supplies, and just two-dozen cars among them—enjoy a wilderness lifestyle. Even on a peak summer season day, only around 200 visitors make the trek here. ⊕ *www.stehekin.com.*

EDUCATIONAL OFFERINGS

RANGER PROGRAMS

In summer, rangers conduct programs at the visitor centers, where you also can find exhibits and other park information. At the North Cascades Visitor Center (in Newhalem) you can learn about rain-forest ecology, while at the Golden West Visitor Center (in Stehekin) there's an arts and crafts gallery as well as audiovisual and children's programs. Check center bulletin boards for schedules.

28

SPORTS AND THE OUTDOORS

BICYCLING

Mountain bikes are permitted on highways, unpaved back roads, and a few designated tracks around the park; however, there is no biking on footpaths. Ranger stations have details on the best places to ride in each season, as well as notes on spots that are closed due to weather, mud, or other environmental factors. It's $27 round-trip to bring a bike on the Lake Chelan ferry to Stehekin.

OUTFITTERS

Discovery Bikes. You can rent mountain bikes at a self-serve rack in front of the Courtney Log Office in Stehekin. Helmets are included. ☎ *509/682–3014* ⊕ *www.stehekindiscoverybikes.com* ⬚ *$4 per hr, $15 per half-day, $20 per day, $25 per 24 hrs; $35 for breakfast ride.*

BOATING

The boundaries of North Cascades National Park touch two long and sinewy expanses: Lake Chelan in the far south, and Ross Lake, which runs toward the Canadian border. Boat ramps, some with speed- and sailboat, paddleboat, kayak, and canoe rentals, are situated all around

Lake Chelan, and passenger ferries cross between towns and campgrounds. Hozomeen, accessible via a 39-mile dirt road from Canada, is the boating base for Ross Lake; the site has a large boat ramp, and a boat taxi makes drops at campgrounds all around the shoreline. Diablo Lake, in the center of the park, also has a ramp at Colonial Creek. Gorge Lake has a public ramp near the town of Diablo.

HIKING

⚠ Black bears are often sighted along trails in the summer; do not approach them. Back away carefully, and report sightings to the Golden West Visitor Center. Cougars, which are shy of humans and well aware of their presence, are rarely sighted in this region. Still, keep kids close and don't let them run too far ahead or lag behind on a trail. If you do spot a cougar, pick up children, have the whole group stand close together, and make yourself look as large as possible.

EASY

FAMILY **Happy Creek Forest Walk.** Old-growth forests are the focus of this kid-friendly boardwalk route, which loops just 0.3 miles through the trees right off the North Cascades Highway. Interpretive signs provide details about flora along the way. *Easy.* ⊠ *Trailhead at milepost 135, North Cascades Hwy. (Hwy. 20)*

Rainy Pass. An easy and accessible 1-mile paved trail leads to Rainy Lake, a waterfall, and glacier-view platform. *Easy.* ⊠ *Trailhead off Hwy. 20, 38 miles east of visitor center at Newhalem.*

River Loop Trail. Take this flat and easy, 1.8-mile, wheelchair-accessible trail down through stands of huge, old-growth firs and cedars toward the Skagit River. *Easy.* ⊠ *Trailhead near North Cascades Visitor Center.*

Sterling Munro Trail. Starting from the North Cascades Visitor Center, this popular introductory stroll follows a short 300-foot path over a boardwalk to a lookout above the forested Picket Range peaks. *Easy.* ⊠ *North Cascades Visitor Center.*

Trail of the Cedars. Only 0.3 miles long, this trail winds its way through one of the finest surviving stands of old-growth western red cedar in Washington. Some of the trees on the path are more than 1,000 years old. *Easy.* ⊠ *Trailhead near North Cascades Visitor Center, milepost 120, Hwy. 20, Newhalem.*

MODERATE

Fodor's Choice **Cascade Pass.** This extremely popular 3.7-mile, four-hour trail is known
★ for stunning panoramas from the great mountain divide. Dozens of peaks line the horizon as you make your way up the fairly flat, hairpin-turn track, the scene fronted by a blanket of alpine wildflowers from July to mid-August. Arrive before noon if you want a parking spot at the trailhead. *Moderate.* ⊠ *Trailhead at end of Cascade River Rd., 14 miles from Marblemount.*

Diablo Lake Trail. Explore nearly 4 miles of waterside terrain on this route, which is accessed from the Sourdough Creek parking lot. An excellent alternative for parties with small hikers is to take the Seattle City Light Ferry one way. *Moderate.* ⊠ *Trailhead at milepost 135, Hwy. 20.*

DIFFICULT

Thornton Lakes Trail. A 5-mile climb into an alpine basin with three pretty lakes, this steep and strenuous hike takes about five to six hours round-trip. *Difficult.* ⊠ *Trailhead at Thornton Lake Rd. and Hwy. 20, 3 miles west of Newhalem.*

HORSEBACK RIDING

Many hiking trails and backwoods paths are also popular horseback-riding routes, particularly around the park's southern fringes.

TOURS AND OUTFITTERS

Cascade Corrals. This subsidiary of Stehekin Outfitters organizes 2½-hour horseback trips to Coon Lake and full-day rides (lunch included) to Moore Point and Bridge Creek. English- and western-style riding lessons are also available. Reservations are taken at the Courtney Log Office at Stehekin Landing. Some rides depart from the Landing, others from Stehekin Valley Ranch. ⊕ *www.cascadecorrals.com* ⊠ *$55–$150* ⊙ *June–mid-Sept., half-day rides daily at 8:15 and 2:15.*

KAYAKING

The park's tangles of waterways offer access to remote areas inaccessible by road or trail; here are some of the most pristine and secluded mountain scenes on the continent. Bring your own kayak and you can launch from any boat ramp or beach; otherwise, companies in several nearby towns and Seattle suburbs offer kayak and canoe rentals, portage, and tours. The upper basin of Lake Chelan (at the park's southern end) and Ross Lake (at the top edge of the park) are two well-known kayaking expanses, but there are dozens of smaller lakes and creeks between. The Stehekin River also provides many kayaking possibilities.

TOURS AND OUTFITTERS

Ross Lake Resort. The resort rents kayaks and offers portage service for exploring Ross Lake. A water-taxi service is also available; the resort is not accessible by road. ⊠ *503 Diablo St., Rockport* ☎ *206/386–4437, 206/708–3980 off-season (Jan.–May)* ⊕ *www.rosslakeresort.com.*

Stehekin Adventure Company. Book a two-hour trip along the lake's upper estuary and western shoreline with Stehekin Adventure Company. ⊠ *Stehekin Landing, Stehekin* ☎ *509/682–4677, 800/536–0745* ⊕ *www. stehekinoutfitters.com* ⊠ *Tour $35* ⊙ *Tours June–Sept., daily at 10.*

RAFTING

June through August is the park's white-water season, and rafting trips run through the lower section of the Stehekin River. Along the way take in views of cottonwood and pine forests, glimpses of Yawning Glacier on Magic Mountain, and placid vistas of Lake Chelan.

28

TOURS AND OUTFITTERS

Downstream River Runners. Check out this outfitter for rafting throughout the Northwest, including floats on the Skagit River in the summer months and again in winter for bald-eagle viewing. ☎ *206/910–7102* ⊕ *www.riverpeople.com.*

North Cascades River Expeditions. June through October, North Cascades River Expeditions focuses on regional rivers; trips are offered on the Upper Skagit year-round. ☎ *800/634–8433* ⊕ *www.riverexpeditions.com.*

Orion River Expeditions. Introductory, family-oriented floats are offered in August on the Skagit River for ages 6 and up. More lively white-water tours run on other area rivers April through September. ☎ *509/548–1401, 800/553–7466* ⊕ *www.orionexp.com.*

Stehekin Valley Ranch. Guided trips on the Class III Stehekin River leave from Stehekin Valley Ranch daily at 2:30. ✉ *Stehekin Valley Rd., 3½ miles from Stehekin Landing, Stehekin* ☎ *509/682–4677, 800/536–0745* ⊕ *www.stehekinvalleyranch.com* 🖃 *$50* ⊙ *June–Sept.*

Wildwater River Guides. Half-day rafting excursions on the Skagit River depart from Goodell Creek Campground near Newhalem. The mild waters are great for beginners and families. ✉ *Goodell Creek Campground, Newhalem* ☎ *509/470–8558, 800/522–9453* ⊕ *www.wildwater-river.com.*

WINTER SPORTS

Mt. Baker, just off the park's far northwest corner, is one of the Northwest's premier skiing, snowboarding, and snowshoeing regions—the area set a world record for most snow in a single season during the winter of 1998–99 (1,140 inches). The Mt. Baker Highway (Route 542) cuts through the slopes toward state sno-parks; Salmon Ridge Sno-Park, 46 miles east of Bellingham at exit 255, has groomed trails and parking. Mt. Baker Ski Area, 17 miles east of the town of Glacier, has eight chairlifts and access to backcountry skiing; its season runs roughly from November to April.

Stehekin is another base for winter sports. The Stehekin Valley alone has 20 miles of trails; some of the most popular are around Buckner Orchard, Coon Lake, and the Courtney Ranch (Cascade Corrals).

Mt. Baker. Off the park's northwest corner, this is the closest winter-sports area, with facilities for downhill and Nordic skiing, snowboarding, and other recreational ventures. The main base is the town of Glacier, 17 miles west of the slopes, where lodging is available. Equipment rental and food service are on site. ✉ *Hwy. 542, 52 miles east of Bellingham, Glacier* ☎ *360/734–6771, 360/671–0211 for snow reports* ⊕ *www.mtbaker.us* 🖃 *All-day lift ticket $50 weekdays, $55 weekends and holidays* ⊙ *Nov.–Apr.*

WHAT'S NEARBY

NEARBY TOWNS

Heading into North Cascades National Park from Seattle on Interstate 5 to Highway 2, **Sedro-Woolley** (pronounced "*see*-droh *wool*-lee") is the first main town you encounter. A former logging and steel-mill base settled by North Carolina pioneers, the settlement still has a 19th-century ambience throughout its rustic downtown area. Surrounded by farmlands, it's a pretty spot to stop and has basic visitor services like hotels, gas stations, and groceries. It's also home to the North Cascades National Park Headquarters. From here, it's about 40 miles to the park's western edges. Along the way, you still have a chance to stop for supplies in **Concrete**, about 20 miles from the park along Highway 2.

Marblemount is 10 miles farther east, about 12 miles west of the North Cascades Visitor Center. It's another atmospheric former timber settlement nestled in the mountain foothills, and its growing collection of motels, cafés, and tour outfitters draw outdoor enthusiasts each summer. The park's base town, though, is **Newhalem**, tucked right along the highway between the north and south regions. This is the place to explore the visitor center and its surrounding trails, view exhibits, and pick up maps, permits, and tour information.

Still traveling east on Highway 20, it's about 5 miles from Newhalem to **Diablo**, where the local lake, dam, and overlook are all good reasons to stop. Keep going until the road turns south along the park's eastern side: this is the famed North Cascades Scenic Highway. From top to bottom, including Rainy Pass and the curve through the chilly Washington Pass overlook, this section is about 20 miles.

Winthrop, a relaxed, riverside rodeo town complete with clapboard cafés and five-and-dime charm, is about a 6-mile drive east of Washington Pass. This is also an outdoor-recreation base, offering activities that range from cross-country skiing to hiking, mountain biking, and whitewater rafting. Less than 10 miles southeast of Winthrop, the tiny town of **Twisp** is settled in the farmlands and orchards, its streets lined with a few small lodgings and eateries.

The resort town of **Chelan**, nestled around its serene namesake lake, lies about 40 miles due south of Winthrop along Highway 153. It's a serene summer getaway for boating and swimming, as well as an access point for small villages and campgrounds along the shoreline. **Stehekin**, at the lake's northern end, is a favorite tourist stop for its peaceful isolation; without road connections, your options for getting here are by boat, floatplane, or trail. A ferry runs between Chelan and Stehekin.

VISITOR INFORMATION

Lake Chelan Chamber of Commerce ✉ *102 E. Johnson, Chelan* ☎ *509/682–3503, 800/424–3526* ⊕ *www.lakechelan.com.* **Sedro-Woolley Chamber of Commerce** ✉ *714-B Metcalf St., Sedro-Woolley* ☎ *360/855–1841, 888/225–8365* ⊕ *www.sedro-woolley.com.* **Twisp Visitor Information Center and**

28

Chamber of Commerce ✉ *201 S. Methow Valley Hwy., Twisp* ☎ *509/997–2020* 🌐 *www.twispinfo.com.* **Winthrop Chamber of Commerce** ✉ *202 Hwy. 20, Winthrop* ☎ *509/996–2125, 888/463–8469* 🌐 *www.winthropwashington.com.*

NEARBY ATTRACTIONS

Lake Chelan. This sinewy, 50.5-mile-long fjord—Washington's deepest lake—works its way from the town of Chelan, at its south end, to Stehekin, at the far northwest edge. The scenery is unparalleled, the flat blue water encircled by plunging gorges, with a vista of snow-slathered mountains beyond. No roads access the lake except for Chelan, so a floatplane or boat is needed to see the whole thing. Resorts dot the warmer eastern shores. ✉ *U.S. 97A, Chelan* ☎ *509/856–5700* 🌐 *www.lakechelan.com.*

Lake Chelan Boat Co. The *Lady of the Lake II* makes journeys from May to October, departing Chelan at 8:30 and returning at 6 ($40.50 round-trip). The *Lady Express,* a speedy catamaran, runs between Stehekin, Holden Village, the national park, and Lake Chelan year-round; schedules vary with the seasons. Tickets are $61 round-trip. The vessels also can drop off and pick up at lakeshore trailheads. ✉ *1418 Woodin Ave., Chelan* ☎ *509/682–4584, 888/682–4584* 🌐 *www.ladyofthelake.com.*

Lake Whatcom Railway. The steam-powered train makes short jaunts through the woods 11 miles north of Sedro-Woolley. Excursions run in July and August and during special events, such as the Christmas train rides with Santa in December. During peak weekends, tours depart at noon and children pay half-price. Note that the schedule changes seasonally. ✉ *Hwy. 9, Wickersham* ☎ *360/595–2218* 🌐 *www.lakewhatcomrailway.com* 🎟 *$25* 🕒 *Call for hrs.*

WHERE TO EAT

IN THE PARK

$ CAFÉ 🍴 **Stehekin Pastry Company.** As you enter this lawn-framed timber chalet, you're immersed in the tantalizing aromas of a European bakery. Glassed-in display cases are filled with trays of homemade baked goods, and the pungent espresso is eye-opening. Sit down at a windowside table and dig into an over-filled sandwich or rich bowl of soup—and don't forget dessert: we're guessing you'll never taste a better slice of pie, made with fruit fresh-picked from local orchards. Although it's outside of town, the shop is conveniently en route to Rainbow Falls. [$] *Average main: $5* ✉ *Stehekin Valley Rd., about 2 miles north of Stehekin Landing, Stehekin* ☎ *509/682–7742* 🌐 *www.stehekinpastry.com* 💳 *No credit cards* 🕒 *Closed mid-Oct.–Memorial Day. Closed Mon.–Thurs. early June and early Oct.*

$$ AMERICAN 🍴 **Stehekin Valley Ranch.** Meals in the rustic log ranch house, served at polished wood tables, include buffet dinners of steak, ribs, hamburgers, salad, beans, and dessert. Note that breakfast is served 7 to 9, lunch is noon to 1, and dinner is 5:30 to 7. Show up later than that and you'll find the kitchen is closed. For guests not staying at the ranch,

dinner reservations are required and transportation from the Stehekin Landing costs $6. [$] *Average main: $18* ✉ *9 miles north of Stehekin Landing, Stehekin Valley Rd., Stehekin* ☎ *509/682–4677, 800/536–0745* 🌐 *www.stehekinvalleyranch.com* ✍ *Reservations essential* 💳 *No credit cards* ⏲ *Closed Oct.–mid-June.*

PICNIC AREAS

Developed picnic areas at both Rainy Pass (Highway 20, 38 miles east of the park visitor center) and Washington Pass (Highway 20, 42 miles east of the visitor center) have a half-dozen picnic tables, drinking water, and pit toilets. The vistas of surrounding peaks are sensational at these two overlooks. More picnic facilities are located near the visitor center in Newhalem and at Colonial Creek Campground, 10 miles east of the visitor center on Highway 20.

BEST BETS FOR FAMILIES

- **Get out on the water.** Take a Lake Chelan ferry, make a kayak exploration of river areas, or run the white water on the Stehekin River.
- **Learn about nature.** Join a guided walk, evening program, or ranger-led children's event—and be sure to stop at the North Cascades Institute's Environmental Learning Center near Diablo Dam.
- **Travel back in time.** Head to Winthrop for pioneer-style family fun.

OUTSIDE THE PARK

28

$$$ AMERICAN 🍴 **Buffalo Run.** Buffalo, venison, elk, and ostrich are the specialties at this little place next to the Marblemount Post Office, but vegetarians will find a few nonmeat options on the menu too. The atmosphere is completely casual, with buffalo heads and Old West memorabilia lining the dining room walls. Outside, the patio adds warm-weather seating and garden views; it's a good spot to kick back with a glass of wine. The adjacent inn, under the same management, is an inexpensive overnight option. [$] *Average main: $22* ✉ *60084 Hwy. 20, Marblemount* ☎ *360/873–2461* 🌐 *www.buffaloruninn.com* ⏲ *Closed Nov.–Apr.*

$$$$ PACIFIC NORTHWEST 🍴 **Dining Room at Sun Mountain Lodge.** In a sylvan hilltop setting overlooking the Methow Valley, intimate tables and a woodsy interior design set the scene for an extraordinary dining experience. The upscale Pacific Northwest cuisine is based on often-organic, locally grown, raised, caught, and crafted ingredients, providing for exquisite flavors to match the artful presentation and elegant yet unpretentious atmosphere. Delicacies include chicken curry soup, melt-in-your-mouth pork chops, eggplant gateaux, and beef tenderloin with foie gras and potato tart. The dessert menu has many tempting choices, including a duo of vanilla and mocha brûlée, individual apple pie with house-made vanilla bean ice cream, and Chocolate Fantasy—a quintet of chocolate delights. The 5,000-bottle wine cellar is one of the best and most extensive in the region. [$] *Average main: $38* ✉ *604 Patterson Lake Rd., Winthrop* ☎ *509/996–2211* 🌐 *www.sunmountainlodge.com/dining* ⏲ *Closed Sun.–Thurs. in winter and spring; closed late-Oct.–early Dec. and Mar.–early Apr. No lunch.*

$$

AMERICAN

✕ **Twisp River Pub.** This popular brewpub produces a range of house beers, including IPA (the most popular), ESB, and porter, hard pear and apple ciders, and seasonal ales. Regional wines are also available. Within the industrial Craftsman-style interior, choose from burgers fashioned from local beef, fish-and-chips, and meaty sandwiches at lunch. Dinners include steak, salmon, coconut curry, and Thai peanut noodles—one of the most frequently requested dishes. Or you can snack on buffalo wings, nachos, and an array of homemade soups. Brunch is served on Sunday. There's live music every weekend and jazz in the riverside beer garden on summer Wednesday evenings. $ *Average main: $13* ⊠ *201 Hwy. 20, 9 miles south of Winthrop, Twisp* ☎ *509/997–6822, 888/220–3360* ⊕ *www.methowbrewing. com* ⊘ *Closed Mon.–Wed. mid-Oct.–mid-May (except Christmas–New Year).*

WHERE TO STAY

IN THE PARK

$$

HOTEL

▦ **North Cascades Lodge at Stehekin.** Large lodge-style buildings welcome you with crackling fires and Lake Chelan views. **Pros:** on the water; recreation center with pool table; tent-to-tent hiking excursions. **Cons:** no air-conditioning. $ *Rooms from: $128* ⊠ *955 Stehekin Valley Rd., Stehekin* ☎ *509/682–4494* ⊕ *www.lodgeatstehekin.com* ➟ *28 rooms, 1 house* ⦿ *No meals.*

$$$

B&B/INN

▦ **Silver Bay Inn Resort.** Perched on a slip of land at the head of Lake Chelan, Silver Bay's accommodations feature water and mountain views; all have their own kitchens. **Pros:** hot tub vistas; free use of boats and bikes. **Cons:** summertime mosquitoes; five-night minimum in summer; not for families with kids under 12. $ *Rooms from: $195* ⊠ *Silver Bay Rd., Stehekin* ☎ *800/555–7781* ⊕ *www.silverbayinn.com* ➟ *1 room, 2 cabins, 1 house* ⊘ *Closed Nov.–Apr.* ⦿ *No meals.*

$$$$

B&B/INN

▦ **Stehekin Valley Ranch.** Alongside pretty meadows at the edge of pine forest, this classic ranch is a center for hikers and horseback riders, who stay in barnlike cabins with cedar paneling, tile floors, and a private bath, or canvas-roof tent cabins with bunk beds, kerosene lamps, and shared bathrooms. **Pros:** many activities; free vehicle use with kitchen cabins. **Cons:** no bathrooms in tent cabins. $ *Rooms from: $250* ⊠ *Stehekin Valley Rd., 9 miles north of Stehekin Landing, Stehekin* ☎ *509/682–4677, 800/536–0745* ⊕ *www.stehekinvalleyranch. com* ➟ *7 tent cabins (shared bathroom), 8 cabins* ⊘ *Closed Oct.–mid-June* ⦿ *All meals.*

OUTSIDE THE PARK

$$$$

RESORT

FAMILY

▦ **Campbell's Resort.** More than a century old, this sprawling resort sits on landscaped grounds alongside Lake Chelan; every room has a balcony with mountain and beach views, and some have a kitchen or fireplace. **Pros:** plenty of summer programs to keep kids busy; on-site day spa; great base for winter sports. **Cons:** tour buses, weddings,

CLOSE UP

Best Campgrounds in North Cascades

Tent campers can choose between forest sites, riverside spots, lake grounds, or meadow spreads encircled by mountains. Here camping is as easy or challenging as you want to make it; some campgrounds are a short walk from ranger stations, while others are miles from the highway. Note that many campsites, particularly those around Stehekin, are completely remote and without road access anywhere, so you have to walk, boat, ride a horse, or take a floatplane to reach them. Most don't accept reservations, and spots fill up quickly May through September. If there's no ranger on-site, you can often sign yourself in—and always check in at a ranger station before you set out overnight. Note that some areas are occasionally closed due to flooding, forest fires, or other factors.

Lake Chelan National Recreation Area. Many backcountry camping areas are accessible via park shuttles or boat. All require a free backcountry permit. Purple Point, the most popular campground due to its quick access to Stehekin Landing, has six tent sites, bear boxes, and nearby road access. ✉ *Stehekin Landing, Stehekin* ☎ *360/854*-7365 Ext. 14.

and conferences bring noisy crowds. [$] *Rooms from: $265* ✉ *104 W. Woodin Ave., Chelan* ☎ *509/682–2561, 800/553–8225* 🌐 *www.campbellsresort.com* 🛏 *163 rooms, 5 suites, 2 cabins* 🍴 *No meals.*

$ B&B/INN 🏨 **Chewuch Inn.** Set on 5 acres just south of Winthrop, lodgings at the inn have modern amenities and luxurious touches. **Pros:** free cookies in afternoon; excellent service; short walk to town. **Cons:** basement rooms have no windows; a bit hard to find off the main highway. [$] *Rooms from: $95* ✉ *223 White Ave., Winthrop* ☎ *509/996–3107, 800/747–3107* 🌐 *www.chewuchinn.com* 🛏 *11 rooms, 7 cabins* 🍴 *Breakfast.*

$$$$ RESORT Fodor's Choice ★ 🏨 **Freestone Inn.** At the heart of the 120-acre, historic Wilson Ranch, amid more than 2 million acres of forest, this upscale mountain retreat embraces luxury along with the pioneer spirit. **Pros:** gorgeous scenery; myriad activities; close to North Cascades National Park (17 miles west). **Cons:** limited cell-phone and TV service; some resort amenities may be limited in shoulder season. [$] *Rooms from: $225* ✉ *31 Early Winters Dr., about 14 miles northwest of Winthop, Mazama* ☎ *509/996–3906, 800/639–3809* 🌐 *www.freestoneinn.com* 🛏 *10 rooms, 7 suites, 15 cabins, 4 lodges* 🍴 *Breakfast.*

$$ B&B/INN 🏨 **Mazama Country Inn.** Ideal as a base for outdoor-recreation enthusiasts, the inn offers clean, no-frills accommodations and nearby access to the Pasayten Wilderness and North Cascades National Park. **Pros:** inclusive meal option available in winter; off-season specials; rooms very clean. **Cons:** no TV; no kids under 10 during winter months. [$] *Rooms from: $110* ✉ *15 Country Rd., Mazama* ☎ *800/843–7951, 509/996–2681* 🌐 *www.mazamacountryinn.com* 🛏 *18 rooms* 🍴 *Breakfast.*

$ B&B/INN **Methow Valley Inn.** Run with family-style friendliness, this historic country inn with lovely gardens has guest rooms furnished with antiques and decorated with a Scandinavian influence. **Pros:** gorgeous gardens in summer; lovely holiday decorations in winter; superb cleanliness. **Cons:** no bathtubs; no in-room TVs; some shared bathrooms; no children under 12 unless you rent the entire inn. [$] *Rooms from: $89* ✉ *234 E. 2nd Ave., about 9 miles south of Winthrop, Twisp* ☎ *509/997–2253* 🌐 *www.methowvalleyinn.com* 🛏 *7 rooms, 5 with private bath, 1 suite* 🍴 *Breakfast.*

$$ B&B/INN **River Run Inn.** The rooms and cabins aren't fancy here, but the inn's riverfront location and amenities—including picnic tables, hammocks, playground, lawn games, and indoor pool—make it a popular place to stay. **Pros:** free use of bikes; serene riverfront setting; free DVD library. **Cons:** hot tub is only big enough for a few people; bathrooms are small. [$] *Rooms from: $120* ✉ *27 Rader Rd., Winthrop* ☎ *800/757–2709, 509/996–2173* 🌐 *www.riverrun-inn.com* 🛏 *10 rooms, 5 cabins* 🍴 *No meals.*

$$$$ RESORT Fodor's Choice ★ **Sun Mountain Lodge.** The stunning North Cascades and all its attractions are the stars of this outdoor-oriented resort set 3,000-feet up in the foothills, with spectacular mountain views and a range of activities that make it a year-round destination, whether the peaks are covered in snow or wildflowers. **Pros:** stunning setting; a wide array of outdoor activities year-round; panoramic views; award-winning dining; warm hospitality. **Cons:** limited cell service; roundabout route from Seattle in winter. [$] *Rooms from: $235* ✉ *604 Patterson Lake Rd., Winthrop* ☎ *509/996–2211, 800/572–0493* 🌐 *www.sunmountainlodge.com* 🛏 *86 rooms, 10 suites, 16 cabins* 🍴 *Breakfast.*

OLYMPIC
NATIONAL PARK

WELCOME TO OLYMPIC

TOP REASONS TO GO

★ **Exotic rain forest:** A rain forest in the Pacific Northwest? Indeed, Olympic National Park is one of the few places in the world with this unique temperate landscape.

★ **Beachcombing:** Miles of rugged, spectacular coastline hemmed with sea stacks and tidal pools edge the driftwood-strewn shores of the Olympic Peninsula.

★ **Nature's hot tubs:** A dip in Sol Duc's natural geothermal mineral pools offers a secluded spa experience in the wooded heart of the park.

★ **Lofty vistas:** The hardy can hike up meadowed foothill trails or climb the frosty peaks throughout the Olympics—or just drive up to Hurricane Ridge for endless views.

★ **A sense of history:** American Indian history is key to this region, where eight tribes have traditional ties to the park lands— there's 12,000 years of human history to explore.

1 Coastal Olympic.
Here the Pacific smashes endlessly into the rugged coastline, carving out some of the park's most memorable scenes in the massive, rocky sea stacks and islets just offshore. Back from the water are beaches and tide pools full of sea stars, crabs, and anemones.

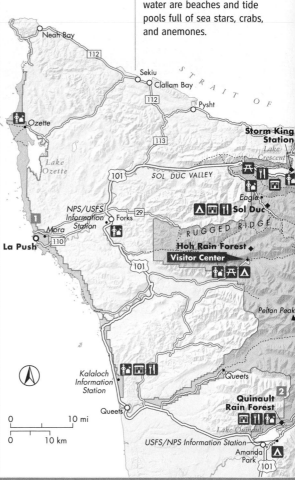

2 The Rain Forest.
Centered on the Hoh, Queets, and Quinault river valleys, this is the region's most unique landscape. Fog-shrouded Douglas firs and Sitka spruces, some more than 300 feet tall, huddle in this moist, pine-carpeted area, shading fern- and moss-draped cedars, maples, and alders.

3 The Mountains. Craggy gray peaks and snow-covered summits dominate the skyline. Low-level foliage and wildflower meadows make for excellent hiking in the plateaus. Even on the sunniest days, temperatures are brisk. Some roads are closed in winter months.

4 Alpine Meadows.
In midsummer, the swath of colors is like a Monet canvas spread over the landscape, and wildlife teems among the honeyed flowers. Trails are never prettier, and views are crisp and vast.

WASHINGTON

GETTING ORIENTED

The Olympic peninsula's elegant snowcapped and forested landscape is edged on all sides by water: to the north the Strait of Juan de Fuca separates the United States from Canada, a network of Puget Sound bays laces the east, the Chehalis River meanders along the southern end, and the massive gray Pacific Ocean guards the west side.

29

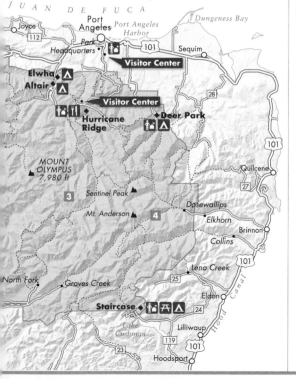

KEY	
🏕	Ranger Station
△	Campground
🔀	Picnic Area
🍴	Restaurant
🏠	Lodge
🚶	Trailhead
🚻	Restrooms
⇗	Scenic Viewpoint
⋯⋯	Walking/Hiking Trails

Updated by
Shelley Arenas

A spellbinding setting is tucked into the country's far-north-western corner, within the heart-shape Olympic Peninsula. Edged on all sides by water, the forested landscape is remote and pristine, and works its way around the sharpened ridges of the snowcapped Olympic Mountains. Big lakes cut pockets of blue in the rugged blanket of pine forests, and hot springs gurgle up from the foothills. Along the coast the sights are even more enchanting: wave-sculpted boulders, tidal pools teeming with sea life, and tree-topped sea stacks.

OLYMPIC PLANNER

WHEN TO GO

Summer, with its long stretches of sun-filled days, is prime touring time for Olympic National Park. June through September are the peak months; Hurricane Ridge, the Hoh Rain Forest, Lake Crescent, and Ruby Beach are bustling by 10 am.

Late spring and early autumn are also good bets for clear weather; anytime between April and October, you'll have a good chance of fair skies. Between Thanksgiving and Easter, it's a toss-up as to which days will turn out fair; prepare for heavy clouds, rain showers, and chilly temperatures, then hope for the best.

Winter is a great time to visit if you enjoy isolation. Locals are usually the only hardy souls during this time, except for weekend skiers heading to the snowfields around Hurricane Ridge. Many visitor facilities have limited hours or are closed from October to April.

AVG. HIGH/LOW TEMPS.

JAN.	FEB.	MAR.	APR.	MAY	JUNE
45/33	48/35	51/36	55/39	60/44	65/48

JULY	AUG.	SEPT.	OCT.	NOV.	DEC.
68/50	69/51	66/48	58/42	50/37	45/34

FESTIVALS AND EVENTS

MAY **Irrigation Festival.** For more than 100 years, the people have Sequim have been celebrating the irrigation ditches that brought life-giving water here. Highlights of the nine-day festival include a beauty pageant, logging demonstrations, arts and crafts, classic car show, strongman competition, parades, and a picnic. ⊕ *www.irrigationfestival.com.*

JUNE–AUGUST **Centrum Summer Arts Festival.** This summer-long lineup of concerts and workshops is held at Fort Worden State Park, a 19th-century army base near Port Townsend. ☎ *360/385–3102* ⊕ *www.centrum.org.*

JUNE–SEPTEMBER **Olympic Music Festival.** A variety of classical concerts are performed in a renovated barn; picnic on the farm while you listen. ☎ *360/732–4800* ⊕ *www.olympicmusicfestival.org.*

JULY **Forks Old-Fashioned Fourth of July.** A salmon bake, parade, demolition derby, arts and crafts exhibits, kids activities, and plenty of fireworks mark Forks' weekend-long celebration. ☎ *360/374–2531, 800/443–6757* ⊕ *www.forkswa.com.*

Sequim Lavender Farm Faire. Held the same weekend as the long-running Sequim Lavender Festival, this newer event features guided farm tours and a free festival in the park. ☎ *360/452–6300* ⊕ *sequimlavender-farmersassociation.org.*

Sequim Lavender Festival. Mid-month, a street fair and free self-guided farm tours celebrate Sequim's many fragrant lavender fields. ☎ *360/681–3035* ⊕ *www.lavenderfestival.com.*

SEPTEMBER **Wooden Boat Festival.** Hundreds of antique boats sail into Port Townsend for the weekend; there's also live music, education programs, and demonstrations. ☎ *360/385–3628* ⊕ *www.woodenboat.org.*

29

PLANNING YOUR TIME
OLYMPIC IN ONE DAY

Start at the **Lake Quinault Lodge,** in the park's southwest corner. From here, drive a half hour into the Quinault Valley via **South Shore Road.** Tackle the forested **Graves Creek Trail,** then head up **North Shore Road** to the Quinault Rain Forest Interpretive Trail. Next, head back to U.S. 101 and drive to **Ruby Beach,** where a shoreline walk presents a breathtaking scene of sea stacks and sparkling, pink-hued sands.

Forks, and its **Timber Museum,** are your next stop; have lunch here, then drive 20 minutes to the beach at **La Push.** Next, head to **Lake Crescent,** around the corner to the northeast, where you can rent a boat, take a swim, or enjoy a picnic next to the sparkling teal waters. Drive through **Port Angeles** to **Hurricane Ridge;** count on an hour's drive from bottom to top if there aren't too many visitors. At the ridge, explore the visitor center or hike the 3-mile loop to **Hurricane Hill,** where you can see over the entire park north to Vancouver Island and south past Mt. Olympus.

GOOD READS

■ Robert L. Wood's *Olympic Mountain Trail Guide* is a great resource for both day hikers and those planning longer excursions.

■ Stephen Whitney's *A Field Guide to the Cascades and Olympics* is an excellent trailside reference, covering more than 500 plant and animal species found in the park.

■ The park's newspaper, the *Olympic Bugler,* is a seasonal guide for activities and opportunities in the park. You can pick it up at the visitor centers.

■ A handy online catalog of books, maps, and passes for northwest parks is available from Discover Your Northwest (⊕ *www.discovernw.org*).

GETTING HERE AND AROUND

You can enter the park at a number of points, but since the park is 95% wilderness, access roads do not penetrate far. The best way to get around and to see many of the park's top sites is on foot.

BOAT TRAVEL

Ferries provide another unique (though indirect) link to the Olympic area from Seattle; contact **Washington State Ferries** (☎ *800/843–3779, 206/464–6400* ⊕ *www.wsdot.wa.gov/ferries*) for information.

BUS TRAVEL

Grays Harbor Transit runs buses on weekdays only from Aberdeen, Hoquiam, and Forks to Amanda Park, on the west end of Lake Quinault. Jefferson Transit operates a Forks–Amanda Park route Monday through Saturday.

Bus Contacts Grays Harbor Transit ☎ *360/532–2770, 800/562–9730* ⊕ *www.ghtransit.com.* **Jefferson Transit** ☎ *800/371–0497, 360/385-4777* ⊕ *www.jeffersontransit.com.*

CAR TRAVEL

U.S. 101 essentially encircles the main section of Olympic National Park, and a number of roads lead from the highway into the park's mountains and toward its beaches. You can reach U.S. 101 via Interstate 5 at Olympia, via Route 12 at Aberdeen, or via Route 104 from the Washington state ferry terminals at Bainbridge or Kingston.

PARK ESSENTIALS
ADMISSION FEES AND PERMITS

Seven-day vehicle admission fee is $15; an annual family pass is $30. Individuals arriving on foot, bike, or motorcycle pay $5. An overnight wilderness permit, available at visitor centers and ranger stations, is $5 (covers registration of your party for up to 14 days), plus $2 per person per night. A frequent-hiker pass, which covers all wilderness-use fees, is $30 per year. Fishing in freshwater streams and lakes within Olympic National Park does not require a Washington state fishing license; however, anglers must acquire a salmon-steelhead punch card when fishing for those species. Ocean fishing and harvesting shellfish and seaweed require licenses, which are available at sporting goods and outdoor supply stores.

ADMISSION HOURS

Six park entrances are open 24/7; gate kiosk hours (for buying passes) vary according to season and location, but most are staffed during daylight hours. Olympic National Park is in the Pacific time zone.

CELL-PHONE RECEPTION

Note that cell reception is sketchy in wilderness areas. There are public telephones at the Olympic National Park Visitor Center, Hoh River Rain Forest Visitor Center, and lodging properties within the park—Lake Crescent, Kalaloch, and Sol Duc Hot Springs. Fairholme General Store also has a phone.

RESTAURANTS

The major resorts are your best bets for eating out in the park. Each has a main restaurant, café, and/or kiosk, as well as casually upscale dinner service, with regional seafood, meat, and produce complemented by a range of microbrews and good Washington and international wines. Reservations are either recommended or required.

Outside the park, small, easygoing cafés and bistros line the main thoroughfares in Sequim, Port Angeles, and Port Townsend, offering cuisine that ranges from hearty American-style fare to more eclectic local flavor.

Prices in the reviews are the average cost of a main course at dinner, or if dinner is not served, at lunch.

HOTELS

Major park resorts run from good to terrific, with generally comfortable rooms, excellent facilities, and easy access to trails, beaches, and activity centers. Midsize accommodations, like Sol Duc Hot Springs Resort, are often shockingly rustic—but remember, you're here for the park, not for the rooms.

The towns around the park have motels, hotels, and resorts for every budget. For high-priced stays with lots of perks, base yourself in the new coastal community of Seabrook (near Pacific Beach). Sequim and Port Angeles have many attractive, friendly B&Bs, plus lots of inexpensive chain hotels and motels. Forks is basically a motel town, with a few guesthouses around its fringes.

Prices in the reviews are the lowest cost of a standard double room in high season. For expanded reviews, facilities, and current deals, visit Fodors.com.

VISITOR INFORMATION

PARK CONTACT INFORMATION

Olympic National Park ⊠ *Olympic National Park Visitor Center, 3002 Mount Angeles Rd., Port Angeles* ☎ *360/565–3130* ⊕ *www.nps.gov/olym.*

VISITOR CENTERS

Forks NPS/USFS Recreation Information Center. The information center has park maps, brochures, and exhibits; they also provide permits and rent bear-proof containers. ⊠ *551 S. Forks Ave. (U.S. 101), Forks* ☎ *360/374–5877* ⊕ *www.nps.gov/olym/planyourvisit/visitorcenters. htm* ☾ *Mid-June–mid-Oct., Thurs.–Sun. 9–4.*

29

Hoh Rain Forest Visitor Center. Pick up park maps and pamphlets, permits, and activities lists in this busy, woodsy chalet; there's also a shop and exhibits on natural history. Several short interpretive trails and longer wilderness treks start from here. ✉ *Hoh Valley Rd., 31 miles south of Forks* ☎ *360/374–6925* ⊕ *www.nps.gov/olym/planyourvisit/ visitorcenters.htm* ⊙ *Mid-June–Aug., daily 9–5:30; Sept.–mid-June, Fri.–Sun. 9–4.*

Hurricane Ridge Visitor Center. The upper level of this visitor center has exhibits and nice views; the lower level has a gift shop and snack bar. Guided walks and programs start in late June. In winter, find details on the surrounding ski and sledding slopes and take guided snowshoe walks. ✉ *Hurricane Ridge Rd., Port Angeles* ☎ *360/565–3131* ⊕ *www. nps.gov/olym/planyourvisit/visitorcenters.htm* ⊙ *May–Dec., daily 9– dusk; late-Dec.–Apr., Fri.–Sun. 10–4 (if road is open).*

Olympic National Park Visitor Center. This modern, well-organized facility, staffed by park rangers, provides everything: maps, trail brochures, campground advice, weather forecasts, listings of wildlife sightings, educational programs and exhibits, information on road and trail closures, and a gift shop. ✉ *3002 Mount Angeles Rd., Port Angeles* ☎ *360/565–3130* ⊕ *www.nps.gov/olym* ⊙ *May–Sept., daily 9–4; Oct.–Apr., daily 10–4.*

South Shore Quinault Ranger Station. The National Forest Service's ranger station near the Lake Quinault Lodge has maps, campground information, and program listings. ✉ *353 S. Shore Rd., Quinault* ☎ *360/288– 2525* ⊕ *www.fs.usda.gov/recarea/olympic* ⊙ *Year-round, weekdays 8–4:30; Memorial Day–Labor Day, also open weekends 9–4.*

Wilderness Information Center (WIC). Located behind Olympic National Park Visitor Center, this facility provides all the information you'll need for a trip in the park, including trail conditions, safety tips, and weather bulletins. The office also issues camping permits, takes campground reservations, and rents bear-proof food canisters. ✉ *3002 Mount Angeles Rd., Port Angeles* ☎ *360/565–3100* ⊕ *www.nps.gov/olym* ⊙ *May– Sept., daily 9–4; Oct.–Apr., daily 10–4.*

EXPLORING

Most of the park's attractions are found either off U.S. 101 or down trails that require hikes of 15 minutes or longer. The west coast beaches are linked to the highway by downhill tracks; the number of cars parked alongside the road at the start of the paths indicates how crowded the beach will be.

SCENIC DRIVES

Port Angeles Visitor Center to Hurricane Ridge. The premier scenic drive in Olympic National Park is a steep ribbon of curves, which climbs from thickly forested foothills and subalpine meadows into the upper stretches of pine-swathed peaks. At the top, the visitor center at Hurricane Ridge has some truly spectacular views over the heart of the

Plants and Wildlife in Olympic

Along the high mountain slopes hardy cedar, fir, and hemlock trees stand tough on the rugged land; the lower montane forests are filled with thickets of silver firs; and valleys stream with Douglas firs and western hemlock. The park's famous temperate rain forests are on the peninsula's western side, marked by broad western red cedars, towering red spruces, and ferns festooned with strands of mosses and patchwork lichens. This lower landscape is also home to some of the Northwest's largest trees: massive cedar and Sitka spruce near Lake Quinault can measure more than 700 inches around, and Douglas firs near the Queets and Hoh rivers are nearly as wide.

These landscapes are home to a variety of wildlife, including many large mammals and 15 creatures found nowhere else in the world. Hikers often come across Roosevelt's elk, black-tailed deer, mountain goats, beavers, raccoons, skunks, opossums, and foxes; Douglas squirrels and flying squirrels populate the heights of the forest. Less common are black bears (most prevalent from May through August); wolves, bobcats,

and cougar are rarely seen. Birdlife includes bald eagles, red-tailed hawks, osprey, and great horned owls. Rivers and lakes are filled with freshwater fish, while beaches hold crabs, sea stars, anemones, and other shelled creatures. Get out in a boat on the Pacific to spot seals, sea lions, and sea otters—and perhaps a pod of porpoises, orcas, or gray whales.

Beware of jellyfish around the shores—beached jellyfish can still sting. In the woods, check for ticks after every hike and after each shower. Biting nasties include black flies, horseflies, sand fleas, and the ever-present mosquitoes. Yellow-jacket nests populate tree hollows along many trails; signs throughout the Hoh Rain Forest warn hikers to move quickly through these sections. If one or two chase you, remain calm and keep walking; these are just "guards" making sure you're keeping away from the hive. Poison oak is common, so familiarize yourself with its appearance. Bug repellent, sunscreen, and long pants and sleeves will go a long way toward making your experience more comfortable.

29

peninsula and across the Strait of Juan de Fuca. (Backpackers note wryly that you have to hike a long way in other parts of the park to get the kinds of views you can drive to here.) A mile past the visitor center, there are picnic tables in open meadows with photo-worthy views of the mountains to the east. Hurricane Ridge also has an uncommonly fine display of wildflowers in spring and summer. In winter, vehicles must carry chains, and the road is usually open Friday–Sunday only (call first to check conditions). ☎ *360/565–3131* ⊕ *www.nps.gov/olym.*

HISTORIC SITES

La Push. At the mouth of Quileute River, La Push is the tribal center of the Quileute Indians. In fact, the town's name is a variation on the French *la bouche,* which means "the mouth." Offshore rock spires known as sea stacks dot the coast here, and you may catch a glimpse of bald eagles nesting in the nearby cliffs. ⊠ *Rte. 110, 14 miles west of Forks, La Push* ⊕ *www.nps.gov/olym/planyourvisit/upload/Mora.pdf.*

Lake Ozette. The third-largest glacial impoundment in Washington anchors the coastal strip of Olympic National Park at its north end. The small town of Ozette, home to a coastal tribe, is the trailhead for two of the park's better one-day hikes. Both 3-mile trails lead over boardwalks through swampy wetland and coastal old-growth forest to the ocean shore and uncrowded beaches. ⊠ *At the end of Hoko-Ozette Rd., 26 miles southwest of Hwy. 112 near Sekiu, Ozette* ☎ *360/963–2725 for Ozette Ranger Station* ⊕ *www.nps.gov/olym/planyourvisit/visiting-ozette.htm.*

SCENIC STOPS

Fodor'sChoice
★ **Hoh River Rain Forest.** South of Forks, an 18-mile spur road links U.S. 101 with this unique temperate rain forest, where spruce and hemlock trees soar to heights of more than 200 feet. Alders and big-leaf maples are so densely covered with mosses they look more like shaggy prehistoric animals than trees, and elk browse in shaded glens. Be prepared for precipitation: the region receives 140 inches or more each year. The visitor center is open daily July through September from 9 to 6, and Friday through Sunday from 10 to 4 in other months. ⊠ *From U.S. 101, at about 20 miles north of Kalaloch, turn onto Upper Hoh Rd. 18 miles east to Hoh Rain Forest Visitor Center* ☎ *360/374–6925* ⊕ *www.nps.gov/olym.*

Fodor'sChoice
★ **Hurricane Ridge.** The panoramic view from this 5,200-foot-high ridge encompasses the Olympic range, the Strait of Juan de Fuca, and Vancouver Island. Guided tours are given in summer along the many paved and unpaved trails, where wildflowers and wildlife such as deer and marmots flourish. ⊠ *Hurricane Ridge Rd., 17 miles south of Port Angeles* ☎ *360/565–3130 for visitor center* ⊕ *www.nps.gov/olym* ☉ *Visitor center: daily in summer; on days road is open rest of year.*

Kalaloch. With a lodge, a huge campground, miles of coastline, and easy access from the highway, this is another popular spot. Keen-eyed beachcombers may spot sea otters just offshore; they were reintroduced here in 1970. ⊠ *U.S. 101, 32 miles northwest of Lake Quinault, Kalaloch* ☎ *360/565–3130 for visitor center* ⊕ *www.nps.gov/olym/planyourvisit/ visiting-kalaloch-and-ruby-beach.htm.*

Lake Crescent. Visitors see Lake Crescent as U.S. 101 winds along its southern shore, giving way to gorgeous views of teal waters rippling in a basin formed by Tuscan-like hills. In the evening, low bands of clouds caught between the surrounding mountains often linger over its reflective surface. ⊠ *U.S. 101, 16 miles west of Port Angeles and 28 miles northeast of Forks* ☎ *360/565–3130 for visitor center* ⊕ *www.nps.gov/ olym/planyourvisit/visiting-lake-crescent.htm.*

DID YOU KNOW?

Encompassing more than 70 miles of beachfront, Olympic is one of the few national parks of the West with an ocean beach (Redwood, Channel Islands, and some of the Alaskan parks are the others). The park is therefore home to many marine animals, including sea otters, whales, sea lions, and seals.

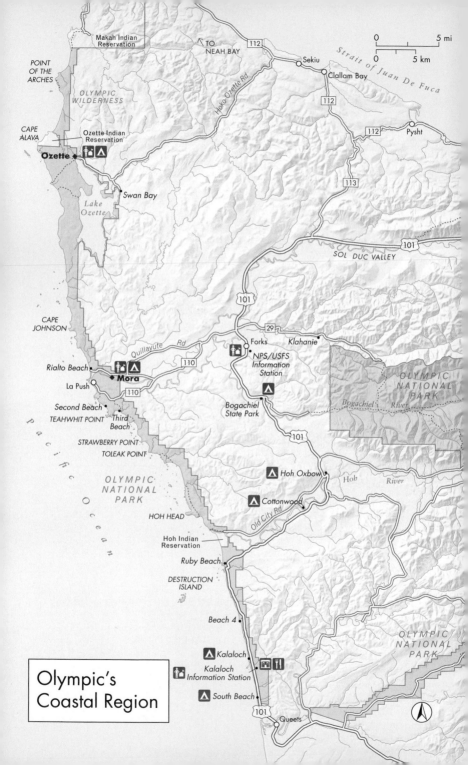

Lake Quinault. This glimmering lake, 4½ miles long and 300 feet deep, is the first landmark you'll reach when driving the west-side loop of U.S. 101. The rain forest is thickest here, with moss-draped maples and alders, and towering spruce, fir, and hemlock. Enchanted Valley, high up near the Quinault River's source, is a deeply glaciated valley that's closer to the Hood Canal than to the Pacific Ocean. A scenic loop drive circles the lake and travels around a section of the Quinault River. ✉ *U.S. 101, 38 miles north of Hoquiam* ☎ *360/288–2444 for Quinault Rain Forest ranger station* ⊕ *www.nps.gov/olym/planyourvisit/visiting-quinault.htm* ☉ *Ranger station open part-time in summer.*

Second and Third Beaches. During low tide these flat, driftwood-strewn expanses are perfect for long afternoon strolls. Second Beach, accessed via an easy forest trail through Quileute lands, opens to a vista of Pacific Ocean and sea stacks; Third Beach offers a 1.3-mile forest hike for a warm-up before reaching the sands. ✉ *U.S. 101, 32 miles north of Lake Quinault* ☎ *360/565–3130 for visitor center* ⊕ *www. nps.gov/olym.*

Sol Duc. Sol Duc Valley is one of those magical places where all the Northwest's virtues seem at hand: lush lowland forests, sparkling river scenes, salmon runs, and serene hiking trails. Here, the popular Sol Duc Hot Springs area includes three attractive sulfuric pools ranging in temperature from 98°F to 104°F. ✉ *Sol Duc Rd., south of U.S. 101, 12 miles past the west end of Lake Crescent* ☎ *360/565–3130 for visitor center* ⊕ *www.nps.gov/olym.*

Staircase. Unlike the forests of the park's south and west sides, Douglas fir is the dominant tree on the east slope of the Olympic Mountains. Fire has played an important role in creating the majestic forest here, as the Staircase Ranger Station explains in interpretive exhibits. ✉ *At end of Rte. 119, 15 miles from U.S. 101 at Hoodsport* ☎ *360/877–5569 Staircase Ranger Station* ☉ *Hrs vary.*

29

EDUCATIONAL OFFERINGS

CLASSES AND SEMINARS

NatureBridge. This rustic educational facility offers talks and excursions focusing on park ecology and history. Trips range from canoe trips to camping excursions, with a strong emphasis on family programs. ✉ *111 Barnes Point Rd., Port Angeles* ☎ *360/928–3720* ⊕ *www.naturebridge. org/olympic-national-park.*

RANGER PROGRAMS

Junior Ranger Program. Anyone can pick up the booklet at visitor centers and ranger stations and follow this fun program, which includes assignments to discover park flora and fauna, ocean life, and Native American lore. Kids get a badge when they turn in the finished work. ☎ *360/565–3130* ⊕ *www.nps.gov/olym/forkids/beajuniorranger.htm.*

SPORTS AND THE OUTDOORS

BEACHCOMBING

The wild, shell-strewn Pacific coast teems with tide pools and crustaceans. Crabs, sand dollars, anemones, sea stars, and all sorts of shellfish are exposed at low tide, when flat beaches can stretch out for hundreds of yards. The most easily accessible sand-strolling spots are Rialto, Ruby, First, and Second beaches, near Mora and La Push, and Kalaloch Beach and Fourth Beach in the Kalaloch stretch.

The Wilderness Act and the park's code of ethics instruct visitors to leave all nonliving materials where they are for others to enjoy.

BICYCLING

The rough gravel car tracks to some of the park's remote sites were meant for four-wheel-drive vehicles, but can double as mountain-bike routes. The Quinault Valley, Queets River, Hoh River, and Sol Duc River roads have bike paths through old-growth forest. Graves Creek Road, in the southwest, is a mountain-bike path; Lake Crescent's north side is also edged by the bike-friendly Spruce Railroad Trail. More bike tracks run through the adjacent Olympic National Forest. Note that U.S. 101 has heavy traffic and isn't recommended for cycling, although the western side has broad roads with beautiful scenery and can be biked off-season. Bikes are not permitted on foot trails.

TOURS AND OUTFITTERS

Mike's Bikes. A bike, gear, and repair shop, Mike's is a great resource for advice on routes around the Olympic Peninsula. Bike rentals cost $30 pe half day, $50 all day, and $60 for 24 hours. ⊠ *150 W. Sequim Bay Rd., Sequim* ☎ *360/681–3868* ⊕ *www.mikes-bikes.net.*

Peak 6. This adventure store on the way to the Hoh Rain Forest Visitor Center rents mountain bikes. ⊠ *4883 Upper Hoh Rd., Forks* ☎ *360/374–5254.*

Sound Bike & Kayak. This sports outfitter rents and sells bikes, kayaks, and related equipment. ⊠ *120 E. Front St., Port Angeles* ☎ *360/457–1240* ⊕ *www.soundbikeskayaks.com.*

CLIMBING

At 7,980 feet, Mt. Olympus is the highest peak in the park and the most popular climb in the region. To attempt the summit, climbers must register at the Glacier Meadows Ranger Station. Mt. Constance, the third-highest Olympic peak at 7,743 feet, has a well-traversed climbing route that requires technical experience; reservations are recommended for the Lake Constance stop, which is limited to 20 campers. Mt. Deception is another possibility, though tricky snows have caused fatalities and injuries in the last decade. Climbing season runs from late June through September. Note that crevasse skills and self-rescue experience are highly recommended. Climbers must register with park officials and purchase wilderness permits before setting out. The best resource for climbing advice is the Wilderness Information Center in Port Angeles.

TOURS AND OUTFITTERS

Alpine Ascents. This company offers a backpacking and wilderness navigation course in the Olympic ranges. ✉ *109 W. Mercer St., Seattle* ☎ *206/378–1927* ⊕ *www.alpineascents.com.*

Mountain Madness. Choose from several adventure trips to summits around the Olympic Peninsula. ☎ *800/328–5925, 206/937–8389* ⊕ *www.mountainmadness.com.*

The Olympia Mountaineers. A branch of the Seattle Mountaineers, this group schedules climbing-oriented activities throughout the park. ☎ *360/570–0296* ⊕ *www.olympiamountaineers.org.*

FISHING

There are numerous fishing possibilities throughout the park. Lake Crescent is home to cutthroat and rainbow trout, as well as petite kokanee salmon; Lake Cushman, Lake Quinault, and Ozette Lake have trout, salmon, and steelhead. As for rivers, the Bogachiel and Queets have steelhead salmon in season. The glacier-fed Hoh River is home to chinook salmon April to November, and coho salmon from August through November; the Sol Duc River offers all five species of salmon, plus cutthroat and steelhead trout. Rainbow trout are also found in the Dosewallips, Elwha, and Skykomish rivers. Other places to go after salmon and trout include the Duckabush, Quillayute, Quinault, and Salmon rivers. A Washington state punch card is required during salmon-spawning months; fishing regulations vary throughout the park. Licenses are available from sporting goods and outdoor supply stores.

TOURS AND OUTFITTERS

Bob's Piscatorial Pursuits. This company, based in Forks, offers salmon and steelhead fishing trips around the Olympic Peninsula from October through mid-May. ☎ *866/347–4232* ⊕ *www.piscatorialpursuits.com.*

29

HIKING

Know your tides, or you might be trapped by high water. Tide tables are available at all visitor centers and ranger stations. Remember that a wilderness permit is required for all overnight backcountry visits.

EASY

FAMILY **Hoh River Trail.** From the Hoh Visitor Center, this rainforest jaunt takes

Fodor'sChoice you into the Hoh Valley, wending its way for 17.4 miles alongside the

★ river, through moss-draped maple and alder trees and past open meadows where elk roam in winter. *Easy.* ✉ *Hoh Visitor Center, 18 miles east of U.S. 101* ⊕ *www.nps.gov/olym/planyourvisit/hoh-river-trail.htm.*

Hurricane Ridge Meadow Trail. A 0.25-mile alpine loop, most of it wheelchair-accessible, leads through wildflower meadows overlooking numerous vistas of the interior Olympic peaks to the south and a panorama of the Strait of Juan de Fuca to the north. *Easy.* ✉ *Hurricane Ridge Rd., 17 miles south of Port Angeles* ⊕ *www.nps.gov/olym/planyourvisit/visiting-hurricane-ridge.htm.*

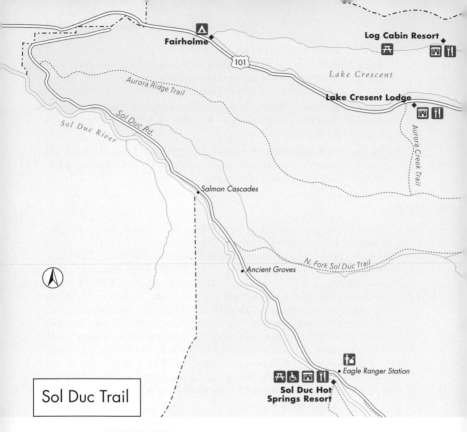

Sol Duc Trail

MODERATE

FAMILY **Cape Alava Trail.** Beginning at Ozette, this 3-mile boardwalk trail leads from the forest to wave-tossed headlands. *Moderate.* ⊠ *End of the Hoko-Ozette Rd., 26 miles south of Hwy. 112, west of Sekiu, Ozette.*

Graves Creek Trail. This 6-mile-long moderately strenuous trail climbs from lowland rain forest to alpine territory at Sundown Pass. Due to spring floods, a fjord halfway up is often impassable in May and June. *Moderate.* ⊠ *End of S. Shore Rd., 23 miles east of U.S. 101.*

FAMILY **Sol Duc River Trail.** The 1.5-mile gravel path off Sol Duc Road winds
Fodor'sChoice through thick Douglas fir forests toward the thundering, three-chute Sol
★ Duc Falls. Just 0.1 mile from the road, below a wooden platform over the Sol Duc River, you'll come across the 70-foot Salmon Cascades. In late summer and autumn, thousands of salmon negotiate 50 miles or more of treacherous waters to reach the cascades and the tamer pools near Sol Duc Hot Springs. The popular 6-mile **Lovers Lane Loop Trail** links the Sol Duc falls with the hot springs. You can continue up from the falls 5 miles to the **Appleton Pass Trail,** at 3,100 feet. From there you can hike on to the 8.5-mile mark, where views at the High Divide are from 5,050 feet. *Moderate.* ⊠ *Sol Duc Rd., 12 miles south of U.S. 101* ⊕ *www.nps.gov/olym/planyourvisit/sol-duc-river-trail.htm.*

DIFFICULT

High Divide Trail. A 9-mile hike in the park's high country defines this trail, which includes some strenuous climbing on its last 4 miles before topping out at a small alpine lake. A return loop along High Divide wends its way an extra mile through alpine territory, with sensational views of Olympic peaks. This trail is only for dedicated, properly equipped hikers who are in good shape. *Difficult.* ⊠ *End of Sol Duc River Rd., 13 miles south of U.S. 101* ⊕ *www.nps.gov/olym/ planyourvisit/high-divide-loop.htm.*

KAYAKING AND CANOEING

Lake Crescent, a serene expanse of teal-color waters surrounded by deep-green pine forests, is one of the park's best boating areas. Note that the west end is for swimming only; no speedboats are allowed here.

Lake Quinault has boating access from a gravel ramp on the north shore. From U.S. 101, take a right on North Shore Road, another right on Hemlock Way, and a left on Lakeview Drive. There are plank ramps at Falls Creek and Willoughby campgrounds on South Shore Drive, 0.1 mile and 0.2 mile past the Quinault Ranger Station, respectively.

Lake Ozette, with just one access road, is a good place for overnight trips. Only experienced canoe and kayak handlers should travel far from the put-in, since fierce storms occasionally strike—even in summer.

TOURS AND OUTFITTERS

Fairholm General Store. Rowboats and canoes on Lake Crescent are available to rent from $20 per hour to $55 per day. The store is at the lake's west end, 27 miles west of Port Angeles. ⊠ *221121 U.S. 101, Port Angeles* ☎ *360/928–3020* ⊘ *Closed after Labor Day–Memorial Day weekend.*

Lake Crescent Lodge. You can rent rowboats, canoes, and kayaks here for $20 per hour and $55 per day. Fishing poles can also be rented and the gift shop sells some fishing tackle. ⊠ *416 Lake Crescent Rd., Olympic National Park* ☎ *360/928–3211* ⊕ *www.olympicnationalparks.com* ⊘ *Closed Jan.-Apr.*

Log Cabin Resort. This resort, 17 miles west of Port Angeles, has paddleboat, kayak, and canoe rentals for $20 per hour and $55 per day. The dock provides easy access to Lake Crescent's northeast section. ⊠ *3183 E. Beach Rd., Port Angeles* ☎ *360/928–3325* ⊕ *www. olympicnationalparks.com* ⊘ *Closed mid-Sept.–mid-May.*

Rainforest Paddlers. This company takes kayakers down the Lizard Rock and Oxbow sections of the Hoh River. They also offer river rafting and rent bikes and kayaks. ⊠ *4882 Upper Hoh Rd., Forks* ☎ *360/374–5254* ⊕ *www.rainforestpaddlers.com.*

RAFTING

Olympic has excellent rafting rivers, with Class II to Class V rapids. The Elwha River is a popular place to paddle, with some exciting turns. The Hoh is better for those who like a smooth, easy float.

DID YOU KNOW?

Olympic National Park is home to 13 species of amphibians (frogs, toads, and salamanders), including the Pacific Tree Frog. The park is a rare refuge for these animals, whose world populations have been declining due to air and water pollution (amphibians live in both environments, making them doubly susceptible).

TOURS AND OUTFITTERS

Olympic Raft and Kayak. Based in Port Angeles, this is the only rafting outfit that offers trips on the restored Elwha River in Olympic National Park. ⊠ *123 Lake Aldwell Rd., Port Angeles* ☎ *360/452–5268, 888/452–1443* ⊕ *www.raftandkayak.com.*

WINTER SPORTS

Hurricane Ridge is the central spot for winter sports. Miles of downhill and Nordic ski tracks are open late December through March, and a ski lift, towropes, and ski school are open 10 to 4 weekends and holidays. A snow-play area for children ages 8 and younger is near the Hurricane Ridge Visitors Center. Hurricane Ridge Road is open Friday through Sunday in the winter season; all vehicles are required to carry chains.

TOURS AND OUTFITTERS

Hurricane Ridge Visitor Center. Rent snowshoes and ski equipment here December through March for $17 to $42. Free 90-minute snowshoe tours depart from here weekends from mid-December through March. Groups of 7–30 people can register in advance by phone for the 10:30 tour. The 2 pm tour is first-come, first-served, with sign-ups beginning at 1:30. A $5 per person donation is requested to cover trail and equipment maintenance. ⊠ *Hurricane Ridge Rd., Port Angeles* ☎ *360/565–3131 for information, 360/565–3136 for tour reservations* ⊕ *www.nps.gov/olym.*

WHAT'S NEARBY

NEARBY TOWNS

Although most Olympic Peninsula towns have evolved from their exclusive reliance on timber, **Forks,** outside the national park's northwest tip, remains one of the region's logging capitals. Washington state's wettest town (100 inches or more of rain a year), it's a small, friendly place with just 3,500 residents and a modicum of visitor facilities. **Port Angeles,** a city of 19,000, focuses on its status as the main gateway to Olympic National Park and Victoria, British Columbia. Set below the Strait of Juan de Fuca and looking north to Vancouver Island, it's an enviably scenic settlement filled with attractive, Craftsman-style homes. The Pacific Northwest has its very own "Banana Belt" in the waterfront community of **Sequim,** 15 miles east of Port Angeles along U.S. 101. The town of 6,000 is in the rain shadow of the Olympics and receives only 16 inches of rain per year (compared with the 40 inches that drench the Hoh Rain Forest just 40 miles away).

VISITOR INFORMATION

Forks Chamber of Commerce Visitor Center ⊠ *1411 S. Forks Ave. (U.S. 101), Forks* ☎ *800/443–6757* ⊕ *www.forkswa.com.* **Port Angeles Chamber of Commerce Visitor Center** ⊠ *121 E. Railroad Ave., Port Angeles* ☎ *360/452–2363* ⊕ *www.cityofpa.com.* **Sequim-Dungeness Valley Chamber of Commerce** ⊠ *1192 E. Washington St., Sequim* ☎ *360/693–6197, 800/737–8462* ⊕ *www.sequimchamber.com.*

29

NEARBY ATTRACTIONS

Fodor's Choice ★ **Dungeness Spit.** Curving 5½ miles into the Strait of Juan de Fuca, the longest natural sand spit in the United States is a wild, beautiful section of shoreline. More than 30,000 migratory waterfowl stop here each spring and fall, but you'll see plenty of birdlife any time of year. The entire spit is part of the **Dungeness National Wildlife Refuge.** ✉ *554 Voice of America Rd., entrance 3 miles north of U.S. 101, 4 miles west of Sequim* ☎ *360/457–8451 for wildlife refuge* 🌐 *www.clallam.net/Parks/Dungeness.html* 🎟 *$3 per family* 🕒 *Daily dawn–dusk.*

Dungeness Lighthouse. At the end of the Dungeness Spit is the towering white 1857 Dungeness Lighthouse; tours are available, though access is limited to those who can hike or kayak out 5 miles to the end of the spit. Guests also have the opportunity to serve as lighthouse keepers for a week at a time. An adjacent, 64-site camping area, on the bluff above the Strait of Juan de Fuca, is open February through September. ✉ *Entrance 3 miles north of Hwy. 101 via Kitchen Dick Rd., Sequim* ☎ *360/683–6638* 🌐 *www.newdungenesslighthouse.com*

Port Angeles Fine Arts Center. This small, sophisticated museum is inside the former home of late artist and publisher Esther Barrows Webster, one of Port Angeles's most energetic and cultured citizens; displays are modern, funky, and intriguing. Outside, Webster's Woods Art Park is dotted with oversize sculptures set before a vista of the city and harbor. Exhibitions emphasize the works of emerging and well-established Pacific Northwest artists. ✉ *1203 W. Lauridsen Blvd., Port Angeles* ☎ *360/417–4590* 🌐 *www.pafac.org* 🎟 *Free* 🕒 *Mar.–Nov., Thurs.–Sun. 11–5; Dec.–Feb., Thurs.–Sun. 10–4 and by appointment; Art Park daily sunrise–sunset.*

Timber Museum. The museum highlights Forks' logging history since the 1870s; a garden and fire tower are also on the grounds. ✉ *1421 S. Forks Ave., Forks* ☎ *360/374–9663* 🌐 *www.forks-web.com/fg/timbermuseum.htm* 🕒 *Open May–Oct., Tues.–Sat. 10–4.*

WHERE TO EAT

IN THE PARK

$$$ AMERICAN 🍴 **Creekside Restaurant.** A tranquil country setting and ocean views at Kalaloch Lodge's restaurant create the perfect backdrop for savoring local dinner specialties like cedar-planked salmon, fresh shellfish, wild mushrooms, meat loaf made with grass-fed beef, and roasted chicken. Tempting desserts include local berry crisp and chocolate espresso bread pudding. Note that seating is every half hour after 5, and reservations are recommended. Hearty breakfasts and sandwich-style lunches are more casual. [$] *Average main: $24* ✉ *157151 U.S. 101, Forks* ☎ *866/525–2562, 360/962–2271* 🌐 *www.thekalalochlodge.com/Dine.aspx.*

$$$ AMERICAN 🍴 **Lake Crescent Lodge.** Part of the original 1916 lodge, the fir-paneled dining room overlooks the lake; you also won't find a better spot for sunset views. Entrées include crab cakes, grilled salmon, seared weathervane

scallops, fish-and-chips, classic burgers and steak, pork loin, and duck breast. Organic chicken breast is prepared with pears and riesling wine sauce and served with sweet potato mash and seasonal vegetables. A good Northwest wine list complements the menu. Note that meals are only offered during set hours, but a more casual menu of appetizers, sandwiches, burgers, and desserts is available from the lounge all day for dining in the lobby or out on the Sun Porch. [$] *Average main: $26* ✉ *416 Lake Crescent Rd., Port Angeles* ☎ *360/928–3211* 🌐 *www.olympicnationalparks.com/activities/dining.aspx* 🕒 *Closed Jan.–Apr.*

$$$ AMERICAN 🍴 **The Springs Restaurant.** The main Sol Duc Hot Springs Resort restaurant is a rustic, fir-and-cedar paneled dining room surrounded by trees. Big breakfasts are turned out daily 7:30 to 10; dinner is served daily between 5:30 and 9 (lunch and snacks are available 11 to 4 at the Poolside Deli or Espresso Hut). Evening choices include Northwest seafood, pork, and beef highlighted by fresh-picked fruits and vegetables. There's also a different macaroni and cheese special offered each day, such as gouda with jalapeños and ham with sweet peas. [$] *Average main: $22* ✉ *12076 Sol Duc Rd., at U.S. 101, Port Angeles* ☎ *360/327–3583* 🌐 *www.olympicnationalparks.com/activities/dining.aspx* 🕒 *Closed mid-Oct.–Apr.*

PICNIC AREAS

All Olympic National Park campgrounds have adjacent picnic areas with tables, some shelters, and restrooms, but no cooking facilities. The same is true for major visitor centers, such as Hoh Rain Forest. Drinking water is available at ranger stations, interpretive centers, and inside campgrounds.

East Beach. Set on a grassy meadow overlooking Lake Crescent, this popular swimming spot has six picnic tables and vault toilets. ✉ *East Beach Rd., off U.S. 101, at far east end of Lake Crescent, 17 miles west of Port Angeles.*

Rialto Beach. Relatively secluded at the end of the road from Forks, this is one of the premier day-use areas in the park's Pacific coast segment. This site has 12 picnic tables, fire grills, and vault toilets. ✉ *Rte. 110, 14 miles west of Forks.*

OUTSIDE THE PARK

$$ ECLECTIC 🍴 **Alder Wood Bistro.** An inventive menu of local and organic dishes makes this one of the most popular restaurants in Sequim. Pizzas from the wood-fired oven include unique creations, like the chicken pesto with organic chicken, basil pesto, blue cheese, black olives, toasted walnuts, pickled red onions, and mozzarella. Some feature Mt. Townsend Creamery cheeses. The menu's sustainably harvested seafood selections highlight whatever is in season, from black cod and mussels to oysters and salmon; they also get the wood-fire treatment. Even the bacon-wrapped meat loaf features local beef, along with buttermilk mashed potatoes and greens. For dessert, try the organic seasonal frangipane fruit tart or panna cotta. On warmer days, enjoy alfresco dining in the pretty garden courtyard. [$] *Average main: $18* ✉ *139 W. Alder St., Sequim* ☎ *360/683–4321* 🌐 *www.alderwoodbistro.com* 🕒 *Closed Sun. and Mon. No lunch.*

$$$ PACIFIC NORTHWEST 🍴 **Blondie's Plate.** This Sequim bistro, which opened in 2013 in a former church, has quickly become a popular spot for both locals and tourists. Many of the menu choices are "small plates," or tapas-style, which makes it easy to mix and match different tastes and share with dining companions. Categories include starters, garden, surf, pasture, and grains; servers can recommend good matches. The grilled pear salad with blue cheese marries well with the crispy-skin salmon, served with ginger miso and sautéed vegetables. Traditional full plates like roast chicken with roasted baby potatoes and asparagus are also available. Cocktails are noteworthy, too, and a changing dessert menu may include flourless chocolate cake or croissant bread pudding. Unlike many of the downtown restaurants in quiet Sequim, Blondie's stays open every night of the week. The restaurant is small, so reserve ahead. [$] *Average main: $25* ✉ *134 S. 2nd Ave., Sequim* ☎ *360/683–2233* ⏲ *No lunch.*

$$$$ FRENCH 🍴 **C'est Si Bon.** Far more Euro-savvy than is typical on the Olympic Peninsula, this longtime, first-rate restaurant stands out for its interior design as well as for its food. The fanciful dining room is done up in bold red hues, with crisp white linens, huge oil paintings, and glittering chandeliers; the spacious solarium takes an equally formal approach. The changing menu highlights housemade French onion soup, escargots, magret de canard with berry sauce, Dungeness crab soufflé, filet mignon, and rack of lamb. The wine list is superb, with French, Australian, and Northwest choices to pair with everything. [$] *Average main: $32* ✉ *23 Cedar Park Rd., Port Angeles* ☎ *360/452–8888* 🌐 *www.cestsibon-frenchcuisine.com* ✍ *Reservations essential* ⏲ *Closed Mon. No lunch.*

$$ PACIFIC NORTHWEST 🍴 **Dockside Grill.** With tremendous views of John Wayne Marina and Sequim Bay, this family restaurant is a fun place to watch ships placidly sail by. The casual menu includes Dungeness crab fritters, steamed clams, cedar-plank salmon, bouillabaisse, cioppino, and pasta. The kitchen also serves up excellent steak, surf 'n' turf *poutine* (fried shrimp and beef tips, served on fries with cheese and a Cabernet demi-glace), and a duck confit burger. [$] *Average main: $18* ✉ *2577 W. Sequim Bay Rd., Sequim* ☎ *360/683–7510* 🌐 *www.docksidegrill-sequim.com* ⏲ *Closed Mon. and Tues.*

$$ ECLECTIC 🍴 **Fountain Café.** Tucked inside a historic clapboard building a block off the main drag, this intimate and eclectic eatery is a local favorite. Artwork lines the walls of the small, funky café where seafood and pasta dishes carry Mediterranean, Morroccan, Indian, and Thai influences, and often include rich cream sauces as well as plenty of garlic. Chicken marsala and paella are mainstays. Full-bodied Pacific Northwest and Italian wines as well as simple sweets like tiramisu and gingerbread round out the menu. Most of the art on the walls is for sale, and the café forms part of the town's monthly gallery walks. [$] *Average main: $17* ✉ *920 Washington St., Port Townsend* ☎ *360/385–1364* ✍ *Reservations not accepted.*

$ THAI 🍴 **Khu Larb Thai.** Some of the state's best Thai food is prepared at this unassuming restaurant, a few steps off the main street. Family-run for more than 20 years, its recipes reflect Chinese, Indian, and Malaysian influences on traditional Thai fare, including savory soups, curries, and fried rice and noodle dishes, many with fresh basil, sliced lime leaves, and hints of lemongrass. There's a wide array of meat and vegetarian dishes as well as seafood like tender scallops in red curry or local Marrowstone Island clams in ginger curry. The signature black rice pudding dessert far surpasses the usual coconut ice cream on Thai menus. $ *Average main: $12* ⊠ *225 Adams St., Port Townsend* ☎ *360/385–5023* ⊕ *www.khularbthai.com* ⊗ *Closed Tues.*

$ ╳ **Oak Table Café.** Carefully crafted breakfasts and lunches, made with
AMERICAN high-grade, fresh ingredients, are the focus of this well-run, family-friendly eatery, a Sequim institution since 1981. Breakfast is served 7 am–3 pm; on Sunday, when the large, well-lighted dining room is especially bustling, it's the only meal, and the selection is extensive. Thickly sliced bacon and eggs are a top seller, but the restaurant is best known for its creamy blintzes, golden-brown waffles, crêpes, and variety of pancakes, particularly the cinnamony sweet soufflé-style apple pancake. Egg dishes include eggs Nicole—a medley of sautéed mushrooms, onions, spinach, and scrambled eggs served over an open-face croissant and covered with hollandaise sauce. Lunches include burgers, salads, and sandwiches. $ *Average main: $12* ⊠ *292 W. Bell St., Sequim* ☎ *360/683–2179* ⊕ *www.oaktablecafe.com* ⊗ *No dinner. No lunch Sun.*

WHERE TO STAY

IN THE PARK

$$$ ▦ **Kalaloch Lodge.** Overlooking the Pacific, Kalaloch has cozy lodge
HOTEL rooms with sea views and separate cabins along the bluff. **Pros:** ranger tours nearby; clam digging; supreme storm watching in winter. **Cons:** no Internet or TV; some units are two blocks from main lodge; cabins can smell like pets. $ *Rooms from: $188* ⊠ *157151 U.S. 101, Forks* ☎ *360/962–2271, 866/662–9928* ⊕ *www.thekalalochlodge.com* ⤶ *10 lodge rooms, 7 motel rooms, 3 motel suites, 42 cabins* ⦿ *No meals.*

$$$$ ▦ **Lake Crescent Lodge.** Deep in the forest at the foot of Mt. Storm King,
HOTEL this 1916 lodge has a variety of comfortable accommodations, from basic rooms with shared baths to spacious two-bedroom fireplace cottages (the latter available even on winter weekends when the rest of the lodge is closed). **Pros:** gorgeous setting; free wireless access in the wilderness. **Cons:** no laundry; Roosevelt Cottages must be booked a year in advance for summer stays. $ *Rooms from: $204* ⊠ *416 Lake Crescent Rd., Port Angeles* ☎ *360/928–3211* ⊕ *www.lakecrescentlodge. com* ⤶ *30 motel rooms, 17 cabins, 5 lodge rooms with shared bath* ⊗ *Closed Nov.–Apr.* ⦿ *No meals.*

$$$$ ▦ **Lake Quinault Lodge.** On a lovely glacial lake in Olympic National For-
HOTEL est, this beautiful early-20th-century lodge complex is within walking distance of the lakeshore and hiking trails in the spectacular old-growth forest. **Pros:** hosts summer campfires with s'mores; family-friendly ambience; year-round pool. **Cons:** no TVs; lake is sometimes closed to fishing and boating. $ *Rooms from: $220* ⊠ *345 South Shore Rd., Quinault* ☎ *360/288–2900, 888/896–3818* ⊕ *www.olympicnationalparks.com* ⤶ *92 rooms* ⦿ *No meals.*

29

Best Campgrounds in Olympic

Note that only a few places take reservations; if you can't book in advance, you'll have to arrive early to get a place. Each site usually has a picnic table and grill or fire pit, and most campgrounds have water, toilets, and garbage containers; for hookups, showers, and laundry facilities, you'll have to head into the towns. Firewood is available from camp concessions, but if there's no store you can collect dead wood within 1 mile of your campsite. Dogs are allowed in campgrounds, but not on most trails or in the backcountry. Trailers should be 21 feet long or less (15 feet or less at Queets Campground) though a few campgrounds can accommodate up to 35 feet. There's a camping limit of two weeks. Nightly rates run $12–$18 per site.

If you have a backcountry pass, you can camp virtually anywhere throughout the park's forests and shores. Overnight wilderness permits are $5—plus $2 per person per night—and are available at visitor centers and ranger stations. Note that when you camp in the backcountry, you must choose a site at least ½ mile inside the park boundary.

Elwha Campground. The larger of the Elwha Valley's two campgrounds, this is one of Olympic's year-round facilities. ⊠ *Elwha River Rd., 7 miles south of U.S. 101* ☏ *No phone.*

Kalaloch Campground. Kalaloch is the biggest and most popular Olympic campground, and it's open all year. Its vantage of the Pacific is unmatched on the park's coastal stretch. ⊠ *U.S. 101, ½ mile north of Kalaloch Information Station, Olympic National Park* ☏ *360/962–2271 for group bookings.*

Lake Quinault Rain Forest Resort Village Campground. Stretching along the south shore of Lake Quinault, this RV campground has many recreation facilities, including beaches, canoes, ball fields, and horseshoe pits. The 31 RV sites, which rent for $30 per night, are open year-round but bathrooms are closed in winter. ⊠ *3½ miles east of U.S. 101, South Shore Rd., Lake Quinault* ☏ *360/288–2535, 800/255–6936* ⊕ *www.rainforestresort.com.*

Mora Campground. Along the Quillayute estuary, this campground doubles as a popular staging point for hikes northward along the coast's wilderness stretch. ⊠ *Rte. 110, 13 miles west of Forks* ☏ *No phone.*

Ozette Campground. Hikers heading to Cape Alava, a scenic promontory that is the westernmost point in the lower 48 states, use this lakeshore campground as a jumping-off point. ⊠ *Hoko-Ozette Rd., 26 miles south of Hwy. 112* ☏ *No phone.*

Sol Duc Campground. Sol Duc resembles virtually all Olympic campgrounds save one distinguishing feature—the famed hot springs are a short walk away. ⊠ *Sol Duc Rd., 11 miles south of U.S. 101* ☏ *360/327–3534.*

Staircase Campground. In deep woods away from the river, this campground is a popular jumping-off point for hikes into the Skokomish River Valley and the Olympic high country. ⊠ *Rte. 119, 16 miles northwest of U.S. 101* ☏ *No phone.*

$$ **Log Cabin Resort.** This rustic resort has an idyllic setting at the northeast end of Lake Crescent with lodging choices that include A-frame chalet units, standard cabins, small camper cabins, motel units, and RV sites with full hookups. **Pros:** boat rentals available on site; convenient general store; pets allowed in some cabins. **Cons:** cabins are very rustic; no plumbing in the camper cabins; no TV. [$] *Rooms from: $110* ✉ *3183 E. Beach Rd., Port Angeles* ☎ *888/896–3818* 🌐 *www.olympicnationalparks.com* 🛏 *4 rooms, 24 cabins, 22 RV sites, 4 tent sites* ⏱ *Closed mid-Sept.–late May* 🍴 *No meals.*
HOTEL

$$$ **Sol Duc Hot Springs Resort.** Deep in the brooding forest along the Sol Duc River and surrounded by 5,000-foot-tall mountains, the main draw of this remote 1910 resort is the pool area, with soothing mineral baths and a freshwater swimming pool. **Pros:** nearby trails; peaceful setting; some units are pet-friendly. **Cons:** units are dated; some guests have complained about cleanliness; pools get crowded. [$] *Rooms from: $172* ✉ *12076 Sol Duc Hot Springs Rd.* ☎ *360/327–3583, 888/476–5382* 🌐 *www.olympicnationalparks.com* 🛏 *27 cabins, 1 suite* ⏱ *Closed mid-Oct.–late-Mar.* 🍴 *No meals.*
HOTEL

OUTSIDE THE PARK

$$$ **Colette's Bed & Breakfast.** A contemporary oceanfront mansion set on a 10-acre sanctuary of gorgeous gardens, this appealing place offers more space, service, and luxury than any other property in the area. **Pros:** water views extend to Victoria, BC; discreet personal service. **Cons:** does not cater to families. [$] *Rooms from: $195* ✉ *339 Finn Hall Rd., 10 miles east of Port Angeles* ☎ *360/457–9197, 888/457–9777* 🌐 *www.colettes.com* 🛏 *5 suites* 🍴 *Breakfast.*
B&B/INN
Fodor's Choice ★

$$$ **Domaine Madeleine.** At this luxury B&B perched on 5 acres on a bluff above the Strait of Juan de Fuca, owner/innkeeper Jeri loves to amaze her guests with inventive, tasty, and artfully presented five-course breakfasts. **Pros:** the mosaic of colorful waterfront blossoms; abundant wildlife; well-appointed rooms; beautifully presented gourmet breakfast. **Cons:** no children under 12. [$] *Rooms from: $195* ✉ *146 Wildflower La., 8 miles east of Port Angeles* ☎ *360/457–4174, 888/811–8376* 🌐 *www.domainemadeleine.com* 🛏 *4 rooms, 1 cottage* 🍴 *Breakfast.*
B&B/INN

$$$$ **Fort Worden State Park Conference Center.** The 330-acre Fort Worden, built as a late-19th-century gun emplacement to guard the mouth of the Puget Sound, gained a new purpose when enterprising souls turned the spacious Victorian homes on officer's row into one of the more memorable lodgings on the Olympic Peninsula. **Pros:** myriad activities; acres of waterfront for play; historic ambience. **Cons:** summer crowds; no TV, Internet, or air-conditioning in the houses. [$] *Rooms from: $201* ✉ *200 Battery Way, Port Townsend* ☎ *360/344–4400* 🌐 *www.parks.wa.gov/fortworden* 🛏 *35 houses, 3 dorms, 80 sites with full hookups* 🍴 *Breakfast.*
RENTAL

$ **Ocean Crest Resort.** Set on a forested bluff above the Pacific Ocean 30 minutes from Olympic National Park and Lake Quinault, Ocean Crest has small budget studios, large studios with ocean views, and one- and two-bedroom units. **Pros:** windows open to hear the ocean's roar;
RESORT

some rooms are pet-friendly; off-season specials. **Cons:** location is remote; rooms are quite dated. $ *Rooms from: $69* ⊠ *4651 Rte. 109, Moclips* ☎ *360/276–4465, 800/684–8439* ⊕ *www.oceancrestresort. com* ⟿ *45 rooms* ⏹️ *No meals.*

$$$
HOTEL

⊡ **Quality Inn Uptown.** South of town, at the green edge of the Olympic Mountain foothills, this inn offers a stunning panorama of mountain and harbor views. **Pros:** central location; great views. **Cons:** basic interior design and amenities; somewhat dated; no elevators. $ *Rooms from: $175* ⊠ *101 E. 2nd St., Port Angeles* ☎ *360/457– 9434, 800/858–3812* ⊕ *www.qualityinnportangeles.com* ⟿ *51 rooms* ⏹️ *Breakfast.*

$$$
B&B/INN
Fodor's Choice
★

⊡ **Sea Cliff Gardens Bed & Breakfast.** A gingerbread-style porch fronts this antiques-furnished waterfront Victorian home on 2 acres of landscaped grounds. **Pros:** sumptuous accommodations with stunning views; gorgeous flower gardens have been featured in a national commercial; very romantic setting. **Cons:** a bit off the beaten path. $ *Rooms from: $175* ⊠ *397 Monterra Dr., Port Angeles* ☎ *360/452–2322, 800/880–1332* ⊕ *www.seacliffgardens.com* ⟿ *5 suites* ⏹️ *Breakfast.*

$$$$
RENTAL
FAMILY
Fodor's Choice
★

⊡ **Seabrook Cottage Rentals.** A range of individually owned rental properties are available in a charming new beach town that has been under development since 2004; choices range from small cottages perfect for a couple to large homes big enough for multiple families. **Pros:** recreational amenities and beach within walking distance; homes are new with full amenities; some are pet-friendly. **Cons:** there is ongoing construction; cleaning fee added to all stays; limited nearby services outside of village. $ *Rooms from: $269* ⊠ *4275 Rte. 109, Pacific Beach* ☎ *360/276–0265, 877/779–9990* ⊕ *www.seabrookcottagerentals.com* ⟿ *138 cottages* ⏹️ *No meals.*

PETRIFIED FOREST
NATIONAL PARK

WELCOME TO PETRIFIED FOREST

TOP REASONS TO GO

★ **Terrific timber:** Be mesmerized by the clusters of petrified (fossilized) wood. The trees look like they're made of colorful stone.

★ **Route 66 kicks:** Put the top down on the Chevrolet. A section of the fabled road is preserved in the park, the only section of the highway protected in a national park.

★ **Triassic treasures:** Find an oasis of water in the desert, or at least evidence that it once existed. Clam fossils in the park indicate that waterways once prevailed where sand, stone, and trees now define the land.

★ **Corps creations:** Say thanks to FDR. The Painted Desert Inn, a National Historic Landmark, was modernized by the Civilian Conservation Corps (CCC) during the throes of the Great Depression. The recently renovated building is now a museum and bookstore.

1 Painted Desert. The main area of the park, in the northern section, is where park headquarters, the Painted Desert Inn, and Route 66 are located. It's also the best place for hiking. A permit is required for overnight camping in the wilderness area, but day users need not obtain one. The 28-mile park road begins here, off Interstate 40.

2 Blue Mesa. In the heart of the Painted Desert, this 1-mile loop trail begins off a loop road accessed from the park road. Petrified trees lie among hills of bluish bentonite clay.

3 Rainbow Forest Museum. Get a trail guide here for the short Giant Logs Trail located behind the museum, and keep an eye out for Old Faithful, a log almost 10 feet wide. The southern terminus for the park road is here.

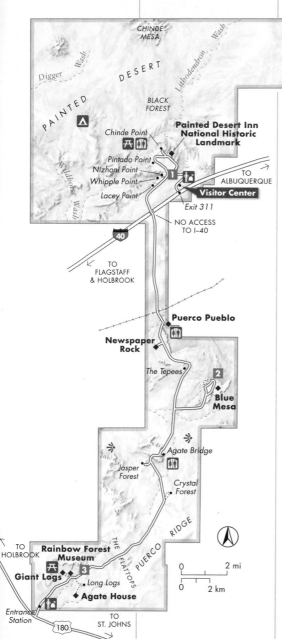

CHINDE MESA

Digger Wash

PAINTED DESERT

Lithodendron Wash

BLACK FOREST

🔺

Chinde Point

🪑 🚻

Pintado Point
Nizhoni Point
Whipple Point

Lacey Point

Painted Desert Inn National Historic Landmark

1

🚻

Visitor Center

TO ALBUQUERQUE

Exit 311

NO ACCESS TO I-40

40

Wildhorse Wash

← TO FLAGSTAFF & HOLBROOK

Puerco Pueblo

🚻

Newspaper Rock ◆

The Tepees •

2

Blue Mesa ◆

🌿

Agate Bridge
🚻

Jasper Forest

Crystal Forest •

PUERCO RIDGE

🧭

0 ——— 2 mi
0 ——— 2 km

← TO HOLBROOK

Rainbow Forest Museum

THE FLATTOPS

🔺 🚻 3

Giant Logs ◆

• *Long Logs*

Agate House ◆

Entrance Station
📷

180

TO ST. JOHNS →

ARIZONA

GETTING ORIENTED

There are few places where the span of geologic and human history is as wide or apparent as it is at Petrified Forest National Park. Fossilized trees and countless other fossils date back to the Triassic Period, while a stretch of the famed Route 66 of more modern lore is protected within park boundaries. Ancestors of the Hopi, Zuni, and Navajo left petroglyphs, pottery, and even structures built of petrified wood. Nine park sites are on the National Register of Historic Places; one, the Painted Desert Inn, is one of only 3% of such sites that are also listed as National Historic Landmarks.

30

KEY	
🚻	Ranger Station
🔺	Campground
🪑	Picnic Area
🍴	Restaurant
📷	Lodge
🏃	Trailhead
🚻	Restrooms
🌿	Scenic Viewpoint
::::::	Walking/Hiking Trails

Updated by
Elise Riley

Petrified logs scattered about a vast pink-hued lunarlike landscape resemble a fairy-tale forest turned to stone at Petrified Forest National Park. The park's 218,533 acres, which include portions of the Painted Desert, are covered with petrified tree trunks whose wood cells were fossilized over centuries by brightly hued mineral deposits—silica, iron oxide, carbon, manganese, aluminum, copper, and lithium. The park holds plenty of other fossils; remnants of humans and their artifacts have been recovered at more than 500 sites in the park.

PETRIFIED FOREST PLANNER

WHEN TO GO

The park is rarely crowded. Weather-wise, the best time to visit is autumn, when nights are chilly but daytime temperatures hover near 70°F. Half of all yearly rain falls between June and August, so it's a good time to spot blooming wildflowers. The park is least crowded in winter, because of cold winds and occasional snow, though daytime temperatures are in the 50s and 60s.

AVG. HIGH/LOW TEMPS.

JAN.	FEB.	MAR.	APR.	MAY	JUNE
48/21	54/25	60/29	70/35	79/43	89/52

JULY	AUG.	SEPT.	OCT.	NOV.	DEC.
92/60	89/59	84/52	72/40	59/28	48/22

FESTIVALS AND EVENTS

MAY **National Wildflower Week.** Activities include wildflower walks and an interactive wildflower display.

DECEMBER **Petrified Forest Park Anniversary.** A national monument since 1906 and a national park since 1962, Petrified Forest throws a party for its birthday, with homemade cider, cookies, and cultural demonstrations.

PLANNING YOUR TIME
PETRIFIED FOREST IN ONE DAY
A nonstop drive through the park (28 miles) takes only 45 minutes, but you can spend a half day or more exploring if you stop along the way. From almost any vantage point you can see the multicolored rocks and hills that were home to prehistoric humans and ancient dinosaurs.

Entering from the north, stop at **Painted Desert Visitor Center** for a 20-minute introductory film. Two miles in, the **Painted Desert Inn National Historic Landmark** provides guided ranger tours. Drive south 8 miles to reach **Puerco Pueblo,** a 100-room pueblo built before 1400. Continuing south, you'll find Puebloan petroglyphs at **Newspaper Rock** and, just beyond, the **Tepees,** cone-shape rock formations.

Blue Mesa is roughly the midpoint of the drive, and the start of a 1-mile, moderately steep loop hike that leads you around badland hills made of bentonite clay. Drive on for 5 miles until you come to **Jasper Forest,** just past **Agate Bridge,** with views of the landscape strewn with petrified logs. **Crystal Forest,** about 20 miles south of the north entrance, is named for the smoky quartz, amethyst, and citrine along the 0.8-mile loop trail. **Rainbow Forest Museum,** at the park's south entrance, has restrooms, a bookstore, and exhibits. Just behind Rainbow Forest Museum is **Giant Logs,** a 0.4-mile loop that takes you to "Old Faithful," the largest log in the park, estimated to weigh 44 tons.

GETTING HERE AND AROUND
AIR TRAVEL
The nearest major airports are in Phoenix, Arizona (259 miles away via U.S. 17 and U.S. 40), and Albuquerque, New Mexico (204 miles via U.S. 40).

CAR TRAVEL
Holbrook, the nearest large town with services such as gas or food, is on U.S. 40, roughly 30 miles from either of the park's two entrances.

Parking is free, and there's ample space at all trailheads, as well as at the visitor center and the museum. The main park road extends 28 miles from the Painted Desert Visitor Center (north entrance) to the Rainbow Forest Museum (south entrance). For park road conditions, call ☎ 928/524–6228.

PARK ESSENTIALS
PARK FEES AND PERMITS
Entrance fees are $10 per car for seven consecutive days or $5 per person on foot, bicycle, motorcycle, or bus. Backcountry hiking and camping permits are free (limit of 15 days) at the Painted Desert Visitor Center or the Rainbow Forest Museum before 4 pm.

PARK HOURS
It's a good idea to call ahead or check the website, since the park's hours vary so much; as a rule of thumb, the park is open daily from sunrise to sunset, and keep in mind that the area does not observe daylight savings

time. Hours are approximately: 8–5 from November to February, daily 7–6:30 in March and April, daily 7 am–7:30 pm from May to August, and daily 7–6 in September and October.

RESTAURANTS

Dining in the park is limited to a cafeteria in the Painted Desert Visitor Center and snacks in the Rainbow Forest Museum. In and around the Navajo and Hopi reservations, be sure to sample Indian tacos, an authentic treat made with scrumptious fry bread, beans, and chilies. If you're searching for burger-and-fries fare, Holbrook is your best bet.

Prices in the reviews are the average cost of a main course at dinner, or if dinner is not served, at lunch.

HOTELS

There is no lodging within Petrified Forest. Outside the park, lodging choices include modern resorts, rustic cabins, and small bed-and-breakfasts. Note that air-conditioning is not a standard amenity in the mountains, where the nights are cool enough for a blanket even in summer. Closer to the Navajo and Hopi reservations many establishments are run by American Indians, tribal enterprises intent on offering first-class service and hospitality. Nearby Holbrook offers most national chain hotels and comfortable accommodations.

Prices in the reviews are the lowest cost of a standard double room in high season. For expanded reviews, facilities, and current deals, visit Fodors.com.

VISITOR INFORMATION

PARK CONTACT INFORMATION

Petrified Forest National Park ⊠ *1 Park Rd., Petrified Forest* ☎ *928/524–6228* ⊕ *www.nps.gov/pefo.*

VISITOR CENTERS

Painted Desert Inn National Historic Landmark. This visitor center isn't as large as the other two, but here you can get information as well as view cultural history exhibits. ⊠ *2 miles north of Painted Desert Visitor Center on the main park road* ☎ *928/524–6228.*

Painted Desert Visitor Center. This is the place to go for general park information and an informative 20-minute film on the park. Proceeds from books purchased here will fund continued research and interpretive activities for the park. ⊠ *North entrance off U.S. 40, 27 miles east of Holbrook* ☎ *928/524–6228.*

Rainbow Forest Museum and Visitor Center. The museum houses artifacts of early reptiles, dinosaurs, and petrified wood. Be sure to see Gurtie, a skeleton of a phytosaur, a crocodile-like carnivore. ⊠ *South entrance off U.S. 180, 18 miles southeast of Holbrook* ☎ *928/524–6228.*

Different minerals in different concentrations cause the rich colors in petrified wood and in the Painted Desert.

EXPLORING

SCENIC DRIVES

Painted Desert Scenic Drive. A 28-mile scenic drive takes you through the park from one entrance to the other. If you begin at the north end, the first 5 miles of the drive take you along the edge of a high mesa, with spectacular views of the Painted Desert. Beyond lies the desolate Painted Desert Wilderness Area. After the 5-mile point, the road crosses Interstate 40, then swings south toward the Puerco River across a landscape covered with sagebrush, saltbrush, sunflowers, and Apache plume. Past the river, the road climbs onto a narrow mesa leading to Newspaper Rock, a panel of Pueblo Indian rock art. Then the road bends southeast, enters a barren stretch, and passes teepee-shaped buttes in the distance. Next you come to Blue Mesa, roughly the park's midpoint and a good place to stop for views of petrified logs. The next stop on the drive is Agate Bridge, really a 100-foot log over a wide wash. The remaining overlooks are Jasper Forest and Crystal Forest, where you can get a further glimpse of the accumulated petrified wood. On your way out of the park, stop at the Rainbow Forest Museum for a rest and to shop for a memento. ⊠ *Begins at Painted Desert Visitor Center.*

HISTORIC SITES

Agate House. This eight-room pueblo is thought to have been built entirely of petrified wood 700 years ago. Researchers believe it might have been used as a temporary dwelling by seasonal farmers or traders from one of the area tribes. ⊠ *Rainbow Forest Museum parking area.*

Newspaper Rock. See huge boulders covered with petroglyphs believed to have been carved by the Pueblo Indians more than 500 years ago. Be sure to look through the binoculars that are provided here—you'll be surprised at what the naked eye misses. ⊠ *On the main park road, 6 miles south of Painted Desert Visitor Center.*

Painted Desert Inn National Historic Landmark. A nice place to stop and rest in the shade, this site offers vast views of the Painted Desert from several lookouts. Inside, cultural-history exhibits, murals, and American Indian crafts are on display. ⊠ *On the main park road, 2 miles north of Painted Desert Visitor Center.*

Puerco Pueblo. This is a 100-room pueblo, built before 1400 and said to have housed Ancestral Puebloan people. Many visitors come to see petroglyphs, as well as a solar calendar. ⊠ *On the main park road, 10 miles south of the Painted Desert Visitor Center.*

SCENIC STOPS

Agate Bridge. Here you'll see a 100-foot log spanning a 40-foot-wide wash. ⊠ *On the main park road, 19 miles south of Painted Desert Visitor Center.*

Crystal Forest. The fragments of petrified wood strewn here once held clear quartz and amethyst crystals. ⊠ *On the main park road, 20 miles south of Painted Desert Visitor Center.*

Giant Logs Interpretive Loop Trail. A short walk leads you past the park's largest log, known as Old Faithful. It's considered the largest because of its diameter (9 feet, 9 inches), as well as how tall it once was. ⊠ *On the main park road, 28 miles south of Painted Desert Visitor Center.*

Jasper Forest. More of an overlook than a forest, this spot has a large concentration of petrified trees in jasper or red. ⊠ *On the main park road, 17 miles south of Painted Desert Visitor Center.*

The Tepees. Witness the effects of time on these cone-shaped rock formations colored by iron, manganese, and other minerals. ⊠ *On the main park road, 8 miles south of Painted Desert Visitor Center.*

EDUCATIONAL OFFERINGS

Ask at either park visitor center for the availability of special ranger-led tours, such as the after-hours lantern tour of the Painted Desert Inn Museum.

CLOSE UP

Plants and Wildlife in Petrified Forest

Engelmann's asters and sunflowers are among the blooms in the park each summer. Juniper trees, cottonwoods, and willows grow along Puerco River wash, providing shelter for all manner of wildlife. You might spot mule deer, coyotes, prairie dogs, and foxes, while other inhabitants, like porcupines and bobcats, tend to hide. Bird-watchers should keep an eye out for mockingbirds, red-tailed and Swainson's hawks, roadrunners, swallows, and hummingbirds. Look for all three kinds of lizards—collared, side-blotched, and southern prairie—in rocks.

Beware of rattlesnakes. They're common but can generally be easily avoided: Watch where you step, and don't step anywhere you can't see. If you do come across a rattler, give it plenty of space, and let it go its way before you continue on yours. Other reptiles are just as common but not as dangerous. The gopher snake looks similar to a rattlesnake, but is nonpoisonous. The collared lizard, with its yellow head, can be seen scurrying out of your way in bursts measured at up to 15 mph. They aren't poisonous, but will bite in the rare instance of being caught.

RANGER PROGRAMS

Ranger Walks and Talks. Park rangers lead regular programs along the Great Logs Trail, inside the Painted Desert Inn Museum, and to the Puerco Pueblo. You can view which ranger programs are currently being offered at the visitor centers or online at ⊕ *www.nps.gov/pefo*.

FAMILY **Junior Ranger.** Children 12 and younger can learn more about the park's extensive human, animal, and geologic history as they train to become a Junior Ranger.

SPORTS AND THE OUTDOORS

Because the park goes to great pains to maintain the integrity of the fossil- and artifact-strewn landscape, sports and outdoor options in the park are limited to on-trail hiking.

30

HIKING

All trails begin off the main road, with restrooms at or near the trailheads. Most maintained trails are relatively short, paved, clearly marked, and, with a few exceptions, easy to moderate in difficulty. Hikers with greater stamina can make their own trails in the wilderness area, located just north of the Painted Desert Visitor Center. Watch your step for rattlesnakes, which are common in the park—if left alone and given a wide berth, they're passed easily enough.

EASY

Crystal Forest Trail. This easy 0.75-mile loop leads you past petrified wood that once held quartz crystals and amethyst chips. *Easy.* ⊠ *Trailhead 20 miles south of the Painted Desert Visitor Center.*

The stones tell a story with ancient etchings on Newspaper Rock.

Giant Logs Trail. At 0.4 mile, Giant Logs is the park's shortest trail. The loop leads you to Old Faithful, the park's largest petrified log—9 feet, 9 inches at its base, weighing an estimated 44 tons. *Easy. ⊠ Trailhead directly behind Rainbow Forest Museum, 28 miles south of Painted Desert Visitor Center.*

Long Logs Trail. Although barren, this easy 1.6-mile loop passes the largest concentration of wood in the park. *Easy. ⊠ Trailhead 26 miles south of Painted Desert Visitor Center.*

FAMILY **Puerco Pueblo Trail.** A relatively flat and interesting 0.3-mile trail takes you past remains of a home of the Ancestral Puebloan people, built before 1400. The trail is paved and wheelchair accessible. *Easy. ⊠ Trailhead 10 miles south of Painted Desert Visitor Center.*

MODERATE

Fodor's Choice **Agate House.** A fairly flat 1-mile trip takes you to an eight-room pueblo
★ sitting high on a knoll. *Moderate. ⊠ Trailhead 26 miles south of Painted Desert Visitor Center.*

Blue Mesa. Although it's only 1 mile long and it's significantly steeper than the rest, this trail at the park's midway point is one of the most popular and worth the effort. *Moderate. ⊠ Trailhead 14 miles south of Painted Desert Visitor Center.*

Painted Desert Rim. The 1-mile trail is at its best in early morning or late afternoon, when the sun accentuates the brilliant red, blue, purple, and other hues of the desert and petrified forest landscape. *Moderate. ⊠ Trail runs between Tawa Point and Kachina Point, 1 mile north of Painted Desert Visitor Center; drive to either point from visitor center.*

DIFFICULT

Kachina Point. This is the trailhead for wilderness hiking. A 1-mile trail leads to the Wilderness Area, but from there you're on your own; with no developed trails, hiking here is cross-country style. Expect to see strange formations, beautifully colored landscapes, and maybe, just maybe, a pronghorn antelope. *Difficult.* ✉ *Trailhead on the northwest side of the Painted Desert Inn National Historic Landmark.*

LOOK AND TOUCH— BUT DON'T TAKE

One of the most commonly asked questions about the Petrified Forest is, "Can I touch the wood?" Yes! Feel comfortable to touch anything, pick it up, inspect it…just make sure you put it back where you found it. It's illegal to remove even a small sliver of fossilized wood from the park.

WHAT'S NEARBY

Located in eastern Arizona just off Interstate 40, Petrified Forest National Park is set in an area of grasslands, overlooked by mountains in the distance. At nearly an hour from **American Indian Nations,** nearly two hours from **Flagstaff,** and three hours from the **Grand Canyon,** the park is relatively remote and separated from many comforts of travel. Just a half-hour away, **Holbrook,** the nearest town, is the best place to grab a quick bite to eat or take a brief rest.

NEARBY ATTRACTIONS

Fodor'sChoice **Canyon de Chelly.** Home to Ancestral Puebloans from AD 350 to 1300,
★ the nearly 84,000-acre Canyon de Chelly (pronounced d'*shay*) is one of the most beautiful natural wonders in the Southwest. On a smaller scale, it rivals the Grand Canyon for beauty. Its main gorges—the 26-mile-long Canyon de Chelly ("canyon in the rock") and the adjoining 35-mile-long Canyon del Muerto ("canyon of the dead")—comprise sheer, heavily eroded sandstone walls that rise to 1,100 feet over dramatic valleys. Ancient pictographs and petroglyphs decorate some of the cliffs, and within the canyon complex there are more than 7,000 archaeological sites. Stone walls rise hundreds of feet above streams, hogans, tilled fields, and sheep-grazing lands.

You can view prehistoric sites near the base of cliffs and perched on high, sheltering ledges, some of which you can access from the park's two main drives along the canyon rims. The dwellings and cultivated fields of the present-day Navajo lie in the flatlands between the cliffs, and those who inhabit the canyon today farm much the way their ancestors did. Most residents leave the canyon in winter but return in early spring to farm.

Canyon de Chelly's South Rim Drive (36 miles round-trip with seven overlooks) starts at the visitor center and ends at **Spider Rock Overlook,** where cliffs plunge nearly 1,000 feet to the canyon floor. The view here is of two pinnacles, Speaking Rock and Spider Rock. Other highlights on the South Rim Drive are Junction Overlook, where

30

Petroglyphs: The Writing on the Wall

Like some other historic sites in Eastern Arizona, Petrified Forest National Park is a great place to view petroglyphs and pictographs—designs pecked or scratched into the stone are called petroglyphs; those that are painted on the surface are pictographs. Few pictographs remain because of the deleterious effects of weathering, but the more durable petroglyphs number in the thousands.

The rock art of early Native Americans is carved or painted on basalt boulders, on canyon walls, and on the underside of overhangs throughout the area. No one knows the exact meaning of these signs, and interpretations vary; they've been seen as elements in shamanistic or hunting rituals, as clan signs, maps, or even indications of visits by extraterrestrials.

WHERE TO FIND IT

Susceptible to (and often already damaged by) vandalism, many rock-art sites aren't open to the public. Two good petroglyphs to check out at **Petrified Forest National Park** are Newspaper Rock, an overlook near mile marker 12, and Puerco Pueblo, near mile marker 11. Other sites in Arizona include **Hieroglyphic Point** in Salt River Canyon, and **Five-Mile Canyon** in Snowflake.

DETERMINING ITS AGE

It's just as difficult to date a "glyph" as it is to understand it. Archaeologists try to determine a general time frame by judging the style, the date of the ruins and pottery in the vicinity, the amount of patination (formation of minerals) on the design, or the superimposition of newer images on top of older ones. Most of Eastern Arizona's rock art is estimated to be at least 1,000 years old, and many of the glyphs were created even earlier.

VARIED IMAGES

Some glyphs depict animals like bighorn sheep, deer, bear, and mountain lions; others are geometric patterns. The most unusual are the anthropomorphs, strange humanlike figures with elaborate headdresses. Concentric circles are a common design. A few of these circles served as solstice signs, indicating the summer and winter solstice and other important dates. At the solstice, when the angle of the sun is just right, a shaft of light shines through a crack in a nearby rock, illuminating the center of the circle. Archaeologists believe that these solar calendars helped determine the time for ceremonies and planting.

Many solstice signs are in remote regions, but you can visit Petrified Forest National Park around June 20 to see a concentric circle illuminated during the summer solstice. The glyph, reached by a paved trail just a few hundred yards from the parking area, is visible year-round, but light shines directly in the center during the week of the solstice. The phenomenon occurs at 9 am, a reasonable hour for looking at the calendar.

■TIP→ Do not touch petroglyphs or pictographs—the oil from your hands can damage the images.

Canyon del Muerto joins Canyon de Chelly; White House Overlook, from which a 2.5-mile round-trip trail leads to the **White House Ruin,** with remains of nearly 60 rooms and several kivas; and Sliding House Overlook, where you can see dwellings on a narrow, sloped ledge across the canyon. The carved and sometimes narrow trail down the canyon side to White House Ruin is the only access into Canyon de Chelly without a guide—but if you have a fear of heights, this may not be the hike for you.

The only slightly less breathtaking **North Rim Drive** (34 miles round-trip with four overlooks) of Canyon del Muerto also begins at the visitor center and continues northeast on Indian Highway 64 toward the town of Tsaile. Major stops include Antelope House Overlook, a large site named for the animals painted on an adjacent cliff; **Mummy Cave Overlook,** where two mummies were found inside a remarkably unspoiled pueblo dwelling; and **Massacre Cave Overlook,** which marks the spot where an estimated 115 Navajo were killed by the Spanish in 1805. (The rock walls of the cave are still pockmarked by the Spaniards' ricocheting bullets.) ✉ *Indian Hwy. 7, 3 miles east of U.S. 191, Chinle* ☎ *928/674–5500 for visitor center* ⊕ *www.nps.gov/cach* 🎫 *Free* ⊙ *Daily 8–5.*

> ## BEST CAMPGROUNDS IN PETRIFIED FOREST
>
> There are no campgrounds in the park. Backpacking or minimal-impact camping is allowed in a designated zone north of Lithodendron Wash in the Wilderness Area; a free permit must be obtained (pick up at the visitor center or museum), and group size is limited to eight. RVs are not allowed. There are no fire pits or designated sites, nor is any shade available. Note that if it rains, that pretty Painted Desert formation turns to sticky clay.

Homolovi Ruins State Park. *Homolovi* is a Hopi word meaning "place of the little hills." The pueblo sites here at Homolovi Ruins State Park are thought to have been occupied between AD 1200 and 1425, and include 40 ceremonial kivas and two pueblos containing more than 1,000 rooms each. The Hopi believe their immediate ancestors inhabited this place, and they consider the site sacred. Many rooms have been excavated and recovered for protection; rangers conduct guided tours. The Homolovi Visitor Center has a small museum with Hopi pottery and Ancestral Puebloan artifacts; it also hosts workshops on native art, ethnobotany, and traditional foods. ✉ *Rte. 87, 5 miles northeast of Winslow* ☎ *928/289–4106* ⊕ *www.azstateparks.com* 🎫 *$7* ⊙ *Visitor center daily 8–5.*

Rock Art Ranch. The Ancestral Puebloan petroglyphs of this working cattle ranch in Chevelon Canyon are startlingly vivid after more than 1,000 years. Ranch owner Brantly Baird will guide you along the 0.25-mile trail, explaining Western and archaeological history. It's mostly easy walking, except for the climb in and out of Chevelon Canyon, where there are handrails. Baird houses his Native American artifacts and pioneer farming implements in his own private museum. It's out of the way and on a dirt road, but you'll see some of the best rock art in northern Arizona. Reservations are required. ✉ *Off Rte. 87, 13 miles southeast of Winslow* ☎ *928/386–5047* 🎫 *$35 per person for 1 or 2 people* ⊙ *By appointment only.*

30

WHERE TO EAT

INSIDE THE PARK

$ ✕ **Painted Desert Visitor Center Cafeteria.** Serving standard (but pretty

AMERICAN decent) cafeteria fare, this is the only place in the park where you can get a full meal. $ *Average main: $7* ✉ *North entrance* ☎ *928/524–6228.*

PICNIC AREAS

Chinde Point. Near the north entrance, this small spot has tables and restrooms. ✉ *2 miles north of Painted Desert Visitor Center.*

Rainbow Forest Museum. There are restrooms and tables at this small picnic area near the south entrance. ✉ *Off U.S. 40, 27 miles east of Holbrook.*

WHERE TO STAY

OUTSIDE THE PARK

HOLBROOK

$ 🏠 **Wigwam Motel.** On the National Register of Historic Places, the

HOTEL Wigwam consists of 15 bright-white concrete tepees. **Pros:** impeccably kitschy; one of the signature spots along Route 66. **Cons:** very sparse accommodations that can fit no more than two. $ *Rooms from: $62* ✉ *811 West Hopi Dr., Holbrook* ☎ *928/524–3048* ⊕ *www.galerie-kokopelli.com/wigwam* ⤳ *15 rooms* ⦿ *No meals.*

WINSLOW

$$ 🏠 **La Posada Hotel.** One of the great railroad hotels, La Posada ("rest-

HOTEL ing place") exudes the charm of an 18th-century Spanish hacienda and

Fodor'sChoice its restoration has been a labor of love. **Pros:** historic charm; unique

★ architecture; impressive restaurant. **Cons:** mazes of staircases aren't very wheelchair-friendly. $ *Rooms from: $119* ✉ *303 E. 2nd St., Winslow* ☎ *928/289–4366* ⊕ *www.laposada.org* ⤳ *53 rooms* ⦿ *No meals.*

PINNACLES
NATIONAL PARK

WELCOME TO PINNACLES

TOP REASONS TO GO

★ **Condor encounters:** There are only 240 California condors alive in the wild today, and Pinnacles is home to more than 30 of the critically endangered bird.

★ **Cave exploring:** The park contains two talus caves—a unique type of cave formed when boulders fall into narrow canyons, creating ceilings, passageways, and small rooms.

★ **Hiking the pinnacles:** There aren't many roads, so the best way to see the otherworldly rock formations of the ancient volcano found in the middle of the park is to hike the over 30 miles of trails.

★ **Climbing sans crowds:** The park's newbie status and remote location means it gets a lot fewer visitors than parks like Yosemite, leaving the hundreds of rock-climbing routes crowd-free.

★ **Star appeal:** Far from cities and smog, the park is a popular star-gazing destination, especially during the annual Perseid meteor shower.

1 East Entrance. There are only two entrances to the park, and this is the family-friendly choice. It has the park's only campground—including a visitor center, a small but welcoming swimming pool that's especially inviting on hot days, and a small store for food, drinks, and other camping essentials. It's also the best way to access Bear Gulch Cave, the most popular hike in the park.

2 West Entrance. This tends to be the more quiet side of the park, with few amenities available. But this is the side to go to if you want to get a good look at the high-peak formations without having to hike—just head to the Chaparral Trailhead parking lot to view them from there. The Balconies Cave Trail is also popular on this side of the park, and the towering rocks tend to keep the canyon trail shady and relatively cool.

North Wilderness Trail

Balconies Trail

BALCONIES

Chaparral Trailhead 🏕🏞🚻

Hawkins Pk 2,720ft

Juniper Canyon Trail

Visitor Center

HIGH PEAKS

Scout Pk 2,605ft

🚻

2 West Entrance

146

Moses Spring Trail

Chalo Tr

N Ch 3,

KEY

🏚	Ranger Station
⛺	Campground
🏞	Picnic Area
🍴	Restaurant
🏨	Lodge
🧍	Trailhead
🚻	Restrooms
⇗	Scenic Viewpoint
⋯⋯	Walking/Hiking Trails

CALIFORNIA

GETTING ORIENTED

Bounded on the west by Steinbeck's Salinas Valley and busy Highway 101 and on the east by pastoral Highway 25, Pinnacles can almost seem like two parks, with the ancient volcanic peaks at its center barring cars from getting from one side to the other (only hikers can make this trek). From San Francisco, it's about 130 miles (2.5 hours) south to either entrance on Highway 146, and about 80 miles (1.75 hours) south of San Jose; from Monterey/Carmel, it's about 50 miles (1 hour) to the west entrance. To drive from one entrance to the other, allow at least an hour and a half. If you're entering the park from the west, Highway 146 becomes very windy and hilly after Soledad, and is only one-lane wide in many places. The park service strongly recommends that RVs, trailers, and large vehicles avoid this road and enter via the east entrance instead.

By Deb Hopewell

Pinnacles may be our nation's newest national park, but Teddy Roosevelt recognized the uniqueness of this ancient volcano—its jagged spires and monoliths thrusting upward from chaparral-covered mountains—when he made it a national monument in 1908. Legends abound of robbers and banditos who used the park's talus caves as hideouts, though undoubtedly the park's most famous denizens today are the singularly magnificent California condors, which were all but extinct just 25 years ago. Though only about two hours from the bustling Bay Area, the outside world seems to recede even before you reach the park's gates.

PINNACLES PLANNER

WHEN TO GO

Summers tend to be very warm, and triple-digit temperatures are not uncommon; luckily this means fewer crowds, especially on weekdays. The spring months, particularly March and April, are the most popular season at the park, as they are prime times for viewing spectacular displays of lupine, poppies, and other California wildflowers. Fall is a great time to visit if you want to enjoy cooler temperatures (though September can still be quite warm) and fewer crowds. Winter months can be cold by California standards, but can also be an opportune time to hike the park, especially the High Peaks, where most of the trails are in the sun (temperatures in the deeply shaded parts of the park, such as the Balconies Trail, can reach below freezing).

One thing to keep in mind: Bear Gulch Cave on the east side is one of the most popular hikes and attractions in the park, and it's also home to the largest colony of Townsend's big-eared bats in the region. This protected species raise its young in the late spring and summer, so the cave is closed each year from about mid-May to mid-July. If your plans include visiting the cave, be sure to check the park's website (⊕ *www.nps.gov/ pinn/planyourvisit/cavestatus.htm*), which provides updates on closures.

31

AVG. HIGH/LOW TEMPS.

JAN.	FEB.	MAR.	APR.	MAY	JUNE
62/27	63/30	67/32	72/33	80/37	88/41
JULY	AUG.	SEPT.	OCT.	NOV.	DEC.
95/45	95/45	90/42	81/36	69/31	61/27

FESTIVALS AND EVENTS

California Salinas Rodeo. More than a century old, this rodeo is the largest in California and one of the best professional rodeos in the country. Watch as more than 700 top-ranked wranglers compete for prizes in events that include bareback riding, saddle bronc riding, steer wrestling, and bull riding. ⊠ *1034 N. Main St., Salinas* ☎ *831/775–3100* ⊕ *www.carodeo.com.*

MAY **Steinbeck Festival.** This annual three-day festival celebrates the life and works of author and Salinas native John Steinbeck, whose Pulitzer- and Nobel-prize-winning novels were often set in the areas of Monterey County he knew and loved so well. Films, tours, talks, and visual/ performing-arts activities take place in both Monterey and Salinas. ⊠ *1 Main St., Salinas* ☎ *831/775–4721* ⊕ *www.steinbeck.org.*

PLANNING YOUR TIME

PINNACLES IN ONE DAY

Begin your day early by arriving at the West Entrance, with a quick stop at the **West Pinnacles Visitor Contact Station** pick up maps. Continue on Highway 146 about 2 miles to the **Chaparral Trailhead** parking lot, where you can get a welcome view of the park's impressive peaks. The best way to experience these peaks is by hiking, so grab your flashlight and some water, and follow the **Balconies Trail** from the parking lot. It's a quick, mostly level 1-mile hike along the shady canyon floor to the **Balconies Cave,** where you must duck under boulders and sometimes squeeze through the talus passages. By adding an extra half-mile you can take the **Balconies Cliff Trail** from the Balconies Trail and climb for about a half-mile for fantastic views looking east to Machete Ridge. Follow the trail down to the back side of the caves, and return through the caves to the original trail. Once you return to your car, head back west to Soledad.

From Soledad follow 101 south about 19 miles to King City, and exit at 1st Street. Going toward King City, drive about 15 miles through Highway 25 until you reach Highway 146 and the east entrance of the park.

Stop at the store (if it's open) adjacent to the **Pinnacles Visitor Center** for a cold drink or snack before continuing on Highway 146 a little more than 2 miles to the turnoff for the Bear Gulch Day Use Area. The **Bear Gulch Nature Center** is open seasonally as staffing permits, so if you can, make a quick stop to take a look at the displays, including an earthquake seismograph (the park lies near the San Andreas Fault). Afterward, just past the nature center, there's a small parking lot with shaded tables, a perfect place for a picnic. Make sure you have your water and flashlight with you as you take the **Bear Gulch Trail** straight from the picnic area to the **Moses Spring Trail** (0.2 miles). Once you get to the caves (about 0.3 miles), you'll scramble through until you come to a long staircase cut into the stone; very shortly the trail will bring you to the **Bear Gulch Reservoir.** Follow the Rim Trail as it leaves the reservoir for views of the peaks to the east and west. After a switchback descent, it connects again with the Moses Spring Trail (0.7 miles), and then back to the parking lot.

GETTING HERE AND AROUND
AIR TRAVEL
The nearest major airport is Mineta San Jose International Airport, about 80 miles north of the park. San Francisco International Airport is about 100 miles north.

CAR TRAVEL
One of the first things you need to decide when visiting Pinnacles is which entrance—east or west—you'll use, because there's no road connecting the two, thanks to the rugged peaks separating them. Entering from Highway 25 on the east is straightforward. The gate is only a mile or so from the turnoff. From the west, once you head east out of Soledad on Highway 146, the road quickly becomes narrow and hilly, with many blind curves. The park service doesn't recommend that RVs, large vehicles, or vehicles towing trailers use this entrance. Drive slowly and cautiously along the 11 miles or so before you reach the west entrance.

PARK ESSENTIALS
PARK FEES AND PERMITS
Park admission is $5 per car or motorcycle, $3 per person on foot or bicycle. The Pinnacles National Park Annual Pass is $15 and valid for one year from the month of purchase.

PARK HOURS
The East Entrance is open 24 hours a day, 7 days a week. The West Entrance opens daily at 7:30 am and closes at 8 pm in summer, 6 pm in winter. If you wish to stay later, an automatic gate allows cars to leave the park after closing time.

CELL-PHONE RECEPTION
The closer you get to Pinnacles, the less reliable service will be; it's nearly nonexistent within the park. There's a pay phone at the visitor center at the east entrance and at the Bear Gulch Nature Center. There are no public phones at the west entrance or in the interior of the park.

RESTAURANTS
There are no restaurants in the park, so it's a good idea to pack a cooler before you arrive, especially if you plan on staying for more than a day. If you're coming from the north, you'll find supermarkets and grocery stores in nearby Hollister; at the southern end, King City is the best option. Soledad, the gateway to the park's west entrance, also has a supermarket. In a pinch, there's a small camp store adjacent to the east entrance visitor center that carries mostly canned goods and snacks, as well as bags of ice. Be warned that there's no food or drink available at the west entrance, and because you can't drive through to the other entrance, you'll need to come prepared.

Plants and Wildlife in Pinnacles

31

Pinnacles doesn't have any of the wildlife superstars you can find at other national parks—bison, bear, elk, bighorn sheep—but here, California condors rule the roost. These magnificent birds, whose wingspans reach nearly 10 feet when fully grown, were nearly extinct in the 1980s when only 22 remained in the world. Thanks to an intensive captive breeding program, there are now more than 400, with 240 of them in the wild. Pinnacles is one of the five release locations for California condors, and about 30 make their home here. It's also the preferred habitat for prairie falcons, which breed here in one of the highest densities in the world.

Bobcats and cougars also roam the park, and California quail are abundant. In addition, there are 14 species of bats, including a colony of Townsend's big-eared bats that live in Bear Gulch Cave, resting in winter and raising their young throughout the summer. Pinnacles also has the most bee species—400 per unit area—of any place ever studied. It's also an essential refuge for a host of native species that have been challenged by nearby human encroachment, such as the big-eared kangaroo rat, Gabilan slender salamander, Pinnacles shield-back katydid, and Pinnacles riffle beetle.

Springtime sets the stage for a wildflower extravaganza, especially March through early May, when more than 80% of the park's plants are in bloom. The most prodigious early bloomers include manzanita, shooting stars, and Indian warriors; by March the park is awash in California poppies, bush poppies, buck brush, fiesta flower, and monkey flower. Late-bloomers include suncups, bush lupine, and Johnny-jump-ups. Most of the park is covered in chaparral growth, which has adapted to high-heat, low-moisture conditions. This particular plant community is mostly shrubs that grow to around 6-feet tall; the dominant species is chamise, which grows alongside buck brush, manzanita, black sage, and holly-leaved cherry.

Prices in the reviews are the average cost of a main course at dinner, or if dinner is not served, at lunch.

HOTELS

There aren't any hotels or lodges within the park, so if you want to stay overnight, camping at the Pinnacles Campground (near the east entrance) is your only option. Nearby, you can find an array of mostly budget-class motels in King City, Hollister, and Soledad.

Prices in the reviews are the lowest cost of a standard double room in high season. For expanded reviews, facilities, and current deals, visit Fodors.com.

VISITOR INFORMATION

PARK CONTACT INFORMATION

Pinnacles National Park ⊠ *5000 Hwy. 146, Paicines* ☏ *831/389–4486* ⊕ *www.nps.gov/pinn/index.htm.*

VISITOR CENTERS

Pinnacles Visitor Center. This is the main visitor center for the park, located at the east entrance. Here you can purchase your admission passes, get maps, browse books, and buy gifts. Because it's adjacent to the campground store, it's a good place to stock up on last-minute snacks and drinks if you're headed out to hike the trails. ⊠ *Hwy. 146, 2 miles west of Hwy. 25, Paicines* ☎ *831/389–4485* ⊕ *www.nps.gov/pinn/planyourvisit/hours.htm.*

West Pinnacles Visitor Contact Station. This station is just past the west entrance to the park, about 14 miles east of Soledad. Here you can get maps and information, watch a 13-minute film about the park, view some displays, and browse a small gift shop. Be advised that there isn't any food or drink available at this entrance, so come prepared. ⊠ *Hwy. 146, about 14 miles east of Soledad* ☎ *831/537–7220* ⊕ *www.nps.gov/ pinn/planyourvisit/hours.htm* ⊘ *Daily 9–4:30.*

EXPLORING

HISTORIC SITES

Bacon and Butterfield Homesteads. These two homesteads are in the heart of the 331-acre Ben Bacon Historic District on the east side of the park, and illustrate what subsistence farming in the area looked like from 1865 to 1941, before large-scale farming and ranching became the norm. ⊕ *www.nps.gov/cultural_landscapes/snp/725493.html.*

SCENIC STOPS

Chaparral Trailhead. This is the end of the road on the west side of the park, but it's also the best view of the Peaks you can get without having to hit the trails. Be sure to spot knifelike Machete Ridge looming in the distance. ⊠ *Hwy. 146, about 2 miles northeast of West Pinnacles Visitor Contact Station.*

Peaks View. If your plans on the east side of the park don't include hiking, the Peaks View area is the best spot to catch a glimpse of the rugged High Peaks to the west. Although it doesn't quite match actually hiking up to the Peaks, it's your best shot at seeing what you're missing if you left your hiking boots at home. The area also has restrooms, a few picnic tables, and drinking water. ⊠ *Hwy. 146 about 1½ miles west of Pinnacles Visitor Center, on east side of park.*

EDUCATIONAL OFFERINGS

INTERPRETIVE PROGRAMS

Illustrated Ranger Talks. Every Friday and Saturday evening from mid-February until Labor Day, rangers give free presentations at the campground amphitheater (at the east entrance). The topics depend on the ranger's particular interests, but always relate to the park's main stories and its geology, plants, or wildlife. Times vary, so be sure to check the website. ⊠ *5000 Hwy. 146, Paicines* ☎ *831/389–4486* ⊕ *www.nps.gov/ pinn/planyourvisit/programs.htm.*

LECTURES

Summer Speaker Series. Each summer Pinnacles presents a Speaker Series that runs from June to August and covers subjects that range from the natural resources of the park to general climate change and sustainability practices. The first Wednesday of the month, the talks are held at the Soledad Library (✉ *401 Gabilan Dr.* ☎ *831/678–2430*) usually at 6 pm, and the next two Saturdays at 2 pm at either the Pinnacles Visitor Center or the West Pinnacles Visitor Contact Station; check the park's event calendar to view the specific talks and where they'll be held. The talks are geared to teens and adults, but a Junior Ranger Book or another youth activity sheet is provided for children. ✉ *5000 Hwy. 146, Paicines* ☎ *831/389–4486* ⊕ *www.nps.gov/pinn/planyourvisit/events.htm.*

RANGER PROGRAMS

Junior Ranger Program. Kids can pick up a free Junior Ranger booklet at the Bear Gulch Nature Center, Pinnacles Visitor Center, or the West Pinnacles Visitor Contact Station. Once they explore the park and complete the activities in the booklet, they'll earn a Junior Ranger Badge. ✉ *5000 Hwy. 146, Paicines* ☎ *831/389–4486* ⊕ *www.nps.gov/pinn/ planyourvisit/events.htm.*

Night Hikes. Throughout the year Pinnacles hosts special night hikes that lead hikers under the full moon or on nighttime cave explorations. These aren't regularly scheduled events (and often depend on volunteer availability), so check the website for any that coincide with your visit. Groups are limited to 25, and reservations are required no more than one week in advance; to reserve a spot, stop into the Pinnacles Visitor Center or call ahead. ✉ *5000 Hwy. 146, Paicines* ☎ *831/389– 4486 for east side, 831/537–7220 for west side* ⊕ *www.nps.gov/pinn/ planyourvisit/programs.htm.*

Ranger-Guided Hikes and Activities. From President's Day weekend through the end of May, park rangers offer free guided hikes, usually on the weekends. On the east side of the park, they typically go to the Bear Gulch Cave; on the west side, they go to the Balconies Cliffs and Caves. When you get to the park, ask a ranger or consult one of the Ranger Activity Boards outside the Pinnacles Visitor Center, the Bear Gulch Nature Center, or the West Pinnacles Visitor Contact Station for the day's opportunities. ✉ *5000 Hwy. 146, Paicines* ☎ *831/389–4486* ⊕ *www.nps.gov/pinn/planyourvisit/programs.htm.*

SPORTS AND THE OUTDOORS

BIRD-WATCHING

You don't have to be an avid bird-watcher to appreciate the diversity of birds at Pinnacles, so don't forget your binoculars, especially for that charged moment when you realize you've spotted a highly rare California condor suspended on a thermal draft. You're most likely to see a condor in the early morning or in the early evening in the relatively remote High Peaks area, or on the Balconies Cliff Trail above the caves as you look toward Machete Peak. Condors are also often seen just southeast of the campground, riding the morning thermals along the ridge and coming in to roost on their favorite trees in the evenings. There are two spotting scopes in the campground (on the Bench Trail near Pinnacles Visitor Center) that may help you get a closer look. But if you do happen to find yourself especially close to one, do not under any circumstances approach it—they are a federally protected species, and you can be fined.

The High Peaks are also a good place to spot other raptors, such as prairie and peregrine falcons, golden eagles, red-tailed haws, and American kestrels. But you don't have to undertake a strenuous uphill hike to catch some of the best bird-watching in the park. The campground and visitor center on the east side is a convergence of habitats—riparian, oak/pine trees, chaparral, and human-made. Many species take advantage of water sources provided by the swimming pool and water fountain, and on the paved road past the parking lot, a riparian corridor is the prime habitat for coveys of California quail and wild turkeys.

HIKING

Hiking is the most popular activity at Pinnacles, with more than 30 miles of trails for every interest and level of fitness. Because there isn't a road through the park, hiking is also the only way to experience the interior of the park, including the High Peaks, the talus caves, and the reservoir.

One thing to note about hiking in the Bear Gulch and Balconies cave systems: flashlights are required, and you won't be able to get through the caves without one. Penlights won't do the job; the best choice is a hands-free, head-mounted light. Also, although the hikes to the caves themselves are easy and short, getting through the caves requires lots of scrambling, ducking, climbing, and squeezing. These caves were formed by giant boulders that broke loose and covered the narrow ravines, and getting around/under/over them takes a certain amount of agility. Make sure you have suitable, closed-toe shoes.

EASY

Balconies Cliffs-Cave Loop. Grab your flashlight before heading out from the Chaparral Trailhead parking lot for this 2.4-mile loop that takes you through the Balconies Caves. This trail is especially beautiful in spring when an abundance of wildflowers carpets the canyon floor. About 0.6 miles from the start of the trail, turn left to begin ascending the Balconies Cliffs Trail, where you'll be rewarded with close-up views of Machete Peak and other steep, vertical formations; you'll probably run across a few rock climbers testing their skills. *Easy.* ⊠ *Trailhead at west side of Chaparral Trailhead parking lot, 2 miles from west Pinnacles Visitor Center.*

FAMILY **Moses Spring-Rim Trail Loop.** This is perhaps the most popular hike at Pinnacles, as it's relatively short (2.2 miles in typically 1½hours) and fun for both kids and adults alike. It takes you to the Bear Gulch cave system and if your timing is right, you'll pass by several seasonal waterfalls inside the caves (if it's been raining, check with a ranger as the caves could be flooded). The caves are usually closed in spring and early summer to protect the Townsend's big-ear bats and their pups. *Easy.* ⊠ *Trailhead at south side of overflow parking lot, just past Bear Gulch Nature Center.*

MODERATE

Condor Gulch Trail. The trailhead starts at the Bear Gulch Day Use area, and it's an easy 1-mile hike up to the Condor Gulch Overlook, where you can get a good view of the High Peaks above and look back down to the trail behind you. Take the moderately easy 2-mile loop back down, or continue another 0.7 mile up to where the Condor Gulch meets the High Peaks Trail and extend your hike by following the trail in either direction. *Moderate.* ⊠ *Trailhead opposite Nature Center at Bear Gulch Day Use Area, on east side of park.*

Pinnacles Visitor Center to Bear Gulch Day Use Area. This 4.6-mile round-trip hike (about three hours) follows the Chalone and Bear creeks first along the Bench Trail for about 1½ miles, where it meets up with the Bear Gulch Trail. Purchase an interpretive map at the visitor center and keep your eyes open for signs pointing out where you might be able to spot the rare red-legged frog or the native three-spined stickleback fish. *Moderate.* ⊠ *From Pinnacles Visitor Center, follow signs to Bench Trail.*

South Wilderness Trail. This 6.5-mile hike, with no elevation gain, is an easy stroll alongside the Chalone River that eventually reaches the eastern boundary of the park. Listen to birds sing along the creek as you meander among magnificent groves of valley oaks. Pick up this unmaintained trail by following the Bench Trail from the campground for 0.6 mile before turning left at the South Wilderness Trail junction. *Moderate.* ⊠ *Follow Bench Trail out of campground for 0.6 miles before turning left onto fireroad.*

DIFFICULT

Chalone Peak Trail. If you choose this strenuous 9-mile round-trip hike (2,040 feet of elevation gain), you'll be rewarded with views of the surrounding valleys from the highest point in the park at 3,304 feet (there are also restrooms). If you want to extend the hike, proceed south along the unmaintained portion of the trail for 1.6 miles to South Chalone Peak (3,269 feet). *Difficult.* ⊠ *Trailhead at Bear Gulch Reservoir where Moses Spring, Rim, and Chalone Peak trails meet just outside of caves.*

Juniper Canyon Loop. This steep 4.3-mile loop climbs into the heart of the dramatic High Peaks with a 1,215-foot elevation gain, often in high temperatures. From the trailhead follow the switchbacks up for 1.2 miles, where the trail veers right; be sure to stop at Scout Peak, where you'll find restrooms and fantastic views in all directions—keep an eye out for the occasional California condor sighting. From there, follow the High Peaks Trail through a steep and narrow section, where you hug the side of rock faces until reaching a short, nearly vertical staircase that has a railing to help you up. *Difficult.* ⊠ *Trail off Chaparral Trailhead parking lot, on west side of park.*

ROCK CLIMBING

Pinnacles has been a favorite of local Bay Area and Central Coast climbers for years, but luckily still remains a relatively quiet spot without the hassle and crowds of better-known parks like Yosemite and Joshua Tree. One important thing to consider is that unlike Yosemite and other granite playgrounds, Pinnacles is largely made of volcanic rock that

Best Campgrounds in Pinnacles

There's only one camping option in Pinnacles, on the east side of the park next to the Pinnacles Visitor Center.

Pinnacles Campground. Set amid a canopy of live oaks that provide welcome shade over most of its 134 sites (83 nonelectric tent-only sites, 14 nonelectric group sites, and 37 electric RV sites), Pinnacles Campground is open year-round. Bathrooms (with flush toilets) are clean but somewhat dated; showers are available for a fee ($0.75 for three minutes). Each site has a picnic table and fire ring, but high fire danger, especially in the dry summer and fall months, often means campfires aren't allowed. There's a swimming pool behind the visitor center open from April 1 to September 30 and leashed pets are allowed in the campground, but not on the trails, so consider leaving them at home. The campground store, which shares space next to the visitor center, carries basic food supplies, snacks, soft drinks, beer, and ice. ⊠ *5000 Hwy. 146, Paicines* ☎ *877/444-6777 for reservations, 831/389-4538 for campground store.*

can be soft and crumbly. The park service suggests that if you've never climbed at Pinnacles before, your first attempts should be well below your usual level in order to get familiar with the strength and character of the rocks. In general, the east side of the park has stronger rock, but the west side has much higher peaks.

If you're a first-time climber, one of the best resources is the Friends of Pinnacles (⊕ *www.pinnacles.org*), a nonprofit that works directly with the park to offer useful tips, guidelines, and updates regarding climbing closures due to nesting raptors. Some formations can also be closed from January through June or July, depending on if there are any nesting falcons or eagles. If you want to know if a specific route is open, check with a ranger, or look for the climbing information boards at both the East and West trailheads. Complying with closures is voluntary, but climbers or hikers who disturb nesting birds will be fined.

STARGAZING

Though the populous Bay Area is only a couple of hours away, Pinnacles remains untouched by light pollution, making it an outstanding place to watch meteor showers, stars, or the full moon come up. It's popular with astronomy clubs, who occasionally come for a night to set up their telescopes for public use. The park itself frequently hosts ranger-guided nighttime events, usually on the weekends, throughout the year. They include activities such as dark-sky and full-moon hikes, and "star parties" to watch meteor showers and other celestial phenomena. Meteor showers are a particularly popular time at the park, and the campsites can fill up well in advance. These activities are usually limited to 25 visitors per program, and reservations are required (no more than one week in advance) by calling ☎ *831/389-4485* or visiting the Pinnacles Visitor Center.

WHAT'S NEARBY

NEARBY TOWNS

Soledad, at the town's west entrance, is most famous for being the setting of John Steinbeck's *Of Mice and Men* but it's also a major wine-growing region in California. There are a large number of good wineries with tasting rooms within about 30 miles, including Hahn, Paraiso Vineyards, Ventana, and Sheid.

To the north is **Hollister,** another farming town that's quickly becoming a bedroom community of San Jose. Though not as large or well-known as a wine area, the nearby San Benito County Wine Trail is a nice, low-key way to pass an afternoon visiting local tasting rooms. All of the wineries are on or near Cienega Road, just south of Hollister off Highway 25.

Other popular California towns, like Monterey and Carmel, are a little more than an hour away and can make a great addition to a Pinnacles vacation.

San Benito County Chamber of Commerce ✉ *243 6th St., Suite 100, Hollister* ☎ *831/637–5315* ⊕ *www.sanbenitocountychamber.com.* **Soledad-Mission Chamber of Commerce** ✉ *641 Front St., Soledad* ☎ *831/678–3941* ⊕ *www.soledadchamber.com.*

WHERE TO EAT

IN THE PARK

PICNIC AREAS

Chaparral Trailhead. This is the only designated picnic area on the west side of the park, but there are great views of the nearby high peaks. There are few trees for shade, however, and it can be quite warm in summer. Restrooms are close by, and drinking water is available. ✉ *Hwy. 146, about 2 miles northeast of West Pinnacles Visitor Contact Station.*

Moses Spring. This is the most pleasant picnic area in the park, located along a seasonal creek with plenty of shade from the nearby live oaks. It's also a convenient spot to picnic before or after a hike to the reservoir via the Moses Spring or Rim trail. The nearby Bear Gulch Day Use Area has bathrooms across from the Bear Gulch Nature Center and drinking water. ✉ *Bear Gulch Trail, about ¼ mile past Bear Gulch Nature Center.*

Peaks View. Peaks View is one of the few places on the east side of the park where you can catch a glimpse of the High Peaks without getting on a trail. If you're on the east side and your plans don't include hiking, this is a nice spot to picnic. There are restrooms and drinking water. ✉ *Hwy. 146, about 1½ miles west of Pinnacles Visitor Center, on east side of park.*

WHERE TO STAY

OUTSIDE THE PARK

$$$$
B&B/INN
Fodor's Choice
★

⌂ **Inn at the Pinnacles.** Set amid 160 acres of hilltop vineyards overlooking the Salinas Valley and the coastal Santa Lucia Mountains, this Mediterranean-style bed-and-breakfast is an oasis of comfort just off the winding road leading to the park's west entrance a mile and a half away. **Pros:** gorgeous vineyard setting and sunset views; tasty breakfast included; close to the park. **Cons:** 20 minutes to closest Soledad restaurants; a better choice for couples than for families. $ *Rooms from: $225* ✉ *3025 Stonewall Canyon Rd., Soledad* ⊕ *www.innatthepinnacles.com* ⌁ *6 rooms* ¡○¡ *Breakfast.*

$
RENTAL

⌂ **Paicines Ranch.** These comfortable, somewhat rustic rooms and cottages are tucked into a corner of a 7,000-acre working ranch—where Judy Garland quietly wed Sid Luft in 1952—and are an easy 30-minute drive to the park's east entrance. **Pros:** easy access to east entrance; good for large groups or families; very peaceful; cooking facilities available. **Cons:** no amenities outside of rooms/cottages; closest restaurants 15 minutes away. $ *Rooms from: $90* ✉ *13388 Airline Hwy., Paicines* ⊕ *www.paicinesranch.com* ⌁ *7 rooms* ¡○¡ *No meals.*

$$
HOTEL
FAMILY

⌂ **Peacock Inn at Casa de Fruta.** You can decide for yourself if the surprisingly pleasant accommodations that sit at one end of a popular fruit-stand-cum-amusement park are either charming or cheesy, but rooms are fairly spacious (especially the two king rooms with private patios), quite clean, and the updated fixtures give it a fresh, contemporary feel. **Pros:** great for families with young kids; reasonably priced; convenient for travel to or from Interstate 5. **Cons:** location near highway means noise; next door to large RV park. $ *Rooms from: $129* ✉ *10021 Pacheco Pass Hwy., Hollister* ⊕ *www.casadefruta.com* ⌁ *14 rooms* ¡○¡ *No meals.*

REDWOOD
NATIONAL PARK

WELCOME TO REDWOOD

TOP REASONS TO GO

★ **Giant trees:** These mature coastal redwoods are the tallest trees in the world.

★ **Hiking to the sea:** The park's trails wind through majestic redwood groves, and many connect to the Coastal Trail running along the western edge of the park.

★ **Rare wildlife:** Mighty Roosevelt elk favor the park's flat prairie and open lands; seldom-seen black bears roam the backcountry; trout and salmon leap through streams; and Pacific gray whales swim along the coast during their biannual migrations.

★ **Stepping back in time:** Hike Fern Canyon Trail and explore a prehistoric scene of lush vegetation and giant ferns.

★ **Cheeps, not beeps:** Amid the majestic redwoods you're out of range for cell-phone service—and in range for the soothing sounds of warblers and burbling creeks.

1 Del Norte Coast Redwoods State Park. The rugged terrain of this far northwest corner of California combines stretches of treacherous surf, steep cliffs, and forested ridges. On a clear day it's postcard-perfect; with fog, it's mysteriously mesmerizing.

2 Jedediah Smith Redwoods State Park. Gargantuan old-growth redwoods dominate the scenery here. The Smith River cuts through canyons and splits across boulders, carrying salmon to the inland creeks where they spawn.

3 Prairie Creek Redwoods State Park. The forests here give way to spacious, grassy plains where abundant wildlife thrives. Roosevelt elk are a common sight in the meadows and down to Gold Bluffs Beach.

4 Orick Area. The highlight of the southern portion of Redwood National and State Parks is the Tall Trees Grove. It's difficult to reach and requires a special pass, but it's worth the hassle—this section has the tallest coast redwood trees, with a new record holder discovered in 2006.

32

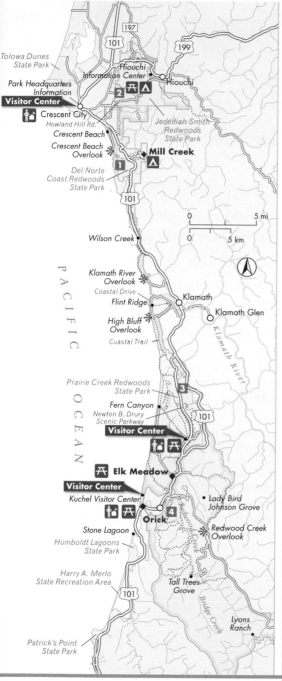

CALIFORNIA

GETTING ORIENTED

U.S. 101 weaves through the southern portion of the park, skirts around the center, and then slips back through redwoods in the north and on to Crescent City. Kuchel Visitor Center, Prairie Creek Redwoods State Park and Visitor Center, Tall Trees Grove, Fern Canyon, and Lady Bird Johnson Grove are all in the park's southern section. In the park's central section, where the Klamath River Overlook is the dominant feature, the narrow, mostly graveled Coastal Drive loop yields ocean vistas. To the north you'll find Mill Creek Trail, Enderts Beach, and Crescent Beach Overlook in Del Norte Coast Redwoods State Park as well as Jedediah Smith Redwoods State Park, Stout Grove, Little Bald Hills, and Simpson-Reed Grove.

KEY	
👫	Ranger Station
🔺	Campground
🌲	Picnic Area
🍴	Restaurant
🏞	Lodge
🚶	Trailhead
🚻	Restrooms
�	Scenic Viewpoint
:::::	Walking/Hiking Trails

Updated
by Christine
Vovakes

Soaring to more than 300 feet, the coastal redwoods that give this park its name are miracles of efficiency—some have survived hundreds of years (a few live for more than 2,000 years). These massive trees glean nutrients from the rich alluvial flats at their feet and from the moisture and nitrogen trapped in their uneven canopy. Their huge, thick-barked trunks can hold thousands of gallons of water, reservoirs that have helped them withstand centuries of firestorms.

REDWOOD PLANNER

WHEN TO GO

Campers and hikers flock to the park from mid-June to early September. Crowds disappear in winter, but you'll have to contend with frequent rains and nasty potholes on side roads. Temperatures fluctuate widely throughout the park: the foggy coastal lowland is much cooler than the higher-altitude interior.

The average annual rainfall here is 90 to 100 inches, and during dry summer months thick fog rolling in from the Pacific veils the forests, giving redwoods a large portion of their moisture intake.

AVG. HIGH/LOW TEMPS.

JAN.	FEB.	MAR.	APR.	MAY	JUNE
54/39	56/40	57/41	59/42	62/45	65/48

JULY	AUG.	SEPT.	OCT.	NOV.	DEC.
67/50	67/51	68/49	64/46	58/43	55/40

32

PLANNING YOUR TIME
REDWOOD IN ONE DAY

From Crescent City head south on U.S. 101. A mile south of Klamath, detour onto the 8-mile-long, narrow, and mostly unpaved **Coastal Drive** loop (motorhomes/RVs and trailers not allowed). Along the way, you'll pass the old **Douglas Memorial Bridge,** destroyed in the 1964 flood. Coastal Drive turns south above Flint Ridge. In less than a mile you'll reach the **World War II Radar Station,** which looks like a farmhouse, its disguise in the 1940s. Continue south to the intersection with Alder Camp Road, stopping at the **High Bluff Overlook.**

From the Coastal Drive turn left to reconnect with U.S. 101. Head south to reach **Newton B. Drury Scenic Parkway,** a 10-mile drive through an old-growth redwood forest with access to numerous trailheads. (This road is open to all noncommercial vehicles.) Along the way, stop at **Prairie Creek Visitor Center,** housed in a small redwood lodge crafted in 1933. Enjoy a picnic lunch and an engaging tactile walk in a grove behind the lodge on the Revelation Trail, which was designed for vision-impaired visitors. Back on the parkway head north less than a mile and drive out unpaved **Cal-Barrel Road** (motorhomes/RVs and trailers not allowed), which leads east through redwood forests. Return to the parkway, continue south about 2 miles to reconnect with U.S. 101, and turn west on mostly unpaved **Davison Road** (motorhomes/RVs and trailers are prohibited). In about 30 minutes you'll curve right to **Gold Bluffs Beach.** Continue north, crossing a narrow creek a number of times, to the **Fern Canyon** trailhead. Return to U.S. 101, and drive south to the turnoff for the **Kuchel Information Center.** Pick up free permits to visit the **Tall Trees Grove,** (only 50 granted per day) and then head north on U.S. 101 to the turnoff for **Bald Hills Road,** a steep route (motorhomes/RVs and trailers are not advised). If you visit the grove, allow at least four hours round-trip from the information center. You could also bypass the turnoff to the grove and continue south on Bald Hills Road to 3,097-foot **Schoolhouse Peak.** For a simpler jaunt, turn onto Bald Hills Road and follow it for 2 miles to the **Lady Bird Johnson Grove Nature Loop Trail.** Take the footbridge to the easy 1-mile loop, which follows an old logging road through a mature redwood forest.

GETTING HERE AND AROUND
CAR TRAVEL

U.S. 101 runs north–south along the park, and Highway 199 cuts east–west through its northern portion. Access routes off 101 include Bald Hills Road, Davison Road, Newton B. Drury Scenic Parkway, Coastal Drive loop, Requa Road, and Enderts Beach Road. From 199 take South Fork Road to Howland Hill Road. Many of the park's roads aren't paved, and winter rains can turn them into obstacle courses; sometimes they're closed completely. Motorhomes/RVs and trailers aren't permitted on some routes. ■TIP➔ **Park rangers say don't rely solely on GPS; closely consult park maps, available at the visitor information centers.**

PARK ESSENTIALS
PARK FEES AND PERMITS
Admission to Redwood National Park is free. There's an $8 day-use fee to enter one or all of Redwood's state parks; for camping at these state parks it's an additional $35. To visit Tall Trees Grove, you must get a free permit at the Kuchel Information Center in Orick. Permits also are needed to camp in all designated backcountry camps.

PARK HOURS
The park is open year-round, 24 hours a day.

CELL-PHONE RECEPTION
It's difficult to pick up a signal in the parks, especially in the camping and hiking areas. If you need a public telephone, go to the Prairie Creek or Jedediah Smith visitor center.

RESTAURANTS
If you're an angler, fresh catch of the day is your best bet, because there are no dining facilities in the park itself. To sample ethnic cuisine, pub fare, and seafood delights, head to the towns north or south of the park. Crescent City and Eureka offer the broadest selections.

Prices in the reviews are the average cost of a main course at dinner, or if dinner is not served, at lunch.

HOTELS
There are no lodging options within park boundaries. Orick and Klamath, the two towns on U.S. 101 near the park, have basic motels, plus the rustic Requa Inn, a two-story B&B on Requa Road beside the Klamath River. In towns north and south of the park you'll find numerous options, from elegant Victorians to seaside inns to no-frills rooms. Reservations at all lodgings should be made in advance for summer visits.

Prices in the reviews are the lowest cost of a standard double room in high season. For expanded reviews, facilities, and current deals, visit Fodors.com.

VISITOR INFORMATION
PARK CONTACT INFORMATION
Redwood National and State Parks ✉ *1111 2nd St., Crescent City* ☎ *707/465–7335* ⊕ *www.nps.gov/redw.*

VISITOR CENTERS
Crescent City Information Center. As the park's headquarters, this center is the main information stop if you're approaching the redwoods from the north. A gift shop and picnic area are here. ✉ *1111 Second St., near K St., off U.S. 101, Crescent City* ☎ *707/465–7335* ⊕ *www.nps.gov/ redw* ☉ *Mid-May–mid-Oct., daily 9–6; mid-Oct.–mid-May, daily 9–4.*

Hiouchi Information Center. Located in Jedediah Smith Redwoods State Park, 2 miles west of Hiouchi and 9 miles east of Crescent City off Highway 199, this center has a bookstore, film, and exhibits about the flora and fauna in the park. It's also a starting point for seasonal ranger programs. ✉ *Hwy. 199* ☎ *707/458–3294, 707/465–7335* ⊕ *www.nps. gov/redw* ☉ *Late May–early Sept., daily 9–6.*

Jedediah Smith Visitor Center. Located off Highway 199, this center has information about ranger-led walks and evening campfire programs in the summer in Jedediah Smith Redwoods State Park. Also here are nature and history exhibits, a gift shop, and a picnic area. ⊠ *Off Hwy. 199, Hiouchi* ☎ *707/458–3496, 707/465-7335* ⊕ *www.parks.ca.gov* ⊗ *Late May–early-Sept., daily 10–6; closed early Sept.–late-May.*

Fodor'sChoice ★ **Prairie Creek Visitor Center.** Housed in a redwood lodge, this center has wildlife displays and a massive stone fireplace that was built in 1933. Several trailheads begin here. Stretch your legs with an easy stroll along Revelation Trail, a short loop behind the lodge. Pick up information about summer programs in Prairie Creek Redwoods State Park. There's a nature museum, gift shop, picnic area, and exhibits on flora and fauna. ■ TIP→ **Roosevelt elk often roam in the vast field adjacent to the center.** ⊠ *Off southern end of Newton B. Drury Scenic Pkwy., Orick* ☎ *707/488–2039* ⊕ *www.parks.ca.gov* ⊗ *Mid-May–mid-Oct., daily 9–5; mid-Oct.–mid-May, daily 9–4.*

Thomas H. Kuchel Visitor Center. If you're approaching the park from the south end, stop here to get brochures, advice, and a free permit to drive up the access road to Tall Trees Grove. Whale-watchers find the deck of the visitor center an excellent observation point, and bird-watchers enjoy the nearby Freshwater Lagoon, a popular layover for migrating waterfowl. Many of the exhibits here are hands-on and kid-friendly. ⊠ *Off U.S. 101, Orick* ☎ *707/465–7765* ⊕ *www.nps.gov/redw* ⊗ *Mid-May–mid-Oct., daily 9–5; mid-Oct.–mid-May, daily 9–4.*

EXPLORING

SCENIC DRIVES

Coastal Drive. This 8-mile, narrow and mostly unpaved road is closed to trailers and RVs and takes about one hour to drive. The slow pace alongside stands of redwoods offers close-up views of the Klamath River and expansive panoramas of the Pacific. From here you'll find access to the Flint Ridge section of the Coastal Trail. Recurring landslides have closed sections of the original road; this loop is all that remains. ⊠ *On U.S. 101, 1 mile south of Klamath* ⊹ *Take the Klamath Beach Rd. exit and follow signs to Coastal Dr.*

Howland Hill Road/Stout Grove. Take your time as you drive this 10-mile route along Mill Creek, which winds through old-growth redwoods and past the Smith River. Trailers and RVs are prohibited on this route. ⊠ *Access via Elk Valley Rd., off U.S. 101.*

Newton B. Drury Scenic Parkway/Big Tree Wayside. This 10-mile track, open to all noncommercial vehicles, threads through Prairie Creek Redwoods State Park and old-growth redwoods. Just north of the Prairie Creek Visitor Center you can make the 0.8-mile walk to Big Tree Wayside and observe Roosevelt elk in the prairie. ⊠ *Off U.S. 101, about 5 miles south of Klamath, Orick.*

SCENIC STOPS

Crescent Beach Overlook. The scenery here includes ocean views and, in the distance, Crescent City and its working harbor; in balmy weather this is a great place for a picnic. From the overlook you can spot migrating gray whales going south November through December and returning north February through April. ⊠ *Off Enderts Beach Rd., 2 miles south of Crescent City.*

Del Norte Coast Redwoods State Park. Seven miles southeast of Crescent City via U.S. 101, this state park contains 15 memorial redwood groves. The growth extends down steep slopes almost to the shore. ⊠ *Crescent City Information Center, 1111 2nd St., off U.S. 101, Crescent City* ☎ *707/465–7335* ⊕ *www.parks.ca.gov* ☉ *Mid-May–mid-Oct., daily 9–6; mid-Oct.–mid-May, daily 9–4.*

Fodor's Choice
★

Fern Canyon. Enter another world and be surrounded by 30-foot canyon walls covered with sword, maidenhair, and five-finger ferns. Allow an hour to explore the ¼-mile-long vertical garden along a 0.7-mile loop. From the north end of Gold Bluffs Beach it's an easy walk, although you'll have to wade across a small stream several times (in addition to driving across streams on the way to the parking area). But the lush surroundings are otherworldly, and worth a visit when creeks aren't running too high. Be aware that motorhomes/RVs and all trailers are prohibited here. ⊠ *Davison Rd., off U.S. 101, 10 miles northwest of Prairie Creek Visitor Center, Orick* ⊕ *www.nps.gov/redw.*

Jedediah Smith Redwoods State Park. Home to the Stout Memorial Grove, Jedediah Smith Redwoods State Park is named after a trapper who, in 1826, became the first white man to explore northern California's interior. You'll find 20 miles of hiking and nature trails here. The park is 2 miles west of Hiouchi and 9 miles east of Crescent City off Highway 199. ⊠ *Jedediah Smith Visitor Center, Hwy. 199, Hiouchi* ☎ *707/458–4396* ⊕ *www.parks.ca.gov* ☉ *Closed mid-Sept.–mid-May* ⊠ *Hiouchi Information Center, Hwy. 199, Hiouchi* ☎ *707/458–3294, 707/465–7335* ☉ *Late-May–mid-Sept., daily 9–6.*

Lady Bird Johnson Grove. This section of the park was dedicated by, and named for, the former first lady. A 1-mile nature loop follows an old logging road through a mature redwood forest. Allow 45 minutes to complete the trail. ⊠ *1 mile north of Orick off U.S. 101 onto Bald Hills Rd., Orick* ✛ *Turn onto Bald Hills Rd. for 2½ miles to trailhead* ⊕ *www.nps.gov/redw.*

Prairie Creek Redwoods State Park. Spectacular redwoods and lush ferns make up this park, 5 miles north of Orick and 50 miles south of Crescent City. Extra space has been paved alongside the parklands, providing fine places to observe herds of Roosevelt elk in adjoining meadows. ⊠ *Prairie Creek Information Center, Newton B. Drury Scenic Pkwy., Orick* ☎ *707/488–2039, 707/465–7335* ⊕ *www.parks.ca.gov* ☉ *Daily 9–5.*

Redwoods State Parks. The three state parks have miles of trails that lead to magnificent redwood groves and overlooks with views of sea lion colonies and migrating whales. Birds inhabit bluffs, lagoons, and

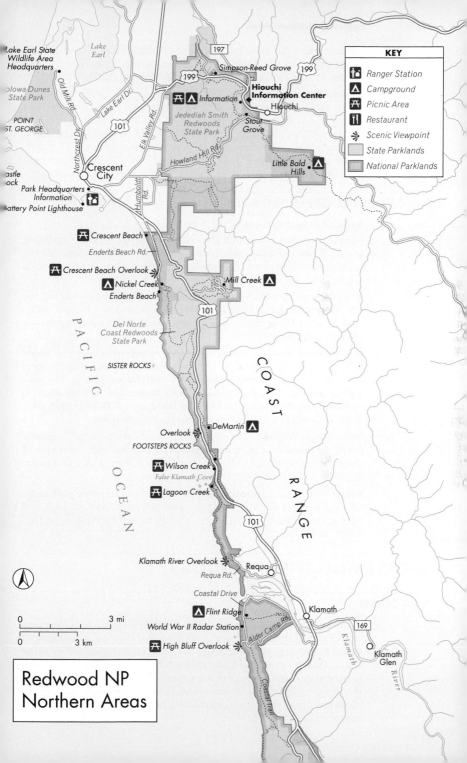

KEY

- 🧍 Ranger Station
- ⛺ Campground
- 🍽 Picnic Area
- 🍴 Restaurant
- ✳ Scenic Viewpoint
- State Parklands
- National Parklands

Lake Earl State Wildlife Area Headquarters

Lake Earl

Tolowa Dunes State Park

POINT ST. GEORGE

Old Mill Rd.

Lake Earl Dr.

Northcrest Dr.

197

199

Simpson-Reed Grove

199

Hiouchi Information Center

Hiouchi

Information

Jedediah Smith Redwoods State Park

Stout Grove

Elk Valley Rd.

Howland Hill Rd.

Little Bald Hills

Castle Rock

Crescent City

Park Headquarters Information

Battery Point Lighthouse

Humboldt Rd.

Crescent Beach

Enderts Beach Rd.

Crescent Beach Overlook

Nickel Creek

Enderts Beach

Mill Creek

101

Del Norte Coast Redwoods State Park

SISTER ROCKS

C O A S T

Overlook

DeMartin

FOOTSTEPS ROCKS

Wilson Creek

False Klamath Cove

Lagoon Creek

R A N G E

101

Klamath River Overlook

Requa

Requa Rd.

Coastal Drive

Flint Ridge

World War II Radar Station

Alder Camp Rd.

Klamath

Klamath

169

High Bluff Overlook

Klamath Glen

Klamath River

P A C I F I C   O C E A N

Coastal Trail

0   3 mi

0   3 km

Redwood NP Northern Areas

offshore rocks. All three parks are open year-round and have seasonal ranger programs for children, as well as ranger-led talks. The fee is $8 per day to visit one or all three parks. ⊕ *www.nps.gov/redw.*

Tall Trees Grove. From the Kuchel Visitor Center, you can get a free permit to make the steep 14-mile drive (the last 6½ miles, on Tall Trees Access Road, are unpaved) to the grove's trailhead (trailers and RVs not allowed). Access to the popular grove is first-come, first-served, and a maximum of 50 permits are handed out each day. ⊠ *On U.S. 101, 1 mile north of Orick* ✛ *Turn right at Bald Hills Rd. and follow signs about 6½ miles to access road, then 6½ miles, unpaved, to trailhead.*

EDUCATIONAL OFFERINGS

RANGER PROGRAMS

How did coastal redwoods grow from fleck-size seeds to towering giants? What are those weird fungi clumped on old stumps? Why is ocean fog so important to redwoods, and what are those green-tentacled creatures floating in tide pools?

Ranger-led programs explore the mysteries of both redwoods and the sea all summer long. Varying campfire programs can include slideshows, storytelling, music, and games. Check with visitor centers for offerings and times.

Field Seminars. State park rangers and other experts conduct seminars with an emphasis on natural history. Subjects may include photography, wildflowers, tide pools, Roosevelt elk, and stargazing. The programs, sponsored by the Redwood Parks Association, are usually free; a few, like the December Candlelight Walk, raise funds for the parks. ☎ *707/465–7325* ⊕ *www.redwoodparksassociation.org.*

FAMILY **Junior Ranger Program.** The state parks run these one-hour programs during the summer season. Rangers instruct children ages 7 through 12 on bird identification, outdoor survival skills, nature walks, and more. ☎ *707/465–7765* ⊠ *Free.*

Ranger Talks. From Memorial Day through Labor Day, state park rangers regularly lead discussions on the redwoods, tide pools, geology, and American Indian culture. Pick up a schedule at one of the visitor centers. ☎ *707/465–7765* ⊠ *Free.*

SPORTS AND THE OUTDOORS

BICYCLING

Besides the roadways, you can bike on several trails. Your best bets include the 11-mile Lost Man Creek Trail that begins 3 miles north of Orick; the 12-mile round-trip Coastal Trail (Last Chance Section) that starts at the south end of Enderts Beach Road and becomes steep and narrow as it travels through dense slopes of foggy redwood forests; and the 19-mile, singletrack Ossagon Trail Loop, where you're likely to see elk as you cruise through redwoods before coasting oceanside near the last leg of the trail.

Plants and Wildlife in Redwood

Coast redwoods, the world's tallest trees (a new record holder, topping out at 379 feet, was found within the park in 2006) grow in the moist, temperate climate of California's North Coast. These ancient giants thrive in an environment that exists in only a few hundred coastal miles along the Pacific Ocean. They commonly live 600 years—though some have been around for 2,000 years.

A healthy redwood forest is diverse and includes Douglas firs, western hemlocks, tan oaks, and madrone trees. The complex soils of the forest floor support a verdant profusion of ferns, mosses, and fungi, along with numerous shrubs and berry bushes. In spring, California rhododendron bloom throughout the forest, providing a dazzling purple and pink contrast to the dense greenery.

Redwood National and State Parks hold 45% of all California's old-growth redwood forests. Of the original 3,125 square miles (2 million acres) in the Redwoods Historic Range, only 4% remain following the logging that began in 1850; 1% is privately owned and managed, and 3% is on public land.

In the park's backcountry, you might spot mountain lions, black bears, black-tailed deer, river otters, beavers, and minks. Roosevelt elk roam the flatlands, and the rivers and streams teem with salmon and trout. Gray whales, seals, and sea lions cavort near the coastline. And thanks to the area's location along the Pacific Flyway, more than 400 species of birds have been recorded in the park.

BIRD-WATCHING

Many rare and striking winged specimens inhabit the area, including chestnut-backed chickadees, brown pelicans, great blue herons, pileated woodpeckers, northern spotted owls, and marbled murrelets.

FISHING

Both deep-sea and freshwater fishing are popular here. Anglers often stake out sections of the Klamath and Smith rivers in their search for salmon and trout. (A single fishing license covers both ocean and river fishing.) Less serious anglers go crabbing and clamming on the coast, but check the tides carefully: rip currents and sneaker waves are deadly.

OUTFITTERS

Coast True Value. This store is a good place to get fishing licenses that are valid for both river and ocean fishing. California residents pay a $45.93 annual fee; nonresidents pay $123.38. Anyone can purchase a two-day license for $22.94. The store sells fishing gear, bait, and tackle. ⊠ *900 Northcrest Dr., Crescent City* ☎ *707/464–3535.*

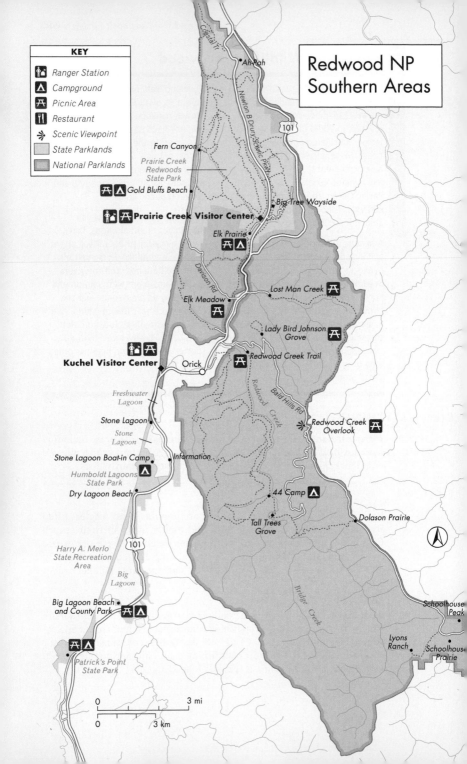

Redwood NP Southern Areas

KEY

- Ranger Station
- Campground
- Picnic Area
- Restaurant
- Scenic Viewpoint
- State Parklands
- National Parklands

Coastal Tr.

Ah-Pah

Newton B Drury Scenic Pkwy

101

Fern Canyon

Prairie Creek Redwoods State Park

Gold Bluffs Beach

Big Tree Wayside

Prairie Creek Visitor Center

Elk Prairie

Davison Rd

Lost Man Creek

Elk Meadow

Lady Bird Johnson Grove

Kuchel Visitor Center

Orick

Redwood Creek Trail

Freshwater Lagoon

Redwood Creek

Bald Hills Rd

Stone Lagoon

Stone Lagoon

Redwood Creek Overlook

Stone Lagoon Boat-in Camp

Information

Humboldt Lagoons State Park

Dry Lagoon Beach

44 Camp

Dolason Prairie

Tall Trees Grove

Harry A. Merlo State Recreation Area

Big Lagoon

Bridge Creek

Big Lagoon Beach and County Park

Schoolhouse Peak

Lyons Ranch

Schoolhouse Prairie

Patrick's Point State Park

101

| 0 | | 3 mi |
| 0 | | 3 km |

HIKING

MODERATE

Coastal Trail. Although this easy-to-difficult trail runs along most of the park's length, smaller sections—of varying degrees of difficulty—are accessible via frequent, well-marked trailheads. The moderate-to-difficult DeMartin section leads past 6 miles of old growth redwoods and through prairie. If you're up for a real workout, you'll be well rewarded with the brutally difficult but stunning Flint Ridge section, a 4.5-mile stretch of steep grades and numerous switchbacks that leads past redwoods and Marshall Pond. The moderate 5.5-mile-long Klamath section, which connects the Wilson Creek picnic area with Hidden Beach tidepools and up to the Klamath Overlook, provides coastal views and whale-watching opportunities. *Moderate.* ⊠ *Shares Flint Ridge trailhead, at Douglas Bridge parking area, north end of Coastal Dr., Klamath.*

> ### GOOD READS
>
> ■ *The Redwood Official National and State Parks Handbook,* by the Redwood Parks Association covers the area's ecology, botany, natural and cultural history, and common wildlife.
>
> ■ *The Tallest Tree,* by Robert Lieber is a beautifully illustrated board book for little ones. If you plan on hiking, stop at one of the visitor centers and purchase an inexpensive *Redwood National Park Trail Guide,* which details more than 200 miles of trails.

DIFFICULT

West Ridge–Friendship Ridge–James Irvine Loop. For a moderately strenuous trek, try this 12.5-mile loop. The difficult West Ridge segment passes redwoods looming above a carpet of ferns. The difficult Friendship Ridge portion slopes down toward the coast through forests of spruce and hemlock. The moderate James Irvine Trail portion winds along a small creek and amid dense stands of redwoods. *Difficult.* ⊠ *Trailhead at Prairie Creek Redwoods State Park information center, off Newton B. Drury Scenic Pkwy., Orick.*

KAYAKING

With many miles of often-shallow rivers and streams in the area, kayaking is a popular pastime in the park.

OUTFITTERS

Humboats Kayak Adventures. Kayak rental and lessons are available here, along with a variety of group kayak tours, including full-moon and sunset tours and popular whale-watching trips (October–June) that get you close enough for photos of migrating gray whales and resident humpback whales. ⊠ *Dock A, Woodley Island Marina, Eureka* ☎ *707/443–5157* ⊕ *www.humboats.com.*

WHALE-WATCHING

Good vantage points for whale-watching include Crescent Beach Overlook, the Kuchel Visitor Center in Orick, points along the Coastal Trail, and the Klamath River Overlook. Late November through January are the best months to see their southward migrations; February through April they return and generally pass closer to shore.

WHAT'S NEARBY

NEARBY TOWNS

Crescent City, north of the park, is Del Norte County's largest town (pop. 7,650) and home to the Redwood National and State Park headquarters. Though it curves around a beautiful stretch of ocean and radiates small-town charm, rain and bone-chilling fog often prevail. The very small town of **Klamath** is outside park boundaries though very near to the middle section of the parks. It has a couple of lodging options but not much dining-wise. Roughly 50 miles south of Crescent City, **Trinidad**'s cove harbor attracts fishermen and photographers, while campers head to nearby Patrick's Point State Park. Farther south, **Arcata** began life in 1850 as a base camp for miners and lumberjacks. Today this town of 17,200 residents is also home to the 8,100 students of Humboldt State University. Activity centers around Arcata Plaza, which is surrounded by restored buildings. Pick up the "Victorian Walking Tour" map at the chamber of commerce. Nearby **Eureka**, a city of 27,200 residents and filled with strip malls, was named after a gold miner's hearty exclamation. Its Old Town has a new waterfront boardwalk, plus a few good restaurants and shops; the chamber of commerce has a free driving map to Victorian homes.

VISITOR INFORMATION

Arcata Chamber of Commerce ✉ *1635 Heindon Rd., Arcata* ☎ *707/822–3619* ⊕ *www.arcatachamber.com.* **Crescent City/Del Norte County Chamber of Commerce** ✉ *1001 Front St., Crescent City* ☎ *707/464–3174, 800/343–8300* ⊕ *www.delnorte.org.* **Eureka/Humboldt County Convention and Visitors Bureau** ✉ *1034 2nd St., Eureka* ☎ *707/443–5097, 800/346–3482* ⊕ *redwoods.info.* **Klamath Chamber of Commerce** ☎ *800/200–2335* ⊕ *www.klamathchamber.com.* **Trinidad Chamber of Commerce** ☎ *707/677–1610* ⊕ *www.trinidadcalif.com.*

NEARBY ATTRACTIONS

Battery Point Lighthouse. At low tide, you can walk from the pier across the ocean floor to this working lighthouse, which was built in 1856. It houses a museum with nautical artifacts and photographs of shipwrecks, and even a resident ghost. Call ahead for guided group tours. ✉ *A St., Crescent City* ☎ *707/464–3089* 💲 *$3* 🕘 *May.–Sept., daily 10–4; Oct.–Mar., weekends at low tide.*

Redwood trees, and the moss that often coats them, grow best in damp, shady environments.

California Western Railroad Skunk Train. Following the same coastal route between Fort Bragg and Willits since 1885, the Skunk Train winds along the Noyo River, crosses some 30 bridges, and passes through two tunnels in this scenic trip into the redwoods. The gas-powered locomotive replaced the steam engine on this train in 1925. Locals say, "You can smell 'em before you can see 'em." Hence, the nickname. Most round trips take 4 hours. ⊠ *100 W. Laurel St., Fort Bragg* ☎ *707/964–6371, 866/457–5865* ⊕ *www.skunktrain.com* 🖃 *$49* 🕓 *Mar.–Nov.; weekends only Dec.–Feb.*

Northcoast Marine Mammal Center. This nonprofit organization rescues and rehabilitates stranded, sick, or injured seals, sea lions, dolphins, and porpoises. This is not a museum per se, but you can see the rescued creatures through a fence enclosing individual pools (even when the center is closed), and learn via placards and information kiosks about marine mammals and coastal ecosystems. ⊠ *424 Howe Dr., Crescent City* ☎ *707/465–6265* ⊕ *www.northcoastmmc.org* 🖃 *Free* 🕓 *Call offfice Fri. 10–3 to check gift shop hrs.*

NEED A BREAK?

Trinidad Bay Eatery and Gallery. A few doors down from the bay, combination diner–gift shop Trinidad Bay Eatery and Gallery is famous for homemade blackberry cobbler. ⊠ *Trinity and Parker sts., Trinidad* ☎ *707/677–3777* ⊕ *www.trinidadeatery.com.*

Best Campgrounds in Redwood

Within a 30-minute drive of Redwood National and State Parks there are nearly 60 public and private camping facilities. None of the four primitive areas in Redwood—DeMartin, Flint Ridge, Little Bald Hills, and Nickel Creek—is a drive-in site. You will need to get a free permit from any visitor center except Prairie Creek before camping in these campgrounds, and along Redwood Creek in the backcountry. Bring your own water, since drinking water isn't available in any of these sites. These campgrounds, plus Gold Bluffs Beach, are first-come, first-served.

If you'd rather drive than hike in, Redwood has four developed campgrounds—Elk Prairie, Gold Bluffs Beach, Jedediah Smith, and Mill Creek—that are within the state-park boundaries. None has RV hookups, and some length restrictions apply. Fees are $35 in state park campgrounds. For details and reservations, call ☎ 800/444–7275 or check ⊕ www.reserveamerica.com.

Elk Prairie Campground. Roosevelt elk frequent this popular campground adjacent to a prairie and old-growth

redwoods. ⊠ On Newton B. Drury Scenic Pkwy., 6 miles north of Orick in Prairie Creek Redwoods State Park ☎ 800/444–7275.

Gold Bluffs Beach Campground. You can camp in tents or RVs right on the beach at this Prairie Creek Redwoods State Park campground near Fern Canyon. ⊠ At end of Davison Rd., 5 miles south of Prairie Creek Visitor Center off U.S. 101 ☎ 707/465–7335.

Jedediah Smith Campground. This is one of the few places to camp—in tents or RVs—within groves of old-growth redwood forest. ⊠ 8 miles east of Crescent City on Hwy. 199 ☎ 800/444–7275.

Mill Creek Campground. Mill Creek is the largest of the state-park campgrounds. ⊠ East of U.S. 101, 7 miles southeast of Crescent City ☎ 800/444–7275.

Nickel Creek Campground. An easy hike gets you to this primitive site, which is near tide pools and has great ocean views. ⊠ On Coastal Trail ½ mile from end of Enderts Beach Rd. ☎ 707/465–7335.

WHERE TO EAT

IN THE PARK

PICNIC AREAS
Crescent Beach. This beach has a grassy picnic area with tables, fire pits, and restrooms. There's an overlook south of the beach. ⊠ 2 miles south of Crescent City Visitor Center, Enderts Beach Rd., Crescent City.

Elk Prairie. In addition to many elk, this spot has a campground, a nature trail, and a ranger station. ⊠ Off Newton B. Drury Scenic Pkwy., Prairie Creek Redwoods State Park, 6 miles north of Orick.

High Bluff Overlook. This picnic area's sunsets and whale-watching are unequaled. A 0.5-mile trail leads from here to the beach. ⊠ Coastal Dr. loop, off U.S. 101 via Alder Camp Rd., Klamath.

OUTSIDE THE PARK

ARCATA

$ 🍴 **Humboldt Brews.** This laid-back watering hole caters to a college crowd
AMERICAN with burgers, sandwiches, and 20 microbrews on tap, plus many bottled beers. There's live music several nights a week. [$] *Average main: $12* ✉ *856 10th St., Arcata* ☎ *707/826–2739* 🌐 *www.humbrews.com.*

CRESCENT CITY

$$ 🍴 **Good Harvest Cafe.** The Good Harvest lives up to its name with ample
AMERICAN use of locally grown and organic ingredients. The restaurant serves one of the best breakfasts in town (along with superb espresso) and offers lunch and dinner menus that feature salads, burgers, sandwiches, vegetarian specialties, and several fish entrées. [$] *Average main: $16* ✉ *575 U.S. 101 S, Crescent City* ☎ *707/465–6028.*

EUREKA

$$ 🍴 **Cafe Waterfront.** This airy local landmark serves a solid basic menu
SEAFOOD of burgers and steaks, but the real standouts are the daily seafood specials—snapper, shrimp, crab, and other treats fresh from the bay across the street. The building, listed on the National Register of Historic Places, was a saloon and brothel until the 1950s. Named after former ladies of the house, Sophie's Suite and Rachel's Room, two Victorian-style B&B rooms, are available upstairs. [$] *Average main: $19* ✉ *102 F St., Eureka* ☎ *707/443–9190.*

WHERE TO STAY

OUTSIDE THE PARK

CRESCENT CITY

$$ 🏨 **Crescent Beach Motel.** Simple and clean, this motel is directly on the
HOTEL beach; most rooms face the water. **Pros:** great sunset views; close to shopping and dining; fabulous location on the beach. **Cons:** noise level can be high in rooms fronting the street side. [$] *Rooms from: $124* ✉ *1455 U.S. 101 S, Crescent City* ☎ *707/464–5436* 🌐 *www.crescentbeachmotel.com* 🛏 *27 rooms* 🍽 *No meals.*

$ 🏨 **Curly Redwood Lodge.** A single redwood tree produced the 57,000
HOTEL board feet of lumber used to build this budget lodge in 1957. **Pros:** large rooms; several restaurants within walking distance. **Cons:** road noise can be bothersome. [$] *Rooms from: $72* ✉ *701 Redwood Hwy. S, Crescent City* ☎ *707/464–2137* 🌐 *www.curlyredwoodlodge.com* 🛏 *36 rooms, 3 suites.*

EUREKA

$$ 🏨 **Abigail's Elegant Victorian Mansion.** Innkeepers Doug and Lily Vieyra
HOTEL have devoted themselves to honoring this National Historic Landmark by decorating it with authentic, Victorian-era opulence; and indeed, it seems that every square inch of the home—once owned by the town's millionaire real-estate sultan—is covered in brocade, antique wallpaper, or redwood paneling, and from every possible surface hangs a painting with gilt frame, or a historical costume. **Pros:** unique; lots of character;

delightful innkeepers. **Cons:** downtown is not within walking distance; bedrooms are a bit worn. [$] *Rooms from: $115* ✉ *1406 C St., Eureka* ☎ *707/444–3144* 🌐 *www.eureka-california.com* 🛏 *4 rooms, 2 with shared bath* 🍴 *No meals.*

$$$ HOTEL Fodor's Choice ★ 🏨 **Carter House.** Owner Mark Carter says he trains his staff always to say yes; whether it's breakfast in bed or an in-room massage, someone here will get you what you want. **Pros:** elegant; every detail in place; excellent dining at Restaurant 301; bar off lobby. **Cons:** kids are allowed, but it's best suited for grown-ups. [$] *Rooms from: $179* ✉ *301 L St., Eureka* ☎ *707/444–8062, 800/404–1390* 🌐 *www.carterhouse.com* 🛏 *22 rooms, 8 suites, 2 cottages* 🍴 *Breakfast.*

$$ B&B/INN 🏨 **Cornelius Daly Inn.** Set in the heart of Eureka's historic area, this three-story B&B was built in 1905 as the home of department store magnate Cornelius Daly. **Pros:** a beautifully furnished Victorian meticulously maintained by husband-and-wife hosts; outstanding breakfast. **Cons:** not within easy walking distance to restaurants; the bedroom with twin beds shares a bath. [$] *Rooms from: $130* ✉ *1125 H St., Eureka* ☎ *707/445–3638, 800/321–9656* 🌐 *www.dalyinn.com* 🛏 *3 rooms, 2 suites* 🍴 *Breakfast.*

KLAMATH

$$ B&B/INN Fodor's Choice ★ 🏨 **Historic Requa Inn.** Neither TVs nor phones disrupt the serenity of this 12-room B&B that overlooks the Klamath River a mile east of where it meets the ocean. **Pros:** the park's most serene lodging choice for noncampers; great central location. **Cons:** walls are thin; not a good choice for children. [$] *Rooms from: $119* ✉ *451 Requa Rd., Klamath* ☎ *707/482–1425, 866/800–8777* 🌐 *www.requainn.com* 🛏 *12 rooms* 🍴 *Breakfast.*

$ HOTEL 🏨 **Ravenwood Motel.** Attentive on-site owners have converted this once dowdy roadside motel into a class act consisting of 10 rooms and five suites—four with full kitchens—beautifully decorated with different themes. **Pros:** great central location; exceptionally clean rooms. **Cons:** nonsuite rooms are a bit small. [$] *Rooms from: $75* ✉ *151 Klamath Blvd., Klamath* ☎ *707/482–5911, 866/520–9875* 🌐 *ravenwoodmotel.com* 🛏 *10 rooms, 5 suites* 🍴 *Breakfast.*

TRINIDAD

$$ HOTEL FAMILY 🏨 **Trinidad Inn.** These quiet cottage rooms nestled in the redwoods are 2 miles north of Trinidad Bay's harbor, restaurants, and shops. **Pros:** idyllic setting with walking path through adjacent redwood grove; good place for kids. **Cons:** older facility. [$] *Rooms from: $110* ✉ *1170 Patrick's Point Dr., Trinidad* ☎ *707/677–3349* 🌐 *www.trinidadinn.com* 🛏 *10 rooms* 🍴 *Breakfast.*

ROCKY MOUNTAIN NATIONAL PARK

WELCOME TO ROCKY MOUNTAIN

TOP REASONS TO GO

★ **Awesome ascents:**
Seasoned climbers can trek to the summit of 14,259-foot Longs Peak or attack the rounded granite domes of Lumpy Ridge. Novices can summit Twin Sisters Peaks or Mount Ida, both reaching more than 11,000 feet.

★ **Continental Divide:**
Straddle this great divide, which cuts through the western part of the park, separating water's flow to either the Pacific or Atlantic Ocean.

★ **Gorgeous scenery:**
Peer out over more than 100 lakes, gaze up at majestic mountain peaks, and soak in the splendor of lush wetlands, pine-scented woods, forests of spruce and fir, and alpine tundra in the park's four distinct ecosystems.

★ **More than 355 miles of trails:** Hike on dozens of marked trails, from easy lakeside strolls to strenuous mountain climbs.

★ **Wildlife viewing:**
Spot elk and bighorn sheep, along with moose, otters, and more than 280 species of birds.

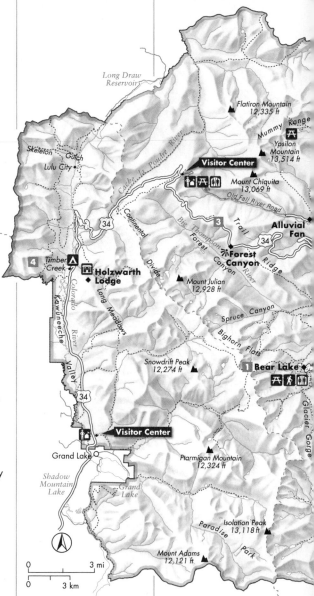

1 **Bear Lake.** One of the most photographed (and crowded) places in the park, Bear Lake is the hub for many trailheads and a major stop on the park's shuttle service.

2 **Longs Peak.** The highest peak in the park and the toughest to climb, this Fourteener pops up in many park vistas. A round-trip trek to the top takes 10 to 15 hours, so most visitors forego summit fever and opt for a (still spectacular) partial journey.

3 **Trail Ridge Road.** The alpine tundra of the park is the highlight here, as the road—the highest continuous highway in the United States—climbs to more than 12,000 feet (almost 700 feet above timberline).

4 **Timber Creek Campground.** The park's far-western area is much less crowded than most other sections, though it has its share of amenities and attractions, including evening programs, 98 camping sites, and a visitor center.

5 **Wild Basin Area.** Far from the crowds, the park's southeast quadrant consists of lovely expanses of subalpine forest punctuated by streams and lakes.

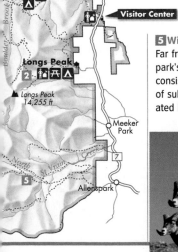

COLORADO

GETTING ORIENTED

33

Rocky Mountain National Park's 416-square-mile wilderness of meadows, mountains, and mirrorlike lakes lies about 70 miles from Denver. The park is roughly an eighth of the size of Yellowstone, yet it receives almost as many visitors—3 million a year.

KEY	
🏠	Ranger Station
▲	Campground
⌂	Picnic Area
🍴	Restaurant
▦	Lodge
🚶	Trailhead
🚻	Restrooms
⇘	Scenic Viewpoint
⋯⋯	Walking/Hiking Trails

Map labels:

Bighorn Mountain 11,463 ft
Black Canyon
Visitor Center
34
Estes Park
36
36
Moraine Park
Park Headquarters
Visitor Center
66
7
Sprague Lake
Visitor Center
Boulder Brook
Longs Peak
2
Longs Peak 14,255 ft
Meeker Park
7
North St. Vrain Creek
5
Allenspark

Updated
by Lindsey
Galloway

Anyone who delights in alpine lakes, dense forests, and abundant wildlife—not to mention dizzying heights—should consider Rocky Mountain National Park. Here, a single hour's drive leads from a 7,800-foot elevation at park headquarters to the 12,183-foot apex of the twisting and turning Trail Ridge Road. More than 355 miles of hiking trails take you to the park's many treasures: meadows flush with wildflowers, cool dense forests of lodgepole pine and Engelmann spruce, and the noticeable presence of wildlife, including elk and bighorn sheep.

ROCKY MOUNTAIN PLANNER

WHEN TO GO

More than 80 percent of the park's annual 3 million visitors come in summer and fall. For thinner high-season crowds, come in early June or September. But there is a good reason to put up with summer crowds: only from Memorial Day to mid-October will you get the chance to make the unforgettable drive over Trail Ridge Road (note that the road may still be closed during those months if the weather turns bad).

Spring is capricious—75°F one day and a blizzard the next (March sees the most snow). June can range from hot and sunny to cool and rainy. July typically ushers in high summer, which can last through September. Up on Trail Ridge Road, it can be 15°F–20°F cooler than at the park's lower elevations. Wildlife viewing and fishing is best in any season but winter. In early fall, the trees blaze with brilliant foliage. Winter, when backcountry snow can be 4 feet deep, is the time for cross-country skiing, snowshoeing, and ice fishing.

AVG. HIGH/LOW TEMPS.

JAN.	FEB.	MAR.	APR.	MAY	JUNE
39/16	41/17	45/21	53/27	62/34	73/41

JULY	AUG.	SEPT.	OCT.	NOV.	DEC.
78/46	76/45	70/38	60/30	46/23	40/18

FESTIVALS AND EVENTS

33

MID-MAY **Jazz Fest & Art Walk.** Pack a picnic and bring the kids for a weekend afternoon of free jazz performances and an art walk at the outdoor theater in downtown Estes Park. ⊠ *Performance Park Amphitheater, 417 W. Elkhorn Ave., Estes Park* ☎ *970/586–6104* ⊕ *www.visitestespark.com/ events-calendar/special-events/jazz-fest-and-art-walk.*

JUNE **Wool Market.** Watch shearing, spinning, and sheepdog herding contests, plus angora goats, sheep, llamas, and alpacas being judged for their wool. Shop for knitting and weaving supplies as well as finished woolen items, such as hats, coats, and mittens. ⊠ *Fairgrounds at Stanley Park, 1209 Manford Ave., Estes Park* ☎ *970/586–6104* ⊕ *www. visitestespark.com/events-calendar/special-events/wool-market.*

JULY **Estes Park Music Festival.** In July and August, the Colorado Music Festival Chamber Orchestra teams with the Estes Park Music Festival for a series of concerts at the historic Stanley Hotel Concert Hall ($30 for adults; children are free). Come winter, concerts featuring a variety of performances are held at 2 on Sunday afternoon from November through April (admission is $7). ⊠ *Stanley Hotel, 333 E. Wonderview Ave., Estes Park* ☎ *970/586–9519, 800/443–7837* ⊕ *www. estesparkmusicfestival.org.*

Rooftop Rodeo. Consistently ranked one of the top small rodeos in the country (and a tradition since 1908), this six-day event features a parade and nightly rodeo events, such as barrel racing and saddle bronc riding. ⊠ *Fairgrounds at Stanley Park, Intersection of U.S 36 and Community Dr., Estes Park* ☎ *970/586–6104* ⊕ *www. rooftoprodeo.com* 🎫 *$10–$17.*

SEPTEMBER **Elk Fest.** In late September, the calls of bull elk fill the forest as the animals make their way down the mountains for mating season. Estes Park celebrates with elk bugle contests, Native American music and performances, and elk educational seminars. For $5, tour buses take visitors to the best elk-viewing spots. ⊠ *Bond Park, E. Elkhorn and MacGregor aves., Estes Park* ⊕ *www.visitestespark.com/events-calendar/ special-events/elk-fest.*

Longs Peak Scottish/Irish Highland Festival. A traditional tattoo (drum- and bugle-filled parade) kicks off this four-day fair of ancient Scottish athletic competitions, including full-armor jousting and throwing contests involving hammers and 20-foot-long, 140-pound wooden poles (called cabers). The festival also features Celtic music, Irish dancing, and events for dogs of the British Isles (such as terrier racing and sheepdog demonstrations). ⊠ *Fairgrounds at Stanley Park, 1209 Manford Ave., Estes Park* ☎ *970/586–6308, 800/903–7837* ⊕ *www.scotfest.com.*

NOVEMBER–
APRIL
Estes Park Music Festival. The storied (and affordable) Estes Park Music Festival stages concerts at 2 pm Sundays from November through April at the Stanley Hotel. ⊠ *Estes Park* ☎ *970/586–9519* ⊕ *www. estesparkmusicfestival.org.*

FAMILY
Estes Park Winter Festival. You'll find plenty of cures for cabin fever during this festival, including chili cook-offs, toboggan races, and ice skating. Be sure to check out the annual Winter Trails Day, which gives families the chance to try out snowshoeing equipment and learn proper techniques from instructors. ⊠ *Fairgrounds at Stanley Park, 1209 Manford Ave., Estes Park* ⊕ *www.visitestespark.com/events-calendar/ special-events/winter-festival.*

PLANNING YOUR TIME
ROCKY MOUNTAIN IN ONE DAY

Starting out in Estes Park, begin your day at the **Bighorn Restaurant,** a classic breakfast spot and a local favorite. While you're enjoying your short stack with apple-cinnamon-raisin topping, you can put in an order for a packed lunch (it's a good idea to bring your food with you, as dining options in the park consist of a single, seasonal snack bar at the top of Trail Ridge Road).

Drive west on U.S. 34 into the park, and stop at the **Beaver Meadows Visitor Center** to watch the orientation film and pick up a park map. Also inquire about road conditions on Trail Ridge Road, which you should plan to drive either in the morning or afternoon, depending on the weather. If possible, save the drive for the afternoon, and use the morning to get out on the trails, before the chance of an afternoon lightning storm.

For a beautiful and invigorating hike, head to Bear Lake and follow the route that takes you to **Nymph Lake** (an easy 0.5-mile hike), then onto **Dream Lake** (an additional 0.6 miles with a steeper ascent), and finally to **Emerald Lake** (an additional 0.7 miles of moderate terrain). You can stop at several places along the way. The trek down is much easier, and quicker, than the climb up. ■ TIP→ If you prefer a shorter, simpler (yet still scenic) walk, consider the **Bear Lake Nature Trail,** a 0.6-mile loop that is wheelchair- and stroller-accessible.

You'll need the better part of your afternoon to drive the scenic **Trail Ridge Road.** Start by heading west toward Grand Lake, stop at the lookout at the Alluvial Fan, and consider taking Old Fall River Road the rest of the way across the park. This single-lane dirt road delivers unbeatable views of waterfalls and mountain vistas. You'll take it westbound from Horseshoe Park (the cutoff is near the Endovalley Campground), then rejoin Trail Ridge Road at its summit, near the Alpine Visitor Center. If you're traveling on to Grand Lake or other points west, stay on Trail Ridge Road. If you're heading back to Estes Park, turn around and take Trail Ridge Road back (for a different set of awesome scenery). End your day with a ranger-led talk or evening campfire program.

GETTING HERE AND AROUND

AIR TRAVEL

The closest commercial airport is **Denver International Airport** (DEN). Its **Ground Transportation Information Center** (☎ *800/247–2336 or 303/342–4059 ⊕ www.flydenver.com*) assists visitors with car rentals, door-to-door shuttles, and limousine services. From the airport, the eastern entrance of the park is 80 miles (about two hours). **Estes Park Shuttle** (☎ *970/586–5151 ⊕ www.estesparkshuttle.com; reservations essential*) serves Estes Park and Rocky Mountain from both Denver International Airport and Longmont/Boulder.

CAR TRAVEL

Estes Park and Grand Lake are the Rocky Mountain's gateway communities; from these you can enter the park via U.S. 34 or 36 (Estes Park) or U.S. 34 (Grand Lake). U.S. 36 runs from Denver through Boulder, Lyons, and Estes Park to the park; the portion between Boulder and Estes Park is heavily traveled—especially on summer weekends. Though less direct, Colorado Routes 119, 72, and 7 have much less traffic (and better scenery). If you're driving directly to Rocky Mountain from the airport, take the E–470 tollway from Peña Boulevard to I–25.

The **Colorado Department of Transportation** (for road conditions ☎ *303/639–1111 ⊕ www.cotrip.org*) plows roads efficiently, but winter snowstorms can slow traffic and create wet or icy conditions. In summer, the roads into both Grand Lake and Estes Park can see heavy traffic, especially on weekends.

CAR TRAVEL WITHIN THE PARK
The main thoroughfare in the park is Trail Ridge Road (U.S. 34); in winter, it's closed from the first storm in the fall (typically in October) through the spring (depending on snowpack, this could be at any time between April and June). During that time, it's plowed only up to Many Parks Curve on the east side and the Colorado River trailhead on the west side. (For current road information: ☎ *970/586–1222 ⊕ www.coloradodot.info*). The spectacular Old Fall River Road runs one-way between the Endovalley Picnic Area on the eastern edge of the park and the Alpine Visitor Center at the summit of Trail Ridge Road, on the western side. It is typically open from July to September, depending on snowfall. It's a steep, narrow road (no wider than 14 feet), and trailers and vehicles longer than 25 feet are prohibited, but a trip on this 90-year-old thoroughfare is well worth the effort. For information on road closures, contact the park: ☎ *970/586–1206 ⊕ www.nps.gov/romo.*

To see Trail Ridge Road the easy way—in a bus, with an expert tour guide pointing out items of interest along the way—$27 ($13 for kids) will get you a ticket with Trail Ridge Road Tours, jointly operated by Rocky Mountain Transit and the park. Tours depart Beaver Meadows Visitor Center at 10 and return at 3 (there's an hourlong break for lunch at the Alpine Visitor Center) (☎ *970/577–7477; reservations essential*).

SHUTTLES
The park has limited parking, but offers two free shuttle buses, which operate daily from 7 to 7, late May to early October. The Moraine Park bus runs every 20 minutes from the Fern Lake Trailhead to the Moraine Park Visitor Center (on Bear Lake Road, by Glacier Basin). The Bear Lake bus runs every 15 minutes from the Moraine Park Visitor Center

to the Bear Lake Trailhead. In addition, the town of Estes Park offers a shuttle bus service, which runs from the Estes Park Visitor Center to the park during the peak summer season (☎ *800/443–7823, 970/577–9900* ⊕ *www.estesparkcvb.com*). Called the Hiker Shuttle, the bus picks up at the Visitor Center and Fairgrounds at Stanley Park and stops at the park's Beaver Meadows Visitor Center and the Moraine Park Visitor Center. The town shuttle buses are free, but you must have a park pass to ride the bus that enters the national park.

TRAIN TRAVEL

Amtrak trains stop in downtown Denver, Winter Park/Fraser (80 miles away), and Granby (66 miles). ☎ *800/872–7245* ⊕ *www.amtrak.com.*

PARK ESSENTIALS

PARK FEES AND PERMITS

Entrance fees are $20 per automobile for a weekly pass, or $10 if you enter on bicycle, motorcycle, or foot. An annual pass costs $40.

Backcountry camping requires a permit that's $20 per party from May through October, and free the rest of the year. Visit ⊕ *www.nps.gov/ romo/planyourvisit/backcntry_guide.htm* before you go for a planning guide to backcountry camping. You can get your permit by mail, by phone, or in person. To get it by mail or in person, you can apply any time after May 1 for a permit for that calendar year (✉ *Backcountry/Wilderness Permits, Rocky Mountain National Park, 1000 Hwy. 36, Estes Park, CO 80517*). By phone, you can reserve a permit for that calendar year between March 1 and May 15 and after October 1 (☎ *970/586–1242*). In person, you can get a day-of-trip permit year-round at one of the park's two backcountry offices, located next to the Beaver Meadows Visitor Center and in the Kawuneeche Visitor Center.

PARK HOURS

The park is open 24/7 year-round; some roads close in winter. It is in the Mountain time zone.

CELL-PHONE RECEPTION

Cell phones work in some sections of the park, and free Wi-Fi can be accessed in and around the Beaver Meadows Visitor Center and the Kawuneeche Visitor Center.

RESTAURANTS

Restaurants in north central Colorado run the gamut from simple diners with tasty, homey basics to elegant establishments with extensive wine lists. Some restaurants take reservations, but many—particularly mid-range spots—seat on a first-come, first-served basis. In the park itself, there are no real dining establishments, though you can get snacks and light fare at the Trail Ridge Store, adjacent to the Alpine Visitor Center at the top of the Trail Ridge Road. The park also has a handful of scenic picnic areas, all with tables and pit or flush toilets.

Prices in the reviews are the average cost of a main course at dinner, or if dinner is not served, at lunch.

HOTELS

Bed-and-breakfasts and small inns in north central Colorado vary from old-fashioned fluffy cottages to sleek, modern buildings with understated lodge themes. If you want some pampering, there are guest ranches and spas.

In Estes Park, Grand Lake, and other nearby towns, the elevation keeps the climate cool, and you'll scarcely need (and you'll have a tough time finding) air-conditioned lodging. For a historic spot, try the Stanley Hotel in Estes Park, which dates to 1909 and features 160 guestrooms. The park has no hotels or lodges.

Prices in the reviews are the lowest cost of a standard double room in high season. For expanded reviews, facilities, and current deals, visit Fodors.com.

33

VISITOR INFORMATION

PARK CONTACT INFORMATION

Rocky Mountain National Park ✉ *1000 U.S. 36, Estes Park* ☎ *970/586–1206* ⊕ *www.nps.gov/romo.*

VISITOR CENTERS

Alpine Visitor Center. At the top of Trail Ridge Road, this visitor center is open only when that road is navigable. There's also a gift shop and snack bar here. ✉ *Fall River Pass, at junction of Trail Ridge and Old Fall River rds., 22 miles from Beaver Meadows entrance* ☎ *970/586–1206* ☽ *Late May–mid-June and Labor Day–Columbus Day, daily 10:30–4:30; mid-June–Labor Day, daily 9–5.*

Beaver Meadows Visitor Center. Housing the park headquarters, this visitor center was designed by students of the Frank Lloyd Wright School of Architecture at Taliesen West using the park's popular rustic style, which integrates buildings into their natural surroundings. Completed in 1966, it was named a National Historic Landmark in 2001. The surrounding utility buildings are also on the National Register and are noteworthy examples of the rustic-style buildings that the Civilian Conservation Corps constructed during the Depression. The center has a terrific 20-minute orientation film and a large relief map of the park. ✉ *U.S. 36, 3 miles west of Estes Park and 1 mile east of Beaver Meadows Entrance Station* ☎ *970/586–1206* ☽ *Daily 8–4:30.*

Fall River Visitor Center. The Discovery Room, which houses everything from old ranger outfits to elk antlers, coyote pelts, and bighorn sheep skulls for hands-on exploration, is a favorite with kids at this visitor center. ✉ *U.S. 34, at the Fall River Entrance Station* ☎ *970/586–1206* ☽ *Daily 9–5.*

Kawuneeche Visitor Center. The only visitor center on the park's far west side, Kawuneeche has exhibits on the plant and animal life of the area, as well as a large three-dimensional map of the park and an orientation film. ✉ *U.S. 34, 1 mile north of Grand Lake and ½ mile south of Grand Lake Entrance Station* ☎ *970/586–1206* ☽ *Daily 8–4:30.*

Plants and Wildlife in Rocky Mountain

Volcanic uplifts and the savage claw-ing of receding glaciers created Rocky Mountain's majestic landscape. You'll find four distinct ecosystems here—a riparian (wetland) environment with 150 lakes and 450 miles of streams; verdant montane valleys teeming with proud ponderosa pines and lush grasses; higher and colder subalpine mountains with wind-whipped trees (krummholz) that grow at right angles; and harsh, unforgiving alpine tundra with dollhouse-size versions of famil-iar plants and wildflowers. Alpine tun-dra is seldom found outside the Arctic, yet it makes up one-third of the park's terrain. Few plants can survive at this elevation of 11,000–11,500 feet, but many beautiful wildflowers—including alpine forget-me-nots—bloom here briefly in late June or early July.

The park has so much wildlife that you can often enjoy prime viewing from the seat of your car. Fall, when many animals begin moving down from higher elevations, is an excel-lent time to spot some of the park's

animal residents. This is also when you'll hear the male elk bugle mating calls (popular spots to see and hear bugling elk are Kawuneeche Valley, Horseshoe Park, Moraine Park, and Upper Beaver Meadows).

May through mid-October is the best time to see the bighorn sheep that congregate in the Horseshoe Park/ Sheep Lakes area, just past the Fall River entrance. If you want to glimpse a moose, try Kawuneeche Valley. Other animals in the park include mule deer, squirrels, chipmunks, pikas, beavers, and marmots. Common birds include broad-tailed and rufous hummingbirds, peregrine falcons, woodpeckers, mountain bluebirds, and Clark's nutcracker, as well as the white-tailed ptarmigan, which live year-round on the alpine tundra.

Mountain lions, black bears, and bobcats also inhabit the park but are rarely seen by visitors. Altogether, the park is home to roughly 60 species of mammals and 280 bird species.

EXPLORING

SCENIC DRIVES

Old Fall River Road. Nearly 100 years old and never more than 14 feet wide, this road stretches for 11 miles, from the park's east side to the Fall River Pass (11,796 feet above sea level) on the west. The drive provides spectacular views and a few white-knuckle moments, as the road is steep, serpentine, and completely lacking in guard rails. Start at West Horseshoe Park, which has the park's largest concentrations of sheep and elk, and head up the gravel road, passing Chasm Falls (there are a few places to park for a quick hike). The road is generally open from July through mid-October. ⊠ *Runs north of and roughly parallel to Trail Ridge Rd. (U.S. 34), starting near Endovalley Campground (to the east) and ending at Fall River Pass/Alpine Visitor Center (to the west)* ⊙ *July–Oct.*

Fodor's Choice ★ **Trail Ridge Road.** This is the park's star attraction and the world's highest continuous paved highway, topping out at 12,183 feet. The 48-mile road connects the park's gateways of Estes Park and Grand Lake. The views around each bend—of moraines and glaciers, and craggy hills framing emerald meadows carpeted with columbine and Indian paintbrush—are truly awesome. As it passes through three ecosystems—montane, subalpine, and arctic tundra—the road climbs 4,300 feet in elevation. As you drive the road, take your time at the numerous turnouts to gaze over the verdant valleys, brushed with yellowing aspen in fall, that slope between the glacier-etched granite peaks. **Rainbow Curve** affords views of nine separate mountain peaks, each more than 10,000 feet high, and of the **Alluvial Fan,** a 42-acre swath of rocks and boulders (some the size of cars) left behind after an earthen dam broke in 1982. ■ TIP→ **You can complete a one-way trip across the park on Trail Ridge Road in two hours, but it's best to give yourself three or four hours to allow for leisurely breaks at the overlooks.** Note that the middle part of the road closes with the first big snow (typically by mid-October) and most often reopens around Memorial Day, though you can still drive up about 10 miles from the west and 8 miles from the east. ⊠ *Trail Ridge Rd. (U.S. 34), Runs between Estes Park and Grand Lake* ☉ *June–mid-Oct.*

> ### GOOD READS
>
> *A Lady's Life in the Rocky Mountains,* by Isabella L. Bird, has long been a favorite with Colorado residents and visitors to the park.
>
> *Hiking Rocky Mountain National Park,* by Kent and Donna Dannen, is what Rocky Mountain rangers use as their park hiking guide.
>
> *The Magnificent Mountain Women,* by Janet Robertson, gives historical accounts of early pioneers.

HISTORIC SITES

Rocky Mountain has more than 1,000 archaeological sites and 150 buildings of historic significance; 47 of the buildings are listed in the National Register of Historic Places, which is reserved for structures that tie in strongly to the park's history in terms of architecture, archaeology, engineering, or culture. Most buildings at Rocky Mountain are done in the rustic style, a design preferred by the National Park Service's first director, Stephen Mather, that works to incorporate nature into these man-made structures.

FAMILY **Holzwarth Historic Site.** A scenic 0.5-mile interpretive trail leads you over the Colorado River to the original dude ranch that the Holzwarth family ran between the 1920s and 1950s. Allow about an hour to view the buildings—including a dozen small guest cabins—and chat with a ranger. It's a great place for families to learn about homesteading. ⊠ *Off U.S. 34, about 8 miles north of Kawuneeche Visitor Center, Estes Park.*

Lulu City. The remains of a few cabins are all that's left of this one-time silver mining town, established around 1880. Reach it by hiking the 3.6-mile Colorado River Trail. Look for wagon ruts from the old Stewart Toll Road and mine tailings in nearby Shipler Park (this is also a good place to spot moose). The Colorado River is a mere stream at this point, flowing south from its headwaters at nearby La Poudre Pass. ⊠ *Off Trail Ridge Rd., 9½ miles north of Grand Lake Entrance Station.*

SCENIC STOPS

Alluvial Fan. In 1982, the 79-year-old dam at Lawn Lake burst, and 220 million gallons of water roared into Estes Park, killing three people and causing millions of dollars in damage to the town. Within the park, the flood created the alluvial fan, a pile of glacial and streambed debris up to 44 feet deep on the north side of Horseshoe Park. A 0.5-mile trail gets you close enough to explore the area. You also can view it from the Rainbow Curve lookout on Trail Ridge Road. ⊠ *Fall River Rd., 3 miles from the Fall River Visitor Center.*

Bear Lake. Thanks to its picturesque location, easy accessibility, and the good hiking trails nearby, this small alpine lake below Flattop Mountain and Hallett Peak is one of the most popular destinations in the park. Free park shuttle buses can take you there May through October. ⊠ *Bear Lake Rd., off U.S. 36, 7 miles southwest of Moraine Park Visitor Center.*

Forest Canyon Overlook. Beyond the classic U-shaped glacial valley lies a high-alpine circle of ice-blue pools (the Gorge Lakes) framed by ragged peaks. ⊠ *Trail Ridge Rd., 6 miles east of Alpine Visitor Center.*

Wild Basin Area. This section in the southeast region of the park consists of lovely expanses of subalpine forest punctuated by streams and lakes. The area's high peaks, along the Continental Divide, are not as easily accessible as those in the vicinity of Bear Lake; hiking to the base of the Divide and back makes for a long day. Nonetheless, a visit here is worth the drive south from Estes Park, and because the Wild Basin trailhead is set apart from the park hub, crowding isn't a problem. ⊠ *Off Rte. 7, 13 miles south of Estes Park.*

EDUCATIONAL OFFERINGS

ART PROGRAM

Artist-in-Residence. Professional writers, sculptors, composers, and visual and performing artists can stay in a rustic cabin for two weeks in summer while working on their art. During their stay, they must make two presentations and donate a piece of original work to the park that relates to their stay. Applications must be received by November for requests for the following summer. ☎ *970/586–1206.*

CLASSES AND SEMINARS

Rocky Mountain Field Seminars. Each year, the Rocky Mountain Nature Association (RMNA) sponsors over 200 hands-on seminars for adults and children on such topics as natural history, fishing, geology, bird-watching, wildflower identification, wildlife biology, photography, and sketching. Classes range from lectures of a few hours to overnight and multiday camping trips. Most are fairly rigorous, incorporating hiking and other outdoor activities as well as instruction. All are taught by expert instructors. ⊠ *1895 Fall River Rd., Estes Park* ☎ *970/586–3262* ⊕ *www.rmna.org* ⌕ *$10–$250 per class* ☉ *Jan.–Nov.*

RANGER PROGRAMS

FAMILY **Junior Ranger Program.** Stop by the Junior Ranger Headquarters off Trail Ridge Road for ranger-led talks during the summer months. You can also pick up a Junior Ranger activity book (in English or Spanish) here or at any visitor center in the park. Program content has been developed for children ages 6 to 12; the material focuses on environmental education, identifying birds and wildlife, and outdoor safety skills. Once a child has completed all of the activities in the book, a ranger will look over his or her work and award a Junior Ranger badge. ☎ *970/586–1206* ⊕ *www.nps.gov/romo/forkids* ⌕ *Free.*

ELK BUGLING

In September and October, there are traffic jams in the park as people drive up to listen to the elk bugling. Rangers and park volunteers keep track of where the elk are and direct visitors to the mating spots. The bugling is high-pitched, and if it's light enough, you can see the elk put his head in the air.

FAMILY **Ranger Programs.** Join in on free hikes, talks, and activities conducted by those who know the park best. Topics may include wildlife, geology, vegetation, or park history. Don't miss special programs like "Skins and Things," a popular hands-on learning experience, and "Exploring with a Camera", which offers photography tips. In the evening, rangers lead twilight hikes, stargazing sessions, and storytelling around the campfire. Look for the extensive program schedule in the park's newspaper available at the main entrances. ☎ *970/586–1206* ⌕ *Free.*

SPORTS AND THE OUTDOORS

BIRD-WATCHING

Spring and summer, early in the morning, are the best times for bird-watching in the park. **Lumpy Ridge** is a nesting ground for several kinds of birds of prey. Migratory songbirds from South America have summer breeding grounds near the **Endovalley Picnic Area.** The **alpine tundra** is habitat for white-tailed ptarmigan. The **Alluvial Fan** is the place for viewing broad-tailed hummingbirds, hairy woodpeckers, ouzels, and the occasional raptor.

FISHING

Rocky Mountain is a wonderful place to fish, especially for trout—German brown, brook, rainbow, cutthroat, and greenback cutthroat—but check at a visitor center about regulations and information on specific closures, catch-and-release areas, and limits on size and possession. No fishing is allowed at Bear Lake. To avoid the crowds, rangers recommend angling in the more-remote backcountry. To fish in the park, anyone 16 and older must have a valid Colorado fishing license, which you can obtain at local sporting-goods stores. See ⊕ *www.wildlife.state.co.us/fishing* for details.

TOURS AND OUTFITTERS

Estes Angler. This popular fishing guide arranges four-, six-, and eight-hour fly-fishing trips—as well as full-day horseback excursions—into the park's quieter

regions, year-round, with a maximum of three people per guide. The best times for fishing are generally from April to mid-November. Equipment is also available for rent. ✉ *338 W. Riverside Dr., Estes Park* ☎ *970/586–2110, 800/586–2110* ⊕ *www.estesangler.com* ⊙ *Daily 8–6.*

Kirks Fly Shop. This Estes Park outfitter offers various guided fly-fishing trips, as well as backpacking, horseback, and llama pack trips. The store also carries fishing and backpacking gear. ✉ *230 E. Elkhorn Ave., Estes Park* ☎ *970/577–0790, 877/669–1859* ⊕ *www.kirksflyshop.com* ⊙ *Daily 7–7.*

Scot's Sporting Goods. This shop rents and sells fishing gear, and provides four-, six-, and eight-hour instruction trips daily from May through mid-October. Clinics, geared toward first-timers, focus on casting, reading the water, identifying insects for flies, and properly presenting natural and artificial flies to the fish. Half-day excursions into the park are available for three or more people. A range of camping and hiking equipment is also for sale. ✉ *870 Moraine Ave., Estes Park* ☎ *970/586–2877 May–Sept., 970/443–4932 Oct.–Apr.* ⊙ *June–Aug., daily 8–8; May and Sept–mid-Oct., daily 9–5* ✉ *870 Moraine Ave., Estes Park* ☎ *970/586–2877* ⊕ *www.scotssportinggoods.com.*

HIKING

Fodor's Choice ★   Rocky Mountain National Park contains more than 355 miles of hiking trails, so you could theoretically wander the park for weeks. Most visitors explore just a small portion of these trails—those that are closest to the roads and visitor centers—which means that some of the park's most accessible and scenic paths can resemble a backcountry highway on busy summer days. The high-alpine terrain around Bear Lake is the park's most popular hiking area, and although it's well worth exploring, you'll get a more frontierlike experience by hiking one of the trails in the less-explored sections of the park, such as the far northern end or in the Wild Basin area to the south. Keep in mind that trails at higher elevations may have some snow on them, even in late summer. And because of afternoon thunderstorms on most summer afternoons, an early morning start is highly recommended: the last place you want to be when a storm approaches is on a peak or anywhere above the tree line. All trail mileages are round-trip unless stated otherwise.

EASY

Bear Lake Trail. The virtually flat nature trail around Bear Lake is an easy, 0.6-mile loop that's wheelchair and stroller accessible. Sharing the route with you will likely be plenty of other hikers as well as songbirds and chipmunks. *Easy.* ⊠ *Trailhead at Bear Lake, Bear Lake Rd.*

FAMILY **Copeland Falls.** The 0.6-mile hike to these Wild Basin Area falls is a good option for families, as the terrain is relatively flat (there's only a 15-foot elevation gain). *Easy.* ⊠ *Trailhead at Wild Basin Ranger Station.*

East Inlet Trail. An easy hike of 0.3 miles from East Inlet trailhead, just outside the park in Grand Lake, will get you to **Adams Falls** in about 15 minutes. The area around the falls is often packed with visitors, so if you have time, continue east to enjoy more solitude, see wildlife, and catch views of **Mount Craig** from near the East Meadow campground. Note, however, that the trail beyond the falls has an elevation gain of between 1,500 and 1,900 feet, making it a more challenging hike. *Easy.* ⊠ *Trailhead at East Inlet, end of W. Portal Rd. (Rte. 278) in Grand Lake.*

Glacier Gorge Trail. The 4.5-mile hike to **Mills Lake** can be crowded, but the reward is one the park's prettiest lakes, set against the breathtaking backdrop of Longs Peak, Pagoda Mountain, and the Keyboard of the Winds. There's a modest elevation gain of 750 feet. On the way, about 1 mile in, you pass **Alberta Falls**, a popular destination in and of itself. The hike travels along Glacier Creek, under the shade of a subalpine forest. Give yourself at least four hours for hiking and lingering. *Easy.* ⊠ *Trailhead off Bear Lake Rd., about 1 mile southeast of Bear Lake.*

Sprague Lake. With virtually no elevation gain, this 1-mile, pine-lined path near a popular backcountry campground is wheelchair accessible and provides views of Hallet Peak and Flattop Mountain. *Easy.* ⊠ *Trailhead at Sprague Lake, off Bear Lake Rd., 4.4 miles southwest of Moraine Park Visitor Center.*

MODERATE

Fodor'sChoice **Bear Lake to Emerald Lake.** This scenic, caloric-burning hike begins with
★ a moderately level, 0.5-mile journey to **Nymph Lake.** From here, the trail gets steeper, with a 425-foot elevation gain, as it winds around for 0.6 mile to **Dream Lake.** The last stretch is the most arduous part of the hike, an almost all-uphill 0.7-mile trek to lovely **Emerald Lake,** where you can perch on a boulder and enjoy the view. All told, the hike is 3.6 miles, with an elevation gain of 605 feet. Allow two hours or more, depending on stops. *Moderate.* ⊠ *Trailhead at Bear Lake, off Bear Lake Rd., 7.9 miles southwest of the Moraine Park Visitor Center.*

HIKERS' SHUTTLE

The many trails in the Bear Lake area of the park are so popular that parking areas at the trailheads usually cannot accommodate all of the hikers' cars. Free shuttle buses connect a large park-and-ride facility at the Moraine Park Visitor Center with the Cub Lake, Fern Lake, Glacier Gorge Junction, and Bear Lake trailheads. Buses run daily between late May and early October, from 7 to 7. The Bear Lake shuttle runs approximately every 15 minutes; the Moraine Park shuttle runs approximately every 20 minutes.

Longs Peak: The Northernmost Fourteener

At 14,259 feet above sea level, **Longs Peak** has long fascinated explorers to the region. Explorer and author Isabella L. Bird wrote of it, "It is one of the noblest of mountains, but in one's imagination it grows to be much more than a mountain. It becomes invested with a personality."

It was named after Major Stephen H. Long, who led an expedition in 1820 up the Platte River to the base of the Rockies. Long never ascended the mountain—in fact, he didn't even get within 40 miles of it—but a few decades later, in 1868, the one-armed Civil War veteran John Wesley Powell climbed to its summit.

Longs Peak is the northernmost of the Fourteeners—the 54 mountains in Colorado that reach above the 14,000-foot mark—and one of more than 114 named mountains in the park that are higher than 10,000 feet. The peak, in the park's southeast quadrant, has a distinctive flat-topped, rectangular summit that is visible from many spots on the park's east side and on Trail Ridge Road.

The ambitious climb to Longs summit is only recommended for those who are strong climbers and well acclimated to the altitude. If you're up for it, be sure to begin before dawn so that you're down from the summit when the typical afternoon thunderstorm hits.

33

Cub Lake. This 4.6-mile, three-hour (round-trip) hike takes you through meadows and stands of aspen trees and up 540 feet in elevation to a lake with water lilies. *Moderate.* ⊠ *Trailhead at Cub Lake, 1.7 miles from Moraine Park Campground.*

Colorado River Trail. This walk to the ghost town of Lulu City on the west side of the park is excellent for looking for the bighorn sheep, elk, and moose that reside in the area. Part of the former stagecoach route that went from Granby to Walden, the 3.1-mile trail parallels the infant Colorado River to the meadow where Lulu City once stood. The elevation gain is 300 feet. *Moderate.* ⊠ *Trailhead at Colorado River, off Trail Ridge Rd., 1.7 miles north of the Timber Creek Campground.*

Continental Divide National Scenic Trail. This 3,100-mile corridor, which extends from Montana's Canadian border to the southern edge of New Mexico, enters Rocky Mountain National Park in two places, at trailheads only about 4 miles apart and located on either side of the Kawuneeche Visitor Center on Trail Ridge Road, at the park's southwestern end. Within the park, it covers about 30 miles of spectacular montane and subalpine terrain and follows the existing Green Mountain, Tonahutu Creek, North Inlet, and East Shore Trails. *Moderate.* ⊠ *Trailheads at Harbison Meadows Picnic Area, off Trail Ridge Rd., about 1 mile inside park from Grand Lake Entrance, and at East Shore Trailhead, just south of Grand Lake.*

Fern Lake Trail. Heading to Odessa Lake from the north involves a steep hike, but on most days you'll encounter fewer other hikers than if you had begun the trip at Bear Lake. Along the way, you'll come to

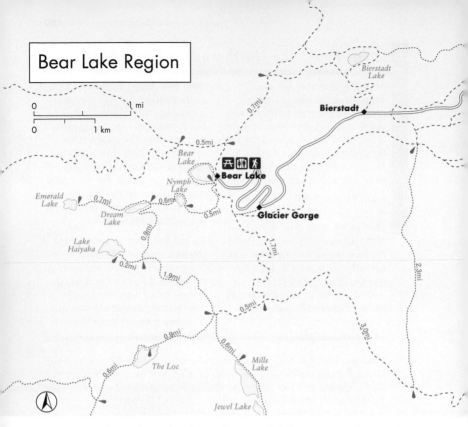

Bear Lake Region

0 ——————— 1 mi
0 ——————— 1 km

Bierstadt Lake

0.7mi

Bierstadt

0.5mi

Bear Lake

Nymph Lake

Bear Lake

Emerald Lake

0.7mi   0.6mi

Dream Lake

0.5mi

Glacier Gorge

Lake Haiyaha

0.9mi

1.7mi

2.3mi

0.2mi

1.9mi

0.5mi

3.0mi

0.9mi

0.6mi

0.6mi

The Loc

Mills Lake

Jewel Lake

---

the Arch Rocks; the Pool, an eroded formation in the Big Thompson River; two waterfalls; and Fern Lake (4.9 miles from your starting point). Odessa Lake itself lies at the foot of Tourmaline Gorge, below the craggy summits of Gabletop Mountain, Little Matterhorn, Knobtop Mountain, and Notchtop Mountain. For a full day of spectacular scenery, continue past Odessa to Bear Lake (9 miles total), where you can pick up the shuttle back to the Fern Lake Trailhead. *Moderate.* ⊠ *Trailhead off Fern Lake Rd., about 2½ miles south of Moraine Park Visitor Center.*

DIFFICULT

Chasm Lake Trail. Nestled in the shadow of Longs Peak and Mount Meeker, Chasm Lake offers one of Colorado's most impressive backdrops, which also means you can expect to encounter plenty of other hikers on the way. The 4.2-mile Chasm Lake Trail, reached via the Longs Peak Trail, has a 2,360-foot elevation gain. Just before the lake, you'll need to climb a small rock ledge, which can be a bit of a challenge for the less surefooted; follow the cairns for the most straightforward route. Once atop the ledge, you'll catch your first memorable view of the lake. *Difficult.* ⊠ *Trailhead at Longs Peak Ranger Station, off Rte. 7, 10 miles from the Beaver Meadows Visitor Center.*

Longs Peak Trail. Climbing this 14,259-foot mountain (one of 53 "Fourteeners" in Colorado) is an ambitious goal for almost anyone—but only those who are very fit and acclimated to the altitude should attempt it. The 16-mile round-trip climb requires a predawn start (3 am is ideal), so that you're off the summit before the typical summer afternoon thunderstorm hits. Also, the last 2 miles or so of the trail are very exposed—you have to traverse narrow ledges with vertigo-inducing drop-offs. That said, summiting Longs can be one of the most rewarding experiences you'll ever have. The Keyhole route is the most popular means of ascent, and the number of people going up it on a summer day can be astounding, given the rigors of the climb. Though just as scenic, the Loft route, between Longs and Mount Meeker from Chasm Lake, is less crowded but not as clearly marked and therefore more difficult to navigate. *Difficult.* ⊠ *Trailhead at Longs Peak Ranger Station, off Rte. 7, 10 miles from Beaver Meadows Visitor Center.*

HORSEBACK RIDING

Horses and riders can access 260 miles of trails in Rocky Mountain.

TOURS AND OUTFITTERS
Hi-Country Stables. The Glacier Creek Stables and Moraine Park Stables are the only liveries located within the borders of the park, and both offer two- to ten-hour guided rides to places like Cub Lake, Beaver Mountain, and Marguerite Falls. ⊠ *Glacier Creek Campground, off Bear Lake Rd. near Sprague Lake* ☎ *970/586–3244 for stables, 970/586–4577 for off-season reservations* ⊕ *www.sombrero.com* ⊠ *Moraine Park Campground, off Fern Lake Rd.* ☎ *970/586–2327 for stables, 970/586–4577 for off-season reservations.* ⊗ *May–mid-Sept.*

ROCK CLIMBING

Expert rock climbers as well as novices can try hundreds of classic and big wall climbs here (there's also ample opportunity for bouldering and mountaineering). The burgeoning sport of ice climbing also thrives in the park. The Diamond, Lumpy Ridge, and Petit Grepon are the places for serious rock climbing, while well-known ice-climbing spots include Hidden Falls, Loch Vale, and Emerald and Black lakes.

TOURS AND OUTFITTERS
Colorado Mountain School. Colorado Mountain School has been guiding climbers since 1877 and is an invaluable resource for climbers in the Rocky Mountain area (they're also the park's only official provider of technical climbing services). They can teach you rock climbing, mountaineering, ice climbing, avalanche survival, and many other skills. Take introductory half-day and one- to five-day courses on climbing and rappelling technique, or sign up for guided introductory trips, full-day climbs, and longer expeditions. Make reservations a month in advance for summer climbs. The school also runs a 16-bed hostel with a full kitchen ($25 a night). ⊠ *341 Moraine Ave., Estes Park* ☎ *800/836–4008, 303/447–2804* ⊕ *www.totalclimbing.com.*

WINTER SPORTS

Each winter, the popularity of snowshoeing in the park increases. It's a wonderful way to experience Rocky Mountain's majestic winter side, when the jagged peaks are softened with a blanket of snow and the summer hordes are nonexistent. You can snowshoe any of the summer hiking trails that are accessible by road; many of them also become well-traveled cross-country ski trails. Two trails to try are Tonahutu Creek Trail (near Kawuneeche Visitor Center) and the Colorado River Trail to Lulu City (start at the Timber Creek Campground).

Backcountry skiing within the park ranges from gentle cross-country outings to full-on, experts-only adventures down steep chutes and open bowls. Ask a ranger about conditions, and gear up as if you were spending the night. If you plan on venturing off trail, take a shovel, probe pole, and avalanche transceiver. Only on the west side of the park are you permitted to snowmobile, and you must register at Kawuneeche Visitor Center before traveling the unplowed section of Trail Ridge Road up to Milner Pass. Check the park newspaper for ranger-guided tours.

TOURS AND OUTFITTERS

Estes Park Mountain Shop. You can rent or buy snowshoes and skis here, as well as fishing, hiking, and climbing equipment. The store is open year-round and gives four-, six-, and eight-hour guided snowshoeing, fly-fishing, and climbing trips to areas in and around Rocky Mountain National Park. ⊠ *2050 Big Thompson Ave., Estes Park* ☎ *970/586–6548, 866/303–6548* ⊕ *www.estesparkmountainshop.com* ☺ *Daily 8 am–9 pm.*

Never Summer Mountain Products. This well-stocked shop sells and rents all sorts of outdoor equipment, including cross-country skis, hiking gear, kayaks, and camping supplies. ⊠ *919 Grand Ave., Grand Lake* ☎ *970/627–3642* ⊕ *www.neversummermtn.com.*

SHOPPING

Trail Ridge Store. This is the park's only official store (though you'll find a small selection of park souvenirs and books at the visitor centers). Trail Ridge stocks sweatshirts and jackets, postcards, and assorted craft items. ⊠ *Trail Ridge Rd., adjacent to Alpine Visitor Center* ☺ *Closed mid-Oct.–late May (when Trail Ridge Rd. is closed).*

WHAT'S NEARBY

NEARBY TOWNS

Estes Park, 5 miles east of Rocky Mountain, is the park's most popular gateway. The town sits at an altitude of more than 7,500 feet, with 14,259-foot Longs Peak and a legion of surrounding mountains as its stunning backdrop. Many of the small hotels lining the roads are mom-and-pop outfits that have been passed down through several generations. Estes Park's quieter cousin, **Grand Lake,** 1½ miles outside the park's west entrance, gets busy in summer, but has a low-key, quintessentially Western graciousness. In winter, it's *the* snowmobiling and ice-fishing destination for Front Range Coloradans. At the park's southwestern entrance are the Arapaho and Roosevelt National Forests, Arapaho National Recreational Area, and the small town of **Granby,** the place to go for big-game hunting and mountain biking. There are also skiing and other mountain activities (both summer and winter varieties) at nearby SolVista Basin and the Winter Park/Mary Jane ski areas.

VISITOR INFORMATION
Estes Park Convention and Visitors Bureau ⊠ *500 Big Thompson Ave., Estes Park* ☎ *970/577–9900, 800/443–7837* ⊕ *www.visitestespark.com.* **Grand Lake Chamber of Commerce Visitor Center** ⊠ *West Portal Rd. and U.S. 34, at the western entrance of Rocky Mountain National Park, Grand Lake* ☎ *970/627–3402, 800/531–1019* ⊕ *www.grandlakechamber.com.* **Greater Granby Area Chamber of Commerce** ⊠ *365 E. Agate, Suite B, Granby* ☎ *970/887–2311, 800/325–1661* ⊕ *www.granbychamber.com.*

33

SCENIC DRIVES

Peak-to-Peak Scenic and Historic Byway. The Peak-to-Peak Scenic and Historic Byway (rtes. 119, 72, and 7), a 55-mile stretch that winds from Central City through Nederland to Estes Park, is not the quickest route to the eastern gateway to Rocky Mountain National Park, but it's certainly the most scenic. You'll pass through the old mining towns of Ward and Allenspark and enjoy spectacular mountain vistas. Mount Meeker and Longs Peak rise magnificently behind every bend in the road. The descent into Estes Park provides grand vistas of snow-covered mountains and green valleys.

An afternoon drive along this route is especially memorable in fall, when the sky is deeper blue and stands of aspens contrast with the evergreen pine forests. ⊠ *From Central City, drive north on 119. From Nederland, drive north on Rte. 72. Turn left at intersection with Rte. 7 and continue to Estes Park, Nederland* ⊕ *www.byways.org.*

AREA ACTIVITIES

SPORTS AND THE OUTDOORS
BIRD-WATCHING
Windy Gap Wildlife Viewing Area. The reservoir at Windy Gap Wildlife Viewing Area is on the waterfowl migration route for geese, pelicans, swans, eagles, and osprey. The park has information kiosks, viewing scopes, viewing blinds, a picnic area, and a nature trail that's also wheelchair accessible. ⊠ *2 miles west of Granby on U.S. 40 where it meets Rte. 125, Granby* ☎ *970/725–6200* ☉ *May–Sept., daily dawn–dusk.*

FISHING
Anglers in the Grand Lake and Granby area enjoy plentiful trout, mackinaw, and kokanee salmon. Ice fishers will not want to miss the big contest held the first weekend in January on Lake Granby, where winners collect $20,000 in cash and prizes. Anyone older than 16 needs a Colorado fishing license, which you can obtain at local sporting-goods stores. See ⊕ *www.wildlife.state.co.us/fishing* for more information.

The Big Thompson River, which runs east of Estes Park along U.S. 34, is popular for its good stock of rainbow and brown trout. See ⊕ *www. wildlife.state.co.us/fishing* for more information on fishing licenses.

TOURS AND
OUTFITTERS **Rocky Mountain Adventures.** From its Fort Collins office, guides from this company can take you fly-fishing on the Big Thompson and other rivers, including those in Rocky Mountain National Park. Call ahead. ✉ *1117 N. U.S. 287, Fort Collins* ☎ *970/586–6191, 800/858–6808* ⊕ *www.shoprma.com.*

Trail Ridge Marina. Visit the Trail Ridge Marina on the western shore of Shadow Mountain Lake to rent a Sea-Doo or motor boat for two to six hours. ✉ *12634 U.S. 34, 2 miles south of Grand Lake* ☎ *970/627–3586* ⊕ *www.trailridgemarina.com.*

GOLF

Grand Elk Ranch & Club. Designed by PGA great Craig Stadler, the challenging mountain course is reminiscent of traditional heathland greens in Britain. ✉ *1300 Tenmile Dr., Granby* ☎ *970/887–9122, 877/389–9333* ⊕ *www.grandelk.com* ⚲ *Reservations essential* ⚑ *18 holes. 7144 yds. Par 71. Green Fee: $95.* ☞ *Facilities: driving range, putting green, golf carts, rental clubs, lessons, restaurant, bar.*

WINTER SPORTS

Many consider Grand Lake to be Colorado's snowmobiling capital, with more than 300 miles of trails (150 miles groomed), many winding through virgin forest. There are several rental and guide companies in the area. If you're visiting during the winter holidays, it's wise to make reservations about three weeks ahead.

Grand Adventures. Guided tours by snowmobile range from $75 for one hour to $195 for four hours, and unguided snowmobile rental fees range from $100 for two hours to $175 for four hours. ✉ *304 W. Portal Rd., Grand Lake* ☎ *970/726–9247, 800/726–9247* ⊕ *www. grandadventures.com.*

Never Summer Mountain Products. Rent cross-country skis, backcountry skis, and snowshoes in the winter, or buy backpacks, tents, and all other camping equipment for summer sports. All backpackers in Rocky Mountain National Park need a manditory bear canister (for overnight food storage), and the friendly staff at Never Summer rents those for $5 per day. ✉ *919 Grand Ave., Grand Lake* ☎ *970/627–3642* ⊕ *www.neversummermtn.com.*

On The Trail Rentals. This outfit a few miles northwest of town rents snowmobiles and organizes unguided trips into Arapaho National Forest. Prices range from $100 for two hours to $240 for eight hours. During the summer, you can rent mountain bikes, ATVs, and side-by-sides here. ✉ *1447 County Rd. 491, Grand Lake* ☎ *970/627–0171, 888/627–2429* ⊕ *www.onthetrailrentals.com.*

ARTS AND ENTERTAINMENT

ARTS

Rocky Ridge Music Center. Relax with some chamber music while taking in views of the mountains at the much respected Rocky Ridge Music Center. Faculty members hold their own classical chamber music concerts June through August. ✉ *465 Longs Peak Rd., off Rte. 7 at the turnoff to Longs Peak Campground, 9 miles south of Estes Park* ☎ *970/586–4031* 🌐 *www.rockyridge.org.*

NIGHTLIFE

Lariat Saloon. A local hot spot, the rustic bar has pinball, pool, darts, and live rock music almost every night. Look for the talking buffalo amid the eclectic Western decor. ✉ *1121 Grand Ave., on Boardwalk 80447, Grand Lake* ☎ *970/627–9965.*

Lonigans Saloon. Blues and rock bands play regularly at the popular Lonigans Saloon. Be sure to check the website for the rotating schedule of live music, karaoke, and open mics. ✉ *110 W. Elkhorn Ave., Estes Park* ☎ *970/586–4346* 🌐 *www.lonigans.com.*

The Tavern. The Tavern (inside Mary's Lake Lodge) has live music on Friday and Saturday nights, offering everything from bluegrass to funk. ✉ *Mary's Lake Lodge, 2625 Mary's Lake Rd., Estes Park* ☎ *970/586–5958* 🌐 *www.maryslakelodge.com.*

SHOPPING

Rocky Mountain Chocolate Factory and Malt Shop. Indulge in fudge, truffles, and caramel apples, plus traditional malts and shakes, at Rocky Mountain Chocolate Factory and Malt Shop. Any walk through town will confirm that Estes is a paradise for sweets and candies, but this storefront stands out for its way with caramel, chocolate, and nuts. ✉ *517 Big Thompson Ave., Estes Park* ☎ *970/586–6601* 🌐 *www.rmcf.com.*

WHERE TO EAT

IN THE PARK

$ AMERICAN 🍴 **Cafe at Trail Ridge.** The park's only source for food is this small café offering snacks and sandwiches, hot dogs, and soups. A coffee bar also serves fair-trade coffee, espresso drinks, and tea, plus water, juice, and salads. The café is in the same building as the Trail Ridge Store, adjacent to the Alpine Visitor Center, and is open seasonally, whenever Trail Ridge Road is open. [$] *Average main: $7* ✉ *Trail Ridge Rd., at Alpine Visitor Center* ☎ *970/586–3097* 🕒 *Late May–mid-June and late Aug.–mid-Oct., daily 10–4:30; mid-June–late Aug., daily 8–5:30.*

PICNIC AREAS

Endovalley. With 32 tables and 30 fire grates, this is the largest picnic area in the park. Here, you'll find aspen groves, nice views of Fall River Pass—and lovely Fan Lake a short hike away. ✉ *Old Fall River Rd., off U.S. 34, 4.4 miles from Fall River Visitor Center.*

Hollowell Park. In a meadow near Mill Creek, this lovely spot for a picnic has nine tables and is open year-round. It's also close to the Hollowell Park and Mill Creek Basin Trailheads. ✉ *Off Bear Lake Rd., 2.4 miles from Moraine Park Visitor Center.*

FAMILY **Sprague Lake.** With 27 tables and 16 pedestal grills, there's plenty of room for the whole gang at this alfresco dining spot. It's open year-round, with flush toilets in the summer and vault toilets the rest of the year. ⊠ *0.6 mile from intersection of Bear Lake Rd. and U.S. 36, 3.9 miles from Bear Lake.*

OUTSIDE THE PARK

ESTES PARK

$$ ✕ **Bighorn Restaurant.** An Estes Park staple since 1972, this family-run
AMERICAN outfit is where the locals go for breakfast—try a double-cheese omelet, huevos rancheros, or grits. Since it opens as early as 6, you can come here before heading into the park. Owners Laura and Sid Brown are happy to pack up a lunch for you—just place your order along with breakfast, and your sandwich, chips, homemade cookie, and drink will be ready to go when you leave. This homey spot also serves lunch and dinner. $ *Average main: $14* ⊠ *401 W. Elkhorn Ave., Estes Park* ☎ *970/586–2792* ⊕ *www.estesparkbighorn.com.*

$ ✕ **Ed's Cantina and Grill.** The fajitas and well-stocked bar make this lively
MEXICAN Mexican restaurant popular with locals and visitors alike. The decor is bright, with light woods and large windows. Try to get patio seating by the river. If you're hungry, try one of the enchilada platters (including mahimahi, chicken mole, and vegetarian); the authentic pork tamales, smothered in green or red chili sauce; or the carne asada. Breakfast is also good here (it's served until 11 on weekends), with both Mexican and all-American options. $ *Average main: $10* ⊠ *390 E. Elkhorn Ave., Estes Park* ☎ *970/586–2919* ⊕ *www.edscantina.com.*

$$ ✕ **Estes Park Brewery.** If you're not sure which beer suits you, head down-
AMERICAN stairs to the tasting area to sample a couple of brews. There is plenty on tap, but take in the region's "Shining" heritage via the Redrum Ale. The Staggering Elk, a crisp lager, and the Estes Park Gold ale come highly recommended. The food is no-frills (beer chili is the specialty here), and the menu includes pizza, burgers, sandwiches, and chicken or steak dinners. ■ TIP➔ **If you're visiting in June, call ahead and ask about the popular Rocky Mountain Brew Fest.** $ *Average main: $15* ⊠ *470 Prospect Village Dr., Estes Park* ☎ *970/586–5421* ⊕ *www.epbrewery.com.*

$$ ✕ **Hunter's Chophouse.** This popular steakhouse fills quickly in the eve-
STEAKHOUSE ning, and for good reason. The locals head here for the savory and spicy barbecue: steaks, venison, buffalo, elk, chicken, and seafood. If you're not hungry enough for 12 ounces of beef (or buffalo), Hunter's has special burgers, like the avocado bacon cheeseburger, and a long list of sandwiches, including a traditional French dip and a grilled salmon fillet on focaccia. There's a good kids' menu, too, with fish-and-chips, a junior sirloin, and a miniburger. $ *Average main: $20* ⊠ *1690 Big Thompson Ave., Estes Park* ☎ *970/586–6962* ⊕ *www. hunterschophouse.com* ⚑ *Reservations essential.*

$$ ✕ **Mama Rose's.** An Estes institution, the friendly staff at Mama Rose
ITALIAN consistently serves good family-style Italian meals. The lasagna with sliced meatballs and sausage and the tricolor baked pasta are popular entrées, and the wine cellar has a good selection of international wines. The spacious Victorian dining room with plenty of fine art harkens

CLOSE UP

Best Campgrounds in Rocky Mountain

Five top-notch campgrounds and one group camping area accommodate campers looking to stay in a tent, trailer, or RV (only three campgrounds accept reservations; the others fill up on a first-come, first-served basis).

Aspenglen Campground. This quiet, eastside spot near the north entrance is set in open pine woodland along Fall River. It doesn't have the views of Moraine Park or Glacier Basin, but it is small and peaceful. There are a few excellent walk-in sites for those who want to pitch a tent away from the crowds but still be close to the car. Reservations are not accepted. ✉ *Drive past Fall River Visitor Center on U.S. 34 and turn left at the campground road.*

Backcountry Permits, Rocky Mountain National Park. Backcountry camping requires advance reservations or a day-of-trip permit; there's a $20 fee during the summer season. It's best to visit the National Park Service's Web site before your trip; definitely contact the Backcountry Permits office before starting out. ✉ *Beaver Meadows Visitor Center, Kawuneeche Visitor Center* ☎ *970/586–1242.*

Glacier Basin Campground. Rest near the banks of Glacier Creek and take in views of the Continental Divide. There's easy access to a network of many popular trails, and rangers come here for campfire programs. Reservations are essential. ✉ *Drive 5 miles south on Bear Lake Rd. from U.S. 36* ☎ *877/444–6777.*

Longs Peak Campground. Hikers going up Longs Peak can stay at this year-round campground. Sites, which are first-come, first-served, are limited to eight people; ice and firewood are sold in summer. ✉ *9 miles south of Estes Park on Rte. 7.*

Moraine Park Campground. This popular campground hosts ranger-led campfire programs and is near hiking trails. You'll hear elk bugling if you camp here in September or October. Reservations are essential from mid-May to late September. ✉ *Drive south on Bear Lake Rd. from U.S. 36, l' mile to campground entrance* ☎ *877/444–6777.*

Timber Creek Campground. Anglers love this spot on the Colorado River, 10 miles from Grand Lake village. In the evening you can sit in on ranger-led campfire programs. Reservations are not accepted. ✉ *1 Trail Ridge Rd., 2 miles west of Alpine Visitor Center.*

33

back to earlier eras in Estes Park, minus the formal dress code. In warm weather diners enjoy the patio with views of the Big Thompson River. [$] *Average main: $18* ✉ *338 E. Elkhorn Ave., Estes Park* ☎ *970/586–3330* 🌐 *www.mamarosesrestaurant.com* 🕒 *No lunch.*

$ PIZZA 🍴 **Poppy's Pizza & Grill.** This casual riverside eatery (owned by the same folks at the nearby Mama Rose's) serves creative signature pizzas. Try the spinach, artichoke, and feta pie made with sundried tomato pesto. You can also create your own pie from the five sauces and 40 toppings on the menu. Options also include sandwiches, wraps, salads, and burgers. Poppy's has patio seating at the river and an extensive selection of wine and beer. [$] *Average main: $10* ✉ *342 E. Elkhorn Ave., Estes Park* ☎ *970/586–8282* 🌐 *www.poppyspizzaandgrill.com* 🕒 *Closed Jan.*

THE GRAND DAYS OF THE SPA

Colorado's scenery has long attracted high-profile personalities like Teddy Roosevelt and Walt Whitman, but many early travelers were asthma, tuberculosis, and arthritis sufferers who came to the dry climate to convalesce. From the early to mid-20th century, healing spas and resorts like Hot Sulphur Springs and Eldorado Springs sprang up in the mountains of north central Colorado, serving as destinations for long-term visitors. The list of rich or famous visitors is long: Robert Frost visited his daughter, Marjorie, in Boulder while she recuperated in the early 1930s; Dwight and Mamie Eisenhower honeymooned at Eldorado Springs.

This therapeutic tradition continues today. Refurbished hot springs and spas are regaining their popularity, and the National Jewish Medical and Research Center in Denver specializes in treatments for respiratory ailments.

$$ ITALIAN FAMILY 🍴 **Sweet Basilico.** This family-owned and family-friendly restaurant is a local favorite for basic Italian classics like lasagna, manicotti, and eggplant Parmesan, as well as home-style entrées like the savory and spicy chicken scarpelli. The calamari fritti are crisp and spicy, sandwiches made with homemade focaccia are delicious, and the minestrone satisfies. Enjoy dinner alfresco on the large covered patio or in the well-lighted, brick-wall dining room accented with photos of Italian scenery. Don't forget the spumoni cheesecake with mascarpone frosting for dessert. [$] *Average main: $15* ✉ *430 Prospect Village Dr., Estes Park* ☎ *970/586–3899* 🌐 *www.sweetbasilico.com* 🕒 *Closed Mon. Oct.–Apr.*

GRAND LAKE

$ CAFÉ Fodor's Choice ★ 🍴 **Fat Cat Cafe.** Located right on the boardwalk, this small one-room breakfast and lunch spot serves delicious food at very reasonable prices. The $12.50 ($6.95 for kids) weekend breakfast buffet is downright amazing, with close to 50 items at a time—everything from biscuits and gravy to scones and Scotch eggs to Mexican-style omelets with beans and green chili. If you have to wait for a table (which you might on a summer Sunday), Fat Cat offers coffee and cinnamon rolls to tide you over. [$] *Average main: $10* ✉ *916 Grand Ave., Grand Lake* ☎ *970/627–0900* 🕒 *Mon. and Wed.–Fri. 7–2, weekends 7–1* 🕒 *Closed Tues.*

$$ AMERICAN 🍴 **Grand Lake Brewing Company.** A handcrafted beer and a bratwurst with the works or a pulled chicken sandwich will hit the spot at this rustic brewpub outfitted with a tin ceiling and wooden bar with brass rails. Eat at the bar or at a table in the small but sunny dining area; the food is standard pub fare, inexpensive if uninspired. The beer's the real draw here. For example, the crisp and light White Cap Wheat is an unfiltered brew that tastes best with a slice of orange or lemon, while the Plaid Bastard, a rich Scotch ale served in a brandy snifter to highlight its deep aromas and flavors, really packs a punch (8% ABV). Can't decide? Try a flight—4 oz. of each of the nine available beers—then take home a 64-oz. growler as a memento of your visit. There's also a second location, at 9921 U.S. 34. [$] *Average main: $15* ✉ *915 Grand Ave., Grand Lake* ☎ *970/627–1711* 🌐 *www.grandlakebrewing.com.*

$$ ✕ **Sagebrush BBQ & Grill.** Falling-off-the-bone, melt-in-your-mouth bar-
SOUTHERN becue pork, chicken, and beef draw local and out-of-town attention to this homey café, where you can munch on old-fashioned peanuts (and toss the shells on the floor) while waiting for your table. Comforting sides such as baked beans, corn bread, coleslaw, and potatoes top off the large plates. The breakfast menu includes omelets, pancakes, and biscuits as well as chicken-fried steak and huevos rancheros platters for heartier appetites. $ *Average main: $18* ✉ *1101 Grand Ave., Grand Lake* ☎ *970/627–1404, 866/900–1404* ⊕ *www.sagebrushbbq.com.*

33

WHERE TO STAY

OUTSIDE THE PARK

ESTES PARK

$$$ ⌂ **Boulder Brook.** Luxury suites at this smart, secluded spot on the river
HOTEL are tucked into the pines, yet close to town and 1½ miles from Rocky Mountain National Park. **Pros:** scenic location; quiet area; attractive grounds. **Cons:** not within walking distance of attractions; no nearby dining. $ *Rooms from: $190* ✉ *1900 Fall River Rd., Estes Park* ☎ *970/586–0910, 800/238–0910* ⊕ *www.boulderbrook.com* ⇱ *19 suites* ⦿ *No meals.*

$$$$ ⌂ **C Lazy U Guest Ranch.** Secluded in a broad, verdant valley, this deluxe
RESORT dude ranch attracts an international clientele, including both Holly-
ALL-INCLUSIVE wood royalty and the real thing. **Pros:** kid- and family-friendly; helpful
FAMILY staff; deluxe in every respect. **Cons:** distant from other area attractions; no pets; very expensive. $ *Rooms from: $2590* ✉ *Granby* ⧊ *3½ miles north on Hwy. 125 from U.S. 40* ☎ *970/887–3344* ⊕ *www.clazyu.com* ⇱ *19 rooms, 20 cabins* ⦿ *All-inclusive.*

$ ⌂ **Estes Park Center/YMCA of the Rockies.** This 890-acre family-friendly
RENTAL property has a wealth of attractive, clean lodging options among its
FAMILY nine lodges and 230 cabins. **Pros:** good value for large groups and for longer stays; lots of family-oriented activities and amenities; stun-ningly scenic setting. **Cons:** very large, busy, and crowded property; fills fast; location requires vehicle to visit town or the national park. $ *Rooms from: $80* ✉ *2515 Tunnel Rd., Estes Park* ☎ *970/586–3341, 303/448–1616, 800/777–9622* ⊕ *www.ymcarockies.org* ⇱ *688 rooms, 220 cabins* ⦿ *Some meals.*

$ ⌂ **Glacier Lodge.** Families are the specialty at this secluded, 19-acre
RESORT guest resort on the banks of the Big Thompson River. **Pros:** great place
FAMILY for families; attractive grounds on the river; on free bus route. **Cons:** not within walking distance of attractions; along rather busy road. $ *Rooms from: $85* ✉ *2166 Hwy. 66, Estes Park* ☎ *970/586–4401, 800/523–3920* ⊕ *www.glacierlodge.com* ⇱ *24 single-family cabins, 4 cabins for 12–30* ⦿ *No meals.*

$$$ ⌂ **Mary's Lake Lodge and Resort.** This 1913 chalet-style lodge sits in
HOTEL the mountains and overlooks peaceful Mary's Lake, a couple of miles south of town. **Pros:** two excellent on-site restaurants; beautiful views. **Cons:** not within walking distance of attractions or other dining; large,

older hotel. $ *Rooms from: $180 ⊠ 2625 Mary's Lake Rd., Estes Park* ☎ *970/586–5958, 877/442–6279* ⊕ *www.maryslakelodge.com* ⌐ *16 rooms, 54 condos* ¹◯¹ *No meals.*

$$ ⊡ **Riverview Pines.** Do some fishing, or just sit and read on the expansive
HOTEL   lawn at this peaceful hotel, the least expensive along the beautiful Fall River Road between Estes and Rocky Mountain National Park. **Pros:** friendly and helpful owner-managers; quiet and scenic location on river; low rates for the area. **Cons:** very basic rooms without much decoration; on a busy road. $ *Rooms from: $120 ⊠ 1150 W. Elkhorn Ave., Estes Park* ☎ *970/586–3627, 800/340–5764* ⊕ *www.riverviewpines. com* ⌐ *18 rooms, 8 cabins* ¹◯¹ *No meals.*

$$ ⊡ **Stanley Hotel.** Perched regally on a hill, with a commanding view of
HOTEL   the town, the Stanley is one of Colorado's great old hotels, impeccably
Fodor's Choice   maintained in its historic state, yet with many modern conveniences,
★   including a spa. **Pros:** historic hotel; many rooms have been updated recently; good restaurant. **Cons:** some rooms are small and tight; building is old; no a/c. $ *Rooms from: $140 ⊠ 333 Wonderview Ave., Estes Park* ☎ *970/577–4000, 800/976–1377* ⊕ *www.stanleyhotel.com* ⌐ *160 rooms* ¹◯¹ *No meals.*

GRAND LAKE

$ ⊡ **Historic Rapids Lodge & Restaurant.** This handsome lodgepole-pine
HOTEL   structure on the Tonahutu River dates to 1915, and a stay here will
Fodor's Choice   give you a dose of history and put you near nature. **Pros:** in-house res-
★   taurant; condos are great for longer stays; quiet area of town. **Cons:** unpaved parking area; lodge rooms are above restaurant; all lodge rooms are on second floor and there's no elevator. $ *Rooms from: $85* ⊠ *209 Rapids La., Grand Lake* ☎ *970/627–3707* ⊕ *www.rapidslodge. com* ⌐ *7 rooms, 8 suites, 6 cabins, 12 condos* ☉ *Closed Apr. and Nov.* ¹◯¹ *No meals.*

$ ⊡ **Mountain Lakes Lodge.** The scent of the pine forest welcomes you to
HOTEL   these charming and comfortable log cabins whimsically decorated with animal and sports themes—down to the curtains and drawer pulls. **Pros:** dog-friendly; close to fishing; good value. **Cons:** 4 miles from town (and services); two-day minimum stay (three-day minimum for holidays and special events). $ *Rooms from: $100 ⊠ 10480 U.S. 34, Grand Lake* ☎ *970/627–8448, 877/627–3220* ⊕ *www.mountainlakeslodge.com* ⌐ *10 cabins, 1 house* ¹◯¹ *No meals.*

SAGUARO
NATIONAL PARK

WELCOME TO SAGUARO

TOP REASONS TO GO

★ **Saguaro sightseeing:** Hike, bike, or drive through dense saguaro stands for an up-close look at this king of all cacti.

★ **Wildlife watching:** Diverse wildlife roams through the park, including such ground dwellers as javelinas, coyotes, and rattlesnakes, and winged residents ranging from the migratory lesser long-nosed bat to the diminutive elf owl.

★ **Ancient artwork:** Get a glimpse into the past at the numerous rock-art sites where ancient peoples etched into the stones as far back as 5000 BC.

1 **Saguaro West: Tucson Mountain District.** This popular district makes up less than one-third of the park. Here you'll find an American Indian video orientation to saguaros at the visitor center, hiking trails, an ancient Hohokam petroglyph site at Signal Hill, and a scenic drive through the park's densest desert growth.

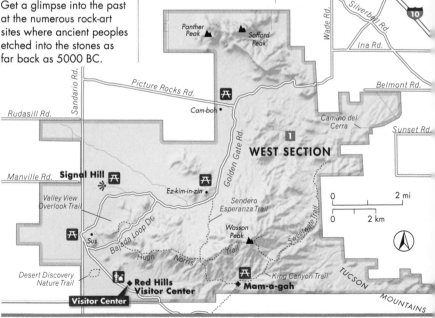

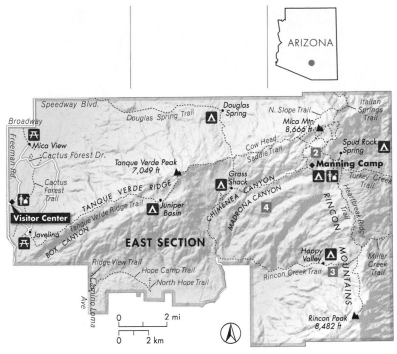

ARIZONA

Speedway Blvd.
Broadway
Freeman Rd.
Mica View
Cactus Forest Dr.
Cactus Forest Trail
Visitor Center
Javelina
Douglas Spring Trail
Tanque Verde Peak 7,049 ft
TANQUE VERDE RIDGE
Tanque Verde Ridge Trail
Juniper Basin
BOX CANYON
EAST SECTION
Ridge View Trail
Hope Camp Trail
North Hope Trail
Camino Loma Ave.
Douglas Spring
N. Slope Trail
Mica Mtn. 8,666 ft
Cow Head Saddle Trail
Grass Shack
CHIMENEA CANYON
MADRONA CANYON
4
Italian Springs Trail
Spud Rock Spring
Manning Camp 2
Turkey Creek Trail
Heartbreak Ridge Trail
RINCON MOUNTAINS
Happy Valley
Rincon Creek Trail
3
Miller Creek Trail
Rincon Peak 8,482 ft

0   2 mi
0   2 km

GETTING ORIENTED

2 Saguaro East: Rincon Mountain District.
In the Rincon Mountains, Saguaro East encompasses 57,930 acres of designated wilderness area, an easily accessible scenic loop drive, several easy and intermediate trails through the cactus forest, and opportunities for adventure and backcountry camping at six rustic campgrounds.

3 Rincon Valley Area.
This 4,011-acre expansion along the southern border of Saguaro's Rincon Mountain District offers access to the riparian area along Rincon Creek.

4 Saguaro Wilderness Area. In the Rincon Mountain District, this backcountry area travels from desert scrublands at 3,000 feet to mixed conifer forests at 9,000 feet.

Saguaro National Park preserves some of the densest stands of these massive cacti, which can live up to 200 years and weigh up to 2 tons. Today more than 90,000 acres include habitats stretching from the arid Sonoran Desert up to high mountain forests. The park is split into two sections, with Tucson, Arizona, sandwiched in the middle. The urban base proves useful, but the park is no less rugged. More than half of it is designated wilderness area.

KEY

- 🏠 *Ranger Station*
- △ *Campground*
- 🌲 *Picnic Area*
- 🍴 *Restaurant*
- 🏨 *Lodge*
- 🚶 *Trailhead*
- 🚻 *Restrooms*
- ⤳ *Scenic Viewpoint*
- ⋯⋯ *Walking/Hiking Trails*

34

Updated by
Mara Levin
and Elise Riley

Standing sentinel in the desert, the towering saguaro is perhaps the most familiar emblem of the Southwest. Known for their height (often 50 feet) and arms reaching out in weird configurations, these slow-growing giants can take 15 years to grow a foot high and up to 75 years to grow their first arm. They are found only in the Sonoran Desert, and the largest concentration is in Saguaro National Park. In late spring (usually May), the succulent's top is covered with tiny white blooms—the Arizona state flower. The cacti are protected by state and federal laws, so don't disturb them.

SAGUARO PLANNER

WHEN TO GO

Saguaro never gets crowded; however, most people visit in milder weather, October through April. December through February can be cool, and are likely to see gentle rain showers. The spring days from March through May are bright and sunny with wildflowers in bloom. Because of high temperatures, from June through September it's best to visit the park in the early morning or late afternoon. The intense summer heat puts off most hikers, at least at lower elevations, but lodging prices are much cheaper—rates at top resorts in Tucson drop by as much as 70%. Cooler temperatures return in October and November, providing perfect weather for hiking and camping throughout the park.

AVG. HIGH/LOW TEMPS.

JAN.	FEB.	MAR.	APR.	MAY	JUNE
63/38	66/40	72/44	80/50	89/57	98/67

JULY	AUG.	SEPT.	OCT.	NOV.	DEC.
98/73	96/72	93/67	84/57	72/45	65/39

PLANNING YOUR TIME

SAGUARO IN ONE DAY

Before setting off, choose which section of the park to visit and pack a lunch (there's no food service in either park district). Also bring plenty of water—you're likely to get dehydrated in the dry climate—or purchase a reusable bottle at the visitor center (there are water stations in both districts of the park).

In the western section, start out by watching the 15-minute video at the **Red Hills Visitor Center,** then stroll along the 0.5-mile-long **Desert Discovery Trail.**

Drive north along Kinney Road, then turn right onto the graded dirt **Bajada Loop Drive.** Before long you'll soon see a turnoff for the **Hugh Norris Trail** on your right. If you're game for a steep 45-minute hike uphill, this trail leads to a perfect spot for a picnic. Hike back down and drive along the Bajada Loop Drive until you reach the turnoff for **Signal Hill.** From here it's a short walk to the **Hohokam petroglyphs.**

Alternatively, in the eastern section, pick up a free map of the hiking trails at the **Saguaro East Visitor Center.** Drive south along the paved **Cactus Forest Drive** to the Javelina picnic area, where you'll see signs for the **Freeman Homestead Trail,** an easy 1-mile loop that winds through a stand of mesquite as interpretive signs describe early inhabitants in the Tucson basin. If you're up for more difficult hiking, you might want to tackle part of the **Tanque Verde Ridge Trail,** which affords excellent views of saguaro-studded hillsides.

Along the northern loop of Cactus Forest Drive is **Cactus Forest Trail,** which branches off into several fairly level paths. You can easily spend the rest of the afternoon strolling among the saguaros.

GETTING HERE AND AROUND

CAR TRAVEL

Both districts are about a half-hour drive from central Tucson. To reach Rincon Mountain District (east section) from Interstate 10, take Exit 275, then go north on Houghton Road for 10 miles. Turn right on Escalante and left onto Old Spanish Trail, and the park will be on the right side. If you're coming from town, go east on Speedway Boulevard to Houghton Road. Turn right on Houghton and left onto Old Spanish Trail.

To reach the Tucson Mountain District (west section) from Interstate 10, take Exit 242 or Exit 257, then go west on Speedway Boulevard (the name will change to Gates Pass Road), follow it to Kinney Road, and turn right.

34

As there's no public transportation to or within Saguaro, a car is a necessity. In the western section, Bajada Loop Drive takes you through the park and to various trailheads; Cactus Forest Drive does the same for the eastern section.

PARK ESSENTIALS

PARK FEES AND PERMITS

Admission to Saguaro is $10 per vehicle and $5 for individuals on foot or bicycle; it's good for seven days from purchase at both park districts. Annual passes cost $25. For camping at one of the primitive campsites in the east district (the closest campsite is 6 miles from the trailhead), obtain a required backcountry permit for $6 nightly from the Saguaro East Visitor Center up to two months in advance.

PARK HOURS

The park opens at sunrise and closes at sunset. It's in the Mountain time zone.

CELL-PHONE RECEPTION

Cell-phone reception is generally good in the eastern district but is unreliable in the western district. The visitor centers have pay phones.

RESTAURANTS

At Saguaro, you won't find more than a sampling of Southwest jams, hot sauces, and candy bars at the two visitor centers' gift shops. Vending machines outside sell bottled water and soda, but pack some lunch for a picnic if you don't want to drive all the way back into town. Five picnic areas in the west district, and two in the east, offer scenery and shade. However, the city of Tucson, sandwiched neatly between the two park districts, offers some of the best Mexican cuisine in the country. A genuine college town, Tucson also has excellent upscale Southwestern cuisine, as well as good sushi, Thai, Italian, and Ethiopian food.

Prices in the reviews are the average cost of a main course at dinner, or if dinner is not served, at lunch.

HOTELS

Although there are no hotels within the park, its immediate proximity to Tucson makes finding a place to stay easy. A couple of B&Bs are a short drive from the park. Some ranches and smaller accommodations close during the hottest months of summer, but many inexpensive B&Bs and hotels are open year-round, and offer significantly lower rates from late May through August.

Prices in the reviews are the lowest cost of a standard double room in high season. For expanded reviews, facilities, and current deals, visit Fodors.com.

VISITOR INFORMATION

PARK CONTACT INFORMATION

Saguaro National Park ✉ 3693 S. Old Spanish Trail, Tucson ☎ 520/733–5158 for Saguaro West, 520/733–5153 for Saguaro East ⊕ www.nps.gov/sagu.

VISITOR CENTERS

The visitor centers in both districts have orientation slide shows and rangers who can answer your questions, as well as loads of books and maps. Both sell bottled water and soda.

Red Hills Visitor Center. Take in gorgeous views of nearby mountains and the surrounding desert from the center's large windows and shaded outdoor terrace. A spacious gallery is filled with educational exhibits, and a lifelike display simulates the flora and fauna of the region. A 15-minute slide show, "Voices of the Desert," provides a poetic, American Indian perspective on the saguaro. Park rangers and volunteers provide maps and suggest hikes to suit your interests. The well-stocked gift shop sells reusable water bottles that you can fill at water stations outside. ✉ *2700 N. Kinney Rd., Saguaro West* ☎ *520/733–5158* ☉ *Daily 9–5.*

34

Saguaro East Visitor Center. Stop here to pick up free maps and printed materials on various aspects of the park, including maps of hiking trails and backcountry camping permits (Red Hills Visitor Center, in Saguaro West, does not offer permits). Exhibits at the center are comprehensive, and a relief map of the park lays out the complexities of this protected landscape.

Two 20-minute slide shows explain the botanical and cultural history of the region, and there is a short self-guided nature walk along the paved Cactus Garden Trail. A small, select variety of books and other gift items are sold here, too. ✉ *3693 S. Old Spanish Trail, Saguaro East* ☎ *520/733–5153* ⊕ *www.nps.gov/sagu* ☉ *Daily 9–5.*

EXPLORING

SCENIC DRIVES

Unless you're ready for a long desert hike, the best way to see Saguaro is from the comfort of your car.

Bajada Loop Drive. This 6-mile drive winds through thick stands of saguaros and past two picnic areas and trailheads to a few short hikes, including one to a petroglyph site. Although the road is unpaved and moderately bumpy, it's a worthwhile trade-off for access to some of the park's densest desert growth. It's one way between Hugh Norris Trail and Golden Gate Road, so if you want to make the complete circuit, travel counterclockwise. The road is susceptible to flash floods during the monsoon season (July and August), so check road conditions at the visitor center before proceeding. This bumpy route is also popular among bicyclists. ✉ *Saguaro West.*

Cactus Forest Drive. This paved 8-mile drive provides a great overview of all Saguaro East has to offer. The one-way road, which circles clockwise, has several turnouts with roadside displays that make it easy to pull over and admire the scenery; you can also stop at two picnic areas and three easy nature trails. This is a good bicycling route as well, but watch out for snakes and javelinas traversing the roads. This road is open from 7 am to sunset daily. ✉ *Saguaro East.*

Plants and Wildlife in Saguaro

The saguaro may be the centerpiece of Saguaro National Park, but more than 1,200 plant species, including 50 types of cactus, thrive in the park. Among the most common cacti here are the prickly pear, barrel cactus, and teddy bear cholla—so named because it appears cuddly, but rangers advise packing a comb to pull its barbed hooks from unwary fingers.

For many of the desert fauna, the saguaro functions as a high-rise hotel. Each spring the Gila woodpecker and gilded flicker create holes in the cactus and then nest there. When they give up their temporary digs, elf owls, cactus wrens, sparrow hawks, and other birds move in, as do dangerous Africanized honeybees.

You may not encounter any of the park's six species of rattlesnake or the Gila monster, a venomous lizard, but avoid sticking your hands or feet under rocks or into crevices. Look where you're walking; if you do get bitten, get to a clinic or hospital as soon as possible. Not all snakes pass on venom; 50% of the time the bite is "dry" (nonpoisonous).

Wildlife, from bobcats to jackrabbits, is most active in early morning and at dusk. In spring and summer, lizards and snakes are out and about but tend to keep a low profile during the midday heat.

HISTORIC SITES

Manning Camp. The summer home of Levi Manning, onetime Tucson mayor, was a popular gathering spot for the city's elite in the early 1900s. The cabin can be reached only on foot or horseback via one of several challenging high-country trails: Douglas Spring Trail to Cow Head Saddle Trail (12 miles), Turkey Creek Trail (7.5 miles), or Tanque Verde Ridge Trail (15.4 miles). The cabin itself is not open for viewing. ⊠ *Saguaro East.*

SCENIC STOPS

FAMILY **Signal Hill.** The most impressive petroglyphs, and the only ones with explanatory signs, are on the Bajada Loop Drive in Saguaro West. An easy five-minute stroll from the signposted parking area takes you to one of the largest concentrations of rock carvings in the Southwest. You'll have a close-up view of the designs left by the Hohokam people between AD 900 and 1200, including large spirals some believe are astronomical markers. ⊠ *Bajada Loop Dr., 4½ miles north of visitor center, Saguaro West.*

EDUCATIONAL OFFERINGS

Orientation Programs. Daily programs at both park districts introduce visitors to the desert. You might find presentations on bats, birds, or desert blooms, naturalist-led hikes (including moonlight hikes), and, in summer only, films. Check online or call for the current week's activities. ⊠ *Saguaro East and Red Hills visitor centers* ☎ *520/733–5153* ✉ *Free* ☉ *Daily.*

RANGER PROGRAMS

Junior Ranger Program. Usually offered during June, a day camp for kids 5–12 includes daily hikes and workshops on pottery and petroglyphs. In the **Junior Ranger Discovery program,** young visitors can pick up an activity pack any time of the year and complete it within an hour or two. ⊠ *Saguaro East and Red Hills visitor centers* ☎ *520/733–5153.*

Ranger Talks. These are a great way to hear about wildlife, geology, and archaeology. ⊠ *Saguaro East and Red Hills visitor centers* ☎ *520/733–5153* 🔁 *Free* ⊙ *Nov.–Apr.*

SPORTS AND THE OUTDOORS

34

BICYCLING

TOURS AND OUTFITTERS

Fair Wheel Bikes. Mountain bikes and road bikes can be rented by the day or week here. They also organize group rides of varying difficulty. ⊠ *1110 E. 6th St., University, Tucson* ☎ *520/884–9018.*

BIRD-WATCHING

To check out the more than 200 species of birds living in or migrating through the park, begin by focusing your binoculars on the limbs of the saguaros, where many birds make their home. In general, early morning and early evening are the best times for sightings. In winter and spring, volunteer-led birding hikes begin at the visitor centers.

The finest areas to flock to in Saguaro East (the Rincon Mountain District) are the Desert Ecology Trail, where you may find rufous-winged sparrows, verdins, and Cooper's hawks along the washes, and the Javelina picnic area, where you'll most likely spot canyon wrens and black-chinned sparrows. At Saguaro West (the Tucson Mountain District), sit down on one of the visitor center benches and look for ash-throated flycatchers, Say's phoebes, curve-billed thrashers, and Gila woodpeckers. During the cooler months, keep a lookout for wintering neotropical migrants such as hummingbirds, swallows, orioles, and warblers.

TOURS

Borderland Tours. Bird-watching tours throughout the state and internationally are led by this company, whose owner, Richard Taylor, has written several photo field guides, including *Birds of Southeastern Arizona.* ⊠ *2550 W. Calle Padilla, Northwest, Tucson* ☎ *520/882–7650* ⊕ *www.borderland-tours.com.*

Wild Bird Store. This shop is an excellent resource for bird-watching information, feeders, books, and trail guides. ⊠ *3160 E. Fort Lowell Rd., Central, Tucson* ☎ *520/322–9466* ⊕ *www.wildbirdsonline.com.*

Wings. A Tucson-based company, Wings leads ornithological expeditions worldwide and locally. ⊠ *1643 N. Alvernon Way, 109, Central, Tucson* ☎ *520/320–9868, 866/547–9868* ⊕ *www.wingsbirds.com.*

A saguaro grows under the protection of another tree, such as a paloverde or mesquite, before superseding it.

HIKING

The park has more than 100 miles of trails. The shorter hikes, such as the Desert Discovery and Desert Ecology trails, are perfect for those looking to learn about the desert ecosystem without expending too much energy.

■TIP→ Rattlesnakes are commonly seen on trails; so are coyotes, javelinas, roadrunners, Gambel's quail, and desert spiny lizards. Hikers should keep their distance from all wildlife.

TOURS

Sierra Club. The Club's local chapter, The Rincon Group, welcomes out-of-towners on weekend hikes, ranging in levels of difficulty. ⊠ *738 N. 5th Ave., University, Tucson* ☎ *520/620–6401* ⊕ *www.arizona. sierraclub.org/rincon.*

SAGUARO WEST

EASY

Cactus Garden Trail. This 100-yard paved trail in front of the Saguaro East Visitor Center is wheelchair accessible, and has resting benches and interpretive signs about common desert plants. *Easy.* ⊠ *Trailhead next to Saguaro East Visitor Center, Saguaro East.*

FAMILY **Desert Discovery Trail.** Learn about plants and animals native to the region on this paved path in Saguaro West. The 0.5-mile loop is wheelchair accessible, and has resting benches and ramadas (wooden shelters that supply shade for your table). *Easy.* ⊠ *Trailhead 1 mile north of Red Hills Visitor Center, Saguaro West.*

Signal Hill Trail. This 0.25-mile trail in Saguaro West is an easy, rewarding ascent to ancient petroglyphs carved a millennium ago by the Hohokam people. *Easy.* ⊠ *Trailhead 4½ miles north of Red Hills Visitor Center on Bajada Loop Dr., Saguaro West.*

MODERATE

Sendero Esperanza Trail. Follow a sandy mine road for the first section of this 6-mile trail in Saguaro West, then ascend via a series of switchbacks to the top of a ridge and cross the Hugh Norris Trail. Descending on the other side, you'll meet up with the King Canyon Trail. The Esperanza ("Hope") Trail is often rocky and sometimes steep, but rewards include ruins of the Gould Mine, dating back to 1907. *Moderate.* ⊠ *Trailhead 1½ miles east of the intersection of Bajada Loop Dr. and Golden Gate Rd., Saguaro West.*

Sweetwater Trail. Though technically within Saguaro West, this trail is on the eastern edge of the district, and affords access to Wasson Peak from the eastern side of the Tucson Mountains. After gradually climbing 3.4 miles it ends at King Canyon Trail (which would then take you on a fairly steep 1.2 mile climb to Wasson Peak). Long and meandering, this little-used trail allows more privacy to enjoy the natural surroundings than some of the more frequently used trails. *Moderate.* ⊠ *Trailhead at western end of El Camino del Cerro Rd., Saguaro West.*

Valley View Overlook Trail. On clear days you can spot the distinctive slope of Picacho Peak from this 1.5-mile trail in Saguaro West. Even on an overcast day you'll be treated to splendid vistas of Avra Valley. *Moderate.* ⊠ *Trailhead 3 miles north of Red Hills Visitor Center on Bajada Loop Dr., Saguaro West.*

DIFFICULT

Fodor's Choice ★ **Hugh Norris Trail.** This 10-mile trail through the Tucson Mountains is one of the most impressive in the Southwest. It's full of switchbacks, and some sections are moderately steep, but at the top of 4,687-foot Wasson Peak you'll enjoy views of the saguaro forest spread across the *bajada* (the gently rolling hills at the base of taller mountains). *Difficult.* ⊠ *Trailhead 2½ miles north of Red Hills Visitor Center on Bajada Loop Dr., Saguaro West.*

King Canyon Trail. This 3.5-mile trail is the shortest, but steepest, route to the top of Wasson Peak in Saguaro West. It meets the Hugh Norris Trail less than half a mile from the summit. The trail, which begins across from the Arizona–Sonora Desert Museum, is named after the Copper King Mine. It leads past many scars from the search for mineral wealth. Look for petroglyphs in this area. *Difficult.* ⊠ *Trailhead 2 miles south of Red Hills Visitor Center, Saguaro West.*

SAGUARO EAST

EASY

Cactus Forest Trail. This 2.5-mile one-way loop drive in the east district is open to pedestrians, bicyclists, and equestrians. It is a moderately easy walk along a dirt path that passes historic lime kilns and a wide variety of Sonoran Desert vegetation. While walking this trail, keep in mind that it is one of the only off-road trails for bicyclists. *Easy.* ⊠ *Trailhead*

34

2 miles south of Saguaro East Visitor Center, off Cactus Forest Dr., Saguaro East.

FAMILY **Desert Ecology Trail.** Exhibits on this 0.25-mile loop near the Mica View picnic area explain how local plants and animals subsist on limited water. *Easy.* ⊠ *Trailhead 2 miles north of Saguaro East Visitor Center.*

Freeman Homestead Trail. Learn a bit about the history of homesteading in the region on this 1-mile loop. Look for owls living in the cliffs above as you make your way through the lowland vegetation. *Easy.* ⊠ *Trailhead at Javelina picnic area, 2 miles south of Saguaro East Visitor Center.*

GOOD READS

■ The *Tucson Hiking Guide,* by Betty Leavengood, is a useful and entertaining book with day hikes in the park.

■ Books that give a general introduction to the park include *Saguaro National Park,* by Doris Evans, and *Sonoran Desert: The Story Behind the Scenery,* by Christopher L. Helms.

■ *All About Saguaros,* by Carle Hodge and published by Arizona Highways Books, includes fabulous color photos of the cactus.

MODERATE

Douglas Spring Trail. This challenging 6-mile trail leads almost due east into the Rincon Mountains. After a half mile through a dense concentration of saguaros you reach the open desert. About 3 miles in is Bridal Wreath Falls, worth a slight detour in spring when melting snow creates a larger cascade. Blackened tree trunks at the Douglas Spring Campground are one of the few traces of a huge fire that swept through the area in 1989. *Moderate.* ⊠ *Trailhead at eastern end of Speedway Blvd., Saguaro East.*

Fodor's Choice **Hope Camp Trail.** Well worth the 7-mile round-trip trek, this Rincon Val-★ ley Area route rewards hikers with gorgeous views of the Tanque Verde Ridge and Rincon Peak. The trail is also open to mountain bicyclists. *Moderate.* ⊠ *Trailhead from Camino Loma Alta trailhead.*

DIFFICULT

Tanque Verde Ridge Trail. Be rewarded with spectacular scenery on this 15.4-mile trail through desert scrub, oak, alligator juniper, and pinyon pine at the 6,000-foot peak, where views of the surrounding mountain ranges from both sides of the ridge delight. *Difficult.* ⊠ *Trailhead at Javelina picnic area, 2 miles south of Saguaro East Visitor Center.*

WHAT'S NEARBY

NEARBY TOWNS

Saguaro stands as a protected desert oasis, with metropolitan **Tucson,** Arizona's second-largest city, lying between the two park sections. Spread over 227 miles, and with a population of nearly a half million, Tucson averages 340 days of sunshine a year.

NEARBY ATTRACTIONS

FAMILY
Fodor's Choice
★

Arizona–Sonora Desert Museum. The name "museum" is a bit misleading, since this delightful site is actually a zoo, aquarium, and botanical garden featuring the animals, plants and, yes, even fish of the Sonoran Desert. Hummingbirds, coatis, rattlesnakes, scorpions, bighorn sheep, bobcats, and Mexican wolves all busy themselves in ingeniously designed habitats.

An Earth Sciences Center has an artificial limestone cave to climb through and an excellent mineral display. The coyote and javelina (wild, piglike mammals with oddly oversize heads) exhibits have "invisible" fencing that separates humans from animals, and at the Raptor Free Flight show (October–April daily at 10 and 2), you can see the powerful birds soar and dive, untethered, inches above your head.

The restaurants are above average, and the gift shop, which carries books, jewelry, and crafts, is outstanding. ■**TIP➜** June through August, the museum stays open until 10 pm every Saturday, which provides a great opportunity to see nocturnal critters. ⊠ *2021 N. Kinney Rd., Westside, Tucson* ☎ *520/883–2702* ⊕ *www.desertmuseum.org* 🖅 *$14.50* ⊗ *Mar.–May, daily 7:30–5; June–Sept., daily 7–5; Oct.–Feb., daily 8:30–5.*

FAMILY
Fodor's Choice
★

Bear Canyon Trail. Also known as Seven Falls Trail, this route in Sabino Canyon is a three- to four-hour, 7.8-mile round trip that is moderately easy and fun, crossing the stream several times on the way up the canyon.

Be sure to bring plenty of water. Kids enjoy the boulder-hopping, and all are rewarded with pools and waterfalls as well as views at the top. The trailhead can be reached from the parking area by either taking a five-minute Bear Canyon Tram ride or walking the 1.8-mile tram route. *Easy.* ⊠ *Sabino Canyon Rd. at Sunrise Dr., Foothills, Tucson* ☎ *520/749–2861* ⊕ *www.fs.usda.gov/coronado.*

FAMILY
Colossal Cave Mountain Park. This limestone grotto 20 miles east of Tucson is the largest dry cavern in the world. Guides discuss the fascinating crystal formations and relate the many romantic tales surrounding the cave, including the legend that an enormous sum of money stolen in a stagecoach robbery is hidden here.

Forty-five-minute cave tours begin every 30 minutes and require a 0.5-mile walk and climbing 363 steps. The park includes a ranch area with trail rides ($30 per hour), a gemstone-sluicing area, a small museum, a desert tortoise habitat, nature trails, a butterfly garden, a snack bar, and a gift shop. Parking is $5 per vehicle. Take Broadway Boulevard or 22nd Street east to Old Spanish Trail. ⊠ *16721 E. Old Spanish Trail, Eastside, Tucson* ☎ *520/647–7275* ⊕ *www.colossalcave.com* 🖅 *Cave tour $13* ⊗ *Oct.–mid-Mar., daily 9–5; mid-Mar.–Sept., daily 8–5.*

FAMILY
Old Tucson. This film studio–theme park, originally built for the 1940 motion picture *Arizona,* has been used to shoot countless movies, such as *Rio Bravo* (1959) and *The Quick and the Dead* (1994), and the TV shows *Gunsmoke, Bonanza,* and *Highway to Heaven.* Actors in Western garb perform and roam the streets talking to visitors.

34

Youngsters enjoy the simulated gunfights, rides, stunt shows, and petting farm, while adults might appreciate the screenings of old Westerns, studio tour, and the little-bit-bawdy Grand Palace Hotel's Dance Hall Revue. There are plenty of places to eat and to buy souvenirs. Horseback riding is available for an additional charge. ⊠ *Tucson Mountain Park, 201 S. Kinney Rd., Westside, Tucson* ☎ *520/883–0100* ⊕ *www. oldtucson.com* 🖃 *$16.95* ☉ *Jan.–Apr., daily 10–5; May and Oct.–Dec., Fri.–Sun. 10-5* ☉ *Closed June–Sept.*

St. Augustine Cathedral. Although the imposing white-and-beige, late-19th-century, Spanish-style building was modeled after the Cathedral of Queretaro in Mexico, a number of its details reflect the desert setting: above the entryway, next to a bronze statue of St. Augustine, are carvings of local desert scenes with saguaro cacti, yucca, and prickly pears—look closely and you'll find the horned toad. Compared with the magnificent facade, the modernized interior is a bit disappointing. ■ **TIP→ For a distinctly Southwestern experience, attend the mariachi mass celebrated Sunday at 8 am.** ⊠ *192 S. Stone Ave., Downtown, Tucson* ☎ *520/623–6351* ⊕ *www.augustinecathedral.org/* 🖃 *Free* ☉ *Daily 7–6.*

AREA ACTIVITIES

SPORTS AND THE OUTDOORS
BALLOONING
Fleur de Tucson Balloon Tours. Operating out of the Northwest from October through April, this company arranges flights over the Tucson Mountains and Saguaro National Park West. ⊠ *4635 N. Caida Pl., Tucson* ☎ *520/403–8547* ⊕ *www.fleurdetucson.net.*

WHERE TO EAT

IN THE PARK

PICNIC AREAS
Mam-A-Gah. This is the most isolated picnic area in Saguaro West. It's on King Canyon Trail, a good area for birding and wildflower viewing. It's about a mile walk to reach the site, and the undeveloped trail isn't wheelchair accessible. ⊠ *King Canyon Trail, 1 mile from Kinney Rd., Saguaro West.*

Mica View. Talk about truth in advertising: This picnic area gives you an eyeful of Mica Mountain, the park's highest peak. None of the tables are in the shade. ⊠ *Cactus Forest Dr., 2 miles north of Saguaro East Visitor Center.*

Signal Hill. Because of the nearby petroglyphs, this is the park's most popular picnic site. Its many picnic tables, sprinkled around palo verde and mesquite trees, can accommodate large groups. ⊠ *Bajada Loop Dr., 4½ miles north of Red Hills Visitor Center, Saguaro West.*

OUTSIDE THE PARK

$ CAFÉ Fodor's Choice ★ 🍴 **Beyond Bread.** Twenty-seven varieties of bread are made at this bustling bakery with Central, Eastside, and Northwest locations, and highlights from the menu of generously-sized sandwiches include Annie's Addiction (hummus, tomato, sprouts, red onion, and cucumber) and Brad's Beef (roast beef, provolone, onion, green chilies, and Russian dressing); soups, salads, and breakfast items are equally scrumptious. Eat inside or on the patio, or order takeout, but be sure to splurge on one of the incredible desserts. The other locations—larger and just as busy—are at 6260 East Speedway Boulevard and 421 West Ina Road. [$] *Average main: $8* ✉ *3026 N. Campbell Ave., Central, Tucson* ☎ *520/322–9965* 🌐 *www.beyondbread.com* 🕒 *No dinner Sun.*

$$$$ SOUTHWESTERN 🍴 **The Grill at Hacienda del Sol.** Tucked into the Foothills and surrounded by spectacular flowers and cactus gardens, this special-occasion restaurant, a favorite among locals hosting out-of-town visitors, provides an alternative to the chili-laden dishes of most Southwestern nouvelle cuisine. Wild-mushroom bisque, grilled buffalo in dark chocolate mole, and pan-seared sea bass are among the menu choices at this luxurious guest ranch resort. Lower-priced tapas such as tequila-steamed mussels and carne asada tacos can be enjoyed on the more casual outdoor patio, accompanied by live flamenco guitar music on weekends. The lavish Sunday brunch buffet is worth a splurge. [$] *Average main: $38* ✉ *Hacienda del Sol Guest Ranch Resort, 5501 N. Hacienda Del Sol Rd., Foothills, Tucson* ☎ *800/728–6514* 🌐 *www.haciendadelsol.com.*

$ MEXICAN 🍴 **Mi Nidito.** A perennial favorite among locals (the wait is worth it), Mi Nidito—"my little nest"—has also hosted its share of visiting celebrities. Following President Clinton's lunch here, the rather hefty Presidential Plate (bean tostada, taco with barbecued meat, chiles rellenos, chicken enchilada, and beef tamale with rice and beans) was added to the menu. Top that off with the mango chimichangas for dessert, and you're talkin' executive privilege. [$] *Average main: $10* ✉ *1813 S. 4th Ave., South, Tucson* ☎ *520/622–5081* 🌐 *www.minidito.net* 🕒 *Closed Mon. and Tues.*

$$$ ITALIAN 🍴 **Vivace.** A nouvelle Italian bistro in the lovely St. Philip's Plaza, Vivace has long been a favorite with Tucsonans. Wild mushrooms and goat cheese in puff pastry is hard to resist as a starter. The fettuccini with grilled salmon is a nice, lighter alternative to such entrées as a rich osso buco. For dessert, the molten chocolate cake with spumoni is worth the 20 minutes it takes to create. Patio seating overlooking the pretty, flower-filled courtyard is especially inviting on warm evenings. [$] *Average main: $26* ✉ *4310 N. Campbell Ave., St. Philip's Plaza, Foothills, Tucson* ☎ *520/795–7221* 🌐 *www.vivacetucson.com* 🕒 *Closed Sun.*

$ AMERICAN 🍴 **Zinburger.** Have a glass of wine or a cocktail with your gourmet burger and fries at this high-energy, somewhat noisy, and unquestionably hip burger joint. Open until 11 pm on Friday and Saturday (late by Tucson standards), Zinburger delivers tempting burgers—try the Kobe beef with cheddar and wild mushrooms—and decadent milk shakes made of exotic combinations like dates and honey or melted chocolate with praline flakes. A few creative salads, including one with ahi tuna, round out the menu. The restaurant also has a second location on the northeast side of town. $ *Average main: $10* ✉ *1865 E. River Rd., Foothills, Tucson* ☎ *520/299–7799* ⊕ *www.foxrc.com.*

$$ ✕ **Zona 78.** Fresh food takes on a whole new meaning at this contempo-
ITALIAN rary bistro emphasizing inventive pizzas, pastas, and salads. The casual interior's focal point is a huge stone oven, where the pies are fired with toppings like Australian blue cheese, kalamata olives, sausage, and even chicken with peanut sauce. Whole-wheat crust is an option, and there are also baked salmon and chicken entrées. The house-made mozzarella is delectable, either on top of a pizza or in a salad with organic tomatoes. The newer eastside location at 7301 East Tanque Verde Road has the same low-key, neighborhood feel. $ *Average main: $15* ✉ *78 W. River Rd., Central, Tucson* ☎ *520/888–7878* ⊕ *www.zona78.com.*

WHERE TO STAY

OUTSIDE THE PARK

$$$$ ⊞ **Arizona Inn.** Although near the University and many sights, the beau-
HOTEL tifully landscaped lawns and gardens of this 1930 inn seem far from
Fodor'sChoice the hustle and bustle. **Pros:** unique historical property; emphasis on
★ service. **Cons:** rooms may not be modern enough for some; close to University Medical Center but long walk (1½ miles) from the main campus. $ *Rooms from: $329* ✉ *2200 E. Elm St., University, Tucson* ☎ *520/325–1541, 800/933–1093* ⊕ *www.arizonainn.com* ⌑ *72 rooms, 20 suites, 3 casitas* ⦵ *No meals.*

$$$ ⊞ **Casa Tierra.** For a real desert experience, head to this B&B on 5 acres
B&B/INN near the Desert Museum and Saguaro National Park West. **Pros:** peace-
Fodor'sChoice ful; great Southwest character. **Cons:** far from town (30-minute drive);
★ two-night minimum stay; closed in summer. $ *Rooms from: $165* ✉ *11155 W. Calle Pima, Westside, Tucson* ☎ *520/578–3058, 866/254–0006* ⊕ *www.casatierratucson.com* ⌑ *3 rooms, 1 suite* ⊙ *Closed mid-June–mid-Aug.* ⦵ *Breakfast.*

$$$$ ⊞ **Hacienda del Sol Guest Ranch Resort.** This 32-acre hideaway in the
RESORT Santa Catalina Foothills is a charming and more intimate alternative
Fodor'sChoice to the larger resorts. **Pros:** outstanding restaurant and bar; build-
★ ings and landscaping are stunningly beautiful. **Cons:** not enough resort amenities for some (no golf or spa, just a few massage rooms). $ *Rooms from: $209* ✉ *5501 N. Hacienda Del Sol Rd., Foothills, Tucson* ☎ *520/299–1501, 800/728–6514* ⊕ *www.haciendadelsol.com* ⌑ *22 rooms, 8 suites* ⦵ *No meals.*

$$ ⊞ **Hotel Congress.** This hotel built in 1919 has been artfully restored to
HOTEL its original Western version of art deco; it's now the center of Tucson's
Fodor'sChoice hippest scene and a great place to stay for younger or more adven-
★ turous visitors. **Pros:** prime location; good restaurant; funky and fun. **Cons:** no elevator to guest rooms; no TVs in rooms; noise from nightclub. $ *Rooms from: $125* ✉ *311 E. Congress St., Downtown, Tucson* ☎ *520/622–8848, 800/722–8848* ⊕ *www.hotelcongress.com* ⌑ *40 rooms* ⦵ *No meals.*

CLOSE UP

Best Campgrounds in Saguaro

There's no drive-up camping in the park. All six primitive campgrounds are in the eastern district and require a hike to reach—the shortest hikes are to Douglas Spring Campground (6 miles) and to Happy Valley (5 miles). All are open year-round. Pick up your backcountry camping permit ($6 per night) at the Saguaro East Visitor Center. Before choosing a camping destination, look over the relief map of hiking trails and the book of wilderness campground photos taken by park rangers. You can camp in the backcountry for a maximum of 14 days. Each site can accommodate up to six people. Reservations can be made via mail or in person up to two months in advance. Hikers are encouraged to set out before noon. If you haven't the time or the inclination to hike in, several more camping opportunities exist within a few miles of the park.

Douglas Spring. Getting to this 4,800-foot-elevation campground takes a not-too-rough 6-mile hike up the Douglas Spring Trail. ✉ *6 miles on Douglas Spring Trail, off Speedway Blvd.* ☎ *No phone.*

Grass Shack. This pretty campground is among juniper and small oak trees in a transitional area midway up Mica Mountain. ✉ *10.3 miles via Douglas Spring Trail to Manning Camp Trail* ☎ *No phone.*

Juniper Basin. Vegetation here is oak forest, and the expansive views are worth the challenging 7-mile ascent. ✉ *7 miles on Tanque Verde Ridge Trail* ☎ *No phone.*

$$$$ HOTEL ALL-INCLUSIVE FAMILY

🏨 **Tanque Verde Ranch.** The most upscale of Tucson's guest ranches and one of the oldest in the country, the Tanque Verde sits on 640 beautiful acres in the Rincon Mountains next to Saguaro National Park East. **Pros:** authentic Western experience; loads of all-inclusive activities; great riding. **Cons:** expensive; at the eastern edge of town; all-inclusive package excludes alcohol. [$] *Rooms from: $350* ✉ *14301 E. Speedway Blvd., Eastside, Tucson* ☎ *520/296–6275, 800/234–3833* 🌐 *www.tanqueverderanch.com* 🛏 *49 rooms, 25 suites* 🍴 *All-inclusive.*

$$$$ HOTEL ALL-INCLUSIVE Fodor's Choice ★

🏨 **White Stallion Ranch.** A 3,000-acre working cattle ranch run by the hospitable True family since 1965, this place is the real deal. **Pros:** solid dude-ranch experience; very charming hosts; satisfying for families as well as singles or couple; airport shuttle. **Cons:** no TV in rooms; alcohol not included in the rate—you must pay extra, or bring your own. [$] *Rooms from: $350* ✉ *9251 W. Twin Peaks Rd., Northwest, Tucson* ☎ *520/297–0252, 888/977–2624* 🌐 *www.wsranch.com* 🛏 *24 rooms, 17 suites* 🍴 *All-inclusive.*

SEQUOIA AND KINGS CANYON NATIONAL PARKS

WELCOME TO
SEQUOIA AND KINGS CANYON

TOP REASONS TO GO

★ **Gentle giants:** You'll feel small—in a good way—walking among some of the world's largest living things in Sequoia's Giant Forest and Kings Canyon's Grant Grove.

★ **Because it's there:** You can't even glimpse it from the main part of Sequoia, but the sight of majestic Mt. Whitney is worth the trek to the eastern face of the High Sierra.

★ **Underground exploration:** Far older even than the giant sequoias, the gleaming limestone formations in Crystal Cave will draw you along dark, marble passages.

★ **A grander-than-Grand Canyon:** Drive the twisting Kings Canyon Scenic Byway down into the jagged, granite Kings River Canyon, deeper in parts than the Grand Canyon.

★ **Regal solitude:** To spend a day or two hiking in a subalpine world of your own, pick one of the 11 trailheads at Mineral King.

1 Giant Forest–Lodgepole Village. The most heavily visited area of Sequoia lies at the base of the "thumb" portion of Kings Canyon National Park and contains major sights such as Giant Forest, General Sherman Tree, Crystal Cave, and Moro Rock.

2 Grant Grove Village–Redwood Canyon. The "thumb" of Kings Canyon National Park is its busiest section, where Grant Grove, General Grant Tree, Panoramic Point, and Big Stump are the main attractions.

3 Cedar Grove. The drive through the high-country portion of Kings Canyon National Park to Cedar Grove Village, on the canyon floor, reveals magnificent granite formations of varied hues. Rock meets river in breathtaking fashion a few miles beyond Cedar Grove in Zumwalt Meadow.

4 Mineral King. In the southeast section of Sequoia, the highest road-accessible part of the park is a good place to hike, camp, and soak up the unspoiled grandeur of the Sierra Nevada.

5 Mount Whitney. The highest peak in the Lower 48 stands on the eastern edge of Sequoia; to get there from Giant Forest you must either backpack eight days through the mountains or drive nearly 400 miles around the park to its other side.

KEY

🏕	*Ranger Station*
⛺	*Campground*
🍱	*Picnic Area*
🍴	*Restaurant*
🏨	*Lodge*
🥾	*Trailhead*
🚻	*Restrooms*
⚜	*Scenic Viewpoint*
⋯⋯	*Walking/Hiking Trails*

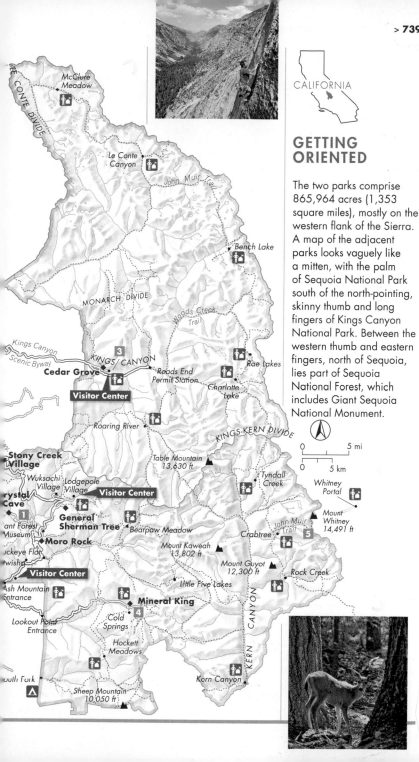

McClure
Meadow

LE CONTE DIVIDE

Le Conte
Canyon

John Muir Trail

CALIFORNIA

Bench Lake

GETTING
ORIENTED

MONARCH DIVIDE

Woods Creek Trail

Kings Canyon
Scenic Byway

KINGS CANYON

3

Cedar Grove

Roads End
Permit Station

Rae Lakes

Charlotte
Lake

Visitor Center

Roaring River

KINGS-KERN DIVIDE

The two parks comprise
865,964 acres (1,353
square miles), mostly on the
western flank of the Sierra.
A map of the adjacent
parks looks vaguely like
a mitten, with the palm
of Sequoia National Park
south of the north-pointing,
skinny thumb and long
fingers of Kings Canyon
National Park. Between the
western thumb and eastern
fingers, north of Sequoia,
lies part of Sequoia
National Forest, which
includes Giant Sequoia
National Monument.

35

**Stony Creek
Village**

Table Mountain
13,630 ft

Tyndall
Creek

0   5 mi

0   5 km

Wuksachi
Village Lodgepole
Village

Visitor Center

Whitney
Portal

**Crystal
Cave**

1

**General
Sherman Tree**

Bearpaw Meadow

Mount
Whitney
14,491 ft

Giant Forest
Museum

Moro Rock

Crabtree

John Muir Trail

5

Buckeye Flat

Mount Kaweah
13,802 ft

twisho

Mount Guyot
12,300 ft

Rock Creek

Visitor Center

Little Five Lakes

Ash Mountain
Entrance

Mineral King

KERN CANYON

Lookout Point
Entrance

4

Cold
Springs

Hockett
Meadows

South Fork

Sheep Mountain
10,050 ft

Kern Canyon

Updated by
Daniel Mangin

Although *Sequoiadendron giganteum* is the formal name for the redwoods that grow here, everyone outside the classroom calls them sequoias, big trees, or Sierra redwoods. Their monstrously thick trunks and branches, remarkably shallow root systems, and neck-craning heights are almost impossible to believe, as is the fact they can live for more than 2,500 years. Many of these towering marvels are in the Giant Forest stretch of Generals Highway, which connects Sequoia and Kings Canyon national parks.

Next to or a few miles off the 43-mile Generals Highway are most of Sequoia National Park's main attractions and Grant Grove Village, the orientation hub for Kings Canyon National Park. The two parks share a boundary that runs from the Central Valley in the west, where the Sierra Nevada foothills begin, to the range's dramatic eastern ridges. Kings Canyon has two portions: the smaller is shaped like a bent finger and encompasses Grant Grove Village and Redwood Mountain Grove (the two parks' largest concentration of sequoias), and the larger is home to stunning Kings River Canyon, whose vast, unspoiled peaks and valleys are a backpacker's dream. Sequoia is in one piece and includes Mt. Whitney, the highest point in the Lower 48 states (although it is impossible to see from the western part of the park and is a chore to ascend from either side).

SEQUOIA AND KINGS CANYON PLANNER

WHEN TO GO

The best times to visit are late spring and early fall, when temperatures are moderate and crowds thin. Summertime can draw hordes of tourists to see the giant sequoias, and the few, narrow roads mean congestion at peak holiday times. If you must visit in summer, go during the week. By contrast, in wintertime you may feel as though you have the parks all to yourself. But because of heavy snows, sections of the main park roads can be closed without warning, and low-hanging clouds can move in and obscure mountains and valleys for days. From mid-November to late April, check road and weather conditions before venturing out.

Temperatures in the chart below are for the mid-level elevations, generally between 4,000 and 7,000 feet.

AVG. HIGH/LOW TEMPS.

JAN.	FEB.	MAR.	APR.	MAY	JUNE
42/24	44/25	46/26	51/30	58/36	68/44
JULY	AUG.	SEPT.	OCT.	NOV.	DEC.
76/51	76/50	71/45	61/38	50/31	44/27

FESTIVALS AND EVENTS

MARCH **Blossom Days Festival.** On the first Saturday of March, communities along Fresno County's Blossom Trail celebrate the flowering of the area's orchards, citrus groves, and vineyards. ☎ *559/262–4271* ⊕ *www.gofresnocounty.com/blossomtrail/blossomindex.asp.*

APRIL **Jazzaffair.** On the second weekend of April, a festival of mostly traditional jazz takes place at several venues just south of the parks. ☎ *559/561–4549* ⊕ *www.jazzaffair.info.*

MAY **Woodlake Rodeo.** The local Lions Club sponsors this rousing rodeo that draws large crowds to Woodlake on Mother's Day weekend. ☎ *559/564–8555* ⊕ *www.woodlakelionsrodeo.com.*

OCTOBER **Big Fresno Fair.** Over 12 days in October, agricultural, home-arts, and other competitions, plus horse racing and a carnival make for a lively county fair. ☎ *559/650–3247* ⊕ *www.fresnofair.com.*

DECEMBER **Annual Trek to the Tree.** On the second Sunday of December, thousands of carolers gather at the base of General Grant Tree, the nation's official Christmas tree. ☎ *559/565–4307.*

PLANNING YOUR TIME

SEQUOIA NATIONAL PARK IN ONE DAY

After spending the night in Visalia or Three Rivers—and provided your vehicle's length does not exceed 22 feet—shove off early on Route 198 to Sequoia National Park's **Ash Mountain entrance.** Pull over at the **Hospital Rock** picnic area to gaze up at the imposing granite formation of Moro Rock, which you later will climb. Heed signs that advise "10 mph" around tight turns as you climb 3,500 feet on **Generals Highway** to the **Giant Forest Museum.** Spend a half hour there, then examine some firsthand by circling the lovely **Round Meadow** on the **Big Trees Trail,** to which you must walk from the museum or from its parking lot across the road.

Get back in your car and continue a few miles north on Generals Highway to see the jaw-dropping **General Sherman Tree.** Then set off on the **Congress Trail** so that you can be further awed by the Senate and House big-tree clusters. Buy lunch at the **Lodgepole** complex, 2 miles to the north, and eat at the nearby **Pinewood** picnic area. Now you're ready for the day's big exercise, the mounting of **Moro Rock.**

You can drive there or, if it is summer, park at the museum lot and take the free shuttle. Count on spending at least an hour for the 350-step ascent and descent, with a pause on top to appreciate the 360-degree view. Get back in the car, or on the shuttle, and proceed past the **Tunnel Log** to **Crescent Meadow**. Spend a relaxing hour or two strolling on the trails that pass by, among other things, **Tharp's Log**. By now you've probably renewed your appetite; head to **Wolverton Barbecue** (summer evenings only) or the restaurant at **Wuksachi Lodge**.

KINGS CANYON NATIONAL PARK IN ONE DAY

Enter the park via the **Kings Canyon Scenic Byway** (Route 180), having spent the night in Fresno or Visalia. Better yet, wake up already in **Grant Grove Village**, perhaps in the **John Muir Lodge**. Stock up for a picnic with takeout food from the **Grant Grove Restaurant,** or purchase prepackaged food from the nearby market. Drive east a mile to see the **General Grant Tree** and compact **Grant Grove's** other sequoias. If it's no later than midmorning, motor on up to the short trail at **Panoramic Point,** for a great view of Hume Lake and the High Sierra. Either way, return to Route 180 and continue east. Stop at Junction View to take in several noteworthy peaks that tower over Kings Canyon. From here, visit **Boyden Cavern** or continue to **Cedar Grove Village,** pausing along the way for a gander at **Grizzly Falls**. Eat at a table by the **South Fork of the Kings River,** or on the deck off the Cedar Grove Snack Bar. Now you are ready for the day's highlight, strolling **Zumwalt Meadow,** which lies a few miles past the village.

After you have enjoyed that short trail and the views it offers of **Grand Sentinel** and **North Dome,** you might as well go the extra mile to **Roads End,** where backpackers embark for the High Sierra wilderness. Make the return trip—with a quick stop at **Roaring River Falls**—past Grant Grove and briefly onto southbound **Generals Highway**. Pull over at the **Redwood Mountain Overlook** and use binoculars to look down upon the world's largest sequoia grove, then drive another couple of miles to the **Kings Canyon Overlook,** where you can survey some of what you have done today. If you've made reservations and have time, have a late dinner at **Wuksachi Lodge**.

GETTING HERE AND AROUND

CAR TRAVEL

Sequoia is 36 miles east of Visalia on Route 198; Grant Grove Village in Kings Canyon is 56 miles east of Fresno on Route 180. There is no automobile entrance on the eastern side of the Sierra. Routes 180 and 198 are connected by Generals Highway, a paved two-lane road that sometimes sees delays at peak times due to ongoing improvements. The road is extremely narrow and steep from Route 198 to Giant Forest, so keep an eye on your engine temperature gauge, as the incline and congestion can cause vehicles to overheat; to avoid overheated brakes, use low gears on downgrades.

If you are traveling in an RV or with a trailer, study the restrictions on these vehicles. Do not travel beyond Potwisha Campground on Route 198 with an RV longer than 22 feet; take straighter, easier Route 180 instead. Maximum vehicle length on Generals Highway is 40 feet, or 50 feet combined length for vehicles with trailers.

Generals Highway between Lodgepole and Grant Grove is sometimes closed by snow. The Mineral King Road from Route 198 into southern Sequoia National Park is closed 2 miles below Atwell Mill either on November 1 or after the first heavy snow. The Buckeye Flat–Middle Fork Trailhead Road is closed from mid-October to mid-April when the Buckeye Flat Campground closes. The lower Crystal Cave Road is closed when the cave closes in November. Its upper 2 miles, as well as the Panoramic Point and Moro Rock–Crescent Meadow roads, close with the first heavy snow. Because of the danger of rockfall, the portion of Kings Canyon Scenic Byway east of Grant Grove closes in winter. For current road and weather conditions, call ☎ 559/565–3341.

■TIP→ Snowstorms are common from late October through April. Unless you have a four-wheel-drive vehicle with snow tires, you should carry chains and know how to install them.

PARK ESSENTIALS

PARK FEES AND PERMITS

35

The admission fee is $20 per vehicle and $10 for those who enter by bus, on foot, bicycle, motorcycle, or horse; it is valid for seven days in both parks. U.S. residents over the age of 62 pay $10 for a lifetime pass, and permanently disabled U.S. residents are admitted free.

If you plan to camp in the backcountry, you need a permit, which costs $15 for hikers or $30 for stock users (e.g., horseback riders). One permit covers the group. Availability of permits depends upon trailhead quotas. Reservations are accepted by mail or fax for a $15 processing fee, beginning March 1, and must be made at least 14 days in advance (☎ 559/565–3766). Without a reservation, you may still get a permit on a first-come, first-served basis starting at 1 pm the day before you plan to hike. For more information on backcountry camping or travel with pack animals (horses, mules, burros, or llamas), contact the Wilderness Permit Office (☎ 530/565–3761).

PARK HOURS

The parks are open 24/7 year-round. They are in the Pacific time zone.

CELL-PHONE RECEPTION

Cell-phone reception is poor to nonexistent in the higher elevations and spotty even on portions of Generals Highway, where you can (on rare clear days) see the Central Valley. Public telephones may be found at the park entrance stations, visitor centers, ranger stations, some trailheads, and at all restaurants and lodging facilities in the park.

RESTAURANTS

In Sequoia and Kings Canyon national parks, you can treat yourself (and the family) to a high-quality meal in a wonderful setting in the Peaks restaurant at Wuksachi Lodge, but otherwise you should keep your expectations modest. A good strategy is to embrace outdoor eating. You can grab bread, spreads, drinks, and fresh produce at one of several small grocery stores, or get take-out food from the Grant Grove Restaurant, the Cedar Grove snack bar, or one of the two small Lodgepole eateries. The summertime Wolverton Barbecue is a hybrid experience between dining in and picnicking out; the all-you-can-eat feast is staged on a patio that overlooks a sublime meadow.

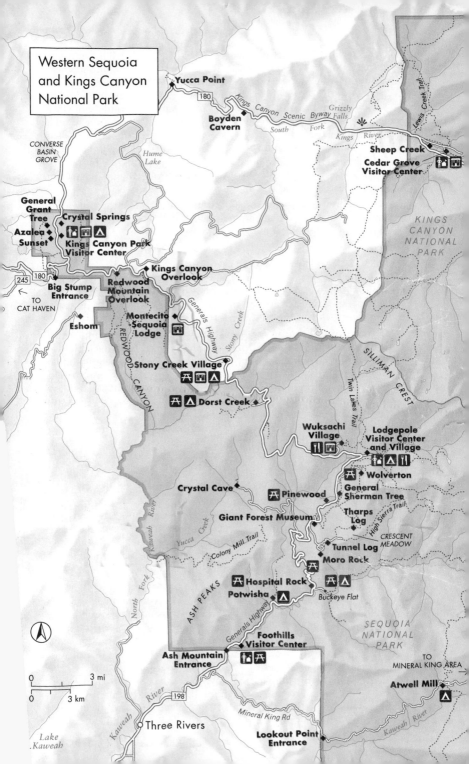

Between the parks and just off Generals Highway, the Montecito Sequoia Lodge has a year-round buffet.

Prices in the reviews are the average cost of a main course at dinner, or if dinner is not served, at lunch.

HOTELS

Hotel accommodations in Sequoia and Kings Canyon are limited, and—although they are clean and comfortable—tend to lack much in-room character. Keep in mind, however, that the extra money you spend on lodging here is offset by the time you'll save by being inside the parks. You won't be faced with a 60- to 90-minute commute from the less-expensive motels in Three Rivers (by far the most charming option), Visalia, and Fresno. Reserve as far in advance as you can, especially for summertime stays.

Prices in the reviews are the lowest cost of a standard double room in high season. For expanded reviews, facilities, and current deals, visit Fodors.com.

VISITOR INFORMATION

NATIONAL PARK SERVICE

Sequoia and Kings Canyon National Parks ⊠ *47050 Generals Hwy. (Rte. 198), Three Rivers* ☎ *559/565–3341* ⊕ *www.nps.gov/seki/planyourvisit/things2know.htm.*

ADDITIONAL CONTACTS

Delaware North Park Services. This concessionaire operates most of the lodgings and visitor services in Sequoia and Kings Canyon. ☎ *559/565–4070* ⊕ *www.visitsequoia.com.*

Sequoia Natural History Association. The association operates Crystal Cave and the Pear Lake Ski Hut, publishes the parks' newspaper, provides educational materials, and conducts daytime and evening programs. ☎ *559/565–3759* ⊕ *www.sequoiahistory.org.*

SEQUOIA VISITOR CENTERS

Foothills Visitor Center. Exhibits here focus on the foothills and resource issues facing the parks. You can pick up books, maps, and a list of ranger-led walks, and get wilderness permits. ⊠ *47050 Generals Hwy. (Rte. 198), 1 mile north of Ash Mountain entrance* ☎ *559/565–4212* ☯ *Daily 8–4:30.*

Lodgepole Visitor Center. Along with exhibits on the area's history, geology, and wildlife, the center screens an outstanding 22-minute film about bears. You can buy books, maps, and tickets to cave tours and the Wolverton barbecue here. ⊠ *Generals Hwy. (Rte. 198), 21 miles north of Ash Mountain entrance* ☎ *559/565–4436* ☯ *Late May–early Sept., daily 7–7; days and hrs vary Apr.–late May and early Sept.–Dec. Closed Jan.–Mar.* ☞ *Shuttle: Giant Forest or Wuksachi-Lodgepole-Dorst.*

Mineral King Ranger Station. The station's small visitor center has exhibits on area history; wilderness permits and some books and maps are available. ⊠ *Mineral King Rd., 24 miles east of Rte. 198, Sequoia National Park* ☎ *559/565–3768* ☯ *Late May–mid-Sept., daily 8–4 or 4:30.*

KINGS CANYON VISITOR CENTERS

Cedar Grove Visitor Center. Off the main road and behind the Sentinel Campground, this small ranger station has books and maps, plus information about hikes and other activities. ⊠ *Kings Canyon Scenic Byway, 30 miles east of Rte. 180/198 junction* ☎ *559/565–3793* ⊙ *Late May–early Sept., Tues.–Sun. 9–5.*

Kings Canyon Park Visitor Center. The center's 15-minute film and various exhibits provide an overview of the park's canyon, sequoias, and human history. Books, maps, and weather advice are dispensed here, as are (if available) free wilderness permits. ⊠ *Grant Grove Village, Generals Hwy. (Rte. 198), 3 miles northeast of Rte. 180, Big Stump entrance* ☎ *559/565–4307* ⊙ *Mid-May–early Sept., daily 8–5; hrs vary rest of year.*

SEQUOIA NATIONAL PARK

EXPLORING

SCENIC DRIVES

Fodor's Choice ★ **Generals Highway.** One of California's most scenic drives, this 43-mile road is the main asphalt artery between Sequoia and Kings Canyon national parks. Some portions are also signed as Route 180, others as Route 198. Named after the landmark Grant and Sherman trees that leave so many visitors awestruck, Generals Highway runs from Sequoia's Foothills Visitor Center north to Kings Canyon's Grant Grove Village. Along the way, it passes the turnoff to Crystal Cave, the Giant Forest Museum, Lodgepole Village, and other popular attractions. The lower portion, from Hospital Rock to the Giant Forest, is especially steep and winding. If your vehicle is 22 feet or longer, avoid that stretch by entering the parks via Route 180 (from Fresno) rather than Route 198 (from Visalia or Three Rivers). ■ TIP→ Take your time on this road—there's a lot to see, and wildlife can scamper across at any time.

Mineral King Road. Vehicles longer than 22 feet are prohibited on this side road into southern Sequoia National Park, and for good reason: it contains 589 twists and turns, according to one reputable source. Anticipating an average speed of 20 mph is optimistic. The scenery is splendid as you climb nearly 6,000 feet from Three Rivers to the Mineral King Area. In addition to maneuvering the blind curves and narrow stretches, you might find yourself sharing the pavement with bears, rattlesnakes, and even softball-size spiders. Allow 90 minutes each way. ■ TIP→ The road is usually open from late May through October. ⊠ *East off Sierra Dr. (Rte. 198), 3.5 miles northeast of Three Rivers, Sequoia National Forest.*

SCENIC STOPS

Sequoia National Park is all about the trees, and to understand the scale of these giants you must walk among them. If you do nothing else, get out of the car for a short stroll through one of the groves. But there is much more to the park than the trees. Try to access one of the vista points that provide a panoramic view over the forested mountains. Generals Highway (on Routes 198 and 180) will be your route to most of the park's sights. A few short spur roads lead from the highway to some sights, and Mineral King Road branches off Route 198 to enter the park at Lookout Point, winding east from there to park's the southernmost section.

Auto Log. Before its wood showed signs of severe rot, cars drove right on top of this giant fallen sequoia. Now it's a great place to pose for pictures or shoot a video. ⊠ *Moro Rock–Crescent Meadow Rd., 1 mile south of Giant Forest.*

35

Crescent Meadow. A sea of ferns signals your arrival at what John Muir called the "gem of the Sierra." Walk around for an hour or two and you might decide that the Scotland-born naturalist was exaggerating a wee bit, but the verdant meadow is quite pleasant and you just might see a bear. ■ TIP➔ Wildflowers bloom here throughout the summer. ⊠ *End of Moro Rock–Crescent Meadow Rd., 2.6 miles east off Generals Hwy.* ⟲ Shuttle: *Moro Rock–Crescent Meadow.*

Fodor'sChoice **Crystal Cave.** One of more than 200 caves in Sequoia and Kings Canyon, Crystal Cave is composed largely of marble, the result of limestone being hardened under heat and pressure. It contains several eye-popping formations. There used to be more, but some were damaged or obliterated by early-20th-century dynamite blasting. You can only see the cave on a tour. The Daily Tour ($15), a great overview, takes about 50 minutes. To immerse yourself in the cave experience—at times you'll be crawling on your belly—book the exhilarating Wild Cave Tour ($130). ■ TIP➔ Purchase Daily Tour tickets at either the Foothills or Lodgepole visitor center; they're not sold at the cave itself. ⊠ *Crystal Cave Rd., off Generals Hwy.* ☎ 559/565–3759 ⊕ *www. sequoiahistory.org* ⊡ $15 ⊙ *Mid-May–Nov., daily 10–4.*

Fodor'sChoice **General Sherman Tree.** The 274.9-foot-tall General Sherman is one of the world's tallest and oldest sequoias, and it ranks no. 1 in volume, adding the equivalent of a 60-foot-tall tree every year to its approximately 52,500 cubic feet of mass. The tree doesn't grow taller, though—it's dead at the top. A short, wheelchair-accessible trail leads to the tree from Generals Highway, but the main trail (0.5 mile) winds down from a parking lot off Wolverton Road. ■ TIP➔ The walk back up the main trail is steep, but benches along the way provide rest for the short of breath. ⊠ *Wolverton Rd., off Generals Hwy. (Rte. 198)* ⟲ Shuttle: *Giant Forest or Wolverton–Sherman Tree.*

Mineral King Area. A subalpine valley of fir, pine, and sequoia trees, Mineral King sits at 7,800 feet at the end of a steep, winding road (⇨ *Scenic Drives, above*). This is the highest point to which you can drive in the park. ⊠ *Mineral King Rd., 25 miles east of Generals Hwy. (Rte. 198).*

Fodor'sChoice **Moro Rock.** Sequoia National Park's best non-tree attraction offers pan-
★ oramic views to those fit and determined enough to mount its 350 or so steps. In a case where the journey rivals the destination, Moro's stone stairway is so impressive in its twisty inventiveness that it's on the National Register of Historic Places. The rock's 6,725-foot summit overlooks the Middle Fork Canyon, sculpted by the Kaweah River and approaching the depth of Arizona's Grand Canyon, although smoggy, hazy air often compromises the view. ⊠ *Moro Rock–Crescent Meadow Rd., 2 miles east off Generals Hwy. (Rte. 198) to parking area ☞ Shuttle: Moro Rock–Crescent Meadow.*

Tunnel Log. This 275-foot tree fell in 1937, and soon a 17-foot-wide, 8-foot-high hole was cut through it for vehicular passage (not to mention the irresistible photograph) that continues today. Large vehicles take the nearby bypass. ⊠ *Moro Rock–Crescent Meadow Rd., 2 miles east of Generals Hwy. (Rte. 198) ☞ Shuttle: Moro Rock–Crescent Meadow.*

EDUCATIONAL OFFERINGS

Educational programs at the parks include museum-style exhibits, ranger- and naturalist-led talks and walks, film and other programs, and sightseeing tours, most of them conducted by either the park service or the nonprofit Sequoia Natural History Association. Exhibits at the visitor centers and the Giant Forest Museum focus on different aspects of the park: its history, wildlife, geology, climate, and vegetation—most notably the giant sequoias. Weekly notices about programs are posted at the visitor centers and elsewhere.

EXHIBITS

Giant Forest Museum. Well-imagined and interactive displays at this worthwhile stop provide the basics about sequoias, of which there are 2,161 with diameters exceeding 10 feet in the approximately 2,000-acre Giant Forest. ⊠ *Generals Hwy., 4 miles south of Lodgepole Visitor Center ☎ 559/565–4480 ☒ Free ☉ Late-May–early-Sept., daily 9–5 (sometimes until 6); days and hrs vary rest of yr; mid-Oct.–mid-May open weekends and holidays only ☞ Shuttle: Giant Forest or Moro Rock–Crescent Meadow.*

PROGRAMS AND SEMINARS

Evening Programs. Film and slide shows and evening campfire lectures about Sequoia and Kings Canyon take place often during the summer. The popular Wonders of the Night Sky programs celebrate the often-stunning views of the heavens experienced at both parks. ☎ 559/565–3341 ⊕ *www.sequoiahistory.org/snhacalendar.asp ☉ Locations and hrs vary.*

Free Nature Programs. Almost any summer day, half-hour to 1½-hour ranger talks and walks explore subjects such as the life of the sequoia, the geology of the park, and the habits of bears. Giant Forest, Lodgepole Visitor Center, Wuksachi Village, and Dorst Creek Campground are frequent starting points. Check bulletin boards throughout the park for the week's offerings.

Seminars. Expert naturalists lead seminars on a range of topics, including birds, wildflowers, geology, botany, photography, park history, backpacking, and pathfinding. Reservations are recommended. Information about times and prices is available at the visitor centers or through the Sequoia Natural History Association. ☎ *559/565–3759* ⊕ *www.sequoiahistory.org.*

TOURS

Fodor's Choice **Sequoia Field Institute.** The Sequoia Natural History Association's
★ highly regarded educational division conducts single-day and multi-day "EdVenture" tours that include backpacking hikes, natural-history walks, and kayaking excursions. ⊠ *47050 Generals Hwy., Unit 10, Three Rivers* ☎ *559/565–4251* ⊕ *www.sequoiahistory.org.*

Sequoia Sightseeing Tours. This operator's friendly, knowledgeable guides conduct interpretive sightseeing tours in a 10-passenger van. Reservations are essential. The company also offers private tours of Kings Canyon. ⊠ *Three Rivers* ☎ *559/561–4489* ⊕ *www.sequoiatours.com* ⊡ *$65 half-day tour, $88 full-day tour.*

35

SPORTS AND THE OUTDOORS

The best way to see Sequoia is to take a hike. Unless you do so, you'll miss out on the up-close grandeur of mist wafting between deeply scored, red-orange tree trunks bigger than you've ever seen. If it's winter, put on some snowshoes or cross-country skis and plunge into the snow-swaddled woodland. There are not too many other outdoor options: no off-road driving is allowed in the parks, and no special provisions have been made for bicycles. Boating, rafting, and snowmobiling are also prohibited.

BICYCLING

Steep, winding roads and shoulders that are either narrow or nonexistent make bicycling here more of a danger than a pleasure. Outside of campgrounds, you are not allowed to pedal on unpaved roads.

BIRD-WATCHING

More than 200 species of birds inhabit Sequoia and Kings Canyon national parks. Not seen in most parts of the United States, the white-headed woodpecker and the pileated woodpecker are common in most mid-elevation areas here. There are also many hawks and owls, including the renowned spotted owl. Species are diverse in both parks due to the changes in elevation, and range from warblers, kingbirds, thrushes, and sparrows in the foothills to goshawk, blue grouse, red-breasted nuthatch, and brown creeper at the highest elevations. Ranger-led bird-watching tours are held on a sporadic basis. Call the park's main information number to find out more about these tours. The Sequoia Natural History Association (☎ *559/565–3759* ⊕ *www.sequoiahistory.org*) also has information about bird-watching in the southern Sierra.

CROSS-COUNTRY SKIING

For a one-of-a-kind experience, cut through the groves of mammoth sequoias in Giant Forest. Some of the Crescent Meadow trails are suitable for skiing as well; none of the trails is groomed. You can park at Giant Forest. Note that roads can be precarious in bad weather. Some advanced trails begin at Wolverton.

Wuksachi Lodge. Rent skis here. Depending on snowfall amounts, instruction may also be available. Reservations are recommended. Marked trails cut through Giant Forest, about 5 miles south of the lodge. ☒ *Off Generals Hwy. (Rte. 198), 2 miles north of Lodgepole* ☎ *559/565–4070* ☾ *Nov.–May (unless no snow), daily 9–4* ☞ *Shuttle: Wuksachi-Lodgepole-Dorst.*

FISHING

There's limited trout fishing in the creeks and rivers from late April to mid-November. The Kaweah River is a popular spot; check at visitor centers for open and closed waters. Some of the park's secluded back-country lakes have good fishing. A California fishing license, required for persons 16 and older, costs about $15 for one day, $23 for two days, and $46 for 10 days (discounts are available for state residents and others). For park regulations, closures, and restrictions, call the parks at ☎ *559/565–3341* or stop at a visitor center. Licenses and fishing tackle are usually available in Lodgepole.

California Department of Fish and Game. The department supplies fishing licenses and provides a full listing of regulations. ☎ *916/653–7661* ⊕ *www.dfg.ca.gov.*

HIKING

The best way to see the park is to hike it. The grandeur and majesty of the Sierra is best seen up close. Carry a hiking map and plenty of water. Visitor center gift shops sell maps and trail books and pamphlets. Check with rangers for current trail conditions, and be aware of rapidly changing weather. As a rule of thumb, plan on covering about a mile per hour.

EASY

Big Trees Trail. This one's a must, as it does not take long to stroll and the setting is spectacular: beautiful Round Meadow surrounded by many mature sequoias, with well-thought-out interpretive signs along the path that explain the ecology on display. The 0.7-mile Big Trees Trail is wheelchair-accessible. Parking at the trailhead lot off Generals Highway is for cars with handicap placards only. The round-trip loop from the Giant Forest Museum is about a mile long. *Easy.* ☒ *Trailhead off Generals Hwy. (Rte. 198), near the Giant Forest Museum* ☞ *Shuttle: Giant Forest.*

Fodor's Choice ★ **Congress Trail.** This 2-mile trail, arguably the best hike in the parks in terms of natural beauty, is a paved loop that begins near General Sherman Tree. You'll get close-up views of more big trees here than on any other Sequoia hike. Watch for the clusters known as the House and Senate. The President Tree, also on the trail, supplanted the General Grant Tree in 2012 as the world's second largest in volume (behind the General Sherman). ■TIP→ An offshoot of the Congress Trail leads to Crescent Meadow, where in summer you can catch a free shuttle back to the Sherman parking lot. *Easy.* ☒ *Trailhead off Generals Hwy. (Rte. 198), 2 miles north of Giant Forest* ☞ *Shuttle: Giant Forest.*

Crescent Meadow Trails. A 1.8-mile trail loops around lush Crescent Meadow past Tharp's Log, a cabin built from a fire-hollowed sequoia. ■TIP→ Brilliant wildflowers bloom here in midsummer. *Easy.* ☒ *Trailhead at the end of Moro Rock–Crescent Meadow Rd., 2.6 miles east off Generals Hwy. (Rte. 198)* ☞ *Shuttle: Moro Rock–Crescent Meadow.*

Muir Grove Trail. You will attain solitude and possibly see a bear or two on this unheralded gem of a hike, a 4-mile round trip from the Dorst Creek Campground. The remote grove is small but indescribably lovely, its soundtrack provided solely by nature. ■ TIP➔ The trailhead is subtly marked. In summer, park in the amphitheater lot and walk down toward the group campsite area. *Easy.* ☒ *Trailhead at Dorst Creek Campground, Generals Hwy. (Rte. 198), 8 miles north of Lodgepole Visitor Center* ☞ *Shuttle: Lodgepole-Wuksachi-Dorst.*

MODERATE

Little Baldy Trail. Climbing 700 vertical feet in 1.75 miles of switchbacking, this trail ends at a granite dome with a great view of the peaks of the Mineral King area and the Great Western Divide. The walk to the summit and back takes about four hours. *Moderate.* ☒ *Trailhead at Little Baldy Saddle, Generals Hwy. (Rte. 198), 9 miles north of General Sherman Tree* ☞ *Shuttle: Lodgepole-Wuksachi-Dorst.*

Tokopah Falls Trail. This trail with a 500-foot elevation gain follows the Marble Fork of the Kaweah River for 1.75 miles one way and dead-ends below the impressive granite cliffs and cascading waterfall of Tokopah Canyon. The trail passes through a mixed-conifer forest. It takes 2½ to 4 hours to make the round-trip journey. *Moderate.* ☒ *Trailhead off Generals Hwy. (Rte. 198), ¼ mile north of Lodgepole Campground* ☞ *Shuttle: Lodgepole-Wuksachi-Dorst.*

DIFFICULT

Marble Falls Trail. The 3.7-mile trail to Marble Falls crosses through the rugged foothills before reaching the cascading water. Plan on three to four hours one way. *Difficult.* ☒ *Trailhead off dirt road across from the concrete ditch near site 17 at Potwisha Campground, off Generals Hwy. (Rte. 198).*

Mineral King Trails. Many trails to the high country begin at Mineral King. Two popular day hikes are Eagle Lake (6.8 miles round-trip) and Timber Gap. (4.4 miles round-trip) ■ TIP➔ At the Mineral King Ranger Station (☏ 559/565–3768) you can pick up maps and check about conditions. *Difficult.* ☒ *Trailheads at end of Mineral King Rd., 25 miles east of Generals Hwy. (Rte. 198).*

HORSEBACK RIDING

Trips take you through forests and flowering meadows and up mountain slopes.

TOURS AND OUTFITTERS

Grant Grove Stables. Grant Grove Stables (⇨ *See Horseback Riding in Kings Canyon National Park)* isn't too far from parts of Sequoia National Park and is perfect for short rides. ⊕ *www.visitsequoia.com/ grant-grove-stables.aspx.*

Horse Corral Pack Station. One- and two-hour trips through Sequoia are available for beginning and advanced riders. ☒ *Big Meadow Rd., 12 miles east of Generals Hwy. (Rte. 198) between Sequoia and Kings Canyon national parks* ☏ *559/565–3404 in summer, 559/564–6429 year-round* ▣ *$40–$75* ☽ *May–Sept.*

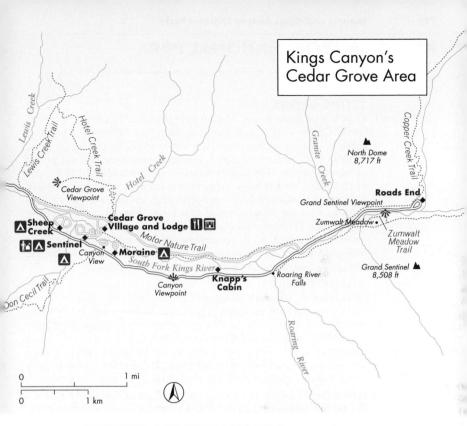

Kings Canyon's Cedar Grove Area

Lewis Creek

Lewis Creek Trail

Hotel Creek Trail

Hotel Creek

Cedar Grove Viewpoint

Sheep Creek

Sentinel

Canyon View

Don Cecil Trail

Cedar Grove Village and Lodge

Motor Nature Trail

Moraine

South Fork Kings River

Canyon Viewpoint

Knapp's Cabin

Granite Creek

North Dome 8,717 ft

Copper Creek Trail

Roads End

Grand Sentinel Viewpoint

Zumwalt Meadow

Zumwalt Meadow Trail

Roaring River Falls

Grand Sentinel 8,508 ft

Roaring River

0   1 mi
0   1 km

SLEDDING AND SNOWSHOEING

The Wolverton area, on Route 198 near Giant Forest, is a popular sledding spot, where sleds, inner tubes, and platters are allowed. You can buy sleds and saucers, with prices starting at $8, at the Wuksachi Lodge (☎ 559/565–4070), 2 miles north of Lodgepole.

You can rent snowshoes for $18–$25 at the Wuksachi Lodge (☎ 559/565–4070), 2 miles north of Lodgepole. Naturalists lead snowshoe walks around Giant Forest and Wuksachi Lodge, conditions permitting, on Saturdays and holidays. Snowshoes are provided for a $1 donation. Make reservations and check schedules at Giant Forest Museum (☎ 559/565–4480) or Wuksachi Lodge.

SWIMMING

Drowning is the number-one cause of death in both Sequoia and Kings Canyon parks. Though it is sometimes safe to swim in the parks' rivers in the late summer and early fall, it is extremely dangerous to do so in the spring and early summer, when the snowmelt from the high country causes swift currents and icy temperatures. Stand clear of the water when the rivers are running, and stay off wet rocks to avoid falling in. Check with rangers if you're unsure about conditions or to learn the safest locations to wade in the water.

KINGS CANYON NATIONAL PARK

EXPLORING

SCENIC DRIVES

Fodor'sChoice **Kings Canyon Scenic Byway.** The 30-mile stretch of Route 180 between
★ Grant Grove Village and Zumwalt Meadow delivers eye-popping
scenery—granite cliffs, a roaring river, waterfalls, and Kings River
Canyon itself—much of which you can experience at vista points
or on easy walks. The canyon comes into view about 10 miles east
of the village at **Junction View.** Five miles beyond at **Yucca Point,**
the canyon is thousands of feet deeper than the more famous Grand
Canyon. **Canyon View,** a special spot 1 mile east of the Cedar Grove
Village turnoff, showcases evidence of the area's glacial history. Here,
perhaps more than anywhere else, you'll understand why John Muir
compared Kings Canyon vistas with those in Yosemite. ■ TIP➡ Driving
the byway takes about an hour each way without stops.

HISTORIC SITES

Fallen Monarch. This toppled sequoia's hollow base was used in the second half of the 19th century as a home for settlers, a saloon, and even
to stable U.S. Cavalry horses. As you walk through it (assuming entry
is permitted, which is not always possible), notice how little the wood
has decayed, and imagine yourself tucked safely inside, sheltered from
a storm or protected from the searing heat. ⊠ *Grant Grove Trail, 1 mile
north of Kings Canyon Park Visitor Center.*

Gamlin Cabin. Despite being listed on the National Register of Historic
Places, this replica of a modest 1872 pioneer cabin is only borderline
historical. The structure, which was moved and rebuilt several times
over the years, once served as U.S. Cavalry storage space and, in the
early 20th century, a ranger station. ⊠ *Grant Grove Trail.*

SCENIC STOPS

Kings Canyon National Park consists of two sections that adjoin the
northern boundary of Sequoia National Park. The western portion,
covered with sequoia and pine forest, contains the park's most visited
sights, such as Grant Grove. The vast eastern portion is remote high
country, slashed across half its southern breadth by the deep, rugged
Kings River Canyon. Separating the two is Sequoia National Forest,
which encompasses Giant Sequoia National Monument. The Kings
Canyon Scenic Byway (Route 180) links the major sights within and
between the park's two sections.

General Grant Tree. President Coolidge proclaimed this to be "the
nation's Christmas tree," and 30 years later President Eisenhower
designated it as a living shrine to all Americans who have died in
wars. Bigger at its base than the General Sherman Tree, it tapers
more quickly. It's estimated to be the world's third-largest sequoia by
volume. ■ TIP➡ A spur trail winds behind the tree, where scars from a
long-ago fire remain visible. ⊠ *Trailhead 1 mile north of Grant Grove
Visitor Center.*

Plants and Wildlife in Sequoia and Kings Canyon

The parks can be divided into three distinct zones. In the west (1,500–4,500 feet) are the rolling, lower elevation foothills, covered with shrubby chaparral vegetation or golden grasslands dotted with oaks. Chamise, red-barked manzanita, and the occasional yucca plant grow here. Fields of white popcorn flower cover the hillsides in spring, and the yellow fiddleneck flourishes. In summer, intense heat and absence of rain cause the hills to turn golden brown. Wildlife includes the California ground squirrel, noisy blue-and-gray scrub jay, black bears, coyotes, skunks, and gray fox.

At middle elevation (5,000–9,000 feet), where the giant sequoia belt resides, rock formations mix with meadows and huge stands of evergreens—red and white fir, incense cedar, and

ponderosa pines, to name a few. Wildflowers like yellow blazing star and red Indian paintbrush bloom in spring and summer. Mule deer, golden-mantled ground squirrels, Steller's jays, mule deer, and black bears (most active in fall) inhabit the area, as does the chickaree.

The high alpine section of the parks is extremely rugged, with a string of rocky peaks reaching above 13,000 feet to Mt. Whitney's 14,494 feet. Fierce weather and scarcity of soil make vegetation and wildlife sparse. Foxtail and whitebark pines have gnarled and twisted trunks, the result of high wind, heavy snowfall, and freezing temperatures. In summer you can see yellow-bellied marmots, pikas, weasels, mountain chickadees, and Clark's nutcrackers.

35

Redwood Mountain Sequoia Grove. One of the world's largest sequoia groves, Redwood contains within its 2,078 acres nearly 2,200 sequoias whose diameters exceed 10 feet. Your can view the grove from afar at an overlook or hike 6 to 10 miles down into the richest regions, which include two of the world's 25 heaviest trees. ⊠ *Drive 5 miles south of Grant Grove on Generals Hwy. (Rte. 198), then turn right at Quail Flat; follow it 1½ miles to the Redwood Canyon trailhead* ⊕ *From Grant Grove, drive south on Generals Hwy. (Rte. 198) 5 miles, turn right (west) at sign for Redwood Canyon, and follow road 2 miles to Redwood Canyon trailhead.*

EDUCATIONAL OFFERINGS

Grant Grove Visitor Center has maps of self-guided park tours. Ranger-led walks and programs take place throughout the year in Grant Grove. Cedar Grove and Forest Service campgrounds have activities from Memorial Day to Labor Day. Check bulletin boards or visitor centers for schedules.

SPORTS AND THE OUTDOORS

The siren song of beauty, challenge, and relative solitude (by national parks standards) draws hard-core outdoors enthusiasts to the Kings River Canyon and the backcountry of the park's eastern section. Backpacking, rock-climbing, and extreme-kayaking opportunities abound, but the park also has day hikes for all ability levels. Winter brings sledding, skiing, and snowshoeing fun. No off-road driving or bicycling is allowed in the park, and snowmobiling is also prohibited.

BICYCLING

Cedar Grove has a designated bike trail. Other than that, bicycles are allowed only on the paved roads in Kings Canyon. Cyclists should be extremely cautious along the steep highways and narrow shoulders.

BIRD-WATCHING

For information about bird-watching in Sequoia and Kings Canyon national parks, see Sports and the Outdoors, in Sequoia National Park.

CROSS-COUNTRY SKIING

Roads to Grant Grove are accessible even during heavy snowfall, making the trails here a good choice over Sequoia's Giant Forest when harsh weather hits.

FISHING

There is limited trout fishing in the park from late April to mid-November, and catches are minor. Still, Kings River is a popular spot. Some of the park's secluded backcountry lakes have good fishing. Licenses are available, along with fishing tackle, in Grant Grove and Cedar Grove. ⇨ *See Sports and the Outdoors, in Sequoia National Park, above, for more information about licenses.*

HIKING

You can enjoy many of Kings Canyon's sights from your car, but the giant gorge of the Kings River Canyon and the sweeping vistas of some of the highest mountains in the United States are best seen on foot. Carry a hiking map—available at any visitor center—and plenty of water. Check with rangers for current trail conditions, and be aware of rapidly changing weather. Except for one trail to Mt. Whitney, permits are not required for day hikes.

Roads End Permit Station. You can obtain wilderness permits, maps, and information about the backcountry at this station, where bear canisters, a must for campers, can be rented or purchased. When the station is closed, complete a self-service permit form. ⊠ *Eastern end of Kings Canyon Scenic Byway, 6 miles east of Cedar Grove Visitor Center* ☉ *Mid-May–Sept., daily 7–4.*

EASY

Big Stump Trail. From 1883 until 1890, logging was done here, complete with a mill. The 1-mile loop trail, whose unmarked beginning is a few yards west of the Big Stump entrance, passes by many enormous stumps. *Easy.* ⊠ *Trailhead near Big Stump Entrance, Generals Hwy. (Rte. 180).*

Grant Grove Trail. Grant Grove is only 128 acres, but it's a big deal. More than 120 sequoias here have a base diameter that exceeds 10 feet, and the **General Grant Tree** is the world's third-largest sequoia by volume. Nearby, the Confederacy is represented by the **Robert E. Lee Tree,** recognized as the world's 11th-largest sequoia. Also along the easy-to-walk trail are the **Fallen Monarch** and the **Gamlin Cabin,** built by 19th-century pioneers. *Easy.* ⊠ *Trailhead off Generals Hwy. (Rte. 180), 1 mile north of Kings Canyon Park Visitor Center.*

Mt. Whitney

At 14,494 feet, Mt. Whitney is the highest point in the contiguous United States and the crown jewel of Sequoia National Park's wild eastern side. The peak looms high above the tiny, high-mountain desert community of Lone Pine, where numerous Hollywood Westerns have been filmed. The high mountain ranges, arid landscape, and scrubby brush of the eastern Sierra are beautiful in their vastness and austerity.

Despite the mountain's scale, you can't see it from the more traveled west side of the park because it is hidden behind the Great Western Divide. The only way to access Mt. Whitney from the main part of the park is to circumnavigate the Sierra Nevada via a 10-hour, nearly 400-mile drive outside the park. No road ascends the peak; the best vantage point from which to catch a glimpse of the mountain is at the end of Whitney Portal Road. The 13 miles of winding road leads from U.S. 395 at

Lone Pine to the trailhead for the hiking route to the top of the mountain. Whitney Portal Road is closed in winter.

Mt. Whitney Trail. The most popular route to the summit, the Mt. Whitney Trail can be conquered by fit and reasonably experienced hikers. If there's snow on the mountain, this is a challenge for expert mountaineers only. All overnighters must have a permit, as must day hikers on the trail beyond Lone Pine Lake, about 2½ miles from the trailhead. From May through October, permits are distributed via a lottery run each February by Recreation.gov. ■TIP→ **The Eastern Sierra Interagency Visitor Center (**☎ **760/876–6222), on Route 136 at U.S. 395 about a mile south of Lone Pine, is a good resource for information about permits and hiking.** ☎ *760/873–2485 for trail information, 760/873–2483 for trail reservations* ⊕ *www.fs.usda.gov/inyo.*

Roaring River Falls Walk. Take a shady five-minute walk to this forceful waterfall that rushes through a narrow granite chute. The trail is paved and mostly accessible. *Easy.* ⊠ *Trailhead 3 miles east of Cedar Grove Village turnoff from Kings Canyon Scenic Byway.*

Fodor's Choice
★
Zumwalt Meadow Trail. Rangers say this is the best (and most popular) day hike in the Cedar Grove area. Just 1.5 miles long, it offers three visual treats: the South Fork of the Kings River, the lush meadow, and the high granite walls above, including those of Grand Sentinel and North Dome. *Easy.* ⊠ *Trailhead 4½ miles east of Cedar Grove Village turnoff from Kings Canyon Scenic Byway.*

MODERATE

Big Baldy. This hike climbs 600 feet and 2 miles up to the 8,209-feet summit of Big Baldy. Your reward is the view of Redwood Canyon. Round-trip the hike is 4 miles. *Moderate.* ⊠ *Trailhead 8 miles south of Grant Grove on Generals Hwy. (Rte. 198).*

Mist Falls Trail. This sandy trail follows the glaciated South Fork Canyon through forest and chaparral, past several rapids and cascades, to one of the largest waterfalls in the two parks. Nine miles round-trip, the hike is relatively flat, but climbs 600 feet in the last 2 miles. It takes

Hiking in the Sierra Mountains is a thrilling experience, putting you amid some of the world's highest trees.

from four to five hours to complete. *Moderate.* ⊠ *Trailhead at end of Kings Canyon Scenic Byway, 5½ miles east of Cedar Grove Village.*

Panoramic Point Trail. You'll get a nice view of whale-shape Hume Lake from the top of this Grant Grove path, which is paved and only 300 feet long. It's fairly steep—strollers might work here, but not wheelchairs. Trailers and RVs are not permitted on the steep and narrow road that leads to the trailhead parking lot. *Moderate.* ⊠ *Trial begins at end of Panoramic Point Rd., 2.3 miles from Grant Grove Village.*

Redwood Canyon Trails. Two main trails lead into Redwood Canyon Grove, the world's largest sequoia grove. The 6.5-mile **Hart Tree and Fallen Goliath Loop** passes by a 19th-century logging site, pristine Hart Meadow, and the hollowed-out Tunnel Tree before accessing a side trail to the grove's largest sequoia, the 277.9-foot-tall Hart Tree. The 6.4-mile **Sugar Bowl Loop** provides views of Redwood Mountain and Big Baldy before winding down into its namesake, a thick grove of mature and young sequoias. *Moderate.* ⊠ *Trail begins off Quail Flat. Drive 5 miles south of Grant Grove on Generals Hwy. (Rte. 198), then turn right at Quail Flat; follow it 1½ miles to the Redwood Canyon trailhead.*

DIFFICULT
Buena Vista Peak. For a 360-degree view of Redwood Canyon and the High Sierra, make the 2-mile ascent to Buena Vista. *Difficult.* ⊠ *Trailhead off Generals Hwy. (Rte. 198), south of Kings Canyon Overlook, 7 miles southeast of Grant Grove.*

Don Cecil Trail. This trail climbs 4,000 feet up the cool north-facing slope of the Kings River Canyon, passing Sheep Creek Cascade and providing several fine glimpses of the canyon and the 11,000-foot Monarch Divide. The trail leads to Lookout Peak, which affords a panorama of the park's backcountry. This strenuous, all-day hike covers 13 miles round-trip. *Difficult.* ⊠ *Trailhead at Sentinel Campground, Cedar Grove Village.*

Hotel Creek Trail. For gorgeous canyon views, take this trail from Cedar Grove up a series of switchbacks until it splits. Follow the route left through chaparral to the forested ridge and rocky outcrop known as Cedar Grove Overlook, where you can see the Kings River Canyon stretching below. This strenuous 5-mile round-trip hike gains 1,200 feet and takes three to four hours to complete. *Difficult.* ⊠ *Trailhead at Cedar Grove Pack Station, 1 mile east of Cedar Grove Village.*

HORSEBACK RIDING

One-day destinations by horseback out of Cedar Grove include Mist Falls and Upper Bubb's Creek. In the backcountry, many equestrians head for Volcanic Lakes or Granite Basin, ascending trails that reach elevations of 10,000 feet. Costs per person range from $35 for a one-hour guided ride to around $250 per day for fully guided trips for which the packers do all the cooking and camp chores.

TOURS AND OUTFITTERS

Cedar Grove Pack Station. Take a day or overnight trip along the Kings River Canyon with Cedar Grove Pack Station. Popular routes include the Rae Lakes Loop and Monarch Divide. ⊠ *Kings Canyon Scenic Byway, 1 mile east of Cedar Grove Village* ☏ *559/565–3464* 🖃 *Call for prices* ☉ *Late May–early Sept.*

Grant Grove Stables. A one- or two-hour trip through Grant Grove leaving from the stables provides a taste of horseback riding in Kings Canyon. ⊠ *Rte. 180, ½ mile north of Grant Grove Visitor Center* ☏ *559/335–9292 mid-June–Sept.* 🖃 *$45–$70* ☉ *June–Labor Day, daily 8–6.*

SLEDDING AND SNOWSHOEING

In winter, Kings Canyon has a few great places to play in the snow. Sleds, inner tubes, and platters are allowed at both the Azalea Campground area on Grant Tree Road, ¼ mile north of Grant Grove Visitor Center, and at the Big Stump picnic area, 2 miles north of the lower Route 180 entrance to the park.

Snowshoeing is good around Grant Grove, where you can take naturalist-guided snowshoe walks on Saturdays and holidays from mid-December through mid-March as conditions permit. For a small donation, you can rent snowshoes at the Grant Grove Visitor Center for the guided walks. Grant Grove Market rents sleds and snowshoes.

35

WHAT'S NEARBY

The already remote Sierra National Forest encircles much of Sequoia and Kings Canyon national parks, making them a wilderness within a wilderness.

NEARBY TOWNS

Numerous towns and cities tout themselves as "gateways" to the parks, with some more deserving of the title than others. One that certainly merits the name is frisky **Three Rivers,** a Sierra foothills hamlet (population 2,200) along the Kaweah River. Close to Sequoia's Ash Mountain and Lookout Point entrances, Three Rivers is a good spot to find a room when park lodgings are full. Either because Three Rivers residents appreciate their idyllic setting or because they know that tourists are their bread and butter, you'll find them almost uniformly pleasant and eager to share tips about the best spots for "Sierra surfing" the Kaweah's smooth, moss-covered rocks or where to find the best cell-phone reception (it's off to the cemetery for Verizon customers).

Visalia, a Central Valley city of about 125,000 people, lies 58 miles southwest of Sequoia's Wuksachi Village and 56 miles southwest of the Kings Canyon Park Visitor Center. Its vibrant downtown contains several good restaurants. Closest to Kings Canyon's Big Stump entrance, **Fresno,** the main gateway to the southern Sierra region, is about 55 miles west of Kings Canyon and about 85 miles northwest of Wuksachi Village. This Central Valley city of nearly a half-million people is sprawling and unglamorous, but it has all the cultural and other amenities you'd expect of a major crossroads.

VISITOR INFORMATION

Fresno/Clovis Convention & Visitors Bureau ⊠ 1550 E. Shaw Ave., Suite 101, Fresno ☎ 559/445–8300, 800/788–0836 ⊕ www.playfresno.org. **Sequoia Foothills Chamber of Commerce** ⊠ 42268 Sierra Dr., Three Rivers ☎ 559/561–3300 ⊕ www.threerivers.com. **Visalia Visitor Center** ⊠ 303 E. Acequia Ave., at S. Bridge St., Visalia ☎ 559/334–0141 ⊕ www.visitvisalia.org ⊗ Weekdays 8–5.

NEARBY ATTRACTIONS

Boyden Cavern. The Kings River has carved out hundreds of caverns, including Boyden, which brims with stalagmite, stalactite, drapery, flowstone, and other formations. In summer, the Bat Grotto shelters a slew of bats. If you can't make it to Crystal Cave in Sequoia, Boyden is a reasonable substitute. ■TIP→ **Reservations aren't taken for regular tours, which take about 45 minutes and start with a steep walk uphill.** ⊠ 74101 E. Kings Canyon Rd.(Rte. 180), between Grant Grove and Cedar Grove ⊕ www.caverntours.com/BoydenRt.htm ☎ $14 ⊗ June–Aug., daily 10–5; May and Sept.–Nov., daily 11–5; tours on the hr.

Exeter Murals. More than two dozen murals in the Central Valley city of Exeter's cute-as-a-button downtown make it worth a quick detour if you're traveling on Route 198. Several of the murals, which depict the area's agricultural and social history, are quite good. All adorn buildings

**OFF THE
BEATEN
PATH**

within a few blocks of the intersection of Pine and E Streets. If you're hungry, the **Wildflower Cafe,** at 121 South E Street, serves inventive salads and sandwiches. ■ TIP→ **Shortly after entering Exeter head west on Pine Street (it's just before the water tower) to reach downtown.** ✉ *Rte. 65, 2 miles south of Rte. 198, about 11 miles east of Visalia, Exeter* ⊕ *cityofexeter.com/about-8187/gallery/murals.*

FAMILY

Fodor'sChoice

★

Forestiere Underground Gardens. Sicilian immigrant Baldasare Forestiere spent four decades (1906–46) carving out an odd, subterranean realm of rooms, tunnels, grottoes, alcoves, and arched passageways that once extended for more than 10 acres between Highway 99 and busy, mall-packed Shaw Avenue. Though not an engineer, Forestiere called on his memories of the ancient Roman structures he saw as a youth and on techniques he learned digging subways in New York and Boston. Only a fraction of his prodigious output is on view, but you can tour his underground living quarters, including bedrooms (one with a fireplace), the kitchen, living room, and bath, as well as a fishpond and auto tunnel. Skylights allow exotic, full-grown fruit trees to flourish more than 20 feet belowground. ✉ *5021 W. Shaw Ave., 2 blocks east of Hwy. 99, Fresno* ☎ *559/271–0734* ⊕ *www.undergroundgardens.com* ✉ *$15* ⊙ *Late May–early Sept., Wed.–Sun. 10–4; days and hrs vary rest of yr.*

Lake Kaweah. The Kaweah River rushes out of the Sierra from high above Mineral King in Sequoia National Park. When it reaches the hills above the Central Valley the water collects in Lake Kaweah, a reservoir operated by the Army Corps of Engineers. You can swim, sail, kayak, water ski, hike, camp, fish, and picnic here. ■ TIP→ **The visitor center at Lemon Cove has interesting exhibits about the dam that created the lake.** ✉ *34443 Sierra Dr. (Rte. 198), about 20 miles east of Visalia* ☎ *559/597–2301, 559/561–3155, 877/444–6777 for campground reservations* ✉ *Free (day use).*

Project Survival's Cat Haven. Take the rare opportunity to glimpse a Siberian lynx, a clouded leopard, a Bengal tiger, and other endangered wild cats at this conservation facility that shelters more than 30 big cats. A guided hour-long tour along a quarter-mile of walkway leads to fenced habitat areas shaded by trees and overlooking the Central Valley. ✉ *38257 E. Kings Canyon Rd. (Rte. 180), 15 miles west of Kings Canyon National Park, Dunlap* ☎ *559/338–3216* ⊕ *www.cathaven. com* ✉ *$9* ⊙ *May–Sept., Wed.–Mon. 10–5; Oct.–Apr., Thurs.–Mon. 10–4. Last tour leaves 1 hr before closing.*

Sequoia National Forest and Giant Sequoia National Monument. Delicate spring wildflowers, cool summer campgrounds, and varied winter-sports opportunities—not to mention more than half of the world's giant sequoia groves—draw outdoorsy types year-round to this sprawling district surrounding the national parks. Together, the forest and monument cover nearly 1,700 square miles, south from the Kings River and east from the foothills along the San Joaquin Valley. The monument's groves are both north and south of Sequoia National Park. One of the most popular is the **Converse Basin Grove,** home of the Boole Tree, the forest's largest sequoia. The grove is accessible by car on an unpaved road.

35

The Hume Lake Forest Service District Office, at 35860 Kings Canyon Scenic Byway (Route 180), has information about the groves, along with details about recreational activities. In springtime, diversions include hiking among the wildflowers that brighten the foothills. The floral display rises with the heat as the mountain elevations warm up in summer, when hikers, campers, and picnickers become more plentiful. The abundant trout supply attracts anglers to area waters, including 87-acre **Hume Lake**, which is also ideal for swimming and nonmotorized boating. By fall the turning leaves provide the visual delights, particularly in the Western Divide, Indian Basin, and the Kern Plateau. Winter activities include downhill and cross-country skiing, snowshoeing, and snowmobiling. ✉ *Northern Entrances: Generals Hwy. (Rte. 198), 7 miles southeast of Grant Grove; Hume Lake Rd. between Generals Hwy. (Rte. 198) and Kings Canyon Scenic Byway (Rte. 180); Kings Canyon Scenic Byway (Rte. 180) between Grant Grove and Cedar Grove. Southern Entrances: Rte. 190 east of Springville; Rte. 178 east of Bakersfield* ☎ *559/784–1500 for forest and monument, 559/338–2251 for Hume Lake* 🌐 *www.fs.usda.gov/sequoia.*

AREA ACTIVITIES

SPORTS AND THE OUTDOORS

BOATING AND RAFTING

Kaweah White Water Adventures. Owner Frank Root's outfit offers three Kaweah River trips: a two-hour excursion (good for families) through Class III rapids, a longer paddle through Class IV rapids, and an all-day trip (Class IV and V rapids). ✉ *Three Rivers* ☎ *559/561–1000, 800/229–8658* 🌐 *www.kaweah-whitewater.com* 🎟 *$50–$140 per person.*

Kings River Expeditions. This Clovis-based outfit arranges one- and two-day white-water rafting trips on the Kings River. ☎ *559/233–4881, 800/846–3674* 🌐 *www.kingsriver.com.*

WHERE TO EAT

IN THE PARKS

SEQUOIA

$ CAFÉ 🍴 **Lodgepole Market and Snack Bar.** The choices here run the gamut from simple to very simple, with the three counters only a few strides apart in a central eating complex. For hot food, venture into the snack bar. The deli sells prepackaged salads, sandwiches, and wraps along with ice cream scooped from tubs. You'll find other prepackaged foods in the market. [$] *Average main: $6* ✉ *Next to Lodgepole Visitor Center* ☎ *559/565–3301* 🕒 *Closed late Sept.–mid-Apr.*

$$$ MODERN AMERICAN 🍴 **The Peaks.** Huge windows run the length of the Wuksachi Lodge's high-ceilinged dining room, and a large fireplace on the far wall warms both body and soul. The diverse dinner menu—by far the best at both parks—includes items such as venison medallions, grilled pork tenderloin, and pan-seared mountain trout. The menu might also

include pastas, a vegan burger or other vegan dish, and ratatouille. The wine selection is serviceable but lacks imagination. Breakfast and lunch are also served. [$] *Average main: $24* ✉ *Wukschi Village* ☎ *559/565–4070* 🌐 *www.visitsequoia.com/the-peaks-restaurant.aspx* ✍ *Reservations essential.*

$$$ BARBECUE 🍴 **Wolverton Barbecue.** Weather permitting, diners congregate nightly on a wooden porch that looks directly out onto a small but strikingly verdant meadow. In addition to the predictable meats such as ribs and chicken, the all-you-can-eat buffet has sides that include baked beans, corn on the cob, and potato salad. Following the meal, listen to a ranger talk and clear your throat for a campfire sing-along. Purchase tickets at Lodgepole Market, Wuksachi Lodge, or Wolverton Recreation Area's office. [$] *Average main: $24* ✉ *Wolverton Rd., 1½ miles northeast off Generals Hwy. (Rte. 198)* ☎ *559/565–4070* ⏲ *Closed early Sept.–mid-June. No lunch.*

PICNIC AREAS

Take care to dispose of your food scraps properly (the bears might not appreciate this short-term, but the practice helps ensure their long-term survival).

Crescent Meadow. A mile or so past Moro Rock, this comparatively remote picnic area has meadow views and, quite handily, is by a lovely trail on which you can burn off those potato chips and cookies. Tables are under the giant sequoias, off the parking area. There are restrooms and drinking water. Fires are not allowed. ✉ *End of Moro Rock–Crescent Rd., 2.6 miles east off Generals Hwy. (Rte. 198).*

Foothills. Near the parking lot at the southern entrance of the park, this area has tables on grass. Drinking water and restrooms are available. ✉ *Across Generals Hwy. from Foothills Visitor Center.*

Hospital Rock. American Indians once ground acorns into meal at this site; outdoor exhibits tell the story. The picnic area's name, however, stems from a Caucasian hunter/trapper who was treated for a leg wound here in 1873. Look up, and you'll see Moro Rock. Grills, drinking water, and restrooms are available. ✉ *Generals Hwy. (Rte. 198), 6 miles north of Ash Mountain entrance.*

Pinewood. Picnic in Giant Forest, in the vicinity of sequoias if not actually under them. Drinking water, restrooms, grills, and wheelchair-accessible spots are provided in this expansive setting near Sequoia National Park's most popular attractions. ✉ *Generals Hwy. (Rte. 198), 2 miles north of Giant Forest Museum, halfway between Giant Forest Museum and General Sherman Tree.*

Wolverton Meadow. At a major trailhead to the backcountry, this is a great place to stop for lunch before a hike. The area sits in a mixed-conifer forest adjacent to parking. Drinking water, grills, and restrooms are available. ✉ *Wolverton Rd., 1½ miles northeast off Generals Hwy. (Rte. 198.)*

KINGS CANYON

$ AMERICAN 🍴 **Cedar Grove Restaurant.** The menu here is surprisingly extensive, with dinner entrées such as pasta, pork chops, trout, and steak. For breakfast, try the biscuits and gravy, French toast, pancakes, or cold cereal. Burgers (including vegetarian patties) and hot dogs dominate the lunch choices. Outside, a patio dining area overlooks the Kings River. [$] *Average main: $14* ✉ *Cedar Grove Village* ☎ *559/565–0100* 🕑 *Closed Oct.–May.*

$$ AMERICAN 🍴 **Grant Grove Restaurant.** In a no-frills, open room, this restaurant offers utterly standard American fare such as pancakes for breakfast or hot sandwiches and chicken for later meals. Take-out service is available year-round, and during the summer, there's also a pizza parlor. [$] *Average main: $17* ✉ *Grant Grove Village* ☎ *559/335–5500.*

PICNIC AREAS

Big Stump. Some trees still stand at this site at the edge of a logged sequoia grove. Near the park's entrance, the area is paved and next to the road. It's the only picnic area in either park that is plowed in the wintertime. Restrooms, grills, and drinking water are available, and the area is entirely accessible. ✉ *Generals Hwy. (Rte. 180), just inside Big Stump entrance.*

Grizzly Falls. This little gem is worth a pull-over, if not a picnic at the roadside tables. A less-than-a-minute trek from the parking lot delivers you to the base of the delightful, 100-foot-plus falls. On a hot day, nothing feels better than dipping your feet in the cool water. An outhouse is on site, but grills are not, and water is unavailable. ✉ *Off Rte. 180, 2½ miles west of Cedar Grove entrance.*

OUTSIDE THE PARKS

$ CAFÉ 🍴 **Antoinette's Coffee and Goodies.** For smoothies, well-crafted espresso drinks, and pumpkin chocolate-chip muffins and other homemade baked goods, stop for a spell at this convivial coffee shop next door to Sierra Subs and Salads. ■ **TIP→ There's Wi-Fi here, too.** [$] *Average main: $5* ✉ *41727 Sierra Dr., Three Rivers* ☎ *559/561–2253* 🌐 *www.antoinettescoffeeandgoodies.com* ✍ *Reservations not accepted* 🕑 *Closed Tues. No dinner.*

$$ MODERN AMERICAN 🍴 **Café 225.** High ceilings and contemporary decor create a relaxed elegance at this popular downtown restaurant. Chef-owner Karl Merten can often be spotted at area markets seeking out locally grown ingredients for his seasonally changing dishes. Meats and fish grilled on a wood-fired rotisserie figure prominently on the menu, which also includes pastas and unusual treats such as artichoke fritters and slow-roasted Kalua pig. The green-chili burger, grilled over oak coals and served with sharp cheddar and chipotle aioli, is a town favorite. [$] *Average main: $19* ✉ *225 W. Main St., Visalia* ☎ *559/733–2967* 🌐 *www.cafe225.com* 🕑 *Closed Sun.*

$$$ AMERICAN 🍴 **Gateway Restaurant and Lodge.** The view's the main draw at this raucous roadhouse that overlooks the roaring Kaweah River as it plunges out of the high country. Taking seriously its role as its town's only true fine-dining establishment, the Gateway serves everything from

panfried trout to osso buco to shrimp in Thai chili sauce. Some menu items are pricey, but you can also order a pizza or a Kobe beef or salmon burger. In general, the simpler the preparation is, the better the result. Dinner reservations are essential on summer weekends. [$] *Average main: $29* ✉ *45978 Sierra Dr., Three Rivers* ☎ *559/561–4133* 🌐 *www.gateway-sequoia.com* 🕒 *No breakfast weekdays.*

$ AMERICAN 🍴 **Irene's Cafe Dining.** Downtown workers pack this Tower District restaurant at lunchtime. Handmade, half-pound burgers are the most popular, and most filling, items on the menu. Other favorites include the smoked ham and melted Swiss cheese sandwich served on a hard roll, and fresh salads. For breakfast, homemade granola, huge buttermilk pancakes, and the Denver omelet (with ham, onions, and green peppers) will fill up even those with the heartiest of appetites. [$] *Average main: $12* ✉ *747 E. Olive Ave., Fresno* ☎ *559/237–9919* 🌐 *irenescafe.com.*

35

$ AMERICAN 🍴 **Sierra Subs and Salads.** This simple but well-run sandwichery satisfies carnivores and vegetarians alike with crispy-fresh ingredients prepared with panache. Depending on your preference, the centerpiece of the Bulls Eye sandwich, for instance, will be roast beef or a Portobello mushroom, but whichever you choose the accompanying flavors—of Ciabatta bread, horseradish-and-garlic mayonnaise, roasted red peppers, Havarti cheese, and spinach—will delight your palate. With quesadillas, pizzas, burgers, hot dogs, and salads also on the menu, there's something for pretty much any appetite. [$] *Average main: $8* ✉ *41717 Sierra Dr., Three Rivers* ☎ *559/561–4810* 🌐 *www.sierrasubsandsalads.com* 🕒 *Closed Mon. No dinner.*

$$$ EUROPEAN Fodor's Choice ★ 🍴 **The Vintage Press.** One of the Central Valley's best restaurants serves California-Continental cuisine in a stylish wood-paneled room lit softly by Tiffany-style ceiling lamps. The seasonally changing menu includes selections such as pistachio-crusted king salmon and filet mignon with mustard and cognac. The chocolate Grand Marnier cake is a standout among the homemade desserts and ice creams, and the wine list has received high praise from *Wine Spectator* and other publications. [$] *Average main: $30* ✉ *216 N. Willis St., Visalia* ☎ *559/733–3033* 🌐 *www.thevintagepress.com.*

WHERE TO STAY

IN THE PARKS

SEQUOIA

$$$$ RESORT 🏨 **Silver City Mountain Resort.** High on Mineral King Road, this privately owned resort has rustic cabins and Swiss-style chalets, all with at least a stove, refrigerator, and sink. **Pros:** rustic setting; friendly staff; "off the grid" ambience. **Cons:** electricity (by generator) available only between noon and 10 pm. [$] *Rooms from: $250* ✉ *Mineral King Rd., 21 miles southeast of Rte. 198* ☎ *559/561–3223* 🌐 *www.silvercityresort.com* 🛏 *11 units, 6 with shared bath* 🕒 *Closed Nov.–late May* 🍴 *No meals.*

$$$ **Wuksachi Lodge.** The striking cedar-and-stone main building here is
HOTEL a fine example of how a structure can blend effectively with lovely
Fodor's Choice mountain scenery. **Pros:** best place to stay in the parks; lots of wildlife.
★ **Cons:** rooms can be small; main lodge is a few-minutes' walk from guest
rooms. $ *Rooms from: $185* ⊠ *64740 Wuksachi Way, Wuksachi Village* ☎ *559/565–4070, 888/252–5757* ⊕ *www.visitsequoia.com* ➪ *102 rooms* |❍| *No meals.*

KINGS CANYON

$$ **Cedar Grove Lodge.** Backpackers like to stay here on the eve of long
HOTEL treks into the High Sierra wilderness, so bedtimes tend to be early. **Pros:**
a definite step up from camping in terms of comfort. **Cons:** impersonal;
not everybody agrees it's clean enough. $ *Rooms from: $138* ⊠ *Kings Canyon Scenic Byway* ☎ *877/522–6966* ⊕ *www.visitsequoia.com/kings-canyon.aspx* ➪ *21 rooms* ☉ *Closed mid-Oct.–mid-May* |❍| *No meals.*

$ **Grant Grove Cabins.** Some of the wood-panel cabins here have heaters,
HOTEL electric lights, and private baths, but most have woodstoves, battery
lamps, and shared baths. **Pros:** warm, woodsy feel; clean. **Cons:** can be
difficult to walk up to if you're not in decent physical shape; costly for
what you get. $ *Rooms from: $94* ⊠ *Kings Canyon Scenic Byway in Grant Grove Village* ☎ *877/522–6966* ⊕ *www.visitsequoia.com/kings-canyon.aspx* ➪ *33 cabins, 9 with bath; 17 tent cabins* |❍| *No meals.*

$$$ **John Muir Lodge.** This modern, timber-sided lodge occupies a wooded
HOTEL area in the hills above Grant Grove Village. **Pros:** open year-round;
common room stays warm; lodge is far enough from the main road to
be quiet. **Cons:** check-in is down in the village. $ *Rooms from: $184* ⊠ *Kings Canyon Scenic Byway, ¼ mile north of Grant Grove Village* ☎ *877/522–6966* ⊕ *www.visitsequoia.com/kings-canyon.aspx* ➪ *36 rooms* |❍| *No meals.*

OUTSIDE THE PARKS

The only lodging immediately outside the parks is in Three Rivers.
Options include inns, chain and mom-and-pop motels, and riverside
cabins. Numerous chain properties operate in Visalia or Fresno (your
favorite is likely represented in one or both cities), about an hour from
the south and north entrances, respectively.

$$ **Buckeye Tree Lodge.** Every room at this two-story motel has a patio fac-
B&B/INN ing a sun-dappled grassy lawn, right on the banks of the Kaweah River.
Pros: near the park entrance; fantastic river views; friendly staff; kitch-
enette in some rooms. **Cons:** can fill up quickly in the summer; could use
a little updating. $ *Rooms from: $144* ⊠ *46000 Sierra Dr., Rte. 198, Three Rivers* ☎ *559/561–5900* ⊕ *www.buckeyetree.com* ➪ *11 rooms, 1 cottage* |❍| *Breakfast* ⚯ *2-night minimum on summer weekends.*

$$ **Lazy J Ranch Motel.** Surrounded by 12 acres of green lawns and a
B&B/INN split-rail fence, the Lazy J is a modest compound of one-story motel
buildings and freestanding cottages near the banks of the Kaweah River.
Pros: lovely landscaping; quiet rooms; friendly staff. **Cons:** on the far
edge of town; can't see the river from most rooms; dated style and fix-
tures. $ *Rooms from: $115* ⊠ *39625 Sierra Dr. (Rte. 198), Three Rivers* ☎ *559/561–4449, 888/315–2378* ➪ *11 rooms, 7 cottages* |❍| *Breakfast.*

Best Campgrounds in Sequoia and Kings Canyon

Campgrounds in Sequoia and Kings Canyon occupy wonderful settings, with lots of shade and nearby hiking trails. Some campgrounds are open year-round, others only seasonally. Except for Bearpaw (just under $200 a night including meals), fees at the campgrounds listed below range from $12 to $35, depending on location and size. There are no RV hookups at any of the campgrounds; expect a table and a fire ring with a grill at standard sites. Only Bearpaw and Lodgepole accept reservations, and for both of these you'll need to book well ahead. The rest are first-come, first served. Campgrounds around Lodgepole and Grant Grove get busy in summer with vacationing families. Keep in mind that this is black-bear country. Carefully follow posted instructions about storing food—you'll be fined if you don't. Bear-proof metal containers are provided at many campgrounds.

IN SEQUOIA

Atwell Mill Campground. At 6,650 feet, this peaceful, tent-only campground is just south of the Western Divide. ⊠ *Mineral King Rd., 20 miles east of Rte. 198* ☏ *559/565–3341.*

Bearpaw High Sierra Camp. Classy camping is the order of the day at this tent hotel and restaurant. Make reservations starting on January 2nd. ⊠ *High Sierra Trail, 11.5 miles from Lodgepole Village* ☏ *888/252–5757* ⊕ *www.visitsequoia.com.*

Dorst Creek Campground. Wildlife sightings are common at this large campground at elevation 6,700 feet. ⊠ *Generals Hwy., 8 miles north of Lodgepole Visitor Center* ☏ *559/565–3341.*

Lodgepole Campground. The largest Lodgepole-area campground is also the noisiest, though things quiet down at night. ⊠ *Off Generals Hwy. beyond Lodgepole Village* ☏ *559/565–3341 or 877/444–6777.*

Potwisha Campground. On the Marble Fork of the Kaweah River, this midsize campground, open year-round, at elevation 2,100 feet gets no snow in winter and can be hot in summer. ⊠ *Generals Hwy., 4 miles north of Foothills Visitor Center* ☏ *559/565–3341.*

IN KINGS CANYON

Azalea Campground. Of the three campgrounds in the Grant Grove area, Azalea is the only one open year-round. It sits at 6,500 feet amid giant sequoias. ⊠ *Kings Canyon Scenic Byway, ¼ mile north of Grant Grove Village* ☏ *559/565–3341.*

Sentinel Campground. At 4,600 feet and within walking distance of Cedar Grove Village, Sentinel fills up fast in summer. ⊠ *Kings Canyon Scenic Byway, ¼ mile west of Cedar Grove Village* ☏ *559/565–3341.*

Sheep Creek Campground. Of the overflow campgrounds, this is one of the prettiest. ⊠ *Off Kings Canyon Scenic Byway, 1 mile west of Cedar Grove Village* ☏ *No phone.*

Sunset Campground. Many of the easiest trails through Grant Grove are adjacent to this large camp, near the giant sequoias at 6,500 feet. ⊠ *Off Generals Hwy., near Grant Grove Visitor Center* ☏ *No phone.*

35

$$$ HOTEL FAMILY **Montecito-Sequoia Lodge.** Outdoor activities are what this year-round family resort is all about, including many that are geared toward teenagers and small children. **Pros:** friendly staff; great for kids; lots of fresh air and planned activities. **Cons:** can be noisy with all the activity; some complaints about cleanliness; not within national park. [$] *Rooms from: $179* ✉ *63410 Generals Hwy., 11 miles south of Grant Grove* ☎ *559/565–3388, 800/227–9900* 🌐 *www.montecitosequoia.com* 🛏 *32 rooms, 13 cabins* 🕓 *Closed 1st 2 wks of Dec.* 🍴 *All meals.*

$$ B&B/INN Fodor's Choice ★ **Rio Sierra Riverhouse.** Guests at Rio Sierra come for the river views, the sandy beach, and the proximity to Sequoia National Park (it's 6 miles away), but invariably end up raving as much about the warm yet laid-back hospitality of proprietress Mars Roberts as they do about location. **Pros:** seductive beach; winning hostess; river views from all rooms; contemporary ambience; full kitchen in one room, kitchenette in another. **Cons:** books up quickly in summer; some road noise audible in rooms. [$] *Rooms from: $150* ✉ *41997 Sierra Dr. (Rte. 198), Three Rivers* ☎ *559/561–4720* 🌐 *www.rio-sierra.com* 🛏 *5 rooms* 🕓 *Closed Jan. and Feb.* 🍴 *No meals* ☞ *2-night minimum stay on summer weekends.*

$ B&B/INN **Sequoia Motel.** An old-fashioned single-story mom-and-pop motel, the Sequoia stands out with such extra touches as country-style quilts and mismatched Americana furnishings that lend a retro charm to the rooms. **Pros:** clean; friendly; comparatively affordable; pool. **Cons:** not especially modern; fills up quickly in the summer. [$] *Rooms from: $105* ✉ *43000 Sierra Dr. (Rte. 198), Three Rivers* ☎ *559/561–4453, 877/672–2327* 🌐 *www.sequoiamotel.com* 🛏 *11 rooms, 3 cottages* 🍴 *No meals.*

$ B&B/INN **The Spalding House.** This restored colonial-revival B&B is decked out with antiques, Oriental rugs, handcrafted woodwork, and glass doors. **Pros:** warm feel; old-time atmosphere; great place for a twilight stroll. **Cons:** only three rooms. [$] *Rooms from: $95* ✉ *631 N. Encina St., Visalia* ☎ *559/739–7877* 🌐 *www.thespaldinghouse.com* 🛏 *3 suites* 🍴 *Breakfast.*

THEODORE ROOSEVELT NATIONAL PARK

WELCOME TO THEODORE ROOSEVELT

TOP REASONS TO GO

★ **The "Granddaddy Trail":** Hike the Maah Daah Hey Trail, which means "grandfather" or "been here long." It's one of the most popular and well-maintained trails in western North Dakota.

★ **Views from above:** Get an encompassing 360-degree view of the badlands from Buck Hill.

★ **History lessons from the frontier:** View Maltese Cross Ranch Cabin, which once belonged to Theodore Roosevelt.

★ **Badlands Broadway:** Come experience a theatrical tribute to the history and personalities that make up the Old West at the *Medora Musical*, located in the town, not the park.

★ **Great clubbing— golf, that is:** Perfect your swing at Bully Pulpit Golf Course in Medora, one of America's premiere courses near the national park.

★ **Away from it all:** As this is not a heavily visited park, you'll likely encounter more wild horses than people here.

1 North Unit. Visitors looking to enjoy the great outdoors should be sure to travel along the 14-mile scenic drive and stop at one of the many hiking trailheads along the way. These trailheads give easy access to the backcountry of the North Unit.

2 South Unit. Often considered the main unit of Theodore Roosevelt National Park and adjacent to the famous town of Medora, the South Unit is the home to some of the former president's personal artifacts and even his cabin.

3 Elkhorn Ranch. This area of the park is the actual location of one of T.R.'s ranches in the badlands. None of the ranch buildings are still standing, but signs show their former location.

GETTING ORIENTED

The Little Missouri River winds throughout this western North Dakota park, and plenty of bison, deer, pronghorn, coyote, prairie dogs, and eagles inhabit the land. Climb the peaks and you will get exceptional views of the canyons, caprocks, petrified forest, and other bizarre geological formations that make up the badlands.

KEY	
🧍	Ranger Station
⛺	Campground
🪑	Picnic Area
🍴	Restaurant
🏠	Lodge
🚶	Trailhead
🚻	Restrooms
⤴	Scenic Viewpoint
┈┈	Walking/Hiking Trails

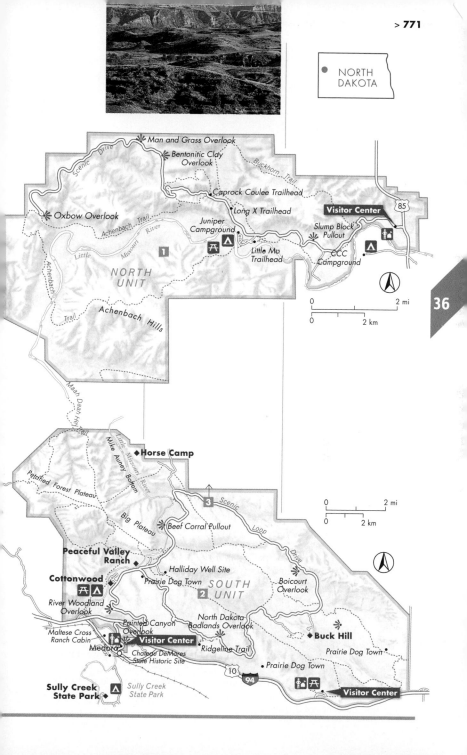

NORTH
DAKOTA

36

Man and Grass Overlook

Bentonitic Clay
Overlook

Scenic Drive

Buckhorn Trail

Caprock Coulee Trailhead

Visitor Center

85

Long X Trailhead

Oxbow Overlook

Achenbach Trail

Juniper
Campground

Slump Block
Pullout

Little Missouri River

Little Mo
Trailhead

CCC
Campground

1

Achenbach

**NORTH
UNIT**

Achenbach Hills

Trail

0   2 mi

0   2 km

Maah Daah Hey Trail

Little Missouri River

◆Horse Camp

Mike Auney Bottom

Petrified Forest Plateau

3 *Scenic*

Big Plateau

Beef Corral Pullout

Loop

**Peaceful Valley
Ranch**

Halliday Well Site

Drive

Cottonwood

Prairie Dog Town

**SOUTH
UNIT**

Boicourt
Overlook

River Woodland
Overlook

2

Maltese Cross
Ranch Cabin

Painted Canyon
Overlook

North Dakota
Badlands Overlook

◆Buck Hill

Visitor Center

Medora

Ridgeline Trail

Prairie Dog Town

Chateau DeMores
State Historic Site

10

Prairie Dog Town

**Sully Creek
State Park ◆**

94

*Sully Creek
State Park*

Visitor Center

0   2 mi

0   2 km

Updated by
T.D. Griffith

Across the open plains of North Dakota, you can travel for miles without seeing a house or business. But today, with some towns doubling in population due to a new landscape formed in the wake of the discovery of the Bakken Oil Field, you are more likely to see one of 8,000 wells and countless drilling rigs on the horizon than you are deer or antelope. That same development is slowly encroaching on the craggy ravines, tablelands, and gorges of the North Dakota badlands.

For a century and a quarter, the terrain remained virtually unchanged from the day Theodore Roosevelt stepped off the train here in 1883, eager to shoot his first bison. Within two weeks, the future 26th president purchased an open-range cattle ranch, and the following year he returned to establish a second, which is part of the 110-square-mile national park that today bears his name.

Roosevelt became dedicated to the preservation of the animals and land he saw devastated by hunting and overgrazing. He established the U.S. Forest Service and signed into law 150 national forests, 51 bird reserves, 4 game preserves, 5 national parks, and established 18 national monuments. Theodore Roosevelt National Park was created in 1947 to commemorate his efforts.

THEODORE ROOSEVELT PLANNER

WHEN TO GO
The park is open year-round, but North Dakota winters can be brutal—very cold and windy. Portions of some roads close during winter months, depending on snowfall. Rangers discontinue their outdoor programs when autumn comes, and they recommend that only experienced hikers do any winter explorations. Check the park's website for current conditions.

■TIP→ **Although July and August tend to be the busiest months, the park is rarely crowded.** About 600,000 people visit each year, with the South Unit receiving the greatest number of visitors. The best times to see wildlife and hike comfortably are May through October. The park is all but desolate December through February, but it's a beautiful time to see the wildlife—also, winter sunsets can be very vivid as the colors reflect off the snow and ice. The park gets an average of 30 inches of snow per year.

AVG. HIGH/LOW TEMPS.

JAN.	FEB.	MAR.	APR.	MAY	JUNE
27/1	34/8	43/18	58/30	71/40	79/50
JULY	AUG.	SEPT.	OCT.	NOV.	DEC.
87/55	87/52	75/41	62/30	43/17	32/7

FESTIVALS AND EVENTS

JULY **Killdeer Mountain Roundup Rodeo.** Begun in 1923, this is North Dakota's oldest rodeo sanctioned by the PRCA. The community goes all out, hosting a parade, street dance, community barbecue, and fireworks display on July 3 and 4. ☎ *701/764–5777* ⊕ *www.kildeer.com.*

AUGUST **Founder's Day.** Each August 25, this holiday commemorates the establishment of the National Park Service in 1916. The visitor centers host special programs and serve cookies and lemonade. ☎ *701/623–4466.*

Stargazing. Without light pollution from nearby towns, Theodore Roosevelt National Park is ideal for astronomical observation any cloudless night of the year. To enjoy the stars with others, come during an annual event when, on a late August weekend, the Northern Sky Astronomical Society sets up telescopes for an all-night star-watching party. ⊕ *www. und.edu/org/nsas* ✉ *Free.*

DECEMBER **Old-Fashioned Cowboy Christmas.** Held the first full weekend in December in downtown Medora, the festivities begin with a wreath-hanging ceremony at the community center, followed by poetry readings, a holiday doll show, sleigh rides, and a dance. ☎ *701/623–4910.*

PLANNING YOUR TIME
THEODORE ROOSEVELT IN ONE DAY

With just one day, focus on the South Unit. Arrive early at the **Painted Canyon Scenic Overlook,** near the visitor center, for a sweeping and colorful vista of the canyon's rock formations. Stay awhile to watch the effect of the sun's progress across the sky, or come back in the evening to witness the deepening colors and silhouettes in the fading sunlight.

Continue to the **South Unit Visitor Center** in Medora, spending about an hour here touring the Theodore Roosevelt exhibit and the Maltese Cross Ranch Cabin. Circle the 36-mile **Scenic Loop Drive** twice: once to stop and walk a few trails and visit the overlooks, and once at night to watch the wildlife. Your first time around, go counterclockwise. Stop at **Scoria Point Overlook** and hike 0.6 mile on **Ridgeline Nature Trail.** Back on the drive, stop next at the North Dakota Badlands and Boicourt overlooks to gaze at the strange, ever-changing terrain. When you pass through Peaceful Valley, look for prairie dogs. Have a packed lunch

36

Plants and Wildlife in Theodore Roosevelt

The park's landscape is one of prairies marked by cliffs and rock chasms made of alternating layers of sandstone, siltstone, mudstone, and bentonite clay. In spring the prairies are awash with tall grasses, wildflowers, and shrubs including the ubiquitous poison ivy. The pesky plant also inhabits the forests, where you find box elders, ash, and junipers among the trees. To avoid the rash-inducing plant—and scrapes and bruises that may come from rocks and thick undergrowth—it's always advisable to hike with long pants and sturdy boots.

More than 400 American bison live in the park. These normally docile beasts look tame, but with a set of horns, up to a ton of weight and legs that will carry them at speeds in excess of 35 mph, they could be the most dangerous animals within park boundaries. Rangers tell visitors repeatedly not to approach them. Some mountain lions also live in the park but are rarely seen. The same goes for prairie rattlers.

On the less threatening side of the park's fauna, a herd of more than 200 to 300 elk live in the South Unit. As many as 150 feral horses are also in the South Unit. The North Unit has some longhorn steers, which are often found in the bison corral area, about 2½ miles west of the visitor center.

---

at the **Cottonwood picnic area,** then use a couple of hours to hike Jones Creek Trail or Coal Vein Nature Trail—or sign up for a horseback ride at **Peaceful Valley Ranch.**

Return to your car at least an hour before sunset, and drive slowly around Scenic Loop Drive, clockwise this time, to view the wildlife. Plan to be at **Buck Hill** for one of the most spectacular sunsets you'll ever see. Bring a jacket, because it's a bit windy and it gets chilly as the sun sets. After dark, drive carefully out of the park—elk and other animals may still be on the road.

GETTING HERE AND AROUND
AIR TRAVEL
Planes fly into the North Dakota towns of Bismarck, Dickinson, and Williston.

CAR TRAVEL
Getting to and from the park is relatively easy due to its close proximity to Medora, as well as exceptional signage. The South Unit entrance and visitor center is just off I–94 in Medora at exits 24 and 27. The Painted Canyon Visitor Center is 7 miles east of Medora at exit 32. The North Unit entrance is south of Watford City on U.S. 85. Bus transportation is available along I–94, with a stop in Medora that is only three blocks from the park entrance.

There's ample parking space at all trailheads, and parking is free. Some roads are closed in winter. You may encounter bison and other wildlife on the roadway.

TRAIN TRAVEL
Amtrak serves Williston.

PARK ESSENTIALS

PARK FEES AND PERMITS

The entrance pass is $10 per vehicle, good for seven days. An annual pass is $20. A backcountry permit, free from the visitor centers, is required for overnight camping away from campgrounds.

PARK HOURS

The park is open year-round. The North Unit is in the Central time zone. The South Unit and the Painted Canyon Visitor Center are in the Mountain time zone.

CELL-PHONE RECEPTION

Cell-phone reception occurs in some areas of the park, but many places receive no signal. Public telephones can be found at the South Unit's Cottonwood Campground, at the Painted Canyon Visitor Center, and at the North Unit Visitor Center.

RESTAURANTS

One does not visit Theodore Roosevelt National Park for the fine dining. In fact, the only venues within the park are the picnic areas, and provided you've prepared, this can be a perfectly simple and satisfying way to experience the open spaces and natural wonder of the badlands. In the towns near the park you'll find casual, down-to-earth family establishments that largely cater to the locals. Expect steak and potatoes, and lots of them. Fortunately, the beef here is among the best in the country.

Prices in the reviews are the average coast of a main course at dinner, or if dinner is not served, at lunch.

HOTELS

If you're set on sleeping within the park, be sure to pack your tent. Outside the park are mostly small chain hotels catering to interstate travelers—largely retired couples in RVs and young families in minivans. However, there is a handful of historic properties and working ranches that offer guests a truly Western experience. Due to the current oil boom in the region, it's essential to book ahead during summer months.

Prices in the reviews are the lowest cost of a standard double room in high season. For expanded reviews, facilities, and current deals, visit Fodors.com.

VISITOR INFORMATION

PARK CONTACT INFORMATION

Theodore Roosevelt National Park. Theodore Roosevelt National Park ☎ *701/842–2333 for North Unit, 701/575–4020 for Painted Canyon, 701/623–4466 for South Unit* ⊕ *www.nps.gov/thro.*

VISITOR CENTERS

North Unit Visitor Center. Here you'll find a bookstore and small auditorium where you can watch park films to acquaint you with the park. ✉ *North Unit entrance, off U.S. 85, North Unit* ☎ *701/842–2333* ⊕ *www.nps.gov/thro* ☉ *Memorial Day–Labor Day, daily 9–5:30; check park website for off-season hrs.*

Painted Canyon Visitor Center. Easily reached off Interstate 94, this South Unit Visitor Center has a bookstore and exhibits. ⊠ *Exit 32 off I–94, South Unit* ☎ *701/575–4020* ⊕ *www.nps.gov/thro* ☉ *Mid-June–Labor Day, daily 8–6; May–mid-June and early Sept. and Oct., daily 8:30–4:30.*

South Unit Visitor Center. This building houses a large auditorium screening films about the park, plus an excellent exhibit on Theodore Roosevelt's life. On display are artifacts such as the clothing Roosevelt wore while ranching in the Dakota Territory, his firearms, and several writings in his own hand reflecting his thoughts on the nation's environmental resources. A bookstore and public restrooms are available. ⊠ *South Unit entrance, exits 24 and 27 off I–94* ☎ *701/623–4466* ⊕ *www.nps.gov/thro* ☉ *June–Sept., daily 8–6; Oct.–May, daily 8–4:30.*

> **BEST BETS FOR FAMILIES**
>
> ■ **Horseback Riding.** Saddling up and riding astride a horse for a while let kids relive the days of the Old West.
>
> ■ **Medora Musical.** This show is a fun summer event with surprisingly diverse acts. For the complete package, hit the Pitchfork Fondue before the show.
>
> ■ **Stargazing Party.** Look upon the seemingly endless stars in the vast North Dakota sky.

EXPLORING

SCENIC DRIVES

North Unit Scenic Drive. The 14-mile, two-way drive follows rugged terrain above spectacular views of the canyons, and is flanked by more than a dozen turnouts with interpretive signs. Notice the slump blocks, massive segments of rock that have slipped down the cliff walls over time. Farther along pass through badlands coulees, deep-water clefts that are now dry. There's a good chance of meeting bison, mule deer, and bighorn sheep along the way, also keep an eye out for longhorn steers, just like the ones you would see in Texas. ⊠ *From the unit entrance to Oxbow Overlook, North Unit.*

South Unit Scenic Loop Drive. A 36-mile, two-way scenic loop takes you past prairie dog towns, coal veins, trailheads, and panoramic views of the badlands. Information on the park's natural history is posted at the various overlooks—stop at all of the interpretive signs to learn about the park's natural and historical phenomena. Some of the best views can be seen from Scoria Point Overlook, Boicourt Overlook, North Dakota Badlands Overlook, Skyline Vista, and Buck Hill. If you hit the road at dusk, be prepared to get caught in a buffalo traffic jam, as the huge creatures sometimes block the road and aren't in any hurry to move. Don't get out of your car or honk at them—they don't like it. ⊠ *Loop begins near Peaceful Valley Ranch, South Unit.*

Don't let these bulky beasts fool you: even though a bison may weigh 2,000 pounds, it can run 35 mph.

HISTORIC SITES

Elkhorn Ranch. This unit of the park is composed of the 218 acres of ranchland where Theodore Roosevelt ran cattle on the open range. Today there are no buildings, but foundation blocks outline the original structures. Check with visitor center staff about road conditions. ✉ *35 miles north of South Unit Visitor Center* ☎ *701/623–4466 for South Unit.*

Maltese Cross Ranch Cabin. About 7 miles from its original site in the river bottom sits the cabin Theodore Roosevelt commissioned to be built on his Dakota Territory property. Inside are Roosevelt's original writing table and rocking chair. Interpretive tours are scheduled every day June–September. ✉ *South Unit entrance, exits 24 and 27 off I–94* ☎ *701/623–4466 for South Unit.*

SCENIC STOPS

Fodor's Choice ★ **Buck Hill.** At 2,855 feet, this is one of the highest points in the park and provides a spectacular 360-degree view of the badlands. Come here for the sunset. ✉ *17 miles east of the South Unit Visitor Center.*

Oxbow Overlook. The view from this spot at the end of the North Unit drive looks over the unit's westerly badlands and the Little Missouri River, where it takes a sharp turn south. This is the place to come for stargazing. ✉ *14 miles west of the North Unit Visitor Center.*

Painted Canyon Scenic Overlook. Catch your first glimpse of badlands majesty here—the South Unit canyon's colors change dramatically with the movement of the sun across the sky. ✉ *Exit 32 off I–94, South Unit.*

Petrified Forest. Although bits of petrified wood have been found all over the park, the densest collection is in the South Unit's west end, accessible on foot or horseback via the Petrified Forest Loop Trail from Peaceful Valley Ranch (10 miles round-trip) or from the park's west boundary (3 miles round-trip). ⊠ *Trailheads: Peaceful Valley Ranch, 7 miles north of the South Unit Visitor Center; west boundary, 10 miles north of exit 23 off I–94/U.S. 10.*

Sperati Point. For a great view of the Missouri River's 90-degree angle, hike a 1½-mile round-trip trail to this spot 430 feet above the river-bed. ⊠ *14 miles west of the North Unit Visitor Center* ⊕ *www.nps. gov/thro.*

EDUCATIONAL OFFERINGS

RANGER PROGRAMS

Evening Campfires. Rangers host hour-long presentations and discussions on such subjects as park history, astronomy, fires, and wildlife. Look for times and subjects posted at park campgrounds. ⊠ *Cottonwood Campground, South Unit; Juniper Campground, North Unit* ⊙ *June–mid-Sept., daily.*

Ranger-Led Talks and Walks. Rangers take visitors on the trails of both units and through the backcountry and Elkhorn Ranch, discussing such subjects as geology, paleontology, wildlife, and natural history. Check at campground entrances or at the visitor centers for times, topics, departure points, and destinations. ☎ *701/623–4466* 🖾 *Free* ⊙ *June–mid-Sept., daily.*

FILM

T.R. Country. All three visitor centers show 13-minute film focusing on the unique beauty and breathtaking landscape of North Dakota's badlands, its wildlife, and its history, narrated with Roosevelt's own words. ⊠ *South Unit, North Unit, and Painted Canyon visitor centers* ☎ *701/623–4466* 🖾 *Free* ⊙ *Daily, every half hr.*

SPORTS AND THE OUTDOORS

During the summer months, the park is best seen by hiking its many trails. If visitors want to take in the park the way the West's original settlers did, there are ample opportunities to saddle up and view the park on horseback.

BICYCLING

Bikes are allowed on interior roads but not off-road. Cyclists on the multiuse Maah Daah Hey Trail aren't allowed on the portions of the trails within the park.

FISHING

Catfish, little suckers, northern pikes, and goldeyes are among the underwater inhabitants of the Little Missouri River. If you wish to fish in the park or elsewhere in the state and are over age 16, you must obtain a North Dakota fishing license. For out-of-state residents, a three-day permit is $15, a 10-day permit is $25, and a one-year permit is $45. For in-state residents, a one-year permit is $10.

Buffalo Gap Guest Ranch. The Buffalo Gap Guest Ranch, 8 miles west of Medora, sells hunting and fishing licenses. ⊠ *3100 Buffalo Gap Rd., Medora* ☎ *701/623–4200* ⊕ *www.buffalogapguestranch.com.*

TOURS AND OUTFITTERS
Greg Simonson Fishing Services. A champion of several regional and state fishing tournaments, the owner of Greg Simonson Fishing Services leads individuals or groups on expeditions through the park and the outlying grasslands. ⊠ *13892 U.S. 85 N, Alexander* ☎ *701/828–3425.*

HIKING

Particularly in the South Unit, there are numerous opportunities to jump on a trail right from the park road. The North and South units are connected by the 96-mile Maah Daah Hey Trail. Backcountry hiking is allowed, but you need a permit (free from any visitor center) to camp in the wild. Park maps are available at all three visitor centers. If you plan to camp overnight, let several people know about where you plan to pitch your tent, and inquire about river conditions, maps, regulations, trail updates, and additional water sources before setting out.

NORTH UNIT
EASY
FAMILY **Buckhorn Trail.** A thriving prairie-dog town is just 1 mile from the trailhead of this 11-mile North Unit trail. It travels over level grasslands, then it loops back along the banks of Squaw Creek. If you're an experienced hiker, you'll complete the entire trail in about half a day. Novices or families might want to plan on a whole day, however. *Easy.* ⊠ *Trailhead at the Caprock Coulee Nature Trail, 1½ miles west of the Juniper Campground.*

FAMILY **Little Mo Nature Trail.** Flat and only 1.1-mile long, this trail in the North Unit passes through badlands and woodlands to the river's edge. The first 0.7 mile is wheelchair accessible. It's a great way to see the park's diverse terrain and wildlife, and because it shouldn't take you longer than an hour, it's a great trail for families with children. *Easy.* ⊠ *Trailhead at Juniper Campground in the North Unit* ⊕ *www.nps.gov/thro.*

DIFFICULT
Upper Caprock Coulee Trail. This 4.3-mile round-trip trail follows a loop around the pockmarked lower-badlands coulees. There's a slow incline that takes you up 300 feet. Portions of the trail are slippery. Beginners should plan a half day for this hike. *Difficult.* ⊠ *Trailhead 8 miles west of North Unit Visitor Center* ⊕ *www.nps.gov/thro.*

36

SOUTH UNIT
MODERATE

Fodor'sChoice **Maah Daah Hey Trail.** Hike, bike, or ride horseback on the 96-mile and
★ growing Maah Daah Hey Trail, the most popular and well-maintained
trail in western North Dakota. An expansion project, completed in
the summer of 2010, opened up new vistas that were previously inaccessible. The trail traverses both park units and the Little Missouri
National Grasslands. Maps are available at the park visitor centers.
Walking the entire trail is a true wilderness adventure and will probably take you at least five days. If you want to do something shorter,
such as a two- or three-hour hike, leave from the South Unit and walk
an hour or hour and a half in one direction, and then return. *Moderate.* ⊠ *Begins at Sully Creek State Park, 3 miles south of South Unit
Visitor Center* ⊕ *www.nps.gov/thro.*

HORSEBACK RIDING

The best way to see many of the park's sights is on horseback. You
are allowed to bring your own horse to the park, or you can sign up
for a guided trip. Horses are allowed only on backcountry trails or
cross-country. Like campers, riders must obtain free backcountry-use
permits. Riders taking multiday trips through the park must also have
a permit. Horses are not allowed on park roadways, in developed
campgrounds, picnic areas, or on developed nature trails. Overnight
parties in the backcountry are limited to a maximum of eight horses
and eight riders per group. Horses must be tied down securely when
not being ridden. Be sure to bring enough water for the animals and
certified weed-free hay.

TOURS AND OUTFITTERS
Peaceful Valley Ranch Horse Rides. Experienced guides at Peaceful Valley
Ranch Horse Rides help you to see the park the way trappers, ranchers,
and pioneers did a century ago. Rides are 90 minutes to 2½ hours long.
⊠ *South Unit* ☎ *701/623–4568* ☉ *Late May–Labor Day.*

WHAT'S NEARBY

NEARBY TOWNS

Medora, gateway to the park's South Unit, may have a population of
only 96, but it is a walkable town with several museums, tiny shops,
and plenty of restaurants and places to stay. Its Wild West history is
reenacted in a madcap musical production each night in summer. To
the east is **Dickinson** (pop. 28,000), the largest town near the national
park. North of Dickinson and about 35 miles east of the park's North
Unit, **Killdeer** (pop. about 825) is known for its Roundup Rodeo—
North Dakota's oldest—and its gorgeous scenery. Killdeer is the place
to fill your tank, because there isn't another gas station around for
40 miles. **Williston** (pop. about 30,000) is 60 miles north of the North
Unit, just over the Missouri River. The Amtrak stop nearest to the
national park is here.

VISITOR INFORMATION

Dickinson Convention and Visitors Bureau ⊠ *72 W. Museum Dr., Dickinson* ☎ *701/483–4988, 800/279–7391* ⊕ *www.visitdickinson.com.* **Killdeer City Hall** ⊠ *165 Railroad St., Killdeer* ☎ *701/764–5295* ⊕ *www.killdeer.com.* **Medora Chamber of Commerce** ⊠ *475 4th St., Medora* ☎ *701/623–4829* ⊕ *www.medorand.com.* **Williston Convention and Visitors Bureau** ⊠ *212 Airport Rd., Williston* ☎ *701/774–9041, 800/615–9041* ⊕ *www.willistonnd.com.*

NEARBY ATTRACTIONS

FAMILY **Dakota Dinosaur Museum.** A huge triceratops greets you at the entrance of this museum, which houses dozens of dinosaur bones, fossilized plants and seashells, and rocks and minerals collected around the world. ⊠ *200 Museum Dr. E, Dickinson* ☎ *701/225–3466* ⊕ *www.dakotadino. com* ☞ *$8* ⊗ *May–Labor Day, daily 9–5.*

Little Missouri State Park. Called *Mako Shika* or "Land Bad" by the Sioux, the unusual land formations here create the state's most awe-inspiring scenery. The beehive-shaped rock formations resulted from the erosion of sedimentary rock deposited millions of years ago by streams flowing from the Rocky Mountains. Undeveloped and rugged, this wilderness area has primitive and modern camping and 50 miles of horse trails. ⊠ *Off Rte. 22, 18 miles north and 2 miles east of Killdeer* ☎ *701/764–5256 in summer, 701/794–3731 in winter* ⊕ *www.parkrec. nd.gov/parks/lmosp/lmosp.html* ☞ *$5 per vehicle* ⊗ *Daily.*

North Dakota Cowboy Hall of Fame. This $4 million museum features six galleries and rotating exhibits, hosts special events, and is dedicated to the horse culture of the plains. ⊠ *250 Main St., Medora* ☎ *701/623–2000* ⊕ *www.northdakotacowboy.com* ☞ *$8* ⊗ *May–Sept., daily 9–6.*

Roadside Art. Known as the "Enchanted Highway," this self-guided 30-mile driving tour on Route 21 south of Dickinson features seven giant metal sculptures designed by a local artist, including a 51-foot Teddy Roosevelt. Massive sculptures include a deer crossing, grasshopper family, pheasants on the prairie, a 150-foot-long gaggle of geese, and a tin family with a 45-foot father, 44-foot mother, and 23-foot son. ⊠ *Exit 72 off I–94, Rte. 21 between Lefor and Regent, Dickinson* ☎ *701/483–4988, 800/279–7391* ☞ *Free.*

AREA ACTIVITIES

SPORTS AND THE OUTDOORS

GOLF

Fodor's Choice ★ **Bully Pulpit Golf Course.** This impressive golf course weaves its way through the badlands buttes, giving players a truly breathtaking backdrop for a round of golf, and some exceptional vertical teeboxes and greens. At 4,750 total yards from the forward tees to a challenging 7,166 at the tips, this course was voted the number-one affordable public golf course in the nation and remains in the top 100 public courses in the United States. ⊠ *East River Rd., Medora* ☎ *701/623–4653* ☞ *$85, includes cart* ⊗ *Mid-Apr.–Oct., daily dawn–dusk.*

36

Best Campgrounds in Theodore Roosevelt

For the adventurous traveler, camping in Theodore Roosevelt is well worth the effort. The unadulterated isolation, epic views, and relationship with nature afforded by the Spartan campgrounds within the park create an experience you'll be hard-pressed to find elsewhere in the United States. Just remember that the park's campgrounds are relatively undeveloped—you'll have to pack in everything you need. If you pick a campsite in the surrounding wilderness, you must obtain a backcountry camping permit (available free) from a visitor center first.

Cottonwood Campground. Nestled under juniper and cottonwood trees on the bank of the Little Missouri River, this is a wonderful place to watch buffalo, elk, and other wildlife drink from the river at sunrise and just before sunset. ⊠ *½ mile north of South Unit Visitor Center* ☎ *701/623–4466.*

Juniper Campground. The sites here are surrounded by junipers, hence the name. Don't be surprised if you see a bison herd wander through on its way to the Little Missouri River. ⊠ *5 miles west of North Unit Visitor Center* ☎ *701/842–2333.*

ARTS AND ENTERTAINMENT

FAMILY **Medora Musical.** Well worth your while in summer is this theatrical tribute to the Old West, its history, and its personalities. ⊠ *3422 Chateau Rd.* ☎ *701/623–4444, 800/633–6721* ⊕ *www.medora.com* ☜ *$35* ☉ *Early June–Labor Day, daily 7:30 pm.*

SHOPPING

Prairie Fire Pottery. Handmade stoneware pottery and terra-cotta tiles with exceptional glazes are displayed and sold in this studio and showroom. The studio also produces 27 different animal-track tiles, all cast from actual tracks. ⊠ *127 Main St. E, Beach* ☎ *701/872–3855, 888/229-9496* ⊕ *www.prairiefirepottery.com.*

Western Edge Books, Artwork, Music. For books on Western regional history and other topics stop by this bookstore in downtown Medora. ⊠ *425 Fourth St., Medora* ☎ *701/623–4345* ⊕ *www.westernedgebooks.com.*

WHERE TO EAT

IN THE PARK

PICNIC AREAS

Cottonwood. This is in a lovely valley near the river. There are fire pits, drinking water, restrooms, eight open tables, and eight covered tables. ⊠ *5½ miles north of South Unit Visitor Center.*

Juniper. This area has restrooms, grills, drinking water, and 28 tables (eight with shelter). ⊠ *5 miles west of North Unit Visitor Center.*

Painted Canyon Scenic Overlook. This area has eight covered tables, drinking water, restrooms, and a spectacular view. ⊠ *Exit 32 off I–94.*

OUTSIDE THE PARK

$$ STEAKHOUSE 🍴 **Boots Bar and Grill.** This watering hole is the type of place your grandpa probably talked about. It's replete with Medora's largest tavern, an upstairs dining room, and breezy patios, as well as live music, dancing, and microbrews. Diners feast primarily on pizzas, burgers, and steak and it's kid-friendly until 10 pm, even friendlier afterward. [$] *Average main: $20* ✉ *300 Pacific Ave., Medora* ☎ *701/623–2668* 🌐 *www.bootsbarmedora.com.*

$$ STEAKHOUSE 🍴 **Buckskin Bar and Grill.** This steakhouse, with a saloon and dance hall, was built in 1915. The building has rough-hewn walls, original wood floors, tin ceilings, and its still the local hangout for the ranching community who saunter in for the prime rib and latest local news. Photos of local cowboy celebrities who dined here line the walls. Steak and seafood are the kitchen's main focus, with prime rib a specialty. For dessert, the homemade peach and cherry cobbler is a must. There is a kids' menu, and the premises are nonsmoking. [$] *Average main: $17* ✉ *64 Central Ave. S, Killdeer* ☎ *701/764–5321.*

$ AMERICAN 🍴 **Cowboy Cafe.** This locally owned-and-operated café specializes in homemade soups, caramel rolls, and delicious roast beef dishes. Be prepared for a (short) wait, since the cozy dining room is popular with both locals and visitors, particularly at breakfast. [$] *Average main: $8* ✉ *215 4th St., Medora* ☎ *701/623–4343* 💳 *No credit cards.*

$$$ AMERICAN Fodor's Choice ★ 🍴 **Theodore's.** Theodore's offers the best fine dining in Medora and, perhaps, in western North Dakota. The lunch menu features salads, prime-rib sandwiches, and buffalo burgers, while dinner fare includes shrimp with pineapple dipping sauce, a crusted South American ribeye, and tenderloin with Gorgonzola cream sauce. The stained glass and wood paneling makes this restaurant inside the Rough Riders Hotel feel like a little hideaway for a quiet lunch or dinner. The fireplace was built from bricks taken from the North Dakota Capitol that burned in 1930. T. R.'s Tavern has a full-service bar. [$] *Average main: $24* ✉ *Rough Riders Hotel, 301 3rd Ave., Medora* ☎ *701/623–4433.*

WHERE TO STAY

OUTSIDE THE PARK

$$$ B&B/INN 🏨 **AmericInn Motel and Suites.** A Western theme, complete with mounted animals, dominates the public areas of this contemporary hotel. **Pros:** near shops and restaurants; indoor pool; ideal after long hikes in the park. **Cons:** right on the railroad tracks; no elevator; chain-hotel feel. [$] *Rooms from: $189* ✉ *75 E. River Rd. S, Medora* ☎ *701/623–4800, 800/634–3444* 🌐 *www.americinn.com* 🛏 *77 rooms, 8 suites* 🍽 *Breakfast.*

$ HOTEL 🏨 **Buffalo Gap Guest Ranch.** Perched on a bluff 8 miles west of Medora, this rustic property commands a view of the Dakota badlands and has access to the Maah Daah Hey Trail. **Pros:** great prices on lodging and food; exceptional view; large outdoor patio. **Cons:** bar can be smoky; 10 minutes from town. [$] *Rooms from: $95* ✉ *3100 Buffalo*

36

Gap Rd., Medora ☎ 701/623–4200 🌐 www.buffalogapguestranch.com 🛏 22 cabins, 10 RV sites 🍴 No meals.

$$ HOTEL 🏨 **Ramada Grand Dakota Lodge & Conference Center.** Across from the Prairie Hills Mall, this three-story motel lets you relax on couches before the fireplace in the huge lobby. **Pros:** full-service restaurant; great customer service. **Cons:** can be busy; pool can be quite popular, particularly in the summer. [$] *Rooms from: $149 ✉ 532 15th St. W, Dickinson ☎ 701/483–5600, 800/422–0949 🌐 www.granddakotalodge.com 🛏 192 rooms, 47 suites 🍴 No meals.*

$$$ HOTEL Fodor's Choice ★ 🏨 **Rough Riders Hotel.** Renovations over the years have made this place decidedly posh, but it retains the red velvet chairs, antique armoires, and iron-rod and oak bed frames that have made this property a favorite for decades. **Pros:** historic, downtown location; dining on the premises. **Cons:** relatively expensive; occasional railroad noise. [$] *Rooms from: $189 ✉ 301 3rd Ave., Medora ☎ 701/623–4444, 800/633–6721 🌐 www.medora.com 🛏 76 rooms 🍴 No meals.*

WIND CAVE NATIONAL PARK

And the Black Hills

WELCOME TO WIND CAVE

TOP REASONS TO GO

★ **Underground exploring:** Wind Cave offers visitors the chance to get their hands and feet dirty on a four-hour guided tour through one of America's longest and most complex caves.

★ **The call of the wild:** Wind Cave National Park boasts a wide variety of animals: bison, coyote, deer, antelope, elk, prairie dogs, and 215 species of birds, to name just a few.

★ **Education by candlelight:** Wind Cave offers numerous educational and interpretive programs, including the Candlelight Cave Tour, which allows guests to explore the cave by candlelight only.

★ **Noteworthy neighbors:** On the north border of Wind Cave sits Custer State Park, one of South Dakota's can't-miss areas. With its close proximity to numerous other national parks, state parks, and other monuments and memorials, Wind Cave is situated perfectly to explore some of America's greatest national treasures.

1 **The Surface.** Wind Cave lies at the confluence of western mountains and central plains, which blesses the park with a unique landscape. A series of established trails weaves in and out of forested hillsides and grassy meadows, providing treks of varying difficulty.

2 **The Cave.** With an explored maze of caverns totaling 141 miles, Wind Cave is considered one of the longest caves in the world. Notably, scientists estimate that only 5% of the cave has been explored to date. It is also estimated that 95% of the world's boxwork formations are found in Wind Cave, which means that visitors here are treated to some of the rarest geological features on the planet.

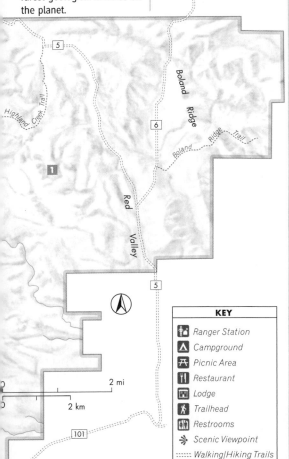

SOUTH
DAKOTA

GETTING ORIENTED

Bounded by Black Hills National Forest to the west and windswept prairie to the east, Wind Cave National Park, in south-western South Dakota, encompasses the transi-tion between two distinct ecosystems: mountain forest and mixed-grass prairie. Abundant wildlife, including bison and elk, roam the 33,851 acres of the park's diverse terrain. Underground, a year-round 53°F temperature gives summer visitors a cool oasis—and winter visitors a warm escape.

37

KEY

🕴️ *Ranger Station*

🏕️ *Campground*

🎋 *Picnic Area*

🍴 *Restaurant*

🏨 *Lodge*

🥾 *Trailhead*

🚻 *Restrooms*

➹ *Scenic Viewpoint*

∷∷∷∷ *Walking/Hiking Trails*

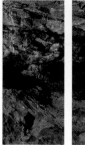

Updated by
T.D. Griffith

If you don't get out of your car at Wind Cave, you haven't scratched the surface—literally. The park has more than 141 miles of underground passageways. Curious cave formations include 95% of the world's mineral boxwork, and gypsum beard so sensitive it reacts to the heat of a lamp. This underground wilderness is part of a giant limestone labyrinth beneath the Black Hills. Wind Cave ranks as the sixth-longest cave in the world, but experts believe 95% of it has yet to be mapped.

WIND CAVE PLANNER

WHEN TO GO

The biggest crowds come to Wind Cave from June to September, but the park and surrounding Black Hills are large enough to diffuse the masses. Neither the cave nor grounds above are ever too packed. Park officials contend it's actually less busy during the first full week in August, when the Sturgis Motorcycle Rally brings roughly a half-million bikers to the region, clogging highways for miles around. Most hotels within a 100-mile radius are booked up to a year in advance.

The colder months are the least crowded, though you can still explore underground, thanks to the cave's constant 53°F temperature. The shoulder seasons are also unpopular, though autumn is a perfect time to visit. The days are warm, the nights are cool, and in late September/early October the park's canyons and coulees display incredible colors.

AVG. HIGH/LOW TEMPS.

JAN.	FEB.	MAR.	APR.	MAY	JUNE
37/8	41/14	49/21	58/30	67/40	77/49

JULY	AUG.	SEPT.	OCT.	NOV.	DEC.
84/55	84/53	76/44	63/32	46/20	39/12

FESTIVALS AND EVENTS

JUNE **Crazy Horse Volksmarch.** This 6.2-mile hike up the mountain where the massive Crazy Horse Memorial is being carved is the largest event of its kind and gives hikers the opportunity to stand on the Lakota leader's outstretched arm. It's held the first full weekend in June. ☎ *605/673–4681* ⊕ *www.crazyhorse.org.*

JULY **Days of '76.** This award-winning PRCA outdoor rodeo includes the usual riding, roping, and bull-riding, two parades with vintage carriages and coaches, and Western arts and crafts. This five-day affair is one of the most popular events in South Dakota. ☎ *800/999–1876* ⊕ *www.daysof76.com.*

Gold Discovery Days. A parade, carnival, car show, stick-horse rodeo, balloon rally and bed races are all part of the fun at this three-day event in late July in Custer. ☎ *800/992–9818* ⊕ *www.golddiscoverydays.com.*

SEPTEMBER **Custer State Park Buffalo Roundup.** The nation's largest buffalo roundup is one of South Dakota's most exciting events. Early on a Monday morning in late September or early October, cowboys and rangers saddle up and corral the park's 1,400 head of bison so they can be vaccinated. ☎ *605/255–4515* ⊕ *www.gfp.sd.gov/state-parks/directory/custer.*

Deadwood Jam. Two decades and still filling the streets of Deadwood with live music, the Black Hills' premiere music festival showcases an ecelectic collection of country, rock, and blues for two days in mid-September. ☎ *800/999–1876* ⊕ *www.deadwood.org/events/deadwoodjam.*

PLANNING YOUR TIME
WIND CAVE IN ONE DAY

Pack a picnic lunch, then head to the visitor center to purchase tickets for a morning tour of Wind Cave. Visit the exhibit rooms in the center afterward. Then drive or walk the quarter mile to the picnic area north of the visitor center. The refreshing air and deep emerald color of the pine woodlands will flavor your meal.

In the afternoon, take a leisurely drive through the parklands south of the visitor center, passing through **Gobbler Pass** and **Bison Flats**, for an archetypal view of the park and to look for wildlife. On the way back north, follow U.S. 385 east toward **Wind Cave Canyon**. If you enjoy bird-watching, park at the turnout and hike the 1.8-mile trail into the canyon, where you can spot swallows and great horned owls in the cliffs and woodpeckers in the trees.

Get back on the highway going north, take a right on Highway 87, and continue a half mile to the turnout for **Centennial Trail**. Hike the trail about 2 miles to the junction with **Lookout Point Trail**, turn right and return to Highway 87. The whole loop is about 4.75 miles. As you continue driving north to the top of Rankin Ridge, a pull-out to the right serves as the starting point for 1.25-mile **Rankin Ridge Trail**. It loops around the ridge, past **Lookout Tower**—the park's highest point— and ends up back at the pull-out. This trail is an excellent opportunity to enjoy the fresh air, open spaces, and diversity of wildlife in the park.

GETTING HERE AND AROUND

AIR TRAVEL

The nearest commercial airport is in Rapid City.

BUS TRAVEL

Bus lines serve Rapid City and Wall.

Gray Line of the Black Hills. This outfit offers bus tours from Rapid City to Mt. Rushmore, Black Hills National Forest, Custer State Park, and the Crazy Horse Memorial, as well as other tours tied to special events. ☎ *605/342–4461, 800/456–4461* ⊕ *www.blackhillsgrayline.com.*

CAR TRAVEL

Wind Cave is 56 miles from Rapid City, via U.S. 16 and Highway 87, which runs through the park, and 73 miles southwest of Badlands National Park.

U.S. 385 and Highway 87 travel the length of the park on the west side. Additionally, two unpaved roads, NPS Roads 5 and 6, traverse the northeastern part of Wind Cave. NPS Road 5 joins Highway 87 at the park's north border.

PARK ESSENTIALS

PARK FEES AND PERMITS

There's no fee to enter the park; cave tours cost $7–$23. The requisite backcountry camping and horseback riding permits are both free from the visitor center.

PARK HOURS

The park is open year-round. It is in the mountain time zone.

CELL-PHONE RECEPTION

Cell-phone reception is hit and miss in the park, and western South Dakota is serviced only by Verizon Wireless and AT&T, so those with other carriers may be charged roaming fees. You will find a public phone outside the visitor center.

Custer Post Office ⊠ *643 Mt. Rushmore Rd., Custer* ☎ *605/673–4248.*
Hot Springs Post Office ⊠ *146 N. Chicago St., Hot Springs* ☎ *605/745–4117.*

RESTAURANTS

If you're determined to dine in Wind Cave National Park, be sure to pack your own meal because, other than vending machines, the only dining venues inside park boundaries are the two picnic areas near the visitor center and Elk Mountain Campground. The towns beyond the park offer additional options. Deadwood claims some of the best-ranked restaurants in South Dakota. Buffalo, pheasant, and elk are relatively common ingredients in the Black Hills. No matter where you go, beef is king.

Prices in the reviews are the average cost of a main course at dinner, or if dinner is not served, at lunch.

HOTELS

While Wind Cave claims a singular campground, you'll have to look outside park boundaries if you want to bed down in something more substantial than a tent. New chain hotels with modern amenities are plentiful in the Black Hills, but when booking accommodations consider a stay at one of the area's historic properties. From grand brick downtown hotels to intimate Queen Anne homes converted to bed-and-breakfasts, historic lodgings are easy to locate. Other distinctive lodging choices include the region's mountain lodges and forest retreats.

It may be difficult to obtain quality accommodations during summer—and downright impossible during the Sturgis Motorcycle Rally, held the first full week of August every year—so plan ahead and make reservations (three or four months out is a good rule of thumb) if you're going to travel during peak season. To find the best value, choose a hotel far from Interstate 90.

Prices in the reviews are the lowest cost of a standard double room in high season. For expanded reviews, facilities, and current deals, visit Fodors.com.

VISITOR INFORMATION

PARK CONTACT INFORMATION

Wind Cave National Park ⊠ *26611 U.S. 385, Hot Springs* ☎ *605/745–4600* ⊕ *www.nps.gov/wica.*

VISITOR CENTERS

Wind Cave Visitor Center. The park's sole visitor center is the primary place to get general information. Located on top of the cave, it has three exhibit rooms, with displays on cave exploration, the Civilian Conservation Corps, park wildlife, and resource management. ■ **TIP**➔ **Other than vending machines, there's no coffee or snacks here or elsewhere in the park, so if you need your morning caffeine fix, pick up your coffee before entering the park.** ⊠ *Off U.S. 385, 3 miles north of park's southern border, 26611 U.S. 385, Hot Springs* ☎ *605/745–4600* ⊕ *www. nps.gov/wica* 🎫 *Free* 🕙 *Mid-Apr.–mid-Oct., daily 8–5; mid-Oct.–early Apr., daily 8–4:30.*

EXPLORING

SCENIC DRIVES

Bison Flats Drive (South Entrance). Entering the park from the south on U.S. 385 will take you past Gobbler Ridge and into the hills commonly found in the southern Black Hills region. After a couple of miles, the landscape gently levels onto the Bison Flats, one of the mixed-grass prairies on which the park prides itself. You might see a herd of grazing buffalo between here and the visitor center. You'll also catch panoramic views of the parklands, surrounding hills, and limestone bluffs. ⊠ *Wind Cave National Park, U.S. 385.*

CLOSE UP

Plants and Wildlife in Wind Cave

About three-quarters of the park is grassland. The rest is forested, mostly by the ponderosa pine. Poison ivy is common in wetter, shadier areas, so wear long pants and boots when hiking. The convergence of forest and prairies makes an attractive home for bison, elk, coyotes, pronghorn antelope, prairie dogs, and mule deer. Wild turkey and squirrels are less obvious in this landscape, but commonly seen by observant hikers.

Mountain lions also live in the park; although usually shy, they will attack if surprised or threatened. Make noise while hiking to prevent chance encounters. Bison appear docile, but can be dangerous. The largest land mammal in North America, they weigh up to a ton and run at speeds in excess of 35 mph.

Rankin Ridge Drive (North Entrance). Entering the park across the north border via Highway 87 is perhaps the most beautiful drive into the park. As you leave behind the grasslands and granite spires of Custer State Park and enter Wind Cave. You see the prairie, forest, and wetland habitats of the backcountry and some of the oldest rock in the Black Hills. The silvery twinkle of mica, quartz, and feldspar crystals dot Rankin Ridge east of Highway 87, and gradually give way to limestone and sandstone formations. ⊠ *Hwy. 87.*

SCENIC STOPS

Rankin Ridge Lookout Tower. Some of the best panoramic views of the park and surrounding hills can be seen from this 5,013-foot tower, which is typically not staffed or open to the public. Hike the 1-mile Rankin Ridge loop to get there. ⊠ *6 miles north of the visitor center on Hwy. 87.*

Wind Cave. Known to American Indians for centuries and named for the strong currents of air that alternately blow in and out of its entrance, Wind Cave was first documented by the Bingham brothers in 1881. The cave's winds are related to the difference in atmospheric pressure between the cave and the surface. When the atmospheric pressure is higher outside than inside the cave, the air blows in, and vice versa. With more than 141 miles of known passageway divided into three different levels, Wind Cave ranks the sixth longest in the world. It's host to an incredibly diverse collection of geologic formations, including more boxwork than any other known cave, plus a series of underground lakes. The cave tours sponsored by the National Park Service allow you to see unusual and beautiful formations with names such as popcorn, frostwork, and boxwork. ⊠ *U.S. 385 to Wind Cave Visitor Center.*

DID YOU KNOW?

Theodore Roosevelt made Wind Cave one of the country's earliest national parks, and the first dedicated to preserving a cave resource, on January 3, 1903. It is now known to be one of the longest caves in the world, with 141 miles of explored passageways.

EDUCATIONAL OFFERINGS

RANGER PROGRAMS

FAMILY **Junior Ranger Program.** Kids 12 and younger can earn a Junior Ranger badge by completing activities that teach them about the park's ecosystems, the cave, the animals, and protecting the environment. Pick up the Junior Ranger guidebook for free at the Wind Cave Visitor Center. ⊠ *Wind Cave National Park, 26611 U.S.* ☎ *605/745–4600* ⊕ *www.nps. gov/wica/forkids/beajuniorranger.htm.*

Prairie Hike. This two-hour exploration of parkland habitats begins with a short talk at the visitor center, then moves to a trailhead. ⊠ *Wind Cave National Park, 26611 U.S. 385* ☎ *605/745–4600* ⊕ *www.nps.gov/wica* ⊙ *Early June–mid-Aug., daily at 9 am.*

SPORTS AND THE OUTDOORS

Many visitors come to Wind Cave solely to descend into the park's underground passages. While there are great ranger-led tours for casual visitors—and more daring explorations for experienced cavers—the prairie and forest above the cave shouldn't be neglected.

MULTISPORT OUTFITTERS

Edge Sports—Lead. On the way to the ski slopes in the northern Black Hills, Edge Sports maintains a good stock of winter-sports equipment, including rental skis and snowboards. It's open in the winter only, although Edge Sports has a Rapid City store at 619 Main Street. ⊠ *11380 Hwy. 14A, Lead* ☎ *605/722–7547* ⊕ *www.grabanedge.com.*

Edge Sports—Rapid City. Rock climbers will find a good selection of equipment at Edge Sports, cavers will find a solid inventory of clothing and gear, while winter-sports lovers can explore an ample inventory of snowboards. ⊠ *619 Main St., Rapid City* ☎ *605/716–9912.*

Granite Sports. Several miles north of the park in Hill City, Granite Sports sells hiking boots, Gore-Tex jackets, packs, water bottles, and they know the best local guides. ⊠ *301 Main St., Hill City* ☎ *605/574–2121* ⊕ *www.granitesports.biz.*

Scheels All Sport. In the 100,000-square-foot Rushmore Crossing Mall, off I–90 at East-North Street or Lacrosse Street exits, Scheels All Sport carries a wide selection of all-weather hiking clothes and binoculars suitable for bird-watchers and has shooting simulators. New in 2014, Sheels will unveil an 18,000-square-foot expansion. ⊠ *1225 Eglin St., Rapid City* ☎ *605/342–9033.*

BICYCLING

Bikes are prohibited on all of the park's trails and in the backcountry. Cyclists may ride on designated roads, and on the 111-mile Centennial Trail, once it passes the park's northern border.

37

OUTFITTERS AND EXPEDITIONS

Two Wheeler Dealer Cycle and Fitness. A full-service bicycle outfitter based in Rapid City, Two Wheeler Dealer carries more than 1,000 different bikes for sale or rent. Service is top-notch, and trail maps for the Black Hills National Forest and Mickelson Trail are available. ⊠ *100 East Blvd. N, Rapid City* ☎ *605/343–0524* ⊕ *www.twowheelerdealer.com.*

BIRD-WATCHING

Rankin Ridge. See large birds of prey here, including turkey vultures, hawks, and golden eagles. ⊠ *6 miles north of the visitor center on Hwy. 87* ⊕ *www.nps.gov/wica.*

Wind Cave Canyon. Here's one of the best birding areas in the park. The limestone walls of the canyon are ideal nesting grounds for cliff swallows and great horned owls, while the standing dead trees on the canyon floor attract red-headed and Lewis woodpeckers. As you hike down the trail, the steep-sided canyon widens to a panoramic view east across the prairies. ⊠ *About ½ mile east of visitor center* ⊕ *www.nps.gov/wica.*

HIKING

There are more than 30 miles of hiking trails within the boundaries of Wind Cave National Park, covering ponderosa forest and mixed-grass prairie. The landscape has changed little over the past century, so a hike through the park is as much a historical snapshot of pioneer life in the 1890s as it is exercise. Be sure to hit the Wind Cave Canyon Trail, where limestone cliffs attract birds like cliff swallows and great horned owls, and the Cold Brook Canyon Trail, a short but fun trip past a prairie-dog town to the park's edge. Besides birds and small animals such as squirrels, you're apt to see deer and pronghorn while hiking, and probably some bison.

Hiking into the wild, untouched backcountry is perfectly safe, provided you have a map (available from the visitor center) and a good sense of direction. Don't expect any developments, however; bathrooms and a water bottle filling station are available only at the visitor center, and the trails are dirt or gravel. There are no easily accessible sources along the trails, and water from backcountry sources must be treated, so pack your own.

EASY

Wind Cave Canyon Trail. This easy 1.8-mile trail follows Wind Cave Canyon to the park boundary fence. The canyon, with its steep limestone walls and dead trees, provides the best opportunity in the park for bird-watching. Be especially vigilant for cliff swallows, great horned owls, and red-headed and Lewis woodpeckers. Deer, least chipmunks, and other small animals also are attracted to the sheltered environment of the canyon. Even though you could probably do a round-trip tour of this trail in less than an hour and a half, be sure to spend more time here to observe the wildlife. *Easy.* ⊠ *Trailhead on east side of U.S. 385, 1 mile north of southern access road to visitor center.*

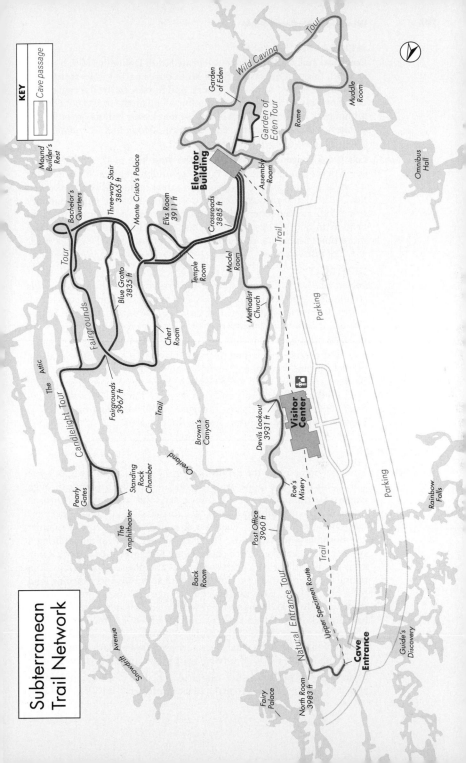

Subterranean Trail Network

KEY

Cave passage

Wild Caving Tour

Garden of Eden

Garden of Eden Tour

Mound Builder's Rest

Muddle Room

Rome

Omnibus Hall

Bachelor's Quarters

Three-way Stair
3865 ft

Monte Cristo's Palace

Elevator Building

Elks Room
3911 ft

Assembly Room

Crossroads
3885 ft

Tour

Fairgrounds

Blue Grotto
3835 ft

Temple Room

Model Room

Trail

The Attic

Candlelight Tour

Chert Room

Methodist Church

Parking

Fairgrounds
3367 ft

Standing Rock Chamber

Trail

Brown's Canyon

Overland

Pearly Gates

The Amphitheater

Devils Lookout
3931 ft

Visitor Center

Back Room

Snowdrift Avenue

Post Office
3960 ft

Roe's Misery

Parking

Rainbow Falls

Natural Entrance Tour

Upper Specimen Route

Trail

Fairy Palace

North Room
3983 ft

Cave Entrance

Guide's Discovery

MODERATE

Centennial Trail. Constructed to celebrate South Dakota's 100th birthday in 1989, this trail bisects the Black Hills, covering 111 miles from north to south. Designed for bikers, hikers, and horses, the trail is rugged but accommodating (note, however, that bicycling on the trail is not allowed within park boundaries). It will take you at least a half day to cover the 6 miles of this trail that traverse the park. *Moderate.* ⊠ *Trailhead off Hwy. 87, 2 miles north of visitor center.*

FAMILY **Cold Brook Canyon Trail.** Starting on the west side of U.S. 385, 2 miles south of the visitor center, this 1.5-mile, mildly strenuous hike runs past a former prairie-dog town, the edge of an area burned by a controlled fire in 1986, and through Cold Brook Canyon to the park boundary fence. Experienced hikers will conquer this trail and return to the trailhead in an hour or less, but more leisurely visitors will probably need more time. *Moderate.* ⊠ *Trailhead on west side of U.S. 385, 2 miles south of visitor center.*

DIFFICULT

Boland Ridge Trail. Get away from the crowds for half a day via this strenuous, 2.5-mile round-trip hike. The panorama from the top is well worth it, especially at night. *Difficult.* ⊠ *Trailhead off Forest Service Rd. 6, 1 mile north of junction with Forest Service Rd. 5.*

Highland Creek Trail. This difficult, roughly 8.5-mile trail is the longest and most diverse trail within the park, traversing mixed-grass prairies, ponderosa pine forests, and the riparian habitats of Highland Creek, Beaver Creek, and Wind Cave Canyon. Even those in good shape will need a full day to cover this trail round-trip. *Difficult.* ⊠ *Southern trailhead stems from Wind Cave Canyon trail 1 mile east of U.S. 385. Northern trailhead on Forest Service Rd. 5.*

SPELUNKING

Fodor's Choice
★
You may not explore the depths of Wind Cave on your own, but you can choose from five ranger-led cave tours, available from June through August; the rest of the year, only one or two tours are available. On each tour you pass incredibly beautiful cave formations, including extremely well-developed boxwork. The least crowded times to visit in summer are mornings and weekends. The cave is 53°F year-round, so bring a sweater. Note that the uneven passages are often wet and slippery. Rangers discourage those with heart conditions and physical limitations from taking the organized tours. However, with some advance warning (and for a nominal fee) park rangers can arrange private, limited tours for those with physical disabilities. For wild caving tours, the park provides hard hats, knee pads, and gloves, and all cavers are required to have long pants, a long-sleeved shirt, and hiking boots or shoes with nonslip soles. If you prefer lighted passages and stairways to dark crawl spaces, a tour other than the Wild Caving Tour might appeal to you.

Tours depart from the visitor center. A schedule can be found online at ⊕ *www.nps.gov/wica*. To make a reservation, call ☎ *605/745–1134.*

EASY

Garden of Eden Cave Tour. You don't need to go far to see boxwork, popcorn, and flowstone formations. Just take the relatively easy, one-hour tour, which covers about 0.25 miles and 150 stairs. It's available four times daily, June through Labor Day, and three times daily, October to early June. (It is unavailable most of September.) The cost is $7. *Easy.*

Natural Entrance Cave Tour. This 1¼-hour tour takes you 0.5 mile into the cave, over 300 stairs (most heading down), and out an elevator exit. Along the way are some significant boxwork deposits on the middle level. The tour costs $9 and leaves 15 times daily from June through Labor Day, and seven times daily for the rest of September. *Easy.*

> ### HATS OFF TO THE CAVE
>
> American Indians knew of Wind Cave long before cowboys Jesse and Tom Bingham stumbled on it when they heard air whistling through the rocky opening. Legend goes that the airflow was so strong that day that it knocked Tom's hat clean off his head. Jesse came back a few days later to show the trick to some friends, but it didn't happen quite as he'd planned. The wind, now flowing in the opposite direction, stole Jesse's hat and vacuumed it into the murky depths of the cave.

MODERATE

Candlelight Cave Tour. Available twice daily, early June through Labor Day, this tour goes into a section of the cave with no paved walks or lighting. Everyone on the tour carries a lantern similar to those used in expeditions in the 1890s. The $9 tour lasts two hours and covers 1 mile; reservations are essential. Children younger than 8 are not admitted. *Moderate.*

Fairgrounds Cave Tour. View examples of nearly every type of calcite formation found in the cave on this 1½-hour tour, available eight times daily, June through Labor Day. There are some 450 steps, leading up and down. The cost is $9. *Moderate.*

DIFFICULT

Fodor's Choice ★ **Wild Caving Tour.** For a serious caving experience, sign up for this challenging four-hour tour. After some basic training in spelunking, you crawl and climb through fissures and corridors, most lined with gypsum needles, frostwork, and boxwork. Expect to get dirty. Wear shoes with good traction, long pants, and a long-sleeve shirt. The park provides knee pads, gloves, and hard hats with headlamps. Parents or guardians must sign a consent form for 16- and 17-year-olds. Tours cost $23 and are available at 1 pm daily, early June through mid-August, and at 1 pm weekends mid-August through Labor Day. Reservations are essential. *Difficult.*

SHOPPING

Wind Cave National Park Bookstore. The only retail establishment on park grounds, this bookstore sells trail maps, guides to the Black Hills, and books on the geology and history of Wind Cave and neighboring Jewel Cave. ⊠ *Wind Cave Visitor Center* ☎ *605/745–4600* ⊘ *Closed Nov.–Mar.*

CAVEMEN SPEAK

Sound like a serious spelunker with this cavemen cheat sheet for various *speleothems* (cave formations).

Boxwork: Composed of interconnecting thin blades that were left in relief on cave walls when the bedrock was dissolved away.

Cave balloons: Thin-walled formations resembling partially deflated balloons, usually composed of hydromagnesite.

Flowstone: Consists of thin layers of a mineral deposited on a sloping surface by flowing or seeping water.

Frostwork: Sprays of needles that radiate from a central point that are usually made of aragonite.

Gypsum beard: Composed of bundles of gypsum fibers that resemble a human beard.

Logomites: Consists of popcorn and superficially resembles a hollowed-out stalagmite.

Pool Fingers: Deposited underneath water around organic filaments.

Stalactites: Carrot-shape formations formed from dripping water that hang down from a cave ceiling.

Stalagmites: Mineral deposits from dripping water built up on a cave floor.

WHAT'S NEARBY

Wind Cave is part of South Dakota's Black Hills, a diverse region of alpine meadows, ponderosa pine forests, and creek-carved, granite-walled canyons covering 2 million acres in the state's southwest quadrant. This mountain range contrasts sharply with the sheer cliffs and dramatic buttes of the badlands to the north and east, and the wide, windswept plains of most of the state. Though anchored by Rapid City—the largest city for 350 miles in any direction—the Black Hills' crown jewel is Mount Rushmore National Memorial, visited by nearly 3 million people each year. U.S. 385 is the backbone of the Black Hills.

NEARBY TOWNS

Custer. About 30 miles north of Hot Springs is the town of Custer, the Mother City of the Black Hills. Near here, George Armstrong Custer and his expedition first discovered gold in 1874, leading to the gold rush of 1875 and '76. ⊕ *www.visitcuster.com.*

Deadwood. In one of America's longest ongoing historic preservation projects, you'll discover brick streets fronted by Victorian architecture, with Main Street shops, restaurants, and gaming halls. Deadwood owes its historical character to gold and gaming halls, just as it did in its late 19th-century heyday. You can walk in the footsteps of Wild Bill Hickok and Calamity Jane, who swore she could outdrink, outspit, and outswear any man—and usually did. Both of the Western legends are buried in Deadwood's Boot Hill–Mt. Moriah Cemetery. ⊕ *www.deadwood.com.*

Hill City. The small, quiet mountain town of Hill City is the gateway to Mt. Rushmore. Despite having just 780 residents, the community claims no fewer than seven art galleries, a natural-history museum, a winery, a vintage steam railroad, and a classy visitor center on its eastern flank. ⊕ *www.hillcitysd.com.*

Hot Springs. Noted for its striking sandstone structures, the small and historic community of Hot Springs is the gateway to Wind Cave National Park. It is also the entry point to scores of other natural and historical sites, including Evans Plunge, a naturally heated indoor-outdoor pool; the Mammoth Site, where more than 50 woolly and Columbian mammoths have been unearthed, the Black Hills Wild Horse Sanctuary, and one of the region's premier golf courses. ⊕ *www. hotsprings-sd.com.*

Keystone. Founded in the 1880s by prospectors searching for gold deposits, the small town of Keystone, 2 miles from Mt. Rushmore, has an abundance of restaurants, shops, and attractions, from wax museums to miniature-golf courses to alpine slides. To serve the millions of visitors passing through the area, there are 700 hotel rooms—more than twice the town's number of permanent residents. ⊕ *www. keystonechamber.com.*

Rapid City. Called the "City of Presidents" because of the life-size bronze statues of U.S. presidents that adorn virtually every downtown street corner, Rapid City is the largest urban center in a 350-mile radius. The city is the area's cultural, educational, medical, and economic hub, and a good base from which to explore the treasures of the state's southwestern corner, including Mount Rushmore (25 miles south) and Wind Cave National Park (50 miles south).

VISITOR INFORMATION
Black Hills, Badlands & Lakes Association. Black Hills, Badlands & Lakes Association ⊠ *1851 Discovery Circle, Rapid City* ☎ *605/355–3600* ⊕ *www.blackhillsbadlands.com.*

> ### PARK PUBLICATION
> Wind Cave publishes a newspaper called *Passages.* Pick it up at the visitor center or at the chambers of commerce in Hot Springs, Custer, Keystone, and Rapid City. Call ☎ 605/745–4600 to have a copy mailed to you, and ask for the Southern Hills Visitor Guide as well.

37

NEARBY ATTRACTIONS

CUSTER
Crazy Horse Memorial. Designed to be the world's largest sculpture, this tribute to the spirit of the North American Indian people depicts Crazy Horse, the legendary Lakota leader who defeated General Custer at Little Bighorn. A work in progress, thus far the warrior's head has been carved from the mountain, and the colossal head of his horse is beginning to emerge. Self-taught sculptor Korczak Ziolkowski started this memorial in 1948. After his death in 1982, his family carried on the project. Near the worksite stands an exceptional orientation center, the Indian Museum of North America, Ziolkowski's home and workshop,

and the Indian University of North America. ✉ *U.S. 385, 5 miles north of Custer* 🕾 *605/673–4681* ⊕ *www.crazyhorsememorial.org* 🔖 *$10* ◔ *May–Sept., daily 7 am–9 pm; Oct.–Apr., daily 8–5.*

Custer State Park. This 71,000-acre park is considered the crown jewel of South Dakota's state park system. Elk, antelope, mountain goats, bighorn sheep, mountain lions, wild turkey, prairie dogs, and the second-largest (behind Yellowstone National Park) publicly owned herd of bison in the world roam this pristine landscape. Scenic drives roll past fingerlike granite spires and panoramic views (try the Needles Highway). Take the 18-mile Wildlife Loop Road to see prairies teeming with animals and some of the beautiful backdrops for countless western films. ✉ *13329 U.S. 16A, 4 miles east of Custer* 🕾 *605/255– 4515* ⊕ *www.custerstatepark.info* 🔖 *$6–$28* ◔ *24/7 year-round.*

Jewel Cave National Monument. Even though its more than 168.25 miles of surveyed passages make this cave the world's third-largest (Kentucky's Mammoth Cave is the longest), it isn't the size of Jewel Cave that draws visitors, it's the rare crystalline formations that abound in the cave's vast passages. Wander the dark passageways and you'll be rewarded with the sight of tiny crystal Christmas trees, hydromagnesite balloons that would pop if you touched them, and delicate calcite deposits dubbed "cave popcorn." Year-round, you can take ranger-led tours for a fee, from a simple half-hour walk to a lantern-light tour. Surface trails and facilities are free. ✉ *U.S. 16, 15 miles west of Custer* 🕾 *605/673–2288* ⊕ *www.nps.gov/jeca* 🔖 *$4–$27* ◔ *Sept.–Apr., daily 8–4:30; May–Aug., daily 8–7.*

DEADWOOD

Adams Museum. Between the massive stone-block post office and the old railroad depot there are three floors of displays, including the region's first locomotive, photographs of the town's early days, and a reproduction of the largest gold nugget ever discovered in the Black Hills. ✉ *54 Sherman St., Deadwood* 🕾 *605/578–1714* ⊕ *www. adamsmuseumandhouse.org* 🔖 *Free* ◔ *Late May–early Sept., Mon.– Sat. 9–7, Sun. noon–5; early Sept.–late May, Mon.–Sat. 10–4.*

FAMILY **Broken Boot Gold Mine.** You can pan for gold, and even if you don't find any you'll leave with a souvenir stock certificate. ✉ *U.S. 14A, Deadwood* 🕾 *605/578–9997* ⊕ *www.brokenbootgoldmine.com* 🔖 *Tour $5, gold panning $7* ◔ *May–Aug., daily 8–5:30.*

HOT SPRINGS

Black Hills Wild Horse Sanctuary. More than 600 wild mustangs inhabit this 11,000-acre preserve of rugged canyons, forests, and grasslands along the Cheyenne River. Take a guided tour or hike, and sign up for a chuck-wagon dinner. From Hot Springs, drive 14 miles south until you see signs off Route 71. ✉ *12165 Highland Rd. (Rte. 71), Hot Springs* 🕾 *605/745–5955, 800/252–6652* ⊕ *www.wildmustangs. com* 🔖 *Tours start at $50* ◔ *Nov.–Apr., Mon.–Sat. 9–5; tours at 10 and 1; Apr.–Oct., daily 8–5.*

In the fall, listen to elk bugling, a high-pitched, whistlelike sound the animals make as they mate.

FAMILY
Fodor's Choice
★

Mammoth Site. While building a housing development in the 1970s, workers uncovered this sinkhole where giant mammoths came to drink, got trapped, and died. In July 2013, the 61st of the fossilized woolly beasts was discovered, and most can still be seen on-site. You can watch the excavation in progress and take guided tours. ⊠ *1800 W. Hwy. 18 Bypass, 15 miles south of Wind Cave National Park, Hot Springs* ☎ *605/745–6017* ⊕ *www.mammothsite.com* ✉ *$10* ⊙ *May–Sept., daily 8–8; Oct., daily 9–5; Nov.–Apr., Mon.–Sat. 9–3:30, Sun. 11–3:30.*

KEYSTONE

Beautiful Rushmore Cave. Stalagmites, stalactites, flowstone, ribbons, columns, helictites, and the "Big Room" are all part of the worthwhile tour into this cave. In 1876, miners found the opening to the cave while digging a flume into the mountainside to carry water to the gold mines below. The cave was opened to the public in 1927, just before the carving of Mt. Rushmore began. In recent years, the attraction added the Soaring Eagle zipline, Gunslinger 7D interactive ride and Xpedition Adventure, a caving adventure tour. ⊠ *13622 Hwy. 40, Keystone* ☎ *605/255–4384* ⊕ *www.rushmorecave.com* ✉ *$14* ⊙ *June–Sept., daily 8–8; May and Oct., daily 9–5.*

RAPID CITY

FAMILY
Fodor's Choice
★

Bear Country U.S.A. Encounter black bear, elk, sheep, and wolves at this drive-through wildlife park, which has been entertaining guests for more than 40 years. There's also a walk-through wildlife center with red foxes, porcupines, badgers, bobcats, and lynx, as well as bear cubs. ⊠ *13820 S. U.S. 16, Rapid City* ☎ *605/343–2290* ⊕ *www.bearcountryusa.com* ✉ *$16* ⊙ *June–Aug., daily 8–6; May and Sept.–Nov., daily 9–4.*

America's Shrine to Democracy

Abraham Lincoln was tall in real life—6 feet, 4 inches, though add a few more for his hat. But at one of the nation's most famous icons, Honest Abe, along with presidents George Washington, Thomas Jefferson, and Theodore Roosevelt, towers over the Black Hills in a 60-foot-high likeness. The four images look especially spectacular at night, June through mid-September, when a lighting ceremony dramatically illuminates them.

Like most impressive undertakings, Mount Rushmore's path to realization was one of personalities and perseverance.

When Gutzon Borglum, a talented and patriotic sculptor, was invited to create a giant monument to Confederate soldiers in Georgia in 1915, he jumped at the chance. The son of Danish immigrants, Borglum was raised in California and trained in art in Paris, even studying under Auguste Rodin, who influenced his style. Georgia's Stone Mountain project was to be massive in scope—encompassing the rock face of an entire peak—and would give Borglum the opportunity to exercise his artistic vision on a grand scale.

But the relationship with the project backers and Borglum went sour, causing the sculptor to destroy his models and flee the state. South Dakota state officials had a vision for another mountain memorial, and Borglum was eager to jump on board. His passion and flamboyant personality were well matched to the project, which involved carving legends of the Wild West on a gigantic scale. In time, Borglum convinced officials to think larger, and the idea of carving a monument to U.S. presidents was born.

On a massive granite cliff, at an elevation of 5,725 feet, Borglum began carving Mount Rushmore in 1927 with the help of some 400 assistants. In consultation with U.S. Senator Peter Norbeck and State Historian Doane Robinson, Borglum chose the four presidents to signify the birth, growth, preservation, and development of the nation. In 6½ years of carving over a 14-year period, the sculptor and his crew drilled and dynamited a masterpiece, the largest work of art on earth. Borglum died in March 1941, leaving his son, Lincoln, to complete the work only a few months later—in the wake of the gathering storm of World War II.

ATTRACTIONS

Follow the Presidential Trail through the forest to gain excellent views of the colossal sculpture, or stroll the Avenue of Flags for a different perspective. Also on site are an impressive museum, indoor theaters where films are shown, an outdoor amphitheater for live performances, and concession facilities. The nightly ranger program and lighting of the memorial is reportedly the most

popular interpretive program in all of the national parks system.

Avenue of Flags. Running from the entrance of the memorial to the museum and amphitheater at the base of the mountain, the avenue represents each state, commonwealth, district, and territory of the United States.

Lincoln Borglum Museum. This giant granite-and-glass structure underneath the viewing platform has permanent exhibits on the carving of the mountain, its history, and its significance. There also are temporary exhibits, a bookstore, and an orientation film. Admission is free.

Presidential Trail. This easy hike along a boardwalk and down some stairs leads to the very base of the mountain. Although the trail is thickly forested, you'll have more than ample opportunity to look straight up the noses of the four giant heads. The trail is open year-round, so long as snow and/or ice don't present a safety hazard.

Sculptor's Studio. Built in 1939 as Gutzon Borglum's on-site workshop, it displays tools used by the mountain carvers, a model of the memorial, and a model depicting the unfinished Hall of Records. It's open May–September only; admission is free.

Youth Exploration Area. Planned for completion in fall 2014, this "kid-friendly" center will be located at the base of the mountain caring, along the Presidential Trail. The shelter, utilizing a natural setting of pine trees and granite, will provide a new home for youth activities and is funded by the nonprofit Mount Rushmore Society.

VISITOR INFORMATION
Mount Rushmore Information Center. The Mount Rushmore Information Center, between the park entrance and the Avenue of Flags, has a small exhibit of photographs detailing the carving of the presidents' faces. The information desk is staffed by rangers who can answer questions about the area. A nearly identical building across from the information center houses restrooms, telephones, soda machines, and an award-winning audio tour by the nonprofit Mount Rushmore History Association. ✉ *Ave. of Flags, Keystone* ☎ *605/574–2523* ⊕ *www.nps.gov/ moru* ✉ *Free* ⊙ *May–Sept., daily 8 am–10 pm; Oct.–Apr., daily 8–5.*

37

FAMILY **Black Hills Caverns.** Amethysts, logomites, calcite crystals, and other specimens fill this cave, first discovered by gold-seekers in 1882. Half-hour and hour tours, as well as panning for gold, are available. ✉ *2600 Cavern Rd., Rapid City* ☎ *605/343–0542, 800/837–9358* ⊕ *www. blackhillscaverns.com* ✉ *Tours start at $9* ⊘ *May–mid-June and mid-Aug.–Sept., daily 8:30–5:30; mid-June–mid-Aug., daily 8–7.*

FAMILY **Reptile Gardens.** In the valley between Rapid City and Mt. Rushmore is western South Dakota's answer to a zoo. In addition to the world's largest private reptile collection, the site also has alligator wrestling, a raptor show, and giant tortoises. Enjoy more than 50,000 orchids, tulips, banana trees on the grounds and in the giant dome. ✉ *8955 S. U.S. 16, Rapid City* ☎ *605/342–5873, 800/335–0275* ⊕ *www. reptilegardens.com* ✉ *$16* ⊘ *May–Sept., daily 8–6; Apr. and Oct., daily 9–4; Nov., 9–3.*

South Dakota Air and Space Museum. See General Dwight D. Eisenhower's Mitchell B-25 bomber, a B-1 Bomber, and nearly three dozen other planes and missiles, as well as a once-operational missile training silo, at this museum. Tours are not available in winter. ✉ *Ellsworth Air Force Base, 2890 Rushmore Dr., Box Elder* ☎ *605/385–5189* ⊕ *www. sdairandspacemuseum.com* ✉ *Museum free; tour $8* ⊘ *Daily, 8:30– 4:30; tours mid-May–mid-Sept.*

SPEARFISH

FAMILY **High Plains Western Heritage Center.** Focusing on a region now covered by five states—the Dakotas, Wyoming, Montana, and Nebraska—this center features artifacts such as a Deadwood-Spearfish stagecoach. Outdoor exhibits include a log cabin, a one-room schoolhouse, and, in summer, an entire farm set up with antique equipment. Often on the calendar are cowboy poetry, live music, and historical talks. ✉ *825 Heritage Dr., Spearfish* ☎ *605/642–9378* ⊕ *www.westernheritagecenter. com* ✉ *$7* ⊘ *Daily 9–5.*

AREA ACTIVITIES

SPORTS AND THE OUTDOORS

The Black Hills are a haven for outdoor enthusiasts, and with good reason. The warmer temperatures of spring and summer make for excellent fishing, hiking, mountain climbing, mountain biking, camping, and horseback riding in the national forest. Autumn's cooler weather and changing colors bring out the leaf peepers, and the hunters aren't far behind. Snow can fall as early as October, but the white stuff really starts coming down in December and January, when snowmobilers and skiers (both downhill and cross-country) come out to play. The northern Black Hills, where there are two ski areas, generally receive the highest accumulations, and have seen up to 180 inches of annual snowfall.

FISHING

The Black Hills are filled with tiny mountain creeks, especially on the wetter western and northern slopes, that are ideal for fly-fishing. Rapid Creek, which flows down from the Central Hills into Pactola

Reservoir and finally into Rapid City, is a favorite fishing venue for the city's anglers, both because of its regularly stocked population of trout and for its easy accessibility.

South Dakota Game, Fish, and Parks. Besides the local chambers of commerce, South Dakota Game, Fish, and Parks is your best bet for updated information on regional fishing locations and their conditions. ✉ *523 E. Capitol Ave., Pierre* ☎ *605/773–3485* ⊕ *www.sdgfp.info.*

HIKING AND BICYCLING

Mickelson Trail. Beginning in Deadwood and running the length of the Black Hills, the Mickelson Trail incorporates more than 100 converted railroad bridges, four tunnels and 15 trailheads along its 108.8-mile-long course. Although the grade is seldom steep, parts of the trail are strenuous. A $3 day pass or $15 annual pass are available at self-service stations along the trail, some state park offices, and from the South Dakota Game, Fish & Parks. A portion of the trail is open for snowmobiling in winter. ✉ *Deadwood* ⊕ *gfp.sd.gov/state-parks/ directory/mickelson-trail.*

WATER SPORTS

Angostura Reservoir State Recreation Area. Water-based recreation is the main draw at this park 10 miles south of Hot Springs. Besides a marina, you'll find a floating convenience store, restaurant, campgrounds, and cabins. Boat rentals are available. ✉ *U.S. 385, off Rte. 79, 13157 N. Angostura Rd., Hot Springs* ☎ *605/745–6996, 800/364–8831* ⊕ *gfp. sd.gov/state-parks/directory/angostura* 💲 *$4 per person, $6 per vehicle; $30 per vehicle annually* ⊙ *Daily dawn–dusk.*

WINTER SPORTS

Heavy snowfalls and lovely views make the Black Hills prime cross-country skiing territory. Many trails are open to snowmobilers as well as skiers. Trade and travel magazines consistently rank the Black Hills among the top snowmobiling destinations in the country for two simple reasons: dramatic scenery and an abundance of snow.

Mystic Miner Ski Resort at Deer Mountain. This resort has an enlarged beginner's area, a redesigned Zero Gravity tube park, skiing, and snowboarding. ✉ *11187 Deer Mt. Rd., 3 miles south of Lead on U.S. 85* ☎ *605/580–1169* ⊕ *www.skimystic.com* 💲 *Full-day lift ticket, $38; 2-hr tubing session, $25.*

Terry Peak Ski Area. Perched on the sides of a 7,076-foot mountain, Terry Peak claims the Black Hills' second-highest summit and high-speed quad lifts. The runs are challenging for novice and intermediate skiers and should also keep the experts entertained. From the top, on a clear day, you can see Wyoming, Montana, and North Dakota. ✉ *21120 Stewart Slope Rd., 2 miles south of Lead on U.S. 85* ☎ *800/456–0524, 605/584–2165* ⊕ *www.terrypeak.com* 💲 *Full-day lift ticket, $49.*

Trailshead Lodge. Near the Wyoming border, this lodge has a small restaurant and bar, a gas station and garage, and dozens of brand-new snowmobiles for rent by the day. A favorite pit-stop for snowmobilers exploring the popular Black Hills' 400-mile trail network. ✉ *22075 U.S. 85 S, 21 miles southwest of Lead on U.S. 85* ☎ *605/584–3464* ⊕ *www. trailsheadlodge.com.*

37

ARTS AND ENTERTAINMENT

THE ARTS

Rushmore Plaza Civic Center Fine Arts Theater. This is the venue for a half-dozen touring Broadway shows and the Vucurevich Speaker Series, which has attracted prominent names such as the humorist Dave Barry, late astronomer Carl Sagan, and former Secretary of State Colin Powell. There's also an ice rink where the Rush hockey team plays in winter months. ⊠ *444 Mt. Rushmore Rd. N, Rapid City* ☎ *800/468–6463, 605/394–4111* ⊕ *www.gotmine.com.*

ENTERTAINMENT

Midnight Star. It doesn't offer live music, but the Midnight Star is owned by actor Kevin Costner and decorated throughout with props and costumes from his movies. The bar on the first floor is named for and modeled after the bar in the film *Silverado,* in which Costner starred. Wood accents, stained glass, and plush carpeting give the structure an elegant Victorian look and there's a sports bar, Diamond Lil's, on the second floor. Jakes, on its top floor, is among the region's finest restaurants. ⊠ *677 Main St., Deadwood* ☎ *605/578–1555, 800/999–6482* ⊕ *www.themidnightstar.com.*

Fodor's Choice ★ **Old Style Saloon No. 10.** Billing itself as "the world's only museum with a bar," the Old Style Saloon No. 10 is where you want to come to drink, listen to music, and socialize. Thousands of artifacts, vintage photos, and a two-headed calf set the scene—plus the chair in which Wild Bill Hickok was supposedly shot. A reenactment of his murder takes place four times daily in summer. Upstairs, there's an exceptional restaurant, the Deadwood Social Club, with the state's premier wine and martini bar. ⊠ *657 Main St., Deadwood* ☎ *605/578–3346* ⊕ *www.saloon10.com.*

Silverado. Sprawling over half a city block at the top of Main Street, and including the historic Franklin Hotel across the street, the Silverado is among Deadwood's largest gaming establishments. Although the wood paneling and brass accents around the bars recall Deadwood's Wild West past, the red carpets, velvet ropes, and bow-tie-clad staff give the place modern polish. ⊠ *709 Main St., Deadwood* ☎ *605/578–1366, 800/584–7005* ⊕ *www.silveradofranklin.com.*

SHOPPING

Fodor's Choice ★ **Prairie Edge Trading Company and Galleries.** One of the world's top collections of Plains Indian artwork and crafts makes Prairie Edge Trading Company and Galleries seem more like a museum than a store. The collection ranges from books and CDs to artwork representing the Lakota, Crow, Cheyenne, Shoshone, Arapaho, and Assiniboine tribes of the Great Plains. ⊠ *6th and Main sts., Rapid City* ☎ *605/342–3086* ⊕ *www.prairieedge.com.*

Best Campgrounds in Wind Cave

Camping is one of this region's strengths. While there is only one primitive campground within the park, there are countless campgrounds in the Black Hills. The public campgrounds in the national forest are accessible by road but otherwise secluded and undeveloped; private campgrounds typically have more amenities.

Elk Mountain Campground.
If you prefer a relatively developed campsite and relative proximity to civilization, Elk Mountain is an excellent choice. You can experience the peaceful pine forests and wild creatures of the park without straying too far from the safety of the beaten path. ⊠ ½ *mile north of visitor center* ☎ *605/745–4600.*

SCENIC DRIVES

Peter Norbeck National Scenic Byway. Although there are faster ways to get from Mt. Rushmore to the southern Black Hills, this scenic drive in the Black Hills is a more stunning route. Take U.S. 16A south into Custer State Park, where bison, bighorn sheep, elk, antelope, and burros roam free. Then drive north on Highway 87 through the Needles, towering granite spires that rise above the forest. A short drive off the highway reaches 7,242-foot Harney Peak, the highest point in North America east of the Rockies. Highway 87 finally brings you to U.S. 16/U.S. 385, where you head south to the Crazy Horse Memorial. Because the scenic byway is a challenging drive (with one-lane tunnels and switchbacks) and because you'll likely want to stop a few times to admire the scenery, plan on spending two to three hours on this drive. Stretches of U.S. 16A and Highway 87 may close in winter.

Spearfish Canyon Scenic Byway. The easiest way to get from Deadwood to Rapid City is east through Boulder Canyon on U.S. 14A. However, it's worth looping north and taking the long way around on this 20-mile scenic route past 1,000-foot limestone cliffs and some of the most breathtaking scenery in the region. Cascading waterfalls quench the thirst of quaking aspen, gnarled oaks, sweet-smelling spruce, and the ubiquitous ponderosa pine. The canyon is home to deer, mountain goats, porcupines, and bobcats. Near its middle is the old sawmill town of Savoy, a jumping-off point for scenic hikes to Spearfish Falls and Roughlock Falls. In fall, changing leaves rival any found in New England. ⊠ *10619 Roughlock Falls Rd* ⊕ *www.spearfishcanyon.com.*

37

WHERE TO EAT

IN THE PARK

PICNIC AREAS

Elk Mountain Campground. You don't have to be a camper to use this well-developed picnic spot, with more than 70 tables, fire pits, and restrooms. Some of the tables are on the prairie, others sit amid the pines. ✉ *½ mile north of visitor center.*

Wind Cave. On the edge of a prairie and grove of ponderosa, this is a peaceful, pretty place. Small and simple, it's equipped with 12 tables and a potable-water pump. ✉ *¼ mile north of visitor center.*

OUTSIDE THE PARK

$$ AMERICAN

🍴 **Blue Bell Lodge and Resort.** Feast on fresh trout or buffalo, which you can have as a steak or a stew, in this rustic log building within the boundaries of Custer State Park. There's a kids' menu. On the property, hayrides and cookouts are part of the entertainment, and you can sign up for trail rides and overnight pack trips on old Indian trails with the nearby stable. [$] *Average main: $19* ✉ *Custer State Park, 25453 Hwy. 87, Custer* ☎ *605/255–4531, 800/658–3530* 🌐 *www.custerresorts.com/blue-bell-lodge* ⏲ *Closed mid-Oct.–mid-May.*

$$ ITALIAN

🍴 **Botticelli Ristorante Italiano.** With a wide selection of delectable veal and chicken dishes as well as creamy pastas, this Italian eatery provides a welcome respite from the traditional Midwestern meat and potatoes. The artwork and traditional Italian music in the background give the place a European air. [$] *Average main: $17* ✉ *523 Main St., Rapid City* ☎ *605/348–0089* 🌐 *www.botticelliristorante.net.*

$ AMERICAN

🍴 **Carvers Cafe.** The only restaurant at the Mount Rushmore Memorial affords commanding views of the memorial and the surrounding ponderosa pine forest. It serves exceptional food at reasonable prices. The menu includes pot roast, buffalo stew, and homemade rhubarb pie. It's open for breakfast, lunch, and dinner, so dine with the presidents. [$] *Average main: $7* ✉ *Ave. of Flags, Keystone* ☎ *605/574–2515* 🌐 *www.mtrushmorenationalmemorial.com/about-xanterra* ⏲ *No dinner mid-Oct.–early Mar.*

$$ ITALIAN
Fodor's Choice ★

🍴 **Deadwood Social Club.** On the second floor of historic Saloon No. 10, this warm restaurant surrounds you with wood and old-time photographs of Deadwood. Light jazz and blues play over the sound system. The decor is Western, but the food is northern Italian, a juxtaposition that keeps patrons coming back. The menu stretches from wild mushroom pasta with seafood to chicken in a lemon-butter sauce, as well as elk, buffalo, and melt-in-your-mouth ribeye steaks. The wine list has nearly 200 selections. Reservations are a good idea. [$] *Average main: $19* ✉ *657 Main St., Deadwood* ☎ *605/578–3346* 🌐 *www.saloon10.com/deadwoodsocialclub.*

$$$ ECLECTIC

🍴 **Jakes.** Owned by actor Kevin Costner, this restaurant is among South Dakota's classiest dining experiences. Cherrywood pillars inlaid with etched glass, white-brick fireplaces, and a pianist add to the elegance of the atrium dining room. Among the menu's eclectic offerings are buffalo roulade, Cajun seafood tortellini, filet mignon, and fresh fish. [$] *Average main: $28* ✉ *677 Main St., Deadwood* ☎ *605/578–1555* 🌐 *www.themidnightstar.com/jakes.html* ✍ *Reservations essential.*

$ AMERICAN 🍴 **Laughing Water.** With windows facing the mountain sculpture, this airy pine restaurant is noted for its fry bread and buffalo burgers. There's a soup-and-salad bar, but you'd do well to stick to the American Indian offerings. Try the Indian taco or "buffaloski" (a Polish-style sausage made with Dakota buffalo). A kids' menu is available. [$] *Average main: $10* ✉ *12151 Ave. of the Chiefs, Custer* ☎ *605/673–4681* 🌐 *www.crazyhorsememorial.com* ⏲ *Closed Nov.–Apr.*

$$ AMERICAN FAMILY 🍴 **Woolly's Western Grill.** Run by a friendly couple, this place caters to families with its modestly priced menu. If you're lucky you'll discover it specializes in smoked ribeyes and New York strip steaks. It's near the Mammoth Site and close to the exceptional Southern Hills Golf Course. [$] *Average main: $17* ✉ *1648 Hwy. 18 Bypass, Hot Springs* ☎ *605/745–6414* 🌐 *www.woollys.com.*

WHERE TO STAY

OUTSIDE THE PARK

$$$ B&B/INN Fodor's Choice ★ 🏨 **Audrie's Bed & Breakfast.** Victorian antiques and the hint of romance greet you at this out-of-the-way B&B, set in a thick woods 7 miles west of Rapid City. **Pros:** great antiques; terrific treats; inspiring isolation. **Cons:** fills up fast; cabins lack a/c and phones; no restaurant within walking distance. [$] *Rooms from: $175* ✉ *23029 Thunderhead Falls Rd., Rapid City* ☎ *605/342–7788* 🌐 *www.audriesbb.com* 🛏 *2 suites, 7 cottages and cabins, 1 vacation home* 💳 *No credit cards* 🍽 *Breakfast.*

$$ B&B/INN 🏨 **Buffalo Rock Lodge B&B.** A native-rock fireplace surrounded by hefty logs adds to the rustic quality of this lodge. **Pros:** quiet location; exceptional furnishings. **Cons:** relatively pricey; drive to shopping and dining; no TVs. [$] *Rooms from: $145* ✉ *24524 Playhouse Rd., Keystone* ☎ *605/666–4781, 888/564–5634* 🌐 *www.buffalorock.net* 🛏 *3 rooms* 🍽 *Breakfast.*

$ RESORT 🏨 **Deadwood Gulch Gaming Resort.** Pine-clad hills, a little creek, and a deck from which to view the mountains are at your disposal at this family-style resort about a mile from Deadwood. **Pros:** away from downtown bustle; spacious rooms; attentive staff. **Cons:** busy with bus tours. [$] *Rooms from: $99* ✉ *304 Cliff St., Deadwood* ☎ *605/578–1294, 800/695–1876* 🌐 *www.deadwoodgulch.com* 🛏 *87 rooms* 🍽 *Breakfast.*

$ HOTEL 🏨 **Franklin Hotel.** Built in 1903, this imposing hotel has welcomed many famous guests, including John Wayne, Teddy Roosevelt, and Babe Ruth. **Pros:** at the top of Main Street; spacious rooms; historic vibe. **Cons:** guest rooms need some attention. [$] *Rooms from: $89* ✉ *700 Main St., Deadwood* ☎ *605/578–2241, 800/688–1876* 🌐 *www.silveradofranklin.com* 🛏 *81 rooms* 🍽 *No meals.*

$$$ RESORT 🏨 **K Bar S Lodge.** This contemporary lodge on 45 pine-clad acres feels as if it's stood here for a century. **Pros:** excellent staff; exceptional food; amid a wildlife preserve. **Cons:** quite a walk to dining options; pricey rates; often full. [$] *Rooms from: $167* ✉ *434 Old Hill City Rd., Keystone* ☎ *866/522–7724, 605/666–4545* 🌐 *www.kbarslodge.com* 🛏 *96 rooms* 🍴 *Breakfast.*

$$ RESORT 🏨 **Spearfish Canyon Lodge.** Midway between Spearfish and Deadwood, this lodge-style hotel commands some of the best views in the Black Hills. **Pros:** wonderful location; snowmobile and bike rentals; as pretty as it gets. **Cons:** remote location; half-hour drive to restaurants; standard rooms. [$] *Rooms from: $152* ✉ *10619 Roughlock Falls Rd., Lead* ☎ *877/975–6343, 605/584–3435* 🌐 *www.spfcanyon.com* 🛏 *54 rooms* 🍴 *No meals.*

$$ RESORT FAMILY 🏨 **Sylvan Lake Resort.** This spacious stone-and-wood lodge in Custer State Park affords fantastic views of pristine Sylvan Lake and Harney Peak. **Pros:** wonderful views; multitude of lodging options; alpine atmosphere: **Cons:** on a winding road; limited dining options; can be pricey. [$] *Rooms from: $139* ✉ *24572 Hwy. 87, Custer* ☎ *605/574–2561, 800/658–3530* 🌐 *www.custerresorts.com* 🛏 *35 rooms, 31 cabins* ⏲ *Closed Oct.–Mother's Day* 🍴 *No meals.*

YELLOWSTONE NATIONAL PARK

WELCOME TO YELLOWSTONE

TOP REASONS TO GO

★ **Hot spots:** Thinner-than-normal crust depth and a huge magma chamber beneath the park explain Yellowstone's abundant geysers, steaming pools, hissing fumaroles, and bubbling mud pots.

★ **Bison:** They're just one of many species that roam freely here. Seemingly docile, the bison make your heart race if you catch them stampeding across Lamar Valley.

★ **Hiking:** Yellowstone has more than 1,000 miles of trails, along which you can summit a 10,000-foot peak, follow a trout-filled creek, or descend into the Grand Canyon of the Yellowstone.

★ **Yellowstone Lake:** Here you can fish, boat, kayak, stargaze, and bird-watch on black obsidian beaches—just don't stray too far into the frigid water.

★ **Canyon:** The Colorado River runs through the park, creating a deep yellow-color canyon with two impressive waterfalls.

1 Grant Village/West Thumb. Named for President Ulysses S. Grant, Grant Village is on the western edge of Yellowstone Lake.

2 Old Faithful area. Famous for its regularity and awesome power, Old Faithful erupts every 94 minutes or so. The most important geyser site in the world is a full-service area with inns, restaurants, campsites, cabins, a visitor center, and general stores.

3 Madison. Here the Madison River is formed by the joining of the Gibbon and Firehole rivers. Fly-fishermen will find healthy stocks of brown and rainbow trout and mountain whitefish.

4 Norris. The Norris area is the hottest and most changeable part of Yellowstone National Park. There are campsites here and a small information center.

5 Mammoth Hot Springs. This full-service fortlike area has an inn, restaurants, campsites, a visitor center, and general stores.

6 Tower-Roosevelt. This least visited area of the park is the place to go for solitude, horseback riding, and animal sightings. There are a lodge, restaurant, and campsites here.

7 Canyon area. The Yellowstone River runs through here, and the yellow walls of the canyon lend the park its name. Two massive waterfalls highlight "downtown" Yellowstone, where cars, services, and natural beauty all converge.

8 Lake area. The largest body of water within the park, Yellowstone Lake is believed to have once been 200 feet higher than it presently is. This is a full-service area with a hotel, lodge, restaurants, campsites, cabins, and general stores.

WYOMING

GETTING ORIENTED

At more than 2.2 million acres, Yellowstone National Park is considered one of America's most scenic and diverse national parks. The park has five entrances, each with its own attractions: the South has the Lewis River canyon; the East, Sylvan Pass; the West, the Madison River valley; the North, the beautiful Paradise Valley; and the Northeast, the spectacular Beartooth Pass.

38

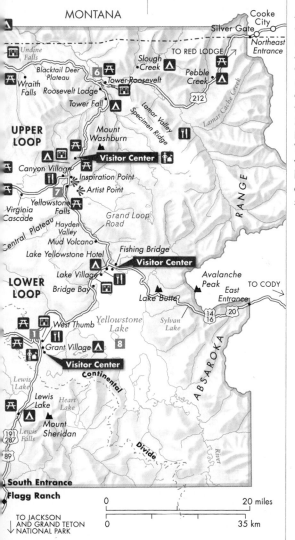

MONTANA

Cooke City
Silver Gate
Northeast Entrance
TO RED LODGE
Undine Falls
Slough Creek
Pebble Creek
Blacktail Deer Plateau
Tower-Roosevelt
Wraith Falls
Roosevelt Lodge
212
Lamar Cache Creek
Tower Fall
Lamar Valley
Specimen Ridge

UPPER LOOP
Mount Washburn
Visitor Center
Canyon Village
Inspiration Point
Artist Point
RANGE
Virginia Cascade
Yellowstone Falls
Hayden Valley
Grand Loop Road
Central Plateau
Mud Volcano
Lake Yellowstone Hotel
Fishing Bridge
Visitor Center

LOWER LOOP
Lake Village
Bridge Bay
Lake Butte
Avalanche Peak
East Entrance
TO CODY
14 16 20
West Thumb
Yellowstone Lake
Sylvan Lake
Grant Village
8
Visitor Center
Continental
ABSAROKA
Lewis Lake
Lewis Lake
Heart Lake
Mount Sheridan
Divide
River
191 287
Lewis Falls
89

South Entrance
Flagg Ranch

0 ——————— 20 miles
0 ——————— 35 km

TO JACKSON AND GRAND TETON NATIONAL PARK

KEY	
	Ranger Station
	Campground
	Picnic Area
	Restaurant
	Lodge
	Trailhead
	Restrooms
	Scenic Viewpoint
::::::	Walking/Hiking Trails

Updated by
T.D. Griffith
and Nyla
Griffith

A trip to Yellowstone has been a rich part of the American experience for five generations now. Though it's remote, we come—more than 3,000,000 strong—year after year. When we arrive, we gasp at the incomparable combination of natural beauty, rugged wilderness, majestic peaks, and abundant wildlife. Indescribable geysers, mud pots, fumaroles, and hot springs make this magma-filled pressure cooker of a park unlike any place else on earth. If you're not here for the geysers, chances are that you've come to spot some of the teeming wildlife, from grazing bison to cruising trumpeter swans.

YELLOWSTONE PLANNER

WHEN TO GO

There are two major seasons in Yellowstone: summer (May–October), the only time when most of the park's roads are open to cars; and winter (mid-December–February), when over-snow travel (snowmobiles, snow coaches, and skis) takes a fraction of the number of visitors to a frigid, bucolic sanctuary. Except for services at park headquarters at Mammoth Hot Springs, the park closes from October to mid-December and from March to late April or early May.

You'll find big crowds from mid-July to mid-August. There are fewer people in the park the month or two before and after this peak season, but there are also fewer facilities open. There's also more rain, especially at lower elevations. Except for holiday weekends, there are few visitors in winter. Snow is possible year-round at high elevations.

AVG. HIGH/LOW TEMPS

JAN.	FEB.	MAR.	APR.	MAY	JUNE
30/10	33/12	42/17	49/28	60/32	71/41

JULY	AUG.	SEPT.	OCT.	NOV.	DEC.
81/45	79/45	67/37	56/30	38/22	30/12

FESTIVALS AND EVENTS

FEBRUARY **Buffalo Bill Birthday Ball.** Hundreds of folks, some of them dressed in turn-of-the-20th-century attire, dance in Cody until the wee hours to celebrate the birthday of William F. Cody. The ball, held on a Saturday in late February, is at Cody Auditorium, which is dressed up as Wolfville Hall for the occasion. Tickets are $20 to $25 per person. ⊠ *1240 Beck Ave., Cody* ☎ *307/527–5520* ⊕ *www.codykc.org.*

JULY **Cody Stampede Rodeo.** The "Rodeo Capital of the World" hosts an annual event around July 4 that is affectionately known as "Cowboy Christmas." The event, held at Cody Stampede Park, is one of the most important stops on the rodeo circuit. Tickets range from $18 to $24. ☎ *307/587–5155, 800/207–0744* ⊕ *www.codystampederodeo.com.*

PLANNING YOUR TIME

YELLOWSTONE IN ONE DAY

If you plan to spend just one full day in the park, your best approach would be to concentrate on one or two of the park's major areas, such as the two biggest attractions: the famous Old Faithful geyser and the Grand Canyon of the Yellowstone. En route between these attractions, you can see geothermal activity and most likely some wildlife.

Plan on at least two hours for Old Faithful, one of the most iconic landmarks in America. Eruptions are approximately 90 minutes apart, though they can be as close as 60 minutes apart. Before and after an eruption you can explore the surrounding geyser basin and Old Faithful Inn. To the north of Old Faithful, make Grand Prismatic Spring your can't-miss geothermal stop; farther north, near Madison, veer off the road to the west to do the short Firehole Canyon Drive to see the Firehole River cut a small canyon and waterfall (Firehole Falls).

If you're arriving from the east, start with sunrise at **Lake Butte, Fishing Bridge,** and the wildlife-rich **Hayden Valley** as you cross the park counterclockwise to **Old Faithful.** To try to see wolves or bears, call ahead and ask when/if rangers will be stationed at roadside turnouts with spotting scopes. Alternatively, hike any trail in the park at least 2 miles—and remember that you're entering the domain of wild and sometimes dangerous animals, so be alert and don't hike alone.

If you're entering through the North or Northeast Entrance, begin at dawn looking for wolves and other animals in Lamar Valley, then head to **Tower-Roosevelt** and take a horseback ride into the surrounding forest. After your ride, continue west to **Mammoth Hot Springs,** where you can hike the **Lower Terrace Interpretive Trail** past Liberty Cap and other strange, brightly colored limestone formations. If you drive 1½ miles south of the visitor center you will reach the **Upper Terrace Drive** for close-ups of hot springs. In the late afternoon, drive south, keeping an eye out for

38

wildlife as you go—you're almost certain to see elk, buffalo, and possibly even a bear. Alternatively, from Tower-Roosevelt you can head south to go through **Canyon Village** to see the north or south rim of the **Grand Canyon of the Yellowstone** and its waterfalls, and then head west through Norris and Madison.

When you reach **Old Faithful,** you can place the famous geyser into context by walking the 1.5-mile **Geyser Hill Loop.** Watch the next eruption from the deck of the **Old Faithful Inn.**

GETTING HERE AND AROUND

AIR TRAVEL

Yellowstone National Park is served by airports in nearby communities, including Cody, Wyoming, one hour east; Jackson, Wyoming, one hour south; Bozeman, Montana, 90 minutes north; and West Yellowstone, Montana, just outside the park's west gate, which has only summer service. The best places to rent cars in the region are at these airports.

BUS TRAVEL

There is no commercial bus service to Yellowstone.

CAR TRAVEL

Yellowstone is well away from the interstates, so drivers make their way here on two-lane highways that are long on miles and scenery. From Interstate 80, take U.S. 191 north from Rock Springs; it's about 177 miles to Jackson, then another 60 miles north to Yellowstone. From Interstate 90, head south at Livingston, Montana, 80 miles to Gardiner and the park's North Entrance. From Bozeman travel south 90 miles to West Yellowstone.

Yellowstone has five primary entrances. Many visitors arrive through the South Entrance, north of Grand Teton National Park and Jackson, Wyoming. Other entrances are the East Entrance, with a main point of origin in Cody, Wyoming; the West Entrance at West Yellowstone, Montana, and the North Entrance at Gardiner, Montana; and the Northeast Entrance at Cooke City, Montana, which can be reached from either Cody, Wyoming, via the Chief Joseph Scenic Highway, or from Red Lodge, Montana, over the Beartooth Pass.

■ TIP→ The best way to keep your bearings in Yellowstone is to remember that the major roads form a figure eight, known as the Grand Loop, which all entrance roads feed into. It doesn't matter at which point you begin, as you can hit most of the major sights if you follow the entire route.

The 370 miles of public roads in the park used to be riddled with potholes and had narrow shoulders—a bit tight when a motor home was pulled over to the side to capture wildlife or scenery on film. But because of the park's efforts to upgrade its roads, most of them are now wide and smooth. Roadwork is likely every summer in some portion of the park—check the *Yellowstone Today* newspaper or ask a ranger. On holiday weekends road construction usually halts, so there are no construction delays for travelers. Remember, snow is possible any time of year in almost all areas of the park.

TOP 10 YELLOWSTONE TIPS

1. Before your trip, go online to get information from the park's official website, ⊕ *www.nps.gov/yell.*

2. On arrival at the park, stop at the nearest visitor center for information and updates.

3. Pack for all types of weather no matter what time of year.

4. Avoid the crowds by getting an early start to your day in the park.

5. Stay at least 75 feet away from wildlife (300 feet for bears).

6. Stay on geyser basin boardwalks to prevent serious thermal burns.

7. Drive defensively, and allow more time than you think you need.

8. Try to be to your destination before dark to avoid hitting wildlife on park roads.

9. Take a friend when you go hiking; it's safer and a lot more fun!

10. Don't try to see and do everything. You need two to three days just to visit the park highlights.

PARK ESSENTIALS
PARK FEES AND PERMITS

Entrance fees of $25 per vehicle, $20 per motorcycle or snowmobile, or $12 per visitor 16 and older entering by foot, bike, ski, and so on, gives you access for seven days to both Yellowstone and Grand Teton. An annual pass to the two parks costs $50.

Fishing permits (available at ranger stations, visitor centers, and Yellowstone general stores) are required if you want to take advantage of Yellowstone's abundant lakes and streams. Live bait is not allowed, and for all native species of fish, a catch-and-release policy stands. Anglers 16 and older must purchase an $18 three-day permit, a $25 seven-day permit, or a $40 season permit. Those under 16 need a free permit or must fish under the direct supervision of an adult with a permit. A state license is not needed to fish in Yellowstone National Park.

All camping outside of designated campgrounds requires a free backcountry permit. Horseback riding also requires a free permit. Day use horseback riding does not require a permit, only overnight trips with stock. All boats, motorized or nonmotorized, including float tubes, require a permit, which is $20 (annual) or $10 (seven days) for motorized boats and $10 (annual) or $5 (seven days) for nonmotorized vessels. Permits from Grand Teton National Park are valid in Yellowstone, but owners must register their vessel in Yellowstone.

PARK HOURS

Depending on the weather, Yellowstone is generally open late April to November and mid-December to early March. In winter, only one road, going from the Northeast Entrance at Cooke City to the North Entrance at Gardiner, is open to wheeled vehicles; other roads are used by over-snow vehicles. The park is in the Mountain time zone. Yellowstone is open 24 hours a day, 365 days per year from the North Entrance at Gardiner, Montana, to Mammoth Hot Springs, and from Mammoth Hot Springs to the Northeast Entrance and the town of Cooke City (with no through-travel beyond Cooke City).

38

CELL-PHONE RECEPTION

A comprehensive cell-phone coverage plan is in process, but currently reception in the park is hit-or-miss and generally confined to developed areas such as Mammoth, Old Faithful, Canyon, and Grant Village areas. In general, don't count on it. Public telephones are near visitor centers and major park attractions. ■ TIP→ **Try to use indoor phones rather than outdoor ones so your conversation doesn't distract you from being alert to wildlife that might approach you while you're on the phone.**

RESTAURANTS

When traveling in Yellowstone it's always a good idea to bring along a cooler—that way you can carry some snacks and lunch items for a picnic or break and not have to worry about making it to one of the more developed areas of the park, where all restaurants and cafeterias are managed by two competing companies (Xanterra and Delaware North). Generally you'll find burgers and sandwiches at cafeterias and full meals (as well as a kid's menu) at restaurants. There is a good selection of entrées such as beef and chicken, game meats such as elk and bison, fish like salmon and trout, plus other sustainably produced foods. At the several delis and general stores in the park you can purchase picnic items, snacks, sandwiches, and desserts like fudge and ice cream. Considering you are in one of the most remote outposts of the United States, selection and quality are above average—but expect to pay more as well. Note that reservations are needed for dinner at the Old Faithful Inn, Lake Yellowstone Hotel, and Grant Village dining rooms during the summer season.

Prices in the reviews are the average cost of a main course at dinner, or if dinner is not served, at lunch.

HOTELS

Park lodgings range from two of the national park system's magnificent old hotels to simple cabins to bland modern motels. Make reservations at least two months in advance for July and August for all park lodgings. Old Faithful Snow Lodge and Mammoth Hot Springs Hotel are the only accommodations open in winter; rates are the same as in summer. Ask about the size of beds, bathrooms, thickness of walls, and room location when you book, especially in the older hotels, where accommodations vary and upgrades are ongoing. Telephones have been put in most rooms, but there are no TVs. There are no roll-away beds available.

Prices in the reviews are the lowest cost of a standard double in high season. For expanded reviews, facilities, and current deals, visit Fodors.com.

TOURS

Historic Yellow Bus Tour. These 13-passenger buses are originals, built between 1936 and 1938. Carefully restored, they are the most elegant way to learn about the park. Your driver, who narrates the trip, will roll back the soft-top convertible for you to bask under the sun if the weather is warm enough. More than a dozen itineraries include wildlife sightings, photo opportunities, and some of the park's favorite landmarks. Buses depart from various in-park locations, including the Old Faithful Inn, Mammoth Hotel, and Canyon Lodge in Canyon. ☎ 866/439–7375 ⊕ *www.yellowstonenationalparklodges.com* ✉ *$26–$90* ☽ *June–Sept.*

Plants and Wildlife in Yellowstone

Eighty percent of Yellowstone is forest, and the great majority of it is lodgepole pine. Miles and miles of the "telephone pole" pines were lost in the massive 1988 fire that burned more than 35% of the park. The fire's heat created the ideal condition for the lodgepole pine's serotinous cones to release their seeds—which now provides a stark juxtaposition between 20-year-old and 100-year-old trees.

Yellowstone's scenery astonishes any time of day, though the play of light and shadow makes the park most appealing in early morning and late afternoon. That's exactly when you should be looking for wildlife, as most are active around dawn and dusk, moving out of the forest in search of food and water. May and June are the best months for seeing baby bison, moose, and other young arrivals. Look for glacier lilies among the spring wildflowers and goldenrod amid the changing foliate of fall. Winter visitors see the park at its most magical, with steam billowing from geyser basins to wreath trees in ice, and elk foraging close to roads transformed into ski trails.

Bison, elk, and coyotes populate virtually all areas; elk and bison particularly like river valleys and the geyser basins. Moose like marshy areas along Yellowstone Lake and in the northeast corner of the park. Wolves are most common in the Lamar Valley and areas south of Mammoth; bears are most visible in the Pelican Valley–Fishing Bridge area, near Dunraven Pass, and near Mammoth. Watch for trumpeter swans along the Yellowstone River and for sandhill cranes near the Firehole River and in Madison Valley.

38

VISITOR INFORMATION
PARK CONTACT INFORMATION
Yellowstone National Park ☎ *307/344–7381* ⊕ *www.nps.gov/yell.*

VISITOR CENTERS
FAMILY **Albright Visitor Center.** Serving as bachelor quarters for cavalry officers from 1909 to 1918, this red-roof building now holds a museum with exhibits on the region's early inhabitants and the park's history. Kids will love the extensive displays of park wildlife, including bears and wolves. Open hours can change yearly and seasonally, so visitors are encouraged to verify hours upon entering the park. ⊠ *Mammoth Hot Springs* ☎ *307/344–2263* ⊙ *Late May–Sept., daily 8–7; Oct.–late May, daily 9–6.*

FAMILY **Canyon Visitor Center.** This gleaming visitor center features elaborate interactive exhibits for adults and kids. The focus here is volcanoes and earthquakes, but there are also exhibits on Native Americans and park wildlife, including bison and wolves. As at all visitor centers, you can obtain park information, backcountry camping permits, etc. The adjacent bookstore is the best in the park, with hundreds of books on the park, its history, and the science surrounding it. ⊠ *Canyon Village* ☎ *307/242–2552* ⊙ *Late May–Aug., daily 8–8; Sept., daily 9–6; early Oct., daily 9–5.*

FAMILY **Fishing Bridge Visitor Center.** This distinctive stone-and-log building, built in 1931, has been designated a National Historic Landmark. If you can't distinguish between a Clark's nuthatch and an ermine (hint: one's a bird, the other a weasel), check out the extensive exhibits on the park's smaller wildlife. Step out the back door to find yourself on one of the beautiful black obsidian beaches of Yellowstone Lake. Adjacent is one of the park's larger amphitheaters, and it features ranger presentations nightly in summer. The bookstore here features books, guides, and other educational materials, but you can't buy coffee. ⊠ *East Entrance Rd., 1 mile from Grand Loop Rd.* ☎ *307/242–2450* ⊙ *Memorial Day–late Sept., daily 8–7.*

Grant Village Visitor Center. Each visitor center relates a small piece of the park's history—this one tells about the 1988 fire that burned more than a third of the total acreage and forced multiple federal agencies to reevaluate their fire-control policies. Watch an informative video, purchase maps or books, and learn more about the 25,000 firefighters from across America who fought the 1988 fire. Bathrooms and a backcountry office are housed here as well. ⊠ *Grant Village* ☎ *307/242–2650* ⊙ *Late May–late Sept., daily 8–7.*

Madison Information Center. In this National Historic Landmark, park rangers share the space with a bookstore featuring books, maps, and learning aids. You may find spotting scopes set up for wildlife viewing out the rear window; if this is the case, look for eagles, swans, bison, and elk. Rangers will answer questions about the park, provide basic hiking information, and issue permits for backcountry camping and fishing. Picnic tables, toilets, and an amphitheater for summer-evening ranger programs are shared with the nearby campground. ⊠ *Grand Loop Rd. at West Entrance Rd.* ☎ *307/344–2821* ⊙ *Late May–late Sept., daily 9–6.*

Old Faithful Visitor Education Center. This $27 million visitor center, opened in 2010, has quickly become one of the jewels of the national park system. Check out the interactive exhibits, then inquire about geyser eruption predictions and ranger-led walks and talks. Backcountry and fishing permits are handled out of the ranger station adjacent to the Old Faithful Snow Lodge. ⊠ *Old Faithful Bypass Rd.* ☎ *307/545–2750* ⊙ *Late Apr.–late May, daily 9–6; late May–late Sept., daily 8–8; Oct.–early Nov., daily 9–5; Dec.–late Apr., daily 9–6.*

West Thumb Information Station. This historic log cabin houses a bookstore and doubles as a warming hut in the winter. There are restrooms in the parking area. Check for informal ranger-led discussions beneath the old sequoia tree in the summer. ⊠ *West Thumb* ⊙ *Late May–late Sept., daily 9–5.*

EXPLORING

SCENIC DRIVES

Firehole Canyon Drive. The 2-mile narrow asphalt road twists through a deep canyon and passes the 40-foot Firehole Falls. In summer look for a sign marking a pullout and swimming hole. This is one of only two places in the park (Boiling River on the North Entrance Road is the other) where you can safely and legally swim in the park's thermally heated waters. Look carefully for osprey and other raptors. ✉ *1 mile south of Madison junction off Grand Loop Rd.*

Firehole Lake Drive. This one-way, 3-mile-long road takes you past Great Fountain Geyser, which shoots out jets of water reaching as high as 200 feet about twice a day. Rangers' predictions have a two-hour window of opportunity. Should you witness it, however, you'll be rewarded with a view of waves of water cascading down the terraces that form the edges of the geyser. This road is not open to over-snow vehicle traffic in winter, only foot, snowshoe, or skies, and is rarely traveled by any of those options because it is not groomed for those uses. ✉ *Firehole Lake Dr., 8 miles north of Old Faithful, Old Faithful.*

Hayden Valley on Grand Loop Road. Bison, bears, coyotes, wolves, and birds of prey all call Hayden Valley home almost year-round. Once part of Yellowstone Lake, the broad valley now features peaceful meadows, rolling hills, and the placid Yellowstone River. There are multiple turnouts and picnic areas on the 16-mile drive, many with views of the river and valley. Ask a ranger about "Grizzly Overlook," an unofficial site where wildlife watchers, including NPS rangers with spotting scopes for the public to use, congregate in the summer. It has 11 turnouts north of Mud Volcano—there's no sign, so look for the timber railings. ✉ *Grand Loop Rd., between Canyon and Fishing Bridge.*

Fodor's Choice ★ **Northeast Entrance Road and Lamar Valley.** The 29-mile road features the richest diversity of landscape of the five entrance roads. Just after you enter the park, you cut between 10,928-foot Abiathar Peak and the 10,404-foot Barronette Peak. Lamar Valley is the melancholy home to hundreds of bison, while the rugged peaks and ridges adjacent to it are home to some of the park's most famous wolf packs (reintroduced in 1995). The main wolf-watching activities in the park occur here during early-morning and late-evening hours year-round. As you exit Lamar Valley, the road crosses the Yellowstone River before leading you to the rustic Roosevelt Lodge. ✉ *From Northeast Entrance to junction with Grand Loop Rd.*

Northeastern Grand Loop. Commonly called Dunraven Pass, this 19-mile segment of Grand Loop Road climbs to nearly 9,000 feet as it passes some of the park's finest scenery, twisting beneath a series of leaning basalt towers 40 to 50 feet high. That behemoth to the east is 10,243-foot Mt. Washburn. ✉ *Between Canyon Village and Roosevelt Falls.*

Upper Terrace Drive. Limber pines as old as 500 years line this 1½-mile loop near Mammoth Hot Springs, where a variety of mosses grow through white travertine, composed of lime deposited by the area's hot springs. ✉ *Grand Loop Rd., 2 miles from Mammoth Hot Springs Hotel.*

38

HISTORIC SITES

OLD FAITHFUL

FAMILY **Old Faithful Inn.** It's hard to imagine how any work could be accom-
Fodor'sChoice plished when snow and ice blanket the region, but this historic hotel
★ was constructed over the course of a single winter in 1903. Open since
1904, this massive log structure is an attraction in its own right. Even
if you don't spend a night at the Old Faithful Inn, walk through or take
the free 45-minute guided tour to admire its massive open-beam lobby
and rock fireplace. There are antique writing desks on the second-floor
balcony. You can watch Old Faithful geyser from two second-floor outdoor decks. ✉ *Old Faithful Bypass Rd., Old Faithful* ☎ *307/344–7311*
🕙 *May–mid-Oct.; tours daily, times vary.*

MAMMOTH HOT SPRINGS

Fort Yellowstone. The oldest buildings here served as Fort Yellowstone
from 1891 to 1918, when the U.S. Army managed the park. The redbrick
buildings cluster around an open area reminiscent of a frontier-era parade
ground. You can pick up a self-guided tour map of the area to make
your way around the historic fort structures. ✉ *Mammoth Hot Springs.*

LAKE AREA

Lake Yellowstone Hotel. Completed in 1891, this structure is on the
National Register of Historic Places and is the oldest lodging in Yellowstone National Park. Casual daytime visitors can lounge in white
wicker chairs in the sunroom and watch the waters of Yellowstone
Lake through massive windows. Robert Reamer, the architect of the
Old Faithful Inn, added its columned entrance in 1903 to enhance the
original facade. ✉ *Lake Village Rd., 1 Grand Loop Rd., Lake Village*
☎ *307/344–7901* ⊕ *www.yellowstonenationalparklodges.com/lodging/*
summer-lodges/lake-yellowstone-hotel-cabins 🕙 *Mid-May–early Oct.*

SCENIC STOPS

Along the park's main drive—the Grand Loop (also referred to as
Yellowstone's Figure Eight)—are eight primary "communities," or
developed areas. On the Western Yellowstone map are five of those
communities—Grant Village, Old Faithful, Madison, Norris, and Mammoth Hot Springs—with their respective sights, while the Eastern Yellowstone map shows the remaining three—Tower-Roosevelt, Canyon,
and Lake (for Yellowstone Lake area)—with their respective sights.

GRANT VILLAGE AND WEST THUMB

Along the western edge of Yellowstone Lake (called the West Thumb),
Grant Village is the first community you encounter from the South
Entrance. It has basic lodging and dining facilities.

FAMILY **West Thumb Geyser Basin.** The primary Yellowstone caldera was created by one volcanic eruption, while West Thumb came about as the
result of another, later volcanic eruption. This unique geyser basin is
the only place to see active geothermal features in Yellowstone Lake.
Two boardwalk loops are offered; take the longer one to see features
like Fishing Cone, where fishermen used to drop their freshly caught
fish straight into boiling water without ever taking it off the hook. This

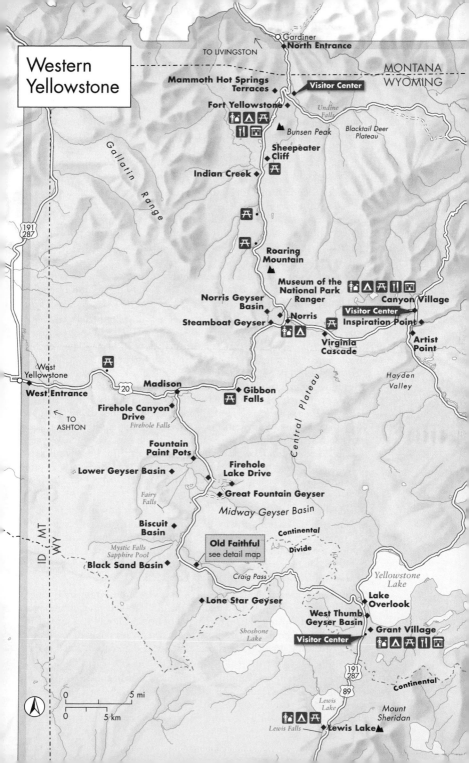

Western Yellowstone

TO LIVINGSTON

Gardiner
North Entrance

MONTANA
WYOMING

Visitor Center

Mammoth Hot Springs Terraces

Undine Falls

Blacktail Deer Plateau

Fort Yellowstone

Bunsen Peak

Sheepeater Cliff

Indian Creek

Gallatin Range

191 287

Roaring Mountain

Museum of the National Park Ranger

Canyon Village

Norris Geyser Basin

Steamboat Geyser

Norris

Visitor Center

Inspiration Point

Hayden Valley

Virginia Cascade

Artist Point

West Yellowstone

West Entrance

20 **Madison**

TO ASHTON

Gibbon Falls

Central Plateau

Firehole Canyon Drive

Firehole Falls

Fountain Paint Pots

Lower Geyser Basin

Firehole Lake Drive

Fairy Falls

Great Fountain Geyser

Midway Geyser Basin

Biscuit Basin

Mystic Falls Sapphire Pool

Continental

Divide

Black Sand Basin

Craig Pass

Old Faithful see detail map

Yellowstone Lake

ID MT WY

Lone Star Geyser

Shoshone Lake

Lake Overlook

West Thumb Geyser Basin

Grant Village

Visitor Center

191 287

Continental

89

0   5 mi

0   5 km

Lewis Lake

Lewis Falls

Lewis Lake

Mount Sheridan

area is particularly popular for winter visitors, who take advantage of the nearby warming hut and a stroll around the geyser basin before continuing their trip via snow coach or snowmobile. ⊠ *Grand Loop Rd., 22 miles north of South Entrance, West Thumb.*

OLD FAITHFUL

Fodor's Choice
★
The world's most famous geyser is the centerpiece of this area, which has extensive boardwalks through the Upper Geyser Basin and equally extensive visitor services, including several choices in lodging and dining, and a new visitor center. In winter you can dine and stay in this area and cross-country ski or snowshoe through the Geyser Basin.

Biscuit Basin. North of Old Faithful, this basin is also the trailhead for the Mystic Falls Trail. The namesake "biscuit" formations were reduced to crumbs when Sapphire Pool erupted after the 1959 Hebgen Lake earthquake. Now, Sapphire is a calm, beautiful blue pool again, but that could change at any moment. ⊠ *Grand Loop Rd., 3 miles north of Old Faithful.*

Black Sand Basin. There are a dozen hot springs and geysers near the cloverleaf entrance from Grand Loop Road to Old Faithful. Emerald Pool is one of the prettiest. ⊠ *North of Old Faithful on Grand Loop Rd.*

FAMILY **Geyser Hill Loop.** Along the 1.3-mile Geyser Hill Loop boardwalk you will see active thermal features such as violent Giantess Geyser. Erupting only a few times each year, Giantess spouts 100 to 250 feet in the air for five to eight minutes once or twice hourly for 12 to 43 hours. Nearby Doublet Pool's two adjacent springs have complex ledges and deep blue waters, which are highly photogenic. Starting as a gentle pool, Anemone Geyser overflows, bubbles, and finally erupts 10 feet or more, every three to eight minutes. The loop boardwalk brings you close to the action, making it especially appealing to children intrigued with the sights and sounds of the basin. To reach Geyser Hill, head counterclockwise around the Old Faithful boardwalk 0.3 miles from the visitor center, crossing the Firehole River and entering Upper Geyser Basin. ⊠ *Old Faithful, ⅓ miles from Old Faithful Visitor Center.*

Grand Prismatic Spring. This is Yellowstone's largest hot spring, 370 feet in diameter. It's in the Midway Geyser Basin, and you can reach it by following the boardwalk. The spring is deep blue in color, with yellow and orange rings formed by bacteria that give it the effect of a prism. For a stunning perspective, look down on in from the Fairy Falls Trail. ⊠ *Midway Geyser Basin, off Grand Loop Rd.*

Great Fountain Geyser. This geyser erupts twice a day; rangers predict when it will shoot some 200 feet into the air, but their prediction has a window of opportunity lasting a couple of hours. Should you see Great Fountain spew, however, you'll be rewarded with a view of waves of water cascading down the terraces that form the edges of the geyser. ⊠ *Firehole Lake Dr., north of Old Faithful.*

Lower Geyser Basin. Shooting more than 150 feet in the air, the Great Fountain Geyser is the most spectacular sight in this basin. Less impressive but more regular is White Dome Geyser, which shoots from a 20-foot-tall cone. You'll also find pink mudpots and blue pools at the

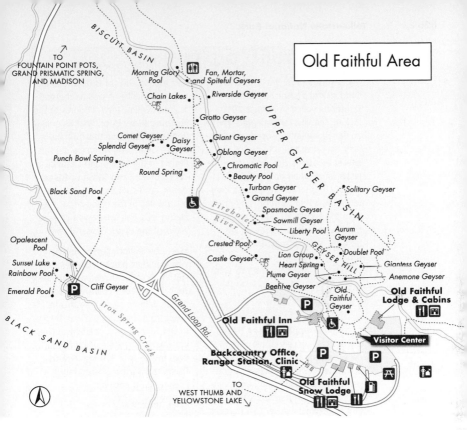

Old Faithful Area

basin's Fountain Paint Pots, a unique spot in the park because visitors discover all four hydrothermal features that are in Yellowstone, including fumaroles, mudpots, hot springs, and geysers. ⊠ *Grand Loop Rd., midway between Old Faithful and Madison*

Midway Geyser Basin. Called "Hell's Half Acre" by writer Rudyard Kipling, Midway Geyser Basin is a more interesting stop than Lower Geyser Basin. A series of boardwalks wind their way to the Excelsior Geyser, which deposits 4,000 gallons of vivid blue water per minute into the Firehole River. Just above Excelsior is Yellowstone's largest hot spring, Grand Prismatic Spring. ⊠ *Grand Loop Rd., between Old Faithful and Madison*

Morning Glory Pool. Shaped somewhat like a morning glory, this pool once was a deep blue, but the color is no longer as striking due to tourists dropping coins and other debris into the hole. To reach the pool, follow the boardwalk past Geyser Hill Loop and stately Castle Geyser, which has the biggest cone in Yellowstone. Morning Glory is the inspiration for popular children's author Jan Brett's story *Hedgie Blasts Off*, in which a hedgehog goes to another planet to unclog a geyser damaged by space tourists' debris. ⊠ *At the north end of Upper Geyser Basin at Old Faithful.*

A GOOD TOUR: OLD FAITHFUL

Begin your tour at the impressive **Old Faithful Visitor Education Center**, unveiled in August 2010. Pick up the Old Faithful–area trail guide (50 cents) and check a board with the latest predictions for six geyser eruptions. You don't need to jostle for position on the boardwalk directly in front of the visitor's center to enjoy Old Faithful—any angle from the boardwalk surrounding the geyser is impressive—or view it from the deck of the **Old Faithful Inn**. And speaking of that famous, century-old inn, make time to stop in to check out its massive log-construction interior.

At Old Faithful Village you're in the heart of the **Upper Geyser Basin**, the densest concentration of geysers on Earth with about 140 geysers in a one square mile. The biggest attraction is where you should begin your tour: **Old Faithful** spouts 130 to 180 feet approximately every 94 minutes. Once you've watched Old Faithful erupt, explore the larger basin with a hike around **Geyser Hill**, where you may see wildlife as well as thermal features. Follow the trail north to the **Morning Glory Pool**, with its unique flower shape. Along this trail are Castle, Grand, and Riverside geysers. Return to the village and continue by car to **Black Sand Basin** or **Biscuit Basin**. At Biscuit Basin, follow the boardwalks to the trailhead for the Mystic Falls Trail, where you can get views of the Upper Geyser Basin.

Take a break from geyser watching with a packed lunch at the Whiskey Flat picnic area. Afterward, continue your drive toward **Lower Geyser Basin**, with its colorful **Fountain Paint Pots**. Then, on the way back to Old Faithful, stop at **Midway Geyser Basin**, where steaming runoff from the colorful 370-foot **Grand Prismatic Spring** crashes into the Firehole River each minute.

Relax and revisit your long day with dinner (advance reservations required!) at the Old Faithful Inn, or enjoy drinks on the second floor.

FAMILY

Fodor'sChoice

★

Old Faithful. Almost every visitor's itinerary includes the world's most famous geyser. Yellowstone's most predictable big geyser—although not its largest or most regular—sometimes reaches 180 feet, but it averages 130 feet. The mysterious plumbing of Yellowstone has lengthened Old Faithful's cycle somewhat in recent years, to every 94 minutes or so. To find out when Old Faithful is likely to erupt, check at the visitor center, at any of the lodging properties in the area, or by calling the geyser prediction line at ☎ *307/344–2751.* You can view the eruption from a bench just yards away, from the dining room at the lodge cafeteria, or the second-floor balcony of Old Faithful Inn. The 1-mile hike to Observation Point yields yet another view—from above—of the geyser and its surrounding basin. ⊠ *Southwest segment of Grand Loop Rd.*

Upper Geyser Basin. With Old Faithful as its central attraction, this mile-square basin contains about 140 different geysers—one-fifth of the known geysers in the world. It's an excellent place to spend a day or more exploring. You will find a complex system of boardwalks and trails—some of them used as bicycle trails—that take you to the basin's various attractions.

MADISON

The area around the junction of the West Entrance Road and the Lower Loop is a good place to take a break as you travel through the park, because you will almost always see bison grazing along the Madison River, and often elk are in the area as well. Limited visitor services are here, and there are no dining facilities.

Gibbon Falls. Water rushes over the caldera rim in this 84-foot waterfall on the Gibbon River. You can see it on your right from the road as you're driving east from Madison to Norris. ⊠ *Grand Loop Rd., 4 miles east of Madison.*

NORRIS

The area at the western junction of the Upper and Lower Loops has the most active geyser basin in the park. The underground plumbing occasionally reaches such high temperatures—the ground itself has heated up in areas to nearly 200°F—that a portion of the basin is periodically closed for safety reasons. There are limited visitor services: two museums, a bookstore, and a picnic area. ■TIP→ **Ask rangers at the Norris Geyser Basin Museum when different geysers are expected to erupt and plan your walk accordingly.**

Back Basin. The trail through Back Basin is a 1.5-mile loop guiding you past Steamboat Geyser. When it erupts fully (most recently in 1985), it's the world's largest, climbing 400 feet above the basin. More often, Steamboat growls and spits constantly, sending clouds of steam high above the basin. Kids will love the Puff 'n' Stuff Geyser and the mysterious cave-like Green Dragon Spring. Ask trangers for an anticipated schedule of geyser eruptions—you might catch the Echinus Geyser, which erupts almost hourly. ⊠ *Grand Loop Rd. at Norris.*

FAMILY **Norris Geyser Basin.** From the Norris Ranger Station, choose Porcelain Basin, Back Basin, or both. These volatile thermal features are constantly changing, although you can expect to find a variety of geysers and springs here at any time. The area is accessible via an extensive system of boardwalks, some of them suitable for people with disabilities. The famous Steamboat Geyser is here. ⊠ *Grand Loop Rd. at Norris.*

Porcelain Basin. In the eastern portion of the Norris Geyser Basin this thermal area is reached by a 0.75-mile, partially boardwalked loop from Norris Geyser Basin Museum. In this geothermal field of whitish geyserite stone, the earth bulges and belches from the underground pressure. You'll find bubbling pools, some milky white and others ringed in orange because of the minerals in the water, as well as small geysers such as extremely active Whirligig. ⊠ *Grand Loop Rd.*

MAMMOTH HOT SPRINGS

This northern community in the park is known for its massive natural terraces, where mineral water flows continuously, building an ever-changing display. (Note, however, that water levels can fluctuate, so if it's late in a particularly dry summer, you won't see the terraces in all their glory.) You will often see elk grazing here. In the early days of the park, it was the site of Fort Yellowstone, and the brick buildings constructed during that era are still used for various park activities.

38

FAMILY **Mammoth Hot Springs Terraces.** Multicolor travertine terraces formed by slowly escaping hot mineral water mark this unusual geological formation. You can explore the terraces via an elaborate network of boardwalks, the best of which is the Lower Terrace Interpretive Trail. If you head uphill from Liberty Cap, at the area's north end, in an hour you'll pass bright and ornately terraced Minerva Spring. Along the way you may spy elk grazing nearby. Alternatively, you can drive up to the Lower Terrace Overlook on Upper Terrace Drive and take the boardwalks down past New Blue Springs to the Lower Terrace. This route, which also takes an hour, works especially well if you can park a second vehicle at the foot of Lower Terrace. ■TIP→ There are lots of steps on the lower terrace boardwalks, so plan to take your time there. ⊠ *Northwest corner of Grand Loop Rd.*

TOWER-ROOSEVELT

The northeast region of Yellowstone is the least visited part of the park, making it a great place to explore without running into as many people. Packs of wolves may be spotted in the Lamar Valley.

Petrified Tree. If you enjoy seeing bears in zoo pens, you'll get the same level of satisfaction as you look at this geological landmark surrounded on all four sides by high wrought-iron gates. Unfortunately, a century of vandalism has forced park officials to completely enclose this 45-million-year-old redwood tree—utterly ruining the experience. ⊠ *Grand Loop Rd., 1 mile west of Tower-Roosevelt.*

FAMILY **Tower Fall.** This is one of the easiest waterfalls to see from the roadside; you can also view volcanic pinnacles here. Tower Creek plunges 132 feet at this waterfall to join the Yellowstone River. While a trail that used to go to the base of the falls has washed out, it will take trekkers down to the river. ⊠ *Grand Loop Rd., 2 miles south of Tower-Roosevelt*

CANYON

The Yellowstone River's source is in the Absaroka Mountains in the southeast corner of the park. It winds its way through the heart of the park, entering Yellowstone Lake, then heading northward under Fishing Ridge through Hayden Valley. When it cuts through the multicolor Grand Canyon of the Yellowstone, it creates one of the most spectacular gorges in the world, enticing visitors with its steep canyon walls and waterfalls. All types of visitor services are here, as well as lots of hiking opportunities.

Artist Point. An impressive view of the Lower Falls of the Yellowstone River can be seen from this point, which has two different viewing levels, one accessible to wheelchairs. The South Rim Trail goes past this point, and there is a nearby parking area open in both summer and winter. ⊠ *East end of South Rim Rd.*

Fodor'sChoice **Grand Canyon of the Yellowstone.** This stunning canyon is 23 miles long, ★ but there is only one trail from rim to base. As a result, a majority of Park visitors clog the north and south rims to see Upper and Lower Falls. Unless you're up for the six-hour strenuous hike called Seven Mile Hole, you have no choice but to join the crowds on the rims to see this natural wonder. The red-and-ochre canyon walls are topped with emerald-green forest. It's a feast of color. Also look for osprey, which nest in the canyon's spires and precarious trees.

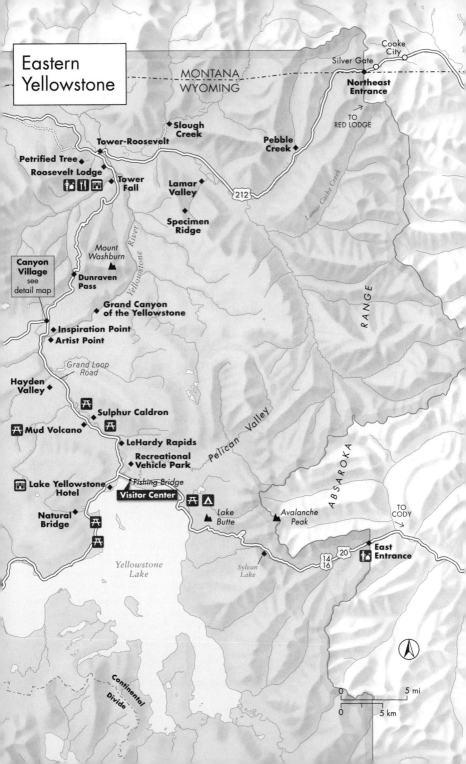

Lookout Point. Midway on the North Rim Trail—or accessible via the one-way North Rim Drive—Lookout Point gives you a view of the Grand Canyon of the Yellowstone. Follow the right-hand fork in the path to descend a steep trail (approximately 500-foot elevation change) for an "eye-to-eye" view of the falls from a half mile downstream. The best time to hike the trail is early morning, when sunlight reflects off the mist from the falls to create a rainbow. ⊠ *Off North Rim Dr.*

Upper Falls View. A spur road off Grand Loop Road south of Canyon gives you access to the west end of the North Rim Trail and takes you down a fairly steep trail for a view of Upper Falls from almost directly above. ⊠ *Off Grand Loop Rd., ¾ miles south of Canyon.*

> **CAUTION: A WILD PLACE**
>
> As you explore the park keep this thought in mind: Yellowstone is not an amusement park. It is a wild place. The animals may seem docile or tame, but they are wild, and every year careless visitors are injured—sometimes even killed—when they venture too close. Particularly dangerous are female animals with their young, and bison, which can turn and charge in an instant. (Watch their tails: when they are standing up or crooked like a question mark, the bison is agitated.)

LAKE AREA

In the park's southeastern segment, the area is permeated by the tranquility of massive Yellowstone Lake. Near Fishing Bridge you might see grizzly bears. They like to hunt for fish spawning or swimming near the lake's outlet to the Yellowstone River. Visitor information may be found at Lake Yellowstone Hotel, Fishing Bridge RV Park (for hardsided vehicles only), and Bridge Bay Campground, the park's largest, with 432 sites.

LeHardy Rapids. Witness one of nature's epic battles as cutthroat trout migrate upstream by catapulting themselves out of the water to get over and around obstacles in the Yellowstone River. The quarter-mile forested loop takes you to the river's edge. Also keep an eye out for waterfowl and bears, which feed on the trout. ⊠ *3 miles north of Fishing Bridge.*

FAMILY **Mud Volcano.** Gasses hissing from vents underscore the volatile nature of this area's geothermal features. The 0.75-mile round-trip Mud Volcano Interpretive Trail loops gently around seething, sulfuric mudpots with names such as Black Dragon's Cauldron and Sizzling Basin before making its way around Mud Volcano itself, a boiling pot of brown goo. ⊠ *Grand Loop Rd., 10 miles south of Canyon, 4 miles north of Fishing Bridge.*

Sulphur Caldron. You can smell the sulfur before you even leave your vehicle to walk to the overlook of Sulphur Caldron, where hissing steam escapes from a moonscape like surface as superheated bubbling mud. ⊠ *Grand Loop Rd., 9½ miles south of Canyon, 4½ miles north of Fishing Bridge.*

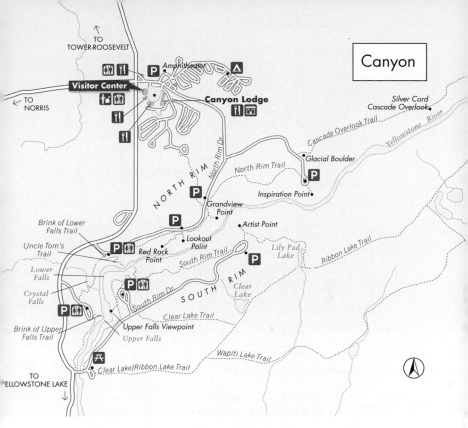

FAMILY
Fodor's Choice
★

Yellowstone Lake. One of the world's largest alpine lakes, 132-square-mile Yellowstone Lake was formed when the glaciers that once covered the region melted into a caldera—a crater formed by a volcano. The lake has 141 miles of shoreline, along which you will often see moose, elk, waterfowl, and other wildlife. In winter you can sometimes see otters and coyotes stepping gingerly onto the ice at the lake's edge. Many visitors head here for the excellent fishing—streams flowing into the lake give it an abundant supply of trout. ⊠ *Intersection of East Entrance and Grand Loop rds., between Fishing Bridge and Grant Village.*

EDUCATIONAL OFFERINGS

CLASSES AND SEMINARS

Expedition: Yellowstone! Since 1985, this four- to five-day residential program for kids in grades four to eight has taught about the natural and cultural history of Yellowstone, as well as issues affecting its ecosystem. The curriculum includes hikes, discussions, journal keeping, and presentations. The historic Lamar Buffalo Ranch is used during the spring and fall. The Youth Conservation Corps facilities are used during winter months. ⊠ *Lamar Buffalo Ranch* ☎ *307/344–7381* ⊕ *www.nps.gov/yell/planyourvisit/expeditionyell.htm* ☉ *Sept.–mid-Dec.; mid-Feb.–May.*

"On a cold and windy evening, walking along Yellowstone Lake, I came across this beautiful shot of a log engulfed by the flowing water." —photo by Brian Mosoff, Fodors.com member

FAMILY **Yellowstone Association Institute.** Learn about the park's ecology, geology, history, and wildlife from park experts, including well-known geologists, biologists and photographers. Classes last one to three days, and rates are reasonable. Some programs are designed specifically for young people and families. ✉ *115 3rd St. S., Gardiner, Montana* ☎ *406/848–2400* ⊕ *www.yellowstoneassociation.org/institute.*

RANGER PROGRAMS

Yellowstone offers a busy schedule of guided hikes, talks, and campfire programs. For dates and times, check the park's *Yellowstone Today* newsletter, available at all entrances and visitor centers.

FAMILY **Daytime Walks and Talks.** Ranger-led programs are available during both the winter and summer seasons. Ranger Adventure Hikes are more strenuous and must be reserved in advance, but anyone can join the regular ranger talks and ranger walks. Winter programs are held at West Yellowstone, Old Faithful, and Mammoth.

FAMILY **Evening Programs.** Gather around to hear tales about Yellowstone's fascinating history, with hour-long programs on topics ranging from the return of the bison to 19th-century photographers. Every major area hosts programs, but check visitor centers or campground bulletin board for updates. ⊙ *June–Aug., nightly at 9 and 9:30.*

FAMILY **Junior Ranger Program.** Children ages 5 to 12 are eligible to earn patches and become Junior Rangers. Pick up the Junior Ranger Newspaper at Madison, Canyon, or Old Faithful for $3, and start the entertaining self-guided curriculum, or download it for free online. ⊕ *www.nps.gov/ yell/forkids/beajuniorranger.htm.*

SPORTS AND THE OUTDOORS

In the winter months, snowmobiling and cross-country skiing are the activities of choice. In summer, hiking, biking, and fishing are the best ways to get out and enjoy the park.

BOATING

Motorized boats are allowed only on Lewis Lake and Yellowstone Lake. Kayaking or canoeing is allowed on all park lakes except Sylvan Lake, Eleanor Lake, Twin Lakes, and Beach Springs Lagoon; however, most lakes are inaccessible by car, so accessing the park's lakes requires long portages. Boating is not allowed on any park river, except for the Lewis River between Lewis Lake and Shoshone Lake, where nonmotorized boats are permitted.

You must purchase a seven-day, $5 permit for boats and floatables, or a $10 permit for motorized boats at Bridge Bay Ranger Station, South Entrance Ranger Station, Grant Village Backcountry Office, and Lewis Lake Ranger Station (at the campground). Nonmotorized permits are available at the Northeast entrance, West Yellowstone Information Center; backcountry offices at Mammoth, Old Faithful, and Canyon; Bechler Ranger Station; and locations where motorized permits are sold. Annual permits are also available for $20.

Boat permits issued in Grand Teton National Park are honored in Yellowstone, but owners must register their vessel in Yellowstone and obtain a no-charge Yellowstone validation sticker from a permit-issuing station.

TOURS AND OUTFITTERS

FAMILY **Bridge Bay Marina.** Watercraft, from rowboats to powerboats, are available for trips on Yellowstone Lake at Bridge Bay Marina. You also can rent 22- and 34-foot cabin cruisers with a guide. ⊠ *Grand Loop Rd., 2 miles south of Lake Village, Lake area* ☎ *307/344–7311* ⊕ *www.xanterra.com/what-we-do/activities* ⊠ *$88/hr for guided cruisers for fishing or sightseeing; $10/hr for rowboat; $47/hr for small boat with outboard motor* ⊙ *June–early Sept., daily 8:30–8:30.*

Yellowstone Lake Scenic Cruises. Yellowstone Lake Scenic Cruises take visitors on one-hour cruises aboard the *Lake Queen II.* The vessel makes its way from Bridge Bay to Stevenson Island and back. Reservations are strongly recommended. ⊠ *Bridge Bay Marina, Lake area* ☎ *307/344–7311* ⊕ *www.xanterra.com/what-we-do/activities* ⊠ *Cruises $15* ⊙ *Late May–mid-Sept., daily 8:30–8:30.*

38

Continued on page 843

YELLOWSTONE'S GEOTHERMAL WONDERS

By Brian Kevin

Steaming, bubbling,
and erupting
throughout the day
like giant teapots.

Yellowstone's geothermal features are constantly putting on a show. The 10,000 hot springs, mud pots, and fumaroles, plus 300 or so active geysers within the park comprise more than half the entire world's thermal features. You'd need to search two or three other continents for as many geysers as you can see during a single afternoon around Old Faithful.

HEATING UP

Past eruptions of cataclysmic volcanoes brought about the steaming, vaporous landscape of Yellowstone today. The heat from the magma (molten rock) under the Yellowstone Caldera, an active volcano, continues to fuel the park's geyser basins, such as the Upper Geyser Basin, where more than 200 spouters cram into less than two square miles; and Norris, where water 1,000 feet below ground is 450° F. The complex underground plumbing in these geyser basins is affected by earthquakes and other subterranean hijinks that geologists are only beginning to understand. Some spouters spring to life, while others fall dormant with little or no warning.

HOT SPOT TIPS

■ **Stay on trails and boardwalks.** In some areas, like in Norris, water boils at temperatures of more than 200°. If you want to venture into the back country, where there are no boardwalks, consult a ranger first.

■ **Leave the area if you feel sick or dizzy.** You might be feeling this way due to overexposure to various thermal gases.

■ **These hot springs aren't for bathing.** The pH levels of some of these features are extremely acidic.

■ **They also aren't wishing wells.** In the past people threw hundreds of coins into the bright blue Morning Glory Pool. The coins clogged the pool's natural water vents, causing it to change to a sickly green color.

(left) Old Faithful. (above) Punch Bowl Spring.

HOW DO GEYSERS WORK?

A few main ingredients make geysers possible: abundant water, a heat source, a certain kind of plumbing system, and rock strong enough to withstand some serious pressure. The layout of any one geyser's underground plumbing may vary, but we know that below each vent is a system of fissures and chambers, with constrictions here and there that prevent hot water from rising to the surface. As the underground water heats up, these constrictions and the cooler surface water "cap" the whole system, keeping it from boiling over and ratcheting up the underground pressure. When a few steam bubbles eventually fight their way through the constrictions, the result is like uncapping a shaken-up soda bottle, when the released pressure causes the soda to spray.

FUN FACTS

A cone geyser (like Lone Star Geyser in Yellowstone's backcountry) has a spout-like formation around its vent, formed by silica particles deposited during eruptions.

A fountain geyser (like Daisy Geyser in the Old Faithful area) erupts from a vent submerged in a hot spring-like pool. Eruptions tend to be smaller and more sporadic.

Yellowstone's tallest geyser is Steamboat, in Norris, shooting up to 350 feet high.

When they erupt, geysers sometimes create rainbows amid their spray.

❶ RECHARGE STAGE

Groundwater accumulates in plumbing and is heated by the volcano. Some hot water flashes to steam and bubbles try to rise toward surface.

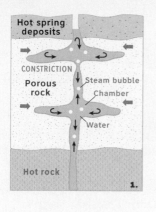

❷ PRELIMINARY ERUPTION STAGE

Pressure builds as steam bubbles clog at constriction. High pressure raises the boiling point, preventing superheated water from becoming steam.

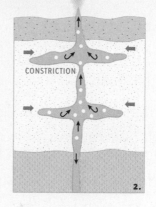

❸ ERUPTION STAGE

Bubbles squeeze through constriction, displacing surface water and relieving pressure. Trapped water flashes to steam, forcing water out of the chambers and causing a chain reaction.

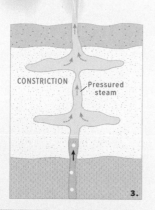

❹ RECOVERY STAGE

Eruption ends when the chambers are emptied or the temperature falls below boiling. Chambers begin to refill with ground water and the process begins again.

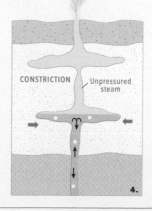

(left) Lone Star Geyser.

HOW DO HOT SPRINGS WORK?

Essentially, what keeps a hot spring from becoming a geyser is a lack of constriction in its underground plumbing. Like their more explosive cousins, hot springs consist of water that seeps into the earth, only to simmer its way back up through fissures after it's heated by hot volcanic rocks. Unlike in constricted geysers, water in a hot spring can circulate by convection. Rising hot water displaces cooling surface water, which then sinks underground to be heated and eventually rise again. Thus the whole mixture keeps itself at a gurgly equilibrium. As it rises, superheated water dissolves some subterranean minerals, depositing them at the surface to form the sculptural terraces that surround many hot springs.

The vivid colors that characterize hot springs and their terraces can be attributed alternately to minerals like sulfur and iron or to thermophiles. Thermophiles are microorganisms that thrive in extremely high temperatures. Blooming in thick bacterial mats, they convert light to energy, like plants, and their bright photosynthetic pigments help give hot springs their rainbow hues. Scientists suppose only a small percentage of Yellowstone's thermophiles have been identified. Still, these microbes have had a big impact on science. In 1965, a microorganism called Thermus aquaticus, or Taq, was discovered in the Lower Geyser Basin. From it, scientists extracted an enzyme that revolutionized molecular biology, ultimately making possible both DNA fingerprinting and the mapping of the human genome. NASA is among those performing research in the park today, studying thermophiles to gain insight on extraterrestrial life.

WHAT'S THAT SMELL?

Most people think hot springs smell like rotten eggs; some even say "burnt gunpowder" and "paper mill smokestack." Whatever similie you settle on, there's no question that hot springs and other thermal features stink to high heaven. Sulphur gases escaping from the volcano produce distinctive smells. Other gases are reduced to the stinky chemical hydrogen sulfide, which bubbles up to the surface. In high concentration, hydrogen sulfide can actually kill you, but the small amounts released by thermals can only kill your appetite. It's because hydrogen sulfide is often present in volcanic areas that we associate brimstone (or sulfur) with the underworld.

DID YOU KNOW?

Grand Prismatic Spring (pictured here) is the world's third-largest hot spring, at more than 370 feet across. The pool's vivid red and orange colors drizzle down its runoff channels, but from the boardwalk you can only glimpse a portion of these psychedelic tentacles. Thank the little guys: heat-loving microorganisms (bacteria and algae) tint the Grand Prismatic Spring with a rainbow of colors.

THE INNER WORKINGS OF HOT SPRINGS

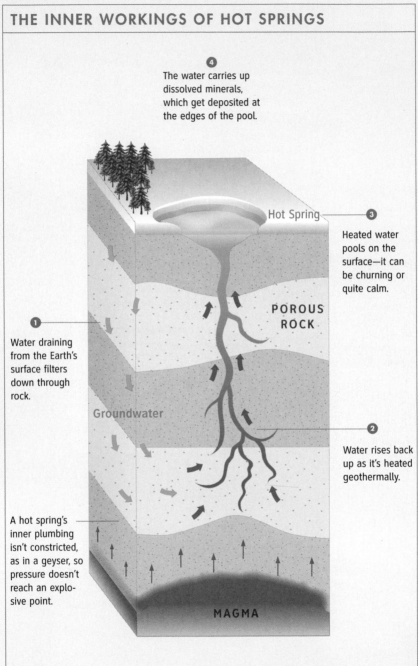

4 The water carries up dissolved minerals, which get deposited at the edges of the pool.

Hot Spring **3**

3 Heated water pools on the surface—it can be churning or quite calm.

POROUS ROCK

1

Water draining from the Earth's surface filters down through rock.

Groundwater

2 Water rises back up as it's heated geothermally.

A hot spring's inner plumbing isn't constricted, as in a geyser, so pressure doesn't reach an explosive point.

MAGMA

WHAT ARE FUMAROLES?

Take away the water from a hot spring and you're left with steam and other gas, forming a fumarole. Often called steam vents, these noisy thermals occur when available water boils away before reaching the surface. All that escapes the vent is heat, vapor, and the whisper-roar of a giant, menacing teakettle. Fumaroles are often found on high ground. The gases expelled from fumaroles might include carbon dioxide, sulfur dioxide, and hydrogen sulfide. Some hot spots, like Red Spouter in the Lower Geyser Basin, can exhibit different behaviors depending on the seasonal water table, so what's a fumarole today could be a hot spring in a few months.

FUN FACTS

■ The word fumarole comes from the Latin *fumus*, which means "smoke."

■ Fumaroles are also known as steam vents and solfataras, from *sulpha terra*, Latin for "land of sulfur."

■ Yellowstone's hottest fumarole is *Black Growler*, at Norris, which heats up to 280°F.

■ About 4,000 fumaroles are in Yellowstone.

fumarole

WHAT ARE MUD POTS?

Mud pots in Lower Geyser Basin.

Might as well say it up front: mud pots are great because their thick, bursting bubbles can sound like a chorus of rude noises or "greetings from the interior." That's why the few places they're found in Yellowstone are usually surrounded by gaggles of giggling visitors with video cameras rolling. A mud pot is basically just a hot spring where the water table results in a bubbling broth of water and clay. The acid gases react with surface rocks, breaking them down into silica and clay. As gases escape from below, bubbles swell and pop, flinging mud chunks onto the banks to form gloppy clay mounds. The mud's thickness varies with rainfall through the seasons.

FUN FACTS

■ Mud pots have been nicknamed "paint pots" due to iron and other metals tinting the mud.

■ The biggest cluster of mud pots in the park is in Pocket Basin in Lower Geyser Basin.

■ Before it exploded in 1872, Mud Volcano was 30 feet tall by 30 feet wide.

PHOTOGRAPHY TIPS

■ Set your alarm clock: generally, the best light for shooting the geothermal features is early in the morning. You'll avoid the thickest crowds then, too. The runner-up time is the late afternoon.

■ Breezy days are good for photographing geysers, since the steam will be blown away from the jetting water. But avoid standing downwind or your view can be clouded with steam.

■ If you get water from a thermal feature on your lens, dry it off as quickly as possible, because the water has a high mineral content that can damage your lens.

Thermal pool in the Rabbit Creek Thermal Area.

FISHING

Anglers flock to Yellowstone beginning the Saturday of Memorial Day weekend, when fishing season begins. By the time the season ends in November, thousands have found a favorite spot along the park's rivers and streams. Native cutthroat trout are one of the prize catches, but four other varieties—brown, brook, lake, and rainbow—along with grayling and mountain whitefish inhabit Yellowstone's waters. Popular sportfishing opportunities include the Gardner and Yellowstone rivers as well as Soda Butte Creek, but the top fishing area in the region is Madison River, known to fly-fishermen throughout the country.

Yellowstone fishing permits are required for people over age 16. Montana and Wyoming fishing permits are not valid in the park. Yellowstone fishing permits cost $18 for a three-day permit, $25 for a seven-day permit, or $40 for a season permit. Anglers ages 15 and younger must have a (no-fee) permit or fish under direct supervision of an adult with a permit. Permits are available at all ranger stations, visitor centers, and Yellowstone general stores.

HIKING

Your most memorable Yellowstone moments will likely take place along a park hiking trail. Encountering a gang of elk in the woods is unquestionably more exciting than watching them graze on the grasses of Mammoth Hot Springs Hotel. Hearing the creak of lodgepole pines on a breezy afternoon feels more authentic than listening to idle tourist chatter as you jostle for the best view of Old Faithful on a recycled-plastic boardwalk for 94 minutes or so.

Even a one-day visitor to Yellowstone can—and should—get off the roads and into the "wilderness." Because the park is a wild place, however, even a half-mile walk on a trail puts you at the mercy of nature, so be sure to prepare yourself accordingly. As a guide on an Old Yellow Bus Tour said, "You don't have to fear the animals—just respect them."

■ TIP➔ Much of Yellowstone lies more than 7,500 feet above sea level—significantly higher than Denver. The most frequent incidents requiring medical attention in the park are respiratory problems, not animal attacks. So be aware of your physical limitations—as well as those of young children or elderly companions.

OLD FAITHFUL
EASY

Fountain Paint Pots Nature Trail. Take the easy 0.5-mile loop boardwalk of Fountain Paint Pot Nature Trail to see fumaroles (steam vents), blue pools, pink mudpots, and minigeysers in this thermal area. It's popular in both summer and winter because it's right next to Grand Loop Road. *Easy.* ⊠ *Trailhead at Lower Geyser Basin, between Old Faithful and Madison.*

FAMILY **Old Faithful Geyser Loop.** Old Faithful and its environs in the Upper Geyser Basin are rich in short-walk options, starting with three connected loops that depart from visitor center. The 0.75-mile loop simply circles the benches around Old Faithful, filled nearly all day long in summer with tourists. *Easy.* ⊠ *Trailhead at Old Faithful Village.*

Fodor's Choice
★

MODERATE

Mystic Falls Trail. From the west end of Biscuit Basin boardwalk, this trail gently climbs 1 mile through heavily burned forest to the lava-rock base of 70-foot Mystic Falls. It then switchbacks up Madison Plateau to a lookout with the park's least-crowded view of Old Faithful and the Upper Geyser Basin. *Moderate.* ⊠ *Trailhead off Grand Loop Rd., 3 miles north of Old Faithful Village.*

MAMMOTH HOT SPRINGS

MODERATE

Bunsen Peak Trail. Past the entrance to Bunsen Peak Road, the moderately difficult trail is a 4-mile, three-hour round trip that climbs 1,300 feet to Bunsen Peak for a panoramic view of Blacktail Plateau, Swan Lake Flats, the Gallatin Mountains, and the Yellowstone River valley. *Moderate.* ⊠ *Trailhead off Grand Loop Rd., 1½ miles south of Mammoth Hot Springs.*

TOWER-ROOSEVELT

MODERATE

Fodor'sChoice **Slough Creek Trail.** Starting at Slough Creek Campground, this trail
★ climbs steeply along a historic wagon trail for the first 1.5 miles before reaching expansive meadows and prime fishing spots, where moose are common and grizzlies occasionally wander. From this point the trail, now mostly level, meanders another 9.5 miles to the park's northern boundary. Anglers absolutely rave about this trail. *Moderate.* ⊠ *Trailhead off Northeast Entrance Rd., 7 miles east of Tower-Roosevelt*

CANYON

MODERATE

Brink of the Lower Falls Trail. Especially scenic, this trail branches off of the North Rim Trail at the Brink of the Upper Falls parking area. The steep 0.5-mile one-way trail switchbacks 600 feet down to within a few yards of the top of the Yellowstone River's Lower Falls. *Moderate.* ⊠ *Trailhead at entrance to North Rim Dr., 300 yards east of Grand Loop Rd., 1 mile south of Canyon.*

North Rim Trail. Offering great views of the Grand Canyon of the Yellowstone, the 3-mile North Rim Trail runs from Inspiration Point to Chittenden Bridge. Especially scenic is the 0.5-mile section of the North Rim Trail from the Brink of the Upper Falls parking area to Chittenden Bridge that hugs the rushing Yellowstone River as it approaches the canyon. This trail is paved and fully accessible between Lookout Point and Grand View. *Moderate.* ⊠ *Trailhead at North Rim Dr. 1 mile south of Canyon.*

South Rim Trail. Partly paved and fairly flat, this 1.75-mile trail along the south rim of the Grand Canyon of the Yellowstone affords impressive views and photo opportunities of the canyon and falls of the Yellowstone River. It starts at Chittenden Bridge and ends at Artist Point. Beyond Artist Point, the trail gives way to a high plateau and high mountain meadows. Although popular with day hikers, this is technically backcountry. Prepare accordingly, make some noise, and carry bear spray. *Moderate.* ⊠ *Trailhead at Chittenden Bridge, off South Rim Dr., Canyon.*

DIFFICULT

Uncle Tom's Trail. Accessed by the South Rim Drive, the spectacular and strenuous 700-step trail ½ mile east of Chittenden Bridge descends 500 feet from the parking area to the roaring base of the Lower Falls of the Yellowstone. Much of this walk is on steel sheeting, which can have a film of ice on early summer mornings or anytime in spring and fall. *Difficult.* ⊠ *Trailhead at South Rim Dr., 1 mile east of Chittenden Bridge, 3 miles south of Canyon.*

LAKE AREA

EASY

FAMILY **Storm Point Trail.** Well marked and mostly flat, this 1.5-mile loop leaves the south side of the road for a perfect beginner's hike out to Yellowstone Lake, particularly with a setting sun. The trail rounds the western edge of Indian Pond, then passes moose habitat on its way to Yellowstone Lake's Storm Point, named for its frequent afternoon windstorms and crashing waves. Heading west along the shore, you're likely to hear the shrill chirping of yellow-bellied marmots, rodents that grow as long as 2 feet. Also look for ducks, pelicans, trumpeter swans, and bison. You will pass several small beaches where kids can explore on warm summer mornings. *Easy.* ⊠ *Trailhead on East Entrance Rd., 3 miles east of Lake Junction, Fishing Bridge.*

DIFFICULT

Fodor's Choice **Avalanche Peak Trail.** On a busy day in summer, maybe six parties will

★ fill out the trail register at the Avalanche Peak trailhead, so you won't have a lot of company on this hike. Starting across from a parking area on the East Entrance Road, the difficult 4-mile, four-hour round trip climbs 2,150 feet to the peak's 10,566-foot summit, from which you'll see the rugged Absaroka Mountains running north and south. Look around the talus and tundra near the top of Avalanche Peak for alpine wildflowers and butterflies. Don't try this trail before late June or after early September—it may be covered in deep snow. Rangers discourage hikers from attempting this hike in September or October because of bear activity. *Difficult.* ⊠ *Trailhead on north side of East Entrance Rd., 2 miles east of Sylvan Lake, Fishing Bridge.*

HORSEBACK RIDING

Advance reservations are recommended. Don't worry about experience, as rangers estimate 90% of riders have not been on a horse in at least 10 years.

Private stock can be brought into the park. Horses are not allowed in frontcountry campgrounds but are permitted in certain backcountry campsites. For information on planning a backcountry trip with stock, call the Backcountry Office (☎ 307/344–2160).

TOURS AND OUTFITTERS

About 50 area outfitters lead horse-packing trips and trail rides into Yellowstone. Expect to pay $250 to $400 per day for a backcountry trip, including meals, accommodations, and guides. A guide must accompany all horseback-riding trips.

FAMILY **Xanterra Parks & Resorts.** Xanterra Parks & Resorts offers one-hour horseback rides at Mammoth, and one- and two-hour rides at Tower-Roosevelt and Canyon Village. ✉ *Mammoth Hot Springs, 1 Grand Loop Rd.* ☎ *307/344–7311, 866/439–7375* ⊕ *www.nps.gov/yell/planyourvisit/horseride.htm* 🎫 *$40–$60.*

Yellowstone Wilderness Outfitters. Exclusively dedicated to trips inside Yellowstone National Park, Yellowstone Wilderness Outfitters employs musically inclined Jett Hitt as its multitalented guide. Trips range from half- and full-day family rides to three- to six-day pack trips in every area of the park. Trips feature wildlife biologists and lecturers. ✉ ☎ *406/223–3300* ⊕ *www.yellowstone.ws* 🎫 *$110 for half-day trips; $190 for full-day trips.*

SKIING, SNOWSHOEING, AND SNOWMOBILING

Yellowstone can be the coldest place in the continental United States in winter, with temperatures of –30°F not uncommon. Still, winter-sports enthusiasts flock here when the park opens for its winter season the last week of December. Until early March, the park's roads teem with over-snow vehicles like snowmobiles and snow coaches. Its trails bristle with cross-country skiers and snowshoers.

Snowmobiling is an exhilarating way to experience Yellowstone. It's also controversial: there's heated debate about the pollution and disruption to animal habitats. The number of riders per day is limited, and you must have a reservation, a guide, and a four-stroke engine (which is less polluting than the more common two-stroke variety). About a dozen companies have been authorized to lead snowmobile excursions into the park from the North, West, South, and East entrances. Prices vary, as do itineraries and inclusions—be sure to ask about insurance, guides, taxes, park entrance fees, clothing, helmets, and meals. Regulations are subject to change.

TOURS AND OUTFITTERS

Xanterra Parks & Resorts. At Mammoth Hot Springs Hotel and Old Faithful Snow Lodge, Xanterra Parks & Resorts rents skis, snowmobiles, and snowshoes. Ski rentals (including skis, poles, gloves, and gaiters) are $15 per half day, $24.50 per full day. Snowshoes rentals are $12 per half day, $20 per full day. Skier shuttles run from Mammoth Hotel to Indian Creek and from Old Faithful Snow Lodge to Fairy Falls and the Continental Divide Overlook. ✉ *Mammoth Hot Springs, 1 Grand Loop Rd.* ☎ *307/344–7311, 866/439–7375, 307/344–5276* ⊕ *www.xanterra.com/activities/skier-shuttles.*

Yellowstone Association Institute. The Yellowstone Association Institute offers everything from daylong wildlife-watching excursions to multi-day skiing and snowshoeing treks. ✉ *115 3rd St. S, Gardiner, Montana* ☎ *406/848–2400* ⊕ *www.yellowstoneassociation.org.*

CLOSE UP

Yellowstone in Winter

To see a spectacularly different Yellowstone than that experienced by 90% of the park's visitors, come in winter. Rocky outcroppings are smoothed over. Waterfalls are transformed into jagged sheets of ice.

The best reason for a visit to Yellowstone between December and March is the opportunity to experience the park without the crowds. The first thing that strikes you during this season is the quiet. The gargantuan snowpack—as many as 200 inches annually at low elevation—seems to muffle the sounds of bison foraging in the geyser basins and of hot springs simmering. Yet even in the depths of a deep freeze, the park is never totally still: the mud pots bubble, geysers shoot skyward, and wind rustles the snow-covered pine trees. Above these sounds, the cry of a hawk, the yip of a coyote, or even on rare occasions the howl of a wolf may pierce the air.

Animals in Yellowstone head *down* when the thermometer falls. Herbivores like elk and bison head to the

warmer, less snowy valleys to find vegetation; predators like wolves and cougars follow them. As a result, you're more likely to see these animals in the frontcountry in winter. The snow also makes it easier to pick out animal tracks.

Snowmobiling is popular but is also controversial (critics cite noise and pollution). At the time of this writing, guided trips with capped speed limits are offered in both Yellowstone and Grand Teton national parks. There are also the options of cross-country skiing and snowshoeing through geyser basins and along the canyon, both excellent ways to see the park. Dogsledding isn't permitted in the park, but outfitters in Jackson lead trips in the nearby national forests.

—Brian Kevin, excerpted from Fodor's *Compass American Guides: Yellowstone and Grand Teton National Parks*

38

WHAT'S NEARBY

Yellowstone National Park is a destination, not something to see as you pass through the area, and it covers a lot of ground; so if you plan on spending several days in the park, we suggest staying overnight in the park itself. If you don't mind the driving, however, or want to spend time outside the park, there are several upscale resorts in nearby towns, as well as literally thousands of possible campsites for those looking to rough it.

NEARBY TOWNS

Because of its airport and its proximity to both Grand Teton and Yellowstone national parks, **Jackson,** the closest town to Yellowstone's South Entrance, is the region's busiest community in summer and has the widest selection of dining and lodging options. Meanwhile, the least well-known gateway, the little town of **Dubois,** southeast of the park, is far from the madding crowds and a good place to stop on the way in or out of the park if you want to visit the National Bighorn Sheep Interpretive Center.

The most popular gateway from Montana, particularly in winter, is **West Yellowstone,** near the park's West Entrance. This is where the open plains of southwestern Montana and northeastern Idaho come together along the Madison River Valley. Affectionately known among winter recreationists as the "snowmobile capital of the world," this town of 1,000 is also a good place to go for fishing, horseback riding, and downhill skiing. There is plenty of culture here, as this is where you'll find the Museum of the Yellowstone, and a small airport.

As the only entrance to Yellowstone that's open the entire year, **Gardiner,** in Montana, is always bustling. The town's Roosevelt Arch has marked the park's North Entrance since 1903, when President Theodore Roosevelt dedicated it. The Yellowstone River slices through town, beckoning fishermen and rafters. The town of 800 has quaint shops and good restaurants. North of Gardiner, along Interstate 90, is **Livingston,** a town of 7,500 known for its charming historic district.

With both Yellowstone and the Absaroka-Beartooth Wilderness at its back door, the Montana village of **Cooke City,** at the park's Northeast Entrance, is a good place for hiking, horseback riding, mountain climbing, and other outdoor activities. Some 50 miles to the east of Cooke City and 60 miles southeast of Billings via U.S. 212 is the small resort town of **Red Lodge.** Nestled against the foot of the pine-draped Absaroka-Beartooth Wilderness and edged by the Limestone Palisades, Red Lodge has a ski area, trout fishing, a golf course, horseback riding, and more options for dining and lodging than Cooke City. Driving along the Beartooth Scenic Byway between Red Lodge and Cooke City, you'll cross the southern tip of the Beartooth range, literally in the ramparts of the Rockies. From Cooke City, the drive into Yellowstone through the Lamar Valley is one of the prettiest routes in the park.

Park Ranger Mary Wilson

For Yellowstone National Park Ranger Mary Wilson, every day is an adventure and, even after two decades of working in some of the nation's most pristine preserves, she never tires of assisting visitors who have come to explore America's natural treasures.

"Almost every day, I am approached by visitors who, in awe of the wonderful and exciting things they have experienced in the parks, tell me that these places are the most beautiful and inspiring places they have ever seen or been," she says. "Somehow, these places help foster memories and feelings that last a lifetime."

Visitors have left lasting impressions that Wilson has incorporated into her instruction of new park rangers. One of the most poignant occurred while she was working in the mid-1980s as an interpretive ranger at Grand Canyon National Park.

"I came across an elderly woman sitting near the south rim of the canyon who was just sobbing," Wilson recalls. "Thinking that she may have been hurt, sick, or missing someone, I approached and asked if I could help her. She told me she was fine, but that she was from New York City, had raised five kids, and that this was the first time she had ventured out of her home state. She told me that the one thing she had wanted to see more than anything else in the world in her entire life was the Grand Canyon. I told her it was so great that she was here now, to which she responded, 'Yes, but it makes me wonder how many other beautiful places I may have missed in my life ... and will never get to see.' I sat down on the bench next to her and began to cry with her. It reminded me of the

power these very special places we call national parks have on our lives; how they offer us a chance to reflect upon our relationship with nature, the importance of beauty and solitude, and how lucky we are to have them preserved for everyone to enjoy."

Wilson's passion for animals, combined with a love for the outdoors and helping people, turned her professional interests toward the National Park Service. "Serving as a park ranger was a way to achieve a little of all of those worlds," says Wilson, who grew up in Muncie, Indiana, before earning her bachelor's and master's degrees from Purdue University.

After serving stints as a student volunteer in South Dakota's Custer State Park and Montana's Glacier National Park, working side by side with rangers, Wilson was hired by the National Park Service in Glacier. Since then, she's taken assignments at Rocky Mountain, Grand Canyon, and Sequoia/Kings Canyon national parks, and Montezuma Castle National Monument. At her job at Yellowstone, she supervises other rangers and assists visitors.

38

GOOD READS

The Yellowstone Story, by Aubrey L. Haines, is a classic.

Yellowstone Place Names, by Lee Whittlesey, tells the stories behind the names of many park destinations.

Yellowstone: The Official Guide to Touring America's First National Park, published by Yellowstone Association, is a magazine-size, full-color, glossy, 80-page "yearbook."

Decade of the Wolf, by Douglas Smith and Gary Ferguson, is the most comprehensive and gripping account of the reintroduction of wolves into the park in the 1990s.

Yellowstone Trails, A Hiking Guide, by Mark C. Marschall, will help you navigate the shortest and longest trails in the park.

Lost In My Own Backyard, by Tim Cahill, is a hilarious account of one person's experience in the park.

Explaining the park's geological processes are William R. Keefer's *The Geologic Story of Yellowstone National Park* and Robert B. Smith and Lee J. Siegel's *Windows into the Earth: The Geologic Story of Yellowstone and Grand Teton National Parks.*

Alston Chase's controversial *Playing God in Yellowstone* chronicles a century of government mismanagement.

Three other excellent titles are:

Roadside History of Yellowstone Park, by Winfred Blevins.

Roadside Geology of the Yellowstone Country, by William J. Fritz.

Yellowstone Ecology: A Road Guide, by Sharon Eversman and Mary Carr.

Named for Pony Express rider, army scout, and entertainer William F. "Buffalo Bill" Cody, the town of **Cody,** in Wyoming, sits near the park's East Entrance. It is a good base for hiking trips, horseback-riding excursions, and white-water rafting on the North Fork of the Shoshone or the Clarks Fork of the Yellowstone. It also is home to dude ranches and, in season, the nightly rodeo.

VISITOR INFORMATION

Cody Country Chamber of Commerce ⊠ *836 Sheridan Ave., Cody* ☎ *307/587–2777* ⊕ *www.codychamber.org.* **Cooke City Chamber of Commerce** ⊠ *406/838–2495* ⊕ *www.cookecitychamber.org.* **Dubois Chamber of Commerce** ⊠ *616 W. Ramshorn St., Dubois* ☎ *307/455–2556* ⊕ *www.duboiswyomingchamber.org.* **Gardiner Chamber of Commerce** ⊠ *222 Park St., Gardiner, Montana* ☎ *406/848–7971* ⊕ *www.gardinerchamber.com.* **Jackson Hole Chamber of Commerce** ⊠ *532 North Cache, Jackson* ☎ *307/733–3316* ⊕ *www.jacksonholechamber.com.* **Livingston Chamber of Commerce** ⊠ *303 E. Park St., Livingston, Montana* ☎ *406/222–0850* ⊕ *www.livingston-chamber.com.* **Red Lodge Chamber of Commerce** ⊠ *601 N. Broadway, Red Lodge, Montana* ☎ *406/446–1718, 888/281–0625* ⊕ *www.redlodgechamber.org.* **West Yellowstone Chamber of Commerce** ⊠ *30 Yellowstone Ave., West Yellowstone, Montana* ☎ *406/646–7701* ⊕ *www.westyellowstonechamber.com.*

NEARBY ATTRACTIONS

CODY

Buffalo Bill Center of the West. This sprawling complex, sometimes called the Smithsonian of the West, contains the Buffalo Bill Museum, the Whitney Gallery of Western Art, the Plains Indian Museum, the Cody Firearms Museum, the Draper Museum of Natural History, and the Harold McCracken Research Library. Plan to spend at least four hours here. ✉ *720 Sheridan Ave., Cody* ☎ *307/587–4771* 🌐 *www.centerofthewest.org* 🎟 *$18* 🕒 *Mar. and Apr., daily 10–5; May–mid-Sept., daily 8–6; mid-Sept.–Oct., daily 8–5; Nov., daily 10–5; Dec.–Feb., Thurs.–Sun. 10–5.*

WEST YELLOWSTONE

FAMILY **Grizzly and Wolf Discovery Center.** Home to eight grizzlies and seven wolves, this center gives you an up-close look at Yellowstone's two most feared predators. In addition, you'll find birds of prey on display during the summer months. The nonprofit center is also home to important scientific research. ✉ *201 S. Canyon, West Yellowstone* ☎ *406/646–7001, 800/257–2570* 🌐 *www.grizzlydiscoveryctr.org* 🎟 *$11.50* 🕒 *Daily 8:30 am–dusk.*

FAMILY **Yellowstone Historic Center.** West Yellowstone's Union Pacific Depot, built in 1909, has been transformed into a museum dedicated to modes of travel—from stagecoaches to trains—used to get to Yellowstone before World War II. Films provide insight on topics such as the fire that devastated Yellowstone in 1988 and the way earthquakes affect the area's hydrothermal features. ✉ *220 Yellowstone Ave., West Yellowstone* ☎ *406/646-7461* 🌐 *www.yellowstonehistoriccenter.org* 🎟 *$6* 🕒 *Mid-May–mid-June and mid-Sept.–Oct., daily 9–6; mid-June–mid-Sept., daily 9–9; mid-Nov.–mid-Apr., weekdays 10–3.*

SHOPPING

Sunlight Sports. Boasting a wide selection of name-brand outdoor gear, this spacious 8,000-square-foot store can set you up with everything from camping gear to downhill and cross-country ski equipment. The staff is friendly and has extensive experience in hiking, climbing, guiding, running, and other outdoor pursuits. ✉ *1131 Sheridan Ave., Cody* ☎ *307/587-9517* 🌐 *www.sunlightsports.com.*

WHERE TO EAT

IN THE PARK

$ FAST FOOD 🍴 **Bear Paw Deli.** You can grab a quick bite and not miss a geyser eruption at this snack shop in the Old Faithful Inn. Tasty salads and sandwiches are available throughout the day, as is hand-dipped ice cream. If you're staying at the inn, fill up your water bottles at the soda fountain. Limited seating is available. [$] *Average main: $8* ✉ *Old Faithful Village, Old Faithful* ☎ *307/344–7311* 🌐 *www.yellowstonenationalparklodges.com/dining/old-faithful-inn-bear-paw-deli* ✍ *Reservations not accepted* 🕒 *Closed mid-Oct.–May.*

$ ✕ **Canyon Lodge Cafeteria.** This busy lunch spot serves such traditional
AMERICAN American fare as country-fried steak and open-faced turkey sandwiches.
There's also a pasta station with cannelloni, tortellini, and manicotti
that makes this a nice dinner option. Grab a tray and get in line. There's
a full breakfast menu for early risers. $ *Average main: $9* ✉ *Canyon
Village* ☎ *307/344–7311* ⊕ *www.yellowstonenationalparklodges.com/
dining* ⟆ *Reservations not accepted* ⊗ *Closed Oct.–late May.*

$ ✕ **Geyser Grill.** The location is the main attraction at this busy grill,
FAST FOOD where hamburgers, hot dogs, and chicken nuggets highlight the kids'
FAMILY menu. Parents can squeak by on an assortment of soup, salads, and
sandwiches. Remember you're here for the geyser, not the grub. $ *Aver-
age main: $6* ✉ *Old Faithful Lodge, at south end of Old Faithful Village*
☎ *307/344–7311* ⊕ *www.yellowstonenationalparklodges.com/dining*
⟆ *Reservations not accepted* ⊗ *Closed Nov.–mid-Apr.*

$$ ✕ **Grant Village Dining Room.** The floor-to-ceiling windows of this water-
AMERICAN front restaurant provide views of Yellowstone Lake through the thick
stand of pines. The most contemporary of the park's restaurants, it
makes you feel at home with pine-beam ceilings and cedar-shake walls.
You'll find dishes ranging from pasta to wild salmon to bison and
elk meat loaf. $ *Average main: $19* ✉ *1 Grand Loop Rd., about 2
miles south of West Thumb junction, Grant Village* ☎ *307/344–7311,
866/439–7375* ⊕ *www.yellowstonenationalparklodges.com/dining*
⟆ *Reservations essential* ⊗ *Closed late Oct.–late May.*

$ ✕ **Lake Lodge Cafeteria.** One of the park's most inspiring views of the lake
AMERICAN is complemented by a revamped menu. Roast turkey and pot roast are
FAMILY typical fare at this cafeteria, but you'll also find more upscale offerings
like trout amandine, prime rib, and poached salmon. It has a full break-
fast menu. $ *Average main: $9* ✉ *At end of Lake Village Rd., about 1
mile south of Fishing Bridge junction* ☎ *307/344–7311* ⟆ *Reservations
not accepted* ⊗ *Closed Oct.–early June.*

$$$ ✕ **Lake Yellowstone Hotel Dining Room.** Opened in 1891, this double-colon-
AMERICAN naded dining room off the lobby of the Lake Yellowstone Hotel is the
Fodor's Choice park's most elegant place to dine. It's superior to the Old Faithful Inn
★ in every way—the view, the service, the menu, and even the gorgeous
china. Arrive early and enjoy a beverage in the airy Reamer Lounge. The
dinner menu includes such attractive starters as an artisan cheese and
dried fruit plate. Main courses include lamb, buffalo, steak, duck, quail,
and fish dishes, as well as at least one imaginative vegetarian entrée. The
wine list focuses on bottles from California, Oregon, and Washington.
Reservations are not needed for breakfast or lunch, but are essential
for dinner. Make them up to a year in advance with hotel reservations;
otherwise, call a month ahead. $ *Average main: $24* ✉ *Lake Village
Rd., 1 mile south of Fishing Bridge, Lake Village* ☎ *307/344–7311,
866/439–7375* ⊕ *www.yellowstonenationalparklodges.com/dining*
⟆ *Reservations essential* ⊗ *Closed early Oct.–mid-May.*

$$ ✕ **Mammoth Hot Springs Dining Room.** A wall of windows overlooks an
AMERICAN expanse of green that was once a military parade and drill field at Mam-
moth Hot Springs. While you enjoy breakfast, lunch, or dinner you may
catch a glimpse of elk grazing on the lawn. The art deco–style restaurant,
decorated in shades of gray, green, and burgundy, has an airy feel with

its bentwood chairs. Montana beef, bison, and fish are featured, and there is always at least one vegetarian dish. A small-plate menu is right for lighter appetites. Dinner reservations are not taken in summer, but are essential in winter. [$] *Average main: $18* ✉ *5 miles south of North Entrance, Mammoth Hot Springs* ☎ *307/344–7311, 866/439–7375* 🌐 *www.yellowstonenationalparklodges.com/dining* ✍ *Reservations not accepted* ⏲ *Closed mid-Oct.–mid-Dec. and mid-Mar.–mid-May.*

$ FAST FOOD 🍴 **Mammoth Terrace Grill.** Although the exterior looks rather elegant, this restaurant in Mammoth Hot Springs serves only simple fare. Expect dishes like biscuits and gravy for breakfast and hamburgers and veggie burgers for lunch and dinner. [$] *Average main: $6* ✉ *Mammoth Springs Hotel, 5 miles south of North Entrance, Mammoth Hot Springs* ☎ *307/344–7311* 🌐 *www.yellowstonenationalparklodges.com/dining* ⏲ *Closed late Sept.–mid-May.*

$$$ STEAKHOUSE Fodor's Choice ★ 🍴 **Obsidian Dining Room.** From the wood-and-leather chairs etched with animal figures to the intricate lighting fixtures that resemble snow-capped trees, there's ample Western atmosphere at this smaller dining room inside the Old Faithful Snow Lodge. The huge windows give you a view of the Old Faithful area, and you can sometimes see the famous geyser as it erupts. Aside from Mammoth Hot Springs Dining Room, this is the only place in the park where you can enjoy a full dinner in winter. The French onion soup will warm you up on a chilly afternoon; among the main courses, look for prime rib, elk, beef, and salmon. [$] *Average main: $21* ✉ *Old Faithful Snow Lodge, south end of Old Faithful Village* ☎ *307/344–7311, 866/439–7375* 🌐 *www.yellowstonenationalparklodges.com/dining* ✍ *Reservations not accepted* ⏲ *Closed mid-Oct.–mid-Dec. and mid-Mar.–early May. No lunch.*

$$ AMERICAN 🍴 **Old Faithful Inn Dining Room.** The Old Faithful Inn's original dining room—designed by Robert Reamer in 1903 and expanded by him in 1927—has lodgepole-pine walls and ceiling beams and a giant volcanic rock fireplace. Note the whimsical etched-glass panels that separate the dining room from the Bear Pit Lounge; the images of partying animals were commissioned by Reamer in 1933 to celebrate the end of Prohibition. A dinner buffet offers quantity over quality, so you're better off choosing from nearly a dozen entrées on the à la carte menu, including grilled salmon, prime rib, and bison ribeye. Expect at least one vegetarian entrée. Save room for a signature dessert such as the Caldera, a chocolate-truffle torte with a molten middle. The park's most extensive wine list offers more than 50 choices. For breakfast, there's a buffet as well as individual entrées. [$] *Average main: $18* ✉ *Take first left off Old Faithful Bypass Rd., Old Faithful Village* ☎ *307/344–7311, 866/439–7375* 🌐 *www.yellowstonenationalparklodges.com/dining/old-faithful* ✍ *Reservations essential* ⏲ *Closed late Oct.–early May.*

$ AMERICAN FAMILY 🍴 **Old Faithful Lodge Cafeteria.** This noisy eatery serves kid-friendly fare like pizza and hamburgers. The cafeteria's one redeeming value is that it has some of the best views of Old Faithful, and while you eat you can watch it erupt. It's not open for breakfast, but the snack shop just outside is, offering a small selection of baked goods. [$] *Average main: $8* ✉ *At the end of Old Faithful Bypass Rd.* ☎ *307/344–7311* ⏲ *Closed mid-Sept.–mid-May.*

$$ AMERICAN FAMILY 🍴 **Roosevelt Lodge Dining Room.** At this rustic log cabin in a pine forest, the menu includes tasty options like sirloin steak, barbecued ribs, and shrimp tacos. If you want something simpler, there are always burgers and fries. Don't miss the killer cornbread muffins. For a real adventure at this tribute to the Old West, reserve ahead to join the popular Roosevelt Old West Dinner Cookout that includes an hour-long trail ride or a stagecoach ride. [$] *Average main: $18* ✉ *Junction of Northeast Entrance Rd. and Grand Loop Rd., Tower-Roosevelt* ☎ *307/344–7311* ✍ *Reservations not accepted* 🕓 *Closed early Sept.–early June.*

PICNIC AREAS

The 49 picnic areas in the park range from secluded spots with a couple of tables to more popular stops with a dozen or more tables and several amenities. Only nine areas—Snake River, Grant Village, Spring Creek, Nez Perce, Old Faithful East, Bridge Bay, Cascade Lake Trail, Norris Meadows, and Yellowstone River—have fire grates. Gas stoves only may be used in the other areas. None have running water; all but a few have pit toilets. You can stock up your cooler at any of the park's general stores. It is also possible to purchase box lunches that include drinks, snacks, sandwiches, and fruit, or vegetarian or cheese-and-crackers selections from some park restaurants.

■ **TIP→ Keep an eye out for wildlife.** You never know when a herd of bison might decide to march through. If that happens, it's best to leave your food and move a safe distance away from them.

FAMILY **Firehole River.** The Firehole River rolls past, and you might see elk grazing along its banks. This picnic area has 12 tables and one pit toilet. ✉ *Grand Loop Rd., 3 miles south of Madison.*

Gibbon Meadows. You are likely to see elk or buffalo along the Gibbon River from one of nine tables at this area, which has a wheelchair-accessible pit toilet. ✉ *Grand Loop Rd., 3 miles south of Norris.*

Sedge Bay. On the northern end of this volcanic beach, look carefully for the large rock slabs pushed out of the lake bottom. Nearby trees offer shade and a table, or you can hop onto the level rocks for an ideal lakeside picnic. You may see bubbles rising from the clear water around the rocks—these indicate an active underwater thermal feature. The only company you may have here could be crickets, birds, and bison. ✉ *East Entrance Rd., 8 miles east of Fishing Bridge Junction.*

OUTSIDE THE PARK

$$ BARBECUE 🍴 **Beartooth Barbecue.** When you taste a rack of the hand-rubbed spare ribs, pulled beef brisket, and zesty baked beans, you'll know why this place has been a favorite with locals for a dozen years. Go early during high season, because it's so popular that it sometimes sells out of ribs. Select from a dozen microbrews crafted in Wyoming and Montana. [$] *Average main: $15* ✉ *111 Canyon St., West Yellowstone, Montana* ☎ *406/646–0227* ✍ *Reservations not accepted.*

$$ AMERICAN 🍴 **Old Piney Dell.** A favorite among locals, this small restaurant on the banks of Rock Creek has good steaks and schnitzels, as well as daily pasta specials. Part of the Rock Creek Resort, the restaurant dates to the early 1940s. [$] *Average main: $19* ✉ *Rock Creek Resort, 6380 Hwy 212 S., Red Lodge, Montana* ☎ *406/446–1111* 🌐 *www.rockcreekresort.com* ✍ *Reservations essential* ⏲ *No lunch. No dinner Sun.*

$ AMERICAN FAMILY 🍴 **Running Bear Pancake House.** All the pies, muffins, and cinnamon rolls are made on the premises at this eatery. There are a lot of choices, but trust the name and go for the buttermilk or buckwheat pancakes topped with blueberries, strawberries, peaches, coconut, walnuts, or chocolate chips. There's also a basic lunch menu with sandwiches and salads and box lunches to go. [$] *Average main: $8* ✉ *538 Madison Ave., West Yellowstone, Montana* ☎ *406/646–7703* ⏲ *Closed Nov.–late Dec. and mid-Mar.–May 1. No dinner.*

$$ PIZZA FAMILY 🍴 **Wild West Pizzeria.** A decade ago, Aaron and Megan Hecht set out to make the best pizza in the region. The combination of a crispy crust, flavorful sauce, and memorable frontier names just seems to work. The Sitting Bull features pepperoni, sausage, salami, and Canadian bacon, while Calamity Jane offers white sauce, mushrooms, artichoke hearts, minced garlic, and fresh tomatoes. There are also sandwiches and pasta dishes. [$] *Average main: $14* ✉ *14 Madison Ave., West Yellowstone, Montana* ☎ *406/646–4400* 🌐 *www.wildwestpizza.com.*

$$ BARBECUE 🍴 **Wyoming's Rib & Chop House.** This place can be packed in the summer with cowboys and tourists searching for the region's best baby-back ribs. Excellent steak, chicken, and seafood dishes complement a wine list of more than 70 selections. There is a limit of two margaritas, and for good reason. It's open for lunch and dinner. [$] *Average main: $19* ✉ *1367 Sheridan Ave., Cody* ☎ *307/527–7731* 🌐 *www.ribandchophouse.com.*

$$ STEAKHOUSE FAMILY 🍴 **Yellowstone Mine.** Decorated with mining equipment like picks and shovels, this is a place for casual family-style dining. Townies come in for the steaks and seafood. A breakfast buffet is available in summer. [$] *Average main: $20* ✉ *905 Scott St. W, Gardiner, Montana* ☎ *406/848–7336* ⏲ *No lunch.*

38

WHERE TO STAY

IN THE PARK

CANYON

$$ HOTEL 🏨 **Canyon Cabins.** Unattractive and unassuming, these pine-frame cabins are arranged in clusters of four, six, and eight. **Pros:** affordability; location; private baths. **Cons:** too much asphalt; too many neighbors; no central lobby area. [$] *Rooms from: $130* ✉ *North Rim Dr. at Grand Loop Rd., Canyon Village* ☎ *307/344–7311, 866/439-7375* 🌐 *www.yellowstonenationalparklodges.com* 🛏 *428 cabins* ⏲ *Closed mid-Sept.–late May* 🍽 *No meals.*

$$$ HOTEL **Dunraven Lodge.** This four-floor lodge sits in the pine trees at the edge of the Grand Canyon of the Yellowstone. **Pros:** canyon location. **Cons:** far from dining and other services. [$] *Rooms from: $195* ✉ *1 Grand Loop Rd., at North Rim Dr., Canyon Village* ☎ *307/344–7311, 866/439–7375* 🌐 *www.yellowstonenationalparklodges.com* 🛏 *44 rooms* ⏲ *Closed mid-Sept.–early June* 🍴 *No meals.*

MAMMOTH HOT SPRINGS

$$ HOTEL **Mammoth Hot Springs Hotel and Cabins.** Built in 1937, this lodge has a spacious art deco lobby. **Pros:** great rates for a historic property; wake up to an elk bugling outside your window. **Cons:** many hotel rooms and cabins lack private bathrooms. [$] *Rooms from: $130* ✉ *Mammoth Hot Springs* ☎ *307/344–7311, 866/439–7375* 🌐 *www.yellowstonenationalparklodges.com* 🛏 *97 rooms, 67 with bath; 2 suites; 115 cabins, 76 with bath* ⏲ *Closed early Oct.–late Dec. and mid-Mar.–early May* 🍴 *No meals.*

OLD FAITHFUL AREA

$$$ HOTEL FAMILY Fodor's Choice ★ **Old Faithful Inn.** Easily earning its National Historic Landmark status, this lovely lodge has been a favorite of five generations of park visitors. **Pros:** a one-of-a-kind property; truly memorable rooms. **Cons:** thin walls; waves of tourists in the lobby; shared baths make you recall college dorm days. [$] *Rooms from: $174* ✉ *First left off Bypass Rd., Old Faithful* ☎ *307/344–7311, 866/439–7375* 🌐 *www.yellowstonenationalparklodges.com* 🛏 *324 rooms, 246 with bath; 6 suites* ⏲ *Closed mid-Oct.–early May* 🍴 *No meals.*

$$ HOTEL **Old Faithful Lodge Cabins.** There are no rooms inside the Old Faithful Lodge, but there are close to 100 cabins sitting at the northeast end of the village. **Pros:** price can't be beat; stone's throw from Old Faithful; services are within walking distance. **Cons:** some cabins lack private bathrooms; pretty basic. [$] *Rooms from: $121* ✉ *South end of Old Faithful Bypass Rd.* ☎ *307/344–7311, 866/439–7375* 🌐 *www.yellowstonenationalparklodges.com* 🛏 *96 cabins, 60 with bath* ⏲ *Closed mid-Sept.–mid-May* 🍴 *No meals.*

$$$$ HOTEL **Old Faithful Snow Lodge.** This massive modern structure brings back the grand tradition of park lodges by making good use of heavy timber beams and wrought-iron accents in its distinctive facade. **Pros:** the park's most modern hotel; lobby is great for relaxing; open in winter. **Cons:** pricey, but you're paying for location. [$] *Rooms from: $241* ✉ *Far end of Old Faithful Bypass Rd., Old Faithful* ☎ *307/344–7311, 866/439–7375* 🌐 *www.yellowstonenationalparklodges.com* 🛏 *100 rooms* ⏲ *Closed mid-Oct.–mid-Dec. and mid-Mar.–early May* 🍴 *No meals.*

$$$ HOTEL **Old Faithful Snow Lodge Cabins.** Just yards from Old Faithful, many of these cabins sprang up after the 1988 fires. **Pros:** price and proximity to the geyser. **Cons:** no amenities beyond the basics. [$] *Rooms from: $165* ✉ *Far end of Old Faithful Bypass Rd., Old Faithful* ☎ *307/344–7311, 866/439–7375* 🌐 *www.yellowstonenationalparklodges.com* 🛏 *100 rooms* ⏲ *Closed mid-Oct.–early May* 🍴 *No meals.*

Best Campgrounds in Yellowstone

Yellowstone has a dozen frontcountry campgrounds scattered around the park, in addition to more than 200 backcountry sites. Most campgrounds have flush toilets; some have coin-operated showers and laundry facilities. The campgrounds run by Xanterra Parks & Resorts—Bridge Bay, Canyon, Fishing Bridge RV Park, Grant Village, and Madison—accept bookings in advance. The rest, operated by the National Park Service, are available on a first-come, first-served basis.

Bridge Bay. The park's largest campground, Bridge Bay rests in a wooded grove above Yellowstone Lake and adjacent to the park's major marina. ⊠ *Grand Loop Rd., 3 miles southwest of Lake Village* ☎ *307/344-7311* ⊕ *www.yellowstonenationalpark-lodges.com.*

Canyon. A massive campground with 250-plus sites, Canyon Campground accommodates everyone from hiker/biker tent campers to large RVs. ⊠ *North Rim Dr., ¼ mile east of Grand Loop Rd., Canyon Village* ☎ *307/344-7311* ⊕ *www.yellowstonenationalparklodges.com.*

Fishing Bridge RV Park. It's more of a parking lot than a campground, but RV services like tank filling/emptying and hookups are available. ⊠ *Grand Loop Rd., 3 miles southwest of Lake Village* ☎ *307/344-7311* ⊕ *www.yellowstonenationalparklodges.com.*

Grant Village. The park's second-largest campground, Grant Village has some sites with great views of Yellowstone Lake. Some sites are wheelchair accessible. ⊠ *South Entrance Rd., Grant Village* ☎ *307/344-7311* ⊕ *www.yellowstonenationalparklodges.com.*

Indian Creek. In a picturesque setting next to a creek, this campground is in the middle of a prime wildlife-viewing area. ⊠ *Grand Loop Rd., 8 miles south of Mammoth Hot Springs* ☎ *307/344-2017.*

Madison. The largest National Park Service–operated campground, where no advance reservations are accepted, Madison has eight loops and nearly 300 sites. ⊠ *Grand Loop Rd., Madison* ☎ *307/344-7311* ⊕ *www.yellowstonenationalpark-lodges.com.*

Norris. Straddling the Gibbon River, this is a quiet, popular campground. A few of its "walk-in" sites are among the best in the park. ⊠ *Grand Loop Rd., Norris* ☎ *307/344-2017.*

Pebble Creek. Beneath multiple 10,000-foot peaks (Thunderer, Barronnette Peak, and Mt. Norris) this easternmost campground in the park is set creekside in a forested canopy. ⊠ *Northeast Entrance Rd., 22 miles east of Tower-Roosevelt Junction* ☎ *307/344-2017.*

Slough Creek. Down the most rewarding 2 miles of dirt road in the park, Slough Creek is a gem. Nearly every site is adjacent to the creek, which is prized by anglers. ⊠ *Northeast Entrance Rd., 10 miles east of Tower-Roosevelt Junction* ☎ *307/344-2017.*

Tower Falls. It's within hiking distance of the roaring waterfall, so this modest-size campground gets a lot of foot traffic. ⊠ *Grand Loop Rd., 3 miles southeast of Tower-Roosevelt* ☎ *307/344-2017.*

38

LAKE AREA

$$$$ HOTEL 🏨 **Lake Yellowstone Hotel.** Dating from 1891, the park's oldest lodge has maintained an air of refinement that Old Faithful Inn can't muster because of its constant visits from tour buses. **Pros:** relaxing atmosphere; the best views of any park lodging. **Cons:** the park's most expensive property; expensive restaurant; not particularly kid-friendly. [$] *Rooms from: $399* ✉ *1 Grand Loop Rd., about 1 mile south of Fishing Bridge, Lake Village* ☎ *307/344–7311, 866/439–7375* 🌐 *www.yellowstonenationalparklodges.com* 🛏 *194 rooms* 🕒 *Closed early Oct.–mid-May* 🍴 *No meals.*

$ HOTEL FAMILY 🏨 **Lake Lodge Cabins.** Just beyond the Lake Yellowstone Hotel lies one of the park's hidden treasures: Lake Lodge, built in 1920. **Pros:** the best porch at a Yellowstone lodge; great lobby; good for families. **Cons:** restaurant can get packed when motor coaches pull in. [$] *Rooms from: $80* ✉ *Lake Village Rd., 1 mile south of Fishing Bridge, Lake Village* ☎ *307/344–7311, 866/439–7375* 🌐 *www.yellowstonenationalparklodges.com* 🛏 *186 rooms, 100 with bath* 🕒 *Closed mid-Sept.–early June* 🍴 *No meals.*

OUTSIDE THE PARK

$$$$ HOTEL 🏨 **The Cody.** This all-suites hotel incorporates Western themes into a thoroughly modern and eco-friendly property. **Pros:** shuttle to airport and downtown attractions; continental breakfast included. **Cons:** luxury has its price. [$] *Rooms from: $209* ✉ *232 W. Yellowstone Ave., Cody* ☎ *307/587–5915* 🌐 *www.thecody.com* 🛏 *90 suites* 🍴 *Breakfast.*

$$ RESORT 🏨 **Pahaska Tepee Resort.** Just 2 miles from Yellowstone's East Entrance, these cabins in a pine forest are a good base for destinations both inside and outside the park. **Pros:** historic property; on a scenic highway. **Cons:** few services between Cody and Fishing Bridge. [$] *Rooms from: $120* ✉ *183 N. Fork Hwy., Cody* ☎ *307/527–7701, 800/628–7791* 🌐 *www.pahaska.com* 🛏 *43 cabins, 1 lodge* 🍴 *No meals.*

$$$ HOTEL 🏨 **Pollard Hotel.** Guns have been banned in the hotel ever since Harry Longbaugh, aka the Sundance Kid, brandished one when he robbed a bank on the corner. **Pros:** full breakfast discounted; historical property. **Cons:** front-desk service can be erratic. [$] *Rooms from: $162* ✉ *2 N. Broadway, Red Lodge, Montana* ☎ *406/446–0001, 800/765–5273* 🌐 *www.thepollard.net* 🛏 *39 rooms, 11 suites* 🍴 *No meals.*

$$$$ HOTEL 🏨 **Three Bear Lodge.** A towering stone fireplace and lots of natural wood greet guests in the lobby of the Three Bear Lodge. **Pros:** family-friendly feel; a block off the main drag; good value rooms, especially in the off-season. **Cons:** no staff at front desk at night. [$] *Rooms from: $219* ✉ *217 Yellowstone Ave., West Yellowstone, Montana* ☎ *406/646–7353, 800/646–7353* 🌐 *www.threebearlodge.com* 🛏 *70 rooms* 🍴 *No meals.*

YOSEMITE NATIONAL PARK

WELCOME TO YOSEMITE

TOP REASONS TO GO

★ **Wet and wild:** An easy stroll brings you to the base of Lower Yosemite Falls, where roaring springtime waters make for misty lens caps and lasting memories.

★ **Tunnel vision:** Approaching Yosemite Valley, Wawona Road passes through a mountainside and emerges before one of the park's most heart-stopping vistas.

★ **Inhale the beauty:** Pause to smell the light, pristine air as you travel about the High Sierra's Tioga Pass and Tuolumne Meadows, where 10,000-foot granite peaks just might take your breath away.

★ **Walk away:** Leave the crowds behind—but do bring along a buddy—and take a hike somewhere along Yosemite's 800 miles of trails.

★ **Powder your nose:** Winter's hush floats into Yosemite on snowflakes. Lift your face to the sky and listen to the trees.

1 Yosemite Valley. At an elevation of 4,000 feet, in roughly the center of the park, beats Yosemite's heart. This is where you'll find the park's most famous sights and biggest crowds.

2 Wawona and Mariposa Grove. The park's southern tip holds Wawona, with its grand old hotel and pioneer history center, and the Mariposa Grove of Big Trees, filled with giant sequoias. These are closest to the South Entrance, 35 miles (a one-hour drive) south of Yosemite Village.

3 Tuolumne Meadows. The highlight of east-central Yosemite is this wild-flower-strewn valley with hiking trails, nestled among sharp, rocky peaks. It's a 1½-hour drive northeast of Yosemite Valley along Tioga Road (closed mid-October–late May).

4 Hetch Hetchy. The most remote, least visited part of Yosemite accessible by auto-mobile, this glacial valley is dominated by a reservoir and veined with wilderness trails. It's near the park's western boundary, about a half-hour drive north of the Big Oak Flat Entrance.

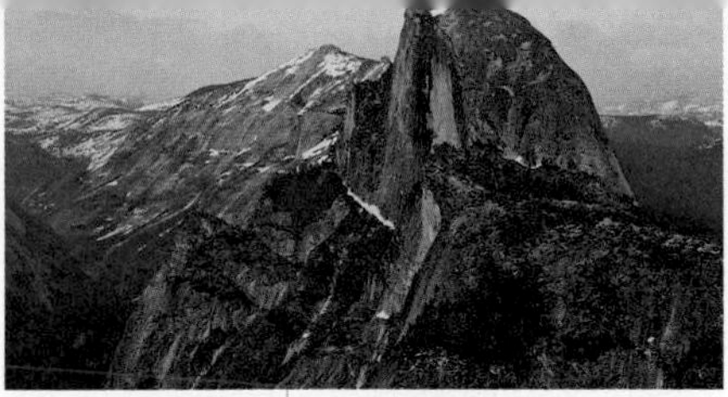

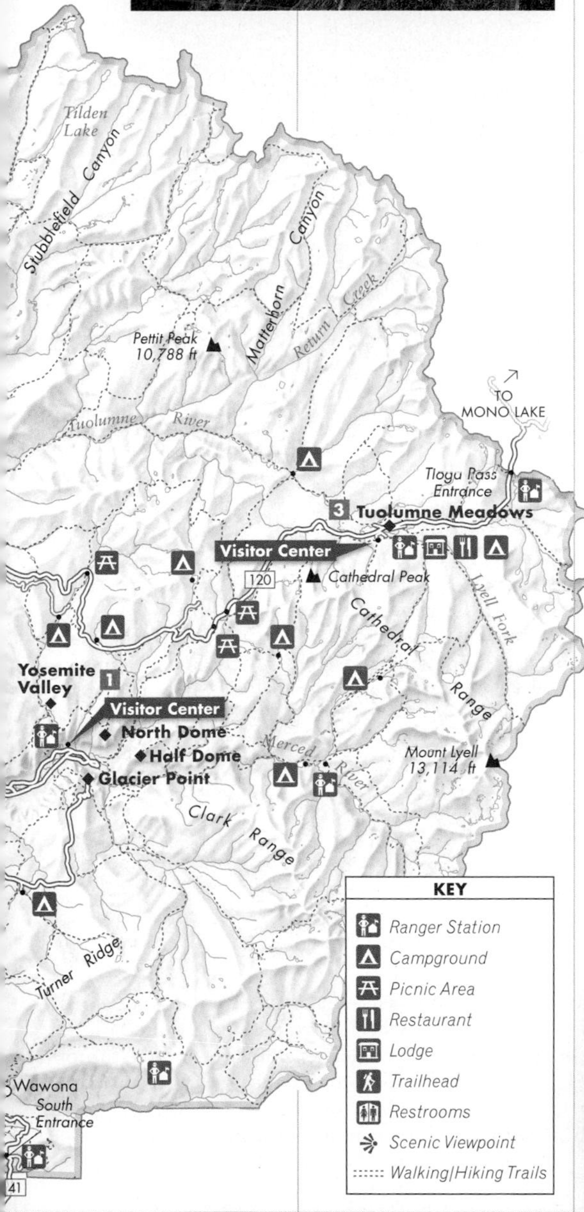

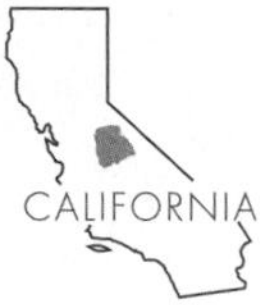

GETTING ORIENTED

Yosemite is so large that you can think of it as five parks. Yosemite Valley, famous for waterfalls and cliffs, and Wawona, where the giant sequoias stand, are open all year. Hetch Hetchy, home of less-used backcountry trails, is most accessible from late spring through early fall. The subalpine high country, Tuolumne Meadows, is open for summer hiking and camping; in winter it's accessible via cross-country skis or snowshoes. Badger Pass Ski Area is open in winter only. Most visitors spend their time along the park's southwestern border, between Wawona and Big Oak Flat Entrance; a bit farther east in Yosemite Valley and Badger Pass Ski Area; and along the east–west corridor of Tioga Road, which spans the park north of Yosemite Valley and bisects Tuolumne Meadows.

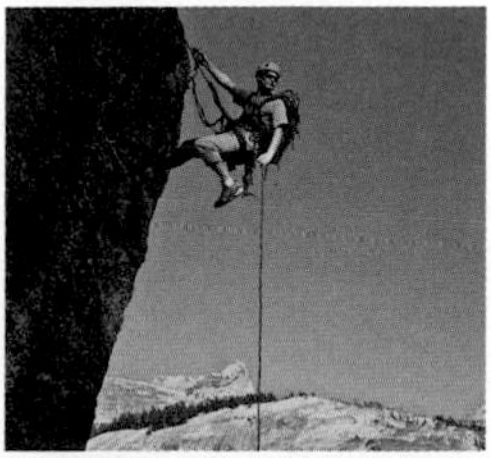

Updated by
Sharron Wood By merely standing in Yosemite Valley and turning in a circle, you can see more natural wonders in a minute than you could in a full day pretty much anywhere else. Half Dome, Yosemite Falls, El Capitan, Bridalveil Fall, Sentinel Dome, the Merced River, white-flowering dogwood trees, maybe even bears ripping into the bark of fallen trees or sticking their snouts into beehives—it's all in Yosemite Valley.

In the mid-1800s, when tourists were arriving to the area, the valley's special geologic qualities and the giant sequoias of Mariposa Grove 30 miles to the south so impressed a group of influential Californians that they persuaded President Abraham Lincoln to grant those two areas to the state for protection. On October 1, 1890—thanks largely to lobbying efforts by naturalist John Muir and Robert Underwood Johnson, the editor of *Century Magazine*—Congress set aside 1,500 square miles for Yosemite National Park.

YOSEMITE PLANNER

WHEN TO GO

During extremely busy periods—such as July 4—you will experience delays at the entrance gates. For smaller crowds, visit midweek. Or come mid-April through Memorial Day or mid-September through October, when the park is a bit less busy and the days usually are sunny and clear.

Summer rainfall is rare. In winter, heavy snows occasionally cause road closures, and tire chains or four-wheel drive may be required on the roads that remain open. The road to Glacier Point beyond the turnoff for Badger Pass is closed after the first major snowfall; Tioga Road is closed from late October through May or mid-June. Mariposa Grove Road is typically closed for a shorter period in winter.

AVG. HIGH/LOW TEMPS.

JAN.	FEB.	MAR.	APR.	MAY	JUNE
48/29	53/30	55/32	61/36	69/43	78/49
JULY	AUG.	SEPT.	OCT.	NOV.	DEC.
85/55	84/55	79/49	70/42	56/34	47/29

FESTIVALS AND EVENTS

JANUARY–FEBRUARY **Chefs' Holidays.** Celebrated chefs present cooking demonstrations and multicourse meals at the Ahwahnee Hotel in Yosemite Village on weekends from mid-January to early February. Two-night packages are $332 to $449 per person, three-night packages $399 to $574 per person. Space is limited. ☎ 559/253–5641 ⊕ www.yosemitepark.com.

MAY **Fireman's Muster.** North of Sonora in the old mining town of Columbia, history springs to life at this festival of antique fire engines, with hose-spraying contests and a parade of the old pumpers. ☎ 209/536–1672.

Mother Lode Roundup Parade and Rodeo. On Mother's Day weekend, the town of Sonora celebrates its gold-mining, agricultural, and lumbering heritage with a parade, rodeo, entertainment, and food. ☎ 209/532–7428 ⊕ www.motherloderoundup.com.

JULY **Mammoth Lakes Jazz Jubilee.** This festival, founded in 1989, features more than 20 different bands that play in a variety of venues, most with dance floors. ☎ 760/934–2478 ⊕ www.mammothjazz.org.

AUGUST **Bluesapalooza.** The first weekend of every August, Mammoth Lakes hosts a blues and beer festival—with an emphasis on the beer tasting. ☎ 888/992–7397 ⊕ www.mammothbluesbrewsfest.com.

OCTOBER **Sierra Art Trails.** The work of more than 100 artists is on display in studios and galleries throughout eastern Madera and Mariposa counties. Purchase the catalog of locations and hours at area shops. ☎ 559/658–8844 ⊕ www.sierraarttrails.org.

NOVEMBER–DECEMBER **Vintners' Holidays.** Free two- and three-day seminars by some of California's most prestigious vintners are held midweek in the Great Room of the Ahwahnee Hotel in Yosemite Village. They culminate with an elegant—albeit pricey—banquet dinner. Arrive early for seats in the free seminars; book early for lodging and dining packages ($664–$1,148). ☎ 559/253–5641 ⊕ www.yosemitepark.com.

DECEMBER **Bracebridge Dinner.** Held at the Ahwahnee Hotel in Yosemite Village every Christmas since 1928, this 17th-century-theme madrigal dinner is so popular that most seats are booked months in advance. Lodging packages start at $975, or $1,269 if you want to stay at the Ahwahnee. ☎ 801/252–4848 ⊕ www.bracebridgedinners.com.

PLANNING YOUR TIME

YOSEMITE IN ONE DAY

Begin at the **Valley Visitor Center,** where you can watch the documentary *Spirit of Yosemite* (which inexplicably shows no animals other than one deer). A minute's stroll from there is the **Indian village of Ahwahneechee,** which recalls American Indian life circa 1870. Take another 20 minutes to see the **Yosemite Museum.** Then, hop aboard the free shuttle to Yosemite Falls and hike the **Lower Yosemite Falls Trail** to the base of the falls. Then proceed via shuttle or a 20-minute walk to lunch at **Yosemite Lodge**.

Next choose one of three things: leisurely exploring **Curry Village**—perhaps going for a swim or ice skating, shopping, renting a bike, or having a beer on the deck; checking out family-friendly **Happy Isles Nature Center** and the adjacent nature trail; or hiking up the **Mist Trail** to the Vernal Fall footbridge to admire the view.

Hop back on the shuttle, then disembark at the **Ahwahnee Hotel.** Step into the Great Lounge, which has a magnificent fireplace and Indian artwork, and sneak a peek into the Dining Room, if you're up for a splurge. Get back on the shuttle, and head to **Yosemite Village,** where you can grab some food. Get back in your car and drive to the **El Capitan picnic area** and enjoy an outdoor evening meal. At this time of day, "El Cap" should be sun-splashed. (You will have gotten several good looks at world-famous **Half Dome** throughout the day.) Any sunlight left? If so, continue driving on around to see **Bridalveil Fall.**

GETTING HERE AND AROUND

BUS TRAVEL

Once you're in Yosemite you can take advantage of the free shuttle buses, which operate on low emissions, have 21 stops, and run from 7 am to 10 pm year-round. Buses run about every 10 minutes in summer, a bit less frequently in winter. A separate (but also free) summer-only shuttle runs out to El Capitan. Also in summer, you can pay to take the morning "hikers' bus" from Yosemite Valley to Tuolumne or the bus up to Glacier Point. Bus service from Wawona is geared for people who are staying there and want to spend the day in Yosemite Valley. Free and frequent shuttles transport people between the Wawona Hotel and Mariposa Grove. During the snow season, buses run regularly between Yosemite Valley and Badger Pass Ski Area.

CAR TRAVEL

Roughly 200 miles from San Francisco, 300 miles from Los Angeles, and 500 miles from Las Vegas, Yosemite takes a while to reach—and its many sites and attractions merit much more time than what rangers say is the average visit: four hours. Most people arrive via automobile or tour bus, but public transportation (courtesy of Amtrak and the regional YARTS bus system) also can get you to the valley efficiently.

Of the park's four entrances, Arch Rock is the closest to Yosemite Valley. The road that goes through it, Route 140 from Merced and Mariposa, is a scenic western approach that snakes alongside the boulder-packed Merced River. Route 41, through Wawona, is the way to come from Los Angeles (or Fresno, if you've flown in and rented a car). Route 120, through Crane Flat, is the most direct route from San Francisco. The only way in from the east is Tioga Road, which may be the best route in terms of scenery—though due to snow accumulation it's open for a frustratingly short amount of time each year (typically early June through mid-October).

There are few gas stations within Yosemite (Crane Flat, Tuolumne Meadows, and Wawona; none in the valley), so fuel up before you reach the park. From late fall until early spring, the weather is especially unpredictable, and driving can be treacherous. You should carry chains.

PARK ESSENTIALS

PARK FEES AND PERMITS

The admission fee, valid for seven days, is $20 per vehicle or $10 per individual.

If you plan to camp in the backcountry or climb Half Dome, you must have a wilderness permit. Availability of permits depends upon trailhead quotas. It's best to make a reservation, especially if you will be visiting May through September. You can reserve two days to 24 weeks in advance by phone, mail, or fax (✉ *Box 545, Yosemite, CA 95389* ☎ *209/372–0740* 🖷 *209/372–0739*); you'll pay $5 per person plus $5 per reservation if and when your reservations are confirmed. Requests must include your name, address, daytime phone, the number of people in your party, trip date, alternative dates, starting and ending trailheads, and a brief itinerary. Without a reservation, you may still get a free permit on a first-come, first-served basis at wilderness permit offices at Big Oak Flat, Hetch Hetchy, Tuolumne Meadows, Wawona, the Wilderness Center in Yosemite Village, and Yosemite Valley in summer. From fall to spring, visit the Valley Visitor Center.

PARK HOURS

The park is open 24/7 year-round. All entrances are open at all hours, except for Hetch Hetchy Entrance, which is open roughly dawn to dusk. Yosemite is in the Pacific time zone.

CELL-PHONE RECEPTION

Cell-phone reception is often just fine in the valley but hit-or-miss elsewhere in the park. There are public telephones at park entrance stations, visitor centers, all restaurants and lodging facilities in the park, gas stations, and in Yosemite Village.

RESTAURANTS

39

Yosemite National Park has a couple of moderately priced restaurants in lovely (which almost goes without saying) settings: the Mountain Room at Yosemite Lodge and Wawona Hotel's dining room. The Ahwahnee Hotel provides one of the finest dining experiences in the country.

Otherwise, food service is geared toward satisfying the masses as efficiently as possible. Yosemite Lodge's food court is the valley's best lower-cost, hot-food option; Curry Village Pavilion's cafeteria-style offerings are overpriced and usually fairly bland. In Valley Village, the Village Grill whips up burgers and fries, Degnan's Deli has $6–$8 made-to-order sandwiches, and Loft Pizzeria has a chaletlike open dining area in which you can enjoy pizza, salads, and desserts until 9 pm.

The White Wolf Lodge and Tuolumne Meadows Lodge—both off Tioga Road and therefore guaranteed open only from early June through September—have small restaurants where meals are competently prepared. Tuolumne Meadows also has a grill, as does the store at Glacier Point. During the ski season you'll also find one at Badger Pass, off Glacier Point Road.

Prices in the reviews are the average cost of a main course at dinner, or if dinner is not served, at lunch.

HOTELS

Indoor lodging options inside the park appear more expensive than initially seems warranted, but that premium pays off big-time in terms of the time you'll save—unless you are bunking within a few miles of a Yosemite entrance, you will face long commutes to the park when you stay outside its borders (though the Yosemite View Lodge, on Route 140, is within a reasonable half-hour's drive of Yosemite Valley).

Because of Yosemite National Park's immense popularity—not just with tourists from around the world but with Northern Californians who make weekend trips here—reservations are all but mandatory. Book up to one year ahead. ■TIP→ If you're not set on a specific hotel or camp but just want to stay somewhere inside the park, call the main reservation number to check for availability and reserve (☎ 801/559–4884).

Prices in the reviews are the lowest cost of a standard double room in high season. For expanded reviews, facilities, and current deals, visit Fodors.com.

TOURS

Fodor'sChoice
★
Ansel Adams Photo Walks. Photography enthusiasts shouldn't miss these 90-minute guided camera walks offered four mornings (Mon., Tues., Thurs., and Sat.) each week by professional photographers. All are free, but participation is limited to 15 people. Meeting points vary, and advance reservations are essential. ☎ 209/372–4413 ⊕ www.anseladams.com ✉ Free.

Big Trees Tram Tour. This 75-minute open-air tram tour of the Mariposa Grove of Big Trees departs from the parking lot every half-hour. Consider parking at the Wawona Hotel and taking advantage of the free shuttle; the ride takes about 15 minutes. ☎ 209/372–1240 ✉ $26.50 ⊙ May–Oct., depending on snowfall.

Glacier Point Tour. This four-hour trip takes you from Yosemite Valley to the Glacier Point vista, 3,214 feet above the valley floor. Some people buy a $25 one-way ticket and hike down. Shuttles depart from the Yosemite Lodge three times a day. ☎ 209/372–1240 ⊕ www.yosemitepark.com ✉ $41 ⚲ Reservations essential ⊙ June–Oct.

Grand Tour. For a full-day tour of the Mariposa Grove and Glacier Point, try the Grand Tour, which departs from the Yosemite Lodge in the valley. The tour stops for lunch at the historic Wawona Hotel, but the cost of the meal is not included. ☎ 209/372–1240 ⊕ www.yosemitepark.com ✉ $82 ⚲ Reservations essential ⊙ Late May–early Nov.

Tuolumne Meadows Tour. For a full day's outing to the high country, opt for this ride up Tioga Road to Tuolumne Meadows. You'll stop at several overlooks, and you can connect with another shuttle at Tuolumne Lodge. This service is mostly for hikers and backpackers who want to reach high-country trailheads, but everyone is welcome. ☎ 209/372–1240 ⊕ www.yosemitepark.com ✉ $23 ⚲ Reservations essential ⊙ July–Labor Day.

CLOSE UP

Plants and Wildlife in Yosemite

Dense stands of incense cedar and Douglas fir—as well as ponderosa, Jeffrey, lodgepole, and sugar pines—cover much of the park, but the stellar standout, quite literally, is the *Sequoiadendron giganteum,* the giant sequoia. Sequoias grow only along the west slope of the Sierra Nevada between 4,500 and 7,000 feet in elevation. Starting from a seed the size of a rolled-oat flake, each of these ancient monuments assumes remarkable proportions in adulthood; you can see them in the Mariposa Grove of Big Trees. In late May the valley's dogwood trees bloom with white, starlike flowers. Wildflowers, such as black-eyed Susan, bull thistle, cow parsnip, lupine, and meadow goldenrod, peak in June in the valley and in July at higher elevations.

The most visible animals in the park—aside from the omnipresent western gray squirrel, which fearlessly attempt to steal your food at every campground and picnic

site—are the mule deer. Though sightings of bighorn sheep are infrequent in the park itself, you can sometimes see them on the eastern side of the Sierra Crest, just off Route 120 in Lee Vining Canyon. You may also see the American black bear, which often has a brown, cinnamon, or blond coat. The Sierra Nevada is home to thousands of bears, and you should take all necessary precautions to keep yourself—and the bears—safe. Bears that acquire a taste for human food can become very aggressive and destructive and often must be destroyed by rangers, so store all your food and even scented toiletries in the bear lockers located at many campgrounds and trailheads, or use bear-resistant canisters if you'll be hiking in the backcountry.

Watch for the blue Steller's jay along trails, near public buildings, and in campgrounds, and look for golden eagles soaring over Tioga Road.

39

Valley Floor Tour. Take a two-hour tour of Yosemite Valley's highlights, complete with narration on the area's history, geology, and flora and fauna. Tours are either in trams or enclosed motor coaches, depending on weather conditions. They run year-round. ☎ *209/372–1240* ⊕ *www. yosemitepark.com* ✉ *$25.*

Moonlight Tour. This after-dark version of the Valley Floor Tour takes place on moonlit nights, depending on weather conditions. ☎ *209/372–1240* ⊕ *www.yosemitepark.com*

FAMILY **Wee Wild Ones.** Designed for kids under 7, this 45-minute program includes animal-theme games, songs, stories, and crafts. The event is held outdoors before the regular Yosemite Lodge or Curry Village evening programs in summer and fall; it moves to the Ahwahnee's big fireplace in winter and spring. All children must be accompanied by an adult. ☎ *209/372–1240* ⊕ *www.yosemitepark.com* ✉ *Free.*

VISITOR INFORMATION
PARK CONTACT INFORMATION
Yosemite National Park ☎ *209/372–0200* ⊕ *www.nps.gov/yose.*

VISITOR CENTERS

Le Conte Memorial Lodge. This small but striking National Historic Landmark, with its granite walls and steeply pitched shingle roof, is Yosemite's first permanent public information center. Step inside to see the cathedral-like interior, which contains a library and environmental exhibits. To find out about evening programs, check the kiosk out front. ⊠ *Southside Dr., about ½ mile west of Curry Village ⊕ www. nps.gov/yose ⊙ May–Sept., Wed.–Sun. 10–4.*

Valley Visitor Center. Learn about Yosemite Valley's geology, vegetation, and human inhabitants at this visitor center, which is also staffed with helpful rangers and contains a bookstore with a wide selection of books and maps. Don't leave without watching *Spirit of Yosemite*, a 23-minute introductory film that runs every half hour in the theater behind the visitor center. ⊠ *Yosemite Village* ☎ *209/372–0299* ⊕ *www.nps.gov/yose* ⊙ *Late May–early Sept., daily 9–7:30; early Sept.–late May, daily 9–5.*

EXPLORING

SCENIC DRIVES

Tioga Road. Few mountain drives can compare with this 59-mile road, especially its eastern half between Lee Vining and Olmstead Point. As you climb 3,200 feet to the 9,945-foot summit of Tioga Pass (Yosemite's sole eastern entrance for cars), you'll encounter broad vistas of the granite-splotched High Sierra and its craggy but hearty trees and shrubs. Past the bustling scene at Tuolumne Meadows, you'll see picturesque Tenaya Lake and then Olmstead Point, where you'll get your first peak at Half Dome. Driving Tioga Road one-way takes approximately 1½ hours. Wildflowers bloom here in July and August. By November, the high-altitude road closes for the winter; it sometimes doesn't reopen until early June.

HISTORIC SITES

Ahwahnee Hotel. Gilbert Stanley Underwood, architect of the Grand Canyon Lodge, also designed the Ahwahnee. Opened in 1927, it is generally considered his best work. You can stay here (for about $500 a night), or simply explore the first-floor shops and perhaps have breakfast or lunch in the bustling and beautiful Dining Room. The Great Lounge, 77 feet long with magnificent 24-foot-high ceilings and all manner of Indian artwork on display, beckons with big, comfortable chairs and relative calm. ⊠ *Ahwahnee Rd., about ¾ mile east of Yosemite Valley Visitor Center, Yosemite Village* ☎ *209/372–1489* ⊕ *www.yosemitepark.com.*

Ahwahneechee Village. This solemn smattering of structures, accessed by a short loop trail behind the Yosemite Valley Visitor Center, is a look at what American Indian life might have been like in the 1870s. One interpretive sign points out that the Miwok people referred to the 19th-century newcomers as "Yohemite" or "Yohometuk," which have been translated as meaning, "some of them are killers." ⊠ *Northside Dr., Yosemite Village* ⊠ *Free* ⊙ *Daily sunrise–sunset.*

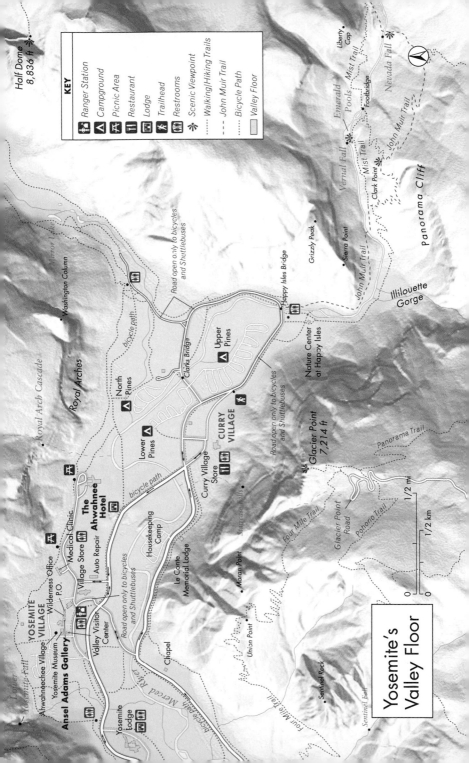

Yosemite's Valley Floor

KEY

- 🏠 Ranger Station
- ⛺ Campground
- 🧺 Picnic Area
- 🍴 Restaurant
- 🏨 Lodge
- 🥾 Trailhead
- 🚻 Restrooms
- ✳ Scenic Viewpoint
- ⋯ Walking/Hiking Trails
- --- John Muir Trail
- ····· Bicycle Path
- Valley Floor

Half Dome
8,836 ft

Liberty Cap

Emerald Pools

Mist Trail

Vernal Fall

Nevada Fall

John Muir Trail

Footbridge

Clark Point

Mist Trail

Panorama Cliff

Grizzly Peak

Sierra Point

Illilouette Gorge

John Muir Trail

Happy Isles Bridge

Nature Center at Happy Isles

Road open only to bicycles and Shuttlebuses

Mirror Lake

Washington Column

Royal Arch Cascade

Royal Arches

bicycle path

Clarks Bridge

Upper Pines

North Pines

Lower Pines

Curry Village Store

CURRY VILLAGE

Glacier Point
7,214 ft

Panorama Trail

Panorama Trail

Housekeeping Camp

bicycle path

The Ahwahnee Hotel

Medical Clinic

Village Store

Auto Repair

P.O.

Wilderness Office

Ansel Adams Gallery

YOSEMITE VILLAGE

Yosemite Museum

Ahwahneechee Village

Yosemite Fall

Lower Yosemite Fall

Le Conte Memorial Lodge

Chapel

Valley Visitor Center

Road open only to bicycles and Shuttlebuses

Road open only to bicycles and Shuttlebuses

Merced River

bicycle path

Yosemite Lodge

Moran Point

Mirror Hills

Union Point

Sentinel Beach

Sentinel Rock

Four Mile Trail

Glacier Point Road

Pohono Trail

1/2 mi

1/2 km

0

Pioneer Yosemite History Center. Some of Yosemite's first structures—those not occupied by American Indians, that is—were relocated here in the 1950s and 1960s. You can spend a pleasurable and informative half-hour walking about them and reading the signs, perhaps springing for a self-guided-tour pamphlet (50¢) to further enhance the history lesson. Weekends and some weekdays in the summer, costumed docents conduct free blacksmithing and "wet-plate" photography demonstrations, and for a small fee you can take a stagecoach ride. ⊠ *Rte. 41, Wawona* ☎ *209/375–9531, 209/379–2646* ✉ *Free* ☉ *Building interiors: mid-June–Labor Day, Wed. 2–5, Thurs.–Sun. 10–1 and 2–5.*

Wawona Hotel. Imagine a white-bearded Mark Twain relaxing in a rocking chair on one of the broad verandas of the park's first lodge, a whitewashed series of two-story buildings from the Victorian era. Plop down in one of the dozens of white adirondack chairs on the sprawling lawn and look across the road at the area's only golf course, one of the few links in the world that does not employ fertilizers or other chemicals. The hotel, an excellent place for lunch, is closed December through March, though it opens for about two weeks around Christmas and New Year's. ⊠ *Rte. 41, Wawona* ☎ *209/375–1425* ⊕ *www. yosemitepark.com.*

SCENIC STOPS

El Capitan. Rising 3,593 feet—more than 350 stories—above the valley, El Capitan is the largest exposed-granite monolith in the world. Since 1958, people have been climbing its entire face, including the famous "nose." You can spot adventurers with your binoculars by scanning the smooth and nearly vertical cliff for specks of color. ⊠ *Off Northside Dr., about 4 miles west of the Valley Visitor Center.*

Fodor'sChoice ★ **Glacier Point.** If you lack the time, desire, or stamina to hike more than 3,200 feet up to Glacier Point from the Yosemite Valley floor, you can drive here—or take a bus from the valley—for a bird's-eye view. You are likely to encounter a lot of day-trippers on the short, paved trail that leads from the parking lot to the main overlook. Take a moment to veer off a few yards to the Geology Hut, which succinctly explains and illustrates what the valley looked like 10 million, 3 million, and 20,000 years ago. ⊠ *Glacier Point Rd., 16 miles northeast of Rte. 41* ☎ *209/372–1240.*

Fodor'sChoice ★ **Half Dome.** Visitors' eyes are continually drawn to this remarkable granite formation that tops out at more than 4,700 feet above the valley floor. Despite its name, the dome is actually about three-quarters intact. You can hike to the top of Half Dome on an 8.5-mile (one-way) trail whose last 400 feet must be ascended while holding onto a steel cable. Permits are required (and checked on the trail), and available only by lottery. Visit ⊕ *www.recreation.gov* well in advance of your trip for details. Back down in the valley, see Half Dome reflected in the Merced River by heading to Sentinel Bridge just before sundown. The brilliant orange light on Half Dome is a stunning sight.

"This is us taking a break before conquering the top of Lembert Dome, while enjoying the beautiful view over Yosemite's high country." —photo by Rebalyn, Fodors.com member

Hetch Hetchy Reservoir. When Congress approved the O'Shaughnessy Dam in 1913, pragmatism triumphed over aestheticism. Some 2.5 million residents of the San Francisco Bay Area continue to get their water from this 117-billion-gallon reservoir. Although spirited efforts are being made to restore the Hetch Hetchy Valley to its former, pristine glory, three-quarters of San Francisco voters in 2012 ultimately opposed a measure to even consider draining the reservoir. Eight miles long, the reservoir is Yosemite's largest body of water, and one that can be seen up close from several trails. ⊠ *Hetch Hetchy Rd., about 15 miles north of the Big Oak Flat entrance station.*

High Country. The above-tree-line, high-alpine region east of the valley—a land of alpenglow and top-of-the-world vistas—is often missed by crowds who come to gawk at the more publicized splendors. Summer wildflowers, which usually pop up mid-July through August, carpet the meadows and mountainsides with pink, purple, blue, red, yellow, and orange. On foot or on horseback are the only ways to get here. For information on trails and backcountry permits, check with the visitor center.

Fodor's Choice
★

Mariposa Grove of Big Trees. Of Yosemite's three sequoia groves—the others being Merced and Tuolumne, both near Crane Flat well to the north—Mariposa is by far the largest and easiest to walk around. Grizzly Giant, whose base measures 96 feet around, has been estimated to be one of the largest in the world. Perhaps more astoundingly, it's about 2,700 years old. Up the hill, you'll find many more sequoias, a small museum, and fewer people. Summer weekends are especially crowded here. Consider taking the free shuttle from Wawona. ⊠ *Rte. 41, 2 miles north of the South Entrance station.*

GOOD READS

■ *The Photographer's Guide to Yosemite*, by Michael Frye, is an insider's guide to the park, with maps for shutterbugs looking to capture perfect images.

■ John Muir penned his observations of the park he long advocated for in *The Yosemite*.

■ *Yosemite and the High Sierra*, edited by Andrea G. Stillman and John Szarkowski, features beautiful reproductions of landmark photographs by Ansel Adams, accompanied by excerpts from the photographer's journals written when Adams traveled in Yosemite National Park in the early 20th century.

■ An insightful collection of essays accompanies the museum-quality artworks in *Yosemite: Art of an American Icon*, by Amy Scott.

■ Perfect for budding botanists, *Sierra Nevada Wildflowers*, by Karen Wiese, identifies more than 230 kinds of flora growing in the Sierra Nevada region.

Sentinel Dome. The view from here is similar to that from Glacier Point, except you can't see the valley floor. A moderately steep 1.1-mile path climbs to the viewpoint from the parking lot. Topping out at an elevation of 8,122 feet, Sentinel is more than 900 feet higher than Glacier Point. ⊠ *Glacier Point Rd., off Rte. 41.*

Tuolumne Meadows. The largest subalpine meadow in the Sierra (at 8,600 feet) is a popular way station for backpack trips along the Pacific Crest and John Muir trails. The setting is not as dramatic as Yosemite Valley, 56 miles away, but the almost perfectly flat basin, about 2½ miles long, is intriguing, and in July it's resplendent with wildflowers. The most popular day hike is up Lembert Dome, atop which you'll have breathtaking views of the basin below. Keep in mind that Tioga Road rarely opens before June and usually closes by mid-October. ⊠ *Tioga Rd. (Rte. 120), about 8 miles west of the Tioga Pass entrance station.*

WATERFALLS

Yosemite's waterfalls are at their most spectacular in May and June. When the snow starts to melt (usually peaking in May), streaming snowmelt spills down to meet the Merced River. By summer's end, some falls, including the mighty Yosemite Falls, trickle or dry up. Their flow increases in late fall, and in winter they may be hung dramatically with ice. Even in drier months, the waterfalls can be breathtaking. If you choose to hike any of the trails to or up the falls, be sure to wear shoes with no-slip soles; the rocks can be extremely slick. Stay on trails at all times.

■TIP➔ **Visit the park during a full moon and you can stroll without a flashlight and still make out the ribbons of falling water, as well as silhouettes of the giant granite monoliths.**

Bridalveil Fall. This 620-foot waterfall is often diverted dozens of feet one way or the other by the breeze. It is the first marvelous site you will see up-close when you drive into Yosemite Valley. ⊠ *Yosemite Valley, access from parking area off Wawona Rd.*

Nevada Fall. Climb Mist Trail from Happy Isles for an up-close view of this 594-foot cascading beauty. If you don't want to hike (the trail's final approach is quite taxing), you can see it—albeit distantly—from Glacier Point. ⚠ **Stay safely on the trail, as people sometimes die when they climb over the railing and onto the slippery rocks.** ⊠ *Yosemite Valley, access via Mist Trail from Nature Center at Happy Isles.*

Ribbon Fall. At 1,612 feet, this is the highest single fall in North America. It's also the first waterfall to dry up in summer; the rainwater and melted snow that create the slender fall evaporate quickly at this height. Look just west of El Capitan for the best view of the fall from the base of Bridalveil Fall. ⊠ *Yosemite Valley, west of El Capitan Meadow.*

Vernal Fall. Fern-covered black rocks frame this 317-foot fall, and rainbows play in the spray at its base. You can get a distant view from Glacier Point, or hike to see it close up. You'll get wet, but the view is worth it. ⊠ *Yosemite Valley, access via Mist Trail from Nature Center at Happy Isles.*

Fodor's Choice ★ **Yosemite Falls.** Actually three falls, they together constitute the highest waterfall in North America and the fifth-highest in the world. The water from the top descends a total of 2,425 feet, and when the falls run hard, you can hear them thunder across the valley. If they dry up—that sometimes happens in late summer—the valley seems naked without the wavering tower of spray. ■ TIP➔ **If you hike the mile-long loop trail (partially paved) to the base of the Lower Falls in May, prepare to get wet.** You can get a good full-length view of the falls from the lawn of Yosemite Chapel, off Southside Drive. ⊠ *Yosemite Valley, access from Yosemite Lodge or trail parking area.*

39

EDUCATIONAL OFFERINGS

CLASSES AND SEMINARS

Art Classes. Professional artists conduct workshops in watercolor, etching, drawing, and other mediums. Bring your own materials or purchase the basics at the Art Activity Center, next to the Village Store. Children under 13 must be accompanied by an adult. ⊠ *Art Activity Center, Yosemite Village* ☎ *209/372–1442* ⊕ *www.yosemitepark.com* ⬛ *Free* ☉ *Early Apr.–early Oct., Mon.–Sat. 10–2.*

Yosemite Outdoor Adventures. Naturalists, scientists, and park rangers lead multi-hour to multiday educational outings on topics from woodpeckers to fire management to pastel painting. Most sessions take place spring through fall, but a few focus on winter phenomena. ⊠ *Various locations* ☎ *209/379–2321* ⊕ *www.yosemitepark.com* ⬛ *$82–$465.*

MUSEUMS

Nature Center at Happy Isles. Designed for children, this old-fashioned museum has dioramas with several stuffed animals, including a baby bear. A rotating selection of hands-on, kid-friendly exhibits teach tykes and their parents about the park's ecosystem. Books, toys, T-shirts, and water bottles are stocked in the small gift shop. ⊠ *Off Southside Dr., about ¾ mile east of Curry Village* ⊡ *Free* ☉ *May–Sept., daily 9:30–5.*

Yosemite Museum. This small museum consists of a permanent exhibit that focuses on the history of the area and the people who once lived here. An adjacent gallery promotes contemporary Yosemite art. A docent demonstrates traditional Native American basket-weaving techniques a few days a week. ⊠ *Yosemite Village* ☎ *209/372–0299* ⊡ *Free* ☉ *Daily 9–5.*

RANGER PROGRAMS

Junior Ranger Program. Children ages 7 to 13 can participate in the informal, self-guided Junior Ranger program. A park activity handbook ($4) is available at the Valley Visitor Center or the Nature Center at Happy Isles. Once kids complete the book, rangers present them with a certificate and a badge. ⊠ *Yosemite Valley Visitor Center or the Nature Center at Happy Isles* ☎ *209/372–0299.*

Ranger-Led Programs. Rangers lead entertaining walks and give informative talks several times a day from spring to fall. The schedule is more limited in winter, but most days you can find a program somewhere in the park. In the evenings at Yosemite Lodge and Curry Village, lectures, slide shows, and documentary films present unique perspectives on Yosemite. On summer weekends, Camp Curry and Tuolumne Meadows Campground host sing-along campfire programs. Schedules and locations are posted on bulletin boards throughout the park as well as in the indispenable *Yosemite Guide,* which is distributed to visitors as they arrive at the park. ⊕ *www.yosemitepark.com.*

SPORTS AND THE OUTDOORS

BICYCLING

One enjoyable way to see Yosemite Valley is to ride a bike beneath its lofty granite monoliths. The eastern valley has 12 miles of paved, flat bicycle paths across meadows and through woods, with bike racks at convenient stopping points. For a greater challenge but at no small risk, you can ride on 196 miles of paved park roads—but bicycles are not allowed on hiking trails or in the backcountry. Kids under 18 must wear a helmet.

TOURS AND OUTFITTERS

Yosemite bike rentals. You can arrange for rentals from Yosemite Lodge and Curry Village bike stands. Bikes with child trailers, baby-jogger strollers, and wheelchairs are also available. The cost for bikes is $11.50 per hour, or $31.50 per day. ⊠ *Yosemite Lodge or Curry Village* ☎ *209/372–1208* ⊕ *www.yosemitepark.com* ☉ *Apr.–Oct.*

DID YOU KNOW?

Waterfalls in Yosemite Valley are especially famous for their heart-stopping drops over sheer granite cliffs. At peak times, hydrologists estimate that almost 135,000 gallons of water tumble down Yosemite Falls' triple cascade every minute.

Q & A with Ranger Scott Gediman

What's your favorite thing to do in the park?
I really enjoy hiking in Yosemite; in my opinion there's no better way to see the park. My favorite is the classic hike up the Mist Trail to Vernal Fall. I've done it literally hundreds of times—I've got family photos of my folks pushing me up the trail in a stroller. If you can only take one hike in Yosemite, do this one, especially in spring and summer.

Which time of year is best for visiting Yosemite?
The spring is wonderful, with the waterfalls going full blast and the meadows so green. The fall colors are beautiful, too. But in winter, the weather is great. The most stunning time in the valley is when a winter storm clears and there are incredible blue skies above the granite rocks, and the snow. There's a feeling you get seeing Half Dome with snow on it, or doing a winter hike on the Four-Mile Trail, Yosemite Falls Trail, or the Glacier Point trails.

What's there to do here in winter?
There's the ice-skating rink at Curry Village, and up at Badger Pass there's a wonderful ski school that specializes in teaching kids. There's cross-country skiing on groomed tracks along Glacier Point Road. Snowshoeing is really catching on. It's fun, it's easy, families can do it. You don't need special skills or a bunch of gear to go hiking through the snow; just put some snowshoes on your sneakers or hiking boots, and you're off. Every morning from about mid-December to mid-March, park rangers lead free snowshoe walks from Badger Pass. We talk about winter ecology and adaptations animals make,

or we hike up to the old Badger Summit for some fantastic views.

What about summer?
There's a misperception that the crowds are unmanageable, but it's not true. It's easy to get away from the crowds in the valley. One easy way is to hike the Valley Loop Trail, which a lot of people don't even know about. It goes all around the valley perimeter. Five minutes from Yosemite Lodge, and you won't see anybody.

How crowded does the valley really get?
At the busiest time, probably Memorial Day weekend, there can be as many as 25,000 people in the park at one time, many of them in the valley. The biggest mistake people make in summer is to drive everywhere. It's frustrating because of the traffic, and it takes longer even than walking. Park your car in the day-use lot or leave it at your hotel and take the free shuttle around. The shuttle goes to all the popular spots in the valley.

BIRD-WATCHING

More than 250 bird species have been spotted in the park, including the sage sparrow, pygmy owl, blue grouse, and mountain bluebird. Park rangers lead free bird-watching walks in Yosemite Valley a few days each week in summer; check at a visitor center or information station for times and locations. Binoculars sometimes are available for loan.

TOURS

Birding seminars. The Yosemite Conservancy organizes day- and weekend-long seminars for beginner and intermediate birders, as well as two-hour birding tram tours ($25) and bird walks a few times a week. ☎ *209/379–2321 ⊕ www.yosemiteconservancy.org ✉ $92–$200 ☉ Apr.–Aug.*

FISHING

The waters in Yosemite are not stocked; trout, mostly brown and rainbow, live here but are not plentiful. Yosemite's fishing season begins on the last Saturday in April and ends on November 15. Some waterways are off-limits at certain times; be sure to inquire at the visitor center about regulations.

A California fishing license is required; in 2013 licenses ran $14.61 for one day, $22.94 for two days, and $45.93 for 10 days. Full season licenses cost $45.93 for state residents and $123.38 for nonresidents. Buy your license in season at **Yosemite Village Sport Shop** (☎ *209/372–1286*) or at the **Wawona Store** (☎ *209/375–6574*).

HIKING

TOURS AND OUTFITTERS

Wilderness Center. This facility provides free wilderness permits, which are required for overnight camping (advance reservations are available for $5 per person plus $5 per reservation and are highly recommended for popular trailheads in summer and on weekends). The staff here also provide maps and advice to hikers heading into the backcountry, as well as rent bear-resistant canisters, which are required if you don't have your own. ☎ *209/372–0308.*

Yosemite Mountaineering School and Guide Service. From April to November, Yosemite Mountaineering School and Guide Service leads two-hour to full-day treks, as well as backpacking and overnight excursions. Reservations are recommended. ✉ *Yosemite Mountain Shop, Curry Village* ☎ *209/372–8344.*

EASY

FAMILY **"A Changing Yosemite" Interpretive Trail.** Take this 1-mile, wheelchair-accessible, looped path around Cook's Meadow to see and learn the basics about Yosemite Valley's past, present, and future. A self-guiding trail guide (available at a kiosk just outside the entrance) explains how to tell oaks, cedars, and pines apart; how fires help keep the forest floor healthy; and how pollution poses significant challenges to the park's inhabitants. *Easy.* ✉ *Trailhead across from the Valley Visitor Center.*

39

Yosemite Falls Trail. This is the highest waterfall in North America. The upper fall (1,430 feet), the middle cascades (675 feet), and the lower fall (320 feet) combine for a total of 2,425 feet and, when viewed from the valley, appear as a single waterfall. The 0.25-mile trail leads from the parking lot to the base of the falls. Upper Yosemite Fall Trail, a strenuous 3½-mile climb rising 2,700 feet, takes you above the top of the falls. Lower trail: *Easy.* Upper trail: *Difficult.* ⊠ *Trailhead off Camp 4, north of Northside Dr.*

MODERATE
Mist Trail. Except for Lower Yosemite Falls, more visitors take this trail (or portions of it) than any other in the park. The trek up to and back from Vernal Fall is 3 miles. Add another 4 miles total by continuing up to 594-foot Nevada Fall; the trail becomes quite steep and slippery in its final stages. The elevation gain to Vernal Fall is 1,000 feet, and to Nevada Fall an additional 1,000 feet. Merced River tumbles down both falls on its way to a tranquil flow through the Valley. *Moderate.* ⊠ *Trailhead at Happy Isles.*

Fodor's Choice ★ **Panorama Trail.** Few hikes come with the visual punch that this 8.5-mile trail provides. The star attraction is Half Dome, visible from many intriguing angles, but you also see three waterfalls up close and walk through a manzanita grove. Before you begin, look down on Yosemite Valley from Glacier Point, a special experience in itself. ⚠ **If you start after taking the last bus from the valley floor to Glacier Point, you might run out of daylight before you finish.** *Moderate.* ⊠ *Trailhead at Glacier Point.*

DIFFICULT
Chilnualna Falls Trail. This Wawona-area trail runs 4 miles one way to the top of the falls, then leads into the backcountry, connecting with miles of other trails. This is one of the park's most inspiring and secluded— albeit strenuous—trails. Past the tumbling cascade, and up through forests, you'll emerge before a panoramic vista at the top. *Difficult.* ⊠ *Trailhead at Chilnualna Falls Rd., off Rte. 41, Wawona.*

Fodor's Choice ★ **John Muir Trail to Half Dome.** Ardent and courageous trekkers continue on from Nevada Fall to the top of Half Dome. Some hikers attempt this entire 10- to 12-hour, 16.75-mile round-trip trek in one day; if you're planning to do this, remember that the 4,800-foot elevation gain and the 8,842-foot altitude will cause shortness of breath. Another option is to hike to a campground in Little Yosemite Valley near the top of Nevada Fall the first day, then climb to the top of Half Dome and hike out the next day. Get your wilderness permit (required for a one-day hike to Half Dome, too) at least a month in advance. Be sure to wear hiking boots and bring gloves. The last pitch up the back of Half Dome is very steep—the only way to climb this sheer rock face is to pull yourself up using the steel cable handrails, which are in place only from late spring to early fall. Those who brave the ascent will be rewarded with an unbeatable view of Yosemite Valley below and the high country beyond. ⚠ **Only 300 hikers per day are allowed atop Half Dome, and they all must have permits, which are distributed by lottery, one in the spring before the season starts and another two days before the climb. Contact** ⊕ *www. recreation.gov* **for details.** *Difficult.* ⊠ *Trailhead at Happy Isles.*

HORSEBACK RIDING

Reservations for guided trail rides must be made in advance at the hotel tour desks or by phone. Scenic trail rides range from two hours to a half day; four- and six-day High Sierra saddle trips are also available.

TOURS AND OUTFITTERS

Tuolumne Meadows Stables. Tuolumne Meadows Stables runs two- and four-hour trips that start at $64, as well as four- to six-day camping treks on mules that start at $1,018. Reservations are mandatory. ⊠ *Off Tioga Rd., 2 miles east of Tuolumne Meadows Visitor Center* ☎ *209/372–8427* ⊕ *www.yosemitepark.com.*

Wawona Stables. Two- and five-hour rides start at $64. Reservations are recommended. ⊠ *Rte. 41, Wawona* ☎ *209/375–6502.*

Yosemite Valley Stables. You can tour the valley on two-hour and four-hour rides starting from the Yosemite Valley Stables. Reservations are strongly recommended for the trips, which start at $64. ⊠ *At entrance to North Pines Campground, 100 yards northeast of Curry Village* ☎ *209/372–8348* ⊕ *www.yosemitepark.com.*

RAFTING

Rafting is permitted only on designated areas of the Middle and South Forks of the Merced River. Check with the Valley Visitor Center for closures and other restrictions.

OUTFITTERS

Curry Village raft stand. The per-person rental fee ($30) at Curry Village raft stand covers the four- to six-person raft, two paddles, and life jackets, plus a return shuttle at the end of your trip. ⊠ *South side of Southside Dr., Curry Village* ☎ *209/372–4386* ⊕ *www.yosemitepark. com* ✉ *$30* ☉ *Late May–July.*

39

ROCK CLIMBING

Fodor's Choice The granite canyon walls of Yosemite Valley are world-renowned for ★ rock climbing. El Capitan, with its 3,593-foot vertical face, is the most famous, but there are many other options here for all skill levels.

TOURS AND OUTFITTERS

Yosemite Mountaineering School and Guide Service. The one-day basic lesson at Yosemite Mountaineering School and Guide Service includes some bouldering and rappelling, and three or four 60-foot climbs. Climbers must be at least 10 years old and in reasonably good physical condition. Intermediate and advanced classes include instruction in first aid, anchor building, multi-pitch climbing, summer snow climbing, and big-wall climbing. There's a nordic program in the winter. ⊠ *Yosemite Mountain Shop, Curry Village* ☎ *209/372–8344* ⊕ *www.yosemitepark. com* ✉ *Starting at $148* ☉ *Apr.–Nov.*

WINTER SPORTS

The beauty of Yosemite under a blanket of snow has long inspired poets and artists, as well as ordinary folks. Skiing and snowshoeing activities in the park center on Badger Pass Ski Area, California's oldest snow-sports resort, which is about 40 minutes away from the valley on Glacier Point Road. Here you can rent equipment, take a lesson, have lunch, join a guided excursion, and take the free shuttle back to the valley after a drink in the lounge.

ICE-SKATING

Curry Village Ice Rink. Winter visitors have skated at this outdoor rink for decades, and there's no mystery why: it's a kick to glide across the ice while soaking up views of Half Dome and Glacier Point. ⊠ *South side of Southside Dr., Curry Village* ☎ *209/372–8319* ✉ *$9.75 per session, $4 skate rental* ☉ *Mid-Nov.–mid-Mar. afternoons and evenings daily, morning sessions weekends (hrs vary).*

SKIING AND SNOWSHOEING

Badger Pass Ski Area. California's first ski resort has five lifts and 10 downhill runs, as well as 90 miles of groomed cross-country trails. Free shuttle buses from Yosemite Valley operate between December and the end of March, weather permitting. Lift tickets are $47, downhill equipment rents for $36, and snowboard rental with boots is $37.50. ⊠ *Badger Pass Rd., off Glacier Point Rd., 18 miles from Yosemite Valley* ☎ *209/372–8430.*

Yosemite Ski School. The gentle slopes of Badger Pass make Yosemite Ski School an ideal spot for children and beginners to learn downhill skiing or snowboarding for as little as $45.50 for a group lesson. ☎ *209/372–8430* ⊕ *www.yosemitepark.com.*

Yosemite Cross-Country Ski School. The highlight of Yosemite's cross-country skiing center is a 21-mile loop from Badger Pass to Glacier Point. You can rent cross-country skis for $25 per day at the Cross-Country Ski School, which also rents snowshoes ($24 per day) and telemarking equipment ($29.50). ☎ *209/372–8444* ⊕ *www.yosemitepark.com.*

Yosemite Mountaineering School. This branch of the Yosemite Mountaineering School, open at the Badger Pass Ski Area during ski season only, conducts snowshoeing, cross-country skiing, telemarking, and skate-skiing classes starting at $35.50. ⊠ *Badger Pass Ski Area* ☎ *209/372–8344* ⊕ *www.yosemitepark.com*

SWIMMING

The pools at **Curry Village** (☎ *209/372–8324* ⊕ *www.yosemitepark. com*) and **Yosemite Lodge** (☎ *209/372–1250* ⊕ *www.yosemitepark. com*) are open to nonguests for $5, late May through early or mid-September. Additionally, several swimming holes with small sandy beaches can be found in midsummer along the Merced River at the eastern end of Yosemite Valley. Find gentle waters to swim; currents are often stronger than they appear, and temperatures are chilling. To conserve riparian habitats, step into the river at sandy beaches and other obvious entry points. ⚠ **Do not attempt to swim above or near waterfalls or rapids; people have died trying.**

CLOSE UP

Ansel Adams's Black-and-White Yosemite

What John Muir did for Yosemite with words, Ansel Adams did with photographs. His photographs have inspired millions of people to visit Yosemite, and his persistent activism helped to ensure the park's conservation.

Born in 1902, Adams first came to the valley when he was 14, photographing it with a Box Brownie camera. He later said his first visit "was a culmination of experience so intense as to be almost painful. From that day in 1916 my life has been colored and modulated by the great earth gesture of the Sierra." By 1919 he was working in the valley, as custodian of LeConte Memorial Lodge, the Sierra Club headquarters in Yosemite National Park.

Adams had harbored dreams of a career as a concert pianist, but the park sealed his fate as a photographer in 1928, the day he shot *Monolith: The Face of Half Dome,* which remains one of his most famous works. Adams also married Virginia Best in 1928, in her father's studio in the valley (now the Ansel Adams Gallery).

As Adams' photographic career took off, Yosemite began to sear itself into the American consciousness. David Brower, first executive director of the Sierra Club, later said of Adams' impact, "That Ansel Adams came to be recognized as one of the great photographers of this century is a tribute to the places that informed him."

In 1934 Adams was elected to the Sierra Club's board of directors; he would serve until 1971. As a representative of the conservation group, he combined his work with the club's mission, showing his photographs of the Sierra to influential officials such as Secretary of the Interior Harold L. Ickes, who showed them to President Franklin Delano Roosevelt. The images were a key factor in the establishment of Kings Canyon National Park.

In 1968, the Department of the Interior granted Adams its highest honor, the Conservation Service Award, and in 1980 he received the Presidential Medal of Freedom in recognition of his conservation work. Until his death in 1984, Adams continued not only to record Yosemite's majesty on film but to urge the federal government and park managers to do right by the park.

In one of his many public pleas on behalf of Yosemite, Adams said, "Yosemite Valley itself is one of the great shrines of the world and—belonging to all our people—must be both protected and appropriately accessible." As an artist and an activist, Adams never gave up on his dream of keeping Yosemite wild yet within reach of every visitor who wants to experience that wildness.

39

ARTS AND ENTERTAINMENT

Vintage Music of Yosemite. A pianist-singer performs four hours of live old-time music at the Wawona Hotel (call for schedule of performances). ⊠ *Wawona Hotel, Rte. 41, Wawona* ☎ *209/375–1425* 🖼 *Free* ☉ *Shows usually Tues.–Sat. at 5:30.*

Yosemite Theatre. Various theater and music programs are held throughout the year, and one of the best loved is Lee Stetson's portrayal of John Muir in *Conversation with a Tramp* and other Muir-theme shows. Purchase tickets in advance at the Conservancy Store at the Valley Visitor Center or the Tour and Activity Desk at Yosemite Lodge. Unsold seats are available at the door at performance time, 7 pm. ⊠ *Valley Visitor Center* ☎ *209/372–0299* 🖼 *$8.*

SHOPPING

Ahwahnee Gift Shop. This shop sells more upscale items, such as American Indian crafts, photographic prints, handmade ceramics, and elegant jewelry. For less expensive gift items, browse the small book selection, which includes writings by John Muir. ⊠ *Ahwahnee Hotel, Ahwahnee Rd.* ☎ *209/372–1409.*

Ansel Adams Gallery. Framed prints of the famed nature photographer's best works are on sale here, as are affordable posters. New works by contemporary artists are available, along with Native American jewelry and handicrafts. The gallery's elegant camera shop conducts photography workshops, from free camera walks a few mornings a week to five-day workshops. ⊠ *Northside Dr., Yosemite Village* ☎ *209/372–4413* ☉ *Apr.–Oct., daily 9–6; Nov.–Mar., daily 10–5.*

WHAT'S NEARBY

NEARBY TOWNS

Marking the southern end of the Sierra's gold-bearing mother lode, **Mariposa** is the last town before you enter Yosemite on Route 140. In addition to a fine mining museum, Mariposa has numerous shops, restaurants, and service stations. Motels and restaurants dot both sides of Route 41 as it cuts through the town of **Oakhurst,** a boomtown during the Gold Rush that is now a magnet for fast-food restaurants and chain stores. Oakhurst has a population of about 3,000 and sits 15 miles south of the park.

The tiny town of **Lee Vining,** near the park's eastern entrance, is home to the eerily beautiful, salty Mono Lake, where millions of migratory birds nest. Visit **Mammoth Lakes,** about 40 miles southeast of Yosemite's Tioga Pass entrance, for excellent skiing and snowboarding in winter, with fishing, mountain biking, hiking, and horseback riding in summer. Nine deep-blue lakes form the Mammoth Lakes Basin, and another hundred dot the surrounding countryside. Devils Postpile National Monument sits at the base of Mammoth Mountain.

DID YOU KNOW?

Yosemite's granite formations provide sturdy ground for climbers of all skill levels. The sheer granite monolith El Capitan—simply "El Cap" to climbers—is the most famous, climbed by even Captain Kirk (if you believe the opening scene of *Star Trek V: The Final Frontier*), but climbers tackle rock faces up in the mountains, too.

VISITOR INFORMATION
Lee Vining Office and Information Center ☎ 760/647–6595
⊕ www.leevining.com. **Mammoth Lakes Visitors Bureau** ✉ 2510 Main St.,
Mammoth Lakes ☎ 760/934–2712, 888/466–2666 ⊕ www.visitmammoth.com.
Mariposa County Visitors Bureau ✉ 5158 Rte. 140, Mariposa ☎ 209/966–
7082 ⊕ www.homeofyosemite.com. **Tuolumne County Visitors Bureau**
☎ 209/533–4420, 800/446–1333 ⊕ www.tcvb.com. **Yosemite Sierra
Visitors Bureau** ✉ 40637 Rte. 41, Oakhurst ☎ 559/683–4636
⊕ www.yosemitethisyear.com.

NEARBY ATTRACTIONS

Fodor's Choice
★
Bodie Ghost Town. The mining village of Rattlesnake Gulch, abandoned
mine shafts, and the remains of a small Chinatown are among the sights
at this fascinating ghost town. The town boomed from about 1878 to
1881, but by the late 1940s all its residents had departed. A state park
was established here in 1962, with a mandate to preserve everything
in a state of "arrested decay." Evidence of Bodie's wild past survives
at an excellent museum, and you can tour an old stamp mill where ore
was crushed into fine powder to extract gold and silver. The town is
23 miles from Lee Vining, north on U.S. 395, then east on Highway
270; the last 3 miles are unpaved. Snow may close Highway 270 from
late fall through early spring. No food, drink, or lodging is available in
Bodie. ✉ *Main and Green sts., Bodie* ☎ *760/647–6445* ⊕ *www.bodie.
com* ➪ *Park $7, museum free* ⊙ *Hrs vary; call ahead.*

California State Mining and Mineral Museum. Displays on gold-rush history here include a faux hard-rock mine shaft, a miniature stamp mill,
and a 13-pound chunk of crystallized gold. In September 2012, thieves
stole almost $2 million in gold and jewels; suspects were soon arrested,
but only some of the items were recovered. ✉ *5005 Fairground Rd.,
off Hwy. 49, Mariposa* ☎ *209/742–7625* ⊕ *www.parks.ca.gov* ➪ *$4*
⊙ *May–Sept., daily 10–5; Oct.–Apr., Wed.–Mon. 10–4.*

Devils Postpile National Monument. East of Mammoth Lakes lies this formation of smooth, vertical basalt columns sculpted by volcanic and
glacial forces. A short, steep trail winds to the top of the 60-foot cliff
for a bird's-eye view of the columns. Follow Highway 203 west from
U.S. 395 to Mammoth Mountain Ski Area to board the shuttle bus
to the monument, which day-use visitors must take from mid-June
to early September. A 2-mile hike past Devils Postpile leads to the
monument's second scenic wonder, **Rainbow Falls**, where a branch of
the San Joaquin River plunges more than 100 feet over a lava ledge.
When the water hits the pool below, sunlight turns the resulting mist
into a spray of color. Scenic picnic spots dot the banks of the river.
✉ *Minaret Rd., Mammoth Lakes* ☎ *760/934–2289, 760/934–0606 for
shuttle* ⊕ *www.nps.gov/depo* ➪ *$7 per person* ⊙ *Shuttle daily mid-
June–early Oct.*

Hot Creek Geologic Site. Forged by an ancient volcanic eruption, the
Hot Creek Geologic Site is a landscape of boiling hot springs, fumaroles, and geysers about 10 miles southeast of the town of Mammoth Lakes. You can stroll along boardwalks through the canyon

to view the steaming volcanic features. Fly-fishing for trout is popular upstream from the springs. ⊠ *Hot Creek Hatchery Rd., east of U.S. 395, Mammoth Lakes* ☎ *760/924–5500* 🌐 *Free* ☉ *Daily sunrise–sunset.*

Fodor'sChoice **Mono Lake.** Since the 1940s Los
★ Angeles has diverted water from this lake, exposing striking towers of tufa, or calcium carbonate. Court victories by environmentalists have meant fewer diversions, and the lake is rising again. Although to see the lake from U.S. 395 is stunning, make time to walk about South Tufa, whose parking lot is 5 miles east of U.S. 395 off Route 120. There in summer you can join the naturalist-guided **South Tufa Walk,** which lasts about 1½ hours. The sensational **Scenic Area Visitor Center,** on U.S. 395, is open from June through September (daily 8–5); it's closed December through March and open weekends the rest of the year. The center's hilltop and sweeping views of Mono Lake, along with its interactive exhibits inside, make this one of California's best visitor centers. Rangers and naturalists lead walking tours of the tufa daily in summer and on weekends (sometimes on cross-country skis) in winter. In town at U.S. 395 and 3rd Street, the **Mono Lake Committee Information Center & Bookstore** has more information about this beautiful area. ⊠ *Rte. 120, east of Lee Vining* ☎ *760/647–3044* 🌐 *www.monolake.org.*

FAMILY **Yosemite Mountain Sugar Pine Railroad.** Travel back to a time when powerful steam locomotives hauled massive log trains through the Sierra. This 4-mile, narrow-gauge railroad excursion takes you near Yosemite's south gate; there's also a moonlight special, with dinner and entertainment ($49). Take Route 41 south from Yosemite about 8 miles to the departure point. ⊠ *56001 Rte. 41, Fish Camp* ☎ *559/683–7273* 🌐 *www.ymsprr.com* 🌐 *$19* ☉ *May–Sept., daily; Apr. and Oct., weekends and selected weekdays.*

> **BEST BETS FOR FAMILIES**
>
> ■ **Bass Lake Recreation Area.** Rent a boat, splash around in the water, and watch bald eagles teach their young how to fish.
>
> ■ **Bodie Ghost Town.** Wander through the once-bustling Gold Rush streets and peer into saloons and miners' shacks at this state historic park.
>
> ■ **Mammoth Mountain.** In winter, schuss through powder, then warm up with a hot chocolate.
>
> ■ **Yosemite Mountain Sugar Pine Railroad.** Listen to the vintage steam engine huff and puff as you ride into logging history on the narrow-gauge railroad.

39

AREA ACTIVITIES

BOATING AND RAFTING
TOURS
Zephyr Whitewater Expeditions. This outfitter conducts half-day to three-day white-water trips on the Tuolumne, Merced, and American rivers for paddlers of all experience levels. ☎ *800/431–3636* 🌐 *www.zrafting.com.*

SKIING

Mammoth Mountain. One of the nation's premier ski resorts, Mammoth Mountain offers more than 3,500 acres of skiable boulevards, canyons, and bowls, and a 3,100-foot vertical drop. Ski season starts in November and can run through June. There's a ski school, cross-country trails, snowboarding, snowmobiling, and dogsledding. The resort has extensive lodging, dining, and shopping options. ✉ *Rte. 203, off U.S. 395, Mammoth Lakes* ☎ *800/626–6684* 🌐 *www.mammothmountain.com.*

WHERE TO EAT

IN THE PARK

In addition to the dining options listed here, you'll find fast-food grills and cafeterias, plus temporary snack bars, hamburger stands, and pizza joints lining park roads in summer. Many dining facilities in the park are open summer only.

$$$$ EUROPEAN Fodor's Choice ★ 🍴 **Ahwahnee Hotel Dining Room.** Rave reviews about the dining room's appearance are fully justified—it features towering windows, a 34-foot-high ceiling with interlaced sugar-pine beams, and massive chandeliers. Although many continue to applaud the food, others have reported that they sense a dip in the quality of both the service and what is being served. Diners must spend a lot of money here, so perhaps that inflates the expectations and amplifies the disappointments. In any event, the lavish $43 Sunday brunch is a popular way to experience the grand room. Reservations are always advised, and the attire is "resort casual." [$] *Average main: $35* ✉ *Ahwahnee Hotel, Ahwahnee Rd., about ¾ mile east of Yosemite Valley Visitor Center, Yosemite Village* ☎ *209/372–1489* 🌐 *www.yosemitepark.com* ✍ *Reservations essential.*

$ AMERICAN 🍴 **Food Court at Yosemite Lodge.** Fast and convenient (if outdated), this food court serves simple fare, ranging from hamburgers and pizzas to pastas and roasted meats. At breakfast, you can get pancakes and eggs made any way you like. Salads are popular at lunch and dinner. There's also a selection of beer and wine. The coffee shop near the entrance keeps longer hours. [$] *Average main: $10* ✉ *Yosemite Lodge, about ¾ mile west of the visitor center, Yosemite Village* ☎ *209/372–1265* 🌐 *www.yosemitepark.com.*

$$$ AMERICAN Fodor's Choice ★ 🍴 **Mountain Room.** Though good, the food becomes secondary when you see Yosemite Falls through this dining room's wall of windows—almost every table has a view. The chef makes a point of using locally sourced, organic ingredients whenever possible, so you can be assured of fresh vegetables to accompany the hearty main courses, such as steaks and seafood, as well as vegetarian and even vegan options. The Mountain Room Lounge, a few steps away in the Yosemite Lodge complex, has about 10 beers on tap. Weather permitting, take your drink out onto the small back patio. [$] *Average main: $23* ✉ *Yosemite Lodge, Northside Dr. about ¾ mile west of the visitor center, Yosemite Village* ☎ *209/372–1281* 🌐 *www.yosemitepark.com* ⏲ *No lunch.*

$$ ✕**Pavillion Buffet.** This cafeteria-style eatery isn't as inexpensive or as
AMERICAN good as it should be. Come early for breakfast or dinner (there's no
lunch), as the food (which runs the gamut from roasted meats to pastas
to burritos and beyond), gets worse as closing time nears. Bring your
tray outside to the deck, and take in the views of the valley's granite
walls. $ *Average main: $16 ⊠ Curry Village ☎ 209/372–8303 ⊙ Closed
mid-Oct.–mid-Apr. No lunch.*

$ ✕**Tuolumne Meadows Grill.** Serving continuously throughout the day until
FAST FOOD 5 or 6, this fast-food eatery cooks up basic breakfast, lunch, and snacks.
It's possible that ice cream tastes better at this altitude. Stop in for a
quick meal before exploring the meadows. $ *Average main: $8 ⊠ Tioga
Rd. (Rte. 120), 1½ miles east of Tuolumne Meadows Visitor Center
☎ 209/372–8426 ⊙ Closed Oct.–Memorial Day.*

$$ ✕**Tuolumne Meadows Lodge.** At the back of a small building that con-
AMERICAN tains the lodge's front desk and small gift shop, this restaurant serves
a menu of hearty American fare at breakfast and dinner. The decor is
ultrawoodsy, with dark-wood walls, red-and-white-checkered tablecloths, and a handful of communal tables, which give it the feeling of
an old-fashioned summer camp. The menu is small, often featuring a
few meat and seafood dishes and one pasta or other special, including
a vegetarian choice. If you have any dietary restrictions, let the front
desk know in advance and the cooks will not let you down. Order box
lunches from here for before hikes. $ *Average main: $20 ⊠ Tioga Rd.
(Rte. 120) ☎ 209/372–8413 ⊕ www.yosemitepark.com ⚑ Reservations
essential ⊙ Closed late Sept.–mid-June. No lunch.*

$ ✕**The Village Grill.** If a burger joint is what you've been missing, head
FAST FOOD to this bustling eatery in Yosemite Village that serves veggie, salmon,
and a few other burger varieties in addition to the usual beef patties.
Order at the counter by 5 pm, then take your tray out to the deck
and enjoy your meal under the trees. Degnan's Deli (open until 6 pm)
and Degnan's Pizza (open until 9 pm) are nearby. $ *Average main: $8
⊠ 100 yards east of Yosemite Valley Visitor Center, Yosemite Village
☎ 209/372–1207 ⊕ www.yosemitepark.com ⊙ Closed Oct.–May.*

$$$ ✕**Wawona Hotel Dining Room.** Watch deer graze on the meadow while
AMERICAN you dine in the romantic, candlelit dining room of the whitewashed
Wawona Hotel, which dates from the late 1800s. The American-style
cuisine favors fresh ingredients and flavors; trout and flatiron steaks
are menu staples. There's also a brunch on some Sunday holidays, like
Mother's Day and Easter, and a barbecue on the lawn Saturday evenings
in summer. $ *Average main: $27 ⊠ Wawona Hotel, Rte. 41, Wawona
☎ 209/559–4935 ⚑ Reservations essential ⊙ Closed Dec.–Mar.*

$$$ ✕**White Wolf Lodge.** Those fueling up for a day on the trail or famished
AMERICAN after a high-country hike will appreciate the all-you-can-eat family-style
breakfasts and dinners in this tiny rustic dining room. Mashed potatoes,
big pots of curried vegetables, and heaps of pasta often grace the tables
in this cozy out-of-the-way place. Lunch is not served, but box lunches
can be ordered the night before. $ *Average main: $23 ⊠ Tioga Rd.
(Rte. 120), 25 miles west of Tuolumne Meadows and 15 miles east of
Crane Flat ☎ 209/372–8416 ⊕ www.yosemitepark.com ⚑ Reservations
essential ⊙ Closed mid-Sept.–mid-June. No lunch.*

39

PICNIC AREAS

Considering how large the park is and how many visitors come here—some 4 million people every year, most of them just for the day—it is somewhat surprising that Yosemite has so few formal picnic areas, though in many places you can find a smooth rock to sit on and enjoy breathtaking views along with your lunch. The convenience stores all sell picnic supplies, and prepackaged sandwiches and salads are widely available. Those options can come in especially handy during the middle of the day, when you might not want to spend precious daylight hours in such a spectacular setting sitting in a restaurant for a formal meal. *None of the below options has drinking water available; most have some type of toilet.*

Cathedral Beach. You may have some solitude picnicking here, as this spot usually has fewer people than picnic areas at the eastern end of the valley. ⊠ *Southside Dr. underneath spirelike Cathedral Rocks.*

Church Bowl. Tucked behind the Ahwahnee Hotel, this picnic area nearly abuts the granite walls below the Royal Arches. If you're walking from the village with your supplies, this is the shortest trek to a picnic area. ⊠ *Behind Ahwahnee Hotel, Yosemite Valley.*

El Capitan. Come here for great views that look straight up the giant granite wall above. ⊠ *Northside Dr., at western end of valley.*

Sentinel Beach. Usually crowded in season, this area is right alongside a running creek and the Merced River. ⊠ *Southside Dr., just south of Swinging Bridge.*

Swinging Bridge. This picnic area is just before the little wooden footbridge that crosses the Merced River, which babbles pleasantly by. ⊠ *Southside Dr., east of Sentinel Beach.*

OUTSIDE THE PARK

$$$$
EUROPEAN
Fodor's Choice
★

✕ **Erna's Elderberry House.** Erna Kubin-Clanin, the grande dame of Château du Sureau, created this culinary oasis, stunning for its understated elegance, gorgeous setting, and impeccable service. Red walls and wood beams accent the dining room's high ceilings, and arched windows reflect the glow of candles. The seasonal six-course prix-fixe dinner can be paired with superb wines, with every course delivered in perfect synchronicity by the elite waitstaff. A short bar menu is served in the former wine cellar. $ *Average main: $95* ⊠ *Château du Sureau, 48688 Victoria La., off Rte. 41, Oakhurst* ☎ *559/683–6800* ⊕ *www.elderberryhouse. com* ⚑ *Reservations essential* ☾ *No lunch Mon.–Sat.*

$$$
STEAKHOUSE
FAMILY

✕ **The Mogul.** This longtime favorite is the place to go when you want a straightforward steak and salad bar. The only catch is that the waiters cook your steak—and the result depends on the waiter's experience. But generally you can't go wrong. And kids love it. The knotty-pine walls lend a woodsy touch and suggest Mammoth Mountain before all the development. $ *Average main: $24* ⊠ *1528 Tavern Rd., off Old Mammoth Rd., Mammoth Lakes* ☎ *760/934–3039* ⊕ *www.themogul. com* ☾ *No lunch.*

$$ AMERICAN FAMILY 🍴 **Nicely's.** Artworks for sale decorate the walls of this vintage diner. The country cooking isn't fancy—think blueberry pancakes for breakfast and chicken-fried steak for dinner—but this is a good spot for families with kids and unfussy eaters looking for a square meal. It's the kind of place where the waitress walks up with a pot of coffee and asks, "Ya want a warm-up, hon?" [$] *Average main: $15* ✉ *U.S. 395 and 4th St., Lee Vining* ☎ *760/647–6477* 🕒 *Closed Tues. and Wed. in winter.*

LODGING TIP

Reserve your room or cabin in Yosemite as far in advance as possible. You can make a reservation up to a year before your arrival (within minutes after the reservation office makes a date available, the Ahwahnee, Yosemite Lodge, and Wawona Hotel often sell out their weekends, holiday periods, and all days between May and September).

$$ AMERICAN Fodor's Choice ★ 🍴 **Tioga Gas Mart & Whoa Nelli Deli.** This might be the only gas station in the United States that serves craft beers and lobster taquitos, but its appeal goes way beyond novelty. Everything on the inventive menu is expertly executed, from the succulent fish tacos with mango salsa to a generous portion of barbecued ribs served with a slightly sweet huckleberry glaze. Order at the counter and grab a seat inside, or, better yet, sit at one of the picnic tables on the lawn outside, which have a distant view of Mono Lake. [$] *Average main: $15* ✉ *Rte. 120 and U.S. 395, Lee Vining* ☎ *760/647–1088* 🌐 *www.whoanelliedeli.com* 🕒 *Closed early Nov.–late Apr.*

WHERE TO STAY

IN THE PARK

$$$$ HOTEL Fodor's Choice ★ 🏨 **Ahwahnee Hotel.** A National Historic Landmark, the hotel is constructed of sugar-pine logs and features American Indian design motifs; public spaces are enlivened with art deco flourishes, oriental rugs, and elaborate iron- and woodwork. **Pros:** best lodge in Yosemite; helpful concierge. **Cons:** expensive rates; some reports that service has slipped in recent years. [$] *Rooms from: $471* ✉ *Ahwahnee Rd., about ¾ miles east of Yosemite Valley Visitor Center, Yosemite Village* ☎ *801/559–4884* 🌐 *www.yosemitepark.com* 🛏 *99 lodge rooms, 4 suites, 24 cottage rooms* 🍽 *No meals.*

$$ HOTEL 🏨 **Curry Village.** Opened in 1899 as a place for budget-conscious travelers, Curry Village has plain accommodations: standard motel rooms, simple cabins with either private or shared baths, and tent cabins with shared baths. **Pros:** close to many activities; family-friendly atmosphere. **Cons:** not that economical after a recent price surge; can be crowded; sometimes a bit noisy. [$] *Rooms from: $124* ✉ *South side of Southside Dr.* ☎ *801/559–4884* 🌐 *www.yosemitepark.com* 🛏 *18 rooms, 389 cabins* 🍽 *No meals.*

$$$$ RENTAL 🏨 **Redwoods Guest Cottages.** This collection of individually owned cabins and homes in the Wawona area is a great alternative to the overcrowded valley. **Pros:** sense of privacy; peaceful setting; full kitchens. **Cons:** remote from the valley; some have no TV. [$] *Rooms from: $270* ✉ *8038 Chilnualna Falls Rd., off Rte. 41, Wawona* ☎ *209/375–6666* 🌐 *www.redwoodsinyosemite.com* 🛏 *130 units* 🍴 *No meals.*

$$ HOTEL 🏨 **Wawona Hotel.** This 1879 National Historic Landmark at Yosemite's southern end is an old-fashioned New England–style estate, with whitewashed buildings, wraparound verandahs, and pleasant, no-frills rooms decorated with period pieces. **Pros:** lovely building; peaceful atmosphere. **Cons:** few modern amenities, such as phones and TVs; an hour's drive from Yosemite Valley. [$] *Rooms from: $159* ✉ *Rte. 41, Wawona* ☎ *801/559–4884* 🌐 *www.yosemitepark.com* 🛏 *104 rooms, 50 with bath* 🕒 *Closed Dec.–Mar., except Dec. 20–Jan. 2* 🍴 *No meals.*

$$ HOTEL 🏨 **White Wolf Lodge.** Set in a subalpine meadow, the rustic accommodations at White Wolf Lodge make it an excellent base camp for hiking the backcountry. **Pros:** quiet location; near some of Yosemite's most beautiful, less crowded hikes; good restaurant. **Cons:** far from the valley. [$] *Rooms from: $124* ✉ *Off Tioga Rd. (Rte. 120), 25 miles west of Tuolumne Meadows and 15 miles east of Crane Flat* ☎ *801/559–4884* 🛏 *24 tent cabins, 4 cabins* 🕒 *Closed mid-Sept.–mid-June* 🍴 *No meals.*

$$$ HOTEL 🏨 **Yosemite Lodge at the Falls.** This 1915 lodge near Yosemite Falls more closely resembles a 1960s resort with its numerous two-story structures tucked beneath the trees, and it doesn't help that the brown buildings are surrounded by large parking lots. **Pros:** centrally located; dependably clean rooms; lots of tours leave from out front. **Cons:** can feel impersonal; appearance is a little dated; prices recently skyrocketed. [$] *Rooms from: $199* ✉ *Northside Dr., about ¾ mile west of the visitor center, Yosemite Village* ☎ *801/559–4884* 🌐 *www.yosemitepark.com* 🛏 *245 rooms* 🍴 *No meals.*

OUTSIDE THE PARK

$$ HOTEL FAMILY 🏨 **Best Western Yosemite Gateway Inn.** Oakhurst's best motel has carefully tended landscaping and rooms with attractive colonial-style furniture and slightly kitschy hand-painted wall murals of Yosemite. **Pros:** close to Yosemite's southern entrance and the Wawona area of the park; clean; indoor and outdoor swimming pools; comfortable. **Cons:** chain property; getting to Yosemite Valley from here is a haul. [$] *Rooms from: $140* ✉ *40530 Rte. 41, Oakhurst* ☎ *800/545–5462, 559/683–2378* 🌐 *www.yosemitegatewayinn.com* 🛏 *121 rooms, 16 suites* 🍴 *No meals.*

$$$$ RESORT Fodor's Choice ★ 🏨 **Château du Sureau.** You'll feel pampered from the moment you drive through the wrought-iron gates of this fairy-tale castle. **Pros:** luxurious; great views. **Cons:** expensive; if you're not really into spas, it might not be worth your while. [$] *Rooms from: $385* ✉ *48688 Victoria La., Oakhurst* ☎ *559/683–6860* 🌐 *www.chateausureau.com* 🛏 *10 rooms, 1 villa* 🍴 *Breakfast.*

CLOSE UP

Best Campgrounds in Yosemite

If you are going to concentrate solely on valley sites and activities, you should endeavor to stay in one of the "Pines" campgrounds, which are clustered near Curry Village and within an easy stroll from that busy complex's many facilities. For a more primitive and quiet experience, and to be near many backcountry hikes, try one of the Tioga Road campgrounds.

National Park Service Reservations Office. Reservations are required at many of Yosemite's campgrounds, especially in summer; you can book a site up to five months in advance, starting on the 15th of the month. Unless otherwise noted, book your site through the central National Park Service Reservations Office. If you don't have reservations when you arrive, many sites, especially those outside Yosemite Valley, are available on a first-come, first-served basis. ☎ 877/436–7275 ⊕ www.recreation. gov ⊙ Daily 7–7.

Bridalveil Creek. This campground sits among lodgepole pines at 7,200 feet, above the valley on Glacier Point Road. From here, you can easily drive to Glacier Point's magnificent valley views. ⊠ From Rte. 41 in Wawona, go north to Glacier Point Rd. and turn right; entrance to campground is 25 miles ahead on right side.

Camp 4. Formerly known as Sunnyside Walk-In, and extremely popular with rock climbers, who don't mind that a total of six are assigned to each campsite, no matter how many are in your group, this is the only valley campground available on a first-come, first-served basis. ⊠ Base of Yosemite Falls Trail, just west of

Yosemite Lodge on Northside Dr., Yosemite Village.

Housekeeping Camp. Composed of three concrete walls and covered with two layers of canvas, each unit has an open-ended fourth side that can be closed off with a heavy white canvas curtain. You can rent "bedpacks," consisting of blankets, sheets, and other comforts. ⊠ Southside Dr., ½ mile west of Curry Village.

Porcupine Flat. Sixteen miles west of Tuolumne Meadows, this campground sits at 8,100 feet. If you want to be in the high country, this is a good bet. ⊠ Rte. 120, 16 miles west of Tuolumne Meadows.

Tuolumne Meadows. In a wooded area at 8,600 feet, just south of its namesake meadow, this is one of the most spectacular and sought-after campgrounds in Yosemite. ⊠ Rte. 120, 46 miles east of Big Oak Flat entrance station.

Upper Pines. This is one of the valley's largest campgrounds and the closest one to the trailheads. Expect large crowds in the summer—and little privacy. ⊠ At east end of valley, near Curry Village.

Wawona. Near the Mariposa Grove, just downstream from a popular fishing spot, this year-round campground has larger, less densely packed sites than campgrounds in the valley. ⊠ Rte. 41, 1 mile north of Wawona.

White Wolf. Set in the beautiful high country at 8,000 feet, this is a prime spot for hikers from early July to mid-September. ⊠ Tioga Rd., 15 miles east of Big Oak Flat entrance.

39

CAMPING IN BEAR COUNTRY

The national parks' campgrounds and some campgrounds outside the parks provide food-storage boxes that can keep bears from pilfering your edibles (portable canisters for backpackers can be rented in most park stores). It's imperative that you move all food, coolers, and items with a scent (including toiletries, toothpaste, chewing gum, and air fresheners) from your car (including the trunk) to the storage box at your campsite; day-trippers should lock food in bear boxes provided at parking lots. If you don't, a bear may break into your car by literally peeling off the door or ripping open the trunk, or ransack your tent. The familiar tactic of hanging your food from high tree limbs is not an effective deterrent, as bears easily can scale trees. In the southern Sierra, bear canisters are the only effective and proven method for preventing bears from getting human food.

$$ HOTEL **Comfort Inn Yosemite Valley Gateway.** This white three-story building with a broad veranda sits on a hill above Mariposa. **Pros:** reasonably priced; good views; pleasant little town. **Cons:** pretty far from Yosemite—the public bus is a good option. [$] *Rooms from: $139* ✉ *4994 Bullion St., Mariposa* ☎ *209/966–4344, 877/742–4371* 🌐 *www.comfortinn.com* 🛏 *59 rooms, 2 suites* 🍴 *Breakfast.*

$$$ RESORT FAMILY **Evergreen Lodge.** The perfect blend of rustic charm and modern comfort, these cabins have sumptuous beds, comfy armchairs, pull-out sofas, and tree-stump end tables. **Pros:** romantic setting; very friendly staff; lots of things to do. **Cons:** far from Yosemite Valley (though close to Hetch Hetchy). [$] *Rooms from: $180* ✉ *33160 Evergreen Rd., 25 miles east of Groveland, 23 miles north of Yosemite Valley, Groveland* ☎ *209/379–2606, 800/935–6343* 🌐 *www.evergreenlodge.com* 🛏 *90 cabins* ⏲ *Closed Jan.–early Feb.* 🍴 *No meals*

$$$ B&B/INN **Homestead Cottages.** Set on 160 acres of rolling hills that once held a Miwok village, these cottages (the largest sleeps six) have gas fireplaces, fully equipped kitchens, and queen-size beds. **Pros:** remote location; quiet setting; friendly owners. **Cons:** might be a little *too* quiet for some. [$] *Rooms from: $159* ✉ *41110 Rd. 600, 2½ miles off Hwy. 49, Ahwahnee* ☎ *559/683–0495, 800/483–0495* 🌐 *www.homesteadcottages.com* 🛏 *6 cottages* 🍴 *No meals.*

$$ B&B/INN **Narrow Gauge Inn.** The well-tended rooms at this family-owned property have balconies with great views of the surrounding woods and mountains. **Pros:** close to Yosemite's south entrance; nicely appointed rooms; wonderful balconies. **Cons:** rooms can be a bit dark; dining options are limited, especially for vegetarians. [$] *Rooms from: $145* ✉ *48571 Rte. 41, Fish Camp* ☎ *559/683–7720, 888/644–9050* 🌐 *www.narrowgaugeinn.com* 🛏 *26 rooms* 🍴 *Breakfast.*

$$ RESORT **Tamarack Lodge Resort.** Tucked away on the edge of the John Muir Wilderness Area, where cross-country ski trails loop through the woods, this 1924 lodge looks like something out of a snow globe. **Pros:** rustic but not run-down; tons of nearby outdoor activities. **Cons:** thin walls; some shared bathrooms. [$] *Rooms from: $119*

✉ Lake Mary Rd., off Rte. 203, Mammoth Lakes ☎ 760/934–2442, 800/237–6879 🌐 www.tamaracklodge.com 🛏 11 rooms, 34 cabins 🍴 No meals.

$$$$ HOTEL 🏨 **Tenaya Lodge.** One of the region's largest hotels, Tenaya Lodge is ideal for people who enjoy wilderness treks by day but prefer creature comforts at night. **Pros:** rustic setting with modern comforts; good off-season deals; very close to Yosemite National Park. **Cons:** so big it can seem impersonal; pricey during summer. [$] *Rooms from: $295 ✉ 1122 Rte. 41, Fish Camp ☎ 559/683–6555, 888/514–2167 🌐 www.tenayalodge.com 🛏 244 rooms, 6 suites 🍴 No meals.*

$$$ HOTEL 🏨 **Yosemite View Lodge.** Two miles outside the park's Arch Rock entrance, this modern property is the most convenient place to spend the night if you are unable to secure lodgings in the valley. **Pros:** great location; good views; lots of on-site amenities. **Cons:** somewhat pricey; it can be a challenge to get the dates you want. [$] *Rooms from: $189 ✉ 11136 Rte. 140, El Portal ☎ 209/379–2681, 888/742–4371 🌐 www.yosemiteresorts.us 🛏 279 rooms 🍴 No meals.*

ZION NATIONAL PARK

WELCOME TO ZION

TOP REASONS TO GO

★ **Eye candy:** Pick just about any trail in the park and it's all but guaranteed to culminate in an astounding viewpoint full of pink, orange, and crimson rock formations.

★ **Auto immunity:** From spring through autumn, cars are generally not allowed in Zion Canyon, allowing for a quiet and peaceful park.

★ **Botanical wonderland:** Zion Canyon is home to approximately 900 species of plants, more than anywhere else in Utah.

★ **Animal tracks:** Zion has expansive hinterlands where furry, scaly, and feathered residents are common. Hike long enough and you'll encounter deer, elk, rare lizards, birds of prey, and other zoological treats.

★ **Unforgettable canyoneering:** Zion's array of rugged slot canyons is the richest place on earth for scrambling, rappelling, climbing, and descending.

1 Zion Canyon. This area defines Zion National Park for most people. Free shuttle buses are the only vehicles allowed during the crowded high season. The backcountry is accessible via the West Rim Trail and the Narrows, and 2,000-foot cliffs rise all around.

2 The Narrows. It's the quintessential slot canyon, and one of the best hiking trails in the national park system. Following the north fork of the Virgin River, there's something for everyone in the Narrows, whether you're a day-tripper or an overnight explorer.

exit 42

exit 40

Horse Ranch Mountain

Visitor Center

Double Arch Alcove

Nagunt Mesa

Kolob Canyons Viewpoint

3 Kolob Canyons

Kolob Arch

La Verkin Creek

15

Firepit Knoll

Lower Kolob Plateau

Spendlove Knoll

0 ___ 2 mi

0 ___ 2 km

Kolob Terrace Road

Virgin

9

3 Kolob Canyons.

The northwestern corner of Zion is a secluded 30,000-acre wonderland that can be reached only via a special entrance. Don't miss the West Temple and the Kolob Arch, and keep looking up to spot Horse Ranch Mountain, the park's highest point.

4 Lava Point.

Infrequently visited, this area has a primitive campground and two nearby reservoirs that offer the only significant fishing opportunities in Zion National Park. Lava Point Overlook provides a view of Zion Canyon from the north.

GETTING ORIENTED

The heart of Zion National Park is Zion Canyon, which follows the North Fork of the Virgin River for 6½ miles beneath cliffs that rise 2,000 feet from the river bottom. The Kolob area is considered by some to be superior in beauty, and because it's isolated from the rest of the park, you aren't likely to run into any crowds here. Both sections hint at the extensive backcountry beyond, open for those with the stamina, time, and the courage to go off the beaten paths of the park.

40

KEY	
🏕	Ranger Station
▲	Campground
🎋	Picnic Area
🍴	Restaurant
🖼	Lodge
🚶	Trailhead
🚻	Restrooms
⚡	Scenic Viewpoint
⋯	Walking/Hiking Trails

Updated by Mike Weatherford

The walls of Zion Canyon soar more than 2,000 feet above the valley below, but it's the character, not the size, of the sandstone forms that defines the park's splendor. Throughout the park, stratigraphic evidence points to the distant past, with fantastically colored bands of limestone, sandstone, and lava. Stripes and spots of greenery high in the cliff walls create a "hanging garden" effect, and invariably indicate the presence of water seepage or a spring. Erosion has left behind a collection of domes, fins, and blocky massifs bearing the names and likenesses of cathedrals and temples, prophets and angels.

Trails lead deep into side canyons and up narrow ledges to waterfalls, serene spring-fed pools, and shaded spots of solitude. So diverse is this place that 85% of Utah's flora and fauna species are found here. Some, like the tiny Zion snail, appear nowhere else in the world.

The Colorado River helped create the Grand Canyon, while the Virgin River—the Colorado's muddy progeny—carved Zion's features. Because of the park's unique topography, distant storms and spring runoff can transform a tranquil slot canyon into a sluice.

ZION PLANNER

WHEN TO GO

Zion is the most heavily visited national park in Utah, receiving nearly 2.5 million visitors each year. Locals used to call the spring and fall the shoulder seasons because traffic would drop off from the highly visited summer months. Not so much anymore. Warmer temperatures mean the park is packed April to October.

Summer in the park is hot and dry, punctuated with sudden cloudbursts that can create flash flooding and spectacular waterfalls. Expect afternoon thunderstorms between July and September. Whether the day starts out sunny or not, wear sunscreen and drink lots of water, even if you aren't exerting yourself or spending much time outside. The sun is very powerful at this elevation.

Winters are mild at lower desert elevations. You can expect to encounter winter driving conditions November through March, and although most park programs are suspended, winter is a wonderful and solitary time to see the canyons.

⚠ Extreme highs in Zion can often exceed 100°F in July and August.

AVG. HIGH/LOW TEMPS.

JAN.	FEB.	MAR.	APR.	MAY	JUNE
52/29	57/31	63/36	73/43	83/52	93/60

JULY	AUG.	SEPT.	OCT.	NOV.	DEC.
100/68	97/66	91/60	78/49	63/37	53/30

FESTIVALS AND EVENTS

JANUARY **St. George Winter Bird Festival.** Serious bird-watchers, along with the merely ornithologically curious, gather in St. George every January to peep at the nearly 400 feathery species. After a Thursday-night kickoff event, join in two full days of field trips, exhibits, lectures, and activities. ✉ *1851 S. Dixie Dr., St. George* ☎ *435/627–4560* ⊕ *www.sgcity. org/birdfestival* ✉ *$5.*

APRIL **Dixie Downs Horse Races.** For more than 40 years, two Saturdays in April are reserved for quarter horse racing at Dixie Downs Track, located at the Washington County Fair Grounds in Hurricane. ☎ *435/673–5553* ⊕ *www.stgeorgelions.com.*

AUGUST **Western Legends Roundup.** This nostalgic festival, held every August, is for FAMILY anyone with a love of all things cowboys and Indians. For three days the small town of Kanab plays host to cowboy poets, musicians, and character actors from Old West TV series of yesteryear, such as *The Virginian* and *Wagon Train.* American Indian dancers and weavers, arts-and-crafts vendors, quilt shows, and a parade are also part of the fun. ☎ *435/644–3444* ⊕ *www.westernlegendsroundup.com.*

SEPTEMBER **Dixie Roundup.** Sponsored by the St. George Lions Club, the Dixie Roundup rodeo has been a tradition for decades. The September event includes both young mutton busters and professional bull riders, and is held in the evenings on the green grass of Sun Bowl Stadium. ☎ *435/673–3301* ⊕ *www.stgeorgelions.com.*

PLANNING YOUR TIME
ZION IN ONE DAY

Begin your visit at the **Zion Canyon Visitor Center,** where outdoor exhibits inform you about the park's geology, wildlife, history, and trails. Get a taste of what's in store by viewing the far off Towers of the Virgin, then head to the **Court of the Patriarchs** viewpoint to take photos and walk the short path. Then take the shuttle (or your car, if it's off-season) to **Zion Canyon Lodge,** where you can take a trail to one of the most beautiful

40

spots in the park, the **Emerald Pools.** The Lower Pool Trail is the second most popular walk at Zion (after the Riverside Walk); the trail branches off into Middle Pool and Upper Pool trails for those who are fit and have more time. Ride the next shuttle to the end of the road, where you can walk to the gateway of the canyon's narrows on the paved, accessible **Riverside Walk.**

Reboard the shuttle to return to the Zion Canyon Visitor Center to pick up your car (or continue driving off-season). Head out onto the beautiful **Zion–Mount Carmel Highway,** with its long, curving tunnels, with your camera at the ready for stops at viewpoints along the road. Once you reach the park's east entrance, turn around, and on your return trip stop to take the short hike up to **Canyon Overlook.** Now you're ready to rest your feet at a screening of *Zion Canyon: Treasure of the Gods* on the giant screen of the **Zion Canyon Theatre.** In the evening, you might want to attend a ranger program at one of the campground amphitheaters or at Zion Lodge. Or you can follow a relaxing dinner in **Springdale** with a stroll downtown.

GETTING HERE AND AROUND
AIR TRAVEL
The nearest commercial airport is 46 miles away in St. George, Utah.

CAR TRAVEL
In southwestern Utah, not far from the Nevada border, Zion National Park is closer to Las Vegas (158 miles) than to Salt Lake City (310 miles). The 46 miles from the interstate to the main entrance has become busier over the years, with more roadside development along the way. From I–15, head east on Route 9. After 21 miles you'll reach Springdale, which abuts the main entrance to the park.

If you're arriving April to October, you can drive your vehicle into the park only if you have reservations at the Zion Lodge. Otherwise, you'll have to park it in Springdale or at the Zion Canyon Visitor Center and take the shuttle. There are no car restrictions November through March.

The Zion Canyon Visitor Center parking lot fills up quickly. You can avoid parking heartburn by leaving your car in Springdale and riding the shuttle to the park entrance. Shuttles are accessible for people with disabilities and have plenty of room for gear. Town shuttle stops are at Eagle's Nest, Driftwood Lodge, Bit & Spur Restaurant, Best Western Zion Park Inn, Bumbleberry Inn, Zion Pizza & Noodle Co., Watchman Cafe, Flanigan's Inn, and Zion Canyon Giant Screen Theatre. Times for the shuttle service vary according to season, but you can generally count on the first bus arriving at 5:45 am and the last bus leaving at 10:30 pm. You won't likely wait more than 15 minutes at any stop before you see one.

PARK ESSENTIALS
PARK FEES AND PERMITS
Entrance to Zion National Park is $25 per vehicle for a seven-day pass. People entering on foot or by bicycle or motorcycle pay $12 per person (not to exceed $25 per family) for a seven-day pass. Entrance to the Kolob Canyons section of the park costs only $10, and you receive credit for this entrance fee when you pay to enter Zion Canyon.

Plants and Wildlife in Zion

Zion Canyon's unique geography—the park is on the Colorado Plateau and bordered by the Great Basin and Mojave Desert provinces—supports more than 900 species of plants in environments that range from desert to hanging garden to high plateau. (Those so inclined can pick up a plant identification guide at the Zion Canyon Visitor Center.) And yes, poison ivy is among the plant species. If you're not sure how to recognize it, take a quick lesson from a ranger prior to your first hike or you'll wind up with an itchy souvenir.

With car traffic having been almost completely replaced by a shuttle bus system between April and October, wildlife has returned in force to the park. Even in high season you can spot mule deer wandering in shady glens as you ride through the park, especially in early morning and near dusk. You'll also see scores of lizards and wild turkeys everywhere you go.

If you're looking for more exotic fauna, hit the hiking trails. Nearly 300 species of birds occupy (either part-time or full-time) the park, from tiny hummingbirds and chickadees to surprisingly large wild turkeys, eagles, and even pelicans. Ringtail cats (which are not cats but are similar to raccoons) prowl the park. Evening hikes may reveal foxes, but you're more likely to spot their tracks than the elusive animals themselves. All animals, from the smallest chipmunk to the biggest elk, should be given plenty of space, but only the extremely rare mountain lion or black bear pose any kind of threat to humans.

Permits are required for backcountry camping and overnight hikes. Depending on which parts of the trails you're going to explore, you'll need a special permit for the Narrows and Kolob Creek or the Subway slot canyon. Climbing and canyoneering parties will also need a permit before using technical equipment.

Zion National Park limits the total number of overnight and canyoneering permits issued per day and has a reservation system with most of the permits now issued in an online lottery to apportion them fairly. Permits to the Subway, Mystery Canyon, the Narrows through-hikes, and West Rim are in short supply during high season. The maximum size of a group hiking into the backcountry is 12 people. The cost for a permit for 1 to 2 people is $10; 3 to 7 people, $15; and 8 to 12 people, $20. Permits and hiking information are available at either visitor center. For more information, visit ⊕ *www.nps.gov/zion* prior to your trip to the park.

40

PARK HOURS

The park, open daily year-round, 24 hours a day, is in the Mountain time zone.

CELL-PHONE RECEPTION

Cell-phone reception is good in Springdale but spotty in Zion Canyon itself. Public telephones may be found at South Campground, Watchman Campground, Zion Canyon Visitor Center, Zion Lodge, and Zion Human History Museum.

RESTAURANTS

There is only one full-service restaurant in Zion National Park, but there are numerous places around the park. Springdale is the obvious choice for family-friendly restaurants.

Prices in the reviews are the average cost of a main course at dinner, or if dinner is not served, at lunch.

HOTELS

The Zion Canyon Lodge is rustic but clean and comfortable. Springdale has dozens of lodging options, from quaint bed-and-breakfasts to modest motels to chain hotels with riverside rooms. Panguitch and Hurricane have some good options for budget and last-minute travelers.

Prices in the reviews are the lowest cost of a standard double room in high season. For expanded reviews, facilities, and current deals, visit Fodors.com.

VISITOR INFORMATION

PARK CONTACT INFORMATION

Zion National Park ⊠ *Rte. 9, Springdale* ☎ *435/772–3256* ⊕ *www.nps. gov/zion.*

VISITOR CENTERS

The visitor center should be the first stop on your itinerary regardless of how deep into the bush you plan to go. Because access to Kolob Canyon is separate from the rest of the park, Zion has a dedicated visitor center in that section of the park in addition to the main facility at the south entrance of the park.

Kolob Canyons Visitor Center. Make the Kolob Canyons Visitor Center your first stop as you enter this remote section of the park. There are books and maps, a small gift shop, and helpful rangers to answer questions about Kolob Canyons exploration. Clean public restrooms can also be found here. ⊠ *Exit 40 off I–15, 17 miles south of Cedar City* ☎ *435/586–9548* ⊕ *www.nps.gov/zion* ۞ *Late May–early Sept., daily 8–6; early Sept.–mid-Oct., daily 8–5; mid-Oct.–Apr., daily 8–4:30; late Apr.–late May, daily 8–5.*

Zion Canyon Visitor Center. Unlike most national park visitor centers, which are filled with indoor displays, Zion's presents most of its information in an appealing outdoor exhibit next to a gurgling runnel shaded by cottonwood trees. These displays introduce you to the area's geology, flora, and fauna. Inside, a large bookstore/gift shop sells everything from field guides to souvenirs. Zion Canyon shuttle buses leave from the center, including ranger-guided shuttle tours that depart twice a day and make several stops along the canyon's beautiful scenic drive. ⊠ *At south entrance, Springdale* ☎ *435/772–3256* ⊕ *www.nps.gov/zion* ۞ *June–early Sept., daily 8–7:30; Sept.–mid-Oct., daily 8–6; mid-Oct.– late Apr., daily 8–5; late Apr.–late May, daily 8–6.*

EXPLORING

SCENIC DRIVES

Zion Canyon's grandeur is best experienced on foot whenever possible, but there is something to be said for covering a lot of ground on wheels. Take the shuttle whenever possible. Driving is the only way to easily access Kolob Canyon, for example, and from November through March, driving your own vehicle is the only way to access the Zion Canyon scenic drive.

Kolob Canyons Road. The beauty starts modestly at the junction with Interstate 15, but as you move along this 5-mile road the red walls of the Kolob finger canyons rise suddenly and spectacularly out of the earth. With the crowds left behind at Zion Canyon, this drive offers the chance to take in incredible vistas at your leisure. Trails include the short but rugged Middle Fork of Taylor Creek Trail, which passes two 1930s homestead cabins then culminates in the Double Arch Alcove after 2.7 miles. During heavy snowfall Kolob Canyons Road may be closed. ⊠ *Kolob Canyons Rd., east of I–15.*

Zion–Mount Carmel Highway and Tunnels. Two narrow tunnels as old as the park itself lie between the east entrance and Zion Canyon on this breathtaking 24-mile stretch of Route 9. One was once the longest man-made tunnel in the world. As you travel the (1.1-mile) passage through solid rock, five arched portals along one side provide fleeting glimpses of cliffs and canyons. When you emerge into the daylight you'll find that the landscape has changed dramatically. Large vehicles require traffic control and a $15 permit, available at the park entrance, and have restricted hours of travel. This includes nearly all RVs, trailers, dual-wheel trucks, campers, and boats. The 0.5-mile Canyon Overlook Trail starts from a parking area between the two tunnels. The road is open April through October. ⊠ *Rte. 9, 5 miles east of Canyon Junction.*

HISTORIC SITES

40

Zion Human History Museum. Enrich your visit with a stop at this quaint museum, which tells the story of the park from the perspective of humans who have lived here throughout history, including Ancestral Puebloans and early Mormon settlers. Permanent exhibits show how inhabitants dealt with wildlife, plants, and other natural forces from prehistory to the present. Temporary art exhibits include finds from more recent archaeological excavations. A 22-minute film on the park's human history screens throughout the day. ⊠ *Zion Canyon Scenic Dr., ½ mile north of south entrance* ☎ *435/772–3256* ⊕ *www. nps.gov/zion/historyculture/zion-human-history-museum.htm* 🆓 *Free* ☉ *Mar.–Nov., daily 10–5.*

Zion Lodge. Built by Union Pacific Railroad in 1925, the original lodge was destroyed by fire in 1966. Today's scenic structure, carefully renovated in 1990, recaptures the look and feel of the first building. Some of the original Western-style cabins are still in use today. Set

"There were great contrasts between the Narrows' red rock, green trees, and cool, clear water. This spot was an ideal swimming hole." —photo by Brad Campbell, Fodors.com member

among a sprawling lawn shaded by giant cottonwoods, the lodge houses a restaurant, snack bar, gift shop, and a spacious patio with rocking chairs that provide both respite and vistas of the canyon walls. ⊠ *Zion Canyon Scenic Dr., 3 miles north of Canyon Junction* ☎ *435/772–7700.*

SCENIC STOPS

The park comprises two distinct sections—Zion Canyon and the Kolob Plateau and Canyons. Most people restrict their visit to the better-known Zion Canyon, especially if they have only one day to explore, but the Kolob area has much to offer and should not be missed if time allows. Though there's little evidence of Kolob's beauty from the entrance point off Interstate 15, once you negotiate the first switchback on the park road, you are hit with a vision of red-rock cliffs shooting out of the earth. As you climb in elevation, you are treated first to a journey through these canyons, then with a view into the chasm. ■TIP➔ **You have to exit the park to get between Zion Canyon and Kolob Canyon, so it is not easy to explore both sections in one day.**

Checkerboard Mesa. The distinctive waffle patterns on this huge, white mound of sandstone were created by eons of freeze/thaw cycles creating vertical fractures, along with the exposure of horizontal bedding planes by erosion. The crosshatch effect is stunning and well worth stopping at the pull-out for a long gaze. ⊠ *Zion–Mount Carmel Hwy., 1 mile west of the east entrance.*

Court of the Patriarchs. This trio of peaks bears the names of, from left to right, Abraham, Isaac, and Jacob. Mount Moroni is the reddish peak on the far right, which partially blocks your view of Jacob. Hike the trail that leaves from the Court of the Patriarchs Viewpoint to get a much better view of the sandstone prophets; you may catch a glimpse of rock climbers camming their way up Isaac's sheer face. ⊠ *Zion Canyon Scenic Dr., 1½ miles north of Canyon Junction.*

Great White Throne. Dominating the Grotto picnic area near Zion Lodge is this massive Navajo sandstone peak, which juts 2,000 feet above the valley floor. The Throne was for decades the most popular formation in the park, while today the arches are what draw visitors in droves. ⊠ *Zion Canyon Scenic Dr., about 3 miles north of Canyon Junction.*

Fodor's Choice ★ **The Narrows.** This sinuous 16-mile crack in the earth where the Virgin River flows over gravel and boulders is one of the most stunning gorges in the world. If you hike through it, you'll find yourself surrounded—and sometimes, nearly closed in by—smooth walls stretching high into the heavens. Plan to get wet, as the river still flows here. ⊠ *Begins at Riverside Walk.*

Weeping Rock. Surface water from the rim of Echo Canyon spends several thousand years seeping down through the porous sandstone before exiting at this picturesque alcove. A hike to see it won't take nearly that long; a paved walkway climbs a quarter mile to this flowing rock face where wildflowers and delicate ferns grow. In fall, the maples and cottonwoods along the trail riot with color, and an abundance of lizards point the way down the path. It's too steep and slippery for wheelchairs. ⊠ *Zion Canyon Scenic Dr., 4½ miles north of Canyon Junction.*

EDUCATIONAL OFFERINGS

CLASSES AND SEMINARS

Zion Canyon Field Institute. The educational arm of the Zion Natural History Association offers one- and two-day workshops on the park's natural and cultural history with an expert instructor. Each session includes classroom time plus a hike into the field to apply what you've learned. Take a deep dive into subjects like edible plants, bat biology, river geology, photography, or adobe-brick making, or general-interest offerings like bird-watching. Classes are limited to small groups; reserve ahead to ensure placement. There are also ongoing park projects visitors can volunteer to help out with, gaining a behind-the-scenes glimpse at Zion's inner workings. ☎ *435/772–3264, 800/635–3959* ⊕ *www.zionpark.org* ⊠ *$25–$80 per day.*

RANGER PROGRAMS

Evening Programs. Held each evening in campground amphitheaters and at Zion Lodge, these entertaining ranger-led talks give you the park's slant on geology, biology, and history. You might learn about wildfires, Zion's migratory birds, or how to observe nature with all your senses. Slide shows and audience participaton are often part of the discussion. Check the park guide for times and locations. ☎ *435/772–3256* ⊕ *www.nps.gov/zion.*

40

Fodor's Choice   **Expert Talks.** These free, informal lectures take place on the Zion
★   Human History Museum patio and Kolob Canyons area of the park.
Recent sessions have included "Animals of Zion," "Water, Rocks, and
Time," and "Snapshots of History," highlighting stories of the early
settlers. There are no reservations, and you can come and go as you
please. Talks are usually scheduled for 20 to 30 minutes, but some
topics run longer. Park bulletin boards and publications have updated
schedules. ☎ *435/772–3256.*

FAMILY   **Junior Ranger Program.** The park offers an array of worthy educational
activities aimed at younger visitors. This includes the chance to earn
their Junior Ranger badge by attending at least one nature program
and completing the free Junior Ranger Handbook, available at visitor
centers, the Zion Human History Museum, and Zion Nature Center.
The ranger-led programs cover topics such as plants, animals, geology, and archaeology through hands-on activities, games, and hikes.
Check the park guide for scheduled talks. ⊠ *Zion Nature Center,
near South Campground entrance, ½ mile north of south entrance*
☎ *435/772–3256* ⊕ *www.nps.gov/zion* 🔁 *Free.*

Ranger-Led Hikes. These guided hikes are perfect if you crave to know
more about the sites and sounds of the trail but don't have the time
to get a degree in botany or zoology prior to the trip. Itineraries vary
between easy 1-mile to moderate 2.5-mile walks and have recently
included a Riverside Ramble, a geologic tour called Rock and Stroll,
and a natural-history walk taking in the incredible vistas of Kolob
Canyons. Inquire at the Zion Canyon and Kolob Canyon visitor centers, or check park bulletin boards for locations and times. Wear
sturdy footgear and bring a hat, sunglasses, sunscreen, and water.
⊕ *www.nps.gov/zion.*

FAMILY   **Ride with a Ranger Shuttle Tours.** Listening to the audiotaped narration
Fodor's Choice   that accompanies every shuttle ride is one thing, but having your very
★   own expert along for the trip is quite another. Twice a day the park
provides ranger-led shuttle tours that stop at various points of interest along Zion Canyon Scenic Drive, offering details on the canyon's
geology, ecology, and history, as well as great photo ops. The two-hour
tours take place in the morning and evening and depart from the Zion
Canyon Visitor Center. Make reservations, in person, at the visitor
center up to three days in advance; seating is limited. ⊠ *Zion Canyon
Visitor Center* ☎ *435/772–3256* ⊕ *www.nps.gov/zion* 🔁 *Free* ☉ *May–
Sept., daily at 9 and 6:30.*

SPORTS AND THE OUTDOORS

Hiking is by far the most popular activity at Zion, with a panoply of
trails leading to rewarding destinations in the hinterlands: extreme slot
canyons, gorgeous overlooks, verdant meadows, and dripping springs.
Some sections of the Virgin River are ideal for canoeing (inner tubes are
not allowed). In winter, hiking boots can be exchanged for snowshoes
and cross-country skis, but check with a ranger to determine backcountry snow conditions.

BICYCLING

Zion National Park has something for every kind of biker. Mountain bikers can cake themselves with mud on the park's trails, and racers will find enough up and down to make their pulse race.

Zion has taken steps to become much more bicycle-friendly, including having bike racks at some of the facilities and on the shuttle buses themselves. If you are renting bikes by the hour from a Springdale outfitter, you can load your bike on the bus, have the shuttle take you to the last stop (Temple of Sinawava), and take an easy one-way pedal back to Springdale. ■ TIP➡ **When you're on the park road, shuttle buses and cars have the right of way and you're expected to pull off to the side and let them pass.**

Within the park proper, bicycles are allowed only on established park roads and on the 3½-mile Pa'rus Trail, which winds along the Virgin River in Zion Canyon. You cannot walk or ride your bicycle through the Zion–Mount Carmel Tunnels; the only way to get your bike past this stretch of the highway is to transport it by motor vehicle.

TOURS AND OUTFITTERS

Bicycles Unlimited. A treasure trove of information on mountain biking in southern Utah, Bicycles Unlimited rents bikes and sells parts, accessories, and guidebooks. ⊠ *90 S. 100 East, St. George* ☎ *888/673–4492* ⊕ *www.bicyclesunlimited.com* ⊘ *Mon.–Sat., 9–6.*

BIRD-WATCHING

More than 200 bird species call Zion Canyon home, and scores more pass through the park on their annual migrations. Some species, such as the white-throated swift and ospreys, make their home in the towering cliff walls. Red-tailed and Cooper's hawks are abundant. Closer to the ground you'll doubtless see the bold Steller's jay and scrub jay rustling around the pinyon thickets. The wild turkey population has been booming in recent years, and some of the flock just might come your way looking for a handout. Five species of hummingbirds are residents of the park, with the black-chinned variety being the most common. The park service says four other species of hummers may zip by you on their way to some nectar-filled destination, but these birds are just tourists here like you. Climb to the top of Angel's Landing and you may catch a glimpse of a bald eagle. The luckiest bird-watchers might even see two of the park's rarest species: the Mexican spotted owl and the enormous California condor. ■ TIP➡ **Ask for a bird checklist at the visitor center.**

40

HIKING

The best way to experience Zion Canyon is to walk beneath, between and, if you can bear it (and have good balance!), along its towering cliffs. Trails vary, from paved and flat river strolls to precarious cliffside scrambles. Whether you're heading out for a day of rock hopping or an hour of meandering, plan on packing and consuming plenty of drinking water throughout your hike to counteract the effects of a high-altitude workout in the arid climate.

DID YOU KNOW?

Hiking the canyons of the Left Fork of North Creek in Zion from the top down involves rappelling, swimming through deep pools, long stretches of wading, and route-finding skills. The goal is to get to the Subway, a spectacular tunnel-like canyon that can quickly fill with water.

Keeping the sun at bay is a real challenge at Zion National Park (though less so by mid-afternoon in the canyon, shielded by steep walls). Put on sunscreen before you set out, and reapply at regular intervals. Because the park's hikes usually include uneven surfaces and elevation changes, wear sturdy shoes or hiking boots. A lot of veteran hikers carry good walking sticks, too, as they're invaluable along trails that ford or follow the Virgin River or its tributaries.

Zion is one of the most popular parks in the country, so it can be hard to envision just how alone you'll be on some of the less traveled trails. If you want to do a backcountry hike, make a reservation and let park rangers know where you're going and when you plan to be back.

■ TIP➔ **Park rangers warn hikers to remain on alert for flash floods; these walls of water can appear out of nowhere, even when the sky above you is clear.**

EASY

FAMILY **Emerald Pools Trail.** Multiple waterfalls cascade (or drip, in dry weather) into algae-filled pools along this trail. The path leading to the lower pool is paved and appropriate for strollers and wheelchairs. If you've got any energy left, keep going past the lower pool. The quarter mile from there to the middle pool gets rocky and steep but offers increasingly scenic views. A less crowded and exceptionally enjoyable return route follows the Kayenta Trail connecting on to the Grotto Trail. Allow 50 minutes for the 1.2-mile round-trip hike to the lower pool, and 2½ hours round trip to the middle (2 miles) and upper pools (3 miles). *Easy. ⊠ Trailhead at Zion Canyon Scenic Dr., about 3 miles north of Canyon Junction.*

FAMILY **Grotto Trail.** This flat trail takes you from Zion Lodge to the Grotto picnic area, traveling for the most part along the park road. Allow 20 minutes or less for the walk along the half-mile trail. If you are up for a longer hike, and have two to three hours, connect with the Kayenta Trail after you cross the footbridge, and head for the Emerald Pools. You will begin gaining elevation, and it's a steady, steep climb to the pools, which you will begin to see after about 1 mile. *Easy. ⊠ Trailhead at Zion Canyon Scenic Dr., about 3 miles north of Canyon Junction.*

Pa'rus Trail. This 2-mile, relatively flat walking and biking path parallels and occasionally crosses the Virgin River, starting at South Campground and proceeding north along the river to the beginning of Zion Canyon Scenic Drive. It's paved and gives you great views of the Watchman, the Sentinel, the East and West temples, and Towers of the Virgin. Dogs are allowed on this trail as long as they are leashed. *Easy. ⊠ Trailhead at Canyon Junction, ½ mile north of south entrance.*

FAMILY **Riverside Walk.** Beginning at the Temple of Sinawava shuttle stop at the end of Zion Canyon Scenic Drive, this easy 1-mile round trip shadows the Virgin River. The river gurgles by on one side of the trail; on the other, spring wildflowers bloom from the canyon wall in fascinating hanging gardens. This is the park's most trekked trail, so be prepared for crowds at high season; it is paved and suitable for strollers and wheelchairs. A round-trip walk takes between one and two hours. The end of the trail marks the beginning of the Narrows Trail. *Easy. ⊠ Trailhead at Zion Canyon Scenic Dr., 5 miles north of Canyon Junction.*

40

MODERATE

FAMILY
Fodor's Choice
★
Canyon Overlook Trail. The parking area just east of Zion–Mount Carmel tunnel leads to this popular 1-mile trail; allow an hour to hike it. The overlook at the trail's end gives you views of the West and East temples, Towers of the Virgin, the Streaked Wall, and other Zion Canyon cliffs and peaks. The elevation change is 160 feet. *Moderate. ⊠ Trailhead at Rte. 9, east of Zion–Mount Carmel Tunnel.*

Taylor Creek Trail. In the Kolob Canyons area of the park, this trail immediately descends parallel to Taylor Creek, sometimes crossing it, sometimes shortcutting benches beside it. The historic Larsen Cabin precedes the entrance to the canyon of the Middle Fork, where the trail becomes rougher. After the old Fife Cabin, the canyon bends to the right and delivers you into Double Arch Alcove, a large, colorful grotto with a high arch towering above. The distance one way to Double Arch is 2.75 miles. Allow about four hours round-trip for this hike. The elevation change on this trail is 440 feet. *Moderate. ⊠ Trailhead at Kolob Canyons Rd., about 1½ miles east of Kolob Canyons Visitor Center.*

Watchman Trail. For a view of the town of Springdale and a look at lower Zion Creek Canyon and the Towers of the Virgin, take this popular but strenuous hike, which begins on a service road east of Watchman Campground. Some springs seep out of the sandstone to nourish hanging gardens and attract wildlife here. There are a few sheer cliff edges on this route, so children should be supervised carefully. Plan on two hours for this 3-mile hike with a 380-foot elevation change. *Moderate. ⊠ Trailhead east of Rte. 9 (main park road), on access road inside south entrance.*

DIFFICULT

Fodor's Choice
★
Angels Landing Trail. As much a trial as it is a trail, this hike beneath the Great White Throne is one of the most challenging in the park. Leave your acrophobia at home as you work your way through Walter's Wiggles, a series of 21 switchbacks built out of sandstone blocks. From here you traverse sheer cliffs with chains bolted into the rock face to serve as handrails in some places. In spite of its hair-raising nature, this trail attracts many people. Allow 2½ hours round-trip if you stop at Scout's Lookout (2 miles), and four hours if you keep going the half mile to where the angels (and birds of prey) play. The trail is 5 miles round-trip and is not appropriate for children; you'll get the heebie-jeebies every time there's a handrail-free drop-off. *Difficult. ⊠ Trailhead at Zion Canyon Scenic Dr., about 4½ miles north of Canyon Junction.*

Narrows Trail. After leaving the paved ease of the Gateway to the Narrows trail behind, the real fun begins. This route does not follow a trail or path; rather, you are walking on the riverbed itself. In places you'll find a pebbly shingle or dry sandbar footpath, but eventually the walls of the canyon close in and you'll be forced into the chilly waters of the Virgin River itself, walking against the current (tack back and forth, don't fight it head-on). The hike is a stunning and unique nature experience, but it's no picnic. A walking stick and shoes with good tread and ankle support are highly recommended and will make hiking the riverbed much more enjoyable. Be prepared to swim, as chest-deep holes may occur even when water levels are low. Like any narrow desert

View stunning vistas on Angels Landing Trail, but take note that it's not for those with acrophobia.

canyon, this one is famous for sudden flash flooding, even when skies are clear. ■TIP→ **Before attempting to hike into the Narrows, check with park rangers about the likelihood of flash floods.** A day trip up the lower section of the Narrows is 6 miles one-way to the turnaround point. Allow at least five hours round-trip. *Difficult.* ⊠ *Trailhead at end of Riverside Walk.*

HORSEBACK RIDING

TOURS AND OUTFITTERS

FAMILY **Canyon Trail Rides.** Grab your hat and boots and see Zion Canyon the way the pioneers did—on the back of a horse or mule. Easygoing, one-hour and half-day guided rides are available, with a minimum age of 7 and 10 years, respectively. Maximum weight on either trip is 220 pounds. These friendly folks have been around for years, and they are the only outfitter for trail rides inside the park. Reservations are recommended and can be made via the company's website. ⊠ *Across the road from Zion Lodge* ☎ *435/679–8665* ⊕ *www.canyonrides.com* ✉ *$40–$80 per person* ⊘ *Late Mar.–Oct.*

SWIMMING

Swimming is allowed in the Virgin River, but be careful of cold water, slippery rock bottoms, and the occasional flash floods whenever it rains. Swimming is not allowed in the Emerald Pools. The use of inner tubes is prohibited within park boundaries, but some companies offer trips on a tributary of the Virgin River just outside the park.

WINTER SPORTS

Cross-country skiing and snowshoeing are best experienced in the park's higher elevations in winter, where snow stays on the ground longer. Inquire at the Zion Canyon Visitor Center for backcountry conditions. Snowmobiling is allowed only for residential access.

WHAT'S NEARBY

NEARBY TOWNS

FAMILY Hotels, restaurants, and shops keep popping up in **Springdale,** population 529, on the southern boundary of Zion National Park, yet the town still manages to maintain its small-town charm—and oh, the view! There are a surprising number of wonderful places to stay and eat, and if you take the time to stroll the main drag you can pick up souvenirs. There's a free shuttle that carries you through town, or you can rent bikes to explore the main drag.

If you have time to explore, there's always **Virgin, La Verkin,** and the ghost town of **Grafton,** which you might recognize from such films as *Butch Cassidy and the Sundance Kid.* Today there's only a stone school and a dusty cemetery. **Hurricane,** population 8,200, has quintupled in size over the last few decades and keeps sprouting new chain restaurants and lodging. (Locals emphasize the first syllable, barely uttering the last.) There are many excellent historical sites, a world-class golf course, and the charming Hurricane Canal, dug by hand and used for 80 years to irrigate the fields around the town.

Heading east from Zion is **Mount Carmel Junction,** an intersection offering some funky small-town lodging and the studio of American West artist Maynard Dixon.

VISITOR INFORMATION
Color Country Travel Region (Hurricane) ⊠ *906 N. 1400 W, St. George* ☏ *800/233–8824* ⊕ *www.utah.com/visitor/travel_offices/color_country.htm.* **Kane County Office of Tourism (Mount Carmel)** ⊠ *78 S. 100 E, Kanab* ☏ *800/733–5263* ⊕ *www.kaneutah.com.* **Zion Canyon Visitors Bureau (Springdale)** ⊠ *Springdale* ☏ *888/518–7070* ⊕ *www.zionpark.com.*

NEARBY ATTRACTIONS

Coral Pink Sand Dunes State Park. This sweeping expanse of pink sand comes from eroding sandstone. Funneled through a notch in the rock, wind picks up speed and carries grains of sand into the area. Once the wind slows down, the sand is deposited, creating this giant playground for dune buggies, ATVs—called "off-highway vehicles" in Utah—and dirt motorcycles. A small area is fenced off for walking, but the sound of wheeled toys is always with you. Children love to play in the sand, but check the surface temperature; it can become very hot. ⊠ *Yellowjacket and Hancock rds., 12 miles off U.S. 89, Kanab* ☏ *435/648–2800* ⊕ *www.stateparks.utah.gov* ⊡ *$6* ⊙ *Daily.*

DID YOU KNOW?

Zion National Park is an outstanding spot for climbing, and has one of the world's largest concentrations of vertical climbing walls exceeding 1,000 feet. If you are used to the solid granite of Yosemite, you're in for a surprise. Zion's sandstone is much more varied, and can behave unpredictably depending on the weather. Always make sure you're accompanied by someone knowledgeable about the area.

Snow Canyon State Park. Named not for winter weather but after a pair of pioneering Utahans named Snow, this overlooked gem of a state park is filled with natural wonders. Hiking trails lead to lava cones, sand dunes, cactus gardens, and high-contrast vistas. From the campground you can scramble up huge sandstone mounds and overlook the entire valley. About an hour from Zion, this state park is near St. George. ✉ *1002 Snow Canyon Dr., Ivins* ☎ *435/628–2255* 🌐 *www.stateparks.utah.gov* 🎟 *$6 per vehicle* 🕑 *Daily 6 am–10 pm.*

AREA ACTIVITIES

SPORTS AND THE OUTDOORS

GOLF

Sky Mountain. Hurricane has Sky Mountain, a scenic 18-hole public course. Many fairways are framed by red-rock outcroppings; the course has a front-tee view of the nearby 10,000-foot Pine Valley Mountains. There's also a snack bar, pro-shop, and driving range on the premises. Peak season at this course is February through April. Green fees range from $10 to walk nine holes in the off-season to $65 for 18 holes with a cart during peak season. ✉ *1030 N. 2600 W, Hurricane* ☎ *435/635–7888* 🌐 *www.skymountaingolf.com* ⛳ *18 holes. Yards: blue 6392; white 6014; gold (ladies) 5044. Par 72. Green Fee: $39–$65* ☞ *Facilities: driving range, putting green, pitching area, golf carts, rental clubs, pro-shop, restaurant.*

ARTS AND ENTERTAINMENT

ART GALLERIES

Fodor's Choice ★ **Worthington Gallery.** Opened in 1980 by a single potter in a pioneer-era home near the mouth of Zion Canyon, Worthington Gallery now features more than 30 artists who create with paper, metal, glass, paint, and pottery. Even if you only have time for a quick stop, it is worth the trip to see some of the best pottery and fine art in the area. ✉ *789 Zion Park Blvd., Springdale* ☎ *435/772–3446* 🌐 *www.worthingtongallery.com* 🕑 *Mar.–Oct., daily 9–9; Nov.–Feb., daily 10–5.*

NIGHTLIFE

Bit & Spur Restaurant and Saloon. A Springdale instititution for more than 30 years, this restaurant is known not only for its unique Southwestern fare, but as an occasional stop for top-flight bands and musicians—in genres such as blues, rock, jam, and reggae—who go out of their way to play here. ✉ *1212 Zion Park Blvd., Springdale* ☎ *435/772–3498* 🌐 *www.bitandspur.com.*

WHERE TO EAT

IN THE PARK

$ AMERICAN 🍴 **Castle Dome Café & Snack Bar.** Next to the Zion Lodge shuttle stop, this small fast-food restaurant is all about convenience. Hikers on the go can grab a banana, burger, smoothie, or salad, or you can while away an hour with ice cream on the shaded patio. Gets quite busy during high-season months. [$] *Average main: $6* ✉ *Zion Canyon Scenic Dr., 3¼ mile north of Canyon Junction* ☎ *435/772–7700* 🌐 *www.zionlodge.com.*

$$ ✕ **Red Rock Grill at Zion Lodge.** This restaurant's monopoly on in-park fine
AMERICAN dining has not made it complacent. The menu is solid American fare, with steaks, seafood, and surprises such as house-made Western bison meat loaf. The spacious dining room is adorned with photos of the area landscape, and a large patio offers dining with views of the canyon and the lodge's parklike setting. Lunch includes a generous selection of salads, sandwiches, and specialties such as the Wrangler cheeseburger with onion straws and chipotle mayo. Breakfast is also served. $ *Average main: $18 ✉ Zion Canyon Scenic Dr., 3¼ miles north of Canyon Junction ☎ 435/772–7760 ⊕ www.zionlodge.com ⚶ Reservations essential.*

PICNIC AREAS

FAMILY **The Grotto.** Get your food to go at the Zion Lodge, take a short walk to this lunch retreat, and dine beneath a shady oak. There are lots of amenities—drinking water, fire grates, picnic tables, and restrooms. A trail leads to the Emerald Pools if you want to walk off your lunchtime calories. ✉ *Zion Canyon Scenic Dr., 3½ miles north of Canyon Junction.*

Kolob Canyons Viewpoint. Take in a shaded meal with a view at this charming picnic site 100 yards down the Timber Creek Trail. ✉ *End of Kolob Canyons Rd., 5 miles from Kolob Canyons Visitor Center.*

FAMILY **Zion Nature Center.** On your way to or from the Junior Ranger Program feed your kids at the nature center picnic area. When the nature center is closed, you can use the restrooms in South Campground. ✉ *Near the entrance to South Campground, ½ mile north of the south entrance ☎ 435/772–3256.*

OUTSIDE THE PARK

$ ✕ **Bear Paw Cafe.** Prepare to wait for a table on busy weekend mornings, but it's worth it at this cozy Western-themed diner where the French toast is nearly two inches thick and tender crêpes come in choices such as cherries jubilee or spiced apples. The lunch menu includes twice-baked potatoes and panini, and don't forget to try an Italian soda or one of their homemade smoothies. $ *Average main: $8 ✉ 75 N. Main St., St. George ☎ 435/634–0126 ⊕ www.bearpawcafe.com ☻ No dinner.*

AMERICAN

Fodor'sChoice
★

40

$ ✕ **Benja Thai and Sushi.** In St. George's charming Ancestor Square, you can dine on exotic Thai soups, salads, and specialty dishes, and choose from an extensive sushi menu. The room's tapestries, intricate wood carvings, and lilting music give it a warmth and tranquility, and large windows provide views of the landscaped courtyard dotted with quaint historic buildings. $ *Average main: $12 ✉ 2 W. St. George Blvd., St. George ☎ 435/628–9538 ⊕ www.benjathai.com.*

THAI

$$ ✕ **Bit & Spur Restaurant and Saloon.** Creative Southwestern fare such as sweet-potato tamales and blue crab and roasted corn cannelloni highlight the menu at this Springdale institution, which has been serving patrons for more than 30 years. An outside dining area with fountain, stone pathways, and shade trees is an oasis, not to mention desserts like the brownie crème brûlée. $ *Average main: $20 ✉ 1212 Zion Park Blvd., Springdale ☎ 435/772–3498 ⊕ www.bitandspur.com ☻ No lunch.*

SOUTHWESTERN

Fodor'sChoice
★

CLOSE UP

Best Campgrounds in Zion

The two campgrounds within Zion National Park—Watchman and South campgrounds—are family-friendly, convenient, and quite pleasant, but in the high season they do fill up fast. Outside the park you'll find a third park-affiliated campground, Lava Point, and a number of private campgrounds.

South Campground. All the sites here are under big cottonwood trees, providing some relief from the summer sun. The campground operates on a first-come, first-served basis, and sites are usually filled before noon each day during high season. ✉ *Rte. 9, ½ mile north of south entrance* ☎ *435/772-3256.*

Watchman Campground. This large campground on the Virgin River operates on a reservation system between April and October, but you do not get to choose your own site. ✉ *Access road off Zion Canyon Visitor Center parking lot* ☎ *435/772-3256, 800/365-2267* 🌐 *www.recreation.gov.*

$ AMERICAN 🍴 **Sol Foods Market and Deli.** Stop by the deli and check out the well-stocked salad bar, or let them rustle you up a quick burger, sandwich, or vegetarian snack. Daily specials include freshly made wraps and sandwiches. The staff can also prepare picnic baskets or box lunches for your day in the park. [$] *Average main: $8* ✉ *995 Zion Park Blvd., Springdale* ☎ *435/772-0277* 🌐 *www.solfoods.com.*

$ AMERICAN 🍴 **TwentyFive Main Cafe and Cake Parlor.** With bird's-egg blue cuckoo clocks and light-hearted Victorian-themed prints along the walls, this café is all about whimsy, including a daily selection of to-die-for homemade cupcakes such as orange blossom or chocolate espresso. Lunch offerings include generous pastas, panini, deli sandwiches, and salads. Breakfast is served until noon on Friday and Saturday. [$] *Average main: $9* ✉ *25 N. Main St., St. George* ☎ *435/628-7110* 🌐 *www.25main.com* 🕒 *Closed Sun.*

$$ PIZZA FAMILY 🍴 **Zion Pizza & Noodle Co.** It may look like a church, but the only thing being worshipped here is beer and incredible pizza. After a long day on the trails, put up your feet and dig into the meat-laden Cholesterol Hiker or Good for You pizza with grilled zucchini and asiago cheese. You can also order pasta dishes like linguine with peanuts and grilled chicken, and chicken Parmesan. A selection of Utah microbrews and wines by the glass are also served. Enjoy dinner indoors or in the beer garden. [$] *Average main: $14* ✉ *868 Zion Park Blvd., Springdale* ☎ *435/772-3815* 🌐 *www.zionpizzanoodle.com* 🕒 *Closed Dec.–Feb. No lunch.*

WHERE TO STAY

IN THE PARK

$$$ HOTEL **Zion Lodge.** Knotty pine and log furnishings re-create the look and feel of the lodge when it was first built in the 1920s; rooms are modern but not fancy, and each has its own balcony or patio. **Pros:** guests can drive their cars here all year; incredible views; gets quiet and dark at night. **Cons:** pathways dimly lit so bring a flashlight to make your way to your cabin; staff seems overwhelmed at busiest times. $ *Rooms from: $185* ✉ *Zion Canyon Scenic Dr., 3¼ miles north of Canyon Junction* ☎ *888/297–2757* 🌐 *www.zionlodge.com* 🛏 *75 rooms, 6 suites, 40 cabins* 🍴 *No meals.*

OUTSIDE THE PARK

$$$ HOTEL **Cliffrose Lodge and Gardens.** The acres of flowers, lush lawns, and canyon views at this riverside hotel make it more than a place to rest your head. **Pros:** expansive, scenic pool area; you could throw a rock and hit the south entrance to the park; bedding and linens are absolutely top-notch. **Cons:** some walls are thin. $ *Rooms from: $159* ✉ *281 Zion Park Blvd., Springdale* ☎ *435/772–3234, 800/243–8824* 🌐 *www.cliffroselodge.com* 🛏 *51 rooms* 🍴 *No meals.*

$$$ HOTEL Fodor's Choice ★ **Desert Pearl Inn.** You're not exactly roughing it at the riverside Desert Pearl, as every room has vaulted ceilings, oversize windows, and soaking tubs. **Pros:** cute gift shop; striking views; rooms facing river have balconies or terraces. **Cons:** bedding is plush but minimalist; cooking smells can permeate the walls (so the wrong neighbor can spoil your retreat). $ *Rooms from: $168* ✉ *707 Zion Park Blvd., Springdale* ☎ *435/772–8888, 888/828–0898* 🌐 *www.desertpearl.com* 🛏 *61 rooms* 🍴 *No meals.*

$ HOTEL **Golden Hills Motel.** Don't judge a book by its cover: this may not be a beautiful resort, but the rooms are comfortable and inexpensive—where else can you get a two-room suite for under $100? **Pros:** clean rooms; affordable rates. **Cons:** books up quickly; crowds appear without warning like a flash flood in the desert. $ *Rooms from: $64* ✉ *4475 S. State St., at the junction of U.S. 89 and Rte. 9, Mount Carmel* ☎ *435/648–2268, 800/648–2268* 🌐 *www.goldenhillsmotel.com* 🛏 *30 rooms* 🍴 *No meals.*

$$ HOTEL **Pioneer Lodge.** It may appear modest on the outside, but the rooms at the renovated Pioneer Lodge have a cozy cabin feel with modern perks such as plush beds. **Pros:** centrally located near Springdale shops; on-site restaurant. **Cons:** limited outdoor space to kick back and relax; rooms a little close together. $ *Rooms from: $140* ✉ *828 Zion Park Blvd., Springdale* ☎ *435/772–3233* 🌐 *www.zionpioneerlodge.com* 🛏 *43 rooms, 2 apartments* 🍴 *No meals.*

INDEX

PHOTO CREDITS

Front cover: Xuan Che/Flickr Select/Getty Images [Description: Grand Prismatic Spring, Yellowstone National Park]. 1, Evan Spiler, Fodors.com member. 2, RRuntsch/shutterstock. 5, Jeff Vanuga. Chapter 1: Experience the National Parks of the West: 12-13, Jeff Vanuga. 15 (left), Christopher Byczko, Fodors. com member. 15 (right), Loic Bernard/iStockphoto. 16 (top), Eric Foltz/iStockphoto. 16 (bottom), NPS (National Park Service). 17 (left), Eric Foltz/iStockphoto. 17 (right), Bill Pofahl, Fodors.com member. 18, Nancy A. Hann, Fodors.com member. 19 (left), Erica L. Wainer, Fodors.com member. 19 (right), Natalia Eliason, Fodors.com member. 20 (left and right), Library of Congress Prints and Photographs Division. 21, texasbookworm, Fodors.com member. 22 (left), Erica L. Wainer, Fodors.com member. 22 (top center), Gene Zdonek, Fodors.com member. 22 (top right), Art_man/Shutterstock. 22 (bottom right), Stephen Fadem, Fodors.com member. 23 (left), Public domain. 23 (top center), Roger Bravo, Fodors.com member. 23 (top right), David Davis/Shutterstock. 23 (bottom right), Debbie Bowles, Fodors.com member. 24 (left), Heather A. Craig/Shutterstock. 24 (top center), Dan King, Fodors.com member. 24 (top right), Mark Yarchoan/Shutterstock. 24 (bottom right), BostonGal, Fodors.com member. 25 (top left), Dan King, Fodors.com member. 25 (bottom left), Blue Ice/Shutterstock. 25 (top center), Darklich14/ Wikimedia Commons. 25 (bottom center), Eric Gevaert/Shutterstock. 25 (right), Bill Perry/Shutterstock. 26 (left), Gary Whitton/Shutterstock. 26 (top center), Steve Bower/Shutterstock. 26 (top right), NPS. 26 (bottom right), Jacom Stephens/Avid Creative, Inc./iStockphoto. 27 (left), Judy Crawford/Shutterstock. 27 (top center), Christina Tisi-Kramer/Shutterstock. 27 (top right), MWaits/Shutterstock. 27 (bottom right), kenkistler/Shutterstock. 28 (left), Andrey Tarantin/Shutterstock. 28 (top right), Caitlin Mirra/ Shutterstock. 28 (bottom right), Gene Lee/Shutterstock. 29 (left), Krzysztof Wiktor/Shutterstock. 29 (top right), NPS. 29 (bottom right), Public Domain. 30, Xanterra Parks & Resorts. 31, Scott Johnson Photography, Inc. 32 (top), Danita Delimont/Alamy. 32 (bottom), Library of Congress Prints and Photographs Division. 33 (top and bottom), Xanterra Parks & Resorts. 34 (top), Roberto Soncin Gerometta/ Alamy. 34 (bottom), Danita Delimont/Alamy. 35 (top), Travel Alberta. 35 (bottom), Carmen Sorvillo/ Shutterstock. Chapter 2: Choosing a Park: 36-37, Daniel McFadden, Fodors.com member. 38, Keith Jorgensen, Fodors.com. 40, Brad Campbell, Fodors.com member. 42, John H. Kim, Fodors.com member. 44, NPS. 45 (left), DebitNM, Fodors.com member. 45 (right), Jennifer Petoff, Fodors.com. 46, Sandy Rubinstein, Fodors.com member. 47 (left), Dan King, Fodors.com member. 47 (right), Rebalyn, Fodors.com member. 48, Luca Moi/Shutterstock. 49 (left), Kimberly Jozwiak, Fodors.com member. 49 (right), cyndyq, Fodors.com member. 50, Evan Spiler, Fodors.com member. Chapter 3: Planning Your Visit: 52-53, Lura Smith, Fodors.com member. 54, NPS. 55, Diego Cervo/Shutterstock. 56, Jim Lopes/ Shutterstock. 57, David Restivo/Glacier National Park/NPS. 58, Kevin Inman, Fodors.com member. 59 (left), Keith Jorgensen, Fodors.com member. 59 (right), David Restivo/Glacier National Park/NPS. 60, Jeffrey Kramer, Fodors.com member. 62, Inc/Shutterstock. 63 (left), Vitalii Nesterchuk/Shutterstock. 63 (right), Michael Svoboda/Shutterstock. 64, Pacific Northwest Photography/Shutterstock. 65 (left), travlingdude, Fodors.com member. 65 (right), Danny Warren/iStockphoto. 66, Erica L. Wainer, Fodors.com member. 67 (left), William A. McConnell, Fodors.com member. 67 (right), travlingdude, Fodors.com member. 68, Carolv, Fodors.com member. 69, David Davis/Shutterstock. Chapter 4: Great Itineraries: 70-71, Som Vembar, Fodors.com member. 72, Jan Paul/iStockphoto. 79, Lorcel/Shutterstock. 89, CarlB9090, Fodors.com member. Chapter 5: Arches National Park: 91, Evan Spiler, Fodors.com member. 92 (all), NPS. 94, David Noton/age fotostock. 109, mlgb, Fodors.com member. Chapter 6: Badlands National Park: 121, Andrew Mace, Fodors.com member. 122 (top and bottom) and 123, South Dakota Tourism. 124, Jim W. Parkin/iStockphoto. 135, National Archives and Records Administration. Chapter 7: Banff National Park: 139, Mayskyphoto/Shutterstock. 140-41 and 142, Travel Alberta. 150, Artifan/ Shutterstock. 161, Travel Alberta. 165, Mayskyphoto/Shutterstock. Chapter 8: Big Bend National Park: 171, Eric Foltz/iStockphoto. 172 (top), Kenny Braun/Texas Tourism. 172 (bottom), Jim Woodard/NPS. 174, Eric Foltz/iStockphoto. 180, Mike Norton/Shutterstock. Chapter 9: Black Canyon of the Gunnison National Park: 195, Tom Till/Alamy. 196, iStockphoto. 197, Tom Stillo/CTO. 198, Lisa Lynch/NPS. 205, Jim Parkin/Shutterstock. Chapter 10: Bryce Canyon National Park: 211, Chris Christensen, Fodors. com member. 212 (all), Public Domain. 214, Ron Yue/Alamy. 219, Pete Foley, Fodors.com member. 225, Inc/Shutterstock. Chapter 11: Canyonlands National Park: 233, Bryan Brazil/Shutterstock. 234-35, NPS. 236, rollie rodriguez/Alamy. 246-47, Doug Lemke/Shutterstock. Chapter 12: Capitol Reef National Park: 255, Luca Moi/Shutterstock. 256 (top), Jacom Stephens/Avid Creative, Inc./iStockphoto. 256 (center and bottom), Frank Jensen/Utah Office of Tourism. 258, imagebroker/Alamy. 267, Kerrick James. Anton Foltin/Shutterstock. 270, Anton Foltin/Shutterstock. Chapter 13: Carlsbad Caverns National Park: 275, W.P. Fleming/viestiphoto.com. 276 and 277, Peter Jones/NPS. 278, Craig Lovell/viestiphoto.com. 284, John Cancalosi/Alamy. Chapter 14: Channel Islands National Park: 293, Christopher Russell/iStockphoto. 294 (top), Yenwen Lu/iStockphoto. 294 (bottom), NatalieJean/Shutterstock. 295

ABOUT OUR WRITERS

Shelley Arenas grew up in eastern Washington and has lived in the Seattle area since college. She's been a regular contributor to *Fodor's Pacific Northwest* and other guidebooks for more than a decade, along with co-authoring a book about Seattle for families and writing for several regional publishers. She updated the Olympic, North Cascades, and Mt. Rainier chapters this edition. She also thanks recent Florida transplant, Andrea Cohen, for help with researching the Mt. Rainier chapter.

Colorado native Ricardo Baca travels internationally each fall, from India to Australia, Laos to Nicaragua, China to Spain, Cambodia to Belize. When he's not on the road, he is the entertainment editor and lead music critic at *The Denver Post*. He updated the Great Sand Dunes chapter this edition.

Writer John Blodgett updated the Joshua Tree National Park chapter. Currently the owner of MyPetDuck Media based in Carlsbad, California, he is a former magazine editor, newspaper reporter, and photojournalist. This is the eighteenth Fodor's guidebook he has contributed to.

Martha Schindler Connors is a freelance writer in Evergreen, Colorado, where she lives with her husband and two dogs. She enjoys hiking and skiing. She updated the Experience, Planning Your Visit, and Great Itineraries chapters.

Native Californian Cheryl Crabtree—who updated the Channel Islands National Park chapter—has worked as a freelance writer since 1987. She has contributed to *Fodor's California* since 2003 and is currently editor of *Montecito Magazine*. Her articles have appeared in many regional and national publications, including *US Airways Magazine* and *Santa Barbara Seasons*, and annual visitor magazines in Santa Barbara and Ventura.

Lindsey Galloway lives in Boulder, Colorado, and frequently overeats at the many restaurants on Pearl Street. She contributes regularly to BBC Travel and AOL Travel, and founded TravelPretty.com to document her perils in packing. Lindsey updated the Rocky Mountain National Park chapter for this edition.

Long-time Fodor's writer Thomas D. Griffith, who's penned articles for such publications as the *New York Times,* the *Chicago Tribune,* the *Denver Post,* and the *Houston Chronicle,* lives with his wife, Nyla, in Deadwood, South Dakota. He's written or co-authored more than 50 books, including Fodor's *Compass American Guides: South Dakota* and *America's Shrine of Democracy,* with a foreword by President Ronald Reagan. This edition, he updated Badlands, Theodore Roosevelt, Wind Cave, and Yellowstone.

Aimee Heckel is a Colorado native who has been working at Colorado newspapers for 13 years. She is currently a features writer at the *Boulder Daily Camera,* as well as a travel and family writer for ShopAtHome.com and a writer and editor for the SpaTravelGal.com. She updated the Mesa Verde chapter this edition.

Deb Hopewell lives, surfs, and cycles in Santa Cruz, Calif. She prefers exploring by foot, whether wandering the streets of Istanbul or traversing the Sentiers de Grande Randonnée in France. Before becoming the travel editor at Yahoo!, she was a longtime writer and columnist at the *San Jose Mercury News.* She wrote the new chapter on Pinnacles National Park this edition, as well as contributing to the Death Valley chapter.

Kellee Katagi is a Colorado resident and a freelance writer/editor specializing in travel, sports, fitness, health, and food in all its glorious forms. A former managing editor of *SKI Magazine,* Katagi loves to explore the Colorado mountains with her husband and three grade-school-age budding adventurers. She updated the Black Canyon of the Gunnison chapter this edition.

Mara Levin divides her time between travel writing, social work, and her role as mom to two daughters. A native of California, Mara now lives in Tucson, where the grass may not be greener, but the mountains, tranquillity, and slower pace of desert life have their own appeal. She contributed to the Grand Canyon and Saguaro chapters this edition.

The day she returned from her first road trip out west in 1995, Johanna Love quit her job at a Mississippi newspaper and never looked back. She's called Wyoming home since 1997 and enjoys hiking, biking, and paddling on public lands when not working as the features and arts editor at the *Jackson Hole News & Guide*. She writes about her adventures at www.johannalove.com. She updated the Grand Teton chapter.

Daniel Mangin has covered California for Fodor's for over two decades. Several times the editor of *Fodor's California* and the author of the current edition of *Fodor's In Focus Napa & Sonoma,* he took a break from his usual beat—Wine Country—to update the Sequoia and Kings Canyon National Parks chapter.

There is no place freelance writer Debbie Olsen would rather be than hiking a beautiful trail in the Rockies. This veteran Fodor's contributor penned the Glacier and Waterton, Banff, and Jasper chapters for this guide and has contributed to seven other Fodor's guides. Her travel adventures appear regularly in the *Red Deer Advocate* and the *Calgary Herald*.

Steve Pastorino has written for Fodor's about Yellowstone, Zion, and Bryce Canyon national parks for years. Steve credits his mother and father (U.S. Ambassador Robert Pastorino, who passed away in 2013) for inspiring his desire to explore at home and abroad. Steve, his wife, Teri, and their three children have a lot of wandering to do to follow in his parents' footsteps. He updated Arches, Canyonlands, and Great Basin this edition.

Marty Racine has been roaming the mountains, canyons and deserts of the American Southwest for most of his life. His award-winning journalism career includes two decades of feature writing for the *Houston Chronicle* and seven years as editor of the *Ruidoso (NM) News*. This edition Marty updated Big Bend, Carlsbad Caverns, and Guadalupe Mountains.

A Phoenix-based freelance writer and editor, Elise Riley left her native Arizona to report for newspapers across the country. She quickly learned that no place had Mexican food like the Valley, and eventually found the way back to her favorite salsas and enchiladas. This edition, she contributed to the Petrified Forest and Saguaro chapters.

Freelance writer Christine Vovakes updated the Crater Lake, Lassen Volcanic and Redwood Parks chapters and has also contributed to *Fodor's California, Fodor's Pacific Northwest,* and *Fodor's Essential USA*. Her travel articles and photographs have appeared in several publications, including the *Washington Post*, the *Christian Science Monitor,* the *Sacramento Bee* and the *San Francisco Chronicle*.

Mike Weatherford has been an entertainment reporter for the *Las Vegas Review-Journal* since about the time The Mirage opened. He is the author of *Cult Vegas—The Weirdest! The Wildest! The Swingin'est Town on Earth!* As a contrast to all that Las Vegas show business, he and his wife Joan like to explore the natural attractions of Nevada and Southern Utah. He updated the Bryce Canyon, Capital Reef, and Zion.

Sharron Wood has contributed to dozens of Fodor's travel guides, writing about everything from hiking in the high Sierra to hitting the nightclubs in San Francisco. When she's not on assignment with Fodor's, she's usually writing about San Francisco restaurants, editing cookbooks, or shaking up cocktails for a houseful of friends in San Francisco. She updated the Yosemite chapter this edition.